# FRESH-WATER

# INVERTEBRATES

## of the United States

# FRESH-WATER INVERTEBRATES
# of the United States

## SECOND EDITION

By

### ROBERT W. PENNAK
EMERITUS PROFESSOR OF BIOLOGY
UNIVERSITY OF COLORADO
BOULDER, COLORADO

A WILEY-INTERSCIENCE PUBLICATION
JOHN WILEY & SONS,   New York   •   Chichester   •   Brisbane   •   Toronto

*Library of Congress Cataloging in Publication Data:*

Pennak, Robert William.
  Fresh-water invertebrates of the United States.

  "A Wiley-Interscience publication."
  Includes bibliographies and index.
    1.  Freshwater invertebrates—United States.
I.  Title.

QL141.P45   1978        592′.09′2973    78-8130
ISBN 0-471-04249-8

Printed in the United States of America

10 9 8 7 6 5 4 3

To the memory of
C. Juday

"What's the use of their having names," the Gnat said, "if they won't answer to them?"

"No use to *them*," said Alice; "but it's useful to the people that name them, I suppose."

LEWIS CARROLL

"All cold-blooded animals . . . spend an unexpectedly large proportion of their time doing nothing at all, or at any rate, nothing in particular."

CHARLES ELTON

# PREFACE TO THE FIRST EDITION

No comprehensive work on American fresh-water invertebrates has appeared since 1918, and in the meantime much new information has steadily accumulated in a wide variety of biological periodicals. To me, therefore, the need for the present volume is obvious. I hope it will prove useful to biologists and zoologists generally, and to aquatic zoologists, limnologists, fish biologists, and entomologists particularly. It will also serve as a text and reference pitched toward the level of the college senior and beginning graduate student.

Original material resulting from my own field and laboratory research forms only a small fraction of this book. Rather, my role as an author has been one of arrangement, organization, and selection from a very large mass of published information. Indeed, my most perplexing problem has been how *much* material on each taxonomic group to include within the covers of a single volume. General policies, however, have been clear from the outset; I have emphasized natural history, ecology, and taxonomy; I have minimized details in the sections on anatomy and physiology; I have tried to be complete, accurate, concise, and consistent from one chapter to another. During the preparation of this volume all of the chapters have been continually revised and kept up to date in accordance with new material appearing in the literature.

For the most part, only free-living, fresh-water invertebrates that occur in the United States are included. Cestodes, trematodes, parasitic nematodes, etc. are all omitted; their inclusion would have necessitated a much more extensive work and additional years of preparation. Furthermore, most aquatic biologists seldom need to refer to parasitic groups as contrasted with free-living groups.

It will be noted that some chapters contain keys to species, while others contain keys only as far as genera. In general, the chapters in the former category deal with small or comparatively stable taxonomic groups that are fairly well known and in which few new species are being described from time to time in the United States. The chapters in the latter category, however, are all concerned with larger taxonomic groups, as well as those that are less well known in the United States and in which new forms are being described so abundantly that any key to species is quickly out of date. It is assumed that users of this manual are familiar with the fundamentals of taxonomy and the construction of keys. Incidentally, each half of a key couplet consists of but a single sentence; changes in subject within a sentence are indicated by semicolons.

The list of references at the end of each chapter consists only of especially significant and comprehensive works; these include older classical papers as well as recent contributions. Except where sections are especially valuable, I have not listed the larger standard reference works such as Hyman's *The Invertebrates*,

Schulze's *Biologie der Tiere Deutschlands*, Bronn's *Tierreich*, Kükenthal and Krumbach's *Handbuch der Zoologie*, Dahl's *Die Tierwelt Deutschlands*, Grassé's *Traité de Zoologie*, and *Faune de France*.

Almost all of the chapters (with or without figures) were sent to at least one specialist for criticisms, corrections, and suggestions. I am deeply grateful to all these specialists, who were most encouraging, generous, and cooperative. Without their help and assurance I would have had much less confidence in my efforts. Following is a list of these specialists, with the sections examined by each.

John L. Brooks (Cladocera); Royal B. Brunson (Gastrotricha); C. F. Byers (Odonata); Fenner A. Chace, Jr. (Crustacea Introduction, Mysidacea); B. G. Chitwood (Nematoda); W. R. Coe (Nemertea); R. E. Coker (Copepoda); Ralph W. Dexter (Eubranchiopoda); W. T. Edmondson (Rotatoria); T. H. Frison [deceased] (Plecoptera); R. E. Gregg (Insecta Introduction); H. H. Hobbs, Jr. (Decapoda); C. C. Hoff (Ostracoda); Leslie Hubricht (Amphipoda, Isopoda); H. B. Hungerford (Hemiptera); Libbie H. Hyman (Coelenterata, Turbellaria); F. P. Ide (Ephemeroptera); O. A. Johannsen (Diptera); M. W. de Laubenfels (Porifera); H. B. Leech (Coleoptera); James E. Lynch (Eubranchiopoda); J. G. Mackin (Isopoda); Ruth Marshall (Hydracarina); H. B. Mills (Collembola); J. Percy Moore (Hirudinea); L. E. Noland (Protozoa); Mary D. Rogick (Bryozoa); H. H. Ross (Plecoptera, Trichoptera); Henry van der Schalie (Gastropoda, Pelecypoda); Waldo L. Schmitt (Crustacea Introduction, Mysidacea); L. H. Townsend (Megaloptera, Neuroptera); H. C. Yeatman (Copepoda).

The introductory chapter was criticized by A. S. Pearse and by several of my graduate students. Other people have helped me in one way or another. A group of eight protozoologists, for example, selected the 300 most appropriate and common genera of Protozoa to be included in the Protozoa key. These men are: William Balamuth, Gordon H. Ball, A. M. Elliot, Harold Kirby [deceased]; J. B. Lackey, L. E. Noland, K. L. Osterud, and D. H. Wenrich.

Obviously, a book of this sort is bound to have errors and ambiguities, and certainly such faults are clearly my own responsiblity. I hope readers will bring them to my attention.

In a sense, this book constitutes a plea and encouragement for more work on our rich but poorly known fresh-water invertebrate fauna. I hope these chapters will kindle sparks and raise questions in the minds of our students and beginning investigators in zoology, for it is among these young people that we shall find our authorities and specialists of tomorrow.

ROBERT W. PENNAK

Boulder, Colorado
1952

# PREFACE TO THE SECOND EDITION

About 25 years have elapsed since the publication of the first edition of this book. During this long interval I have done my best to gather the pertinent references and literature that would be necessary for the production of this second edition. This period has been characterized by a greatly increased interest in the biology of our fresh-water invertebrates. As a result, the germane literature since 1952 amounts to more than 5000 titles in technical journals. Colleagues and professional acquaintances everywhere have been generous in sending me reprints of their works, and I am greatly in their debt for such thoughtfulness. I am grateful to Dr. John Bushnell for his comments and patience in helping me with anatomical and nomenclatural problems in the Ectoprocta. Dr. Perry Holt generously supplied the key to the genera of Branchiobdellida.

Several of the shortest chapters have required only few changes, but most chapters have had a major overhaul. Nearly all keys have been rewritten and made longer in accordance with maturing systematics. A few of the old figures have been deleted, especially where I could find or make more suitable illustrations. Many new figures have been added, especially to clarify difficult key couplets. Lists of references at the end of each chapter have been revised and enlarged; about half of the citations are new.

When we refer to fresh-water invertebrates of the United States, we are including complete data only for the 48 contiguous states. In general, however, this volume covers essentially all the Alaskan fauna. The Hawaiian fresh-water fauna is impoverished and poorly known.

The Ronald Press Co. and I have been surprised and continuously gratified by the acceptance of the first edition by such a very broad spectrum of users. We hope this second edition will receive similar acceptance.

My greatest personal reward derived from producing the two editions of this book is the host of professional acquaintances I have made, not only in the United States but also in many foreign countries.

ROBERT W. PENNAK

Boulder, Colorado
March 1978

# CONTENTS

# FRESH-WATER

# INVERTEBRATES

## of the United States

# Chapter 1

# INTRODUCTION

EXCLUDING Protozoa and all parasitic classes but including aquatic insects, it is estimated that the fresh-water invertebrate fauna of the United States consists of about 10,000 described species. Twenty-five years ago the figure was 8,500 species. Probably no aquatic biologist is of the opinion that this fauna is well known; certainly the total is bound to increase markedly in coming years, especially when the aquatic fauna of the western half of the country is more thoroughly studied. Although a few groups are fairly well known and reasonably stabilized, such as the Cladocera, Decapoda, Odonata, Gastropoda, and Pelecypoda, the majority of American fresh-water invertebrate groups are in the process of taxonomic refinement. In expanding taxa composed mostly of non-cosmopolitan species we are lagging behind European fresh-water taxonomy by about 10 to 20 years. All taxonomic questions aside, we are seriously lacking in our understanding of geographic distribution patterns, physiology, natural history, and ecology of fresh-water invertebrates in the United States. In a few groups, however, some remarkable progress has been made since the publication of the first edition of this book.

The organization of an introductory chapter to a text such as this one is a problem because of the wide variety of major topics that might profitably be considered. However, to avoid becoming too involved, the subject matter of this chapter is restricted to brief discussions of (1) origins of the fresh-water fauna, (2) fresh-water emigrants to the sea, (3) major distinctions between fresh-water and marine invertebrates, (4) atypical fresh-water habitats, (5) dispersal and barriers, and (6) food webs. This particular selection was made only after considerable indecision. For the most part, these are important topics *not* generally discussed in other texts dealing with fresh-water biology. It also appears advisable to eliminate topics more strictly of a limnological nature.

## ORIGINS OF THE FRESH-WATER FAUNA

The generalization that most major fresh-water invertebrate groups originated from marine ancestors is firmly established. Only a few groups, such as insects, mites, and pulmonate snails, are presumed to have clearly originated from terrestrial habitats. The fresh-water fauna is therefore appropriately termed an immigrant fauna.

The fundamental problem that must be solved before any marine animal can make its way into fresh water involves major physiological readjustments. Body fluids of most marine invertebrates are roughly isotonic with sea water; that is, the internal dissolved salt concentrations are similar to or slightly higher than the 3.5 percent average salt concentration of sea water. It is further true that the majority of marine invertebrates cannot endure much dilution of sea water. Fresh waters commonly contain about 0.01 as much salts as the ocean, and the internal fluids of fresh-water invertebrates usually contain 0.03 to 0.40 as much salts as the ocean. From an osmotic standpoint, water therefore tends to pass into the hypertonic tissues of fresh-water animals.

1

TABLE I. A COMPARISON OF THE TOTAL DISSOLVED SALT CONTENT OF FRESH WATERS, BRACKISH WATERS, AND SEA WATER. Maximum and minimum values are merely approximations. The most abundant salts in brackish waters are chlorides, carbonates, or bicarbonates, depending on the degree of brackishness. In fresh waters the most abundant salts are usually carbonates and bicarbonates. In alkali and saline lakes they are usually carbonates, bicarbonates, chlorides, and sulphates in varying proportions.

| | Percent concentration | | Milligrams per liter | |
|---|---|---|---|---|
| | Minimum | Maximum | Minimum | Maximum |
| Sea water | 3.5 | | 35,000 | |
| Brackish waters | 0.05 | 3.2 | 500 | 32,000 |
| Fresh waters | 0.001 | 0.05 | 10 | 500 |
| Alkali and saline lakes | 0.05 | 25.0 | 500 | 250,000 |

Consequently any successful fresh-water animal must have developed physiological mechanisms for maintaining a proper salt and water balance against this strong gradient.

It is difficult to imagine the appearance of such mechanisms de novo, and it is assumed that the transitions from marine to fresh-water environments were not sudden and rapid processes, but rather series of slow evolutionary processes occurring by way of psammolittoral and phreatic waters, littoral zones, marshes, swamps, and river estuaries where there are transition zones between salt and fresh water.

It should be borne in mind, however, that a river estuary is not a constant environment. Salinities, currents, tides, food, temperatures, and other ecological factors vary widely from time to time, and these conditions are by no means favorable to the evolution and gradual development of forms suited to fresh water. Pearse (1950) has stated the problem well:

An estuary has been called the doorway by which marine forms have populated fresh water. This statement is perhaps in part true, but an estuarine doorway is not wide open and easily passed. There are many difficulties to be surmounted. Many animals struggle long ages to get through and fail. Only a few attain fresh water by this route.

Ideal conditions for the invasion of fresh water are afforded by such places as the Baltic Sea, where there is a large area involved and where there is a permanent and very gradual transition from the sea to fresh water. Yet the Baltic has not a single endemic brackish water species of metazoan that has evolved since the most recent glaciation, although there are a very few subspecies or physiological varieties that may be endemic.

The generalization that marine invertebrates are isotonic with sea water is actually a slight exaggeration. Even pelagic, deep-sea, and the most primitive marine species maintain a dynamic steady state by which a difference in concentration of several ions commonly obtains across external membranes and which must be maintained through physiological regulatory processes. The internal concentrations of magnesium and sulfate ions are often much lower than those in sea water. Potassium concentrations may be considerably higher or lower than in sea water, and calcium and chloride are also variable. Many marine invertebrates have the remarkable ability to concentrate astonishing amounts of elements that are present in the sea water only as traces. Examples are vanadium, iodine, strontium, and bromine.

A wide range in type and degree of osmoregulatory control is found among littoral and estuarine invertebrates. Many species have limited ability to regulate the relative amounts of internal salt and water; their membranes are easily permeable so that the body fluids become more or less isotonic in diluted sea water, and death occurs rather promptly. A few stenohaline species can endure some dilution of sea water by regulating body volume and taking up more water into the tissues. A few other species can regulate their internal osmotic concentration only to a limited degree and venture into slightly brackish water; these species have a slight ability to remain hypertonic in diluted sea water. "Typical" brackish water species are euryhaline and can persist in habitats containing 30 to 85 percent fresh water. Most of these invertebrates maintain a more or less hypertonic internal salt concentration, regardless of the degree of brackishness of their surroundings. They include representatives of many groups, especially arthropods, mollusks, and various kinds of worms. The active absorption of salts is an important mechanism, and perhaps in some species there is actually physiological control of the amounts of water absorbed. Marine and brackish species transferred directly to fresh water usually live a few hours at most, but when the transition is made very slowly, over days or weeks, they may live for weeks or months in fresh water.

Figure 1 is a diagram showing the relative composition of the aquatic fauna in relation to salinity. It is one of the most striking paradoxes of fresh-water, brackish, and marine faunas that animals thrive well in either an environment that is very low in salts or one that is high in salts, but environments of intermediate salinities (brackish) have a poor fauna. From the standpoint of total number of all types of species present, it should be noted that the minimum appears at a salinity of $7^0/_{00}$ (7 parts per thousand), which is well toward the fresh-water end of the diagram in Fig. 1. This situation results from the fact that the number of fresh-water species drops very rapidly with a slight rise in salinity, whereas the number of marine species drops less rapidly with a decrease in salinity.

This diagram also poses a second paradox. It shows that specific brackish-water species, which occur chiefly or exclusively in such environments, are most abundant at salinities of 7 to $10^0/_{00}$ or about the place where the fresh-water forms decrease abruptly and where the total number of all species is smallest. This condition is not to be expected since most brackish-water species have obviously been derived from marine relatives and not from fresh-water relatives. It would be more logical to expect the maximum number of brackish species much farther toward the right in the diagram.

The invasion of fresh waters is a con-

tinuing process, and some American species are undoubtedly new arrivals or are in the process of becoming adapted to fresh waters. The colonial coelenterate *Cordylophora* and a few species in each of the following groups are all typical examples: polychaetes, grapsoid crabs, shrimps, isopods, clams, and snails. A comparable list may be cited for Europe, where a few species are known to have invaded fresh waters within historical times. The mitten crab of the Old World has taken up permanent residence in rivers and returns to the sea only to breed. With few exceptions, the new fresh-water forms are thought to be physiological varieties of their close marine relatives.

Several species of European crustaceans are marine in northern Europe and both brackish and fresh, or fresh alone, in central and southern Europe. Certain tropical areas, especially around the Bay of Bengal, Indonesia, the Malay Archipelago, Madagascar, and tropical America are relatively rich in species that have only recently made their way into fresh waters from the sea. It is presumed that constant temperatures and heavy rainfalls facilitate fresh-water invasions via estuaries. An alternate, newer theory emphasizes temperate and subarctic regions as more likely areas for entry into fresh water, chiefly because lower temperatures minimize the physiological effects of the various ions.

One other item should be discussed briefly in this section. The present writer (Pennak, 1963) has postulated a means by which micrometazoans could colonize fresh waters from the sea via the psammolittoral and phreatic habitats. As shown in Fig. 2, micrometazoans could possibly move from intertidal and subtidal zones into the marine psammolittoral and (1) thence into the phreatic ground water and thereafter inland to distant ponds or lakes via their psammolittoral, or (2) into the psammolittoral of an estuary, and thence progressively "upstream" in the river psammolittoral or deeper phreatic zone to inland fresh-water localities. Porous substrates below typical stream beds have long been known to have well-developed phreatic currents.

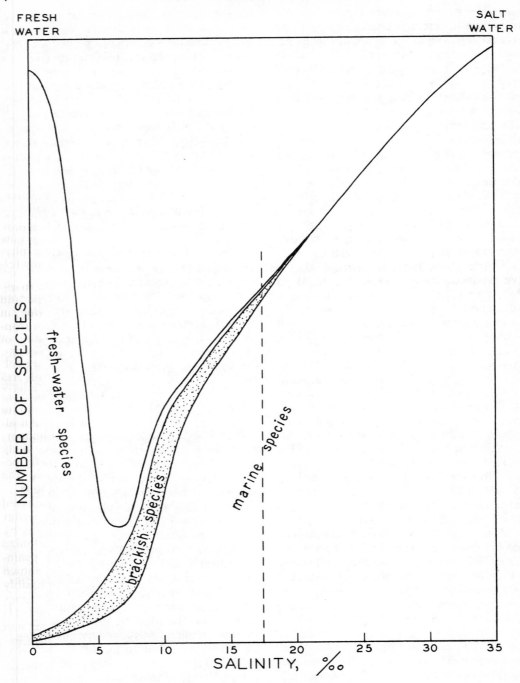

FIG. 1.–The composition of the aquatic fauna in relation to salinity of the environment. (Modified from Remane.)

FIG. 2.–Diagrammatic section of a marine shoreline in an area where the fresh phreatic waters are seeping into the salt water. *HTL,* high tide level; *LTL,* low tide level; brackish zone of mixing shown by stippling; thick, open, and thin arrows show relative amounts of salt, brackish, and fresh waters, respectively. (From Pennak, 1963, after Delamare Deboutteville, 1960.)

The phreatic brackish interstitial zone of mixing at the edge of the sea is relatively thin, but it is also relatively constant in position, and species in this habitat are in a much less hazardous situation than those species that must swim or crawl about on the substrate of an estuarine area. Pennak (1963) also emphasizes the relative rarity of the invasion of fresh waters from the standpoint of mutations and genetics. Ax and Ax (1970) discuss other aspects of the marine–fresh-water transition.

## FRESH-WATER EMIGRANTS TO THE SEA

Once established in fresh water, few invertebrates have returned to brackish water and only rarely to undiluted sea water. Little is known about the major barriers to such migrations, but presumably they are physiological, and perhaps chiefly osmoregulatory. Potassium salts, which are abundant in the sea, are toxic to fresh-water invertebrates, but this effect may be partly neutralized by magnesium compounds. An impervious exoskeleton is advantageous for migrations into salt waters.

Only a few rotifers, hemipterans, beetle larvae and adults, dipteran larvae and pupae (especially Culicidae, Ephydridae, and Chironomidae), and several caddis larvae have successfully invaded estuaries, brackish waters, and the intertidal zone. Diptera larvae have occasionally been dredged from 10 to 15 fathoms off the coast of England. In Samoa there is a peculiar dipteran that is submarine for its entire life cycle. A few marine water striders occur regularly on the surface film of the seas far away from land.

Biologically, insects are considered a most successful group. They exhibit endless adaptations, occur in enormous numbers, and are found in almost every type of habitat. Yet they have not been successful in colonizing the seas. With the exception of some of the groups noted above, a salt content in excess of 2.5 percent appears to be toxic. However, brackish ponds with salt contents ranging up to 1.0 percent are quickly colonized by "fresh-water" insects.

Occasionally typical fresh-water mollusks are reported from brackish estuaries. A few species of *Physa* and *Goniobasis* can endure up to 50 percent sea water, *Amnicola* and *Planorbis* up to 30 percent, and *Lymnaea* up to 25 percent.

# MAJOR DISTINCTIONS BETWEEN MARINE AND FRESH-WATER INVERTEBRATES

**Osmoregulation.** Continuing the discussion of the foregoing sections, one of the basic physiological distinctions centers around the occurrence of more specialized osmoregulatory mechanisms in fresh-water organisms. Since their internal fluids are hypertonic to the greatly dilute surrounding water, there is a continuous and rapid inflow of water through all permeable surfaces of the body. Such surfaces may be epithelia, cuticle, chitin, gills, and other structures. The relative amounts of water absorbed through these various types of surfaces differ greatly from one taxonomic group to another. In general, chitin and thick cuticle are relatively impermeable.

Contractile vacuoles, flame bulb systems, nephridia, and different types of glandular structures have the function of forming a highly dilute urine, which is excreted to the outside in considerable quantities. This urine is greatly hypotonic to the body fluids. By such means excessive water is prevented from accumulating in the body, and the relative concentrations of internal salts and water remain essentially constant. In a general way, fresh-water invertebrates are specialized for retaining their low ionic concentrations, even during long periods of inactivity. Figure 3 shows these relationships in a diagrammatic fashion.

Marine invertebrates usually have excretory organs that are basically more or less similar to those of their fresh-water relatives, but the urine they secrete is approximately isotonic with sea water and their body fluids. The fundamental problem that must be solved when a euryhaline animal invades fresh water is the physiological conversion of the osmoregulatory process to one that secretes dilute urine from hypertonic body fluids. Other things being equal, fresh-water invertebrates use more oxygen than their close marine relatives, probably because of the greater energy needed to maintain the proper internal osmotic pressure.

It is significant to note that contractile vacuoles are absent from most marine protozoans. Fresh-water isopods, amphipods, and decapods have larger excretory (osmoregulatory) glands than their marine relatives, and presumably this indicates greater activity and greater physiological and histological complexity.

Although the urine excreted by fresh-water invertebrates is highly dilute, it does contain traces of body salts. In most animals this loss is negligible, and is apparently made up from food and by the slow selective absorption of ions through body surfaces. In a few groups of fresh-water invertebrates, however, it has been shown that there is active absorption of ions by special parts of the body, particularly in snails, mussels, leeches, dragonfly nymphs, crayfish, and some Diptera larvae. At the same time the ability to retain body salts is sometimes quite striking. Many insects and crustaceans may be placed in distilled water and kept there for weeks at a time without any apparent harm.

Although fresh-water invertebrates are generally considered stenohaline organisms, this generalization is true only in the gross sense. "Fresh water" is highly variable in total salt content and in the relative quantities of different ions present, but many common species in almost all orders of fresh-water invertebrates may be found in waters whose total salt content ranges from 0.002 to 0.04 percent. This is actually a twentyfold difference in dissolved salts! With the exception of a few species adapted to highly saline inland waters, however, the osmoregulatory mechanisms of most fresh-water invertebrates quickly break down when they are placed in solutions containing in excess of 25 percent sea water (0.9 percent salt).

**Eggs.** Fresh-water macrozoans regularly produce much smaller numbers of eggs than their marine counterparts. This difference is especially notable among mollusks and crustaceans. Fresh-water snails produce only about 20 to 500 eggs at a time, whereas most marine species produce thousands or tens of thousands. A large oyster

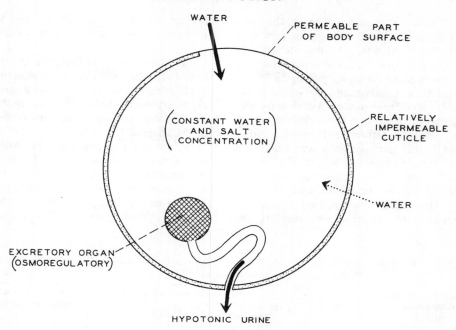

WATER

PERMEABLE PART
OF BODY SURFACE

CONSTANT WATER
AND SALT
CONCENTRATION

RELATIVELY
IMPERMEABLE
CUTICLE

WATER

EXCRETORY ORGAN
(OSMOREGULATORY)

HYPOTONIC URINE

FIG. 3.–Diagram showing the osmoregulatory water balance mechanism in a typical fresh-water invertebrate. (Greatly modified from Baldwin.)

produces up to 500 million eggs per year, but fresh-water mussels produce only several thousand to a maximum of 3 million. A large marine crab may carry several million eggs, a crayfish only 10 to 800. Correlated with this difference in numbers is a further difference in size, fresh-water eggs generally being larger than marine eggs.

In fresh-water species eggs are often carried by the parent until they hatch and the young are released. This is true of certain rotifers, and essentially all cladocerans, mussels, copepods, amphipods, and isopods, in addition to some species in other groups. The egg-carrying habit is also true of some marine species, but it is by no means as frequent as in fresh-water forms. Internal fertilization is much more common among fresh-water organisms.

With the exception of some cladocerans and insects, floating and planktonic eggs are almost unknown among fresh-water species; eggs are usually heavy and sink or remain on the bottom. In marine forms, however, the production of planktonic eggs is a common occurrence. It is also generally true that fresh-water eggs are

more yolky than marine eggs. A dense, tough covering or a gelatinous sheath is much more frequent among the former; many marine species have completely naked eggs.

**Larval stages.** The marine biologist is acquainted with a wealth of fascinating free-swimming larval forms produced by most worms, coelenterates, crustaceans, mollusks, echinoderms, and so on. Familiar examples are ciliated trochophores, pilidia, auriculariae, planulae, and an abundance of crustacean larval types. The fresh-water biologist, on the other hand, sees few larval forms. Larval fresh-water sponges and those of a few bryozoans and coelenterates are free swimming for only a very short time. Mussel glochidia are active only briefly. Copepods, Ostracoda, and Eubranchiopoda have series of free-swimming nauplius larvae. With the addition of certain insects, these few groups practically exhaust the list. In most fresh-water metazoans the young that hatches from the egg is a miniature unspecialized counterpart of the adult. Undoubtedly the greater abundance of yolky stored food in fresh-water eggs is correlated with the general lack of special larval stages. In marine groups where there is little yolk the newly hatched larvae must begin foraging promptly.

One theory advanced to explain the infrequency of fresh-water invasion by marine species is based on the vulnerability of marine larvae. Although free-swimming, they are unable to make their way upstream against river currents. Even if the adults were to breed in an estuary or river, the unattached larvae would be swept downstream. It is also thought that the larval metabolism and hypertonic tissues are un-

able to withstand the severe and variable ecological conditions in fresh waters.

**Phylogenetic differences.** It is quite true that the seas are phylogenetically much richer than fresh waters, and there are many major taxonomic categories that are confined to salt water or are predominantly marine (lists A and B of Table II). Only four small groups, on the other hand, are exclusively fresh-water. These are the Eubranchiopoda, the Syncarida, the several species of Thermosbaenacea, and one species of Spelaeogriphacea (known only from southern Africa). The Eubranchio-

TABLE II.   A Classification of the Invertebrate Kingdom According to Environments. Various taxa are listed, including phyla, classes, and orders.

A.   Exclusively marine
    Amphineura
    Anthozoa
    Archiannelida (?)
    Brachiopoda
    Cephalopoda
    Chaetognatha
    Cirripedia
    Ctenophora
    Cumacea
    Echinodermata
    Echiuroidea
    Enteropneusta
    Euphausiacea
    Gnathostomulida
    Kinorhyncha
    Leptostraca
    Monoplacophora
    Mystacocarida
    Nebaliacea
    Phoronidea
    Pogonophora
    Priapuloidea
    Pterobranchia
    Pycnogonida
    Scaphopoda
    Scyphozoa
    Sipunculoidea
    Stomatopoda
    Tanaidacea
    Xiphosura

B.   Predominantly marine, with few to rare fresh-water species
    Amphipoda
    Bryozoa
    Hydrozoa
    Mysidacea
    Polychaeta
    Porifera

C.   Chiefly marine but well represented in fresh waters
    Decapoda
    Pelecypoda

D.   Abundant representatives in both marine and fresh waters
    Copepoda
    Gastrotricha
    Ostracoda
    Sarcodina
    Suctoria

E.   Abundant representatives in both marine and fresh waters; terrestrial species rare
    Turbellaria

F.   With more fresh-water species than marine
    Ciliata
    Mastigophora
    Tardigrada

G.   Predominantly fresh-water; marine species few to rare
    Cladocera
    Hydracarina
    Nematomorpha
    Rotatoria

H.   Exclusively fresh-water species
    Eubranchiopoda
    Spelaeogriphacea
    Syncarida
    Thermosbaenacea

J.   Chiefly marine but with a few fresh-water and terrestrial species
    Nemertea

K.   Numerous marine, fresh-water, and terrestrial species
    Gastropoda
    Hirudinea
    Isopoda
    Nematoda
    Oligochaeta

L.   Chiefly terrestrial, but with many fresh-water representatives; few marine species
    Insecta

M.   Exclusively terrestrial
    Acarina (excluding Hydracarina in the broad sense)
    Other arachnid orders
    Chilopoda
    Onychophora
    Progoneata (a few rare marine millipedes)

N.   Exclusively parasitic
    Acanthocephala
    Cestoidea
    Linguatulida
    Mesozoa
    Myzostoma
    Sporozoa
    Trematoda

poda are unusual because some species are found in salt-poor waters (e.g., tundra ponds), whereas others are restricted to highly saline inland waters. The Rotatoria, Nematomorpha, Cladocera, and Hydracarina have so few marine representatives, however, that these might just as well be considered fresh-water groups. Because colonization of fresh waters probably began earlier than Devonian times, it is significant that a longer list of fresh-water groups has not made its appearance.

With few exceptions, those taxonomic categories that are well represented in both environments are much richer in species in marine waters than in fresh waters. This is especially true of the Porifera, Hydrozoa, Bryozoa, Polychaeta, Mysidacea, Amphipoda, Decapoda, Pelecypoda, Copepoda, Isopoda, and Gastropoda.

For the sake of completeness, Table II also includes strictly terrestrial and parasitic groups, and it is notable that these lists are quite short.

**Size.** As a whole, the marine fauna consists of a much greater percentage of large species. To anyone who has collected in both environments this is a striking difference, especially among coelenterates, worms, crustaceans, and mollusks. Possibly this size difference is the chief reason why marine invertebrate experimental physiology is so far advanced over the physiology of fresh-water invertebrates, since larger species are much more adaptable for many kinds of laboratory investigations.

**Coloration.** In general, fresh-water invertebrates are a rather monotonously colored lot. Most of the coloration is drab and subdued. Notable exceptions are a few brightly colored bryozoans, decapods, copepods, ostracods, amphipods, water mites, and leeches. This situation is in striking contrast to the bright coloration and distinctive patterns that are so common among marine coelenterates, worms of all kinds, crustaceans, and mollusks. No logical explanations seem to have been suggested to account for this fundamental genetic and physiological distinction.

**Devices for withstanding unfavorable environmental conditions.** A further striking difference between marine and freshwater animals is the frequent and regular occurrence in the latter of resting eggs, cysts, and desiccation adaptations and habits to withstand exceptionally unfavorable environmental conditions.

Such special adaptations as occur among marine animals are restricted chiefly to intertidal species and are for the most part merely special behavior patterns rather than distinctive morphological or life history adaptations. To withstand unfavorable periods when the tide is out and when heavy rain may be falling or when the temperature is unfavorable, marine intertidal species close their shells, burrow into the substrate, hide in crevices or macroalgae, or remain in tide pools.

Many special resistant and dormant devices among fresh-water invertebrates are multipurpose. The same one may withstand desiccation, sometimes for long periods; it may overwinter; it may be blown about and thus increase the geographic range of the species; or it may withstand adverse chemical conditions, such as lack of oxygen, high concentrations of dissolved salts, or high temperatures. Protozoan cysts, sponge gemmules, desiccated tardigrades, bryozoan statoblasts, and desiccated bdelloid rotifers are all examples of special resistant devices. Under appropriate conditions, dormant and resistant eggs or cysts of comparable functions may also be produced by coelenterates, some turbellarians, nemerteans, gastrotrichs, rotifers, many crustaceans, and some oligochaetes.

Another common measure taken by fresh-water invertebrates is the habit of burying themselves in the substrate in a torpid state during dry or cold conditions. Some species secrete a protective layer of mucus. Examples are leeches, some snails, some copepods, a few ostracods, and some water mites.

**Neuston.** The surface film of salt water is virtually uninhabited by small metazoans, but the numerous fresh-water organisms associated with the surface film either constantly or intermittently constitute a special community, the neuston. Many hemipterans, collembolans, and even a few spiders run about on the upper face of the surface film, and some cladocerans and Protozoa are regularly attached to the underface of the film. Visitors to the film for varying lengths of time include dipteran larvae and pupae, hemipterans, beetles, planarians, hydras, a few ostracods, and some snails. The surface film is visited chiefly for food or to make brief contact with air in order to renew the supply of gaseous oxygen held on the surface of the body or in the tracheal system.

**Bioluminescence.** The phenomenon of bioluminescence is common in a variety of animals, including representatives of about 40 different and widely scattered orders. Most of these animals are marine, but there are a few terrestrial groups. In fresh waters, however, the physiological mechanisms responsible for bioluminescence have almost never evolved, and the process is very rare. Only four species of semi-aquatic firefly larvae, one New Zealand fresh-water limpet, and a fresh-water shrimp in western People's Republic of China are bioluminescent.

**Euroky of fresh-water invertebrates.** If estuarine habitats are omitted, even the most casual comparison of marine and fresh-water environments emphasizes the much greater variations in ecological factors in the latter. This generalization holds true from one comparable fresh-water habitat to another as well as from time to time within the same habitat. Seasonal and vertical temperature gradients in lakes and the greater variations in quiet shallows of ponds are much more pronounced than in salt water. Currents may vary seasonally from imperceptible to torrential in the same stream with accompanying variations in suspended silt. Stream invertebrates in general are capable of withstanding the severity of violent spring runoffs, intermittent cloudburst waters, and even short-term industrial pollution incidents produced by ions that are normally considered highly toxic. Other chemical conditions, including dissolved salts, dissolved organic matter, dissolved oxygen, and pH are highly variable and cannot be compared with the more monotonous conditions in typical marine habitats. Drying up of the habitat is a frequent and important hazard.

In general, therefore, our fresh-water invertebrates consist of a group of euroxkous species that are physiologically, morphologically, and behavioristically adapted for maintaining themselves under trying circumstances that would be disastrous or impossible for the great majority of marine forms.

## ATYPICAL FRESH-WATER HABITATS

As a whole, fresh-water habitats are greater in variety (and often in complexity) than those of the marine environment, especially when the former include the complete series of running water habitats and many small, peculiar types of bodies of water.

If one is interested in collecting a wide variety of fresh-water invertebrates, the most favorable locations are small, weedy lakes and ponds. Such habitats afford large numbers of niches occupied by a correspondingly large variety of animals, especially mollusks, aquatic insects, crustaceans, and many representatives of the worms and wormlike groups. Food and population relationships are intricate, and presumably this complexity is the chief reason why so little comprehensive ecological work has been done on ponds and small lakes.

At the other extreme are highly specialized bodies of water in which one or more ecological conditions are so severe that the fauna is restricted to a small number of species. Frequently, however, these few species attain great population densities, perhaps because of the lack of interspecific competition.

There is little advantage to be gained

here by outlining the many divisions and subdivisions of fresh-water communities. Several such outlines may be found in certain standard ecology texts. It may be worth while, nevertheless, to characterize some of the more peculiar habitats that represent extremes in ecological conditions. As compared with the usual sort of fresh-water habitat, these peculiar habitats are characterized by less variable ecological conditions.

**Alkali and salt lakes.** Alkali and salt lakes and ponds are common in many areas of the western states, especially where there are closed drainage basins, semiarid conditions, and soils containing large quantities of soluble salts. Depending on surrounding soil chemistry, these waters may contain large quantities of chlorides, sulfates, or carbonates, especially those of sodium, potassium, and calcium. The expressions "salt" and "alkali" lakes are by no means sharply defined and are often interchangeable, but in general where the dissolved salts are of such composition and concentration as to produce persistent pH readings in excess of 9.0, a body of water is referred to, in common usage, as an "alkali lake."

At low concentrations, up to about 1 to 3 percent dissolved salts, the fauna is still varied in species but much more restricted than in nonalkaline waters. Above this concentration species diminish rapidly in numbers, and the metazoan plankton becomes characterized by a few copepods and highly alkaline rotifers, particularly some species of *Brachionus* and *Hexarthra,* which may be extremely abundant. The insect fauna becomes highly restricted and consists mostly of Chironomidae, occasionally one species of *Aedes,* and a few beetles.

Great Salt Lake, which contains about 25 percent dissolved salt (chiefly sodium chloride), has been studied relatively carefully and has an extremely limited fauna. Protozoa include several ciliates, flagellates, and amoeboid forms; metazoans consist of only two species of *Ephydra* (the brine fly) and *Artemia salina* (the brine shrimp). *Artemia* populations sometimes attain an average density of 50 individuals per liter. In contrast to the situation in most normal lake beaches, no interstitial micrometazoan fauna has been found in the sandy beaches of Great Salt Lake.

**Polluted waters.** Waters grossly polluted with organic matter, especially domestic or "city" sewage, likewise have a highly restricted fauna, one capable of thriving in very low concentrations of oxygen and high concentrations of dissolved and particulate organic matter. The chief metazoans are a few species of tubificid oligochaetes, red chironomid dipteran larvae, psychodid larvae, and the rat-tailed maggot larva, *Eristalis.* Sometimes the bottom of polluted rivers is literally covered with a waving, writhing mass of tubificids. This habitat also supports large populations of ciliates and colorless flagellates.

At a certain distance below the entry of domestic pollutants a river enters a "zone of recovery" in which the dissolved oxygen progressively increases and the polluting materials are oxidized or otherwise sufficiently removed from the water, especially as the result of bacterial action, so that the pollution fauna is slowly replaced by a "normal" river fauna. Depending on the intensity of pollution, size of the river, and so on, the zone of recovery may begin anywhere between one-quarter mile and 100 miles downstream from the source of pollution.

Biologists are prone to overlook the fact that the zone of recovery is frequently the most productive part of a flowage. It is here that the periphyton is most dense. Dense metazoan populations include such forms as *Physa*, isopods, planarians, leeches, amphipods, dipterans, caddis larvae, and mayfly nymphs.

In addition to organic pollution, the situation has been further severely aggravated by industrial toxicants, continuous silting, and more and more irrigation system water withdrawals. The history lesson of Lake Erie demonstrates the inherent recovery potential of our fresh-water fauna, but many of our waters have been continuously fouled for such long periods, especially by industry, that they are beyond recovery and are simply biological deserts.

For this reason those species indicated

as having highly restricted ranges in this volume should not be taken at face value, especially in areas where the tradition of lake and stream despoliation has had a long and continuing history.

Aquatic biologists have been searching many years for the ideal common species or group of "indicator" species that would be (1) present unequivocally in the absence of pollution and (2) absent unequivocally in the presence of pollution. Unfortunately, this search appears to be a lost cause chiefly because of the eurokous nature of most species and because of individual differences within the same species. We are therefore forced to rely on facies or clusters of clean-water species and polluted-water species, differing in composition from one area to another, but nevertheless serving as rough indicators of relative purity or pollution.

**Subterranean waters.** Subterranean streams, cave ponds, and artesian wells sometimes contain endemic, primitive, or highly specialized amphipods. isopods, decapods, copepods, and turbellarians. The Ozarks and similar limestone areas are particularly rich in underground aquatic habitats. Most subterranean species are colorless, translucent, or whitish; eyes are nonfunctional or absent; tactile structures are often well developed and include long antennae and abundant long setae. The subterranean environment is completely monotonous, with constant ecological conditions. Basic food materials consist of fungi and small bits of organic debris washed underground. Populations are generally small, owing to the greatly limited food supply.

Endemic subterranean species are thought to have been derived from ancestral surface species that underwent evolutionary change and specialization concomitantly with the gradual submergence of their surface drainage habitats. Compared with Europe, little is known of the subterranean microcrustacean fauna of the United States, but we do have a rich fauna. It should be added that accessible subterranean streams and ponds usually also contain common species that are regular members of aquatic communities on the surface of the ground.

**Phreatic and psammolittoral waters** These waters are ecologically closely related to subterranean waters, but are characterized by species that are generally smaller, including rotifers, tardigrades, gastrotrichs, mites, copepods, syncarids, and microturbellarians. These groups form the "interstitial community" living in the capillary water between sand and gravel particles 10 to 30 cm deep on the sandy beaches of lakes and streams (Fig. 4), and also in the waters of the phreatic zone below the surface of stream beds. Unfortunately, little work is being done on these habitats in the United States.

**Cold springs, spring brooks.** Typical cold spring communities are restricted to a small area at and just below the point where the water issues from the ground. As soon as it flows any distance as a spring brook it becomes warmer, loses its characteristic growth of water cress, and contains a different animal community. Depending on local conditions, the typical spring and spring brook fauna zone usually extends from 10 to 200 m below the source. Cold springs have an average temperature of about 8° in temperate areas, and the associated animals are mostly cold stenotherms. The list of characteristic animals is relatively small, including planarians, amphipods, and some of the following: beetles, caddis larvae, leeches, isopods, sphaeriid clams, small snails, and blackfly larvae. Frequently two or more of these species are numerically dominant. If the spring emerges from appropriate underground water courses in limestone areas it occasionally brings up typical subterranean species. The ecology of springs and spring brooks has been sadly neglected in the United States.

**Hot springs.** In addition to their high temperatures (about 35°), hot springs are often characterized by large quantities of dissolved salts. Sometimes the water is also high in dissolved carbon dioxide, hydrogen sulfide, or sulfur dioxide. Thus it is often difficult to distinguish between the limiting effects of temperature and the limiting effects of other ecological factors. In general, however, 25° to 30° seems to be the dividing

FIG. 4.–Optical section of a small portion of a sandy beach, 15 cm deep and 150 cm from the water's edge, showing relative sizes of sand grains and some of the common micrometazoans. *1*, rotifers; *2*, gastrotrichs; *3*, tardigrade; *4*, nematode; *5*, harpacticoid copepod. (From Pennak, 1939.)

line between a rich fauna at lower temperatures and a poor fauna at higher temperatures. Unlike cold springs, there do not seem to be any typical genera or species in hot springs, nor are hot spring animals ever abundant. Beetles are among the most characteristic metazoan inhabitants, many species having been reported from a wide variety of hot springs in the western states. Diptera larvae, especially Chironomidae, are also common inhabitants, along with an occasional culicid or stratiomyid. Sometimes a few Hemiptera and Odonata may be collected. Most such records of insects are from springs whose temperatures range from 37° to 50°. Other arthropods include amphipods, ostracods, and Hydracarina reported from springs with temperatures between 32° and 51°. Micrometazoans are often present in exceptionally hot water, a few nematodes and rotifers having been taken as high as 60°. Since the thermal death point of most fresh-water invertebrates is between 30° and 40°, many hot spring animals must have developed considerable thermal acclimation.

## DISPERSAL AND BARRIERS

The successful establishment of the ancient marine ancestors of fresh-water animals in swamps and near estuaries was actually only the beginning of the story. From such footholds they must have developed a higher degree of euroky as they expanded to occupy new inland habitats.

Migration up and downstream throughout a single drainage system is comparatively easy for many fresh-water invertebrates over a long period of time. Superficially, it would appear that they are "landlocked" in separate drainage systems, with little migration from one to another. In the long-time viewpoint, however, land barriers between different lakes and rivers are not effective for most groups within the confines of a single continental land mass. The ability of almost all microscopic species to form thick-shelled eggs, cysts, or resting stages that withstand partial drying or desiccation is a primary factor in ease of dispersal. Such small resting bodies are easily picked up and wind blown overland for long distances. If they drop into a favorable aquatic habitat with the appropriate combination of ecological conditions, they again become active and may produce a new population nucleus.

The literature contains scattered but authentic records of live fish being transported overland by storms, tornadoes, and other strong winds, and there is no reason to doubt that plankton and bottom invertebrates are transported in the same manner. Much of the "dust" of dust storms is organic debris, and it is not improbable that a small fraction consists of cysts and eggs. Ducks, shore birds, and aquatic insects are now known to be important for increasing the ranges of many groups, and the literature contains many accounts of such transport. Both resting and active stages are transported in the detritus and mud that frequently sticks to the appendages. Snails are frequently found on migratory birds, and there is one authentic record of a 2½-ounce live mussel being transported overland by a duck! Many microzoan cysts are carried to new habitats via the intestinal tract of birds.

Adult aquatic insects capable of flight easily migrate overland, often in what appears to be a completely random fashion, and come to occupy suitable new areas. Sometimes such flights are greatly aided by winds. Entomologists report collecting adult aquatic beetles and hemipterans five miles or more from the nearest open ponds. Occasionally such reports are for desert or semiarid regions. The surface of a concrete walk near the writer's home has a slight depression about 80 cm in diameter which fills with water with every shower. On several occasions aquatic beetles have been found in this puddle, and the nearest spot from which they could have come is a pond more than a kilometer distant.

Anyone who follows the biological development of a new, man-made reservoir is bound to be impressed with the promptness with which the reservoir becomes colonized with aquatic animals. Stock tanks and stock ponds, newly constructed in grazing lands where the nearest water is 10 km away, quickly acquire a varied invertebrate population.

Some highly eurokous and vagile species, mostly microscopic, have spread so effectively that they are essentially cosmopolitan and occur the world over in suitable habitats. The list includes a great many Protozoa and Rotatoria, several sponges, *Paracyclops fimbriatus,* perhaps *Plumatella repens,* a few oligochaetes, some Tardigrada, and several Cladocera, such as *Daphnia longispina* and *Chydorus sphaericus.* Many more species could be added to this list.

The fresh-water invertebrate faunas of North America and Europe, and to some extent northern Asia, have many of the species in the following groups in common: Protozoa, Rotatoria, Tardigrada, Bryozoa, Oligochaeta, and Cladocera. American gastrotrichs and nematodes are so poorly known that their European affinities are not established. In all the other major taxonomic groups with low vagility, however, the great majority of species that occur in the United States are endemic and are not found in Europe.

The zoogeographic distribution of fresh-water invertebrates has been rather well investigated in Europe, and zoogeographic regions have been suggested for several taxonomic groups, especially some of the orders of crustaceans and insects, and the mollusks. Numerous distribution patterns have been correlated with the effects of the advances and retreats of glaciers on the European continent. In the United States, however, comprehensive studies of fresh-water invertebrate zoogeography are largely lacking, with the notable exceptions of the mollusks, decapods, and perhaps several other groups.

Europe, Asia, and Africa have certain very ancient lakes where primitive species have been preserved and where geographic isolation has been effective for such a long time that independent speciation has resulted in many unique and endemic species, especially among Porifera, Turbellaria, Oligochaeta, Gastropoda, and crustaceans. Some of the better known lakes of this type are Baikal in Asia, Tanganyika and Nyasa in Africa, Ochrid in Jugoslavia, and the lakes of the Malili River system in the central Celebes. No such ancient lakes occur in the United States.

## FOOD WEBS

During the past generation the literature of aquatic biology has been replete with "productivity" and "trophic level" studies. It is unfortunate that most of these studies are misleading because they (1) are seasonal rather than year-round, (2) have been conducted on complex (rather than simple) ecosystems, and (3) are based on only a fraction of the species making up a particular ecosystem. As a consequence, the generalizations postulated in many of these investigations are open to doubt and modification. Actually a much more fruitful approach of population dynamics and interrelationships involves habitats characterized by few species and few niches. Examples are alkali and saline ponds, relatively barren alpine lakes, spring brooks, very small ponds, warm springs, small mountain streams. Using such bodies of water, it should be relatively easy to determine food habits of individual species and to make quantitative estimates of populations. Productivity indexes, food cycles, energy transfers from one trophic level to another, species interactions, and seasonal population fluctuations are all important ecological concepts that should be derived from such studies on a *year-round basis*. It is important to note that the measurement of associated physical and chemical factors in small streams, lakes, and ponds is simpler than in more complex types of aquatic habitats and in terrestrial habitats.

Nevertheless, even in the simplest aquatic habitats the determination of pyramids of numbers and food chains (or better "food webs") is an involved problem, and only a very few thorough and inclusive studies have been attempted. The great majority of trophic investigations are concerned with only a few energy or biomass transpositions, the remainder being only roughly estimated. In any such study the basic role played by detritus and bacterial action should not be minimized. In a schematic fashion Fig. 5 shows the fundamental food interrelationships for any aquatic habitat, regardless of size and complexity. Only recently have aquatic ecologists come to realize the overwhelming role of detritus in the food web. The significance of the various segments of this diagram vary enormously from one habitat to another. Some habitats, for example, have few or no fishes; other habitats have no rooted aquatics or a poor substrate fauna.

The solid lines in Fig. 5 indicate consumption or utilization as food. Broken lines indicate death and disintegration, or defecation by animals. The dotted line indicates disintegration of detritus as the result of certain bacterial activities. The circle arrows originating and ending at "zooplankton," "fish," and "substrate fauna" are meant to show that certain species in each of these categories are carnivorous and feed on other individuals within the same category. Actually each such category may represent two, three, or more trophic levels. "Substrate fauna" includes all bottom invertebrates as well as the protozoans, micrometazoans, and macrometazoans associated with the surface of rooted aquatic plants and other objects. By inference, "bacteria" also includes molds and their activities.

For simplicity, certain minor aspects of this food web have been omitted. For example, the contribution of excretory ma-

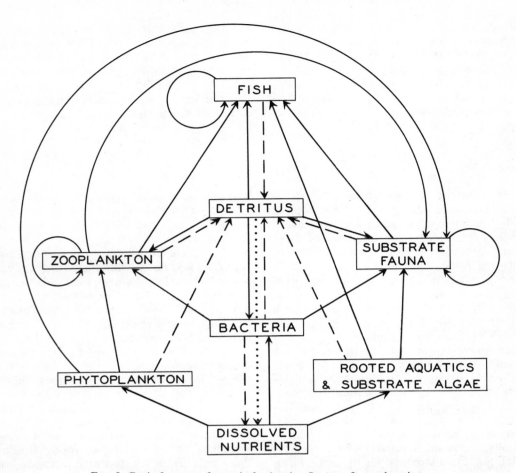

FIG. 5.–Basic features of aquatic food webs. See text for explanation.

terials to the main reservoir of dissolved nutrients is not shown. By inference, "fish" should include other vertebrates such as frogs, salamanders, and turtles.

Not shown, but nevertheless intimately concerned with the continuing balance within the web, are the nitrogen, sulfur, and phosphorus cycles. These are fundamentally similar to the same cycles operating in terrestrial habitats.

Following is a selected list of general references. It includes (1) items referring specifically to the content of this introductory chapter, (2) texts covering some of the same fields as the present manual, (3) important accessory texts covering fields relating to the study of fresh-water invertebrates, (4) periodical references and texts covering major phases of fresh-water invertebrate biology, and (5) a few references giving laboratory and field methods. Some references are recent; others are old classics.

## GENERAL REFERENCES

ADOLPH, E. F. 1925. Some physiological distinctions between fresh-water and marine organisms. *Biol. Bull.* **48**:327-335.

AMERICAN PUBLIC HEALTH ASSOCIATION. 1971. *Standard Methods for the Examination of Water and Sewage*. 13th ed. 874 pp. New York.

AX, P., and R. AX. 1970. Das Verteilungsprinzip des subterranen Psammon am Übergang Meer—Susswässer. *Mikrofauna des Meeresbodens* **1**:1–51.

BADE, E. (n.d). *Das Süsswasseraquarium. Die Flora und Fauna des Süsswasser und ihre Pflege im Zimmer-Aquarium.* 5th ed. 1212 pp. Berlin.

BALDWIN, E. 1948. *An introduction to comparative biochemistry.* 164pp., Cambridge Univ. Press, Cambridge, England.

BARNES, T. C., and T. L. JAHN. 1934. Properties of water of biological interest. *Quart. Rev. Biol.* **9**:292–341.

BEADLE, L. C. 1943. Osmotic regulation and the faunas of inland waters. *Biol. Rev.* **18**:172–183.

———. 1969. Osmotic regulation and the adaptation of freshwater animals to inland saline waters. *Proc. Int. Assoc. Theor. Appl. Limnol.* **17**:421–429.

BICK, H., et al. 1972. Das Zooplankton der Binnengewässer. *Die Binnengewässer* **26**(1):1–294.

BOND, R. M. 1933. A contribution to the study of the natural food cycle in aquatic environments. *Bull. Bingham Oceanogr. Coll.* **4**:1–89.

BRAUER, A. 1909–1912. *Die Süsswasserfauna Deutschlands.* 19 vols. by 32 authors. Jena, Germany.

BROOKS, J. L. 1950. Speciation in ancient lakes. *Quart. Rev. Biol.* **25**:30–60, 131–176.

BRUES, C. T. 1932. Further studies on the fauna of North American hot springs. *Proc. Am. Acad. Arts Sci.* **67**:185–303.

CAIRNS, J., and K. L. DICKSON (eds.). 1973. *Biological methods for the assessment of water quality.* A.S.T.M. Special Tech. Publ. **528**:1–256.

CARPENTER, K. E. 1928. *Life in inland waters.* 267 pp. Sidgwick and Jackson, London.

COKER, R. E. 1954. *Streams lakes ponds.* 327 pp. Univ. North Carolina Press, Chapel Hill.

DOUGHERTY, E. C., and L. G. HARRIS. 1963. Antarctic micrometazoa: fresh-water species in the McMurdo Sound area. *Science* **140**:497–498.

DUNDEE, D. S., et al. 1967. Snails on migratory birds. *Nautilus* **80**:89–91.

EDMONDSON, W. T., and G. G. WINBERG. 1971. *Secondary productivity in fresh waters.* I.B.P. Handbook **17**:1–358.

ELLIS, M. M., B. A. WESTFALL, and M. D. ELLIS. 1946. Determination of water quality. *U. S. Fish and Wildlife Serv. Res. Rep.* **9**:1–122.

EYFERTH, B. 1900. *Einfachste Lebensformen des Tier- und Pflanzenreiches,* 3d ed. 584 pp. Braunschweig, Germany.

FREY, D. G. (ed.). 1962. *Limnology in North America.* 734 pp. Univ. Wisconsin Press, Madison.

FURNEAUX, W. 1906. *Life in ponds and streams.* 406 pp. Longmans, New York.

GALTSOFF, P. W., et al. 1937. *Culture methods for invertebrate animals.* 590 pp. Dover, New York.

GOLTERMAN, H. L. 1969. *Methods for chemical analysis of fresh waters.* I.B.P. Handbook **8**:1–166.

HARNISCH, O. 1951. Hydrophysiologie der Tiere. *Die Binnengewässer* **19**:1–299.

HART, C. W., and S. L. H. FULLER (eds). 1974. *Pollution ecology of freshwater invertebrates.* 389 pp. Academic, New York.

HENTSCHEL, E. 1909. *Das Leben des Süsswassers.* 336 pp. Munich, Germany.

HORA, G. L. 1930. Ecology, economics, and evolution of the torrential fauna. *Philos. Trans. Roy. Soc. Lond.* **218B**:171–282.

HUBALT, E. 1927. Contribution a l'étude des invertebres torrenticoles. *Bull. Biol. Fra. Belg., Suppl.* **9**:1–390.

HUSMANN, S. 1967. Klassifizierung mariner, brackiger und limnischer Grundwasserbiotope. *Helgolander wiss. Meeresunters.* **16**:271–278.

———. 1975. *First international symposium on groundwater ecology.* 232 pp. Swets Publ. Service, Amsterdam.

HUTCHINSON, G. E. 1957. *A treatise on limnology. Vol. I. Geography, physics, and chemistry.* 1015 pp. Wiley, New York.

———. 1967. *Vol. II. Introduction to lake biology and the limnoplankton.* 1115 pp. Wiley, New York.

———. 1975. *Vol. III. Limnological botany.* 660 pp. Wiley, New York.

HYNES, H. B. N. 1960. *The biology of polluted waters.* 199 pp. Liverpool Univ. Press, Liverpool.

———. 1970. *The ecology of running waters.* 555 pp. Univ. Toronto Press, Toronto.

ILLIES, J. (ed.). 1967. *Limnofauna Europaea.* 474 pp. Gustav Fischer Verlag, Stuttgart.

JACOBS, W. 1935. Das Schweben der Wasserorganismen. *Erg. Biol.* **11**:131–218.

JOHANNES, R. E., and M. SATOMI. 1967. Measuring organic matter retained by aquatic invertebrates. *J. Fish. Res. Board Can.* **24**:2467–2471.

KENK, R. 1949. The animal life of temporary and permanent ponds in southern Michigan. *Misc. Publ. Mus. Zool. Univ. Mich.* **71**:1–66.

KROGH, A. 1939. *Osmotic regulation in aquatic animals.* 242 pp. Cambridge, England.

———. 1941. *The comparative physiology of respiratory mechanisms.* 172 pp. Univ. Pennsylvania Press, Philadelphia.

LAMPERT, K. 1925. *Das Leben der Binnengewässer.* 3d ed. 892 pp. Leipzig.

LUCAS, C. E. 1947. The ecological effects of external metabolites. *Biol. Rev.* **22**:270–295.

MACAN, T. T. 1961. Factors that limit the range of freshwater animals. *Biol. Rev.* **36**:151–198.

———. 1963. *Freshwater ecology.* 338 pp. Longmans, London.

———. 1975. *Life in lakes and rivers.* 3rd ed. 320 pp. Collins New Naturalist, London.

MACKENTHUN, K. M. 1973. *Toward a cleaner aquatic environment.* 273 pp. U.S.E.P.A. Office of Air and Water Programs.

MAGUIRE, B. 1963. The passive dispersal of small aquatic organisms and their colonization of isolated bodies of water. *Ecol. Monogr.* **33**:161–175.

MELCHIORRI-SANTOLINI, and J. W. HOPTON (eds.). 1972. Detritus and its role in aquatic ecosystems. *Mem. Ist. Ital. Idrobiol.* **29** (suppl.):1–540.

MORGAN, A. H. 1930. *Field book of ponds and streams.* 448 pp. G. P. Putnam's Sons, New York.

NAUMANN, E. 1931. Limnologische. Terminologie, *Handbuch der biol. Arbeitsmeth.,* Sect. 9, Part 8, Nos. 1–5:1–776.

NEEDHAM, J. 1930. On the penetration of marine organisms into freshwater. *Biol. Zentralbl.* **50**:504–509.

NICHOL, E. A. T. 1935. The ecology of a salt marsh. *J. Mar. Biol. Assoc. U.K.* **20**:203–261.

NIELSEN, A. 1950. The torrential invertebrate fauna. *Oikos* **2**:176–196.

PARK, T., et al. 1946. Dynamics of production in aquatic populations. *Ecol. Monogr.* **16**:311–391.

PAX, F. 1951. Die Grenzen tierischen Lebens in mitteleuropäischen Thermen. *Zool. Anz.* **147**:275–284.

PEARSE, A. S. 1928. On the ability of certain marine invertebrates to live in diluted sea water. *Biol. Bull.* **54**:405–409.

————. 1932. Animals in brackish water ponds and pools at Dry Tortugas. *Publ. Carnegie Inst. Wash.* **435**:125–142.

————. 1950. *The emigrations of animals from the sea.* 210 pp. Dryden, New York.

PENNAK, R. W. 1939. The microscopic fauna of the sandy beaches. In: *Problems of Lake Biology, Publ. Am. Assoc. Adv. Sci.* **10**:94–106.

————. 1963. Ecological affinities and origins of free-living acelomate fresh-water invertebrates. In: *The Lower Metazoa,* pp. 435–551, ed. by E. C. Dougherty, 478 pp. Univ. California Press, Berkeley.

PRESCOTT, G. W. 1969. *How to know the aquatic plants.* 171 pp. Brown, Dubuque, Iowa.

————. 1970. *How to know the freshwater algae.* 348 pp. Ibid.

PROCTOR, V. W. 1964. Viability of crustacean eggs recovered from ducks. *Ecology* **45**:656–658.

PROCTOR, V. W., et al. 1967. Dispersal of aquatic organisms: viability of disseminules recovered from the intestinal tract of captive killdeer. Ibid. **48**:672–676.

REMANE, A., and C. SCHLIEPER. 1971. Biology of brackish water. *Die Binnengewässer* **25**:1–372.

RUSSELL-HUNTER, W. D. 1970. *Aquatic Productivity.* 306 pp. Macmillan, New York.

SCHWOERBEL, J. 1967. Das hyporheische Interstitial als Grenzbiotop zwischen oberirdischem und subterranem Ökosystem und seine Bedeutung für die Primar-Evolution von Kleinsthöhlenbewornern. *Arch. Hydrobiol. Suppl.* **33**:1–62.

SEGERSTRÅLE, S. G. 1957. Baltic Sea. Pp. 751–800, in Treatise on marine ecology and paleoecology. *Mem. Geol. Soc. Am.* **67**:1–1296.

STEUER, H. 1910. *Planktonkunde.* 723 pp. Leipzig and Berlin.

STEWART, K. W., L. E. MILLIGER, and B. M. SOLON. 1970. Dispersal of algae, protozoans, and fungi by aquatic Hemiptera, Trichoptera, and other aquatic insects. *Ann. Entomol. Soc. Am.* **63**:139–144.

SUDIA, W. D. 1951. A device for rearing animals requiring a flowing water environment. *Ohio J. Sci.* **51**:197–202.

THIENEMANN, A. 1950. Verbreitungsgeschichte der Süsswassertierwelt Europas. *Die Binnengewässer* **18**:1–809.

THORPE, W. H. 1932. Colonization of the sea by insects. *Nature* **130**:629–630.

VALKANOV, A. 1968. Das Neuston. *Limnologica* **6**:381–404.

VON BRAND, T. 1946. *Anaerobiosis in invertebrates.* 328 pp. Normandy, Mo.

WARD, H. B., and G. C. WHIPPLE (ed. by W. T. Edmondson). 1959. *Fresh-water biology.* 1248 pp. Wiley, New York.

WARREN, C. F. 1971. *Biology and water pollution.* 434 pp. Saunders, Philadelphia.

WELCH, P. S. 1948. *Limnological methods,* 381 pp. Blakiston, Philadelphia.

WESENBERG-LUND, C. 1939. *Biologie der Süsswassertiere.* 817 pp. Vienna, Austria.

WETZEL, R. G. 1975. *Limnology.* 743 pp. Saunders, Philadelphia.

WHITTON, B. A. 1975. *River ecology.* 725 pp. Univ. California Press, Berkeley.

WOODBURY, A. M. 1949. Animals and salinity in the Great Basin. *Am. Nat.* **82**:171–187.

ZACHARIAS, O. 1891. *Die Tier- und Pflanzenwelt des Süsswassers.* 2 vols. 1–380, 1–369. Leipzig, Germany.

# Chapter 2

# PROTOZOA

BEGINNING with the observations on *Vorticella*, reported in 1675 in a letter to the Royal Society by the pioneer Dutch microscopist Leeuwenhoek, an enormous literature on the Protozoa has accumulated. There are, for example, more than 3000 papers on the genus *Tetrahymena* alone. Unquestionably this phylum has received more attention by zoologists than has any other fresh-water group. Because of the fact that a protozoan cell embodies all the fundamental properties of living matter, it has long been a convenient object for the study of numerous phases of anatomy, cytology, physiology, behavior, and heredity; taxonomy has also been rather thoroughly investigated, but ecology is a relatively neglected phase of protozoan biology, and is only recently receiving emphasis.

Protozoa occur in an extraordinary variety of habitats. Free-living species are found wherever there is water, from an accumulation of a few drops to the largest lakes and seas, and over a wide range of chemical and physical conditions. Parasitic species live in certain organs of most of the larger Metazoa that have been carefully examined. It is estimated that 25,000 valid species of Protozoa have been described, of which more than 7500 are ciliates.

The following discussion is based almost exclusively on free-living fresh-water Protozoa, and emphasis is placed on features that are utilized as key characters, but most of the generalizations apply to the phylum and classes as a whole. Physiology, morphology, and anatomy are discussed only briefly; these phases of protozoan biology are thoroughly covered in many texts and review articles. Indeed, electron microscopy has, in recent years, been responsible for an enormous increase in protozoan literature and countless reinterpretations of detailed protozoan anatomy.

**General characteristics.** All Protozoa are single-celled organisms, though many species form colonies consisting of several to thousands of individuals. With the exception of certain reproductive individuals, however, all the cells in a colony are fundamentally independent and similar in structure and function.

The physical nature of protoplasm is perhaps best studied in Protozoa. Essentially it consists of water in which are dissolved a wide variety of organic and inorganic materials and in which is suspended a variety of minute droplets and solid particles, the whole constituting a complex colloidal system. Fibrils, networks, alveoli, Golgi bodies, chondriosomes, and other granules and droplets larger than colloidal size serve to increase further the physical complexity. Viscosity is more or less variable and reversible from sol to gel states. Typical protozoan protoplasm is translucent and colorless or faintly tinted, but many species are colored by ingested foods, stored materials, or pigments such as chlorophyll. Thus green, yellowish, brown, gray, bluish, and reddish are common colorations.

Size ranges from about 5 microns to 5 mm, but the great majority of species are more than 30 microns and less than 300 microns long. Body shape is highly variable, but spherical, oval, elongated, and more or less flattened are the most common body forms. In flattened species the ventral surface is arbitrarily defined as that surface nearest the substrate and usually bearing the cytostome. Symmetry includes spherical, radial, and bilateral patterns, and asymmetry.

The major subdivisions of the Phylum Protozoa are as follows:

Subphylum Sarcomastigophora. Flagella, pseudopodia, or both types of locomotor organelles; one type of nucleus; sexuality syngamic, if present.

Superclass Mastigophora (flagellates). One or more flagella; solitary or colonial; asexual reproduction by binary fission; nutrition phototrophic, heterotrophic, or both. Key on page 36.

Class Phytomastigophorea. Usually with chromatophores; one or two flagella; amoeboid forms in some groups; mostly free-living.

Class Zoomastigophorea. No chromatophores; one to many flagella; amoeboid forms in some groups; free-living and parasitic.

Superclass Opalinata. Numerous rows of cilialike organelles; no cytostome; two to many nuclei of one type; all parasitic. Not treated in this manual.

Superclass Sarcodina (amoeboid forms). Pseudopodia typically present; flagella sometimes in developmental stages; cell naked or with external or internal supporting tests of skeletal elements; asexual reproduction by fission. Key on page 52.

Subphylum Sporozoa (sporozoans). With spores in the life cycle; single type of nucleus; cilia and flagella absent; all parasitic. Not treated in this manual.

Subphylum Ciliophora (ciliates and suctorians). With simple cilia or composite ciliary organelles; two types of nuclei; binary fission and several types of sexual reproduction. Key on p. 58.

Class Ciliata. Characters as above.

Subclass Holotrichia. Ciliation simple and uniform.

Subclass Peritrichia. Somatic ciliation absent in mature form, but oral ciliation conspicuous as rings around the cytostome; body often with a long contractile stalk; migratory ciliated larvae.

Subclass Suctoria. No ciliation in mature stage; sessile; attached to substrate by a noncontractile stalk; ingestion by means of suctorial tentacles; migratory larvae produced by budding.

Subclass Spirotrichia. Ciliation sparse; cirri common; buccal ciliation conspicuous, with adoral zone of membranelles.

The external surface of Sarcodina is usually a naked, thin, living plasmalemma, but in the ciliates and many flagellates there is also a protective pellicle of varied composition. In addition, both flagellates and Sarcodina often have a thicker shell, case, or armor composed of cellulose, jelly, tectin (pseudochitin), calcium carbonate, or silicon dioxide. Frequently an outer protective sheath or lorica is distinctly separated from the periphery of the cell. Sometimes the outer case consists of foreign particles imbedded in a homogeneous matrix.

In ciliates and Sarcodina the layer of protoplasm just below the bounding membrane is usually a relatively clear ectoplasm in contrast to the more granular endoplasm internal to it.

The nucleus is nearly always difficult to distinguish in living, unstained material. In the ciliates the macronucleus is granular, large, and of variable shape, ranging from round or oval to elongated, beaded, branched, or horseshoe shaped; the one or more micronuclei are very small. Sarcodina have a single type of nucleus; a few genera, such as *Pelomyxa* and *Actinosphaerium*, are multinucleate. The nucleus of free-living flagellates is single, vesicular, and usually more or less centrally located.

**Locomotion.** Typical Sarcodina move about by means of streaming movements and temporary extensions of the cell called pseudopodia. The mechanics of pseudopodial movement have been most extensively studied by Mast and his students, and by Jahn and Bovee. Adequate descriptions are included in most standard zoology texts and reference books.

Four types of pseudopodia are generally recognized, though there are intergradations and none of them can be clearly sep-

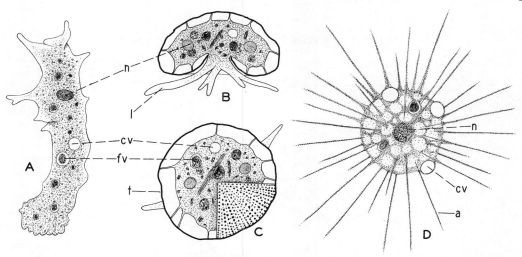

FIG. 6.–Typical Sarcodina. A, *Amoeba*; B, vertical optical section of *Arcella*; C, *Arcella*, showing partial horizontal section and partial external surface of test; D, *Actinophrys sol* Ehr. *a*, axopodium; *cv*, contractile vacuole; *fv*, food vacuole; *n*, nucleus; *l*, lobopodium; *t*, test.

arated from the others. Lobopodia are fingerlike, tonguelike, rounded, or branched; they contain both ectoplasm and endoplasm (Figs. 6A, C). Filopodia are more or less filamentous, usually pointed, and consist of ectoplasm only (Figs. 29E–G). Reticulopodia, or rhizopodia, are also filamentous and composed of ectoplasm but they are branching and anastamosing (Fig. 30D). Axopodia are semipermanent, owing to a relatively stiff axial rod, which in most cases ends internally in a small granule (Fig. 33).

In general, those Sarcodina having lobopodia move most rapidly, usually 0.5 to 3.0 microns per second, whereas those having other types of pseudopodia are more sluggish or do not move at all.

A flagellum is esentially a long, fine, whiplike protoplasmic thread that produces forward locomotion by spiral or undulating movements. Sometimes, however, the basal region is more or less rigid and only the distal half or tip moves about. Many Mastigophora have two flagella, both of which function in locomotion, but in some genera there are one to several accessory flagella that have little or no locomotor function. Accessory posteriorly directed flagella are thought to have a slight pushing or steering function in a few species.

The axial filament, or axoneme, typically consists of nine fibrils arranged in two compact, parallel bundles. The axoneme is surrounded by a sheath and a limiting membrane.

Flagella are commonly inserted at or near the anterior end of the cell, often in a groove, pit, or cytopharynx. The attachment is variable, complex, and sometimes double, but it is not visible in unstained specimens. Usually the flagellum originates in a basal granule just within the periphery of the cell. The basal granule may or may not be combined with another granule, the blepharoplast, just below. A fine fibril, or rhizoplast, sometimes connects the basal granule and blepharoplast with the edge of the nucleus.

Flagellates usually move at the rate of 15 to 300 microns per second. Under adverse environmental conditions the flagella may be lost, but regeneration occurs promptly when conditions are again favorable.

Fundamentally, cilia are similar to flagella, but there are several important differences. Cilia are much shorter, very abundant, and have only a single basal granule. They are arranged in longitudinal, diagonal, or oblique rows, and their movements are often coordinated so that waves of beats

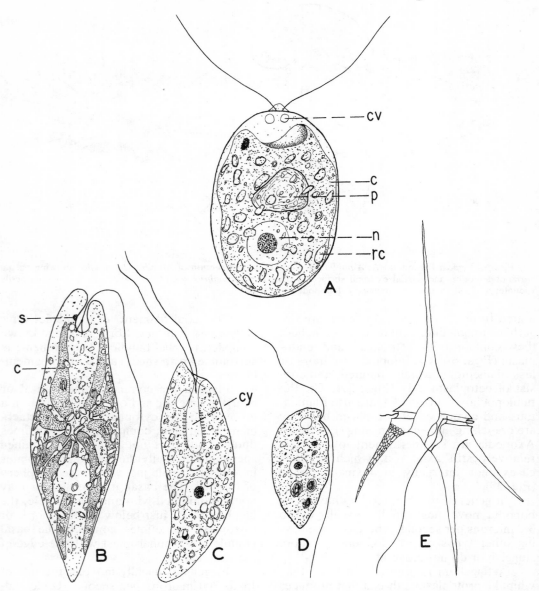

Fig. 7.–Typical Mastigophora. A, *Chlamydomonas*; B, *Euglena viridis*, Ehr. (chromatophores very difficult to distinguish in living animal); C, *Chilomonas paramecium* Ehr.; D, *Bodo*; E, *Ceratium hirundinella* (O.F.M.) with only a portion of shell sculpturing shown. *c*, chloroplast; *cy*, cytopharynx; *cv*, contractile vacuole; *n*, nucleus; *p*, pyrenoid; *rc*, reserve carbohydrate granules; *s*, stigma.

pass along the entire animal. In electron micrographs a cilium commonly appears to consist of a bundle of 11 (double) fibrils. A single cilium is thought to have a pendular or side-to-side movement, usually in one plane or with an oval pattern at the tip.

Ciliates move more rapidly than other Protozoa, the usual speed being 200 to 1000 microns per second.

Cilia may also be fused to form more complex structures. A membranelle, for example, is a double lamella of cilia completely fused into a flexible plate and found in the region of the cytostome, oral groove, or peristome (Figs. 9F, 41–44). Adoral membranelles occur in all ciliates except the Holotrichia.

Undulating membranes of ciliates range in size from delicate aggregates no broader than the length of an ordinary cilium to enormous balloonlike structures (Figs. 9F, 40E). An undulating membrane is composed of a single longitudinal row of fused cilia, but there is often a group of from two to as many as five or six such membranes in the peristomial area near the cytostome or in the cytopharynx.

Cirri are the most specialized ciliary organs and are particularly characteristic of the Hypotrichida. They are highly variable in size and are located more or less definitely on the ventral surface (Fig. 9G). According to their location, they are known as frontal, marginal, ventral, anal, and caudal cirri. A cirrus has an elongated conelike shape and consists of a tuft of fused cilia. Unlike other locomotor organelles, cirri move about in any direction, and consequently they are used for walking, running, jerking, and jumping movements.

In addition to true locomotion, many Protozoa possess pronounced powers of contraction and extension. These movements are usually the result of contractility of unspecialized protoplasm, but in many ciliates there are fine contractile fibrils, or myonemes, in the ectoplasm just below the surface of the body.

Many genera of ciliates, flagellates, and amoeboid Protozoa are normally sessile and attached to the substrate, either with or without a stalk, but frequently these Protozoa metamorphose into temporary "swarmer" stages that are capable of moving to new locations where they again attach to the substrate and assume the usual body form. A temporary, motile telotroch of a stalked, sessile ciliate is shown in Fig. 46C.

**Feeding, nutrition.** Those Protozoa that ingest solid particles of food, including bacteria, algae, other Protozoa, small Metazoa, or debris, are said to be holozoic. Many flagellates possess chromatophores

Fig. 8.–*Volvox*, a large colonial flagellate (×100); note mature colonies, young and old daughter colonies, and clusters of microgametes.

and chlorophyll and are plantlike, or photosynthetic, in their nutrition; carbon dioxide and water are absorbed from the surroundings and synthesized into carbohydrates in the presence of light and chlorophyll; this photosynthetic type of nutrition is called holophytic. From carbohydrates, and especially with the addition of absorbed nitrogen, phosphorus, and sulfur compounds, the other organic constituents of the cell are synthesized. Saprozoic nutrition involves absorbing dissolved salts and simple organic materials from the surrounding medium and synthesizing them into protoplasmic materials; this type of nutrition occurs in all classes of Protozoa. Parasitic nutrition is sometimes placed in a separate category, but since it usually involves the absorption of dissolved materials, it is essentially a specialized type of saprozoic nutrition. However, some parasites ingest particulate matter and might therefore be considered holozoic. Many Protozoa are mixotrophic; that is, they exhibit two of the preceding types of nutri-

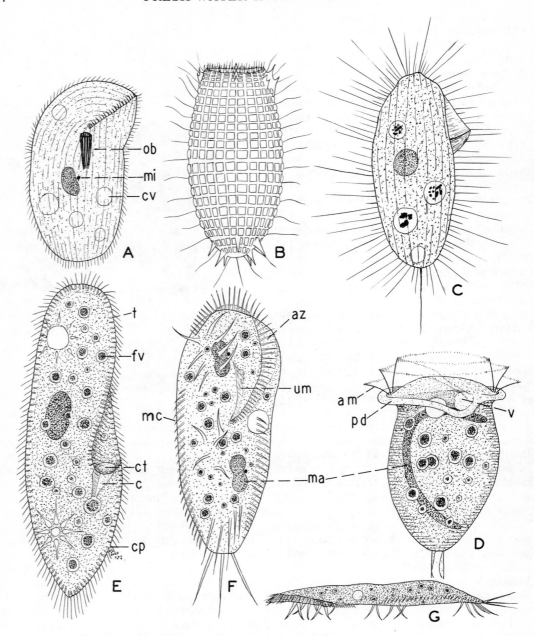

Fig. 9.–Typical Ciliata. A, *Chilodonella cucullula* (O.F.M.); B, *Coleps octospinus* Noland; C, *Cyclidium*; D, *Vorticella*; E, *Paramecium*; F, ventral view of *Stylonychia mytilus* (O.F.M.), showing eight frontal, five ventral, five anal, and three caudal cirri; G, lateral view of *S. mytilus*. *am*, adoral membrane; *az*, adoral zone; *c*, cytopharynx; *cp*, cytopyge; *ct*, cytostome; *cv*, contractile vacuole; *fv*, food vacuole; *ma*, macronucleus; *mc*, marginal cirrus; *mi*, micronucleus; *ob*, oral basket; *t*, trichocyst; *um*, undulating membrane; *v*, vestibule. (B modified from Geiman.)

tion. Some ciliates, for example, are both holozoic and saprozoic, and some flagellates are both holophytic and saprozoic. *Ochromonas* is a flagellate in which holozoic, holophytic, and saprozoic nutrition all occur.

Some protozoans, such as *Chilomonas, Polytoma, Polytomella,* and *Astasia,* are entirely saprozoic and ingest no particulate food; they depend entirely on organic and inorganic nutrients in solution, usually in the vicinity of decaying organic matter.

Holozoic Protozoa may be conveniently classified according to their general food habits. *Spathidium, Dileptus, Didinium,* and *Actinobolina,* for example, are all carnivorous ciliates that feed on other Protozoa, usually only certain species. *Frontonia, Chilodon,* and most Sarcodina are herbivores that feed on algae; many other genera are bacterial feeders. *Blepharisma, Spirostomum,* and *Stentor* are examples of omnivores that feed on all kinds of particulate matter, both living and dead. There are convincing data to show "selection" of certain types of food by some omnivorous ciliates, but in general such observations are variable and inconclusive.

Lobopodia commonly advance in such a way as to surround and enclose a food particle. The latter is then within the cell in a droplet of water, the whole constituting a food vacuole. Sometimes amoeboid Protozoa ingest particles by an invagination process when the particles come in contact with the general body surface. Occasionally large particles, such as algal filaments, are seen to "glide" into the cell by an "import" process. Pseudopodia of many amoeboid groups are sticky so that a food particle sticks to the general body surface on making contact and is then drawn within to form a food vacuole.

With few exceptions, the chlorophyll of holophytic flagellates is localized in chromoplasts (chloroplasts) which may be disc-, band-, bowl-, or cup-shaped, but sometimes the green color is masked by accessory yellow, orange, or brown pigments. A red pigment, hematochrome, often appears in some green flagellates, but it is distributed throughout the cytoplasm and is thought to be formed as a response to low concentrations of nitrogen and phosphorus. Pyrenoids are small proteinaceous bodies that are imbedded in chloroplasts and around which the carbohydrate products of photosynthesis accumulate as laminae or granules. After they are formed, these particles (glycogen, paramylum, or starch) are evidently available to the general cytoplasm as reserve foods. Green flagellates vary widely with respect to their specific nitrogen requirements. Most species can use ammonium and nitrate compounds, others require amino acids, and some are even able to use peptones. These three groups of green flagellates are sometimes termed photoautotrophic, photomesotrophic, and photometatrophic, respectively.

Although many green flagellates are obligate phototrophs, there are numerous species that can also be grown in the dark, provided the correct dissolved nutrients are available in the culture medium. The Zoomastigophorea and many nonphotosynthetic Phytomastigophorea are holozoic, saprozoic, or mixotrophic. Like green flagellates, the colorless saprozoic species differ widely in their nitrogen requirements. In the holozoic species small food particles come in contact with the surface of the cell and sink or are drawn inward, sometimes by definite pseudopodial action. Many flagellates, both green and nongreen, possess an anterior cytostome, cytopharynx, and reservoir through which the flagellum projects, but particulate food is taken into the cell through this opening in only a very few holozoic forms.

Though many ciliates are saprozoic or mixotrophic, the great majority are holozoic. Movement through the water as well as beating of cilia, membranelles of the peristome, and undulating membranes all serve to collect the food and bring it into the cytostome and cytopharynx. In raptorial genera, however, such as *Coleps, Didinium, Prorodon,* and *Lacrymaria,* the prey is relatively large, and current production has little to do with food getting. At the lower end of the cytopharynx the particles enter the cell proper as food vacuoles. In some ciliates, especially gymnostomes, the wall of the cytopharynx is stiffened by minute rodlike trichites that collectively form the cytopharyngeal basket (Figs. 36, 37).

Though the Suctoria are all holozoic and feed mostly on living ciliates, much remains to be learned about the precise mechanisms of feeding. The struggling prey is held tightly at the tips of the tentacles, and contact with the tentacles often (but not always) kills the prey in a matter of seconds, the rigid tentacles being presumed to secrete a potent toxin. American fresh-water species have only one type of tentacles; they are suctorial and often knobbed. Only a few of the tentacles attached to the prey serve as cytostomes and these enlarge to a diameter twice or more that of the nonsucking tentacles. The protoplasm flows through these hollow tentacles and is formed into food vacuoles as it enters the cell proper. The entire contents of even large ciliates may be sucked up in as little as 20 minutes. Suction is said to approxi-

mate 0.2 atm, although some investigators postulate mechanisms other than suction (Rudzinska, 1973). Tentacles may be localized in bundles or more generally over the body surface. Figure 11 shows a large suctorian feeding on *Paramecium*.

Many ciliates regularly or occasionally harbor minute intracellular green zoochlorellae in a symbiotic relationship. In a few species, and especially in *Paramecium bursaria*, this has been shown to be an obligatory association. There are also numerous holozoic flagellates and rhizopods that contain intracellular green symbionts.

**Digestion.** In holozoic species the ingested food organisms may be killed in a few seconds after being taken into the food vacuole or they may stay alive for as long as an hour. Digestive enzymes are released into the food vacuoles from the surrounding cytoplasm. A variety of protein- and carbohydrate-digesting enzymes have been demonstrated, but the occurrence of fat-digesting enzymes is difficult to prove though they are undoubtedly present.

In most Protozoa that have been carefully studied the hydrogen-ion concentration of the food vacuoles is variable but usually within the range of pH 4.0 to 7.6, most digestion being under acid conditions. Depending on the food supply and the activity of a protozoan, there may be few to many contained food vacuoles. As digested materials are absorbed into the cytoplasm through the membrane of the food vacuole the contents of the vacuole become progressively smaller, and the indigestible residue is voided through a temporary rupture in the cell membrane, though in ciliates and flagellates there is often a permanent pore, the cytopyge, for this purpose.

**Reserve foods.** Depending on ecological and physiological conditions, a protozoan cell may contain little to much reserve food. The type of reserve food materials depends largely on the mode of nutrition. In holozoic and saprozoic species it is usually glycogen or paraglycogen. Holophytic species variously store starch, paramylum, and lipids. Paramylum can be easily distin-

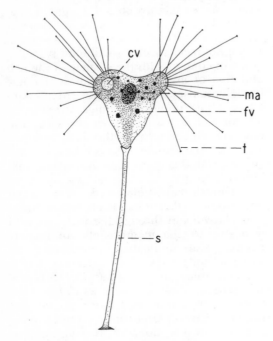

FIG. 10.–*Tokophrya lemnarum* Stein, a typical suctorian. *cv*, contractile vacuole; *fv*, food vacuole; *ma*, macronucleus; *s*, stalk; *t*, tentacle.

FIG. 11.–*Heliophrya* feeding on *Paramecium*. A, *Paramecium* escaping from a small *Heliophrya*; B, *Paramecium* caught by the tentacles of two different *Heliophrya*; C, D, F, and G, various feeding stages; G, deciliation of *Paramecium*; H, remnant of *Paramecium*; L, *Paramecium* about to escape from a tentacle. Note the wide variation in tentacular structure. (From Spoon et al., 1976.)

guished from starch by the fact that it does not stain blue with iodine.

**Respiration.** The great majority of Protozoa are aerobic, the oxygen being absorbed from the surroundings through the cell membranes. Nevertheless, it is probable that more than 90 percent of our freshwater species are capable of thriving in water that is less than 10 percent saturated with oxygen. Indeed, a great many species have been reported from anaerobic habitats such as sewage, the debris and mud of stagnant ponds, and the bottoms of lakes during periods of oxygen exhaustion, but these species are thought to be mostly facultative and temporary anaerobes capable of tolerating anaerobic conditions for variable periods but not able to maintain themselves indefinitely. The following genera, however, are known to have some obligatory anaerobic representatives: *Chlamydophrys, Vahlkampfia, Saprodinium, Mastigamoeba, Bodo, Holophrya, Trepomonas,* and *Metopus*. Under both permanent and temporary anaerobic conditions it is thought that energy is derived from reactions similar to fermentation processes.

**Excretion.** As in higher animals, the chief metabolic excretory products are water, carbon dioxide, and nitrogenous materials. Sometimes the latter are retained as granules or crystals for a variable time within the cell. It is now the general opinion that there are no special excretory organelles in Protozoa, but that dissolved excretory materials, notably urea, simply diffuse through the cell membranes into the surroundings.

**Contractile vacuoles.** These organelles are osmoregulatory devices that remove excess water from the cell. Since the internal salt concentration of fresh-water Protozoa is much higher than that of their surroundings, there is a continuous osmotic uptake of water through the cell membranes. The accumulation of water from the general cytoplasm and the release of water to the outside by the vacuoles therefore serve to maintain a constant internal salt-water balance.

Contractile vacuoles are found in all fresh-water Sarcodina and Mastigophora, and in all Ciliophora regardless of habitat. They do not occur in the Sporozoa or in most parasitic and marine Sarcodina and Mastigophora.

The Sarcodina have one or more contractile vacuoles of indefinite location. Each one starts out as a coalescence of several minute adjacent droplets. The small vacuole then grows, reaches a certain size, and bursts and releases its contents to the outside through a temporary rupture in the plasmalemma. New vacuoles appear in any part of the cell. In the Mastigophora there is a single small contractile vacuole. It is constant in location and usually anterior in the Phytomastigophorea and posterior in the Zoomastigophorea. Ciliophora have one to many contractile vacuoles, all constant in position and opening through permanent pores in the pellicle; sometimes these vacuoles are supplied by a complex system of collecting canals in the cytoplasm.

The rate of pulsation of a contractile vacuole is dependent on such factors as temperature, age, physiological state, food, salt concentration, and so on. In some Protozoa a volume of water equivalent to the volume of the entire cell may be voided in as short a time as two minutes; under other conditions and in other species an equivalent amount of water may be voided in 24 to 48 hours.

It is probable that insignificant quantities of dissolved nitrogenous wastes leave the cell in the expelled fluid of the vacuole, but this is merely incidental to the main osmoregulatory function.

**Irritability, behavior.** Basic perception and response to contact, food, gravity, light, chemicals, and so on are probably all due to the general irritability of protozoan protoplasm. Nevertheless many Protozoa have special receptors. The stigma, or eyespot, of some flagellates is a minute clump of granules with an adjacent light-sensitive area of cytoplasm; such stigmata commonly produce a directional locomotion toward a light source, as shown, for example, by the accumulation of *Euglena* along the lighted side of a culture jar set in a north window. Special cilia or bristles are thought to be touch receptors in some ciliates.

A great many observations have been made on protozoan behavior, but only a few general examples can be cited here. Favorable environmental conditions elicit no visible responses, but under unfavorable circumstances, especially where there are gradients, Protozoa generally move away from the unfavorable and toward the favorable conditions. *Paramecium* and many other ciliates exhibit "trial and error" or "avoiding" reactions. On coming in contact with an unfavorable medium or object, they stop, retreat, turn slightly, and resume locomotion in a new direction; such movements may be repeated until the protozoan reaches favorable conditions. A few ciliates exhibit negative geotaxis.

As a group, only the stigma-bearing flagellates show reactions to light. They are generally photopositive to weak or medium light sources but photonegative to strong lights. Other Protozoa are mostly indifferent to usual light sources, though some are photonegative to exceptionally strong light.

Transmission of impulses is a regular function of the protoplasm, but in many ciliates a special neuromotor system of conducting fibrils has been demonstrated. Essentially, such a system consists of very fine longitudinal and transverse fibrils connecting the basal granules of the cilia. Many fibrils come together and are more or less centralized in the region of the cytopharynx. The neuromotor system functions as a coordinating apparatus for movements of the cilia, but elasticity, support, and contraction are also suggested functions.

In addition to (or in place of) the neuromotor system, many ciliates possess a silverline system in the ectoplasm. This is a latticework or irregular network of granules and fibrils that can be detected only when the protozoan is subjected to dry fixation and impregnation with silver nitrate.

Trichocysts are minute, cigar-shaped pockets of material, which are symmetrically arranged and abundant in the ecto-plasm of numerous ciliates (about 4000 in *Paramecium*). When such ciliates are stimulated by pressure or various chemical substances, the trichocysts are discharged through minute surface pores, and on contact with water the substance of each trichocyst forms instantaneously into a long, rigid, needlelike projection from the cell. Little is known about the functions of trichocysts. In a few species they are used for anchoring to a substrate; perhaps they are useful in carnivorous species for capturing prey; possibly they function in warding off predators.

**Reproduction.** The usual method of reproduction involves mitosis and binary fission, resulting in two new individuals that quickly reconstitute themselves and form new organelles where necessary. Amitosis is probably limited to the macronucleus of Ciliophora. A few free-living fresh-water Protozoa exhibit multiple fission and plasmotomy.

Most protozoans have 4 to 12 chromosomes, but some have as few as 2 and *Amoeba proteus* has 500 to 600.

Syngamy is best developed in some of the colonial green flagellates where certain

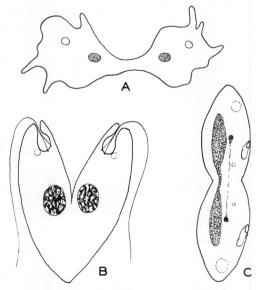

FIG. 12.–Binary fission in Protozoa, diagrammatic. A, *Amoeba*; B, *Euglena*; C, *Paramecium*.

of the vegetative cells become specialized as gametes. In some genera the uniting gametes are apparently identical, and the condition is called isogamy. At the other extreme, such as in *Volvox,* the condition is clearly heterogamous, one of the gametes being small, motile, and spermlike and the other being very large, nonmotile, and egglike. In all cases, however, the zygote eventually gives rise to a new individual or colony.

Conditions most favorable for growth are also most favorable for rapid division, but under unfavorable, crowded conditions and in old cultures many ciliates commonly exhibit one of the two complex phenomena-conjugation and autogamy.

Conjugating ciliates come together in pairs and unite temporarily along their lateral edges. Then follows a complex series of nuclear phenomena that differ from one species to another. In general, however, the process involves disintegration of the macronuclei, a series of mitotic and meiotic divisions of the micronuclei, and an exchange of micronuclear material. The migrating and stationary micronuclei then unite to form a single nucleus in each of the two conjugants. The animals separate, and there is a series of rapid nuclear and cell divisions accompanied by the reappearance of macronuclei derived from micronuclear material. Complex series of "mating types" have been found for several ciliates.

Autogamy involves nuclear changes within a single individual and inclues segmentation and absorption of the macronucleus and a series of divisions of the micronuclei. Subsequent fusion of a pair of micronuclei is accompanied by reconstitution of the macronucleus. Like conjugation, the process of autogamy is completed within one to several days.

Basically, conjugation and autogamy seem to be rejuvenation phenomena by which there is a reshuffling of chromosomes and genes. General physiological vigor and fission rates appear to be increased in a population as a result of these processes. Figures of conjugation and autogamy are available in most elementary zoology textbooks.

Budding is almost restricted to the Suctoria, where it is the common method

FIG. 13.–Reproduction in *Tokophrya lemnarum*. A, animal containing larva within brood pouch; B, released larva. (Modified from Noble.)

of reproduction. In exogenous budding one to several ciliated buds, each with a nucleus, are constricted off from the external surface of the parent cell. Endogenous buds are liberated into internal spaces, or brood chambers, from which they soon escape to the outside. The ciliated embryos swim about for several hours, then become attached to the substrate, lose their cilia, and grow to mature size.

The capacity to regenerate lost parts of the cell is highly variable. In general, however, a bit of cytoplasm with no nuclear material soon dies, but if either a whole or part of a nucleus is present in a cell fragment, then that fragment often grows into a complete normal cell.

**Encystment.** The formation of resistant, protective cysts is rare among marine Protozoa but very common in fresh-water species. Cyst formation may be induced by any one of a variety of adverse environmental conditions, including drying, heat, cold, lack of food, and various chemical substances. The protozoan first rounds up and loses its flagella, cilia, and sometimes other organelles. The cyst wall that is then secreted around the periphery is usually

double, consisting of a thin inner and a tough outer capsule. Sometimes a third innermost albuminous membrane is also formed.

Such cysts are extremely resistant to desiccation, freezing, and high temperatures. Dry cysts commonly remain viable for several months to several years, though there are records of some that were kept for more than 40 years. Protozoans inhabiting damp soil are especially adapted for rapid encystment and excystment. Altogether, about 250 species have been reported from soil habitats.

Excystment of dry cysts and reconstitution of the cells are induced in a few minutes when the cysts come in contact with suitable natural waters or culture solutions. Encysted Protozoa in old culture solutions will excyst when fresh water, salts, hay extracts, and various organic materials are added.

A few Protozoa are known to form reproductive cysts, in which fission occurs, or digestion cysts, which are formed after a large food intake.

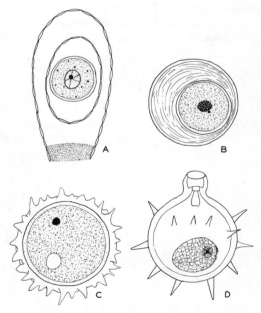

FIG. 14.–Typical protozoan cysts. A, *Euglypha* (amoeboid); B, *Colpoda* (ciliate); C, *Pleurotricha* (ciliata); D, *Ochromonas* (flagellate). (A modified from Kühn, 1926; B and D modified from Doflein, 1923; C modified from Ilowaisky.)

The review of Corliss and Esser (1974) emphasizes our lack of information about the precise details of cyst biology, especially as exemplified by their comment "Recall that *Paramecium,* though widely dispersed, has no cysts of any kind."

**Ecology.** In general, ponds and pools contain the greatest numbers of species though not necessarily the greatest numbers of individuals. Such waters consist of a large number of microhabitats and afford a wide variety of niches. The open waters of lakes contain a characteristic assemblage but small number of species, including representatives of the following genera: *Dinobryon, Mallomonas, Peridinium, Ceratium, Gymnodinium, Trachelomonas,* and *Eudorina.* Sometimes summer populations of plankton species in lakes may reach more than 5 million individuals per liter.

Trickling filters, polluted waters, and Imhoff tanks have a rich and characteristic fauna. Certain species of *Euglypha, Epistylis, Amoeba, Vorticella, Aspidisca, Trachellophyllum, Monas, Tokophrya, Opercularia, Litonotus, Difflugia, Paraglaucoma, Podophrya, Microthorax, Trepomonas, Hexamita, Anthophysis, Carchesium,* and *Bodo* are commonly known as "sewage Protozoa." Colonial green flagellates, on the other hand, are usually most abundant in waters with a high oxygen content. Euglenoids are dominant in small ponds with a high organic content, while testate rhizopods are abundant and varied in sphagnum bogs. Even tree holes and the water held in large leaves and flowers have their characteristic faunas.

Chromatophore-bearing protozoans require light for photosynthesis and are therefore restricted to surface waters of lakes and to small bodies of water.

Owing to ease of transport, especially in the dry, cyst condition, most species are cosmopolitan, but local distribution seems to be governed by such factors as light, temperature, food, dissolved oxygen, acidity or alkalinity, and many chemical substances. Seldom can ecological generalizations be based on genera, only on species. Consequently an ecological classification of fresh-water Protozoa can be only of the most general sort. Following is such a classification suggested about 60 years ago:

1. Katharobic Protozoa are found in springs, brooks, rivers, and ponds that are rich in oxygen and low in organic matter. Such habitats usually have a sparse fauna.

2. Oligosaprobic Protozoa occur in habitats that are relatively high in dissolved salts but low in organic matter; these habitats include the open waters of most lakes and reservoirs.

3. Mesosaprobic Protozoa occur in habitats where there is active oxidation and decomposition. The majority of Protozoa thrive under these conditions.

4. Polysaprobic Protozoa live in habitats where there is much organic matter and carbon dioxide and often quantities of hydrogen sulfide and methane. Pollution, sewage, and anaerobic Protozoa belong in this category.

Coprozoic species grow abundantly in "cultures" or suspensions of fecal matter, which is rich in decomposing organic matter. Such species demonstrate a striking ability to adapt to unusual and abnormal conditions.

Most free-living species show wide ranges of tolerance to single environmental factors, but at the same time it is thought that their activities may be affected by relatively slight environmental changes. In general, flagellates react more directly to single factors than do ciliates, whereas amoebae are intermediate.

The abundance of particulate or dissolved nutrients is important for the distribution of most species, but food is restrictive only when feeding is selective, as it is for carnivorous species. Otherwise food is only a quantitative limiting factor. As might be expected, euryphagous species are most common and widely distributed.

Noland (1925) stressed the distribution of ciliates with respect to food supply. Bacterial growth is most vigorous in acid habitats and where there are small quantities of dissolved oxygen and large quantities of dissolved carbon dioxide; under such circumstances forms feeding on bacteria become abundant. On the other hand, in alkaline habitats where dissolved oxygen is high and dissolved carbon dioxide low, the growth of algae is favored; in such habitats ciliates that feed on algae are abundant. Although certain physical and chemical factors may not in themselves determine the presence or absence of specific ciliates, the sum of these interdependent factors produces bacterial and algal growths in varying degrees, and the precise make-up of the ciliate populations is correspondingly determined.

Picken (1937) has emphasized the fact that an assemblage of Protozoa is not a collection of individuals depending on one source of food, but a complex of herbivores, carnivores, omnivores, and detritus feeders, forming a closed social structure. He analyzed the food chains in several protozoan communities characterized by widely different proportions of diatoms, blue-green algae, and bacteria. *Stentor* and *Dileptus* were at the ends of these chains.

The most pronounced seasonal population changes are quantitative, and temperatures below 10° and above 28° markedly affect the numbers of individuals present but not the numbers of species; summer and winter species lists from the same habitat are often strikingly similar. A few species have become adapted to hot springs where temperatures remain as high as 50°, but most species have a thermal death point somewhere between 30° and 43°. Optimum temperatures generally lie between 10° and 20°. Under experimental conditions many protozoans become accustomed to very high temperatures if the transition is made gradually. Though trophic forms are killed by freezing, a great many species are active in water under ice throughout the winter.

The majority of species tolerate the wide range of ionic concentrations occurring in natural fresh waters, and although some species live in both fresh and marine waters, only a few can be transferred directly from one to the other. The transition is often successful, however, if it is carried

out gradually in the laboratory. Seven species are known from the highly saline waters of Great Salt Lake.

Laboratory experiments have shown that many species can maintain themselves over a wide range in hydrogen-ion concentration. *Euglena viridis* Ehr., for example, has been cultivated in hydrogen-ion concentrations ranging from pH 2.3 to 11.0, *E. gracilis* Klebs in 3.0 to 9.9, *Glaucoma* sp. in 4.0 to 8.9, and *Chilomonas paramecium* Ehr. in 4.1 to 8.4. *Stylonychia pustulata* Ehr., however, will grow only between pH 6.0 and 8.0, and *Spirostomum ambiguum* Ehr. between 6.8 and 7.5. A few species are restricted to highly acid peat bogs in the range of pH 2.0 to 4.0; *Euglena mutabilis* is found in acid coalmine pits in the range of pH 1.8 to 3.9 and has been cultured in the range of pH 1.4 to 7.9. Nevertheless, the great majority of Protozoa have optimum conditions between pH 6.5 and 8.0. It should be borne in mind that pH is a gross measurement of a combination of many chemical factors, any of which, singly or collectively, may be limiting.

Noland and Gojdics (1969) is a recent summary of protozoan ecology; it contains an excellent list of references.

**Succession.** Anyone who has kept hay infusions or other types of mixed cultures in the laboratory is aware that such cultures exhibit a rapid, complex, overlapping series of population growths and declines for the various species. Typically, the dominant hay infusion forms appear and become abundant in the following sequence: small flagellates, *Colpoda*, hypotrichs, *Paramecium*, *Vorticella*, and *Amoeba*. *Paramecium* does not usually become abundant until 8 to 14 days after the culture is begun, and *Amoeba* 2 to 6 weeks later when the culture is "dying out." No equilibrium is reached in such mixed cultures, and as yet sufficient information is not available to explain the sequence of species. Undoubtedly, such factors as food, temperature, light, dissolved oxygen, dissolved carbon dioxide, acidity, and the specific nature of the culture are important; and certainly the more intangible factors such as competition for food, available particulate and dissolved nutrients, and reproductive potential are also significant. Some investigators have presented evidence to indicate that a period of intensive growth of one species is brought to a halt by the accumulation of its own excretory products, and perhaps the growth cycle of one species may result in a favorable medium for another species. Seasonal and cyclic populations of Protozoa have also been studied in natural habitats, especially in the plankton, but these are likewise only poorly understood. The fundamental difficulty involved in protozoan succession studies is our inability to measure, control, and assess the relative significance of many interacting ecological factors.

**Ectocommensal Protozoa.** Many freshwater Metazoa have Protozoa living on their general external surfaces or gills, and some species are thought to be obligatory commensals, although it is sometimes difficult to decide just what special benefits the protozoan derives from such an association. Certain species of Suctoria, for example, are known only from the carapace of turtles; others are often abundant on the gills and appendages of Crustacea. Peritrichida and sessile flagellates are also especially common on Crustacea. The curiously modified ciliates *Kerona* and *Trichodina* are common on the external surface of hydras, where they run about rapdily in search of bits of food. However, some species of *Trichodina* are external parasites of fish, especially in hatcheries, but since they are frequently associated with other protozoan parasites such as *Chilodon, Costia,* and *Ichthyophthirius*, it is difficult to determine the relative importance of *Trichodina* as a true parasite.

**Organisms Living in and on Protozoa.** Although there are a few Phycomycetes and many bacteria that are internal parasites of Protozoa, there are also some bacteria that are internal symbionts, or commensals, especially in amoeboid Protozoa, as well as some bacteria that are epiphytic on the external surface of Protozoa. Certain ciliates, including some species of *Paramecium, Stentor,* and others,

commonly contain internal commensal green, blue-green, or yellow algae (therefore called zoochlorellae, zoocyanellae, and zooxanthellae, respectively). Such algae are ordinarily free-living and autotrophic species, but when they occur as symbionts they are presumed to obtain carbon dioxide and nitrogen and phosphorus compounds resulting from the protozoan metabolism and to contribute oxygen and carbohydrates to the protozoan. *Proales parasita* is a common parasitic or predatory rotifer in the interior of *Volvox* colonies.

**Economic importance.** Although parasitic Protozoa are of inestimable importance because of their adverse effects on the well-being and economic status of man, the free-living species are of little significance. During the summer months, however, some species become so abundant in municipal water supplies in rivers, lakes, and reservoirs as to impart an offensive odor to the water. Blooms of *Dinobryon, Chlamydomonas, Eudorina, Pandorina, Volvox, Glenodinium,* and *Peridinium* produce fishy odors. *Synura* smells like cucumber or muskmelon and has a bitter taste. *Mallomonas* has an aromatic, violet, or fishy odor. *Ceratium* produces a "vile stench." Such disagreeable odors and tastes are more or less eliminated from water supplies by copper sulfate treatment, filtration, or aeration.

Of considerable theoretical importance is the role played by Protozoa in aquatic food chains. Holophytic and saprozoic species are producers that utilize dissolved nutrients and serve as food for small Metazoa. Holozoic species are consumers that form an essential link between particulate living and dead material, on the one hand, and rotifers, Crustacea, and other small Metazoa, on the other hand.

**Collecting.** Plankton and littoral species may be collected with a fine townet, but other free-living species are best obtained by collecting submerged green and rotting vegetation, bottom debris and ooze, and surface scum. A useful device for collecting on and above soft substrates is a long sucking tube attached to a collecting bottle. Materials should be brought back to the laboratory in a quantity of water in which they occur. If desirable, they may be concentrated in a smaller volume by pouring off a part of the water through bolting silk. Stacked laboratory finger bowls are convenient containers. Collections should be allowed to stand in moderate diffuse light where the temperature is not too high. Stigma-bearing species then migrate toward the side facing the strongest light; amoeboid forms remain in the debris, but ciliates often swim about in the water above. If such containers are kept in the laboratory for one to several weeks, additional species often appear.

**Cultures.** Mixed cultures for general study are easily made with hay, lettuce powder, wheat, and rice infusions that are inoculated with pond water. The most successful cultures are obtained by excluding small Metazoa such as oligochaetes and entomostraca, and by adjusting light, food, temperature, and pH to favorable conditions. Moldy cultures should be discarded. Detailed directions for mixed and pure cultures are given in Kudo (1966) and Needham et al. (1937). *Tetrahymena* can be raised in sterile cultures containing the proper nutrients, and for this reason it is probably now the most favored protozoan for laboratory experimentation.

**Examination, preparation.** There is no substitute for the study of *living* Protozoa; killing and fixing agents almost invariably distort specimens badly and make them unfit for accurate identification. Furthermore, instead of using an ordinary glass slide, it is better to use one that has a small, shallow concavity. If a drop of culture solution is placed in the concavity, covered with a Number 1 cover slip, and sealed with vaseline, evaporation is prevented and the living specimens may be studied with the high power of the microscope for hours at a time. Sometimes similar hanging-drop preparations are advantageous. For making careful observations on cilia and flagella dark-field illumination is occasionally useful. It is always important that clean slides, cover slips, and pipettes be used for working with live Protozoa.

Most ciliates move about so rapidly that they cannot be studied with the high powers of the microscope. Their movements may be impeded with cotton fibers or lens paper fibers. Narcotics, such as chloretone, isopropyl alcohol, nickel sulfate, or nickel chloride, are unsatisfactory because they usually alter body shape and physiology. Viscous agents such as agar, gelatin, tragacanth, or quince seed jelly are at best only moderately successful, but a viscous solution of methyl cellulose is excellent. This reagent is made up by dissolving 10 g of methyl cellulose (viscosity rating of 15 centipoises) in 90 ml of water. A drop of this syrupy solution is mixed with a drop of the protozoan culture on a slide before putting on the cover slip. A little experience will determine the relative amounts of culture solution and methyl cellulose that should be used. Movements of ciliates in this mixture are reduced to a minimum, and they may be carefully studied with the high powers. Furthermore, there is no distortion or detectable impairment of the activities of the organelles or physiological processes.

The nucleus and certain organelles can best be distinguished in living Protozoa with the aid of vital stains. Methylene blue is perhaps the best general vital stain; a small amount is placed on the slide and allowed to dry before water containing the Protozoa is placed on it. One percent aqueous solutions of Bismarck brown and neutral red are also good.

Noland's combined fixative and stain in excellent for demonstrating flagella and cilia in temporary mounts; it has the advantage of producing a minimum of distortion.

| | |
|---|---:|
| Phenol, saturated aqueous solution | 80 ml |
| Formalin | 20 ml |
| Glycerin | 4 ml |
| Gentian violet | 20 mg |

The dye should be moistened with 1 ml of water before adding the other ingredients. A drop of this reagent should be mixed with a drop of the culture solution before putting on the cover slip.

Permanent, stained slides are mandatory for careful cytological work; a variety of fixatives, stains, and procedures are given in Kudo (1966) and in microtechnique handbooks. Schaudinn's fluid is perhaps the most generally used fixative. It is made as follows:

| | |
|---|---|
| Saturated aqueous mercuric chloride | 66 ml |
| Absolute or 95 percent alcohol | 33 ml |
| Glacial acetic acid | 1 ml |

The first two ingredients can be kept mixed without deterioration, but the acid should be added just before using. After fixation, specimens can conveniently be brought through changes of 50, 70, 95 percent, and absolute alcohol in a centrifuge tube with gentle centrifuging between changes. A drop of the alcohol containing the concentrated Protozoa is then dropped with a pipette from a height of about 1 in. onto a slide coated with egg albumen. Following this, the slides are placed in absolute alcohol and thereafter treated as ordinary sections for staining.

**Taxonomy.** Unlike some metazoan phyla, the great majority of Protozoa die and disintegrate without leaving any fossil record, the only important exceptions being the skeleton-bearing Foraminifera and Radiolaria, both marine groups. Consequently, our ideas concerning the natural taxonomic relationships of the major groups must be based on existing morphological traits, physiology, and development.

The old idea of amoeboid Protozoa being ancestral to the other groups has been discarded, and most protozoologists believe that the flagellates, especially green flagellates, are most primitive. This conviction is based on the fact that holophytic organisms utilizing dissolved nutrients must necessarily have preceded holozoic forms feeding on particulate organic materials. Furthermore, it is comparatively easy to derive the Sarcodina from holozoic flagellates. The origin of the sporozoans (all parasitic), however, is obscure; they are probably polyphyletic, with flagellate and amoeboid ancestry. Both ciliates and suctorians are highly evolved and complex in structure. The former probably originated from some of the more advanced flagellates, whereas the Suctoria undoubtedly

arose from ciliated ancestors by loss of cilia and development of tentacles during the adult stage.

Morphologically, the ciliates and suctorians are sharply defined groups, but many flagellates are known that are more or less amoeboid, and some amoeboid forms have flagella. The flagellate order Rhizomastigida, for example, has holozoic representatives with well-developed pseudopodia, including *Mastigamoeba* and *Mastigella*. Many representatives of other flagellate orders also have pseudopodia in varying degrees; some of these are *Rhizochrysis, Oikomonas, Chrysamoeba,* and *Bodo*. On the other hand, some Sarcodina such as *Pseudospora* and *Dimastigamoeba* are flagellated swarmers during a short period of their life history.

The criteria to be used for subdividing the Mastigophora and distinctions between "true flagellate algae" and "true flagellate protozoa" are kindred and highly controversial problems which have been discussed for many years. Many members of the Phytomastigophorea of the zoologist are classified by the botanist as members of the Chrysophyceae, Dinophyceae, Chlorophyceae, Euglenophyceae, and Cryptophyceae, and all of these classes of algae also include nonmotile genera. Most of the discussion has centered around the Phytomastigophorea, a group that contains pigmented and colorless forms, as well as holophytic, holozoic, saprozoic, and mixotrophic forms. At one extreme, a few investigators have advocated placing all chlorophyll-containing species with the Algae and all nonpigmented forms with the Protozoa. Most protistologists, however, have a broader viewpoint of these questions; they maintain that a sharp division of flagellates into "plant" and "animal" species is purely an artificial device and serves no useful purpose. Indeed, there is much to be said for considering flagellates as a mutual and primitive stage of organization of both the plant and animal kingdoms, and there is no real reason why many flagellates cannot be claimed by both zoologists and botanists. The widely accepted opinion emphasizes the fact that the flagellates do not constitute a natural taxonomic group but represent diverse branches in a stage of cellular organization, that some orders are quite artificial, and that the majority of orders contain both pigmented and nonpigmented forms. Some holozoic and saprozoic colorless forms are easily linked with their pigmented relatives, but in other cases few indications of affinities can be found. The following respective pairs of pigmented and nonpigmented genera appear to be closely related: *Cryptomonas* and *Chilomonas, Euglena* and *Astasia, Chlamydomonas* and *Polytoma*.

About 450 genera of free-living Protozoa are known to occur in the fresh waters of the United States, but many of these are uncommon and have been reported only once or a few times. Such rare genera are mainly of interest only to the specialist. In order to determine just what genera should be included in this volume, however, the complete list of genera was sent to a group of American protozoologists along with a request that they strike from the list about 150 genera that they considered as being least likely to be encountered in field collections and laboratory cultures. For the first edition of this book, eight protozoologists collaborated in this effort, and as the result of their "votes" the complete list was cut to 303 genera, all of which are included in the following key. In this revised edition many additional genera are added to the keys.

With few exceptions this key is drawn up for the identification of *living* Protozoa. Measurements are given chiefly for general information and should not usually be used as key characters. In each case the greatest dimension is noted; it is given for the cell proper and does not include stalk, flagella, cilia, cirri, tentacles, or case. In colonial species the measurements are given for single individuals of the colony. Except where size ranges are given, lengths are rough averages and are subject to a plus or minus one-third variation. In general, a representative common species is figured for each genus. Most of these figures are diagrammatic optical sections or surface views intended to emphasize key characters. Nuclei are often shaded, but it should be remembered that they are generally translucent in living Protozoa. Some of the figures have been drawn especially for this manual, but a large number are modified, simplified, or composites from a great many literature sources. Almost without exception, these latter figures are so considerably modified from their antecedents as to make acknowledgments unnecessary and superfluous. All figures have been drawn free hand.

The numbers of species known for the various genera are not usually included in the following key, chiefly because few genera have been thoroughly monographed. A few genera are monospecific; examples are *Uroglena, Distigma, Teuthophrys, Urocentrum,* and *Bursaria*. The great majority of genera, however, are represented by more than three species, and some, such as the following, are represented by twenty species: *Euglena, Peridinium, Trachelomonas, Vorticella, Lionotus, Chilodonella, Cyclidium, Metopus, Euplotes, Epistylis, Spathidium,* and *Opercularia*.

In general, we are following the classification proposed by Honigberg et al. (1964), but it should be emphasized that many specialists disagree with certain of the categories included in this scheme. Our main purpose in this key, however, is to enable the student to identify to family or genus those protozoans likely to be encountered in fresh-water aquatic work. To keep key numbers within reason, we are subdividing the Protozoa into separately numbered keys. The Mastigophora begin on this page, the Sarcodina on page 52, and the Ciliophora on page 58.

## KEY TO COMMON GENERA OF MASTIGOPHORA

**1.** Usually with three chromatophores; one or two flagella (rarely three or four), but cell additionally amoeboid in some groups.
Class **PHYTOMASTIGOPHOREA, 2**
No chromatophores; one to many flagella, but cell additionally amoeboid in some groups . . . . . . . . . . . . . . . . . . . . . . . . . . . . . . . . . . . . . . . . . . . . . . . . . **86**

2. With two flagella, of which one extends transversely around the cell; body grooved; chromatophores variously colored; starch and lipid food reserves.

                                                                  Order **DINOFLAGELLIDA, 3**

    With one to four flagella, directed anteriorly or trailing . . . . . . . . . . . . . . . . . . . . . . .11

3. Naked or covered with a thin exoskeleton (Figs. 15A–E) . . . . . . . . . . . . . . . . . . . . . .4

    Covered with a thick exoskeleton (Figs. 15F–H). . . . . . . . . . . . . . . . . . . . . . . . . . . . . .8

4. Covered with a thin exoskeleton; several yellow to brown chromatophores; annulus complete (Fig. 15A); 40 microns; common . . **CYSTODINIIDAE, Glenodinium**

    Naked; numerous chromatophores . . . . . . . . . . . . . . . . . . . . . . . . **GYMNODINIIDAE, 5**

5. Annulus anterior (Fig. 15B); 30 microns . . . . . . . . . . . . . . . . . . . . . . . . . .**Amphidinium**

    Annulus not anterior . . . . . . . . . . . . . . . . . . . . . . . . . . . . . . . . . . . . . . . . . . . . . . . . . . . . .6

6. Annulus spiral (Fig. 15J); 25 microns . . . . . . . . . . . . . . . . . . . . . . . . . . . . **Gyrodinium**

    Annulus not spiral . . . . : . . . . . . . . . . . . . . . . . . . . . . . . . . . . . . . . . . . . . . . . . . . . . . . . . .7

7. Annulus complete (Fig. 15D); 40 microns; common. . . . . . . . . . . . . . . **Gymnodinium**

    Annulus incomplete (Fig. 15E); 28 microns . . . . . . . . . . . . . . . . . . . . . . . **Hemidinium**

8. Exoskeleton with transverse and longitudinal grooves and divided into plates (Figs. 15G, H) . . . . . . . . . . . . . . . . . . . . . . . . . . . . . . . . . . . . . . . . . . . . . **PERIDINIIDAE, 9**

    Exoskeleton without grooves; plates absent; spherical or ellipsoidal (Fig. 15F); 45 microns. . . . . . . . . . . . . . . . . . . . . . . . . . . . . . . . . .**PHYTODINIIDAE, Phytodinium**

Fig. 15.–Representative Dinoflagellata. A, *Glenodinium*; B, *Amphidinium* (chromatophores present or absent); C, ventral view of *Gymnodinium*; D, lateral view of *Gymnodinium*; E, *Hemidinium*; F, *Phytodinium*; G, *Gonyaulax*; H, *Peridinium*; J, *Gyrodinium*. (A and H modified from Eddy; C and D modified from Thompson.)

9. Flattened and with one anterior and three long posterior hornlike processes (Fig. 7E); shape highly variable; 100 to 500 microns; very common in lakes and ponds. . . . . . . . . . . . . . . . . . . . . . . . . . . . . . . . . . **Ceratium hirundinella** (Müller)
   Not flattened; without hornlike processes; 40 microns . . . . . . . . . . . . . . . . . . . . . . .**10**
10. Annulus displaced (Fig. 15G) . . . . . . . . . . . . . . . . . . . . . . . . . . . . . **Gonyaulax**
    Annulus not displaced (Fig. 15H); common in plankton. . . . . . . . . . . . . .**Peridinium**
11. With yellow, brown, or orange chromatophores; usually quite small . . . . . . . . . . . .**12**
    With green chromatophores, or chromatophores absent . . . . . . . . . . . . . . . . . . . . . .**37**
12. With lipid and starch storage bodies; pellicle absent; body without a longitudinal furrow; one or two flagella inserted at or near the anterior end; many species form pseudopodia. . . . . . . . . . . . . . . . . . . . . . Order **CHRYSOMONADIDA, 13**
    With stored carbohydrate granules; pellicle present; body with an oblique furrow; mostly holophytic, a few saprozoic or holozoic; two flagella, inserted anteriorly or laterally; no pseudopodia . . . . . . . . Order **CRYPTOMONADIDA, 32**
13. With one or two flagella; motile stage dominant; with a calcareous or siliceous shell or skeleton . . . . . . . . . . . . . . . . . . . . . .Suborder **EUCHRYSOMONADINA, 15**
    Flagella absent or transient; naked . . . . . . . . . . . . . . . . . . . . . . . . . . . . . . . . . . .**14**

FIG. 16.–Representative Chromulinidae. A, *Chrysapsis*; B, *Chrysopyxis*; C, *Chrysococcus*; D, *Mallomonas*; E, colony of *Chrysosphaerella*; F, individual *Chrysosphaerella*; G, *Chromulina*; H, *Chrysamoeba*; J, *Kephyrion*. (D modified from Smith, 1920.)

Fig. 17.–Representative Syncryptidae. A, *Hymenomonas*; B, *Snycrypta* colony; C, *Synura* colony; D, individual *Synura*; E, *Derepyxis*. (A modified from Conrad; C and D modified from Smith, 1920.)

14. Body amoeboid and solitary, with one or two chromatophores; not colonial (Fig. 19A) .......................Suborder **RHIZOCHRYSIDINA, Rhizochrysis**
    Colonial; cells imbedded in a branching mass, 2 to 30 cm long; attached to substrate in gelatinous mosslike strands in cold mountain streams; with an acrid odor; recently divided cells often forming flagellated zoospores.
                        Suborder **CHRYSOCAPSINA, Hydrurus foetidus** (Vill.)
15. With a single flagellum ............................. CHROMULINIDAE, 16
    With two flagella..............................................................23
16. Cells in spherical colonies; each cell with two, long, siliceous rods (Fig. 16F); 15 microns; plankton.....................................**Chrysosphaerella**
    Not colonial ................................................................17
17. Cell with a lorica (Figs. 16B, C, J); 9 microns .............................18
    Cell without a lorica .......................................................20
18. Lorica more or less flattened; attached to algae (Fig. 16B)...........**Chrysopyxis**
    Lorica not flattened (Figs. 16C, J) .........................................19
19. Body filling lorica (Fig. 16C) ...................................**Chrysococcus**
    Body not filling lorica (Fig. 16J) ................................ **Kephyrion**
20. Elongated; with siliceous scales and spines (Fig. 16D); 30 microns; plankton.
                                                                       **Mallomonas**
    Not elongated; without siliceous scales and spines ...........................21
21. Chromatophore diffuse or branching; amoeboid (Fig. 16A); 12 microns . **Chrysapsis**
    Chromatophore not diffuse or branching (Figs. 16G, H) .......................22
22. Without pseudopodia, or with short, blunt pseudopodia (Fig. 16G) .... **Chromulina**
    With long, slender pseudopodia (Fig. 16H); flagellate stage transient; 20 microns.
                                                                       **Chrysamoeba**
23. With two apical flagella of equal length; usually in acid waters.
                                                            SYNCRYPTIDAE, 24
    With two apical flagella of unequal length............. OCHROMONADIDAE, 27
24. Colonial (Figs. 17B, C) ....................................................26
    Solitary; 35 microns .......................................................25

FIG. 18.–Representative Ochromonadidae. A, *Dinobryon* colony; B, *Dinobryon* individual; C, *Hyalobryon*; D, free-swimming *Ochromonas*; E, sessile *Ochromonas*; F, *Uroglenopsis* colony; G, *Uroglenopsis* individual; H, *Uroglena volvox* colony; J, *U. volvox* single individual. (A modified from Smith, 1920.)

25. Membrane brownish, often sculptured; two chromatophores (Fig. 17A).
......................................................................................... **Hymenomonas**
    With a flimsy lorica, with or without a stalk; one or two chromatophores (Fig.
    17E) ......................................................... **Derepyxis**
26. Cells imbedded in a gelatinous mass (Fig. 17B); 11 microns ............**Syncrypta**
    Cells not imbedded in a gelatinous mass (Figs. 17C, D); 35 microns; common.**Synura**
27. Each cell enclosed within a delicate lorica (Figs. 18A–C) ......................**28**
    Each cell not enclosed within a lorica ......................................**29**
28. Lorica homogeneous, without growth rings (Figs. 18A, B); extremely common in
    plankton ............................................... **Dinobryon**
    Lorica with growth rings (Fig. 18C); epiphytic; sometimes solitary .... **Hyalobryon**
29. Cells arranged in a flat, wheel-like colony composed of 10 to 20 wedge-shaped cells;
    cell 15 microns ......................................... **Cyclonexis**
    Cells arranged otherwise ....................................................**30**
30. Solitary or colonial; individuals not arranged on periphery of a gelatinous mass (Figs.
    18D, E); 22 microns ......................................**Ochromonas**
    Colonial; individuals arranged on periphery of gelatinous mass .................**31**
31. Center of colony without dichotomously branched strands (Figs. 18F, G); 6 microns;
    when abundant imparts an offensive odor to water ........... **Uroglenopsis**
    Center of colony with dichotomously branched strands, which are best seen in
    stained specimens (Figs. 18H, J); 16 microns .........**Uroglena volvox** Ehr.

**32.** With two anterior flagella and an oblique furrow near anterior end (Figs. 7C, 19C–F) . . . . . . . . . . . . . . . . . . . . . . . . . . . . . . . . . . . . . . . . **CRYPTOMONADIDAE, 33**

With two lateral flagella and an equatorial furrow (Fig. 19B).

NEPHROSELMIDAE, **Nephroselmis**

**33.** With one or more chromatophores of various coloration . . . . . . . . . . . . . . . . . . . . . .**34**

Without chromatophores; common in stagnant waters and infusions . . . . . . . . . . .**36**

**34.** One red chromatophore; body often spindle-shaped; furrow strongly granulated (Fig. 19E) . . . . . . . . . . . . . . . . . . . . . . . . . . . . . . . . . . . . . . . . . . . . . . . **Rhodomonas**

Two chromatophores; body not spindle-shaped; furrow lightly granulated . . . . . .**35**

**35.** Gullet present (Fig. 19C) . . . . . . . . . . . . . . . . . . . . . . . . . . . . . . . . . . . . . . .**Cryptomonas**

Gullet absent (Fig. 19F) . . . . . . . . . . . . . . . . . . . . . . . . . . . . . . . . . . . . . . .**Cryptochrysis**

**36.** Body oval, flattened, and obliquely truncate at anterior end (Fig. 19D); holozoic.

**Cyathomonas truncata** Ehr.

Body cylindrical and elongated (Fig. 7C); saprozoic . . . . . . . . . . . . . . . . . **Chilomonas**

**37.** Body more or less spherical; usually two or four apical flagella but three in one family and five in another family; glycogen reserve food; solitary or colonial; few chromatophores, usually shell- or cup-shaped; stigma present or absent . . . . . . . . . . . . . . . . . . . . . . . . . . . . . . . . . . . . . . . .Order **VOLVOCIDA, 39**

Body more or less elongated; always solitary; many chromatophores, not cup-shaped, sometimes absent; with another combination of other characters . . . . . . . .**38**

**38.** Uncommon genera; with one flagellum or with two flagella, of which one is trailing; flagella originating beside a superficial apical cavity or furrow; reserve foods lipids and glycogen; stigma absent . . . . . . . .Order **CHLOROMONADIDA, 83**

Very common genera; with one, two, or three flagella, one trailing in one suborder; flagella originating in a definite reservoir; reserve food paramylum; stigma present . . . . . . . . . . . . . . . . . . . . . . . . . . . . . . . . . . . . . Order **EUGLENIDA, 65**

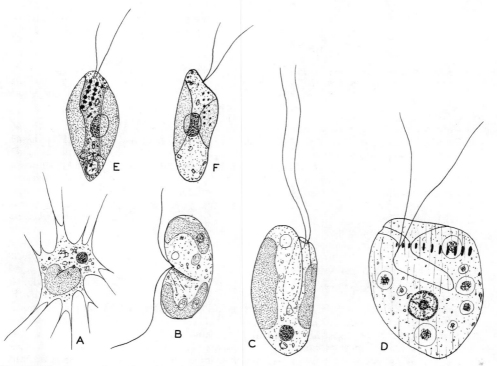

FIG. 19.–Representative Rhizochrysodina, Nephroselmidae, and Cryptomonadidae. A, *Rhizochrysis*; B, *Nephroselmis*; C, *Cryptomonas*; D, *Cyathomonas truncata* Ehr.; E, *Rhodomonas*; F, *Cryptochrysis*.

FIG. 20.–Representative Volvocida. A, *Phacotus*; B, *Pteromonas*; C, *Trichloris*; D, *Chloraster*; E, *Pocillomonas*; F, *Lobomonas*; G, *Gloeomonas*; H, *Thorakomonas*.

**39.** Solitary ..................................................................**40**
Colonial ..............................................................VOLVOCIDAE, **46**
**40.** With an external bivalve membrane (Figs. 20A, B); 16 microns. PHACOTIDAE, **41**
Without a bivalve membrane ...........................................................**42**
**41.** Bivalve membrane sculptured, halves evident in vegetative cell (Fig. 20A); stagnant water ......................................................................**Phacotus**
Bivalve membrane not sculptured, halves evident only in dividing cell (Fig. 20B) ...................................................................... **Pteromonas**
**42.** With two flagella .............................CHLAMYDOMONADIDAE, **53**
More than two flagella ..............................................................**43**
**43.** With three flagella; bean-shaped (Fig. 20C); 14 microns.

                                                      TRICHLORIDIDAE, **Trichloris**
More than three flagella ...............................................................**44**
**44.** With four flagella ....................................... CARTERIIDAE, **62**
With more than four flagella..............................................................**45**
**45.** With five flagella; four anterior wings (Fig. 20D). CHLORASTERIDAE, **Chloraster**
With six flagella (Fig. 20E); 13 microns ... POLYBLEPHARIDIDAE, **Pocillomonas**
**46.** Colony a flat plate (Figs. 21A, B); cell 13 microns ...........................**47**
Colony spherical or subspherical ..............................................................**48**
**47.** Colony in a gelatinous envelope with anterior–posterior differentiation; 16 or 32 cells (Fig. 21A) ........................................................... **Platydorina**
Colony in a gelatinous envelope without anterior–posterior differentiation; 4 to 16 cells (Fig. 21B) .................................................**Gonium**

FIG. 21.–Representative Volvocidae. A, *Platydorina*; B, *Gonium*; C, *Pleodorina*; D, *Pandorina*; E, *Eudorina*; F, *Chlamydobotrys*; G, *Spondylomorum*. (D to E modified from Smith, 1920.)

**48.** Colony with at least 500 cells; colony up to 600 microns in diameter (Fig. 8). **Volvox**
Colony with not more than 256 cells ........................................**49**

**49.** With cells of two different sizes; 32, 64, or 128 cells per colony (Fig. 21C). **Pleodorina**
Cells all of same size ..................................................**50**

**50.** Cells more or less spherical ...........................................**51**
Cells pear-shaped; 8 or 16 cells per colony ..............................**52**

**51.** Cells close together; 4, 8, 16, or 32 cells per colony (Fig. 21D); cells 12 microns. **Pandorina**
Cells farther apart; 16, 32, or 64 cells per colony (Fig. 21E); cells 17 microns. **Eudorina**

**52.** Cells with two flagella (Fig. 21F); cell 15 microns............... **Chlamydobotrys**
Cells with four flagella (Fig. 21G); cell 19 microns .............. **Spondylomorum**

**53.** With chromatophores..................................................**54**
Without chromatophores; saprozoic ....................................**60**

**54.** Spindle-shaped (Fig. 22A); 50 microns.......................... **Chlorogonium**
Cell not spindle-shaped ................................................**55**

**55.** Cell apparently naked (Fig. 7A); 8 to 22 microns ............... **Chlamydomonas**
Cell not naked ........................................................**56**

**56.** Cell covered with thick gelatinous envelope (Fig. 22B); sometimes red pigmented; 10
to 50 microns; mostly in ephemeral ponds ................ **Haematococcus**
Cell not covered with a thick gelatinous sheath .........................**57**

**57.** With blunt, irregular processes (Fig. 20F)..........................**Lobomonas**
Without blunt processes ................................................**58**

**58.** Cell not filling subcapsular space (Fig. 22C); 21 microns............. **Coccomonas**
Cell filling subcapsular space .........................................**59**

FIG. 22.–Representative Chlamydomonadidae, Carteriidae, and Euglenidae. A, *Chlorogonium*; B, *Haematococcus*; C, *Coccomonas*; D, *Hyalogonium*; E, *Polytoma*; F, *Parapolytoma*; G, *Spermatozopsis*; H, *Pyramimonas*; J, *Polytomella*; K, *Carteria*; L, *Ascoglena*.

59. Capsule thin and gelatinous (Fig. 20G) ............................ **Gloeomonas**
    Capsule crustose, brown to black (Fig. 20H) .....................**Thorakomonas**
60. Spindle-shaped (Fig. 22D); 30 to 80 microns ..................... **Hyalogonium**
    Not spindle-shaped ............................................**61**
61. Ovoid (Fig. 22E); 23 microns ........................................ **Polytoma**
    Anterior margin obliquely truncate (Fig. 22F); 15 microns .......... **Parapolytoma**
62. Sickle-shaped (Fig. 22G); rarely biflagellated; 8 microns .......... **Spermatozopsis**
    Not sickle-shaped .............................................**63**
63. Pyramidal or heart-shaped (Fig. 22H); 20 microns .................**Pyramimonas**
    Ovoid or ellipsoid ............................................**64**
64. Colorless (Fig. 22J); 14 microns ................................ **Polytomella**
    Green (Fig. 22K); 6 to 25 microns ................................ **Carteria**
65. With stigma; chromatophores almost invariably present (Figs. 7B, 23B–F).
                                            **EUGLENIDAE, 67**
    Stigma and chromatophores absent ...................................**66**
66. With one flagellum ..................................... **ASTASIIDAE, 74**
    With two flagella...................................... **ANISONEMIDAE, 79**

FIG. 23.–Representative Euglenidae and Astasiidae. A, *Urceolus*; B, *Phacus*; C, *Lepocinclis*; D, *Colacium*; E, *Cryptoglena*; F, *Euglena*; G, *Trachelomonas*; H, *Petalomonas*; J, *Menoidium*; K, *Scytomonas*; L, *Astasia*; M, *Peranema*. (A modified from Senn.)

**67.** Highly flattened, asymmetrical, and often longitudinally striated and twisted (Fig. 23B); 30 to 170 microns . . . . . . . . . . . . . . . . . . . . . . . . . . . . . . . . . . . . . . . . . . . **Phacus**
   Not highly flattened and asymmetrical . . . . . . . . . . . . . . . . . . . . . . . . . . . . . . . . . . . . . .**68**
**68.** Encased in a lorica . . . . . . . . . . . . . . . . . . . . . . . . . . . . . . . . . . . . . . . . . . . . . . . . . . . . . .**69**
   Not encased in a lorica . . . . . . . . . . . . . . . . . . . . . . . . . . . . . . . . . . . . . . . . . . . . . . . . . . .**70**
**69.** Sessile; lorica flexible, colorless to brown (Fig. 22L) . . . . . . . . . . . . . . . . . **Ascoglena**
   Motile; lorica often spinous (Fig. 23G) . . . . . . . . . . . . . . . . . . . . . . . . . **Trachelomonas**
**70.** With a short posterior spinous projection (Fig. 23C); pellicle spirally striated; 30 microns . . . . . . . . . . . . . . . . . . . . . . . . . . . . . . . . . . . . . . . . . . . . . . . . . . . . . . . **Lepocinclis**
   Without a short posterior spinous projection . . . . . . . . . . . . . . . . . . . . . . . . . . . . . . . .**71**
**71.** Stalked and colonial (Fig. 23D); flagellum present only in motile stage; often epizoic on copepods; 25 microns . . . . . . . . . . . . . . . . . . . . . . . . . . . . . . . . . . . . . . . . **Colacium**
   Not stalked and colonial . . . . . . . . . . . . . . . . . . . . . . . . . . . . . . . . . . . . . . . . . . . . . . . . . .**72**
**72.** Rigid, ovate, and somewhat compressed (Fig. 23E); 13 microns; uncommon.
                                                                                                    **Cryptoglena**
   Elongated and plastic . . . . . . . . . . . . . . . . . . . . . . . . . . . . . . . . . . . . . . . . . . . . . . . . . . . . .**73**

73. With chromatophores; often striated (Figs. 7B, 23F); stagnant water, about 60 species; 25 to 500 microns; very common . . . . . . . . . . . . . . . . . . . . . . . . . . . .**Euglena**
    Without chromatophores but otherwise similar to *Euglena;* saprozoic; 45 microns . . . . . . . . . . . . . . . . . . . . . . . . . . . . . . . . . . . . . . . . . . . . . . .**Khawkinea**

74. Flask-shaped, with a funnellike neck (Fig. 23A); holozoic and saprozoic; 40 microns . . . . . . . . . . . . . . . . . . . . . . . . . . . . . . . . . . . . . . . . . . . . . . . . **Urceolus**
    Not flask-shaped . . . . . . . . . . . . . . . . . . . . . . . . . . . . . . . . . . . . . . . . . . . . . . . . .**75**

75. With one or more longitudinal keels or grooves along one side (Fig. 23H); holozoic or saprozoic; 23 microns . . . . . . . . . . . . . . . . . . . . . . . . . . . .**Petalomonas**
    Without longitudinal keels or grooves . . . . . . . . . . . . . . . . . . . . . . . . . . . . . .**76**

76. Rigid, more or less curved; pellicle delicately striated (Fig. 23J); 15 to 80 microns . . . . . . . . . . . . . . . . . . . . . . . . . . . . . . . . . . . . . . . . . . . . . .**Menoidium**
    Plastic; pellicle not striated . . . . . . . . . . . . . . . . . . . . . . . . . . . . . . . . . . . . . . . .**77**

77. Elongated (Figs. 23L, M); holozoic and saprozoic; stagnant water; 20 to 70 microns. **78**
    Not elongated but oval or pyriform (Fig. 23K); holozoic; 15 microns . . **Scytomonas**

78. More or less spindle-shaped; posterior end drawn out (Fig. 23L) . . . . . . . . . . **Astasia**
    Posterior end broad, rounded, or truncate during locomotion (Fig. 23M); very common . . . . . . . . . . . . . . . . . . . . . . . . . . . . . . . . . . . . . . . . . . . **Peranema**

79. Both flagella directed forward; plastic (Fig. 24A); holozoic; 15 to 70 microns.
                                                                                 **Distigma proteus** Ehr.
    One flagellum trailing . . . . . . . . . . . . . . . . . . . . . . . . . . . . . . . . . . . . . . . . . . . . .**80**

80. With a long, slitlike furrow (Figs. 24B, C) . . . . . . . . . . . . . . . . . . . . . . . . . . . .**81**
    Without a furrow . . . . . . . . . . . . . . . . . . . . . . . . . . . . . . . . . . . . . . . . . . . . . . . .**82**

81. Trailing flagellum long (Fig. 24B); 15 to 60 microns . . . . . . . . . . . . . . . .**Anisonema**
    Trailing flagellum short (Fig. 24C); 8 to 25 microns . . . . . . . . . . . . . . .**Notosolenus**

82. Oval, flattened, and furrowed; with a long pharyngeal rod apparatus (Fig. 24E); 25 microns . . . . . . . . . . . . . . . . . . . . . . . . . . . . . . . . . . . . . . . . . . . . . . .**Entosiphon**
    Rounded to elongated; sometimes ridged or striated; pharyngeal rod apparatus short or absent (Fig. 24D); 50 to 250 microns . . . . . . . . . . . . . . . . . . . . . .**Heteronema**

83. With many highly refractile trichocystlike bodies (Fig. 24F); 50 microns; acid waters . . . . . . . . . . . . . . . . . . . . . . . . . . . . . . . . . . . . . . . . . . . . . . **Gonyostomum**
    Without such bodies . . . . . . . . . . . . . . . . . . . . . . . . . . . . . . . . . . . . . . . . . . . . . .**84**

84. Cell with projecting hairlike setae, and sometimes pseudopodia (Fig. 24J).
                                                                            **Thaumatomastix**
    Without setae and pseudopodia . . . . . . . . . . . . . . . . . . . . . . . . . . . . . . . . . . . .**85**

85. Anterior end narrow; body not flattened (Fig. 24H); 100 microns . . . . . . .**Vacuolaria**
    Anterior end not especially narrow; body flattened (Fig. 24G); 60 microns. **Trentonia**

86. Cell with annulus and sulcus (Figs. 15B, D, E, J). Class **PHYTOMASTIGOPHOREA,**
                           Order **DINOFLAGELLIDA,** GYMNODINIIDAE, **5**
    Cell without annulus and sulcus . . . . . . . . . . . . . . . . . . . . . . . . . . . . . . . . . . .**87**

87. Cell with cytostome and cytopharynx . . . . . . Class **PHYTOMASTIGOPHOREA, 88**
    Cell without cytostome and cytopharynx; holozoic or saprozoic . . . . . . . . . . . . .**90**

88. With stored carbohydrate granules; two flagella, both projecting forward.
                         Order **CRYPTOMONADIDA,** CRYPTOMONADIDAE, **33**
    With stored paramylum granules, sometimes oil droplets also; one flagellum, or two flagella with one usually trailing . . . . . . . . . . . . . . . . . Order **EUGLENIDA, 89**

89. Stigma present; saprozoic; similar to *Euglena* but colorless; 45 microns.
                                            EUGLENIDAE, **Khawkinea**
    Stigma absent . . . . . . . . . . . . . . . . . . . . . . . . . . . . . . . . . . . . . . . . . . . . . . . . . .**66**

90. With well-defined pseudopodia in addition to flagella (Figs. 27G–L).
                       Class **ZOOMASTIGOPHOREA,** Order **RHIZOMASTIGIDA, 123**
    With flagella only; only occasionally with one or two small blunt pseudopodia . . .**91**

91. With one or two flagella . . . . . . . . . . . . . . . . . . . . . . . . . . . . . . . . . . . . . . . . . .**92**
    With three to eight flagella . . . . . . . . . . . . . . . . Class **ZOOMASTIGOPHOREA, 128**

92. With two flagella . . . . . . . . . . . . . . . . . . . . . . . . . . . . . . . . . . . . . . . . . . . . . . .**93**
    With one flagellum . . . . . . . . . . . . . . . . . . . . . . Class **ZOOMASTIGOPHOREA, 101**

93. Flagella equally long . . . . . . . . . . . . . . . . . . . . . . . . . . . . . . . . . . . . . . . . . . . . .**94**
    Flagella of unequal length . . . . . . . . . . . . . . . . Class **ZOOMASTIGOPHOREA, 113**

FIG. 24.–Representative Anisonemidae and Chloromonadina. A, *Distigma proteus*; B, *Anisonema*; C, *Notosolenus*; D, *Heteronema*; E, *Entosiphon*; F, *Gonyostomum*; G, *Trentonia*; H, *Vacuolaria*; J, *Thaumatomastix*.

94. Naked or with gelatinous envelope; solitary or colonial; motile or sessile; sometimes with small pseudopodia. Class **MASTIGOPHOREA**, AMPHIMONADIDAE, 95
    Naked; solitary; motile; without pseudopodia.
                    Class **PHYTOMASTIGOPHOREA**, CHLAMYDOMONADIDAE, 53
95. Without lorica or gelatinous covering.........................................96
    With a lorica or gelatinous covering .........................................98
96. Oval or rounded amoeboid; free-swimming or attached by a long stalk (Fig. 25A); 13 microns .................................................. **Amphimonas**
    Not oval or rounded amoeboid; stagnant waters ............................97
97. Spirally twisted (Fig. 25B); 10 microns ......................... **Spiromonas**
    Ovate or pyriform plastic; anterior end pointed (Fig. 25C); 15 microns .. **Dinomonas**
98. Each cell with a stalk and individual lorica (Fig. 25D); 15 microns ...... **Diplomita**
    Cells in gelatinous masses or tubes (Figs. 25E, F); 6 to 12 microns ............99
99. Individuals in dichotomously branching gelatinous tubes ............. **Cladomonas**
    Tubes or mass not dichotomously branched ...............................100
100. Branched tubes united laterally (Fig. 25E) ..................... **Rhipidodendron**
     Individuals imbedded in granular gelatinous masses that are not united laterally (Fig. 25F) ................................................. **Spongomonas**

FIG. 25.–Representative Amphimonadidae, Phalansteriidae, and Oikomonadidae. A, *Amphimonas*; B, *Spiromonas*; C, *Dinomonas*; D, *Diplomita*; E, small part of colony of *Rhipidodendron*; F, small part of colony of *Spongomonas*; G, small part of colony of *Phalansterium*; H, *Oikomonas*.

101.  Cell with collar (Fig. 26) . . . . . . . . . . . . . . . . . . . . . . . . . . . . . . . . . . . . . . . . .**102**
     Cell without collar; flagellum anterior; spherical or oval (Fig. 25H); 10 microns;
        stagnant water (usually included in the flagellated algaelike protozoans).
           Suborder **EUCHRYSOMONADINA**, CHROMULINIDAE, **Oikomonas**
102.  Entire animal enclosed in a gelatinous mass (Fig. 25G); 17 microns.
                             PHALANSTERIIDAE, **Phalansterium**
     No gelatinous mass, or cell body only imbedded in gelatinous mass (Fig. 26); free-
        swimming or sedentary; colonial or solitary . . . . . . . . . . . . . . . . . . . . . . . . .**103**
103.  Without lorica (Figs. 26A, B, F, M, N); stalked; holozoic or saprozoic; 5 to 15
        microns . . . . . . . . . . . . . . . . . . . . . . . . . . . . . . . . . . . . . CODOSIGIDAE, **104**
     With lorica (Figs. 29C, G, H, J, O); stalked or unstalked; holozoic.
                                 BICOSOECIDAE, **109**
104.  With a double collar (Fig. 26B); solitary or clustered . . . . . . . . . . . . . . . . . . . .**Diplosiga**
     With a single collar . . . . . . . . . . . . . . . . . . . . . . . . . . . . . . . . . . . . . . . . . . . . . . .**105**
105.  Solitary (Fig. 26F) . . . . . . . . . . . . . . . . . . . . . . . . . . . . . . . . . . . . . . . . . **Monosiga**
     Colonial . . . . . . . . . . . . . . . . . . . . . . . . . . . . . . . . . . . . . . . . . . . . . . . . . . . . . .**106**

FIG. 26.–Representative Codosigidae, Bicosoecidae, and Bodonidae. A, colony of *Codosiga*; B, *Diplosiga*; C, colony of *Poteriodendron*; D, *Phyllomitus*; E, *Pleuromonas*; F, *Monosiga*; G, *Bicosoeca*; H, *Salpingoeca*; J, *Codonoeca*; K, *Rhynchomonas*; L, *Cercomonas*; M, two cells of a *Sephaeroeca* colony; N, one cell of a colony of *Desmarella*; O, *Histiona*; P, *Colponema*.

106. Cells (except collar) imbedded in a gelatinous mass (Fig. 26M) ..............**107**
     Cells not imbedded in a gelatinous mass (Figs. 26A, N) ....................**108**
107. Colony spherical (Fig. 26M) ..........................................**Sphaeroeca**
     Colony irregular and amorphous, usually flat ...................... **Protospongia**
108. Individuals clustered at end of a simple or branching stalk (Fig. 26A) .....**Codosiga**
     Cells united laterally (Fig. 26N)......................................**Desmarella**
109. Lorica with a fine outer basal stalk (Figs. 26C, J)............................**112**
     Lorica without a fine outer basal stalk (Figs. 26G, H, O) .....................**110**
110. Body small compared with lorica and attached to base of lorica with a fine stalk (Fig. 26G); sessile or free-swimming; often in clusters; 23 microns ..... **Bicosoeca**
     Body almost filling lorica .................................................**111**
111. Distal end with lips and saillike projection (Fig. 26O) ................... **Histiona**
     Distal end a cylindrical cone (Fig. 26H) ........................... **Salpingoeca**
112. Colonial (Fig. 26C); 35 microns ............................ **Poteriodendron**
     Solitary (Fig. 26J); 23 microns ................................... **Codonoeca**

113. One flagellum trailing (Figs. 26D, E, K, L, P); somewhat amoeboid; stagnant water .............................................. BODONIDAE, **114**
    Both flagella directed anteriorly (Figs. 27A–E); attached or free-swimming; (usually included in the flagellated algaelike protozoans).
           Suborder **EUCHRYSOMONADINA**, OCHROMONADIDAE, **119**
114. With an anterior projection (Fig. 26K); 6 microns ................. **Rhynchomonas**
    Without an anterior projection ........................................... **115**
115. Trailing flagellum originating at middle of body; cytoplasm highly granular (Fig. 26P) ........................................................ **Colponema**
    Trailing flagellum originating at anterior end of body ......................... **116**
116. Trailing flagellum about as long as body or slightly longer (Fig. 26L); 10 to 35 microns ................................................... **Cercomonas**
    Trailing flagellum much longer than body (Figs. 26D, E) ..................... **117**
117. Cytostome conspicuous (Fig. 26D); 25 microns ..................... **Phyllomitus**
    Cytostome inconspicuous .................................................. **118**
118. Usually attached by trailing flagellum (Fig. 26E); 8 microns ......... **Pleuromonas**
    Not attached; plastic (Fig. 7D); 15 microns .............................. **Bodo**
119. Solitary ................................................................ **120**
    Colonial ............................................................... **121**
120. Without lorica; stalked or unstalked (Fig. 27A); 5 to 16 microns ............ **Monas**
    With lorica; stalked (Fig. 27B); 22 microns ......................... **Stokesiella**
121. Each individual attached at the end of a branch (Fig. 27C); 8 microns. **Dendromonas**
    Individuals attached in clusters ...................................... **122**
122. Stalks colorless and rigid (Fig. 27D); often attached to plankton crustaceans; 8 microns ............................................... **Cephalothamnium**
    Stalks yellow or brown, usually bent (Fig. 27E); stagnant waters; 6 microns.
                                                       **Anthophysis**

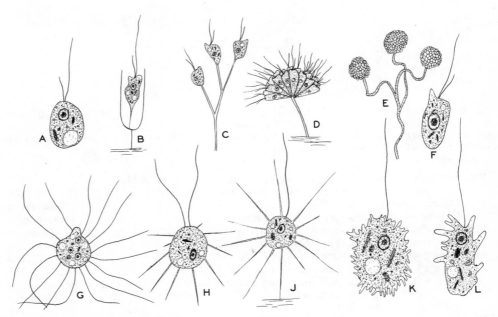

FIG. 27.–Representative Monadidae, Multiciliidae, and Mastigamoebidae. A, *Monas*; B, *Stokesiella*; C, portion of a *Dendromonas* colony; D, portion of a *Cephalothamnium* colony; E, small portion of an *Anthophysis* colony; F, single individual of *Anthophysis*; G, *Multicilia*; H, *Dimorpha*, J, *Actinomonas*; K, *Mastigella*; L, *Mastigamoeba*.

123. With many flagella; generally spherical but amoeboid (Fig. 27G); 35 microns.
       **MULTICILIIDAE, Multicilia**
     With one or two flagella; holozoic or saprozoic......**MASTIGAMOEBIDAE, 124**

124. With two flagella and numerous fine radiating filopodia (Fig. 27H); pseudopodia
       occasionally withdrawn; 18 microns..........................**Dimorpha**
     With one flagellum and exopodia or filopodia.............................**125**

125. With a ring of fine axopodia around flagellum base (Fig. 28G); 10 microns wide.
       **Pteridomonas**
     Without such a ring....................................................**126**

126. With filopodia; usually spheroidal and attached (Fig. 27J) 10 microns. **Actinomonas**
     With lobopodia........................................................**127**

127. Pseudopodia very numerous; flagellum apparently not originating at nucleus (Fig.
       27K); 130 microns.................................................**Mastigella**
     Pseudopodia not so numerous; flagellum originating at nucleus (Fig. 27L); 20 to 200
       microns.............................................................**Mastigamoeba**

Fig. 28.–Representative Mastigamoebidae, Trimastigidae, Tetramitidae, and Hexamitidae. A, *Dallingeria*; B, *Costia*; C, *Collodictyon*; D, *Tetramitus*; E, *Hexamita*; F, *Trepomonas*; G, *Pteridomonas*; H, *Macromastix*; J, *Gyromonas*; K, *Trigonomonas*; L, *Urophagus*.

128. With three flagella, two of which are trailing (Figs. 28A, H); free-swimming or attached; 5 microns; stagnant water . . . . . . . . . . . . . . TRIMASTIGIDAE, **129**
   With four to eight flagella . . . . . . . . . . . . . . . . . . . . . . . . . . . . . . . . . . . . . . . . .**130**
129. Anterior end drawn out (Fig. 28A) . . . . . . . . . . . . . . . . . . . . . . . . . . . . . . **Dallingeria**
   Anterior end not drawn out (Fig. 28H) . . . . . . . . . . . . . . . . . . . . . . . **Macromastix**
130. With four flagella originating in one area . . . . . . . . . . . . . . . . . TETRAMITIDAE, **131**
   With four, six, or eight flagella, not all originating in one area; anaerobic in stagnant water . . . . . . . . . . . . . . . . . . . . . . . . . . . . . . . . . . . . . . . HEXAMITIDAE, **133**
131. Flagella attached at or near anterior end; free-swimming in stagnant water . . . . .**132**
   Flagella attached at base of a funnellike depression (Fig. 28B); ectoparasitic on fish; 10 microns . . . . . . . . . . . . . . . . . . . . . . . . . . . . . . . . . . . . . . . . . . . . . . . . . **Costia**
132. Spherical, ovoid, or heart-shaped (Fig. 28C); 45 microns . . . . . . . . . . . .**Collodictyon**
   Pyriform, with pointed posterior end (Fig. 28D); 12 microns . . . . . . . . . . . **Tetramitus**
133. Posterior end truncate; six flagella near anterior end, two posterior (Fig. 28E); 20 microns . . . . . . . . . . . . . . . . . . . . . . . . . . . . . . . . . . . . . . . . . . . . . . . . . **Hexamita**
   Posterior end not truncate; with another arrangement of flagella . . . . . . . . . . . . . .**134**
134. Body broadly oval and flattened (Figs. 28F, J) . . . . . . . . . . . . . . . . . . . . . . . . . . .**135**
   Posterior end more or less tapered (Figs. 28 K, L) . . . . . . . . . . . . . . . . . . . . . . . .**136**
135. With two anterior pairs of flagella (Fig. 28J) . . . . . . . . . . . . . . . . . . . . . . . .**Gyromonas**
   With four flagella on each side (Fig. 28F); 10 microns . . . . . . . . . . . . . . . **Trepomonas**
136. With two cytostomes and six flagella (Fig. 28K) . . . . . . . . . . . . . . . . . . **Trigonomonas**
   With one cytostome and eight flagella; two body furrows (Fig. 28L) . . . . **Urophagus**

■ ■ ■

## KEY TO COMMON GENERA OF SARCODINA

1. Without chromatophores; with lobopodia, filopodia, or axopodia; pseudopodia the chief means of locomotion throughout the life history; the true amoeboid forms. **3**
   With one or two chromatophores and filopodia; 10 to 40 microns (usually classified with flagellates). Superclass **MASTIGOPHORA,** Class **PHYTOMASTIGOPHO-REA,** Order **CHRYSOMONADIDA, 2**
2. Filopodia branching; one or two chromatophores (Fig. 19A).
   Suborder **RHIZOCHRYSIDINA, Rhizochrysis**
   Filopodia not branching; two chromatophores; usually solitary (Fig. 16H).
   Suborder **EUCHRYSOMONADINA,** CHROMULINIDAE, **Chrysamoeba**
3. With spherical symmetry and axopodia (Figs. 33A–E) . . . . . Class **ACTINOPODA, 47**
   With spherical symmetry; lobopodia or filopodia (Figs. 29, 31, 32).
   Class **RHIZOPODA, 4**
4. Naked, without a test or shell . . . . . . . . . . . . . . . . . . . . . . . . . . . . . . . . . . . . . . . . .**5**
   With a sclerotized test or shell . . . . . . . . . . . . . . . . . . . . . . . . Order **TESTACIDA, 16**
5. With radiating reticulopodia (Fig. 29) . . . . . . . . . . . . . . . . Order **PROTEOMYXIDA, 6**
   With lobopodia (Figs. 6A, 29H, 30A,B) . . . . . . . . . . . . . . . . . . Order **AMOEBIDA, 12**
6. Small individuals grouped in a network of slightly branched and anastomosing reticulopodia (Fig. 29A); often colored by ingested algae; on *Vaucheria.* . . . . . . . . . . . . . . . . . . . . . . LABRYRINTHULIDAE, **Labyrinthula**
   Cells solitary . . . . . . . . . . . . . . . . . . . . . . . . . . . . . . . . . . . . . . . . . . . . . . . . . . . . . .**7**
7. With many reticulopodia that branch freely and anastomose; body shape and size inconstant; many small contractile vacuoles (Fig. 29C).
   VAMPYRELLIDAE, **Biomyxa**
   Reticulopodia not anastomosing . . . . . . . . . . . . . . . . . . . . . . . . . . . . . . . . . . . . . . . .**8**
8. Parasitic and completely within cells of algae and Volvocidae (Fig. 29B); 20 microns . . . . . . . . . . . . . . . . . . . . . . . . . . . . . PSEUDOSPORIDAE, **Pseudospora**
   Not completely within cells of algae and Volvocidae . . . . . . . . . . . . . . . . . . . . . . . .**9**

FIG. 29.–Representative Proteomyxida. A, *Labyrinthula* within an algal cell; B, *Pseudospora* within an algal cell; C, *Biomyxa*; D, *Hyalodiscus*; E, *Vampyrella* on a filamentous alga; F, *Protomonas*; G, *Nuclearia*; H, *Dinamoeba*.

**9.** Generally disc-shaped, with reddish endoplasm and clear ectoplasm (Fig. 29D); 65 microns . . . . . . . . . . . . . . . . . . . . . . . . . . . . . . VAMPYRELLIDAE, **Hyalodiscus**
Not generally disc-shaped; endoplasm reddish or not . . . . . . . . . . . . . . . . . . . . . . . .**10**
**10.** Heliozoa-like; when feeding on filamentous algae, body shape may change markedly (Fig. 29E); 50 to 700 microns . . . . . . . . . . . . VAMPYRELLIDAE, **Vampyrella**
Not Heliozoa-like; not feeding on filamentous algae . . . . . . . . . . . . . . . . . . . . . . . .**11**
**11.** Stored food consisting of starch granules (Fig. 29F). PSEUDOSPORIDAE, **Protomonas**
With other types of food inclusions; with or without mucous envelope (Fig. 29G); 45 microns . . . . . . . . . . . . . . . . . . . . . . . . . . . . . . . . VAMPYRELLIDAE, **Nuclearia**
**12.** With amoeboid and flagellated stages (Fig. 30A); stagnant water.
NAEGLERIIDAE, **Trimastigamoeba**
Without a flagellate stage . . . . . . . . . . . . . . . . . . . . . . . . . . . . . . AMOEBIDAE, **13**
**13.** Large, from 0.5 to 5.0 mm; many small contractile vacuoles and refringent bodies; many nuclei; on bottom in stagnant waters . . . . . . . . . . . . . . . . . . . . . . **Pelomyxa**
Smaller, from 25 to 500 microns; a single nucleus . . . . . . . . . . . . . . . . . . . . . . . . .**14**
**14.** With one broad pseudopodium (Fig. 30B); 35 microns . . . . . . . . . . . . . . . **Vahlkampfia**
With numerous pseudopodia, never anastomosing (Figs. 6A, 29H); 25 to 500 microns. **15**
**15.** Temporary posterior end often with retractile papillae; body surface with many tapering pseudopodia and papillae (Fig. 29H) . . . . . . . . . . . . . . . . . . . .**Dinamoeba**
Body with fewer typical pseudopodia (Fig. 6A) . . . . . . . . . . . . . . . . . . . . . . . . **Amoeba**
**16.** Shell simple and membranous but sometimes with bits of adhering debris (Fig. 30). **17**
Shell composed of scales, plates, sand grains, or bits of debris (Figs. 31,32) . . . . . .**18**
**17.** With numerous branching reticulopodia, usually anastomosing (Figs. 30C, D; 31K, L) . . . . . . . . . . . . . . . . . . . . . . . . . . . . . . . . . . . . . . . . . . . . . . . . . . . . . GROMIIDAE, **19**
With lobopodia or a few, simple, branched filopodia (Figs. 30F–M).
ARCELLIDAE, **23**

FIG. 30.–Representative Rhizopoda and Testacida. A, *Trimastigamoeba* (with and without flagella); B, *Vahlkampfia*; C, *Diplophrys*; D, *Lieberkühnia*; E, *Gromia*; F, *Hyalosphenia*; G, *Pseudochlamys*; H, *Pyxidicula*; J, *Difflugiella*; K, *Cochliopodium*; L, *Pamphagus*; M, *Chlamydophrys*.

18. Shell composed of foreign materials (Figs. 31A–D; 32 A–E) .. DIFFLUGIIDAE, **32**
     Shell composed of symmetrical and similar plates or scales (Figs. 31E–J; 32G,
       H) . . . . . . . . . . . . . . . . . . . . . . . . . . . . . . . . . . . . . . . . . . . EUGLYPHIDAE, **40**
19. Test with one aperture . . . . . . . . . . . . . . . . . . . . . . . . . . . . . . . . . . . . . . . . . . . . . **.20**
     Test with two apertures, thin, spherical (Fig. 30C); 14 microns . . . . . . . . . **Diplophrys**
20. Aperture lateral or subterminal (Fig. 30D); 110 microns . . . . . . . . . . . . **Lieberkühnia**
     Aperture terminal (Figs. 31K, L) . . . . . . . . . . . . . . . . . . . . . . . . . . . . . . . . . . . . **.21**
21. Filopodia branching but not anastomosing; test thin, flexible, colorless; diameter 20
       to 45 microns (Fig. 31K) . . . . . . . . . . . . . . . . . . . . . . . . . . . . . . **Lecythium**
     Filopodia anastomosing (Fig. 31L) . . . . . . . . . . . . . . . . . . . . . . . . . . . . . . . . . . **.22**
22. Filopodia arising from a peduncle; up to 50 microns in diameter (Fig. 31L). **Microgromia**
     Filopodia not arising from a peduncle; test 100 to 400 microns long . . . . . . . . **Gromia**
23. Aperture circular, central, and inverted like a funnel (Fig. 6C); 30 to 250 microns;
       common in ponds; many species . . . . . . . . . . . . . . . . . . . . . . . . . . . . . . . **Arcella**
     Aperture otherwise . . . . . . . . . . . . . . . . . . . . . . . . . . . . . . . . . . . . . . . . . . . . . . **24**

FIG. 31.–Representative Difflugiidae, Gromiidae, Arcellidae, and Euglyphidae. A, *Pseudodifflugia*; B, *Campascus*; C, a spiny *Centropyxis*; D, *Difflugia*; E, *Cyphoderia*; F, *Trinema*; G, a spiny *Euglypha*; H, *Nebela*; J, *Quadrulella*; K, *Lecythium*; L, *Microgromia*; M, *Diplochlamys*; N. *Lesquereusia*.

24. Aperture very large (Figs. 30H, M) ........................................**25**
    Aperture not especially large ............................................**26**
25. Test patelliform and rigid (Fig. 30H); 20 microns ....................**Pyxidicula**
    Test hemispherical or cup-shaped, with an inner membranous sac with an elastic
        aperture (Fig. 31M) ....................................**Diplochlamys**
26. Test disclike, flexible, sometimes rolled up (Fig. 30G); 40 microns .. **Pseudochlamys**
    Test otherwise ...........................................................**27**
27. Test semispiral, composed of curved rods or sand grains (Fig. 31N) ... **Lesquereusia**
    Test not semispiral ......................................................**28**
28. With blunt pseudopodia only; test ovoid or pyriform; protoplasm partly filling test
        (Fig. 30F); 125 microns ....................................**Hyalosphenia**
    Not with blunt pseudopodia only; protoplasm filling test .....................**29**

29.  Median pseudopodia lobate or digitate and with pointed tips; lateral pseudopodia long, fine, and tapering to a point; test ovoid and flexible (Fig. 30J); 40 microns.
**Difflugiella apiculata** Cash

All pseudopodia similar . . . . . . . . . . . . . . . . . . . . . . . . . . . . . . . . . . . . . . . . . . . . . . . . . . . .**30**

30.  Aperture large; test thin and flexible; pseudopodia blunt or pointed (Fig. 30K); 25 to 60 microns . . . . . . . . . . . . . . . . . . . . . . . . . . . . . . . . . . . . . . . **Cochliopodium**

Aperture small (Figs. 30L, M); pseudopodia long and branching . . . . . . . . . . . . . . . .**31**

31.  Test hyaline and flexible; aperture very small (Fig. 30L); 40 to 100 microns. . . . . . . . . . . . . . . . . . . . . . . . . . . . . . . . . . . . . . . . . . . . . . . . . . .**Pamphagus**

Test rigid; aperture not so small (Fig. 30M); 20 microns . . . . . . . . . . .**Chlamydophrys**

32.  Test with a curved neck, covered with small sand particles; filopodia (Fig. 31B); 25 microns . . . . . . . . . . . . . . . . . . . . . . . . . . . . . . . . . . . . . . . . . . . . . . . . .**Campascus**

Test without a curved neck . . . . . . . . . . . . . . . . . . . . . . . . . . . . . . . . . . . . . . . . . . . . .**33**

33.  Test a transparent membrane with two apertures at opposite ends (Fig. 32A).
**Amphitrema**

Test with a single aperture . . . . . . . . . . . . . . . . . . . . . . . . . . . . . . . . . . . . . . . . . . . . .**34**

34.  With long, straight or branching filopodia; test ovoid; aperture terminal (Fig. 31A); 25 to 70 microns . . . . . . . . . . . . . . . . . . . . . . . . . . . . . . . . . . . . . . **Pseudodifflugia**

Pseudopodia not filopodia . . . . . . . . . . . . . . . . . . . . . . . . . . . . . . . . . . . . . . . . . . . . .**35**

35.  Aperture eccentric; test circular, discoid, or ovoid (Fig. 31C); 125 microns.
**Centropyxis**

Aperture not eccentric (Figs. 32) . . . . . . . . . . . . . . . . . . . . . . . . . . . . . . . . . . . . . . . .**36**

FIG. 32.–Representative Difflugiidae and Euglyphidae. A, *Amphitrema*; B, *Cucurbitella*; C, *Pontigulasia*; D, *Phryganella*; E, *Heleopera*; F, *Placocista*; G, *Assulina*; H, *Sphenoderia*.

36. Aperture surrounded by a four-lobed collar; test composed of sand grains (Fig. 32B) . . . . . . . . . . . . . . . . . . . . . . . . . . . . . . . . . . . . . . . . . . . . . . . . . . . . . . **Cucurbitella**
    Aperture without a four-lobed collar . . . . . . . . . . . . . . . . . . . . . . . . . . . . . . . . . .**37**
37. Test with a necklike constriction; test composed of sand grains (Fig. 32C). **Pontigulasia**
    Test without a necklike constriction . . . . . . . . . . . . . . . . . . . . . . . . . . . . . . . . . .**38**
38. Pseudopodia drawn out to points (Fig. 32D) . . . . . . . . . . . . . . . . . . . . . . **Phryganella**
    Pseudopodia not drawn out to points . . . . . . . . . . . . . . . . . . . . . . . . . . . . . . . .**39**
39. Distal end of test covered with especially rough sand grains (Fig. 32E) . . . .**Heleopera**
    Distal end of test not covered with especially rough sand grains; test variable in shape; extremely common (Fig. 31D) . . . . . . . . . . . . . . . . . . . . . . . . . . . . . . . **Difflugia**
40. Test with a curved neck, thin and covered with discs or scales; pseudopodia long and thin (Fig. 31E); 60 to 200 microns . . . . . . . . . . . . . . . . . . . . . . . . . . . **Cyphoderia**
    Test without a curved neck . . . . . . . . . . . . . . . . . . . . . . . . . . . . . . . . . . . . . . . . . **41**
41. Test lenticular in cross section and with projecting spinous scales . . . . . . . **Placocista**
    Test without projecting scales . . . . . . . . . . . . . . . . . . . . . . . . . . . . . . . . . . . . . . . **42**
42. Test compressed anteriorly; circular siliceous scales (Fig. 31F); 30 to 100 microns.
    **Trinema**
    Test not compressed anteriorly . . . . . . . . . . . . . . . . . . . . . . . . . . . . . . . . . . . . . . **43**

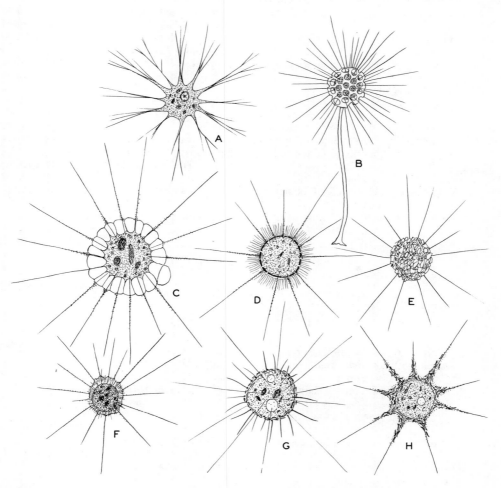

FIG. 33.–Representative Actinopoda. A, *Actinocoma*; B, *Clathrulina*; C, *Actinosphaerium*; D, *Myriophrys*; E, *Lithocolla*; F, *Heterophrys*; G, *Acanthocystis*; H, *Raphidiophrys*.

43. With filopodia ............................................... **45**
    With lobopodia ............................................... **44**
44. Test composed of circular or oval plates (Fig. 31H); 130 microns ........... **Nebela**
    Test composed of quadrangular plates (Fig. 31J); 80 to 140 microns .... **Quadrulella**
45. Aperture bordered by a dentate membrane; test colorless or brown, with elliptical
       scales arranged in diagonal rows; pseudopodia divergent, seldom branched
       (Fig. 32G) .................................................. **Assulina**
    Aperture not bordered by a dentate membrane; test hyaline, membranous; scales
       arranged in alternating series; pseudopodia often branched .............. **46**
46. Test globular or oval, without spines; aperture relatively large (Fig. 32H). **Sphenoderia**
    Test ovoid, often with scales; aperture relatively small (Fig. 31G) ........ **Euglypha**
47. Without scales, spicules, capsule, or an envelope of sand grains or diatoms ...... **48**
    With scales, spicules, capsule, or an envelope of sand grains or diatoms ......... **50**
48. Pseudopodia branched and with thickened bases (Fig. 33A); 20 microns.
                                   ACTINOCOMIDAE, **Actinocoma**
    Pseudopodia unbranched and without thickened bases ....ACTINOPHYRIDAE, **49**
49. Granular endoplasm clearly set off from vacuolar ectoplasm (Fig. 33C); 70 to 300
       microns ............................................... **Actinosphaerium**
    Endoplasm and ectoplasm not clearly divided (Fig. 6D); 40 microns .... **Actinophrys**
50. With a chitinoid, perforated capsule and a stalk (Fig. 33B); 75 microns.
                                   CLATHRULINIDAE, **Clathrulina**
    With chitinoid or siliceous spicules or scales, or with an envelope of sand grains or
       diatoms .................................................. **51**
51. With numerous flagella among axopodia; siliceous scales (Fig. 33D); 40 microns.
                                   MYRIOPHRYIDAE, **Myriophrys**
    Without flagella ............................................... **52**
52. With an outer envelope of sand grains, diatoms, or debris (Fig. 33E); 45 microns.
                                   LITHOCOLLIDAE, **Lithocolla**
    With chitinous or siliceous scales or spicules ................................. **53**
53. Without siliceous scales; with indistinct radially arranged spicules projecting beyond
       the peripheral mucilaginous layer (Fig. 33F); 15 to 80 microns.
                                   HETEROPHYRIDAE, **Heterophrys**
    With siliceous scales ............................ACANTHOCYSTIDAE, **54**
54. With tangentially arranged siliceous scales and radiating siliceous spines (Fig. 33G);
       40 microns ............................................... **Acanthocystis**
    With scales clustered around basal portions of pseudopodia; radiating siliceous spines
       absent (Fig. 33H); 55 microns ............................. **Raphidiophrys**

■  ■  ■

# KEY TO COMMON GENERA OF CILIOPHORA

1. With cilia; free-swimming or sessile ....................................... **2**
   Adult with suctorial tentacles (Fig. 47); cilia only in uncommon immature stages;
      usually sessile .............................. Subclass **SUCTORIA, 156**
2. Without adoral zone of membranelles .............. Subclass **HOLOTRICHIA, 4**
   With adoral zone of membranelles ................................... **3**
3. With adoral zone winding clockwise to cytostome (Figs. 41–43).
                                   Sublcass **SPIROTRICHIA, 96**
   With adoral zone winding counterclockwise to cytostome (Figs. 45, 46).
                                   Subclass **PERITRICHIA, 135**
4. Not commensal in mussels; without large ventral cilia........................ **5**
   Commensal in mantle cavity and gill chambers of mussels; flattened; with large
      ventral cilia for attachment (Fig. 35A); 60 to 250 microns.
              Order **THIGMOTRICHIDA**, CONCHOPHTHIRIDAE, **Conchophthirus**

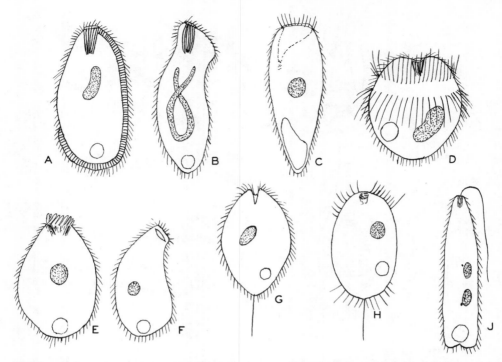

FIG. 34.–Representative Gymnostomatida. A, *Penardiella*; B, *Cranotheridium*; C, *Pelatractus*; D, *Askenasia*; E, *Spasmostoma*; F, *Platyophrya*; G, *Microregma*; H, *Pithothorax*; J, *Ileonema*.

FIG. 35.–Representative Thigmotrichida and Gymnostomatida. A, *Conchophthirus*; B, *Teuthophrys*; C, *Homalozoon*; D, *Perispira*; E, *Spathidium*; F, *Enchelydium*; G, *Vasicola*; H, *Mesodinium*; J, *Didinium*; K, *Actinobolina*; L, *Ichthyophthirius*; M, *Chilophyra*; N, *Bursella*; O, *Placus*; P, *Rhopalophrya*.

16. With large posterior cilia; without a large posterior contractile vacuole (Fig. 35G) .................................................. **Vasicola**
    Without large posterior cilia; with a large posterior contractile vacuole (Fig. 34C) .................................................. **Pelatractus**
17. Cytostome at tip of an apical cone; one to several girdles of cilia (Figs. 34D; 35 H, J) .................................................. DIDINIIDAE, **18**
    Cytostome not at tip of an apical cone .................................................. **20**
18. With an equatorial furrow and tentaclelike processes around cytostome (Fig. 35H); 30 microns .................................................. **Mesodinium**
    Without an equatorial furrow and tentaclelike processes around cytostome (Figs. 34D, 35J) .................................................. **19**
19. Two differing ciliary wreaths before midlength (Fig. 34D); uncommon ...**Askenasia**
    With two or more similar ciliary wreaths, one beyond midlength (Fig. 35J); 60 to 200 microns; feeds on other ciliates; common .................................................. **Didinium**
20. Covered with regularly arranged, perforated plates; barrel-shaped; often spinous (Fig. 9B); 40 to 100 microns .................................................. COLEPIDAE, **Coleps**
    Not covered with plates .................................................. **21**

21. With tentacles scattered among cilia; ovate or spherical (Fig. 35K); 150 microns.
    ACTINOBOLINIDAE, **Actinobolina**
    Without tentacles ....................................HOLOPHRYIDAE, **22**
22. Parasitic on the integument of many fresh-water fishes; oval (Fig. 35L); 100 to 1000
    microns; become mature on host within small pustules ..... **Ichthyophthirius**
    Not parasitic .........................................................**23**
23. With a fingerlike process in front of cytostome; ovoid or ellipsoid (Fig. 35M); 40
    microns .............................................................**Chilophrya**
    Without a fingerlike process in front of cytostome ..........................**24**
24. Cytostome with various special processes (Figs. 34E, J).....................**25**
    Cytostome without special processes........................................**26**
25. Cytostome surrounded by flaplike structures (Fig. 34E) .............**Spasmostoma**
    Cytostome with a long flagellumlike device (Fig. 34J) ................**Ileonema**
26. With a large anterior groovelike pit (Fig. 35N); 250 to 550 microns ....... **Bursella**
    Without a large anterior groovelike pit .....................................**27**
27. With prominent longitudinal grooves; 30 to 80 microns .....................**28**
    Without prominent longitudinal grooves .....................................**29**
28. Grooves spiral; body ellipsoid or ovoid; cytostome a narrow slit (Fig. 35O) . **Placus**
    Grooves not spiral; body not ovoid or ellipsoid; with few cilia (Fig. 35P).
    **Rhopalophrya**
29. Cytopharynx terminating anteriorly in a small more or less distinct conelike process;
    macronucleus spherical to oval; body ovoid to short cylindrical; one side
    convex, the other somewhat flattened (Fig. 36A); 80 microns .. **Lagynophrya**
    Cytopharynx not terminating anteriorly in a small cone; with other
    characteristics. ....................................................**30**
30. Pharyngeal trichites present (Figs. 36B, C, D, K) ..........................**31**
    Pharyngeal trichites absent................................................**34**
31. Body elongated (Fig. 36K) ........................................ **Enchelyodon**
    Body ovoid, glubose, or ellipsoidal (Figs. 36B, C, D) .......................**32**
32. Trichites long (Fig. 36B) ........................................ **Pseudoprorodon**
    Trichites shorter (Figs. 36C, D).............................................**33**
33. Body 80 to 200 microns long ....................................... **Prorodon**
    Body less than 60 microns long ...................................... **Holophrya**
34. Body asymmetrical, compressed, and flasklike or ovoid; (Fig. 34F).... **Platyophrya**
    Body radially symmetrical ...............................................**35**
35. Body elongated (Figs. 36G–J) ..............................................**36**
    Body not especially elongated ............................................**38**
36. Greatly flattened, lancet-shaped or flask-shaped; sometimes ribbonlike (Fig.
    36G) ............................................................**Trachelophyllum**
    Not greatly flattened .....................................................**37**
37. With a ringlike constriction around cytostome bearing long cilia; polymorphic and
    highly contractile (Fig. 36H); 70 to 1000 microns ............. **Lacrymaria**
    Without such a ringlike constriction; with a furrowed headlike structure (Fig. 36J);
    50 to 300 microns .......................................... **Chaenea**
38. Cytostome entirely or partially fringed with small tentaclelike processes (Figs.
    36E, F) ................................................................**39**
    Cytostome without such processes ........................................**40**
39. Small tentaclelike processes surrounding cytostome; one or more long caudal cilia
    (Fig. 36E); 15 to 30 microns .................................. **Urotricha**
    Small tentaclelike processes only partially surrounding cytostome; with or without
    long caudal cilium (Fig. 36F); 30 to 40 microns ................**Plagiocampa**
40. Flask-shaped; anterior end obliquely truncate (Fig. 36L); 40 to 200 microns. **Enchelys**
    Not flask-shaped .......................................................**41**
41. Dorsal side convex; ventral side flat; cytostome small and slitlike (Fig. 34G); up to
    60 microns .................................................. **Microregma**
    Dorsal side not convex; ventral side not flat; no slitlike cytostome ............**42**
42. Ciliation uniform (Fig. 36D); 35 microns ........................... **Holophrya**
    Ciliation coarse and not uniform (Fig. 34H) ....................... **Pithothorax**

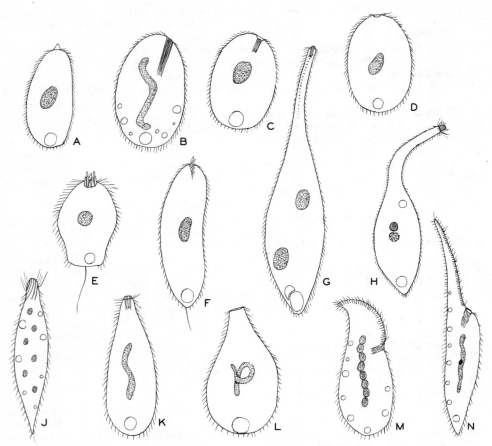

FIG. 36.–Representative Gymnostomatida. A, *Lagynophrya*; B, *Pseudoprorodon*; C, *Prorodon*; D, *Holophrya*; E, *Urotricha*; F, *Plagiocampa*; G, *Trachelophyllum*; H, *Lacrymaria*; J, *Chaenea*; K, *Enchelyodon*; L, *Enchelys*; M, *Branchiocoetes*; N, *Dileptus*.

**43.** Cytostome lateral, slitlike or circular (Figs. 36M, N; 37A–G) . . . . . . . . . . . . . . . . .**44**
   Cytostome on the flat ventral surface, in anterior half (Figs. 37H–N) . . . . . . . . . .**52**
**44.** Cytostome circular, at base of a long neck (Figs. 36M, N; 37A,B).
                                                         TRACHELIIDAE, **45**
   Cytostome a longitudinal cleft (Figs. 37C–G) . . . . . . . . . . . . . . . . . . . . . . . . . . . . . . . .**48**
**45.** Anterior end narrow and drawn out . . . . . . . . . . . . . . . . . . . . . . . . . . . . . . . . . . . . . . . .**46**
   Anterior end not narrow and drawn out (Fig 36M); 150 microns; ectocommensals on
      aquatic isopods and amphipods . . . . . . . . . . . . . . . . . . . . . . . . . . . . .**Branchiocoetes**
**46.** Elongated and narrow (Fig. 36N); 200 to 600 microns; often feeds on small and
      injured metazoans . . . . . . . . . . . . . . . . . . . . . . . . . . . . . . . . . . . . . . . . . . **Dileptus**
   Not especially narrow (Figs. 37A, B) . . . . . . . . . . . . . . . . . . . . . . . . . . . . . . . . . . . . .**47**
**47.** Anterior end in the form of a short fingerlike process; small peristomial field; cytostome in neck region (Fig. 37A); 300 microns . . . . . . . . . . . . . . . . . . . . **Trachelius**
   Anterior end drawn out into a long process; wide peristomial field; body broad at
      level of cytostome (Fig. 37B); 100 to 450 microns . . . . . . . . . . . . . .**Paradileptus**
**48.** Cytostome on convex side of anterior portion of body (Figs.
      37D–G) . . . . . . . . . . . . . . . . . . . . . . . . . . . . . . . . . . . . . . . AMPHILEPTIDAE, **49**
   Cytostome on concave side of anterior end of body; lancet shaped; anterior end
      curved ventrally (Fig. 37C); 100 to 700 microns . . . . LOXODIDAE, **Loxodes**

FIG. 37.–Representative Gymnostomatida. A, *Trachelius*; B, *Paradileptus*; C, *Loxodes*; D, *Bryophyllum*; E, *Amphileptus*; F, *Litonotus*; G, *Loxophyllum*; H, *Nassula*; J, *Chilodontopsis*; K, *Trochilia*; L, *Dysteria*; M, *Chlamydodon*; N, *Cyclogramma*; O, *Orthodonella*.

**49.** Both left and right sides of body ciliated . . . . . . . . . . . . . . . . . . . . . . . . . . . . . . . . . . . . .**50**
Without cilia on the left side . . . . . . . . . . . . . . . . . . . . . . . . . . . . . . . . . . . . . . . . . . . .**51**
**50.** With a prominent ventral ridge bearing trichocysts (Fig. 37D); 130 microns.
**Bryophyllum**
Flask-shaped, without such a ridge (Fig. 37E); often on other colonial Protozoa; sometimes parasitic on gills of fishes and tadpoles; 40 to 135 microns.
**Amphileptus**
**51.** Without trichocyst borders; flask-shaped, elongated, and flattened; cilia only on right side (Fig. 37F); 80 to 500 microns . . . . . . . . . . . . . . . . . . . . . . . . . . . . **Litonotus**
Ventral side with a trichocyst border; dorsal side with trichocyst border or clumps of trichocysts (Fig. 37G); shape variable; 100 to 700 microns . . . **Loxophyllum**
**52.** Ciliation complete; dorsal cilia less dense than those on flat ventral surface; 50 to 250 microns . . . . . . . . . . . . . . . . . . . . . . . . . . . . . . . . . . . . . . . . . . . NASSULIDAE, **53**
Ciliation incomplete; dorsal surface without cilia or with only a few sensory bristles. . . . . . . . . . . . . . . . . . . . . . . . . . . . . . . . . . . . . . . . . . . . . . . . . . . . . . . . . . . .**56**
**53.** Brightly colored because of food vacuoles and symbiotic algae . . . . . . . . . . . . . . .**54**
Not brightly colored . . . . . . . . . . . . . . . . . . . . . . . . . . . . . . . . . . . . . . . . . . . . . . . . . .**55**

**54.** Trichocyst layer indistinct; often swims with a rolling motion; more than 70 microns long (Fig. 37H) ...............................................................**Nassula**

Heavy trichocyst layer; glides on substrate; less than 70 microns long (Fig. 37N) ................................................................ **Cyclogramma**

**55.** Cytopharynx nearly longitudinal (Fig. 37J) .......................**Chilodontopsis**

Cytopharynx at an angle (Fig. 37O) .............................. **Orthodonella**

**56.** Posterior ventral surface with a spinelike process (Figs. 37K, L). DYSTERIIDAE, ...............................................................**57**

Posterior end without such a process .............. CHLAMYDODONTIDAE, 58

**57.** Ciliated portion of ventral surface free (Fig. 37K); 30 microns ..........**Trochilia**

Ciliated portion of ventral surface more or less covered by a fold of the unciliated portion (Fig. 37L); 35 to 160 microns ........................... **Dysteria**

**58.** Variously shaped; dorsal surface without a transverse row of bristles; cytostome more or less elongated (Fig. 37M); 100 microns; rare ......... **Chlamydodon**

Ovoid; dorsal surface with a transverse row of bristles; cytostome round (Fig. 9A); very common; 50 to 300 microns ..........................**Chilodonella**

**59.** With a gelatinous lorica (Fig. 38A); 40 microns ..... MARYNIDAE, **Mycterothrix**

Without a gelatinous lorica ...............................................**60**

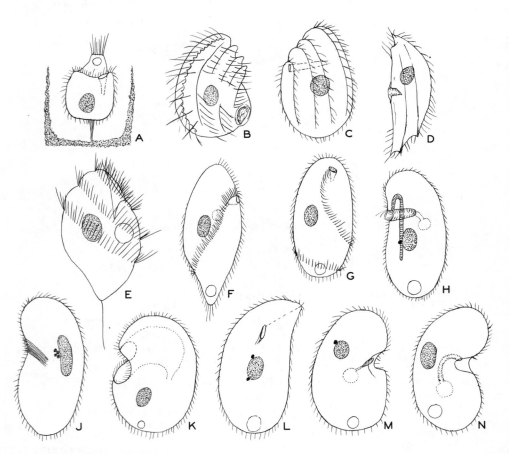

FIG. 38.–Representative Trichostomatida. A, *Mycterothrix*; B, *Microthorax*; C, *Leptopharynx*; D, lateral view of *Drepanomonas*; E, *Trimyema*; F, *Spirozona*; G, *Trichospira*; H, *Plagiopyla*; J, lateral view of *Clathrostoma*; K, *Bresslaua*; L, *Bryophrya*; M, *Colpoda*; N, *Tillina*.

**60.** Ciliation sparse; with two to nine keellike ridges; compressed (Figs. 38B–D) ........................................MICROTHORACIDAE, **61**
Ciliation dense; without keellike ridges .....................................**63**

**61.** Cytostome one-third to one-half of way from anterior end ....................**62**
Cytostome near posterior end (Fig. 38B); 20 to 70 microns ...........**Microthorax**

**62.** Cytopharynx long and tubular (Fig. 38C); 40 microns .............. **Leptopharynx**
Cytopharynx simple and short, near middle of body (Fig. 38D); 40 microns.
**Drepanomonas**

**63.** With a long cilium at the posterior end; cilia in a few spiral rows (Fig. 38E); 65 microns; usually in sewage ..................TRIMYEMIDAE, **Trimyema**
Without a single long posterior cilium; usually larger ........................**64**

**64.** With a spiral zone of special cilia extending from cytostome to posterior end (Figs. 38F, G); 90 microns ...............................................**65**
Without such special cilia .................................................**66**

**65.** Spiral zone of special cilia extending from right anterior to left posterior (Fig. 38F); spindle-shaped; usually in sewage ............ SPIROZONIDAE, **Spirozona**
Spiral zone of special cilia extending from left anterior to right posterior; cylindrical (Fig. 38G) ............................TRICHOSPIRIDAE, **Trichospira**

**66.** Peristome a ciliated cross furrow leading to cytostome; with a curved dorsal band originating in peristome (Fig. 38H); 100 microns.
PLAGIOPYLIDAE, **Plagiopyla**
Peristome otherwise ......................................................**67**

**67.** Cytostome slitlike and in a small, flat, oval groove bearing a ciliated ridge (Fig. 38J); 70 to 180 microns ..................CLATHROSTOMIDAE, **Clathrostoma**
Cytostome funnellike and deep ...........................COLPODIDAE, **68**

**68.** Cytopharynx very large, occupying anterior half of animal (Fig. 38K); 80 to 250 microns; stagnant water .................................... **Bresslaua**
Cytopharynx not particularly large .........................................**69**

**69.** Ovoid to ellipsoid, anterior end slightly bent (Fig. 38L); 50 to 120 microns. **Bryophrya**
Kidney-shaped..............................................................**70**

**70.** Cytopharynx short (Fig. 38M); 20 to 120 microns ., .................. **Colpoda**
Cytopharynx long and curved (Fig. 38N); 80 to 400 microns .............. **Tillina**

**71.** Peristome lined with rows of free cilia; cigar- or slipper-shaped (Fig. 9E); 60 to 300 microns ................................PARAMECIIDAE, **Paramecium**
Peristome with membrane; with or without free cilia ........................**72**

**72.** Cytostome not connected with peristome.
TETRAHYMENIDAE and FRONTONIIDAE, **73**
Cytostome at end or bottom of peristome ..................................**88**

**73.** Without long caudal cilia.................................................**80**
With one or more long caudal cilia ........................................**74**

**74.** Body constricted in middle (Figs. 39L, M) ................................**75**
Body not constricted in middle; with a single large posterior cilium ........**76**

**75.** Two ciliary bands; cluster of fused cilia at posterior end (Fig. 39M); 75 microns.
**Urocentrum turbo** (O.F.M.)
Single ciliary band around anterior half of body; with a single posterior cilium (Fig. 39L); 30 microns ........................................... **Urozona**

**76.** Body cylindrical, with pluglike ends.............................. **Balanonema**
Body not cylindrical; no pluglike ends .....................................**77**

**77.** Body flat and with deep longitudinal furrows (Fig. 39B) ............ **Platynematum**
Body without deep furrows ...............................................**78**

**78.** Cytostome 0.7 to 0.8 as long as body; ventral side concave (Fig. 39K); 140 microns ..............................................................**Lembadion**
Cytostome shorter .......................................................**79**

**79.** Body compressed; with cilia along anterior margin (Fig. 39O); 40 microns; often in decaying animal matter .....................................**Saprophilus**
Body not compressed; without cilia along anterior margin (Fig. 39P); 50 to 200 microns ..............................................................**Loxocephalus**

FIG. 39.–Representative Hymenostomatida. A, *Frontonia*; B, *Platynematum*; C, *Colpidium*; D, *Glaucoma*; E, *Monochilum*; F, *Cyrtolophosis*; G, *Balanonema*; H, *Tetrahymena*; J, *Dichilum*; K, *Lembadion*; L, *Urozona*; M, *Urocentrum*; N, *Cinetochilum*; O, *Saprophilus*; P, *Loxocephalus*; Q, *Uronema*; R, *Disematostoma*; S, *Stokesia*.

**80.** Body an oblique cone with rounded angles; 100 to 160 microns in diameter (Fig. 39S) ..................................................................... **Stokesia**
Body shaped differently ...............................................................81
**81.** Cytostome opening pointed at anterior end (Fig. 39A) ................. **Frontonia**
Cytostome opening more or less rounded at anterior end ......................82
**82.** Posterior end bluntly pointed (Fig. 39R) ....................... **Disematostoma**
Posterior end not pointed .............................................................83
**83.** Cytostome clearly oblique (Figs. 39C, D) ....................................84
Cytostome not clearly oblique (Figs. 39E, F, H, J) ..........................85

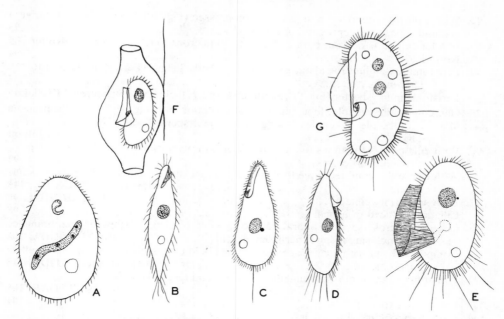

FIG. 40.–Representative Hymenostomatida. A, *Ophryoglena*; B, *Cohnilembus*; C, *Philaster*; D, *Cristigera*; E, *Pleuronema*; F, *Calyptotricha*; G, *Histiobalantium*.

**84.** Ovoid or ellipsoid; with seven postoral ciliary meridians (Fig. 39D); 55 microns.
    **Glaucoma**
   Elongate reniform; usually with a single postoral ciliary meridian (Fig. 39D); 50 to
    150 microns ............................................... **Colpidium**
**85.** Cytostome and cytopharynx with a single membranelle (Fig. 39E); 75 microns.
    **Monochilum**
   Cytostome and cytopharynx with two to four membranelles (Figs. 39F, H, J)....**86**
**86.** Within a mucilaginous envelope; cytostome with a pocket-forming membrane (Fig.
    39F); 30 microns ..........................................**Cyrtolophosis**
   Without a mucilaginous envelope .........................................**87**
**87.** Cytostome about 0.1 or less the body length from the anterior end; pyriform or
    variable body shape; cytostome in median line (Fig. 39H); 40 to 200 microns;
    often a facultative parasite in aquatic invertebrates ...........**Tetrahymena**
   Cytostome about 0.2 the body length from anterior end; ellipsoid; cytostome slightly
    to left of median line (Fig. 39J); 40 microns .....................**Dichilum**
**88.** Peristome a small sickle-shaped slit; ellipsoid to cylindrical (Fig. 40A); some species
    parasitic in fresh-water invertebrates; 80 to 500 microns.
    OPHRYOGLENIDAE, **Ophryoglena**
   Peristome long, beginning at anterior end of body ..........................**89**
**89.** Peristome with a prominent membrane forming a pocket surrounding cytostome;
    with one to several stiff posterior cilia (Figs. 40 D–G).
    PLEURONEMATIDAE, **92**
   Peristome without such a prominent membrane ...........................**90**
**90.** With double undulating membrane on right side of peristomial furrow.
    COHNILEMBIDAE, **91**
   Membrane at right of oral furrow not double; 70 to 150 microns (Fig.
    40C) ................................... PHILASTERIDAE, **Philaster**
**91.** Anterior end not ciliated (Fig. 39Q) .................................**Uronema**
   Anterior end ciliated (Fig. 40B) .................................. **Cohnilembus**

**92.** With a postoral depression or groove; compressed (Fig. 40D); 50 microns. **Cristigera**
   Without a postoral depression or groove . . . . . . . . . . . . . . . . . . . . . . . . . . . . . . . . . .**93**
**93.** In a lorica that is open at both ends; body 50 microns long (Fig. 40F). **Calyptotricha**
   No lorica . . . . . . . . . . . . . . . . . . . . . . . . . . . . . . . . . . . . . . . . . . . . . . . . . . . . . . .**94**
**94.** Peristome extending for about two-thirds of body length (Figs. 40E, G); 70 to 180
   microns . . . . . . . . . . . . . . . . . . . . . . . . . . . . . . . . . . . . . . . . . . . . . . . . . . . . . . . . . .**95**
   Peristome much shorter (Fig. 9C); with refractive pellicle; 20 to 50 microns. **Cyclidium**
**95.** One contractile vacuole; long cilia only at posterior end (Fig. 40E) . . . . **Pleuronema**
   Many contractile vacuoles; long cilia interspersed all over body (Fig.
   40G) . . . . . . . . . . . . . . . . . . . . . . . . . . . . . . . . . . . . . . . . . . . . . . . .**Histiobalantium**
**96.** With cilia only, sometimes reduced or absent; rarely with additional small groups of
   cirruslike structures . . . . . . . . . . . . . . . . . . . . . . . . . . . . . . . . . . . . . . . . . . . . . . .**97**
   With cirri only, confined to ventral surface; dorsal surface usually with rows of short
   bristles . . . . . . . . . . . . . . . . . . . . . . . . . . . . . . . . . . Order **HYPOTRICHIDA, 115**
**97.** Body uniformly ciliated . . . . . . . . . . . . . . . . . . . . . . . .Order **HETEROTRICHIDA, 99**
   Ciliation reduced or absent . . . . . . . . . . . . . . . . . . . . . . . . . . . . . . . . . . . . . . . . . .**98**
**98.** Circular in cross section; adoral zone consisting of cirri, bristles, or membranelles
   and enclosing a spiral peristomial field . . . . . . Order **OLIGOTRICHIDA, 108**
   Compressed and with a carapace; peristomial field consisting of eight membranelles;
   anaerobic . . . . . . . . . . . . . . . . . . . . . . . . . Order **ODONTOSTOMATIDA, 113**
**99.** Peristome sunken into the funnellike anterior end (Figs. 41A,B).
                                                                    **BURSARIIDAE, 100**
   Peristome exposed . . . . . . . . . . . . . . . . . . . . . . . . . . . . . . . . . . . . . . . . . . . . . . .**101**
**100.** Cytopharynx curved to the left (Fig. 41A); 500 to 1000 microns.
                                                         **Bursaria truncatella** O.F.M.
   Cytopharynx curved to the right (Fig. 41B); 60 to 100 microns . . . . . . .**Bursaridium**
**101.** With a narrow nonciliated zone to the right of the adoral zone (Figs. 41C–G) . . .**102**
   Without such a nonciliated zone . . . . . . . . . . . . . . . . . . . . . . . . . . . . . . . . . . . . .**106**
**102.** Adoral zone extending diagonally to right and posterior on ventral surface (Figs.
   41C, E); anaerobic . . . . . . . . . . . . . . . . . . . . . . . . . . . . . . **METOPIDAE, 103**
   Adoral zone longitudinal on flat ventral surface and turning to right before cytostome
   (Figs. 41D, F, G) . . . . . . . . . . . . . . . . . . . . . . . . . . . . .**SPIROSTOMIDAE, 104**
**103.** Body shape variable but more or less oblong or fusiform (Fig. 41C); 80 to 300
   microns . . . . . . . . . . . . . . . . . . . . . . . . . . . . . . . . . . . . . . . . . . . . . . . . . . .**Metopus**
   Bell-shaped and with long, pointed posterior end (Fig. 41E); 185 microns.
                                                                        **Caenomorpha**
**104.** Cylindrical and very much elongated; large posterior contractile vacuole (Fig. 41D);
   150 to 3000 microns . . . . . . . . . . . . . . . . . . . . . . . . . . . . . . . . . . . **Spirostomum**
   Not especially elongated; not cylindrical; contractile vacuole smaller . . . . . . . . . .**105**
**105.** With marked grooves on body surface; cilia in cirruslike fused groups; oval (Fig.
   41F); 100 microns . . . . . . . . . . . . . . . . . . . . . . . . . . . . . . . . . . . . **Phacodinium**
   Without grooves; without fused cilia; spindle-shaped or ellipsoid (Fig. 41G); 80 to
   200 microns . . . . . . . . . . . . . . . . . . . . . . . . . . . . . . . . . . . . . . . . . .**Blepharisma**
**106.** With a large undulating membrane; peristomial field not ciliated; ellipsoid (Fig. 41H);
   100 to 400 microns . . . . . . . . . . . . . . . .CONDYLOSTOMIDAE, **Condylostoma**
   Without a large undulating membrane; peristomial field ciliated.
                                                                    **STENTORIDAE, 107**
**107.** Highly contractile, trumpet-shaped or cylindrical when extended but oval to pyriform
   while swimming; adoral zone encircling peristome in a spiral (Fig. 41K); 200
   to 3000 microns . . . . . . . . . . . . . . . . . . . . . . . . . . . . . . . . . . . . . . . . . . . **Stentor**
   Flattened and oval; adoral zone otherwise (Fig. 41J); 100 to 300 microns.
                                                                        **Climacostomum**
**108.** Oral portion of peristome free on ventral surface; ovoid to spherical (Figs. 42A,B);
   35 microns . . . . . . . . . . . . . . . . . . . . . . . . . . . . . . . . . . . . . . . **HALTERIIDAE, 109**
   Oral region enclosed by adoral zone (Figs. 42C, F) . . . . . . . . . . . . . . . . . . . . . .**110**
**109.** With body bristles or cirri (Fig. 42A) . . . . . . . . . . . . . . . . . . . . . . . . . . . . **Halteria**
   Without body bristles or cirri (Fig. 42B) . . . . . . . . . . . . . . . . . . . . . . **Strombidium**

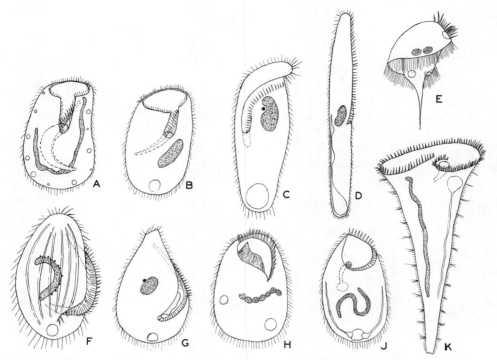

FIG. 41.–Representative Heterotrichida. A, *Bursaria*; B, *Bursaridium*; C, *Metopus*; D, *Spirostomum*; E, *Caenomorpha*; F, *Phacodinium*; G, *Blepharisma*; H, *Condylostoma*; J, *Climacostomum*; K, *Stentor*.

**110.** Without lorica; pyriform (Fig. 42C); 55 microns ..STROBILIDIIDAE, **Strobilidium**
  With lorica or test, usually covered with debris .............TINTINNIDAE, **111**
**111.** Lorica divided into collar and basal portions (Fig. 42D); 65 microns .....**Codonella**
  Lorica not so divided ...................................................**112**
**112.** Lorica viscous, irregular in form, usually elongated, and translucent (Fig. 42F); 40
  to 200 microns ........................................... **Tintinnidium**
  Lorica not viscous, thin, bowl-shaped (Fig. 42E); 50 microns ........ **Tintinnopsis**
**113.** With frontal cilia; with posterior marginal teeth or ridges (Figs.
  42H,J) ........................................... EPALXELLIDAE, **114**
  Without frontal cilia; oval; without marginal posterior teeth or ridges (Fig. 42G); 80
  microns ........................... DISCOMORPHIDAE, **Discomorpha**
**114.** Some posterior teeth spiny (Fig. 42H); 50 microns ................. **Saprodinium**
  Posterior teeth not spiny (Fig. 42J); 25 to 80 microns ................... **Epalxella**
**115.** Adoral zone reduced or rudimentary; seven frontoventral cirri (Fig. 43A); 35
  microns .................................... ASPIDISCIDAE, **Aspidisca**
  Adoral zone well developed; usually larger ..............................**116**
**116.** With two rows of marginal cirri........................OXYTRICHIDAE, **117**
  Without marginal cirri; ovid; macronucleus band-shaped (Fig. 43B); 80 to 200
  microns ................................... EUPLOTIDAE, **Euplotes**
**117.** Anal cirri absent (Figs. 43C–E) ..........................................**118**
  Anal cirri present (Figs. 43,44) .........................................**121**
**118.** Ventral and marginal cirri spirally arranged (Figs. 43D, E); sometimes in gelatinous
  tubes and colonial.....................................................**119**
  Ventral and marginal cirri not spirally arranged; elongated; taillike region (Fig. 43C);
  175 microns ............................................. **Uroleptus**

Fig. 42.–Representative Oligotrichida and Odontostomatida. A, *Halteria*; B, *Strombidium*; C, *Strobilidium*; D, lorica of *Codonella*; E, *Tintinnopsis*; F, *Tintinnidium*; G, *Discomorpha*; H, *Saprodinium*; J, *Epalxella*.

119. Peristome about one-fourth of body length (Fig. 43D); 80 to 250 microns.
         **Strongylidium**
     Peristome about one-half of body length (Fig. 43E); 50 to 200 microns ........**120**
120. Peristome-bearing part not flexible (Fig. 43E) .....................**Stichotricha**
     Peristome-bearing part flexible .................................**Chaetospira**
121. Frontal field without any special cirri (Figs. 43F, G, H, L, M) ...............**122**
     Frontal field with a few strong cirri (Figs. 43J, K; 44A–G)...................**126**
122. Ellipsoid ...............................................................**123**
     Not ellipsoid ..........................................................**124**
123. One row of ventral cirri (Fig. 43F); 30 to 80 microns .................**Balladyna**
     Three rows of ventral cirri (Fig. 43L) ..............................**Trichotaxis**
124. Elongated and spoon-shaped (Fig. 43G); free-swimming; 375 microns .... **Epiclintes**
     Not spoon-shaped.......................................................**125**
125. Reniform (Fig. 43H); commensal or parasitic on hydras; 160 microns.
         **Kerona polyporum** Ehr.
     Elongated, with two ventral rows of setae reaching frontal field (Fig. 43M).
         **Keronopsis**
126. Ventral cirri numerous and always arranged in long longitudinal rows (Figs. 43J,
         K).....................................................................**127**
     Ventral cirri not particularly numerous and at least partly arranged in groups (Figs.
         44A–G) ................................................................**128**
127. Ventral cirri in four or more rows (Fig. 43J); 200 to 800 microns ........ **Urostyla**
     Ventral cirri in one to three rows (Figs. 43K); 80 to 350 microns ....... **Holosticha**
128. Ventral cirri arranged in one to three distinct longitudinal rows (Figs. 44A–D) ..**129**
     Ventral cirri not arranged in rows (Figs. 44E–G) ..........................**132**
129. With one to three longitudinal and parallel rows of cirri (Figs. 44A, B).........**130**
     With one or two oblique ventral rows of cirri (Figs. 44C, D) .................**131**
130. With two of the seven anal cirri more posterior (Fig. 44A); 170 to 400 microns.
         **Pleurotricha**
     With a different arrangement of the anal cirri (Fig. 44B); 110 microns.
         **Onychodromopsis**

FIG. 43.–Representative Hypotrichida; ventral views. A, *Aspidisca*; B, *Euplotes*; C, *Uroleptus*; D, *Strongylidium*; E, *Stichotricha*; F, *Balladyna*; G, *Epiclintes*; H, *Kerona*; J, *Urostyla*; K, *Holosticha*; L, *Trichotaxis*; M, *Keronopsis*.

131. With a long row of ventral cirri (Fig. 44C); 150 to 320 microns . . . . . . . .**Gastrostyla**
    With one or two short rows of ventral cirri (Fig. 44D); 120 microns . . **Gonostomum**
132. With 12 to 17 strong frontal cirri; four to eight macronuclei (Fig. 44E); 100 to 300 microns . . . . . . . . . . . . . . . . . . . . . . . . . . . . . . . . . **Onychodromus grandis** Stein
    With no more than 10 frontal cirri; 1 to 4 macronuclei (Figs. 44F, G) . . . . . . . . .**133**
133. Posterior end taillike (Fig. 44F); 110 to 250 microns . . . . . . . . . . . . . . . . . .**Urosoma**
    Posterior end not taillike; 50 to 300 microns . . . . . . . . . . . . . . . . . . . . . . . . .**134**
134. Body soft and flexible; caudal cirri short (Fig. 44G) . . . . . . . . . . . . . . . . .**Oxytricha**
    Body stiff; caudal cirri usually long (Fig. 9F) . . . . . . . . . . . . . . . . . . . . .**Stylonychia**
135. Usually attached; rarely with body cilia . . . . . . . . . . . . . . . . . . Order **SESSILIA, 136**
    Free-swimming but with highly developed attachment disc on basal (aboral) surface . . . . . . . . . . . . . . . . . . . . . . . .Order **MOBILIA**, URCEOLARIIDAE, **154**
136. Without a lorica but sometimes with a gelatinous envelope (Fig. 45) . . . . . . . . . .**137**
    With a well-developed lorica . . . . . . . . . . . . . . . . . . . . . . . . . . . . . . . . . . . . . . . .**148**
137. Posterior end usually with one or two short spines; free-swimming (Figs. 45A, B) . . . . . . . . . . . . . . . . . . . . . . . . . . . . . . . . . . . . . ASTYLOZOONIDAE, **138**
    Posterior end without spines; sessile . . . . . . . . . . . . . . . . . . . . . . . . . . . . . . . . .**139**

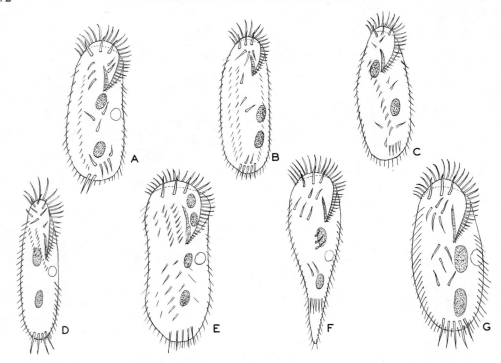

FIG. 44.–Representative Hypotrichida; ventral views. A, *Pleurotricha*; B, *Onychodromopsis*; C, *Gastrostyla*; D, *Gonostomum*; E, *Onychodromus grandis*; F, *Urosoma*; G, *Oxytricha*.

138. Body with two to four rings of long, conical processes (Fig. 45A); 40 microns; common in rivers .......................................... **Hastatella**
     Body without such processes; conical, ends broadly rounded; ring of cilia near aboral end (Fig. 45B); 160 microns ............................... **Opisthonecta**
139. With a long, cylindrical contractile neck; colonial; individuals imbedded in common gelatinous mass (Figs. 45C, D); 200 to 500 microns; colonies up to 15 cm in diameter .................................. OPHRYDIIDAE, **Ophrydium**
     Without a necklike region ............................................... **140**
140. Without stalk, with posterior attachment disc (Fig. 45E); attached to debris, or epizoic; 40 to 100 microns .................. SCYPHIDIIDAE, **Scyphidia**
     Stalk present ......................................................... **141**
141. Stalk not retractile ...................................... EPISTYLIDAE, **142**
     Stalk retractile; bell-shaped; attached to plants and aquatic invertebrates. VORTICELLIDAE, **146**
142. Stalk branched; colonial (Figs. 45F–H) ................................. **143**
     Stalk not branched; attached to vegetation and a wide variety of aquatic invertebrates; 25 to 100 microns ......................................... **145**
143. Adoral zone with four to six turns (Fig. 45F); 130 to 350 microns ..... **Campanella**
     Adoral zone simpler; attached to vegetation and many aquatic invertebrates; 40 to 150 microns .................................................... **144**
144. Peristome small, separated from peristome border and protrusible through it (Fig. 45G); often in polluted waters ............................. **Opercularia**
     Peristome nearly as wide as body, attached to peristome border at margin (Fig. 45H); colonies often macroscopic; common in polluted waters ........... **Epistylis**
145. Frontal disc supported by stylelike process (Fig. 45J) .................. **Pyxidium**
     Frontal disc not supported by stylelike process (Fig. 45K) ............ **Rhabdostyla**
146. Solitary but often gregarious (Fig. 9D); 35 to 160 microns .............. **Vorticella**
     Colonial; colonies up to 6 mm long ................................... **147**

FIG. 45.–Representative Peritrichia. A, *Hastatella*; B, *Opisthonecta*; C, *Ophrydium*; D, very small colony of *Ophrydium*; E, *Scyphidia*; F, *Campanella*; G, *Opercularia*; H, *Epistylis*; J, *Pyxidium*; K, *Rhabdostyla*.

**147.** Myonemes not continuous; individual stalks contract singly (Fig. 46A); 50 to 130 microns . . . . . . . . . . . . . . . . . . . . . . . . . . . . . . . . . . . . . . . . . . . . **Carchesium**
Myonemes continuous; entire colony contracting or expanding simultaneously (Fig. 46B); 40 to 90 microns . . . . . . . . . . . . . . . . . . . . . . . . . . . . . . . **Zoothamnium**
**148.** Distal margin not attached to lorica; with a posterior stalk (Figs. 46E–H) . . . . . . . . . . . . . . . . . . . . . . . . . . . . . . . . . . VAGINICOLIDAE, **149**
Distal margin attached to aperture of lorica; unstalked; lorica with flattened attachment surface (Fig. 46D); often ectocommensal on invertebrates; 75 microns . . . . . . . . . . . . . . . . . . . . . . . . . . . . LAGENOPHRYIDAE, **Lagenophrys**
**149.** Lorica with a stalk (Figs. 46E, F, N) . . . . . . . . . . . . . . . . . . . . . . . . . . . . . . . . . .**150**
Lorica without a stalk (Figs. 46G, H, M) . . . . . . . . . . . . . . . . . . . . . . . . . . . . . .**152**
**150.** With a discoidal corneous operculum that closes lorica when animal contracts (Figs. 46F, N) . . . . . . . . . . . . . . . . . . . . . . . . . . . . . . . . . . . . . . . . . . . . . . .**151**
Without an operculum (Fig. 46E); 50 to 100 microns . . . . . . . . . . . . . . . .**Cothurnia**
**151.** Operculum attached to lorica (Fig. 46N) . . . . . . . . . . . . . . . . . . . . . . . . . . . . **Caulicola**
Operculum attached to body (Fig. 46F) . . . . . . . . . . . . . . . . . . . . . . . . . . . . **Pyxicola**
**152.** Lorica decumbent (Fig. 46M) . . . . . . . . . . . . . . . . . . . . . . . . . . . . . . . . . . .**Platycola**
Lorica upright . . . . . . . . . . . . . . . . . . . . . . . . . . . . . . . . . . . . . . . . . . . . . . . . .**153**
**153.** With a valvelike apparatus that closes the opening of the lorica when the animal is contracted (Fig. 46H); 160 to 220 microns . . . . . . . . . . . . . . . . . . . . . . **Thuricola**
Without such a valvelike apparatus (Fig. 46G); 50 to 200 microns . . . . . . **Vaginicola**
**154.** Peristome obliquely placed (Fig. 46J); 100 microns; commensal on Turbellaria; feeds on bacteria and unicellular forms . . . . . . . . . . . . . . . . . . . . . . . . . . . **Urceolaria**
Peristome not obliquely placed; barrel-, bell-, or saucer-shaped . . . . . . . . . . . . . .**155**

FIG. 46.–Representative Peritrichia. A, *Carchesium*; B, *Zoothamnium* colony; C, free-swimming telotroch stage of a vorticellid; D, *Lagenophrys*; E, *Cothurnia*; F, *Pyxicola*; G, *Vaginicola*; H, *Thuricola*; J, *Urceolaria*; K, *Trichodina*; L, *Cyclochaeta*; M, *Platycola*; N, *Caulicola*.

155. Outer row of cilia of attachment disc not bent upward (Fig. 46K); 55 microns; commensal on *Hydra,* fishes, and amphibians; sometimes thought to be true parasites on fishes ......................................... **Trichodina**
Outer row of cilia of attachment disc stiff and bent upward (Fig. 46L); 45 microns; commensal on sponges and fishes .......................... **Cyclochaeta**
156. Body asymmetrical or branched ...........................................**157**
Body more or less symmetrical ...........................................**161**
157. Without special arms ................................ DENDROSOMIDAE, **158**
With special arms (Figs. 47A,E); commensal on isopods, amphipods, etc.
DENDROCOMITIDAE, **160**
158. Body dendritic, often large (Fig. 47B); up to 2.5 mm high; on vegetation. **Dendrosoma**
Body not dendritic ....................................................**159**
159. Body not rounded or elongated; tentacles knobbed; nucleus band-shaped (Fig. 47C); 30 to 240 microns; on vegetation and various invertebrates; also reported from gills of largemouth black bass ..........................**Trichophrya**
Body rounded and with six processes; tentacles not knobbed; nucleus round (Fig. 47D); 50 microns; often in suspension as a plankter ...........**Staurophrya**
160. With branched arms (Fig. 47A); 75 microns ..................... **Dendrocometes**
Arms not branched (Fig. 47E); 90 microns ...................... **Stylocometes**
161. Without a stalk ....................................................**162**
With a stalk of variable length ...........................................**163**

FIG. 47.–Representative Suctoria. A, *Dendrocometes*; B, *Dendrosoma*; C, *Trichophrya*; D, *Staurophrya*; E, *Stylocometes*; F, *Sphaerophrya*; G, *Solenophrya*; H, *Choanophrya*; J, *Discophrya*; K, *Metacineta*; L, *Podophrya* feeding on a ciliate; M, *Paracineta*; N, *Acineta*; O, *Hallezia*.

162. Without a lorica; spherical (Fig. 47F); 75 microns; stagnant water.
            PODOPHRYIDAE, **Sphaerophrya**
    With a lorica; tentacles in fascicles (Fig. 47G); 40 microns.
            ACINETIDAE, **Solenophrya**
163. With 5 to 12 tubular expansible tentacles used for engulfing large food particles (Fig. 47H); 65 microns......................DISCOPHRYIDAE, **Choanophrya**
    With normal type of tentacles ...........................................**164**
164. With a large attachment plate at the base of the stalk; tentacles evenly distributed or in fascicles (Fig. 47J); 70 microns .........DISCOPHRYIDAE, **Discophrya**
    Without such a plate ................................................**165**
165. Lorica drawn out, funnel-shaped, and attached to stalklike lower end (Fig. 47K); 550 microns .................................PODOPHRYIDAE, **Metacineta**
    Lorica otherwise or absent ...........................................**166**
166. Body spherical to ellipsoidal (Figs. 47L, M) ............. PODOPHRYIDAE, **167**
    Body not spherical to ellipsoidal (Figs. 47N, O) .............ACINETIDAE, **168**

**167.** Without test or cup; tentacles distributed or in fascicles (Fig. 47L); 10 to 50 microns . . . . . . . . . . . . . . . . . . . . . . . . . . . . . . . . . . . . . . . . . . . . . . . . . . . . **Podophrya**

With a close-fitting cup or gelatinous envelope without a visible rim (Fig. 47M); tentacles distributed; 40 microns . . . . . . . . . . . . . . . . . . . . . . . . . . . **Paracineta**

**168.** Body completely or partly filling the delicate cup-shaped lorica; tentacles in one to three fascicles (Fig. 47N); 30 to 180 microns . . . . . . . . . . . . . . . . . . . . . **Acineta**

Lorica absent; tentacles in one to four fascicles . . . . . . . . . . . . . . . . . . . . . . . . . .**169**

**169.** Stalk long (Fig. 10); 55 microns . . . . . . . . . . . . . . . . . . . . . . . . . . . . . . . . . . . **Tokophrya**

Stalk short (Fig. 47O) . . . . . . . . . . . . . . . . . . . . . . . . . . . . . . . . . . . . . . . . . . . . . .**Hallezia**

# PROTOZOA REFERENCES

AHLSTROM, E. H. 1937. Studies on variability in the genus Dinobryon. *Trans. Am. Microsc. Soc.* **56**:139–159.

ALLEGRE, C. F., and T. L. JAHN. 1943. A survey of the genus Phacus (Protozoa: Euglenoidina). Ibid. **62**:233–244.

BALAMUTH, W. 1940. Regeneration in protozoa: a problem of morphogenesis. *Quart. Rev. Biol.* **15**:290–337.

BARKER, A. N. 1946. The ecology and function of Protozoa in sewage purification. *Ann. Appl. Biol.* **33**:314–325.

BHATIA, B. L. 1936. Protozoa: Ciliophora. *Fauna Br. India.* 493 pp.

BICK, H. 1973. Population dynamics of Protozoa associated with the decay of organic materials in fresh waters. *Am. Zool.* **13**:149–160.

BICK, H., and S. KUNZE. 1971. Eine Zusammenstellung von autökologischen und saprobiologischen Befunden an Süsswasserciliaten. *Int. Rev. ges. Hydrobiol.* **56**:337–384.

BORROR, A. C. 1972. Revision of the Order Hypotrichida (Ciliophora, Protozoa). *J. Protozool.* **19**:1–23.

BOVEE, E. C., and T. L. JAHN. 1965. Mechanisms of movement in taxonomy of Sarcodina. II. The organization of subclasses and orders in relationship to the Classes Autotractea and Hydraulea. *Am. Midl. Nat.* **73**:293–298.

BROWN, H. P., and M. M. JENKINS. 1962. A protozoan (Dileptus; Ciliata) predatory upon Metazoa. *Science* **136**:710.

BÜTSCHLI, O. 1887–1889. Protozoa. *Kl. Ord. Thier-Reichs* **1**:1–2035.

CAIRNS, J. 1964. The chemical environment of common fresh-water Protozoa. *Not. Nat.* **365**:1–6.

———. 1971. Factors affecting the number of species in fresh-water protozoan communities. In Cairns, *The structure and function of fresh-water microbial communities.* Va. Polytech. Inst. State Univ. Press, Blacksburg, Va., pp. 219–247.

CAIRNS, J., G. R. LANZA, and B. C. PARKER. 1972. Structural and functional changes in algal and protozoan communities related to pollution. *Proc. Acad. Nat. Sci. Phila.* **124**:79–127.

CAIRNS, J., and J. A. RUTHVEN. 1972. A test of the cosmopolitan distribution of fresh-water protozoans. *Hydrobiologia* **39**:405–427.

CAIRNS, J., and W. H. YONGUE. 1974. Protozoan colonization rates on artificial substrates suspended at different depths. *Trans. Am. Microsc. Soc.* **93**:206–210.

CAIRNS, J., et al. 1969. The relationship of fresh-water protozoan communities to the Macarthur-Wilson equilibrium model. *Am. Nat.* **103**:439–454.

CALAWAY, W. T., and J. B. LACKEY. 1962. Waste treatment Protozoa. Flagellata. *Fla. Eng. Ser.* **3**:1–140.

CALKINS, G. N., and F. M. SUMMERS (eds.). 1941. *Protozoa in biological research.* 1148 pp. Columbia University Press, New York.

CANELLA, M. F. 1957. Studi e ricerche sui tentaculiferi nel quadro della biologia generale. *Ann. Dell' Univ. Ferrara (N.S.) Sezione III, Biol. Anim.* **1**:259–716.

CASH, J., J. HOPKINSON, and G. H. WAILES. 1905–1921. *The British freshwater Rhizopoda and Heliozoa.* 5 vols. London.

CHEN, T.-T. (ED.) 1967–1969. *Research in protozoology.* 3 vols. 1564 pp. Oxford University Press, Oxford, England

COLLIN, B. 1912. Études monographique sur les Acinétiéns. *Arch. Zool. Exp. Gen.* **51**:1–457.

CORLISS, J. O. 1956. Evolution and systematics of ciliates. *Syst. Zool.* **5**:68–91.

———. 1956a. On the evolution and systematics of ciliated Protozoa Part II. Ibid. 121–140.

———. 1959. An illustrated key to the higher groups of the ciliated Protozoa, with definition of terms. *J. Protozool.* **6**:265–281.

———. 1959a. Comments on the systematics and phylogeny of the Protozoa. *Syst. Zool.* **8**:169–190.

———. 1961. *The ciliated protozoa: characterization, classification and guide to the literature.* 310 pp. Pergamon Press, New York.

———. 1974. The changing world of ciliate systematics: historical analysis of past efforts and a newly proposed phylogenetic scheme of classification for the protistan Phylum Ciliophora. *Syst. Zool.* **23**:91–137.

———. 1975. Taxonomic characterization of the suprafamilial groups in a revision of recently proposed schemes of classification for the Phylum Ciliophora. *Trans. Am. Microsc. Soc.* **94**:224–267.

———. 1977. Annotated assignment of families and genera to the orders and classes currently comprising the Corlissian scheme of higher classification for the Phylum Ciliophora. *Trans. Am. Microsc. Soc.* **96:**104–140. (This paper arrived too late to receive adequate consideration.)

CORLISS, J. O., and S. C. ESSER. 1974. Comments on the role of the cyst in the life cycle and survival of free-living protozoa. Ibid. **93:**578–593.

CURDS, C. R. 1966. An ecological study of the ciliated Protozoa in activated sludge. *Oikos* **15:**282–289.

———. 1969. An illustrated key to the British fresh-water ciliated protozoa commonly found in activated sludge. *Water Pollut. Res. Tech. Pap.* **12:**1–90.

———. 1973. The role of Protozoa in the activated-sludge process. *Am. Zool.* **13:**161–169.

DEFLANDRE, G. 1928. Le genre Arcella Ehrenberg. *Arch. Protistenk.* **64:**152–287.

———. 1929. Le genre Centropyxis Stein. Ibid. **67:**322–375.

DILLON, R. D., G. L. WALSH, and D. A. BIERLE. 1968. A preliminary survey of Antarctic meltwater and soil amoebae. *Trans. Am. Microsc. Soc.* **87:**486–492.

DOFLEIN, F., and E. REICHENOW. 1928–1929. *Lehrbuch der Protozoenkunde.* 5th ed. 1262 pp. Jena.

DOYLE, W. L. 1943. The nutrition of the Protozoa. *Biol. Rev.* **18:**119–136.

EDDY, S. 1930. The fresh-water armored or thecate dinoflagellates. *Trans. Am. Microsc. Soc.* **49:**277–321.

EDMONDSON, C. H. 1906. The Protozoa of Iowa. *Proc. Davenport Acad. Sci.* **11:**1–124.

FINLEY, H. E. 1930. Toleration of freshwater Protozoa to increased salinity. *Ecology* **11:**337–346.

FJERDINGSTAD, E. J. 1961. Ultrastructure of the collar of the choanoflagellate Codonosiga botrytis (Ehrenb.). *Z. Zellforsch.* **54:**499–510.

FRITSCH, F. E. 1935. *The structure and reproduction of the algae. I.* 791 pp. Cambridge University Press, Cambridge, England.

———. 1944. Present-day classification of algae. *Bot. Rev.* **10:**233–277.

GEIMAN, Q. M. 1931. Morphological variations in Coleps octospinus. *Trans. Am. Microsc. Soc.* **50:**136–143.

GILL, D. E. 1972. Density dependence and population regulation in laboratory cultures of Paramecium. *Ecology* **53:**701–708.

GOJDICS, M. 1953. *The genus Euglena.* 268 pp. Univ. Wisconsin Press, Madison.

GOULDER, R. 1974. The seasonal and spatial distribution of some benthic ciliated Protozoa in Esthwaite Water. *Freshwater Biol.* **4:**127–147.

GREISER, D. 1974. Ökologische Untersuchungen an Ciliaten in einer Modellselbstreinigungsstrecke. *Int. Rev. ges. Hydrobiol.* **59:**543–555.

GRELL, K. G. 1973. *Protozoology.* 554 pp. Springer, Berlin.

GRIMSTONE, A. V. 1961. Fine structure and morphogenesis in Protozoa. *Biol. Rev.* **36:**97–150.

GRUCHY, D. F. 1955. The breeding system and distribution of Tetrahymena pyriformis. *J. Protozool.* **2:**178–185.

HALL, R. P. 1939. The trophic nature of the plant-like flagellates. *Q. Rev. Biol.* **14:**1–12.

HAMILTON, J. M. 1952. Studies on loricate Ciliophora. I. Cothurnia variabilis Kellicott. *Trans. Am. Microsc. Soc.* **71:**382–392.

HIRSCHFIELD, H. I. 1959. The Biology of the Amoeba. *Ann. N.Y. Acad. Sci.* **78:**1–303.

HOLLANDE, A. 1942. Étude cytologique et biologique de quelques flagellés libres. *Arch. Zool. Exp. Gen.* **83** (Suppl.) :1–268.

HONIGBERG, B. M., et al. 1964. A revised classification of the Phylum Protozoa. *J. Protozool.* **11:**7–20.

JAHN, T. L. 1934. Problems of population growth in the Protozoa. *Cold Spring Harbor Symp. Quant. Biol.* **2:**167–180.

———. 1946. The euglenoid flagellates. *Q. Rev. Biol.* **21:**246–274.

JAHN, T. L., and F. F. JAHN. 1949. *How to know the Protozoa.* 234 pp. W. C. Brown Co., Dubuque, Iowa.

JAKUS, M. A. 1945. The structure and properties of the trichocysts of Paramecium. *J. Exp. Zool.* **100:**457–476.

JENNINGS, H. S. 1906. *Behavior of the lower organisms.* 366 pp. Columbia University Press, New York.

JOHNSON, L. P. 1944. Euglenae of Iowa. *Trans. Am. Microsc. Soc.* **63:**97–135.

JOHNSON, W. H. 1941. Nutrition in the Protozoa. *Q. Rev. Biol.* **16:**336–348.

———. 1941a. Populations of ciliates. *Am. Nat.* **75:**438–457.

KAHL, A. 1930–1935. Urtiere oder Protozoa. I: Wimpertiere oder Ciliata (Infusoria). *Tierwelt Deutschlands* **18, 21, 25, 30:**1–886.

KIDDER, G. W., and V. C. DEWEY. 1945. Studies on the biochemistry of Tetrahymena. III. Strain differences. *Physiol. Zool.* **18:**136–157.

KIMBALL, R. F. 1943. Mating types in the ciliate Protozoa. *Q. Rev. Biol.* **18:**30–45.

KING, R. L., and T. L. JAHN. 1948. Concerning the genera of amebas. *Science* **107:**293–294.

KITCHING, J. A. 1938. Contractile vacuoles. *Biol. Rev.* **13:**403–444.

KOFOID, C. A., and O. SWEZY. 1921. The freeliving, unarmored dinoflagellates. *Mem. Univ. Calif.* **5:**1–562.

KUDO, R. R. 1966. *Protozoology.* 5th ed. 1174 pp. C. C. Thomas, Springfield, Ill.

LACKEY, J. B. 1925. The fauna of Imhoff tanks. *Bull. N.J. Exp. Sta.* **417:**1–39.

———. 1932. Oxygen deficiency and sewage protozoa: with descriptions of some new species. *Biol. Bull.* **63:**287–295.

———. 1936. Some freshwater protozoa with blue chromatophores. Ibid. **71:**492–497.

———. 1938. Protozoan plankton as indicators of pollution in a flowing stream. *Publ. Health Rep. Wash.* **53:**2037–2058.

———. 1938a. A study of some ecologic factors affecting the distribution of Protozoa. *Ecol. Monogr.* **8:**501–527.

———. 1940. The microscopic flora and fauna of tree holes. *Ohio J. Sci.* **40:**186–192.

LEEDALE, G. F. 1967. *Euglenoid flagellates.* 242 pp. Prentice-Hall, New York.

LEIDY, J. 1879. Fresh-water rhizopods of North America. *Rep. U.S. Geol. Surv. Terr.* 12:1–324.

LOWNDES, A. G. 1944. The swimming of unicellular flagellate organisms. *Proc. Zool. Soc. Lond.* 113A:99–107.

MACKINNON, D. L., and R. S. J. HAYES. 1961. *An introduction to the study of Protozoa.* 506 pp. Clarendon Press, Oxford, England.

MANWELL, R. D. 1961. *Protozoology.* 642 pp. St. Martin's Press, New York.

MARQUARDT, W. C., et al. 1966. Preservation of Colpoda steinii and Vahlkampfia sp. from an ice tunnel in Greenland. *Trans. Am. Microsc. Soc.* 85:152–156.

MAST, S. O. 1925. Structure, movement, locomotion, and stimulation in Amoeba. *J. Morph.* 41:347–426.

———. 1947. The food-vacuole in Paramecium. *Biol. Bull.* 92:31–72.

MAST, S. O., and W. J. BOWEN. 1944. The food vacuole in the Peritricha, with special reference to the hydrogen-ion concentration of its contents and of the cytoplasm. Ibid. 87:188–222.

MILLIGER, L. E., K. W. STEWART, and J. K. G. SILVEY. 1971. The passive dispersal of viable algae, protozoans, and fungi by aquatic and terrestrial Coleoptera. *Ann. Entomol. Soc. Am.* 64:36–45.

MORISHITA, I. 1976. Protozoa in sewage and waste water treatment systems. *Trans. Am. Microsc. Soc.* 95:373–377.

NOBLE, A. E. 1932. On Tokophrya lemnarum Stein (Suctoria) with an account of its budding and conjugation. *Univ. Calif. Publ. Zool.* 37:477–520.

NOLAND, L. E. 1925. A review of the genus Coleps with descriptions of two new species. *Trans. Am. Microsc. Soc.* 44:3–13.

———. 1925a. Factors influencing the distribution of fresh water ciliates. *Ecology* 6:437–452.

NOLAND, L. E., and H. E. FINLEY. 1931. Studies on the taxonomy of the genus Vorticella. *Trans. Am. Microsc. Soc.* 50:81–123.

NOLAND, L. E., and M. GOJDICS. 1967. Ecology of free-living Protozoa. *Res. Protozool.* 2:215–266.

PAGE, F. C. 1976. An illustrated key to freshwater and soil amoebae. *Sci. Publ. Freshwater Biol. Assoc.* 34:1–155.

PASCHER, A. 1927. Volvocales. *Süsswasserfl. Dtschl.* 4:1–506.

PENARD, E. 1902. *Faune rhizopodique du bassin du Léman.* 714 pp. Geneva, Switzerland.

———. 1904. *Les héliozoaires d'eau douce.* 341 pp. Geneva, Switzerland.

———. 1922. *Études sur les infusoires d'eau douce.* 331 pp. Geneva, Switzerland

PICKEN, L. E. R. 1937. The structure of some protozoan communities. *J. Ecol.* 25:368–384.

POCHMANN, A. 1942. Synopsis der Gattung Phacus. *Arch. Protistenk.* 95:81–252.

PRINGSHEIM, E. G. 1941. The interrelationships of pigmented and colourless Flagellata. *Biol. Rev.* 16:191–204.

———. 1942. Contributions to our knowledge of saprophytic algae and flagellata. III. Astasia, Distigma, Menoidium, and Rhabdomonas. *New Phytol.* 41:171–205.

———. 1948. Taxonomic problems in the Euglenineae. *Biol. Rev.* 23:46–61.

RIEDER, J. 1936. Beitrag zur Kenntnis der Süsswasser-Suktorien und Revision der Schweizer Suktorien-Fauna. *Rev. Suisse Zool.* 43:359–395.

———. 1936a. Biologische und ökologische Untersuchungen an Süsswasser-Suktorien. *Arch. Naturgesch.* 5:137–214.

ROUX, J. 1901. *Fauna infusorienne des eaux stagnantes des environs de Génève.* 149 pp. Geneva, Switzerland.

RUDZINSKA, M. A. 1973. Do Suctoria really feed by suction? *BioScience* 23:87–94.

SAWYER, T. K., and J. L. GRIFFIN. 1975. A proposed new Family, Acanthamoebidae n. fam. (Order Amoebida), for certain cyst-forming filose amoebae. *Trans. Am. Microsc. Soc.* 94:93–98.

SCHAEFFER, A. A. 1926. Taxonomy of the amoebas with descriptions of thirty-nine new marine and freshwater species. *Publ. Carnegie Inst. Wash.* 345:1–116.

SHAWHAN, F. M., and T. L. JAHN. 1947. A survey of the genus Petalomonas Stein (Protozoa: Euglenidae). *Trans. Am. Microsc. Soc.* 66:182–189.

SLATER, J. V. 1955. Some observations on the cultivation and sterilization of Protozoa. Ibid. 74:80–85.

SLEIGH, M. 1973. *The biology of Protozoa.* 315 pp. Arnold, London.

SMALL, E. B., et al. 1971. A survey of ciliate surface patterns and organelles as revealed with scanning electron microscopy. Ibid. 90:283–294.

SMITH, G. M. 1920. Phytoplankton of the inland lakes of Wisconsin. Part I. *Bull. Wis. Geol. Nat. Hist. Surv.* 57:1–243.

———. 1950. *The fresh-water algae of the United States.* 2nd ed. 719 pp. McGraw-Hill New York.

———. 1944. A comparative study of the species of Volvox. *Trans. Am. Microsc. Soc.* 63:265–310.

SPOON, D. M., et al. 1976. Observations on the behavior and feeding mechanisms of the suctorian Heliophrya erhardi (Rieder) Matthes preying on Paramecium. *Trans. Am. Microsc. Soc.* 95:443–462.

STOUT, J. D. 1956. Reaction of ciliates to environmental factors. *Ecology* 37:178–191.

STUMP, A. B. 1935. Observations on the feeding of Difflugia, Pontigulasia, and Lesquereusia. *Biol. Bull.* 69:136–142.

TARTAR, V. 1961. *The biology of Stentor.* 413 pp. Pergamon Press, New York.

THOMPSON, R. H. 1947. Fresh-water dinoflagellates of Maryland. *Publ. Chesapeake Biol. Lab.* 67:1–28.

UNGER, W. B. 1931. The protozoan sequence in five plant infusions. *Trans. Am. Microsc. Soc.* 50:144–153.

VALKANOV, A. 1940. Die Heliozoen und Proteomyxien. *Arch. Protistenk.* 93:225–254.

VON BRAND, T. 1935. Der Stoffwechsel der Protozoen. *Ergeb. Biol.* 12:161–220.

WALTON, L. B. 1915. A review of the described

species of the Order Euglenoidina Bloch. Class Flagellata (Protozoa) with particular reference to those found in the city water supplies and in other localities in Ohio. *Bull. Ohio Biol. Surv.* **1**:341–449.

WANG, C. C. 1928. Ecological studies of the seasonal distribution of Protozoa in a fresh-water pond. *J. Morphol. Physiol.* **46**:431–478.

WEBB, M. C. 1961. The effects of thermal stratification on the distribution of benthic Protozoa in Esthwaite Water. *J. Anim. Ecol.* **30**:137–152.

WICHTERMAN, R. 1953. *The biology of Paramecium.* 527 pp. Blakiston, New York.

WINKLER, R. H., and J. O. CORLISS. 1965. Notes on the rarely described, green colonial protozoan Ophrydium cersatile (O.F.M.) (Ciliophora, Peritrichida). *Trans. Am. Microsc. Soc.* **84**:127–137.

WOODRUFF, L. L. 1912. The origin and sequence of the protozoan fauna of hay infusions. *J. Exp. Zool.* **12**:205–264.

YONGUE, W. H., and J. CAIRNS. 1971. Colonization and succession of fresh-water protozoans in polyurethane foam suspended in a small pond in North Carolina. *Not. Nat.* **443**:1–13.

# Chapter 3

# PORIFERA (SPONGES)

THE GREAT MAJORITY of the 4500 species of sponges are marine, only a single family, the Spongillidae, being represented in fresh waters. This family consists of about 150 species, of which about 25 have been reported from the United States.

Fresh-water sponges are common in clean ponds, lakes, streams, and rivers. Because they are sessile and because of their inconspicuous green, brown, gray, or yellowish coloration, however, they are frequently unnoticed. Indeed, until their morphology and physiology were first partially understood (beginning 1825), sponges were often considered as plants. Syngamic reproduction has been known only since 1856. A suitable substrate for the matlike sponge growth may be provided by almost any stable submerged object, including rocks, pebbles, aquatic vegetation, logs, branches, and twigs. Sponges may be found on the upper surfaces, sides, or lower surfaces.

The Phylum Porifera may be divided into three classes, which are distinguished on the basis of their skeletal structure. The Class Calcarea consists of small marine sponges having a skeleton composed of calcium carbonate spicules which may be one-, three-, or four-rayed. Hexactinellida are the glass sponges, likewise all marine; their skeleton is an openwork structure of siliceous triaxon spicules or some modification of triaxon. In the Demospongea the skeleton may consist of horny fibers (spongin), siliceous spicules (not triaxon), or both. Sponges of commercial importance are in the Order Keratosa of the Demospongea; the skeleton consists entirely of spongin, spicules being absent. In four other orders there is no spongin, the skeleton being composed entirely of tetraxon spicules. In the three remaining orders, however, the skeleton consists of both monaxon spicules and variable amounts of spongin. One of these orders, the Haplosclerina, contains the Spongillidae. In addition to the skeletal materials already mentioned, it should be emphasized that the noncellular matrix, or mesoglea, of all sponges also functions in support and cohesion of the living tissues.

**General characteristics.** The size of a single fresh-water sponge is enormously variable, depending on the species, age, and various ecological conditions. Some species, for example, even when mature may consist of a thin, slimy, delicate mat having a surface area of only a few square centimeters. Other species may cover an area of as much as 40 m² under highly favorable conditions. The thickness of a sponge growth is likewise variable; sometimes it may be only 1 or 2 mm thick, but under other circumstances it may be as much as 4 cm thick. The growth form may be typically encrusting and matlike, or there may be numerous papillae, fingerlike outgrowths, branches, or an extremely irregular lobed growth form (Figs. 48, 49).

Furthermore, few of our American species are limited to one type of growth form, so that field identification by this character is usually not feasible. *Eunapius fragilis*, for example, may be found as a fine-textured uniform crust; or it may be more robust, with an irregular surface and loose texture; or it may consist of luxuriant branching lobes. *Spongilla lacustris* has every variation, from a simple encrustation to tufts of long fingerlike processes, and

FIG. 48.–Colonies of *Spongilla lacustris* on twigs, ×0.3.

FIG. 49.–*Ephydatia muelleri*. A, growth form on a branched twig, ×0.3; B, proliferating growth on a single unbranched twig, ×0.8.

*Ephydatia muelleri* has a similar range. The more common growth forms for most of our species are indicated in the key that follows. In general individuals of a particular species are usually more lobed and luxuriant in standing waters than in running waters.

Sponges are often collected in which the apparent thickness is as much as 30 to 60 mm, but if such growths are examined carefully it is usually found that the living portion of the mass forms only an outermost stratum 4 to 20 mm thick, all the underlying material being composed of the dead remains of the previous one or more years' growth.

Coloration of sponges may be produced by several factors. Most species found growing on the upper sides of objects are some shade of green, owing to contained algal cells (see page 84). If these same species occur in deep waters or on the undersides of objects, however, there is little chlorophyll, and the coloration may be some shade of dark brown, tan, gray, flesh color, or reddish (rarely). On the other hand, there are a few species that are seldom or never green, even when growing in bright light. Coloration may be modified by the ingestion of food and inorganic particles of a certain shade or by the presence of pigmented metabolic materials in the tissues.

The sponge body is simply constructed. There are no organs, and the tissues are relatively unspecialized and loosely organized. The external surface bears openings of two general sizes. The very abundant microscopic ostia are merely more or less circular openings in the epidermal membrane. The few oscular openings are scattered over the sponge surface. Usually they are 0.5 to 2.0 mm in diameter but may be as wide as 5 to 10 mm. An osculum is typically located at the distal end of a small, chimneylike projection. By means of a carmine suspension it can be easily shown that minute currents of water pass into the sponge through the ostia and out through the oscula.

Internally, the sponge is a maze of interconnected and ramifying spaces, channels, and chambers (Figs. 51, 52). In typical fresh-water species the ostia open into an extensive subdermal cavity from which an abundance of minute narrow incurrent canals lead more deeply into the sponge. At their inner ends these incurrent canals open into small, more or less spherical cavities, the flagellated chambers. At the opposite side each flagellated chamber empties into another minute canal, the excurrent canal, which, along with many other excurrent canals, empties into a much larger irregular central cavity. Each central cavity opens to the outside through an osculum. The opening of the incurrent canal into the flagellated chamber is called the prosopyle; the larger opening from the chamber into the excurrent canal is called the apopyle. The entire arrangement of canals and chambers in the Spongillidae is the rhagon type.

Judging from the available literature, there seems to be some variation in the structure of the thin, flat, outer epidermis. In some species it is apparently a syncitium with scattered nuclei, whereas in others there are definite cells with separating membranes. The ostia may be openings within special pore cells, but some workers maintain that the remnants of the pore cells eventually disappear, leaving the ostium as a simple opening in the epidermis.

In contrast to the situation in some marine sponges, the flagellated chambers of the Spongillidae are minute and lined with only a small number of collar cells, or choanocytes. Except for the flagellated chambers, all internal chambers and canals of a sponge are lined with a flat layer variously characterized as a syncitium, semi-

Fig. 50.–Young spring sponges on bits of charred wood, ×1.6.

Fig. 51.–Diagrammatic section of peripheral portion of a typical fresh-water sponge. Heavy black lines represent layers of choanocytes lining flagellated chambers. Delicate matrix of spongin not shown. *cc*, central cavity; *ec*, excurrent canal; *fc*, flagellated chamber; *fm*, fascicle of megascleres; *ic*, incurrent canal; *o*, ostium; *oc*, oscular chimney; *os*, osculum; *sc*, subdermal cavity.

Fig. 52.–Detailed structure of Spongillidae, semidiagrammatic, showing two flagellated chambers. Spicules and delicate spongin matrix omitted. *a*, apopyle; *ac*, amoebocyte; *ec*, exhalent canal; *ep*, epithelial cell; *ic*, inhalent canal; *m*, mesoglea matrix; *p*, prosopyle. (Modified from Brien, 1936).

syncitium, or layer of colloidal material with contained cells.

The space between layers of epithelium is filled with a gelatinous noncellular matrix, or mesoglea, containing an abundance of several kinds of mesenchymal amoebocytes that have a wide variety of functions. Some secrete the skeleton; some function in nutrition, storage, transport, and excretion; others function in reproduction. Many amoebocytes are motile and move about slowly in the mesogleas.

**Skeleton.** Fresh-water sponges contain great numbers of needlelike microscopic spicules that aid in supporting the flimsy tissues. Such spicules are of two general types. The larger spicules, or megascleres (skeletal spicules), form a reticulate network through and in the tissues, and around and through the many cavities and channels. In addition to many megascleres arranged haphazardly, there are loose overlapping fascicles of megascleres radiating outward from the center or base of the sponge and frequently extending through the external epithelium to the outside. There are also transverse fascicles that run between the radiating fascicles. More or less minute amounts of fibrous and veillike spongin bind the megascleres together.

The smaller type of spicules, or microscleres (flesh, or dermal spicules), are most abundant in the peripheral and epidermal portion of the sponge body, although there are also some lining the deeper channels. Microscleres are arranged in a scattered fashion, rarely in fascicles. Microscleres are lacking in some species.

Megascleres and microscleres may be sharp pointed or blunt and with few to many spines of variable size, depending on the species. A few species have spherical, stellate, or birotulate microscleres.

Additional types of spicules are found associated with the special reproductive bodies, or gemmules, and these are discussed on page 86.

Unfortunately, the details of spicular structure are not always invariable taxonomic characters, especially because ecomorphic malformations are frequent in adverse habitats.

The siliceous material of sponge spicules is often said to have the composition of "hydrated silica" or "opal." Analyses show about 92 percent silicon dioxide, 7 percent water, and small amounts of magnesium, potassium, and sodium oxides.

Small and simple spicules are formed within single specialized amoebocytes, called silicoblasts, but large and complex spicules are formed by two or more silicoblasts. The first sign of a spicule is an extremely thin organic axial thread within the silicoblast, the siliceous material being deposited around it in every-increasing thickness.

**Nutrition.** Fundamentally, a sponge efficiently strains minute particles from the water in which it lives. The flagella of the choanocytes are directed more or less toward the apopyles of the flagellated chambers. Their spiral or undulating movements collectively produce weak water currents that enter the sponge through the ostia and leave through the oscula. As the water traverses the flagellated chambers, bacteria and bits of detritus are caught on the outer sticky surface of the collars of the collar cells as well as on the exposed surface of the cells proper. The collar has been likened to a thin pseudopodial membrane. All digestion is intracellular, but little or no digestion occurs within the choanocytes. Food particles are passed on to the adjacent mesoglea and into the amoebocytes where digestion is completed and where there may be considerable storage.

Prosopyles are so small that they frequently become plugged, and in such cases the particles are carried off to one side by slow "flowing" movements of the epidermal protoplasm. They may later sink below the surface and be taken up by amoebocytes.

It is now thought that the inter- and intracellular "zoochlorellae" of Spongillidae are not essential to sponge metabolism, but there is some evidence to show that their presence results in better sponge growth. Such algae are certain ingested plankton species, including *Pleurococcus*, *Chlorella*, and other minute genera, that persist in the tissues, multiply, and are digested very slowly. In dim light or darkness they are digested much more rapidly than in bright light.

**Circulation.** There is no special circulatory mechanism in sponges. Materials are transferred by diffusion and amoebocytic transport.

**Respiration.** The exchange of oxygen and carbon dioxide occurs everywhere in exposed tissues of sponges, both externally and internally. Diffusion of these dissolved gases is probably rapid and efficient, since all sponge cells are either directly in contact with water or only a few cells distant from it.

**Excretion.** Dissolved metabolic waste materials simply diffuse into the water surrounding and passing through the sponge body. Granular metabolic materials are usually given off from amoebocytes into the excurrent canals but may also be retained by the cells for varying periods of time.

Choanocytes and many amoebocytes sometimes contain one or two contractile vacuoles, and it is probable that they function mainly in keeping the proper osmotic pressure in the tissues.

**Contractile elements, impulse conduction.** Although sponges are completely sessile and there is no definite muscle system, a few specialized amoebocytes, or myocytes, have the ability to contract or relax. A few bipolar and multipolar "nervous type" cells have been described by some investigators, but nothing is known about their role in the transmission of impulses.

The oscular chimneys are normally kept open by the excurrents, but if environmental conditions become unfavorable, the oscula will slowly close in several minutes. Such contraction is produced by the action of fusiform myocytes around the openings. In *Ephydatia fluviatilis* it has been shown that even under normal circumstances the oscular chimneys (1 to 3 mm high) continuously and slowly change in form, from high to low and wide to narrow. The osculum will close and the chimney will collapse in several seconds if the latter is struck a sharp blow with a needle. Complete recovery takes 20 to 30 seconds. Sticking a needle into the tissues 2 mm from the chimney base, however, has no effect on the chimney.

Some workers report that under unfavorable conditions ostia will slowly close as a result of contractility of the surrounding protoplasm, but there are no special sensory or nerve cells, and there is no coordination and no transmission of impulses (or perhaps transmission for 2 to 3 mm at most).

**Reproduction, growth.** Many details of syngamic reproduction are still obscure and confused. Some investigators maintain that the Spongillidae are hermaphroditic and a single individual may produce eggs and sperm simultaneously, but others are convinced that the sexes are separate or that an individual may produce sperm at one time and eggs at another. Perhaps both conditions prevail, depending on the species. Recently one investigator has found that *Spongilla lacustris* may exhibit alternative hermaphroditism, in which a sponge may be exclusively male one year and exclusively female the next year.

Sperm and egg production are thought to occur mostly during July and August, and to a lesser extent in June and September. The oogonia are amoebocytes that grow by absorbing and ingesting many adjacent cells. By the time the egg is mature it is large and lies loosely in one of the internal cavities of the sponge.

Although earlier investigators thought that sperm developed from amoebocytes, more recent work has shown that in at least two species they develop from choanocytes that lose their collars and flagella, become more or less amoeboid, migrate into the mesoglea, and function as spermatogonia. Mature flagellated sperm are formed in abundance in baglike "follicles." These sperm are released into the chambers of the sponge and out through the oscula into the surrounding water. Some of them are eventually drawn into the chambers of the same or other sponges where they fertilize the mature ova.

Several different and peculiar types of

early embryology occur in the Spongillidae, but in all of them a flagellated embryo is formed that is released from the parent and swims about for a few hours or days before settling to the substrate and metamorphosing to form a minute young sponge.

Growth is mainly a process of proliferation and accretion with accompanying development of additional orifices, channels, and chambers. Usually most of the sponge body dies or becomes dormant in the autumn and partly disintegrates during the winter, and although it sometimes does not revive in the following spring, it is more common for the surviving remnant to revive and continue growth during the following season. In this way a specimen may remain more or less intact from year to year, growing in thickness, but with only the outermost layer being alive and active. This persistence of sponges occurs especially on firm, broad substrates and where there is little ice action.

Many times, however, a sponge may remain active and green throughout the winter, even under ice.

**Reduction bodies.** Under highly unfavorable conditions a large sponge forms numerous "reduction bodies," and a small sponge may form a single reduction body. The tissues shrink into the skeleton and the canal system disappears, leaving the epidermis surrounding a mixture of mesenchyme cells, mesoglea, choanocytes, and spicules. Under favorable conditions such a reduction body may grow and regenerate a new sponge. Reduction bodies have been observed for only a few species, and it is not known whether they are produced regularly throughout the Spongillidae.

**Regeneration.** Like certain marine species, the Spongillidae have remarkable powers of regeneration. If bits of *Ephydatia* or *Spongilla* are macerated and dissociated by squeezing through fine bolting silk, small clumps of cells will coalesce within a few hours, slowly reconstitute, and within several days grow into a new minute sponge.

**Gemmules.** The formation of gemmules is one of the most characteristic features of fresh-water sponges. These are highly resistant resting stages similar in function to the statoblasts of fresh-water bryozoans. Briefly, a gemmule is a spherical structure with a multiple, dead, secreted outer layer, a covering of spicules, and an internal mass of undifferentiated mesenchymal amoebocytes. Gemmule diameter ranges from about 150 to 1000 microns. Coloration may be whitish or various shades of yellow or brown.

Formerly it was thought that gemmules appeared only at the close of the growing season, but it is now known that they may be formed at any time during the growing season. *Spongilla lacustris* is the only common species that regularly forms gemmules in September and October. In this species, and perhaps in others also, the control of gemmulation is influenced by endogenous factors during the summer and then triggered by environmental factors in the autumn. Because of autumn disintegration of superficial tissues, it is much easier to observe gemmules in any species at that time.

Gemmules may be deposited in a compact basal layer in a sponge, or they may be scattered throughout the sponge body. The first sign of gemmule development is the grouping of many food-filled amoebocytes into discrete masses. A thin inner sclerotized membrane is formed around each mass of amoebocytes, followed by a heavier, middle (or outer) sclerotized membrane that has a single small foraminal area. The latter sometimes has a narrow, projecting foraminal tubule. Except for the location of the foraminal aperture or foraminal tubule, the gemmule is covered with a complete, crustlike, thick, honeycombed coating, or pneumatic layer. Sometimes a third thin, outer sclerotized membrane covers the pneumatic layer. *Spongilla lacustris* produces two distinctly different kinds of gemmules without reference to time of year, one thin-walled and the other thick-walled. In some species many more or less cylindrical spicules are imbedded in the pneumatic layer and cover its outer surface. Such gemmule spicules are arranged

FIG. 53.–Disintegrated winter appearance of sponges. A, crust of gemmules on bit of bark, X1; B, gemmules of *Spongilla lacustris* on rock, X3. (B from K. Berg, 1948, by permission.)

tangentially or in a heterogeneous manner; they differ markedly from the megascleres and microscleres. In other species, however, the pneumatic layer contains an abundance of radially arranged birotulate spicules, or amphidiscs. One of the wheel-like ends of a birotulate is called a rotule.

Gemmules may remain attached to the substrate or become freed and rise to the surface or sink to the bottom. They winter over easily, withstand repeated freezings and thawings, and have been found to be viable after being kept dried for one to three years or more.

Germination may occur any time at water temperatures of about 13° to 23°, but the process requires two weeks or more in the autumn and only a few days in the spring. Some investigators maintain that gemmules require a quiescent dormant period of one or two months or more before they will germinate. When a gemmule germinates the membrane covering the foramen disappears, and the inner creamy mass of amoebocytes slowly flows out of the foraminal aperture and more or less covers the empty gemmule shell. This process is usually completed in two to six days. The amoebocytes undergo histological differentiation and form the first cells of the several tissue types. Some spicules, channels, and subdermal spaces may be formed as early as the third day, and choanocytes may be functioning as early as the fifth day. Further development and growth result in typical sponge structure.

Gemmules commonly contain zoochlorellae, and it has been found that such zoochlorellae, in both light and dark, initiate gemmule germination at lower temperatures and increase the speed of germination.

It is usually difficult to tell whether renewed growth of an old sponge in the spring is initiated by gemmule germination or by resumption of growth by dormant tissues, but probably both mechanisms are responsible.

**Ecology.** Sponges are most common in waters less than 2 m deep. They are seldom found as deep as 4 m although there are records of collections as deep as 50 m. In very favorable habitats sponge growths may almost obscure all suitable substrates. They are rarely found on a mud bottom, in silty water, or in small puddles. Contrary to Potts (1887), they are seldom found in extremely rapid waters. In general, individuals in running waters are smaller and more encrusting, and show little or no branching.

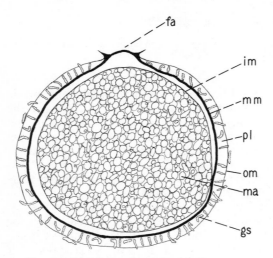

FIG. 54.–Diagrammatic section of a sponge gemmule, X100. *fa*, foraminal area; *gs*, gemmule spicule; *im*, inner sclerotized membrane; *ma*, mesenchymal amoebocytes; *mm*, middle sclerotized membrane; *om*, outer sclerotized membrane (absent in some species); *pl*, pneumatic layer (containing spicules).

*Spongilla lacustris* may often be found in both the branching and encrusting forms in the same body of water, but it is thought that the encrusting form is merely the earlier growth form that becomes branching as the sponge matures. Compared with most groups of fresh-water invertebrates, sponges are quite sensitive to variations in environmental conditions. *Ephydatia fluviatilis* will tolerate a minor amount of pollution, and a few other species a lesser degree.

Most species are more or less photopositive. *Eunapius ingloviformis, Trochospongilla pennsylvanica,* and *Ephydatia fluviatilis,* however, prefer dim light and are usually on the undersides of objects in clear water.

Much of our detailed information about the effects of dissolved inorganic materials has been provided by Jewell (1935, 1939). The most important limiting factors seem to be calcium, silicon, bound carbon dioxide, and pH (the last as a rough measurement of the general suitability of water). The following species are acid (soft) water forms seldom occurring where the pH is above 7.0 or 7.3: *Heteromeyenia baileyi, Anheteromeyenia argyrosperma, Trochospongilla pennsylvanica, Eunapius ingloviformis,* and *Corvomeyenia everetti.* Alkaline species include *Heteromeyenia tubisperma, Ephydatia muelleri,* and *E. fluviatilis.* A few species, such as *Spongilla lacustris* and *Eunapius fragilis,* tolerate a wide range in bound carbon dioxide and hydrogen-ion concentration, although they fare better under alkaline conditions.

All common species regularly occur in waters having less than 12.0 ppm of calcium. *Spongilla lacustris,* however, has been found where the calcium concentration was as high as 33.0 ppm, and *Heteromeyenia baileyi* where there was 53.4 ppm. The distribution of *Ephydatia muelleri* and *Eunapius fragilis* appears to be restricted by low calcium. The former has not been reported from waters containing less than 5.6 ppm and the latter 2.1 ppm. *Eunapius ingloviformis* and *Corvomeyenia everetti,* on the other hand, appear to grow only where there are small quantities of calcium present; the former is restricted to waters having less than 3.2 ppm of calcium, and

FIG. 55.–Gemmules of some common species of sponges, X130. A, *Ephydatia fluviatilis*; B, *Spongilla lacustris*; C, *Heteromeyenia baileyi*.

the latter 2.5 ppm. *Spongilla lacustris* is independent of ordinary calcium concentrations and grows luxuriantly in waters containing from 0.16 to 32.4 ppm.

In view of the fact that sponges require large amounts of silicon for spicule formation, it is surprising to find that most species attain good growth in waters that may contain only a trace of silicon. The only important exception is *Ephydatia muelleri*, which requires a minimum of 1.6 ppm of silicon dioxide. Nevertheless, some species show certain variations in spicule abundance and morphology, depending on the amount of silicon present. *Eunapius fragilis* has a poorly developed skeleton in water containing less than 1.0 ppm of silicon dioxide. In *Spongilla lacustris* both microscleres and megascleres become progressively attenuated in specimens collected in waters ranging from 13.0 ppm of silicon dioxide down to only a trace. In fact, a concentration of 0.56 ppm is the lowest value at which there is full microsclere development; there is no greater development above 0.56, but the microspines are absent below this concentration. In soft-water lakes this species has an abundance of spicules intermediate in size between megascleres and microscleres. *Trochospongilla pennsylvanica* has progressively heavier spicules and closer approximation in the size of the two rotules in lakes of increasing mineralization.

It is common to find three different species in the same lake, less common to find four, and rare to find five or six. Often there are definite associations of certain species, suggesting similar but obscure habitat requirements. The following pairs of species are commonly associated in the same lake or stream: *Ephydatia muelleri* and *Eunapius fragilis*, *Ephydatia muelleri* and *Spongilla lacustris*, *Eunapius fragilis* and *Spongilla lacustris*, *S. lacustris* and *Trochospongilla pennsylvanica*.

Larvae of Sisyridae (page 591) pierce the cells and suck out the contents and are entirely dependent on sponges as a food source, but no animals have been reported to devour healthy sponges bodily. Nevertheless the irregular growth form of many sponges affords a favorable substrate for a wide variety of metazoans, including insects, crustaceans, water mites, annelids, nematodes, and even mollusks.

Spongillidae have occasionally been reported to clog water pipes and conduits, but otherwise they are of no economic importance to man.

**Dispersal, geographic distribution.** Sponges easily spread throughout single drainage systems, and by virtue of their resistant gemmules they are probably transported overland by wind, insects, and birds.

*Spongilla lacustris, Eunapius fragilis,* and *Ephydatia fluviatilis* are essentially cosmopolitan and have been found the world over wherever intensive collecting has been done in suitable areas. *Trochospongilla pennsylvanica, Anheteromeyenia ryderi, Radiospongilla crateriformis,* and probably several other species are widely

distributed in the Northern Hemisphere. The four most common American species are *Spongilla lacustris, Eunapius fragilis, Ephydatia muelleri,* and *Heteromeyenia tubisperma.*

Certain other species, however, are rare and poorly known in the United States. *Spongilla wagneri, Ephydatia subdivisa, E. millsi, E. subtilis, E, robusta,* and *Anheteromeyenia biceps* are each known only from only a single or several localities.

**Collecting.** Hand-picking in the shallows and using a long-handled rake in deeper waters will produce an abundance of specimens. Sponges should be handled gingerly because of their fragility.

**Culturing.** Small *Ephydatia* and *Spongilla* have been kept alive in aquaria up to five or six months, but these are exceptionally long periods. Usually sponges remain in good condition for only one to three weeks, then begin to lose color and disintegrate. Death occurs in such short periods even if there is a continuous flow of water through the aquarium.

Some investigators have had success using a dead bacterial suspension for food.

If a small sponge or a bit of a larger one (about a cubic centimeter) is placed cut surface downward on a glass slide submerged under 5 to 10 cm of water, the sponge will often adhere and grow for a time, especially if the water is changed frequently. Never use tap water.

Germination of gemmules and early growth may be easily studied in the laboratory. Gemmules should be brought in and placed on slides or cover slips in shallow pans of water from the natural habitat. Germination will usually begin in 7 to 25 days, but sometimes the process may be hastened by first "vernalizing" the gemmules in water in a refrigerator at 5° to 10° for a day or two. After germination is completed and the young sponge securely attached, the slide should be removed to an aquarium in which the water is frequently renewed. Under favorable conditions the sponge may grow and cover as much as half of the slide and live for a month or two.

**Preserving, preparing.** If a whole large specimen is to be preserved, it should be removed from the water with or without its substrate and placed in a warm, shaded place to dry out completely. Incidentally, anyone who works with fresh or drying sponges never forgets their peculiar odor, which is sometimes likened to that of garlic. Dried specimens must be stored and handled very carefully because of their fragility. Soft tissue paper, not cotton, should be used for shipping. Do not rub the eyes after handling dry sponges. Bits of sponge tissue and gemmules should be killed and preserved in 70 percent alcohol.

For rapid identification place a small bit of sponge on a slide, add two drops of concentrated nitric acid, heat over a flame until dry, and add mounting medium and cover slip. This treatment destroys essentially everything except the spicules. A fragment of dry epidermis mounted in balsam will usually show the presence or absence of microscleres.

Permanent mounts require more care, and the following method is one of several suitable ones. Place 4 or 5 ml of sponge in a small test tube, add 10 ml of concentrated nitric acid, and heat to boiling. Let stand for one day, remove most of the supernatant acid with a pipette, and *carefully* add water to half fill the test tube. Let stand for one hour with occasional agitation and draw off most of the supernatant. Repeat this washing process twice more. Replace the water with 95 percent alcohol and two changes of absolute alcohol (15 minutes each). Draw up some of the spicules and alcohol in a pipette and place on a slide, burn off the alcohol and add mounting medium and a cover slip.

Permanent mounts of gemmules are made by a slightly different technique. Place the gemmules in cold concentrated nitric acid in a test tube for one to six hours until they turn a translucent orange or yellow color, indicating that most of the pneumatic layer is dissolved away. Then wash with water several times, dehydrate, and mount as indicated in the preceding paragraph.

Glycerin jelly mounts are not desirable because the refractive index of this substance does not result in sufficient differentiation of the sponge spicules.

**Taxonomy.** American fresh-water sponges have been studied by only a few investigators, some off the more important contributors being Potts, Smith, Old, Penney, and Jewell. Much therefore remains to be done, especially from taxonomic, distributional, physiological, and ecological viewpoints.

Since general growth form is usually so variable within a species, it is a poor character for species identification. The detailed anatomy of gemmules, gemmule spicules, megascleres, and microscleres is essential for accurate identification.

There is still considerable disagreement among specialists concerning dividing lines between genera. Indeed, there is evidence of intergeneric or parazoan species mixtures in some forms. In this manual the nomenclature of Penney and Racek (1968) has been followed for most species.

Rough average or typical lengths of spicules are given in the key that follows, and it should be borne in mind that in most species these figures are subject to a variation of plus or minus 20 to 50 percent. It should also be noted that the various spicule types for a particular species are not drawn to the same scale in Figs. 56 to 60. Furthermore, the spicule figures represent only typical specimens, and it must be noted that there is considerable variation even in the same sponge or same gemmule.

## KEY TO SPECIES OF PORIFERA

1. Gemmule spicules elongated and more or less cylindrical, or gemmule spicules absent. 2
   Gemmule spicules always present and more or less birotulate (amphidisks) . . . . . . .6
2. Microscleres present . . . . . . . . . . . . . . . . . . . . . . . . . . . . . . . . . . . . . . . . . . . . . **Spongilla, 3**
   Microscleres absent . . . . . . . . . . . . . . . . . . . . . . . . . . . . . . . . . . . . . . . . . . . . **Eunapius, 5**

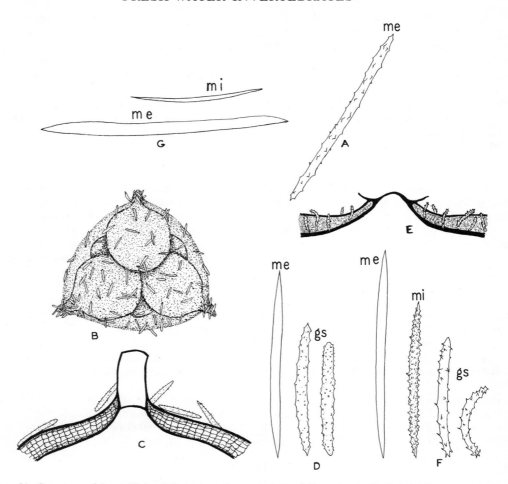

Fig. 56.–Structure of *Spongilla* and *Eunapius*. A, megasclere of *Eunapius ingloviformis*; B, group of gemmules of *E. fragilis* invested in a common pneumatic layer, ×50; C, section of foraminal region of gemmule of *E. fragilis*; D, typical spicules of *E. fragilis*; E, section of foraminal region of gemmule of *Spongilla lacustris*; F, typical spicules of *S. lacustris*; G, typical spicules of *S. aspinosa*. *gs*, gemmule spicules; *me*, megascleres; *mi*, microscleres. (B, C, and E modified from Sasaki.)

3. Microscleres spined ..................................................................4
   Microscleres smooth and small (Fig. 56G); an encrusting species reported only from
       Virginia and New Jersey .......................... **Spongilla aspinosa** Potts
4. Gemmule spicules slightly to strongly curved (Fig. 56F); branched or unbranched
       growth form; in both standing and running waters; common and very widely
       distributed ........................................**Spongilla lacustris** (L.)
   Gemmule spicules not curved; southeastern coastal areas, sometimes in brackish
       waters; growth form a thin crust ...................**Spongilla wagneri** Potts
5. Gemmules either forming a distinct pavement layer or also present in groups of two
       to eight scattered throughout the sponge body (Fig. 56B); growth form variable;
       common and widely distributed in running and standing waters.
                                                              **Eunapius fragilis** (Leidy)
   Gemmules not forming a distinct pavement layer, in compact hemispherical groups of
       seven to 20; soft algalike encrusting growth form; often in highly colored
       standing waters; generally distributed but not common.
                                                              **Eunapius ingloviformis** (Potts)

FIG. 57.–Spicules of *Trochospongilla*. A, spicules of *T. pennsylvanica*; B, spicules of *T. leidyi*; C, spicules of *T. horrida. bi,* gemmule birotulate; *me*, megasclere.

6. Gemmules with one kind of birotulate ........................................7
Gemmules with two types of birotulates, one long and the other short (Fig. 60) ...**17**
7. Margins of rotules entire, not serrate; birotulates short (Figs. 57A–C); encrusting growth form; running or standing waters................ **Trochospongilla, 8**
Margins of rotules serrated or incised; birotulates short to long (Figs. 58A–C) ....**10**
8. Rotules of gemmule spicules unequal in size, the proximal being much the larger; megascleres long, abundantly spined, and ends rounded or pointed (Fig. 57A); slimy and thin growth form, seldom more than 5 mm thick, gray or flesh-colored; generally distributed .......... **Trochospongilla pennsylvanica** (Potts)
Rotules of gemmule spicules equal in size (Figs. 57B,C) ........................**9**
9. Megascleres not spined (Fig. 57B); gemmules formed in a basal layer; color grayish or drab; rare, reported from New Jersey, Pennsylvania, Ohio, Kentucky, Illinois, Louisiana, and West Virginia ....... **Trochospongilla leidyi** (Bowerbank)
Megascleres spined (Fig. 57C); color gray, yellow, or brown; cold-temperate states ....................................**Trochospongilla horrida** Weltner
10. With minute, slender, birotulate microscleres about 10 microns long (Fig. 58A); skeleton poorly developed; finely branched growth form; most common in bogs; northeastern states .........................**Corvomeyenia everetti** (Mills)
Microscleres absent, if present then never birotulate .........................**11**
11. Birotulates many times longer than diameter of rotules (Fig. 58B); gemmules small, white, numerous; thin, encrusting growth form, usually in running waters; generally distributed but not common .... **Radiospongilla crateriformis** (Potts)
Birotulates no more than three times as long as the diameter of rotules (Figs. 58C,E,F)............................................... **Ephydatia, 12**
12. Rays and spines of gemmule birotulates covered with microspines; megascleres smooth or microspined; massive, encrusting growth form; known only from Florida and Louisiana ..........................**Ephydatia subdivisa** Potts
Rays and spines of gemmule birotulates without microspines ..................**13**
13. Margins of rotules finely serrate; megascleres entirely microspines; reported only from Sherwood Lake, near De Land, Florida .............. **Ephydatia millsi** Potts
Margins of rotules coarsely toothed (Figs. 58C, E, F) ........................**14**
14. Megascleres smooth (Fig. 58E); color and growth form highly variable but usually flat and encrusting; more common in standing waters; generally distributed. **Ephydatia fluviatilis** (L.)
Megascleres with small and inconspicuous spines (Fig. 58F) ...................**15**
15. Birotulate length equal to or less than diameter of rotules, which are irregularly serrate or dentate, and with few rays (Fig. 58C); growth form highly variable but most luxuriant in standing waters where a single individual may cover as much as a square meter; usually in alkaline waters; common and generally distributed. **Ephydatia muelleri** (Lieberkühn)
Birotulates longer than diameter of rotule ....................................**16**
16. Rotules split nearly to the center, and with 10 to 20 blunt rays; encrusting growth form; reported only from Kissimmee Lake, Florida. **Ephydatia subtilis** (Weltner)
Rotules not split nearly to the center, with numerous large spines, often malformed (Fig. 58F); reported only from eastern states and California. **Ephydatia robusta** (Potts)

FIG. 58.–Structure of *Corvomeyenia, Radiospongilla,* and *Ephydatia.* A, spicules of *C. everetti*; B, spicules of *R. crateriformis*; C, spicules of *E. muelleri*; D, section of foraminal region of gemmule of *E. fluviatilis*; E, spicules of *E. fluviatilis*; F, spicules of *E. robusta. bi,* gemmule birotulates; *me*, megascleres; *mi*, microscleres.

17. Microscleres stellate (Fig. 60E); generally distributed but rare.
   **Dosilia radiospiculata** (Mills)
   Microscleres absent, or acerate if present ....................................**18**
18. Microscleres present, acerate ............................... **Heteromeyenia, 19**
   Microscleres absent ...................................... **Anheteromeyenia, 22**
19. Foraminal tubule with one or two very long tendrils, often enveloping the tubule (Fig. 59A); shorter birotulates with rotules bearing deeply cut rays; longer birotulates with a smooth or sparsely macrospined shaft, rotules bearing deeply cut rays (Fig. 59B); usually thin and encrusting in running waters; northeastern quarter of the United States ........................ **Heteromeyenia latitenta** (Potts)
   Foraminal tubule with three or more tendrils of varying length; megascleres sparsely microspined ..................................................**20**

FIG. 59.–Structure of *Heteromeyenia*. A, foraminal region of gemmule of *H. latitenta*; B, spicules of *H. latitenta*; C, foraminal region of gemmule of *H. tubisperma*; D, spicules of *H. tubisperma*; E, foraminal region of gemmule of *H. baileyi*; F, spicules of *H. baileyi*. *lb*, longer birotulates; *me*, megascleres; *mi*, microscleres; *sb*, shorter birotulates. (A and C modified from Potts, 1887; E modified from Sasaki.)

20. Foraminal tubule one-half to once the diameter of the gemmule body, with four to six long tendrils (Fig. 59C); shorter birotulates with smooth shaft and with rotules composed of three to five rays; longer birotulates usually with a thinner smooth shaft, and with rotules composed of three to five rays (Fig. 59D); encrusting form with soft papillate projections; usually in running waters; eastern half of the United States ........................**Heteromeyenia tubisperma** (Mills)

   Foraminal tubule one-fourth or less as long as diameter of gemmule body (Figs. 59A, C); both types of birotulates with macrospined shafts (Figs. 59F; 60A); encrusting growth form .......................................................................21

21. Rays of rotules of both types of birotulates deeply cleft and slightly incurved; longer birotulates 80 microns long; shorter birotulates 60 microns long (Fig. 59F); foraminal tubule variable, usually with 6 to 10 irregular and sometimes branched tendrils (Fig. 59E); but tendrils sometimes fewer, reduced, or absent; widely scattered in eastern states ..............**Heteromeyenia baileyi** (Bowerbank)

   Rays of rotules of both types of birotulates less deeply cleft and arranged so as to give the rotule a burlike appearance (Fig. 60A); foraminal tubule with about three to five long, irregular tendrils (Fig. 60B); reported from northeastern states ...............................**Heteromeyenia tentasperma** (Potts)

Fig. 60.–Structure of *Heteromeyenia, Dosilia,* and *Anheteromeyenia.* A, spicules of *H. tentasperma*; B, foraminal region of gemmule of *H. tentasperma*; C, megasclere of *A. pictovensis*; D, spicules of *A. ryderi*; E, spicules of *D. radiospiculata*; F, spicules of *A. biceps*; G, spicules of *A. argyrosperma. lb,* longer birotulates; *me,* megascleres; *mi,* microscleres; *sb,* shorter birotulates. (B modified from Potts, 1887; D modified from Stephens.)

22. Rotules of long birotulates in the form of small knobs; megascleres smooth (Fig. 60F); encrusting growth form, seldom more than 5 cm in diameter; reported only from two streams near Douglas Lake, Michigan; perhaps only a variety of *Ephydatia muelleri.* . . . . . . . . . . . . . . . . **Anheteromeyenia biceps** Lindenschmidt
    Rotules of long birotulates not in the form of knobs; megascleres spined (Figs. 60D, G) . . . . . . . . . . . . . . . . . . . . . . . . . . . . . . . . . . . . . . . . . . . . . . . . . . . . . . . . . .**23**
23. Rotules of short birotulates with a few large rays (Fig. 60G); encrusting growth form; eastern United States . . . . . . . . . . . . . . . **Anheteromeyenia argyrosperma** (Potts)
    Rotules of short birotulates dislike, with numerous small teeth (Fig. 60D) . . . . . . .**24**
24. Megascleres finely spined (Fig. 60D); averaging 200 microns long; standing and running waters in eastern half of the United States . . . . **Anheteromeyenia ryderi** (Potts)
    Megascleres coarsely spined (Fig. 60C); averaging 165 to 210 microns long; extreme northeastern United States . . . . . . . . . . . . . **Anheteromeyenia pictovensis** (Potts)

## PORIFERA REFERENCES

ANKEL, W. E. 1949. Über Fragen der Formbildung und der Zelldetermination bei Süsswasserschwammen. *Verh. Dtschl. Zool. Kiel* (1948):58–66.

ANNANDALE, N. 1909. Fresh-water sponges in the collection of the United States National Museum. Part II. Specimens from North and South America. *Proc. U.S. Nat. Mus.* 37:401–406.

ARNDT, W. 1928. Porifera, Schwämme, Spongien. *Tierwelt Dtschl.* 4:1–94.

BOWERBANK, J. S. 1863. A monograph of the Spongillidae. *Proc. Zool. Soc. Lond.* (1863):440–472.

BRIEN, P. 1932. Contribution à l'étude de la régénération naturelle chez les Spongillidae. *Arch. Zool. exp. gén.* 74:461–506.

———. 1936. La réorganisation de l'éponge après dissociation par filtration et phénomènes d'involution chez Ephydatia fluviatilis. *Arch. Biol.* 48:185–268.

BRØNSTED, A., and H. V. BRØNSTED. 1953. The effects of symbiotic zoochlorellae on the germination rate of gemmules of Spongilla lacustris (L.). *Vidensk. Medd. Dansk Naturhist. For København* 115:133–144.

DE LAUBENFELS, M. W. 1936. A discussion of the sponge fauna of the Dry Tortugas in particular and the West Indies in general, with material for a revision of the families and orders of the Porifera. *Publ. Carnegie Inst. Wash.* 467:1–225.

ESHLEMAN, S. K. 1949. A key to Florida's fresh-water sponges, with descriptive notes. *Quart. J. Fla. Acad. Sci.* 12:35–44.

GEE, N. G.. 1932. Genus Trochospongilla of the fresh water sponges. *Peking Nat. Hist. Bull.* 6:1–32.

———. 1932a. The known fresh-water sponges. Ibid. 25–51.

GILBERT, J. J. 1975. Field experiments on gemmulation in the fresh-water sponge Spongilla lacustris. *Trans. Am. Microsc. Soc.* 94:347–356.

JEWELL, M. E. 1935. An ecological study of the fresh-water sponges of northern Wisconsin. *Ecol. Monogr.* 5:461–504.

———. 1939. An ecological study of the fresh-water sponges of Wisconsin, II. The influence of calcium. *Ecology* 20:11–28.

———. 1952. The genera of North American fresh-water sponges. Parameyenia, new genus. *Trans. Kans. Acad. Sci.* 55:445–457.

JORGENSEN, C. B. 1944. On the spicule-formation of Spongilla lacustris (L.). I. The dependence of the spicule-formation on the content of dissolved and solid silicic acid of the milieu. *Biol. Medd. Kjøbenhavn* 19:1–45.

LEVEAUX, M. 1939. La formation des gemmules chez les Spongillidae. *Ann. Soc. Roy. Zool. Belg.* 70:53–96.

———. 1941, 1942. Contribution à l'étude histologique de l'ovogénèse et de la spermatogénèse des Spongillidae. Ibid. 72:251–269; 73:33–50.

LINDENSCHMIDT, M. J. 1950. A new species of fresh-water sponge. *Trans. Am. Microsc. Soc.* 69:214–216.

McNAIR, G. T. 1923. Motor reactions of the fresh-water sponge, Ephydatia fluviatilis. *Biol. Bull.* 44:153–166.

NEIDHOFER, J. R. 1940. The fresh-water sponges of Wisconsin. *Trans. Wis. Acad. Sci. Arts Lett.* 32:177–197.

OLD, M. C. 1931. A new species of fresh-water sponge. *Trans. Am. Microsc. Soc.* 50:298–299.

———. 1931a. Taxonomy and distribution of the fresh-water sponges (Spongillidae) of Michigan. *Pap. Mich. Acad. Sci. Arts Lett.* 15:439–476.

———. 1932. Environmental selection of the fresh-water sponges (Spongillidae) of Michigan. *Trans. Am. Microsc. Soc.* 51:129–137.

———. 1932a. Contribution to the biology of fresh-water sponges (Spongillidae). *Papers Mich. Acad. Sci. Arts Lett.* 17:663–679.

PENNEY, J. T. 1933. Reduction and regeneration in fresh water sponges (Spongilla discoides). *J. Exp. Zool.* 65:475–495.

———. 1933a. A new fresh-water sponge from South Carolina. *Proc. U.S. Nat. Mus.* 82:1–5.

———. 1954. Ecological observations on the fresh-water sponges of the Savannah River Project area. *Univ. S.C. Publ. Ser.* 3, **1**:156–192.

———. 1960. Distribution and bibliography (1892–1957) of the freshwater sponges. Ibid. **3**:1–97.

PENNEY, J. T., and A. A. RACEK. 1968. Comprehensive revision of a world-wide collection of fresh-water sponges (Porifera: Spongillidae). *Bull. U.S. Nat. Mus.* **272**:1–184.

POTTS, E. 1887. Fresh water sponges. A monograph, *Proc. Acad. Nat. Sci. Phila.* (1887):157–279.

———. 1889. Report upon some fresh-water sponges collected in Florida by Jos. Willcox, Esq. *Trans. Wagner Inst. Phil.* **2**:5–7.

RASMONT, R. 1961. Une technique de culture des éponges d'eau douce en milieu controlé. *Ann. Soc. Roy. Zool. Belg.* **91**:147–155.

SASAKI, N. 1934. Report on the fresh-water sponges obtained from Hokkaido. *Sci. Rep. Tohoku Imp. Univ. (Ser. 4)* **9**:219–248.

SCHRÖDER, K. 1936. Beiträge zur Kenntnis der Spiculabildung und der Larvenspiculation und der Variationsbreite der Gerüstnadeln von Süsswasserschwämmen. *Z. Morphol. Oekol. Tiere* **31**:245–267.

SIMON, L. 1953. Uber die Spezifität der Nadeln und die Variabilität der Arten bei den Spongilliden. *Zool. Jahrb. Abt. allg. Zool. Physiol. Tiere* **64**:207–234.

SIMPSON, T. L., and P. E. FELL. 1974. Dormancy among the Porifera: gemmule formation and germination in fresh-water and marine sponges. *Trans. Am. Microsc. Soc.* **93**:544–577.

SMITH, D. G. 1976. An intergeneric fresh-water sponge mixture (Demospongiae: Spongillidae). Ibid. **95**:235–236.

SMITH, F. 1918. A new species of Spongilla from Oneida Lake, New York. *N.Y. State Coll. For. Syracuse Univ., Tech. Publ.* **9**:239–243.

———. 1921. Data on the distribution of Michigan fresh-water sponges. *Pap. Mich. Acad. Sci. Arts Lett.* **1**:418–421.

———. 1921a. Distribution of the fresh-water sponges of North America. *Bull. Ill. Nat. Hist. Surv.* **14**:9–22.

STEPHENS, J. 1920. The freshwater sponges of Ireland. *Proc. Roy. Irish Acad.* **35** (*Sect. B*): 205–254.

VAN TRIGT, H. 1919. A contribution to the physiology of the fresh-water sponges. (Spongillidae). *Tijd. Ned. Dierkd. Vereen. (II.)* **17**:1–220.

WELTNER, W. 1895. Spongillidenstudien. III. Katalog und Verbreitung der bekannten Süsswasserschwämme. *Arch. Naturgesch.* **61**:114–144.

WIERZEJSKI, A. 1935. Süsswasserspongien. Monographische Bearbeitung. *Mem. Acad. Polon. Sci. Lett., Ser. B*, **9**:1–242.

# Chapter  4

# COELENTERATA (HYDROIDS, JELLYFISH)

ALTHOUGH the Phylum Coelenterata contains in excess of 9000 species, the vast majority are marine. Two classes, the Scyphozoa (true jellyfish) and the Anthozoa (corals, sea anemones, etc.), are exclusively marine, and in the third class, the Hydrozoa, only about 18 species are known from the fresh waters of the United States. These include 14 hydras, one uncommon "fresh-water jellyfish," one uncommon species of colonial polyp, and one rare protohydroid from brackish coastal waters.

Although not conspicuous, hydras are typical representatives of the fauna of ponds, spring brooks, unpolluted streams and rivers, and the littoral zone of lakes. They are all sessile and may be found attached to stones, twigs, vegetation, or debris, occasionally in enormous numbers, but rarely at depths exceeding 1.5 m. When there is a food shortage, however, a hydra often secretes a gas bubble beneath the pedal disc and floats to the surface film, where the bubble bursts, leaving the hydra hanging downward from the surface film.

**General characteristics.** Hydras should be familiar to all who have had an elementary college biology or zoology course. Like other coelenterates, they are radially symmetrical, the main body, or column, being an elongated cylinder from 2 to 25 mm long. Attachment to the substrate is effected by a pedal disc that consists largely of special secretory cells. The distal end of the column has a circlet of tentacles whose length varies from one-half to five times the length of the column. Usually there are 5 or 6 tentacles, sometimes 4, 7, or 8, and rarely up to 12. The end of the column in the center of the circlet of tentacles is raised and domelike to form a hypostome that bears a single opening, the combined mouth and anus. The single, continuous, internal body cavity is a gastrovascular cavity; it continues out into the hollow tentacles.

Although some hydras have a characteristic green or brown color, others have a variable coloration depending on age and the kind and amount of ingested food. Thus there may also be various shades of translucent whitish, grayish, tan, or red.

The body wall is simply constructed. Externally it consists of a layer of epidermis, and internally there is a layer of gastrodermis lining the gastrovascular cavity. Several different histological types of epidermal and gastrodermal cells can be distinguished. Between these two epithelia is a very thin, secreted, noncellular, cementlike mesoglea.

All coelenterates have minute stinging capsules, or nematocysts, imbedded in certain epidermal cells. Each nematocyst contains a coiled capillary thread, which, on proper stimulation, can be "exploded" and extruded. Nematocysts function in food getting and protection by means of their entangling, adhesive, and paralyzing properties. Nematocysts are especially abundant on the tentacles and distal part of the column.

Although metagenesis and the alternation of medusoid and polyp stages are typical of marine hydrozoans, the hydras have only the polyp stage in their life history.

**Locomotion.** Hydras are usually considered sessile creatures; when they are undisturbed the column is extended, the ten-

FIG. 61.–*Hydra* with two buds (partially contracted, ×12. (Courtesy General Biological Supply House, Inc., Chicago, Ill.)

tacles are spread out, and there is no movement visible to the naked eye. Occasionally, however, the tentacles wave about or the whole animal contracts and expands unaccountably. But hydras are also capable of moving slowly on the substrate. Most commonly they have a very slow, gliding locomotion on the pedal disc. Occasionally they exhibit somersaulting or inchwormlike looping movements. More rarely they attach the distal end of the body to the substrate and pull themselves along by contractions and elongations. The central part of the basal disc may secrete a small gas bubble that enables the hydra to rise to the surface and remain suspended at the surface film in quiet waters.

**Feeding, digestion.** Hydrozoans are strictly carnivorous and eat many kinds of small metazoans, including cladocerans, copepods, insects, and annelids (but not ostracods). Occasionally hydras become a hatchery nuisance by killing fish fry, but

*Hydra oligactis* is probably the only species large enough to be of any real importance. When a food organism is swimming or creeping about and by chance comes in contact with the tentacles or column, it is paralyzed and killed in a few seconds by the nematocysts that are discharged from those parts of the column or tentacles contacted. The organism is then manipulated so that it is taken into the mouth. The latter is variously described as star-shaped or circular; both it and the column are capable of great distension, and a cladoceran four times the diameter of the column may be ingested. When the usual food supply is insufficient, hydras may feed on the organic material of the substrate, but this is certainly not a normal means of feeding. The feeding reaction of hydras (writhing and twisting of the tentacles toward the proctostome) is induced by reduced glutathione (and perhaps by other substances). Presumably this is the key mechanism in the feeding process of hydras.

Digestion is both extra- and intracellular. Preliminary extracellular digestion occurs in the gastrovascular cavity, resulting in the maceration of the food organisms into a mush within several hours. These small particles are then taken up by pseudopodial action of many of the gastrodermal cells. Further digestion is intracellular. Only the gastrodermal cells in the upper part of the column appear to function in digestion; those in the more basal part of the column (stalk) are highly vacuolated and have no digestive power.

Excess food is stored in the gastrodermal cells as fat and glycogen. Indigestible material is voided from the mouth.

*Chlorohydra viridissima* is the so-called green hydra because of the abundance of algal cells (probably mostly *Chlorella*) in the gastrodermis. Such living algae probably have a true symbiotic relationship with the hydra, but dead and disintegrating cells are digested and used as food. The algae are passed from one generation to the next in the egg cytoplasm.

**Nematocysts.** A nematocyst is a spherical to elongated, capsular, sclerotized organoid ranging from 5 to 25 microns in

FIG. 62.–Sexually mature hydras, ×17. A, female; B, male. (Courtesy General Biological Supply House, Inc., Chicago, Ill.)

length in fresh-water species. It is contained within a special epidermal cell, the cnidoblast. Inside of the nematocyst is a minute, coiled, hollow thread, or tubule, whose base is attached to the inner distal wall of the nematocyst. A lid, or opercu-lum, covers the distal opening of the capsule, and a tiny, triggerlike bristle, or cnidocil, projects into the surrounding water from the surface of the cnidoblast near the edge of the operculum. In the Phylum Coelenterata as a whole there are many differ-

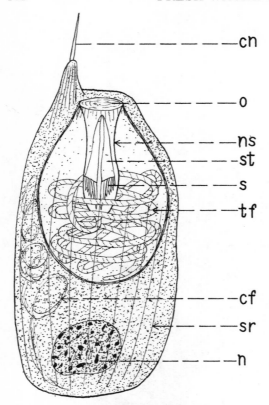

cn

o

ns

st

s

tf

cf

sr

n

FIG. 63.–Undischarged stenotele nematocyst within its cnidoblast. *cf*, cnidoblast filament; *ns*, nematocyst shaft (butt); *o*, operculum; *s*, spines; *sr*, supporting rods of cnidoblast; *st*, stylet; *tf*, tubular filament (actually much longer than shown.)

ent types of nematocysts, but in the fresh-water hydras there are only four types as follows:

Desmonemes (volvents) are small, pyriform, or spherical nematocysts. The tubule forms only one loop, is closed at the distal end, and is usually unarmed but may have extremely fine spinules (Figs. 64D, E). Desmonemes appear to function mainly in entangling and wrapping around bristles of the prey.

Stenoteles (penetrants) are large, spherical nematocysts. The coiled tubule is open at the tip and has a definite butt, or enlarged basal portion, which bears three spines and three spiral rows of minute spinules (Figs. 63, 64F). Exploding stenoteles pierce the prey and inject a paralyzing material.

There are two types of isorhiza (glutinant) nematocysts, but both are characterized by a tubule which is open at the tip, by the absence of a butt, and by the secretion of a paralyzing material. Holotrichous isorhizas are larger and have the tubule covered with minute spinules (Fig. 64C); they function mainly in defense. Atrichous isorhizas are smaller and have a smooth tubule (Figs. 64A, B); they appear to function mainly in locomotion by discharging and sticking when the tentacles are placed in contact with a substrate.

Nematocysts have an unusual mode of origin and migration. They are formed within special interstitial cnidoblast cells of the epidermis. Most cnidoblasts first appear in the distal third of the column. Before their contained nematocysts are fully formed, many cnidoblasts pass through the mesoglea and gastrodermis into the gastrovascular cavity. Here they circulate about briefly before being taken up again by gastrodermal cells, especially in the tentacles. Then they are transported back through the mesoglea to their final location in the epidermis.

According to one theory, when the projecting cnidocil is touched, the operculum springs open and the nematocyst tubule instantaneously turns inside out as it whips out of the capsule. The base of the tubule emerges first and the rest follows from base to tip. According to a more recently elaborated theory, the external tubule is formed by the rapid extrusion of a fluid that hardens on contact with water. At the same time the internal coiled tubule disintegrates. Discharged nematocysts are lost and are of no further use to the hydra.

It is thought that stenotele and desmoneme discharge is usually dependent on a combined chemical and mechanical stimulus. The juice and body fluids of the normal prey will not in themselves discharge nematocysts, nor will a fine glass rod touched to the cnidocils. In addition, these nematocysts of satiated animals do not react when food organisms touch the tentacles.

The physiological mechanisms of nematocyst action are poorly understood, but it is thought that the discharge is produced by an increased pressure within the capsule caused by increased permeability of the capsule wall. Perhaps a chemical stimulus acts first by reducing surface tension and lowering the resistance of the cnidoblast and cnidocil to mechanical stimuli.

One of the most unusual phenomena centering around nematocyst biology is the use of nematocysts by certain species of *Microstomum* for their own protection and food getting. When one of these turbellarians feeds on a hydra only the desmonemes and atrichous isorhizas are digested, and the other two types of nematocysts are passed through the mesenchyme of the *Microstomum* and into the epidermis. Here they are correctly oriented by associated phagocytes and discharged when touched by other animals.

**Physiology.** Circulation of materials within the gastrovascular cavity is effected by movements of the whole animal and by beating of the flagella of some of the gastrodermal cells. Such cells usually have one or two flagella.

Respiration occurs through the general body surface. None of the hydrozoans are active in the presence of reduced quantities of dissolved oxygen.

There seems to be no special excretory mechanism, and it is presumed that metabolic wastes simply diffuse out into the surrounding water. A few workers, however, have reported a small "aboral" or "excretory" pore in the center of the basal disc. Osmoregulation seems to be a function of the individual cells.

When strongly stimulated, and under adverse environmental conditions, hydras contract markedly and assume a barrellike shape with small, budlike contracted tentacles. Though there are no special bands or sheets of muscle tissue to produce such contractions and elongations, many of the epidermal cells and some gastrodermal cells have one or a few strandlike myonemes associated with their basal portions. Most of the longitudinal fibers are restricted to the epidermis and the circular fibers to the gastrodermis; the former are more abundant.

Elongated sensory cells are numerous

FIG. 64.–Typical hydra nematocysts. A, undischarged atrichous isorhiza; B, discharged atrichous isorhiza; C, discharged holotrichous isorhiza; D, undischarged desmoneme; E, discharged desmoneme; F, discharged stenotele. A to E, ×2000; F, ×1000. (Cnidoblasts not shown.)

in the epidermis of the tentacles and oral region. They are generalized receptors for touch, temperature, and substances in solution, and pass basally into one or more processes of the nervous system, which is a nerve net ramifying everywhere at the base of the epidermis. The neurones are bi- and multipolar ganglion cells and their neurites, and the entire system has the appearance of a continuous network. There are no coordinating or relay centers, and stimuli simply diffuse throughout the nerve net in all directions. The nervous system has no connections with nematocysts.

**Reproduction, development.** Budding is the common asexual method of reproduction. Such buds usually originate at the junction of the gastric and stalk regions. A bud first appears as a hemispherical outpouching that later elongates, becomes cylindrical, and develops tentacles. Subsequent buds appear spirally. The gastrovascular cavity of the budding individual and parent are continuous, but soon the base of the bud pinches off completely and the new individual becomes separated and independent. Under favorable conditions a new bud may be produced every two or three days.

Both transverse and longitudinal fission are occasionally observed in hydras, but these methods of reproduction are not normal and usually follow injuries or depression periods (page 107). Powers of regeneration and susceptibility to grafting are well developed, and a large amount of experimental work has been done on these phases of hydra biology.

Syngamic reproduction is usually limited to the autumn months when water temperatures are dropping, but in a few species it may appear in spring or summer when the habitat is drying up. In hermaphroditic species the testes are distal and the ovaries proximal; sometimes ovaries and testes mature simultaneously, sometimes at different periods. In dioecious species the ovaries or testes may be distributed throughout most of the distal half or three-quarters of the column. In general, males far outnumber females, in striking contrast to the situation in most fresh-water invertebrate groups.

A gonad consists of an accumulation of epidermal interstitial cells between mesoglea and epidermis, but in a developing ovary these cells fuse or engulf each other, leaving a single large food-filled ovum. A mature testis is usually hemispherical or helmet-shaped. It usually has a "nipple"; if present, many of the sperm escape to the outside through this small area. Ovaries are hemispherical or bulbous swellings.

When an egg is mature, the covering epidermis ruptures and withdraws, forming a small cup or cushion under the egg. If not fertilized promptly, the egg dies. Sperm may come from the same or a different individual.

During late cleavage the embryo secretes a sclerotized yellowish shell, the embryonic theca. When the theca is being formed it is somewhat sticky, and at this stage the whole embryo drops off the parent or is fastened to the substrate by bending movements of the parent. It sticks to the substrate while the theca hardens. Such thecated embryos may be spherical or planoconvex, spinous or smooth. The diameter ranges from 0.40 to 1.00 mm. They are highly resistant to adverse environmental conditions and endure drying and freezing temperatures. After a dormant period of 3 to 10 weeks or more, the theca softens and splits, permitting the exit of an embryo that already has a gastrovascular cavity and tentacles.

Little is known about the length of life under normal conditions. Under favorable conditions in the laboratory, however, hydras live for 3 to 12 months or more. A few specimens have been kept alive for more than two years, during which time they produced scores of buds.

**Fresh-water jellyfish.** Although hydras are by far the most familiar fresh-water hydrozoans, there is one American species of "jellyfish," *Craspedacusta sowerbyi*. Unlike large marine jellyfish, however, it has a velum and its life history includes a colonial (but simple) polyp.

*C. sowerbyi* was first found in England

FIG. 65.–Mature medusae of *Craspedacusta sowerbyi*, ×5. A, subumbrellar view of stained specimen; B, lateral view of living specimen. (B from Dejdar.)

in 1880; more recently it has been noted many times in Europe and on other continents. It has been found in about 50 localities in the United States since 1908, when it was discovered in this country. It has been reported mostly from small lakes, ponds, fishponds, and old water-filled quarries, especially between July and October.

A mature medusa stage of *C. sowerbyi* has the typical umbrella or bell shape, manubrium, and four radial canals and one circular canal forming the gastrovascular cavity. The diameter of the bell is about 5 to 22 mm, and the circumference bears 50 to 500 solid tentacles of varying length and arranged in three to seven series, depending on the medusa size. Only short tentacles are involved in feeding; long tentacles are presumably stabilizers for swimming. The bell margin also bears many statocysts, often 60 to 100 or more. The velum is rather thick. Nematocysts are especially abundant around the mouth, at the edge of the bell, and on the tentacles. *Craspedacusta* actively swims up, down, or sideways in a dancing sort of movement produced by varying contractions of the bell.

Most populations appear to consist of all males or all females, the occurrence of mixed populations having been observed only a few times. The four gonads consist of convoluted or flaplike masses on the subumbrellar surface of the bell in the vicinity of the radial canals. Both eggs and sperm

are released into the surrounding water, where fertilization occurs.

The zygote develops into a simple, branching, colonial hydroid, 2 to 8 mm long, usually consisting of two to four individuals (seldom up to 10). Single individuals are usually less than 2 mm long, and tentacles are absent. The hydroid creeps about slowly on the substrate, feeding on small metazoans. The region around the mouth bears clumps of nematocysts. The body secretes a sticky, mucous material to which debris adheres and more or less covers the body. During the winter months the hydroids contract and secrete a sclerotized protective coat.

The hydroid stage has three methods of asexual reproduction. Ordinary budding is similar to that of the hydras, and new individuals may remain attached or constrict off from the parent. Nonciliated planulalike buds (frustules) may also be produced. These constrict off, elongate, and creep about slowly on the substrate for a time, and then develop into new polyps. The third method involves the production of medusa buds. When these break free from the parent the bell diameter is about 0.4 mm, and there are only eight tentacles, but rapid growth and development follow, resulting in the large, sexually mature medusae. Both polyps and medusae feed on a wide variety of small invertebrates.

The appearance of the medusae is

FIG. 66.–Stages in the life history of *Craspedacusta sowerbyi*. A, typical colony of hydroids, ×12; B, hydroid with a maturing planulalike bud, ×15; C, hydroid with a maturing medusa bud, ×15; D, newly released medusa with eight tentacles, ×100. (A and D greatly modified from Payne.)

highly sporadic and unpredictable. In some years they may be found in abundance in certain ponds, but in subsequent years they may be absent, only to reappear several years later or in several successive years. In other ponds they have been found only once and have never reappeared, in spite of careful searching. There is some evidence to show that the medusae are positively phototropic.

The hydroid generation has been found only a few times, probably chiefly because of its small size and inconspicuous nature. It is possible that the hydroids live undetected for long periods, only occasionally giving rise to the medusoid generation. For many years the hydroid was called *Microhydra ryderi,* and it was not until 1924 that it was definitely associated with *Craspedacusta sowerbyi.*

The fresh-water jellyfish has been reported from nearly all of the states east of the Mississippi River, but is not known from northern New England. West of the Mississippi it has been found in Iowa, Missouri, Kansas, Oklahoma, Colorado, Arkansas, Louisiana, Texas, California, Washington, and Oregon.

Several related species of fresh-water medusae have been reported from other continents, including one species in China, two or three in Africa, one in India, and one in Trinidad.

**Colonial polyps.** Another unusual fresh-water coelenterate is *Cordylophora lacustris.* It is a profusely branching, mosslike colonial hydrozoan superficially similar to the marine *Obelia* and its many relatives. It does best at 15⁰/₀₀ salinity and occurs in brackish inlets and estuaries from New Jersey to the Gulf of the St. Lawrence, but has also been found in inland rivers in Illinois, Arkansas, and Louisana. This species is probably cosmopolitan. It is widely distributed in northern Europe and has been found in numerous other parts of the world. Some taxonomists believe this species should be called *Cordylophora caspia.*

During the summer months brackish water colonies attain a height of 20 to 100 mm from the substrate, but in fresh waters growths seldom exceed 30 mm in height. There are two kinds of polyps making up such colonies; hydranths are spindle shaped feeding individuals with a prominent manubrium and 10 to 20 thin scattered tentacles, and gonophores are ovoid reproductive polyps. It is notable that only a few gonophores are produced on colonies growing in strictly fresh waters. A single female gonophore usually produces 6 to 20 ova in brackish waters, but only three to six in fresh waters. Mature ova are retained on the gonophores, but the sperm from male gonophores are released into the water, and after swimming about for a short time they penetrate through the covering of the female gonophores and fertilize the eggs. The embryo develops on the gonophore and forms a free-swimming ciliated planula that is released from the colony. The planula attaches to the substrate and by growth and differentiation gives rise to a new colony.

FIG. 67.–*Cordylophora lacustris*, ×5. A, small portions of summer growth of colony; B, colony in winter condition (lower portion of colony covered with detritus). (B from K. Berg, 1948, by permission.)

Thus there is no true medusoid generation in *Cordylophora*.

In the autumn the hydranths disintegrate and only a few horizontal and more basal upright portions of the colony winter over (Fig. 67B).

**Protohydroids.** A third unusual type of hydroid is *Protohydra leuckarti* (Fig. 69). Although not a true fresh-water species, it occurs in brackish estuaries, swamps, and creeks, some of which are almost fresh. It has the general appearance of a hydra but has no tentacles. The body is usually less than 2 mm long but may attain a maximum of 5 mm. The species exhibits dioecious syngamic reproduction and also reproduces by transverse and longitudinal fission. *Protohydra* has been reported several times along the New England coast and from numerous places in Great Britain and northwestern Europe.

**Ecology.** Although hydroids are typical members of the littoral and shallow stream associations, they have occasionally been reported from waters as deep as 40 to 350 m. It is not unusual to find them in swift streams or in the wave-swept rocky littoral of large lakes. Unless there are large pieces of debris present, however, they do not occur on fine, muddy bottoms. Greatest populations are usually found in late spring and early summer, followed by a marked decrease in July or August. Sometimes there is also an autumn maximum in September or October. Populations may be vigorous in midwinter but are usually scanty by the time of the ice melt in late winter.

Gonad production is often induced in two or three weeks by lowered laboratory temperatures, usually 10° to 15°, but often a culture becomes sexual without any apparent stimulus. Medium hard waters with pH readings of 7.6 to 8.4 seem to be especially favorable for most species. Although little is known about minimal oxygen concentrations, about 3.0 ml per liter seems to be a typical value. Hydras do not occur in oxygen-deficient depths of lakes. In general, any lasting contraction of the tentacles is an indication of unfavorable environmental conditions.

Periods of "depression" are often observed in laboratory cultures and are presumably induced by a variety of unfavorable conditions, including temperatures above 20°, lack of sufficient dissolved oxygen, toxic salts, transfer to clean water, and accumulation of metabolic materials. The bodies of hydras undergoing depression rapidly shorten and the tentacles contract and then disappear. The column then further shortens into a small brownish mass that soon disintegrates. If not too far gone, hydras may recover on being placed in more favorable conditions.

FIG. 68.–Small portion of colony of *Corylophora lacustris*, ×15, showing one hydranth and one immature gonophore.

**Commensals, enemies.** Commensal or parasitic ciliates, such as *Kerona* (page 70) and *Trichodina* (page 74), are common on the external surface of hydras where they feed on small bits of food. They do not discharge the nematocysts, although most free-living ciliates, both smaller and larger than *Kerona* and *Trichodina,* do easily discharge them.

Carnivorous enemies are not abundant or important but include a few turbellarians, nemertines, crustaceans, and aquatic insects. *Anchistropus minor* is a cladoceran that feeds exclusively on hydras. Epidemics of an external amoeboid parasite, *Hydramoeba hydroxena*, sometimes decimate vigorous hydra growths.

**Geographic distribution, dispersal.** *Chlorohydra viridissima* is known from North America, Europe, Greenland, South America, and New Zealand. *Hydra oligactis* is widely distributed in the Northern Hemisphere and has been recorded in Australia. The other species of hydras oc-

curring in the United States, however, have not been reported from continents other than North America. About 20 species are recorded in the literature as occurring outside of the continent of North America, but about half of these are so sketchily described as to be unrecognizable. Europe has eight species. Four American hydras are known from single localities, and several others have been reported from a few scattered areas. Undoubtedly when more intensive collecting is done, especially in the western half of the country, the geographical ranges of most species will be greatly extended.

Hydras attached to mollusk shells may be easily distributed through single drainage systems, and thecated embryos are probably easily blown or transported overland.

**Collecting.** Unless hydras are exceedingly abundant, they may be collected most easily by bringing small objects and aquatic plants into the laboratory where they may be picked off. If the containers are placed in semidarkness, the hydras will migrate to the surface film as the dissolved oxygen in the water decreases. The grayish or brown-

FIG. 69.–*Protohydra leuckarti*, ×35.

ish thecated embryos should be sought for on aquatic vegetation or debris with the low powers of a binocular dissecting microscope.

**Culturing.** Specimens keep well in aquaria in moderate light if the temperature is below 20° and if they are well fed with cladocerans, copepods, or brine shrimp. Three or four daphnids per day per hydra will produce prolific budding. A fraction of the aquarium water should be changed frequently, and only pond water should be used, not tap water.

Periods of depression may be overcome by changing the culture water. If necessary, hand feed depressed individuals by holding (with fine forceps) a freshly killed daphnid in contact with the hydra.

**Preserving, preparing.** In order to kill hydras in an expanded condition they should first be squirted off their normal substrate into a dish. After they are fully expanded in about 2 ml of water, dash a copious quantity of hot Bouin's fixative into the dish. After a few minutes place the specimens in cold Bouin's fluid for 10 hours. Then wash in several changes of alkaline 30 percent alcohol, stain, dehydrate, and mount permanently. Hance (1957) gives an alternate excellent method for killing hydras in an expanded condition.

Dissociation of the tissues to permit an examination of the nematocysts may be accomplished by placing hydras in a few drops of Hertwig-Schneider's fluid on a slide for 15 to 20 minutes. This solution consists of one part 0.02 percent osmic acid and four parts 5.0 percent glacial acetic acid. Dilute Bouin's fluid and 1 percent nitric acid are also fairly useful for dissociation.

**Taxonomy.** Modern taxonomic concepts and generic designations date back to the important work of Schulze (1917). Essential characteristics for identification include shape of testes, form of the theca, relative body and tentacle length, hermaphroditism or the dioecious condition, and the shape, size, and structure of the nematocysts. The detailed anatomy of nematocysts can best be distinguished on macerated or dissociated specimens with an oil immersion objective. Preserved nematocysts are of little value.

Most of the information on our American hydras has been gained through the extensive and careful investigations of Dr. Libbie H. Hyman.

The following key includes all American species that have been adequately described in the literature. All lengths and proportions are based on measurements of the living, expanded animal. Ordinarily only living hydras can be accurately identified.

## KEY TO SPECIES OF COELENTERATA

**1.** Solitary polyps with tentacles; with a medusa stage in the life history.
Order **HYDROIDA**, HYDRIDAE, **2**
Colonial polyps, free-swimming medusae, or solitary polyps without tentacles ....**15**
**2.** Gastrodermis containing green algae; hermaphroditic; holotrichous isorhizas narrowed as base (Fig. 70L); tentacles always shorter than the column; green hydras (the taxonomic status of this genus is questionable; possibly it should lapse, with the species being included in the genus *Hydra*.) ............ **Chlorohydra, 3**
Gastrodermis without green algae; hermaphroditic or dioecious .................**4**
**3.** Embryonic theca two-chambered (Fig. 70M); column of mature individuals less than 15 mm long; usually six to ten tentacles; ovaries and testes develop simultaneously; reported only from Pennsylvania and New Jersey but undoubtedly common elsewhere in the eastern states ........ **Chlorohydra hadleyi** Forrest
Embryonic theca with a single chamber; column up to 30 mm. long but usually less than 15 mm; usually from four to 12 tentacles; ovaries and testes do not develop simultaneously; widely distributed and common.
**Chlorohydra viridissima** (Pallas)

FIG. 70.–Structure of hydras. A, male *Hydra cauliculata*, ×4; B, optical section of thecated embryo of *H. cauliculata*; C, *H. oligactis*, ×2; D, holotrichous isorhiza of *H. oligactis*; E, male *H. oligactis* with testes, ×3; F, male *H. pseudoligactis* with testes, ×3; G, holotrichous isorhiza of *H. pseudoligactis*; H, sexually mature *H. utahensis*, showing basal ovaries and distal testes, ×7; J, holotrichous isorhiza of *H. utahensis*; K, theca and contained zygote of *H. utahensis*; L, holotrichous isorhiza of *Chlorohydra viridissima*; M, cross section of theca of *Chlorohydra hadleyi*. (A and B modified from Hyman, 1938; C to E modified from Hyman, 1930; F to K modified from Hyman, 1931b.)

4. Tentacles exceptionally long, up to five times column length; column up to 17 mm long; reported only from lakes near Edmonton, Alberta, Canada.
**Hydra canadensis** Rowan
Tentacles shorter .................................................5
5. Tentacles shorter than column length....................................6
Tentacles longer than column length .....................................7

F<small>IG</small>. 71.–Structure of *Hydra*. A, mature *Hydra carnea*, ×8, with four distal testes, three ovaries, one basal testis, and one bud; B, spines of embryonic theca of *H. carnea*; C, mature male *H. littoralis,* with eight testes and two buds, ×5; D, optical section of thecated embryo of *H. littoralis*; E, holotrichous isorhiza of *H. littoralis*; F, mature male *H. americana,* ×6; G, portion of embryonic theca of *H. americana*; H, thecated embryo of *H. hymanae*; J, sexually mature *H. hymanae* with two testes and two ovaries, ×6. (A and B modified from Hyman, 1931; C and D modified from Hyman, 1938; E modified from Hyman, 1931b; F and G modified from Hyman, 1929; H and J modified from Hadley and Forrest.)

**6.** Tentacles one-half column or more; theca spined and helmet-shaped (Fig. 71H); hermaphroditic; in ponds and brooks; variable coloration, depending on contents of gastrovascular cavity; reported only from New Jersey.

**Hydra hymanae** Hadley and Forrest

Tentacles one-half column or less; theca spined and spherical (Fig. 71G); dioecious, rarely hermaphroditic; in standing or slowly flowing waters; whitish or tan coloration; the white hydra; probably widely distributed throughout the eastern states . . . . . . . . . . . . . . . . . . . . . . . . . . . . . . . . . . . . . . . . **Hydra americana** Hyman

**7.** Holotrichous isorhizas broadly oval (Fig. 70J) . . . . . . . . . . . . . . . . . . . . . . . . . . . . .8

Holotrichous isorhizas narrowly oval or cylindrical (Figs. 70G, L) . . . . . . . . . . . . . .9

**8.** Column 2 to 6 mm long, usually less than 4 mm; known only from a brook in Millburn Township, New Jersey . . . . . . . . . . . . . . . . . . . . . . . . . . . . . .**Hydra minima** Forrest

Column 10 mm or more long; known only from a pond near Salem, Utah.

**Hydra utahensis** Hyman

9. Tentacles more than three times column length .............................. **10**
   Tentacles less than three times column length ............................... **12**
10. Theca spherical and spineless; testes without nipples, or pumpkin-shaped and with
    nipples (Figs. 70E, F); brownish; common ........................... **11**
    Theca spherical and spined; testes pumpkin-shaped, with nipples; reported only from
    ponds near Portland, Oregon ............. **Hydra oregona** Griffin and Peters
11. Holotrichous isorhizas with lengthwise loops (Fig. 70D); testes without nipples (Fig.
    70E); column up to 20 mm long; the true brown hydra; common in northern
    states from Montana, Wyoming, and Colorado east to New England, north of
    the Ohio River ..................................... **Hydra oligactis** (Pallas)
    Holotrichous isorhizas with transverse loops (Fig. 70G); testes pumpkin-shaped, with
    nipples (Fig. 70F); column up to 25 mm long; the false brown hydra; most
    common in central states, scattered elsewhere . **Hydra pseudoligactis** (Hyman)
12. Column slightly stalked; brownish; in standing waters; probably common in the At-
    lantic coast states ............................. **Hydra cauliculata** Hyman
    Column not stalked ..................................................... **13**
13. Buds usually in opposite pairs; column to 18 mm; known only from brooks in New
    Jersey ........................................ **Hydra rutgersensis** Forrest
    Buds not usually in opposite pairs ........................................... **14**
14. Column to 10 mm; hermaphroditic; theca with short, thick spines, in standing waters
    as far west as Nebraska ........................... **Hydra carnea** Agassiz
    Column to 15 mm; dioecious; theca with long branching spines; in swift waters or on
    wave-swept shores; reported from scattered localities as far west as
    Oklahoma ......................................... **Hydra littoralis** Hyman
15. Macroscopic colonial polyps 10 to 100 mm high and consisting of feeding hydranths
    and reproductive gonophores (Figs. 67, 68); uncommon in brackish waters of
    Atlantic and Pacific coasts; also reported from rivers in Illinois, Arkansas,
    Ohio, Oklahoma, Tennessee, and Louisiana.
    Order **HYDROIDA**, CLAVIDAE, **Cordylophora lacustris** Allman
    Not macroscopic colonial polyps ....................................... **16**
16. Free-swimming bell-shaped medusae with numerous peripheral tentacles; bell diam-
    eter ranging from 0.4 to 22 mm (Fig. 65); sporadic and uncommon, especially
    in man-made ponds, small lakes, fishponds, and old flooded quarries.
    Order **TRACHYLINA**, PETASIDAE, **Craspedacusta sowerbyi** Lankester
    Sessile solitary or simple colonial hydroids without tentacles .................. **17**
17. Simple colonial hydroids, 2 to 8 mm long, usually consisting of two to four individuals
    and seldom up to 12 (Fig. 66); rare in ponds, small lakes, fishponds, and old
    flooded quarries.
    Order **TRACHYLINA**, PETASIDAE, **Craspedacusta sowerbyi** Lankester
    Solitary hydroid up to 3 mm long (Fig. 69); in brackish estuaries, swamps, and creeks,
    some of which are almost fresh; rare along New England coast.
    Order **HYDROIDA**, HYDRIDAE, **Protohydra leuckarti** Greeff

# COELENTERATA REFERENCES

BRYDEN, R. R. 1952. Ecology of Pelmatohydra oligactis in Kirkpatricks Lake, Tennessee, *Ecol. Monogr.* **22**:45–68.

BYERS, C. F. 1944. The fresh-water jellyfish in Florida. *Proc. Fla. Acad. Sci.* **7**:173–180.

DEJDAR, E. 1934. Die Süsswassermeduse Craspedacusta sowerbii Lankester in monographischer Darstellung. *Z. Morphol. Oekol. Tiere* **28**:595–691.

EWER, R. F. 1947. On the function and mode of action of the nematocysts of Hydra. *Proc. Zool. Soc. Lond.* **117**:365–376.

——— 1948. A review of the Hydridae and two new species of Hydra from Natal. Ibid. **118**:226–244.

FORREST, H. 1963. Taxonomic studies on the hydras of North America. VIII. Description of two new species, with records and a key to the North American hydras. *Trans. Am. Microsc. Soc.* **82**:6–17.

GRAYSON, R. F. 1971. The freshwater hydras of Europe. I. A review of the European species. *Arch. Hydrobiol.* **68**: 436–449.

HADLEY, C. E., and H. FORREST. 1949. Taxonomic studies on the hydras of North America. 6. Description of Hydra hymanae, new species. *Am. Mus. Novit.* **1423**:1–14.

HANCE, R. T. 1957. Mass fixation of Hydra. *Trans. Am. Microsc. Soc.* **76**:387–389.

HYMAN, L. H. 1929. Taxonomic studies on the hydras of North America, I. General remarks and description of Hydra americana, new species. **48**:242–255.

——. 1930. Studies on hydras, II. The characters of Pelmatohydra oligactis (Pallas). Ibid. **49**:322–333.

——. 1931. Studies on hydras, III. Rediscovery of Hydra carnea L. Agassiz (1850) with a description of its characters. Ibid. **50**:20–29.

——. 1931a. Studies on hydras, IV. Description of three new species with a key to the known species. Ibid. 302–315.

——. 1938. Taxonomic studies on the hydras of North America. V. Description of Hydra cauliculata, n. sp., with notes on other species, especially Hydra littoralis. *Am. Mus. Novit.* **1003**:1–9.

JONES, C. S. 1941. The place of origin and the transportation of cnidoblasts in Pelmatohydra oligactis (Pallas). *J. Exp. Zool.* **87**:457–476.

——. 1947. The control and discharge of nematocysts in Hydra. Ibid. **105**:25–60.

KEPNER, W. A., W. C. GREGORY, and R. J. PORTER. 1935. The manipulation of Hydra's nematocysts by Microstomum. *Science* **82**:621.

KEPNER, W. A., B. D. REYNOLDS, L. GOLDSTEIN, and J. H. TAYLOR. 1943. The structure, development and discharge of the penetrant of Pelmatohydra oligactis (Pall.). *J. Morphol.* **72**:561–587.

KEPNER, W. A., and others. 1951. The discharge of nematocysts of the hydra, with special reference to the penetrant. Ibid. **88**:23–48.

LENHOFF, H. M. 1968. Behavior, hormones, and Hydra. *Science* **161**:434–442.

LOOMIS, W. F. 1954. Environmental factors controlling growth in hydra. *J. Exp. Zool.* **126**:223–234.

MILLER, D. E. 1936. A limnological study of Pelmatohydra with special reference to their quantitative seasonal distribution. *Trans. Am. Microsc. Soc.* **55**:123–193.

MUELLER, J. F. 1950. Some observations on the structure of Hydra, with particular reference to the muscular system. Ibid. **69**:133–147.

PAULY, R. 1902. Untersuchungen über den Bau und die Lebensweise der Cordylophora lacustris Allman. *Jena. Z. Naturwiss.* **36**:737–780.

PAYNE, F. 1924. A study of the fresh-water medusa, Craspedacusta ryderi. *J. Morphol.* **38**:387–430.

PENNAK, R. W. 1956. The fresh-water jellyfish Craspedacusta in Colorado with some remarks on its ecology and morphological degeneration. *Trans. Am. Microsc. Soc.* **75**:324–331.

ROWAN, W. 1930. On a new Hydra from Alberta. *Trans. Roy. Soc. Can., Sect. 5, Biol. Sci.* **24**:165–170.

SCHMITT, W. L. 1939. Freshwater jellyfish records since 1932. *Am. Nat.* **73**:83–89.

SCHULZE, P. 1917. Neue Beiträge zu einer Monographie der Gattung Hydra. *Arch. Biontologie* **4**:33–119.

WELCH, P. S., and H. A. LOOMIS. 1924. A limnological study of Hydra oligactis in Douglas Lake, Michigan. *Trans. Am. Microsc. Soc.* **43**:203–235.

# Chapter 5

# TURBELLARIA (FLATWORMS)

CONSIDERING the Phylum Platyhelminthes as a whole, only a small fraction of the described species are free-living in fresh-water habitats. The classes Cestoidea (tapeworms) and Trematoda (flukes) are entirely parasitic, but the Class Turbellaria is amost exclusively a free-living group. Many of the species of turbellarians are marine and a few (about six in the U.S.) are terrestrial in warm, damp habitats or parasitic on marine invertebrates; the remainder are fresh-water forms.

The Class Turbellaria is customarily divided into seven orders. Two of these orders, the Acoela and Polycladida, are essentially marine. The Alloeocoela is a marine and fresh-water order, but the Tricladida, Catenulida, Macrostomida, and Neorhabdocoela have fresh-water, marine, and terrestrial representatives.

Fresh-water turbellarians are found everywhere, usually on or closely associated with a substrate. The larger species are sometimes confused with small leeches, which they resemble somewhat in shape and color; the microscopic species resemble large ciliates in size, shape, and general habits.

**General characteristics.** All fresh-water flatworms are more or less elongated. They may be highly flattened and leaflike, cylindrical, or spindle-shaped. Almost invariably, however, there is some evidence of flattening on the ventral surface. In many species the anterior end is differentiated and sufficiently specialized to resemble a "head."

Tricladida are usually 5 to 30 mm long, but the other orders are seldom more than 4 mm in length, the majority being micro-scopic. Because of their habit of reproducing by fission, some small species customarily occur in chains of several individuals, or zooids. The general surface of the body is usually more or less covered with cilia, and the term "Turbellaria" was coined by Ehrenberg in 1831, when he detected the minute vortical currents of water generated at the anterior end by ciliary action. In the familiar species of planarians, to which every zoology student is exposed in college, cilia are absent from the dorsal surface and edges of the body.

The body cavity of flatworms is a typical gastrovascular cavity having but a single external opening which functions as both mouth and anus. In the Tricladida the gastrovascular cavity has three main irregular branches, one median and anterior and the others posterior and lateral (Fig. 72). The other orders have a single median gastrovascular chamber, but in a few representatives its outline is more irregular, owing to small lateral caeca.

In a few Turbellaria the mouth is terminal or subterminal. More characteristically it is ventral and somewhere between one-fifth and three-fifths of the way back from the anterior end. A protrusible or non-protrusible muscular pharynx surrounds that portion of the gastrovascular cavity just inside the mouth. If protrusible, the pharynx often lies in a separate pharyngeal chamber.

Almost all species are hermaphroditic and reproduce sexually. One or two genital pores are found on the ventral surface, usually posterior to the mouth.

A wide range of coloration occurs in fresh-water Turbellaria, although the brilliant patterns of marine species are never

114

FIG. 72.–Gross anatomy of a typical planarian, showing the three divisions of the gastrovascular cavity, ×15. *a*, auricle; *e*, eyespot; *m*, mouth (on ventral surface of body); *p*, pharynx (lying in pharyngeal chamber).

Other species are a bright green, owing to internal symbiotic zoochlorellae. In all naturally light-colored Turbellaria the body may take on a variety of darker shades, depending on the particular contents of the gastrovascular cavity.

Two darkly pigmented eyespots are usually present near the anterior end, but in some species eyespots are absent, and in a few others they are numerous.

Epidermal and subepidermal glands secrete an abundance of mucus that usually covers the body. Minute rodlike rhabdites are produced in the epidermis and subepidermal tissues of many genera, and these, on being extruded to the surface of the body, disintegrate and produce an additional adhesive mucus.

Thin layers of circular and oblique, and a thicker layer of longitudinal muscle fibers lie below the basement membrane of the epidermis. The cells that line the gastrovascular cavity are large and phagocytic. Between the inner gastrodermis and the outer muscle fibers and epidermis the body consists largely of an undifferentiated mass of parenchyma cells. A few muscle fibers are found in the parenchyma, but otherwise it appears to function as a loose packing material between the excretory and reproductive organs. In the smaller turbellarians the parenchyma is often highly vacuolated, glandular, and watery.

**Locomotion.** Triclad flatworms cannot swim but are only capable of locomotion on a substrate or on the underside of the surface film of the water. Smooth gliding movements are produced by the action of cilia on the thin coat of mucus secreted onto the substrate by cyanophilous glands in the ventral parenchyma. Faint waves of muscular contractions pass longitudinally down the body and supplement ciliary action. On strong stimulation, planarians may crawl actively by means of pronounced waves of muscular contraction that pass from anterior to posterior. A few species have anterior adhesive organs, which may be used as a leech uses its anterior sucker for locomotion.

Catenulids, macrostomids, neorhabdocoels, and alloeocoels move on a sub-

approached. The more familiar planarians (Tricladida) are various shades of gray, brown or black; often there are dorsal stripes, spots, or mottlings. The ventral surface, however, is usually lighter in color or gray and without a color pattern. Some species have a highly variable coloration. *Dugesia tigrina,* for example, may be dark yellow, olive, brown, or brownish-black, and the pattern may range from lightly mottled to dense coloration (Fig. 73). The lighter shades usually develop in laboratory cultures. Cave species and a few noncave species are whitish.

The other four orders are characteristically grayish or colorless, but some are brilliant yellow, gold, orange, red, or rose.

FIG. 73.–Variations in color pattern of *Dugesia tigrina*. A, striped form; B, spotted form; C, dark spots on uniform brown background; D, E, and F, enlarged views of similar patterns. (From Hyman, 1939.)

strate as do planarians, but many are also capable of swimming about freely in the water, owing to their abundant cilia.

When conditions are unfavorable, when the water is too warm, or when fully fed, planarians are not active but remain more or less contracted for days at a time.

**Feeding, digestion.** The most familiar type of feeding occurs in the planarians. Here the pharynx is long, highly muscular, and protrusible through the mouth. When

the presence of food (usually living, dead, or crushed animal matter) is detected in the water, the animals quickly move toward it and place the ventral surface of the body in contact with it. The pharynx is then extruded through the mouth, and its tip is placed against the food (Fig. 74). Sometimes the pharynx may be extended to as much as one-half of the body length. There appears to be no appreciable secretion of digestive juices from the tip of the pharynx, and apparently only soft or disintegrating tissues are capable of being sucked up into the main gastrovascular cavity by the muscular action of the pharynx. The gastrovascular cavity becomes filled with fluid and small bits of tissues after 30 to 80 minutes of feeding. There is no good evidence for extracellular digestion in planarians. Instead, individual particles are ingested by pseudopodial action of the large gastrodermal cells, and digestion is intracellular. Evidence based on the small amount of work that has been done on microturbellarians, however, indicates that it is probable that they have considerable extracellular digestion.

Some species of *Phagocata* (Tricladida) are interesting in that they are polypharyngeal (Fig. 84F). In microturbellarians the pharynx is short and generally not greatly protrusible, but the normally small mouth may be expanded to a marked degree during feeding.

Although some flatworms are sometimes said to be vegetarians, the great majority of Turbellaria are zoophagous and feed on small living invertebrates. Nevertheless, dead animal matter may often be ingested, and the microscopic species subsist on fresh corpses of larger metazoans as well as on whole living or dead Protozoa, rotifers, nematodes, and gastrotrichs. Small individuals, such as *Catenula* and *Macrostomum,* are especially abundant in decaying organic matter and perhaps are essentially omnivorous. Some species of *Phaenocora* and *Macrostomum,* however, prefer animal tissues and eject plant material from the pharynx. Many substrate species prefer a diatom diet.

Some few species are so voracious that they will exterminate other species in a mixed culture. Cannibalism has occasionally been observed, especially in crowded cultures where there are injured specimens.

A few microturbellarians have been

FIG. 74.–Planarian with extruded pharynx, just beginning to feed on a bit of food.

FIG. 75.–Dorsal views of head of *Procotyla fluviatilis.* A, with adhesive organ retracted; B, with adhesive organ grasping a hydra. (Modified from Redfield.)

found to form an adhesive layer or mass on the substrate by the discharge of rhabdites at the anterior end. Such mucus with its entangled detritus, bacteria, algae, and protozoans is then gathered into a ball and ingested. Some investigators suggest that this method of feeding may be more common than is suspected. Planarians also exude rhabdites, which form a mucus on coming in contact with water. Small crustaceans get caught in this material, as well as in the usual slime track, and are thus easy prey.

Some Dendrocoelidae have an interor, adhesive, suckerlike organ that is used in feeding. Such species pounce on small crustaceans and hydras and grasp them firmly by bringing the lateral edges of the sucker together. The prey is then held against the substrate in the pharyngeal region while feeding proceeds. *Procotyla fluviatilis* feeds chiefly on living crustaceans; it cannot be cultured on raw meat.

When reared in the laboratory, planarians should be fed one to three times per week. They may be kept for months without any food, however, while the body gets progressively smaller and more simplified in structure. No reproduction occurs during such periods of starvation.

*Microstomum* and a few other genera have become curiously adapted for retaining the undischarged nematocysts of ingested hydras. Within 10 to 20 hours after ingestion, the nematocysts are found distributed over the body surface between the epidermal cells. Such nematocysts are retained as defense devices for the remainder of the life of the turbellarian.

There is no special circulatory system in flatworms. Materials are distributed throughout the gastrovascular cavity by means of general muscular and body movements. The tissues are nowhere thick or bulky, and diffusion of materials from cell to cell is easily facilitated.

**Respiration.** The respiratory exchange of oxygen and carbon dioxide occurs through the general epidermis and perhaps to a slight extent through the gastrodermis also. Many microturbellarians are characteristic of habitats where there is much decay and low concentrations of dissolved oxygen; some are able to withstand anaerobic conditions for variable lengths of time, although there is little definite information on this phase of flatworm biology in the literature. Planarians, however, all require high concentrations of oxygen and occur only in well-oxygenated habitats.

Symbiotic zoochlorellae occur in the parenchyma and gastrodermis of many microturbellarians, although they are not necessarily consistently present in a particular species. Photosynthesis releases oxygen to the turbellarian tissues, while the worm contributes carbon dioxide and nitrogenous compounds for algal metabolism. Algae may be passed on to the succeeding generation in the turbellarian egg.

**Excretion.** The flame bulb, or protonephridial, system of flatworms has a variable pattern. There may be few to many flame bulbs, but their ducts usually empty into two longitudinal collecting ducts (Fig. 76). *Stenostomum* and *Catenula* are exceptional in having a single median collecting duct. Collecting ducts open to the ventral surface by means of one or two pores, which are variable in position.

As in certain other phyla, the excretory process is a function of the ducts rather than the flame bulbs themselves. Nevertheless the physiological significance of the whole flame bulb system appears to vary from one species to another. Sometimes the system has an important excretory function; sometimes it is apparently unimportant. Often it is of great importance in osmoregulation; in other species it appears to be relatively unimportant.

*Gyratrix hermaphroditus* occurs in fresh-water, brackish, and marine habitats. In the former it has a highly developed flame bulb system. In brackish habitats the system is less highly developed, with the bladder and ampullae lacking. In marine habitats, however, it is poorly developed or absent.

It is probable that a large fraction of the excretory materials are disposed of through the general epidermal surface and also perhaps to a slight extent through the gastrodermis into the gastrovascular cavity. Some excretory granules are commonly retained and stored in the tissues until the animal dies.

**Nervous system.** The brain consists of two more or less well-defined lobes, or ganglia, near the anterior end. Usually there are two prominent longitudinal nerve trunks, one originating in each ganglion, but often there are one to several additional, smaller trunks. Many cross commissures and small lateral nerves originate from the longitudinal trunks and innervate all of the organs and tissues. An abundance of sensory fibers are given off from the brain and innervate the anterior end (Fig. 77).

**Sensory receptors.** Eyespots are the most highly developed sense organs, especially in planarians. Each eyespot is shaped like a bean or a pigmented cup containing translucent light-sensitive receptor cells, which are attached to nerve fibers at the outer portion of the cup. Some spring and most cave species of Tricladida have no eyespots. The majority of microturbellarians have one pair, but some are blind, and a few have multiple eyespots (Figs. 87–89).

Such eyespots are relatively simple in structure and are sometimes unpigmented and called light-refracting bodies rather than eyes. In *Stenostomum*, for example, the so-called eyespot is colorless and consists of a few to many basal refractive spherules and a distal low cone-shaped vesicle. Actually a visual function has not yet

Fig. 76.–Diagrams of protonephridial structures. A, protonephridial system of *Mesostoma* (the two proximal pores are located just inside the mouth); B, three flame bulbs at terminal endings of tubules.

been definitely established for this structure.

Althout eyespots may be well developed, most turbellarians are photonegative, especially in moderate to strong light, and as a consequence are usually found in shaded areas or under objects.

Some species have a pair of anterior sensory pits, often ciliated, which are presumably chemoreceptors. They may be rounded, oblong, slitlike, and shallow or deep (Fig. 86D)

Larval *Rhynchoscolex* and adult *Catenula* and *Otomesostoma* have a median anterior statocyst (Figs. 86A, 90B), but none of the other American fresh-water genera have such a structure.

In addition to the general coat of short cilia, many have a few long sensory cilia, especially at the anterior and posterior ends

FIG. 77.–Structure of *Mesostoma ehrenbergi* Focke, ×20, ventral view. *b*, brain; *e*, eyespot; *fb*, flame bulb (distributed over entire body); *gvc*, gastrovascular cavity; *m*, mouth; *nt*, longitudinal nerve trunk; *o*, ovum; *ov*, ovary; *p*, penis (projected into genital atrium); *pd*, protonephridial duct; *ph*, pharynx; *r*, rhabdites in epidermis; *sr*, seminal receptacle; *t*, testes (shown only on left side of body); *yg*, yolk gland. (Modified from Ruebush, 1940.)

(Figs. 79, 80). These move independently of each other and of the short cilia. In some species they are relatively stiff and are called "spines."

Other receptors, mostly in the epidermis, function in the detection of currents, in olfaction, and in response to contact. The pharynx and anterior end are especially sensitive.

**Reproduction, development.** With reference to their reproductive habits, there are three general groups of turbellarians: (1) species that reproduce only asexually, by budding or fission; (2) species that reproduce solely by sexual methods; and (3) species that are capable of reproducing sexually or asexually, depending on the genetic strain, physiological strain, and prevailing ecological conditions.

Fission does not occur in the majority of triclads, though certain common species are in the third category. Among these latter species the relative frequency of sexual and asexual reproduction varies greatly from one species to another. In *Dugesia tigrina*, for example, there appear to be at least two physiological varieties. One variety reproduces only asexually. Under appropriate conditions of temperature and food supply individuals pinch in at about midlength on each edge. The pinching in proceeds rapidly until the two halves are completely separated. Then the anterior end of the posterior individual reconstitutes a head, and the posterior end of the anterior individual forms a tail. External factors may change the rate of fission or inhibit it, but they do not change the reproduction to the sexual type. Fission occurs only above 10°, with frequency increasing to a maximum at 25° to 28°. Such fission strains have been kept as long as five years in the laboratory without development of sex organs.

In other physiological races of *D. tigrina* there may be an alternation of reproductive methods according to water temperature. Sex organs may develop during the winter and early spring, and egg capsules are deposited in May and June. As the water temperature increases, however, the reproductive organs degenerate, and in July, August, and September reproduction may be entirely by fission. By late autumn the sex organs are again beginning to develop. If the water temperature remains low throughout the year, however, sexual reproduction may be continuous.

It has also been suggested that there are still other strains of *D. tigrina* that reproduce sexually regardless of normal seasonal temperature variations.

*Dugesia dorotocephala* and a few other triclads also appear to exist in several physiological varieties comparable to the situation in *D. tigrina*. Nevertheless *D. dorotocephala* is rarely observed to reproduce sexually under natural conditions.

*Procotyla fluviatilis* is incapable of asexual reproduction; it is sexual and deposits egg cocoons during the winter months. Asexual reproduction is also unknown in *Cura foremanii*, but it reproduces sexually at all seasons. In *Phagocata vernalis* and *P. velata*, however, sexual reproduction is rare and apparently occurs only during the winter months in permanent bodies of water.

The seasonal reproductive habits of microturbellarians are poorly known, but most of the genera reproduce solely by the sexual method. *Catenula, Rhynchoscolex, Suomina, Microstomum,* and *Stenostomum* are the only genera capable of reproducing asexually. In these forms fission proceeds rapidly and often along several transverse planes so that there may be a series of two to eight zooids in a chain (Fig. 78). Occasionally a few species in this group of five genera have been observed to develop sex organs and reproduce sexually. At least one species of *Phaenocora* spends about seven months in a diapause egg stage.

Asexual reproduction in triclads involves either fission or fragmentation. In fission the posterior part of the body tears itself away; each of the two resulting individuals then grows and regenerates the lost parts. In fragmentation the animal breaks into several parts, each of which encysts in a slime mass. After an inactive period, a small individual emerges from the cyst, becomes active, and grows to normal size.

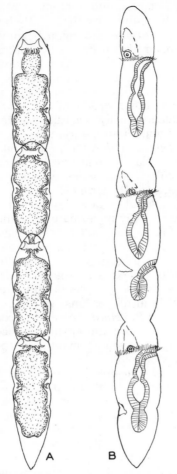

FIG. 78.–Chains of zooids in microturbellarians. A, dorsal view of four zooids of *Stenostomum*, ×24 (gastrovascular cavity stippled); B, lateral view of three zooids of *Catenula*, ×85. (Modified from Marcus, 1945.)

Triclads have seldom been observed dividing, and there is some evidence to show that the process occurs at night and is completed within 30 minutes to several hours. In microturbellarian fission a full complement of organs is usually developed before separation. Under favorable conditions divisions may occur as frequently as every 5 to 10 days in triclads, but in microturbellarians the time interval is much shorter.

All American fresh-water turbellarians are hermaphroditic, and the male and female organ systems are unusually complex in many genera. They are not present during periods of fission but develop later, presumably from undifferentiated parenchyma cells. The male organs sometimes mature before the female organs. Various types of reproductive systems are diagrammed in Figs. 77, 79, 80, and 81, and only a typical planarian arrangement will be described here (Fig. 81).

In the female reproductive system the two ovaries are on either side of the body near the anterior end. A longitudinal oviduct (or ovovitelline duct) proceeds posteriorly from each ovary and collects yolk cells from numerous lateral yolk glands. The two ovovitelline ducts unite near the midline, posterior to the mouth, and enter a common cavity, the female atrium. A saclike bursa copulatrix connects with the female atrium by means of a bursal canal.

The testes are small round bodies arranged roughly in two longitudinal rows. Each one connects with one of the two vasa deferentia by means of a minute duct. As the vasa deferentia proceed posteriorly they are widened and convoluted to form spermiducal vesicles where ripe sperm are stored. The spermiducal vesicles, either with or without uniting into a common duct, enter the basal portion of the highly muscular penis, and the tip of the latter projects into a cavity, the male atrium. Male and female atria unite ventrally to form a common atrium, which opens externally as a common genital pore.

Additional cement glands, copulatory glands, and other accessory reproductive structures occur in many turbellarians. Other orders often have the distal end of the penis modified to form a stylet, and sometimes the basal part is a prostatic vesicle, which secretes a granular material vital to the sperm. Many microturbellarians have two genital pores.

As is the case in most hermaphroditic animals, two turbellarians usually copulate and exchange sperm. The penis of each animal is elongated and protruded from its genital pore and through the genital pore of the other animal, the sperm being discharged into the bursal canal in planarians. Both animals exude quantities of mucus from the genital pore region during copulation. On completion of copulation, sperm

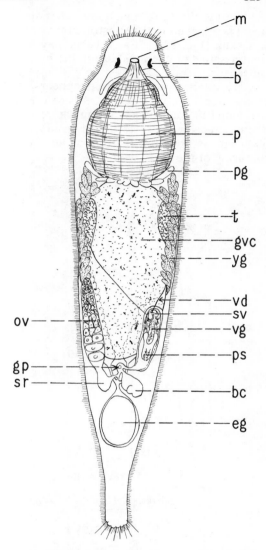

FIG. 79.–Structure of *Macrostomum appendicu-latum* (Fabr.), ×140, a species common everywhere in fresh, brackish, and salt waters. *br*, brain; *e*, eye-spot; *eg*, egg; *fb*, flame bulb; *fg*, female genital pore; *gvc*, gastrovascular cavity; *m*, mouth; *mg*, male genital pore; *od*, oviduct; *ov*, ovary; *p*, pharynx; *ps*, penis stylet; *s*, spine; *sv*, spermiducal vesicle; *t*, testes; *vd*, vas deferens; *vg*, prostatic vesicle. (Modified from Ferguson, 1939.)

FIG. 80.–Structure of *Dalyellia*, ×70, diagrammatic. *b*, brain; *bc*, bursa copulatrix; *e*, eyespot; *eg*, egg; *gp*, genital pore; *gvc*, gastrovascular cavity; *m*, mouth; *ov*, ovary; *p*, pharynx; *pg*, pharyngeal gland; *ps*, penis stylet; *sr*, seminal receptacle; *sv*, spermiducal vesicle; *t*, testes; *yg*, yolk glands; *vd*, vas deferens; *vg*, prostatic vesicle. (Modified from Ruebush and Hayes, 1939.)

are stored in the bursa copulatrix for a short time and then leave and migrate up the oviducts to the region of the ovaries. After a variable interval, the eggs are fertilized as they leave the ovaries.

As the zygote moves down the oviduct it accumulates yolk cells, and in the male atrium aggregates of zygotes and yolk cells become surrounded by a proteinaceous capsule. Such a cocoon usually contains 2 to 20 zygotes and thousands of yolk cells. It leaves the body through the genital pore, and in *Dugesia, Cura,* and a few other species it is attached to the substrate by means of a stalk (Fig. 82A). Each worm may deposit a series of cocoons during the breeding season.

Hypodermic impregnation appears to be the rule in *Stenostomum.* A single egg is ripened in each ovary during the reproductive season. It is fertilized inside the body and is liberated to the outside by a rupturing of the body wall.

FIG. 81.–Diagrammatic ventral view of a typical triclad reproductive system, ×16. (The relationships of the male and female atria are distinct only in a lateral view.) *bc*, bursa copulatrix; *ca*, common atrium; *gp*, genital pore; *o*, ovary; *od*, ovovitelline duct; *p*, penis; *sv*, spermiducal vesicle; *t*, testis, *vd*, vas deferens; *yg*, yolk gland.

More commonly, however, microturbellarians copulate and exchange sperm in the usual fashion. Fertilized eggs are usually laid singly, each enclosed in a capsule or shell which is sometimes stalked (Fig. 82B). Many of the Typhloplanidae produce two kinds of eggs. Thin-shelled "summer" eggs hatch promptly after deposition, but the larger, thick-shelled "winter" eggs have delayed hatching and may be dormant during the winter; they are capable of withstanding unfavorable environmental conditions. Winter eggs may be extruded from the parent body in the customary way or they may be liberated on the death and disintegration of the parent. Some species are regularly viviparous; the summer eggs hatch within the body and the young break out of the posterior region of the parent to the outside. In microturbellarians other than the Typhloplanidae only eggs of the winter type are produced.

Self-fertilization is rare in the Tricladida and has been definitely demonstrated only for *Cura foremanii.* Certain species sometimes produce sterile cocoons. Some investigators think that summer eggs of typhlopanids are self-fertilized.

Cocoons of triclad turbellarians are 2 to 4 mm in diameter and light-colored when recently deposited but soon become dark brown or blackish. Although they are resistant to low temperatures, they cannot withstand isolated drying. Depending on the season, a cocoon may winter over or hatch in about two weeks. The several worms that emerge are only 1 to 3 mm long. Development is direct and there are no special larvae stages in the American fresh-water species. With the exception of reproductive structures, the newly hatched worm often has the full complement of organ systems.

*Phagocata velata* and *P. vernalis* have an unusual habit of fragmenting, especially when their habitat becomes warm in late spring and summer. When a worm reaches a length of 12 to 15 mm, the internal organs degenerate and the whole worm fragments into numerous small bits. Each piece secretes mucus, which hardens to form a small cyst, and a whole miniature individual is reconstituted within the cyst. En-

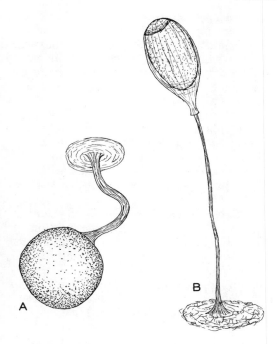

FIG. 82.–Turbellarian cocoon and microturbellarian encapsulated egg. A, stalked planarian cocoon, ×7; B, stalked encapsulated egg of *Gyratrix*, ×100 (note operculum).

axis being maintained. Worms cut into two along the median line regenerate respective right and left halves to form two new worms. Partial longitudinal cuts at the anterior end often produce worms with two or more complete heads. Regeneration potentialities are most highly developed in the anterior half or three-quarters of the body.

In spite of this regeneration capacity, planarians are rather delicate, and when handled roughly in the laboratory they easily develop breaks and irregularities in the body.

**Ecology.** Springs, spring brooks, ditches, marshes, pools, ponds, lakes, and caves all have their characteristic turbellarian populations. Most species, and especially triclads, are photonegative and are found under objects or in debris during the daytime. Flatworms thrive on any kind of substrate where there is an appropriate food supply. Although they are most characteristic of the shallows, a few species have been collected from lake bottoms as deep as 100 m.

Triclads are typical of brooks and streams; the other four orders are never abundant in such habitats. Rheophile forms are also usually cold stenotherms; common species are *Cura foremanii, Dugesia dorotocephala, Polycelis coronata, Phagocata velata,* and *P. morgani.* The last-named species is restricted to water between 4° and 14°. *Procotyla fluviatilis* occurs in all kinds of habitats, including running waters, standing waters, and even brackish areas. In general, specimens from running waters attain greater size than those from standing waters. *Dugesia tigrina* and *Phagocata vernalis* are both standing-water triclads, but whereas the former species is a eurytherm, the latter is active only during the cold months in temperate zone ponds and ditches.

Small colonies of a well-known European species, *Crenobia alpina,* are restricted to cold brooks of the Alps, the Scandinavian countries, and Great Britain. The species is seldom found in water that becomes warmer than 12°, and 7° is the optimum temperature. Sexual reproduction is most rapid in the winter, but fission may

cystment of a whole mature animal has also been reported. Such cysts may hatch in a few weeks or may winter over.

Length of life is known chiefly from laboratory cultures. Sexually reproducing species live for only a few weeks or months, usually dying in summer or autumn after producing winter eggs. A few species, however, may survive a year or more by encysting during unfavorable conditions. Species capable of fission can presumably continue indefinitely under appropriate conditions. Such laboratory cultures have been kept going from 2 to 11 years.

The larger species of planarians, especially *Dugesia,* have long been classical objects for regeneration and grafting experiments. A great deal of such work was done in the United States, especially between 1910 and 1930. If extended specimens are carefully cut transversely into two or several pieces with a razor blade, a large percentage of the pieces will regenerate into whole new worms, the original longitudinal occur in spring and early summer. Encystment is unknown. Because of its peculiar stenothermal distribution, this species is thought to be a glacial relict. No species of comparable habits are known from the United States.

The nontriclads are especially abundant during the warm months in pools and ponds containing quantities of algae, other vegetation, and organic debris. In a single lake, where many microhabitats or niches exist, as many as 30 species have been recorded, especially in hard-water lakes and ponds. Almost any stagnant pool will contain one or more species of *Dalyellia*, and usually one or more additional species in each of *Stenostomum, Macrostomum, Catenula, Microstomum*, and *Mesostoma*. Such species are eurythermal since they occur in habitats having a wide daily and seasonal temperature range. *Gyratrix, Phaenocora*, and *Otomesostoma* are also chiefly eurythermal. *Rhynchomesostoma rostratum* and certain species of *Macrostomum, Dalyellia*, and *Castrada*, however, are some of the few genera known to be cold stenotherms.

The great majority of turbellarian genera occurring in fresh waters are restricted to that environment. *Macrostomum*, however, is the most distinct exception, with many species in brackish and marine environments. As implied in a previous section, *Gyratrix hermaphroditus* is one of the very few euryhaline species; it is found in freshwater, brackish, and marine environments.

In those microturbellarian genera occurring in both standing and running waters there is often a correlation of size and activity with habitat. Still waters are characterized by larger, more sedentary species, whereas the small, faster-moving species are more abundant in waters where there is a current, however slow.

Some species of *Pseudophaenocora* thrive in the presence of only a trace of oxygen, and many other small species occur in water where the concentrations are as low as 5 to 40 percent saturation. Most triclads, however, are restricted to water whose oxygen concentration does not fall below 70 percent saturation.

**Enemies, parasites.** Turbellaria are seldom an important element in the diet of other animals. Odonata nymphs consume a few planarians, and members of the other orders appear to be taken occasionally by nematodes, annelids, and a few crustaceans and aquatic insects.

Internal parasites of turbellarians include ciliates, gregarines, and (rarely) larval mermithid nematodes. Some turbellarians may be found in the brood pouch of isopods and amphipods, but they are probably commensals rather than true parasites.

**Geographical Distribution.** So far as flatworms are concerned, that portion of the United States west of the Great Plains is almost a *terra incognita*. A few triclad records have been published for this region, but microturbellarians have been even more greatly neglected. East of the Mississippi the triclads have been extensively studied, especially by Hyman, and although the nontriclads have been studied to a considerable degree by Kepner, Ferguson, and Ruebush, an enormous amount of work yet remains to be done. The number of microscopic species appears to be very large, and each new investigation turns up new species. As shown in the key beginning on page 130, some triclads are common and widely distributed, whereas others are known from only one or two localities. Cave species are highly endemic, each form being restricted to a single cave or cave system, or to a group of caves in the same general area.

Although many microturbellarians have thus far been reported from only one or several collecting areas, a few appear to be common and essentially cosmopolitan in the Holarctic region. Typical examples are *Macrostomum appendiculatum, Stenostomum leucops* (Dugès), *Castrella truncata* (Abildgaard), *Phaenocora unipunctata* (Ørsted), and *Bothromesostoma personatum* (Schmidt).

Little definite information is available concerning the dissemination of turbellarians. *Dugesia dorotocephala* is generally distributed in spring brooks and marshy springs, yet it probably is unable to migrate actively throughout a single drainage system because of its ecological preference for headwaters. The same is true of *Phagocata morgani,* which is widely distributed east of the Mississippi. *Dugesia tigrina,* however, is never found in springs or spring brooks, but it does occur in a wide variety of other lotic and lentic habitats and presumably can migrate actively through drainage systems over wide areas. *Procotyla fluviatilis* and *Cura foremanii* also probably spread by active migration. Species such as *Phagocata vernalis,* however, which occur in temporary ponds and ditches, must rely entirely on passive means of distribution.

Even less is known about the dissemination of microscopic species, but the mechanisms of distribution must be fairly efficient, since the same species may be found everywhere in suitable habitats, even in temporary ponds and puddles that are dry during the late summer and early autumn.

Undoubtedly the cyst stages, winter eggs, and perhaps even cocoons are transported from place to place by natural agencies and larger animals that are capable of moving or flying overland from one pond, lake, or stream to another.

*Oligochoerus,* a fresh-water acoel turbellarian, has recently been found in several European fresh-water canals, rivers, and lakes. We predict that this group will also eventually be found in U.S. fresh waters.

**Collecting.** Spring brooks may be "baited" for planarians with cubes of raw, lean beef. After 15 minutes the meat should be examined and the worms shaken off into a container of water. Otherwise they may be washed or picked off the undersides of objects with a large pipette. If planarians are abundant in water cress, the plants should be placed in containers in the laboratory. As oxygen decreases, the worms will migrate to the top, where they may be picked off with a glass rod or pipette.

Planarians may be taken from pond and lake substrates by placing the bait in a glass jar with a well-perforated lid. Retrieve the jar after 24 hours.

Because of their small size, the other orders are more difficult to obtain and concentrate in numbers. The uppermost 1 or 2 cm of bottom debris as well as algae and rooted vegetation from any body of water will yield these forms if such material is placed in wide-mouthed jars or aquaria in the laboratory. In 6 to 12 hours many of the specimens will migrate to the surface film and may be picked up with a pipette. Such containers should also be allowed to stand undisturbed for 2 to 20 days. As decomposition increases, more individuals and additional species will be found.

Sometimes a Birge cone net drawn through dense vegetation will take large numbers. Small species are common inhabitants of the under surface of lily pads.

**Culturing.** Planarians may be kept in standing water, provided it does not become too warm and is changed every other day. Tap water is often toxic. Enameled pans and glass or crockery containers are all suitable. Since they are photonegative animals, it is best to put objects into the container, such as pebbles or bits of broken flowerpots, in order to provide shaded places. Also, the whole container may be covered. Cubes of fresh meat (especially beef liver), earthworm fragments, or chopped meal worms are suitable foods and should be supplied once or twice a week. *Procotyla fluviatilis,* however, requires small living crustaceans. After two or three hours any remaining food fragments should be removed, and if the cultures are in standing water, the water should be changed. Planarians will live for 3 to 12 weeks without any food but they get progressively smaller.

Most planarians are seldom found reproducing sexually, but if sexual specimens of *Dugesia tigrina* are collected in the field, they will usually continue producing egg capsules in the laboratory. *Procotyla fluviatilis* is especially useful for a study of sexual reproduction because of its translucency. Its sexual period extends from autumn through winter and sometimes into early spring. Nevertheless, *Cura foremanii* is about the only species that can really be depended on to produce egg capsules regularly under laboratory conditions.

Temporary cultures of microturbellarians may develop and be kept for several weeks in the original containers of decaying aquatic vegetation and debris in the laboratory. More or less permanent cultures may be maintained in Petri dishes or finger bowls in a variety of ways. *Stenostomum* and certain other genera may be cultured in boiled wheat, rice, or rye grain infusions similar to those used for other micrometazoans and Protozoa. Subcultures should be started every five or six weeks. Pablum or cultures of similar foods are often successful. Some cold stenothermal species of *Macrostomum* can be cultured only in a refrigerator. Food may be crushed entomostracans, chopped meal worms, or chopped aquatic oligochaetes.

**Preparing, preserving.** There are several suitable methods of killing and fixing planarians, but all methods should begin with the animals extended in a very small amount of water. Hot saturated mercuric chloride in 0.9 percent sodium chloride is good. Two percent nitric acid for one minute followed by 70 percent alcohol is also fairly good. Two percent nitric acid may be dropped on the planarians, and then they should be flooded with hot saturated mercuric chloride in 0.9 percent sodium chloride. A biological supply company advocates narcotizing in strychnine water for a few minutes and then flooding with hot Gilson's fluid. The latter solution consists of the following: 5 g mercuric chloride, 5 ml 80 percent nitric acid, 1 ml glacial acetic acid, 25 ml 70 percent alcohol, and 220 ml water; filter after three days.

Because of their greater translucency, microturbellarians are advantageously studied alive with the 4, 8, or 16 mm objective in a hollow-ground slide or by placing them between two square cover slips sealed at the edges with petroleum jelly. Such a mount may be turned over on a slide and both sides of the specimens examined. Slight pressure compresses the worms slightly so that they move about only

slowly. If the preparation is carefully made, even an oil immersion lens may be used.

Nontriclads should usually be anesthetized with 0.1 percent chloretone, 10 percent alcohol, 1 percent hydroxylamine hydrochloride, or near-freezing temperatures. Fixation with Helly's fluid produces little shrinkage. This reagent consists of the following: 2.5 g potassium dichromate, 5 g mercuric chloride, 1 g sodium sulphate, 100 ml water, and 5 ml formalin. Hayes (1942) recommends Harper's modification of Allen's B-15 fixative. It consists of two solutions, which should be mixed immediately before use. Solution A contains 380 ml saturated picric acid, 40 ml glacial acetic acid, and 8 g chromic acid. Solution B contains 220 ml saturated picric acid, 200 ml formalin, and 8 g urea.

Flatworm fixation usually takes 30 to 60 minutes. If the fixative contains mercuric chloride, the specimens should be washed several times in 50 percent alcohol containing a little tincture of iodine. Pigmented specimens may be bleached in undiluted hydrogen peroxide. Seventy percent alcohol and dioxan are suitable preservatives. Stained whole mounts of rhabdocoels are sometimes useful, orange G and Delafield's hematoxylin being suitable stains.

**Taxonomy.** If serial sections are not available, identification of triclads to genus or species should be made on living specimens whenever possible. Shape, and especially the shape of the anterior end, is highly variable in preserved specimens, even though carefully prepared.

Generic identification of nontriclads is usually possible with live specimens, but they must be mature.

On the other hand, species identification of almost all nontriclads and species identification of some triclads are entirely dependent on serial sections, and especially on the detailed anatomy of the reproductive system of the mature individual. It is unfortunate that such work can be done only by the experienced specialist, and the considerable effort involved in making species identifications will probably always maintain a dearth of investigators.

The turbellarian fauna of the United States is poorly known, especially in the western half of the country, and therefore a species name should never be given to a specimen simply because it is the only one previously reported from a particular region.

Many of our species have a long history of taxonomic confusion and synonomy, chiefly as the result of variable characters, poor fixation, and identification by inexperienced workers. The section of the key that includes the microturbellarian genera has been greatly modified from Ruebush (1941). There are so many undescribed and unreported species of microturbellarians that it is fruitless to carry this part of the key beyond the generic level. The triclad section is greatly modified from Kenk (1972). Both the triclad and microturbellarian sections are constructed with practicability in mind, without strict attention to fundamental generic criteria. Several rare genera are omitted. Following is an outline of the taxonomic relationships recognized in this manual.

Order Tricladida
  Planariidae
    *Cura*
    *Dugesia*
    *Hymanella*
    *Kenkia*
    *Phagocata*
    *Planaria*
    *Polycelis*
    *Sphalloplana*
  Dendrocoelidae
    *Dendrocoelopsis*
    *Macrocotyla*
    *Procotyla*
    *Rectocephala*
Order Catenulida
  Catenulidaé
    *Catenula*
    *Rhynchoscolex*
    *Suomina*
  Stenostomidae
    *Stenostomum*

Order Macrostomida
  Macrostomidae
    *Macrostomum*
  Microstomidae
    *Microstomum*

Order Neorhabdocoela
  Provorticidae
    *Provortex*
  Dalyelliidae
    *Castrella*
    *Dalyellia*
    *Gieysztoria*
    *Microdalyellia*
  Typhloplanidae
    *Amphibolella*
    *Bothromesostoma*
    *Castrada*
    *Krumbachia*
    *Mesostoma*
    *Olisthanella*
    *Opistomum*
    *Phaenocora*
    *Prorhynchella*
    *Protoascus*
    *Pseudophaenocora*
    *Rhynchomesostoma*
    *Strongylostoma*
    *Typhloplana*
  Gyratricidae
    *Gyratrix*
  Polycystidae
    *Klattia*
    *Polycystis*
  Koinocystidae
    *Koinocystis*
    *Microkalyptorhynchus*

Order Alloeocoela
  Prorhynchidae
    *Geocentrophora*
    *Prorhynchus*
  Otomesostomidae
    *Otomesostoma*
  Bothrioplanidae
    *Bothrioplana*
  Plagiostomidae
    *Hydrolimax*

The figures associated with this key are all diagrammatic, and usually all anatomical details except significant key characters are omitted. Wherever possible, characters are used that do not require serial sections.

## KEY TO TURBELLARIA

1. Large species, living animal longer than 5 mm; gastrovascular cavity consisting of three main branches, one anterior and two posterior and lateral (Fig. 72).
   Order **TRICLADIDA, 2**
   Small species, rarely longer than 4 mm; gastrovascular cavity almost invariably a single, median, longitudinal cavity (Figs. 77, 79, 80); collectively, the "microturbellarians". Orders **CATENULIDA, MACROSTOMIDA, NEORHABDO-COELA, ALLOEOCOELA, 37**
2. Dorsal surface more or less opaquely pigmented, usually grayish to brownish or black; eyes present ................................................................3
   Dorsal surface translucent, whitish, or creamy; eyes present or absent ..........18
3. With many eyespots forming an anterior band (Figs. 83D, E); up to 19 mm long; cold streams in Rocky Mountain area. ................ **Polycelis coronata** (Girard)
   With two eyespots ................................................................**4**
4. With multiple pharynges (Fig. 84F); three polytypic species, very difficult to distinguish ............................................................... **Phagocata, 5**
   With a single pharynx ................................................................**6**
5. Poorly defined auricles (Fig. 84F); penis papilla long, conical; northeastern states.
   **Phagocata gracilis** (Haldeman)
   Without auricles (Fig. 84K); penis papilla short, truncate; southeastern states.
   **Phagocata woodworthi** Hyman
6. Anterior end with adhesive organ (Fig. 75) ....................................**7**
   Anterior end without adhesive organ ........................................**8**
7. In springs, streams, and lakes west of the Continental Divide; 14 to 22 mm long.
   **Dendrocoelopsis vaginata** Hyman
   Known only from one lily pond in Washington, D.C., apparently introduced; 14 mm long ........................................ **Rectocephala exotica** Hyman
8. Auricles elongated, sharply pointed (Fig. 83A); up to 30 mm long; in running and standing waters everywhere ............ **Dugesia dorotocephala** (Woodworth)
   Auricles not especially elongated and sharply pointed ........................**9**
9. Anterior end more or less triangular (Fig. 73) ..............................**10**
   Anterior end truncated (Fig. 83G) ........................................**12**
10. Eyes close to anterior end; up to 20 mm long; a European species now found in the St. Lawrence River system and New York ..... **Dugesia polychroa** (Schmidt)
    Eyes not especially close to anterior end ....................................**11**
11. Coloration highly variable but patterned (Fig. 73); pharynx with white tip; 6 to 18 mm long; generally distributed and very common ........**Dugesia tigrina** (Girard)
    Color uniformly gray, brown, or blackish; pharynx all white; 7 to 15 mm long (Fig. 83F); eastern half of the United States ............. **Cura foremanii** (Girard)
12. Dorsal surface brown, but faded marginally; up to 12 mm long; known only from Lake Tahoe, California ........................**Phagocata tahoena** Kawakatsa
    Coloration extending to margin of body ....................................**13**
13. Lateral corners of head rounded, no distinct necklike constriction behind them (Fig. 83G); up to 14 mm long; vernal pools and seepages in eastern states.
    **Hymanella retenuova** Castle
    Lateral corners of head not rounded ........................................**14**
14. Darkly pigmented gray, brown, or black; with an adenodactyl (a dense prostate gland behind the gonopore); up to 13 mm long; rare in springs and streams of southeastern states ............................... **Planaria dactyligera** Kenk
    Pigment light to dark; up to 22 mm long; adenodactyl absent ..................**15**

FIG. 83.–Structure of Planariidae. A, *Dugesia dorotocephala,* ×6; B and C, *D. tigrina,* ×7; D, *Polycelis coronata,* ×5; E, anterior end of *P. coronata*; F, *Cura foremanii,* ×6; G, *Hymanella retenuova,* ×6. (B redrawn from Hyman, 1931b; D and E modified from Hyman, 1931; F modified from Kenk, 1935.)

15. A high-altitude species, restricted to cold streams and springs in western states; up to
     22 mm long; gray to black coloration . . . . . . . . **Phagocata crenophila** Carpenter
     Not a high-altitude species . . . . . . . . . . . . . . . . . . . . . . . . . . . . . . . . . . . . . . . . . . . . .**16**
16. Up to 20 mm long; coloration dark gray to almost black; widely distributed and
     common in permanent waters. . . . . . . . . . . . . . . . . . . . **Phagocata velata** Stringer
     Up to 12 mm long; coloration gray; distribution more restricted . . . . . . . . . . . . . .**17**
17. Known only from seepage springs in North Carolina . . . . . . .**Phagocata bulbosa** Kenk
     In temporary ponds and ditches in early spring in midwestern states; male phase of
     a protandrous species . . . . . . . . . . . . . . . . . . . . . . . . .**Hymanella retenuova** Castle
18. Auricles long, thin, and pointed; body up to 14 mm long and 1 mm wide; cave waters
     in Georgia and Alabama . . . . . . . . . . . . . . .**Phagocata bursaperforata** Darlington
     Auricles absent . . . . . . . . . . . . . . . . . . . . . . . . . . . . . . . . . . . . . . . . . . . . . . . . . . . . .**19**
19. Adhesive organ in the form of a large, permanent, anterior snout (Fig. 85A); known
     only from Malheur Cave, Harney County, Oregon . .**Kenkia rhynchida** Hyman
     Snout absent . . . . . . . . . . . . . . . . . . . . . . . . . . . . . . . . . . . . . . . . . . . . . . . . . . . . . . . .**20**
20. Eyes present . . . . . . . . . . . . . . . . . . . . . . . . . . . . . . . . . . . . . . . . . . . . . . . . . . . . . . . . .**21**
     Eyes absent . . . . . . . . . . . . . . . . . . . . . . . . . . . . . . . . . . . . . . . . . . . . . . . . . . . . . . . . . .**23**

Fɪɢ. 84.–Structure of Planariidae and Dendrocoelidae. A, *Dendrocoelopsis americana*, ×18; B, longitudinal section of anterior end of *D. americana*, showing adhesive organ; C, *Procotyla typhlops*, ×7; D, *Phagocata morgani*, ×7; E, *P. velata*, ×5; F, *P. gracilis*, ×5; G, *P. woodworthi*, ×7; H, anterior end of *Planaria dactyligera*; J, anterior end of *Phagocata gracilis*; K, anterior end of *P. woodworthi*.

**21.** One pair of eyes; adhesive organ absent (Fig. 84D); up to 14 mm long; eastern states, rare in California (one rare subspecies from Virginia has two parallel rows of eyespots near the midline) ........ **Phagocata morgani** (Stevens and Boring)
Usually more than one pair of eyes; adhesive organ present (Fig. 75) ...........**22**
**22.** One to eight eyes on each side (Fig. 75); up to 20 mm long; widely distributed and common in eastern half of the United States .......**Procotyla fluviatilis** Leidy
Eyes numerous (Fig. 84A); up to 18 mm long; caves and springs of Oklahoma and Arkansas ......................... **Dendrocoelopsis americana** (Hyman)
**23.** Restricted to surface waters ..............................................**24**
Restricted to caves, or caves and springs; (about eight recently described rare species are not keyed out here) ...........................................**25**
**24.** Known only from Lake Tahoe deep waters; up to 14 mm long.
**Dendrocoelopsis hymanae** Kawaktsu
Known only from a spring in Kansas; up to 20 mm long.
**Sphalloplana kansensis** Hyman
**25.** Adhesive organ absent; up to 12 mm long; subterranean in Virginia.
**Procotyla typhlops** Kenk
Adhesive organ present ...............................................**26**
**26.** Coloration a very light reddish-brown or orange; up to 30 mm long; caves and springs in Missouri and Iowa .....................**Macrocotyla glandulosa** Hyman
Coloration creamy or white ............................................**27**
**27.** Anterior end bluntly rounded; body margin with a row of large rhabdites (Fig. 85B). **28**
Anterior end truncate; with large rhabdites (Figs. 85F, J) ......................**30**

Fig. 85.–Structure of Kenkiidae. A, *Kenkia rhynchida*, ×11; B, *Sphalloplana virginiana*, ×4; C, *S. buch-anani*, ×4; D, longitudinal section of anterior end of *S. buchanani*, showing the invaginated adhesive gland; E, *S. hubrichti*, ×3 (penis stippled); F, *S. pricei*, ×5; G, longitudinal section of anterior end of *S. pricei*, showing partly protruded adhesive gland; H, same, showing retracted adhesive gland; J, *S. percoeca*, ×6. *a*, anterior end. (A, C, D, and F to H modified from Hyman, 1937a; B and E modified from Hyman, 1945; J modified from Buchanan.)

**28.** Caves and springs in Illinois and Missouri; up to 17 mm long (Fig. 85E).
                                          **Sphalloplana hubrichti** Hyman
      With another distribution; smaller ........................................**29**
**29.** Known only from a Virginia cave; up to 12 mm long (Fig. 85B).
                                          **Sphalloplana virginiana** Hyman
      Known only from West Virginia caves; up to 11 mm long.
                                          **Macrocotyla hoffmasteri** Hyman
**30.** Maximum length of live worm less than 10 mm ..............................**31**
      Maximum length of live worm more than 10 mm ..........................**33**
**31.** Known only from an Indiana cave; up to 9 mm long. **Sphalloplana weingartneri** Kenk
      With another distribution ...........................................**32**
**32.** Known only from a Georgia cave; up to 8 mm long .. **Sphalloplana georgiana** Hyman
      Known only from an Alabama cave; up to 6 mm long. **Sphalloplana alabamensis** Hyman
**33.** Known only from Texas caves; up to 35 mm long, variable, may be a group of
            species ....................................... **Sphalloplana mohri** Hyman
      Known only from other states ...........................................**34**
**34.** Found only in Pennsylvania caves; up to 28 mm long (Fig. 85F).
                                          **Sphalloplana pricei** (Hyman)
      Found in other cave systems ...............................................**35**
**35.** Found only in Kentucky caves .............................................**36**
      Found only in Missouri caves; up to 30 mm long .........**Macrocotyla lewisi** Kenk
**36.** Head with rounded auricles; up to 16 mm long (Fig. 85J).
                                          **Sphalloplana percoeca** (Packard)
      Anterior end truncate, no auricles; up to 15 mm long. **Sphalloplana buchanani** (Hyman)
**37.** Body usually composed of a series of two to eight zooids whose anterior and posterior
            extremities appear as paired lateral indentations; eyes usually absent (Fig. 78). **38**
      Body composed of a single individual; eyes present or absent ...................**41**

FIG. 86.–Structure of Catenulida and Macrostomida. A, single zooid of *Catenula,* ×230, showing statocyst, mouth, and gastrovascular cavity; B, two zooids of *Rhynchoscolex,* ×55; C, lateral view of four zooids of *Microstomum,* ×35; D, dorsal view of single zooid of *Stenostomum,* ×220; E, ventral view of *Suomina,* ×200, showing mouth, gastrovascular cavity, and ciliated anterior transverse groove. (A modified from Heinlein and Wachowski.)

**38.** With a statocyst at the anterior end of each zooid; each zooid composed of a cephalic
lobe and body (Fig. 86A); two species . . . . . . . . . . . . . . . . . . . . . . . . . . . . **Catenula**
Without a statocyst . . . . . . . . . . . . . . . . . . . . . . . . . . . . . . . . . . . . . . . . . . . . . . .**39**
**39.** With a narrow, proboscislike structure at the anterior end (Fig. 86B) .**Rhynchoscolex**
Without such a structure . . . . . . . . . . . . . . . . . . . . . . . . . . . . . . . . . . . . . . . . . . .**40**
**40.** With a preoral blind pouch at the anterior end of the gastrovascular cavity (Fig. 86C);
common; many species . . . . . . . . . . . . . . . . . . . . . . . . . . . . . . . **Microstomum**
Without such a pouch; with a ciliated pit on either side of the head (Fig. 86D); the
most common of all microturbellarians; generally distributed in a wide variety
of habitats; many species . . . . . . . . . . . . . . . . . . . . . . . . . . . . . . . . .**Stenostomum**
**41.** With a simple pharynx (Figs. 79, 86E) . . . . . . . . . . . . . . . . . . . . . . . . . . . . . . . . .**42**
With a complex pharynx (Figs. 87, 90) . . . . . . . . . . . . . . . . . . . . . . . . . . . . . . .**43**
**42.** With a ciliated groove encircling the anterior part of the body (Fig. 86E) . . . **Suomina**
Without such a groove; dorsoventrally flattened and posterior end somewhat broad-
ened and with adhesive papillae; spatulate (Fig. 79); 0.7 to 3.5 mm long; many
common species . . . . . . . . . . . . . . . . . . . . . . . . . . . . . . . . . . . . . . . . . . .**Macrostomum**

FIG. 87.–Structure of Neorhabdocoela and Alloeocoela. A, *Hydrolimax grisea*, ×4.5; B, *Castrella*, ×60, showing pharynx and eyespots; C, *Provortex*, ×125, showing eyespots, pharynx, and gastrovascular cavity; D, *Microdalyellia*, ×50, showing eyespots, pharynx, gastrovascular cavity, zoochlorellae, and single egg; E, *Phaenocora*, ×37, showing eyespots, pharynx, gastrovascular cavity, and zoochlorellae; F, cuticular apparatus of male copulatory organ of *Gieysztoria*; G, Cuticular apparatus of male copulatory organ of *Dalyellia* and *Microdalyellia*. (A modified from Hyman, 1938; B, D, and E modified from Ruebush, 1941; C modified from Ruebush, 1935a.)

43. Pharynx more or less bulbous (Fig. 87) . . . . . . . . . . . . . . . . . . . . . . . . . . . . . . . . . . . . . . . . . . . . .**44**
   Pharynx not bulbous (Figs. 90C, D) . . . . . . . . . . . . . . . . . . . . . . . . . . . . . . . . . . . . . . . . . . . .**66**
44. Pharynx at anterior end of gastrovascular cavity, directed anteroventrally, and cask-shaped (Figs. 87B, C) . . . . . . . . . . . . . . . . . . . . . . . . . . . . . . . . . . . . . . . . . . . . . . . .**45**
   Pharynx not at anterior end of gastrovascular cavity, directed ventrally, and rosulate in shape (Figs. 88A, E) . . . . . . . . . . . . . . . . . . . . . . . . . . . . . . . . . . . . . . . . . . .**52**
45. A large species, up to 15 mm long; dorsal surface dark gray, ventral surface whitish; body plump and cylindroid; reported from New Jersey and eastern Pennsylvania (Fig. 87A) . . . . . . . . . . . . . . . . . . . . . . . . . .**Hydrolimax grisea** Haldeman
   Usually no more than 5 mm long . . . . . . . . . . . . . . . . . . . . . . . . . . . . . . . . . . . . . . . . . . . . . .**46**
46. Body nearly cylindrical and more or less tapering to a pointed tail (Fig. 87B); usually free-swimming . . . . . . . . . . . . . . . . . . . . . . . . . . . . . . . . . . . . . . . . . . . . . . . . . .**47**
   Body triangular in section; posterior end truncate, with a small tail (Fig. 87E); usually creeping . . . . . . . . . . . . . . . . . . . . . . . . . . . . . . . . . . . . . . . . . . . . . . . . . . . . . . .**51**
47. Each eye consisting of two pigmented spots connected by a pigmented band; anterior end truncate (Fig. 87B); body usually darkly pigmented with blue or black.
   **Castrella**
   Each eye a single concave mass; anterior end more rounded (Figs. 80, 87C); brownish or green pigmentation . . . . . . . . . . . . . . . . . . . . . . . . . . . . . . . . . . . . . . . . . . . .**48**

**48.** Mature animals about 0.5 mm long; not pigmented; posterior end slightly rounded (Fig. 87C); each egg containing two embryos; only one or two species reported from the United States .................................... **Provortex**

　　　Mature animals 0.5 to 3 mm long; usually brown or green coloration; posterior end more or less pointed; each egg with a single embryo .....................**49**

**49.** Cuticular apparatus of male copulatory organ consisting of a collar with stout spines at the distal end (Fig. 87F); one pair of dark eyes................ **Gieysztoria**

　　　Cuticular apparatus of male copulatory organ consisting of a long tongue and two spinous processes (Fig. 87G) .........................................**50**

**50.** Mature animals 2 to 3 mm long (Fig. 80); one to many eggs present and scattered throughout the body; with zoochlorellae and brownish pigment in parenchyma; several species in the United States ............................. **Dalyellia**

　　　Mature animals only 1 to 2 mm long; only one egg carried at a time (Fig. 87D), rarely two to four; zoochlorellae, if present, restricted to the gastrovascular cavity; about 30 species ......................................... **Microdalyellia**

**51.** Mature animals up to 4.8 mm long; without zoochlorellae; in sulfur springs. **Pseudophaenocora sulfophila** Gilbert

　　　Mature animals 1 to 3 mm long; often with zoochlorellae in gastrovascular cavity and parenchyma (Fig. 87E); about five species ..................... **Phaenocora**

**52.** Anterior end with a heavy, muscular proboscis contained in a sheath; body usually cylindrical (Fig. 88A); free-swimming ..................................**53**

　　　Without such a proboscis; body usually flattened; usually creeping .............**55**

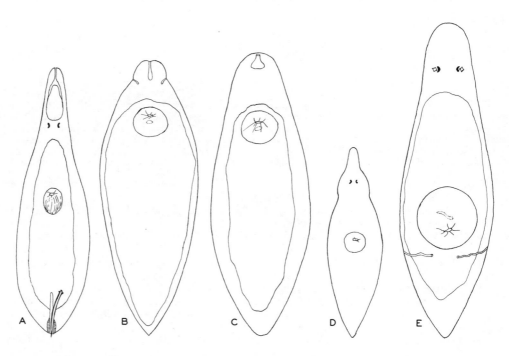

Fig. 88.–Structure of Neorhabdocoela. A, ventral view of *Gyratrix hermaphroditus*, ×40, showing proboscis, eyespots, mouth, pharynx, gastrovascular cavity, and penis stylet; B, ventral view of *Prorhynchella*, ×100, showing anterior sensory pit, anterolateral ciliated pits, mouth, pharynx, and gastrovascular cavity; C, ventral view of *Microkalyptorhynchus*, ×80, showing anterior sensory pit, mouth, pharynx, and gastrovascular cavity; D, ventral view of *Rhynchomesostoma*, ×70, showing eyespots, mouth, and pharynx; E, ventral view of *Krumbachia minuta*, ×180, showing eyespots, mouth, pharynx, gastrovascular cavity, protonephridial tubules, and protonephridial pores. (B modified from Ruebush, 1939; C modified from Ruebush, 1935; D modified from Ruebush, 1941; E modified from Ruebush, 1938.)

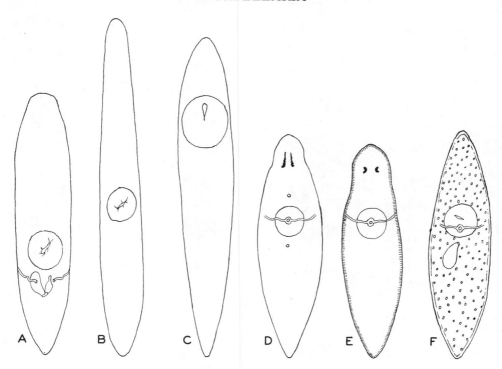

FIG. 89.–Structure of Neorhabdocoela. A, ventral view of *Krumbachia virginiana*, ×30, showing mouth, pharynx, penis, bursa copulatrix, protonephridial tubules, and protonephridial pores; B, ventral biew of *Amphibolella*, ×125; C, *Protoascus wisconsinensis*, ×95; D, ventral view of *Bothromesostoma*, ×11, showing eyespots, pore of sensory pouch, protonephridial tubules, mouth, pharynx, and common genital pore; E, ventral view of *Strongylostoma*, ×50, showing eyespots, protonephridial tubules, mouth, pharynx, and epidermal rhabdites; F, ventral view of *Typhloplana*, ×65, showing zoochlorellae in parenchyma, mouth, pharynx, protonephridial tubules, protonephridial pore, and penis. (A, D, E, and F modified from Ruebush, 1941; B modified from Kepner and Ruebush, 1937.)

**53.** With a posterior penis stylet; eyes black (Fig. 88A); body coloration whitish; 2 mm
    long; common ............................**Gyratrix hermaphroditus** Ehr.
    Without a posterior penis stylet.................................................**54**
**54.** Up to 2 mm long; colorless anteriorly, reddish posteriorly; proboscis opening terminal;
    one rare species .......................................... **Polycystis**
    Up to 1.5 mm long; white to gray coloration; proboscis opening subterminal; one rare
    species.......................................................**Klattia**
**55.** With a median anterior sensory pit (Figs. 88B, C) ...........................**56**
    Without a sensory pit.........................................................**57**
**56.** With a pair of anterolateral ciliated pits (Fig. 88B) ................. **Prorhynchella**
    Without a pair of anterolateral ciliated pits (Fig. 88C) ........ **Microkalyptorhynchus**
**57.** With a retractile and sensory anterior end (Fig. 88D)........... **Rhynchomesostoma**
    Without such a structure at the anterior end ...............................**58**
**58.** Protonephridial tubules opening separately on the ventral surface of the body (Fig.
    88E) ......................................................**59**
    Protonephridial tubules opening into the mouth cavity (Figs. 89D, E) ...........**62**
**59.** With a large refractive rectangle in each eye (Fig. 88E); with a bursa copulatrix; 0.5
    mm long ..................................... **Krumbachia minuta** Ruebush
    Eyes absent; without a bursa copulatrix ....................................**60**
**60.** Body 2 to 3 mm long, opaque (Fig. 89A). **Krumbachia virginiana** (Kepner and Carter)
    Body up to 1.5 mm long, more or less translucent; rare ......................**61**

Fig. 90.–Structure of Neorhabdocoela and Alloeocoela. A, *Castrada*, ×48; B, *Otomesostoma*, ×35; C, *Prorhynchus*, ×17; D, *Geocentrophora*, ×25; E, *Opistomum*, ×16; F, *Bothrioplana*, ×16. (A modified from Kepner, Ruebush, and Ferguson; D modified from Ruebush, 1941.)

61. Pharynx near middle of body (Fig. 89B) .......................... **Amphibolella**
    Pharynx near anterior end (Fig. 89C); reported only from Wisconsin.
                                       **Protoascus wisconsinensis** Hayes
62. With a ventral pore leading into the sensory pouch anterior to mouth; common genital
        pore present (Fig. 89D); 5 to 7 mm long ............... **Bothromesostomum**
    Without a ventral sensory pouch; common genital pore present or combined with the
        mouth (Fig. 89E) ........................................................63
63. With rhabdites in the epidermis (Figs. 77, 89E) ...............................64
    Without rhabdites in the epidermis ..........................................65
64. Large species, usually 2 to 4 mm long, but a few species as long as 10 mm; with long
        parenchymal rhabdites; eyes, when present, black (Fig. 77); coloration pale
        brown, gray, or gold; very common in temporary ponds and puddles; about 10
        species.................................................... **Mesostoma**
    Small species, only 1 to 1.5 mm long; without parenchymal rhabdites; eyes red (Fig.
        89E); several species ..................................... **Strongylostoma**
65. About 1 mm long; without bursa copulatrix; with abundant zoochlorellae in paren-
        chyma (Fig. 89F)..........................................**Typhloplana**
    About 1 to 2 mm long; with bursa copulatrix (Fig. 90A); body whitish or yellowish;
        with or without zoochlorellae; several species ....................**Castrada**
66. With an anterior statocyst (Fig. 90B) .............................**Otomesostoma**
    Without a statocyst .........................................................67
67. Pharynx located at anterior end of the gastrovascular cavity (Figs. 90C, D).......68
    Pharynx behind middle of body and directed posteriorly (Figs. 90E, F) .........69

**68.** Penis stylet straight or slightly bent (Fig. 90C) ..................... **Prorhynchus**
Penis stylet bent almost at a right angle (Fig. 90D); several species up to 8 mm long,
including one from Kentucky caves ....................... **Geocentrophora**
**69.** Pharynx not connected with gastrovascular cavity; penis near posterior end of body
and heavily spined; without ciliated pits (Fig. 90E) ............. **Opistomum**
Pharynx connected with gastrovascular cavity; with two pairs of anterior ciliated pits
(Fig. 90F) ............................................. **Bothrioplana**

# TURBELLARIA REFERENCES

AX, P., and J. DÖRJES. 1966. Oligochoerus limno-philus, nov. spec., ein kaspisches Faunenelement als erster Süsswasservertreter der Turbellaria Acoela in Flussen Mitteleuropas. *Int. Rev. ges. Hydrobiol.* **51**:15–44.

BAUCHHENSS, J. 1971. Die Kleinturbellarien Frankens. Ein Beitrag zur Systematik und Ökologie der Turbellaria excl. Tricladida in Süddeutschland. Ibid. **56**:609–666.

BRØNSTED, H. V. 1955. Planarian regeneration. *Biol. Rev.* **30**:65–126.

CARPENTER, J. H. 1970. Geocentrophora cavernicola n. sp. (Turbellaria, Alloeocoela): first cave alloeocoel. *Trans. Am. Microsc. Soc.* **89**:124–133.

CASTLE, W. A. 1928. An experimental and histological study of the life-cycle of Planaria velata. *J. Exp. Zool.* **51**:417–483.

CASTLE, W. A., and L. H. HYMAN. 1934. Observations on Fonticola velata (Stringer), including a description of the anatomy of the reproductive system. *Trans. Am. Microsc. Soc.* **53**:154–171.

CHANDLER, C. M. 1966. Environmental factors affecting the local distribution and abundance of four species of stream-dwelling triclads. *Invest. Ind. Lakes and Streams* **7**:1–56.

CHODOROWSKI, A. 1959. Ecological differentiation of turbellarians in Harsz-Lake. *Pol. Arch. Hydrobiol.* **6**:33–73.

———. 1960. Vertical stratification of Turbellaria species in some littoral habitats of Harsz Lake. Ibid. **8**:153–163.

CURTIS, W. C. 1902. The life history, the normal fission, and the reproductive organs of Planaria maculata. *Proc. Boston Soc. Nat. Hist.* **31**:515–559.

FERGUSON, F. F. 1939–1940. A monograph of the genus Macrostomum O. Schmidt 1848. Parts I to VIII. *Zool. Anz.* **126**:7–20; **127**:131–144; **128**:49–68; 188–205, 274–291; **129**:21–48, 120–146, 244–266.

———. 1954. Monograph of the macrostomine worms of Turbellaria. *Trans. Am. Microsc. Soc.* **73**:137–164.

FERGUSON, F. F., and W. J. HAYES, Jr. 1941. A synopsis of the genus Mesostoma Ehrenberg 1835. *J. Elisha Mitchell Sci. Soc.* **57**:1–52.

GRAFF, L. VON. 1911. Acoela, Rhabdocoela, und Alloeocoela des Ostens der Vereinigten Staaten von Amerika. *Z. wiss. Zool.* **99**:1–108.

———. 1913. Turbellaria. II. Rhabdocoelida. *Das Tierreich* **35**:1–484.

HAYES, W. J., Jr. 1941. Rhabdocoela of Wisconsin. I. Morphology and taxonomy of Protoascus

wisconsinensis n. g., n. sp. *Am. Midl. Nat.* **25**:388–401.

HEINLEIN, E., and H. E. WACHOWSKI. 1944. Studies on the flatworm Catenula virginiana. Ibid. **31**:150–158.

HYMAN, L. H. 1925. The reproductive system and other characters of Planaria dorotocephala. *Trans. Am. Microsc. Soc.* **44**:51–89.

———. 1928. Studies on the morphology, taxonomy, and distribution of North American triclad Turbellaria, I. Procotyla fluviatilis, commonly but erroneously known as Dendrocoelum lacteum. Ibid. **47**:222–255.

———. 1931. Studies on triclad Turbellaria, III. On Polycelis coronata (Girard). Ibid. **50**:124–135.

———. 1931a. Studies on triclad Turbellaria, IV. Recent European revisions of the triclads, and their application to the American forms, with a key to the latter and new notes on distribution. Ibid. **50**:316–335.

———. 1937. Studies on triclad Turbellaria, VIII. Some cave planarians of the United States. Ibid. **36**:457–477.

———. 1938. North American Rhabdocoela and Alloeocoela. II. Rediscovery of Hydrolimax grisea Haldeman. *Am. Mus. Novit.* **1004**:1–19.

———. 1939. North American triclad Turbellaria. IX. The priority of Dugesia Girard 1850 over Euplanaria Hesse 1897 with notes on American species of Dugesia. *Trans. Am. Microsc. Soc.* **58**:264–275.

———. 1939a. North American triclad Turbellaria, X. Additional species of cave planarians. Ibid. 276–284.

———. 1945. North American triclad Turbellaria, XI. New, chiefly cavernicolous, planarians. *Am. Midl. Nat.* **34**:475–484.

———. 1951. North American triclad Turbellaria, XII. Synopsis of the known species of freshwater planarians of North America. *Trans. Am. Microsc. Soc.* **70**:154–167.

JENKINS, M. M., and H. P. BROWN. 1963. Cocoon-production in Dugesia dorotocephala (Woodworth) 1897. Ibid. **82**:167–177.

JOHNSON, W. H., C. A. MILLER, and J. H. BRUMBAUGH. 1962. Induced loss of pigment in planarians. *Physiol. Zool.* **35**:18–26.

KARLING, T. G. 1963. Die Turbellarien Ostfennoskandiens. V. Neorhabdocoela. 3. Kalyptorhynchia. *Fauna Fenn.* **17**:1–59.

KENK, R. 1937. Sexual and asexual reproduction

in Euplanaria tigrina (Girard). *Biol. Bull.* **73:**280–294.

———. 1941. Induction of sexuality in the asexual form of Dugesia tigrina (Girard). *J. Exp. Zool.* **87:**55–70.

———. 1944. The fresh-water triclads of Michigan. *Misc. Publ. Mus. Zool. Univ. Mich.* **60:**1–44.

———. 1969. Freshwater triclads (Turbellaria) of North America. I. The genus Planaria. *Proc. Biol. Soc. Wash.* **82:**539–558.

———. 1970. Freshwater triclads (Turbellaria) of North America. II. New or little known species of Phagocata. Ibid. **83:**13–34.

———. 1972. Freshwater planarians (Turbellaria) of North America. *Biota of Freshwater Ecosystems, E.P.A. Identification Manual No.* **1:**1–81.

———. 1973. Freshwater triclads (Turbellaria) of North America, V: The genus Polycelis. *Smithson. Contrib. Zool.* **135:**1–15.

———. 1973a. Freshwater triclads (Turbellaria) of North America, VI: the genus Dendrocoelopsis. Ibid. **138:**1–16.

———. 1974. Index of the genera and species of the freshwater triclads (Turbellaria) of the world. Ibid. **183:**1–90.

———. 1975. Fresh-water triclads (Turbellaria) of North America. VII. The genus Macrocotyla. *Trans. Am. Microsc. Soc.* **94:**324–339.

———. 1975a. Freshwater triclads (Turbellaria) of North America. VIII. Dugesia arizonensis, new species. *Proc. Biol. Soc. Wash.* **88:**113–120.

———. 1977. Freshwater triclads (Turbellaria) of North America. X. Three species of Phagocata from the Eastern United States. *Proc. Biol. Soc. Wash.* **89:**645–652.

———. 1977a. Freshwater triclads (Turbellaria) of North America. IX. the genus Sphalloplana. *Smithson. Contrib. Zool.* **246:**1–38.

KEPNER, W. A., and J. L. BARKER. 1924. Nematocysts of Microstoma. *Biol. Bull.* **47:**239–251.

KEPNER, W. A., E. D. MILLER, and A. W. JONES. 1934. Observations upon Rhynchomesostomum rostratum. *Zool. Anz.* **107:**188–192.

KEPNER, W. A., and T. K. RUEBUSH. 1935. Microrhynchus virginianus n. gen. n. sp. Ibid. **111:**257–261.

KEPNER, W. A., T. K. RUEBUSH, and F. F. FERGUSON. 1937. Castrada virginiana n. sp. Ibid. **119:**307–314.

KOLASA, J., and A. FAUBEL. 1974. A preliminary description of a freshwater Acoela (Turbellaria): Oligochoerus polonicus nov. spec. *Boll. Zool.* **41:**81–85.

KROMHOUT, G. A. 1943. A comparison of the protonephridia of fresh-water, brackish-water, and marine specimens of Gyratrix hermaphroditus. *J. Morphol.* **72:**167–169.

LUTHER, A. 1955. Die Dalyelliiden (Turbellaria Neorhabdocoela). Eine Monographie. *Acta Zool. Fenn.* **87:**1–337.

———. 1960. Die Turbellarien Ostfennoskandiens. I. Acoela, Catenulida, Macrostomida, Lecithoepitheliata, Prolecithophora und Proseriata. *Fauna Fenn.* **7:**1–154.

———. 1962. Die Turbellarien Ostfennoskandiens. IV. Neorhabdocoela I. Ibid. **12:**1–71.

———. 1963. Die Turbellarien Ostfennoskandiens. IV. Neorhabdocoela 2. Ibid. **16:**1–163.

MAGUIRE, B. 1963. Population regulation by ectocrines in Cura foremanii (Turbellaria). *Proc. XVI Int. Cong. Zool.* **1:**64.

MARCUS, E. 1945. Sôbre Catenulida brasileiros. *Univ. Sao Paulo, Bol. Fac. Filos. Cienc. Lett., Zool.* No. **10:**8–100.

———. 1946. Sôbre Turbellaria limnicos brasileiros. Ibid. **11:**5–253.

MITCHELL, R. W. 1968. New species of Sphalloplana (Turbellaria; Paludicola) from the caves of Texas and a reexamination of the genus Speophila and the Family Kenkiidae. *Ann. Speleol.* **23:**597–620.

MONTGOMERY, J. R., and S. J. COWARD. 1974. On the minimal size of a planarian capable of regeneration. *Trans. Am. Microsc. Soc.* **93:**386–391.

NUTTYCOMBE, J. W. 1956. The Catenula of the eastern United States. *Am. Midl. Nat.* **55:**419–433.

NUTTYCOMBE, J. W., and A. J. WATERS. 1938. The American species of the genus Stenostomum. *Proc. Am. Philos. Soc.* **79:**213–284.

PEARL, R. 1903. The movements and reactions of fresh-water planarians: a study in animal behaviour. *Quart. J. Microsc. Sci.* **46:**509–714.

PÖRNER, H. 1966. Die rhabdocoeliden Turbellarien der Gewässer von Jena und Umgebung. *Limnologica* **4:**27–44.

REDFIELD, E. S. P. 1915. The grasping organ of Dendrocoelum lacteum. *J. Anim. Behav.* **5:**375–380.

REISINGER, E. 1923. Turbellaria. *Biol. Tiere Dtschl.* **4:**1–64.

REYNOLDSON, T. B. 1958. The quantitative ecology of lake-dwelling triclads in northern Britain. *Oikos* **9:**94–138.

———. 1964. Evidence for intra-specific competition in field populations of triclads. *J. Anim. Ecol.* **33:**187–201.

———. 1967. A key to the British species of freshwater triclads. *Sci. Publ. Freshwater Biol. Assoc.* **23:**1–28.

———. 1968. Shrinkage thresholds in freshwater triclads. *Ecology* **49:**584–586.

REYNOLDSON, T. B., and L. S. BELLAMY. 1971. Intraspecific competition in lake-dwelling triclads. *Oikos* **22:**315–328.

———. 1973. Interspecific competition in lake-dwelling triclads. Ibid. **24:**301–313.

RISER, N. W., and M. P. MORSE. 1974. *Biology of the Turbellaria.* 530 p. McGraw-Hill, New York.

RIXEN, J.-U. 1961. Kleinturbellarien aus dem Litoral der Binnengewässer Schleswig-Holsteins. *Arch. Hydrobiol.* **57:**464–538.

———. 1968. Beitrag zur Kenntnis der Turbellarienfauna des Bodenseegebietes. Ibid. **64:**335–365.

RUEBUSH, T. K. 1935. The genus Olisthanella in the United States. *Zool. Anz.* **112:**129–136.

———. 1935a. The occurrence of Provortex affinis Jensen in the United States. Ibid. **111:**305–308.

———. 1937. The genus Dalyellia in America. Ibid. **119:**237–256.

———. 1939. A new North American rhabdocoel turbellarian, Prorhynchella minuta n. gen., n. sp. Ibid. **127:**204–209.

————. 1940. Mesostoma ehrenbergii wardii for the study of the turbellarian type. *Science* **91**:531–532.

————. 1941. A key to the American freshwater turbellarian genera, exclusive of the Tricladida. *Trans. Am. Microsc. Soc.* **60**:29–40.

RUEBUSH, T. K., and W. J. HAYES, Jr. 1939. The genus Dalyellia in America. II. A new form from Tennessee and a discussion of the relationships within the genus. *Zool. Anz.* **128**:136–152.

SANDERS, O., and R. M. SANDERS. 1970. Webs secreted by planarians. *J. Biol. Psych.* **12**:65–70.

STEINBÖCK, O. 1926. Zur Ökologie der alpinen Turbellarien. *Z. Morphol. Oekol. Tiere* **5**:424–446.

TAYLOR, M. C., and T. B. REYNOLDSON. 1962. The population biology of lake-dwelling Polycelis species with special reference to P. nigra (Müll.) (Turbellaria, Tricladida). *J. Anim. Ecol.* **31**:273–291.

YOUNG, J. O. 1970. British and Irish freshwater microturbellaria: historical records, new records and a key for their identification. *Arch. Hydrobiol.* **67**:210–241.

————. 1975. The population dynamics of Phaenocora typhlops (Vejdovsky) (Turbellaria: Neorhabdocoela) living in a pond. *J. Anim. Ecol.* **44**:251–262.

YOUNG, J. O., and T. B. REYNOLDSON. 1965. A laboratory study of predation on lake-dwelling triclads. *Hydrobiologia* **26**:307–313.

# Chapter 6

# NEMERTEA (PROBOSCIS WORMS)

THE MAJORITY of fresh-water biologists never have the experience of observing living fresh-water nemerteans. One reason is that they are seldom sought intentionally and are usually overlooked or disregarded in collections made with other taxonomic categories uppermost in mind. Another reason is their extremely "spotty" and local abundance. Weedy ponds, masses of filamentous algae, the undersides of lily pads, and the general substrate of littoral areas are preferred habitats, but often nemerteans may be taken from only one restricted area in a pond and are apparently absent elsewhere.

Nemerteans have been badly neglected in the United States, but presumably there is only one well-known fresh-water species. It is called *Prostoma graecense* (Böhmig) by Gibson and Moore (1976) but is also generally known as *P. rubrum* Leidy. This species is widely distributed in the United States. About six valid species in monotypic genera are found in fresh waters in other parts of the world. This situation is in striking contrast to that prevailing in the marine littoral where many species are found.

**General characteristics.** *Prostoma graecense* is elliptical in cross section, somewhat flattened ventrally, up to 30 mm long, and 0.6 to 2.0 mm in diameter. Coloration is highly variable. Young specimens are whitish or pale yellow, but mature specimens are yellowish-red, orange, or deep red. There is also a rare green variety. The anterior end is rounded and without a definite head; the posterior end is tapered to a point. Three pairs of ocelli are usually present, but occasionally there are two or four pairs. They are arranged in two longitudinal rows on the dorsal surface of the anterior end and are sometimes placed asymmetrically. The body is smooth, unsegmented, and covered with a columnar ciliated epithelium.

Owing to a well-developed longitudinal and circular muscle tissues, these worms are highly contractile. A smooth, gliding type of locomotion is produced by cilia acting on a slime track secreted by the epidermis.

**Digestive system, feeding.** The subterminal mouth opens into a buccal cavity, which is followed by an esophagus, stomach, intestine, and terminal anus. The entire length of the long intestine has pairs of small lateral diverticula, and from the anterior end of the intestine a pair of pyloric caeca extend forward. The digestive tract has no musculature of its own.

The proboscis apparatus is a unique feature of nemerteans. A fluid-filled longitudinal cavity, the rhynchocoel, runs throughout most of the body length dorsal to the digestive tract. The muscular wall of the rhynchocoel is called the proboscis sheath. Lying within the rhynchocoel is a tubular muscular proboscis, which can be protruded anteriorly and withdrawn back into the rhynchocoel by a long retractor muscle. The proboscis is very long, sometimes two or three times the body length, and when not in use it is strongly contracted and coiled within the rhynchocoel. The rhynchodaeum is the cavity of the proboscis and it has an opening to the outside in common with the mouth. There are actually three parts to the proboscis. Anteriorly it is a thick-walled tube. Farther back

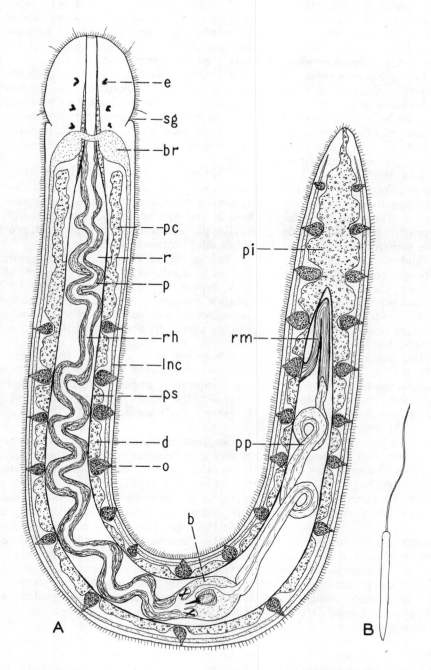

FIG. 91.–Structure of *Prostoma graecense,* semidiagrammatic. A, general anatomy, dorsal view, ×16; B, with protruded proboscis, ×1.5. *b,* bulbous portion of proboscis; *br,* brain; *d,* diverticulum of intestine; *e,* ocellus; *lnc,* lateral nerve cord; *o,* ovotestis; *p,* anterior portion of proboscis; *pc,* pyloric caecum; *pi,* posterior portion of intestine; *pp,* posterior portion of proboscis; *ps,* proboscis sheath; *r,* rhynchocoel; *rh,* rhynchodaeum; *rm,* retractor muscle of proboscis; *sg,* sensory groove.

is a middle bulbous portion bearing a functional sclerotized stylet set in a heavy base along with two lateral pockets containing accessory stylets in various stages of development (Figs. 91, 93). The functional stylet is frequently lost and is then replaced by one from the lateral pockets. Posterior to the bulb is a blind tube. When the proboscis is protruded, the bulb and posterior blind tube are everted through the anterior thick-walled tube and out of the mouth in such a fashion that the stylet is at the tip of the extended proboscis. Proboscis eversion is effected by muscle contraction exerting pressure on the fluid in the rhynchocoel.

The proboscis functions in both defense and food getting. While *Prostoma* creeps about on the substrate its extended proboscis probes and darts about constantly. If the proboscis comes in contact with a small metazoan, the stylet may be used to stab the animal repeatedly. A toxic material is thought to be secreted from the posterior chamber of the proboscis and discharged through the stylet apparatus. The proboscis is also coiled around the prey and quantities of sticky mucus are secreted, thus further immobilizing the prey. The mouth and buccal cavity are capable of great distension, and most food organisms are ingested intact. If the prey is too large, however, only the body juices are sucked out. *Prostoma* is chiefly carnivorous and feeds on all kinds of small metazoans, and especially on small oligochaetes. It may also feed on recently dead animals, and a few times it has been observed ingesting organic detritus.

Preliminary digestion occurs in the stomach and further digestion in the intestine and its diverticula. Specimens may be kept for six months or more without food, but the metabolic requirements during this period may produce a shrinkage to one-tenth or less of normal size.

**General anatomy, physiology.** Below the epidermis *Prostoma* has a thick connective tissue dermis and well-defined layers of longitudinal and circular muscle. Visceral organs are separated by mesenchymal connective tissue.

A closed circulatory system is present, the main vessels being a dorsal longitudinal contractile vessel and two lateral longitudinal contractile vessels. The blood is clear, sometimes faintly yellowish-reddish.

Excretion is effected by a protonephridial system consisting of many branched tubules with clusters of terminal flame bulbs and several nephridiopores along each side of the body. Presumably this apparatus also functions in osmoregulation.

The brain is dark-colored and four-lobed and surrounds the esophagus. Two prominent lateroventral nerve cords pass from it and extend to the posterior end. Smaller paired nerves supply the head, proboscis, and proboscis sheath.

The ocelli lie beneath the epidermis and are irregular cup-shaped masses of black, brown, or reddish pigment granules. Anterior sensory grooves are presumably chemotactile, and sensory cells with long cilia are especially abundant at the extremities.

There are no special respiratory structures or adaptations. It is possible that some respiratory exchange occurs through the wall of the digestive tract in addition to the general body surface.

**Reproduction, life history.** *Prostoma graecense* is hermaphroditic and generally protandric; saclike ovotestes alternate with the intestinal diverticula. Each ovotestis opens to the outside by a lateral genital pore and produces many sperm but only a single ripe egg. The additional oocytes degenerate. Breeding may occur at any time between May and November or December, provided the water temperature is above 10°. A sexually mature individual secretes a mucous sheath around itself, releases sperm and a double row of eggs into the sheath, and then crawls out of the sheath. Not infrequently two individuals, one of which is at the time functionally male and the other female, occupy the same mucous sheath and cross-fertilization occurs. Contact with water causes dissolution of the germinal vesicles around the eggs and they become fertilized. Development is direct and there is no special larval stage. Young worms leave the mucous mass and become independent.

*Prostoma* has considerable powers of regeneration. The whole posterior portion of the body may be regenerated provided the remaining anterior portion contains at least half of the esophageal region. A new proboscis may be regenerated if the old one is lost.

**Ecology** *Prostoma graecense* can be most easily found in autumn when it is relatively abundant. It occurs only in well-oxygenated shallow and littoral standing waters and sluggish streams, especially in

FIG. 92.–Diagrammatic longitudinal section of *Prostoma*, ×7.5. *b*, bulbous portion of proboscis; *bc*, buccal cavity; *d*, diverticulum of intestine; *e*, esophagus; *fg*, frontal gland; *i*, intestine; *p*, anterior portion of proboscis; *pc*, pyloric caecum; *pp*, posterior portion of proboscis; *ps*, proboscis sheath; *r*, rhynchocoel; *rm*, retractor muscle of proboscis; *s*, stomach; *vc*, ventral commissure of brain. (Modified from Reisinger.)

FIG. 93.–Bulbous portion of proboscis and adjacent structures of *Prostoma*. *bs*, base of stylet; *rh*, rhynchodaeum; *rs*, accessory stylet; *s*, functional stylet; *ug*, unicellular glands. (Greatly modified from Reisinger.)

masses of filamentous algae, on rooted aquatics, or in the debris of the general substrate. No explanation is known for its localized distribution in such places. It is especially active at night, when it does most of its feeding and egg deposition. It is highly thigmotactic and reacts positively to water currents. With the approach of autumn and freezing temperatures *Prostoma* migrates to deeper waters and returns to the shallows in spring.

Under adverse environmental conditions, such as insufficient oxygen, high temperature, abnormal substrate, and lack of food, *Prostoma* forms resting cysts by rounding up within a secreted outer layer of mucus, which soon hardens and becomes covered with detritus. The worm may remain alive within such a cyst for a few days to a few weeks, emerging when ecological conditions are again appropriate. Cysts cannot withstand complete drying and are of limited value in dissemination.

*Prostoma* is preyed upon by larger worms and carnivorous insects and crustaceans.

*Prostoma graecense* is widely distributed throughout the United States, though usually in small numbers. It is also found in Central and South America.

**Culturing, preserving.** *Prostoma* may be cultured in an aquarium that has a thin layer of soil on the bottom and plenty of rooted aquatics. Excessive bacterial decomposition inhibits nemerteans and should

be avoided. Feed the worms bits of liver, earthworms, or small metazoans.

Because it is so highly contractile, *Prostoma* should always be anesthetized before killing. Chloretone and other solutions may be used with varying success. Kill in 80 percent alcohol or hot FAA. Preserve in 70 percent alcohol.

**Taxonomy** About 600 valid species of nemerteans are known. The great majority are marine, but a few occur on land and in fresh waters. The genus *Prostoma* is essentially cosmopolitan.

Because of wide variations in color, number of reserve stylets, length of rhynchocoel, number of ocelli and size, the taxonomy of *Prostoma* is confused and difficult. The situation has become especially involved because some of the descriptions and identifications have been based on contracted and faded alcoholic specimens. *Prostoma graecense* has also gone under the generic designations of *Emea, Tetrastemma,* and *Stichostemma* and under the species designations of *asensoriatum, aquarium,* and *rubrum.*

Although it is probably true that European species have been introduced into this country on imported aquatic plants, it is not known how widespread they have become. Furthermore, it is quite possible that additional native species await discovery. Indeed, the present writer has collected several nemerteans that are obviously undescribed species.

## NEMERTEA REFERENCES

Böhmig, L. 1898. Beiträge zur Anatomie und Histologie der Nemertinen. *Z. wiss. Zool.* **64**:479–564.

Child, C. M. 1901. The habits and natural history of Stichostemma. *Am. Nat.* **35**:975–1006.

Coe, W. R. 1943. Biology of the nemerteans of the Atlantic coast of North America. *Trans. Conn. Acad. Arts and Sci.* **35**:129–328.

Cordero, E. H. 1943. Hallazgos en diversos paises de Sud América de nemertinos de agua dulce del género "Prostoma." *An. Acad. Brasil Cien.* **15**:125–134.

Gibson, R., and J. O. Young. 1974. First records of Prostoma (Haplonemertea) from East Africa. *Zool. Anz.* **193**:103–109.

———. 1976. Freshwater nemerteans. *Zool. J. Linn. Soc.* **58**:177–218.

Montgomery, T. 1896. Stichostemma asensoriatum n. sp., a fresh-water nemertean from Pennsylvania. *Zool. Anz.* **19**:436–438.

Reisinger, E. 1926. Nemertini. *Biol. Tiere Dtsch.* **7**:1–24.

Rioja, E. 1941. Estudios hidrobiologicos. V. Hallazgo en Xochimilco de Stichostemma rubrum (Leidy), nemerte de agua dulce. *Mex. An. Inst. Biol.* **12**:663–668.

Stiasny-Wijnhoff, G. 1938. Das Genus Prostoma Dugès, eine Gattung von Süsswasser-Nemertinen. *Arch. Neerl. Zool., Suppl.* **3**:219–230.

# Chapter 7

# GASTROTRICHA

---

IN COMPANY with protozoans, rotifers, nematodes, and small oligochaetes, the Gastrotricha are a part of the characteristic assemblage of microorganisms on aquatic vegetation and on the debris (periphyton) commonly forming the substrates of standing waters.

Formerly it was thought that gastrotrichs were almost restricted to fresh waters, but they are now known to be abundant in marine habitats. The phylum consists of only two orders; the Order Macrodasyoidea is strictly marine, and the Order Chaetonotoidea is predominantly freshwater.

**General characteristics.** Most freshwater gastrotrichs range from 100 to 300 microns in length, although a few are as small as 70 microns or as large as 600 microns. The body is short to long and wormlike, with a flat ventral surface. Head and arched trunk regions are obvious, and often there is a more or less distinct neck. Two toelike projections, forming the furca, are commonly present at the posterior end.

The margin of the head is variable, even within the same genus. Sometimes the entire margin is smooth, sometimes it has a median anterior lobe and one or two pairs of variously developed lateral lobes. Tufts of sensory cilia are customarily situated in the depressions between lobes. The mouth is terminal, subterminal, or ventral, and is often surrounded by short delicate bristles. In fresh-water species the anus lies in a dorsal position at the base of the furca; rarely is it terminal or subterminal.

Locomotor cilia occur chiefly on the ventral surface of the head and trunk. Most commonly there are several patches on the head and two longitudinal bands running throughout most of the body length (Figs. 96H,J).

Coloration is variable, usually light gray to reddish-brown, and mostly determined by the contents of the digestive tract. A starved gastrotrich is grayish and translucent.

Internal organization is relatively uncomplicated. The digestive tract is tubular and without diverticula. The space between the digestive tract and thin body wall is a pseudocoel and it contains the simple muscle, protonephridial, nervous, and reproductive systems (Fig. 94). There are no special circulatory or respiratory structures.

Many workers have discussed the phylogenetic relationships with the Nematoda, Rotatoria, Kinorhyncha, Turbellaria, and other groups, but the Gastrotricha are here considered sufficiently distinctive to constitute a separate phylum

**Cuticular structures.** The general body surface of gastrotrichs is covered with a cuticle secreted by the underlying syncytial hypodermis. In the great majority of species, however, the cuticle is not simple and thin but patterned and with a variety of outgrowths, especially dorsally and laterally (Figs. 95, 99, 100).

In a few species the cuticle is locally thickened to form variously arranged plates, but more commonly there are series of cuticular scales that usually overlap more or less. Both plates and scales may have small keels or spines; the latter range from very short to exceedingly long and robust. In the absence of plates and scales,

FIG. 94.–Diagrammatic internal structure of a typical gastrotrich. A, dorsal; B, ventral. *a*, anus; *b*, brain; *cg*, cement gland; *de*, developing egg; *i*, intestine; *ms*, muscle strand; *ns*, longitudinal nerve strand; *o*, ovary; *p*, pharynx; *pr*, protonephridium; *ps*, pseudocoel; *r*, rectum; *sg*, salivary gland; *xo*, "X organ." (Greatly modified from Zelinka.)

spines are often attached directly to the thin cuticle. Sometimes spines are barbed and have a triradiate or platelike base. A few species have midventral scales or plates. Size and shape of plates, scales, and spines commonly vary within the same individual, depending on the location on the body. A few simple setae are often present, especially near the anterior and posterior ends of the body. The cephalic shield is a thick-

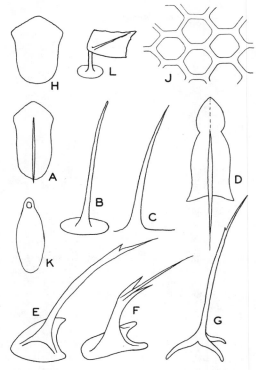

FIG. 95.–Cuticular structures of Gastrotricha. A to G, *Chaetonotus*; H and J, *Lepidodermella*; K, *Polymerurus*; L, *Aspidiophorus*. H, J, and K, simple cuticular plates; A, keeled plate; B, D, E, and F, spined plates; C and G, cuticular spines. (J from Brunson, 1950.)

ened cuticular plate covering the anterior end of the head above the mouth (Fig. 96G). Sometimes there are less distinct special plates posterior to the mouth and laterally on the head.

**Locomotion.** Beating movements of the ventral cilia against the substrate produce a characteristic smooth, graceful, gliding type of locomotion, that is sometimes quite rapid; presumably the lateral tufts of head cilia are also of some importance. Such gliding locomotion is especially notable in the Chaetonotidae.

The long spines of the Dasydytidae are used in springing and leaping. Although the spines are not supplied with special muscles, they are moved vigorously toward the plane of the body when the arched body is straightened.

Most gastrotrichs may temporarily leave the substrate and swim about in the water with the ventral and head cilia, but they seldom go far above the substrate.

*Polymerurus* is said to have a sinuous type of locomotion characteristic of nematodes.

A cement gland is usually found in the base of each process of the furca, with its duct opening at or near the tip. The adhesive secreted material is used for temporary attachment to objects. A similar arrangement is found in rotifers. In the marine order Macrodasyoidea there is often an abundance of small lateral and posterior adhesive tubues.

**Feeding, digestive system.** Gastrotrichs browse about on the substrate, ingesting bacteria, algae, small protozoans, and organic detritus. Currents induced by head cilia aid in concentrating and bringing food particles to the mouth.

Often the mouth opening is surrounded by a projecting cuticular collarlike lip bearing the oral bristles. The mouth cavity opens directly into the pharynx, which is remarkably similar to the nematode pharynx. It is a long, cylindrical, muscular organ, usually slightly larger toward the inner end and sometimes with one or two indistinct bulbs. Its cavity is more or less triquetrous and lined with thin cuticle. Four small unicellular salivary glands are closely associated with the pharynx, one pair anteriorly and one posteriorly.

The intestinal wall consists of only four longitudinal rows of cells. There are no caeca, although a short rectum is distinguishable just before the anus.

One investigator has reported that reserve food materials are stored in special subepidermal cells, which break loose and float about in the pseudocoel.

**Excretion.** The Chaetonotidae, including the great majority of fresh-water species, all have a single pair of flame bulbs at about midlength. The two protonephridial tubules are considerably coiled in the pseudocoel and open ventrally near the midline. Undoubtedly the protonephridial system functions in both excretion and osmoregu-

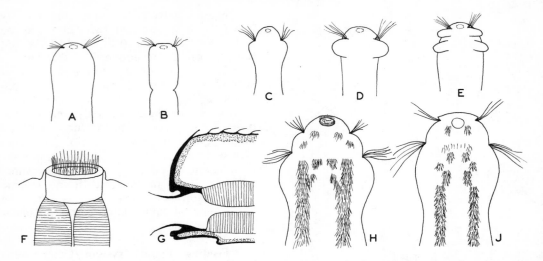

FIG. 96.–Structure of head region of Gastrotricha. A to E, dorsal view of typical heads, showing general shape and head lobes; F, semidiagrammatic ventral view of mouth region, showing circular collar, oral bristles, and anterior portion of pharynx; G, diagrammatic longitudinal section of anterior end, showing oral bristles, oral cavity, anterior portion of pharynx, and the cephalic shield; H, ventral view of anterior end of a typical *Chaetonotus*, showing arrangement of cilia; J, ventral view of anterior end of a typical *Ichthydium*, showing arrangement of cilia. (A to E modified from Brunson, 1950; F to J modified from Remane, 1935–1936.)

lation. Although there is some disagreement, it is probable that the other families of the Chaetonotoidea also have a protonephridial system. Some investigators state that the marine species of Chaetonotidae have a protonephridial system; others maintain that it is absent. In the marine order Macrodasyoidea, however, the system is lacking. It is possible that the intestine of all gastrotrichs has an accessory excretory function.

**Muscle system** The longitudinal muscle strands are quite prominent, especially ventrally. Usually there are about six pairs, with origins and insertions on the body wall. Their contraction produces shortening, curving, and partial rolling up of the body. A few delicate circular fibers in the body wall have recently been demonstrated for a few species, but they are thought to be of little importance in movement. In addition to the radial pharyngeal musculature, there are a few circular fibers on the outside of the pharynx and in the region of the rectum.

**Nervous system.** A large, dorsal, lobed, saddled-shaped brain covers the an-

terior portion of the pharynx, and two lateral nerve strands extend almost to the posterior end of the body. Fine branches innervate the body wall and viscera.

**Sensory receptors.** One or two pairs of pigmented "eyespots" have been seen on the lateral surfaces of the brain in a few species, but their function is questionable.

The tufts of cilia on the head are thought to function in touch, current detection, and the detection of dissolved materials. They are inserted in special thick glandular cells of the hypodermis.

Pairs of anterior and posterior tactile bristles are of common occurrence.

**Reproduction, life history.** Most marine gastrotrichs are hermaphroditic, and a few are protandrous. Fresh-water species, however, are all parthenogenetic females, males being unknown. The two parts of the ovary are more or less lateral to the intestine. Each portion consists of a few oocytes and eggs in various stages of development. The oviduct is so skimpy that some investigators doubt its existence as a definite duct. The genital pore is ventral. A single ventral saclike "X organ" lies just inside the genital pore; possibly it represents a vestigial copulatory bursa.

A gastrotrich usually produces one to five eggs during its lifetime. A mature egg is quite large, and before leaving the parent it distends the body greatly. Nevertheless, it is plastic, and as it emerges from the genital pore it is momentarily constricted into a dumbbell shape. On coming in contact with the water an outer shell hardens. Sometimes the shell bears spines or other protuberances. Eggs are usually attached to some small object on the substrate.

Brunson (1949) distinguishes two definite types of eggs, differing slightly in size. Tachyblastic eggs begin cleavage as soon as deposited and hatch 12 to 70 hours later. Opsiblastic eggs are slightly larger and are produced in old cultures and when environmental conditions become unfavorable. They have a heavier shell and survive desiccation, freezing, and unusually high temperatures. The duration of dormancy is variable, depending on ecological conditions, but it is known to last as long as two years. Opsiblastic eggs are usually the last ones laid by a particular gastrotrich, but there are some exceptions.

Gastrulation begins at the 32-cell stage. Development is direct. On emergence from the egg a gastrotrich is quite large, and during the ensuing several hours it grows by 20 to 30 percent to attain mature size. As compared with the Macrodasyoidea, the Chaetonotoidea are composed of relatively few cells; perhaps the number is constant within each species. Little is known about

the normal length of life; individuals in cultures live for 3 to 22 days, depending on the species and ecological conditions. Like the situation in rotifers, the cuticle is never shed during the life history.

**Ecology.** Only seven genera of gastrotrichs are restricted to fresh waters, including *Dasydytes, Dichaetura, Heterolepidoderma, Kijanebalola, Lepidodermella, Neogossea,* and *Proichthydium.* Four genera occur in both marine and fresh waters, or brackish and fresh waters. These are *Aspidiophorus, Chaetonotus, Ichthydium,* and *Polymerurus.* Only a very few species are known to occur in both types of environments, and some investigators believe that these are all actually pairs of varieties. About 30 genera are restricted to marine habitats.

Gastrotrichs are typical of puddles, marshes, wet bogs, and the shallow litoral, especially where there is detritus and decaying material. Old laboratory protozoan cultures or aquaria with disintegrating aquatic plants commonly have gastrotrich populations. They are uncommon in running waters generally and perhaps absent from swift streams. For some unknown reason, tropical gastrotrichs are often found swimming about above the substrate.

Most species remain closely associated with the substrate, although the Neogosseidae and Dasydytidae may swim about above it. Their occurrence in the plankton of the shallows, however, is atypical and fortuitous. Little is known about the depth distribution and concentrations of freshwater species, although *Chaetonotus* has been found in bottom deposits as deep as 36 m. Recently it has been found that the capillary water of sandy beaches a meter or two from the water's edge supports a considerable population of gastrotrichs.

Although maximum numbers are usually found in summer and autumn, gastrotrichs may be collected at any time of the year. Other than opsiblastic eggs, no special desiccation or overwintering mechanisms are known.

Many species may be collected from habitats where there is much decay, and where the dissolved oxygen content con-

FIG. 97.–Opsiblastic egg of *Chaetonotus.* (Redrawn from Zelinka.)

sequently may be less than 1 ppm. Minimal oxygen concentrations are not definitely known, however, although it is probable that gastrotrichs may withstand at least temporary anaerobiosis.

**Geographical distribution, dispersal.** Except for some areas in Europe and three or four in the United States, there has been almost no intensive, systematic collection of gastrotrichs. Most records are the result of incidental or superficial studies, often associated with collections of other groups of fresh-water invertebrates. As a result, we know little about the geographical distribution of individual species. Most fresh-water genera, however, appear to be cosmopolitan and occur the world over in suitable habitats; these are *Aspidiophorus, Chaetonotus, Dasydytes, Ichthydium, Lepidodermella, Neogossea,* and *Polymerurus.* Overland dispersal is undoubtedly effected by the resistant opsiblastic eggs.

**Enemies.** In addition to the toll taken by browsing insects and crustaceans, gastrotrichs are also devoured by amoeboid protozoans, hydras, oligochaetes, turbellarians, and perhaps by tardigrades and nematodes.

**Collecting.** Sandy beach washings, and rinsings of aquatic vegetation often yield good collections. Specimens may be concentrated by straining the wash water through fine bolting silk. For bottom species the thin layer of surface mud and debris should be carefully scooped up and placed in a suitable container with water. After standing for a time in the laboratory, material at the debris and water interface should be sucked up with a long pipette and examined under the high power of the binoculars.

**Culturing.** Old protozoan cultures are sometimes suitable if gastrotrichs are seeded into them, and one investigator recommends using two drops of uncooked egg yolk in 100 ml spring or pond water. In either case it is best to add a little bottom debris to the culture.

One-tenth percent malted milk in well water is especially useful for pure cultures. After the water is brought to a boil, malted milk powder is added, and the solution is then further boiled for about a minute. Let stand a week before inoculating with gastrotrichs.

Regardless of the culture method used, about one-half the volume of fluid should be renewed every one to three weeks.

**Preserving, preparing.** Two percent osmic acid is an excellent fixative. Place the living specimens in a drop of water on a slide and invert for 5 to 10 seconds over the mouth of the bottle of osmic acid. Saturated mercuric chloride, 10 percent formalin, and Bouin's fluid are alternative fixatives that often give good results. Specimens may be stored in 70 percent alcohol or 5 percent formalin. If glycerin is to be used for mounting, transfer the gastrotrichs to a concave watch glass containing 5 percent glycerin in 50 percent alcohol. Cover loosely to keep out dust and permit evaporation. After about a week the water and alcohol will all have evaporated and the specimens will be in concentrated glycerin. Any of the several mounting methods for rotifers may be used (page 183). Glycerin is excellent for permanent storage.

Some species require narcotization before fixing, and a wide variety of substances may be tried with varying success, including a concentrated aqueous menthol solution, chloretone, 2 percent benzamine lactate, 2 percent butyn, and 2 percent hydroxylamine hydrochloride.

Scales, plates, and spines may be isolated by the judicious use of dilute acetic acid. Stain with fuchsin. Oil immersion is essential for critical work and species identification. An Irwin loop is ideal for sorting and handling individual gastrotrichs.

**Taxonomy.** Only two investigators have made important contributions to the biology of American gastrotrichs. Stokes published the results of his New Jersey observations in 1887 and 1888, and Brunson began his series of papers in 1947. Obviously, therefore, an enormous amount of work remains to be done in this country.

Some of the most important European investigations are those of Zelinka (1889), Grünspan (1910), and Remane (1935–1936). By way of contrast, a great deal of research is being done on marine gastrotrichs.

The most reliable and significant char-acteristics for distinguishing genera are the nature of the furca, and the presence or absence and detailed structure and arrangement of cuticular plates, scales, and spines.

The majority of American species are unreported or undescribed. As a conse-

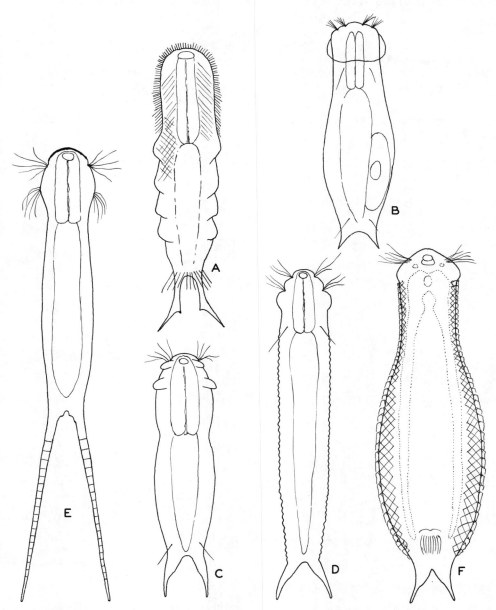

FIG. 98.–Structure of Gastrotricha. A, *Dichaetura*; B, *Ichthydium*, showing cephalic shield; C and D, *Ichthydium*; E, *Polymerurus*; F, ventral view of *Aspidiophorus*, showing arrangement of cilia. (A modified from Metschnikoff; B modified from Konsuloff; C modified from Brunson, 1949; D and E modified from Brunson, 1950; F modified from Saito.)

quence, almost every study, however superficial, turns up new species. It is therefore fruitless to include a key to the approximately 30 American species known to date.

About 250 species have been described from the fresh waters of the world, but they may all be grouped into only 11 genera. The key that follows includes only nine genera; two of these have not yet been reported from the United States (*Aspidiophorus* and *Dichaetura*), but they are widely distributed and will undoubtedly be found here eventually. Three other rare fresh-water genera are not included in the key; *Proichthyidium* has been collected only once in the Argentine, *Kijanebalola* is known only from central Africa, and *Metadasydytes* has been collected only in Poland.

Remane (1935–1936) gives good evidence for grouping *Dasydytes*, *Setopus*, *Anacanthoderma*, *Stylochaeta*, and so on, into a single genus, *Dasydytes*, and this practice is followed in the present manual. *Lepidoderma* is preoccupied and *Lepidodermella* is used instead.

Fig. 99.–Structure of various species of *Chaetonotus*. (A to C modified from Brunson, 1950; D modified from Saito; E from Brunson, 1950; F from Saito.)

# KEY TO GENERA OF GASTROTRICHA

1. Caudal furca present (Figs. 98, 99) ..............................................2
   True caudal furca absent, but sometimes with rudimentary protuberances, long spines, or setose styloid processes (Figs. 100D–J) ..............................8
2. Caudal furca not forked; cuticle smooth, or with spines, plates, simple scales, or spined scales or plates; head usually with two to four tufts of cilia; cephalic shield present or absent; usually with one pair of posterior bristles (Figs. 98B–F; 99; 100A, B); two longitudinal bands of cilia; common and widely distribuated; includes about 90 percent of the known fresh-water species......CHAETONOTIDAE, 3

Fɪɢ. 100.–Structure of Gastrotricha. A, *Lepidodermella*; B, posterior end of *Heterolepidoderma*; C, keeled plates of *Heterolepidoderma*; D, *Neogossea*; E to H, dorsal views of *Dasydytes*; J, lateral view of *Dasydytes*. (A, B, C, and J modified from Remane, 1935–1936; E and F modified from Brunson, 1950; D, modified from Daday; G modified from Voigt; H modified from Greuter.)

Caudal furca forked; cuticle covered with spined plates; head without tufts of cilia but with many single cilia; cephalic shield absent; four to many posterior bristles (Fig. 98A); several rare and poorly known species reported from Europe; not known in the United States ............... DICHAETURIDAE, **Dichaetura**

3. Caudal furca very long and jointed; body usually with spines or spines and scales (Fig. 98E); several species ........................................ **Polymerurus**
   Caudal furca not especially long, not jointed ...................................4

4. Cuticle smooth, without plates, scales, or spines, but sometimes with setae (Figs. 98C,D); about 20 species......................................**Ichthydium**
   Cuticle not smooth ......................................................5

5. Body covered with complex stalked plates, each consisting of a circular basal plate, a short stalk, and a rhombic end plate (Fig. 98F); several uncommon species; not yet reported from the United States ........................ **Aspidiophorus**
   Body with simple plates, scales, or spines ......................................6

6. Body with spines or spined scales (Fig. 99); very common; about 100 species. **Chaetonotus**
   Body without spines or scales but covered with plates .........................7

7. With flat broad plates or scales (Figs. 95H, J; 100A); about 10 species. **Lepidodermella**
   With small, keeled plates (Fig. 100C); several uncommon species; rare in the United States ............................................... **Heterolepidoderma**

8. Head with two club-shaped tentacles; body with long spines, with or without basal plates; two long spines or two styloid processes at posterior end of body; several uncommon species (Fig. 100D); rare in the United States.
   NEOGOSSEIDAE, **Neogossea**
   Head without tentacles; body with long spines, arranged singly or grouped; no plates or scales; ventral ciliation in two longitudinal bands or two longitudinal rows of tufts; head ciliation usually with three ventral transverse bands of cilia (Figs. 100E–J); a highly variable genus; about 20 species. DASYDYTIDAE, **Dasydytes**

## GASTROTRICHA REFERENCES

BRUNSON, R. B. 1947. Gastrotricha of North America. II. Four new species of Ichthyidium from Michigan. *Pap. Mich. Acad. Sci. Arts and Lett.* **33**:59–62.

———. 1948. Chaetonotus tachyneusticus. A new species of gastrotrich from Michigan. *Trans. Am. Microsc. Soc.* **67**:350–351.

———. 1949. The life history and ecology of two North American gastrotrichs. Ibid. **68**:1–20.

———. 1950. An introduction to the taxonomy of the Gastrotricha with a study of eighteen species from Michigan. Ibid. **69**:325–352.

DAVISON, D. B. 1938. A new species of gastrotrichan-Chaetonotus robustus, new species. *Am. Mus. Novit.* **972**:1–6.

DE BEAUCHAMP, P. M. 1934. Sur la morphologie et l'ethologie des Neogossea (gastrotriches). *Bull. Soc. Zool. Fr.* **58**:331–342.

FAUCON, A. S., and W. D. HUMMON. 1976. Effects of mine acid on the longevity and reproductive rate of the Gastrotricha Lepidodermella squammata (Dujardin). *Hydrobiologia* **50**:265–269.

GRÜNSPAN, T. 1910. Die Süsswassergastrotrichen Europas. Eine zusammenfassende Darstellung ihrer Anatomie, Biologie und Systematik. *Ann. Biol. lacustre* **4**:211–365.

HATCH, M. H. 1939. Notes on two species of Gastrotricha from Washington. *Am. Midl. Nat.* **21**:257–258.

MOLA, P. 1932. Gastrotricha delle acque dolci italiane. *Int. Rev.* **26**:397–423.

MURRAY, J. 1913. Gastrotricha. *J. Quekket Microsc. Club* **12**:211–238.

PACKARD, C. E. 1936. Observations on the Gastrotricha indigenous to New Hampshire. *Trans. Am. Microsc. Soc.* **55**:422–427.

REMANE, A. 1927. Beiträge zur Systematik der Süsswassergastrotrichen. *Zool. Jahrb. Abt. Syst.* **53**:269–320.

———. 1935-1936. Gastrotricha. *Klassen u. Ordnungen des Tierreich* **4** (Abt. 2, Buch 1, Teil 2, Lfg. 1–2):1–242.

SAITO, I. 1937. Neue und bekannte Gastrotrichen der Umgebung von Hiroshima (Japan). *J. Sci. Hiroshima Univ., Ser. B, Div. 1,* **5**:245–265.

VOIGT, M. 1960. Gastrotricha. *Die Tierwelt Mitteleur.* **1**:4a:1–74.

ZELINKA, C. 1890. Die Gastrotrichen. Eine monographische Darstellung ihrer Anatomie, Biologie und Systematik. *Z. wiss. Zool.* **49**:209–384.

# Chapter 8

# ROTATORIA (ROTIFERS)

IF WE were to designate a single major taxonomic category that is most characteristic of fresh waters, it could only be the Phylum Rotatoria. For the rotifers are one of the few groups that have unquestionably originated in fresh waters, and it is here that they have attained their greatest abundance and diversity. Probably 1800 species have been described, but less than 5 percent of these are restricted to marine and brackish waters. Only two species occur in the mid-Atlantic.

Rotifers were first studied and described by Leeuwenhoek in 1703, and since his time they have become classical objects for study by the amateur microscopist and professional hydrobiologist alike. They are essentially all microscopic, the length range for the phylum being about 40 microns to 2.5 mm, but the great majority are between 100 microns and 500 microns long. These fascinating creatures have long been called Rotifera, or rotifers, because in some species the disclike ciliated anterior end, or corona, has a fancied and illusory resemblance to a pair of revolving wheels owing to the synchronized beating of the coronal cilia. Rotifers occur in an endless variety of aquatic and semiaquatic habitats, including the limnetic and deepest regions of the largest lakes and the smallest puddles. They are found in damp soil and vegetable debris, in mosses that may be wetted or dampened only occasionally, in the interstices between the sand grains of lake beaches, from the Arctic and Antarctic to the tropics, in small rock depressions, and even in cemetery flower urns and eaves troughs.

The vast majority of rotifers encountered under natural conditions are females.

Males are definitely known for relatively few species; they are much smaller than the females, degenerate, and seldom live for more than two or three days. Most of the remarks in this chapter concern only female rotifers; the biology of males is discussed in a special section on page 173.

**General characteristics.** The Phylum Rotatoria is commonly divided into two classes, the Digononta and the Monogononta. The female members of the former class are characterized by paired ovaries, a ramate mastax, and the absence of a secreted tube or lorica. The Class Digononta is subdivided into two orders, the Seisonidea and the Bdelloidea. The Seisonidea includes only a single genus, *Seison,* occurring as commensals on marine Crustacea; the ovaries have no vitellaria, males are well developed, and the corona is rudimentary. Almost all Bdelloidea, however, occur in fresh waters; the ovaries have vitellaria, males are unknown, reproduction is exclusively by parthenogenesis, and the corona is well developed. The Bdelloidea are appropriately named since the body is highly contractile and they creep about on the substrate in a leechlike manner.

The members of the Class Monogononta constitute about 90 percent of the known species of rotifers and are characterized by a single ovary, by a mastax that is not ramate, and by the presence or absence of a lorica or a secreted tube. Males are known for some species and not for others; they are small and degenerate. This class is divided into three orders: Ploima, Flosculariacea, and Collothecacea.

The Order Ploima includes most of the free-swimming, limnetic plankton, and lit-

FIG. 101.–Diagrammatic structure of *Epiphanes senta* (Müller), ×400. A, ventral view; B, lateral view. (Musculature and coronal ciliation not shown; see Fig. 102.) *b*, brain; *de*, developing egg; *e*, esophagus; *eb*, excretory bladder; *gg*, gastric gland; *hc*, hypodermal cell of head; *i*, intestine; *m*, mastax; *o*, ovary; *ov*, oviduct; *p*, pharynx; *pg*, pedal gland; *pt*, protonephridial tubule; *rs*, retrocerebral sac; *s*, stomach; *t*, toe; *v*, vitellarium.

toral species. These rotifers typically have a posterior "foot" and two "toes." The corona is not especially large.

The Order Flosculariacea includes some species that are free-swimming and many more that are sessile as adults. The foot, when present, has no toes. Often there is a secreted gelatinous envelope or case. The corona is not especially large.

The Order Collothecacea includes those rotifers with a very large, lobed corona and a mouth that is centrally located at the lower end of a funnellike infundibulum; they are usually solitary and sessile.

As a group, the rotifers display an amazing range of morphological variations and adaptations. Yet the great majority have several fundamental features in common. The body is usually elongated and cylindrical, though the complete range of shape extends from linear attenuation to spherical. Usually three main body regions may be distinguished: head, trunk, and foot. The head is more or less distinctly set off from the large trunk region, although there is rarely an elongated neck region. In the bdelloid rotifers the body appears to be composed of segments, but these are only

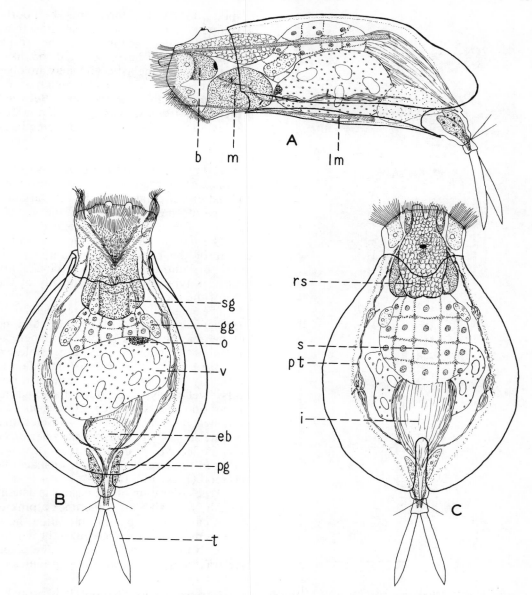

FIG. 102.–Structure of *Euchlanis dilatata* Ehr., ×320, a typical loricate rotifer, semidiagrammatic. A, lateral; B, ventral; C, dorsal. *b*, brain; *eb*, excretory bladder; *gg*, gastric gland; *i*, intestine; *lm*, longitudinal muscle; *m*, mastax; *o*, ovary; *pg*, pedal gland; *pt*, protonephridial tubule; *rs*, retrocerebral sac; *s*, stomach; *sg*, salivary gland; *t*, toe; *v*, vitellarium. (Modified from Myers, 1930.)

superficial annuli indicating the zones of folding and telescoping of the cuticle when the animal contracts; typically there are 15 to 18 such annuli. There is no true segmentation in rotifers. The posterior tapering foot usually consists of two or more superficial segmentlike parts, or it may be highly

retractile and annulated or creased; sometimes it is absent. When present, the foot usually has two (sometimes none, one, three, or four) terminal "toes."

The general body surface of a rotifer is covered with a cuticle that is secreted by a syncytial hypodermis. The hypodermis

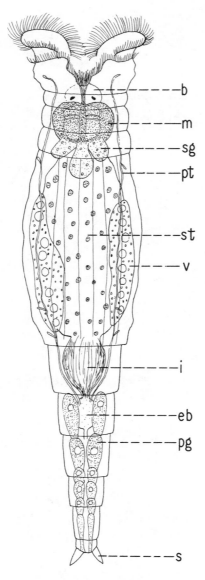

termed a lorica. The lorica may be poorly developed and consists of several thin, elastic, platelike sections of the trunk cuticle, or it may be thick, rigid, boxlike, sculptured, and inelastic and may involve the entire surface of the trunk, much of the foot, and even a part of the head. Between these two extremes, every gradation in lorica development is to be found, sometimes even within a single genus (e.g., *Cephalodella*).

The periphery and more or less of the corona surface are ciliated, but the density and pattern of ciliation are highly variable. In general, these cilia serve the double function of locomotion and feeding.

The mouth may be anterior and in the center of the corona, peripheral, subterminal, or ventral. The anus, or cloacal aperture, is typically located dorsally at the base of the foot.

The mastax is a structure peculiar to the digestive system of rotifers, and no comparable device is known elsewhere in the animal kingdom, with the possible exception of the marine Gnathostomulida. Superficially, it has the appearance of a bulbous swelling lying between the pharynx proper and the esophagus. It consists of a complicated arrangement of muscles that activate a set of translucent sclerotized jaws (collectively called the trophi), which are used to seize, tear, grind, or macerate the food (Figs. 107–109).

True coloration of the tissues is usually grayish, yellowish, or sometimes a pink or bluish cast. The apparent coloration, however, is more often tan, green, or brownish, owing to the varied contents of the digestive tract and stored excretory granules.

Fig. 103.—Ventral view of *Philodina*, a typical bdelloid rotifer, ×375, semidiagrammatic. *b*, brain; *eb*, excretory bladder; *i*, intestine; *m*, mastax; *pg*, pedal gland; *pt*, protonephridial tubule; *s*, spur (toes are completely retracted); *sg*, salivary gland; *st*, stomach; *v*, vitellarium. (Modified from Hickernell.)

**Corona and its ciliation.** It is probable that the most primitive type of corona is that of the creeping and browsing notommatid Ploima. It consists merely of an anterior, ventral, or oblique surface more or less densely covered with cilia; the buccal area, which surrounds the mouth, is always densely ciliated, but this buccal field may be extended so that it covers some or all of the corona (Fig. 104A). From this simple type, all the more complicated and intergrading arrangements are presumed to be derived. In addition to the dense, short cilia

forms a thin layer under most of the cuticle, but at the anterior end it is thick, cushionlike, and inwardly lobed. In some rotifers the cuticle is very thin and flexible, but in many genera a portion of the cuticular surface is thickened, more or less rigid, and is

FIG. 104.–Examples of coronal ciliation. Membranelles and large cilia shown by large dots, smaller cilia by small dots. A, *Dicranophorus,* ventral; B, *Floscularia,* lateral, showing the ventral pellet-making concavity; C, *Philodina,* lateral; D, *Conochilus,* lateral; E, *Cyrtonia,* ventral; F, *Synchaeta,* dorsal.

of the coronal surface, for example, there may be a peripheral wreath of large, strong cilia (Figs. 104B–E). On the other hand, with the exception of the buccal and peripheral areas, some genera, such as *Eosphora* (Fig. 133K), have little or no ciliation on the coronal surface. *Epiphanes* and many other genera have a small buccal field, a strong peripheral wreath, and several transverse rows of long cilia and clumps of cilia located on protuberances on the corona. *Synchaeta* has several long sensory coronal bristles in addition to ordinary cilia (Fig. 104F). In many Notommatidae, *Synchaeta,* and a few other genera the corona bears a pair of lateral ciliated earlike processes, or auricles (Fig. 133D). In the Bdelloidea and Flosculariacea the surface of the corona is usually bare, but it has two peripheral concentric wreaths of long, strong cilia with a densely ciliated furrow between (Figs. 136–140). In *Stephanoceros* and *Collotheca* the corona is a greatly concave infundibulum and its upper edge is folded and developed into prominent lobes or arms. These protuberances bear long, stiff setae. The mouth, at the bottom of the infundibulum, is surrounded by bands of

cilia. In *Acyclus, Cupelopagis,* and *Atrochus* there are no coronal cilia.

In addition to these several types of corona, there are other arrangements and intergradations involving sparse to dense ciliation.

**Locomotion.** Movements through the water are mostly dependent on the beating of the peripheral cilia, and many plankton and limnetic species remain in permanent suspension throughout life without ever coming in contact with a substrate. Such locomotion is often a combination of twisting on the longtudinal axis and spiral movements of the whole animal. A few plankton genera, such as *Filinia, Hexarthra,* and *Polyarthra,* also move by sudden jerks and leaps, owing to sudden beating movements of their long appendages. Most of the free-swimming, nonplankton species having a foot and toes are able to creep about and browse on substances as a result of the beating of the coronal cilia against the substrate combined with a pushing action of the toes. It is quite possible that the toes are useful in steering during both creeping and swimming.

FIG. 105.–Coronal ciliation of *Epiphanes senta*. (Modified from de Beauchamp, 1909.)

In the Bdelloidea, however, the corona is retracted during creeping and in such a manner as to produce an anterior terminal suckerlike proboscis that functions in the leechlike movements. The toes of bdelloids are usually everted only during active creeping (Figs. 138C, F; 139K; 140C).

Most rotifers with a foot and toes have pedal glands. The Ploima usually have two pedal glands in the base of the foot or in the posterior part of the trunk, whereas the Bdelloidea have from 4 to 20 such glands. Pedal glands open via ducts at the tips of the toes, at the base of the toes, or, in some Bdelloidea, also into the spurs. The secretion is used for anchoring the animal to the substrate temporarily by the tips of the toes or spurs.

Most of the Collothecacea and Flosculariacea are sessile as adults, but their newly hatched young swim about actively for a short time before attaching to the substrate.

**Tube Construction.** A wide variety of protective tubes are constructed or secreted by many general of sessile rotifers, and even by a few free-swimming species. In *Ptygura* the tube is usually gelatinous, sometimes flocculose, colorless to brown, and it appears to be secreted by the general body surface; in many species it is more or less covered with bits of adherent debris, and in one species the tube is supplemented with fecal pellets. *Stephanoceros* secretes a thin, hyaline tube, and most species of *Limnias* form a thin, firm, and sometimes annulated tube.

Several species of *Floscularia* construct their tubes of small pellets of debris, and needless to say, it is a fascinating process to watch. The newly settled young *Floscularia* secretes a rough gelatinous tube that is to form the base of the main tube. On the ventral side of the body, just posterior to the mouth, there is a conical, ciliated depression into which a large gland secretes gelatinous material. As an accessory part of the coronal cilia action, small bits of detritus are collected and concentrated in the ciliated cup. This detritus is thoroughly mixed with the gelatinous secretion, and by means of ciliary action in the cup the mass is rotated on its axis and is formed into a hard symmetrical pellet having the shape of a pistol bullet. By appropriate movements of the head and trunk, the pellet is pushed into place at the top of the tube with the tip pointed outward. The upper edge of the tube is always level with the pellet-making cup, and as the animal elongates, it continuously manufactures pellets so that growth closely corresponds with the length of the tube (Edmondson, 1945).

According to the specific constituents of the pellets, the tubes are usually yellow,

FIG. 106.–Dorsal view of anterior end of *Macrotrachela*, a typical bdelloid rotifer. *a*, antenna; *lp*, lamella of proboscis; *p*, proboscis; *ul*, upper lip.

green, or brown, although in one species they are almost colorless and composed largely of the gelatinous secretion. Another species of *Floscularia* constructs its tube out of fecal pellets.

**Mastax and trophi.** The anatomy and action of the mastax and its contained trophi are so variously modified for special feeding habits that it is best to consider these structures before discussing feeding and the digestive system.

Food is brought into the mouth by ciliary action, down the short pharynx, and into the mastax. Only the anterior, dorsal, or anterodorsal part of the mastax contains a cavity through which the food passes. The greater, basal part of this organ consists of minute muscles and the sclerotized trophi, whose movements the muscles bring about. In traversing the mastax, however, the food must pass through the moving, distal, toothlike portions of the trophi.

The trophi consist of one median piece and three paired lateral pieces, all of which are subject to morphological variation and specialization. The fulcrum is basal and median and serves as an attachment for the two rami; these three pieces collectively form the incus. The two unci are usually toothed to a varying degree, and each of these pieces is attached laterally to a manubrium. An uncus and its associated manubrium collectively form a malleus. Thus the trophi consist of one incus (composed of one fulcrum and two rami) plus two mallei (each composed of one manubrium and one uncus) (Figs. 107A, B). Eight basic, but variable, types of mastax are recognized according to the relative development and specialization of their parts. These are characterized briefly below, and their occurrence in the various families of rotifers is given in the taxonomic outline on pages 184–185.

Malleate (Fig. 107B). Specialized for horizontal grinding of plankton and particulate detritus. Feebly prehensile.

Virgate (Fig. 109). The fulcrum is long and expanded at the base for the attachment of the hypopharynx, a powerful domelike mastax muscle; the upper (dorsal) end of the hypopharynx is free and covered with cuticle, and when it contracts it acts as a piston and sucks food into the mouth and mastax cavity. Rotifers with a virgate

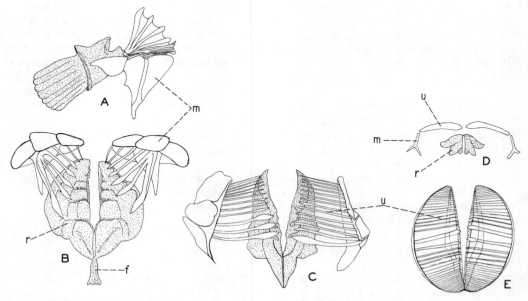

Fig. 107.–Typical trophi. A, left side view of malleate trophi of *Epiphanes senta*; B, anterior view of trophi of *E. senta*; C, anterior view of malleoramate trophi of *Floscularia*; D, optical section of ramate trophi of a bdelloid rotifer; E, anterior view of ramate trophi of a bdelloid rotifer. Inci are stippled. *f*, fulcrum; *m*, manubrium; *r*, ramus; *u*, uncus. (Modified from de Beauchamp, 1909.)

FIG. 108.–Typical trophi. A, lateral view of cardate trophi of *Lindia*; B, ventral view of trophi of *Lindia*; C, lateral view of incudate trophi of *Asplanchna*; D, anterior view of trophi of *Asplanchna*; E, anterior view of forcipate trophi of *Dicranophorus*; F, anterior view of uncinate trophi of *Stephanoceros*. Inci are stippled. *f*, fulcrum; *m*, manubrium; *r*, ramus; *s*, subuncus; *u*, uncus. (A and B modified from Harring and Myers, 1922; C to F modified from de Beauchamp, 1909; E modified from Harring and Myers, 1928.)

mastax commonly extract the fluids of plant cells and the body fluids of microscopic animals by this suction mechanism. In addition to suction, the trophi of the virgate mastax may be used for biting or nibbling preliminary to ingestion and the grinding action. Plankton, periphyton, and particulate detritus are also used as the chief food by many rotifers with a virgate mastax.

Cardate (Figs. 108A, B). This type of mastax occurs only in the Subfamily Lindiinae. Like the virgate type, the cardate mastax functions by suction, but the whole mastax is able to oscillate on a transverse axis, and a complicated epipharynx supports the mouth. The Lindiinae are only incidentally predatory, the chief food being periphyton and particulate detritus.

Forcipate (Fig. 108E). The trophi of this type of mastax are elongated, strongly compressed dorsoventrally, and adapted for protrusion through the mouth and the capture and tearing of the prey (Protozoa and micrometazoa). The trophi can sometimes be protruded for half their length.

Incudate (Figs. 108C, D). The trophi are prehensile and all parts are reduced except the pincerlike protrusile rami. The mastax musculature is likewise reduced. Food consists mostly of zooplankton.

Ramate (Figs. 107D, E). This mastax is specialized for the grinding of plankton, periphyton, and detritus. All parts of the trophi are reduced or vestigial except the semicircular unci, which have opposing linear teeth. The fulcrum is usually absent.

Malleoramate (Fig. 107C). This type is much like the ramate mastax, but the first few ventral teeth are larger, more highly developed, and detached, while the remaining teeth are progressively smaller striations. The fulcrum is present but small.

Uncinate (Fig. 108F). Sepcialized for laceration of ingested plankton, periphyton, and detritus. An intermediate piece, or subuncus, facilitates greater movement of the unci on the rami.

The trophi of all types of mastax are minutely sculptured, ridged, and barred. These complex markings can be discerned to advantage only with the oil immersion lens and they are mostly omitted in the trophi figures in this chapter.

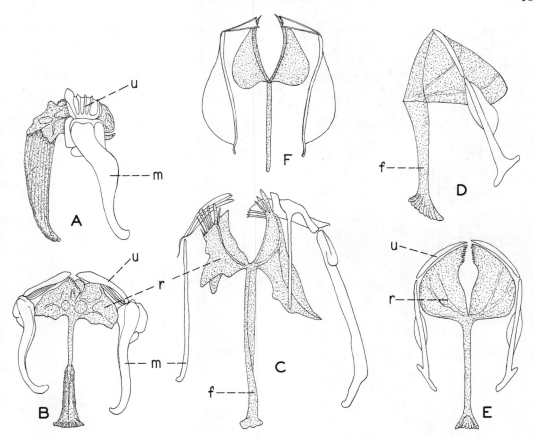

FIG. 109.–Typical virgate trophi. A, lateral view of trophi of *Notommata*; B, ventral view of trophi of *Notommata*; C, ventral view of trophi of *Trichocerca*; D, lateral view of trophi of *Cephalodella*; E, ventral view of trophi of *Cephalodella*; F, ventral view of trophi of *Synchaeta*. Inci are stippled. *f*, fulcrum; *m*, manubrium; *u*, uncus; *r*, ramus. (A and B modified from Harring and Myers, 1922; C modified from de Beauchamp, 1909; D and E modified from Harring and Myers, 1924.)

**Food, feeding.** In both sessile and free-swimming nonpredatory rotifers the coronal cilia are of primary importance in creating localized currents that guide and concentrate the loose periphyton, small plankton organisms, and detritus at the region of the mouth. Indeed, the great majority of species are omnivorous and ingest all organic particles of the appropriate size. Common examples are *Cephalodella, Filinia, Keratella, Lecane, Proales, Euchlanis, Epiphanes, Brachionus,* the Bdelloidea, and most sessile species.

Predatory species probably detect their prey by touch or by biochemical stim-uli. The following common genera feed on other rotifers and all kinds of small Metazoa, either in the plankton or on a substrate: *Asplanchna, Dicranophorus, Ploesoma, Synchaeta,* and *Trichocerca*. A careful investigation has shown that *Asplanchna* will usually ingest all plankton organisms larger than 15 microns.

Many notommatids, as well as a few genera in other families, feed mostly on the fluid contents of filamentous algal cells.

*Cupelopagis, Acyclus,* and *Atrochus* are all sessile and without coronal cilia. They have a large funnellike corona, or infundibulum, however, and when the prey

Fig. 110.–Structure of *Philodina,* diagrammatic. A, ventral view; B, dorsal view with most internal organs not shown; C, lateral view with reproductive system not shown; D, dorsal view with corona retracted; E, lateral view with corona retracted. (From Calaway, 1968, by permission.)

wander into this cavity, they are quickly enclosed and ingested.

A few free-living rotifers have highly specialized food habits. *Acyclus inquietus,* for example, lives among *Sinantherina* colonies and eats the motile young. *Dicranophorus isothes* is thought to subsist entirely on small Cladocera, and *D. thysanus* feeds on dead copepods, Cladocera, and oligochaetes.

**Digestive system.** Most Flosculariacea, Bdelloidea, and Ploima have similar digestive systems (Figs. 112A, B, D–F). The

mouth opens into a narrow, ciliated pharynx which leads to the cavity of the mastax. A variable number of small salivary glands are closely associated with the mastax. After the food has been macerated in the mastax, it passes into the short to long esophagus, which leaves the dorsal or posterodorsal surface of the mastax. The esophagus extends to the large, thick-walled, ciliated stomach, where most of the digestion and absorption are thought to occur. Usually there is a pair of oval or bean-shaped gastric glands on the anterior margin of the stomach. The intestine may

Fig. 111.–*Asplanchna* about to ingest a *Brachionus*. (From Halbach, 1971.)

be distinctly or indistinctly set off from the stomach. It is much smaller, sometimes very narrow, thin-walled, and often ciliated. The cloaca is short and seldom ciliated; it opens to the outside dorsally at the base of the foot.

The anterior end of the Collothecacea digestive tract is much different (Fig. 112C). The buccal area is situated at the base of the large funnellike infundibulum. Food taken into the mouth at the bottom of the infundibulum passes through a narrow esophageal tube, which hangs freely in a very large cavity, the proventriculus. The small mastax is situated at the bottom of the proventriculus.

Digestion is regularly extracellular, but in a few genera, such as *Chromogaster, Ascomorpha,* and a few others, it is clearly intracellular. No gastric glands are present in these rotifers, but the stomach has large gastric caeca that fill much of the pseudocoel.

Although many rotifers have true symbiotic zoochlorellae in the stomach wall, it is now believed that some instances previously reported as symbiosis are in reality ingested algal cells that persist for several days during their very slow intracellular digestion in the cells of the stomach wall.

In members of the bdelloid family Habrotrochidae there is no stomach cavity and the stomach is a continuous syncytial mass. As food leaves the esophagus it enters the stomach protoplasm in the form of food pellets, or food vacuoles, which circulate about and become digested.

**Respiration.** Most littoral and plankton rotifers normally have rather high oxygen requirements, but it is well known that certain genera are capable of withstanding anaerobic conditions for short periods and very low concentrations of dissolved oxygen (0.1 to 1.0 ppm, for example) for extended periods.

Limnetic plankton genera, such as *Asplanchna, Filinia, Polyarthra,* and *Keratella,* commonly occur in the oxygen-poor hypolimnion of lakes during midsummer and midwinter. Rotifers living at a depth of a few centimeters in the interstices of sandy beaches likewise are in a region of low oxygen. Trickling filters of sewage plants and oxygen-deficient bottom muds and hay infusions characteristically contain species of *Lecane, Monostyla, Lepadella,* and many bdelloids. Undoubtedly the creation of water currents by ciliary action ensures an adequate supply of oxygen to rotifers under most circumstances.

**Osmotic control, excretion.** Like most small fresh-water organisms, rotifers are readily permeable to water, but the internal osmotic pressure is kept constant by the action of the protonephridial system (Fig. 113). There are from four to 50 symmetrically arranged flame bulbs throughout much of the body. These are connected to a long, convoluted collecting tubule on each side, a part of the tubule being thin-walled, another part thick-walled and glandular. The two collecting tubules empty into an excretory bladder that has a very short duct leading to the ventral side of the cloaca. Excess water and probably a certain amount of metabolic waste are absorbed from the fluid of the pseudocoel by the flame bulbs and wall of the collecting

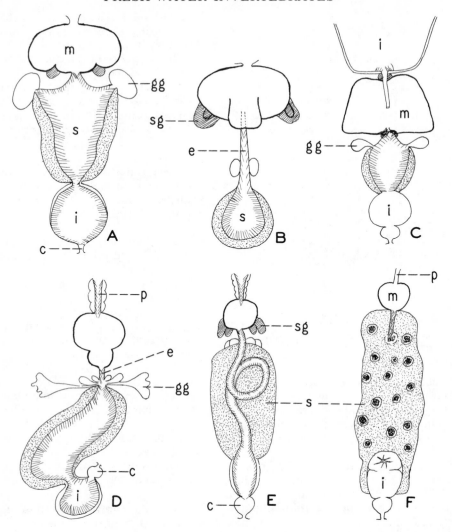

FIG. 112.–Diagrams of typical rotifer digestive systems. A, *Epiphanes*; B, *Asplanchna*; C, *Stephanoceros*; D, *Testudinella*; E, *Mniobia*; F, *Habrotrocha*. *c,* cloaca; *e*, esophagus; *gg*, gastric gland; *k*, intestine; *inf*, infundibulum; *m*, mastax; *p*, pharynx; *s*, stomach; *sg*, salivary gland. (A to E greatly modified from de Beauchamp, 1909; F modified from Burger.)

ducts and are excreted into the cavity of the ducts. The weak pressure produced by the beating of the tufts of cilia in the flame bulbs creates a slight current, which aids in carrying the excretory fluid through the tubules to the bladder. Here it is stored only temporarily, since the bladder normally contracts and empties its contents to the outside through the cloacal aperture (anus) one to six times per minute. In a few Ploima and in typical Bdelloidea there is no separate bladder; the collecting tubules merely empty into the thin-walled posterior part of the cloaca, which is modified into a bladder.

Old rotifers are usually distinguished by their darker pigmentation, most of which consists of accumulated excretory granules retained in the tissues.

**Muscles.** Both smooth and striated muscle fibers occur in rotifers, the latter

FIG. 113.–Protonephridial system of *Euchlanis*. (Modified from Stossberg.)

A few delicate visceral and cutaneo-visceral muscles help move and hold the internal organs in place.

**Nervous system.** The arrangement of the rotifer nervous system is nonlinear. The largest mass of nervous tissue is the sac-shaped cerebral ganglion, or "brain," lying on the dorsal surface of the mastax and esophagus and sometimes more or less obscured by the hypodermal syncytium of the corona. By means of fine paired nerve fibers it is connected with the mastax ganglion (sometimes absent) on the ventral surface of the mastax and with the caudal ganglion in the foot region. A few additional fine connecting fibers and associated nerve cell bodies innervate the sensory areas, muscles, and viscera (Fig. 115).

**Sense organs.** Perhaps the most conspicuous sensory area is the cervical eyespot. Characteristically it lies at the lower end of the brain or is imbedded in the brain and consists of a cup- or bowl-shaped mass of red pigment granules containing a refractile globule. Occasionally it is double. Many rotifers have two additional frontal eyespots located on the corona and widely separated. Eyespots are lacking in the adults of most sessile species, but they are present in the active immature stages.

A small, median, dorsal, setose antenna is usually present; rarely it is paired. In addition, the Monogononta have a pair of lateral antennae in the posterior third of the body and often a minute caudal antenna on the dorsal surface of the foot. Special tufts of cilia, membranelles, setae, and sensory protuberances or papillae are of common occurrence on the corona of many Monogononta.

For many years the retrocerebral organ of rotifers went almost unnoticed. It consists of two parts: a pigmented retrocerebral sac situated dorsal or posterior to the brain and opening on two coronal papillae by a paired duct, and a small paired subcerebral gland on either side of the sac with ducts alongside those of the sac (Fig. 116). Either of these two components may be lacking, but usually it is the latter. "Bacteroids" often occur in the retrocerebral sac and occasionally in the subcerebral

often associated with the rapid movement of long spines and special appendages, as in *Polyarthra* and *Hexarthra*.

Muscles are always arranged in small, bandlike groups of fibers, never in flat sheets. The circular muscle system consists of 4 to 15 bands attached just beneath the hypodermis. These bands are typically complete in the Monogononta, but in the Bdelloidea the bands usually have a ventral gap. One set of posterior longitudinal muscle bands are inserted in the foot or posterior part of the trunk. An anterior set of longitudinal bands have their insertions in the coronal region and their origins near the middle of the trunk. *Testudinella* has short dorsoventral muscles, no circular ones. *Cupelopagis* has a remarkably complex system of muscles.

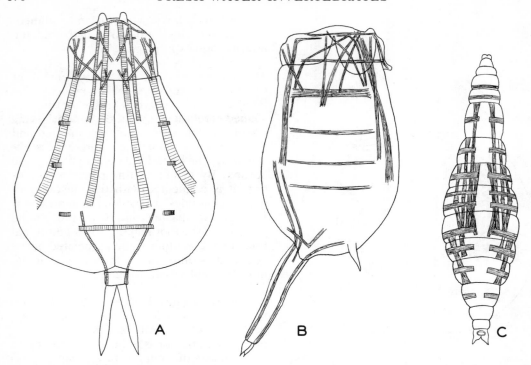

Fɪɢ. 114.–Rotifer musculature, semidiagrammatic. A, *Euchlanis,* dorsal; B, *Brachionus,* lateral; C, typical bdelloid, ventral. (A and B modified from Stossberg; C modified from Zelinka.)

glands. A variety of functions have been postulated for the retrocerebral organ, none of them conclusive. The most plausible suggestion is that it is a special sense organ.

**Reproduction.** The Monogononta have a simple, ventral, elongated, saclike reproductive system (Figs. 101, 102). Just within the distal end of the sac is a small ovary consisting of a clump of developing oocytes. The vitellarium is a syncytium with a few large nuclei; it occupies half or more of the capacity of the sac, and as eggs in the ovary mature one at a time and move downward slightly, the vitellarium contributes a large mass of yolk to the egg so that it becomes relatively large. On maturing, the egg passes down the short oviduct, into the cloaca, and out the cloacal aperture. The egg is quite elastic and is momentarily constricted and elongated as it passes through these small ducts.

The Bdelloidea reproductive system is similar to that of the Monogononta except that it is V- or Y-shaped and has two ovaries and two vitellaria (Fig. 117). The two oviducts are very delicate or rudimentary.

Males are unknown in the bdelloids, and reproduction is solely by parthenogenesis. In the Monogononta, however, males have been reported or described for most species whose biology has been carefully worked out, and it is thought that males occur regularly in this group, although there are a few genera in which males have never been seen, and perhaps in these groups reproduction is also exclusively parthenogenetic. It is commonly stated that males are rare, but this belief has arisen simply because the occurrence of males in most species is restricted to only one to three weeks during the year. If one collects during the brief time of male occurrence, they can be found in abundance.

Ploimate rotifers have two distinct types of females, which, with the exception of two or three species, are morphologi-

FIG. 115.–Diagram of rotifer nervous system. (Greatly modified from Remane, 1932.)

FIG. 116.–Diagram of a typical retrocerebral organ (dorsal view). Retrocerebral sac clear, subcerebral glands stippled, and brain with parallel diagonal lines.

impregnated, she deposits eggs that promptly hatch into males. Fundamentally, a resting egg is a potential male-producing egg that has been fertilized and that, on hatching, produces an amictic female.

One mictic female may produce both fertilized eggs and male eggs, but males and

cally indistinguishable. During the greater part of the year the females reproduce exclusively by parthenogenesis. These females are said to be amictic, and both their body cells and their amictic eggs all have the diploid number of chromosomes. Their eggs undergo only one, nonreductional division during maturation in the ovary. The second type of female is called mictic. Such females appear only at critical times of the year, especially when there are marked changes in the factors of the environment (see page 175). The eggs of a mictic female undergo the usual double meiotic division and are therefore haploid. In contrast to amictic females, the mictic females are capable of being fecundated by the males. If fecundation does occur, the fertilized eggs (also called winter eggs, or resting eggs) they deposit are thick-walled and highly resistant to adverse environmental conditions. If, however, a mictic female is not

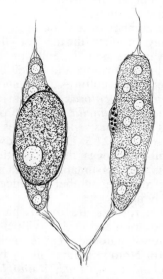

FIG. 117.–Diagram of typical bdelloid reproductive system, showing two vitellaria, two ovaries, two vestigial oviducts, and one developing egg.

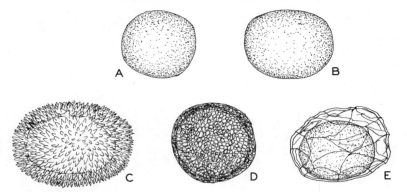

FIG. 118.–Rotifer eggs. A and B, amictic eggs; C to E, fertilized (resting) eggs.

females, or fertilized eggs and females, are never produced by the same parent. In fact mictic females are commonly seen carrying both male eggs and fertilized eggs at the posterior end of the body. Fecundation of an amictic female by a male has no effect. The two kinds of female are always physiologically distinct, not interchangeable. A typical sequence of generations is shown in Fig. 119. Under natural conditions, there are usually only one or two mictic generations per year, whereas there may be up to 20 or 40 amictic generations. The female that hatches from a resting egg is always amictic, but the following generation may be amictic or mictic.

The number of amictic eggs that a female may produce during her lifetime is highly variable and depends on both the species and environmental conditions. Specific laboratory cultures have shown that *Brachionus calyciflorus* averages only 3.6 eggs and *Testudinella elliptica* only 5.0, whereas *Epiphanes senta* averages 45.4 and *Proales sordida* 24.3. Little is known about the number of eggs that a mictic female produces, but presumably it does not differ greatly from the number produced by an amictic female.

Some rotifers are ovoviviparous, the eggs being retained in the oviduct or pseudocoel until hatched. These include two species of Notommatidae, many bdelloids, *Asplanchna, Conochilus, Rhinoglena,* and a few others. Their young are usually released through the cloaca, but many bdelloids are known to release the young

through ruptures in the body wall. In *Asplanchna* the male may fecundate its own mictic mother before it is released from the body of the mother.

Amictic, or summer, eggs are usually released from the body of the female and hatch within a day or two. The summer eggs of some plankton species contain large oil droplets, which facilitate suspension and flotation. In the following genera, however, the summer eggs are usually carried loosely attached to the posterior end of the body until hatching: *Polyarthra, Pompholyx, Keratella, Hexarthra, Brachionus,* and *Filina.*

Resting (or winter, or fertilized) eggs are heavy, thick-shelled, and often sculptured. On release from the female they usually sink to the bottom, but in the autumn they may sometimes be found floating on the surface or blown ashore. They are remarkably resistant to desiccation, high temperatures, low temperatures, and adverse chemical conditions for long periods. Many species winter over in the resting egg stage. Unlike summer eggs, the resting eggs require a latent period of several weeks to several months before they can hatch. Hatching is stimulated by changes in temperature, osmotic pressure, water chemistry, and aeration.

A curious fourth type of rotifer egg has recently been reported from cultures of *Keratella quadrata* and *K. hiemalis.* It is an unfertilized "pseudosexual resting egg" produced by parthenogenesis in the absence of males. The morphology and de-

FIG. 119.–Diagrammatic sequence of generations in a typical ploimate rotifer.

velopment are similar to those of ordinary resting eggs.

**Biology of males.** With few exceptions, male rotifers are minute, degenerate, and short-lived. Commonly they are about a third as long as the female. The digestive tract is absent or vestigial, although a few species have a mastax and stomach. Mouth and anus are never present. The males have no well-developed lorica or spines, and the corona is always anterior and well supplied with cilia. They are very rapid swimmers, never sessile.

The simple reproductive system occupies most of the pseudocoel. The testis is pear-shaped or globular and is held in place by a small strand supposed to be a remnant of the digestive tract. The vas deferens is short to long and sometimes has two or four associated prostate glands. Some species have no true penis, the vas deferens being

FIG. 120.–Typical male rotifers, semidiagrammatic and with musculature omitted (except in D). A, dorsal view of *Notommata*; B, dorsal view of *Filinia*; C, lateral view of *Brachionus*; D, *Asplanchna*; E, *Lecane*. (A to C greatly modified from Wesenberg-Lund, 1923; D from Sudzuki, 1956; E from Sudzuki, 1959.)

everted through a small ciliated orifice during copulation. Other species have a well-developed penis that is everted continually; sometimes it is larger than the foot. In a few males the whole posterior end of the body is tubelike and specialized for copulation.

Males of plankton species are the most strongly reduced. Some are not much more than a sperm sac surrounded by protoplasm and a cuticle, and having an anterior tuft of cilia.

Males are ready for copulation within an hour after hatching. They are extremely active, especially in the presence of females, and swim about erratically until they come in contact with one. Copulation and sperm transfer occur either through the cloacal aperture of the female or through the body wall (*Asplanchna*), and the male dies immediately thereafter. If a female is not located, the male lives for only two or three days; *Asplanchna* males, however, are known to live for as long as four to seven days.

Males have been reported for only

about 10 percent of the species of Mono-gononta. Few have been carefully studied and figured. Males have been reported for only three or four species in each of the large genera *Lecane* and *Monostyla,* and there are only three or four records for the family Trichocercidae.

In the so-called perennial species of rotifers, males usually appear in spring and autumn; in "summer" species they appear in autumn; and in "winter" species they ordinarily occur in spring.

**Development and longevity.** The rotifer zygote undergoes unequal and regular cleavage, and the gastrula consists of an outer layer of cells (ectoderm) enclosing an inner cell mass (mesoderm and endoderm). Cell division and differentiation proceed rapidly, with each organ developing from a definite cell complex. When all organs have received their full complement of cells, cell division ceases.

Most plankton and littoral species grow rapidly during the several hours after hatching, but thereafter very slowly if at all. Many sessile species, however, grow throughout life, chiefly as a result of the elongation of the posterior end. Although rotifers have no ecdyses, the mature adult may be 3 to 10 times as large as the newly hatched young.

Although there may be considerable size variations among the individuals of a single species, it has been found, for the several species carefully studied, that there is an approximately constant number of cells in all adults of the same species. In *Epiphanes senta,* for example, there are about 959 nuclei. Each organ in the great majority of specimens has the same number of nuclei, though a few tissues, especially the vitellarium, show slight variations in the number of nuclei.

Length of life, from hatching until death, is highly variable. *Epiphanes senta* averages about 8 days, *Lecane inermis* 7.4 days, *Brachionus calyciflorus* 6 days, and *Proales decipiens* only 5.5 days. At the other extreme, *Euchlanis incisa* averages 21 days, *Keratella quadrata* 22 days, *Cupelopagis vorax* 6 weeks, and many bdelloids are active for 3 to 6 weeks.

As might be expected, the ability to regenerate lost or damaged organs is poorly developed. Amputation of the coronal lobes of *Stephanoceros* results in regeneration only in immature specimens; regeneration is lacking or very slow in full-grown individuals.

**Syngamic reproduction.** Since about 1904 there has been a vigorous and many-sided controversy over the relative significance of physiological, ecological, and genetic factors in the production of mictic females and males, and bisexual reproduction. Scores of papers dealing with a wide variety of field observations and controlled laboratory experiments have appeared. Reduced to simplest terms, the chief problem may be stated as follows: most ploimate rotifers reproduce by a series of partheno-genetic generations throughout most of the year; yet suddenly mictic females and males may appear in the population, and resting eggs are produced, usually in the autumn, but sometimes in the spring, or both. How may this phenomenon be explained? What factors are responsible for male production?

Most of the important observations and experimental work centering around this involved problem have stemmed from the laboratories of Shull, Whitney, Tauson, Wesenberg-Lund, and (recently) Gilbert. Their many papers should be consulted for a complete account. For our purposes, however, it is sufficient to summarize the present status of the matter and to mention some of the more significant items relating to sexual periodicity that have appeared as side issues in these studies.

To begin, it is obvious that species differ considerably from one another with respect to the nature and degree of ecological factors that instigate their bisexual periods. Furthermore, some species behave differently from one body of water to another and from one year to another. In one lake, for example, a species may regularly produce males in the autumn; in another lake it may have both spring and autumn bisexual periods; in a third lake the occurrence of bisexual periods may be sporadic. *Polyarthra,* for example, sometimes produces males at almost any time of the year, in both ponds and lakes.

In general, it has been shown that small populations of rotifers usually remain parthenogenetic, and that bisexuality appears during population increases. External factors, rather than genetic makeup, control sexual periodicity, but these factors are nonspecific. Careful experimental work indicates that the chief factors responsible for the appearance of males in a population are (1) a change in the type of food (green to nongreen, and vice versa), (2) an increase in food supply, and (3) a decrease in food supply. Other factors that have been shown to be of importance in instigating male production are crowding, addition of fresh culture medium, addition of distilled water, making the culture medium more alkaline, changing the temperature (rarely), and starving (rarely). Sometimes, however, even if measurable conditions remain unaltered, males unaccountably appear in a population.

The solution of the problem must, of course, be sought in a study of the amictic female, for whether she produces eggs that will hatch into more amictic females or eggs that will hatch into mictic females is a matter determined by her physiology. The decision as to which type of egg she will deposit is made in the three-hour period before she releases the egg from her oviduct. Eggs hatching into mictic females are slightly smaller than eggs hatching into amictic females, and several investigators contend that in this difference lies the crux of the whole problem. The production of a large or small egg might very well depend on the available amount of yolk in the ovary, which in turn, might indirectly depend on environmental conditions. It is known, for example, that the appearance of mictic females is in part brought on by a change in the photoperiod, by greater population densities, and by minute quantities of vitamin C in the water.

This matter is further complicated by the fact that some species produce polymorphic resting eggs that may show a considerable range of size, shell sculpture, and color.

*Epiphanes senta* invariably has a sexual period under natural conditions, but experimentally this species has been carried through more than 500 successive parthenogenetic generations; such old cultures are characterized by a considerably lowered vigor and reproductive rate. *Proales decipiens,* however, has been carried through more than 250 successive parthenogenetic generations with no changes in vigor or fecundity, and it is interesting to note that the male is unknown in this species. Such facts appear to constitute some evidence that periodic bisexuality may have a rejuvenating effect on rotifer populations through the associated meiotic and fertilization processes.

**Periodicity.** Like so many other plankton and littoral organisms, rotifers exhibit periodic and sometimes quite striking cycles of abundance during the year, a fact familiar to anyone who has done seasonal plankton work. Various investigators have designated certain species as monocyclic, dicyclic, polycyclic, or acyclic and perennial, according to whether their annual population curves have one, two, several, or no pronounced peaks. *Kellicottia longispina* and *Conochilus unicornis* are usually considered monocyclic, although they are both perennial in certain lakes. *Euchlanis dilatata* commonly has an autumn maximum. *Brachionus angularis* and *Keratella cochlearis* are often considered dicyclic, with spring and autumn maxima, but are sometimes perennial. Other species are more variable. *Polyarthra* is dicyclic (summer and autumn), polycyclic, or perennial. *Keratella quadrata* may be most abundant in spring, summer, or autumn, or it may be perennial. *Asplanchna priodonta* is variously considered monocyclic, dicyclic, or perennial.

There has been an unfortunate tendency on the part of some investigators to generalize on the periodicity of a species on the basis of their observations of a few large lakes during only one or two years. As emphasized by Pennak (1949), however, the cycles of abundance for plankton species are highly variable within each species, variable from year to year within a single lake, and especially variable from one small lake to another.

**Variation, cyclomorphosis.** Like the cladocerans, many species of plankton rotifers exhibit a remarkable range of variation in size and lorica development from one habitat to another. The most striking examples of these local "races" occur in *Keratella* and *Brachionus*. In *Brachionus calyciflorus*, for instance, all degrees of development in the four posterior spines have been reported, ranging from long and well developed to very short or absent (Figs. 128B–D). At least in part, the production of spines in this species is induced by starvation, low temperatures, and substance(s) elaborated into the water by the predatory *Asplanchna*. Comparable variations in posterior spine development occur in *B. quadridentata* (Fig. 128H), *B. caudatus* (Fig. 128F), and *Platyias patulus*; to some extent the anterior spines are also variable. Until about 1915 these variations were often described as distinct species, and more recently taxonomists have had to contend with the resultant confusing synonymy. Now, however, they are recognized as forms or races comprising relatively few species.

Variations in the size of races from different localities are also striking. Ahlstrom (1940) gives the average width of the lorica of *Brachionus calyciflorus* for 21 localities all over the world, and the variation is 124 to 300 microns. This is a remarkable range of average size for a species having determinate cell division.

Superimposed on the confusion of varieties in some loricate plankton species is an annual cyclomorphic series, that is, a sequence of generations in the same strain marked by progressive modifications in morphology through a long parthenogenetic series. In *Keratella cochlearis* (Figs. 124A–D), for example, the lorica has a long posterior spine during the cold months followed by a gradual reduction in length until July and August when there is a very short spine or no spine. At this point syngamic reproduction often occurs, followed by a gradual reversal in spine length during the remainder of the year. Such well-defined cycles usually occur in small lakes that become quite warm in summer. In Lake Michigan there is no cycle, and in other bodies of water only a partial cycle. Sometimes the two extreme lorica forms have no transitional forms.

In *Keratella quadrata* (Figs. 124H–L) a form with long posterior spines initiates

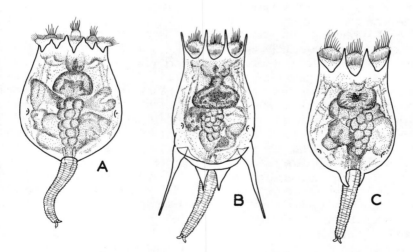

Fig. 121.–A, *Brachionus rubens*; B, *B. calyciflorus* with large posterolateral spines; C, *B. calyciflorus* without posterolateral spines. (From Halbach, 1971.)

the cycle. The spines are progressively reduced in successive generations until a form with very short spines or no spines is dominant. Syngamic reproduction may then occur, and the cycle starts all over again with a long-spined form. But often this species is long-spined the year round even in small ponds.

From these examples, and judging from the occurrence of two or three widely differing varieties in the same population, it is obvious that cyclomorphosis is a variable phenomenon within a single species. Certainly it cannot be ascribed to an inherent mechanism or simply to changes in environmental factors, but rather to a complicated interaction between organism and environment. In fact, the problems of cyclomorphosis, population fluctuations, local races, and bisexual reproduction all seem to be inextricably bound up with each other and with a multitude of ecological factors. Although this complex is a most difficult one, it is probably capable of solution by means of careful field and laboratory observation and experimentation. Gilbert (1973), for example, has shown that the lateral humps of male and female *Asplanchna sieboldi* protect them from cannibalism.

**General ecology.** As emphasized earlier, rotifers occur in an extreme variety of habitats. They are poorly represented only in hot and cold springs, rushing streams, brackish waters, and extremely saline waters. Some common species are usually present in the same pond year after year, but sometimes unaccountably disappear for one or more years, then suddenly reappear. Approximately 75 percent of the known species occur in the littoral areas of lakes and ponds, but only about 100 species are limnetic or planktonic enough in their habits to be completely emancipated from a substrate. The Bdelloidea are most characteristic of mosses and sphagnum. These habitats may be submerged, emergent, or terrestrial and only occasionally wet. Only a few species of the following genera of bdelloids regularly occur in the littoral zone: *Rotaria, Embata, Philodina,* and *Dissotrocha;* two or three other genera are uncommon in littoral waters. On the other hand, only a few ploimate species occur commonly in moss and only if it is kept wet.

A few free-living species are highly specific in their habitat preferences. *Acyclus inquietus* is invariably found among colonies of *Sinantherina. Collotheca algicola* appears to be restricted to clusters of *Gloeotrichia* filaments, and one or two other sessile species are also common on this alga. *Brachionus plicatilis* and *B. pterodinoides* are confined to extremely alkaline ponds and lakes, especially in the western states. *Proales rheinardti* is unusual in that it occurs in mountain springs and among *Fucus* in marine bays and inlets! Only two genera, *Seison* and *Zelinkiella,* are known to be restricted to marine habitats.

Brackish waters contain many euryokous fresh-water species, as well as some species that are restricted to this habitat. The genus *Synchaeta* is remarkable for its many brackish and estuarine species.

Although the Rotatoria are primarily free-living organisms, a few species have become specialized for a parasitic existence. *Notommata trypeta* is parasitic in colonies of the alga *Gomphosphaeria. Proales parasitica* is a common parasite inside *Volvox* colonies. A few species of *Albertia* are ecto- and endoparasites of aquatic oligochaetes. *Drilophaga judayi* has been found only in the free-living state, but a second species in this genus is parasitic on *Lumbriculus,* and a third on *Erpobdella.*

Aside from such true parasites, many free-living rotifers live as commensals or epizoics on a wide variety of fresh-water invertebrates, especially crustaceans and insects. Common examples include certain species of Bdelloidea, *Pleurotrocha, Lepadella,* and *Testudinella.*

The limnologist often collects plankton species that have much of the pseudocoel filled with peculiar sausage-shaped bodies. These are parasitic fungus growths that occasionally become epidemic.

Judging from the large plankton literature, it is obvious that most plankton communities average between 40 and 500 rotifers per liter, with populations in excess of 1000 per liter being unusual. The waters of mountain lakes and large oligotrophic lakes, however, sometimes contain less than 20 rotifers per liter, especially during the cold months. The most dense plankton rotifer population ever recorded from unpolluted waters is 5800 specimens per liter, cited by Pennak (1949).

Within ordinary limits, the density of natural rotifer populations appears to be governed by the amount of available food.

The maximum density of rotifer populations appears to be closely correlated with the relative amount of available substrate and exposed surfaces. Using 5800 per liter as a maximum for plankton, the corresponding maximum for sessile species inhabiting finely divided littoral plants is about 25,000 per liter (Edmondson, 1946). Furthermore, rotifers inhabiting the wet interstices of sandy beaches are reported to attain a maximum density of 1.155 million individuals per liter of damp sand (Pennak, 1940). The greater the surface, therefore, the greater the population. Presumably this phenomenon is associated with more food, more attachment space, more nooks for protection, and reduced predation loss.

Sandy beaches as a habitat for rotifers have only recently been investigated. Below the water's edge the sand contains a negligible rotifer population, but the top 3 or 4 cm of sand extending from the water's edge as far as 3 or 4 m landward is a favorable habitat. Although many of the sandy beach rotifers occur regularly in the littoral, about 40 psammobiotic species are known to be restricted to the sand habitat, especially species of *Trichocerca, Encentrum, Monostyla, Lecane,* and *Wierzejskiella.*

In contrast to littoral forms, the limnetic, or open-water, plankton genera occur over a wide depth range, even as deep as 100 or 200 m. *Asplanchna, Filinia, Polyarthra,* and *Keratella* are all good examples.

If open-water limnetic plankton samples from many lakes are analyzed statistically, the following rotifers will be found to be most abundant and generally distributed: *Keratella cochlearis, K. quadrata, Kellicottia longispina, Filinia longiseta,*

*Asplanchna* spp., and *Conochilus unicornis. Brachionus* spp., *Synchaeta* spp., and *Conochiloides* spp. will be next most common. As shown by Halbach (1973), there are positive association coefficients involved between most of these species cooccurrences.

Those pond and lake plankters having eyespots exhibit, in varying degrees, a 24-hour cycle of vertical movements in accordance with the variations in subsurface illumination. Beginning late in the afternoon a slow drift upward begins, and maximum abundance occurs near the surface in the early morning. Around dawn a reverse drift downward begins, until maximum concentrations in the deep waters are attained about noon. Such movements are also of general occurrence among copepods and cladocerans, but in rotifers they are of course much less pronounced, average amplitudes of only 1 to 3 m being common and amplitudes as high as 8 or 10 m being very unusual.

**Ecology of sessile rotifers.** The work of Edmondson (1944, 1945) has contributed much information to the ecology of sessile rotifers (Flosculariidae and Collothecidae). For the most part, sessile species are never present in quantities below a temperature of 15°, the largest populations always being present at temperatures above 20°. They are usually most plentiful in late spring, especially in small bays and littoral nooks in ponds and lakes. Although any substrate may be used, sessile species are by far the most abundant on submerged aquatic vegetation. *Utricularia vulgaris* var. *americana* has the most extensive, dense, and varied rotifer fauna of all species. Other favored plants are *Myriophyllum,* sphagnum, potamogetons, *Anacharis,* and *Vallisneria.*

Some species occur on a wide variety of plants, but others exhibit striking preferences. Thus *Collotheca gracilipes* is almost invariably on *Utricularia vulgaris americana, Ptygura melicerta* inhabits *Gloeotrichia* and *Coleochaete,* whereas *Collotheca campanulata* and *Ptygura barbata* are usually found on epiphytic algae. *Cupelopagis vorax,* however, is restricted to broad, flat leaf surfaces. Edmondson concludes that species distribution is determined mostly by water chemistry and available plant substrates.

**Hydrogen-ion effect.** Harring and Myers (1928) first pointed out that there are some striking correlations between the pH of a body of water and the composition of its ploimate rotifer fauna. In general, alkaline waters (above pH 7.0) contain relatively few species but large numbers of individuals, whereas acid waters (below pH 7.0) contain large numbers of species and few individuals. In the hard-water lakes around Madison, Wisconsin, Myers identified 100 species in a week of collecting, but he found the same number of species in only one hour of collecting in a small acid lake in northern Wisconsin. In the alkaline Yahara basin of southern Wisconsin he collected 138 species, but in the acid waters of Mount Desert Island in Maine he collected 497 species (Myers, 1931–1934).

As the result of his extensive field collecting, Myers distinguished three ecological groups of species with reference to their occurrence in waters of various hydrogen-ion concentrations. (1) Alkaline water species are those that are confined to waters having pH readings above 7.0. *Asplanchna, Asplanchnopus, Mytilina, Brachionus, Filinia, Lacinularia, Sinantherina, Eosphora,* and *Notholca* are all alkaline genera, but there are also species in other genera that are restricted to alkaline waters. (2) Transcursion species are those that occur in both alkaline and acid waters. By far the large majority of rotifers belong in this category. (3) Acid water species are those that are confined to lakes, ponds, and bogs having an acid reaction. There are no genera restricted to acid waters, only certain species in genera that also have transcursion and alkaline representatives. The following genera contain numerous acid water species: *Cephalodella, Lepadella, Lecane, Monostyla, Trichocera,* and *Dicranophorus.*

Most genera contain representative species in each of these three groups, but a specialist can tell at a glance whether a particular collection came from an acid or alkaline body of water. Even though an acid lake and an alkaline lake may be separated by a ridge of land only 50 m wide, the rotifer faunas are completely different.

In a study of many areas in Wisconsin and New England, Edmondson (1944) lists 8 alkaline, 36 transcursion, and 12 acid species of sessile rotifers. In an investigation of many ponds and lakes (mostly acid) of the Pocono Plateau in Pennsylvania, Myers (1940) found 4 alkaline species, 313 transcursion, and 75 acid water species. In a study of the acid waters of the Adirondacks, Myers (1937) found 42 acid water species and 171 transcursion species. On the other hand, he found (1936) a total of only 106 alkaline and transcursion species in the alkaline waters of southern California, even though he collected almost daily for three months.

To be sure, pH 7.0 is by no means a sharp dividing line between acid or alkaline water species; it is only an approximation. Some acid species, for example, are found in waters giving readings as high as pH 7.1 or 7.2, and alkaline species likewise occur as low as pH 6.9 or 6.8. It is not meant to imply that the hydrogen-ion concentration itself is a governing factor in ecological distribution, since pH is a reflection of a whole complex of physical and chemical variables, and actually the limiting factor may be one or more of these ecological variables. Total dissolved salts, calcium, and bicarbonate, for example, have been suggested as being fundamentally important. Acid water rotifers can easily be transferred to alkaline waters where they will live, and vice versa, but their parthenogenetic eggs will not hatch in the unfavorable environment.

The preceding remarks relating to pH refer only to ploimate rotifers; they do not apply to the Bdelloidea, which are apparently all transcursional and capable of tolerating a relatively wide range of ecological conditions.

**Desiccation.** Even certain modern textbooks include the statement or inference that all rotifers can be dried to form a resistant cyst, which when returned to water will excyst and become active again. In the first place, true desiccation is re-

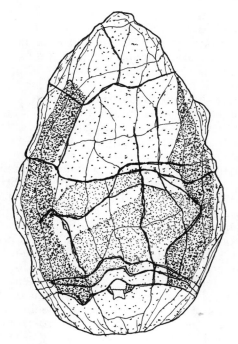

Fig. 122.–Desiccated *Philodina*. (Modified from Hickernell.)

and interstices where drying occurs more gradually and where there is a protective effect, such as in debris, sand, or among moss or sphagnum. When drying begins, the bdelloid draws both ends of the body into the central portion of the trunk and then puckers the two ends as though they were drawn up by purse strings (Fig. 122). This globular body mass then becomes wrinkled and loses much water. The pseudocoel is almost nonexistent, and the volume of the animal is only one-third or one-fourth of its normal size.

A remarkable rearrangement of chromatin occurs during desiccation. Instead of remaining in its usual large karyosome mass in the center of the cell, it fragments, becomes highly dispersed, and adheres to the inner surface of the cell membrane. Presumably this adjustment facilitates suspended animation and the utilization of oxygen at a greatly retarded rate.

Desiccated rotifers may be kept dry as dust for months or even years. There is one record of specimens being revived from moss kept dry for 27 years. When the dried rotifers are placed in water, they quickly absorb water and become extended and normally active. Sometimes complete recovery occurs in only 10 minutes, but under other circumstances it may take a whole day.

Desiccation always produces some mortality, even under favorable conditions, and only a fraction of a group of desiccated rotifers are viable and can be revived. Rapid drying is injurious, and, in general, the longer the interval of desiccation, the lower will be the percentage of recovery. Nevertheless, even under natural conditions, bdelloids are able to survive several alternating periods of activity and desiccation.

stricted to the majority of Bdelloidea and does not occur at all in the much larger ploimate group. Second, in the great majority of bdelloids desiccation involves drying and shrinking of the body contents and cuticle without the formation of a true cyst. Only a few bdelloids are known to form true secreted cysts; when subjected to drying, these species secrete a surrounding gelatinous material that quickly hardens and becomes resistant.

Bdelloids typically inhabit moss on old walls, bark, or ground; they are much more abundant on emergent sphagnum than on submerged sphagnum. Such habitats are wet only intermittently from rains, wave action, or high water, and the process of desiccation allows the rotifer to tide over the frequent unfavorable periods of dryness. Very few truly aquatic bdelloids are able to undergo desiccation.

Bdelloids that are isolated in a little water on a smooth, bare surface are unable to undergo desiccation and they die. They must be associated with irregular surfaces

**Dispersal, geographic distribution.** Overland transport of resting eggs or desiccated bdelloids is easily effected by winds and animals, and all rotifers are potentially cosmopolitan. By "cosmopolitan" we mean that similar habitats all over the world have similar rotifer faunas, and whether a given species is present in a particular body of water depends not on geographic location, but on the precise complex of ecological conditions prevailing there. As Jennings (1900) has said, "The problem of the distribution of the Rotifera is, then, a problem of the conditions of existence, not a problem of the means of distribution." The same species of rotifers are found in limnetic areas, in moss, in sandy beaches, in sphagnum bogs, in comparable farm ponds, and so on, the world over. Even the "rare" species are being reported from localities everywhere that appropriate habitats prevail and where the collector is diligent.

A very few species appear to be generally distributed in restricted areas. *Pseudoploesoma formosum* and *Trichocerca platessa,* for example, are common in the acid waters of the northeastern states but have never been collected anywhere else in the world. Such instances are difficult to explain on the basis of our present knowledge of rotifer ecology.

**Collecting.** Plankton species are easily taken with a townet, thrownet, or a fine dipnet with a vial or centrifuge tube fastened to the lower open end.

Vegetated littoral areas are much richer collecting grounds, especially for browsing species, but nets are of little use there. Instead, masses of the plant material should be carefully placed in large screw-top jars along with water from the same habitat. The jars should be no more than half filled with plant material. When the jars are brought to the laboratory, they should be uncapped and placed in a north window. As the oxygen slowly decreases the rotifers will gather at the top of the water and usually toward the lighted side, where they may be pipetted out. Sessile species may be found with the dissecting binoculars on bits of plants. Such temporary culture jars will keep well for a week or more if the lowermost third of the water is changed daily.

Bdelloids may be brought to the laboratory in handfuls of wet or dry moss, which may be stored dry. When the material is to be studied it should be soaked for a few hours in water, then washed vigorously several times. The wash water and sediment should be kept in covered watch glasses or petri dishes for weeks or months and examined periodically under the microscope. Some bdelloids appear promptly, others not for two or three weeks.

**Culturing.** Many rotifer culture methods are suggested in the literature. Some methods are better for certain species than others, and if an investigator wishes to culture a previously uncultured species, he should try a variety of methods and modifications in order to get best results. Species of *Lecane* have been raised in 0.1 percent malted milk in pond water, the solution being changed daily. The same genus has been cultured in rye extract prepared by grinding 20 grains of rye in a mortar and boiling in 100 ml of water for 20 minutes; the rotifers should be kept in drops of this solution and changed daily. Beef cube extract prepared by boiling one cube in 400 ml of tap water is sometimes good. Dried breakfast oats may be used by boiling 8 to 30 flakes for three minutes in 100 ml of water, filtering, and using after 24 hours. *Epiphanes* and certain other pond genera may be cultured in hay infusions that have been inoculated with a suitable protozoan or algal food organism. "Stable tea" is prepared by boiling 800 ml of horse manure in 1000 ml of water for one hour; cool, strain, dilute with two parts boiled rain water, inoculate with a food organism, and age a week or 10 days before inoculating with the rotifer. Bdelloids may be cultured easily in 0.1 percent nonfat dried milk in tap or pond water. Sessile species are extremely difficult to culture.

Aloia and Moretti (1973) describe a pure culture sequence of *Aerobacter-Paramecium-Asplanchna.*

The most important precaution to be observed in culturing rotifers is to change the culture solution frequently and prevent excessive bacterial activity.

Several species, especially *Lecane,* have been successfully cultured in sterile media containing various mixtures of liver extract, vitamins, salts, and peptones.

**Preparing, preserving.** Since the identification of loricate rotifers depends largely on the details of the lorica, they are conveniently killed and fixed by placing directly in 10 percent formalin. This causes the soft parts of the animal to contract strongly, leaving the lorica well exposed for easy study.

The illoricate, free-swimming Ploima, however, require a much different technique. The identification of these forms depends largely on anatomical details that can be studied only in an uncontracted, natural state. As a consequence, these rotifers must be narcotized before killing and fixing. The following method is adapted from Myers (1942) and should be performed under dissecting binoculars. With a fine pipette place the rotifers in about 3 ml of water in a concave watch glass. If the specimens are from acid waters, add three or four drops of 1 percent neosynephrin hydrochloride; repeat at five-minute intervals until the rotifers are all lying on the bottom and ciliary action has about stopped. Kill and fix by adding three drops of 0.5 or 1.0 percent osmic acid from a dropping bottle and quickly stirring into the water. Pour the contents of the watch glass into a small vial, and after five minutes decant or pipette off most of the fluid; then add water. Repeat the decantation and addition of wash water three times at 15-minute intervals.

If the rotifers are from alkaline waters, a 5 percent solution of novocain or cocaine hydrochlorate in 50 percent methyl alcohol gives better results than the neosynephrin. Usually, however, these narcotics are very difficult to obtain, even for such scientific purposes, and other more readily available substitutes must be used. Chloretone and 2 percent benzamine lactate are useful, and the writer has had considerable success with 2 percent butyn and 2 percent hydroxylamine hydrochloride.

The osmic acid solution will last much longer without deteriorating if it is dissolved in 1 percent chloroplatinic acid (platinic chloride) and kept in a dropping bottle that is painted black. If rotifers are exposed to osmic acid too long, they will blacken but they can be bleached in weak potassium hydroxide.

Many illoricate species, especially No-

tommatidae and bdelloids, are so delicate and sensitive that narcotization is not successful, and in such cases it is advisable to flood the specimens with an equivalent amount of *boiling* water in a watch glass; this treatment kills a large fraction of the animals in a well-expanded and lifelike condition. Formalin or other fixative should then be added.

Hanley (1949) strongly recommends the following procedure. Narcotize by adding several drops of 2 percent benzamine hydrochloride to a small amount of water containing the rotifers, the time being variable from one species to another. Kill in 10 percent formalin. Wash at least six times in 5 percent formalin to remove all the benzamine hydrochloride, which might later crystallize out.

After killing and fixing, all rotifers can be stored in 2 to 5 percent formalin containing 2 percent glycerin. Many workers add a little eosin as this colors the rotifers and makes them easier to study and handle.

Preserved specimens can be studied and kept for several days in a shallow, hollow-ground slide, provided the cover slip is sealed with petroleum jelly.

Permanent mounts are best made with glycerin or glycerin jelly. In either case the rotifers should be slowly run up to pure glycerin. This is done by placing the perserved specimens in 5 percent glycerin in a depression embryology slide or concave watch glass and leaving it loosely covered for about a week so that all the water evaporates. In this way the specimens are penetrated slowly and partially cleared, and they retain their turgidity and natural shape.

Individual specimens in glycerin should never be picked up with a pipette since they usually stick to the inner surface of the glass and are easily lost. Instead, they may be readily picked out of glycerin under the dissecting binoculars with an Irwim loop or a flat toothbrush bristle glued to the tip of a matchstick. The bristle is simply slid under the specimen and quickly lifted straight upward and out of the glycerin; usually the specimen adheres to the tip of the bristle in a droplet of glycerin. Specimens handled in this way may be conveniently set aside while other preparations are being made. Glycerin jelly slides are made by placing a drop of melted jelly on a slide, touching the drop with the tip of the bristle holding the rotifer, and quickly orienting the specimen under the binoculars before putting on the round cover slip. The glycerin jelly should be allowed to set for several hours. Then the excess may be trimmed from the edge of the cover slip and several coats of Murrayite applied to its edge with a camel's hair brush and turntable at 24-hour intervals.

Fluid glycerin mounts are much more difficult to prepare but are superior for some purposes. Detailed directions for one method are given in Harring and Myers (1928). An alternative method is as follows. Three or four bits of *passe partout* or gummed paper are fixed symmetrically to a 1 × 3 slide and spaced about 10 or 12 mm apart to act as supports for the cover slip and thus prevent crushing of the specimen. The rotifer is then placed in a droplet of glycerin in the center of the slide and midway between the supports. The cover slip is next lowered into place very carefully, and by touching a camel's hair brush of Murrayite to the edge of the cover slip, capillarity will draw the Murrayite between the cover slip and slide and it will surround the glycerin droplet and completely fill the capillary space. Such slides should be set aside to dry for several hours and then given several rings of Murrayite at 24-hour intervals for greater permanence.

**Trophi mounting.** Since genus and species identifications are often dependent on the anatomical details of the trophi, it is sometimes essential that permanent or semipermanent mounts of these jaws be made. The following method, requiring some skill and practice and much patience, is modified from Myers (1937). Place a drop of 1:10 Clorox, or similar caustic alkali, just inside the concavity of a shallow concavity slide, and place a similar drop just outside the concavity. Then place a 22 mm square cover slip on the outside drop and push it over the concavity until it is almost in contact with the inside drop. Next place the rotifer in the inner drop by means of a bris-

tle. If the cover slip is pushed slowly over the inner drop, the rotifer will be drawn under. And by working the cover slip over the concavity by short pushes, and adding small quantities of solution after each advance, the rotifer will be forced into the acute angle formed by the edge of the concavity and the under surface of the cover slip. The edges of the cover slip should then be carefully dried and painted with petroleum jelly or Murrayite. The position of the rotifer should be noted, and in about a half hour it will all have dissolved except the trophi. Such trophi slides will last for several to many months, and if a petroleum jelly seal is used, the trophi may be oriented by tapping or moving the cover slip slightly.

**Taxonomy.** Rotifer taxonomy owes much to Harring's painstaking *Synopsis of the Rotatoria,* which appeared in 1913, bringing order out of chaotic nomenclature. Nevertheless, with the exception of specialists, many aquatic biologists still clung to old, ambiguous, and confused nomenclature. Even to this day, much outdated terminology still persists.

The arrangement of genera and families used here is a modification of the plan given by Remane in *Das Tierreich* (1929–1933). It is based primarily on the fundamental structure and modifications of the mastax. The outline presented below includes the genera given in the key that follows.

Class Digononta
  Order Seisonidea
  Order Bdelloidea (ramate mastax)
    Philodinidae
      *Dissotrocha, Embata, Macrotrachela, Mniobia, Philodina, Pleuretra, Rotaria*
    Habrotrochidae
      *Ceratotrocha, Habrotrocha, Scepanotrocha*
    Philodinavidae
      *Philodinavus*
    Adinetidae
      *Adineta, Bradyscela*

Class Monogononta
 Order Flosculariacea (malleoramate mastax)
  Flosculariidae
   *Beauchampia, Floscularia, Lacinularia, Limnias, Octotrocha, Pseudoecistes, Ptygura, Sinantherina*
  Conochilidae
   *Conochilus, Conochiloides*
  Hexarthridae
   *Hexarthra*
  Testudinellidae
   *Filinia, Pompholyx, Testudinella, Tetramastix, Trochosphaera*
 Order Collothecacea (uncinate mastax)
  Collothecidae
   *Acyclus, Atrochus, Collotheca, Cupelopagis, Stephanoceros*
 Order Ploima
  Notommatidae
   Notommatinae (virgate or virgate-forcipate mastax)
    *Cephalodella, Dorria, Drilophaga, Enteroplea, Eosphora, Itura, Monommata, Notommata, Pleurotrocha, Pseudoploesoma, Resticula, Rousseletia, Scaridium, Sphyrias, Taphrocampa*
   Proalinae (modified malleate mastax)
    *Bryceella, Proales, Proalinopsis*
   Tetrasiphoninae (modified virgate mastax)
    *Tetrasiphon*
   Lindiinae (cardate mastax)
    *Lindia*
   Birgeinae (aberrant mastax, with a pair of pseudunci)
    *Birgea*
   Dicranophorinae (forcipate mastax)
    *Albertia, Aspelta, Dicranophorus,*

*Encentrum, Erignatha, Myersinella, Pedipartia, Streptognatha, Wierzejskiella*
  Synchaetidae (virgate or virgate-forcipate mastax)
   *Polyarthra, Synchaeta*
  Microcodonidae (forcipate mastax)
   *Microcodon*
  Ploesomatidae (virgate mastax)
   *Pleosoma*
  Gastropodidae (virgate mastax)
   *Ascomorpha, Chromogaster, Gastropus*
  Trichocercidae (virgate mastax)
   *Ascomorphella, Elosa, Trichocerca*
  Asplanchnidae (incudate mastax)
   *Asplanchna, Asplanchnopus, Harringia*
  Brachionidae (malleate mastax)
   Brachioninae
    *Anuraeopsis, Argonotholca, Brachionus, Cyrtonia, Dipeuchlanis, Epiphanes, Euchlanis, Kellicottia, Keratella, Lophocharis, Macrochaetus, Mikrocodides, Mytilina, Notholca, Platyias, Rhinoglena, Trichotria, Tripleuchlanis*
   Colurinae
    *Colurella, Lepadella, Paracolurella, Squatinella*
   Lecaninae
    *Lecane, Monostyla*

The following key includes all genera likely to be encountered in the United States. It does not include about 30 rare fresh-water genera that have been found only on other continents and that may eventually be found in the United States. Numbers of species are only approximations for the numbers reported or likely to be reported for the United States.

## KEY TO GENERA OF ROTATORIA

1. With a single ovary (Figs. 101, 102); mastax not ramate; lorica or secreted tube present or absent .......................... Class **MONOGONONTA, 3**
   With paired ovaries (Figs. 103, 110); mastax ramate (Fig. 107E); without a lorica or secreted tube ................................. Class **DIGONONTA, 2**

2. Ovaries without a vitellarium; male well developed; corona disc rudimentary; one genus and several species commensal on marine Crustacea.

Order **SEISONIDEA**

Each ovary with a vitellarium (Fig. 117); males absent; reproduction entirely by parthenogenesis; corona usually well developed; body cylindrical, highly contractile, and telescopic; free-swimming or with leechlike creeping movements; with a dorsal proboscis; toes, when present, usually retracted within foot except when creeping; two nonretractile spurs usually present.

Order **BDELLOIDEA, 94**

3. Female almost invariably free-swimming or creeping; lorica present or absent; without a secreted tube; corona not especially large; foot, when present, typically with two toes; solitary . . . . . . . . . . . . . . . . . . . . . . . . . . . . . . . . . . . . . . . . . . . . .**5**

Female usually sessile; without a lorica but often in a secreted tube; corona large; foot, when present, long and annulated and without toes but with a terminal attachment disc; solitary or colonial . . . . . . . . . . . . . . . . . . . . . . . . . . . . . . . . .**4**

4. Corona surrounded by two concentric wreaths of cilia with a ciliated furrow between (Figs. 104B, D); cilia of outer wreath always shorter than inner; mouth not central; usually with one or two well-developed antennae; mastax malleoramate (Fig. 107C); solitary or colonial . . . . . . . .Order **FLOSCULARIACEA, 81**

Corona very large, without such a double wreath of cilia; without well-developed antennae; mouth central; mastax uncinate or poorly developed; buccal field horseshoe-shaped and located at the bottom of a large concave infundibulum (Fig. 137); solitary, often sessile.

Order **COLLOTHECACEA**, COLLOTHECIDAE, **90**

5. Foot and toes always absent . . . . . . . . . . . . . . . . . . . . . . . . . . . . . . . . . . . . . . . .**6**

Foot always present; toes usually present . . . . . . . . . . . . . . . . . . . . . . . . . . . . . .**20**

6. With 12 transparent, movable, sword- or blade-shaped lateral appendages (Fig. 123B); body short and more or less cylindrical; about 10 species, of which several are common plankton forms. Order **PLOIMA**, SYNCHAETIDAE, **Polyarthra**

Without 12 such appendages . . . . . . . . . . . . . . . . . . . . . . . . . . . . . . . . . . . . . . . . .**7**

7. With six stout, muscular, setose appendages; body conical; with a double ciliary wreath and a ciliated groove between (Fig. 123A); the "jumping rotifer"; usually in small alkaline lakes and ponds during the summer months; several species.

Order **FLOSCULARIACEA**, HEXARTHRIDAE, **Hexarthra**

Without such appendages . . . . . . . . . . . . . . . . . . . . . . . . . . . . . . . . . . . . . . . . . . .**8**

8. Without a lorica but with three or four long movable spines (Figs. 123E, F).

Order **FLOSCULARIACEA**, TESTUDINELLIDAE, **9**

Lorica present or absent; spines, if present, rigid and confined to anterior and posterior margins of lorica . . . . . . . . . . . . . . . . . . . . . . . . . . . . . . . . . . . . . . .**10**

9. With two lateral and one posterior spine (Fig. 123E); several common limnetic species, one very common . . . . . . . . . . . . . . . . . . . . . . . . . . . . . . . . . . **Filinia**

With two unequal lateral and two unequal posterior spines (Fig. 123F); one uncommon plankton species . . . . . . . . . . . . . . . . . . . . . . . **Tetramastix opoliensis** Zach.

10. With a spinous lorica composed of two plates immovably fused laterally.

Order **PLOIMA**, BRACHIONIDAE, **11**

Lorica absent, or present and not spinous . . . . . . . . . . . . . . . . . . . . . . . . . . . . .**14**

11. With one very long posterior spine and four or six anterior spines, of which three are very long (Figs. 123H, J); two limnetic species, one of which is very common . . . . . . . . . . . . . . . . . . . . . . . . . . . . . . . . . . . . . . . . . . . . . .**Kellicottia**

With one, two, or no posterior spines, and with six short to medium anterior spines; highly variable plankton and limnetic species . . . . . . . . . . . . . . . . . . . . .**12**

12. Dorsal surface of lorica with a pattern of polygonal facets (Figs. 124A–L); cyclomorphic; about 10 species, of which several are very common . . . . .**Keratella**

Dorsal surface of lorica plain, pustulose, or longitudinally striated; usually in ponds. **13**

13. With a broad ventral bulbous keel (Figs. 123K, L); rare . . . . . . . . . . . . .**Argonotholca**

Without such a keel (Figs. 124M, N); about 10 species . . . . . . . . . . . . . . . .**Notholca**

14. Large transparent species, usually 400 to 2000 microns long . . . . . . . . . . . . . . . . .**15**

Small, more opaque species, less than 200 microns long . . . . . . . . . . . . . . . . . . . . .**16**

FIG. 123.–Structure of Ploima and Flosculariacea. A, right side of *Hexarthra*; B, dorsal view of *Polyarthra*; C and D, single appendages of *Polyarthra*; E, lateral view of *Filinia*; F, *Tetramastix opoliensis* with anterior spines in normal position; G, *T. opoliensis* with anterior spines retracted forward; H, dorsal view of lorica of *Kellicottia bostoniensis*; J, dorsal view of *K. longispina*; K, ventral view of *Argonotholca*; L, side view of *Argonotholca*. (K and L modified from Donner, 1964.)

**15.** Sac-shaped, with a well-developed corona; intestine and anus lacking; mastax incudate; vitellarium horseshoe-shaped or globose (Figs. 125A, B); often viviparous; predatory; morphology variable; body of one species with humps or winglike processes; several very common plankton species.
Order **PLOIMA**, ASPLANCHNIDAE, **Asplanchna**
Spherical and without a true corona, the body being divided into unequal hemispheres by a ciliary band; intestine and anus present; mastax malleoramate (Fig. 125C); up to 750 microns in diameter; very rare in small polluted ponds; more likely to be found in southern states; two species.
Order **FLOSCULARIACEA**, TESTUDINELLIDAE, **Trochosphaera**

FIG. 124.–Lorica of typical species of *Keratella* and *Notholca* (dorsal views). A to D, *Keratella cochlearis*; E, *K. taurocephala* (an acid water species); F, *K. gracilenta*; G, *K. serrulata* (common in acid waters); H to L, *K. quadrata*; M and N, *Notholca*. Dorsal plates shown only for A, E, F, G, and J; small amount of pustulation shown only in A and F. (A to L modified from Ahlstrom, 1943.)

16. With a thin lorica, or lorica absent; sac-shaped; with a very large lobed stomach filling much of the body cavity; anus absent; usually densely colored or opaque (Fig. 125D); mastax virgate; several plankton species.
    Order **PLOIMA**, GASTROPODIDAE, **Ascomorpha**
    With a thick lorica; not sac-shaped.........................................**17**
17. Lorica composed of a single cylindrical piece, trilobate in section and with a crescentic opening posteriorly on the left side (Fig. 125E); trophi asymmetrical; one uncommon species.
    Order **PLOIMA**, TRICHOCERCIDAE, **Elosa worrali** Lord
    Lorica composed of a dorsal and a ventral plate (Figs. 125F–K); trophi symmetrical. **18**

FIG. 125.–Structure of Ploima and Flosculariacea. A, ventral view of *Asplanchna* (muscle fibers not shown); B, *Asplanchna* with winglike processes; C, lateral view of *Trochosphaera*; D, lateral view of *Ascomorpha* showing lobed stomach; E, lateral view of *Elosa worralli*; F, dorsal view of *Chromogaster*; G, cross section of *Chromogaster*; H, dorsal view of *Pompholyx*; J, cross section of *Pompholyx*; K, lateral view of *Anuraeopsis fissa* carrying egg. (H and J modified from Wulfert.)

**18.** Corona with one to three fingerlike processes in addition to ciliated papillae; lorica composed of two convex plates fused laterally (Figs. 125F, G); mastax virgate; probably two species .. Order **PLOIMA**, GASTROPODIDAE, **Chromogaster**
Corona without fingerlike processes . . . . . . . . . . . . . . . . . . . . . . . . . . . . . . . . . . . . . . . .**19**

**19.** Lateral edges of dorsal and ventral plates of lorica closely confluent; flat or four-lobed in cross section; two frontal eyespots (Figs. 125H, J); mastax malleo-ramate; several species, including only two in the U.S.
Order **FLOSCULARIACEA**, TESTUDINELLIDAE, **Pompholyx**
Lateral edges of dorsal and ventral plates of lorica connected by infolded cuticle; ventral plate flat, dorsal plate arched (Fig. 125K); mastax malleate; one rare and variable species.
Order **PLOIMA**, BRACHIONIDAE, **Anuraeopsis fissa** (Gosse)

**20.** With a well-developed rigid lorica . . . . . . . . . . . . . . . . . . . . . . . . . . . . . . . . . . . . . . . .**21**
Lorica absent, or present and poorly developed and flexible . . . Order **PLOIMA, 43**

**21.** Foot attached to the ventral surface; lorica composed of one rigid piece, never dorsoventrally flattened; foot usually annulated (Figs. 126A, B); mastax virgate . . . . . . . . . . . . . . . . . . . . . . . . . . . . . . . . . . . . . . . Order **PLOIMA, 22**
Foot terminal or subterminal . . . . . . . . . . . . . . . . . . . . . . . . . . . . . . . . . . . . . . . . .**24**

FIG. 126.–Structure of ploimate rotifers. A, lateral view of *Gastropus*; B, lateral view of *Ploesoma*; C, lateral view of *Pseudoploesoma formosum*; D to J, common species of *Trichocerca* (contracted). (B modified from Wesenberg-Lund, 1930; C modified from Myers, 1934; G and H modified from Ahlstrom, 1938.)

22. Surface of lorica plain; body laterally compressed; lorica with a small ventral opening for the foot; foot with one or two toes (Fig. 126A); three species.

GASTROPODIDAE, **Gastropus**

Surface of lorica marked with ridges or vesicles; body not laterally compressed; lorica usually open along the midventral line; foot with two toes (Figs. 126B, C) . . . . . . . . . . . . . . . . . . . . . . . . . . . . . . . . . . . . . . . . . . . . . . . . . . . . . . . . . . . . . . . . **23**

23. Corona with frontal palps; foot annulated; lorica open along the midventral line (Fig. 126B); mastax virgate and adapted for prehension; about four species.

PLOESOMATIDAE, **Ploesoma**

Corona without frontal palps but with two unique juxta-buccal protuberances; foot composed of two telescoping segments and emerging from an oval opening in the lorica (Fig. 126C); mastax virgate but not adapted for prehension; one rare species in acid waters. NOTOMMATIDAE, **Pseudoploesoma formosum** (Myers)

24. Body cylindrical, more or less curved, and asymmetrical; lorica a single cylindrical piece, often with teeth and longitudinal grooves or ridges; toes spinelike, of unequal length, and with several small spinules at their base (Figs. 126D–J); creeping or free-swimming; mastax virgate; trophi asymmetrical (Fig. 109C); common; many species. Order **PLOIMA**, TRICHOCERCIDAE, **Trichocerca**
   Without another combination of characters; rarely asymmetrical; toes not spinelike . . . . . . . . . . . . . . . . . . . . . . . . . . . . . . . . . . . . . . . . . . . . . . . . . . . . . . . .**25**

25. Foot long, retractile, annulated, and terminating in a tuft of cilia; dorsal and ventral plates of lorica completely fused laterally; greatly flattened dorsoventrally and sometimes nearly circular (Fig. 127B); mastax malleoramate; 120 to 300 microns long; about 15 littoral species.
   Order **FLOSCULARIACEA**, TESTUDINELLIDAE, **Testudinella**
   Foot ending in one or two toes . . . . . . . . . . . . . . . . . . . . . . . . . Order **PLOIMA, 26**

26. Entire margin spiny; lorica heavy, with 4 to 10 long dorsal spines and six posterior spines; foot short (Fig. 127A); mastax malleate; about six littoral species.
   BRACHIONIDAE, **Macrochaetus**
   Entire margin of body not spiny . . . . . . . . . . . . . . . . . . . . . . . . . . . . . . . . . . . . . . .**27**

27. Head bearing a wide, circular shield; lorica cylindrical or pyriform, often with one or two median dorsal spines, or several spines on posterior margin of lorica; sometimes with a spine at the base of the toes (Figs. 127C, D); mastax malleate; about 10 species . . . . . . . . . . . . . . . .BRACHIONIDAE, **Squatinella**
   Head without a wide circular shield . . . . . . . . . . . . . . . . . . . . . . . . . . . . . . . . . . .**28**

28. Usually with two spines at base of foot, or rarely with two posterior dorsolateral spines on the lorica; lorica composed of one boxlike piece, usually thick and with large facets (Figs. 127E, K); mastax malleate; about six species.
   BRACHIONIDAE, **Trichotria**
   Without two such spines . . . . . . . . . . . . . . . . . . . . . . . . . . . . . . . . . . . . . . . . . . . . . .**29**

29. Body moderately flattened dorsoventrally; dorsal and ventral plates of lorica completely fused laterally; anterior dorsal margin of lorica usually with four or six spines; posterior margin with or without spines; two toes; mastax malleate . . . . . . . . . . . . . . . . . . . . . . . . . . . . . . . . . . . . . . . BRACHIONIDAE, **30**
   With another combination of characters; mastax usually malleate or submalleate; never dorsoventrally flattened and never with four or six spines on anterior dorsal margin of lorica . . . . . . . . . . . . . . . . . . . . . . . . . . . . . . . . . . . . . . . . . .**31**

30. Foot segmented and retractile (Fig. 128N); three species . . . . . . . . . . . . . . . .**Platyias**
   Foot long, annulated, retractile, not segmented (Fig. 128K); about 20 plankton species, some of which are common and highly variable, especially in hard waters; sometimes in dense populations . . . . . . . . . . . . . . . . . . . . . . . . . . . .**Brachionus**

31. Strongly compressed laterally; lorica composed of two lateral plates; frontal head hood present; toes long and tapering; lorica open along anterior, ventral, and posterior margins (Figs. 127F, G); small species . . . . . BRACHIONIDAE, **32**
   Not strongly compressed laterally; lorica of different construction; frontal hood absent . . . . . . . . . . . . . . . . . . . . . . . . . . . . . . . . . . . . . . . . . . . . . . . . . . . . . . . .**33**

32. Terminal foot segment long (Fig. 127F); three rare species . . . . . . . . . . . **Paracolurella**
   Terminal foot segment short; about 15 species, some common (Figs. 127G, H) . . . . . . . . . . . . . . . . . . . . . . . . . . . . . . . . . . . . . . . . . . . . . . . . . . . . .**Colurella**

33. Foot long; toes long; lorica without spines or plates . . . . . . . . . . . . . . . . . . . . . . .**34**
   Foot short; toes short to long . . . . . . . . . . . . . . . . . . . . . . . . . . . . . . . . . . . . . . . . .**35**

34. Lorica vase-shaped and thin; toes shorter than rest of body (Fig. 129B); mastax virgate; one species . . .NOTOMMATIDAE, **Scaridium longicaudum** (Müller)
   Lorica pear-shaped; toes about as long as rest of body (Fig. 129A); mastax malleate; one rare species . . . . .BRACHIONIDAE, **Manfredium eudactylotum** (Gosse)

35. Lorica composed of a ventral plate and two lateral plates, the edges of the latter forming two dorsal ridges; often with anterior and posterior spines (Figs. 129C–E); about 10 littoral species, usually in hard waters.
   BRACHIONIDAE, **Mytilina**
   Lorica constructed differently . . . . . . . . . . . . . . . . . . . . . . . . . . . . . . . . . . . . . . . . .**36**

Fig. 127.–Structure of Testudinellidae and Brachionidae. A, dorsal view of contracted *Macrochaetus*; B, ventral view of *Testudinella*; C, dorsal view of *Squatinella*; D, lateral view of a spined species of *Squatinella*; E, lateral view of contracted *Trichotria*; F, lateral view of contracted *Paracolurella*; G, lateral view of contracted *Colurella*; H, ventral view of contracted *Colurella*; J, dorsal view of *Squatinella*; K, dorsal view of *Trichotria*. (D modified from Hauer, 1935; F modified from Myers, 1934.)

36. Lorica composed of one piece, capacious, rigid, boxlike, and with a prominent dorsal keel or low ridge extending the entire length of the lorica (Figs. 129F, G); several littoral species .....................BRACHIONIDAE, **Lophocharis**
Lorica usually composed of a dorsal and a ventral plate ......................37
37. Dorsal and ventral plates rigidly united at the edges; with an anterior opening for the protrusion of the head and a posterior opening through which the foot projects; foot well developed (Figs. 129H–K); about 30 very small species, 60 to 180 microns long; littoral ...................... BRACHIONIDAE, **Lepadella**
Dorsal and ventral plates not united at the edges; foot not well developed; associated with the substrate but occasionally found in the plankton ...............38
38. With a single long toe; strongly compressed dorsoventrally and oval to ovate in outline (Figs. 129L–N); many small littoral species.
BRACHIONIDAE, **Monostyla**
With two toes .....................................................39

FIG. 128.–Structure of lorica of some common species of *Brachionus* and *Platyias*. A, dorsal view of *Brachionus plicatilis*, a species characteristic of highly alkaline waters; B, ventral view of *B. calyciflorus*; C and D, dorsal views of *B. calyciflorus*; E, dorsal view of *B. angularis*; F, ventral view of *B. caudatus*; G, dorsal view of *B. havanaensis*; H, dorsal view of *B. quadridentata*; J, ventral view of *B. quadridentata*; K, ventral view of *B. pterodinoides*, a species characteristic of highly alkaline waters; L, dorsal view of *B. rubens*; M, ventral view of *B. urceolaris*; N, ventral view of *Platyias quadricornis*; O, ventral view of *P. patulus*. (Redrawn and modified from Ahlstrom, 1940.)

**39.** Prismatic or spindle-shaped; toes tapering, usually curved; lorica thin and poorly developed (Figs. 130A–C); mastax virgate; many littoral species.

                                                       NOTOMMATIDAE, **Cephalodella**

More or less flattened dorsoventrally; toes long and slightly fusiform or parallel-sided and straight; lorica rigid and well developed (Figs. 130D–K); mastax malleate or submalleate ................................. BRACHIONIDAE, **40**

FIG. 129.–Structure of ploimate rotifers. A, contracted *Manfredium eudactylotum*; B, lateral view of *Scaridium longicaudum*; C, lateral view of contracted *Mytilina*; D, dorsal view of contracted *Mytilina*; E, cross section of *Mytilina*; F, lateral view of contracted *Lophocharis*; G, cross section of *Lophocharis*; H, ventral view of contracted *Lepadella*; J, dorsal view of contracted *Lepadella*; K, cross section; L to N, ventral views of three contracted species of *Monostyla*.

**40.** Dorsal plate much smaller than ventral plate (Fig. 130D); cuticle connecting the dorsal and ventral plates in the form of a deep groove dividing the body cavity into two unequal portions (Fig. 130E); one species . . . . . . . . . . . . **Dipeuchlanis**
Dorsal plate the same size or larger than the ventral plate . . . . . . . . . . . . . . . . . . . . .**41**

**41.** Foot with two rudimentary segments, of which only the posterior is movable; toes parallel-sided; strongly compressed dorsoventrally (Figs. 130H–K); many small littoral species; 150 to 250 microns long . . . . . . . . . . . . . . . . . . . . **Lecane**
Foot with two or three obscure segments; toes usually slightly fusiform; ventral plate flat; dorsal plate arched and convex, sometimes keeled (Fig. 102) . . . . . . . .**42**

**42.** Lateral sulci very wide, with a stiff flange (Figs. 130O, P); in brackish waters.
**Tripleuchlanis plicata** Levander
Lateral sulci without a flange (Figs. 102; 130F, G); about 10 large species, some very common . . . . . . . . . . . . . . . . . . . . . . . . . . . . . . . . . . . . . . . . . . . . . . . . . **Euchlanis**

**43.** Foot rudimentary; body saccate (Fig. 131G); one species parasitic in *Volvox* colonies . . . . . . . . . . **TRICHOCERCIDAE, Ascomorphella volvocicola** (Plate)
Foot not rudimentary; body not saccate; free-living . . . . . . . . . . . . . . . . . . . . . . . . .**44**

**44.** With four long, prominent sensory bristles on the corona; body conical; toes small (Fig. 130L); mastax virgate; about 10 plankton species, several of which are common . . . . . . . . . . . . . . . . . . . . . . . . . . . . . **SYNCHAETIDAE, Synchaeta**
Without four such bristles . . . . . . . . . . . . . . . . . . . . . . . . . . . . . . . . . . . . . . . . . . . .**45**

FIG. 130.–Structure of ploimate rotifers. A to C, three typical species of *Cephalodella*; D, dorsal view of retracted *Dipeuchlanis*; E, cross section of *Dipeuchlanis*; F and G, cross sections of *Euchlanis*; H to K, ventral views of typical species of *Lecane* (contracted); L, dorsal view of *Synchaeta*; M, cross section of *Euchlanis*; N, anterior edge of *Euchlanis*; O, lateral view of lorica of *Tripleuchlanis*; P, cross section of *Tripleuchlanis*. (D to G modified from Myers, 1930; H to K modified from Harring and Myers, 1926; M to P from Myers, 1930.)

**45.** Foot very long, about half of total length; a single toe; corona flat and circular (Fig. 131B); mastax forcipate; a single uncommon species, 200 microns long.
MICRODONIDAE, **Microcodon clavus** Ehr.
Foot much shorter, almost invariably with two toes...........................**46**
**46.** Corona complex, with an outer band of cilia and an inner band of cilia, sometimes also with accessory rows of cilia and ciliated protuberances (Figs. 101; 131A, C, D); mastax malleate; large species .............. BRACHIONIDAE, **47**
Corona simple, with a single peripheral band of cilia; general surface of corona without cilia, with few scattered cilia, or with cilia more or less covering the corona; corona occasionally with two slight sensory protuberances .......**50**

Fig. 131.–Structure of ploimate rotifers. A, *Mikrocodides chlaena*; B, *Microcodon clavus*; C, ventral view of *Rhinoglena frontalis*; D, *Cyrtonia tuba*; E, *Harringia*; F, *Asplanchnopus*; G, lateral view of *Ascomorphella volvocicola*.

47. With a single toe; sometimes a small spur at the base of the toe; foot thick (Fig. 131A); one U.S. species . . . . . . . . . . . . . . . . . . . **Mikrocodides chlaena** (Gosse)
    With two toes . . . . . . . . . . . . . . . . . . . . . . . . . . . . . . . . . . . . . . . . . . . . . . . . .**48**
48. With a large dorsal proboscis at the anterior end bearing two eyespots (Fig. 131C); one littoral species, 270 to 400 microns long . . . . . . **Rhinoglena frontalis** Ehr.
    Without such a proboscis . . . . . . . . . . . . . . . . . . . . . . . . . . . . . . . . . . . . . . . . . . .**49**
49. Eyespot absent; body not strongly tapered posteriorly (Fig. 101); common during spring in stock ponds and puddles containing much organic matter; probably five species; 300 to 600 microns long . . . . . . . . . . . . . . . . . . . . . . . . .**Epiphanes**
    Eyespot present; body strongly tapered posteriorly (Fig. 131D); one littoral species; 250 to 300 microns long . . . . . . . . . . . . . . . . . . . . . . . . . . . . . .**Cyrtonia tuba** Ehr.

50. Large, globular species; mastax incudate (Figs. 131E, F); carnivorous.

ASPLANCHNIDAE, **51**

Smaller species, more or less opaque; mastax not incudate; mostly illoricate or weakly loricate (see couplet 61) .................. NOTOMMATIDAE, **52**

51. Intestine and anus absent (Fig. 131F); three rare littoral species; up to 1 mm long ............................................... **Asplanchnopus**

Intestine and anus present (Fig. 131E); two rare littoral species ........ **Harringia**

52. Mastax forcipate; trophi strongly compressed dorsoventrally and adapted for protrusion and tearing prey (Fig. 108E); corona oval and ventral, or subcircular and strongly oblique; marginal cilia short, with the exception of two lateral, auriclelike tufts of cilia; rostrum large; buccal field evenly ciliated; retrocerebral sac present .............................................................**73**

Mastax not forcipate; corona frontal or oblique ..............................**53**

53. Mastax virgate or virgate-forcipate, adapted for sucking out the contents of plant cells and animals (Fig. 109); a pair of lateral auricles often present; retrocerebral sac present .......................................................**54**

Mastax not virgate or virgate-forcipate; retrocerebral sac rudimentary or absent .**55**

54. Lateral antennae located near base of foot, long, knobbed, and with excessively long setae; ovary long, slender, and ribbonlike; auricles absent; dorsal antenna double and very long (Fig. 132C); corona oblique; total length 750 to 1000 microns; one rare species in acid waters ........ **Tetrasiphon hydrocora** Ehr.

Lateral antennae not located near base of foot; ovary not long, slender, and ribbonlike; auricles present or absent; dorsal antenna not especially long; corona frontal or oblique ......................................................**57**

55. Mastax modified malleate; unci adapted for crushing and grinding; corona oblique, with two lateral tufts of cilia but no auricles (Figs. 134D–F); total length 90 to 400 microns ...........................................................**71**

Mastax not modified malleate or malleate-virgate; corona oblique or frontal; auricles present or absent ....................................................**56**

56. Body cylindrical and tapering posteriorly, sometimes indistinctly annulated; foot not set off sharply from body (Fig. 132B); mastax cardate (Fig. 108A); total length 250 to 1200 microns; about 10 species ............................ **Lindia**

Foot slender and sharply set off from the wide body (Fig. 132A); trophi aberrant, with a pair of pseudunci; 240 to 275 microns long; one rare littoral species.

**Birgea enantia** Harring and Myers

57. Toes longer than rest of body, usually unequal in length (Fig. 132D); about 20 species, usually in acid waters ......................................**Monommata**

Toes short .............................................................**58**

58. Gastric glands long, ribbonlike, and bifurcated; with four slender accessory gastric appendages; body short and saclike (Fig. 132E); one uncommon littoral species; 600 microns long ......................... **Enteroplea lacustris** Ehr.

Without such glands....................................................**59**

59. Head very broad and truncate anteriorly; two eyespots widely separated on protuberances; foot annulated (Fig. 132F); one carnivorous littoral species.

**Sphyrias lofuana** (Rousselet)

With other characters ...................................................**60**

60. Body marked with transverse folds or annuli; elongated and spindle-shaped; foot rudimentary (Fig. 132G); several littoral species; 200 microns long.

**Taphrocampa**

Body not so marked.....................................................**61**

61. Toes relatively long, pointed, and usually curved; foot rudimentary and unjointed; body prismatic or spindle-shaped (Figs. 130A–C); retrocerebral sac absent; lorica present, more or less sclerotized and composed of a dorsal and a ventral plate; both rami and unci of very simple construction (Figs. 109D, E); more than 50 U.S. species, some of which are very common ....... **Cephalodella**

Toes comparatively short; foot present and distinct; retrocerebral sac present; lorica absent; rami and unci more complicated ..............................**62**

Fig. 132.–Structure of Notommatidae. A, *Birgea enantia*; B, *Lindia*; C, *Tetrasiphon hydrocora*; D, *Monommata*; E, *Enteroplea lacustris*; F, *Sphyrias lofuana*; G, *Taphrocampa*. (A to C modified from Harring and Myers, 1922; D to G modified from Harring and Myers, 1924.)

62. Foot unsegmented, though sometimes annulated (Figs. 133A–C) ...............63
    Foot segmented (Figs. 133D–K) .........................................65
63. With a single toe; retrocerebral sac absent (Fig. 133A); trophi highly specialized virgate; one rare species in ponds and reservoirs; 250 microns long.
                                           **Tylotrocha monopus** (Jennings)
    With two toes; retrocerebral sac present or absent; trophi not highly specialized virgate .......................................................**64**
64. Retrocerebral sac absent; eyespot absent; foot short (Fig. 133B); one species ectoparasitic on oligochaetes, a second ectoparasitic on *Erpobdella,* and one other (U.S.) possibly free-living; often covered by a gelatinous secretion. **Drilophaga**
    Retrocerebral sac present; eyespot present; foot long (Fig. 133C); one littoral species; 130 microns long ........................ **Rousseletia corniculata** Harring
65. With a projecting auricle on each side of the head, each auricle bearing long cilia; trophi usually asymmetrical (Figs. 109A, B; 133E) ......................**66**
    Without definite auricles but often with a tuft of long cilia in the usual location of an auricle; trophi symmetrical ..........................................**67**
66. Rami roughly hemispherical (Figs. 109A, B); with a cervical eyespot only (Fig. 133D); total length 100 to 1000 microns, usually more than 300 microns; a few species covered by a gelatinous secretion; many littoral species, some very common and spectacular ......................................... **Notommata**
    Rami lyrate, broad, and strongly divergent at the base, continuing as parallel rods toward the tips (Fig. 133E); with a cervical eyespot and two frontal eyespots (Fig. 133F); about four uncommon littoral species ................... **Itura**

FIG. 133.–Structure of Notommatidae. A, *Tylotrocha monopus*; B, *Drilophaga*; C, *Rousseletia corniculata*; D, dorsal view of *Notommata*; E, ventral view of *Itura* trophi; F, *Itura*; G, *Dorria dalecarlica*; H, *Pleurotrocha*; J, ventral view of *Pleurotrocha* trophi (mallei stippled); K, *Eosphora*; L, lateral view of *Eosphora* trophi (malleus stippled). (A, C, H, and J modified from Harring and Myers, 1924; B, D, K, and L modified from Harring and Myers, 1922; E and F modified from Harring and Myers, 1928; G modified from Myers, 1933.)

**67.** Eyespot absent (Fig. 133G); in mountain brooks among submerged moss; one species; 200 microns long .............................. **Dorria dalecarlica** Myers

One or three eyespots present; not in mountain brooks in moss ................**68**

**68.** Retrocerebral sac absent (Fig. 133H); rami without teeth (Fig. 133J); toes separate or fused; total length 110 to 250 microns; eight littoral species  . **Pleurotrocha**

Retrocerebral sac present (Fig. 133K); rami with one or more teeth; toes separate. **69**

**69.** Each uncus with a single simple tooth; rami bent at right angles and with one or two teeth at midlength and many small ones more distally (Fig. 133L); total length 300 to 500 microns; about five littoral species ................... **Eosphora**

One or both unci with a single main tooth plus accessory teeth (Fig. 134B); rami more or less bent at right angles but with a different arrangement of teeth; total length 170 to 400 microns ......................................**70**

**70.** With one eyespot, or eyespot absent (Fig. 134A); each uncus with one main tooth and with accessory teeth on either the left or right uncus; probably five littoral species ...............................................**Resticula**

With three eyespots (Fig. 134C); both unci with one main tooth and accessory teeth (Fig. 134B); about six littoral species ........................... **Eothinia**

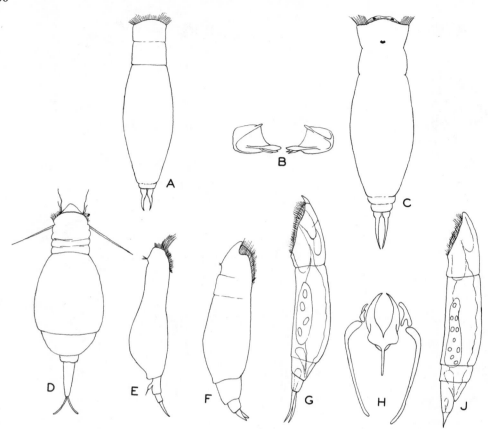

FIG. 134.–Structure of Notommatidae. A, *Resticula*; B, frontal view of unci of *Eothinia*; C, *Eothinia*; D, *Bryceella*; E, *Proalinopsis*; F, *Proales*; G, *Aspelta*; H, trophi of *Aspelta*; J, *Pedipartia gracilis*. (A, E, and F modified from Harring and Myers, 1922; B and C modified from Harring and Myers, 1924; G and H modified from Harring and Myers, 1928; J modified from Myers, 1936.)

71. With a very long stylet on each side of the head (Fig. 134D); two littoral and sandy
       beach species; 130 microns long ...............................**Bryceella**
    Without such stylets ...................................................**72**
72. Tail region or basal foot segment with a knoblike papilla bearing a tuft of setae or a
       spine (Fig. 134E); five littoral species ....................... **Proalinopsis**
    Without such a tuft of setae or spine (Fig. 134F); one species with a single toe; about
       30 littoral species, some quite common ......................... **Proales**
73. Trophi asymmetrical (Fig. 134H)............................................**74**
    Trophi symmetrical (Figs. 135C, E, G, L) ................................**75**
74. Corona ventral; retrocerebral sac present; toes long (Fig. 134G); about 12 species,
       usually in acid waters and sphagnum bogs ........................ **Aspelta**
    Corona oblique; retrocerebral sac absent; toes short (Fig. 134J); one rare species
       known from sandy beaches ................... **Pedipartia gracilis** (Myers)
75. Foot one-fourth to one-third the total length, composed of one to four segments (Fig.
       135A); three uncommon species; most common in sandy beaches. **Wierzejskiella**
    Foot shorter ..........................................................**76**
76. Incus Y-shaped and composed of rods; with a long naviculoid sclerite attached to
       the tip of each uncus (Fig. 135C); a single acid water species.
                                          **Streptognatha lepta** Harring and Myers
    With incus and unci of different construction ..............................**77**

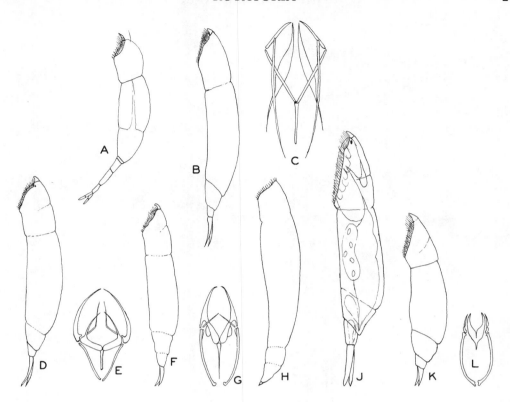

FIG. 135.–Structure of Dicranophorinae. A, *Wierzejskiella*; B, *Streptognatha lepta*; C, trophi of *S. lepta*; D, *Erignatha*; E, trophi of *Erignatha*; F, *Myersinella*; G, trophi of *Myersinella*; H, *Albertia*; J, *Dicranophorus*; K, *Encentrum*; L, trophi of *Encentrum*. (B to L modified from Harring and Myers, 1928.)

**77.** Rami slender and bent at nearly a right angle at midlength and terminating in long, slender, single teeth (Fig. 135E); about five littoral species .......**Erignatha**
  Rami not slender and bent at nearly a right angle at midlength; retrocerebral sac present or absent; corona oblique or ventral .........................**78**

**78.** With a posterior projection at the external angles of the rami (Fig. 135G); retrocerebral sac absent; corona oblique or ventral (Fig. 135F); two sandy beach species; 130 microns long ..................................... **Myersinella**
  Without such projections on the rami ......................................**79**

**79.** Toes minute and fused, or lacking; corona oblique; eyespots lacking; rostrum minute; retrocerebral sac absent (Fig. 135H); several species, most or all of which are ecto- or endoparasites of oligochaetes ......................... **Albertia**
  Toes prominent, not fused; corona oblique or ventral; eyespots present or absent; rostrum conspicuous; retrocerebral sac present or absent; not parasitic ...**80**

**80.** Corona essentially ventral; two frontal eyespots; retrocerebral sac present and large (Fig. 135J); rami often with shearing teeth; unci robust (Fig. 108E); about 50 littoral species ........................................**Dicranophorus**
  Corona oblique; one eyespot, or eyespots absent; retrocerebral sac present or absent (Fig. 135K); rami never with shearing teeth; unci weak and needlelike (Fig. 135L); about 15 species; chiefly littoral ......................**Encentrum**

**81.** With a ventral gap in the ciliary wreath; mouth on the corona, nearer the dorsal edge; gelatinous case (Figs. 136A–C); limnetic species ..... **CONOCHILIDAE, 82**
  Ciliary wreath with a dorsal gap or without a gap; mouth ventral to the corona; eyespots usually absent (Figs. 136D–L); adults usually sessile.

FLOSCULARIIDAE, **83**

FIG. 136.–Structure of Flosculariacea. A, lateral view of *Conochilus*; B, sketch of a small colony of *Conochilus* showing common gelatinous case; C, lateral view of a solitary *Conochiloides* in gelatinous case; D, lateral view of *Sinantherina*; E, *Lacinularia* in gelatinous matrix of colony; F, cluster of empty *Floscularia* tubes; G, lateral view of *Floscularia* (note pellet-making concavity on ventral surface of head); H and J, dorsal views of *Limnias*; K, *Pseudoecistes rotifer*; L, *Ptygura*. (All greatly modified from various sources.)

**82.** With one or two antennae on the corona; colonies composed of radiating individuals inhabiting coherent gelatinous tubes; two common species (Figs. 136A, B).

**Conochilus**

With one or two ventral antennae below the corona; solitary or colonial; probably four limnetic species, of which two are common (Fig. 136C) ...**Conochiloides**

**83.** Adults in spherical, sessile colonies attached to aquatic plants ................**84**

Adults solitary or colonial, but colonies never spherical ......................**85**

**84.** Colonies without tubes; trunk usually with two to four opaque protuberances; corona roughly kidney-shaped (Fig. 136D); about five species ........ **Sinantherina**

Colonies with adhering gelatinous tubes; trunk without protuberances; corona heart-shaped and with the sinus ventral (Fig. 136E); about 10 species ..**Lacinularia**

**85.** Corona with eight prominent lobes and one small median dorsal lobe; in a gelatinous tube; one poorly known species .............. **Octotrocha speciosa** Thorpe

Corona with less than eight lobes, or not lobed .............................**86**

FIG. 137.–Structure of Collothecacea. A, *Stephanoceros*; B, dorsal view of *Collotheca* (gelatinous tube omitted); C, lateral view of *Acyclus inquietus*; D, lateral view of *Cupelopagis vorax*; E, dorsal view of *Atrochus tentaculatus*. (C modified from Leidy, 1882; E modified from Wierzejski, 1893.)

FIG. 138.–Structure of Bdelloidea. A, posterior end of *Embata* while swimming (toes retracted); B, dorsal view of *Philodina* (toes retracted); C, foot of *Philodina* (toes protruded); D, contracted *Philodina*; E, dorsal view of partly contracted *Dissotrocha*; F, dorsal view of foot of *Philodina* (toes protruded); G, toes and spurs of *Embata*. (A modified from Murray, 1906; B and E modified from Murray, 1911; C and D modified from Hickernell.)

**86.** Corona four-lobed; two large ventral antennae; with a tube composed of gelatinous material, pellets of debris, or fecal pellets (Figs. 136F, G); about six species...............................................**Floscularia**
Corona two-lobed and elliptical, circular, or kidney-shaped .....................**87**
**87.** Tube chitinoid, often opaque and more or less covered with debris; corona of two distinct lobes, or nearly circular; dorsal antenna short to long (Figs. 136H, J); about six species.............................................**Limnias**
Tube not chitinoid, or tube absent ........................................**88**
**88.** Tube absent (Fig. 136K); able to leave substrate and swim about; one rare species...................................**Pseudoecistes rotifer** Stenroos
Tube present .............................................................**89**
**89.** Dorsal antenna small or apparently absent; ventral (lateral) antennae short to long; corona a wide oval or nearly circular, indistinctly bilobed; tube made of debris, fecal pellets, or gelatinous and more or less covered with debris (Fig. 136L); one species free-swimming; 20 species; 200 to 1000 microns long ....**Ptygura**
Dorsal antenna very long; corona of two distinct lobes; tube irregular, translucent, and gelatinous; one rare species up to 500 microns long.
**Beauchampia crucigera** (Dutrochet)
**90.** With setae but no cilia on the corona; sessile; in a gelatinous tube; foot terminated by a long, nonretractile peduncle, ending in an adhesive disc ............**91**
Without setae or cilia on the corona; gelatinous case present or absent ........**92**
**91.** Corona drawn out into long, pointed arms, which bear whorls of setae (Fig. 137A); two species.........................................**Stephanoceros**
Corona circular, lobed, or pointed (Fig. 137B); setae not arranged in whorls; some species free-swimming; many species ........................**Collotheca**

FIG. 139.–Structure of Bdelloidea. A, lateral view of contracted *Pleuretra*; B, dorsal view of *Mniobia* (toes retracted); C, ventral view of spurs and disc of *Mniobia*; D, dorsal view of *Macrotrachela* (toes retracted); E, end view of foot of *Macrotrachela* (toes retracted); F, lateral view of foot of *Macrotrachela* (toes retracted); G, lateral view of head of creeping *Rotaria*; H, dorsal view of anterior end of creeping *Rotaria*; J, dorsal view of swimming *Rotaria* (toes shown extruded); K, lateral view of foot of *Habrotrocha* (toes extruded); L, distal end of *Beauchampia crucigera*. (A to J modified from Murray, 1911.)

**92.** Body long, with a long, annulated, tapering stalk and with or without a gelatinous case; corona produced into a large dorsal lobe, and bordered by a thin, festooned membrane (Fig. 137C); lives in *Sinantherina* colonies; one rare species . . . . . . . . . . . . . . . . . . . . . . . . . . . . . . . . . . . . . . . . . **Acyclus inquietus** Leidy
Body shorter, without a gelatinous case; foot absent . . . . . . . . . . . . . . . . . . . . . . . .**93**
**93.** Body saclike, with a flat attachment disc on the ventral surface; corona a large concave chamber (Fig. 137D); usually on broad, flat leaves of aquatic plants; up to 800 microns long; one rare species . . . . . . . . **Cupelopagis vorax** (Leidy)
Body spindle-shaped; corona with numerous small peripheral tentacles (Fig. 137E); one species . . . . . . . . . . . . . . . . . . . . . . . . . . . **Atrochus tentaculatus** Wierzejski
**94.** With a well-developed rostrum and corona, the latter always capable of being retracted into the mouth . . . . . . . . . . . . . . . . . . . . . . . . . . . . . . . . . . . . . . . . . . . **95**
With rostrum imperfect or corona absent . . . . . . . . . . . . . . . . . . . . . . . . . . . . . . .**104**

FIG. 140.–Structure of Bdelloidea. A, anterior end of *Scepanotrocha*; B, dorsal view of anterior end of *Ceratotrocha*; C, *Philodinavus paradoxus* with protruded toes; D, ventral view of anterior end of *P. paradoxus*; E, posterior end of *Adineta* with protruded toes; F, ventral view of posterior end of *Bradyscela clauda* showing papilliform lobes and region of three retracted toes; G, ventral view of anterior end of *B. clauda*. (A modified from Bryce, 1910; C and D modified from Murray, 1906.)

95. Stomach with a true lumen (Fig. 112E); intestine ciliated; oviparous or viviparous . . . . . . . . . . . . . . . . . . . . . . . . . . . . . . . . . . . . . . . . . PHILODINIDAE, 96
    Stomach without a lumen (Fig. 112F); food formed into vacuoles in the stomach protoplasm; intestine unciliated; oviparous . . . . . . HABROTROCHIDAE, 102
96. With four plain toes, of which two are dorsal and two terminal (Figs. 138C, F) . .97
    Toes otherwise . . . . . . . . . . . . . . . . . . . . . . . . . . . . . . . . . . . . . . . . . . . . . . . . .100
97. Cuticle smooth . . . . . . . . . . . . . . . . . . . . . . . . . . . . . . . . . . . . . . . . . . . . . . . . . .98
    Cuticle coarse or leathery, and folded (Figs. 138E; 139A) . . . . . . . . . . . . . . . . . .99
98. Spurs long (Fig. 138G); ectocommensals on many aquatic invertebrates; about three species . . . . . . . . . . . . . . . . . . . . . . . . . . . . . . . . . . . . . . . . . . . . . . . . . **Embata**
    Spurs not particularly long (Figs. 138B, C); not usually commensals; about 20 species; common in sewage treatment processes and in old protozoan cultures. **Philodina**
99. Cuticle coarse, with few or no transverse folds but often with few to many spines, or spines absent (Fig. 138E); viviparous; about four species . . . . **Dissotrocha**
    Cuticle leathery, with many transverse folds (Fig. 139A); oviparous; probably four rare species on mosses . . . . . . . . . . . . . . . . . . . . . . . . . . . . . . . . . . . . . . **Pleuretra**

**100.** With three plain toes, one dorsal and two terminal (Figs. 139D–J) ............**101**

With toes bearing cuplike suckers or united to form a broad disc or twin discs (Figs. 139B, C); about 15 species; up to 1 mm long ....................**Mniobia**

**101.** Eyes absent; oviparous; about 25 species (Figs. 139D–F); in mosses. **Macrotrachela**

Two eyes usually present on proboscis; viviparous; some species greatly elongated; about 10 species (Figs. 139G–J); up to 1.5 mm long ...............**Rotaria**

**102.** Corona of the normal type; with three toes (Fig. 139K); many species. **Habrotrocha**

Corona modified (Fig. 140A, B) ........................................**103**

**103.** Corona with two hornlike processes (Fig. 140B); several rare species in mosses.

**Ceratotrocha**

Corona screened by a wide dorsal membranous plate (Fig. 140A); several uncommon species, chiefly in mosses ..............................**Scepanotrocha**

**104.** Rostrum present and perfect but no corona; with four toes (Figs. 140C, D); one uncommon species not yet reported from the United States.

PHILODINAVIDAE, **Philodinavus paradoxus** (Murray)

Rostrum imperfect; corona cannot be retracted within mouth; no ciliary wreaths but only with cilia distributed on corona (Fig. 140G); unable to swim.

ADINETIDAE, **105**

**105.** Foot slender, with two spurs and three toes (Fig. 140E); about 10 species in mosses and shallow littoral .........................................**Adineta**

Foot stout; spurs absent and replaced by a row of papilliform lobes (Figs. 140F, G); one species, not yet reported from the United States. **Bradyscela clauda** (Bryce)

# ROTATORIA REFERENCES

AHLSTROM, E. H. 1934. Rotatoria of Florida. *Trans. Am. Microsc. Soc.* **53**:251–256.

———. 1934a. A quantitative study of Rotatoria in Terwilliger's Pond, Put-In-Bay, Ohio. *Bull. Ohio State Univ. Nat. Hist. Surv.* **6**:1–36.

———. 1938. Plankton Rotatoria from North Carolina. *J. Elisha Mitchell Sci. Soc.* **54**:88–110.

———. 1940. A revision of the rotatorian genera Brachionus and Platyias with descriptions of one new species and two new varieties. *Bull. Am. Mus. Nat. Hist.* **77**:143–184.

———. 1943. A revision of the rotatorian genus Keratella with descriptions of three new species and five new varieties. Ibid. **80**:411–457.

ALOIA, R. C., and R. L. MORETTI. 1973. Sterile culture techniques for species of the rotifer Asplanchna. *Trans. Am. Microsc. Soc.* **92**:364–371.

BARTOS, E. 1948. On the Bohemian species of the genus Pedalia Barrois. *Hydrobiologia* **1**:63–77.

———. 1951. The Czechoslovak Rotatoria of the Order Bdelloidea. *Vestn. Cs. zool. spol.* **15**:241–500.

BEACH, N. W. 1960. A study of the planktonic rotifers of the Ocqueoc River system, Presque Isle County, Michigan. *Ecol. Monogr.* **30**:339–357.

BÉRZINŞ, B. 1951. On the collothecacean Rotatoria. With special reference to the species found in the Aneboda district, Sweden. *Ark. Zool.* **1**:565–592.

———. 1972. Eine Mikrobenthosstudie an Rotatorien. *Hydrobiologia* **40**:447–452.

BRAKENHOFF H. 1937. Zur Morphologie der Bdelloidea. *Zool. Jahrb. Abt. Anat. Ont. Tiere* **63**:125–182.

BUCHNER, H. 1941. Experimentelle Untersuchungen über den Generationswechsel der Rädertiere. II. *Zool. Jahrb. Abt. Allg. Zool. Physiol. Tiere* **60**:279–344.

BUDDE, E. 1925. Die parasitischen Rädertiere mit besonderer Berücksichtigung der in der Umgegend von Minden I. W. beobachteten Arten. *Z. Morphol. Oekol. Tiere* **3**:706–784.

BURGER, A. 1948. Studies on the moss dwelling bdelloids (Rotifera) of Eastern Massachusetts. *Trans. Am. Microsc. Soc.* **67**:111–142.

CALAWAY, W. T. 1968. The Metazoa of waste treatment processes—rotifers. *J. Water Pollut. Control Fed.* **40**:R412–R422.

CAMPBELL, R. S. 1941. Vertical distribution of the plankton Rotifera in Douglas Lake, Michigan, with special reference to depression individuality. *Ecol. Monogr.* **11**:1–19.

CARLIN, B. 1939. Über die Rotatorien einiger Seen bei Aneboda. *Medd. Lunds Univ. Limnol. Inst.* **2**:1–68.

———. 1943. Die Planktonrotatorien des Motalaström. Ibid. **5**:1–255.

CORI, C. 1925. Zur Morphologie und Biologie von Apsilus vorax Leidy. *Z. wiss. Zool.* **125**:557–584.

DE BEAUCHAMP, P. M. 1909. Recherches sur les rotiféres: les formations tégumentaires et l'appareil digestif. *Arch. Zool. Exp. Gen.* (4) **10**:1–410.

———. 1912. Instructions for collecting and fixing rotifers in bulk. *Proc. U.S. Nat. Mus.* **42**:181–185.

———. 1928. Coup d'oeil sur les recherches récentes relatives aux rotifères et sur les méthodes qui leur sont applicables. *Bull. Biol. Fr. Belg.* **62**:51–125.

———. 1932. Contribution á l'étude du genre Ascomorpha et des processus digestifs chez les rotifères. Bull. *Soc. Zool. Fr.* **57**:428–449.

DOBERS, E. 1915. Über die Biologie der Bdelloidea. *Int. Rev.* **7** (Suppl. 1):1–128.

DONNER, J. 1951. Erste Übersicht über die Rotorienfauna einiger Humusboden. *Oesterreich. Zool. Z.* **3**:175–240.

———. 1966. Ordnung Bdelloidea. Rotatoria, Radertiere. *Bestimmungsbucher zur Bodenfauna Eur.* **6**:1–297.

———. 1966a. *Rotifers.* 80 pp. Warne, New York.

———. 1970. Die Rädertierbestande submerser Moose der Salzach und anderer Wasser-Biotope des Flussgebietes. *Arch. Hydrobiol. Suppl.* **36**:109–254.

———. 1972. Die Rädertierebestände submerser Moose und weiterer Merotope im Bereich der Stauräume der Donau an der deutsch-Österreichischen Landesgranze. *Arch. Hydrobiol. Suppl.* **44**:49–114.

EDMONDSON, W. T. 1935. Some Rotatoria from Arizona. *Trans. Am. Microsc. Soc.* **54**:301–306.

———. 1936. Fixation of sessile Rotatoria. *Science* **84**:444.

———. 1939. New species of Rotatoria, with notes on heterogonic growth. *Trans. Am. Microsc. Soc.* **58**:459–472.

———. 1940. The sessile Rotatoria of Wisconsin. Ibid. **59**:433–459.

———. 1944. Ecological studies of sessile Rotatoria. Part I. Factors affecting distribution. *Ecol. Monogr.* **14**:31–66.

———. 1945. Ecological studies of sessile Rotatoria. Part II. Dynamics of populations and social structures. Ibid. **15**:141–172.

———. 1946. Factors in the dynamics of rotifer populations. Ibid. **16**:357–372.

———. 1948. Ecological applications of Lansing's physiological work on longevity in Rotatoria. *Science* **108**:123–126.

———. 1949. A formula key to the rotatorian genus Ptygura. *Trans. Am. Microsc. Soc.* **68**:127–135.

———. 1965. Reproductive rate of planktonic rotifers as related to food and temperature in nature. *Ecol. Monogr.* **35**:61–111.

FINESINGER. J. E. 1926. Effects of certain chemical and physical agents on fecundity and length of life, and on their inheritance in a rotifer Lecane (Distyla) inermis (Bryce). *J. Exp. Zool.* **44**:63–94.

GILBERT, J. J. 1970. Monoxenic cultivation of the rotifer Brachionus calyciflorus in a defined medium. *Oecologia* **4**:89–101.

———. 1973. The adaptive significance of polymorphism in the rotifer Asplanchna humps in males and females. Ibid. **13**:135–146.

———. 1974. Dormancy in rotifers. *Trans. Am. Microsc. Soc.* **93**:490–513.

———. 1975. Polymorphism in the rotifer Asplanchna sieboldi. Variability in the body-wall-outgrowth response to dietary tocopherol. *Physiol. Zool.* **48**:404–419.

———. 1976. Polymorphism in the rotifer Asplanchna sieboldi: biomass, growth, and reproductive rate of the saccate and campanulate morphotypes. *Ecology* **57**:542–551.

HALBACH, U. 1970. Die Ursachen der Temporalvariation von Brachionus calyciflorus Pallas (Rotatoria). *Oecologia* **4**:262–318.

———. 1970a. Einfluss der Temperatur auf die Populations dynamik des planktischen Rädertieres Brachionus calyciflorus Pallas. Ibid. 176–207.

———. 1971. Zum Adaptivwert der zyklomorphen Dornenbildung von Brachionus calyciflorus Pallas (Rotatoria). I. Räuber-Beute-Beziehung in Kurzzeit-Versuchen. Ibid. **6**:267–288.

———. 1973. Quantitative Untersuchungen zur Assoziation von planktischen Rotatorien in Teichen. *Arch. Hydrobiol.* **71**:233–254.

HANLEY, J. 1949. The narcotization and mounting of Rotifera. *Microscope* **7**:154–159.

HARRING, H. K. 1913. Synopsis of the Rotatoria. *Bull. U.S. Nat. Mus.* **81**:1–226.

———. 1914. A list of the Rotatoria of Washington and vicinity with descriptions of a new genus and ten new species. *Proc. U.S. Nat. Mus.* **46**:387–405.

———. 1916. A revision of the rotatorian genera Lepadella and Lophocharis with descriptions of five new species. Ibid. **51**:527–568.

HARRING, H. K., and F. J. MYERS. 1922. The rotifer fauna of Wisconsin. *Trans. Wis. Acad. Sci. Arts and Lett.* **20**:553–662.

———. 1924. The rotifer fauna of Wisconsin, II. A revision of the notommatid rotifers, exclusive of the Dicranophorinae. Ibid. **21**:415–549.

———. 1926. The rotifer fauna of Wisconsin, III. A revision of the genera Lecane and Monostyla. Ibid. **22**:315–423.

———. 1928. The rotifer fauna of Wisconsin, IV. The Dicranophorinae. Ibid. **23**:667–808.

HAUER, J. 1924. Zur Kenntnis des Rotatorien genus Colurella Bory de St. Vincent. *Zool. Anz.* **59**:177–189.

HICKERNELL, L. M. 1917. A study of desiccation in the rotifer Philodina roseola, with special reference to cytological changes accompanying desiccation. *Biol. Bull.* **32**:343–407.

HLAVA, S. 1904. (Monograph of the Melicertidae.) *Arch. Prir. Prozk. Cech.* **13**:1–79.

HUDSON, C. T., and P. H. GOSSE. 1889. *The Rotifera; or wheel-animalcules, both British and foreign.* 2 vols. 272 pp. London.

JACOBS, M. H. 1909. The effects of desiccation on the rotifer Philodina roseola. *J. Exp. Zool.* **6**:207–265.

JENNINGS, H. S. 1903. Rotatoria of the United States. II. A monograph of the Rattulidae. *Bull. U.S. Fish Comm.* (1902):273–352.

JENNINGS, H. S., and R. S. LYNCH. 1928. Age, mortality, fertility, and individual diversities in the rotifer Proales sordida Gosse. I. *J. Exp. Zool.* **50**:345–407.

———. 1928a. Age, mortality, fertility, and individual diversities in the rotifer Proales sordida Gosse. II. Ibid. **51**:339–381.

KING, C. E. 1967. Food, age, and the dynamics of a laboratory population of rotifers. *Ecology* **48**:111–128.

LANSING, A. I. 1942. Some effects of hydrogen ion

concentration, total salt concentration, calcium and citrate on longevity and fecundity of the rotifer. *J. Exp. Zool.* **91**:195–212.

LUCKS, R. 1929. Rotatoria. Rädertiere. *Biol. Tiere Dtschl.* **10**:1–176.

LUNTZ, A. 1926. Untersuchungen über den Generations-wechsel der Rotatorien. I. Die Bedingungen des Generations-wechsels. *Biol. Zentralbl.* **46**:233–278.

MALY, E. J. 1975. Interactions among the predatory rotifer Asplanchna and two prey, Paramecium and Euglena. *Ecology* **56**:346–358.

MILLER, H. M. 1931. Alternation of generations in the rotifer Lecane inermis Bryce. Life histories of the sexual and non-sexual generations. *Biol. Bull.* **60**:345–381.

MONTGOMERY, T. H. 1903. On the morphology of the rotatorian family Floscularidae. *Proc. Acad. Nat. Sci. Phila.* **55**:363–395.

MURRAY, J. 1905. On a new family and twelve new species of Rotifera of the order Bdelloidea, collected by the Lake Survey. *Trans. Roy. Soc. Edinburgh* **41**:367–386.

MYERS, F. J. 1930. The rotifer fauna of Wisconsin, V. The genera Euchlanis and Monommata. *Trans. Wis. Acad. Sci. Arts and Lett.* **25**:353–411.

———. 1931. The distribution of Rotifera on Mount Desert Island. *Am. Mus. Novit.* **494**:1–12.

———. 1933. The distribution of Rotifera on Mount Desert Island. III. New Notommatidae of the genera Pleurotrocha, Lindia, Eothinia, Proalinopsis, and Encentrum. *Am. Mus. Novit.* **660**:1–18.

———. 1934. The distribution of Rotifera on Mount Desert Island. Part V. A new species of the Synchaetidae and new species of Asplanchnidae, Trichocercidae, and Brachionidae. Ibid. **700**:1–16.

———. 1934. The distribution of Rotifera on Mount Desert Island. Part VII. New Testudinellidae of the genus Testudinella and a new species of Brachionidae of the genus Trichotria. Ibid. **761**:1–8.

———. 1936. Psammolittoral rotifers of Lenape and Union lakes, New Jersey. Ibid. **830**:1–22.

———. 1937. A method of mounting rotifer jaws for study. *Trans. Am. Microsc. Soc.* **56**:256–257.

———. 1937a. Rotifera from the Adirondack region of New York. *Am. Mus. Novit.* **903**:1–17.

———. 1941. Lecane curvicornis var. miamiensis, new variety of Rotatoria, with observations on the feeding habits of rotifers. *Not. Nat.* **75**:1–8.

———. 1942. The rotatorian fauna of the Pocono plateau and environs. *Proc. Acad. Nat. Sci. Phila.* **94**:251–285.

NACHTWEY, R. 1925. Untersuchungen über die Keimbahn, Organogenese und Anatomie von Asplanchna priodonta Gosse. *Z. wiss. Zool.* **126**:239–492.

PAWLOWSKI, L. K. 1938. Materialen zur Kenntnis der mossbewohnenden Rotatorien Polens. I. *Ann. Mus. Zool. Pol.* **13**:115–159.

———. 1970. Les Rotifères de le Rivière Grabia. *Soc. Sci. Lodz, Pr. Wydz. III - Nauk. Mat.-Pryzr.* **110**:1–127.

PAX, F., and K. WULFERT. 1941. Die Rotatorien

deutscher Schwefelquellen und Thermen. *Arch. Hydrobiol.* **38**:165–213.

PEJLER, B. 1956. Introgression in plankton Rotatoria with some points of view on its causes and conceivable results. *Evolution* **10**:246–261.

———. 1957. On variation and evolution in planktonic Rotatoria. *Zool. Bidr. fran Uppsala* **32**:1–66.

———. 1962. Morphological studies on the genera Notholca, Kellicottia and Keratella (Rotatoria). Ibid. **33**:295–309.

PENNAK, R. W. 1940. Ecology of the microscopic Metazoa inhabiting the sandy beaches of some Wisconsin lakes. *Ecol. Monogr.* **10**:537–615.

———. 1949. Annual limnological cycles in some Colorado reservoir lakes. Ibid. **19**:233–267.

POURRIOT, R. 1965. Recherches sur l'écologie des rotifères. *Vie et Milieu, Suppl.* **21**:1–224.

PREISSLER K. 1977. Do rotifers show "avoidance of the shore"? *Oekologia* **27**:253–260.

RAUH, F. 1963. Untersuchungen über die Variabilität der Radertiere. III. Die experimentelle Beeinflussung der Variation von Brachionus calyciflorus und Brachionus capsuliflorus. *Z. Morphol. Oekol. Tiere* **53**:61–106.

REMANE, A. 1929. Intrazellulare Verdauung bei Rädertieren. *Z. Vgl. Physiol.* **11**:146–154.

———. 1929a. Rotatoria. *Tierwelt der Nord- und Ostsee.* **7**:1–156.

———. 1929–1933. Rotatorien. *Klassen und Ordnungen des Tier-Reichs* 4 (Abt. 2, Buch 1) Lief. 1–4:1–576.

ROUSSELET, C. F. 1902. The genus Synchaeta: a monographic study, with descriptions of five new species. *J. Roy. Microsc. Soc.* (1902):269–290, 393–411.

RUDESCU, L. 1960. Rotatoria. *Fauna Rep. Pop. Rom.* **2**(2):1–1192.

RUTTNER-KOLISKO, A. 1946. Über das Auftreten unbefruchteter "Dauereier" bei Anuraea aculeata (Keratella quadrata). *Oesterreich. Zool. Z.* **1**:179–181.

———. 1969. Kreuzungsexperimente zwischen Brachionus urceolaris und Brachionus quadridentatus, ein Beitrag zur Fortpflanzungsbiologie der heterogonen Rotatoria. *Arch. Hydrobiol.* **65**:397–412.

———. 1972. Das Zooplankton der Binnengewässer. 1. Teil. Rotatoria. *Die Binnengewasser* **26**:99–234.

SEEHAUS, W. 1930. Zur Morphologie der Rädertiergattung Testudinella Bory de St. Vincent. *Z. wiss. Zool.* **137**:175–273.

STOSSBERG, K. 1932. Zur Morphologie der Rädertiergattungen Euchlanis, Brachionus und Rhinoglena. Ibid. **142**:313–424.

SUDZUKI, M. 1955. Life history of some Japanese rotifers. I. Polyarthra trigla Ehrenberg. *Sci. Rep. Tokyo Kyoiku Daigaku, Sect. B,* **8**:41–63.

———. 1956. (On the general structure and the seasonal occurrence of the males in some Japanese rotifers. IV.) *(Zool. Mag.)* **65**:1–6.

———. 1959. (On the general structure and the seasonal occurrence of the males in some Japanese rotifers. VIII.) Ibid. **68**:1–7.

VALKANOV, A. 1936. Beitrag zur Anatomie und

Morphologie der Rotatoriengattung Trochosphaera Semper. *Trav. Soc. Bulg. Sci. Nat.* **17**:177–195.

VARGA, L. 1966. Kerekesférgek I. Rotatoria I. *Fauna hung.* **80**:1–144.

VIAUD, G. 1940. Recherches experimentales sur le phototropisme des rotifères. *Bull. Biol. Fr. Belg.* **74**:249–308; **77**:68–93, 224–242.

WATZKA, M. 1928. Die Rotatorienfauna der Cakowitzer Zuckerfabriksteiche und Versuche über das Auftreten von Rotatorien-Männchen und über die Entwicklungszeit der Dauereier. *Int. Rev.* **19**:430–451.

WEBER, E. F. 1898. Faune rotatorienne du bassin de Léman. *Rev. Suisse Zool.* **5**:263–785.

WESENBERG-LUND, C. 1923. Contributions to the biology of the Rotifera. I. The males of the Rotifera. *Det. Kgl. Vidensk. Selsk. Skr. Naturv. Math.* (8) **4**:189–345.

———. 1930. Contributions to the biology of the Rotifera. II. The periodicity and sexual periods. *Ibid.* (9) **2**:1–230.

WILLIAMS L. G. 1966. Dominant planktonic rotifers of major waterways of the United States. *Limnol. Oceanogr.* **11**:83–91.

Wiszniewski, J. 1934. Les rotifères psammiques. *Ann. Mus. Zool. Pol.* **10**:339–399.

WULFERT, K. 1938. Die Rädertiergattung Cephalodella Bory de St. Vincent. *Arch. Naturgesch.* **7**:137–152.

———. 1964. Unsere gegenwärtige Kenntnis der Rotatoriengattung Macrochaetus Perty 1850. *Limnologica* **2**:281–309.

———. 1965. Revision der Rotatorien-Gattung Platyias Harring 1913. *Ibid.* **3**:41–64.

ZACHARIAS, O. 1902. Zum Kapital der "wurstförmigen Parasiten" bei Räderthieren. *Zool. Anz.* **25**:647–649.

# Chapter 9

# NEMATODA (ROUNDWORMS)

ALMOST any collection of sand, mud, debris, or vegetation from the bottom or margin of a pond, lake, brook, or river will be found to contain small roundworms, or nematodes, sometimes in great abundance. Yet as a group the fresh-water species are poorly known, and few American investigators have been concerned with them since the extensive taxonomic and ecological studies of N. A. Cobb, of the U. S. Department of Agriculture, whose many papers appeared during the first third of the present century. Nematodes have been generally avoided by aquatic biologists because of their small size and difficulties in identification. Although most fresh-water nematodes can be readily assigned to the proper genus, there are a great many undescribed species.

Most of the available information about the Phylum Nematoda is concerned with the thousands of parasitic species, some of which are of extreme importance to the health and economic well-being of man. Probably no more than 2000 free-living species have been reported from the fresh waters of the world, but this figure must represent only a small fraction of the actual number of species living in this environment. They occur in such widely differing habitats as pools of polar ice, hot springs, puddles, the bottoms of streams, and the deepest and largest lakes.

The account of the Nematoda as given in this chapter is written specifically from the standpoint of the free-living fresh-water species of the United States, but most of the generalizations apply also to the phylum as a whole.

**General characteristics.** Nematodes occurring in the substrates of fresh waters are almost invariably less than a centimeter long. Their nearly constant and rapid whiplike movements in a dorsoventral plane are quite characteristic, there being no changes in body diameter and proportions. These thrashing, serpentine movements usually produce little or no locomotion in water alone, but debris and vegetation afford sufficient friction to result in forward locomotion. A few species move along the substrate like an inchworm, and the rare free-swimming forms are able to move through the water just above the substrate.

Most aquatic species have three unicellular glands in the tail. Their secretion is carried to the posterior end by one to three minute ducts, and the flow to the outside is regulated by a special pore, or spinneret, at the tip of the body (Figs. 146A, B, D). This secretion is sticky and is used for temporary attachment to objects.

Some nematodes have a pair of lateral caudal pores, or phasmids, of uncertain function (Fig. 146C).

In cross section the nematode body is more or less circular. The mouth is terminal, but the transverse slitlike anus is subterminal. Though coloration ranges from colorless to blackish, the great majority of species are translucent and therefore fascinating objects for study under the microscope. Most of the coloration of nematodes is determined by the contents of the digestive tract and intestinal cell inclusions. The body is slightly tapered, truncate, or bluntly rounded at the anterior end, where there is sometimes a poorly defined head

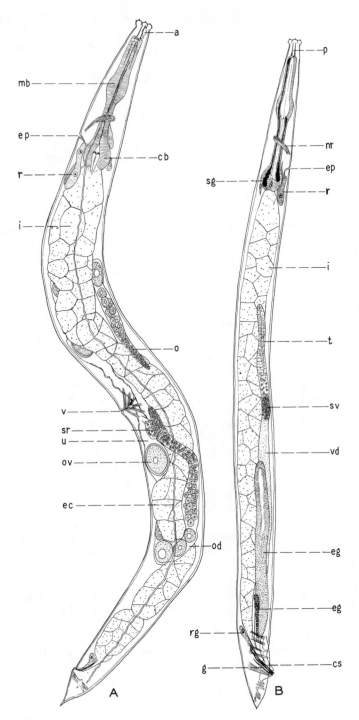

FIG. 141–Structure of *Rhabditis*, a typical fresh-water nematode, ×95. A, female; B, male. A genital bursa is shown in the male, but this structure is rare in free-living species. *a*, amphid; *cb*, cardiac bulb of esophagus; *cs*, copulatory spicule; *ec*, excretory canal; *eg*, ejaculatory gland; *ep*, excretory pore; *g*, gubernaculum; *i*, intestine; *mb*, middle bulb of esophagus; *nr*, nerve ring; *o*, ovary; *od*, oviduct; *ov*, mature fertilized ovum; *p*, pharynx; *r*, renette; *rg*, rectal gland; *sg*, salivary gland (glands and ducts solid black; present in both sexes but shown only in figure of male); *sr*, seminal receptacle; *sv*, seminal vesicle; *t*, testis; *u*, uterus; *v*, vulva and genital pore; *vd*, vas deferens. (Modified from Chitwood, 1937, by permission.)

Fig. 142.–Diagrammatic cross section of a typical female nematode. *c*, cuticle; *dc*, dorsal chord of hypodermis containing dorsal nerve cord; *ec*, excretory canal; *h*, hypodermis; *i*, intestine, showing rodlike layer on inner surface; *lc*, lateral chord of hypodermis; *mf*, muscle fibers of muscle cell; *o*, oviduct with four developing eggs; *p*, pseudocoel.

region, but the posterior end generally tapers to a point.

The outermost layer of the body is a dead, secreted proteinaceous cuticle, which is variously marked, sculptured, or scaly. Sometimes the transverse striations are composed of lines or rows of dots so fine that they may be detected only with critical illumination and the oil immersion lens. At the other extreme, the cuticle may have prominent transverse grooves, rows of dots, or even scalelike folds (Fig. 147C). Some species have longitudinal striations or long, low, keellike wings, or alae, which appear to aid in stiffening the animal. In the males of a few fresh-water species there is a caudal bursa composed of two more or less prominent alae (Fig. 141B). Setae are sometimes present, especially at the anterior end; these are simply elongated projections of the general cuticular exoskeleton. The cuticle extends inward and lines the mouth cavity, esophagus, vulva, and posterior portion of the digestive tract.

The hypodermis, or subcuticle, is usually a syncytial tissue; it secretes the cuticle and lies just below it. This layer is thin except dorsally, ventrally, and laterally, where it is greatly thickened and protruded inward to form the four chords. (Fig. 142).

The remainder of the body wall consists of an innermost layer of muscle cells comprising four groups, or fields, of cells separated by the four chords. In meromyarian nematodes there are usually only two to four cells per field, but in polymyarian nematodes each field has numerous cells. A muscle cell is long and spindle-shaped, and contains numerous ribbon-shaped muscle fibrils. The fibrils may all lie at the base of the cell and adjacent to the hypodermis (platymyarian arrangement), or the fibrils may extend varying distances up the sides of the cells and partially enclose the sarcoplasm (coelomyarian arrangement) (Fig. 142).

The body cavity of a nematode is properly called a pseudocoel and contains only a few connective tissue cells. There is no true mesodermal epithelium covering the digestive tract.

A nematode grows by periodically shedding the cuticle, including the cuticular lining of the stomodaeum and proctodaeum.

**Digestive System.** The mouth is characteristically surrounded by lips, each with a small papilla on its summit. Six appears to be the basic number of lips, but often there is fusion to form three, and sometimes distinct lips are absent. The lips show innumerable modifications. In some species they are muscular, mobile, and modified for sucking or gripping; in others they are modified for ripping (*Ironus*); sometimes they form toothlike odontia (*Mononchus*).

The mouth opening is minute to large, circular or triangular, and often capable of great distension. The mouth cavity is lined with cuticle and varies enormously in size and structure. Sometimes it is inconspicuous or absent; in other species it is capacious. It may be cylindrical, subglobular, cup-shaped, conoid, or some other shape. Its wall is often supplied with stiffening rods or plates; rasps and special teeth, or onchia, are common. In some herbivorous and carnivorous species the pharynx is supplied with a solid or hollow stilettolike protrusile spear (Fig. 147).

The structure of the esophagus is an important taxonomic character. It is circular in cross section, is lined with cuticle, is composed mostly of radial muscle fibers, and has a small triquetrous cavity. Three unicellular salivary glands are usually imbedded in the esophageal wall; their ducts open into the lumen of the stoma or esophagus. In some species the esophagus is elongated, plain, and more or less cylindrical, but more commonly there are one or two ellipsoid or spherical bulbar swellings. If a single bulb is present, it is usually located at the posterior end of the esophagus and is termed the cardiac bulb, whereas the second (middle) bulb is located somewhere near midlength. The esophagus is a suctorial and peristaltic organ, with the bulbs serving to increase the pumping action. Sometimes esophageal valves are present that aid in sucking and prevent regurgitation.

The long intestine extends from esophagus to rectum and is devoid of caeca or loops in fresh-water species. It consists of a single layer of epithelial cells, though rarely there is a flimsy covering of connective tissue or muscle fibers. The inner surface of the intestine is lined with a layer of curious minute rodlike outgrowths, or microvilli, constituting the brush border (Fig. 142). These are sometimes mistaken for cilia, but true cilia (with basal bodies) are unknown in this phylum. Most intestinal digestion is thought to occur in the anterior half of this organ.

The junction of esophagus and intestine is supplied with an obscure valvular apparatus, and there is often a comparable structure separating the intestine proper form its short, narrow, muscular posterior end, the rectum. Several unicellular rectal and anal glands are characteristic of this region of the body.

**Feeding.** All varieties of food habits are represented in free-living fresh-water nematodes. Some feed only on dead plant material, others only on dead animal material. A third group are detritus feeders, consuming both dead plant and dead animal material. Herbivorous species are variously specialized for biting and chewing living plant tissues, and others are equipped with a rigid hollow stylet that pierces plant cells and through which the protoplasm is sucked by the action of the esophagus. Similarly, the predaceous and carnivorous forms, such as *Mononchus, Dorylaimus,*

FIG. 143.–Esophagus shapes. A, *Hirschmanniella*; B, *Aphelenchoides*; C, *Rhabditis*; D, *Butlerius*; E, *Plectus*; F, *Leptolaimus*; G, *Achromadora*; H, *Cylindrolaimus*; I, *Ironus*; J, *Aphanolaimus*; K, *Alaimus*; L, *Tripyla*. (Modified from Ferris, Ferris, and Tjepkema.)

*Nygolaimus,* and *Actinolaimus,* show a variety of anatomical modifications for feeding. The lips may be specialized for seizing or tearing the prey, and the pharynx is often partially eversible and supplied with onchia or rasps for crushing, rasping, or macerating. Many carnivorous species have the hollow stylet type of feeding. The prey consists of Protozoa and all types of small Metazoa, including oligochaetes, rotifers, gastrotrichs, tardigrades, and other nematodes.

Material digested in the alimentary canal is absorbed into the fluid of the surrounding hemocoel and carried to all the single ventral excretory cell, or renette, which opens through an excretory pore on the midventral line in the region of the esophagus by way of a short to long duct. In other nematodes there are two lateral excretory canals imbedded in the lateral chords of the hypodermis throughout most of the body length. They are connected anteriorly and ventrally by a transverse canal, thus forming an H or U shape. A very short duct connects the transverse duct with the excretory pore. There may or may not be two special cells (the renette) associated with the transverse duct (Fig. 141).

In a few genera, including *Dorylaimus*, no excretory system has been found. Considerable excretion through the digestive tract may occur in all nematodes.

**Nervous system.** A ring of nerve fibers and associated indistinct ganglia encircle the esophagus. From this mass six small nerves are given off which innervate the anterior end. Four or more longitudinal nerves extend posteriorly in the hypodermis, of which the dorsal and ventral nerves are usually the most prominent. Especially at the extremities of the body, there are scattered small ganglia and numerous branch nerves that connect the longitudinal nerves with each other. In general, the nervous system is considerably more complicated than most elementary textbooks indicate.

**Sense organs.** Paired eyespots occur in some species of *Punctodora* and *Monhystera*, as well as in a few other genera. Such eyespots are small clumps of reddish, violet, or blackish granules imbedded in the esophagus or between the esophagus and body wall. A minute lenslike device may be present in front of each clump of pigment, or it may be absent. There appears to be some difference of opinion as to whether there are nervous connections between eyespots and nervous system.

Tactile receptors are mainly associated with the cephalic papillae and setae and with the caudal setae. The somatic setae, often present between anterior and posterior ends, are probably also tactile.

Amphids are peculiar nematode structures, and though there is still considerable

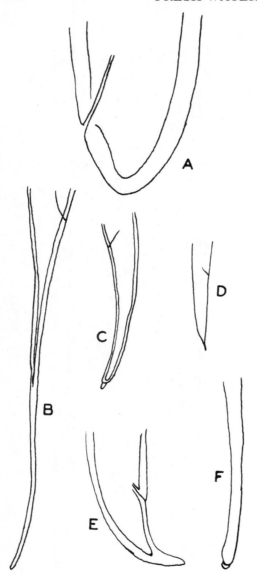

FIG. 144.–Posterior end. A, *Labronema*; B, *Mesodorylaimus*; C, *Achromadora*; D, *Aphelenchoides*; E, *Eudorylaimus*; F, *Labronema*. (Modified from Ferris, Ferris, and Tjepkema.)

internal organs and body wall by circulation resulting from the incessant body movements. There is no special circulatory system.

**Excretion.** The excretory system presents a varied picture in the phylum as a whole. In its simplest condition there is a controversy about their function, it appears most likely that they are chemoreceptors rather than organs of equilibration. A typical fresh-water nematode has two amphids, one on each side of the body near the anterior end. Externally, an amphid may have the shape of a narrow slit, an oval, a circle, or spiral grooves and ridges on the cuticle. Internally, it consists of a small pouch and often a minute longitudinal posterior canal. The pouch has recently been shown to be innervated. Chitwood (1937) maintains that amphids are always present, but often they are so minute, reduced, or vestigial as to be indistinguishable to the average observer.

**Reproduction, development.** Both males and females are known for most species of nematodes, and reproduction is syngamic, but in many species males are rare or unknown, and reproduction is usually parthenogenetic, as in *Rhabdolaimus*, *Monhystera*, and *Alaimus*. Hermaphroditic species occur in *Mononchulus*, *Aphanolaimus*, *Ironus*, *Tobrilus*, *Mononchus*, and a

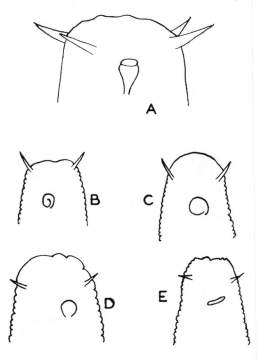

FIG. 145.–Amphid shapes. A, *Tobrilus*; B, *Achromadora*; C, *Prodesmodora*; D, *Plectus*; E, *Anaplectus*. (Modified from Ferris, Ferris, and Tjepkema.)

few other genera. The female is usually the larger, but the sexes can be distinguished by the sex characters.

In general, the reproductive systems are simpler and less extensive than those of parasitic species and produce relatively few gametes. In the mature female the genital pore, or vulva, can be seen as a transverse slit on the ventral midline near the middle of the body. There is a short muscular vagina, which may connect with a single thin-walled tapering reproductive tubule or, more typically, may branch to form two tubules, one anterior and one posterior. Beginning at the vagina, each tubule consists of a wide uterus, an oviduct, and a fine terminal ovary composed of very small oocytes. Sometimes the uterus has a small associated seminal receptacle (Fig. 141). A reproductive tubule may be outstretched or reflexed. Thus the reproductive system of a female nematode may have one of four configurations: double and outstretched, double and reflexed, single and outstretched (Fig. 149D), or single and reflexed

The male reproductive system is ordinarily a single tapering tubule, which opens ventrally into the posterior part of the digestive tract. Beginning basally, the tubule consists of a long vas deferens, short seminal vesicle, and thin testis (Fig. 141B). Rarely the testis is bifurcated or reflexed. Ejaculatory glands sometimes open into the basal part of the vas deferens. Since the rectum of the male is common to both the reproductive and digestive ducts, it is more appropriately called a cloaca. A pair of sclerotized copulatory spicules are contained within a delicate pouch on the dorsal side of the cloaca. During copulation these spicules are extruded through the cloacal aperture, or anus, of the male and into the vulva. They are moved back and forth by muscles so that the vulva and vagina are kept open and so that sperm are more easily propelled into the vagina. The gubernaculum is a sclerotized thickening in the dorsal wall of the male cloaca that acts as a spicular guide and prevents the spicules from rupturing the spicular pouch and cloaca when exserted.

A clasping device, or copulatory bursa (Fig. 141B), is common in parasitic species but is rare in the males of fresh-water species. It consists of two thin, transparent, longitudinal flaps of cuticle near the posterior end. It is widest opposite the anus and may or may not be long enough to encompass the posterior tip of the animal.

Fertilization occurs in the upper end of the uterus and the egg shell is laid down in the lower uterus. The fertilized eggs usually leave the body before the onset of segmentation, but some species are viviparous or ovoviviparous. The embryo is formed and hatches in a few hours to a few weeks, depending on the particular species and ecological conditions. The newly hatched young are fully developed except for size, reproductive system, and certain specializations of the lips, pharynx, and esophagus. It is thought that there is almost always a series of four molts (five instars) in the complete life history. In addition to the general body covering, a molt also includes shedding of the cuticular lining of pharynx, esophagus, vulva, and rectum. The secondary sex characters are not apparent until after either the penultimate molt or the last molt. Little is known about the longevity of free-living nematodes, but males are thought to be much shorter lived than females.

**Ecology.** The eggs of soil and parasitic nematodes are highly resistant to desiccation (even for periods up to 10 or 20 years) and to high and low temperatures; they are easily transported by animals and blown about as dust. The larvae and adults of many soil species likewise are viable after being dried and shriveled up in a state of anabiosis. Nevertheless, there seems to be very little information about encystment and desiccation among aquatic nematodes, and it is not known how important these mechanisms are for dissemination. Judging from the available scanty distribution records, however, most aquatic genera and many species are cosmopolitan and worldwide.

Furthermore, some species show an amazing ability to thrive in a wide variety of habitats and a wide range of ecological conditions. Among all the metazoan phyla, nematodes are perhaps the most highly adaptable from ecological and physiological standpoints. The same species, for example, may be found from the tropics to the subarctic, from warm springs to cold alpine lakes, and on many types of substrates. Only a few genera appear to be restricted to fresh waters; examples are *Cryptonchus*, *Chronogaster*, and *Anonchus*. *Oncholaimus* and *Chromadorita* are both marine and fresh-water genera. The following genera, among others, occur in both fresh waters and terrestrial soils: *Prismatolaimus*, *Mononchus*, *Tobrilus*, *Tripyla*, and *Ironus*. *Monhystera*, however, is a genus with terrestrial, marine, and fresh-water representatives. In addition to being found in fresh waters and soils, *Rhabditis* and *Cephalobus* also have parasitic representatives. A few genera show specific habitat preferences in fresh waters, and some of these are mentioned in the key that follows. Many soil nematodes often occur in fresh waters as the result of wash.

Present ideas emphasize the probable origin of nematodes in fresh waters and their subsequent migration and colonization of salt water and terrestrial environments.

As pointed out long ago by Cobb, nematode populations often reach tremendous numbers both in terrestrial soils and in the substrates of bodies of water, where they are of great mechanical importance in continuously working over and mixing soils in much the same way as oligochaetes. Even in the wet sand of lake beaches near the water's edge, which is not an especially favorable habitat for nematodes, the writer has found up to eight adult nematodes per milliliter of sand. Some of the most dense populations, especially species of *Mononchus, Ironus,* and *Tripyla,* occur in the sand and gravel filter beds of sewage disposal plants. A wide variety of species occur around the roots of aquatic plants. In natural fresh-water habitats most specimens are confined to the uppermost 5 cm of the substrate.

Although populations of aquatic nematodes can be maintained indefinitely in low concentrations of dissolved oxygen, 2 to 10 percent saturation, for example, it is thought that active nematodes are capable of withstanding anaerobic conditions only for one to several weeks at a time. The eggs, however, are highly resistant and may remain viable after many months in the absence of oxygen and after repeated freezing and thawing.

**Collecting, preparing, preserving.** Perhaps the chief reason for the general neglect of the nematodes by investigators in aquatic zoology is the fact that they almost invariably occur in quantities of bottom mud and fine organic debris from which it is difficult to separate them. If a small quantity of the material containing nematodes is placed in a petri dish of water, they can be detected by their movements and picked out with a fine pipette under the dissecting binoculars and transferred to clean water. This is a tedious method, however, and if a relatively large quantity of nematode-containing material is available, many worms may be concentrated by the following method: (1) wash the material through a sieve of 2 or 3 mm mesh and then (2) through a 1 mm mesh sieve to remove the larger pieces of debris; (3) wash the material through number 20 bolting silk, which will retain the nematodes and allow the fine debris to pass; (4) transfer the retained nematodes and debris to a small container of water, agitate, and decant quickly as soon as the heavy sand particles settle out; repeat this step if desirable; (5) agitate and allow to stand two to four minutes, which is sufficient time to allow the nematodes to sink to the bottom, and then decant off the muddy water. The residue will then contain most of the nematodes with a minimum of fine debris; specimens should be picked up individually with a fine pipette, bristle, or Irwin loop for further treatment. Ferris et al. (1973) give directions for a similar method of separating nematodes from large quantities of aquatic substrate debris.

Live nematodes are so active that it is useless to study them with a compound microscope. They should first be narcotized with chloroform, chloral hydrate, magnesium sulfate, or other narcotic.

Hot saturated mercuric chloride or hot 70 to 80 percent alcohol are probably the best fixatives, but for routine fixation in the field cold 85 percent alcohol and 5 percent formalin are quite reliable. Good results are also possible by killing the worms by placing them in a water bath for 10 minutes at 57°. Warm water prevents coiling.

Simple temporary formalin mounts ringed with petroleum jelly are excellent for routine purposes.

For permanent mounts and identification there is probably no better or more convenient mounting medium than glycerin jelly. But glycerin, like most substances, penetrates the nematode cuticle very slowly. If, however, the worms are placed in an open concave watch glass of 5 percent glycerin in 50 percent alcohol, the alcohol and water will evaporate in 3 to 10 days and the worms will be infiltrated in concentrated glycerin. They may be stored thus or mounted directly in glycerin jelly. Like all other glycerin jelly slides, the circular cover slips should be ringed with Murrayite, "Zut," or similar cement.

Stained balsam mounts are tedious to prepare and often exasperating, because unless meticulous care is taken in the reagent transfers, the final mounted nematodes collapse or become distorted and opaque. Cobb (1918) devised a glass "differentiator" for gradually transferring nematodes from one fluid to another so as to avoid distortion. Chatterji (1935) reports success with the following brief procedure: 70 percent alcohol, dioxan overnight, fresh dioxan 1 hour, clove oil 2 hours, and balsam. Chitwood and Chitwood (1930) give detailed directions for imbedding in paraffin.

Many aquatic nematodes may be cultured in the laboratory in 3 percent agar in tap water with a little added soil and debris.

**Taxonomy.** The taxonomic relationships of free-living nematodes, especially with respect to family designations, are uncertain and in a state of flux. The literature, furthermore, is badly scattered, often in obscure journals. Of the several modern plans that have been proposed, that of Ferris et al. (1973) is used in this manual. Following is a list of orders and genera included in the key.

Chromadorida
  *Achromadora*
  *Chromadorita*
  *Ethmolaimus*
  *Monochromadora*
  *Paracyatholaimus*
  *Punctodora*
Araeolaimida
  *Anaplectus*
  *Anonchus*
  *Aphanolaimus*
  *Bastiania*
  *Chronogaster*
  *Cylindrolaimus*
  *Euteratocephalus*
  *Paraphanolaimus*
  *Plectus*
  *Teratocephalus*
Monhysterida
  *Monhystera*
  *Monhystrella*
  *Odontolaimus*
Desmodorida
  *Prodesmodora*
Enoplida
  *Cryptonchus*
  *Ironus*
  *Oncholaimus*
  *Prismatolaimus*
  *Rhabolaimus*
  *Tobrilus*
  *Tripyla*
Dorylaimida
  *Actinolaimus*
  *Alaimus*
  *Amphidelus*
  *Aulolaimoides*
  *Dorylaimus*
  *Eudorylaimus*
  *Labronema*

  *Mesodorylaimus*
  *Microlaimus*
  *Nygolaimus*
  *Thornia*
Mononchida
  *Anatonchus*
  *Miconchus*
  *Mononchulus*
  *Mononchus*
  *Mylonchulus*
  *Prionchulus*
Tylenchida
  *Apelenchoides*
  *Atylenchus*
  *Criconema*
  *Criconemoides*
  *Hemicycliophora*
  *Hirschmanniella*
  *Tylenchus*
Rhabditida
  *Acrobeloides*
  *Butlerius*
  *Cephalobus*
  *Eucephalobus*
  *Goffartia*
  *Mononchoides*
  *Panagrolaimus*
  *Rhabditis*

After considerable experience, identifications to genus can sometimes be made with the 4 mm objective of the microscope, but critical illumination and the oil immersion objective are usually essential in order to study the smaller details.

The following key is greatly modified from Ferris et al. (1973). It includes the great majority of genera reported from U.S. fresh waters and should be reliable for more than 98 percent of all specimens collected. Some of the genera are quite rare. Family designations are not included because of the many taxonomic uncertainties among the Nematoda.

## KEY TO GENERA OF NEMATODA

1. Stoma large, cup-shaped; width and depth of stoma at least one-half of lip region; stoma strongly cuticularized (Figs. 147A, F, K, N) .......................2
   Stoma not both wide and cup-shaped, and either weakly or strongly cuticularized. 15
2. Cephalic setae long (Fig. 146G) ...............................................3
   Cephalic setae short or absent (setose papillae may be present) ..................5

F<small>IG</small>. 146.–Structure of nematodes. A, posterior end of *Rhabdolaimus*, showing caudal glands and spinneret; B, posterior end of *Aphanolaimus*, showing caudal glands, spinneret, and phasmid; C, posterior end of male *Tylenchus*, showing phasmid; D, posterior end of *Tobrilus*, showing spinneret; E, female *Achromadora*, ×350; F, anterior end of *Plectus*; G, anterior end of *Punctodora*; H, anterior end of *Prismatolaimus*; J, anterior end of *Butlerius*; K, anterior end of *Mononchoides*; L, anterior end of *Nygolaimus*.

3. Posterior end elongate-clavate, with spinneret; four large cephalic setae (Fig. 146G). **4**
   Posterior end filiform and without spinneret; six large and four short cephalic setae
   (Fig. 146H); common . . . . . . . . . . . . . . . . . . . . . . . . . . . . . . . . . . . **Prismatolaimus**
4. Stoma in two parts: an anterior cup-shaped region with a large tooth, and a posterior
   part with elongated conical cavity (Fig. 146G); rare . . . . . . . . . . . . . .**Punctodora**
   Stoma not in two parts, without a large tooth (Fig. 148B) . . . . . . . . . . . . . . . . **Anonchus**
5. Esophagus with two bulbs (Fig. 143D) . . . . . . . . . . . . . . . . . . . . . . . . . . . . . . . . . . . . . . . .**6**
   Esophagus cylindrical, or with only a posterior bulb . . . . . . . . . . . . . . . . . . . . . . . . . . .**7**

6. Stoma very wide and deep; anterior edge of stoma not marked and not bearing grooves
   or riblike structure (Fig. 146J); uncommon ........................**Butlerius**
   Stoma deep and moderately wide; anterior edge of stoma bearing riblike structures;
   slender tubular section of stoma extending posterior to large tooth in stoma
   (Fig. 146K) .................................................. **Mononchoides**
7. Spinneret absent ...............................................................**8**
   Spinneret present (Figs. 144C, F) ...........................................**9**
8. Pharynx with a spear and four large teeth (Fig. 150C); common ....... **Actinolaimus**
   Pharynx without a spear and four large teeth; common in decaying material.
                                                              **Panagrolaimus**
9. Spinneret subterminal (Fig. 147M) ...............................**Mononchulus**
   Spinneret at tip of body...................................................**10**
10. Stoma with three large teeth (Fig. 147F); rare ..................... **Oncholaimus**
    Stoma with another arrangement of teeth ...................................**11**
11. Dorsal tooth posteriorly directed in stoma (Fig. 147K); rare in marshy areas.
                                                                 **Anatonchus**
    Dorsal tooth anterior directed in stoma .......................................**12**
12. Large dorsal tooth posteriorly placed in stoma; two large subventral teeth opposite
    (Fig. 147N); uncommon....................................... **Miconchus**
    Dorsal tooth anteriorly placed in stoma; subventral teeth absent or small........**13**
13. Stoma with transverse rows of denticles opposite dorsal tooth (Fig. 152G). **Mylonchulus**
    Without transverse rows of denticles opposite dorsal tooth ....................**14**
14. Longitudinal ridge without denticles opposite dorsal tooth (Fig. 152E); common.
                                                                  **Mononchus**
    Longitudinal denticulate ridge opposite dorsal tooth (Fig. 152F) ........ **Prionchulus**
15. Stoma armed with a spear (Figs. 150E, 148L) or spearlike tooth (Fig. 150A) ......**16**
    Stoma lacking a spear or spearlike tooth ......................................**29**
16. Cuticle strongly annulated (Figs. 147C, D); body stout; swamps and acid waters; large
    genera ..............................................................**17**
    Cuticle not strongly annulated ..............................................**18**
17. Annules with spines or accessory scales (Fig. 147C) .................. **Criconema**
    Annules without spines or scales (Fig. 147D) .....................**Criconemoides**
18. Esophagus with one bulb; amphid stirrup-shaped and distinct (Fig. 145A) ........**19**
    Esophagus with two bulbs; amphid obscure .................................**25**
19. Posterior end of both sexes short and blunt or elongate, never filiform (Fig. 144A). **20**
    Posterior end of female, or both female and male, filiform (Fig. 144B) ...........**23**
20. "Tail" blunt and approximately twice as long as the anal body diameter (Fig. 147J);
    anterior end of body nearly square (Fig. 147H); esophagus expanding sharply
    at middle (Fig. 147G); uncommon.................................**Thornia**
    "Tail" pointed, or if blunt then distinctly shorter than twice anal body diameter;
    anterior end of body somewhat rounded; esophagus expanding gradually ...**21**
21. Toothlike spear attached to stoma wall, but stoma wall cuticularized and separated
    from tooth; esophagus often expanded anterior to middle (Figs.
    150A, B) .................................................... **Nygolaimus**
    With a true spear in the stoma; walls of stoma weakly developed; esophagus usually
    expanded at middle ...............................................**22**
22. Anterior portion of esophagus much narrower than posterior portion (Fig. 148H); total
    length up to 2 mm; very large genus ...................... **Eudorylaimus**
    Anterior portion of esophagus nearly as wide as posterior portion (Fig. 148G); total
    length usually more than 2 mm; rare ..........................**Labronema**
23. Enlarged basal portion of esophagus short, barely longer than wide (Fig. 148J);
    rare ...................................................... **Aulolaimoides**
    Basal portion of esophagus considerably longer than wide ....................**24**
24. Cuticle with longitudinal ridges; more than 2 mm long; abundant and common (Fig.
    150E) ....................................................**Dorylaimus**
    Cuticle without longitudinal ridges; less than 2 mm long; many common species.
                                                              **Mesodorylaimus**

FIG. 147.–Structure of nematodes. A, anterior end of *Panagrolaimus*; B, anterior end of *Aphelenchus*; C, anterior end of *Criconema*; D, posterior end of *Criconemoides*; E, anterior end of *Tylenchus*; F, anterior end of *Oncholaimus*; G, anterior end of *Thornia*; H, anterior end of *Thornia*; J, posterior end of female *Thornia*; K, anterior end of *Anatonchus*; L, anterior end of *Mononchulus*; M, posterior end of female *Mononchulus*; N, anterior end of *Miconchus*. (A modified from Thorne, 1937; B modified from Chitwood, 1937; C modified from Cobb, 1915; G–J modified from Ferris, Ferris, and Tjepkema; K–N from Ferris, Ferris, and Tjepkema.)

FIG. 148.–Anterior end of nematodes. A, *Aphanolaimus*; B, *Anonchus*; C, *Rhabdolaimus*; D, *Euteratocephalus*; E, *Teratocephalus* (annulations not shown); F, *Bastiana* (annulations not shown); G, *Lebronema*; H, *Eudorylaimus*; J, *Aulolaimoides*; K, *Atylenchus*; L, *Hemicycliophora*; M, posterior end of *Tylenchus*. (A, C, D, and E modified from Cobb, 1914; B modified from Cobb, 1913; F modified from Chitwood, 1937; G to M modified from Ferris, Ferris, and Tjepkema.)

25. Cephalic setae present; cuticle with longitudinal ridges and coarse annulations (Fig. 148K); rare ............................................ **Atylenchus**
     Cephalic setae absent; cuticular ridges lacking; cuticle annulations not coarse ....**26**
26. Worm with an accessory loose outer cuticular layer; spear long, approximately same length as esophagus (Fig. 148L); uncommon .............. **Hemicycliophora**
     Without an accessory cuticular layer; spear not nearly as long as esophagus (Fig. 149F) ....................................................**27**

27. Posterior end filiform (Fig. 148M); esophagus not overlapping intestine; median bulb
     of esophagus small and ovate (Fig. 147E); often associated with roots. **Tylenchus**
     Posterior end conical, not filiform (Fig. 144D); esophagus overlapping intestine, and
     median bulb of esophagus prominent and spherical (Figs. 143A, B) . . . . . . . .28
28. Spear slender, with or without modified basal knobs (Fig. 149F); very large genus.
                                                                     **Aphelenchoides**
     Spear stout, with large basal knobs (Fig. 149G) . . . . . . . . . . . . . . . . . **Hirschmanniella**
29. Spinneret present (Figs. 151C, G, H) . . . . . . . . . . . . . . . . . . . . . . . . . . . . . . . . . . . . . . . .30
     Spinneret absent or obscure . . . . . . . . . . . . . . . . . . . . . . . . . . . . . . . . . . . . . . . . . . . . .47
30. Esophagus with basal bulb (Fig. 151D) . . . . . . . . . . . . . . . . . . . . . . . . . . . . . . . . . .31
     Esophagus cylindrical, with no basal bulb (Fig. 143H) . . . . . . . . . . . . . . . . . . . . . . .40

Fig. 149.–Structure of nematodes. A, anterior end of *Microlaimus*; B, anterior end of *Achromadora*; C, anterior end of *Ethmolaimus*; D, female *Monhystera*, ×110; E, anterior end of *Monhystera*; F, anterior end of *Aphelenchoides*; G, anterior end of *Hirschmanniella*; H, anterior end of *Chromadorita*; J, posterior end of female *Hirschmanniella*; K, anterior end of *Tylenchus*. (A modified from Chitwood, 1937; B and D modified from Cobb, 1914; E modified from Micoletzky; C and F to K modified from Ferris, Ferris, and Tjepkema.)

31. Amphid multispiral (Fig. 149C), slitlike (Fig. 149H), or obscure ................32
    Amphid large, unispiral, circular, or open circle (Figs. 149A; 151E, J) ..........37
32. Amphid spiral (Fig. 145B) .....................................................33
    Amphid slitlike or obscure (Fig. 145E) ......................................34
33. Dorsal tooth and opposing subventral teeth large; tubular section of stoma extending
    posterior to teeth (Fig. 149C); one common species ........... **Ethmolaimus**
    Dorsal tooth large, but opposing subventral teeth small or obscure; stoma ending just
    posterior to teeth; tubular section posterior to teeth lacking (Fig. 149B);
    common ...............................................**Achromadora**
34. Stoma with large, sharp dorsal tooth and obscure subventral teeth (Fig. 149H); cuticle
    marked with punctations; uncommon ....................... **Chromadorita**
    Stoma with two or three small teeth or no teeth; cuticle smooth.................35
35. Cephalic setae present; cuticle distinctly annulated (Fig. 151A)......... **Anaplectus**
    Cephalic setae absent; cuticle weakly annulated or smooth ....................36
36. Inconspicuous peglike spinneret (Fig. 151C); stoma funnel-shaped (Fig. 151B);
    rare ................................................. **Monochromadora**
    Prominent long, conical spinneret (Fig. 146A); stoma tubular (Fig. 148C);
    common ..............................................**Rhabdolaimus**
37. Basal bulb of esophagus divided transversely in two places (Fig. 151D). **Prodesmodora**
    Basal bulb of esophagus not divided transversely ...........................38
38. Cuticle smooth (Fig. 151E); rare ................................. **Monhystrella**
    Cuticle annulated or striated ............................................39
39. Head slightly offset and rounded; stoma with a tooth and two denticles (Fig. 149A);
    uncommon .............................................**Microlaimus**
    Head not offset; stoma without teeth (Fig. 151J) ......................... **Plectus**
40. Spinneret located ventrally at posterior end (Fig. 147M); stoma with large subventral
    tooth (Fig. 147L) ......................................**Mononchulus**
    Spinneret terminal; no large tooth, or large tooth dorsal in stoma...............41
41. Anterior end narrow and rounded (Figs. 143H) ..............................42
    Anterior end broad and square (Figs. 149E, 151M).........................44
42. Stoma distinct, elongate, and cylindrical; weak cuticular annulations (Fig. 143H); a
    single ovary ..........................................**Cylindrolaimus**
    Stoma a short broad cylinder or obscure; two ovaries .......................43
43. Stoma greatly reduced; amphid circular and prominent (Fig. 148A) ... **Aphanolaimus**
    Stoma a short, broad cylinder; amphid unispiral and prominent (Fig.
    151K)...............................................**Paraphanolaimus**
44. Amphid multispiral; stoma with large dorsal tooth (Fig. 151M); rare. **Paracyatholaimus**
    Amphid stirrup-shaped (Fig. 145A), circular (Fig. 149E), or obscure; dorsal tooth
    lacking or inconspicuous; many species; common ......................45
45. Amphid circular (Fig. 149E); single outstretched ovary anterior to posterior vulva.
    **Monhystera**
    Amphid stirrup-shaped or obscure; two ovaries, one anterior and one posterior to the
    median vulva .......................................................46
46. Stoma funnel-shaped; amphid stirrup-shaped (Fig. 152A) ................ **Tobrilus**
    Stoma obscure, narrow; amphid reduced and obscure (Figs. 152B, C) ...... **Tripyla**
47. With six sharply pointed, strongly cuticularized, incurved lips (Figs. 148D, E) ....48
    Lips not pointed, strongly cuticularized, and incurved ......................49
48. Cuticle strongly annulated; amphid obscure (Fig. 148E); ovary single. **Teratocephalus**
    Cuticle marked only by punctations; amphid spiral (Fig. 148D); two ovaries;
    uncommon .........................................**Euteratocephalus**
49. Stoma tubular, poorly cuticularized ......................................50
    Stoma not tubular, or if tubular then distinctly cuticularized ...................54
50. Anterior margin of body almost flat; small tooth located dorsally in stoma (Figs. 152B,
    C); large genus; common ...................................... **Tripyla**
    Anterior end of body rounded; no tooth in stoma ..........................51
51. With cephalic setae and distinct cuticular annulations (Fig. 148F); uncommon. **Bastiania**
    Without cephalic setae; cuticular annulations faint or absent; uncommon species ..52
52. Enlarged basal portion of esophagus sharply set off (Fig. 148J) ....... **Aulolaimoides**
    Basal portion of esophagus tapered (Fig. 150F) ...........................53

FIG. 150.–Anterior end of nematodes. A, *Nygolaimus*; B, *Nygolaimus* with protruded spear; C, *Actinolaimus*; D, *Cryptonchus*; E, *Dorylaimus*; F, *Alaimus*; G, *Ironus*. (A and B modified from Thorne, 1930; C and D modified from Cobb, 1913; E modified from Micoletzky; F and G modified from Cobb, 1914.)

**53.** Amphid large, slitlike or crescent-shaped (Fig. 151L) ................. **Amphidelus**
Amphid obscure ........................................................ **Alaimus**
**54.** Esophagus cylindrical, without a basal bulb (Fig. 150G) ........................**55**
Esophagus with a basal bulb (Fig. 151S) ....................................**57**
**55.** Three large, hooklike teeth at anterior end of stoma (Fig. 151N); two ovaries, one anterior and one posterior to vulva; common ...................... **Ironus**
Without teeth at anterior end of stoma; single ovary ........................**56**
**56.** Posterior end bluntly rounded (Fig. 151O); amphid circular (Fig. 151F). **Cylindrolaimus**
Posterior end pointed (Fig. 151P); amphid stirrup-shaped (Fig. 150D); uncommon.
**Cryptonchus**
**57.** Basal bulb of esophagus nonmuscular and lacking valves; median bulb present (Fig. 151X); uncommon...............................................**58**
Basal bulb of esophagus muscular and valvate; median bulb present or absent ....**59**
**58.** Stoma moderately wide and deep; anterior edge of stoma with riblike structures; slender tubular section of stoma extending posterior to large tooth in stoma (Fig. 146K); amphids obscure ............................. **Mononchoides**
Stoma slender, barrel-shaped or tubular; anterior edge of stoma without riblike structures; without tooth in stoma; large oval amphids (Fig. 151X) .......**Goffartia**

FIG. 151.–Anterior and posterior ends of nematodes. A, *Anaplectus*; B, *Monochromadora*; C, *Monochromadora*; D, *Prodesmodora*; E, *Monhystrella*; F, *Cylindrolaimus*; G, *Plectus*; H, *Plectus* female; J, *Plectus*; K, *Paraphanolaimus*; L, *Amphidelus*; M, *Paracyatholaimus*; N, *Ironus*; O, *Cylindrolaimus*; P, *Cryptonchus*; Q, *Odontolaimus*; R, *Chronogaster*; S, *Chronogaster*; T, *Rhabditis*; U, *Acrobeloides*; V, *Acrobeloides*; W, *Eucephalobus*; X, *Goffartia*. (All modified from Ferris, Ferris, and Tjepkema.)

**59.** Amphid large and circular (Figs. 145C, D); uncommon . . . . . . . . . . . . . . . . . . . . . .**60**
　　　Amphid small, slitlike or porelike . . . . . . . . . . . . . . . . . . . . . . . . . . . . . . . . . . . . . . .**61**
**60.** Stoma elongate, cylindrical, and strongly cuticularized (Fig. 151Q); two ovaries, one
　　　anterior and one posterior to vulva. . . . . . . . . . . . . . . . . . . . . . **Odontolaimus**
　　　Stoma short, funnel-shaped, and moderately cuticularized (Fig. 151E); a single ovary
　　　anterior to vulva . . . . . . . . . . . . . . . . . . . . . . . . . . . . . . . . . . . . . . . . . . **Monhystrella**

FIG. 152.–Anterior and posterior ends of nematodes. A, *Tobrilus*; B and C, *Tripyla*; D, *Cephalobus*; E, *Mononchus*; F, *Prionchulus*; G, *Mylonchulus*; H, *Cephalobus*. (A and B modified from Micoletzky; C modified from Cobb, 1914; E to G modified from Cobb, 1917; D and H modified from Ferris, Ferris, and Tjepkema.)

**61.** Cephalic setae present (Fig. 151R); esophagus uniformly cylindrical anterior to basal bulb (Fig. 151S); body slender and tapering very gradually anteriorly and posteriorly ............................................**Chronogaster**
Cephalic setae absent; esophagus narrows between anterior portion and basal bulb (Figs. 151T, U, V); body spindle-shaped, considerably thicker in middle ...**62**
**62.** Stoma elongate, open, cylindrical (Fig. 151T); one anterior and one posterior ovary, or single anterior ovary; cuticle weakly annulated; a terrestrial family (Rhabditidae) having several genera occasionally found in semiaquatic and aquatic habitats; most common genus ................................. **Rhabditis**
Stoma with small, widely separated plates at anterior end followed by a slender moderately cuticularized tube (Figs. 151U, V); single ovary extending anterior to vulva, then reflexed and extending posterior to vulva; cuticle distinctly annulated ....................................................................**63**
**63.** With three cuticularized plates extending beyond lip region (Fig. 151U); esophagus expanded in middle (Fig. 151V); posterior end blunt; usually in decaying vegetation ............................................... **Acrobeloides**
Without cuticularized plates extending beyond lip region; esophagus not expanded in middle; posterior end blunt or pointed ................................**64**
**64.** Posterior end pointed (Fig. 151W) ................................**Eucephalobus**
Posterior end blunt (Fig. 152D) .................................... **Cephalobus**

# NEMATODA REFERENCES

BASTIAN, H. C. 1865. Monograph on the Anguillulidae, or free nematodes, marine, land, and fresh water; with descriptions of 100 new species. *Trans. Linn. Soc. Lond.* **25**:74–184.

BAYLIS, H. A., and R. DAUBNEY. 1926. *A synopsis of the families and genera of Nematoda.* 277 pp. British Museum of Natural History, London.

CHATTERJI, R. C. 1935. Permanent mounts of nematodes. *Zool. Anz.* **109**:270.

CHITWOOD, B.G. 1931. A comparative histological study of certain nematodes. *Z. Morph. Oekol. Tiere* **23**:237–284.

CHITWOOD, B. G., and M. B. CHITWOOD. 1930. A technique for the embedding of nematodes. *Trans. Am. Microsc. Soc.* **49**:186–187.

——. 1974. *Introduction to Nematology.* 315 p. University Park Press, Baltimore, Md.

COBB, M. V. 1915. Some fresh-water nematodes of the Douglas Lake region of Michigan, U.S.A. *Trans. Am. Microsc. Soc.* **34**:21–47.

COBB, N. A. 1913. New nematode genera found inhabiting fresh water and non-brackish soils. *J. Wash. Acad. Sci.* **3**:432–444.

——. 1914. The North American free-living fresh-water nematodes. *Trans. Am. Microsc. Soc.* **33**:69–134.

——. 1914–1935. *Contributions to the science of nematology.* 490 pp. Baltimore, Md. (Issued in 26 parts, bound in one volume; some parts are reprints of previously published articles, others are original.)

——. 1915. Nematodes and their relationships. *Yearbook U.S.D.A for 1914*, pp. 453–490.

——. 1917. The mononchs. A genus of freeliving predatory nematodes. *Soil Sci.* **3**:431–486.

——. 1918. Estimating the nema population of soil. *U.S.D.A. Bur. Plant Ind. Agric. Tech. Circ.* **1**:1–48.

——. 1918a. Filter-bed nemas: nematodes of the slow sand filter beds of American cities (including new genera and species) with notes on hermaphroditism and parthenogenesis. *Contrib. Sci. Nematol.* **7**:189–212.

——. 1919. The orders and classes of nemas. Ibid. **8**:213–216.

——. 1935. A key to the genera of free-living nemas. *Proc. Helminth. Soc. Wash.* **2**:1–40.

FERRIS, V. R., J. M. FERRIS, and J. P. TJEPKEMA. 1973. Genera of freshwater nematodes (Nematoda) of eastern North America. *Biota of Freshwater Ecosystems Identification Manual* **10**:1–38.

FILIPJEV, I. N. 1934. The classification of the free-living nematodes and their relation to the parasitic nematodes. *Smithson. Misc. Coll.* **89**:1–63.

——. 1936. On the classification of the Tylenchinae. *Proc. Helminth. Soc. Wash.* **3**:80–82.

GOODEY, J. B. 1963. *Soil and freshwater nematodes.* 544 pp. Wiley, New York.

GRUNDMANN, A. W. 1955. Improved methods for preparing and mounting nematodes for study. *Turtox News* **33**:152–153.

HOEPPLI. R. J. C. 1926. Studies of free-living nematodes from the thermal waters of Yellowstone Park. *Trans. Am. Microsc. Soc.* **45**:234–255.

LINFORD, N. B. 1937. The feeding of some hollow-stylet nematodes. *Proc. Helminth. Soc. Wash.* **4**:41–46.

MAN, J. G. DE. 1884. *Die frei in der reinen Erde und im süssen Wasser lebenden Nematoden der Niederländischen Fauna.* 206 pp. Leiden.

MEYL, A. 1960. Freilebenden Nematoden. *Tierwelt Mitteleuro.* **1**:(5a):1–164.

MICOLETZKY, H. 1925. Die freilebenden Süsswasser- und Moornematoden Dänemarks. *Det. Kgl. Danske Vidensk. Selsk. Skr. Naturv. Math. Afd.* **10**:57–310.

PREJS, K. 1970. Some problems of the ecology of benthic nematodes (Nematoda) of Mikołajskie Lake. *Ekol. Polska* **18**:225–242.

SCHNEIDER, W. 1937. Freilebende Nematoden der Deutschen Limnologischen Sundaexpedition nach Sumatra, Java, und Bali. *Arch. Hydrobiol.* **15** (Suppl):30–108.

STEFANSKI, W. 1938. Les nematodes libres des lacs Tatra Polonaises, leur distribution et systematique. *Arch. Hydrobiol.* **33**:585–687.

STEINER, G. 1914. Freilebende Nematoden aus der Schweiz. Ibid. **9**:259–276, 420–438.

——. 1915. Beiträge zur geographischen Verbreitung freilebender Nematoden. *Zool. Anz.* **46**:311–335, 337–349.

THORNE, C. 1935. Notes on free-living and plant-parasitic nematodes. II. *Proc. Helminth. Soc. Wash.* **2**:96–98.

——. 1937. A revision of the nematode family Cephalobidae Chitwood and Chitwood. Ibid. **4**:1–16.

——. 1939. A monograph of the nematodes of the superfamily Dorylaimoidea. *Capita Zool.* **8**:1–261.

# Chapter 10

# NEMATOMORPHA (HORSEHAIR WORMS, GORDIAN WORMS)

BECAUSE of their fancied resemblance to animated horsehairs, members of the Phylum Nematomorpha have long been known as "horsehair worms," and because of their habit of becoming inextricably entangled in masses of two to many individuals they are also commonly called "gordian worms," after the Gordian knot episode of antiquity.

The adults swim clumsily by slow undulations or writhe about in puddles and in the shallows of marshes, ponds, lakes, and streams. Sometimes they occur on the shore near the water's edge, especially if the substrate is wet. The immature stages are internal parasites of insects, usually crickets, terrestrial beetles, and grasshoppers.

**General characteristics.** Adult gordian worms range from about 10 to 70 cm in length with a diameter of 0.3 to 2.5 mm. The diameter is the same throughout the body length except for slight tapering at the extremities, especially anteriorly. Coloration includes opaque yellowish, gray, tan, dark brown, or blackish. There is considerable variation in size and coloration within single species. Males are consistently smaller than females and often exhibit slight coiling of the posterior end. The two sexes occur in about equal numbers.

The small mouth is terminal or subterminal, and sometimes absent. The cloacal aperture is terminal, subterminal, or ventral. Sexes of several genera can be distinguished by the structure of the posterior end. Females of *Paragordius* have three lobes. Males of *Gordius, Parachordodes,* *Paragordius,* and *Gordionus* have two lobes. In females of *Gordius, Gordionus,* and *Parachordodes* the posterior end is simple and rounded, and this is also the situation in both sexes for *Pantachordodes, Chordodes,* and *Pseudochordodes.* In some species the posterior end of the female is slightly bulbous.

These worms were not separated from the nematodes until 1886, and they are often confused with mermithid nematodes. Externally, however Mermithidae are easily differentiated by their pointed ends, tapered body, smooth cuticle, and location of the anus.

**Cuticle.** The gordian cuticle is unusually complex, lamellated, and fibrous (Figs. 155, 158). Areoles are irregular, rounded, or polygonal thickened surface areas of the cuticle that are present in most species. Sometimes they are poorly differentiated or flat and project only slightly from the general surface of the cuticle; in other species they may be papillate to a varying degree. Often the areoles bear small pore canals, granules, setae, or filamentous processes. The furrows or flat areas between areoles likewise may contain setae, granules, papillae, or filamentous processes. In the cloacal region of the male there are often special tracts of setae, thorns, or adhesive wartlike structures that presumably aid in copulation.

**Internal anatomy, physiology.** In addition to cuticle, the body wall consists of a flat to columnar hypodermis and an innermost layer of longitudinal muscle fibers.

231

FIG. 153.–Three female gordians, ×1.

There are no circular fibers, and consequently the diameter of the body cannot be varied. Locomotion consists of localized bending and writhing movements produced by contractions of the longitudinal muscle fibers in one or two quadrants at a time. Males are able to swim in an undulatory manner, but such locomotion is not to be compared with the rapid wriggling of small nematodes.

Food is never ingested at any time during the life history, the digestive tract being degenerate and completely functionless. A pharynx is usually differentiated but has no cavity, and the midgut is a simple narrow tubule. The posterior end of the digestive tract is a cloaca into which the two genital ducts open.

The gonads consist of a pair of long, cylindrical bodies that fill most of the pseudocoel in mature animals. Ripe eggs and sperm pass posteriorly through short paired oviducts and sperm ducts, respectively, into the cloaca, and thence to the outside. In the female there is a median ventral seminal receptacle extending forward from the anterior end of the cloaca.

A cerebral mass, or brain, encircles the digestive tract at the anterior end, and a longitudinal ventral nerve cord extends throughout the body.

One or two ocelli have been described at the anterior end of some species, but otherwise sensory receptors are limited to tactile areas near the brain and perhaps also to some of the cuticular outgrowths on the general body surface.

There are no special circulatory, respiratory, or excretory structures. The residual pseudocoel space between body wall and visceral organs is filled with loose mesenchyme.

**Reproduction, life history.** Probably depending on the species and ecological conditions, copulation usually occurs in spring, early summer, or autumn. Although it is not uncommon to find up to 10 or 20 worms aggregated in a single writhing mass in the springtime, only one female and one male are involved in a copulation. A male coils the posterior tip of his body around the posterior end of the female and deposits sperm at her cloacal opening. The sperm then migrate into the female cloaca, and may be stored for a short time in the seminal receptacle. Fertilization is internal, and presumably the eggs are fertilized just be-

FIG. 154.–Cross section of a typical gordian, ×60. c, cuticle (partly torn away from underlying hypodermis); e, developing eggs; h, hypodermis; i, intestine; lm, longitudinal muscle; nc, nerve cord.

FIG. 155.–Various types of areoles, diagrammatic. (Partly modified from Müller.)

water's edge. The colder the water, the more readily encystment occurs. Such cysts may remain viable for two months in water and up to one month in a moist habitat such as grass and other vegetation along the waterside. The latter condition may result when the water level of a stream or pond is falling.

Assuming favorable cirumstances, a wide variety of crickets, grasshoppers, and terrestrial and aquatic beetles and other aquatic insects accidentally ingest these cysts along with the vegetation to which they are attached. Within the digestive tract

fore being extruded from the cloacal opening of the female. Eggs are deposited in long gelatinous strings that swell and may exceed the size of the parent. Such masses contain up to several million eggs. Males die after copulation and females after egg deposition.

Depending on water temperature, the incubation period is usually 15 to 80 days. The resulting larva (Fig. 156) is unlike the adult and has a very brief free-swimming existence. It is cylindrical, often annulated, only about 250 microns long, and divided into a trunk and large muscular presoma. The anterior end of the presoma has an eversible proboscis bearing three long stylets and three circlets of hooks. The anterior portion of the trunk contains a large glandular mass that opens at the tip of the presoma via a long duct. Posteriorly the trunk contains a blind nonfuctional intestine which opens to the outside by means of a pore.

The immediate and ultimate fates of this larval stage have been the subject of a long and confusing controversy, and even the most recent investigations do not seem to have cleared up the problem. Within 24 hours after hatching, the larva is usually thought to encyst on vegetation or any other convenient substrate at or near the

FIG. 156.–Diagram of a typical gordian larva, ×500, with protruded proboscis.

the cyst wall disintegrates, and the released larva bores its way through the wall of the intestine and into the hemocoel of the host.

Large numbers of cysts are undoubtedly ingested by abnormal hosts (snails, oligochaetes, aquatic insects, fish, etc.), but in these hosts the larva dies or re-encysts in the tissues instead of developing further. If such an abnormal host is eaten by an omnivorous insect that is a normal host, the contained larva then burrows through the wall of the digestive tract to the hemocoel of the latter and undergoes further development.

There is also the possibility (but one that is losing favor) that motile larvae actively penetrate through the body wall of almost any small aquatic or waterside animal but develop further only within such insects as crickets, grasshoppers, and beetles.

Within the host the worm digests and absorbs the surrounding tissues as a source of nourishment. Metamorphosis and development to the adult stage are completed in several weeks to several months, by which time the worm is a tightly coiled mass in the hemocoel. Usually there are one to several worms per host. Sometimes gordians overwinter in the host body.

If the host falls into water or becomes wetted at a time when the contained worm is mature or nearly mature, the latter breaks through the body wall and is thenceforth free-living. There is some evidence that hosts tend to seek water when their worms are ready to emerge. Newly released worms that do not have access to water soon die. If emergence from the host occurs in spring or summer, copulation usually soon follows. Sometimes emergence occurs in the autumn and then the worms remain solitary, customarily hibernating in waterside grass and roots, and become active and copulate in the water in the following spring. Length of the complete life cycle is variable, ranging from about 2 to 15 months.

Unlike most parasites, gordians generally have little host specificity, and the same species may develop in a variety of grasshoppers or beetles. A few gordians have even been reported emerging from caddis flies and dragonflies.

Adults have occasionally been recorded as human parasites, but such cases are undoubtedly fortuitous and produced by accidental ingestion of worms in food or water.

**Ecology.** Little is known about gordian ecology. The worms occur in suitable habitats wherever appropriate hosts are found, from the tropics to cold-temperate latitudes, and to altitudes above timberline in mountainous areas. Some species are widely distributed throughout North and South America, and a few occur in both Europe and the United States or are Holarctic. The genus *Gordius* is essentially cosmopolitan. The most common and widely distributed species in the United States are *Gordius robustus* Leidy and *Paragordius varius* (Leidy)

There seem to be few habitat preferences, and the same species may be found in both running and standing waters. Occasionally they are on the shore just above the water's edge but more usually in water 2 to 20 cm deep. Even small puddles and stock tanks are fruitful collecting areas. A few observations indicate that the worms are more active at night, but there is no evidence for a true negative phototaxis. Males are much more active than females and move about in a serpentine manner for hours in the water and on the bottom. Females are sluggish and move about but little.

**Preparing.** Seventy to 90 percent alcohol is a suitable fixative and preservative, but for more critical work hot saturated mercuric chloride containing 5 to 10 percent acetic acid is much better, especially if histological sections are contemplated.

For a study of the extremities, cut anterior to the cloacal aperture and posterior to the dark ring near the anterior end; mount in lactophenol, clarite, or balsam after dehydrating. Small bits of cuticle should be sliced from the middle third of the body with a sharp razor blade by stretching the worm firmly over the left forefinger. Such pieces should be placed in a drop of glycerin for about an hour. Then gently scrape off the soft tissues from the underside with needles. Rinse the cleaned cuticle in a change of glycerin and mount, outer surface up, in glycerin jelly on a slide. Lactophenol and clarite mounts are often preferable for certain cuticular structures.

**Taxonomy.** The Phylum Nematomorpha is divided into the Nectonematoidea and Gordioidea. The former category contains a single marine species whose larvae are parasitic in crustaceans. All the other species are fresh-water, totaling about 100 for the world, and belong in the Gordioidea. This category consists of 5 families and about 16 genera. The following taxa occur in the United States: Chordodidae *(Chordodes, Pantachordodes, Pseudochordodes, Euchordodes)*, Parachordodidae *(Parachordodes, Gordionus, Paragordius)*, and Gordiidae *(Gordius)*.

Some generic characters and most species characters are based largely on the surface pattern and sculpturing of the cuticle. For studying some of these details it is often necessary to use oil immersion.

Only a negligible amount of work on American gordians has been published since the papers of Montgomery and May, and the taxonomy and distribution of our species are very poorly known. Many of the descriptions published prior to 1910 were quite brief and did not include sufficient fine details, and for this reason some such descriptions are not trustworthy. Until the gordian fauna of the United States is more thoroughly investigated, therefore, it seems fruitless to draw up a key to species that would be unreliable and soon out of date. For this reason the following key includes only generic categories. Most of the delimitations and suggestions of Carvalho and Heinze have been followed.

## KEY TO GENERA OF NEMATOMORPHA

1. Posterior end with three lobes (Fig. 157B); cuticle with scattered aeroles of one kind (Fig. 158A); widely distributed and common; several species; females.
   **Paragordius**
   Posterior end blunt or bilobed (Figs. 157C, F, G) ...............................2
2. Posterior end clearly bilobed and often with a tendency toward coiling (Figs. 157C, D, G); males ........................................................3
   Posterior end blunt and without lobes; males and females ......................7
3. Postcloacal region with a crescentic fold; aeroles present and indistinct (Fig. 158B); or absent; widely distributed; several species .....................**Gordius**
   Postcloacal region without a crescentic fold ..................................4
4. With two kinds of aeroles (Fig. 158E); poorly known in the United States ........5
   With one kind of areole (Figs. 158A, C) ......................................6
5. Anterior end rounded ............................................**Paragordius**
   Anterior end truncate ..........................................**Parachordodes**
6. Posterior lobes about two and one-half to three times as long as wide; without rows of hairs or papillae lateral to cloacal aperture (Fig. 157C); widely distributed and common; several species ...............................**Paragordius**
   Posterior lobes about twice as long as wide; with rows of long papillae on either side of cloacal aperture (Fig. 157G); several species ..................**Gordionus**
7. Posterior end with a ventral furrow; males ...................................8
   Posterior end without a ventral furrow ......................................9
8. With two kinds of areoles; not known from the United States ........**Paragordionus**
   With one kind of areoles .....................................................10
9. Areoles grouped; interareolar furrows with spines; not known from the United States ...................................................**Euchordodes**
   Areoles not grouped; interareolar furrows without spines; poorly known in the United States .................................................**Pantachordodes**
10. Interareolar furrows clear and without setae, pore canals, or large granulations; areoles often absent or indistinct; only one kind of areole (Fig. 158B); common and widely distributed; several species; females ......................**Gordius**
    Interareolar furrows usually with setae, pore canals, granulations, or other structures; one, two, or more kinds of areoles present ..........................11

FIG. 157.–Extremities of Nematomorpha. A, anterior end of *Paragordius*; B, posterior end of female *Paragordius*; C, posterior end of male *Paragordius*; D, posterior end of male *Gordius*; E, anterior end of *Gordius*; F, posterior end of female *Gordius*; G, posterior end of male *Gordionus*.

11. With one kind of areole . . . . . . . . . . . . . . . . . . . . . . . . . . . . . . . . . . . . . . . . . . . . . . . . . . . . **12**
    With two or more kinds of areoles; pore canals in areoles or between adjacent areoles (Figs. 158E–H), sometimes absent . . . . . . . . . . . . . . . . . . . . . . . . . . . . . . . . . . . . . **14**
12. With a few pore canals in furrows between areoles (Fig. 158C); several species; females . . . . . . . . . . . . . . . . . . . . . . . . . . . . . . . . . . . . . . . . . . . . . . . . . . . . **Gordionus**
    Without pore canals in furrows between areoles (Fig. 158D) . . . . . . . . . . . . . . . . . . . . **13**
13. Areoles not grouped; interareolar spines absent; males and females; poorly known in the United States . . . . . . . . . . . . . . . . . . . . . . . . . . . . . . . . . . . . . . **Pantachordodes**
    Areoles grouped; interareolar spines present; females; not known in the United States . . . . . . . . . . . . . . . . . . . . . . . . . . . . . . . . . . . . . . . . . . . . . . . . . . . . **Euchordodes**
14. Pore canals in center of large areoles (Fig. 158E); body of mature individuals usually less than 1 mm thick; poorly known in the United States; females. **Parachordodes**
    Pore canals absent, or between large areoles (Figs. 158F, H); body of mature individuals usually more than 1 mm thick; males and females . . . . . . . . . . . . . . . . . . **15**
15. Cuticle with two or more types of prominent papillate areoles, the highest ones often bearing a tuft of slender filaments; interareolar furrows with scattered tubercles, bristles, and granules (Figs. 158F, G); several species . . . . . . . . . . . **Chordodes**
    Cuticle with two types of nonpapillate areoles; interareolar furrows free of tubercles, bristles, and granules (Fig. 158H); uncommon in the United States.
    **Pseudochordodes**

FIG. 158.–Areoles and other cuticular structures of Nematomorpha, semidiagrammatic. (Pore canals shown in solid black.) A, *Paragordius*; B, *Gordius*; C, *Gordionus*; D, *Pantachordodes*; E, *Parachordodes*; F, surface view of *Chordodes* areoles; G, side view of *Chordodes* areoles; H, *Pseudochordodes*. (E modified from Heinze, 1935; F and G modified from Camerano, 1897; H modified from Carvalho.)

## NEMATOMORPHA REFERENCES

CAMERANO, L. 1897. Monografia dei Gordii. *Mem. Roy. Accad. Sci. Torino* (2) **47**:339–419.

———. 1915. Revisione dei Gordii. Ibid. **66**:1–66.

CARVALHO, J. C. M. 1942. Studies on some Gordiacea of North and South America. *J. Parasitol.* **28**:213–222.

DORIER, A. 1930. Recherches biologiques et systématiques sur les Gordiacés. *Trav. Lab. Hydrobiol. Piscicult. Grenoble* **22**:1–180.

HEINZE, K. 1935. Über das genus Parachordodes Camerano 1897 nebst allgemeinen Angaben über die Familie Chordodidae. *Z. Parasitenk.* **7**:657–678.

———. 1935a. Über Gordiiden. *Zool Anz.* **111**:23–32.

———. 1937. Die Saitenwürmer (Gordioidea) Deutschlands. Eine systematisch-faunistische Studie über Insektenparasiten aus der Gruppe der Nematomorpha. *Z. Parasitenk.* **9**:263–344.

————. 1941. Saitenwürmer oder Gordioidea. *Tierwelt Dtschl.* **39**:1–78.

————. 1952. Über Gordioidea, eine systematische Studie über Insektenparasiten aus der Gruppe der Nematomorpha. *Z. Parasitenk.* **15**:183–202.

MÜLLER, G. W. 1927. Über Gordiaceen. *Z. Morphol. Oekol. Tiere* **7**:134–219.

MONTGOMERY, T. H., JR. 1898. The Gordiacea of certain American collections with particular reference to the North American fauna. *Bull. Mus. Comp. Zool. Harvard Univ.* **32**:23–59.

————. 1898a. The Gordiacea of certain American collections, with particular reference to the North American fauna. II. *Proc. Calif. Acad. Sci.* (3) **1**:333–344.

————. 1899. Synopses of North American invertebrates. II. Gordiacea (hair worms). *Am. Nat.* **33**:647–652.

SCHUURMANS STEKHOVEN, J. H., JR. 1943. Contribution a l'étude des gordiides de la fauna Belge. *Bull. Mus. roy. Hist. nat. Belg.* **19**:1–28.

# Chapter  11

# TARDIGRADA (WATER BEARS)

ALTHOUGH tardigrades are strictly aquatic animals, they are seldom abundant in the usual types of habitats harboring fresh-water invertebrates. They are not plankton organisms; they are only occasionally collected in aquatic mosses and algae, on rooted aquatics, or in the mud and debris of puddles, ponds, and lakes. More typically, active tardigrades are found in the droplets and film of water on terrestrial wet mosses, liverworts, and certain angiosperms with a rosette growth form. They also occur in the capillary water between the sand grains of sandy beaches up to 2 or 3 m from the water's edge.

Mature individuals range from 50 to 1200 microns in length but are usually less than 500 microns long. Many species have a considerable size variation. The short, stout, cylindrical body, the four pairs of stumpy lateroventral legs, and a deliberate "pawing" sort of locomotion produce a fancied resemblance to a miniature bearlike creature, and the Tardigrada have been generally called "water bears" since they were given that name by Huxley in 1869.

The great majority of species have been reported from lichens, liverworts, and terrestrial and fresh-water mosses. All other species have been reported from marine habitats.

Nearly all of what we know about tardigrade biology has been contributed through the efforts of British, German, Italian, and French investigators. Water bears have been badly neglected in the United States, even though we undoubtedly have a rich fauna. Only about 70 species have been reported from this country, and this figure includes marine, moss, and fresh-

water forms. About 350 species have been described the world over.

**General characteristics.** Tardigrades are fascinating objects for electron and low-power microscopy investigations. The body consists of a distinct head and four indefinite "body segments." Each leg is armed with four claws or two pairs of double claws. Crawling and creeping are more or less sluggish, the claws being used for clinging to vegetation and debris. The mouth is anterior, subterminal, or ventral, and the cloacal aperture, or anus, lies between the bases of the last legs. The entire surface of the body is covered with a cuticle secreted by the thin hypodermis, which consists of polygonal cells. Depending on the species, the cuticle may be variously thickened and marked. Cilia do not occur in this phylum. Only liquid materials are ingested, and the anterior part of the digestive tract has a sucking pharynx and a pair of long, piercing stylets.

Sexes are separate, but the great majority of individuals are females. Usually there are four to six ecdyses in the life history.

A remarkable feature of most aquatic and semiaquatic fresh-water tardigrades is their ability to tide over dry periods in a shriveled, rounded, anabiotic state. When normal moisture conditions return, the animal resumes its normal appearance and activity.

Coloration is variously produced by the pigmentation of the cuticle and hypodermis, dissolved materials in the body fluid, reserve food bodies, and the contents of the digestive tract. Gray, bluish, yellow-

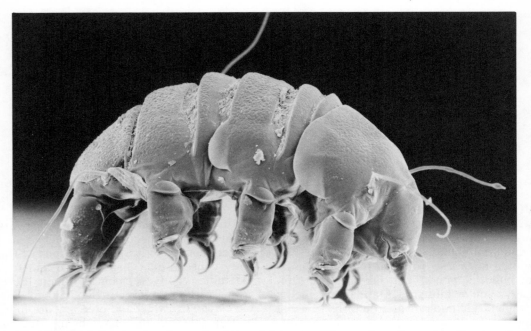

FIG. 159.–Scanning electron micrograph of *Parechniniscus*, ×600, a semiaquatic species. (Courtesy R. O. Schuster, University of California, Davis.)

brown, reddish, or brown are common colors. Some species are relatively dark and opaque, especially among older individuals; others are translucent and pale.

There are no special circulatory or respiratory systems. Materials diffuse and circulate about easily in the body fluid, and respiration occurs through the general body surface.

**Feeding, digestive system.** Tardigrades are mostly plant feeders. The cellulose wall

FIG. 160.–Scanning electron micrograph of *Macrobiotus*, ×150. (Courtesy of R. O. Schuster, University of California, Davis.)

FIG. 161.–Semidiagrammatic dorsal view of *Macrobiotus,* ×220; trunk and leg muscle not shown. *b*, brain; *cg*, claw gland; *deg*, dorsal excretory gland; *e*, esophagus; *es*, eyespot; *l*, leg; *me*, mature egg in saclike ovary; *mt*, Malpighian tubule; *o*, oviduct; *s*, stomach; *sr*, seminal receptacle; *sg*, salivary gland; *sp*, sucking pharynx. (Greatly modified from Marcus, 1928b.)

of moss leaflet cells and algal filaments are pierced with the stylets and the fluid contents are sucked out by pharyngeal pumping action. Occasionally, however, the body fluids of small metazoans, such as nematodes and rotifers, are used as food. *Milnesium tardigradum* is said to be chiefly carnivorous.

The periphery of the mouth is stiffened and surrounded by two or three folded and superimposed rings of cuticle. That portion of the digestive system extending from the small mouth cavity to the anterior end of the esophagus is called the buccal apparatus (Fig. 163). It consists of the tubular pharynx, the muscular or sucking pharynx, and the stylet mechanism. The tubular pharynx is narrow and sclerotized and extends into the mass of the sucking pharynx. The latter is football-shaped, with thick walls composed of radial muscle fibers; its small triquetrous cavity is lined with a thin epithelium. Six longitudinal ridges or fragmented sclerotized bars give stiffness to the sucking pharynx and provide for insertions of muscle fibers. The individual sclerotized

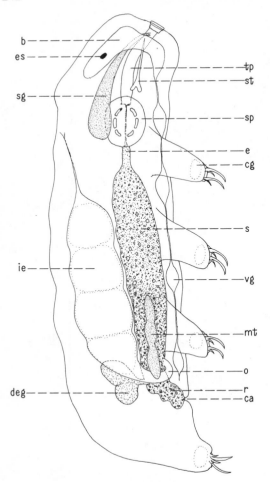

FIG. 162.–Semidiagrammatic lateral view of a typical tardigrade, ×220; all musculature omitted. *b*, brain; *ca*, cloacal aperture; *cg*, claw gland; *deg*, dorsal excretory gland; *e*, esophagus; *es*, eyespot; *ie*, immature egg in saclike ovary; *mt*, Malpighian tubule; *o*, oviduct; *r*, rectum; *s*, stomach; *sg*, salivary gland; *sp*, sucking pharynx; *st*, stylet; *tp*, tubular pharynx; *vg*, ventral ganglion.

small muscles extending from the base of the stylets to the tubular pharynx and the sucking pharynx are capable of withdrawing and protruding the stylets a considerable distance out of the mouth.

A pair of large salivary glands open into the mouth cavity. They also function in the secretion of new stylets and stylet supports at molting and for this reason are sometimes called stylet glands. Some investigators believe that they have an excretory function, especially in the Heterotardigrada. A few small unicellular glands of unknown function occur near the mouth. They are ingrowths of the hypodermis.

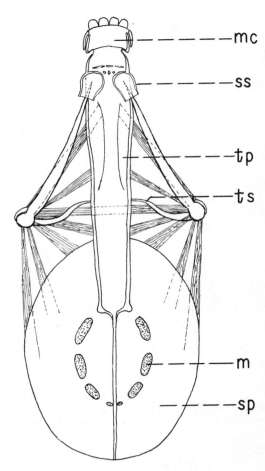

pieces in the pharynx are called macroplacoids (Figs. 163, 164). Sometimes there is a single small posterior piece, called a microplacoid or comma.

The two stylets lie at an angle on either side of the tubular pharynx and the sharp tips project into the anterior end of the pharyngeal cavity through special lateral slots, or stylet sheaths. A transverse support extends from the tubular pharynx to the basal portion of each stylet. Several pairs of

FIG. 163.–Semidiagrammatic dorsal view of buccal apparatus and associated musculature; stylets are shown retracted. *m*, macroplacoids; *mc*, mouth cavity; *sp*, sucking pharynx; *ss*, stylet sheath; *tp*, tubular pharynx; *ts*, transverse support.

FIG. 164.–Diagrammatic cross section of a typical tardigrade sucking pharynx showing radial muscle fibers. *c*, triquetrous cavity; *m*, macroplacoid.

The esophagus ranges from long to very short. It empties into the capacious stomach, or midgut, which is usually without diverticula but may have slight lateral caeca. The hindgut, or rectum, is short and has a small cavity. In the Class Eutardigrada it is a true cloaca. The anus or cloacal aperture is a longitudinal or transverse slit.

Digestion in the anterior portion of the stomach is acid; posteriorly it is alkaline. Reserve food may be stored in hypodermal cells or in special reserve food bodies which float about in the body cavity. Feces are often released into the old cuticle during molting, especially in *Echiniscus*.

**Excretion.** In the Eutardigrada there are three small glands situated at the junction of midgut and hindgut, each of which consists of only three cells. One gland is dorsal and two are lateral. All supposedly have an excretory function, and perhaps they are also osmoregulatory. The paired glands are commonly called Malpighian tubules. Some excretory material is stored in the hypodermal cells, some excretory granules are left within the old exoskeleton at ecdysis, and some are given off at the anterior end when the stylet mechanism is shed just preceding an ecdysis.

**Muscle system.** In addition to the pharynx and the stylet muscles, a tardigrade usually has from about 40 to 140 long, thin body muscles, the number depending on the species. Each such muscle is merely a single fibrillar cell with one nucleus, or several such cells. Most origins and insertions are on the body wall (Fig. 165). Contractions of the dorsal and ventral longitudinal muscles bring about a slight shortening or curvature of the body. Each leg is moved by a set of muscles originating on the dorsal and ventral body wall and inserting near the tip of the leg. The body wall is devoid of circular muscle fibers, but the turgor of the body fluid presumably acts as an antagonist to the longitudinal and leg muscles. Muscles extending from the body wall to the cloaca facilitate egg deposition and defecation. A few species have longitudinal fibers associated with the stomach.

**Nervous system.** The large dorsal brain commonly has two long lateral lobes and two or three median lobes; it covers much of the tubular pharynx (Fig. 166). Two broad circumpharyngeal connectives pass around the pharynx and unite with a subpharyngeal ganglion. In the trunk there is a chain of four conspicuous ventral ganglia united by two longitudinal nerve strands. Frequently these ganglia are slightly bilobed. Paired nerve strands originating in the brain and ganglia innervate all parts of the body. Some of the longer strands, especially those extending into the legs, have small terminal ganglionic masses.

**Sense organs.** The great majority of tardigrades have a pair of eyespots in the lateral lobes of the brain. Each consists of a cup-shaped mass of black or red pigment granules.

Head cirri are usually tactile, but there is some question about the presumed sensory function of body cirri and filaments.

**Cuticular structures.** Fresh-water species usually have a thicker cuticle than marine species, and semiaquatic species have a thicker cuticle than aquatic species. The surface may be smooth or variously sculptured, granular, or papillate. Often there are long cirri. Some species of Eutardigrada have transverse grooves or folds, but *Echiniscus* and *Pseudechiniscus* have dor-

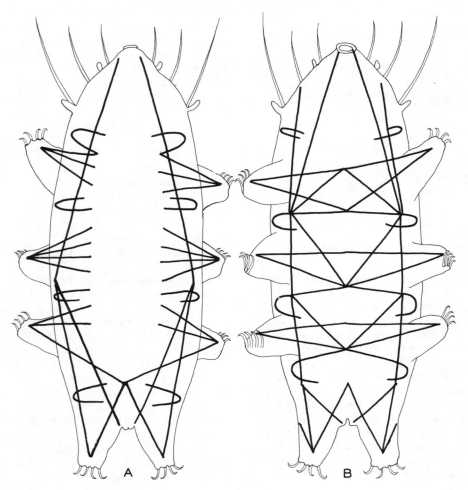

Fig. 165.–Trunk and leg musculature of *Echiniscus,* ×350, semidiagrammatic. A, dorsal view; B, ventral view. (Greatly modified from Marcus, 1928b.)

sal armorlike thickened plates. Beginning at the anterior end, these are as follows (Fig. 170F): head plate, shoulder plate (first trunk plate), a small median first intercalary, second trunk plate (divided longitudinally), second intercalary, third trunk plate (usually divided longitudinally), third intercalary (often indistinct), and the anal plate (usually grooved).

**Reproduction, growth.** The bulk of a population is always composed of females, and males reach their peak of abundance during the winter or early spring. Males are unknown in *Oreella, Parechiniscus,* and

*Echiniscus,* and these genera probably reproduce exclusively by parthenogenesis.

Some species show sexual dimorphism in the shape and cuticular structure of the last legs, in the size and curvature of the claws, and in the smaller size of the males.

The gonad is an unpaired sac dorsal to the digestive tract and with one or two attachment fibers at the anterior end. In the male there are two vasa deferentia which curve around each side of the intestine and have a small swollen portion which acts as a seminal vesicle. The female has a single oviduct on the right side of the intestine. On the other side a blind seminal receptacle may sometimes be found in *Hypsibius* and *Macrobiotus,* especially in the late fall, winter, and early spring. In the Eutardigrada the genital ducts open into the rectum, which is therefore more appropriately a cloaca. In the Heterotardigrada there is a separate preanal genital pore.

Two distinct types of eggs have been observed in some species, thin-shelled and thick-shelled, and perhaps they are similar to the tachyblastic and opsiblastic eggs produced by gastrotrichs, or the summer and winter eggs produced by rotifers. At least there is some evidence to show that thick-

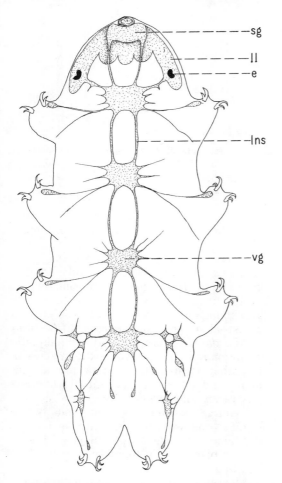

FIG. 166.–Ventral view of nervous system of *Macrobiotus,* ×220. *e*, eyespot; *ll*, lateral lobe of brain; *lns*, longitudinal nerve strand; *sg*, subpharyngeal ganglion; *vg*, ventral ganglion. (Modified from various sources.)

shelled eggs are produced when environmental conditions are unfavorable; there is the further possibility that thin-shelled eggs are parthenogenetic and thick-shelled eggs are fertilized. The peak of the reproductive period is from November to May, but females with eggs may be found at any time of the year.

In most of the true aquatic species "external" fertilization is the rule. One or more males clamber about on the body of a female before she is ready to release her eggs but after the old cuticle has become loosened in preparation for a molt. The males release sperm through the cloacal aperture or genital pore of the old cuticle, and the eggs are fertilized when they are released into the cavity between the new and old cuticle.

In typical semiaquatic species fertilization is "internal" and does not necessarily occur just before an ecdysis. Sperm enter the genital pore or cloacal aperture and fertilize the eggs before their release from the body of the female. Sometimes the sperm may be stored in the seminal receptacle.

Most female Echiniscoidea produce only two to six eggs, but in other groups a female produces anywhere from one to 30 eggs. Sometimes the whole complement may be released in 15 to 30 minutes.

In *Macrobiotus* and some species of *Hypsibius* the eggs are deposited freely and singly, or in groups. In other fresh-water forms they are contained in the newly shed cuticle. Free eggs are often sticky for attachment to the substrate and frequently faceted, spinous, tuberculate, or variously sculptured. Eggs released into the old cuticle usually have a smooth surface. Inside the true shell a thin membrane surrounds the developing embryo.

Depending on the species and ecological conditions, a thin-shelled egg usually completes development in 3 to 12 days and a thick-shelled egg in 10 to 14 days.

The young emerge from the egg by rupturing the shell with their stylets. Newly hatched individuals are one-third to one-fifth the size of mature specimens, and all growth occurs by enlargement of cells already present. Aside from their smaller size, immature tardigrades may be recog-

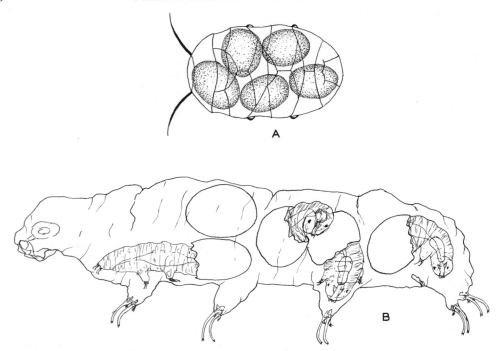

FIG. 167.–Cast tardigrade exoskeletons containing eggs. A, dorsal view of *Pseudechiniscus*; B, lateral view of *Milnesium tardigradum* (four of five eggs in process of hatching). (A modified from Ramazotti; B greatly modified from Marcus, 1929.)

nized by their underveloped reproductive system, slight differences in the details of the buccal apparatus, and sometimes by the fact that there are only two claws per leg.

Most investigators indicate four to six molts during the life history, and sexual maturity is usually attained sometime after the second or third molt. The old cuticle is usually shed after a period of growth, but it may also be shed as a response to hunger and unfavorable environmental conditions. Several days before a molt the sclerotized portions of the buccal apparatus are ejected and new ones (attached to the old muscles) promptly begin to be formed by the salivary glands. A day or two before a molt, the animal shrinks temporarily and slightly. Then the old cuticle ruptures at the anterior end and the animal crawls out. The lining of the rectum and the claws are lost at molting, and new claws are secreted by special claw glands in the tip of each leg.

There appears to be considerable variation in longevity, assuming that the animal is continuously active. Two months and 20 months are perhaps the extremes.

**General ecology.** A few species of *Macrobiotus* and *Hypsibius* are truly aquatic and some are both aquatic and semiaquatic, but the majority of species in these genera are semiaquatic only and occur chiefly on terrestrial mosses and lichens. *Milnesium tardigradum* occurs in both semiaquatic and aquatic habitats. All of the species in the other fresh-water genera are semiaquatic and occur in true aquatic habitats only rarely and fortuitously.

Active tardigrades can usually be found if one searches diligently in masses of filamentous algae, washings of higher aquatic plants, or in the debris on the bottom of ponds and pools. The semiaquatic species, however, are active only when the plant has been wetted by rain or when it is splashed at streamside. Many mosses, liverworts, lichens, and rosette angiosperms contain large tardigrade populations.

Mosses on rocks or on the bark of trees contain tardigrades, even though they may be wet enough to allow them to be active for less than 5 percent of the time. Concentrations up to 22,000 dry and inactive anabiotic tardigrades per gram of dry moss have been reported. Mosses with especially thick cellulose cell walls, such as *Polytrichum,* usually do not harbor tardigrades. Presumably their stylets cannot penetrate such walls. Favorable portions of sandy beaches sometimes contain 300 to 400 tardigrades per 10 cm³ of wet sand. Sometimes they occur as deep as 15 cm in the sand.

Most species appear to be eurythermal and are normally active anywhere between near-freezing temperatures and 25° to 30°. Some forms have been found in warm springs where they are continuously exposed to temperatures of 40°.

Although aquatic species are generally characteristic of the littoral, there are records of collections as deep as 100 m on lake bottoms. Semiaquatic species occur from the tropics to the Arctic and Antarctic and from sea level to mountain tops up to 6000 m high. The annual period of activity varies correspondingly, from the year round to only a week or two.

Little is known about minimal oxygen requirements, but it is usually inferred that tardigrades cannot endure low dissolved oxygen concentrations as do many other small aquatic metazoans.

Aquatic species are usually most abundant between January and May, and sometimes there is a second maximum in the autumn months. Moss dwellers do not have pronounced seasonal maxima. Individuals are active as long as the moss is damp.

Tardigrades are chiefly preyed on by amoeboid protozoans, nematodes, and perhaps by each other to a certain extent.

**Anhydrobiosis.** When a bit of moss dries, many of the associated Tardigrada have the unusual ability to assume an inactive anabiotic (cryptobiotic) state that may persist for as long as four to seven years. When normal ecological conditions again prevail, the tardigrades come out of their quiescent state and resume normal activity. Most marine species and true aquatic

FIG. 168.–Dorsal view of a tardigrade "tun" in the anhydrobiotic state, ×300.

fresh-water species do not apparently have the ability to assume an anabiotic condition.

Under drying conditions the head, posterior end, and legs are retracted, and the whole body becomes more or less rounded into a "tun." Considerable water is lost from the body cavity and the anabiotic animal is therefore shriveled and wrinkled (Fig. 168). Internal visceral structures are not greatly modified. Although drying is almost always responsible for bringing on anabiosis, a lack of sufficient dissolved oxygen and perhaps other unfavorable conditions may also be responsible. Tuns can be formed only when the drying process occurs slowly, and when the relative humidity is high.

Metabolic processes proceed very slowly, but the length of time a specimen can remain in continuous anabiosis depends on the amount of stored food in the body. Death occurs as soon as the supply is exhausted.

Anabiotic tardigrades are highly resistant to abnormal environmental conditions. Some remain viable even after being kept experimentally in strong brine solutions, at 100° for six hours, and at −190° for as long as 20 months.

Revival from anabiosis takes but a short time when individuals are properly wetted. Usually the interval is four minutes to several hours, and occasionally a day or two. The animal absorbs water, swells, and promptly becomes active. Revival is more rapid at higher temperatures, with higher dissolved oxygen, and in animals having more stored food material. Moss species usually go through numerous alternating periods of activity and anabiosis during their life cycle, depending on the nature of their habitat. One author states that the life cycle may be as long as 60 years, including anabiotic periods. Laboratory animals can easily be dried and revived ten times or more.

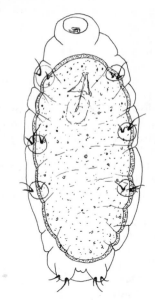

FIG. 169.–Cyst of *Hypsibius*, semidiagrammatic, ×75. (Greatly modified from Marcus, 1928.)

**Cysts.** Damage, hunger, and other abnormal ecological conditions sometimes bring about the formation of resistant cysts, especially in true aquatic species of *Macrobiotus* and *Hypsibius*. The animal contracts inside the old wrinkled cuticle and forms a dark-colored, thick-walled inner cyst (Fig. 169). The internal organs undergo a variable degree of degeneration. When ecological conditions are favorable the animal becomes reconstituted, the cyst wall ruptures, and the tardigrade emerges.

A "simplex" stage has been observed in many tardigrades, especially in species of *Macrobiotus*. Such animals are inactive and have a more or less reduced buccal apparatus. The macroplacoids are abortive, the esophagus is very slender, and the stylets are nonfunctional and reduced; sometimes all of the digestive system anterior to the stomach disappears and there is no mouth. Little is known about the factors responsible for the appearance of the simplex stage, but it is thought that it may occur in animals about to encyst or in those just emerged from a cyst.

**Anoxybiosis.** A third type of inactive condition in tardigrades is called anoxy-

biosis. It usually comes about when there is insufficient oxygen. The body swells and becomes rigid and turgid. There are no movements, and it is difficult to decide whether the animal is alive. After a maximum of about five days in this condition the animal dies, but if food and oxygen are supplied promptly the animal again resumes normal activity. Sometimes individuals emerging from anabiosis go into the state of anoxybiosis.

Crowe (1975) recognizes two other kinds of latency among tardigrades, both of which have been only superficially investigated. One is cryobiosis, which is closely associated with tun formation and is a state of suspended animation assumed on freezing and other exceptionally low temperatures. The second is osmobiosis, a cryptobiotic or tun state induced by exceptionally high osmotic pressures when the animals are placed in abnormal salt concentrations.

**Geographical distribution, dispersal.** The great majority of tardigrades are undoubtedly widely distributed, and an abundance of species first found in Europe have since been found scattered over a broad range.

Some are Holarctic, generally distributed in the Northern Hemisphere, or even cosmopolitan (*Macrobiotus hüfelandi* Schultze, *Hypsibius oberhäuseri* (Doyère), and *Milnesium tardigradum*). Other species, of course, have been reported only from single mainland or island localities. The tropics contain notably few species and few individuals.

Passive distribution is effected by currents, animals (usually insects), waves, and wind, especially in the anabiotic and cyst stages. There is considerable positive evidence for wind as an important distributive agency.

**Collecting.** Almost any bit of suitable moss will yield tardigrades. If the moss is wet, simply rinse it out in water and examine the washings. Masses of filamentous algae and rooted aquatics may be treated similarly. Dry mosses and lichens should be soaked for 30 minutes to several days. At intervals rinse such plant material, and the tardigrades will be found as they emerge from cysts and the anabiotic state.

**Culturing.** Tardigrades are easy to culture, although little actual culture work seems to have been done. They may be kept in masses of filamentous algae or wet moss. Change a large fraction of the water every three or four days.

**Preserving, preparing.** Unlike many other small fresh-water metazoans, tardigrades are easy to fix in extended form. A large percentage will be suitable when killed and fixed in 5 percent formalin or 85 percent alcohol. Especially fine specimens may be secured by inducing anoxybiosis under a cover slip sealed with petroleum jelly before killing and fixing. This procedure usually requires 10 minutes to 3 hours. Some investigators recommend the use of one of a variety of narcotics before fixation. Fixatives that are particularly useful for staining and histological work are osmic acid, saturated mercuric chloride, and 2 percent acetic acid. Piercing the body wall with a fine needle permits better staining and dehydration. Simple unstained permanent mounts may be made in glycerin jelly.

The sclerotized parts of the buccal apparatus may be isolated on a slide by the judicious use of 10 percent potassium hydroxide.

**Taxonomy.** The phylogenetic affinities of tardigrades are highly debatable. During early embryology five coelomic pouches are formed from the mesoderm, but only one posterior pair persists as the gonads and their ducts; the others degenerate. The main body cavity is therefore probably a hemocoel.

Often they are placed near the mites in the Phylum Arthropoda, especially because of their indistinct segmentation, four pairs of legs, and piercing stylets. Some workers consider them crustaceans, and a further suggestion places them near the Onychophora. Other workers, however, consider the Phylum Tardigrada one of the wormlike groups of various affinities and place it after the Nematoda and either before or after the Chaetognatha and Bryozoa in the phylogenetic series. For the time being and until more definite evidence is forthcoming, this last suggestion is the one followed in the present manual.

Only about 28 genera are recognized in the whole phylum of which 14 contain a total of about 400 semiaquatic and aquatic fresh-water species. Nine of these genera have been reported from the United States; they are *Echiniscus, Pseudechiniscus, Milnesium, Macrobiotus, Itaquascon, Haplomacrobiotus, Hexapodibius, Diphascon,* and *Hypsibius.* Five other genera have not yet been reported from the United States, but are included in the following key for the sake of completeness; these include *Oreella* (three species), *Thermozodium esakii, Necopinatum mirabile, Parechiniscus chitonides* and *Mopsechiniscus imberbis.*

The chief taxonomic structures used in generic and specific determinations include details of the buccal apparatus (especially macroplacoids), armor, claws, cirri, filaments, and eggs. *Echiniscus, Macrobiotus,* and *Hypsibius* are large genera that are often subdivided into species groups or subgenera for taxonomic convenience. Most of the earlier descriptions are insufficient, owing to the false supposition that the structures of the claws alone were sufficient and trustworthy characters. The Ra-

mazotti (1972) monograph and supplement (1974) are the most complete references.

The following key includes data for all well-established and valid fresh-water genera of the world.

## KEY TO GENERA OF TARDIGRADA

1. Each leg with four claws or two double claws .................................2
   Each leg with six similar long claws; one species known from Japanese hot springs ........... Class **MESOTARDIGRADA, Thermozodium esakii** Rahm
2. Head with anterior cirri (rarely absent) and lateral filaments; with four separate but similar claws on each leg (Fig. 170); semiaquatic.
   Class **HETEROTARDIGRADA**, Order **ECHINISCOIDEA, 3**
   Head without anterior cirri and lateral filaments (Figs. 171O–Q); each leg with two double claws or two unlike pairs of claws (Figs. 171C–E, L–N); semiaquatic and aquatic) ........Class **EUTARDIGRADA**, Order **MACROBIOTOIDEA, 7**
3. Posterior legs stout and not set off from body by cuticular folds. ECHINISCIDAE, 4
   Posterior legs slender and set off from body by distinct cuticular folds (Fig. 170A); up to 230 microns long; one species reported from Alps and New South Wales, another from Chile and Germany, and a third from Chile.
   OREELLIDAE, **Oreella**
4. Body with thick dorsal plates, variously sculptured; with a variable number of cirri and filaments (Figs. 170D–G); eggs deposited in shed exoskeleton (Fig. 167A). 5
   Body with thin dorsal plates (Fig. 170B); up to 200 microns long; one species reported from Europe ............................. **Parechiniscus chitonides** Cuénot
5. Armor consisting of head plate, three trunk plates, and anal plate (plus intercalaries) (Fig. 170D–F); up to 350 microns long; about 100 species ........ **Echiniscus**
   Armor consisting of head plate, four trunk plates, and anal plate (plus intercalaries) (Fig. 170G) .........................................................6
6. Head with anterior cirri (Fig. 170G); up to 500 microns long; about 30 species; widely distributed ............................................. **Pseudechiniscus**
   Head without anterior cirri; one species reported from South Georgia Island and the state of São Paulo, Brazil .............. **Mopsechiniscus imberbis** (Richters)
7. Sucking pharynx with macroplacoids (Figs. 161, 162); eyes present or absent; each leg with two double claws (Figs. 171C–E, L–N) ...... MACROBIOTIDAE, 8
   Sucking pharynx elongated and without macroplacoids (Fig. 171B); mouth surrounded by six prominent papillae; eyes present; each set with two long, slender claws and two short, heavy claws (Figs. 171A, C); up to 1200 microns long; one cosmopolitan species ....... MILNESIIDAE, **Milnesium tardigradum** Doyère
8. Each of two claws of each leg indistinctly double, with one of the hooks reduced to a small nub; a single species known from Sonora, Mexico and California.
   **Haplomacrobiotus hermosillensis** May
   Each of the two claws of each leg clearly double .............................9
9. Sucking pharynx elongated and without placoids; one species reported from Poland, another from Brazil, Illinois, and Virginia, and a third from Sicily. **Itaquascon**
   Sucking pharynx not especially elongated, with placoids ......................**10**
10. Claws of second and third legs lacking; one species known from terrestrial mosses in Sicily ..................................... **Necopinatum mirabile** Pilato
    Claws present on second and third legs....................................**11**
11. Fourth legs rudimentary; claws at posterior end lacking or vestigial; in wet mosses; one species in Italy and another reported from Georgia and Michigan.
    **Hexapodibius**
    Fourth legs not rudimentary; claws at posterior end present and normal ........**12**

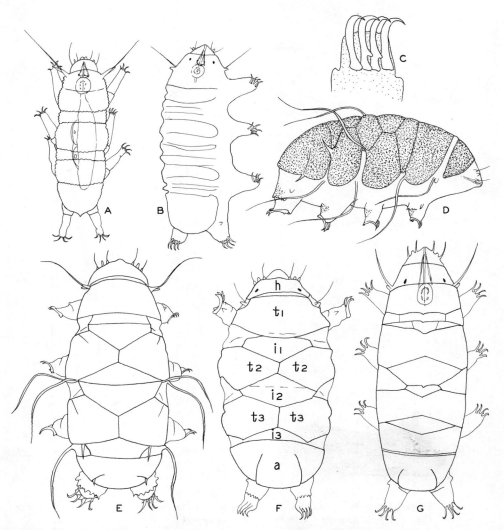

FIG. 170.–Structure of Heterotardigrada. A, dorsal view of *Oreella mollis*, ×280; B, *Parechiniscus chitonides*, ×430; C, claws of *Echiniscus*; D to F, typical species of *Echiniscus*, ×240; G, dorsal view of *Pseudechiniscus*, ×340. Armor sculpturing omitted on D, F, and G. *a*, anal plate; *h*, head plate; *i1*, *i2*, and *i3*, intercalaries; *t1*, first trunk plate; *t2*, second trunk plate (divided); *t3*, third trunk plate (divided). (Modified from various sources.)

**12.** The two double claws of each leg similar in shape; the two larger claws of each leg more or less parallel; the two smaller claws more or less turned away from each other (Figs. 171D, E); cuticle smooth; eggs mostly free and sculptured (Figs. 171F, G); up to 1100 microns long; about 80 species . . . . . .**Macrobiotus**
The two double claws of each leg usually dissimilar; the two larger claws of each leg more or less parallel; the two smaller claws more or less parallel (Figs. 171L–N); cuticle smooth or sculptured; eggs smooth or sculptured and deposited in the shed exoskeleton (Figs. 171H–J); up to 700 microns long . . . . . . . . . . . .**13**

FIG. 171.–Structure of Macrobiotoidea. A, *Milnesium tardigradum*, ×75; B, buccal apparatus of *M. tardigradum*; C, claws of *M. tardigradum*; D and E, claws of *Macrobiotus*; O to Q, dorsal view of typical species of *Hypsibius*, ×220. (Modified from various sources.)

13. With a long, tubular pharynx between the stylet mechanism and the sucking pharynx (Fig. 171Q); about 40 species; often considered a subgenus of *Hypsibius*.

**Diphascon**

Sucking pharynx and stylet mechanism not separated by a long, tubular pharynx; about 90 species .......................................... **Hypsibius**

## TARDIGRADA REFERENCES

BARTOS, E. 1941. Studien über die Tardigraden des Karpathengebietes. *Zool. Jahrb. Abt. Syst. Oekol. Geogr. Tiere* **74**:435–472.

BAUMANN, H. 1921. Beiträge zur Kenntnis der Anatomie der Tardigraden (Macrobiotus hüfelandi). *Z. wiss. Zool.* **68**:637–652.

———. 1922. Die Anabiose der Tardigraden. *Zool. Jahrb. Abt. Syst. Geogr. Biol. Tiere* **45**:501–556.

CROWE, J. H. 1975. The physiology of cryptobiosis in tardigrades. *Mem. Ist. Ital. Idrobiol. Suppl.* **32**:37–59.

CROWE, J. H., and R. P. HIGGINS. 1967. The revival of Macrobiotus areolatus Murray (Tardigrada) from the cryptobiotic state. *Trans. Am. Microsc. Soc.* **86**:286–294.

DOYÈRE, L. 1840, 1842. Mémoire sur less Tardigrades. *Ann. Sci. Nat. Zool.* (2) **14**:269–361; **17**:193–205; **18**:5–35.

HENNECKE, J. 1911. Beiträge zur Kenntnis der Biologie und Anatomie der Tardigraden (Macrobiotus macronyx Duj.). *Z. wiss. Zool.* **97**:721–752.

HIGGINS, R. P. 1959. Life history of Macrobiotus

islandicus Richters with notes on other tardigrades from Colorado. *Trans. Am. Microsc. Soc.* **78**:137–154.

———. (ed.). 1975. International symposium on tardigrades. *Mem. Ist. Ital. Idrobiol. Suppl.* **32**:1–469.

MARCUS, E. 1928. Spinnentiere oder Arachnoidea. IV. Bärtierchen (Tardigrada). *Tierwelt Dtschl.* **12**:1–230.

———. 1928a. Zur Ökologie und Physiologie der Tardigraden. *Zool. Jahrb. Abt. Allg. Zool.* **44**:323–370.

———. 1928b. Zur vergleichenden Anatomie und Histologie der Tardigraden. Ibid. **45**:99–158.

———. 1929. Tardigrada. *Tierreich* **5**, Abt. 4, Buch 3:1–608.

———. 1929a. Zur Embryologie der Tardigraden. *Zool. Jahrb. Abt. Anat.* **50**:333–384.

———. 1935. Über die Verdauung bei den Tardigraden. *Zool. Jahrb. Abt. Allg. Zool.* **54**:385–404.

———. 1936. Tardigrada. *Das Tierreich* **66**:1–340.

MATHEWS, G. B. 1938. Tardigrada from North America. *Am. Midl. Nat.* **19**:619–626.

MAY, R.-M. 1948. La vie des Tardigrades. *Hist. Nat.* **8**:1–133.

MORGAN, C. I., and P. E. KING. 1976. *British tardigrades*. 132 pp. Academic, London.

MÜLLER, J. 1935. Zur vergleichenden Myologie der Tardigraden. *Z. wiss. Zool.* **147**:171–204.

MURRAY, J. 1907. Scottish Tardigrada, collected by the Lake Survey. *Trans. Roy. Soc. Edinburgh* **45**:641–668.

———. 1907a. Encystment of Tardigrada. Ibid. 837–854.

———. 1910. Tardigrada. *Sci. Rep, Brit. Antarctic Exped. 1907–1909* **1**:81–185.

PETERSON, B. 1951. The tardigrade fauna of Greenland. A faunistic study with some few ecological remarks. *Medd. Grønland* **150**:1–94.

PIGON, A., and B. WEGLARSKA. 1955. Rate of metabolism in tardigrades during active life and anabiosis. *Nature* **176**:121–122.

RAMAZOTTI, G. 1972. Il phylum Tardigrada. *Mem. Ist. Ital. Idrobiol. Dott. Marco de Marchi* **28**:1–732.

———. 1974. Supplemento a "Il phylum Tardigrada," seconda edizione. Ibid. **31**:69–179.

RIGGIN, G. T. 1962. Tardigrada of southwest Virginia: with the addition of a description of a new marine species from Florida. *Tech. Bull. Va. Agric. Exp. Sta.* **152**:1–145.

RUDESCU, L. 1964. Tardigrada. *Fauna Rep. Pop. Rom.* **4**:1–401.

SCHUSTER, T. R., and A. A. GRIGARICK. 1965. Tardigrada from Western North America: with emphasis on the fauna of California. *Univ. Calif. Publ. Zool.* **76**:1–67.

THULIN, G. 1911. Beiträge zur Kenntnis der Tardigradenfauna Schwedens. *Ark. Zool.* **7**:1–60.

———. 1928. Über die Phylogenie und das System der Tardigraden. *Hereditas* **11**:207–266.

# Chapter 12

# BRYOZOA (MOSS ANIMALCULES)

UNPOLLUTED and unsilted waters, especially ponds and the shallows of lakes and slow streams, characteristically contain colonies of Bryozoa. To the casual observer such colonies are often mistaken for a mat of moss, and certainly some of the common species do have a superficial plantlike appearance. A large, encrusting, sessile colony may consist of thousands of individuals covering an area in excess of a square meter, and a massive gelatinous species may attain the size of a grapefruit or a small watermelon. Usually bryozoans occur on the undersides of logs and stones, or on twigs and other objects where the light is dim.

Bryozoa are more generally distributed and obvious in salt-water habitats than in fresh waters, and about 4000 marine species have been described the world over, as contrasted with about 50 fresh-water species. Only about 21 species have been reported from American fresh waters.

We use "Bryozoa" and "Ectoprocta" as equivalent names for the same phylum, taxonomists being generally divided in their preferences. The term "Polyzoa" has been discarded except in Great Britain. This chapter also includes the Phylum Entoprocta (with a single fresh-water species in the United States).

**General characteristics.** The unit of organization is a microscopic, more or less cylindrical zooid (Figs. 175, 176). Superficially it resembles certain coelenterate polyps, and it wasn't until 1830 that the Bryozoa were distinguished from the Coelenterata as a separate phylum. The living body wall (cystid) is very thin, and the

Y-shaped digestive tract is suspended in the extensive coelomic cavity. The mouth is situated on a large, distal, circular, oval, or horseshoe-shaped lophophore bearing numerous ciliated tentacles, but the anus is located posterior to or below the lophophore rather than on it. Sometimes the lophophore and its tentacles are collectively called the tentacular crown. The lophophore, its tentacles, and the base of the lophophore form a polypide (collectively, the protruded living parts of an individual bryozoan). Typically the individuals of a colony are all connected in a highly branched, twiglike manner. The coelom is more or less continous from one zooid to another, depending on the relative development of the septum.

Only the tentacular crown and distal portion of the body are exposed to the water, the rest of the body and the whole colony being invested by a zooecium, which is secreted by the body wall. This protective layer may be thin to massive, corneous, cuticular, gelatinous, delicate, or tough, depending on the particular species and variety. According to the mode of growth and type of zooecium, there are three general but intergrading growth forms: (1) branching and threadlike, (2) matlike or crustlike, and (3) gelatinous and massive. In addition, *Plumatella casmiana* and *P. fungosa* occasionally form "honeycomb" colonies 2 to 20 mm thick (Fig. 174). In the older portions of colonies the zooecium is commonly opaque, brownish, and more or less covered with detritus, algae, and microzoa. But the cystid proper, which comprises the living portions of the zooid (exclusive of the polypide), is delicate,

FIG. 172.–*Plumatella repens*. A, bit of colony on piece of burned wood, ×1.5; B, bit of colony, ×6.

leased from the colony, statoblasts are distributed at random by currents and winds; they may float or remain on the bottom. A statoblast is highly resistant to drying, cold, and other adverse environmental conditions, but under appropriate conditions it germinates to produce a new colony.

The Phylum Bryozoa is divided into two classes, the Phylactolaemata and the Gymnolaemata. All species in the former are restricted to fresh waters, but the much larger Class Gymnolaemata is almost exclusively marine. Four of the five orders in this class are marine, and in the fifth order, the Ctenostomata, only two American species occur in fresh waters. Unlike many marine species, fresh water bryozoans exhibit no polymorphism.

The Entoprocta is a phylum that is mainly marine and possibly closely related to the Bryozoa. In addition to the true Bryozoa, the key on page 267 includes the one American fresh-water species of Entoprocta. The differentiating features of this peculiar and uncommon species are given in the key.

**Locomotion.** Although bryozoan colonies are generally sessile, a few fresh-water species are capable of sluggish creeping movements. *Cristatella mucedo* (Fig. 188B) is the most active form, and a colony may progress as much as 1 to 10 cm per day. The small colonies of *Lophopus crystallinus* and *Lophopodella carteri*, as well as young colonies of *Pectinatella magnifica*, also move but usually less than 2 cm per day.

The mechanism of colony locomotion if obscure, but it is probable that ciliary action on the tentacles, the musculature of the body wall, and perhaps polypide retractor muscle action are of some importance.

**Feeding, digestive system.** When the lophophore is expanded under normal conditions, the tentacles are almost motionless, but their abundant cilia beat constantly and create miniature currents along the lophophore that bring algae, protozoans, micrometazoa, and detritus to the region of the mouth. If large and inedible

translucent, and only slightly pigmented. Internal structures can therefore usually be observed only in younger individuals.

When undisturbed, the bryozoan tentacular crown is extended through the distal aperture of the zooecium. It is large and beautifully expanded, and a colony has the appearance of a patch of tiny and delicate flowers, but at the slightest disturbance the tentacular crowns are retracted within the zooecia in a flash. After a few minutes they are again slowly extruded and expanded.

Growth and proliferation of a colony is a matter of simple asexual budding. Sexual reproduction, when evident, is restricted to a few weeks during the year. Each individual is hermaphroditic, and early development takes place within the coelom. On being released to the outside, the ciliated embryo soon becomes fixed to the substrate and gives rise to a new colony.

Statoblasts are asexual internal buds whose functional cells are enclosed by two tightly fitting convex sclerotized and sculptured valves (Figs. 180–183). On being re-

FIG. 173.–Massive colonies of *Pectinatella magnifica* photographed in natural habitat; relative size can be judged from the two tree trunks at the water's edge in the immediate background. (Photo courtesy of Percy Viosca, Jr.)

particles reach the mouth, the individual tentacles may bend over in such a way as to brush the particles away and alter the ciliary currents. In all Phylactolaemata the base of the lophophore is surrounded by a membranous cup, or calyx, which is festooned or scalloped; presumably this structure increases the efficiency of feeding. The distal end of the animal may extend upward from the substrate or downward from the underside of an object, but feeding goes on effectively regardless of position. Phylactolaemata have a flaplike epistome over the mouth. It may cover the mouth or aid in rejecting or warding off undesirable particles.

The anterior portion of the esophagus is slightly modified to form a somewhat muscular pharynx. Food passes through the mouth and pharynx and into the esophagus, and when a sufficient quantity has accumulated in the esophagus, the esophageal valve relaxes and the food passes into the stomach, where most of the digestion occurs. Below the stomach and corresponding to the basal leg of the Y is a long, baglike absorptive organ, the caecum. Connecting the lower end of the caecum and

Fig. 174.–Bit of a massive colony of *Plumatella fungosa,* showing zooecium. Upper, diagram of mass of upright parallel tubes; lower, preserved material showing lower surface and upright tubes, ×1. (Lower, courtesy of John Bushnell; upper from Allman.)

the body wall is a long strand of tissue, the funiculus. The tubular intestine passes from the upper end of the caecum to the anus; its terminal portion is slightly modified to form a rectum. The anus is located just below the lophophore. The feces are released as pellets surrounded by a peritrophic membrane.

The Phylactolaemata alimentary canal is ciliated only around the mouth and in the pharynx but in the Gymnolaemata cilia extend as far as the upper portion of the stomach.

Much of the polypide coloration is determined by the specific contents of the alimentary canal, and by changing the diet experimentally it is possible to get yellow, green, and brown coloration all in the same day.

**Circulation.** There is no circulatory mechanism in bryozoans, but materials are undoubtedly distributed quickly and efficiently via the coelomic fluid owing to the movements of the alimentary canal and retractions and extrusions of the tentacular crown.

**Respiration.** No special respiratory devices are present. The greater portion of the carbon dioxide and oxygen exchange undoubtedly occurs through the basal portion of the lophophore.

**Excretion.** No excretory system occurs in the bryozoans, although some investigators claim otherwise. Coelomic amoebocytes containing engulfed excretory granules supposedly make their way through the body wall to the outside. In *Urnatella gracilis* (an entoproct) there is a simple protonephridial system.

In *Cristatella, Lophopus, Plumatella,* and possibly some other genera the epidermal cells of the tentacles apparently accumulate excretory substances and liberate them to the outside. In addition, quantities of metabolic wastes are undoubtedly retained in many of the body tissues until the animal dies and disintegrates. A true intertentacular organ is unknown in fresh-water bryozoans.

A few Phylactolaemata, including *Hyalinella, Lophopus, Cristatella,* and *Lophopodella,* sometimes undergo partial disintegration similar to true "brown-body" formation in marine forms, especially under unfavorable conditions. It is thought that this phenomenon is at least partially excretory in nature. The polypides (especially older individuals) first retract permanently and then begin to undergo degeneration. The lophophore, tentacles, digestive tract, and nervous system degenerate (Fig. 176). Such a body remains unchanged, or it may further disintegrate into small fragments that circulate about in the coelom. Sometimes, in *Plumatella casmiana,* a new polypide is then regenerated from an internal bud on the body wall; it comes to occupy the space vacated by the old polypide. Sometimes the same zooid may undergo "brown-body" formation two times a season. In spite of certain textbook statements

Fig. 175.–Structure of a *Plumatella* zooid, diagrammatic. Tentacles and retractor muscle shown for only one side. *a*, anus; *b*, brain; *bw*, body wall; *c*, caecum; *ca*, calyx; *ds*, developing statoblasts (3); *e*, cuticula; *es*, esophagus; *f*, funiculus; *i*, intestine; *o*, ovary; *rm*, retractor muscle; *s*, stomach; *t*, testis.

to the contrary, a "brown body" has never been seen to regenerate a new cystid.

**Muscle system.** The most prominent muscles are the two retractors, which are somewhat stringy and not at all compact. They originate at the base of the zooecium and are inserted on the base of the lophophore and uppermost portion of the digestive tract, one on each side (Fig. 175). Their contraction pulls the whole distal end of the polypide back into the coelom and cystid. Some short indistinct fibers connect the upper part of the polypide with the nearby body wall, and a few associated fibers aid in rotating the tentacular crown and depressing the lobes.

The thin body wall contains a few loosely arranged circular and longitudinal fibers, which are effective in everting the polypide. Other indistinct muscles elevate the epistome, move the alimentary canal slightly, and act as dilators and sphincters.

FIG. 176.–Semidiagrammatic view of a small portion of a *Lophopodella carteri* colony, ×25, showing two "brown bodies." *bb*, "brown bodies"; *bw*, body wall; *c*, caecum; *e*, zooecium; *f*, funiculus; *i*, intestine. (Greatly modified from Rogick, 1938.)

**Nervous system.** A single large ganglion, or "brain," is situated at the distal end between the mouth and anus. From it a series of flimsy fibers with a few associated nerve cell bodies radiate out to all tissues and organs. There are no proven nervous connections between adjacent zooids.

Special sense organs are absent, but bryozoans are remarkably sensitive to light and other stimuli, certain epidermal cells being specialized as receptors.

**Reproduction, development.** Growth of a colony is an asexual form of proliferation, often dichotomous, whereby a part of the body wall grows outward and eventually forms a new zooid. In this way, beginning with a single zooid in the spring, the resulting colony may consist of thousands of living and dead individuals by autumn. Developing *Pectinatella, Cristatella,* and *Lophopodella* colonies often undergo fission, thus giving rise to two or more new colonies (Fig. 177). A fission or fragmentation of portions of a colony has been observed in *Fredericella sultana*.

The period of sexual reproduction in a colony usually lasts only about one to four weeks, most often some time between May and July. Individual zooids are hermaphroditic in all species except for *Urnatella,* which is dioecious. The single ovary develops from the peritoneum of the body wall near the distal end of the zooid, and the testis develops from the peritoneum of the funiculus. Unlike the situation in the great majority of hermaphroditic animals, there seems to be no current evidence for cross-fertilization in fresh-water Bryozoa. Mature eggs and sperm are produced either simultaneously or in rapid succession. Ordinarily only a single ovum matures at a time and is fertilized by sperm in the coelomic fluid just as it leaves the ovary. The zygote then becomes implanted in a special pouchlike ooecium, which develops from the body wall in the immediate vicinity of the ovary. Here the embryo develops into a pear-shaped, oval, or round ciliated larva 1 to 2 mm long and usually containing one to five immature polypides. A *Cristatella* larva, however, may have up to 25 polypides or polypide buds. This larva breaks out of the parent through a special large pore at the base of the lophophore, or it escapes when the parent degenerates (Fig.

FIG. 177.–Diagram of dividing colony of *Lophopodella carteri,* ×5. Polypides are shown contracted; 10 statoblasts present. (Redrawn from Rogick, 1935.)

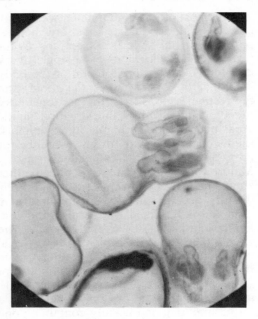

FIG. 178.–Ciliated free-swimming larvae of *Plumatella*, ×27. Center embryo contains three developing zooids.

several stages of development may be found. A mature statoblast is roughly biconvex, but the central portion is considerably thickened into a capsule owing to its contained mass of undifferentiated germinative cells. The peripheral portion (annulus, or float) consists of air cells and is relatively thin; sometimes it bears spiny, barbed, or hooked process (Fig. 180). Except for the germinative cells, a statoblast therefore consists of two sclerotized, dead valves that are tightly attached to each other in the region of the annulus. Early stages in statoblast development are almost smooth; older ones are strongly ridged or mammillate and tan, brown, or black. Usually each zooid produces two to eight statoblasts, although more than 20 per zooid have been reported.

The literature distinguishes six general and specific types of statoblasts. Floatoblasts are free or become floating after the zooecium disintegrates. In some species the floatoblasts are released from the living zooid by means of a hyaline collarlike protrusion (Fig. 184). They have no peripheral

178). It is free-swimming for only a few minutes or for as long as 20 to 24 hours and then settles on the substrate, evaginates, and eventually gives rise to a mature colony.

Little specific information is available concerning the natural longevity of individual zooids, but presumably the great majority live for three to eight weeks in temperate climates. Large, old colonies contain many dead zooids in the parts of the colony that were first formed.

Although colonies customarily die out in the late summer or autumn, there are records of *Paludicella, Fredericella,* and *Lophopus* colonies being active throughout the winter, especially if it is mild and the water temperature does not drop below 2°.

**Statoblasts.** The production of highly resistant statoblasts is a unique feature of fresh-water Phylactolaemata. They function mainly in tiding the species over unfavorable environmental conditions and in geographic dissemination.

Statoblasts develop by asexual budding from the funiculus, and in some zooids

FIG. 179.–Young colony of *Pectinatella magnifica,* ×33.

processes; they are annulated when mature and are 0.2 to 1.0 mm long. All Phylactolaemata except *Fredericella* produce floatoblasts (Figs. 190A, B; 191B, C).

There are several specialized kinds of floatoblasts. Spinoblasts are free or float-

FIG. 181.–Bryozoan statoblasts, all ×60. Top, pyknoblasts of *Plumatella casmiana*; middle, piptoblasts of *Fredericella sultana;* bottom, floatoblasts of *Plumatella emarginata*. (Photos courtesy of T. S. Wood.)

FIG. 180.–Bryozoan statoblasts. Top, *Hyalinella orbisperma,* ×160; middle, *Cristatella mucedo* spinoblast, ×40; bottom, edge view of *C. mucedo* spinoblast, ×75, showing suture zone. (SEM photos courtesy of K. S. Rao.)

ing, but are provided with spined, barbed, or hooked processes. Length ranges from 0.7 to 1.8 mm. *Cristatella, Lophopodella, Lophopus,* and *Pectinatella* produce spinoblasts (Figs. 180, 182, 185). A leptoblast is a fragile floatoblast that germinates without a diapause. A pyknoblast is thick-walled and germinates only after a diapause (Fig. 181, top). *Plumatella casmiana* produces leptoblasts, pyknoblasts, and an "intermediate form." All other species have a single morphotype.

Fig. 182.–Diagrammatic section of statoblast of *Pectinatella magnifica*, showing the two valves, hooked spines, central capsule filled with germinative cells, and float.

Sessoblasts are sessile, fixed, or attached to the zooecium wall with cement; an annulus may be present or absent, well developed or reduced. The length is 0.3 to 0.6 mm. *Fredericella, Hyalinella, Plumatella,* and *Stolella* produce sessoblasts (Fig. 183). Some species of *Plumatella* produce both sessoblasts and floatoblasts. The two species of *Fredericella* produce piptoblasts (Fig. 181, middle), which are neither cemented to the substrate nor capable of floating. They lack an annulus and usually sink to the bottom when the zooecium disintegrates.

Formerly it was thought that statoblast production is limited to late summer and autumn just before the colonies die off, but it is now well established that statoblasts may also be regularly produced during the earlier portion of the growing season. In the tropics statoblasts usually appear with the onset of hot weather. Sexual reproduction and statoblast production may occur simultaneously in the same zooid; there is little evidence for alternation of the two methods.

On disintegration of the zooids, the floatoblasts are released to the vagaries of currents, waves, and wind. Some of them sink or remain on the bottom. Others float to the surface, and under appropriate conditions may be found in such abundance as to form windrows on the shore, especially in spring and autumn. Sessoblasts, however, remain attached to the substrate until the last bit of old zooecium has disintegrated. A few species actively release statoblasts (Fig. 184).

The length of the statoblast dormant period is highly variable, depending on the species, the individual, temperature, and other environmental conditions. In high latitudes there is usually only one generation per year, and the majority of statoblasts

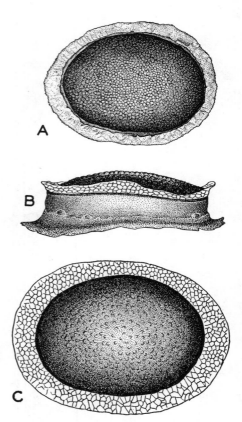

Fig. 183.–Sessoblasts of *Plumatella,* ×120. A, unattached surface view of sessoblast of *P. emarginata*; B, side view of sessoblast of *P. repens* (note sclerotized lamella that resembles the float of floatoblasts); C, unattached surface view of same. (From Rogick, 1940.)

FIG. 184.–Sequence of release of two statoblasts in *Stolella*. (From Marcus, 1942.)

winter over and germinate the following spring, but south of the 50th parallel it appears that the growing season is often sufficiently long for two or three main crops of statoblasts. Colonies mature in the spring, and their statoblasts hatch out and produce a second group of mature colonies by late summer or early autumn. These individuals, in turn, give rise to statoblasts that winter over. In spite of their ability to survive drying and freezing temperatures, it should be borne in mind that statoblasts have a very high natural mortality rate.

Under natural conditions the period of statoblast dormancy or desiccation extends from the end of one growing season to the beginning of the next, which is usually four to nine months, and most workers are agreed that a majority of statoblasts of all species are viable for the duration of such periods.

The natural period of dormancy and germination is usually 30 to 150 days, the chief governing factors being low temperatures and desiccation. Germination begins in the spring when the water reaches 10° to 19°. The first evidence of germination is the gradual separation of the two statoblast valves along the equator, a process that may take one to eight days. A mass of undifferentiated yolky cells slowly grows and protrudes from between the valves. These cells are whitish or grayish, very contractile, and they adhere to the substrate. The primary zooid meanwhile develops between the valves, hidden from view. It utilizes the abundant stored food of the undifferentiated yolk cells, and as it enlarges it protrudes, pushes the valves farther apart, and absorbs and incorporates more and more of the yolk mass so that the latter soon becomes an indistinguishable part of the zooid. As growth proceeds, additional zooids appear by budding, and eventually a colony results.

A large amount of experimental laboratory work has been conducted on the viability of statoblasts, but the results vary so much from one species to another and from one investigator to another that it is difficult to generalize. Most workers, however, seem to agree that natural freezing

FIG. 185.–Germinating statoblasts of *Lophopodella carteri*, ×33. A, valves separating and mass of undifferentiated yolky cells extruded; B, primary polypide emerging; C, primary zooid almost mature (note small bud on left side near distal end). (Modified from Rogick, 1935.)

and normal winter temperatures have little effect on the percentage of later germination, but little is known about the lethal effects of unusually low temperatures.

Viability of statoblasts dried and kept at room temperature differs widely from one species to another. Rogick (1940) found that all *Hyalinella, Pectinatella,* and *Plumatella* statoblasts died within 23 to 34 months under such conditions. *Fredericella,* on the other hand, showed 50 to 100 percent germination after 24 months. Seventy percent of *Lophopodella* statoblasts were capable of germinating after being dry for 50 months, but none germinated after 74 months. In general, wet storage in the refrigerator produces a lower statoblast mortality than drying at room temperature for the same length of time. Statoblasts die within a few days when kept in a laboratory desiccator.

When statoblasts are placed in water and germinated in the laboratory the period of incubation is highly variable. Some individuals and species germinate in four to ten days; others require one to four months for germination.

**Hibernacula.** The Paludicellidae, including *Paludicella* and *Pottsiella,* do not form statoblasts, but rather hibernacula, which are similar to statoblasts in function. A hibernaculum is a specially modified external winter bud. Like statoblasts, they consist of masses of cells protected by a thick sclerotized coat (Fig. 186).

**Ecology.** Quiet ponds, backwaters, bays, and slow streams, especially where there are sunken logs, twigs, rocks, and aquatic vegetation, are ideal places for Bryozoa. Sandy and pebbly bottoms are poor

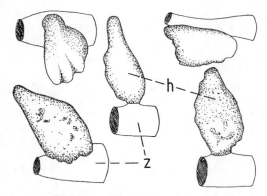

FIG. 186.–Hibernacula of *Paludicella articulata*, ×50. *h*, hibernaculum; *z*, bits of old zooecium. (Modified from Rogick, 1935.)

habitats, but certain species of *Plumatella, Fredericella,* and *Paludicella* are often found in turbulent waters. Although they are common in stagnant waters, bryozoans are never found under markedly polluted conditions and only sparingly where the quantity of dissolved oxygen falls below 30 percent saturation. Silting also discourages establishment and growth, and strongly acid waters and bogs almost never contain bryozoans. *Lophopodella carteri* is probably the species that is most tolerant of decay and stagnation.

Light is not necessary for development and growth, as shown by the occurrence of bryozoans in water pipes and closed conduits. On the other hand, they are seldom present in bright light, although *Cristatella mucedo* occurs regularly on the upper sides of objects in the shallows. All other species found in shallow water are attached to the undersides or shaded sides of rocks, logs, vegetation, and boards.

Most Bryozoa are collected in waters less than 1 m deep, but they commonly occur at considerably greater depths, and if appropriate collecting equipment is used, almost all of our common species may be taken in lakes at depths up to 5 or 10 m. *Paludicella* has been taken as deep as 36 m and *Fredericella* up to 214 m. *F. sultana* is sometimes found in marl lakes; it also occasionally grows up from sandy substrates in an arborescent form.

*Lophopodella* and *Lophopus* are generally restricted to standing waters. *Paludicella, Cristatella, Pectinatella, Fredericella,* and *Hyalinella* are more common in standing waters but are found also in slowly running waters. *Urnatella* and *Plumatella* may, in addition, be found in fairly rapid waters. *Pottsiella* is restricted to rapid waters. Sometimes *Fredericella, Plumatella, Pectinatella,* and *Cristatella* are all found in the same pond or lake at the same time. Up to eight species have been found in a single lake.

Most American species attain their greatest abundance in the summer when the water temperature reaches 19° to 23° and begin to die off in the autumn when the water cools to 10°. *Pectinatella*, however, tolerates a much smaller range of temperature and usually dies when the water temperature goes below 16°. *Fredericella* and *Lophopus*, on the other hand, are unusually tolerant and do well anywhere between 2° and 23°. *Plumatella* is sometimes collected at water temperatures as high as 37°.

**Economic importance.** Occasional summer plagues of large floating gelatinous colonies of *Pectinatella magnifica* clog the screens of water intakes and the grates of hydroelectric plants so effectively that it requires a full-time man to keep them clear.

In communities using unfiltered and unchlorinated water, bryozoans sometimes become established in the pipes, and dead and living masses clog the valves and meters. Occasionally fishermens' trap-nets accumulate large growths. The usual offenders are *Paludicella, Fredericella,* and *Plumatella.*

Bryozoa are an element in the diet of many fresh-water invertebrates, including planarians, snails, oligochaetes, Hydracarina, crustaceans, and especially Trichoptera. Statoblasts and colonies are often eaten by small fish. The zooecium forms an excellent substrate for a variety of commensals and browsers, especially ciliates and rotifers.

**Geographical distribution, dispersal.** *Plumatella repens, Fredericella sultana, Plumatella emarginata,* and *Hyalinella punctata* are the only known truly cosmopolitan species; they occur in suitable habitats all over the world. At the other extreme, some North American species have greatly restricted and often puzzling distributions. *Hyalinella orbisperma* is Nearctic; *Stolella evelinae* and *Pottsiella erecta* are Nearctic and Neotropical; *Cristatella mucedo* and *Plumatella fungosa* are circumpolar; *Pectinatella magnifica* is probably native only to North America but has been recently introduced into Japan and Germany; *Hyalinella vaihiriae* is peculiar to the Nearctic and Australian regions.

Unquestionably the paucity of records for some of the American species is a reflection of the fact that little systematic and intensive collecting has been done. Future collecting, especially in the South, and west of the Mississippi River, will probably show that some of our "rare" species are actually widely distributed.

Chiefly by virtue of their resistant statoblasts and hibernacula, bryozoans are one of the few fresh-water groups that are clearly capable of being transported overland from one body of water to another by animals. There are definite records of statoblast occurrence in mud on the feet and feathers of waterfowl, and in the fur of mammals. Some statoblasts are capable of germinating after passing through the alimentary canal of waterfowl, turtles, frogs, salamanders, and fish (see Bushnell, 1973).

**Collecting.** Bits of colonies, sessoblasts, and hibernacula should be carefully removed from their substrate with forceps, spatula, and scalpel, but if the colonies are on small pieces of wood, twigs, or stones, they may be brought to the laboratory intact. A dredge or double rake is necessary for collecting below a depth of 1 m.

Floating statoblasts may often be obtained in abundance at the right season by skimming the surface of the water with a net or by scooping them up from windrows.

**Culturing.** Bryozoa are among the most difficult of all fresh-water invertebrates to culture in the laboratory. If intact colonies are used, they may sometimes be kept alive in finger bowls for 5 to 15 days, provided the water is replaced frequently with fresh pond water, preferably from their natural habitat. Sometimes a small quantity of fresh yeast is beneficial to the culture.

Rogick reports some success using water from aquatic plant aquariums along with a bit of the organic debris from the bottom of such aquariums. Such debris usually contains an abundance of suitable microorganisms for food. Both water and debris should be changed every two or three days.

Wood (1971) presents a simple and highly successful method of culturing in the laboratory. Statoblasts are first allowed to germinate in petri dishes. Once the ancestrulae (young colonies) are formed, they stick to the glass, and the petri dish is then placed in an aquarium where it is held upside down by Plexiglas strips. Fecal pellets and detritus fall away and leave the colony clean. The most reliable food source is the suspended organic matter normally present in a large, thriving aquarium.

**Preparing, preserving.** Bryozoans are highly sensitive to foreign substances, and if ordinary methods of fixation are used the tentacular crown contracts into the zooecium so strongly as to make the whole animal useless for study. Consequently some method of narcotization must first be used so that the animals can be killed and fixed with the lophophore expanded.

The colonies and a part of their substrate should be placed in a finger bowl one-third to one-half full of water from their habitat, and the subsequent narcotization must be done very gradually and patiently. If chloretone, methol, or chloral hydrate is used, a saturated solution should be added slowly over a period of one to three hours. When the animals no longer respond appreciably to jarring or touching, most of the fluid should be withdrawn with a large pipette. Then Bouin's fixative or 50 percent formalin should be poured over the animals, and if the narcotization has been successful, they will be killed in a beautifully expanded condition.

The following effective method is modified from Hurrell (1936). Place the colonies and a bit of their substrate in a finger bowl of water. Sprinkle a teaspoonful of menthol crystals on top of the water, cover the finger bowl with a glass plate, and let stand overnight. By morning the bryozoans should be fully narcotized. Then withdraw most of the fluid from the finger bowl, add concentrated formalin equivalent to the amount of water remaining in the finger bowl, and let stand for one hour.

Five percent formalin and 70 percent alcohol with 5 percent glycerin are suitable preservatives.

Bryozoa may be mounted either unstained or stained with hematoxylin or borax carmine. Before mounting or staining, however, the zooecium should be gently brushed as free of debris as possible. If glycerin jelly mounts are to be made, the animals must first be run up into glycerin. Place them in a watch glass containing a solution of 5 percent glycerin in 50 percent alcohol and cover with a loose cover to keep out dust and permit evaporation of the alcohol and water. When nearly pure glycerin remains, they are ready for mounting.

**Taxonomy.** Fresh-water Bryozoa are one of many groups of American freshwater invertebrates greatly in need of much more systematic collecting and critical work. Indeed, between 1904 and 1935, this group was almost completely forgotten, but in more recent years much fundamental work has been accomplished by two outstanding American investigators, John Bushnell and Mary Rogick. Dr. Bushnell contributed much toward the details of this chapter.

Most of our species are distinctive, especially if both the colonies and their statoblasts are available for identification. Indeed, the genera are easily distinguished with the naked eye or hand lens. The most common and widely distributed species, *Plumatella repens,* is extremely variable and puzzling. At least six different varieties and two "phases" of this species have been reported from the United States, and although all of them are perhaps best placed in the single species, there are some investigators, especially Europeans, who prefer to consider these several varieties as distinct species. Some of the more striking intergrading and variable characters are (Rogick, 1935): colony composed of two discrete masses or not, branching compact to open, zooecia furrowed or not furrowed, tubes attached to the substrate along their entire length or tubes more or less erect, keel present or absent, and statoblasts relatively long or short. Sometimes the variations differ according to the age of the animals, but often they are apparently controlled and induced by certain obscure factors of the many different types of habitats in which *P. repens* occurs. The problem awaits solution by means of controlled laboratory cultures.

## KEY TO SPECIES OF BRYOZOA

1. Anus outside the lophophore; zooids not stalked; tentacular crown capable of being retracted within zooecium; without a protonephridial system; statoblasts present or absent .....................Phylum **BRYOZOA (ECTOPROCTA), 2**
   Anus on the lophophore; each zooid on a flexible stalk composed of sclerotized urn-shaped segments; one to six such stalks arising from one basal plate; stalks may be branched or unbranched and up to 5 mm long; lophophore circular, with 8 to 16 tentacles, and incapable of being retracted into zooecium (Fig. 187A); with a simple protonephridial system; without statoblasts; on objects in running waters or in large lakes; one uncommon species reported from scattered localities in eastern half of the United States, but there are also records from Texas, Oklahoma, and Gulf coast rivers, including mildly polluted waters.
   Phylum **ENTOPROCTA, Urnatella gracilis** Leidy

FIG. 187.–Structure of Entoprocta and Paludicellidae. A, small portion of a colony of *Urnatella gracilis*, ×32; B, zooid of *Paludicella articulata*, ×33; C, portion of a young colony of *P. articulata* showing three retracted individuals and two buds; D, young colony of *Pottsiella erecta*, ×33, showing two hibernacula. (A modified from Leidy, 1884; B and C modified from Rogick, 1940; D modified from Kraepelin, 1887.)

2. Lophophore circular and without an epistome (Fig. 187B); colony covered with a corneous or membranous cuticle; statoblasts absent; hibernacula produced (Fig. 186)................... Class **GYMNOLAEMATA**, PALUDICELLIDAE, 3
   Lophophore horseshoe-shaped, oval, or circular, and with an epistome (Figs. 188– 190); statoblasts produced................ Class **PHYLACTOLAEMATA, 4**
3. Colony threadlike and consisting of a series of club-shaped zooecia arranged end to end and separated from each other by partitions; 16 to 18 tentacles; zooecium openings on upper surface; zooids about 2 mm long; colony recumbent or partially erect (Figs. 187B,C); standing and slowly flowing waters; reported from scattered localities chiefly east of the Mississippi River but probably cosmopolitan in the United States .............. **Paludicella articulata** (Ehr.)
   Colony consisting of a stolon from which single individuals arise; zooecium openings terminal; 19 to 21 tentacles; zooids about 1.5 mm long (Fig. 187D); on upper surface of stones in rapid water; reported only from streams in Louisiana, Ohio, Pennsylvania, Virginia, Tennessee, and Texas .. **Pottsiella erecta** (Potts)
4. Statoblasts all free, annulated, and with processes (Figs. 182; 185; 188C,D; 189D,E); colony soft, gelatinous, transparent, without septa, and not dendritic (Figs. 188B, E; 189H, J) .................................................5
   Often with two types of statoblasts; one attached and without float cells (sessoblasts); the other unattached, funicular, and annulated (floatoblasts) (except *Frederi-cella);* statoblasts without processes; colony most often dendritic ..........8
5. Case a transient secretion elaborated by flat base of colony; colony elongated and slowly motile (Fig. 188B); statoblasts with two circlets of hooked spines; dorsal circlet with 10 to 34 hooks and ventral circlet with 20 to 50 hooks (Figs. 188C,D); zooids on upper surface and arranged marginally in three rows; all

Fig. 188.–Structure of *Cristatella* and *Pectinatella*. A, colony of *Cristatella mucedo*, ×5; B, colony of *C. mucedo*, ×40; C, edge view of *C. mucedo* statoblast, ×50; D, surface view of *C. mucedo* statoblast; E, rosette of *Pectinatella magnifica*; F, edge of colony of *Cristatella mucedo* showing three rows of marginal polypides. (A to D from Allman; E and F from Kraepelin, 1887.)

polypides retracted into a common cavity; usually 80 to 90 tentacles; long dimension of colony sometimes as much as 10 to 30 cm but more typically 2 to 6 cm; in standing water or slow currents, on upper side of submerged objects and vegetation; widely distributed but not common.

CRISTATELLIDAE, **Cristatella mucedo** Cuvier

Case present throughout life of colony and sometimes very well developed; colony not usually motile; statoblasts never with two circlets of hooked spines . . . . . **6**

**6.** Colonies in the form of rosettes on gelatinous base or surrounding a gelatinous core; very young colonies motile; colonies commonly investing twigs and other submerged objects, especially in shaded places in quiet waters (Fig. 188E); 60 to 84 tentacles; free statoblasts with single row of marginal anchorlike spines (Fig. 182); widely distributed but uncommon west of the Mississippi Valley.

PECTINATELLIDAE, **Pectinatella magnifica** Leidy

Colonies in the form of small gelatinous masses with radiate branching; a few to 70 zooids per colony; free statoblasts pointed or with hooked spines at each end (Figs. 185; 189D,E). . . . . . . . . . . . . . . . . . . . . . . . . . . . . . . LOPHOPODIDAE, **7**

FIG. 189.–Structure of Plumatellidae. A, cuticula enclosing sessoblast of *Fredericella australiensis*, ×100; B, branching in colony of *F. australiensis*, ×12 (polypides shown retracted); C, sessoblast of *F. sultana*, ×85; D, edge view of statoblast of *Lophopus crystallinus*, ×40; E, surface view of same statoblast; F, zooid of *Fredericella sultana*, ×15; G, small colony of *F. sultana*, ×3; H and J, small colonies of *Lophopus crystallinus*, ×7. (A and B modified from Rogick, 1945; C modified from Rogick, 1937; D to G, and J from Allman; H from Kraepelin, 1887.)

7. Free statoblasts broadly oval, with one or several hooked polar spines (Fig. 185);
zooecium translucent; colonies small, circular to oval, and mound-shaped when
only a few polypides are present, but radiating lobate when many polypides
are present; average colony 5 mm wide, 8 mm long, and with 20 to 45 polypides;
52 to 82 tentacles; rare, reported from Lake Erie, New Jersey, Ohio, Pennsylvania, Kentucky, and Michigan . . . . . . . . . . . . . . . **Lophopodella carteri** (Hyatt)
    Free statoblasts elongated, attenuated to a point at each pole (Figs. 189D,E); colony
sac-shaped, erect, often lobed, and usually less than 1 cm across; zooecium
gelatinous (Figs. 189H,J); with about 60 tentacles; usually attached to vegetation in standing water; rare in eastern states . . . . .**Lophopus crystallinus** Pallas
8. Lophophore circular or elliptical; colony tubular, branched, and antlerlike (Fig. 189B);
zooecium usually opaque and brown; all statoblasts (piptoblasts) free, without
annulus (Fig. 189A); no floatoblasts . . . FREDERICELLIDAE, **Fredericella, 9**
    Lophophore horseshoe-shaped; floatoblasts present; sessoblasts also present in most
species . . . . . . . . . . . . . . . . . . . . . . . . . . . . . . . . . . . . . PLUMATELLIDAE, **10**
9. With 24 to 30 tentacles; polypides short; zooecium not especially slender; cuticula
thin, chitinoid, and opaque (Fig. 189B); most sessoblasts circular or broadly
elliptical (Fig. 189A); reported from a pond in Uinta County, Wyoming, and
otherwise known only from Mexico in North American.
                                                **Fredericella australiensis** Goddard
    With 17 to 27 tentacles; polypides longer; zooecium slender, with antlerlike branching
(Fig. 189G); most sessoblasts reniform or elongated (Fig. 189C); on submerged
objects and vegetation in standing and slowly flowing waters; common and
widely distributed . . . . . . . . . . . . . . . . . . . . **Fredericella sultana** (Blumenbach)
10. Zooecium in the form of elongated pseudostolons (Figs. 190H, J) . . . . . . .**Stolella, 11**
    Zooecium not in the form of elongated pseudostolons . . . . . . . . . . . . . . . . . . . . .**12**
11. Basal portion of the zooecium of each zooid slender and strongly tapered (Fig. 190H);
reported only from Pennsylvania and Michigan . . . . . **Stolella indica** Annandale
    Basal portion of the zooecium of each zooid not slender and strongly tapered (Fig.
190J); reported only from Michigan . . . . . . . . . . . . . . . **Stollela evelinae** Marcus
12. With soft, hyaline, gelatinous cuticula; horizontal branches only; thickly branched,
often completely covering the substrate (Fig. 190D) . . . . . . . . . . . **Hyalinella, 13**
    With thin, firm, and sometimes horny cuticula; zooecium long and tubular, pale and
transparent to dark brown; in masses up to 5 cm high or closely adherent to
substrate (Fig. 191); in a variety of habitats . . . . . . . . . . . . . . . . **Plumatella, 15**
13. Floatoblasts circular, diameter about 0.34 mm; colony flat and massive; reported only
from Michigan . . . . . . . . . . . . . . . . . . . . . . . **Hyalinella orbisperma** (Kellicott)
    Floatoblasts not circular . . . . . . . . . . . . . . . . . . . . . . . . . . . . . . . . . . . . . . . . . . . .**14**
14. Floatoblasts averaging 0.37 mm wide and 0.54 mm long (Fig. 190B); cuticula soft,
swollen, colorless, or yellowish (Fig. 190D); widely distributed and
common . . . . . . . . . . . . . . . . . . . . . . . . . . . . . . . . .**Hyalinella punctata** (Hancock)
    Floatoblasts averaging 0.25 mm wide and 0.36 mm long (Fig. 190A); reported only
from Bear River, Utah . . . . . . . . . . . . . . . . . . . . . **Hyalinella vaihiriae** Hastings
15. With sessoblasts and two types of floatoblasts; the more common type is somewhat
narrow, very thin-walled, and has the annulus the same width all around the
capsule (Fig. 191E); the less common type is the usual thick-walled capsuled
form similar to those of the other forms in this genus; occasionally this species
forms a fourth type of elongate and fragile statoblast; colony without free,
upright branches; zooecium often keeled (Fig. 191D); reported only from Lake
Erie, Indiana, Michigan, and Colorado . . . . . . . . . . . **Plumatella casmiana** Oka
    With sessoblasts plus only thick-walled capsuled floatoblasts; annulus not of the same
width all around capsule (Figs. 191B,C); on underside of vegetation and ob-
jects . . . . . . . . . . . . . . . . . . . . . . . . . . . . . . . . . . . . . . . . . . . . . . . . . . . . . . . . . . . .**16**
16. Floatoblasts twice or more as long as wide; sessoblasts with wide, lacy annulus;
zooids keeled; zooecia slender and adherent; Rocky Mountains, Illinois, Michigan, and Pennsylvania. . . . . . . . . . . . . . . . . . . . . . **Plumatella fruticosa** Allman
    Length of floatoblasts less than twice the width; sessoblasts not as above . . . . . . .**17**

Fig. 190.–Structure of Plumatellidae. A, floatoblast of *Hyalinella vaihiriae*, ×60; B and C, surface view of floatoblast of *H. punctata*, ×65; D, entire colony of *H. punctata*, ×6; E, twin polypides of *H. punctata*; F, three developing statoblasts on funiculus of *H. punctata*; G, immature sperm mass on funiculus of *H. punctata*; H, outline of colony of *Stolella indica*, ×6 (all polypides shown retracted); J, portion of a colony of *S. evelinae* (all polypides retracted). (A from Rogick, 1942; B and C from Rogick, 1940; D to G from Rogick, 1935; H modified from Rogick, 1943a; J from Bushnell, 1965.)

17. Zooecium strongly keeled, furrowed, and with an emarginate orifice (Fig. 191G); cuticula dark; dorsal surface of floatoblasts largely covered by float cells; common and widely distributed . . . . . . . . . . . . . . .**Plumatella emarginata** Allman
Zooecium not strongly keeled; floatoblasts not as above . . . . . . . . . . . . . . . . . . . . . . .**18**

FIG. 191.–Structure of *Plumatella*. A, small colony of *Plumatella repens*, ×4; B and C, opposite surfaces of floatoblasts of *P. repens*, ×100; D, colony of *P. casmiana*, ×5; E, floatoblast of *P. casmiana*, ×65; F, diagram of small portion of colony of *P. repens* (polypides all retracted); G, small portion of colony of *P. emarginata* (only one polypide partially expanded); H, small portion of colony of *P. repens* (all polypides retracted); J, diagram of small portion of colony of *P. repens* (all polypides retracted); K, diagram of small portion of colony of *P. fruticosa* (all polypides retracted). (A from Allman; B to D from Rogick, 1941; E from Rogick, 1943; F modified from Newcomer; G and H modified from Rogick, 1935; J modified from Rogick, 1940.

**18.** Colony translucent to light-colored; zooecium adherent for only part of the length of each zooid; colony loosely branched (Figs. 191A,H,J); the most common U.S. bryozoan . . . . . . . . . . . . . . . . . . . . . . . . . . . . . . . . . . . . . . . . . . . . . .**Plumatella repens** (L.)
Colony dark-colored; zooecium extending upright and cemented together into masses of parallel tubes (Fig. 174); Illinois, Maine, Colorado, Massachusetts; some investigators report overlapping of morphological features between this form and *P. repens*, and accordingly consider this form a variety of *P. repens*.
**Plumatella fungosa** (Pallas)

## BRYOZOA REFERENCES

ALLMAN, J. 1856. *A monograph of the fresh-water Polyzoa*. 119 pp. Ray Society, London.

ANNANDALE, N. 1911. Freshwater sponges, hydroids, and Polyzoa. *Fauna Br. India,* 251 pp.

BROWN, C. J. D. 1933. A limnological study of certain fresh-water Polyzoa with special reference to their statoblasts. *Trans. Am. Microsc. Soc.* **52:**271–316.

BUSHNELL, J. H. 1965. On the taxonomy and distribution of fresh-water Ectoprocta in Michigan. Part I. *Trans. Am. Microsc. Soc.* **84:**231–244.

——. 1965a. On the taxonomy and distribution of fresh-water Ectoprocta in Michigan. Part II. Ibid. 339–358.

——. 1965b. On the taxonomy and distribution of freshwater Ectoprocta in Michigan. III. Ibid. 529–548.

——. 1966. Environmental relations of Michigan Ectoprocta, and dynamics of natural populations of Plumatella repens. *Ecol. Monogr.* **36:**95–123.

——. 1968. Aspects of architecture, ecology, and zoogeography of freshwater Ectoprocta. *Atti Soc. Ital. Sci. Nat. Mus. Civ. St. Nat. Milano* **108:**129–151.

——. 1973. The freshwater Ectoprocta: a zoogeographical discussion. *In: Living and fossil bryozoa: Recent advances in research,* pp. 503–521. E. P. Larwood (ed), Academic, London.

BUSHNELL, J. H., and K. S. RAO. 1974. Dormant or quiescent stages and structures among the Ectoprocta: Physical and chemical factors affecting viability and germination of statoblasts. *Trans. Am. Microsc. Soc.* **93:**524–543.

BUSHNELL, J. H., and T. S. WOOD. 1971. Honeycomb colonies of Plumatella casmiana Oka (Ectoprocta: Phylactolaemata). Ibid. **90:**229–231.

DAVENPORT, C. B. 1893. On Urnatella gracilis. *Bull. Mus. Comp. Zool. Harvard Coll.* **24:**1–44.

——. 1904. Report on the fresh-water Bryozoa of the United States. *Proc. U.S. Nat. Mus.* **27:**211–221.

DENDY, J. W. 1963. Observations on bryozoan ecology in farm ponds. *Limnol. Oceanogr.* **8:**478–482.

GEISER, S. W. 1937. Pectinatella magnifica Leidy an occasional river-pest in Iowa. *Field & Laboratory* **5:**65–76.

HARMER, S. F. 1913. The Polyzoa of water-works. *Proc. Zool. Soc. Lond.* 426–457.

JULLIEN, J. 1885. Monographie des Bryozoaires d'eau douce. *Bull. Soc. zool. Fr.* **10:**91–207.

KRAEPELIN, K. 1887. Die deutschen S;üsswasser-Bryozoen. Eine Mongraphie. I. Anatomisch-systematischer Teil. *Abh. natw. Vereins. Hamburg* **10:**1–168.

——. 1892. Die deutschen Süsswasserbryozoen. Eine Monographie. II. Entwicklungsgeschichtlicher Teil. Ibid. **12:**1–68.

LACOURT, A. W. 1968. A monograph of the freshwater Bryozoa-Phylactolaemata. *Uitg. Rijksmus. Nat. Hist. Leiden* **93:**1–159.

LEIDY, J. 1884. Urnatella gracilis, a fresh-water polyzoan. *J. Acad. Nat. Sci. Phila.* **9:**5–16.

MARCUS, E. 1925. Bryozoa. *Biol. Tiere Deutschl.* **47:**1–46.

——. 1926. Beobachtungen und Versuche an lebenden Süsswasserbryozoen. *Zool. Jahrb. Abt. Syst. Oekol. Geogr. Tiere* **52:**279–350.

——. 1942. Sôbre Bryozoa do Brasil II. *Univ. Sao Paulo. Bol. Zool.* **6:**57–96.

MAYR, E. 1968. Bryozoa versus Ectoprocta. *Syst. Zool.* **17:**213–216.

ODA, S. 1959. Germination of the statoblasts in freshwater Bryozoa. *Sci. Rep. Tokyo Kyoiku Daigaku, B,* **135:**90–135.

ROGICK, M. D. 1935. Studies on freshwater Bryozoa. II. The Bryozoa of Lake Erie. *Trans. Am. Microsc. Soc.* **54:**245–263.

——. 1937. Studies on fresh-water Bryozoa. VI. The finer anatomy of Lophopodella carteri var. typica. Ibid. **56:**367–396.

——. 1938. Studies on fresh-water Bryozoa. VII. On the viability of dried statoblasts of Lophopodella carteri var. typica. Ibid. **57:**178–199.

——. 1940. Studies on fresh-water Bryozoa. IX. Additions to New York Bryozoa. Ibid. **59:**187–204.

——. 1940a. Studies on fresh-water Bryozoa. XI. The viability of dried statoblasts of several species. *Growth* **4:**315–322.

——. 1945. Studies on fresh-water Bryozoa. XV. Hyalinella punctata growth data. *Ohio J. Sci.* **45:**55–79.

ROGICK, M. D., and C. J. D. BROWN. 1942. Studies on fresh-water Bryozoa. XII. A collection from various sources. *Ann. N.Y. Acad. Sci.* **43:**123–144.

ROGICK, M. D., and H. VAN DER SCHALIE. 1950. Studies on fresh-water Bryozoa. XVII. Michigan Bryozoa. *Ohio J. Sci.* **50:**136–146.

TORIUMI, M. 1956. Taxonomical study on freshwater Bryozoa. XVII. General consideration: interspecific relation of described species and phylogenetic consideration. *Sci. Rep. Tohoku Univ. Ser. 4, Biol.* **22:**57–88.

——. 1971. Additional observations on Plumatella repens (L.) (a fresh-water bryozoan), IV. Reexamination on the field materials of P. repens and P. fungosa. *Bull. Mar. Biol. Sta. Asamuschi* **14:**117–126.

TWITCHELL, G. B. 1934. Urnatella gracilis Leidy, a living Trepostomatous bryozoan. *Am. Midl. Nat.* **15:**629–655.

WILLIAMS, S. R. 1921. Concerning "larval" colonies of Pectinatella. *Ohio J. Sci.* **21:**123–127.

WOOD, T. S. 1971. Laboratory culture of freshwater Ectoprocta. *Trans. Am. Microsc. Soc.* **90:**92–94.

# Chapter 13

# ANNELIDA (AQUATIC EARTHWORMS, BRANCHIOBDELLIDA, POLYCHAETES, ARCHIANNELIDA, LEECHES)

TYPICAL segmented worms, constituting the Phylum Annelida, are constructed on a tube-within-tube plan. The body wall is soft, muscular, and covered with a very thin cuticle. The specialized digestive tract has a terminal mouth and anus and is supported in the coelom by thin transverse septa that mark the internal segmental divisions. Unlike the condition in arthropods, segmentation is homonomous. There is an extensive closed circulatory system, and a few to most segments have a pair of long, tubular nephridia, or excretory organs. The two ventral nerve cords and their segmental ganglia are fused along the median line; the brain typically consists of a pair of cerebral ganglia, and these connect with the nerve cord by two circumpharyngeal connectives. Anterior eyespots are present in some genera. Except for certain aquatic species that reproduce by budding, reproduction is syngamic, and individuals are hermaphroditic. Cross-fertilization is the rule.

Five classes of annelids are represented in fresh waters. Oligochaeta, or earthworms, have many fresh-water representatives; the Hirudinea, or leeches, are dominantly a fresh-water group; the Poly-

chaeta, however, which are so varied and richly represented in salt water, occur in fresh water only as a few rare and sporadic species. The Branchiobdellida are highly modified commensals or parasites of crayfishes. Fresh-water Archiannelida are extremely rare. These five classes are easily distinguished from each other, and because they are so different they are considered in separate sections of this chapter.

Polychaeta have muscular, paired, lateral projections from the body wall, called parapodia; these are absent in the other four classes occurring in fresh water. Groups of setae accompany the parapodia of polychaetes, and setae are also present in the Oligochaeta and archiannelids, though not in the Hirudinea and branchiobdellids. Polychaetes usually have accessory tentacles or other appendages at the anterior end but these are absent in the other two groups. Leeches are dorsoventrally flattened, have an oral and a caudal sucker, and the body segments are subdivided into superficial annuli. None of these features occur in the oligochaetes, polychaetes, archiannelids, and branchiobdellids, although the branchiobdellids have a caudal sucker.

## OLIGOCHAETA (AQUATIC EARTHWORMS)

Aquatic oligochaetes have the same fundamental structure as the common terrestrial earthworms, and the anatomy, physiology, and behavior of the latter are

so familiar to everyone who has been exposed to an elementary course in college zoology that it would be superfluous to repeat these details here. Instead, the various

275

specializations and peculiarities of aquatic oligochaetes will be emphasized.

**General characteristics.** Representatives of 10 families of oligochaetes occur in the fresh waters of the United States. The Aeolosomatidae, Naididae, Tubificidae, and Lumbriculidae are strictly aquatic. Some species of Haplotaxidae are semiaquatic or amphibious and occur especially in debris at the edges of streams, ponds, or in marshes and soggy ground; other species, however, are essentially terrestrial and never occur in water. One genus in the family Glossoscolecidae is regularly found in fresh waters, but other genera, as well as the Megascolecidae and Lumbricidae, are terrestrial and may be accidental in aquatic habitats. The Opistocystidae are extremely rare.

The great majority of true aquatic species are common in the mud and debris substrate of stagnant pools and ponds and in streams and lakes everywhere. They are sometimes especially abundant in masses of filamentous algae. Tubificidae occur even in the deepest parts of large lakes, but the shallows down to a depth of a meter are the usual habitat for the great majority of species.

Compared with amphibious and terrestrial forms, the true aquatic oligochaetes are much more delicately constructed and small, the usual length range being 1 to 30 mm. The body wall is thin, and the internal organs can be easily seen in living specimens.

The prostomium is a half-segment at the extreme anterior end of the body; it projects in a rooflike fashion above the mouth and is sometimes elongated into a proboscis. In locating various external and internal structures of oligochaetes it is customary to designate the body segments serially by Roman numerals, beginning at the anterior end. Thus the first complete body segment immediately behind the prostomium is designated as I.

The number of segments is quite variable, even in mature individuals, and commonly there is a plus or minus 25 percent variation from the average for various specimens of a particular species. The thread-

like Haplotaxidae have the largest number of segments, sometimes up to 500. At the opposite extreme the Aeolosomatidae and Naididae usually have between 7 and 40 segments. The other families have an intermediate number of segments, tubificids, for example, usually consisting of 40 to 200 segments.

The chitinoid setae are arranged in four bundles, two dorsolateral and two ventrolateral. Setae are never found on segment I, but usually begin on II, although in some genera they are absent from several successive segments, either dorsally, ven-

FIG. 192.–Dorsal view of *Aeolosoma leidyi*, a typical aquatic oligochaete, ×50. Note formation of posterior zooid behind zone of fission. (Modified from Kenk.)

FIG. 193.–Scanning electron micrograph of *Chaetogaster diastrophus*, ×240. Anterior end in ventral view; posterior end in lateroventral view. The fission zone separates the two zooids. Background ripples are the gold-plated surface of the stud. (Photo courtesy of Donald L. Elrick.)

as *Pristina* and *Stylaria,* are effective swimmers that move along just above the substrate in a serpentine manner. Some species of *Aeolosoma* swim about with the aid of the beating of the cilia of the anterior end.

**Feeding.** The great majority of aquatic oligochaetes obtain nutriment by ingesting quantities of the substrate after the manner of the earthworm, the organic component being digested as it passes through the alimentary canal. Sometimes the food is ingested at a depth of 2 or 3 cm below the water-substrate interface. Under some circumstances the food may consist largely of filamentous algae, diatoms, or simply miscellaneous plant and animal detritus. *Chaetogaster* is one of the few carnivorous forms. It feeds on entomostraca, insect larvae, and other oligochaetes. *Aeolosoma* feeds on particulate debris and microorganisms, which are swept toward the mouth by ciliary currents set up at the anterior end and by a type of suction feeding.

trally, or both. Detailed structure of the setae and their arrangement are important as taxonomic characters. A bundle may consist of from 1 to as many as 20 setae, and the number in a particular bundle may be constant from one specimen to another within a species, or it may vary. Setae may be long, short, straight, curved, sigmoid, hair (capilliform), aciculate, pectinate, bifurcate, hooked bifurcate, or uncinate (Fig. 194). Two-thirds or more of the total length of a capilliform seta usually projects from the body wall, but only about a quarter or less of an aciculate seta is exposed. Sigmoid or crotchet setae are usually called needle setae when the nodule is small or absent and when they are more or less straight.

**Locomotion.** Usually locomotion is a crawling movement on or in the superficial layers of the substrate; it is similar to that of the earthworm and involves contractions of the muscular body wall and obtaining a purchase with the setae. A few naids, such

FIG. 194.–Typical setae of aquatic Oligochaeta. A and B, capilliform; C through L, aciculate; B, serrate; C and D, sigmoid; D, H, and J, bifurcate; G, uncinate; J, hooked; K, pectinate; L, biuncinate.

Fig. 195.–*Tubifex*, a typical tube builder, ×3.

**Respiration.** Because the body wall is thin and often well supplied with capillaries, most of the carbon dioxide and oxygen exchange occurs through the general body surface. In most naids and in some tubificids water is taken into the anus and passed forward for a variable distance by antiperistalsis and ciliary action, and these processes are thought to constitute an accessory respiratory mechanism.

*Dero* and *Aulophorus* have handsome ciliated gills surrounding the anal region. The posterior extremity has the form of a shallow cup, and the gills originate within the cup or from its margin. *Branchiura* has a fingerlike dorsal and ventral gill on each of the posterior segments. All oligochaete gills are well supplied with blood vessels. Gilled species remain quietly in position with the anterior portion of the body hidden in the substrate and in a tube constructed of fine debris and projecting up from the substrate for a variable distance. The posterior end projects vertically out of the tube and into the water. When disturbed, the worm withdraws into its tube and the substrate in a fraction of a second.

Most tubificids also build tubes, the projecting posterior end of the animal being waved about vigorously in the water, presumably to circulate the water and make more oxygen available to the body surface. Tubificids are commonly red, owing to dissolved erythrocruorin in the blood.

**Epidermal sensory structures.** Many species of Naididae have a pair of eyespots. They are entirely epidermal, the overlying cuticle being unmodified. Each eye consists of a transverse row of five or six small visual cells and a large number of pigment granules that cover the sensory cells medially and posteriorly. Other epidermal sense organs, consisting of either single cells or aggregates and often arranged symmetrically, occur over the general body surface of all oligochaetes but are especially concentrated at the anterior end. Sensory hairs are common in the Naididae, and in *Slavina appendiculata* they are borne on prominent sensory papillae. Epidermal sensory cells are generally assumed to be sensitive to tactile, thermal, and chemical stimuli.

**Reproduction.** According to the published literature, asexual reproduction by budding is the rule in the Aeolosomatidae and Naididae, only a few instances of syngamic reproduction having been reported. It is our experience, however, that sexual reproduction may sometimes be very common, especially in *Chaetogaster*. In asexual reproduction, the budding zone is localized in one of the segments toward the posterior end (Fig. 193), and the number of segments anterior to the budding segment is often designated by $n$. The location of the budding segment is usually constant within a single individual, but under experimental conditions it is possible to alter its position slightly; favorable temperature, food, and oxygen conditions will move the zone anteriorly a segment or two; unfavorable conditions may move it posteriorly a segment or two. On the other hand, the specific location of the fission zone varies greatly from one individual to another within a species. Thus, in *Nais elinguis*, $n$ varies from 12 to 20, and in *Stylaria fossularis*, $n$ varies from 8 to 23 but is usually 18.

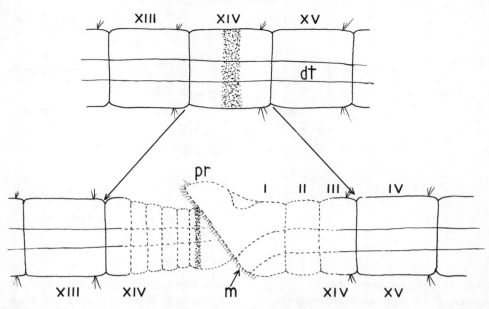

FIG. 196.–Budding in *Aeolosoma*, showing segmental derivatives in daughter zooids. *dt*, digestive tract; *m*, mouth; *pr*, prostomium. (Modified from Marcus, 1944.)

The budding segment grows and undergoes repeated transverse divisions that result in four or more anterior segments of a new posterior worm and several new posterior segments of the anterior parent worm. These regions rapidly become differentiated (Fig. 196). The two animals remain attached for a variable length of time, and the more posterior individual may in turn produce a third individual posterior to its budding zone. This process may be repeated so that in some species there may be chains of as many as four to eight zooids in various stages of development. After an interval, however, two adjacent and mature zooids separate and become completely independent individuals. Under favorable conditions most naids reproduce a new individual every two or three days. In *Dero* it is unusual to find a chain of more than two zooids. In general, zooid chains are longest in spring and autumn.

Syngamic reproduction is essentially similar to the familiar story in the earthworm. In the true aquatic species, however, the clitellum is often thin and inconspicuous. Cocoons containing embryos are deposited on rocks, vegetation, and debris, especially in the late summer and early autumn, but syngamic reproduction has often been reported as early as July. Under rare circumstances reproduction in isolated tubificids indicates self-fertilization. Life cycles of macroscopic species usually take one or two years.

The capacity to regenerate lost or damaged anterior or posterior segments varies within the aquatic oligochaetes, but it is best developed in the Naididae and Tubificidae.

**Ecology.** Aquatic oligochaetes occupy a niche equivalent to that occupied by terrestrial species, and they feed on bottom mud and mix it much as earthworms effectively mix the surface layers of garden and meadow soils.

Temperature is not usually a limiting factor, but it often determines the relative abundance of oligochaetes. Some amphibious species, especially enchytraeids and lumbriculids, are notable because they are found on the shores of cold mountain streams and brooks originating from snowbanks and glaciers.

Some species of *Aeolosoma* are known

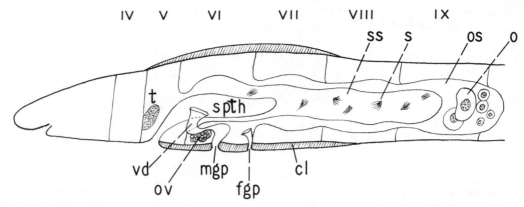

FIG. 197.–Diagram of typical Naididae sex organs. *cl*, clitellum; *fgp*, female genital pore; *mgp*, male genital pore; *o*, ovum; *os*, ovisac; *ov*, ovary; *s*, sperm; *spth*, spermatheca; *ss*, sperm sac; *t*, testis; *vd*, vas deferens. (Modified from Stephenson.)

to encyst when the water temperature is 6° or lower. A translucent, hardened coat of mucus is formed around the tightly coiled worm. Emergence from the cyst occurs at about 20°.

Tubificidae are the dominant forms at depths exceeding 1 m, and in the deep waters of lakes there are sometimes more than 8000 individuals per square meter. By far the most concentrated populations are found in streams and rivers that are polluted with sewage. Here tubificids, especially the common and cosmopolitan *Tubifex tubifex,* occur in dense waving masses. In fact, this species is usually considered an "indicator" of organic pollution, especially where the water is between 10 and 60 percent saturated with oxygen. *Tubifex,* some enchytraeids, and a few other macroscopic forms are common inhabitants of sewage settling tanks and trickling filters.

Two to four species of *Chaetogaster* may commonly be found in the same collection, but, in general, little is known about interspecies competition.

Most of the true aquatic species are able to thrive in low concentrations of dissolved oxygen, and many are also able to withstand the complete absence of oxygen for extended periods. Tubificids, for example, can endure the summer and winter periods of stagnation in lakes. Nevertheless, populations cannot be maintained indefinitely in the absence of oxygen. Dau-

send (1931) found that only one-third of the specimens of *Tubifex* that he used were able to survive anaerobic conditions for 48 days at 0° to 2°, and at higher temperatures the fraction was progressively smaller. Other workers report the survival of very

FIG. 198.–Cocoon of *Stylaria* deposited on a bit of debris, ×60.

FIG. 199.–Mixed colony of *Tubifex* (long, flexible individuals) and *Lumbriculus* (shorter, less flexible individuals), ×1. (From Von Wagner.)

small percentages of *Tubifex* populations after 120 days under anaerobic conditions. In general, the lower the oxygen concentration the more the animal projects from its tube and the move vigorous are the waving aeration movements of the posterior part of the body, but when the oxygen concentration nears complete exhaustion most tubificids become relatively quiescent.

By way of summary, it seems obvious that many aquatic oligochaetes are typically euryokous.

**Dispersal, geographic distribution.** Oligochaetes undoubtedly migrate easily throughout whole drainage systems, but passive and accidental overland transport presumably is most effective during the cocoon stage in those species that have syngamic reproduction. *Aeolosoma*, however, forms a resistant mucus cyst stage that may be easily transported from place to place.

The aquatic oligochaete fauna of the United States is poorly known. Collecting has been scanty and sporadic, and there have been less than 25 major American papers published since 1900. Nevertheless, as additional records slowly accumulate, it is becoming increasingly apparent that many of our species are cosmopolitan and occur the world over or are widely distributed in the Northern Hemisphere. *Aeolosoma variegatum*, several species of *Chaetogaster*, *Nais obtusa*, *Slavina appendiculata*, *Dero limosa*, and *Tubifex tubifex* are all examples of common and cosmopolitan species. Of the species of Aeolosomatidae and Naididae occurring in the United States, less

than 20 percent have not yet been reported from other continents.

The Lumbricidae are restricted to temperate and cold-temperate zones, and most of the Megascolecidae and Glossoscolecidae are tropical to subtropical. Some few species have an interesting sporadic distribution. The "rare" *Branchiura sowerbyi*, for example, has been collected only one to several times in most states. A few "freshwater" genera also have salt-water representatives, especially *Peloscolex*, *Tubifex*, and *Clittelio*.

**Collecting.** If the bottom material is finely divided, a sieve or strainer may be used for field collecting. Otherwise, the bottom debris should be brought into the laboratory where it may be examined immediately or allowed to stand until the worms can be seen at the surface of the debris or crawling up the sides of the container. Masses of filamentous algae can be rinsed or washed out with a stream of water. The small species can best be found with the aid of dissecting binoculars. Amphibious and large species can usually be picked up with tweezers by sorting stream and lakeside trash.

**Culturing.** The success of a laboratory culture often depends on the amount and kind of water supply and the available oxygen, but many species can be grown in their natural substrate when it is kept in shallow pans into which water drips or slowly flows. Water should never be changed rapidly. Needham et al. (1937) give directions for raising Naididae in rice-agar cultures. Naids often become abundant in old protozoan cultures.

**Preparation.** For gross structure and even for many fine details of small oligochaetes there is no substitute for the examination of living specimens. Nevertheless, preserved specimens are unavoidable for lengthy examinations and comparisons. Perhaps the greatest difficulty encountered in working with Aeolosomatidae, Naididae, Tubicifidae, and Lumbriculidae is the usual strongly contracted and distorted condition, which makes careful anatomical work impossible. Chloretone, chloroform vapors, and magnesium sulfate have all been suggested as narcotic agents, but almost invariably the posterior end of the worm being narcotized disintegrates long before the anterior end has become quiet. Nevertheless, the writer has had some success with 2 percent hydroxylamine hydrochloride. Regardless of the method used, it is almost impossible to kill *Dero* and *Aulophorus* with expanded gills.

Most investigators advocate killing and fixing small oligochaetes without the use of a narcotic. Some tubificids will die in an extended condition if diluted fixatives are used. Stephenson recommends placing a glass slide on edge along the center of the flat surface of another slide, thus making a right angle. When one to several worms are placed in the angle in a small quantity of water, they usually extend and begin to crawl, and at that point they are flooded with Schaudinn's fixative. If many specimens are being fixed, they may be placed in a shallow dish, and then the water is poured off. The worms thereupon elongate and crawl about, and if they are flooded with hot Schaudinn's fixative, a good percentage of the worms will remain elongated and in good condition. Seventy percent alcohol is a suitable preservative, and permanent glycerin jelly mounts are generally satisfactory, either with or without staining.

Large amphibious or terrestrial species are best killed and preserved in an extended condition in accordance with standard methods. If the specimens are to be sectioned, they should be first kept in water or on wet filter paper until the digestive tract is free of grit.

The number, arrangement, and structural details of the setae are essential for the identification of Aeolosomatidae, Naididae, Tubificidae, and some Lumbriculidae, but whole mounts do not often allow an examination of the finer details. If living specimens are available, it is best to place one in water on a slide with a circular cover slip. Then remove most of the water at the edge of the cover slip with blotting paper and allow the mount to dry. The worm will be compressed, and then it will burst and flatten, leaving the body wall and setae nicely in place. If a drop of glycerin is placed at the edge of the cover slip, capillarity will draw it under, and such a slide can be made semipermanent by ringing with Murrayite.

Similar preparations of larger dead or preserved specimens of Tubificidae and some Lumbriculidae may be made if they are left in water for a day or two until they begin to decompose and are soft enough for setae preparations.

**Taxonomy.** In addition to setae, other characters of taxonomic significance in small species are the location of the budding zone, gill structure, shape and size of the prostomium, and the arrangement of certain blood vessels. Body length is of little value since preserved specimens exhibit varying degrees of contraction. In addition, the published literature is often confusing because it is not made clear whether lengths refer to a single anterior zooid or a whole chain of zooids.

It is unfortunate that the identification of Lumbricidae, Megascolecidae, Glossoscolecidae, and some Lumbriculidae depends on internal details of the reproductive system, and though careful dissections are often adequate, it is frequently necessary to make stained serial sections of the segments containing the reproductive structures. Usually cross sections are sufficient, but some workers advocate longitudinal sections in addition. It is chiefly this tedious procedure that has discouraged taxonomic investigations of these annelids.

Because of the fact that the aquatic oligochaetes of the United States are relatively poorly known, the following key has certain limitations. Nevertheless, with the exception of a few very rare and poorly described and unrecognizable species, this key includes all known Aeolosomatidae and Naididae. The Tubificidae are keyed to some genera and some species. Opistocystidae and Lumbriculidae are carried to genera. The Lumbricidae, Megascolecidae, Enchytraeidae, and Glossoscolecidae are almost exclusively terrestrial and are not considered beyond the family characters.

## KEY TO GENERA AND SPECIES OF OLIGOCHAETA

1. Reproduction normally by fission, producing chains of individuals, but sexual reproduction may occur occasionally; living animals more or less translucent and delicate; with one to six setae per bundle; less than 25 mm long; cosmopolitan and common on the substrate of pools, ponds, and lakes. (part).
   Order **HAPLOTAXIDA, 2**
   Reproduction always sexual; no chains of individuals; living animal more or less opaque; more than 25 mm long . . . . . . . . . . . . . . . . . . . . . . . . . . . . . . . . . . . . .**4**
2. Single zooids usually less than 5 mm long, but a few species sometimes reaching 10 mm; usually with minute red, yellow, or greenish pigment globules in the epithelium of living animals; with cilia on ventral and sometimes lateral surfaces of prostomium (Figs. 192, 200D); cerebral ganglia permanently connected with epidermis; this family has uncertain fundamental taxonomic affinities.
   AEOLOSOMATIDAE, **Aeolosoma, 10**
   Usually 5 to 25 mm long; without colored oil globules in epithelium of living animals; without cilia anteriorly; with septa; cerebral ganglia free in coelom.
   Order **HAPLOTAXIDA, 3**
3. Posterior end with two lateral and one median process; extremely rare.
   OPISTOCYSTIDAE, **Opistocysta**
   Posterior end not with two lateral and one median process; common and abundant everywhere . . . . . . . . . . . . . . . . . . . . . . . . . . . . . . . . . . . . . . . . . . . . NAIDIDAE, **14**
4. Body threadlike, 0.5 to 1.0 mm in diameter and 100 to 300 mm long; with two large ventral and two small dorsal sigmoid setae per segment; up to 500 segments; semiaquatic; in wet earth, marshes, ditches, mud, and under rocks at streamside. . . . . . . . . . . . . . . . . . . . . . . . . . . . . . . . . . . . . . . . . . Order **HAPLOTAXIDA,**
   HAPLOTAXIDAE, **Haplotaxis gordioides** (Hartmann)
   Not threadlike; with a different pattern of setae . . . . . . . . . . . . . . . . . . . . . . . . . . . . . .**5**
5. Large, thick-bodied worms that are essentially terrestrial but occasionally occur in mud or debris of stream and lake margins or in trickling filters of sewage plants; setae sigmoid; true earthworms; usually 5 to 30 cm long.
   Order **HAPLOTAXIDA, 8**
   Smaller, thin worms, mostly aquatic; setae sigmoid or some other shape; usually less than 8 cm long but a few up to 15 cm . . . . . . . . . . . . . . . . . . . . . . . . . . . . . . . . . . .**6**
6. Whitish to pinkish; spermathecae opening on IV or V; without a tube; usually two to six setae per bundle; setae all similar; usually 10 to 30 mm long; terrestrial; many species; common in debris along margins of streams and lakes.
   Order **HAPLOTAXIDA,** ENCHYTRAEIDAE
   Red to brown; spermathecae opening behind VI; anterior end of worm sometimes hidden in a tube that projects vertically from the substrate and is composed of mud and debris; two setae per bundle, or an indeterminate number per bundle; dorsal and ventral setae similar or dissimilar; typically aquatic . . . . . . . . . . . . .**7**
7. Setae all of one form, single-pointed or sometimes more or less distinctly bifurcate; four bundles of two setae each per segment; usually reddish or brownish worms; up to 8 cm long; in mud or debris of pools, ponds, and lakes.
   Order **LUMBRICULIDA,** LUMBRICULIDAE, **61**
   Dorsal and ventral setae different; ventral setae bifurcate, dorsal setae bifurcate or a mixture of two or three types; four bundles of an indeterminate number each per segment; worm usually reddish. Order **HAPLOTAXIDA,** TUBIFICIDAE, **48**

Fɪɢ. 200.–Structure of *Aeolosoma*. A, setal bundle of *Aeolosoma hemprichi*; B, setal bundle of *A. leidyi*; C, setal bundle of *A. headleyi*; D, ventral view of anterior end of *A. leidyi*. *b*, brain; *cp*, ciliated pit; *dbv*, dorsal blood vessel; *e*, esophagus; *m*, mouth; *n*, nephridium; *pg*, pigment globules. (B to D redrawn from Kenk.)

   8. With a well-formed gizzard at the beginning of the intestine; four pairs of setae per segment; clitellum beginning at or behind XVIII . . . . . . . . . . LUMBRICIDAE
      Without a gizzard at the beginning of the intestine; clitellum beginning before XVIII; mostly tropical and subtropical . . . . . . . . . . . . . . . . . . . . . . . . . . . . . . . . . . . .9
   9. Male genital pores on XVII, XVIII, or XIX; 8, 12, or more setae per segment, in the latter case forming rings that may be either closed or broken dorsally and ventrally; clitellum beginning with or in front of XV . . MEGASCOLECIDAE
      Male genital pores in anterior portion of clitellum or in front of it; eight setae per segment; clitellum beginning with or in front of XXV. GLOSSOSCOLECIDAE
  10. Setae bundles composed of long, flexible hair setae and short, stiff sigmoid setae (Fig. 200B) . . . . . . . . . . . . . . . . . . . . . . . . . . . . . . . . . . . . . . . . . . . . . . . . . . . . . . . .11
      Sigmoid setae absent (Fig. 200C) . . . . . . . . . . . . . . . . . . . . . . . . . . . . . . . . . . . . . . .12
  11. Sigmoid setae may occur in all bundles but mostly absent from II; epidermal glands green . . . . . . . . . . . . . . . . . . . . . . . . . . . . . . . . . . . **Aeolosoma leidyi** Cragin
      Sigmoid setae only in V and posteriorly; epidermal glands greenish yellow to olive green . . . . . . . . . . . . . . . . . . . . . . . . . . . . . . . . . . .**Aeolosoma tenebrarum** Vejd.
  12. Longest hair setae more than 175 microns; body 150 to 300 microns wide.
                                                    **Aeolosoma headleyi** Beddard
      Longest hair setae less than 160 microns; body 40 to 175 microns wide . . . . . . . . . .13
  13. Epidermal glands orange-red . . . . . . . . . . . . . . . . . . . . . . . **Aeolosoma hemprichi** Ehr.
      Epidermal glands green or yellow . . . . . . . . . . . . . . . . . . . **Aeolosoma variegatum** Vejd.

14. Dorsal setae completely lacking; carnivorous; mouth and pharynx large (Figs. 193; 201E, F) ............................................... **Chaetogaster, 28**
    Dorsal setae present in nearly all segments ...................................**15**
15. All dorsal setae aciculate; capilliform setae lacking ...........................**16**
    Some capilliform setae in dorsal bundles (Fig. 202H) ........................**18**
16. Segment III two or three times as long as other anterior segments; rare.
                                                        **Amphichaeta americana** Chen
    Segment III not elongated ................................................**17**
17. Dorsal and ventral setae both bifurcate at the tips; several species in fresh and brackish waters; uncommon ...................................... **Paranais**
    Dorsal and ventral setae with different tips; the ventral setae hooked bifurcate, the dorsal weakly bifurcate or uncinate (Fig. 201B); four dark anterior pigment bands; pair of eyespots (Fig. 201A); body more or less covered with debris; usually in mud substrates; up to 30 mm long. **Ophidonais serpentina** (O.F.M.)
18. With ciliated posterior gills surrounding the anus (Fig. 202) .............. **Dero, 32**
    Without ciliated posterior gills ..........................................**19**
19. Hair setae absent ................................... **Uncinais uncinata** (Ørsted)
    Hair setae present.......................................................**20**
20. Dorsal setae beginning in II; prostomium forming a proboscis; often in tubes; about 10 species ............................................... **Pristina, 37**
    Dorsal setae beginning behind II ..........................................**21**
21. Dorsal setae shed anteriorly after budding; retained from about XVIII.
                                                        **Haemonais waldvogeli** Bret.
    Dorsal setae beginning on IV, V, or VI....................................**22**
22. Anterior end forming a proboscis (Figs. 204E, F) ..........................**23**
    Without proboscis.......................................................**24**
23. Dorsal bundles with up to 30 setae each .............. **Arcteonais lomondi** (Martin)
    Fewer setae, mostly less than 10 per bundle ................ **Stylaria lacustris** (L.)
24. Body wall covered with foreign particles ............ **Slavina appendiculata** (Udek.)
    Body wall naked .......................................................**25**
25. Capilliform setae of dorsal bundles with a series of prominent teeth (Fig. 201H); rare ................................... **Vejdovskyella comata** (Vejd.)
    Capilliform setae of dorsal bundles without teeth .............................**26**
26. Needle setae similar to ventral setae..................... **Specaria josinae** (Vejd.)
    Needle setae distinctly different from ventral setae ..........................**27**
27. Eyes absent ................................. **Allonais paraguayensis** (Mich.)
    Eyes present ................................................... **Nais, 41**
28. Epizoic on surface or in mantle cavity of aquatic snails and fingernail clams (*Sphaerium*); chain of zooids 2 to 6 mm long; usually eight segments in first animal of a chain................................... **Chaetogaster limnaei** v. Baer
    Not epizoic on snails or clams............................................**29**
29. Prostomium conspicuous (Fig. 201D) ............. **Chaetogaster diastrophus** (Gruit.)
    Prostomium inconspicuous (Fig. 201E) .....................................**30**
30. Prostomium with median cleft; chains of zooids 2.5 to 7.0 mm long; up to six setae per bundle in II .......................... **Chaetogaster crystallinus** Vejd.
    Prostomium without median cleft ..........................................**31**
31. Setae more than 145 microns long in II; with more than six setae per bundle in II ................................... **Chaetogaster diaphanus** (Gruit.)
    Setae less than 100 microns long ................. **Chaetogaster langi** (Bretscher)
32. Branchial fossa with two long palps (Figs. 202E, F, G) ......................**33**
    Branchial fossa without long palps (Figs. 202A–D)..........................**34**
33. Dorsal setae beginning on V............................. **Dero furcatus** (Müller)
    Dorsal setae beginning on VI............................... **Dero vagus** Leidy
34. Asexual reproduction by fragmentation; ventral setae all of one shape; Pennsylvania; rare ........................................... **Dero bilongata** Chen
    Asexual reproduction by budding; ventral setae of II to V sharply differentiated from those of other segments.............................................**35**

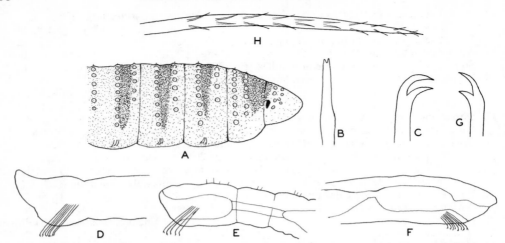

FIG. 201.–Structure of Naididae. A, anterior end of *Ophidonais serpentina*; B, dorsal seta of *O. serpentina*; C, tip of seta of *Chaetogaster limnaei*; D, anterior end of *C. diastrophus*; E, anterior end of *C. langi*; F, anterior end of *C. limnaei*; G, terminal bifurcation of seta of *C. diaphanus*; H, tip of dorsal capilliform seta of *Vejdovskyella comata*.

35. Branchial fossa elongated (Fig. 203J); three pairs of gills or two pairs and one pair of ciliated swellings; rare ............................... **Dero nivea** Sperber
    Branchial fossa not elongated ............................................... **36**
36. With four pairs of gills or gill-like structures (Figs. 202A, B); very common.
    **Dero digitata** (Müller)
    With two pairs of gills (Fig. 202C) ........................... **Dero obtusa** Udek.
37. Needles with a single point; proboscis present .............. **Pristina longiseta** Ehr.
    Needles bifid or pectinate (Fig. 203D) ....................................... **38**

FIG. 202.–Structure of Naididae. A, dorsal view of posterior end of *Dero digitata*; B, lateral view of posterior end of *D. digitata*; C, dorsal view of posterior end of *D. obtusa*; D, dorsal view of *Dero* sp.; E, lateral view of posterior end of *D. furcatus*; F, dorsal view of posterior end of *D. furcatus*; G, dorsal view of posterior end of *D. vagus*; H, dorsal bundle of setae of *D. vagus*. (B and E modified from Bousfield; D modified from Chen, 1940; F modified from Marcus, 1943; H modified from Walton.)

FIG. 203.–Structure of Naididae. A, dorsal bundle of *Pristina osborni*; B, anterior end of *Dero bilongata*; C, ventral seta of *Pristina aequiseta*; D, dorsal seta of *P. aequiseta*; E and F, extreme variations in anterior end of *P. breviseta*; G, anterior end of *P. longiseta*; H, thick seta from VI of *Nais pardalis*; J, branchial apparatus of *Dero nivea*; K, anterior end of *Pristina plumaseta*; L, ventral seta of II of *Nais behningi*; M, dorsal seta of *Nais elinguis*; N, dorsal seta of *N. simplex*; O, ventral seta of II of *N. barbata*; P, posterior seta of *N. barbata*; Q, dorsal seta of *N. barbata*. (A modified from Walton; B modified from Chen, 1944; G modified from Marcus, 1943; K modified from Leidy, 1880; C, D, H, J, L to Q modified from Brinkhurst et al.)

38. Prostomium with proboscis (Figs. 203E, F, K) ................................**39**
    Prostomium without proboscis......................... **Pristina osborni** (Walton)
39. Needle teeth short, of equal length ..................... **Pristina aequiseta** Bourne
    Needle teeth long, equal or unequal in length ................................**40**
40. Needle teeth unequal in length (Fig. 203K); rare ..........**Pristina plumaseta** Turner
    Needle teeth equal in length; prostomium variable (Figs. 203E, F).
                                                      **Pristina breviseta** Bourne
41. Needles single-pointed (Fig. 203N) ...........................................**42**
    Needles bifid (Fig. 203M) ................................................**45**
42. Ventral setae of II to V with long thin teeth (Fig. 203L) ........**Nais behningi** Mich.
    Ventral setae with relatively short teeth (Fig. 203O) ........................**43**
43. Needle setae hairlike, with fine tip (Fig. 203Q) .............................**44**
    Needle setae with a more blunt tip (Fig. 203N) ............... **Nais simplex** Piguet
44. Hair and needle setae each up to five per bundle ..............**Nais barbata** Muller
    Hair and needle setae each one to three per bundle ........ **Nais pseudobtusa** Piguet

FIG. 204.–Structure of Naididae. A, dorsal view of anterior end of *Nais communis*; B, dorsal bundle of setae of *N. communis*; C, ventral bundle of setae of *N. communis*; D, dorsal bundle of setae of *N. elinguis*; E and F, anterior end of *Stylaria lacustris*; G, dorsal bundle of setae of *S. lacustris*.

45. Ventral setae of at least some segments behind V with some thickened setae or a
    single giant seta (Fig. 203H) ...........................**Nais pardalis** Piguet
    Ventral setae posterior to V not especially thickened .........................**46**
46. Needle teeth long and almost parallel (Fig. 204D) .............**Nais elinguis** O.F.M.
    Needle teeth short and divergent (Fig. 204B) .................................**47**
47. Stomach widening gradually; very common; cosmopolitan .... **Nais communis** Piguet
    Stomach widening abruptly; uncommon ....................**Nais variabilis** Piguet
48. Coelomocytes abundant ................................................**49**
    Coelomocytes sparse or absent .........................................**51**
49. Prostomium with dorsal ciliated pit; rare; one species known ....... **Bothrioneurum**
    Prostomium without ciliated pit .........................................**50**

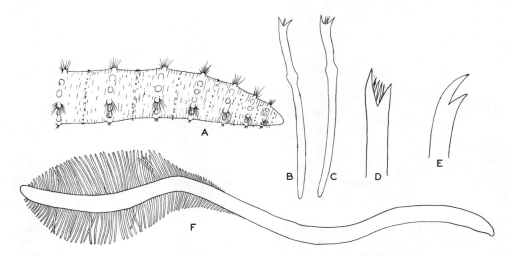

FIG. 205.–Structure of Tubificidae. A, anterior end of *Peloscolex*; B and C, dorsal pectinate setae of *Tubifex tubifex*; D, distal end of dorsal pectinate seta of *Ilyodrilus*; E, tip of seta of *Limnodrilus*; F, lateral view (diagrammatic) of *Branchiura sowerbyi,* ×1.1, showing dorsal and ventral gills.

50. Vasa deferentia long, distinct from their wide atria; about four rare species.
     **Rhyacodrilus**
     Vasa deferentia short, scarcely distinguishable from their tubular atria; usually among roots of aquatic plants; several brackish species, one fresh-water species.
     **Monopylephorus**
51. With a dorsal and a ventral gill on each segment in the posterior 25 to 40 percent of the body; 40 to 140 pairs of such gills (Figs. 205F); 20 to 185 mm long; pinkish gray; reported from many scattered stations, especially on lake bottoms.
     **Branchiura sowerbyi** Bedd.
     Without gills . . . . . . . . . . . . . . . . . . . . . . . . . . . . . . . . . . . . . . . . . . . . . . .52
52. Single solid prostates attached to atria by a narrow stalk . . . . . . . . . . . . . . . . . . . .53
     Prostates and atria of different form; rare and uncommon species . . . . . . . . . . . . . .59
53. Vasa deferentia much shorter than atria; about four rare species . . . . . . .**Potamothrix**
     Vasa deferentia as long as or longer than atria . . . . . . . . . . . . . . . . . . . . . . . . . . . .54
54. Tubular atria only slightly wider than vasa deferentia; one rare species in Lake Tahoe . . . . . . . . . . . . . . . . . . . . . . . . . . . . . . . . . . . . . . . . . . **Isochaeta**
     Atria much wider than vasa deferentia . . . . . . . . . . . . . . . . . . . . . . . . . . . . . . . . .55
55. Penis sheaths thick-walled, cuticular, and surrounded by spiral muscles; common and widely distributed; in stagnant water; often in tubes; about seven species.
     **Limnodrilus**
     Penis sheaths never thick-walled, without spiral muscles . . . . . . . . . . . . . . . . . . . . .56
56. Body papillate, often with a sheath of mucus and detritus (Fig. 205A); among roots of aquatic plants or in vegetable debris; about 10 uncommon species. **Peloscolex**
     Body not papillate . . . . . . . . . . . . . . . . . . . . . . . . . . . . . . . . . . . . . . . . . . . . . . .57
57. Atria at the opening of a long internal duct . . . . . . . . . . . . . . . . . . . . . **Psammoryctides**
     Atria without a long internal duct (Fig. 206C) . . . . . . . . . . . . . . . . . . . . . . . . . . . .58
58. Living worm 30 to 100 mm long; several species reported from the United States, but only one is common; it has the anterior end imbedded in mud bottoms, sometimes in a special tube, and waves the posterior end about in the water for aeration; especially common in polluted waters; sometimes present in enormous numbers . . . . . . . . . . . . . . . . . . . . . . . . . . . . . . . . . . . . . **Tubifex tubifex** (O.F.M.)
     Living worm 10 to 30 mm long; several rare species described from western states.
     **Ilyodrilus**

FIG. 206.–Structure of Tubificidae. A, ventral seta from posterior part of body of *Lumbriculus*; B, anterior end of *Rhynchelmis*; C, male duct of *Tubifex*. (B modified from Altman; C modified from Brinkhurst et al.)

59. Atrium with numerous prostate glands ........................... **Telmatodrilus**
    Atrium with one or two prostate glands, or prostate glands diffuse ..............**60**
60. Prostates diffuse; two species .........................................**Clitellio**
    Prostates solid; about four species .................................. **Aulodrilus**
61. One pair of male gonopores on X (Fig. 206B); prostomium present or absent; 20 to
        100 mm long; setae single-pointed or bifid ..............................**62**
    One pair of male gonopores on VII to XII; prostomium present or absent; 8 to 100
        mm long; setae single or bifid ......................................**64**
62. Fifty to 100 mm long; two rare species .......................... **Rhynchelmis**
    Twenty to 50 mm long..............................................**63**
63. Prostomium without a proboscis; setae single-pointed, bifid, or both; one rare
        species.......................................................... **Stylodrilus**
    Prostomium rounded or with a proboscis; setae single-pointed; widely distributed;
        five uncommon species ....................................**Eclipidrilus**
64. Setae single-pointed or bifid; two rare species ...................... **Kincaidiana**
    Setae bifid but with upper tooth reduced (Fig. 206A); several species but only one
        common ................................. **Lumbriculus variegatus** (Müller)

# BRANCHIOBDELLIDA

In these commensals of crayfishes there is always a distinct head region. They are so similar to leeches that they were considered a leech family until 1884. From a morphological standpoint, however, the Branchiobdellida form a connecting link between typical oligochaetes and true leeches.

The body ranges from 1 to 12 mm in length and consists of head, trunk, and muscular caudal sucker. The cylindrical head consists of four fused segments, which are sometimes superficially annulated. A prostomium is absent. The mouth is surrounded by a dorsal and a ventral lip, and just inside the mouth is a pair of sclerotized jaws.

The trunk consists of 11 segments, al-

though the last three are often indistinct and somewhat fused into the base of the sucker. Trunk segments are usually subdivided externally by transverse sulci. Setae are absent, and there are only two pairs of nephridia. The anus is on the dorsal side of segment X. In most species a spermatheca opens on the ventral midline of V, and there is a male genital pore on the ventral midline of VI. There is a pair of testes in each of V and VI. At maturity, the testes disassociate into clumps of spermatids, which, with developing and mature spermatozoa, fill the coelomic cavities of V and VI in American members of the group. A pair of ovaries is present in VII, and there are two lateroventral female genital pores. Large eggs may be seen in sexually mature specimens.

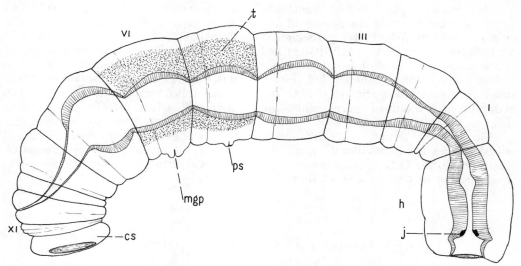

FIG. 207.–Diagram of *Cambarincola*, lateral view, showing digestive tract, ×70. *cs*, caudal sucker; *h*, head; *j*, jaw; *mgp*, male genital pore; *ps*, pore of spermatheca; *t*, testes (shaded areas).

The glandular clitellum forms around V, VI, and VII. Cocoons are formed, but almost nothing is known about the embryological development.

Branchiobdellids in the United States are always associated with crayfish, except for some species of *Cambarincola* that are found on cavernicolous *Asellus* and on *Callinectes sapidus* acclimated to fresh water. They occur on the gills, on the inner surface of the gill chambers, and on the general anterior external surface of the body and appendages. Sometimes a single crayfish may harbor as many as 200 or 300 worms. It is thought that the worms are essentially commensals since their digestive tracts usually contain only diatoms, other algae, and organic debris. Nevertheless, some species almost surely feed on blood of the host taken from gills or intersegmental membranes, and the species found on *Asellus* apparently feed on the eggs of the host. Branchiobdellids have survived up to 240 days in the laboratory, separated from their hosts, but have never been observed to produce cocoons under such conditions.

Except for *Xironogiton*, species of branchiobdellids reported from western crayfish (*Pacifastacus*) in Pacific drainages have never been found on eastern crayfish (Cambaridae), and vice versa; otherwise

there seems to be no host specificity. One species of *Cambarincola*, for example, has been reported from at least 11 species of Cambaridae. Nevertheless, most species are known only from small geographic areas, often only one state, or one cave.

FIG. 208.–Ventral view of reproductive organs of V and VI of *Ankyrodrilus* (testes not shown). *b*, bursa; *sf*, sperm funnel (4); *sg*, spermiducal gland; *s*, spermatheca. (Modified from Holt, 1965.)

A convenient place to find branchiobdellids is in the debris at the bottom of jars of preserved crayfish. If living specimens are collected, they are best killed and fixed in a solution consisting of 4 parts formalin and 96 parts of 70 percent alcohol. Either stained or unstained specimens may be dehydrated and mounted permanently on slides in a suitable medium.

Because of the rate at which undescribed species are being found by specialists, a key to the U.S. species now known would be out of date in a short time. We are therefore including a key that goes only to the generic level. Unfortunately, the determination of genera in this key is based chiefly on differences in the anatomy of the male reproductive system. In many cases this requires careful observation of the internal reproductive organs, which can be done with whole mounts or by dissection of large worms. Even so, considerable experience and effort is required. See Holt (1960a) for methods and definitions of anatomical terms.

## KEY TO GENERA OF BRANCHIOBDELLIDA*

1. Body dorsoventrally flattened (depressed); paired nephridiopores on dorsal surface of
   segment III . . . . . . . . . . . . . . . . . . . . . . . . . . . . . . . . . . . . . . . . . . . . . . . . . . . . . . . . . .2
   Body cylindrical (terete); single nephridiopore opening on dorsal surface of segment
   III . . . . . . . . . . . . . . . . . . . . . . . . . . . . . . . . . . . . . . . . . . . . . . . . . . . . . . . . . . . . . . . . . .4
2. Spermiducal gland with ental bifurcation; vasa deferentia enter spermiducal gland near
   ectal end; spermatheca prominent (Fig. 208); body 2 to 3 mm† long; two species
   in Virginia and Tennessee . . . . . . . . . . . . . . . . . . . . . . . . . . . . . . . . . . . **Ankyrodrilus**
   Spermiducal gland not bifurcated entally . . . . . . . . . . . . . . . . . . . . . . . . . . . . . . . . . . . . . .3

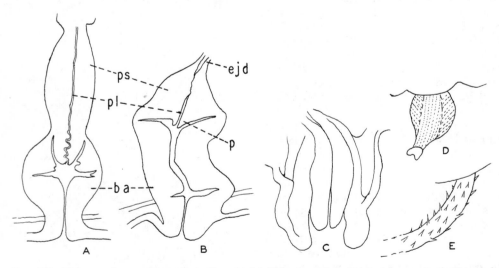

FIG. 209.–Male copulatory structures in Branchiobdellida. A, male copulatory apparatus in *Triannulata*; B, male copulatory apparatus in *Magmatodrilus*; C, protrusible penis in shape of a muscular cone; D, eversible penis with internal strands; E, cuticular tube type of penis. *ba*, bursal atrium; *ejd*, ejaculatory duct; *p*, penis; *pl*, lumen of penis; *ps*, penial sheath. (A and B modified from Holt, 1974; C to E courtesy of Perry C. Holt.)

*Prepared by Perry C. Holt.

†Lengths given are of preserved specimens and are approximate; extended living worms may be two or three times as long.

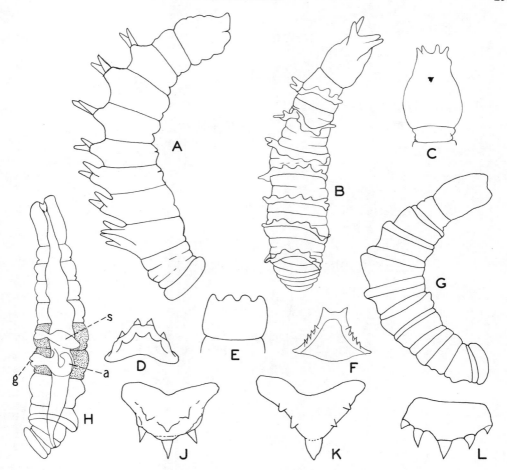

FIG. 210.–Structure of Branchiobdellida. A, lateral view of *Pterodrilus,* ×85; B, dorsal view of *Ceratodrilus,* ×35; C, dorsal view of head of *Cambarincola*; D to L, structure of *Cambarincola*; D, lower jaw; E, upper lip; F, lower jaw; G, lateral view, ×24; H, lateral view, ×30; J, upper jaw; K, upper jaw; L, upper jaw. *a*, accessory sperm duct; *g*, male genital pore; *s*, spermatheca; testes shown as shaded area in H. (B modified from Hall, 1915; D, J, and L modified from Ellis, 1920; F redrawn from Moore, 1893; G modified from Goodnight, 1941; H modified from Goodnight, 1940; K modified from Ellis, 1912.)

**3.** Vasa deferentia enter tubular spermiducal gland near ectal end; spermatheca disproportionately small; 2 to 8 mm long (Fig. 211B); five species on crayfishes of both eastern and western mountains .......................... **Xironogiton**

    Vasa deferentia enter tubular or subspherical spermiducal gland basally; spermatheca prominent; up to 6 mm long; six species on eastern crayfish ..... **Xironodrilus**

**4.** Penis eversible (Figs. 209D, E) ............................................. **5**

    Penis a protrusible muscular cone (Fig. 209C) ................................ **12**

**5.** Eversible penis a cuticular tube, often very long, with or without spines (Fig. 209E). **6**

    Eversible penis with internal strands (Fig. 209D), or an epithelial or muscular wall or both .......................................................................... **7**

**6.** Vasa deferentia enter spermiducal gland ectad to ental end of latter; prostate absent; about 2 mm long; one species in Tennessee ................... **Cronodrilus**

    Vasa deferentia enter ental end of spermiducal gland; prostate present, often rudimentary; 1 to 3 mm long; two species in Tennessee and Kentucky. **Oedipodrilus**

FIG. 211.–Structure of Branchiobdellida. A, lateral view of fourth trunk segment of *Bdellodrilus* showing lateral gland; B, ventral view of *Xironogiton*, ×18; C, dorsal view of *Triannulata*, ×21; D, lateral view of *Magmatodrilus*, ×30; E to H, upper jaws of *Xironodrilus*. (B redrawn from Moore, 1893; C and D modified from Goodnight, 1940; E and F modified from Ellis, 1919; G and H modified from Goodnight, 1943.)

7. With cylindrical projections borne dorsally on transverse folds of segments II to VIII (Fig. 210B); upper lip with four tentacles; 3 mm long; two species in Utah, Idaho, and Oregon . . . . . . . . . . . . . . . . . . . . . . . . . . . . . . . . . . . . . . .**Ceratodrilus**
   Without such dorsal projections . . . . . . . . . . . . . . . . . . . . . . . . . . . . . . . . . . . . . . . .**8**
8. With pairs of large, clear glands in lateral body wall of segments I to IX (Fig. 211A); upper jaw a longitudinal ridge fitting concavity of lower jaw; bifid spermatheca; gill-inhabiting delicate worms; 2 to 3 mm long; one widely distributed species . . . . . . . . . . . . . . . . . . . . . . . . . . . . . . . . . . . . . . . . . . . . . **Bdellodrilus**
   Without lateral glands; spermatheca not bifid . . . . . . . . . . . . . . . . . . . . . . . . . . . . .**9**
9. Penis and ejaculatory duct a continuous heavily muscular eversible tube (Fig. 209A); 4 to 5 mm long (Fig. 211C); one California species . . . . . . . . . . . . . . **Triannulata**
   Penis and ejaculatory duct distinct regions; ejaculatory duct not eversible . . . . . . . .**10**

10. Bursal atrium long and heavily muscular (Fig. 209B); penial sheath and eversible penis short; spermiducal gland very long with prominent anterior deferent lobe; prostate absent (Fig. 211D); about 3 mm long; one species in California.
**Magmatodrilus**
Bursal atrium shorter than penial sheath; noneversible penial sheath . . . . . . . . . . . . **11**
11. Spermiducal gland small and slender, subequal to ejaculatory duct in length and diameter; prostate short; penis cuticular, enclosed when retracted by muscular extension of ejaculatory duct, which projects into bursal atrium; 2 to 3 mm long; one species in Tennessee . . . . . . . . . . . . . . . . . . . . . . . . . . . . . . . **Tettodrilus**
Spermiducal gland various but always larger than ejaculatory duct; prostate present or absent; penis eversible, cuticular with strands connecting its outer everted surface to wall of penial sheath; 1 to 5 mm long; several species; Florida to Washington . . . . . . . . . . . . . . . . . . . . . . . . . . . . . . . . . . . . . . . . **Sathodrilus**
12. Spermatheca absent; bursa asymmetrically subglobular; about 1.5 mm long; two species; Kentucky, Indiana, and Michigan . . . . . . . . . . . . . . . . . . . . . . **Ellisodrilus**
Spermatheca present . . . . . . . . . . . . . . . . . . . . . . . . . . . . . . . . . . . . . . . . . . .**13**
13. Large worms; without dorsal appendages, though peristomial lobes or tentacles may be present; dorsal ridges, if present, not confined to segment VIII; 2.5 to 8 mm long; many species; generally distributed . . . . . . . . . . . . . . . . . . . . . **Cambarincola**
Small worms; usually with finger- or fanlike projections on some dorsal ridges (Fig. 210A), but sometimes a single prominent dorsal ridge on segment VIII; 1 to 2 mm long; eight species; uplands of eastern United States and Ozark Mountains . . . . . . . . . . . . . . . . . . . . . . . . . . . . . . . . . . . . . . . . . . . . . . . **Pterodrilus**

# POLYCHAETA

Polychaetes are almost exclusively marine annelids, and an amazing variety of species and enormous numbers of individuals are found in many types of marine habitats. Some species (especially Nereidae) are euryhaline and occur also in estuaries and brackish waters, but less than 50 species of polychaetes are known to be restricted to the fresh waters of the world.

The colonization of inland waters by these few polychaetes is by no means restricted to one family or a few genera. Eight families are represented, and all species have close marine relatives. In addition to being found in the United States, fresh-water polychaetes have been reported sporadically from Yugoslavia, Lake Baikal in Asia, Viet Nam, Gabon, Java, Sumatra, China, Great Britain, Trinidad, and Brazil. With few exceptions, they have been collected from fresh-water rivers, lakes, and springs within 20 miles of the seacoast, and this seems to be an indication that polychaetes, in spite of their phylogenetic antiquity, are relative newcomers to fresh waters. Presumably the physiological and morphological adjustments necessary for the marine-brackish-freshwater transition

constitute almost insurmountable barriers. Perhaps the most striking incidence of polychaete distribution is the occurrence of two fresh-water species in Lake Baikal, a body of water that is geologically ancient and more than 1600 km from the nearest salt water.

Most fresh-water polychaetes look similar to the familiar *Nereis* of invertebrate zoology courses. Eight species have been reported from the United States. *Nereis limnicola* Johnson, one of the Nereidae, was first collected in 1895 from Lake Merced near San Francisco, a body of fresh water less than 0.4 km from the ocean and formed in very recent geological times. It may be taken as far north as Oregon. *N. succinea* Frey and Leuckart is widely distributed in brackish to fresh waters on both east and west coasts. Another nereid, *Lycastoides alticola* Johnson, was described from a single specimen collected in 1892 in a mountain stream at an altitude of 2100 m in "Sierra Laguna, Lower California." It has apparently not been collected since. *Laeonereis culveri* (Webster) occurs in brackish to fresh waters along the east coast, and *Lycastopsis hummelincki* Au-

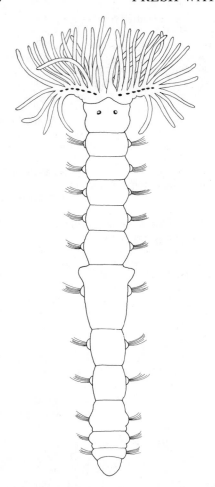

FIG. 212.–*Manayunkia speciosa*, ×37, a fresh-water polychaete. (Modified from Leidy, 1883.)

gener is in similar habitats on the west coast of Florida. *Namanereis hawaiiensis* (Johnson), however, has been taken from only a single pond in southern California.

A single serpulid, *Mercierella enigmatica* Fauvel, is known from marine to brackish and fresh waters near Oakland,

California, and from a few streams entering the Gulf of Mexico. It builds a calcareous tube.

In 1859 and in several later papers the great microscopist Leidy described an interesting sabellid polychaete, *Manayunkia speciosa* Leidy, from the Schuylkill River near Philadelphia; it was later found in other areas in southeastern Pennsylvania and New Jersey. In 1939 Krecker described another species in the same genus, *M. eriensis* Krecker, from mud samples taken at a depth of 17 m in Lake Erie, near Put-in-Bay, Ohio. More recently this species has been considered a synonym of *M. speciosa*. It has since been found to be widely distributed in the Great Lakes, Georgia, New York, Oregon, California, Alaska, North Carolina, and South Carolina. This is undoubtedly the polychaete most likely to be found by the fresh-water biologist, and undoubtedly it is widely distributed in the United States.

*Manayunkia speciosa* is 3 to 5 mm long and inhabits a tube built of mud or sand and mucus. The head bears two large lateral lophophorelike structures, each of which has about 18 long, ciliated tentacles used in feeding. There is a pair of eyes near the median line of the head, and also a linear group of pigmented spots on each half of the lophophore, which are presumed to be light sensitive. Each of the first 11 of the 12 trunk segments has a pair of reduced, knoblike parapodia bearing a bundle of 4 to 10 setae. The circulatory system is well developed, and the bright green chlorocruorin of the blood colors the whole body. Leidy showed that development is direct and that there is no free-swimming trochophore larva. The large size and lateral swellings of the sixth trunk segment may be an indication that these polychaetes also reproduce by budding.

## ARCHIANNELIDA

One of the most remarkable recent phylogenetic discoveries among fresh-water invertebrates is the collection of what are presumably two species of archiannelids. *Troglochaetus beranecki* Delachaux

was first described from underground waters of caverns in Switzerland (Delachaux 1921), and more recently this worm has been taken in Hungary, Romania, Austria, and Germany. In 1969 the writer found

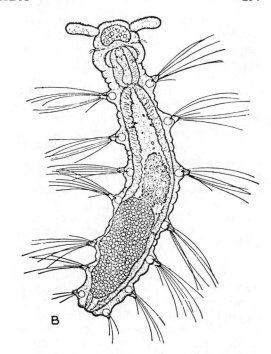

Fig. 213.–*Troglochaetus beranecki*, ×100. A, retouched photograph; B, showing general anatomy. (B from Andrassy, 1956.)

what is thought to be the same species in the interstitial water 20 cm below the surface of gravels of mountain streams in Colorado at altitudes of 2640 and 3050 m. Undoubtedly, however, this species will be found elsewhere in the United States. *Troglochaetus* averages only 630 microns in length. There are two blunt prostomial tentacles and seven pairs of parapodia. Each parapodium has a dorsal and a ventral fascicle of long, thin setae that are easily broken off during field collecting. There are no

segmental septa. The species is closely related to several marine genera, especially the littoral genus *Thalassochaetus,* from the North Sea.

A problematical microannelid, *Rheomorpha neiswestnovae* Lastochkin, has been found in the interstitial zone of freshwater sandy beahces in Russia, Poland, and Italy. It may be an archiannelid, but the worm also has certain oligochaete affinities.

## HIRUDINEA (LEECHES)

The leeches are predominantly a freshwater group, although there are many marine as well as numerous terrestrial species, the latter mostly in the tropics. About 44 fresh-water species are known from the United States, and they are common inhabitants of ponds, marshes, lakes, and slow streams, especially in the northern half of the country. To the layman, leeches are

collectively known as "bloodsuckers," but many forms are predators and scavengers, and only a minority of our species will take blood from warm-blooded animals. Unlike the great majority of fresh-water invertebrates, leeches are often brightly colored and patterned, and in some species the coloration is highly variable. The length of mature leeches ranges from minute species only 5 mm long to some of the giant *Haemopis* that have been reported to reach a length of 45 cm when extended and swimming.

**General characteristics.** Unlike oligochaetes, the Hirudinea are dorsoventrally flattened. The mouth is surrounded by an oral sucker that may be large, or small, fused with the anterior end, and liplike. The caudal sucker usually faces ventrally and is much larger, discoid, powerful, and expanded over a short central attachment pedestal. The anus is dorsal and in front of the sucker. The surface of the body may be smooth, wrinkled, tuberculate, or papillated. Although most genera have characteristic shapes, it should be borne in mind that leeches are highly muscular and contractile, and the body outline may vary greatly with locomotion, reaction to stimuli, and method of killing and fixation.

From the standpoint of basic body segmentation, external appearances are deceiving. All leeches are composed of only 34 true segments, but each segment is subdivided into a definite and constant number of superficial annuli. In the middle portion of the body a segment typically has three, five, or six annuli, but in some of the Piscicolidae (fish leeches) there are 7, 12, or 14 annuli. Toward the extremities of the body annulation is incomplete so that there are fewer annuli per segment than in the midbody segments. In *Haemopis marmorata,* for example, midbody segments all have five annuli, but segments I through VII are represented by 1, 1, 1, 2, 2, 3, and 4 or 5 annuli, respectively; and XXIII through XXVII are represented by 5, 4, 3, 2, and 1 annuli. Furthermore, in all leeches there is considerable fusion of the true segments of the body at the extremities, and especially at the posterior end. In *H. marmorata* segments XXVIII through XXXIV are all fused to form the caudal sucker.

The true body segmentation has been precisely established by a study of the nervous system. Each of the 34 segments is represented by a ganglion and paired nerves, but these structures are crowded together and partially fused at the anterior and posterior ends.

Some investigators distinguish the following major body regions in leeches: head (I to VI), preclitellar (VII to IX), clitellar (X to XIII), postclitellar (XIV to XXIV), anal (XXV to XXVII), and caudal sucker (XXVIII to XXXIV). The degree of differentiation of these regions is highly variable from one species to another.

The Class Hirudinea is divided into three orders. Each member of the Order Rhynchobdellida has a small, porelike mouth in the oral sucker through which a muscular proboscis can be protruded; jaws are absent; the blood is colorless; and there are three or six or more annuli per segment in the middle of the body. Members of the orders Gnathobdellida and Pharyngobdellida have a medium to large mouth, no proboscis, jaws present or absent, red blood, and usually five annuli per segment in the middle of the body.

The Order Rhynchobdellida is subdivided into two American families. The Glossiphoniidae generally have a flattened body, the anterior sucker more or less fused with the body, one to four pairs of eyes, and typically three annuli in each of the midbody segments. The American Piscicolidae, on the other hand, are somewhat cylindrical, with a distinct anterior sucker, one or two pairs of eyes, and usually six or more annuli per midbody segment; these leeches are almost invariably found as parasites on the body of fish or crustaceans.

The Order Gnathobdellida contains only the Family Hirudinidae in North America. The Family Erpobdellidae in the Order Pharyngobdellida have three or four pairs of eyes (never arranged in an arch), no jaws, and no gastric caeca. The Hirudinidae, however, have five pairs of eyes (forming a regular arch), toothed jaws, and one to several pairs of gastric caeca.

**Color.** When collecting specimens in the field, notes on coloration should always be taken, since leeches quickly fade in preservatives, with only red, brown, and black pigments persisting. Uniform coloration is a rare condition, most leeches being

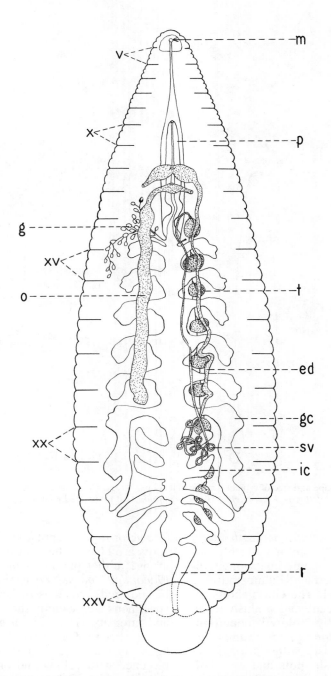

FIG.214.–Ventral diagram of *Glossiphonia complanata*, ×10, showing annulations, reproductive system, and digestive system. Reproductive system stippled; female organs shown only on the left; male organs shown only on the right. *ed*, ejaculatory duct; *ic*, intestinal caecum (second); *g*, salivary glands; *gc*, gastric caecum (sixth); *m*, mouth; *o*, ovary; *p*, proboscis; *r*, rectum; *t*, testis; *sv*, seminal vesicle. (Modified from Harding and·Moore.)

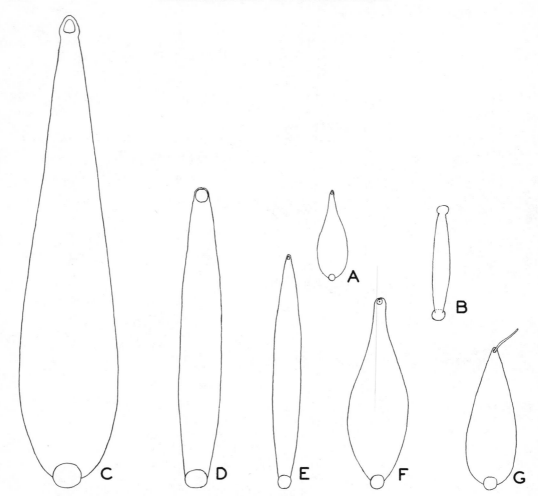

FIG.215.–Relative shape and size of typical American leeches, ×1. A, *Helobdella*; B, *Piscicola*; C, *Haemopis*; D, *Macrobdella*; E, *Erpobdella*; F, *Placobdella*; G, *Glossiphonia,* with extruded proboscis.

brightly mottled, spotted, or segmentally striped; sometimes the color pattern is arranged transversely, sometimes longitudinally. The ventral surface is almost always paler than the dorsal. The Glossiphoniidae range from translucent and pinkish to an opaque and brightly colored condition. *Glossiphonia complanata,* for example, is dull green to brownish, with six longitudinal rows of yellowish spots and two dark longitudinal paramedian lines. *Macrobdella decora,* the American medicinal leech, is very showy; the general coloration is green with obscure longitudinal stripes or short median lines; in the midline are bright

orange or reddish spots, while the marginal spots are black. The ventral surface is rich orange, either plain or spotted with black. *Placobdella parasitica* is richly and variably colored, and it is difficult to find two specimens with exactly the same coloration and intensity. The general ground color is some shade of greenish-brown, but the body is variously spotted, striped, or blotched with yellow and orange. A histological study of this species has revealed three types of pigment granules: (1) a pale yellowish granular reflecting substance, (2) chromatophores that range from black (contracted) to green (expanded), and (3 reddish-brown chromatophores that form a fine network in the expanded state. Leeches show no background color adaptation, but usually become paler in darkness and darker under illumination. Color changes are thought to be governed through the central nervous system.

**Locomotion.** All leeches can move about on the substrate with characteristic creeping, looping, or inchworm movements, by getting a firm grip alternately with the oral and caudal suckers. The body shape changes greatly during such locomotion. The Hirudinidae and Erpobdellidae are excellent swimmers, moving along rapidly with graceful up-and-down or side-to-side undulations. The Glossiphoniidae are poor swimmers, however, and when disturbed they usually roll up like a pillbug and fall to the substrate.

**Feeding, digestive system.** The structure of the digestive system is partially correlated with food habits. In the Rynchobdellida there are no jaws, and the mouth is normally a small pore in the oral sucker. The anterior portion of the digestive tract contains an elongated, muscular, protrusible proboscis that lies in a proboscis sheath and is thrust forward and out of the mouth during feeding. There is a very short esophagus at the base of the proboscis, but the unicellular salivary glands in this region have long ducts that carry their secretion through the proboscis to its tip. The large stomach extends approximately through the middle third of the body and has from 1 to 10 pairs of lateral gastric caeca (often branched), in which quantities of ingested food may be stored for long periods prior to digestion. The gastric caeca are capable of great distension, and after a large meal a leech may weigh two to four times as much as it did before the meal. Digestion occurs in the intestine, and this part of the digestive tract is also supplied with caeca; usually, however, there are only four small pairs. The rectum is an unspecialized part of the digestive tract just before the anus. The Glossiphoniidae have a wide variety of food habits; many species are scavengers, feeding on dead animal matter, but more

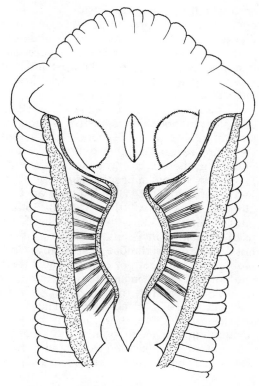

FIG. 216.–Diagrammatic ventral dissection of the anterior end of *Hirudo*. Stippling denotes cut edges of oral chamber, pharynx, and body wall. (Greatly modified from Pfurtscheller.)

commonly they are carnivorous and feed on snails, insects, oligochaetes, and other small invertebrates. *Glossiphonia complanata* and *Helobdella stagnalis* are almost always associated with snails on which they feed and are consequently commonly called "snail leeches." *Placobdella* and *Helobdella* are often temporary parasites on fish, frogs, and turtles, and they have occasionally been reported as taking a blood meal from man, especially from an open abrasion on the skin. Except during the breeding season, the Piscicolidae are almost invariably found as parasites on fish or crustaceans; they feed on the surface mucus as well as on blood and tissue fluids. The fact that certain Rynchobdellida are capable of taking blood from vertebrates does not seem to have been satisfactorily explained, especially since these leeches have no teeth with which to make an incision in the host epidermis. It is probable, however, that digestive enzymes are released through the pore at the tip of the proboscis where it is in contact with the skin of the host and that these enzymes digest the superficial layers and permit blood to flow.

The general plan of the Gnathobdellida and Pharyngobdellida digestive system is similar to that of the Rynchobdellida, but there are several striking differences. For one thing, there is no proboscis, and in its place is a strong, muscular, sucking pharynx. Some of the Hirudinidae, or true bloodsuckers, have three sharp-toothed jaws behind the large mouth. These are used in making incisions in the skin of the host. Other Hirudinidae, especially *Haemopis,* have no teeth or only vestigial teeth and normally feed on small invertebrates or dead animal matter, though *H. marmorata* will occasionally attack man. The latter species is called the "horse leech" because it commonly lives in ponds and troughs, where it attacks drinking cattle and horses. The Pharyngobdellida never have true jaws. They are scavengers or feed mostly on small invertebrates, which they sometimes swallow whole; occasionally they suck blood from fish, frogs, and man, especially at bleeding epidermal abrasions. None of the American Gnathobdellida and Pharyngobdellida have intestinal caeca. The Hirudinidae have one to several pairs of gastric caeca, but the Erpobdellidae have none.

*Macrobdella* and *Philobdella* are the only common American leeches that regularly take human blood. Like all other bloodsuckers, they attach to the host with the caudal sucker and explore with the anterior end until a suitable spot is located, especially where the skin is thin. The oral sucker is then attached tightly and three fine painless incisions are made by back-and-forth rotary motions of the jaws. Sufficient blood is taken to distend the stomach and its caeca greatly so that the leech may be five times as heavy as it was when it began feeding. Much of the fluid of the ingested blood is excreted by the nephridia during feeding, the stored organic components, both cellular and noncellular, being considerably concentrated. When the leech has filled its digestive tract, it leaves the host voluntarily, but the incisions keep on bleeding for a variable time because of the persistence of small quantities of the salivary anticoagulant, hirudin, in the adjacent tissues.

True bloodsucking leeches require only an occasional full meal, the stored blood being digested and utilized very slowly. Specimens have been kept for more than two years without feeding.

**Circulatory system.** Unlike the condition in oligochaetes, where there is a spacious coelom regularly divided by transverse septa, the coelom of leeches is largely obliterated and reduced by greatly developed muscular, botryoidal, and parenchymatous tissues. The remaining sinuslike cavities consist of several longitudinal canals interconnected by smaller branch canals. The nerve cord, larger blood vessels, and reproductive organs are located in these sinuses.

The main portion of the circulatory system of typical Rynchobdellida consists of a large dorsal longitudinal blood vessel and a large ventral longitudinal blood vessel, which are connected near the two extremities by a series of convoluted branch vessels. The muscular wall of the anterior portion of the dorsal vessel acts as a heart. Near the posterior end the dorsal vessel is greatly expanded into an intestinal blood sinus that envelops the intestine and its caeca, and muscular contractions of the intestine are thought to aid in forcing the blood anteriorly out of this sinus and through the dorsal vessel proper. All the body tissues are well supplied with capillaries. In addition to the blood circulatory system, the coelomic sinuses contain a lymphlike fluid that circulates slowly. The two systems are unconnected, blood flowing in one and lymph in the other, both fluids being colorless. In some of the Piscicolidae the lymphatic system has a series of paired lateral pulsating vesicles that force the lymph around the body.

In the other two orders the true blood vascular system has disappeared, and the system of coelomic sinuses alone remains in a modified form. It contains blood that is red because of dissolved erythrocruorin.

**Respiration.** Some marine leeches have special lateral gill-like structures, but none of the American fresh-water species have any special respiratory structures. The oxygen and carbon dioxide exchange readily occurs through the general body surface since there is a rich network of capillaries just below the epidermis. Many species attach to the substrate with one or both suckers and undulate the body, probably to facilitate respiration. Little is known about the ability of active leeches to tolerate low concentrations of dissolved oxygen, but many species will live through several days without free oxygen. They do not appear to be able to tolerate highly acid conditions or decomposition gases at low oxygen concentrations.

**Excretion.** There are never more than 17 pairs of nephridia and these are all segmentally arranged in the middle body segments. The internal openings, located in the sinus system, are simple ciliated funnels in some species and simple to complex, variable "ciliated organs" in others. The paired external openings, or nephridiopores, are in the ventral furrows between annuli.

**Nervous system.** The brain is in the region of segments V and VI and consists of the fused ganglia and basal portions of the nerves of the first six body segments. There is a small suprapharyngeal mass, a small connective passing around each side of the pharynx, and a very large subpharyngeal mass. The posterior ganglionic mass, in segments XXV and XXVI, represents the more or less fused ganglia of XXV through XXXIV. The ventral nerve cord connects brain and posterior ganglionic mass, and each of VII through XXIV has a ganglion with three pairs of nerves.

**Sense organs.** Typical leeches have a variable number of small papillae arranged in transverse rows or extending completely around the body. These are of two general types. Ordinary cutaneous papillae are tac-

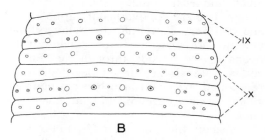

FIG. 217.–Arrangement of sensillae and papillae in typical segments in two species of *Placobdella*. Sensillae are shown with central dots; all other areas are cutaneous papillae. Note that sensillae occur only on the middle annulus of each segment and that they are symmetrically arranged.

tile and possibly chemical receptors. Sensillae, however, are more specialized, light-colored or whitish, and sensitive to light. Although there may be numerous transverse rows or rings of cutaneous papillae in a single segment, there is never more than one row or ring of sensillae per segment. Usually a ring of sensillae consists of a dorsal transverse row of six or eight sensillae and a ventral row of six sensillae. Such a ring of sensillae is often called the neural ring, or sensory ring, and is always situated on the neural or sensory annulus of every somite. The term is usually applied to the annulus and not to the sense organs themselves.

True paired eyes are found at the anterior end of the body. Each eye consists of a clump of dark-colored pigment granules, often cup-shaped, and an adjacent sensory area. Glossiphoniidae have one to four pairs of eyes, Piscicolidae one or two or more, Erpobdellidae three or four, and Hirudinidae five. A few leeches have eyespots on the caudal sucker or body somites.

**Reproduction.** In a very few leeches there is a common genital pore for both sets of reproductive organs, but usually there are two genital pores located on the median ventral line in XI and XII and separated by one to five or more annuli, the male genital pore always being more anterior than the female.

The female reproductive system is much simpler than that of the male. It consists of two saclike ovaries of variable size and two very short, narrow oviducts that unite to form a vagina. The vagina, in turn, opens to the outside through the female genital pore. In the Hirudinidae the female reproductive system also has an albumen gland, vaginal caecum, and muscular vagina.

Usually there are 5 to 12 pairs of segmentally arranged spherical testes, but in some of the Erpobdellidae they may be minutely subdivided like linear bunches of grapes. On each side of the body the testes are connected to a long vas deferens by means of short vasa efferentia. Each vas deferens has a modified seminal vesicle region that, in turn, becomes an ejaculatory duct. The two ejaculatory ducts unite to form a median atrium that is often complex and glandular.

The relative development and size of the seminal vesicles and ejaculatory ducts vary greatly from one species to another. They may be short to long, straight or much convoluted, and small to massive. In the seminal vesicles sperm become cemented together and stored for future use.

An eversible muscular bursa is associated with the male atrium. In the Glossiphoniidae it is rudimentary, but in the other families it is generally larger and functional. In the Hirudinidae, however, the bursa region contains a coiled filamentous tubular penis, often having a complicated structure.

As the sperm leave the seminal vesicle and pass down the ejaculatory ducts into the region of the atrium, they are formed into spermatophores (except in the Hirudinidae) for conveyance to another individual during copulation. These double club-shaped structures, which have a chitinoid covering, consist of two more or less adherent tubes containing sperm bundles (Fig. 217). Spermatophores are formed by glandular areas of the atrium and adjacent portions of the ejaculatory ducts.

Like most hermaphroditic animals, an individual leech does not fertilize itself, but copulates with another individual and exchanges sperm. In the Rhynchobdellida and Erpobdellidae copulating pairs implant spermatophores on the ventral or dorsal surface of each other, usually in the clitellar region, but sometimes only one member of a copulating pair releases spermatophores. The sperm issue out of the spermatophores and penetrate the superficial tissues to the sinuses of the recipient leech with the aid of local histolysis. Soon the sperm reach the ovaries in the ventral sinuses and fertilize the eggs.

In the Hirudinidae the penis of each member of a copulating pair is extruded so that sperm are deposited at the genital pore or in the vagina of the recipient.

The clitellum of a leech is relatively inconspicuous, but in the breeding season it secretes ringlike structures that slip off the anterior end of the body to form cocoons, just as in the earthworm. As the cocoon passes the female genital pore it receives and encloses from one to several

FIG. 218.–Spermatophore of *Glossiphonia,* showing two oval bundles of sperm. (Modified from Brumpt.)

fertilized eggs. The Piscicolidae and most Gnathobdellida and Pharyngobdellida fasten their cocoons to the substrate, but some of the Hirudinidae superficially bury their cocoons in soft substrates, often in or on exposed mud along the shores of bodies of water. Cocoons are usually 2 to 15 mm long, more or less oval, and flattened on the attachment surface. The outer surface may be gelatinous, spongy, tough and membranous, horny, or chitinoid (Figs. 219, 220). After a variable period of growth, the young leeches emerge from the cocoons and become independent.

The Glossiphoniidae do not form true cocoons but carry their fertilized eggs in membranous capsules on the ventral surface of the body. After hatching, the young remain on the body of the parent in the same area. They are attached by means of mucous threads and probably feed on mucus until they attain quite a large size, at which time they leave the parent.

Copulation usually begins in the spring after a good meal has been obtained, and most cocoons are deposited between May and August. Some species produce batches of eggs for periods of five to six months, and empty cocoons may be found as late as October or November.

Little is known about the length of life of leeches. *Macrobdella decora* takes two to three years to mature, certain other Hirudinidae may require four to five years, and it is claimed that some specimens may live for 10 to 15 years. *Helobdella stagnalis,* on the other hand, may have two generations per year.

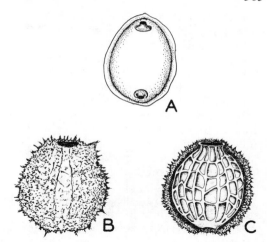

FIG. 220.—Leech cocoons. A, *Erpobdella*; B, complete cocoon of *Cystobranchus*; C, cocoon of *Cystobranchus* with spongy layer removed from upper surface. (A from Mann, 1964; B and C modified from Hoffmann, 1955.)

**Ecology.** Leeches abound in warm, protected shallows where there is little wave action and where plants, stones, and debris afford concealment. In such habitats population densities of 700 leeches per square meter of bottom have been reported. Superficial daylight examination of a likely body of water may be disappointing, but it must be borne in mind that leeches are chiefly nocturnal, and that they are hidden under stones, vegetation, and debris during the hours of daylight. The great majority of specimens are collected between the water's edge and depths of 2 m, but a few species have been collected as deep as 50 m. Leeches require substrates to which they can adhere and consequently are uncommon on pure mud or clay bottoms.

Few species and few individuals occur in strongly acid lakes, and they are generally absent from sphagnum bogs. There is some evidence indicating that low calcium content of waters may be a limiting factor in leech distribution

Unlike most groups of fresh-water invertebrates, there is very little habitat preference among leeches. The same species (*Helobdella stagnalis,* for example) may occur in lakes, ponds, springs, slow

FIG. 219.—Cocoons of *Haemopis,* ×1.5.

streams, marshes, and on all kinds of suitable substrates. A few species of Erpobdellidae and Glossiphoniidae may be collected in swift streams, and some of them even tolerate some degree of pollution.

The leech fauna of intermittent ponds persists because some species are able to tide over dry periods by burrowing into the mud bottom, losing considerable weight, and constructing a small mucus-lined cell. Leeches have been known to aestivate in this manner for more than four weeks at a time. Winters are spent in a lethargic dormant state buried in the upper parts of the substrate but below the frost line.

Although American leeches are all considered aquatic organisms, there are some that are actually amphibious. *Haemopis*, for example, commonly crawls out of the water and wanders about on the moist shore and ground, sometimes as much as a quarter of a mile from the water, where it feeds on living and dead invertebrates, especially earthworms.

Semipermanent and permanent parasites, such as the Piscicolidae and *Placobdella parasitica,* remain on the body of the host except during the breeding season when they become free-living long enough to deposit their eggs on the substrate. But some of the fish leeches are completely dependent and deposit their cocoons on the host fish.

**Economic importance.** The common medical practice of bloodletting as treatment for a wide variety of human ills supported a considerable leech industry in eighteenth- and nineteenth-century Europe. *Hirudo medicinalis* was raised commercially in so-called leech ponds, especially in France, Hungary, and Russia, and it is estimated that 25 million leeches were used in France in 1846 and 7 million in London hospitals in 1863.

Leeching never attained such great importance in the United States, and between 1840 and 1890 it is doubtful if more than 1.5 million leeches were used in any one year, including both the imported and native species (usually *Macrobdella decora*). The maximum wholesale price was about one hundred dollars per thousand. By 1890 the use of leeches had dwindled greatly and by the turn of the century it was difficult to find a drugstore that still carried leeches in stock. Bloodletting by the use of leeches is now extremely rare in this country and is confined to a few older European elements of our population. The practice is mostly resorted to as a home remedy for boils, contusions, and abscessed teeth.

Leeches sometimes become so abundant in northern lake resort areas as to constitute a nuisance for bathers. Disturbances in the water, such as splashing and currents, are known to attract bloodsuckers quickly. Unfortunately there are usually no effective remedial measures that can be taken to reduce leech populations, but if the water level of a lake can be lowered at least a meter in the late fall, dormant leeches in the exposed muddy shallows will be killed by temperatures of −6°C or less. Leeches may be temporarily controlled in localized bathing beach areas by applying 100 lb of powdered lime per acre per day in the shallows.

With reference to fish populations, the Glossiphoniidae, Hirudinidae, and Erpobdellidae can be dismissed as being of no real importance as parasites. Heavy infestations of Piscicolidae, however, have sometimes caused considerable mortality in both hatcheries and the natural habitat. Meyer (1969) summarizes the generally unsuccessful methods for treating fish infestations.

**Dispersal, geographic distribution.** Since many leeches temporarily attach to or definitely parasitize ducks and shore birds, they are easily transported overland from

FIG. 221.–A small carp heavily infected with *Piscicola,* ×0.5. (From Plehn, 1924.)

one body of water or drainage system to another. In fact, the leeches are one of the few fresh-water groups in which such transport is definitely known to occur. Within a single drainage system, however, passive dispersal by attachment to fish is undoubtedly of great importance.

In addition, leeches actively and readily spread from place to place and colonize suitable habitats within individual drainage systems. Peculiar seasonal upstream mass migrations of great numbers of leeches have been reported several times. As shown in the key, some American leeches are known from only one or two states, whereas others are generally distributed in suitable habitats. Two species of *Glossiphonia* occur throughout Europe and much of Asia; *Helobdella stagnalis* and *Theromyzon tessulatum* are widely distributed in the north and south temperate zones. The common European bloodsucker, *Hirudo medicinalis,* has been recorded a few times from the northeastern states, but is probably not well established.

**Collecting, preparing.** Usually specimens are collected individually with forceps by turning over rocks, logs, and debris in the shallows. A small dipnet should be carried to capture the rapid swimmers and to retrieve sluggish glossiphoniids as they roll up and fall to the bottom. Some collectors have had success by placing the body of a dead and bleeding small animal as bait in the water where there is a slight current.

If leeches are kept in aquariums, they must be provided with food, especially the Hirudinidae, which otherwise have a habit of crawling out and wandering about on the floor.

For close examination in the living state leeches should be narcotized. Carbonated water, chloretone, chloroform vapors, chloral hydrate, nicotine sulfate, and magnesium sulfate are all variously successful for different species. Specimens to be killed and preserved should receive similar treatment until they no longer respond to pinching. If carefully done, exceptionally good specimens may require one to five hours or more for narcotization. They are then placed in a flat dish and flooded with the killing agent, which may be any one of a variety of standard fixatives. Schaudinn's fluid, 0.5 percent chromic acid, and 2 percent formalin in 50 percent alcohol are all suitable. If an acid-containing fixative is used, care must be exercised to remove all acid after fixation; otherwise the connective tissues swell greatly. Permanent preservation should be in 80 percent alcohol or 5 percent formalin. Preserved leeches should be straight, moderately extended, undistorted, and not too hard or too soft.

Bennike (1943) advises narcotizing leeches in 15 percent alcohol for 15 minutes. Then they should be removed, stretched to normal size, and placed in 10 percent formalin or 70 percent alcohol. If they bend or contract, they have not been kept in the weak alcohol long enough. Zinn and Kneeland (1964) obtained best results with 1 percent eucaine hydrochloride.

**Laboratory cultures.** With the exception of the Piscicolidae, laboratory cultures can be easily maintained, especially since leeches need to be fed only infrequently. It is most important that the culture water be kept cool and clean. Although leeches are tolerant of a wide range of temperatures, they do not usually survive in the laboratory in direct sunlight or water that is too warm. A wide variety of common substances are toxic, even in minute quantities; copper and chlorine are especially harmful. Dead leeches, feces, and unused food material should always be removed promptly. Water should be changed as soon as it shows signs of becoming foul.

Small Glossiphoniidae may be kept in finger bowls or similar dishes of pond water containing a few shoots of *Anacharis* or other aquatic plants. Pieces of shell or pebbles afford additional concealment and protection. Small balanced aquariums also make excellent containers for leeches in the laboratory. Living snails should be added occasionally for food. Large bloodsucking glossiphoniids should be kept in larger containers and require a feeding of turtle, frog, or toad blood every month or two. Glossiphoniids thrive and readily reproduce under suitable conditions, but care should be taken to prevent overcrowding.

Erpobdellidae are very active, especially at night, and require large containers with tightly fitting covers or screens so that they will not crawl out. Stones and pieces of shell are a suitable substrate for the deposition of cocoons. Earthworms, immature insects, and ground fresh meat are appropriate foods for maintaining satisfactory cultures.

Hirudinidae may be kept in large, low aquariums or eathernware jars, but similar precautions must be taken against wandering. They do not require vegetation, but since they are somewhat amphibious there should be room for them to crawl up on the side of the container above the water level, and it is well to have a sloping bank of sandy soil at one end with a partial cover of moss, stones, or sticks. A vertebrate blood meal should be supplied at intervals of about six months, but the diet may be varied with frog eggs, immature insects, and earthworms. Cocoons are mostly deposited in wet soil just above the water's edge.

**Taxonomy.** Most of the United States has had only sporadic collecting, and much remains to be done. Extensive work has been accomplished only in the northeastern quarter of the country. Consequently, aside from those leeches that are undoubtedly generally distributed throughout much of the country, geographic distributions are necessarily uncertain.

External key characters are used wherever possible, but in a few couplets it has been necessary to use internal anatomical features that require dissection. Lengths are for average specimens when at rest. The 55 species listed in this key are believed to be essentially a complete list for the United States. Only a few poorly described, unrecognizable, and rare species are not included. The key is modified from Sawyer (1972) and Klemm (1972).

## KEY TO SPECIES OF HIRUDINEA

1. Mouth a small pore in the oral sucker through which a muscular proboscis can be protruded; jaws absent (Figs. 214, 215 G); blood colorless.
   Order **RHYNCHOBDELLIDA, 2**
   Mouth medium to large, without a proboscis (Figs. 215C–E); blood red . . . . . . . . . . .3
2. Body flat and much wider than head, never cylindrical (Figs. 214, 223); oral sucker ventral and more or less fused to body; eggs in membranous sacs on ventral surface of body; young clinging to ventral side of adult; poor swimmers.
   GLOSSIPHONIIDAE, 4
   Body clylindrical, often divided into a narrow anterior and a wide posterior region; oral sucker distinctly separated from body (Fig. 224); 6 to 30 mm long; almost invariably found as parasites on fishes; fish leeches . . . . . PISCICOLIDAE, 28
3. Five pairs of eyes forming a regular arch (Fig. 222B); jaws typically present and toothed, but may be toothless or absent; one to several pairs of large gastric caeca; medium to very large size.
   Order **GNATHOBDELLIDA,** HIRUDINIDAE, **36**
   Three or four pairs of eyes (rarely absent) never arranged in a regular arch (Fig. 222C); jaws absent; gastric caeca absent; body linear.
   Order **PHARYNGOBDELLIDA,** ERPOBDELLIDAE, **47**
4. With three or four pairs of eyes (Figs. 223G–J) . . . . . . . . . . . . . . . . . . . . . . . . . . . . .10
   With one or two pairs of eyes (except for *Placobdella hollensis,* which has accessory eyes) (Figs. 223B, L) . . . . . . . . . . . . . . . . . . . . . . . . . . . . . . . . . . . . . . . . . . . . .5
5. Mouth within anterior sucker cavity, not on rim . . . . . . . . . . . . . . . . . . . . . . . . . . . .9
   Mouth on rim of anterior sucker (Figs. 223M) . . . . . . . . . . . . . . . . . . . . . . . . . . . . .6
6. Caudal sucker with marginal papillae and glands, their positions marked by faint radiating ridges (Fig. 223F); uncommon in northeastern states; usually found on fish . . . . . . . . . . . . . . . . . . . . . . . . . . . . . . . . . . . . . . . . . . . . **Actinobdella, 11**
   Caudal sucker without marginal papillae and glands . . . . . . . . . . . . . . . . . . . . . . . . .7

FIG. 222.–Structure of Gnathobdellida and Pharyngobdellida. A, typical midbody segment of *Nephelopsis obscura,* showing subdivided annuli; B, anterior and posterior ends of *Macrobdella decora*; C, anterior end of *Dina parva*; D, dorsal view of part of reproductive system of *Mooreobdella parva*; E, dorsal view of part of reproductive system of *D. fervida*; F, ventral view of XII and XIII of *Philobdella gracilis,* showing copulatory gland region and genital pores; G, edge view of median jaw of *P. gracilis*; H, segments VII and VIII of *Haemopis marmorata*; J, edge view of teeth of median jaw of *H. terrestris*; K, ventral view of anterior end of *H. plumbea*; L, ventral view of anterior end of *H. grandis*; M, N, and O, arrangement of copulatory gland pores in *Macrobdella decora, M. sestertia,* and *M. ditetra,* respectively. gXI, eleventh ganglion; *ej,* ejaculatory duct; nerve tissue stippled. (B to D, K, and L modified from Moore, 1912; E to G, and J modified from Moore, 1901; M to O modified from Klemm.)

7. With one pair of separated eyes; 15 to 22 mm long; reported only from Michigan.
             **Marvinmeyeria lucida** (Moore)
  With one pair of fused eyes (Figs. 223K) or almost fused (Fig. 223L) . . . . . . . . . . . . .**8**
8. Body papillate or tuberculate . . . . . . . . . . . . . . . . . . . . . . . . . . . . . . . . . **Placobdella, 12**
  Body smooth, without conspicuous tubercles; translucent, pale green; parasitic on amphibians; North Carolina, South Carolina; rare.
             **Oligobdella biannulata** (Moore)
9. One or two pairs of eyes; if only one pair of eyes, they are fused or close together; parasitic on amphibians, occasionally on fish; seldom free-living; widely distributed but rare . . . . . . . . . . . . . . . . . . . . . . . . . . . . . . . . . **Batrachobdella, 18**
  One pair of eyes, well separated . . . . . . . . . . . . . . . . . . . . . . . . . . . . . . . **Helobdella, 20**
10. Three pairs of eyes (Figs. 223G, H) . . . . . . . . . . . . . . . . . . . . . . . . **Glossiphonia, 25**
  Four pairs of eyes (Fig. 223J); widely distributed but not common. **Theromyzon, 26**
11. Five rows of dorsal tubercles; three annuli per segment; parasitic on cold-blooded vertebrates; rare in northeastern states (may be a synonym of *A. inequiannulata* . . . . . . . . . . . . . . . . . . . . . . . . . . . .**Actinobdella triannulata** Moore
  One middorsal row of tubercles; six unequal annuli per segment; host unknown; rare in northeastern states . . . . . . . . . . . . . . . . . . . .**Actinobdella inequiannulata** Moore
12. Anterior segments forming a discoid "head" (Fig. 223B); body with three dorsal ridges; widely distributed but uncommon . . . . . . . **Placobdella montifera** Moore
  Without a separate discoid "head" . . . . . . . . . . . . . . . . . . . . . . . . . . . . . . . . . .**13**

13. Caudal sucker set off from the body by a peduncle (Fig. 223C); parasitic on fish; rare midwestern species.....................**Placobdella pediculata** Hemingway
Caudal sucker not set off from the body ....................................**14**

14. Accessory eyes present (Fig. 223E); main coloration olive-green with small brown, yellow, and colorless areas; usually free-living; rare in eastern half of the United States....................................**Placobdella hollensis** (Whitman)
Without accessory eyes.................................................**15**

15. With ventral stripes of blue, brown, or green; dorsal coloration variable, usually greenish-brown; dorsal tubercles inconspicuous or absent; 35 to 65 mm long; commonly found clinging to the legs of the common snapping turtle; widely distributed ................................. **Placobdella parasitica** (Say)
Without ventral stripes; dorsal tubercles prominent; smaller ...................**16**

16. Dorsal surface warty; papillae large, numerous, and randomly arranged; dorsal surface a mixture of brown, green, and yellow, with or without a median interrupted stripe; ventral surface unstriped; free-living or parasitic; widely distributed and common .....................................**Placobdella ornata** (Verrill)
Dorsal surface with more uniform tubercles and papillae ......................**17**

17. Dorsal surface uniformly brown with a darker brown median longitudinal stripe; ventral surface with about 30 dark lines; 40 to 55 mm long; widely distributed .............................. **Placobdella multilineata** Moore
Dorsal surface brownish but with five longitudinal rows of tubercles; ventral surface with two bluish longitudinal stripes; 15 to 45 mm long.
**Placobdella papillifera** (Verrill)

18. With white patches in eye, neck, genital, and anal areas; body translucent, with conspicuous middorsal and lateral segmental dots or papillae .............**19**
Without white patches in genital and anal areas; slight and variable patches sometimes in eye and neck areas; body smooth, opaque; parasitic on amphibians, especially in small ponds.......................... **Batrachobdella picta** Verrill

19. Body convex, thick; three longitudinal rows of papillae; uncommon, widely distributed ............................... **Batrachobdella phalera** (Graf)
Body very thin and flat; five longitudinal rows of papillae; Michigan.
**Batrachobdella michiganensis** Sawyer

20. With a brown chitinoid plate on the dorsal surface of VIII (Fig. 223A); brown, pink, or green color; 9 to 14 mm long; the most cosmopolitan of all American leeches ........................................ **Helobdella stagnalis** (L.)
Without a chitinoid plate .................................................**21**

21. Dorsal surface smooth .................................................**22**
Dorsal surface with three to seven longitudinal series of papillae ................**24**

22. Body translucent, elongate, and cylindrical; lateral margins almost parallel; feeds on aquatic insects; common east of the Continental Divide.
**Helobdella elongata** (Castle)
Body pigmented, flattened ...............................................**23**

23. Dorsal surface with transverse brown bands alternating with white bands; Michigan ............................... **Helobdella transversa** Sawyer
Dorsal surface with six major longitudinal white stripes alternating with brown stripes; widely distributed and common .....................**Helobdella fusca** Castle

24. Dorsal surface with three (incomplete) series of small, black-tipped papillae; a common, variable species..................... **Helobdella triserialis** (Blanchard)
Dorsal surface with five to seven longitudinal series of papillae; lightly pigmented; uncommon in northeastern states .............. **Helobdella papillata** (Moore)

25. Eyes arranged in a roughly triangular pattern of three groups of two each (Fig. 223G); body translucent, with little pigmentation; body 6 to 9 mm long.
**Glossiphonia heteroclita** (L.)
Eyes in two nearly parallel rows near the median line (Fig. 223H); body opaque, deeply pigmented; 14 to 25 mm long; very common.
**Glossiphonia complanata** (L.)

26. With two annuli between genital pores; olive-green to brown, translucent, flecked with black spots; 20 to 26 mm long ........**Theromyzon maculosum** (Rathke)
With three or four annuli between genital pores ...........................**27**

FIG. 223.–Structure of Rhynchobdellida. A, dorsal view of anterior end of *Helobdella stagnalis* also showing position of genital pores on ventral surface; B, dorsal view of anterior end of *Placobdella montifera*; C, ventral view of posterior end of *P. pediculata* (annulations not shown); D, lateral view of same; E, dorsal view of anterior end of *P. hollensis* (note transitions between well-developed pair of eyes and sensillae); F, caudal sucker of *Actinobdella inequiannulata*; G, eyes of *Glossiphonia heteroclita*; H, eyes of *G. complanata*; J, eyes of *Theromyzon*; K and L, anterior end of *Placobdella*, showing eyes fused and adjacent; M to O, ventral views of anterior suckers of Rhynchobdellida showing various locations of the porelike mouth. (A, C to E modified from Moore, 1912; B and F modified from Moore, 1901; K to O modified from Klemm.)

27. With three annuli between gonopores; color variable, with spots of yellow, orange, or brown; 20 to 30 mm long ........................ **Theromyzon rude** (Baird)
    With four annuli between gonopores; transparent amber or greenish color; 15 to 30 mm long ............................... **Theromyzon tessulatum** (O.F.M.)
28. Caudal sucker flattened, as wide or wider than the widest part of body; vesicles on margin of trunk; suckers distinctly set off from body (Figs. 224A–C, G, H). **29**
    Caudal sucker concave, weakly developed, and narrower than widest part of body; vesicles absent..................................................**34**
29. Vesicles small, difficult to see on preserved leeches; body not divided into anterior and posterior parts (Fig. 224C) ............................. **Piscicola, 30**
    Vesicles large, obvious after preservation; body divided into anterior and posterior parts (Figs. 224A, B); uncommon ...................... **Cystobranchus, 32**
30. With eyespots on caudal sucker (Figs. 224G, H)...............................**31**
    Without eyespots on caudal sucker (Fig. 224F); translucent greenish color; 14 to 16 mm long; east of the Rocky Mountains ........... **Piscicola punctata** (Verrill)
31. Crescent-shaped spots on caudal sucker (Fig. 224G); 10 to 31 mm long; Washington .................................... **Piscicola salmositica** Meyer
    Oculiform spots on caudal sucker (Fig. 224H); 16 to 24 mm long; northern states.
                                                                        **Piscicola milneri** (Verrill)
32. Segments in middle of body with six annuli, northeastern states.
                                                        **Cystobranchus vividus** Verrill
    Segments in middle of body with seven annuli ...............................**33**

33. Gonopores separated by two annuli; 10 to 30 mm long; northeastern states.
     **Cystobranchus verrilli** Meyer
     Gonopores separated by one or two annuli; 9 to 15 mm long; Virginia.
     **Cystobranchus virginicus** Hoffman
34. Body divided into narrow anterior region and wider posterior region (Fig. 224J); one
     pair of eyes; colorless or with scattered pigment cells; 24 to 26 mm long; widely
     distributed . . . . . . . . . . . . . . . . . . . . . . . . . . . . . . . .**Myzobdella lugubris** Leidy
     Body not divided into two regions . . . . . . . . . . . . . . . . . . . . . . . . . . . . . . . . .**35**
35. Body thin, without pigment; 9 to 30 mm long; scattered distribution; one variable
     species, may be identical with *Myzobdella lugubris*. **Illinobdella moorei** Meyer
     Body thicker; six longitudinal rows of brown-black pigments; 6 to 8 mm long; scattered
     distribution in eastern half of United States . . . . . . . **Piscicolaria reducta** Meyer
36. Copulatory glands behind gonopores on ventral surface (Figs. 222M–O).
     **Macrobdella, 37**
     Copulatory glands absent . . . . . . . . . . . . . . . . . . . . . . . . . . . . . . . . . . . . .**39**
37. With about 21 red or orange spots in middorsal line . . . . . . . . . . . . . . . . . . . . . . .**38**
     Without red spots in middorsal line; eight copulatory gland pores (Fig. 222O); 100 to
     150 mm long; widely distributed, uncommon . . . . . .**Macrobdella ditetra** Moore
38. With four copulatory gland pores (Fig. 222M); five annuli between gonopores; ventral
     surface red or orange; 110 to 150 mm long; the ''American medicinal leech'';
     feeds almost exclusively on vertebrate blood; widely distributed and
     common . . . . . . . . . . . . . . . . . . . . . . . . . . . . . . .**Macrobdella decora** (Say)
     With 24 copulatory gland pores (Fig. 222N); two and one-half annuli between gono-
     pores; ventral surface reddish-brown with a few black flecks; 50 to 100 mm
     long; rare in eastern states . . . . . . . . . . . . . . . . . **Macrobdella sestertia** Whitman
39. Dorsal surface with one or more colored stripes . . . . . . . . . . . . . . . . . . . . . . . . .**40**
     Dorsal surface without colored stripes . . . . . . . . . . . . . . . . . . . . . . . . . .**Haemopis, 44**
40. Dorsal surface with a single median stripe . . . . . . . . . . . . . . . . . . . . . . . . . . . .**41**
     Dorsal surface with longitudinal reddish-yellow stripes and color pattern; ventral
     surface black with white and gray markings; each jaw with about 50 small teeth
     (Fig. 216); up to 100 mm long; the introduced European medicinal leech; rare,
     probably not established. . . . . . . . . . . . . . . . . . . . . . . . . **Hirudo medicinalis** L.
41. Dorsal surface with a median black stripe . . . . . . . . . . . . . . . . . . . . . . . .**Haemopis, 42**
     Dorsal surface with a median stripe of another color . . . . . . . . . . . . . . .**Philobdella, 43**
42. Each jaw with 9 to 12 pairs of teeth; 60 to 110 mm long; uncommon; scattered
     distribution . . . . . . . . . . . . . . . . . . . . . . . . . . . . . . . . .**Haemopis kingi** (Mathers)
     Each jaw with 20 to 25 pairs of teeth (Fig. 222J); 150 to 200 mm long; one variety has
     been found as much as 1 km from water; feeds on aquatic invertebrates and
     earthworms; widely distributed and common . . . . **Haemopis terrestris** (Forbes)
43. Each jaw with 20 teeth; 40 to 85 mm long; known only from southern Florida.
     **Philobdella floridana** ( (Verrill)
     Each jaw with 35 to 50 teeth (Fig. 222G); 40 to 85 mm long; widely distributed east
     of the Continental Divide but uncommon . . . . . . . . **Philobdella gracilis** Moore
44. Jaws and teeth absent or vestigial; incapable of taking vertebrate blood; often found
     away from water . . . . . . . . . . . . . . . . . . . . . . . . . . . . . . . . . . . . . . . . . .**45**
     Jaws small, with few teeth . . . . . . . . . . . . . . . . . . . . . . . . . . . . . . . . . . . .**46**
45. Lip broad and flat (Fig. 222K); dorsal surface grayish, with few or no blotches;
     margins with reddish or orange band; 140 to 200 mm long.
     **Haemopis plumbea** (Moore)
     Lip narrow and arched (Fig. 222L); dorsal surface usually green, gray, or plain, but
     always more or less blotched with black; 150 to 300 mm long.
     **Haemopis grandis** (Verrill)
46. Each jaw with 10 or 14 pairs of teeth; caudal sucker about three-quarters of the body
     width; 50 to 85 mm long; known only from Iowa and Minnesota.
     **Haemopis lateromaculata** (Mathers)
     Each jaw with 10 to 16 pairs of teeth; caudal sucker about one-half of body width; 75
     to 100 mm long; often in mud at edge of water; the common ''horse leech'';
     occasionally attacks man . . . . . . . . . . . . . . . . . . . . **Haemopis marmorata** (Say)

FIG. 224.–Structure of Piscicolidae. A, *Cystobranchus verrilli*, ×10; B, *Cystobranchus vivida* ×4; C, *Piscicola punctata*, ×6.5; D to F, anterior, middle, and posterior portions of *P. punctata*; G, posterior end of *P. salmositica*; H, posterior end of *P. milneri*; J, *Myzobdella lugubris*, ×6.5; K, *Illinobdella moorei*, ×8. (A, C, J, and K modified from Meyer, 1940; D to F, and H modified from Meyer, 1946; B modified from Moore, 1899; G modified from Meyer, 1946a.)

47. Segments mostly composed of five annuli; dorsal surface with two or four longitudinal stripes, but some forms are barred with black or lightly pigmented; three pairs of eyes . . . . . . . . . . . . . . . . . . . . . . . . . . . . . . . . . . . . . . . . . . . . . . . . .**Erpobdella, 49**
    Segments mostly composed of six or seven annuli; three or four pairs of eyes . . . .**48**
48. With four eyes arranged in an anterior horizontal linear fashion, and the posterior four eyes similarly arranged in a horizontal line; feeds on aquatic invertebrates, also a scavenger; up to 100 mm long; widely distributed. **Nephelopsis obscura** Verrill
    With six or eight eyes arranged in a different manner . . . . . . . . . . . . . . . . . . . . . . . .**50**

49. With two annuli between gonopores; common and widely distributed; feeds on aquatic invertebrates, fish, and frogs; sometimes a scavenger; occasionally attacks man; 80 to 100 mm long ...................... **Erpobdella punctata** (Leidy)
    With three annuli between gonopores; 25 to 30 mm long; rare and widely distributed ............................... **Erpobdella triannulata** Moore
50. With three pairs of eyes ................................................**51**
    With four pairs of eyes (Fig. 222C); 25 to 50 mm long; widely distributed but uncommon .................................................. **Dina, 54**
51. Gonopores separated by two annuli ....................................**52**
    Gonopores separated by two and one-half to four annuli .....................**53**
52. Atrium globular, with prominent horns projecting anteriorly (Fig. 222E); 25 to 50 mm long; common and widely distributed.......... **Mooreobdella fervida** (Verrill)
    Atrium globular, but with horns projecting laterally; reported only from Michigan.
    **Mooreobdella bucera** (Moore)
53. Gonopores separated by three annuli; no rows of black spots on dorsal surface; 30 to 50 mm long; common and widely distributed. **Mooreobdella microstoma** (Moore)
    Gonopores separated by three and one-half annuli; two longitudinal rows of black spots on the dorsal surface; 25 to 50 mm long; common and widely distributed ........................................ **Dina lateralis** (Verrill)
54. With few dark spots or no pigmentation ..................... **Dina parva** Moore
    With dark brown or blackish median dorsal stripe obvious in anterior half, fading posteriorly ................................. **Dina dubia** Moore and Meyer

# ANNELIDA REFERENCES

ALSTERBERG, G. 1922. Die respiratorischen Mechanismen der Tubificiden. *Lunds Univ. Årsskr., N. F. Avd 2* **18**:1–176.

ALTMAN, L. C. 1936. Oligochaeta of Washington. *Univ. Wash. Publ. Biol.* **4**:41–137.

APPLEBY, A. G., and R. O. BRINKHURST. 1970. Defecation rates of three tubificid oligochaetes found in the sediment of Toronto Harbour, Ontario. *J. Fish. Res. Board of Can.* **27**:1971–1982.

ASTON, R. J. 1968. The effect of temperature on the life cycle, growth and fecundity of Branchiura sowerbyi (Oligochaeta: Tubificidae). *J. Zool. Lond.* **154**:29–40.

———. 1973. Tubificids and water quality; a review. *Environ. Pollut.* **5**:1–10.

BECKER, C. D., and M. KATZ. 1965. Distribution, ecology, and biology of the salmonid leech, Piscicola salmositica (Rhynchobdellae: Piscicolidae). *J. Fish. Res. Board of Can.* **22**:1175–1195.

BEDDARD, E. F. 1892. A new branchiate oligochaeta (Branchiura sowerbyi). *Q. J. Microsc. Sci.* **33**:325–340.

———. 1895. *A monograph of the Order Oligochaeta.* 769 pp. Oxford, England.

BOLDT, W. 1940. Oligochaeta. *Biol. Tiere Deutschl.* **12a**:1–39.

BOUSFIELD, E. C. 1887. The natural history of the genus Dero. *J. Linn. Soc. (Zool.)* **20**:91–107.

BRINKHURST, R. O. 1963. A guide for the identification of British aquatic Oligochaeta. *Sci. Publ. Freshwater Biol. Assoc.* **22**:1–52.

———. 1964. Studies on the North American aquatic Oligochaeta. I. Naididae and Opistocystidae. *Proc. Acad. Nat. Sci. Phila.* **116**:195–230.

———. 1966. The Tubificidae (Oligochaeta) of polluted waters. *Proc. Int. Assoc. Theor. Appl. Limnol.* **16**:854–859.

———. 1970. Distribution and abundance of tubificid (Oligochaeta) species in Toronto harbour, Lake Ontario. *J. Fish. Res. Board of Can.* **27**:1961–1969.

BRINKHURST, R. O., and B. G. M. JAMIESON. 1971. *Aquatic Oligochaeta of the World.* 860 pp. Univ. Toronto Press, Toronto.

BRINKHURST, R. O., et al. 1972. Interspecific interactions and selective feeding by tubificid oligochaetes. *Limnol. Oceanogr.* **17**:122–133.

BUNKE, D. 1967. Zur Morphologie und Systematik der Aeolosomatidae Beddard 1895 und Potamodrilidae nov. fam. (Oligochaeta). *Zool. Jahrb. Abt. Syst. Oekol. Geogr. Tiere* **94**:187–368.

CASTLE, W. E. 1900. Some North American freshwater Rhynchobdellidae, and their parasites. *Bull. Harvard Mus. Comp. Zool.* **36**:15–64.

CHEN, Y. 1940. Taxonomy and faunal relations of the limnetic Oligochaeta of China. *Contr. Biol. Lab. Sci. Soc. China, Zool. Ser.* **14**:1–132.

———. 1944. Notes on naidomorph Oligochaeta of Philadelphia and vicinity. *Not. Nat.* **136**:1–8.

COOK, D. G. 1975. Cave-dwelling aquatic Oligochaeta (Annelida) from the Eastern Unites States. *Trans. Am. Microsc. Soc.* **94**:24–37.

DAUSEND, K. 1931. Über die Atmung der Tubificiden. *Z. vgl. Physiol.* **14**:557–608.

DAVIES, R. W. 1971. A key to the freshwater Hirudinoidea of Canada. *J. Fish. Res. Board of Can.* **28**:543–552.

DAVIES, R. W., and R. P. EVERETT. 1975. The

feeding of four species of freshwater Hirudinoidea in southern Alberta. *Proc. Int. Assoc. Theor. Appl. Limnol.* **19**:2816–2827.

DELACHAUX, T. 1921. Un Polychète d'eau douce cavernicole. Troglochaetus beranecki nov. gen. nov. spec. (Note Prél.). *Bull. Soc. Sci. Nat. Neuchatel* **45**:3–11.

EISEN, G. 1885. Oligochaetological researches. *Rept. U.S. Fish. Comm. for 1883* **11**:879–964.

ELLIS, M. M. 1912. A new discodrilid worm from Colorado. *Proc. U.S. Nat. Mus.* **42**:481–486.

———. 1919. The branchiobdellid worms in the collections of the United States National Museum, with descriptions of new genera and new species. Ibid. **55**:241–265.

FOSTER, N. 1972. Freshwater polychaetes (Annelida) of North America. *Biota of Freshwater Ecosystems Identification Manual* **4**:1–15.

FOWLER, D. J., and C. J. GOODNIGHT. 1965. The effect of environmental factors on the respiration of Tubifex. *Am. Midl. Nat.* **74**:418–428.

GALLOWAY, T. W. 1911. The common fresh-water Oligochaeta of the U.S. *Trans. Am. Microsc. Soc.* **30**:285–317.

GOODNIGHT, C. J. 1940. The Branchiobdellidae (Oligochaeta) of North American crayfishes. *Ill. Biol. Monogr.* **17**:1–75.

———. 1941. The Branchiobdellidae (Oligochaeta) of Florida. *Trans. Am. Microsc. Soc.* **60**:69–74.

———. 1943. Report on a collection of Branchiobdellidae. *J. Parasitol.* **29**:100–102.

GREENE, K. L. 1974. Experiments and observations on the feeding behavior of the freshwater leech Erpobdella octoculata (L.) (Hirudinea: Erpobdellidae). *Arch. Hydrobiol.* **74**:87–99.

GRUFFYDD, LL. D. 1965. Notes on a population of the leech, Glossiphonia heteroclita, infesting Lymnaea periger. *Ann. Mag. Nat. Hist.* **8**:144–150.

HALL, M. C. 1914. Description of a new genus and species of the discodrilid worms. *Proc. U.S. Nat. Mus.* **48**:187–193.

HARDING, W. A., and J. P. MOORE. 1927. Hirudinea. *Fauna Br. India.* 302 pp.

HARTMAN, O. 1936. New species of polychaetous annelids of the family Nereidae from California. *Proc. U.S. Nat. Mus.* **83**:467–480.

———. 1938. Brackish and freshwater Nereidae from the northeast Pacific with the description of a new species from central California. *Univ. Calif. Publ. Zool.* **43**:79–82.

———. 1959. Capitellidae and Nereidae (marine annelids) from the Gulf side of Florida, with a review of freshwater Nereidae. *Bull. Mar. Sci. Gulf Carib.* **9**:153–168.

HERLANT-MEEWIS, H. 1950. Cyst-formation in Aeolosoma hemprichi (Ehr.). *Biol. Bull.* **99**:172–180.

HERRMANN, S. J. 1970. Systematics, distribution, and ecology of Colorado Hirudinea. *Am. Midl. Nat.* **83**:1–37.

HERTER, K. 1932. Hirudinea. *Biol. Tiere Deutschl.* **12b**:1–158.

———. 1968. *Der Medizinische Blutegel und seine Verwandten.* 199 pp. Ziemsen Verlag, Wittenberg, East Germany.

HILTUNEN, J. K. 1967. Some oligochaetes from Lake Michigan. *Trans. Am. Microsc. Soc.* **86**:433–453.

HOBBS, H. H., et al. 1967. The crayfishes and their epizootic ostracod and branchiobdellid associates of the Mountain Lake, Virginia, Region. *Proc. U.S. Nat. Mus.* **123**:1–84.

HOFFMAN, R. L. 1963. A revision of the North American annelid worms of the genus Cambarincola (Oligochaeta: Branchiobdellidae). *Proc. U.S. Nat. Mus.* **114** (3470):271–371.

HOLMQUIST, C. 1973. Fresh-water polychaete worms of Alaska with notes on the anatomy of Manayunkia speciosa Leidy. *Zool. Jahrb. Syst.* **100**:497–516.

HOLT, P. C. 1953. Characters of systematic importance in the Family Branchiobdellidae (Oligochaeta). *Va. J. Sci.* **4**:57–61.

———. 1960. On a new genus of the Family Branchiobdellidae (Oligochaeta). *Am. Midl. Nat.* **64**:169–176.

———. 1960a. The genus Ceratodrilus Hall (Branchiobdellidae, Oligochaeta) with the description of a new species. *Va. J. Sci.* **11**:53–77.

———. 1965. On Ankyrodrilus, a new genus of branchiobdellid worms (Annelida). Ibid. **16**:9–21.

———. 1967. Oedipodrilus oedipus, n. g., n. sp. (Annelida, Clitellata: Branchiobdellida). *Trans. Am. Microsc. Soc.* **86**:58–60.

———. 1967a. Status of genera Branchiobdella and Stephanodrilus in North America with description of a new genus (Clitellata: Branchiobdellida). *Proc. U.S. Nat. Mus.* **124**:1–10.

———. 1968. The Branchiobdellida: epizootic annelids. *The Biologist* **50**:79–94.

———. 1968a. New genera and species of branchiobdellid worms (Annelida: Clittellata). *Proc. Biol. Soc. Wash.* **81**:291–318.

———. 1968b. The genus Pterodrilus (Annelida: Branchiobdellida). *Proc. U.S. Nat. Mus.* **125**:1–44.

———. 1969. The relationships of the branchiobdellid fauna of the Southern Appalachians. *Va. Polytech. Inst. Res. Div. Monogr.* **1**:191–219.

———. 1973. Branchiobdellids (Annelida: Clitellata) from some eastern North American caves, with descriptions of new species of the genus Cambarincola. *Int. J. Speleol.* **5**:219–256.

———. 1973a. Epigean branchiobdellids (Annelida: Clitellata) from Florida. *Proc. Biol. Soc. Wash.* **86**:79–104.

———. 1974. An emendation of the genus Triannulata Goodnight, 1940, with the assignment of Triannulata montana to Cambarincola Ellis 1912 (Clitellata: Branchiobdellida). Ibid. **87**:57–72.

———. 1974a. The genus Xironogiton Ellis, 1919 (Clitellata: Branchiobdellida). *Va. J. Sci.* **25**:5–19.

HOTZ, H. 1938. Protoclepsis tesselata (O. F. Müller); ein Beitrag zur Kenntnis von Bau und Lebensweise der Hirudineen. *Rev. Suisse Zool.* (Suppl.) **45**:1–380.

JENNINGS, J. B., and V. M. VAN DER LANDE. 1967. Histochemical and bacteriological studies on digestion in nine species of leeches (Annelida: Hirudinea). *Biol. Bull.* **133**:166–183.

KALBE, L. 1966. Zur Ökologie und saprobiewertung der Hirudineen im Habelgebiet. *Int. Rev. ges. Hydrobiol.* **51**:243–277.

KENK, R. 1941. Notes on three species of Aeolosoma (Oligochaeta) from Michigan. *Occas. Pap. Mus. Zool. Univ. Mich.* **435**:1–7.

KENNEDY, C. R. 1966. The life history of Limnodrilus hoffmeisteri Clap. (Oligochaeta: Tubificidae) and its adaptive significance. *Oikos* **17**:158–168.

KEYL, F. 1913. Beiträge zur Kenntnis von Branchiura sowerbyi Bedd. *Z. wiss. Zool.* **107**:199–304.

KLEMM, D. J. 1972. Freshwater leeches (Annelida: Hirudinea) of North America. *Biota of Freshwater Ecosystems Identification Manual* **5**:1–53.

KOSIOREK, D. 1974. Development cycle of Tubifex tubifex Müll. in experimental culture. *Pol. Arch. Hydrobiol.* **21**:411–422.

LASTOCHKIN, D. A. 1935. Two new river Aeolosomatidae (Oligochaeta limicola). *Ann. Mag. Nat. Hist.* **15**:636–645.

LEIDY, J. 1883. Manayunkia speciosa. *Proc. Phila. Acad. Nat. Sci.* (1883):204–212.

MANN, K. H. 1955. The ecology of the British freshwater leeches. *J. Anim. Ecol.* **24**:98–119.

———. 1962. Leeches (Hirudinea). Their structure, physiology, ecology and embryology. 201 pp. Pergamon, New York.

———. 1964. A key to the British freshwater leeches with notes on their ecology. *Sci. Publ. Freshwater Biol. Assoc.* **14**:1–50.

MARCUS, E. 1942. Sôbre algumas Tubificidae do Brasil. *Univ. Sao Paulo, Bol. Fac. Filos. Cien. Lett. Zool.* **6**:153–228.

———. 1943. Sôbre Naididae do Brasil. Ibid. **7**:1–247.

———. 1944. Sôbre Oligochaeta limnicos do Brasil. Ibid. **8**:5–135.

MEYER, F. P. 1969. A potential control of leeches. *Prog. Fish-Cult.* **31**:160–163.

MEYER, M. C. 1940. A revision of the leeches (Piscicolidae) living on fresh-water fishes of North America. *Trans. Am. Microsc. Soc.* **59**:354–376.

———. 1946. Further notes on the leeches (Piscicolidae) living on fresh-water fishes of North America. Ibid. **65**:237–249.

———. 1946a. A new leech, Piscicola salmositica n. sp. (Piscicolidae), from steelhead trout (Salmo gairdneri gairdneri Richardson, 1838). *J. Parasitol.* **32**:467–473.

MILLER, J. A. 1929. The leeches of Ohio. *Contrib. Franz Theodore Stone Lab.* **2**:1–38.

———. 1937. A study of the leeches of Michigan with key to orders, suborders and species. *Ohio J. Sci.* **37**:85–90.

MOORE, J. P. 1895. The anatomy of Bdellodrilus illuminatus, an American discodrilid. *J. Morphol.* **10**:497–540.

———. 1898. The leeches of the U.S. National Museum. *Proc. U.S. Nat. Mus.* **21**:543–563.

———. 1898a. The Hirudinea of Illinois. *Bull. Ill. State Lab. Nat. Hist.* **5**:479–547.

———. 1923. The control of blood-sucking leeches, with an account of the leeches of Palisades Interstate Park. *Roosevelt Wild Life Bull.* **2**:1–53.

———. 1924. The leeches (Hirudinea) of Lake Nipigon. *Univ. Toronto Studies, Biol. Ser.* **25**:15–31.

———. 1951. Leeches (Hirudinea) from Alaskan and adjacent waters. *Wasmann J. Biol.* **9**:11–77.

NACHTREIB, H. F., E. E. HEMINGWAY, and J. P. MOORE. 1912. The leeches of Minnesota. *Geol. Nat. Hist. Surv. Minn. Zool. Ser.* **5**:1–150.

PENNAK, R. W. 1971. A fresh-water archiannelid from the Colorado Rocky Mountains. *Trans. Am. Microsc. Soc.* **90**:372–375.

POE, T. P., and D. C. STEFAN. 1974. Several environmental factors influencing the distribution of the fresh-water polychaeta, Manayunkia speciosa Leidy. *Chesapeake Sci.* **12**:235–237.

REYNOLDSON, T. B. 1947. An ecological study of the enchytraeid worm population of sewage bacteria beds. *J. Anim. Ecol.* **16**:26–37.

RUPP, R. W., and M. C. MEYER. 1954. Mortality among brook trout, Salvelinus fontinalis, resulting from attacks of freshwater leeches. *Copeia* (1954):294–295.

SAPKAREV, J. A. 1967–1968. The taxonomy and ecology of leeches (Hirudinea) of Lake Mendota, Wisconsin. *Trans. Wis. Acad.* **56**:225–253.

SAWYER, R. T. 1970. Observations on the natural history and behavior of Herpobdella punctata (Leidy) (Annelida: Hirudinea). *Am. Midl. Nat.* **83**:65–80.

———. 1970. North American freshwater leeches, exclusive of the Piscicolidae, with a key to all species. *Ill. Biol. Monogr.* **46**:1–154.

RICHARDSON, L. R. 1969. A contribution to the systematics of the hirudinid leeches, with description of new families, genera and species. *Acta Zool. Acad. Sci. Hung.* **15**:97–149.

SMITH, R. I. 1942. Nervous control of chromatophores in the leech Placobdella parasitica. *Physiol. Zool.* **15**:410–417.

———. 1959. The synonymy of the viviparous polychaete Neanthes lighti Hartman (1938) with Nereis limnicola Johnson (1903). *Pac. Sci.* **13**:349–350.

SOOS, A. 1963. Identification key to the species of the genus Dina R. Blanchard, 1892 (emend. Mann, 1962) (Hirudinea: Erpobdellidae). *Acta Univ. Szeged. Acta Biol.* **9**:253–261.

———. 1965. Identification key to the leech (Hirudinoidea) genera of the world, with a catalogue of the species. I. Family: Piscicolidae. *Acta Zool. Acad. Sci. Hung.* **11**:417–463.

———. 1966. On the genus Glossiphonia Johnson, 1816, with a key and catalogue to the species. *Ann. Hist.-Nat. Mus. Nat. Hung. Zool.* **58**:271–279.

———. 1966a. Identification key to the leech (Hirudinoidea) genera of the world, with a catalogue of the species. III. Family: Erpobdellidae. *Acta Zool. Acad. Sci. Hung.* **12**:371–407.

———. 1967. On the genus Batracobdella Viguier, 1879, with a key and catalogue to the species. *Ann. Hist.-Nat. Mus. Nat. Hung. Zool.* **59**:243–257.

———. 1969. Identification key to the leech (Hirudinoidea) genera of the world, with a catalog of the species: V. Family: Hirudinidae. *Acta Zool. Acad. Sci. Hung.* **15**:151–201.

SPENCER, D. R. 1976. Occurrence of Manayunkia speciosa (Polychaeta: Sabellidae) in Cayuga Lake, New York, with additional notes on its North American distribution. *Trans. Am. Microsc. Soc.* **95**:127–128.

SPENCER, W. P. 1932. A gilled oligochaete Branchiura sowerbyi new to America. *Trans. Am. Microsc. Soc.* **51**:267–272.

SPERBER, C. 1948. A taxonomical study of the Naididae. *Zool. Bidrag f. Uppsala* **28**:1–296.

STEPHENSON, J. 1923. Oligochaeta. *Fauna Br. India,* 518 pp.

———. 1930. *The Oligochaeta.* 978 pp. Oxford, England.

STIMPSON, K. S., et al. 1975. Distribution and abundance of inshore oligochaetes in Lake Michigan. *Trans. Am. Microsc. Soc.* **94**:384–394.

VON WAGNER, P. 1916. Zur Oecologie des Tubifex und Lumbriculus. *Zool. Jahrb. Abt. Syst.* **23**:295–318.

WALKER, J. G. 1970. Oxygen poisoning in the annelid Tubifex tubifex. I. Response to oxygen exposure. *Biol. Bull.* **138**:235–244.

WALTON, L. B. 1906. The Naididae of Cedar Point, Ohio. *Am. Nat.* **40**:683–706.

WAVRE, M., and R. O. BRINKHURST. 1971. Interactions between some tubificid oligochaetes and bacteria found in the sediments of Toronto Harbour, Ontario. *J. Fish. Res. Board of Can.* **28**:335–341.

WILKIALIS, J. 1964. On the ecology and biology of the leech Glossiphonia heteroclita f. hyalina (O. F. Müll.). *Ekol. Polska—Ser. A,* **12**:315–323.

———. 1970. Investigations on the biology of leeches of the Glossiphoniidae Family. *Zool. Pol.* **20**:29–54.

YOUNG, W. 1966. Ecological studies of the Branchiobdellida (Oligochaeta). *Ecology* **47**:571–577.

ZINN, D. J., and I. R. KNEELAND. 1964. Narcotization and fixation of leeches (Hirudinea). *Trans. Am. Microsc. Soc.* **83**:275–276.

# Chapter 14

# INTRODUCTION TO THE CRUSTACEA

FOUR obvious features clearly distinguish the members of the Class Crustacea: With few exceptions, they are all aquatic arthropods; respiration occurs through gills or through the general body surface; they all have two pairs of antennae; most of the body segments, or at least the more anterior ones, bear paired, jointed appendages that are fundamentally biramous.

The great majority of the 35,000 known species of the world are marine, and of the 26 orders occurring in the United States and surrounding waters, 13 are represented in fresh waters, but only 5 are restricted to our fresh waters. The number of species represented for each of the 13 orders in the United States ranges from one (Thermosbaenacea) to about 330 (Decapoda), the total number being about 1130. Eleven orders are treated in detail in Chapters 15 to 22, so the present chapter is merely a summary and tabulation of their chief distinguishing characteristics and affinities.

Table III shows the environmental affinities of major groups of Crustacea in the area of the continental United States. On a worldwide basis, however, some of these entries are not strictly true because of exceptional rarities. For example, several species of Cumacea are known from freshwater habitats in Kerala; and several freshwater species of Tanaidacea have been found in South America and the Kurile Islands.

A few carcinologists distinguish fine gradations in meaning in the usage of "somite," "metamere," and "body segment" to denote the primary body divisions of adult Crustacea. Nevertheless, these expressions are more generally used interchangeably and without confusion; in this manual "body segment," "trunk segment," or simply "segment" are used consistently.

In the primitive condition the trunk segments are distinct, but the segments forming the head are completely fused. The trunk is usually subdivided into thorax and abdomen so that there are three body regions, though fusion of some thoracic and abdominal segments is the common condition. One or more thoracic segments, for example, are often fused with the head to form a cephalothorax, which in many crustaceans is completely or partly covered by a shieldlike carapace. In groups such as the Cladocera and Ostracoda body segmentation has disappeared. The general body plan of the various orders is outlined in Table IV.

In the strict sense, the most posterior division of the body, which bears the anus, is not considered a true body segment and is usually referred to as the telson. This term is universally used in the orders of Malacostraca, where this structure is comparatively small and flattened and does not bear any processes. In the other orders, however, the telson typically resembles the preceding body segment; furthermore, it bears a pair of terminal caudal rami, cercopods, or heavy claws. In common usage it is often referred to as a "segment" in the nonmalacostracan orders. The writer can see no real objection to this practice.

The paired appendages are serially homologous; each is fundamentally biramous and consists of a basal protopod, a segmented endopod, and a segmented exopod. They are usually more or less specialized for a widy variety of functions, many such modifications being figured and considered rather completely in Chapters 15 to 22.

TABLE III. FUNDAMENTAL ENVIRONMENTAL AFFINITIES OF THE GROUPS OF CRUSTACEA FOUND IN THE UNITED STATES AND SURROUNDING WATERS

| Restricted to marine waters | Chiefly marine; few fresh-water representatives | Well represented in both marine and fresh waters | Chiefly in fresh waters; few marine representatives | Exclusively fresh water | Approximate number of species occurring in U.S. fresh waters |
|---|---|---|---|---|---|
| Myodocopa | Mysidacea | | | | 3 |
| Cladocopa | | | | | |
| Platycopa | | | | | |
| Thoracica | | Podocopa | | | 200 |
| Ascothoracica | | Eucopepoda | | | 180 |
| Acrothoracica | | Branchiura | | | 15 |
| Rhizocephala | | Isopoda | | | 100 |
| Nebaliacea | | Amphipoda | | | 100 |
| Cumacea | | Decapoda | | | 330 |
| Tanaidacea | | | | | |
| Euphausiacea | | | Cladocera | | 135 |
| Stomatopoda | | | | Anostraca | 32 |
| Mystacocarida | | | | Notostraca | 6 |
| | | | | Conchostraca | 28 |
| | | | | Thermosbaenacea | 1 |
| | | | | Bathynellacea | ? |

Because of variations in early embryology from one order to another and because of the variety of interpretations that may be drawn from such embryological material, the "head problem" of arthropods is still unsettled. Some investigators maintain that the adult crustacean head represents the fusion of five segments or four segments plus a large anterior cephalic lobe (Snodgrass, 1951); others hold to an older theory that the head represents six fused segments. Henry (1948) maintains that the older theory is the more acceptable and that none of the six segments forming the head are "preoral." Aside from this controversy, the typical adult crustacean head bears five pairs of serially homologous appendages. Beginning at the anterior end, these are first antennae, second antennae, mandibles, first maxillae, and second maxillae. Compound eyes are not considered true segmental appendages. In the Cladocera and Ostracoda the second maxillae are lacking. More posteriorly the situation is variable, with some groups having an additional complement of thoracic or body appendages modified as mouthparts, and others not. Further, the number of thoracic and abdominal appendages and their modifications vary widely from one group to another, even within single genera.

The Crustacea may be conveniently divided into two groups, Entomostraca and Malacostraca. The latter group is a clearly defined and natural section of the Crustacea, all of its members having abdominal appendages, a gastric mill, an eight-segmented thorax, and an abdomen of six (rarely seven or eight) segments. The Entomostraca, however, is a heterogeneous assemblage of orders that differ from one another as widely as each of them does from the Malacostraca, and for this reason the use of "Entomostraca" as a specific taxonomic category should be discouraged. Nevertheless, "entomostraca" is a convenient general descriptive term that might be legitimately used to designate collectively all small fresh-water Crustacea. It is interesting, however, to note that hemoglobin has been reported from all entomostracan orders, but is unknown in the Malacostraca.

Carcinologists differ in their ideas about systematic arrangement and hierarchical terminology for the many major taxa of Crustacea. From the student's standpoint it is often a disturbing melange of groups, divisions, superorders, and suborders. We are avoiding a discussion of this whole problem and are restricting our systematic array to the plan shown in Table

TABLE IV.  GROSS MORPHOLOGICAL FEATURES OF THE ORDERS OF FRESH-WATER CRUSTACEA OF THE UNITED STATES

| Order | Main body features | Length range, in mm | Number of thoracic segments fused with head to form cephalothorax | Number of free thoracic segments | Number of abdominal segments | Number of pairs of thoracic appendages | | Number of pairs of abdominal appendages | Common terminology for posterior end |
|---|---|---|---|---|---|---|---|---|---|
| | | | | | | modified for use as mouth parts | not used as mouth parts | | |
| Anostraca | Head and trunk; body cylindrical | 7–100 | 0 | 19 trunk segments | | 0 | 11 pairs of trunk appendages | 0 | telson and caudal rami |
| Notostraca | Head and trunk; shieldlike carapace covering most of body; depressed dorsoventrally | 10–58 | 0 | 25 to 44 trunk segments | | 0 | 35 to 71 pairs of trunk appendages | 0 | telson and caudal rami |
| Conchostraca | Head and trunk; body enclosed in a bivalve carapace; laterally compressed | 2–16 | 0 | 10 to 32 trunk segments | | 0 | 10 to 32 pairs of trunk appendages | 0 | telson and caudal rami |
| Cladocera | Head, trunk, and postabdomen; segmentation obscure; body laterally compressed and covered with a folded carapace | 0.2–18.0 | – | – | – | 0 | 5 or 6 | 0 | postabdomen and claws |
| Podocopa | Head indistinctly set off from trunk; segmentation obscure; body laterally compressed and covered with a bivalve shell | 0.3–4.2 | – | – | – | – | 3 | 0 | caudal rami |
| Eucopepoda | Cephalothorax, thorax, and abdomen; body cylindrical | 0.3–3.2 | 1 or 2 | usually 5 | 3 to 5 | 1 | 5 | 0 | caudal rami |

| | Body regions | Size (mm) | | | | | | | Terminal structure |
|---|---|---|---|---|---|---|---|---|---|
| Branchiura | Cephalothorax, thorax, and abdomen; large, expanded cephalothoracic carapace; body strongly depressed; parasitic | 5–25 | 1 or 2 | 3 (4th and 5th fused with abdomen) | fused | 1 | 4 | 0 | caudal rami |
| Mysidacea | Cephalothorax, thorax, and abdomen; carapace covering cephalothorax and most of thorax; body slightly compressed laterally | 10–30 | 1 | 7 | 6 | 2 | 6 | 6 | telson |
| Isopoda | Cephalothorax, thorax, and abdomen; body depressed | 5–20 | 1 | 7 | 6 (usually fused) | 1 | 7 | 6 | telson (obscure) |
| Amphipoda | Cephalothorax, thorax, and abdomen; body slightly compressed laterally | 5–25 | 1 | 7 | 6 | 1 | 7 | 6 | telson |
| Decapoda | Cephalothorax and abdomen; carapace covering all of cephalothorax; body subcylindrical | 15–130 | 8 | 0 | 6 | 3 | 5 | 6 | telson |
| Thermosbaenacea (*Monodella*) | Cephalothorax, thorax, and abdomen; body cylindrical | 1–3.5 | 1–2 | 6–7 | 6 | 1 | 7 | 3 | telson may or may not be fused with last abdominal segment |
| Bathynellacea | Head, thorax, and abdomen | 0.5–2.0 | 0 | 8 | 6 | 0 | 8 | 1–3 | telson and caudal rami |

TABLE V. ARRANGEMENT AND TERMINOLOGY OF

| Body region | Eubranchiopoda | Cladocera | Copepoda | Ostracoda | Mysidacea |
|---|---|---|---|---|---|
| Head | 1st antennae<br>2d "<br>mandibles<br>1st maxillae<br>2d " | 1st antennae<br>2d "<br>mandibles<br>maxillae<br>– | 1st antennae<br>2d "<br>mandibles<br>1st maxillae<br>2d " | 1st antennae<br>2d "<br>mandibles<br>maxillae<br>– | 1st antennae<br>2d "<br>mandibles<br>1st maxillae<br>2d " |
| 1 | | 1st legs | maxillipeds† | 1st legs | 1st maxillipeds |
| 2 | | 2d " | 1st legs | 2d " | 2d " |
| 3 | | 3d " | 2d " | 3d " | 1st legs |
| 4 | | 4th " | 3d " | | 2d " |
| 5 | | 5th "* | 4th " | | 3d " |
| 6 | | 6th " | 5th " | | 4th " |
| 7 | 10 to 71 pairs of | – | – | | 5th " |
| 8 | appendages on 10 to<br>44 trunk segments | – | – | | 6th " |
| 9 | | – | – | | 1st pieopods |
| 10 | | | – | | 2d " |
| 11 | | | | | 3d " |
| 12 | | | | | 4th " |
| 13 | | | | | 5th " |
| 14 | | | | | uropods |

(Body region: "Trunk segments" labels rows 1–14)

* These appendages are present only in three small families of Cladocera.
† Some copepod specialists consider the maxillipeds as head appendages.

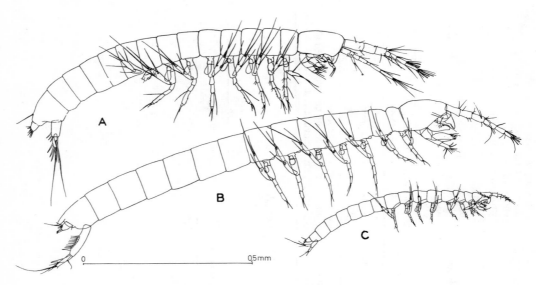

FIG. 225.–Typical Bathynellacea. A, *Bathynella*; B, *Parabathynella*; C, *Leptobathynella*. (From Noodt, 1964.)

SEGMENTAL APPENDAGES OF TYPICAL FRESH-WATER CRUSTACEA

| Isopoda | Amphipoda | Decapoda | Thermosbaenacea | Bathynellacea |
|---|---|---|---|---|
| 1st antennae | 1st antennae | 1st antennae | 1st antennae | 1st antennae |
| 2d " | 2d " | 2d " | 2nd " | 2nd " |
| mandibles | mandibles | mandibles | mandibles | mandibles |
| 1st maxillae | 1st maxillae | 1st maxillae | 1st maxillae | 1st maxillae |
| 2d " | 2d " | 2d " | 2nd " | 2nd " |
| maxillipeds | maxillipeds | 1st maxillipeds | maxillipeds | 1st legs (pereiopods) |
| 1st legs (gnathopods) | 1st legs (gnathopods) | 2d " | 1st legs (pereiopods) | 2nd " " |
| 2d " (pereiopods) | 2d " " | 3d " | 2nd " " | 3rd " " |
| 3d " " | 3d " (pereiopods) | 1st legs (pereiopods) | 3rd " " | 4th " " |
| 4th " " | 4th " " | 2d " " | 4th " " | 5th " " |
| 5th " " | 5th " " | 3d " " | 5th " " | 6th " " |
| 6th " " | 6th " " | 4th " " | 6th " " | 7th " " |
| 7th " " | 7th " " | 5th " " | 7th " " | 8th " " |
| 1st pleopods | 1st pleopods | 1st pleopods | 1st pleopods | 1st pleopods (often absent) |
| 2d " | 2d " | 2d " | 2nd " | 2nd " " " |
| 3d " | 3d " | 3d " | – | – |
| 4th " | 1st uropods | 4th " | – | – |
| 5th " | 2d " | 5th " | – | – |
| uropods | 3d " | uropods | uropods | uropods |

VI, which involves only those taxa found in the fresh waters of the United States.

**Crustacean rarities.** Among the Syncarida, the fresh-water Order Stygocaridacea is known only from sand and gravel interstitial stream habitats in Argentina, Chile, and New Zealand. The Order Anaspidacea occurs only in ponds and streams of Tasmania and Australia. The Order Bathynellacea, however, is almost worldwide in temperate and tropical latitudes, chiefly in wells, subterranean waters, artesian systems, and interstitial waters of streams. The bathynellid literature is very large and chiefly European. Only very recently (Noodt, 1974) have bathynellids been reported from the United States (in California). Dr. David R. Cook has found

500 μ

FIG. 226.–Dorsal view of *Monodella argentarii* Stella, a typical member of the Thermosbaenacea. (From Fryer, 1964.)

TABLE VI. CLASSIFICATION OF CRUSTACEA OCCURRING IN THE FRESH WATERS OF THE UNITED STATES

Class Crustacea
  Subclass Branchiopoda
    Division Eubranchiopoda
      Order Anostraca (fairy shrimps)
      Order Notostraca (tadpole shrimps)
      Order Conchostraca (clam shrimps)
    Division Oligobranchiopoda
      Order Cladocera (water fleas)
  Subclass Ostracoda
    Order Podocopa (seed shrimps)
  Subclass Copepoda
    Order Eucopepoda (copepods)
    Order Branchiura (fish lice)
  Subclass Malacostraca
    Division Peracarida
      Order Mysidacea (opossum shrimps)
      Order Isopoda (aquatic sow bugs)
      Order Amphipoda (scuds, sideswimmers)
    Division Eucarida
      Order Decapoda (fresh-water shrimps, crayfish)
    Division Pancarida
      Order Thermosbaenacea
    Division Syncarida
      Order Bathynellacea

them in the phreatic waters of Wyoming mountain trout streams, and the writer has also found them in similar Colorado habitats. Undoubtedly they are widely distributed in this country. Bathynellids are microscopic, blind, vermiform, and well adapted to interstitial situations. Some typical species are shown in Fig. 225.

Another crustacean rarity in fresh waters is the Order Thermosbaenacea. These are likewise small crustaceans, normally found in interstitial and subterranean waters and in springs. The earliest representative, *Thermosbaena mirabilis,* was first found in saline hot springs near Gabes, Tunisia, in 1924. Four other species have more recently been described from Italy, Yugoslavia, and Israel. All five of these species occur in salty or brackish waters relatively close to the sea, but Fryer (1964) reports keeping thermosbaenaceans in fresh water for long periods. In 1965, however, Maguire described *Monodella texana* from fresh, cool water in a cave near San Marcos, Texas, about 200 km from the sea. Undoubtedly, careful searching should reveal Thermosbaenacea in other subterranean habitats. Superficially, they are similar to bathynellids, but they have a shieldlike carapace that roofs the anterior part of the thorax (Fig. 226). The female uses this device as a marsupium.

## GENERAL CRUSTACEA REFERENCES

BARKER, D. 1959. The distribution and systematic position of the Thermosbaenacea. *Hydrobiologia* 13:209–237.

———. 1962. A study of Thermosbaena mirabilis (Malacostraca, Peracarida) and its reproduction. *Q. J. Microsc. Sci.* 103:261–286.

CRAMPTON, G. C. 1928. The evolution of the head region in lower arthropods and its bearing upon the origin and relationships of the arthropodan groups. *Can. Ent.* 40:284–302.

FRYER, G. 1964. Studies on the functional morphology and feeding mechanism of Monodella argentarii Stella (Crustacea, Thermosbaenacea). *Trans. Roy. Soc. Edinburgh* **66**:51–90.

GLEDHILL, T., T. W. SUTCLIFFE, and W. D. WILLIAMS. 1976. Key to British freshwater Crustacea: Malacostraca. *Sci. Publ. Freshwater Biol. Assoc.* **32**:1–72.

GORDON, I. 1957. On Spelaeogriphus, a new cavernicolous crustacean from South Africa. *Bull. Br. Mus. (Nat. Hist.) Zool.* **5**:29–47.

HENRY, L. M. 1948. The nervous system and the segmentation of the head in the Annulata. *Microentomology* **13**:1–26.

HUSMANN, S. 1967. Ökologie, Systematik und Verbreitung zweier in Norddeutschland sympatrisch lebender Bathynella-Arten (Crustacea, Syncarida). *Int. J. Speleol.* **3**:111–114.

KURIAN, C. V. 1962. Three species of Cumacea from the lakes of Kerala. *Bull. cent. Res. Inst. Trivandrum 8C,* **1961**:55–61.

MAGUIRE, B. 1965. Monodella texana n. sp., an extension of the range of the crustacean order Thermosbaenacea to the Western Hemisphere. *Crustaceana* **9**:149–154.

MAÑÉ-GARZÓN, F. 1943. Tres especies de Tanais de las aquas dulces de Sud América. *Com. Zool. mus. Hist. Nat. Montevideo* **1**:(4):1–15.

NOODT, W. 1964. Natürliches System und Biogeographie der Syncarida (Crustacea Malacostraca). *Gewässer und Abwässer* **37**:77–186.

———. 1967. Biogeographie der Bathynellacea (Syncarida). *Proc. Symp. Crustacea* **1**:411–417.

———. 1968. Deuten die Verbreitungsbilder reliktärer Grundwasser-Crustaceen alte Kontinentzusammenhänge an? *Naturwiss. Rundschau* **21**:470–476.

———. 1974. Bathynellacea (Crustacea, Syncarida) auch in Nord-Amerika. *Naturwissenschaften* **61**:132.

SCHMINKE, H. K. 1976. The ubiquitous telson and the deceptive furca. *Crustaceana* **30**:292–299.

SIEWING, R. 1957. Anatomie und Histologie von Thermosbaena mirabilis. *Akad. Wiss. Lit. Abh. Math.-Naturwiss. Kl.* 1957, **7**:195–270.

SNODGRASS, R. E. 1938. Evolution of the Annelida, Onychophora, and Arthropoda. *Smithson. Misc. Coll.* **97**:1–159.

———. 1951. *Comparative studies on the head of mandibulate arthropods.* 118 pp. Comstock, Ithaca, N.Y.

———. 1956. Crustacean metamorphoses. *Smithson. Misc. Coll.* **131**:1–78.

ZILCH, R. 1972. Beitrag zur Verbreitung und Entwicklungsbiologie der Thermosbaenacea. *Int. Rev. ges. Hydrobiol.* **57**:75–107.

# Chapter 15

# EUBRANCHIOPODA (FAIRY, TADPOLE, AND CLAM SHRIMPS)

THE EUBRANCHIOPODA are among the most characteristic inhabitants of temporary ponds and pools, especially during spring and early summer. They move along the bottom or swim and glide about gracefully, often with the ventral side uppermost. They are absent from running waters, and there are no true marine representatives, although one species, *Artemia salina*, is restricted to highly saline lakes and evaporation basins used for the commercial production of salt.

Except for the immature stages in some families of insects, this is the only major taxonomic category found exclusively in fresh waters in the United States. All others have marine representatives, terrestrial representatives, or both.

**General characteristics.** All members of this primitive group are distinctly segmented and have 10 to 71 pairs of delicate, flat, lobate swimming and respiratory appendages. Because of the leaflike appearance of these appendages, the members of this division are collectively known as phyllopods. The last body segment bears a pair of short to long cercopods. Body length, exclusive of cercopods, ranges between 2 and 100 mm. Females are usually more abundant than males in natural populations, and sometimes males are rare.

The Division Eubranchiopoda consists of three sharply defined orders (Figs. 227, 229). The Anostraca (fairy shrimps) have stalked compound eyes, 11 pairs of swimming legs (in American species), and no carapace. The Notostraca (tadpole shrimps)

have sessile compound eyes, a large, shieldlike carapace covering most of the body, and 35 to 71 pairs of legs. Neither the number of legs nor the number of segments is constant within a species. The Conchostraca (clam shrimps) are laterally compressed, have sessile compound eyes, 10 to 32 pairs of legs, and are enclosed in a carapace consisting of two lateral valves. This carapace is flexible along the middorsal line, but rarely is there a well-defined hinge line. Many species have concentric growth lines that are important in taxonomy. Opening and closing of the valves are governed by a short transverse adductor muscle.

Coloration ranges from translucent or whitish through gray, blue, green, orange, and reddish. Coloration of some species is highly variable and probably governed to a large extent by the type of food being ingested. All the individuals in a particular pond usually have the same general coloration at any one time, although some species exhibit progressive color changes during the adult instars.

The first antennae are small, uniramous, and often unsegmented (Figs. 229, 230). In female Anostraca the second antennae are cylindrical and elongated, but in the males they are greatly enlarged and specialized for clasping the females during copulation (Figs. 230, 239). The males of some species of Anostraca have a median frontal appendage on the head (Fig. 240B), or an antennal appendage arising near the base of each second antenna (Figs. 230, 240E). In the Notostraca the second antennae are

FIG. 227.–Typical Eubranchiopoda. A, female *Branchinecta gigas,* ×1; B, large clam shrimps, ×2.5; C, *Triops longicaudatus,* ×1.5.

minute or absent in both sexes, but in the Conchostraca they are long, biramous, and setose (Fig. 229C).

In ventral view the mouthparts are largely concealed by the labrum. The mandibles have undivided molar surfaces and no palp, the first maxillae are triangular plates with setose biting edges, and the second maxillae are small simple plates that are of little importance in feeding (Fig. 228).

According to prevailing usage, the boundary between head and trunk of phyllopods lies immediately behind the segment that bears the second maxillae, the first trunk segment being the one that bears the first pair of legs. Although the head forms a well-defined body region, the trunk is not clearly divisible into thorax and abdomen as it is in most entomostraca. The trunk segments are all similar morphologically and vary widely in number from one genus to another. Furthermore, the number of pairs of legs and the proportion of trunk segments bearing them also vary widely. The location of the genital pores, however, is sometimes used as a basis for loosely designating a "thorax" (pregenital segments) and an "abdomen" (postgenital segments) in some families. In the Anostraca the first two abdominal segments (collectively the genital segment) are partially fused and bear the external uterine chamber and base of the ovisac in the female, and penes in the male.

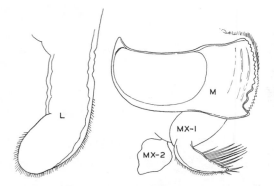

FIG. 228.–Mouthparts of *Lynceus brachyurus*. L, lateral view of labrum; M, MX-1, and MX-2, right mandible, first maxilla, and second maxilla as seen from below. (Modified from Sars).

All Anostraca of the United States have 20 trunk segments, including 11 that bear legs, the two genital segements, and seven other posterior segments, the last of which is the telson. The Conchostraca have 10 to 32 trunk segments and 10 to 32 pairs of legs.

The body divisions, segmentation, and leg arrangement of the Notostraca represent a peculiar situation among fresh-water crustaceans. Posterior to the second maxillae there are 25 to 44 so-called segments, not counting the terminal telson. Unlike typical segments, however, many of them have two or more pairs of legs, and especially posteriorly some of them bear 5, 10, or more pairs of legs per segment (Figs. 227C, 231). The total number of pairs of legs ranges from 35 to 71 among the American species of Notostraca. Following the suggestions of Linder (1952), it therefore seems preferable to refer to "body rings" in the Notostraca rather than "segments." The first 11 rings are sometimes considered the thorax, the remainder being the abdomen. In general, all body rings are of comparable length. A variable number of posterior abdominal rings are without legs. A single species usually shows considerable variation with respect to: number of body rings, total number of legs, number of legs on a particular body ring, number of leg-bearing abdominal rings, and number of legless abdominal rings. In *Triops longicau-*

*datus*, for example, the number of legless abdominal rings varies from 4 to 16. The number of body rings is usually more constant in a parthenogenetic population than in one containing males.

Tadpole shrimps sometimes have an incomplete body ring just anterior to the telson. Only the dorsal or ventral part of the ring may be present. About 1 percent of the specimens in many collections show "spiral rings" (Fig. 232), usually near the telson. These consist of one to four spirals, running either to the left or to the right.

The telson of the fairy shrimps bears two terminal platelike plumose cercopods (caudal rami, furcal rami). In the tadpole shrimps the cercopods are very long, filamentous, segmented, and spiny. In the clam shrimps the telson is laterally compressed and bears two flattened upward curved processes and two stout anal spines (Fig. 243F).

Most phyllopod trunk appendages, or swimming legs, are basically similar (Fig. 233). They are biramous, flat, translucent, lobed, and setose. The median margin bears a series of small lobes, or endites, the basal endite of the Notostraca and Conchostraca being a more robust gnathobase. Near the base of the lateral margin are one or two large lobes, the proepipodites, and more distally is the thin, oval or elongated, nonsetose branchia (epipodite). The two large distal lobes are the exopodite (flabellum) and endopodite.

A few of the legs of all phyllopods are modified from this basic plan. In the Anostraca the more posterior pairs are definitely smaller and less lobate than preceding pairs. In the Notostraca the first one or two pairs of legs have elongated filamentous rami that probably serve as tactile structures (Fig. 234A). The flabellum of the eleventh pair of legs of the female is modified into a cuplike brood pouch that carries the eggs after they leave the reproductive tract (Fig. 234C). The more posterior legs of the Notostraca taper progressively to a very small size. The first one or two pairs of legs of male Conchostraca are hooked and prehensile (Fig. 234D), and in the female elongated flabella of two or three pairs

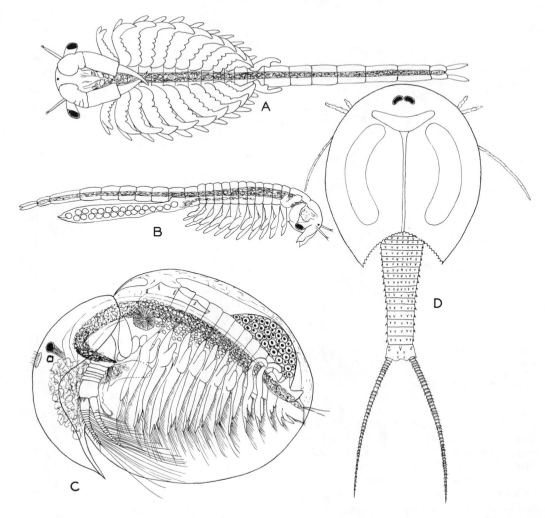

FIG. 229.–Typical Eubranchiopoda. A, ventral view of male *Branchinecta paludosa*, ×8 (setation omitted); B, lateral view of female *B. paludosa*, ×6 (setation omitted) showing brood sac; C, female *Lynceus brachyurus*, ×25, with left valve removed (diagrammatic); D, dorsal view of *Triops*, ×3. (A to C modified from Sars.)

of posterior legs aid in keeping the developing eggs in place between body and carapace (Fig. 229C).

**Locomotion.** Fairy shrimps and tadpole shrimps glide or swim gracefully by means of complex beating movements of the legs that pass in a wavelike anterior-posterior direction. Sometimes they drift along slowly; other times they dart rapidly or come to rest on the bottom. Lowndes (1933) presents evidence to show that locomotion in the Anostraca is not produced by beating of the legs as a whole, but rather by propellerlike movements of the exopodites, the speed of the animal being determined by the angle at which the exopodites are held. In the clam shrimps locomotion is accomplished mainly by "rowing" movements of the large biramous second antennae, the legs being of little importance. Fairy shrimps habitually swim with the

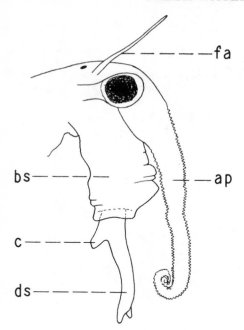

FIG. 230.–Diagrammatic lateral view of head of male *Eubranchipus bundyi*. *ap*, antennal appendage; *bs*, basal segment of second antenna; *c*, calcar of distal segment of second antenna; *ds*, distal segment of second antenna; *fa*, first antenna.

ventral side upward, but members of the other two orders are often seen swimming with the ventral side downward. Tadpole shrimps creep or burrow superficially in soft substrates much of the time. Clam shrimps also burrow or move along the surface of the substrate in a clumsy manner. When the antennae stop beating they fall on their side.

**Food, feeding.** Food consists mostly of algae, bacteria, Protozoa, rotifers, and bits of detritus. Movements of the legs serve as a food-getting mechanism, plankton and materials from the substrate being strained nonselectively from the water by the setose appendages (especially by the basal endites) and concentrated and agglutinated in a median ventral groove running most of the length of the body. This stream of food moves forward, activated chiefly by the gnathobases, and is further agglutinated at the anterior end by a sticky secretion produced by labral glands. Mastication occurs

FIG. 231.–Ventral view of a portion of the right side of a female *Lepidurus lemmoni* from which the last 25 legs have been removed. The small rectangles represent the attachment areas of the removed legs. (Redrawn from Linder, 1952.)

outside the digestive tract in an atrium formed by the overhanging labrum. It is probable that phyllopods feed continuously, but all the food reaching the mouth is not necessarily ingested, the excess being sloughed off. Although microscopic orga-

FIG. 232.–Ventral view of telson and a portion of the abdomen of *Triops longicaudatus* showing a spiral of two rounds located between normal body rings and beginning and ending in the midventral line. (Modified from Linder, 1952.)

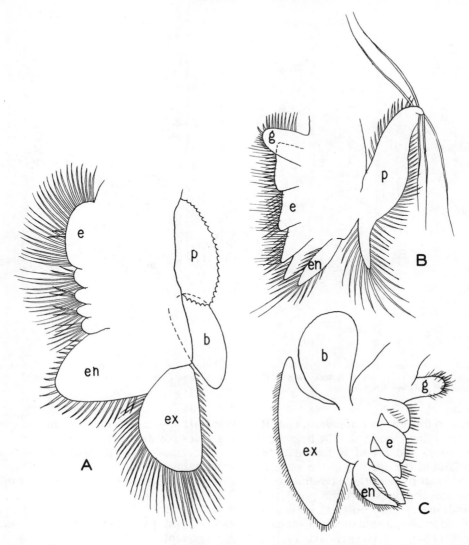

FIG. 233.–Trunk appendages of typical Eubranchiopoda. A, *Branchinecta paludosa*; B, *Lynceus brachyurus*; C, *Lepidurus*. *b,* branchia; *e,* endite; *en,* endopodite; *ex,* exopodite; *g,* gnathobase; *p,* proepipodite. (A and B modified from Sars; C modified from Packard.)

nisms and detritus constitute the sole food of Anostraca and Conchostraca, the Notostraca also utilize larger particles and have even been observed gnawing on dead tadpoles, earthworms, mollusks, and frog eggs. They are best characterized as omnivores. *Branchinecta gigas* is unique among American Anostraca. It is not a filter-feeder and subsists on large food masses as a carnivore, chiefly other crustaceans.

**Internal anatomy, physiology.** The digestive tract consists of a vertical esophagus, a small lobate stomach lying in the head, a long intestine, a short rectum, and an anus. Two digestive glands in the head empty into the stomach.

A dorsal tubular heart extends throughout most or all of the body segments in the Anostraca, but in the Notostraca and Conchostraca it is much shorter, sometimes extending through only four seg-

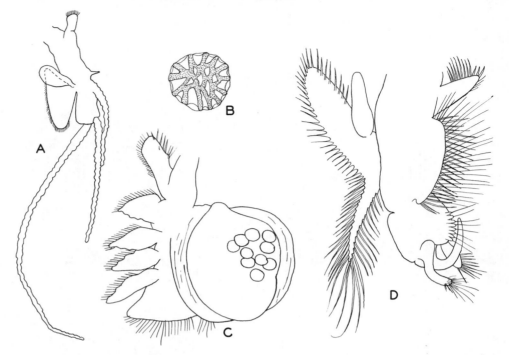

FIG. 234.–Specialized reproductive structures of Eubranchiopoda. A, first leg of male *Triops*; B, resting egg of *Eulimnadia*; C, eleventh leg of female *Triops*; D, first leg of male *Lynceus brachyurus*. (A and C modified from Packard; B redrawn from Mattox, 1939; D modified from Sars.)

ments. A variable number of paired, lateral, slitlike ostia bring blood from the hemocoel into the heart, and blood is forced anteriorly and out of the opening at the anterior end of the heart by peristaltic contractions. Colorless amoebocytes occur in phyllopod blood, and an erythrocruorin is known to be dissolved in the plasma of some species.

The exchange of oxygen and carbon dioxide probably takes place through all exposed surfaces of the body but especially through the surfaces of the legs and their branchiae.

The chief excretory organs are the two coiled shell glands that empty their contents at the base of the second maxillae. It is possible that the paired antennal glands and mandibular glands also function in excretion during the early instars of some species. Osmotic regulation presumably occurs chiefly through the wall of the digestive tract and through the branchiae of the first 10 pairs of legs. In some species there is an active uptake of sodium by the gills. *Artemia* continually swallows water, regardless of its salt concentration.

The ladderlike nervous system is diagrammatic and primitive (Fig. 235). The two widely separated nerve cords run the full length of the body, and except for the more posterior segments, there are two ganglia and two transverse commissures per segment.

In the Anostraca the compound eyes are stalked and far apart, but in the other two orders they are quite close together, sometimes touching or partially fused. A small median ocellus of the nauplius persists in the adult. Experiments have shown that the upside-down swimming position of some species is a phototropic response governed by stimuli received by both the ocellus and compound eyes, and if the upper side of the container is covered and weak illumination is supplied from below, many of the animals will turn over and swim with the ventral side downward. Swimming on the back is normal in darkness. Immature

individuals usually react more strongly to
a light source than do the mature animals.
Taste areas appear to be concentrated in
the region of the mouthparts, and touch is
distributed over the whole body. The "dorsal organ" is a small patch of modified cephalic epithelium of unknown function, but
it is probably sensory.

**Reproduction.** None of the Eubranchiopoda are known to be hermaphroditic.
Testes and ovaries are two posterior tubules, one on each side of the digestive tract;
in the Notostraca the gonads are ramified.
Males have two short vasa deferentia and
two small seminal vesicles in the genital

FIG. 236.–Genital segments of male *Branchinecta
paludosa*. A, dorsal view; B, ventral view showing
penes. (Redrawn from Linder.)

FIG. 235.–Nervous system of *Branchinecta*.
(Modified from Sars.)

segment; sperm leave the body through two
simple genital pores in the Notostraca and
Conchostraca, but through penes in the
Anostraca (Fig. 236).

Many of the reproductive phenomena
in the phyllopods are poorly understood.
The occurrence of males, for example, cannot usually be correlated with any seasonal,
ecological, or reproductive events. In many
species males are not abundant in natural
populations. Parthenogenesis is therefore
common, and, in a few species of Notostraca, sometimes the rule. Even in a mixed
population, however, both parthenogenetic
and syngamic reproduction may occur at
the same time.

Clasping, paired males and females
may swim about firmly united together for
several days at a time. In the Anostraca the
male assumes a dorsal position with the
second antennae clasped around the female
in the region of the genital segment. The
actual processes of copulation and transfer
of sperm are completed in a few seconds or
minutes. In the fairy shrimps the male turns
the body at an angle to that of the female
and recurves the posterior end so that the
genital segment is brought into contact with
the external uterine chamber of the female.
The process is somewhat similar in the tadpole shrimps, and in the clam shrimps the
body of the male is placed at a right angle
and vertical to that of the female before
sperm can be transferred. Males usually die
a few hours after copulation.

Both fertilized and parthenogenetic

eggs are retained externally for one to several days on the body of the female before being released. The eggs of Anostraca are carried in an oval or elongated ventral brood sac. In the Notostraca they are carried in a curious receptacle formed by modified and overlapping flabellum and branchia on each eleventh trunk appendage. In the Conchostraca the eggs are held together in a mucous mass between body and shell (Fig. 229C).

The number of eggs produced by a single female varies widely. They are released in a series of fertilized or unfertilized clutches at intervals of two to six or more days. Usually there are one to six clutches per female and 10 to 250 eggs per clutch, depending on the species. In syngamic reproduction, each clutch of eggs is fertilized by a separate copulation. The female carries the eggs for one to several days, during which time they undergo early development. Thereafter they may be dropped to the bottom or remain attached until the female dies and sinks to the bottom.

It appears that some phyllopods pro-duce two distinct types of eggs: (1) thin-shelled "summer" eggs, which hatch almost immediately, and (2) thick-shelled, brown "resting" or "winter" eggs, which are capable of withstanding unusual heat, cold, and prolonged desiccation (Fig. 234B); the thick shell affords protection from mechanical injury and sunlight. Both types are produced in either the presence or absence of males in the population. There is some evidence to indicate that the type of egg depends on the nature and amount of secretion coming out of the shell glands at the time of egg formation. A copious brown secretion results in thick-shelled resting eggs; slightly less secretion produces thinner shells, and the eggs hatch within several days after deposition; if the secretion is scanty and colorless, the shell is thin and transparent, and development is so rapid that the larva may hatch before the egg is released from the body of the female. It is thought that both thin-and thick-shelled eggs may produce either males or females; the genetic and physiological mechanisms involved are not clear.

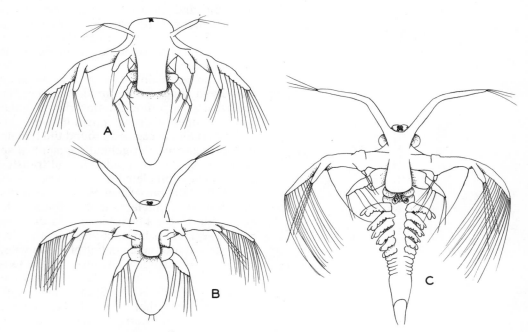

FIG. 237.–Immature Eubranchiopoda. A, first instar of *Artemia salina,* ×110; B, first instar (nauplius) of *Linderiella occidentalis,* ×80; C, third instar of *L. occidentalis,* ×30. (Modified from Heath.)

**Resting eggs.** When it is recalled that phyllopods are chiefly inhabitants of vernal pools and ponds, which dry up completely in the dry, warm months, it is obvious that resting eggs constitute the sole device for tiding a population over from one season to another. It is probable that resting eggs of all species are capable of withstanding desiccation. During the summer the resting eggs become dried in the bottom mud, and during the winter they are frozen for varying periods. Until rather recently it was commonly believed that *both* drying and freezing were necessary prerequisites for further development and hatching of these eggs, but experimental evidence has been accumulated to show that this is sometimes not the case. Resting eggs have. been hatched in the laboratory after drying without freezing and freezing without drying as well as after both freezing and drying. Groups of eggs subjected to rapid or slow freezing and thawing all showed hatching. There is also some evidence to show that resting eggs of a few species will hatch without either drying or freezing.

The observation is sometimes made that phyllopods occur in ponds that never dry up completely during the summer months. This is unquestionably true, but it must be borne in mind that the active phyllopod population disappears with the onset of warm or cool weather and that the animals appearing in the following spring have undoubtedly hatched from resting eggs that overwintered on the bottom or in the dried mud along the pond margin above the lowered water level.

Although freezing and drying usually occur naturally, neither is indispensable. The resting period usually lasts from 6 to 10 months in temperate latitudes, but such a long interval is neither necessary nor inhibitory; dry eggs of certain species may be placed in water and hatched at any time of the year in the laboratory. The viability of resting eggs is very striking. Some species have been described from adults reared from eggs in dried mud sent from distant parts of the world. Viable eggs have been kept in dried pond mud on the laboratory shelf for as long as 15 years. Viable eggs of *Artemia* have withstood a temperature of

81° for one hour, $-190°$ for 24 hours, and an air pressure of 0.000001 mm of mercury for six months. Eggs are more viable when stored in the refrigerator, as compared with room temperature.

**Development, life cycle.** Depending on the species, the eggs hatch into the typical nauplius or the more advanced metanauplius larvae with three pairs of appendages representing the first antennae, second antennae, and mandibles of the adults (Fig. 237). A metanauplius usually shows the faint beginning of two or three trunk segments. Although summer eggs hatch while they are still held on the body of the female or on the bottom shortly after their release, development of resting eggs is much slower. It is thought that early segmentation begins soon after the eggs reach the bottom of the drying pond and before the water temperature gets too low. Development ceases or is greatly retarded by desiccation and low temperatures, however, and is not resumed until early the following spring, when water is available and temperatures become favorable. Hatching of resting eggs in temperate latitudes therefore normally occurs sometime between late January and early May. Development proceeds comparatively rapidly in the early spring, and phyllopods may often be collected immediately after the ice melts. They have even been seen swimming about under ice, especially after an early thaw and subsequent freeze, or in the winter months in deep pools.

Beginning with the newly hatched nauplius, there is a long series of instars, each following a complete ecdysis, or shedding of the exoskeleton. Changes in size from one instar to the next are gradual, and there is progressive appearance of more segments, more appendages, and increasing complexity of appendages. *Linderiella occidentalis*, for example, has 17 instars in the life history. By the third instar the length averages 1.1 mm and all appendages through the fifth or sixth trunk segments are represented to some degree. By the sixth instar the average length is 2.1 mm, and all appendages are present, though most of the more posterior ones are incompletely developed. Complete development, sexual maturity, and copulation are attained in the 16th instar. *Artemia salina* probably has 14 instars, sexual maturity being attained in the twelfth instar. *Streptocephalus seali* has 18 preadult instars. Some investigators have found that the number of instars is variable for each species, depending on temperatures and food conditions.

The active portion of the life cycle may be completed in a surprisingly short time. Mattox (1937), for example, found that the life history of *Eulimnadia diversa* from hatching until death was completed during the 15 days that a small pond had water in it. He also found (1939) that *Lynceus brachyurus* lived about 26 days and *Cyzicus mexicanus* about two months. *Artemia salina*, on the other hand, reaches sexual maturity in 18 to 21 days after hatching and has a normal life span of four months, although specimens have been kept alive for nine months in the laboratory. *Eubranchipus oregonus* has an exceptionally long natural life span, sometimes up to 25 weeks.

In small ponds that contain water for only a few weeks during the spring and early summer, phyllopods usually have one generation per year. The resting eggs hatch early in the spring, and the animals mature rapidly and produce resting eggs that fall to the bottom and do not hatch until the following spring. Some summer eggs are usually produced during the short period of activity, and although they may hatch, there is not sufficient time for the second generation to mature, and such immature individuals and any remaining summer eggs are presumably destroyed by the adverse conditions accompanying the disappearance of water from the pond.

In Great Salt Lake, in permanent ponds, and in ponds that persist for several months, however, there are usually two or more complete generations per year, the summer generations being completed in a short time because the summer eggs hatch almost immediately.

**Ecology.** It seems quite clear that the development of phyllopod populations in the spring and their sudden disappearance in summer or early autumn are governed largely by temperature conditions. Most species do not appear until water temperatures exceed 4°, and 13° to 30°, depending on the species, is the upper limit beyond which individuals die quickly. In Great Salt Lake, *Artemia salina* disappears in the autumn when the water temperature drops below 6°; *Eubranchipus bundyi* and *Eubranchipus serratus* are seldom found in water warmer than 15°.

Most species exhibit little in the way of specific habitat preferences. The widely distributed *Eubranchipus vernalis*, for example, occurs in roadside ditches, grassy vernal ponds, cattail marshes, and woodland pools. Some species, however, appear to be generally restricted to clear or muddy waters. *Eubranchipus bundyi*, *Eubranchipus oregonus*, and *Branchinecta coloradensis* occur only in clear ponds and pools, while many clam shrimps, *Triops*, *Branchinecta gigas*, and *Thamnocephalus platyurus* are almost invariably found in muddy, alkaline waters.

A curious feature about phyllopod ecology is their absence from lakes. Seldom are they collected from bodies of water having areas exceeding one hectare. Phyllopods are almost defenseless, and it is also notable that they are not often abundant in ponds containing carnivorous insects, and are rarely present along with carnivorous fishes. In fact they attain greatest densities in vernal ponds and prairie pools that are generally lacking in other macrometazoans.

In keeping with widely fluctuating water levels and the consequent rapid changes in the dissolved salt content of pond waters, phyllopods have highly efficient but poorly known means of making physiological adjustments to varying osmotic pressures. In prairie pools, for example, the total salt or alkali content may vary between 0.05 and 1.00 percent within several weeks, yet their phyllopod populations maintain themselves successfully. Similarly, prairie phyllopods are usually capable of tolerating wide ranges in hydrogen-ion concentration. *Eubranchipus serratus* has been found in a pH range of 6.6 to 9.5, *E. vernalis* from 5.2 to 7.4, and *Streptocephalus seali* in 5.2 to 10.0. As a whole, however, phyllopods have alkaline affinities; pH 6.8 seems to be about the usual lower limit for most species.

Excellent cultures of *Artemia salina* can be maintained in the laboratory, using natural or synthetic sea water, and much experimental work has been done on this species. Mature specimens will tolerate salinities ranging from the saturation point of sodium chloride down to about 3 percent sea water, though they will not reproduce in salinities below 3 percent sodium chloride. Adults reared in high salt concentrations reach a larger size than those reared in lower salt concentrations, and sexual maturity is attained more rapidly in populations reared at low salt concentrations. Europeans have found that the pregenital:postgenital body-length ratio and relative development of the cercopods and their setation are correlated with salinity, but these results have not been duplicated with American strains. *Artemia* populations have variously been found to be parthenogenetic, bisexual, diploid, triploid, tetraploid, pentaploid, or octoploid.

Year-to-year field notes on the occurrence of phyllopods in particular ponds present a puzzling problem. Sometimes a species is abundant for several successive years, and then one year it is unaccountably absent. Other ponds may have populations present or absent from year to year in a completely sporadic manner. Furthermore, where there is a group of small ponds and pools in a restricted area, phyllopods are usually present only in certain scattered pools and absent from most or all of the bodies of water immediately surrounding each inhabited one. With few exceptions, a pond never contains more than one species of a particular genus at a time.

The bodies and appendages of phyllopods sometimes become so completely covered with sessile ciliates and green algae that they swim sluggishly and with difficulty.

**Geographical distribution.** A few genera and species of Eubranchiopoda are truly cosmopolitan. *Artemia salina* is found on all continents, and in the United States is best known from Great Salt Lake and man-made California salterns. *Lepidurus* occurs everywhere except in South America. The species of *Streptocephalus* are quite restricted; there are several species in Asia, 21 in Africa and Madagascar, 1 in Europe, 2 in the West Indies, and 6 in continental North America. The species of *Eubranchipus* are all restricted to North America, and, as extreme examples of endemism, *Eulimnadia diversa* is known only from a single Illinois pond and *E. stoningtonensis* was found year after year in a single small pool in Connecticut. Similar examples are evident from the key that follows. Temporary ponds and pools of the Great Plains constitute a rich collecting ground, the majority of the species reported from the United States occurring in this area.

Phyllopods are probably effectively distributed through their resting eggs, which may be blown about as dust or transported by birds and insects. The presence of populations of *Branchinecta coloradensis* above timberline in rock pools have a volume of only a few liters and may be easily attibuted to both of these agencies.

**Enemies.** Amphibia, dytiscid larvae, caddis larvae, and perhaps a few other insects are the chief predators of phyllopods. They are of no importance in the diet of fish since they occur in bodies of water too alkaline, too small, or too temporary to support fish.

**Economic importance.** Many years ago, the Indians in the vicinity of Great Salt Lake are said to have used dried *Artemia* extensively as food, and *Triops* is at present said to be used as food by a few natives of the Federal District in Mexico. Occasionally *Triops* becomes a pest in rice fields, notably in California. There are several reports of clam shrimps becoming a nuisance in fish rearing ponds, especially where the fish do not feed on the shrimp (goldfish and pike). Shrimp become so numerous as to clog outlet screens.

**Collection, preparation.** A coarse dipnet is the only necessary implement for collecting adults, but a plankton net is required for the early immature stages. Either 4 percent formalin or 70 to 80 percent alcohol is a satisfactory killing agent and preservative.

With few exceptions, phyllopods are usually difficult to maintain and rear in the laboratory. *Artemia,* however, is easy to culture; dry brine shrimp eggs are simply added to sea water or a 0.1 to 6.0 percent brine solution. The salt should not be iodized. Best results are obtained at 20° to 30°. See Galtsoff et al. (1937), Cole and Brown (1967), and Dempster (1953) for more details about salt tolerances. *Artemia salina* is one of the very few species of metazoans that can be raised in axenic cultures (Provasoli and Shiraishi, 1959).

Dissection is not often necessary for identification, but specimens being studied for any length of time should be manipulated in glycerin. Conchostraca and isolated appendages may be permanently mounted in glycerin jelly.

**Taxonomy.** The Anostraca, Notostraca, Conchostraca, and Cladocera constitute the Subclass Branchiopoda and have the following characters in common: leafy trunk appendages, compound eyes, reduced mouthparts, and usually parthenogenesis, fertilized eggs, and a carapace. The Anostraca, Notostraca, and Conchostraca, however, form a convenient taxonomic group, the Division Eubranchiopoda, having several fundamental characters in common and differing from the Cladocera (Division Oligobranchiopoda) in some important features. The bodies of Eubranchiopoda are elongated, distinctly segmented, and have 10 or more pairs of trunk appendages, whereas the Cladocera are short and compact, with no sign of segmentation, and have only five or six pairs of trunk appendages. The abdomen of Cladocera is greatly reduced, but in Eubranchiopoda the abdomen (postgenital region) is prominent. It is also significant that the phyllopods have nauplius stages, whereas the Cladocera have direct development. Other less important differences are the occurrence of ephippia in the Cladocera and

a single compound eye in Cladocera as compared with two in phyllopods.

Instead of Branchiopoda, the name "Phyllopoda" is occasionally used for the whole subclass; other references use "Phyllopoda" to include all Branchiopoda exclusive of Cladocera. Preuss uses the term "Phyllopoda" to include all Branchiopoda except Anostraca. Because of this ambiguity "Phyllopoda" is best not used in systematic nomenclature to designate a definite taxonomic category. On the other hand, there is no such serious objection to using "phyllopod" as a common, descriptive, inclusive term for Anostraca, Notostraca, and Conchostraca.

Because of brief descriptions, inadequate figures, and a reluctance to recognize wide variations within a species as to size, color, and the number and arrangement of spines and spinules, many phyllopods have an uncertain and controversial taxonomy. Formerly most investigators maintained that there were four to six species of *Triops* in the United States. These presumed species are represented by surprisingly few collections and specimens, and furthermore their differentiation was based on size, the number of exposed trunk segments behind the carapace, and the number and disposition of spinules on the telson. The revision of Linder (1952), however, has shown that none of these characters are reliable taxonomically, and that it is quite likely that there is only a single highly variable species of *Triops* in the United States. *T. longicaudatus. Lepidurus,* the only other American notostracan genus, is represented by five recognizable species.

Morphological variations within single species of Notostraca are so pronounced that Linder has been led to make the following statement: "A new species should never be described from less than 100 specimens from the same district, preferably taken at varying times of the year."

Unfortunately the general outline of the conchostracan shell is somewhat variable and does not have the taxonomic importance formerly attributed to it. Furthermore, the original descriptions of many American conchostracans are too generalized to be used for critical work. Hence this section of the following key is subject to considerable revision.

The taxonomic status of *Artemia* has long been controversial, especially in Europe, where *Artemia* shows much greater variability than it does in the United States. The reproductive habits of different populations vary markedly. In parts of Europe parthenogenesis is the rule, males being rare or absent; some such populations are diploid, but others are tetraploid and octo-

ploid. *Artemia* in Great Salt Lake is diploid and males are common. The present consensus is that there is a single cosmopolitan species, *Artemia salina,* which has numerous intergrading physiological and morphological varieties.

To use the following key effectively, mature males and females are required. The scanty and spotty distribution records are usually the result of inadequate collecting; undoubtedly such ranges will eventually be greatly extended.

## KEY TO SPECIES OF EUBRANCHIOPODA

1. Eyes stalked; no carapace; body elongated; 11 pairs of swimming legs; second antennae uniramous, greatly enlarged and used as clasping organs in male; some genera with one frontal appendage or two antennal appendages in male (Figs. 227A, 229A, B) (most of the Anostraca couplets are based on detailed morphology of the male second antennae). Order **ANOSTRACA** (fairy shrimps), **3**
   Eyes sessile; with a large carapace . . . . . . . . . . . . . . . . . . . . . . . . . . . . . . . . . . . . . . . . . . **2**
2. With a low, arched, univalve carapace covering head and much of trunk; 35 to 71 pairs of trunk appendages; second antennae minute or absent; two long cercopods (Figs. 227C, 229D); living animals often brightly colored, blue-green, red, brown, or marbled; total body length 11 to 58 mm, not including supraanal plate; not known east of the Mississippi River.
   Order **NOTOSTRACA** (tadpole shrimps), **59**
   Body compressed laterally and completely enclosed in a carapace composed of two lateral, shell-like valves; 10 to 32 pairs of legs; second antennae large and biramous (Figs. 227B, 229C). . . . Order **CONCHOSTRACA** (clam shrimps), **33**
3. Second antennae of male long and with a long, folded cheliform outgrowth on basal segment (Fig. 238C); with a small median frontal appendage between the bases of the second antennae . . . . . . . STREPTOCEPHALIDAE, **Streptocephalus, 5**
   Second antennae of male shorter and more simply constructed . . . . . . . . . . . . . . . . . .**4**
4. Frontal and antennal appendages small or absent (Fig. 239A) . . . . . . . . . . . . . . . . . .**10**
   Male with a long, branched, median frontal appendage (Fig. 240B); females with a long, unbranched frontal appendage (Fig. 240C); up to 50 mm long; central and southwestern states.
   THAMNOCEPHALIDAE, **Thamnocephalus platyurus** Packard
5. Male cercopods bowed and with setae along proximal half and with short, curved spines distally (Fig. 238A). . . . . . . . . . . . . . . . . . . . . . . . . . . . . . . . . . . . . . . . . . . .**6**
   Male cercopods straight and setose along entire margins (Fig. 238B) . . . . . . . . . . . . . .**7**
6. Inner branch of male second antenna with two basal teeth on anterior margin; up to 45 mm long; widely distributed in pools and ponds. **Streptocephalus seali** Ryder
   Inner branch of male second antenna with three basal teeth; known only from Texas . . . . . . . . . . . . . . . . . . . . . . . . . . . . . . . . . . . . . **Streptocephalus similis** Baird
7. Distal tooth at base of finger shorter than proximal tooth; tip of finger serrate (Fig. 238F); southwestern Texas . . . . . . . . . . . . . . . . . **Streptocephalus linderi** Moore
   Distal tooth at base of finger longer than proximal tooth; tip of finger variously formed . . . . . . . . . . . . . . . . . . . . . . . . . . . . . . . . . . . . . . . . . . . . . . . . . . . . . . . . .**8**
8. Inner branch of male second antenna without a process near distal end (Fig. 238D); 10 to 18 mm long; Oklahoma, Texas, and New Mexico.
   **Streptocephalus dorothae** Mackin
   Inner branch of male second antenna notched, or with a posterior process or spine. **9**

FIG. 238.–Structure of *Streptocephalus*. A, cercopods of *Streptocephalus seali*; B, cercopods of *S. texanus*; C, lateral view of anterior part of head and appendages of male *S. texanus*; D, inner branch of male second antenna of *S. dorothae*; E, second antenna of male *S. mackini*; F, second antenna of male *S. linderi*. (B to D modified from Mackin, 1942; E and F modified from Moore, 1966.)

**9.** Distal end of finger as in Fig. 238C; up to 23 mm long; in pools and ponds of the plains in the southwest quarter of the United States.

**Streptocephalus texanus** Packard

Distal end of finger as in Fig. 238E; rare in Texas and Arizona.

**Streptocephalus mackini** Moore

**10.** Male second antennae somewhat fused basally and with a laminate terminal segment (Fig. 239A); average length 10 mm; in saline lakes and salterns of Utah, Nevada, California, Oregon, Washington, North Dakota, Connecticut, Arizona, and Nebraska .......................... ARTEMIIDAE, **Artemia salina** Leach

Male second antennae not fused basally and terminal segment not laminate (Fig. 241); common and widely distributed west of the Mississippi River .............**11**

**11.** Frontal appendage complex and longer than second antennae (Figs. 241 A, B) ........................ THAMNOCEPHALIDAE, **Branchinella, 12**

Frontal appendage shorter than second antennae or absent ....................**13**

**12.** Frontal appendage with two terminal branches (Fig. 241 B); 8 to 11 mm long; known only from rock pools in De Kalb County, Georgia. **Branchinella lithaca** (Creaser)

Frontal appendage with three terminal branches (Fig. 241 A); 6 to 7 mm long; Florida ................................... **Branchinella alachua** Dexter

**13.** Each abdominal segment with one spine on each side; 6 to 10 mm long; known only from west Texas. ...THAMNOCEPHALIDAE, **Branchinella sublettei** Sissom

Without such abdominal spines ...........................................**14**

**14.** With antennal appendages (Fig. 242) .........................................**15**

Without antennal appendages........................ BRANCHINECTIDAE, **25**

**15.** Basal antennal appendages conical, with short median spines (Fig. 239D); California ............LINDERIELLIDAE, **Linderiella occidentalis** (Dodds)

Basal antennal appendages lamelliform, with conical projections along at least part of one or both edges (Figs. 242 A–E). ............. CHIROCEPHALIDAE, **16**

FIG. 239.–Structure of Artemiidae, Branchinectidae, and Linderiellidae. A, head of male *Artemia salina*; B, head of male *Branchinecta paludosa*; C, head of male *B. lindahli*; D, head of male *Linderiella occidentalis*; E, head of female *L. occidentalis*; F, head of male *Branchinecta packardi*; G, head of male *B. coloradensis*; H, second antenna of male *B. cornigera*; J, second antenna of male *B. dissimilis*. (A modified from Heath; B modified from Sars; C modified from Shantz; D and E modified from Dodds; H modified from Lynch, 1958; J from Lynch, 1972.)

16. Basal antennal appendage not extending beyond distal end of basal segment of second
    antenna (Fig. 242A) . . . . . . . . . . . . . . . . . . . . . . . . . . . . . . . . . . . . . . . . . . . . . . . . .**17**
    Basal antennal appendage longer than basal segment of second antenna (Fig. 242B). **19**
17. Teeth on either side of male antennal appendage not greatly different in size (Figs.
    242A, E) . . . . . . . . . . . . . . . . . . . . . . . . . . . . . . . . . . . . . . . . . . . . . . . . . . . . . . . . . . .**18**
    Teeth on one side of male antennal appendage much longer than those on the other
    side (Fig. 242C); average length 23 mm; known only from Kentucky and Ohio
    (this may not be a good species) . . . . . . . . . . . . **Eubranchipus neglectus** Garman
18. Basal antennal appendage of male with large, separate teeth (Fig. 242E); 12 to 18 mm
    long; Washington, Oregon, and Oklahoma . . . **Eubranchipus oregonus** Creaser
    Basal antennal appendage of male with small teeth (Fig. 242A); 20 to 26 mm long;
    widely distributed and common in northern states. **Eubranchipus vernalis** (Verrill)
19. Basal antennal appendage without conical processes along lateral margin (Fig. 240F). **20**
    Basal antennal appendage with conical processes along at least part of lateral and
    median margins (Figs. 242B–E) . . . . . . . . . . . . . . . . . . . . . . . . . . . . . . . . . . . . . . . .**21**
20. Basal antennal appendage robust (Fig. 241C); a rare species known only from
    Louisiana . . . . . . . . . . . . . . . . . . . . . . . . . . . . . . . . . **Eubranchipus moorei** Brtek
    Basal antennal appendage slim (Fig. 240F); 8 to 17 mm long; Connecticut, New Jersey,
    Virginia, Long Island, North Carolina, Georgia, Tennessee, Ohio, Maryland,
    and Louisiana . . . . . . . . . . . . . . . . . . . . . . . . . . . . . **Eubranchipus holmani** Ryder
21. Basal antennal appendage long, tapering, and with small serrations on medial and
    lateral margins (Fig. 240D) . . . . . . . . . . . . . . . . . . . . . . . . . . . . . . . . . . . . . . . . . . .**22**
    Basal antennal appendage with a different shape . . . . . . . . . . . . . . . . . . . . . . . . . . . .**24**

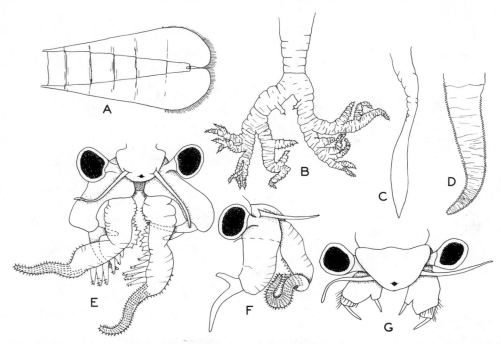

FIG. 240.–Structure of Thamnocephalidae and Chirocephalidae. A, posterior end of *Thamnocephalus platyurus*; B, frontal appendage of male *T. platyurus*; C, frontal appendage of female *T. platyurus*; D, antennal appendage of *Eubranchipus bundyi*; E, anterior view of head of male *Eubranchipus holmani*; F, lateral view of head of male *E. holmani*; G, anterior view of head of female *E. holmani*. (C redrawn from Packard; E to G modified from Mattox, 1936.)

22. Labrum with a knoblike protuberance at anterior end (Fig. 241D); 10 to 18 mm long; widely distributed in northern states ...........**Eubranchipus bundyi** Forbes
    Labrum without such a protuberance......................................**23**
23. Basal segment of second antenna with a fingerlike process on the median surface near midlength; Florida ..........................**Dexteria floridana** (Dexter)
    Basal segment of second antenna without such a process; uncommon but widely distributed in temporary pools of low salinity.
                                                 **Eubranchipus intricatus** Hartland-Rowe
24. Terminal segment of male second antenna with a calcar half as long as the segment (Fig. 242B); 10 to 35 mm long; Illinois, Indiana, Missouri, Nebraska, Kansas, Oklahoma, Montana, Washington, and Oregon. **Eubranchipus serratus** Forbes
    Terminal segment of male second antenna with a calcar about one-eighth or less as long as the segment (Fig. 242F); average length 12 mm; Wisconsin, Minnesota, North Dakota, Montana, and Nebraska........**Eubranchipus ornatus** Holmes
25. Length 50 to 100 mm (Fig. 227A); known only from a few temporary alkali ponds in Washington, Nevada, Utah, and Montana .........**Branchinecta gigas** Lynch
    Usually 8 to 25 mm long ..............................................**26**
26. Basal segment of second antenna with a prominent dorsally directed peglike process just below midlength of the median surface (Fig. 239F); Colorado, Texas, Oklahoma, Wyoming, Kansas, Nebraska, New Mexico, and Arizona.
                                                     **Branchinecta packardi** Pearse
    Basal segment of second antenna otherwise ...................................**27**
27. Distal segment of second antenna tapering to a point (Figs. 239B, H) ............**28**
    Distal segment of second antenna otherwise ...............................**29**

FIG. 241.–Structure of *Branchinella* and *Eubranchipus*. A, half of frontal appendage of *Branchinella alachua*; B, half of frontal appendage of *B. lithaca*; C, antennal appendage of *Eubranchipus moorei*; D, ventral view of labrum of *E. bundyi*. (A modified from Dexter, 1953; B modified from Creaser, 1940; C modified from Brtek, 1967; D modified from Brtek, 1966.)

28. Basal segment of male second antenna with a row of spines along much of the median margin (Fig. 239B); a subarctic species, reported only from Wyoming mountains in the United States . . . . . . . . . . . . . . . . . . . . . . **Branchinecta paludosa** (O.F.M.)
   Basal segment of male second antenna with a spinous pad, a median protuberance, and many small distal spines (Fig. 239H); 21 to 35 mm long; known only from Washington . . . . . . . . . . . . . . . . . . . . . . . . . . . . . . **Branchinecta cornigera** Lynch

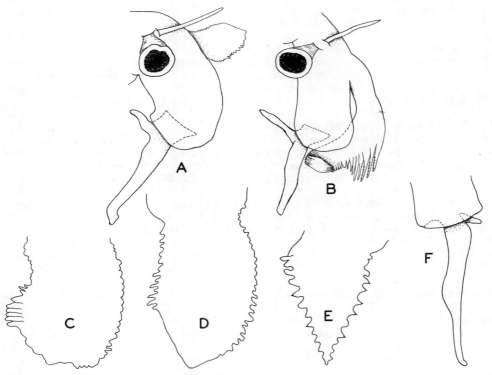

FIG. 242.–Structure of *Eubranchipus*. A, lateral view of head of *Eubranchipus vernalis*; B, lateral view of head of *E. serratus* (antennal appendage partly coiled); C, antennal appendage of *E. neglectus*; D, antennal appendage of *E. vernalis*; E, antennal appendage of *E. oregonus*; F, male second antenna of *E. ornatus*. (A and B modified from Mattox, 1939; C to F redrawn from Creaser, 1930.)

29. Basal segment of second antenna with a basal pad covered with minute spines (Fig. 239C); a eurythermal and euryhaline species reported from Iowa, Kansas, Nebraska, North Dakota, Wyoming, Colorado, Arizona, Nevada, Washington, and New Mexico.........................**Branchinecta lindahli** Packard
Basal segment of second antenna otherwise .................................**30**

30. Distal segment of second antenna curved medially, laterally flattened, and slightly concave on the lateral (anterior) surface (Fig. 239J); 11 to 24 mm long; known only from ponds in Oregon..................**Branchinecta dissimilis** Lynch
Distal segment of second antenna otherwise ................................**31**

31. Basal segment of second antenna with a spinous tubercle at about midlength, and usually with a small cylindrical process at the base of the segment (Fig. 239G); usually in ponds and pools at elevations of 1500 to 4000 m; California, Texas, Utah, Colorado, Wyoming, and Oregon ...**Branchinecta coloradensis** Packard
Basal segment of second antenna otherwise ...............................**32**

32. Female first antenna equal to or shorter than second antenna; 15 to 30 mm long; known only from alkali ponds in Washington and Wyoming.
**Branchinecta campestris** Lynch
Female first antenna longer than second antenna; Nevada, Washington, and California ................................**Branchinecta mackini** Dexter

33. Shell without growth lines ...............................................**34**
Shell with growth lines ..................................................**35**

34. Head not entirely covered by carapace ...............LYNCEIDAE, **Lynceus, 37**
Head entirely covered by carapace; known only from Arkansas rice fields.
**Eulimnadia alineata** Mattox

35. Head with a frontal appendage (Fig. 243E)...................LIMNADIIDAE, **40**
Head without a frontal appendage .......................................**36**

36. Apex of rostrum armed with a heavy spine (Fig. 243C); about 11 mm long; Kansas, Texas, Colorado, Utah, Oklahoma, and California.
LEPTESTHERIIDAE, **Leptestheria compleximanus** (Packard)
Apex of rostrum unarmed.........................CAENESTHERIIDAE, **51**

37. Second antennae 29-segmented; 4 to 6 mm long; Kansas, Colorado, New Mexico, and Texas......................................**Lynceus brevifrons** (Packard)
Second antennae with 20 segments or less .................................**38**

38. Second antennae 20-segmented; 4.2 mm long; rare, reported only from Texas.
**Lynceus gracilicornis** (Packard)
Second antennae with less than 20 segments ...............................**39**

39. Front of head of male narrow (Fig. 243B); second antennae 16-segmented; 2 to 6 mm long; the only common species in this genus; often in permanent ponds; widely distributed in the northeastern quarter of the United States, but reported as far west as Colorado, Oregon, Washington, and California.
**Lynceus brachyurus** Müller
Front of head of male broad and square; rami of second antennae 14- to 17-segmented; 4 mm long; Montana and Kansas ............**Lynceus mucronatus** (Packard)

40. Shell with about 7 to 18 growth lines, broadly oval, and 10 to 17 mm long; Massachusetts ................................**Limnadia lenticularis** (L.)
Shell with 2 to 11 growth lines (Fig. 243D); narrow, oval, and 3 to 11 mm long.
**Eulimnadia, 41**

41. Shell with one to four growth lines .......................................**42**
Shell with 5 to 12 growth lines..........................................**46**

42. Telson with 9 or 10 dorsal spines ........................................**43**
Telson with 12 to 16 dorsal spines .......................................**44**

43. Shell 5 to 6 mm long and 3 to 4 mm wide; rostrum rounded; known only from Louisiana ................................**Eulimnadia antillarum** (Baird)
Shell 4.3 mm long and 2.5 mm wide; rostrum pointed; known only from Maryland.
**Eulimnadia francescae** Mattox

44. Shell with two growth lines (Fig. 243D); male 4.2 mm long and 2.5 mm wide; forked filament between third and fourth spinules; known only from Illinois.
**Eulimnadia diversa** Mattox
Shell with three or four growth lines; 6 to 7.5 mm long.......................**45**

Fig. 243.–Structure of Conchostraca. A, frontal view of female *Lynceus brachyurus*; B, frontal view of male *L. brachyurus*; C, lateral view of head of *Leptestheria compleximanus*; D, lateral view of male shell of *Eulimnadia diversa*, ×9; E, head of female *E. diversa*; F, telson of *E. texana*; G, telson and dorsal portion of abdomen of *Cyzicus mexicanus*; H, lateral view of *Caenestheriella belfragei*, ×3.5; J, head of male *Cyzicus mexicanus*; K, head of female *C. mexicanus*; L, telson of *C. mexicanus*; M, anterior end of *Caenestheriella* showing acute rostrum; N, anterior end of *Eocyzicus concavus* showing shallow occipital notch. (A, B, D, G, H, J, and K redrawn from Mattox, 1939; C, F, and L modified from Packard.)

45. Telson with 12 dorsal spines; forked filament between first and second spines; shell averages 6.2 by 3.8 mm; Woods Hole, Massachusetts, area.
    **Eulimnadia agassizi** Packard
    Telson with 16 dorsal spines; forked filament between sixth and seventh spines; shell averages 7.3 by 4.3 mm; Illinois and Ohio ....... **Eulimnadia inflecta** Mattox
46. Female with five growth lines; less than 8 mm long when mature ...............**47**
    Female with 7 to 12 growth lines; more than 8 mm long when mature ............**48**
47. Seven to nine telson spines; shell averages 5 by 3 mm; Oklahoma.
    **Eulimnadia antlei** Mackin
    Sixteen to 20 telson spines (Fig. 243F); shell averages 7 by 4 mm; widely distributed in Florida, Texas, Kansas, Arizona, Louisiana, Nebraska, and Oklahoma.
    **Eulimnadia texana** Packard
48. Forked filament of telson between third and fourth spines; male first antenna exceeds scape of second antenna ............................................**49**
    Forked filament of telson between fifth and sixth spine; male first antenna reaches only to end of scape of second antenna; Connecticut.
    **Eulimnadia stoningtonensis** Berry
49. Male first antennae reach to second segment of second antennae; average of seven growth lines; Illinois.......................**Eulimnadia thompsoni** Mattox
    Male first antennae reach to third segment of second antennae; 10 to 12 growth rings. **50.**

50. Shell length–height ratio 1.3:1.0; transparent amber color; Maryland, Virginia, and
    Georgia ................................... **Eulimnadia ventricosa** Mattox
    Shell length–height ratio 1.5:1.0; transparent colorless; Arkansas rice fields.
    **Eulimnadia oryzae** Mattox
51. Occipital notch shallow and inconspicuous (Fig. 243N); rare .......... **Eocyzicus, 52**
    Occipital notch acute and pronounced (Fig. 243M) ........................... **53**
52. Shell with 18 to 22 growth lines; telson with 16 or 17 spines; Oklahoma and Texas.
    **Eocyzicus concavus** (Mackin)
    Shell with 14 to 16 growth lines; telson with 12 to 15 spines; reported only from
    Kansas, Nevada, and California ................. **Eocyzicus digueti** (Richard)
53. Rostrum of both male and female acute (Fig. 243M); second antennae 14- or 15-
    segmented ........................................... **Caenestheriella, 54**
    Rostrum of male spatulate (Fig. 243J); rostrum of female acute (Fig. 243K); second
    antennae 16- to 22-segmented ............................... **Cyzicus, 56**
54. Shell compressed ...................................................... **55**
    Shell thick and globose, with 21 to 25 growth lines (Fig. 243H); telson with 17 to 25
    spines; total length up to 11 mm; Kansas, Oklahoma, Texas, South Dakota,
    Montana, and Nebraska ................. **Caenestheriella belfragei** (Packard)
55. Umbones one-third length from anterior end; 13 to 21 growth lines; up to 8 mm long;
    Nebraska, Oklahoma, Oregon, South Dakota, Texas, and Missouri.
    **Caenestheriella setosa** (Pearse)
    Umbones one-fifth length from anterior end; 15 to 26 growth lines; up to 11 mm long;
    reported only from Ohio ................... **Caenestheriella gynecia** Mattox
56. With 35 or more crowded, indistinct growth lines; shell globose, 5 to 6 mm thick and
    9 to 13 mm long; South Dakota, Nebraska, Iowa, Colorado, Oklahoma, and
    North Dakota ................................. **Cyzicus morsei** (Packard)
    Growth lines distinct; shell not globose; umbo near anterior end ................ **57**
57. With 25 to 35 growth lines; shell swollen; hinge line short and straight; 9 to 12 mm
    long; telson with 40 to 50 spines (Fig. 243L); common from east coast to the
    Rockies and Canada to Mexico ................. **Cyzicus mexicanus** (Claus)
    With less than 25 growth lines; shell not swollen; rare, known only from California. **58**
58. Hinge line in an arc; 15 to 25 growth lines; up to 16 mm long; telson with 30 to 50
    dorsal spines ........................... **Cyzicus californicus** (Packard)
    Hinge line straight; with about 18 growth lines; average length 7 mm; telson with
    about 31 dorsal spines ......................... **Cyzicus elongatus** Mattox
59. Telson extended as a flat, paddle-shaped protuberance (supra-anal plate) (Figs. 244A–
    D); 25 to 34 body rings, of which two to eight are legless; second maxillae well
    developed ........................................... **Lepidurus, 60**
    Telson not extended as a supra-anal plate; 35 to 44 body rings, of which 5 to 13 are
    legless; second maxillae reduced in adult; a single highly variable species
    generally distributed west of meridian 99 or 100; temporary waters and rice
    fields......................................... **Triops longicaudatus** (LeConte)
60. Anterior part of nuchal organ between posterior part of eye tubercles, not far from
    hind margin of eyes (Figs. 244F–H) ..................................... **61**
    Nuchal organ considerably behind eye tubercles (Fig. 244E); 30 to 34 body rings; 60
    to 78 pairs of legs; supra-anal plate simple or bilobed; alkali ponds in Washing-
    ton, Nevada, Montana, California, Oregon, and Wyoming.
    **Lepidurus lemmoni** Holmes
61. With 9.5 to 13 leg–bearing abdominal rings; usually 26 to 29 body rings .......... **62**
    With 16 or 17 leg-bearing abdominal rings; 33 body rings; supra-anal plate slightly
    bilobed (Fig. 244C); about 60 pairs of legs; males unknown; a poorly known
    species reported from Colorado, Arizona, and Utah.
    **Lepidurus bilobatus** Packard
62. Third to fifth endites of first leg rather similar in size, projecting very little or not at
    all beyond edge of carapace; 41 to 46 pairs of legs; reported from temporary
    pools in subarctic America and not known from the United States.
    **Lepidurus arcticus** (Pallas)
    Third to fifth endites of first leg dissimilar in size, the fifth endite projecting well
    beyond the carapace margin (Fig. 244J)................................ **63**

FIG. 244.–Structure of Notostraca. A, dorsal view of telson and last two body rings of *Lepidurus couesi*; B, dorsal view of telson and last two body rings of *L. lemmoni*; C, dorsal view of telson of *L. bilobatus*; D, dorsal view of telson and last two body rings of *L. packardi*; E, eyes and nuchal organ of *L. lemmoni*; F, eyes and nuchal organ of *L. packardi*; G, eyes and nuchal organ of *L. couesi*; H, eyes and nuchal organ of *Triops longicaudatus*; J, first leg of *Lepidurus couesi* (note long fifth endite). (A to H modified from Linder, 1952.)

**63.** Median spines of supra-anal plate similar in size, few in number, and not placed on a keel (Fig. 244D); about 35 pairs of legs; a poorly known species reported from only two California localities .................... **Lepidurus packardi** Simon
Median spines of supra-anal plate dissimilar in size, numerous, and placed on a keel (Fig. 244A); about 35 to 40 pairs of legs; reported from alkali ponds in western states ........................................ **Lepidurus couesi** Packard

## EUBRANCHIOPODA REFERENCES

BAQUI, I. U. 1963. Studies on the postembryonic development of the fairy shrimp Streptocephalus seali Ryder. *Tulane Stud. Zool.* **10:**91–120.

BELK, D. 1973. *Key to the Anostraca of North America.* 12 pp. mimeographed.

BRTEK, J. 1967. Eubranchipus (Creaseria) moorei n. sp. *Annot. Zool. Bot.* **36:**1–7.

CANNON, H. G., and F. M. C. LEAK. 1933. On the feeding mechanism of the Branchiopoda. *Philos. Trans. Roy. Soc. Lond. B,* 222:267–352.

COLE, G. A., and R. J. BROWN. 1967. The chemistry of Artemia habitats. *Ecology* **48:**858–861.

CREASER, E. P. 1930. Revision of the phyllopod genus Eubranchipus with description of a new species. *Occas. Pap. Mus. Zool. Univ. Mich.* **208:**1–13.

——. 1930a. The North American phyllopods of the genus Streptocephalus. Ibid. **217:**1–10.

——. 1940. A new species of phyllopod crustacean from Stone Mountain, Georgia. *J. Wash. Acad. Sci.* **30:**435–437.

DADAY DE DEÉS, E. 1910. Monographie systématique des phyllopodes anostracés. *Ann. Sci. Nat. Zool. (9)* **11:**91–492.

——. 1915. Monographie systématique des phyllopodes conchostracés. Ibid. **20:**39–330.

——. 1923. Monographie systématique des phyllopodes conchostracés (2ᵉ partie). Ibid. (10) **6:**255–390.

——. 1925. Monographie systématique des phyllopodes conchostracés. Troisième partie. Ibid. **8:**143–184.

————. 1926. Monographie systématique phyllopodes conchostracés. Troisième partie (suite). Ibid. 9:1–81.

————. 1927. Monographie systématique des phyllopodes conchostracés. Troisième partie (fin.). Ibid. 10:1–112.

DEMPSTER, R. P. 1953. The use of larval and adult brine shrimp in aquarium fish culture. Calif. Fish and Game 39:355–364.

DEXTER, R. W. 1946. Further studies on the life history and distribution of Eubranchipus vernalis (Verrill). Ohio J. Sci. 46:31–44.

————. 1953. Studies on North American fairy shrimps with the description of two new species. Am. Midl. Nat. 49:751–771.

————. 1956. A new fairy shrimp from Western United States, with notes on other North American species. J. Wash. Acad. Sci. 46:159–165.

DEXTER, R. W., and M. S. FERGUSON, 1943. Life history and distributional studies on Eubranchipus serratus Forbes (1876). Am. Midl. Nat. 29:210–222.

DEXTER, R. W., and C. H. KUEHNLE. 1951. Further studies on the fairy shrimp populations of northeastern Ohio. Ohio J. Sci. 51:73–86.

DEXTER, R. W., and D. B. McCARRAHER. 1967. Clam shrimps as pests in fish rearing ponds. Prog. Fish-Cult. 29:105–107.

ERIKSSON, S. 1936. Studien über die Fangapparate der Branchiopoden nebst einigen phylogenetischen Bemerkungen. Zool. Bidr. Uppsala 15:23–287.

FRYER, G. 1966. Branchinecta gigas Lynch, a non-filter-feeding raptatory anostracan, with notes on the feeding habits of certain other anostracans. Proc. Linn. Soc. Lond. 177:19–34.

HARTLAND-ROWE, R. 1967. Eubranchipus intricatus n. sp., a widely distributed North American fairy-shrimp, with a note on its ecology. Can. J. Zool. 45:663–666.

HEATH, H. 1924. The external development of certain phyllopods. J. Morphol. 38:453–483.

HORNE, F. R. 1974. Phyllopods of some southern high plains saline playas. Southwest Nat. 18:475–479.

JENNINGS, R. H., and D. M. WHITAKER. 1941. The effect of salinity upon the rate of excystment of Artemia. Biol. Bull. 80:194–201.

JENSEN, A. C. 1918. Some observations on Artemia gracilis, the brine shrimp of Great Salt Lake. Ibid. 34:18–32.

KUENEN, D. J. 1939. Systematical and physiological notes on the brine shrimp, Artemia. Arch. Neerl. Zool. 3:365–449.

LINDER, F. 1941. Contributions to the morphology and the taxonomy of the Branchiopoda Anostraca. Zool. Bidr. Uppsala 20:101–302.

————. 1952. Contributions to the morphology and taxonomy of the Branchiopoda Notostraca, with special reference to the North American species. Proc. U.S. Nat. Mus. 102:1–69.

LITTLEPAGE, J. L., and M. N. McGINLEY. 1965. A bibliography of the genus Artemia (Artemia salina) 1812-1962. Spec. Publ. San Francisco Aquarium Soc., Calif. Acad. Sci. 1:1–73 (mimeographed).

LOCHHEAD, J. H., and M. S. LOCHHEAD. 1941.

Studies on the blood and related tissues in Artemia (Crustacea, Anostraca). J. Morphol. 68:593–632.

LONGHURST, A. R. 1955. A review of the Notostraca. Bull. Br. Mus. (Nat. Hist.), Zool. 3:1–57.

LOWNDES, A. G. 1933. The feeding mechanism of Chirocephalus diaphanus Prévost, the fairy shrimp. Proc. Zool. Soc. Lond. (B) (1933): 1093–1118.

LYNCH, J. E. 1937. A giant new species of fairy shrimp of the genus Branchinecta from the State of Washington. Proc. U.S. Nat. Mus. 84:555–562.

————. 1958. Branchinecta cornigera, a new species of Anostracan phyllopod from the state of Washington. Ibid. 108:25–37.

————. 1960. The fairy shrimp Branchinecta campestris from northwestern United States (Crustacea: Phyllopoda). Ibid. 112:549–561.

————. 1964. Packard's and Pearse's species of Branchinecta: analysis of a nomenclatural involvement. Am. Midl. Nat. 71:466–488.

————. 1966. Lepidurus lemmoni Holmes: a redescription with notes on variation and distribution. Trans. Am. Microsc. Soc. 85:181–192.

————. 1972. Lepidurus couesii Packard (Notostraca) redescribed with a discussion of specific characters in the genus. Crustaceana 23:43–49.

————. 1972a. Branchinecta dissimilis n. sp. a new species of fairy shrimp, with a discussion of specific characters in the genus. Trans. Am. Microsc. Soc. 91:240–243.

MACKIN, J. G. 1940. A new species of conchostracan phyllopod, Eulimnadia antlei, from Oklahoma. Am. Midl. Nat. 23:219–221.

————. 1942. A new species of phyllopod crustacean from the southwestern short-grass prairies. Proc. U.S. Nat. Mus. 92:33–39.

————. 1952. On the correct specific names of several North American species of Branchinecta Verrill. Am. Midl. Nat. 47:61–65.

MATHIAS, P. 1937. Biologie des Crustacés Phyllopodes. Actual. Sci. Ind. 447:1–107.

MATTOX, N. T. 1937. Studies on the life history of a new species of fairy shrimp, Eulimnadia diversa. Trans. Am. Microsc. Soc. 56:249–255.

————. 1939. Descriptions of two new species of the genus Eulimnadia and notes on the other Phyllopoda of Illinois. Am. Midl. Nat. 22:642–653.

————. 1950. Notes on the life history and description of a new species of conchostracan phyllopod, Caenestheriella gynecia. Trans. Am. Microsc. Soc. 69:50–53.

————. 1953. A new conchostracan phyllopod, Eulimnadia alineata, from Arkansas. Am. Midl. Nat. 49:210–213.

————. 1953a. Two new species of Eulimnadia from Maryland and Virginia (Crustacea: Conchostraca) J. Wash. Acad. Sci. 43:57–60.

————. 1954. A new Eulimnadia from the rice fields of Arkansas with a key to the American species of the genus. Tulane Stud. Zool. 2:1–10.

————. 1954a. Description of Eocyzicus concavus (Mackin) with a review of other North American species of the genus (Crustacea: Conchostraca). J. Wash. Acad. Sci. 44:46–49.

————. 1957. A new estheriid conchostracan with a review of the other North American forms. *Am. Midl. Nat.* **58**:367–377.

MCCARRAHER, D. B. 1970. Some ecological relations of fairy shrimps in alkaline habitats of Nebraska. *Am. Midl. Nat.* **84**:59–68.

MOORE, W. G. 1951. Observations on the biology of Streptocephalus seali. *Proc. La. Acad. Sci.* **14**:57–65.

————. 1957. Studies on the laboratory culture of Anostraca. *Trans. Am. Microsc. Soc.* **76**:159–173.

————. 1966. New World fairy shrimps of the genus Streptocephalus (Branchiopoda, Anostraca). *Southwest Nat.* **1**:24–48.

MOORE, W. G., and J. B. YOUNG. 1964. Fairy shrimps of the genus Thamnocephalus (Branchiopoda, Anostraca) in the United States and Mexico. *Ibid.* **9**:68–77.

PACKARD, A. 1883. A monograph of the phyllopod Crustacea of North America, with remarks on the Order Phyllocarida. *12th Ann. Rept. U.S. Geol. and Geog. Surv. of the Terr.* 1878 (*Hayden Survey*), Part I:295–592.

PREUSS, G. 1951. Die Verwandtschaft der Anostraca und Phyllopoda. *Zool. Anz.* **147**:49–64.

PROVASOLI, L., and K. SHIRAISHI. 1959. Axenic cultivation of the brine shrimp Artemia salina. *Biol. Bull.* **117**:347–355.

RELYEA, G. M. 1937. The brine shrimp of Great Salt Lake. *Am. Nat.* **71**:612–616.

ROSENBERG, L. E. 1946. Fairy shrimps in California rice fields. *Science* **104**:111–112.

SARS, G. O. 1896. Phyllocarida og Phyllopoda. *Fauna Norv.* **1**:1–140.

SHANTZ, H. L. 1905. Notes on North American species of Branchinecta and their habits. *Biol. Bull.* **9**:249–264.

SISSOM, S. L. 1976. Studies on a new fairy shrimp from the playa lakes of West Texas (Branchiopoda Anostraca, Thamnocephalidae). *Crustaceana* **30**:39–42.

WARREN, H. S. 1938. The segmental excretory glands of Artemia salina Linn. var. principalis Simon. (The brine shrimp.) *J. Morphol.* **62**:263–298.

WEAVER, C. R. 1943. Observations on the life cycle of the fairy shrimp. Eubranchipus vernalis. *Ecology* **24**:500–502.

WHITAKER, D. M. 1940. The tolerance of Artemia for cold and high vacuum. *J. Exp. Zool.* **83**:391–399.

# Chapter 16

# CLADOCERA (WATER FLEAS)

BECAUSE of their interesting habits, their availability in nearly all types of fresh-water habitats, and their complex but easily studied anatomy, the water fleas have been favorite objects of observation by both amateur and professional biologists ever since the invention of the microscope.

**General characteristics.** Most members of the Order Cladocera are between 0.2 and 3.0 mm long. The body is not clearly segmented, and in the great majority of species the thoracic and abdominal regions are covered by a secreted shell or carapace that has a general bivalved appearance but is actually a single folded piece that gapes ventrally. In lateral view the shell is variously shaped; it may be oval, circular, elongated, or angular. There are often surface reticulations, striations, or other types of markings. In many species the posterior end has a spinule or spine, and the ventral edges of the valves usually bear setae. The inner surface of the valves is lined with the delicate body wall.

The head is a compact structure and does not open ventrally as the valves do. It is bent downward and dorsally it is sometimes indistinctly set off from the body by a cervical sinus or notch. The most conspicuous internal structure of the head is the large compound eye. It consists of a few to many small hyaline lenses surrounding a mass of pigment granules. It is rotated constantly and jerkily by three pairs of small muscles. A single small ocellus lies posterior or ventral to the compound eye. The first antennae (antennules) are inserted on the ventral side of the head near its posterior margin. They are usually inconspicuous, unsegmented, and bear olfactory setae. The second antennae, however, are very large and are inserted laterally near the posterior margin of the head. Each consists of a stout basal segment, a segmented dorsal ramus, and a segmented ventral ramus. The two rami bear a variable number of plumose setae. Setation formulas are often used as a means of identifying genera and species. Thus the setation formula for *Daphnia* is 0–0–1–3/1–1–3; it indicates that the dorsal ramus of the antenna is four-segmented and that the basal, second, third, and fourth segments bear 0, 0, 1, and 3 setae, respectively; it also indicates a three-segmented ventral ramus of which the basal, second, and third segments bear 1, 1, and 3 setae, respectively. The antennae are activated by a set of powerful muscles that originate dorsally in the "neck" region. Externally, there is a strengthening ridge, or fornix, above the base of each antenna. The beak, or rostrum, is a more or less well defined projection of the head between or in front of the antennules. The vertex of the head is that part that lies anterior to the compound eye.

The small mouthparts are situated near the junction of head and body. Beginning at the anterior end, they consist of (1) a median labrum; (2) a pair of stout, sclerotized, toothed, or ridged grinding mandibles; (3) a pair of small, pointed maxillae, used in pushing food between the mandibles; and (4) a single median labium. In some of the Macrothricidae and Chydoridae the labium bears a median keel that is of systematic value.

There are five or six pairs of lobed, leaflike thoracic legs, bearing numerous hairs and setae (Fig. 249). Although the legs are fundamentally biramous, this condition

350

FIG. 245.–Anatomy of female *Daphnia pulex,* ×70, diagrammatic, muscles not shown. *B*, brain; *BC*, brood chamber; *C*, digestive caecum; *CE*, compound eye; *F*, fornix; *FA*, first antenna (antennule); *H*, heart; *INT*, intestine; *O*, ocellus; *OV*, ovary; *R*, rostrum or beak; *SG*, shell gland. (Greatly modified from Storch, 1925.)

is not clearly evident because of their considerable modification. In the Sididae and Holopedidae all legs are similar, but in the other families the first two pairs are more or less prehensile and may aid in clinging to a substrate.

The true abdomen is suppressed, but there is a large postabdomen at the posterior end of the body. It is usually bent forward so that the dorsal side is downward. It bears two long abdominal setae, two ter-

minal claws, and usually a series of marginal or lateral teeth or denticles. The postabdomen seems to be used chiefly for cleaning debris from the thoracic legs, although it may aid in locomotion.

During the greater part of the year Cladocera populations consist almost exclusively of females, the males being abundant only in the autumn or spring. In many species, however, males are rare or unknown. Anatomically, males are distinguished from periods of active swimming and often use the antennae incidentally for obtaining a purchase on vegetation and bottom debris. The postabdomen is also useful for locomotion in bottom-inhabiting species. A cladoceran may literally kick itself along, sometimes by quite respectable hops.

**Feeding.** Complex movements of the highly setose thoracic legs (Figs. 247, 248) produce a constant current of water between the valves. These movements further serve to filter food particles from the water and collect them in a median ventral groove at the base of the legs. This stream of food is fed forward to the mouth parts where the particles may be ground between the surfaces of the mandibles before being taken into the mouth.

Algae and Protozoa have often been assumed to be the chief foods, to the exclusion of other materials, but is is now well known that organic detritus of all kinds, as well as bacteria, are very important and commonly form the great bulk of material ingested. It has also been successfully demonstrated that the feeding movements of the legs of plankton species are so efficient that they separate some colloidal organic particles from the water. Although there is a little evidence that certain types of food, such as particular groups of algae, Protozoa, or bacteria may be selected by some species, it is generally believed that all organic particles of suitable size are ingested without any selective mechanism. When undesirable material or large tangled masses are introduced between the mandibles, they may be removed by spines at the base of the first legs and then kicked out of the shell by the postabdomen. Although the food stream in the median groove is continuous, ingestion may cease for varying periods. Minute amounts of dissolved organic materials may be absorbed by the general body surface, but they are of no metabolic significance.

A few genera, such as *Polyphemus* and *Leptodora,* are predaceous and have the legs modified for seizing. Their prey consists mostly of other entomostraca and rotifers.

The finely divided food is passed from

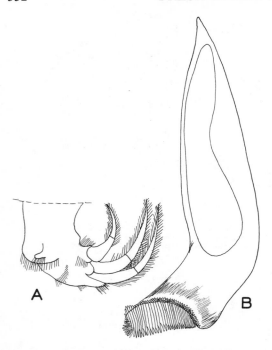

FIG. 246.–Mouthparts of *Daphnia pulex.* A, maxilla; B, mandible. (Redrawn from Lilljeborg.)

females by their smaller size, larger antennules, modified postabdomen, and first legs armed with a stout hook used in clasping (Fig. 250E).

Limnetic species are usually light-colored and translucent. Pond, littoral, and bottom species are darker in color, ranging from light yellowish-brown to reddish-brown, grayish, or almost black. Pigmentation occurs in both the carapace and general body tissues.

**Locomotion.** For the most part, Cladocera keep intermittently in motion, the antennae being the chief organs of locomotion. In some genera, such as *Latona,* single vigorous strokes of the antennae produce powerful leaps. *Daphnia* and its relatives move by a series of "hops," produced by more rapid and less vigorous strokes. In some other genera the swimming movements have been characterized as "uncertain" and "tottering." A few genera, including *Holopedium* and *Scapholeberis,* habitually swim upside down. Species occurring on a substrate have less frequent

FIG. 247.–Ventral view of female *Acantholeberis curvirostris,* showing the complex setation. (Modified from Fryer, 1974.)

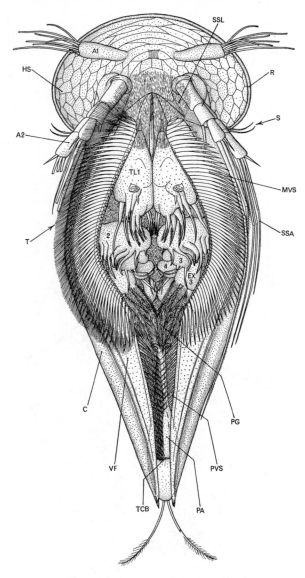

FIG. 248.–*Graptoleberis testudinaria* seen from below as it glides over a surface. The medium ventral setae (MVS) form a tight chamber between the body and the substrate surface. The first and second trunk limbs scrape food particles from the surface, and there are no significant currents within the carapace chamber. (From Fryer, 1968.)

the mouth parts to the esophagus in small masses of definite size. The time required to fill the digestive tract varies considerably, depending on the species, temperature, concentration of food, and other factors. Laboratory observations show a range of 10 to 240 minutes. Hasler (1937) demonstrated the presence of fat, carbohydrate, and protein digesting enzymes in *Daphnia* and *Polyphemus*. He found the pH of the digestive tract of *Daphnia* to range between 6.8 and 7.2. The indigestible

FIG. 249.–Legs of adult female *Daphnia pulex*. A, first leg; B, second leg; C, third leg; D, fourth leg; E, fifth leg. (Modified from Uéno.)

residue leaves the body through the anus, which is usually situated on the lower (dorsal) border of the postabdomen.

**Internal anatomy.** Although the complex muscular system obscures some of the smaller anatomical features, the essential parts of most of the organ systems can be easily distinguished. The digestive system is relatively unspecialized. In the head region the narrow esophagus opens into a stomach that, however, is often indistinguishable from the remainder of the tubular digestive tract, the intestine. In some genera there are one or two digestive caeca that open into the anterior part of the intestine. The course of the intestine may be relatively straight or convoluted. It can always be distinguished in both living and preserved specimens because of its contained dark food mass. In some of the Chydoridae there is a posterior ventral caecum.

The posterior part of the digestive tract is somewhat specialized as a rectum. It is now known that many algae cells are still viable after traversing the cladoceran digestive tract. Many chydorids and macrothricid cladocerans exhibit "anal drinking," which would appear to prevent loss of digestive products and to increase the efficiency of food utilization.

The simple oval or football-shaped heart lies behind the head on the dorsal side. Blood enters the heart through two lateral ostia and leaves through an anterior opening. At room temperature the heart beats about as rapidly as one can open and close his fist. There are no blood vessels, the blood being roughly guided about in the hemocoel by a series of thin mesenteries. The blood plasma is usually colorless or has a faint yellowish cast; it contains numerous colorless corpuscles.

Some pond species, however, are

Fig. 250.–Sex characters of Cladocera. A, rostrum region of female *Daphnia pulex*; B, rostrum region of male *D. pulex*; C, postabdomen of male *Simocephalus exspinosus*; D, postabdomen of female *S. exspinosus*; E, first leg of male *D. pulex*. (C and D redrawn from Banta; E modified from Uéno.)

pinkish, owing to dissolved hemoglobin that may be formed when dissolved oxygen concentrations are low. This appears to be associated with an increased life span, more energetic swimming, and faster embryonic development. Presumably the hemoglobin functions in the respiration of embryos that are retained in a more or less closed brood pouch with little access to the outside water.

The exchange of oxygen and carbon dioxide occurs through the general body surface but especially along the inner surfaces of the valves and through the surfaces of the legs.

Irregular or looped shell glands, situated near the anterior end of the valves, are thought to function as excretory organs. In some of the Chydoridae there is a long tubular gland that arises from the rectum and lies freely in the hemocoel. Its function is unknown.

The nervous system consists of the usual ventral double nerve cord, relatively few ganglia, paired nerves, and a brain just anterior (dorsal) to the esophagus. Both the compound eye and the ocellus appear to be important in orientation to light sources and light intensity. Olfactory stimuli are thought to be received by the setae at the edges of the valves, by the antennules, and by areas around the mouth. The sense of touch is centered particularly in the abdominal setae and sensory hairs on the basal segment of the antennae.

All Cladocera have small structures on or near the middorsal line known as "head pores." These are borne on the head shield, an unpaired plate covering the frontal and lateral surfaces of the head. In adult Chydoridae there are one to five minute head pores on the midline of the posterior portion of the head shield (Frey, 1959). The number and arrangement of these struc-

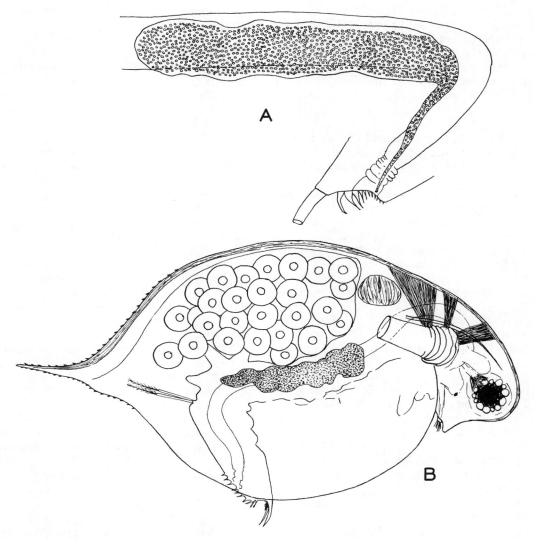

FIG. 251.–Cladoceran structures. A, postabdomen region of male *Simocephalus exspinosus* showing testis, sperm duct, intestine, and rectum; B, mature female *Daphnia pulex* (×70) showing ovary, parthenogenetic eggs in brood chamber, heart, antennal muscles, and compound eye. (A modified from Banta; B modified from Uéno.)

tures may be used as taxonomic characters in the Chydoridae. All the other families of Cladocera have (larger) head pores, at least in some stage of their ontogeny, but here they are associated with certain underlying tissues. Such structures have variously been called, for example, neck organs, dorsal organs, and cervical glands. It is possible that they have a special respiratory function in early instars.

Gonads are easily distinguished only in sexually mature specimens. The two elongated ovaries lie lateral or somewhat ventral to the intestine in the thoracic region of the body (Fig. 251B). Depending on the stage in reproduction, an ovary is densely granular, with large oogonial nuclei, or it contains a mass of large, pigmented, granular, yolky eggs. Each oviduct is located dorsally at the posterior end; it is so delicate that it cannot be distinguished except when an egg is passing through it. The testes are smaller and contain small, semi-transparent, granulelike sperm (Fig. 251A). The sperm ducts are posterior continuations of the testes, which pass laterally to the intestine and rectum and open on the postabdomen near the anus or claws. A part of the postabdomen is sometimes specialized to form a copulatory organ.

**Reproduction in general.** Reproduction is parthenogenetic during the greater part of the year in most habitats, and only female young are produced. The eggs undergo a single maturation division in the ovary and a number are released at a time via the oviducts into the brood chamber. The latter is a cavity dorsal to the body proper and between the valves; it is effectively closed posteriorly by the abdominal processes. Depending on the species and environmental conditions, the number of eggs per clutch varies considerably; usually there are between 2 and 40, and most frequently between 10 and 20. The parthenogenetic eggs undergo further development in the brood chamber and hatch into young similar in form to the adult. The parent then liberates them to the outside by moving the postabdomen downward. Normally, one clutch of eggs is released into the brood chamber during each adult instar.

**Seasonal abundance.** In early spring relatively few cladocerans are to be found in lakes and ponds. Such populations consist of females that survived over the winter or recently hatched from winter (resting) eggs. As the water reaches a temperature of 6° to 12°, active reproduction begins and subsequently speeds up tremendously so that large populations result (in exceptional cases as high as 200 to 500 individuals per liter of water). Populations in ponds then soon begin to wane, so that few individuals can be found during the summer months. In the autumn there may or may not be a second population pulse, but during the winter the population is invariably low, with little or no reproduction. Thus in a pond where the common species is *Daphnia pulex* or *D. magna* the population may be monocyclic or dicyclic, that is, hav-

ing one or two population maxima during the year.

In larger bodies of water, however, seasonal variations in the abundance of Cladocera are not usually so pronounced. There is commonly a spring maximum and sometimes a less well defined fall maximum, but summer and winter populations are large compared with those of ponds. In some lakes *D. pulex* is monocyclic, in others dicyclic. *Daphnia rosea* may be monocyclic, dicyclic, and in some cold lakes, acyclic, that is, without any pronounced population maxima during the entire year. Other common forms exhibiting monocycly or dicycly are *Simocephalus* and *Ceriodaphnia*. Occasionally, as in *Sida crystallina* in some lakes, there may be a single autumn pulse. There are also many Cladocera that exhibit single long population pulses during the warmer months in certain lakes. Examples are *Diaphanosoma brachyurum*, *Chydorus sphaericus*, *Bosmina longirostris* and *Moina*.

It is useless to predict or formulate any preconceived notions concerning the seasonal abundance of Cladocera in a particular lake or pond. Species differ greatly from one another in their seasonal abundance; a single species may have quite different population curves in two adjacent bodies of water; furthermore, relative abundance and the specific time of maximum and minimum populations may vary considerably within a single species in the same lake from one year to the next.

**Male production, resting eggs.** Numbers of males begin to appear in ponds in the spring, late in the intensive reproductive cycle. Sometimes only 5 percent of the population may consist of males; sometimes more than half are males. The factors responsible for the appearance of males in cladoceran populations have been the object of long and intensive studies by many investigators. We do not as yet have a detailed explanation of the phenomenon. By way of partial explanation, however, it is probable that a complex interplay of factors is responsible. Production of male eggs seems to be induced mostly by (1) crowding

FIG. 252.–Ephippium of *Daphnia pulex*.

of the females and the subsequent accumulation of excretory products, (2) a decrease in available food, (3) a water temperature of 14° to 17°, and (4) light intensity. These conditions (and probably others also), by altering the metabolism, appear to affect the chromosome mechanism in such a way that parthenogenetic male eggs rather than parthenogenetic female eggs are released into the brood chamber.

The same conditions responsible for male production, if continued for a longer time, appear to induce the appearance of sexual eggs. Females producing such eggs are morphologically similar to parthenogenetic females, but they produce only one, two, or sometimes several large opaque "resting" eggs, and, unlike the parthenogenetic females, they are capable of copulation with males. The fertilized eggs pass into the brood chamber, the walls of which then become thickened and darkened to form an ephippium (Fig. 252). In the Daphnidae the ephippium separates from the rest of the shell at the subsequent molt. In the Chydoridae it remains attached to the shell at the molt. Sometimes as many as a third or half of the females in a population may bear ephippia.

On being released, the ephippia sink to the bottom, become attached to the substrate (certain Macrothricidae), or float on the surface. In the last event, they may be blown ashore and accumulated in diminutive windrows. Ephippia and their contained eggs are capable of withstanding drying and freezing, and their production is clearly an adaptation to adverse environmental conditions. It has been shown that ephippia are sometimes viable even after passing through the digestive tract of fish. Ephippia are of special value in small ponds that dry up during the summer months. When such basins become filled with water in the early autumn, a large percentage of the ephippial eggs hatch into parthenogenetic females. Then there may be an autumn pulse followed by the appearance of males, sexual females, and ephippia that winter over and give rise to at least a part of the small seed population in the following spring.

Thus it is seen that during most of the year the population consists entirely of parthenogenetic females, but for short periods the population may be complex, consisting of parthenogenetic females, males, unfertilized sexual females, and fertilized sexual females.

In bodies of water larger than ponds, ephippia are produced by smaller percentages of the populations, and in limnetic populations in large lakes it is thought that reproduction may be entirely parthenogenetic the year round, especially in *Daphnia rosea*.

The expressions "monocyclic" and "dicyclic" are really used in two different ways in the literature. They may refer to an annual population curve having one or two pronounced maxima, without reference to types of reproduction, or they may be used to designate populations having one or two periods of syngamic reproduction during the year.

The older idea of internal genetic or physiological "rhythms" being responsible for the periodic occurrence of syngamic reproduction has been discarded. The experimental work of Banta and others has demonstrated conclusively that the mode of reproduction is influenced by environmental factors. By changing the culture solutions frequently, Banta reared several common Cladocera for 800 to 1600 successive parthenogenetic generations (more than 27 years). Males, sexual females, and subsequent ephippia may be easily produced by crowding the mothers in a small amount of culture solution or by chilling the culture.

Laboratory observations have shown that under appropriate conditions a mature parthenogenetic female may begin to produce sexual eggs, or a sexual female may change over and produce parthenogenetic eggs. Males usually appear in both natural and controlled populations before females begin the formation of sexual eggs in the ovary. When a female passes an unfertilized sexual egg into the developing ephippium it disintegrates. There are, however, a few records in the literature of such eggs developing into parthenogenetic females.

Wood (1938) has contributed much to our understanding of the induction of hatching of ephippial eggs. Working with *Daphnia*, she found that (1) the considerable majority of eggs died when stored either wet or dry for one to many weeks; (2) the longer the period of storage, the greater the mortality; (3) a few eggs stored wet for seven years were viable; (4) exposure to low temperatures decreased the percentage of hatch; (5) placing eggs in fresh culture medium or allowing them to dry out only a day or two gave the highest percentage of hatch, usually 35 to 45 percent; and (6) aeration and changing the culture solution frequently induced hatching of a comparable percentage of eggs that had not been allowed to dry out.

**Development, life cycle.** Length of life, from release of the egg into the brood chamber until the death of the adult, is highly variable, depending on the species and environmental conditions. *Daphnia rosea* usually lives for 28 to 33 days in laboratory cultures. MacArthur and Baillie (1929) found that *D. magna* lived an average of 26, 42, and 108 days at 28°, 18°, and 8°, respectively. Limnetic individuals undoubtedly live through the entire winter at low temperatures, although high-latitude and high-altitude populations overwinter by means of ephippial eggs. Poor food supply also increases length of life.

Four distinct periods may be recognized in the life history of a cladoceran: egg, juvenile, adolescent, and adult. When a clutch of eggs is released into the brood chamber, segmentation begins promptly; the young, in the first juvenile instar and similar in form to the adult, are released from the brood chamber in about two days. There are but few juvenile instars, although greatest growth occurs during these stages. *Moina macrocopa* has two juvenile instars, *Daphnia rosea* has three, *D. pulex* has three or four, and *D. magna* three to five. The adolescent period is a single instar between the last juvenile instar and the first adult instar; during this instar the first clutch of eggs reaches full development in the ovary. As soon as the animal molts at the end of the adolescent instar and enters the first adult instar, the first clutch of parthenogenetic eggs is released into the brood chamber. During the first adult instar the second clutch of eggs is developing in the ovary. Successive adult instars and new clutches of young are produced in a similar manner. However, there is often a sterile period during the last few instars of life.

As in all other Crustacea, growth, in terms of increase in size, becomes apparent only immediately after each molt. During juvenile instars there may be almost a doubling of size after each molt, the increase in volume occurring within a few seconds or minutes and before the new exoskeleton hardens and loses its elasticity.

The number of adult instars is much more variable than the number of juvenile instars. *Daphnia pulex* usually has 18 to 25 adult instars; *D. rosea*, 10 to 19; and *D. magna*, 6 to 22. As already inferred, the duration of a single adult instar is highly variable, from a day to several weeks, though about two days under favorable conditions. At the close of each adult instar four events follow one another in rapid succession, usually in a few minutes to a few hours. These are the release of young from the brood chamber to the outside, molting, increase in size, and the release of a new clutch of eggs to the brood chamber.

**Cyclomorphosis.** One of the most intriguing and puzzling of all cladoceran problems is the matter of cyclomorphosis, or seasonal changes in morphology, especially in females of limnetic species such as *Daphnia pulex* and *D. rosea*. A population

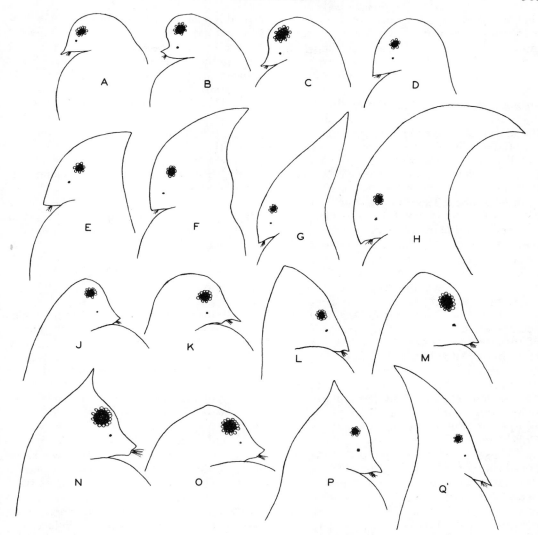

FIG. 253.–Some variations in head form in *Daphnia*. A to C, J, and K, *D. pulex*; D to H, *D. retrocurva*; L, M, *D. galeata mendotae*; N, O, *D. ambigua*; P, Q, *D. dubia*.

of a cyclomorphic species has a homogeneous "normal," or round-headed, form during the late fall, winter, and early spring. As the water becomes warmer and the population develops, however, there is commonly a progressive increase in the longitudinal axis produced by a general elongation of the head and the appearance of a "helmet" (Figs. 253E, P, Q). Characteristically, the helmets become fully developed by midsummer, when they may be quite bizarre (Figs. 253G, H, Q). Beginning in the late summer or early autumn, the morphology of the head progressively reverts so that the "normal" head condition prevails by late autumn. In addition to changes in the shape of the head, cyclomorphosis may also involve changes in size of eye and length of the posterior spine.

The problem is greatly complicated by the fact that the degree of summer helmet development differs widely in the same species, even in two neighboring lakes. Cyclomorphosis is less pronounced in ponds and shallow lakes, and the degree of helmet development is relatively consistent from one individual to another at any one time, but in larger and deeper lakes cyclomorphosis and the degree of helmet development in a population is much more variable, and both strongly developed and poorly developed helmets, as well as intergrades, may be found in the same townet sample.

Explanations of these seasonal changes in form have naturally long been sought for in the changing seasonal ecological conditions in bodies of water. Between 1900 and 1910 Wesenberg-Lund and Ostwald elaborated their "Buoyance Theory," which attempted to explain the occurrence of helmets as a flotation adaptation to decreased viscosities of water at summer temperatures. Subsequent observations and experimental work have discredited this viewpoint. More recent proposals have centered around nutrition, internal cycles, and the accumulation of waste products, but none of these now receives favorable consideration by investigators in this field.

One of the more logical explanations of cyclomorphosis appears to center around temperature, and particularly the temperature during the early stages of development. The controlled experiments of Coker and Addlestone (1938) are illuminating. These investigators found that the last one-third of the period of development of the first juvenile instar in the brood chamber was the critical period. *Daphnia rosea* raised at a temperature of 10° or below during this period all had round heads; 15 percent of those raised at 12° had pointed heads; 33 percent of those raised at 13° had pointed heads; 87 percent at 14° had pointed heads; and all of those raised at 16° or more had pointed heads. In general, the higher temperatures produced more prominent helmets. Brooks (1946) found comparable temperature relationships for helmet formation in *Daphnia retrocurva* and head spine formation in *D. galeata*. Kiang (1942) demonstrated a relation between mean temperature of a lake and relative head length in *D. rosea*.

Nevertheless, the work of Banta (1938) indicates that temperature is by no means the whole story and that genetic factors probably play an important role. He collected 10 distinct morphological types of *Daphnia pulex* in the field and cultured them in the laboratory. Under such circumstances the pronounced helmets were lost or minimized, but each of the 10 types remained recognizable and peculiar to itself. Other workers have shown that turbulence and high light intensities may increase the degree of helmet formation. By selective predation on larger individuals, plankton-feeding fish may also influence helmet development in a population.

In the words of Coker (1939), "The changes in form are not simple functions of external conditions or of any inherent cycle, but rather of a combination of internal and external conditions in a way that becomes exceedingly baffling the more we know about it."

**Vertical migrations.** Most limnetic cladocerans undergo vertical migratory movements during each 24-hour period. These "drifting" movements of the general population are commonly upward with the onset of darkness and downward with the coming of the light of dawn. In some species, however, and in some habitats, there is a rapid upward and downward cycle near dusk and a similar upward and downward cycle around dawn. In rare instances some species show "reverse" migratory movements. The average amplitude ranges from 2 to 10 m, depending on the species and many environmental factors. This whole phenomenon defies a simple explanation, since the vertical movements of the cladocerans appear to be variously governed by species, age, size, temperature, food supply, water chemistry, water color, season of year, light intensity, and turbulence.

Much of the experimental work on vertical migrations has been done with *Daphnia magna*, and the results have been transposed to other species. This is an unwarranted generalization because *D. magna* is a species of shallow ponds, and it is likely that the responses of this species differ from those of species inhabiting deep, limnetic habitats.

Most of the conclusions about vertical migrations have been based on light sensitivity plus a cluster of environmental variables. The recent discovery that experimentally blinded *Daphnia* still exhibit vertical movements suggests that some part of the body other than the eyes may be light sensitive. Furthermore, some recent investigators have revived the "endogenous rhythm" explanation because they have found that *Daphnia* migrates even when kept in continuous darkness.

**General ecology.** Cladocera are primarily fresh-water organisms, the several American marine species belonging to *Evadne* and *Podon* (Polyphemidae). Aside from rapid streams, brooks, and grossly polluted waters, they are abundant everywhere. Common open-water and limnetic forms are *Daphnia rosea*, *D. pulex*, *Bosmina*, *Diaphanosoma*, *Chydorus sphaericus*, *Ceriodaphnia*, and *Holopedium*. Such forms are seldom found in vegetated areas. The greatest abundance of species may be collected in the vegetation at margins of lakes and rivers, including *D. pulex*, *Sida crystallina*, *Ophryoxus gracilis*, most Chydoridae, and most Macrothricidae. A careful collector may find as many as 25 species in a single day's collecting. The two most common inhabitants of ponds, permanent pools, and temporary pools are *D. pulex* and *D. magna*. *Alona quadrangularis*, *Drepanothrix*, *Ilyocryptus*, and *Monospilus* are among the most common forms to be found on or near the bottom in weedy littoral areas. Specific affinities are indicated for most species in the key at the end of this chapter.

The great majority of species and nearly all the common ones are eurythermal. Only a few appear to have distributions limited by temperature. *Latona*, *Holopedium gibberum* and *Daphnia longiremis* are cold stenotherms, whereas *Pseudosida bidentata*, *Ceriodaphnia rigaudi*, and *Euryalona occidentalis* are restricted to warm waters of southern states.

Little information is available concerning chemical limiting factors. Dissolved oxygen is seldom of any significance except in the hypolimnion of lakes during summer and winter periods of complete oxygen exhaustion. Many species can withstand oxygen concentrations of less than one part per million. Most Cladocera occur in waters containing a wide range of concentrations of calcium. *Holopedium*, however, is widely distributed and confined to calcium-poor waters. Hutchinson (1932) found that magnesium may act as a limiting factor by inhibiting reproduction; critical concentrations for *Daphnia magna*, *D. pulex*, and *D. rosea* were found to be 240, 120, and 30 to 60 mg per liter. Although a few species are restricted to acid and bog waters, most Cladocera occur over a wide range in pH, nearly all species being found in the range 6.5 to 8.5.

In littoral and substrate environments two or more species in the same genus usually coexist in the same local habitat. In the open-water limnetic environment, however, it is unusual to find two species of *Daphnia* coexisting. But occasionally when two (or more) species are found in the same limnetic sample, then one of them is always much more abundant than the other(s).

There is increasing evidence to show that fishes are selectively predaceous on populations by ingesting larger and more obvious individuals in preference to smaller individuals. In this way the species makeup in lakes and ponds may be significantly altered.

Many laboratories have used *Daphnia*, especially *D. magna*, as an assay organism for the detection of toxic substances in water. Unfortunately, however, most such laboratories have evolved their own techniques, and we do not as yet have a "standard method" for such assays.

There is an enormous literature dealing with many phases of the ecology and reproductive phenomena of cladocerans. Unfortunately, space does not permit a discussion of these problems in this volume.

**Geographical distribution.** Because of their resistant ephippial eggs, Cladocera are easily transported overland to new habitats. As a result, the great majority of species are very widely distributed, some being truly cosmopolitan. The general occurrence of a few common species is indicated in Table VII. Less than 20 species are known only from the United States, and

TABLE VII. General Geographic Distribution
of Some Common Species of Cladocera

Cosmopolitan
  *Alona guttata, A. rectangula*
  *Ceriodaphnia laticaudata*
  *Chydorus sphaericus*
  *Daphnia magna, D. pulex*

North America, Europe, Asia, and South America
  *Alona affinis*
  *Bosmina longirostris*
  *Ceriodaphnia quadrangula*
  *Macrothrix laticornis*
  *Simocephalus vetulus*

North America, Europe, and Asia
  *Acroperus harpae*
  *Bosmina coregoni*
  *Camptocercus rectirostris*
  *Daphnia rosea*
  *Diaphanosoma brachyurum*
  *Eurycerus lamellatus*
  *Holopedium gibberum*
  *Leptodora kindti*
  *Moina macrocopa*
  *Pleuroxus strictus*
  *Polyphemus pediculus*
  *Scapholeberis mucronata*
  *Sida crystallina*

most of these have been collected in only one or two localities. Intensive collecting has been done in relatively few areas, however, and our knowledge of the geographical limits of many species in the United States is decidedly incomplete.

**Culturing.** Several species of *Daphnia* are among the most easily cultured of all fresh-water invertebrates. Fish hatcheries and tropical fish fanciers raise them in tanks or in concrete or plastic outdoor wading pools. Cottonseed meal, animal manure, some kinds of commercial agricultural fertilizers, dried yeast, dried milk, dried and chopped hay are all suitable foods, especially for the suspended organic particles and the bacteria that become abundant. It is important to avoid adding too much food to the cultures; otherwise the medium becomes foul. The writer has kept 20 cultures of *Daphnia rosea* going continuously in 1- to 10-gal aquariums for eight years. Once per week each aquarium receives dried yeast suspended in 20 to 200 ml of water. Each aquarium is then thoroughly stirred for a few seconds.

**Economic significance.** The great importance of Cladocera in the aquatic food chain as food for both young and adult fish was emphasized first by Forbes in 1883, and since then by innumerable investigators. Various studies of the stomach contents of young fish show from 1 to 95 percent Cladocera by volume, and very few studies show less than 10 percent. Other groups of less importance that utilize Cladocera in the diet are *Hydra* and immature and mature insects. Goulden (1971), for example, found that midsummer populations of littoral Chydoridae were greatly reduced by Diptera larvae predation.

**Collecting, preserving.** An ordinary plankton townet is suitable for limnetic species but is of little use for collecting in littoral vegetation. For such habitats the Birge cone net does an excellent job. Bottom forms may be taken by bringing the top centimeter of mud and debris into the laboratory and allowing it to settle. By looking horizontally along the surface toward a light source, the Cladocera may be located and picked up with a long pipette. In small ponds and pools, and to some extent in vegetation, a small dipnet is convenient.

The best general killing agent is undoubtedly 95 percent ethyl alcohol. Because of their delicate body and strong muscles, however, *Moina* and most of the Sididae are badly distorted when placed in alcohol. These forms should first be narcotized with chloral hydrate or a similar deadening agent. Seventy percent alcohol is the standard preservative. The writer always adds 5 percent glycerin to his storage vials so that specimens will not be destroyed through evaporation if the corks dry out or the vials break.

Fortunately, little or no dissection is necessary for identification purposes, but permanent slide mounts in glycerin or glycerin jelly are highly desirable. Cover slips should be supported by bits of cardboard of appropriate thickness so that specimens will not be crushed. Sometimes it is necessary to disarticulate and clear the exoskeletons of cladocerans in order to make out minute anatomical details. Judicious use of cold hydrochloric acid for 24 hours or hot acid for a few minutes usually will give the desired results.

**Taxonomy.** Brooks (1957) has given the genus *Daphnia* its most thorough treatment, and his suggestions have been generally followed in this chapter. Nevertheless, much work still remains to be done on this troublesome taxon. Most of the species are featured by irksome seasonal and geographic variations in carapace and head morphology, and details of setation and the postabdomen. The *retrocurva, carinata, rosea-longispina,* and *pulex-pulicaria* problems, as well as several other questions, deserve further consideration. The situation is confused by what seems to be "hy-

bridization" in some geographical areas. Our major difficulty is the fact that definitive species descriptions are often based on specimens collected from only a limited number of field sites. We need widely distributed massive collecting and careful analyses of large numbers of specimens.

Aside from the *Daphnia* problem, certain other genera will be clarified as more specimens are collected from many additional field sites, notably *Ceriodaphnia, Diaphanosoma, Moina, Alonella, Alona, Pleuroxus,* and *Chydorus.*

In the key that follows, lengths refer only to females and do not include spines or antennae. Some species appear in two different places in the key because of variable anatomical characters.

## KEY TO SPECIES OF CLADOCERA

1. Body and legs covered with a bivalve carapace; legs foliaceous, not clearly segmented ..............................................................2
   Body and legs not covered with a carapace; legs subcylindrical or somewhat flattened, clearly segmented, and prehensile; northern states ..............141
2. With six pairs of foliaceous legs; first and second pairs not prehensile (Figs. 254, 255) ..............................................................3
   With five or six pairs of legs; first and second pairs more or less prehensile (Figs. 256 ff.) ..............................................................12
3. Carapace of the usual type; antennae of female biramous and flattened (Figs. 254F; 255A, C) ..............................................SIDIDAE, 5
   Animal enclosed in a large gelatinous mantle, open ventrally and forming two valves (Fig. 254A); the mantle is shed during ecdysis but regenerated within two hours; antennae of female simple and cylindrical; swims ventral side up; found in low-calcium waters; 1 to 2 mm long ....HOLOPEDIDAE, **Holopedium, 4**
4. Ventral margins of valves with fine spines; up to 25 anal spines and spinules; anal claws with a basal spine (Fig. 254B); spotty distribution in open waters of northern states and southward in mountains. **Holopedium gibberum** Zaddach
   Ventral margins of valves smooth; 7 to 13 anal spines and spinules; anal claws without basal spine (Fig. 254D); east of Louisiana and south of northern tier of states ..............................**Holopedium amazonicum** Stingelin
5. Dorsal ramus of antenna three-segmented (Fig. 254E); 3 to 4 mm long; common among aquatic plants in lakes and ponds .......... **Sida crystallina** (O.F.M.)
   Dorsal ramus of antenna two-segmented ..............................................6
6. With a lateral expansion on basal segment of dorsal ramus of antenna; with a tonguelike projection on ventral surface of head (Figs. 254F, G); 2 to 3 mm long; in littoral vegetation; chiefly in northern states and mountainous areas ..............................................**Latona, 7**
   Without lateral expansion on antenna ..............................................8
7. Antennal expansion very large (Fig. 254F) ..............**Latona setifera** (O.F.M.)
   Antennal expansion small (Fig. 254G) ..................**Latona parviremis** Birge
8. Without spines on postabdomen; ocellus absent; 0.8 to 1.2 mm long; common and widely distributed (Fig. 255A) ......................**Diaphanosoma, 9**
   With spines on postabdomen (Fig. 255B); ocellus present; about 2 mm long .....10

FIG. 254.–Structure of Holopedidae and Sididae. A, *Holopedium gibberum,* ×40; B, postabdomen of *H. gibberum*; C, first leg of *H. gibberum*; D, postabdomen of *H. amazonicum*; E, *Sida crystallina,* ×14; F, antenna of *Latona setifera*; G, anterior end of *L. parviremis.* (B and D modified from Ward and Whipple, 1918; C modified from Sars; E and F modified from Lilljeborg.)

**9.** Head about two-thirds the valve length; eye in the middle of the head near the ventral margin; limnetic ................ **Diaphanosoma leuchtenbergianum** Fischer
Head not more than half the valve length; eye anterior (Fig. 255A); littoral.
**Diaphanosoma brachyurum** (Liéven)

**10.** Rostrum present (Fig. 255B); southern states ........ **Pseudosida bidentata** Herrick
Rostrum absent (Fig. 255C); usually in vegetation ................ **Latonopsis, 11**

**11.** Postabdomen with about nine small spines; common in Gulf states, sporadic farther north (Fig. 255C).......................... **Latonopsis occidentalis** Birge
Postabdomen with 12 to 14 small clusters of lancet-shaped anal spines (Fig. 255D); Gulf states ............................... **Latonopsis fasciculata** Daday

**12.** Antennules attached to ventral side of head, not covered by fornices (Figs. 256–264) ..................................................................**13**
Fornices extended so as to cover antennules more or less, and united with rostrum into a beak that projects ventrally in front of antennules (Figs. 265 ff.) ............................................... CHYDORIDAE, **70**

**13.** Antennules of female small, often rudimentary; if large, then never inserted at anterior end of ventral edge of head (Figs. 256–260) ....................**15**
Antennules of female large, inserted at anterior end of ventral edge of head (Figs. 261–264) ........................................................**14**

**14.** Antennules of female fixed (Fig. 261); intestine simple; 0.3 to 0.5 mm long.
BOSMINIDAE, **49**
Antennules of female freely movable (Fig. 262); intestine simple or convoluted.
MACROTHRICIDAE, **54**

**15.** Rostrum present ......................................... DAPHNIDAE, **16**
Rostrum absent ..................................................**35**

FIG. 255.–Structure of Sididae. A, *Diaphanosoma brachyurum*, ×45; B, *Pseudosida bidentata*, ×27; C, *Latonopsis occidentalis*, ×22; D, *L. fasciculata*. (A modified from Lilljeborg; B modified from Birge, 1910; C and D modified from Ward and Whipple, 1918.)

**16.** Without a cervical sinus .............................................**Daphnia, 17**
With a cervical sinus (Figs. 259B–D) ....................................**31**

**17.** Carapace extends anteriorly along middorsal line as a broad strip between halves of head shield (Fig. 257H); thick-bodied; up to 5 mm long; scattered distribution in western half of the United States ...................................**18**
Median line of head shield continues along middorsal line onto carapace; marked lateral compression; up to 3 mm long, usually less than 2 mm long ......**19**

**18.** Margin of postabdomen sinuate (Figs. 257E); up to 5 mm long; usually in ponds containing much suspended organic matter.......... **Daphnia magna** Straus
Margin of postabdomen not sinuate; up to 3 mm long; usually in temporary, saline, or alkaline ponds.................................. **Daphnia similis** Claus

**19.** Teeth of proximal and middle pectens of postabdominal claw larger than teeth of distal pecten (Figs. 258G, H, K) ......................................**20**
Teeth of all three pectens of claw about the same size (Fig. 258J) ..............**25**

**20.** Teeth of middle pecten of postabdominal claw stout, the largest at least three times as long as teeth of distal pecten (Figs. 258G, K); ocellus present .........**21**
Teeth of middle pecten of postabdominal claw not more than twice as long as teeth of distal pecten (Fig. 258H); ocellus absent ...........................**24**

**21.** Ventral margin of head concave; optic vesicle touching margin of head (Figs. 256B–E) ...............................................................**22**
Ventral margin of head sinuate or more or less straight; optic vesicle not touching margin of head...............................................**23**

**22.** Head longest over optic vesicle; ventral margin of head separated from anterior margin of valves by a prominent gap (Fig. 256E); dorsal part of head usually dark brownish; up to 3 mm long; ponds and lakes; Texas to Montana and westward; easily confused and sometimes hybridized(?) with *D. pulex*; perhaps a variety of *D. pulex*; not common ........**Daphnia middendorffiana** Fischer
Head longest near midline; ventral part of head close to anterior margin of valves (Figs. 256B–D); entire body occasionally brownish, but head alone never dark brown; up to 2.5 mm long; extremely common and generally distributed in lakes and ponds; a variable species; easily confused and sometimes hybridized(?) with *D. middendorffiana* ....................**Daphnia pulex** Leydig

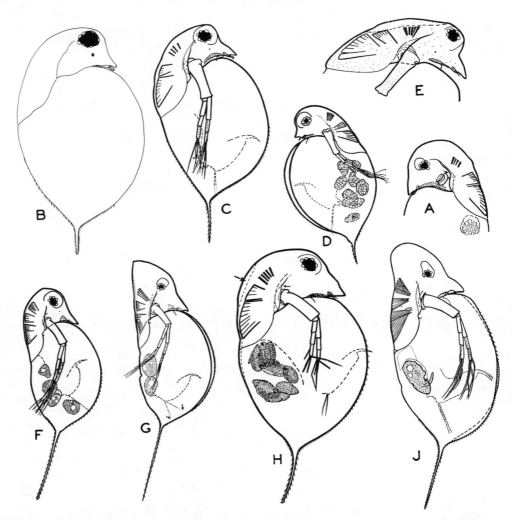

FIG. 256.–Structure of *Daphnia*. A, head of *D. schødleri*; B and C, *D. pulex*; D, *D. parvula*; E, head of *D. middendorffiana*; F, *D. laevis*; G, *D. dubia*; H, *D. rosea*; J, *D. thorata*. (A, C to J from Brooks, 1957; B from Brandlova, Brandl, and Fernando.)

23. Spinules on dorsal margin of body long, interspinule distance less than 1.5 times spinule length (Fig. 258B); middle pecten of claw with three to seven teeth (Fig. 258K); up to 2 mm long; uncommon; found west of the Mississippi River but occurs also in the Great Lakes . . . . . . . . . . . . . . . . . **Daphnia schødleri** Sars
    Spinules on dorsal margin of body short, interspinule distance two to three times spinule length (Fig. 258A); middle pecten of claw with two to five teeth (Fig. 258G); up to 1.5 mm long; uncommon; in eastern states. **Daphnia catawba** Coker
24. Anterior margin of head broadly rounded; if a small crest is present, it is longest in the midline; posterior spine less than one-quarter of valve length (Fig. 256D); up to 1.2 mm long; lakes and ponds; widely distributed except for Rocky Mountain ranges (often confused with *D. retrocurva*). **Daphnia parvula** Fordyce
    Anterior margin of head with small to large helmet, longest dorsal to midline (Figs. 253D–H); posterior spine at least one-third valve length; northeastern quarter of the United States, and Washington and Oregon (often confused with *D. parvula*) . . . . . . . . . . . . . . . . . . . . . . . . . . . . . . . . . **Daphnia retrocurva** Forbes

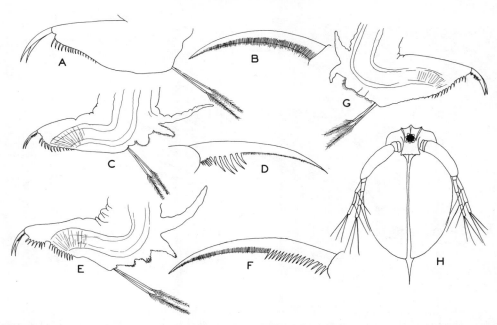

FIG. 257.–Structure of *Daphnia*. A, postabdomen of *D. rosea*; B, claw of *D. laevis*; C, postabdomen of *D. pulex*; D, claw of *D. pulex*; E, postabdomen of *D. magna*; F, claw of *D. magna*; G, postabdomen of *D. middendorffiana*; H, ventral view of *D. magna*, diagrammatic, ×11.

**25.** Swimming hair at base of second segment of three-segmented ramus does not reach end of ramus (Fig. 258C); ocellus absent; swimming hairs of antennae extend beyond posterior margin of valves; limnetic, confined to hypolimnion during stratification; up to 1.2 mm long; northeastern states, but as far west as Minnesota . . . . . . . . . . . . . . . . . . . . . . . . . . . . . . . . . . **Daphnia longiremis** Sars

Swimming hair at base of second segment of three-segmented ramus extends beyond tip of ramus (Fig. 258D); ocellus present; swimming hairs of antennae not extending beyond posterior margins of valves . . . . . . . . . . . . . . . . . . . . . . . .**26**

**26.** Small, head and valves up to 1.3 mm long; almost circular in outline; head often with a small anterior point (Fig. 253N, O); highly variable morphological details; may not be a good species; ponds and lakes east of the Continental Divide, but also along the Pacific coast . . . . . . . . . . . . . . **Daphnia ambigua** Scourfield

Medium to large; head and valves more than 1.3 mm long . . . . . . . . . . . . . . . . . . . .**27**

**27.** Second abdominal process about one-quarter as long as first abdominal process (Fig. 258E) . . . . . . . . . . . . . . . . . . . . . . . . . . . . . . . . . . . . . . . . . . . . . . . . . . . . .**28**

Second abdominal process about one-half as long as first abdominal process (Fig. 258F) . . . . . . . . . . . . . . . . . . . . . . . . . . . . . . . . . . . . . . . . . . . . . . . . . . . . . . . .**29**

**28.** With spines over slightly more than half of ventral margin of valve; anterior margin of head rounded or with a low, blunt crest (Fig. 256F); up to 1.7 mm long; ponds in southern states but extending up along both coasts.

**Daphnia laevis** Birge

With spines over posterior three-quarters of ventral margin of valve; head usually helmeted (Fig. 256G); up to 1.8 mm long; extreme northeastern states, west to Wisconsin . . . . . . . . . . . . . . . . . . . . . . . . . . . . . . . **Daphnia dubia** Herrick

**29.** Anterior margin with a low, rounded crest; head twice as deep as long (Fig. 256H); posterior spine usually less than one-third valve length; morphological details variable; up to 2 mm long; common in ponds and lakes of western states (usually referred to in the past as *D. longispina*) . . . . . . . **Daphnia rosea** Sars

Anterior margin usually helmeted; head length more than half its greatest depth (Fig. 256J); posterior spine more than one-third valve length . . . . . . . . . . . . . . . . . .**30**

Fig. 258.–Structure of *Daphnia*. A, spinules on dorsal margin of carapace of *D. catawba*; B, same for *D. schødleri*; C, second antenna of *D. longiremis*; D, same for *D. ambigua*; E, abdominal processes of *D. dubia*; F, same for *D. rosea*; G, postabdominal claw of *D. catawba*; H, same for *D. retrocurva*; J, same for *D. rosea*; K, same for *D. schødleri*. (B from Brandlova, Brandl, and Fernando; G to K from Brooks, 1957.)

**30.** Dorsal margin of head with a concavity; anterior margin of head not pointed (Fig. 256J); ventral spines of valves extend over at least the posterior two-thirds; up to 1.8 mm long; large lakes of Washington, Oregon, Idaho, and Montana ..................................... **Daphnia thorata** Forbes

Dorsal margin of head without a concavity; anterior margin of head usually pointed; head more or less helmeted except during early spring (Figs. 253L, M); ventral spines of valves extending over less than the posterior two-thirds; up to 3 mm long; northeastern states and Pacific coast states.
**Daphnia galeata mendotae** Birge

**31.** Valves transversely striated (Fig. 259B); up to 3 mm long ...... **Simocephalus, 32**

Valves not transversely striated; up to 1 mm long; usually in vegetation.
**Scapholeberis, 34**

**32.** Claws with a pecten (Fig. 259A); uncommon; reported from scattered localities in the eastern half of the United States ....... **Simocephalus exspinosus** (Koch)

Claws without a pecten ................................................**33**

**33.** Vertex evenly rounded about the eye and without serrations or spinules (Fig. 259B); widely distributed but not common ........ **Simocephalus vetulus** (O.F.M.)

With serrations or spinules in front of or below the eye; vertex more or less angulate (Fig. 259C); common everywhere ..........**Simocephalus serrulatus** (Koch)

**34.** Color usually dark, often nearly black; common and widely distributed (Fig. 259D); a variety with a frontal horn is rare in the United States.
**Scapholeberis mucronata** (O.F.M.)

Color whitish or greenish, translucent or opaque; uncommon; northern states.
**Scapholeberis aurita** (Fischer)

**35.** Antennules small; head small and depressed (Figs. 259F, H–K); up to 1.4 mm long ................................. DAPHNIDAE, **Ceriodaphnia, 36**

Antennules large; head large and extended (Figs. 260A, B, D) .... MOINIDAE, **43**

**36.** Head with a short spine (Fig. 259E); a variable species, 0.4 to 0.5 mm long; pools; in southern states ........................ **Ceriodaphnia rigaudi** Richard

Head without a spine .................................................**37**

FIG. 259.–Structure of Daphnidae. A, claw of *Simocephalus exspinosus*; B, *S. vetulus,* showing a portion of transverse striations, ×15; C, head of *S. serrulatus*; D, *Scapholeberis mucronata*, ×50; E, head of *Ceriodaphnia rigaudi*; F, *C. reticulata*, ×25; G, postabdomen of *C. megalops*; H, head of *C. lacustris*; J, head of *C. rotunda*; K, *C. laticaudata*, ×50; L, postabdomen of *C. quadrangula*; M, postabdomen of *C. pulchella*. (B to H, and L modified from Ward and Whipple, 1918; J and M modified from Lilljeborg.)

37. Claws with pecten (Fig. 259F); up to 1.4 mm long; common and widely distributed .............................. **Ceriodaphnia reticulata** (Jurine)
   Claws without pecten...................................................**38**
38. Postabdomen abruptly incised (Fig. 259G); widely distributed but uncommon.
                                                          **Ceriodaphnia megalops** Sars
   Postabdomen not incised...............................................**39**
39. Fornices projecting to form spinous processes (Fig. 259H); 0.8 to 0.9 mm long; limnetic; scattered east of the Mississippi River. **Ceriodaphnia lacustris** Birge
   Fornices of the usual form; up to 1 mm long ...............................**40**
40. Vertex with spines (Fig. 259J); in aquatic vegetation; reported only from Wisconsin...................................**Ceriodaphnia rotunda** Sars
   Vertex without spines; widely distributed ..................................**41**
41. General form round (Fig. 259K); up to 1 mm long; in vegetation.
                                                   **Ceriodaphnia laticaudata** P. E. Müller
   General form not especially round; littoral and limnetic ......................**42**
42. With seven to nine anal spines (Fig. 259L); up to 1 mm long.
                                                   **Ceriodaphnia quadrangula** (O.F.M.)
   With 7 to 10 anal spines plus 3 to 5 anal setae (Fig. 259M); up to 0.7 mm long.
                                                          **Ceriodaphnia pulchella** Sars
43. Body laterally compressed; valves completely covering body (Fig. 260A); up to 1 mm long; on bottom and in vegetation; reported only from Louisiana.
                                                   **Moinodaphnia macleayi** (King)
   Body thick and heavy; valves not completely covering body (Figs. 260B, D); usually in pools and ponds .........................................**Moina, 44**

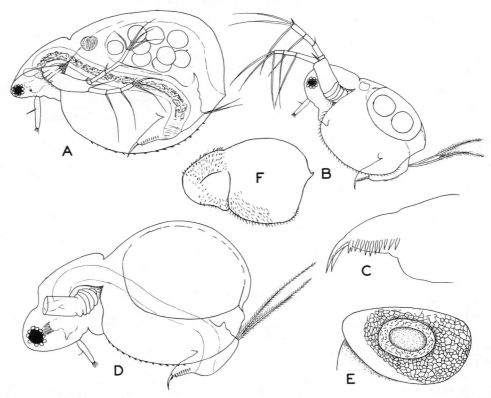

FIG. 260.–Structure of Daphnidae. A, *Moinodaphnia macleayi* with parthenogenetic eggs, ×60; B, *Moina macrocopa* with ephippium, ×24; C, postabdomen of same; D, *M. micrura,* ×40; E, ephippium of *M. micrura*; F, head and carapace of *Moina affinis* showing distribution of hairs. (A, D, and E modified from Ward and Whipple, 1918; B and C modified from Uéno.)

**44.** Postabdomen without a distal bident tooth; up to 1.6 mm long; highly saline basins; Washington, California, and Nevada . . . . . . . . . . . . .**Moina hutchinsoni** Brehm
Postabdomen with a distal bident tooth (Fig. 260C) . . . . . . . . . . . . . . . . . . . . . . . . .**45**
**45.** Head almost invariably with a supraocular depression (Fig. 260D); first leg of female with anterior setae on penultimate and ultimate segments feathered or with fine hairs . . . . . . . . . . . . . . . . . . . . . . . . . . . . . . . . . . . . . . . . . . . . . . . . . . . . .**46**
Head without a supraocular depression (Fig. 260B); first leg of female with anterior setae of penultimate and ultimate segments toothed; widely distributed but not common . . . . . . . . . . . . . . . . . . . . . . . . . . . . . . . . . . . . . .**Moina macrocopa** Straus
**46.** Female with long hairs on head and carapace (Fig. 260F) . . . . . . . . . . . . . . . . . . . . .**47**
Female with long hairs only on ventral surface of head, or hairs absent . . . . . . . .**48**
**47.** Ephippium reticulated and with a single egg; up to 1.2 mm long; widely distributed . . . . . . . . . . . . . . . . . . . . . . . . . . . . . . . . . . . . . . . . . .**Moina affinis** Birge
Ephippium knobby and with two eggs; up to 1.5 mm long; reported only from Arizona, California, Colorado, Kansas, and Texas. **Moina wierzejskii** Richard
**48.** Head narrow and with a distinct supraocular depression (Fig. 260D); up to 1.2 mm long; one ephippial egg (Fig. 260E); widely distributed and common.

**Moina micrura** Kurz

Head large and broad, without a supraocular depression; up to 1.4 mm long; two ephippial eggs; one record from the southern California desert.

**Moina brachycephala** Goulden

# CLADOCERA 373

FIG. 261.—Structure of Bosminidae. A, lateral view of *Bosminopsis dietersi*; B, dorsal view of same; C, *Bosmina longirostris*, ×140; D, anterior end of *Eubosmina coregoni*; E, mucro of *B. longirostris*; F, mucro of *E. hagmanni*; G, mucro of *E. longispina*; H, postabdomen of *B. longirostris*; J. postabdomen of *E. longispina*; K, *E. coregoni*; L, anterior end of *E. tubicen*; M, anterior end of *E. hagmanni*. (J to M modified from Deevey and Deevey.)

49. Antennules united at base and diverging at apex (Fig. 261B); widely distributed in southern states; uncommon .................. **Bosminopsis dietersi** Richard
Antennules not united at base, parallel; highly variable; littoral and limnetic; widely distributed and common .............................................**50**

50. Female postabdominal claw with a very fine distal pecten (Fig. 261H); frontal sensory bristle near midpoint between eye and tip of rostrum (Fig. 261C); widely distributed and common ................... **Bosmina longirostris** (O.F.M.)
Female postabdominal claw with proximal pecten only, emarginate near tip (Fig. 261J); frontal sensory bristle near tip of rostrum, near or at base of antennule (Fig. 261D) .............................................**Eubosmina, 51**

FIG. 262.–Structure of Macrothricidae. A, *Ophryoxus gracilis,* ×30; B, *Streblocerus serricaudatus,* ×100; C, posterior end of *Parophryoxus tubulatus*; D, *Drepanothrix dentata,* ×60; E, *Acantholeberis curvirostris,* ×26. (Modified from Ward and Whipple, 1918.)

**51.** Mucro absent (Fig. 261K); Great Lakes and northeastern states.

                   **Eubosmina coregoni** (Baird)

  Mucro present (Figs. 261E–G) . . . . . . . . . . . . . . . . . . . . . . . . . . . . . . . . . . . . . . . .**52**

**52.** Mucro with minute ventral notches, at least on immature forms (Fig. 261G); reported
    only from extreme northeastern states . . . . . . . **Eubosmina longispina** (Leydig)

  Mucro with minute dorsal notches, at least on immature forms (Fig. 261F) . . . . . .**53**

**53.** Rostrum becomes relatively shorter with age; mucro grows longer with age; frontal
    bulge present at base of antenna (Fig. 261L); reported from northeastern
    states . . . . . . . . . . . . . . . . . . . . . . . . . . . . . . . . . **Eubosmina tubicen** (Brehm)

  Rostrum becomes longer with age; mucro grows shorter with age; frontal bulge
    absent (Fig. 261M); western states . . . . . . . . .**Eubosmina hagmanni** (Stingelin)

**54.** Intestine convoluted (Figs. 262A, B) . . . . . . . . . . . . . . . . . . . . . . . . . . . . . . . . . . . .**55**

  Intestine simple . . . . . . . . . . . . . . . . . . . . . . . . . . . . . . . . . . . . . . . . . . . . . . . . . . . . .**60**

**55.** Valves with spine at posterior dorsal angle (Fig. 262A); up to 2 mm long; in vege-
    tation; widely distributed . . . . . . . . . . . . . . . . . . . . . . . .**Ophryoxus gracilis** Sars

  Valves without such a spine . . . . . . . . . . . . . . . . . . . . . . . . . . . . . . . . . . . . . . . . . . . .**56**

**56.** Antennal setae 0–0–1–3/1–1–3; 0.2 to 0.5 mm long . . . . . . . . . . . . . . **Streblocerus, 57**

  With another antennal setae formula; more than 0.5 mm long . . . . . . . . . . . . . . . . .**58**

**57.** Dorsal margin of valves smooth (Figs. 262B, 263A); uncommon but widely distributed
    in littoral zones . . . . . . . . . . . . . . . . . . . . . . .**Streblocerus serricaudatus** (Fischer)

  Dorsal margin of valves serrate; in vegetation in pools; Louisiana.

                   **Streblocerus pygmaeus** Sars

**58.** Valves narrowed posteriorly and prolonged into a short tube (Fig. 262C); up to 1.2
    mm long; in vegetation; New England states and rare farther west.

                **Parophyroxus tubulatus** Doolittle

  Valves not narrowed posteriorly; widely distributed . . . . . . . . . . . . . . . . . . . . . . . . .**59**

FIG. 263.–Structure of Macrothricidae. A, *Streblocerus serricaudatus*; B, *Ilyocryptus sordidus*. (From Fryer, 1974.)

**59.** Dorsal and posterior margin arched; with a conspicuous dorsal tooth (Fig. 262D); up to 0.7 mm long; in littoral zones; uncommon in northern states.
                                               **Drepanothrix dentata** (Eurén)
    Without a dorsal tooth (Fig. 262E); up to 1.8 mm long; in littoral, especially in *Sphagnum* bogs .................... **Acantholeberis curvirostris** (O.F.M.)

**60.** With a wide crest on dorsal margin of valves (Fig. 264B); up to 1 mm long; reported from Maine, Wisconsin, and other northern states. **Bunops serricaudata** (Daday)
    Without such a crest ..................................................... **61**

**61.** Postabdomen with numerous long spines (Figs. 264C–E); antennal setae 0–0–0–3/1–1–3; often more or less covered with detritus; usually found creeping about on the substrate, especially in vegetated areas .............. **Ilyocryptus, 63**
    Postabdomen without numerous long spines; with another setae formula ....... **62**

**62.** Hepatic caeca present: 0.9 mm long; in vegetation in shallow water; Louisiana.
                                               **Grimaldina brazzai** Richard
    Hepatic caeca absent .................................................... **65**

Fig. 264.–Structure of Macrothricidae. A, postabdomen of *Grimaldia brazzai*; B, *Bunops serricaudata*, ×35; C, *Ilyocryptus spinifer*, ×40; D, postabdomen of *I. sordidus*; E, postabdomen of *I. acutifrons*; F, *Lathonura rectirostris*, ×38; G, *Macrothrix rosea*, ×55; H, anterior end of *M. borysthenica*; J, postabdomen of *M. laticornis*; K, anterior end of *M. montana*. (B to H and K modified from Ward and Whipple, 1918; J modified from Lilljeborg.)

63. Anus on dorsal margin of postabdomen (Fig. 264D); molting imperfect; widely distributed . . . . . . . . . . . . . . . . . . . . . . . . . . . . . . . . . . . . . . . . . . . . . . . .**64**
   Anus terminal (Fig. 264E); molting perfect; widely distributed but uncommon.
                                             **Ilyocryptus acutifrons** Sars
64. With eight or more preanal spines (Fig. 263B, 264D); uncommon.
                                             **Ilyocryptus sordidus** (Liéven)
   With five to seven preanal spines (Fig. 264C); common and widely distributed.
                                             **Ilyocryptus spinifer** Herrick
65. Antennal setae 0–0–1–3/1–1–3; setae of basal segment of lower ramus stout (Fig. 264G) . . . . . . . . . . . . . . . . . . . . . . . . . . . . . . . . . . . . . . . . **Macrothrix, 66**
   Antennal setae 0–1–1–3/1–1–3; all setae slender; 1 mm long (Fig. 264F); widely distributed but uncommon in vegetation of littoral.
                                             **Lathonura rectirostris** (O.F.M.)
66. Dorsal margin of head evenly rounded . . . . . . . . . . . . . . . . . . . . . . . . . . . . . . . . . . .67
   Dorsal margin of head not evenly rounded (Fig. 264G); 0.7 mm long; in vegetation; widely distributed . . . . . . . . . . . . . . . . . . . . . . . . . . . . **Macrothrix rosea** (Jurine)
67. Head depressed, rostrum close to margin of valves (Fig. 264H); up to 1.1 mm long; southwestern . . . . . . . . . . . . . . . . . . . . . . . . . . . .**Macrothrix borysthenica** Matile
   Head extended, rostrum far from margin of valves (Fig. 264K) . . . . . . . . . . . . . . . .**68**
68. Postabdomen not bilobed (Fig. 264J); up to 0.7 mm long; widely distributed.
                                             **Macrothrix laticornis** (Jurine)
   Postabdomen bilobed; 0.55 mm long . . . . . . . . . . . . . . . . . . . . . . . . . . . . . . . . . . . .**69**

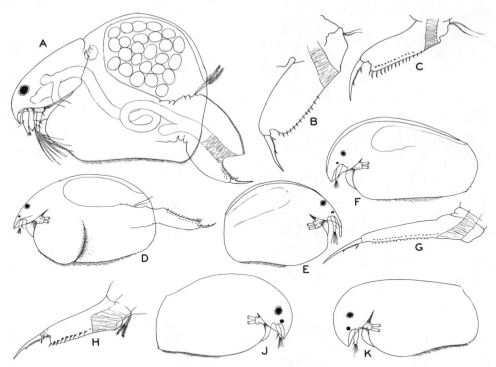

FIG. 265.–Structure of Eurycercinae and Chydorinae. E, *Eurycercus lamellatus*, ×17; B, postabdomen of *Alonopsis aureola*; C, postabdomen of *A. elongata*; D, *Euryalona occidentalis*, ×38; E, *Kurzia latissima*, ×48; F, *Camptocercus rectirostris*, ×40; G, postabdomen of same; H, postabdomen of *Acroperus harpae*; J, *A. harpae*, ×42; K, *A. angustatus*, ×46. (A modified from Lilljeborg; B and C modified from Doolittle; D, E, F, J, and K modified from Ward and Whipple, 1918; G and H modified from Uéno.)

**69.** With conspicuous folds at cervical sinus (Fig. 264K); Rocky Mountains.
                **Macrothrix montana** Birge
 Without such folds; New England to Colorado.
            **Macrothrix hirsuticornis** Norman and Brady
**70.** Anus terminal; 3 mm long (Fig. 265A); common everywhere in shallows.
        EURYCERCINAE, **Eurycercus lamellatus** (O.F.M.)
 Anus on dorsal side of abdomen (Figs. 265B, C). . . . . . . . . . . . . .CHYDORINAE, **71**
**71.** Compound eye present . . . . . . . . . . . . . . . . . . . . . . . . . . . . . . . . . . . . . . . . . . . . . .**72**
 Compound eye absent; 0.5 mm long; rare; northern states . . **Monospilus dispar** Sars
**72.** Eye and ocellus of usual size . . . . . . . . . . . . . . . . . . . . . . . . . . . . . . . . . . . . . . . . .**73**
 Compound eye and ocellus extremely large and of similar size; rare in southern
  states . . . . . . . . . . . . . . . . . . . . . . . . . . . . . . . . . . **Dadaya macrops** (Daday)
**73.** Posterior margin of valves not greatly less than maximum height (Figs. 265, 266). **74**
 Posterior margin of valves considerably less than maximum height (Figs. 268, 269). **104**
**74.** Claws with secondary tooth in the middle (Figs. 265C, G); secondary tooth sometimes
  very small . . . . . . . . . . . . . . . . . . . . . . . . . . . . . . . . . . . . . . . . . . . . . . . .**75**
 Claws without secondary tooth in the middle . . . . . . . . . . . . . . . . . . . . . . . . . . . . .**83**
**75.** Postabdomen with both marginal and lateral denticles (Figs. 265C, G) . . . . . . . . . .**77**
 Postabdomen without both marginal and lateral denticles . . . . . . . . . . . . . . . . . . . . .**76**
**76.** Postabdomen with lateral denticles only, sometimes inconspicuous (Fig. 265H); 0.8
  to 0.9 mm long (Fig. 265J); common everywhere in vegetation.
                 **Acroperus harpae** Baird
 Postabdomen with marginal denticles only (Fig. 265B); up to 1.9 mm long; in littoral
  vegetation; known only from an old Maine record. **Alonopsis aureola** Doolittle

Fig. 266.–Structure of Chydorinae. A, *Graptoleberis testudinaria,* ×80; B, postabdomen of *Leydigia quadrangularis*; C, *L. quadrangularis,* ×45; D, postabdomen of *Oxyurella tenuicaudis*; E, postabdomen of *Alonella diaphana*; F, postabdomen of *Alona guttata*; G, *A. monacantha,* ×100; H, *Alonella karua,* ×75; J, claw of *Alona affinis*; K, postabdomen of *A. costata*; L and M, postabdomen of *A. rectangula*; N, claw of *A. quadrangularis.* (A, E, G, and H modified from Ward and Whipple; B and L modified from D'Ancona; C, F, K, and M modified from Lilljeborg; D modified from Birge, 1910.)

77. Postabdomen relatively broad (Fig. 265C).................................**78**
    Postabdomen relatively narrow (Fig. 265G) ..............................**79**
78. Terminal claw with two medium-sized teeth (Fig. 265C); 0.8 mm long.
    **Alonopsis elongata** Sars
    Terminal claw with one large tooth; 0.4 mm long; reported only from Mississippi.
    **Alonopsis fitzpatricki** Chien
79. Anterior portion of valves swollen (Fig. 265D); 1 mm long; in vegetation; southern
    states ..................................... **Euryalona occidentalis** Sars
    Anterior portion of valves not swollen; usually in vegetation in shallows .......**80**
80. Crest on head and valves (Fig. 265F); about 1 mm long .........**Camptocercus, 81**
    Crest on valves only (Fig. 265E); 0.6 mm long; common everywhere.
    **Kurzia latissima** (Kurz)
81. Postabdomen with 15 to 17 marginal denticles (Fig. 265G); common everywhere in
    vegetation ...........................**Camptocercus rectirostris** Schödler
    Postabdomen with 20 or more marginal denticles ...........................**82**
82. Postabdomen with 20 to 30 marginal denticles; widely distributed but rare.
    **Camptocercus macrurus** (O.F.M.)
    Postabdomen with 45 to 65 minute marginal denticles; in temporary ponds in Okla-
    homa and Kansas ....................**Camptocercus oklahomensis** Mackin
83. Rostrum not greatly exceeding antennules (Figs. 266A, G, H)..................**84**
    Rostrum much longer than antennules (Fig. 268B) ...........................**103**
84. Rostrum abruptly narrowed and pointed near tip (Figs. 266G, H)...............**86**
    Rostrum not abruptly narrowed near tip (Fig. 266A) .........................**85**
85. Ventroposterior angle with teeth (Fig. 266A); 0.5 to 0.7 mm long; usually on bottom
    in shallows; common and widely distributed.
    **Graptoleberis testudinaria** (Fischer)
    Ventroposterior angle without teeth; up to 0.4 mm long; reported from Wisconsin,
    Indiana, Florida, Georgia, and Minnesota ...........**Alona setulosa** Megard

FIG. 267.–Structure of *Alona*. A, anterior end of *A. setulosa*; B, postabdomen of *A. costata*; C, postabdomen of *A. rustica*; D, anterior end of *A. rustica*; E, anterior end of *A. bicolor*. (B and C from Frey, 1965; D and E modified from Frey, 1965.)

86. Ventroposterior angle without teeth . . . . . . . . . . . . . . . . . . . . . . . . . . . . . . . . . . . . . . . . .87
    Ventroposterior angle with one to four small teeth . . . . . . . . . . . . . . . . . . . . . . . . . . . .94
87. Postabdomen with clusters of large spines (Fig. 266B); about 1 mm long;
    uncommon . . . . . . . . . . . . . . . . . . . . . . . . . . . . . . . . . . . . . . . . . . . . . . . . . . . . . **Leydigia, 88**
    Postabdomen without clusters of large spines . . . . . . . . . . . . . . . . . . . . . . . . . . . . . . .89
88. Valves without markings (Fig. 266C); widely distributed but uncommon among
    vegetation . . . . . . . . . . . . . . . . . . . . . . . . . . . . . . . **Leydigia quadrangularis** (Leydig)
    Valves with longitudinal striations; rare, in southern states.
                                                      **Leydigia acanthocercoides** (Fischer)
89. Postabdomen with marginal and lateral denticles (Figs. 266D, L) . . . . . . . . . . . . . . .90
    Postabdomen with marginal denticles only (Figs. 266E, F) . . . . . . . . . . . . . . . . . . . .92
90. Marginal denticles markedly longer distally (Fig. 266D); about 0.5 mm long.
                                                                          **Oxyurella, 91**
    Marginal denticles not markedly longer distally . . . . . . . . . . . . . . . . . . . . . . . **Alona, 96**
91. Penultimate marginal denticle largest (Fig. 266D); widely distributed but not
    common . . . . . . . . . . . . . . . . . . . . . . . . . . . . . . . . . . . . . . . **Oxyurella tenuicaudis** (Sars)
    Ultimate marginal denticle largest, serrate; rare, in southern states.
                                                         **Oxyurella longicaudis** (Birge)
92. Denticles minute (Fig. 266E); 0.5 mm long; rare; southern states.
                                                            **Alonella diaphana** (King)
    Denticles of usual size (Fig. 266F); 0.4 mm long . . . . . . . . . . . . . . . . . . . . . . . . . . . . . .93
93. Postabdomen with 8 to 10 marginal denticles (Fig. 266F); common everywhere.
                                                                  **Alona guttata** Sars
    Postabdomen with more than 10 marginal denticles; known only from
    Mississippi . . . . . . . . . . . . . . . . . . . . . . . . . . . . . . . . . . . . . . . . . **Alonella leei** Chien
94. With a fringe of setae along most of the ventral margin (Figs. 266G, H); southern
    states . . . . . . . . . . . . . . . . . . . . . . . . . . . . . . . . . . . . . . . . . . . . . . . . . . . . . . . . . . . . . . . .95
    With a fringe of setae confined to the posterior ventral margin; up to 0.4 mm long;
    rare; reported from Minnesota, Indiana, South Carolina, Florida, and New
    Mexico . . . . . . . . . . . . . . . . . . . . . . . . . . . . . . . . . **Alona circumfimbriata** Megard
95. Valves with longitudinal striae (Fig. 266G); 0.4 mm long; in vegetation in pools.
                                                              **Alona monacantha** Sars
    Valves with oblique striae (Fig. 266H); about 0.5 mm long . . . **Alonella karua** (King)
96. Postabdomen with marginal denticles only (Fig. 266F); 0.4 mm long; common
    everywhere . . . . . . . . . . . . . . . . . . . . . . . . . . . . . . . . . . . . . . . . . . . **Alona guttata** Sars
    Postabdomen with both marginal and lateral denticles (Figs. 266L; 267B) . . . . . . .97
97. With 14 or more marginal denticles; up to 1 mm long . . . . . . . . . . . . . . . . . . . . . . . .98
    With less than 14 marginal denticles; up to 0.5 mm long . . . . . . . . . . . . . . . . . . . . . .99
98. With a cluster of fine spinules at base of claw (Fig. 266J); 1 mm long; abundant
    everywhere in vegetation of littoral . . . . . . . . . . . . . . . . . . **Alona affinis** (Leydig)
    Without spinules at base of claw (Fig. 266N); up to 0.9 mm long; in vegetation of
    littoral and on bottom in deeper water; common everywhere.
                                                     **Alona quadrangularis** (O.F.M.)

Fig. 268.–Structure of Chydorinae. A, postabdomen of *Rhynchotalona falcata*; B, *Pleuroxus procurvatus*, ×70; C, *Alonella dentifera*, ×95; D, *Pleuroxus striatus*, ×55; E, claw of *P. striatus*; F, *Dunhevedia crassa*, ×75; G and H, anterior end of *Pleuroxus uncinatus*; J, posterior end of *P. hastatus*; K, *P. denticulatus*, ×85; L, postabdomen of *P. trigonellus*; M, postabdomen of *P. aduncus*. (A modified from Lilljeborg; B, C, and F to M modified from Ward and Whipple, 1918; D and E redrawn from Uéno.)

99. Lateral denticles long, extending beyond dorsal margin of postabdomen (Figs. 266L, M) .................................................. **Alona rectangula** Sars
Lateral denticles not extending beyond dorsal margin of postabdomen (Fig. 267B); cryptic species ...................................................**100**
100. Anal groove of postabdomen unarmed (Fig. 267B) ...........................**101**
Anal groove of postabdomen completely edged by groups of spinules (Fig. 267C). **102**
101. Female postabdomen with about 12 subequal marginal denticles; common and widely distributed ......................................... **Alona costata** Sars
Female postabdomen with about seven subequal marginal denticles; Wyoming and Minnesota....................................**Alona barbulata** Megard
102. Rostrum not projecting beyond setae of antennae (Fig. 267D); carapace unicolored; widely distributed ..................................**Alona rustica** Scott
Rostrum projecting beyond tips of setae of antennae (Fig. 267E); carapace strongly amber or straw-colored, brood chamber area colorless; reported only from New England ....................................**Alona bicolor** Frey
103. Postabdomen with marginal denticles only (Fig. 266E) ..............**Alonella, 113**
Postabdomen with numerous lateral denticles, only two to four marginal denticles (Fig. 268A); 0.5 mm long; northern states ...... **Rhynchotalona falcata** (Sars)
104. Body elongated ...............................................................**105**
Body spherical or broadly ellipsoidal .......................................**122**
105. Posterior margin with teeth along entire length (Fig. 268D); 0.5 mm long. **Pleuroxus, 106**
Posterior margin without teeth along entire length .........................**107**

106. Rostrum bent sharply into a hook (Fig. 268B); common in vegetation in northern states . . . . . . . . . . . . . . . . . . . . . . . . . . . . . . . . . . . . . . **Pleuroxus procurvatus** Birge
Rostrum not bent; rare in northern states . . . . . . . . . . **Pleuroxus truncatus** (O.F.M.)

107. Without teeth at the ventroposterior angle . . . . . . . . . . . . . . . . . . . . . . . . . . . . . . **108**
With one or more teeth at the ventroposterior angle . . . . . . . . . . . . . . . . . . . . . . . **114**

108. Claws with two basal spines (Figs. 268L, M) . . . . . . . . . . . . . . . . . . . . **Pleuroxus, 109**
Claws with one basal spine (Fig. 266E) . . . . . . . . . . . . . . . . . . . . . . . . . . . **Alonella, 112**

109. Postabdomen long and slender; ventroposterior angle rounded (Fig. 268D); 0.8 mm long; common in vegetation . . . . . . . . . . . . . . . . . . . **Pleuroxus striatus** Schödler
Postabdomen of moderate length (Figs. 268L, M); 0.5 to 0.6 mm long . . . . . . . . **110**

110. Angle of postabdomen sharp; in pools and vegetation; probably generally distributed . . . . . . . . . . . . . . . . . . . . . . . . . . . . . . . . **Pleuroxus hamulatus** Birge
Angle of postabdomen rounded (Figs. 268L, M) . . . . . . . . . . . . . . . . . . . . . . . . . . **111**

111. With the row of marginal denticles longer than anal emargination (Fig. 268L); widely distributed but uncommon . . . . . . . . . . . . . . . . **Pleuroxus trigonellus** (O.F.M.)
With the row of marginal denticles about equal to anal emargination (Fig. 268M); in vegetation; reported from several northern and western states.

**Pleuroxus aduncus** (Jurine)

112. Postabdomen with marginal and lateral denticles; in vegetation; Louisiana.

**Alonella globulosa** Daday
Postabdomen with marginal denticles only (Fig. 266E) . . . . . . . . . . . . . . . . . . . . . . **113**

113. Marginal denticles minute (Fig. 266E); rostrum reaching not more than two-thirds the distance to the ventral margin; rare; southern states.

**Alonella diaphana** (King)
Marginal denticles of usual size; rostrum long, recurved, and reaching the ventral margin (Fig. 270D) . . . . . . . . . . . . . . . . . . . . . . . . . **Disparalona rostrata** (Koch)

114. Claws with two major basal spines . . . . . . . . . . . . . . . . . . . . . . . . . . . . . . . . . . . . . . **115**
Claws with one major basal spine . . . . . . . . . . . . . . . . . . . . . . . . . . . . . . . . . . . . . . . **135**

115. Rostrum long, extending well beyond the tips of the terminal olfactory setae (Figs. 268G, H); teeth on ventroposterior angle variable . . . . . . . . . . . . **Pleuroxus, 117**
Rostrum shorter, extending only slightly, if at all, beyond the tips of the olfactory setae; lowermost part of posterior margin excised or notched, or ventroposterior angle with one or two prominent teeth (Fig. 268C) . . . . . . **Alonella, 116**

116. Postabdomen angled at apex (Fig. 270F); common everywhere in vegetation.

**Alonella excisa** (Fischer)
Postabdomen rounded at apex (Fig. 270G); rare; northern states. **Alonella exigua** (Lillj.)

117. Rostrum curved forward (Figs. 268G, H); two to four long, curved teeth at inferoposterior angle; 0.7 to 0.9 mm long; rare; northern states.

**Pleuroxus uncinatus** Baird
Rostrum not curved forward . . . . . . . . . . . . . . . . . . . . . . . . . . . . . . . . . . . . . . . . . . . . . **118**

118. Postabdomen long and slender (Fig. 268D) . . . . . . . . . . . . . . . . . . . . . . . . . . . . . . . **119**
Postabdomen of moderate length (Figs. 268K–M); 0.5 to 0.6 mm long . . . . . . . . **120**

119. Ventroposterior angle a sharp point, with a very small tooth (Fig. 268J); 0.6 mm long; rare but widely distributed . . . . . . . . . . . . . . . . . . **Pleuroxus hastatus** Sars
Ventroposterior angle rounded, with a small tooth anterior to it (Fig. 268D); 0.8 mm long; common everywhere in vegetation . . . . . . . . **Pleuroxus striatus** Schödler

120. Angle of postabdomen sharp; ventroposterior angle with teeth (Fig. 268K); a highly variable species, common everywhere in vegetation.

**Pleuroxus denticulatus** Birge
Angle of postabdomen rounded (Figs. 268L, M) . . . . . . . . . . . . . . . . . . . . . . . . . . . **121**

121. With a row of marginal denticles longer than anal emargination (Fig. 268L); two to three small teeth on inferoposterior angle; widely distributed but uncommon . . . . . . . . . . . . . . . . . . . . . . . . . . . . . **Pleuroxus trigonellus** (O.F.M.)
With a row of marginal denticles about equal to anal emargination (Fig. 268M); occasionally two or three small teeth on inferoposterior angle; in vegetation; reported from several northern and western states. **Pleuroxus aduncus** (Jurine)

122. With a small to large spine at ventroposterior angle (Fig. 269A) . . . . . . . . . . . . . . **123**
Without a spine at ventroposterior angle . . . . . . . . . . . . . . . . . . . . . . . . . . . . . . . . . **124**

FIG. 269.–Structure of Chydorinae. A, *Alonella nana* with only part of striations shown, ×200; B, *Anchistropus minor,* ×160; C, postabdomen of *Pseudochydorus globosus*; D, *Chydorus bicornutus,* ×120; E, *C. gibbus,* ×110; F, *C. sphaericus,* ×130; G, postabdomen of *C. sphaericus*; H, antennule of *C. sphaericus*; J, antennule of *C. piger*; K, antennule of *C. ovalis.* (A to E modified from Ward and Whipple, 1918; G to K modified from Lilljeborg.)

**123.** Valves conspicuously striated (Fig. 269A); 0.2 to 0.3 mm long; rare; northern states . . . . . . . . . . . . . . . . . . . . . . . . . . . . . . . . . . . . . . . . . . . . . . .**Alonella nana** (Baird)
    Valves not striated . . . . . . . . . . . . . . . . . . . . . . . . . . . . . . . . . . . . . . . . . . . . .**Chydorus, 134**
**124.** Valves with conspicuous projection at anteroventral margin (Fig. 269B); 0.35 mm long; widely distributed . . . . . . . . . . . . . . . . . . . . . . .**Anchistropus minor** Birge
    Valves without such a projection . . . . . . . . . . . . . . . . . . . . . . . . . . . . . . . . . . . . .**125**

Fig. 270.–Structure of Chydorinae and Polyphemidae. A, anterior end of *Chydorus poppei*; B, *C. barroisi*, ×140; C, anterior end of *C. hybridus*; D, *Disparalona rostrata* with only a portion of valve reticulations shown, ×110; E, *Alonella dadayi* with only a portion of valve reticulations shown, ×200; F, postabdomen of *Alonella excisa*; G, postabdomen of *A. exigua*; H, *Polyphemus pediculus*, ×50; J and K, ventroposterior angle of *Alonella excisa*. (A to E modified from Ward and Whipple, 1918; F to H modified from Lilljeborg.)

**125.** Animal spherical or ovate; postabdomen with prominent preanal angle (Fig. 269); 0.3 to 0.8 mm long . . . . . . . . . . . . . . . . . . . . . . . . . . . . . . . . . . . . . . . . . . . . . . . . . . **126**

Animal more elongated; postabdomen without prominent preanal angle; 0.2 to 0.5 mm long . . . . . . . . . . . . . . . . . . . . . . . . . . . . . . . . . . . . . . . . . . . . . . . . . . . . **135**

**126.** Postabdomen long, narrow (Fig. 269C); widely distributed; in vegetation.

**Pseudochydorus globosus** (Baird)

Postabdomen short, broad (Fig. 269G) . . . . . . . . . . . . . . . . . . . . . . . . . . **Chydorus, 127**

**127.** Carapace deeply sculptured . . . . . . . . . . . . . . . . . . . . . . . . . . . . . . . . . . . . . . . . . **128**

Carapace not deeply sculptured . . . . . . . . . . . . . . . . . . . . . . . . . . . . . . . . . . . . . . **129**

**128.** Carapace covered with deep polygonal cells; widely distributed but uncommon.

**Chydorus faviformis** Birge

Shell covered with deep polygonal cells and ridges (Fig. 269D); northern states.

**Chydorus bicornutus** Doolittle

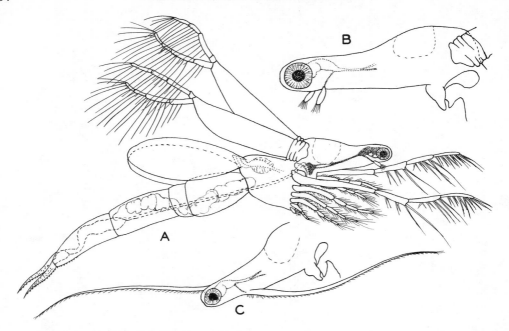

FIG. 271.–Structure of *Leptodora kindti*. A, adult female with winter eggs, ×85; B, anterior end of female; C, anterior end of male. (Modified from Sebestyén.)

129. Ventral edge of keel of labrum smooth ....................................**130**
     Ventral edge of keel of labrum toothed (Figs. 270A–C); rare ..................**133**
130. Dorsoanterior surface of head and valves somewhat flattened (Fig. 269E); rare;
     northern states....................................**Chydorus gibbus** Lillj.
     Dorsoanterior surface of head and valves not flattened ......................**131**
131. All olfactory setae inserted at end of antennule (Fig. 269H); 0.3 to 0.5 mm long; the
     most common of all Cladocera; widely distributed.
                                              **Chydorus sphaericus** (O.F.M.)
     All olfactory setae not inserted at end of antennule; rare ....................**132**
132. With two olfactory setae on side of antennule (Fig. 269J); 0.4 mm long; Maine.
                                              **Chydorus piger** Sars
     With one olfactory seta on side of antennule (Fig. 269K); 0.5 mm long;
     Nebraska ...................................... **Chydorus ovalis** Kurz
133. Without a spine at the ventroposterior angle; one tooth on labrum (Fig. 270A);
     Louisiana and California; rare ................... **Chydorus poppei** Richard
     With a spine at the ventroposterior angle; one or several teeth on labrum ......**134**
134. With several teeth on keel of labrum (Fig. 270B); Louisiana.
                                              **Chydorus barroisi** (Richard)
     With one tooth on keel of labrum (Fig. 270C); widely distributed but rare.
                                              **Chydorus hybridus** Daday
135. Rostrum short, extending only slightly, if at all, beyond the tips of the terminal
     olfactory setae (Figs. 268C, F); lateral denticles present on postabdomen. **136**
     Rostrum long, extending well beyond the tips of the terminal olfactory setae (Figs.
     269A; 270E); lateral denticles absent ...................... **Alonella, 140**
136. Postabdomen bent abruptly behind anus; one or two teeth at inferoposterior
     angle ................................................. **Dunhevedia, 137**
     Postabdomen not bent abruptly behind anus ............................**138**

137. Ventral margin of keel of labrum smooth; dorsal margin of body arched (Fig. 268F); up to 0.5 mm long; widely distributed . . . . . . . . . . . . **Dunhevedia crassa** King
Ventral margin of keel of labrum toothed; dorsal margin of body only slightly arched; up to 0.7 mm long; Louisiana, Texas . . . . . . . . . . . **Dunhevedia serrata** Daday

138. Valves reticulated; one to three larger teeth at inferoposterior angle (Fig. 268C); Louisiana, Texas . . . . . . . . . . . . . . . . . . . . . . . . . . . . . . . **Alonella dentifera** Sars
Valves striated; usually one to four small teeth at inferoposterior angle (Fig. 266H); up to 0.5 mm long . . . . . . . . . . . . . . . . . . . . . . . . . . . . . . . . . . . . . . **139**

139. Postabdomen expanded beyond anus; one to four (usually three) small teeth at inferoposterior angle (Fig. 266H); Louisiana, Texas, and Arkansas.

**Alonella karua** (King)

Postabdomen not especially expanded beyond anus; usually one minute tooth at inferoposterior angle; rostrum variable; rare but probably widely distributed . . . . . . . . . . . . . . . . . . . . . . . . . . . . . . .**Disparalona rostrata** (Koch)

140. Rostrum very long and strongly recurved; valves reticulated; inferoposterior angle rounded, with several minute teeth (Fig. 270E); up to 0.3 mm long; in pools in vegetation; Louisiana and Texas . . . . . . . . . . . . . . . . .**Alonella dadayi** Birge
Rostrum shorter and only slightly recurved; one small tooth at inferoposterior angle (Fig. 269A); up to 0.3 mm long; rare; northern states . . . **Alonella nana** Baird

141. Body short; with four pairs of stout legs bearing branchial appendages (Fig. 270H); up to 1.5 mm long; common in northern lakes, ponds, and marshes.

POLYPHEMIDAE, **Polyphemus pediculus** (L.)

Body long; with six pairs of legs; branchial appendages absent; up to 17 mm long (Fig. 271); limnetic; common in northern states.

LEPTODORIDAE, **Leptodora kindti** (Focke)


## CLADOCERA REFERENCES

ANDERSON, B. G., and J. C. JENKINS. 1942. A time study of events in the life span of Daphnia magna. *Biol. Bull.* **83**:260–272.

ANGINO, E. E., K. E. ARMITAGE, and B. SAXENA. 1973. Population dynamics of pond zooplankton. II. Daphnia ambigua Scourfield. *Hydrobiologia* **42**:491–507.

APPLEGATE, E. R., and J. W. MULLAN. 1970. Ecology of Daphnia in Bull Shoals Reservoir. *Res. Rept. U.S. Bur. Sport Fish. Wildlife* **74**:1–23.

BANTA, A. M. 1939. Studies on the physiology, genetics, and evolution of some Cladocera. *Publ. Carnegie Inst. Wash.* **513**:1–285.

BERG, K. 1931. Studies on the genus Daphnia O. F. Müller with especial reference to the mode of reproduction. *Vidensk. Medd. Dansk. naturhist. Foren.* **92**:1–222.

———. 1934. Cyclic reproduction, sex determination and depression in the Cladocera. *Biol. Rev.* **9**:139–174.

BRANDLOVA, J. 1972. The Cladocera of Ontario with remarks on some species and distribution. *Can. J. Zool.* **50**:1373–1403.

BREHM, V. 1937. Zwei neue Moina-Formen aus Nevada, U.S.A. *Zool. Anz.* **117**:91–96.

BROOKS, J. L. 1946. Cyclomorphosis in Daphnia. I. An analysis of D. retrocurva and D. galeata. *Ecol. Monogr.* **16**:409–447.

———. 1953. A re-description of typical Daphnia clathrata Forbes and Daphnia arcuata Forbes. *Am. Midl. Nat.* **49**:193–209.

———. 1953a. Re-description of Daphnia pulex var. pulicaria Forbes, D. thorata F. and D. dentifera F. Ibid. 772–800.

———. 1957. The systematics of North American Daphnia. *Mem. Conn. Acad. Arts and Sci.* **13**:1–180.

CANNON, H. G., and F. M. C. LEAK. 1933. On the feeding mechanism of the Branchiopoda. *Philos. Trans. Roy. Soc. Lond. B*, **222**:267–352.

CHIEN, S. M. 1970. Alonella fitzpatricki sp. n. and A. leei sp. n.: new Cladocera from Mississippi. *Trans. Am. Microsc. Soc.* **89**:532–538.

COKER, R. E. 1939. The problem of cyclomorphosis in Daphnia. *Quart. Rev. Biol.* **14**:137–148.

COKER, R. E., and H. H. ADDLESTONE. 1938. Influence of temperature on cyclomorphosis of D. longispina. *J. Elisha Mitchell Sci. Soc.* **54**:45–75.

DAVISON, J. 1969. Activation of the ephippial egg of Daphnia pulex. *J. Gen. Physiol.* **53**:562–575.

DEEVEY, E. S., and G. B. DEEVEY. 1971. The American species of Eubosmina Seligo (Crustacea, Cladocera). *Limnol. Oceanogr.* **16**:201–218.

EDMONDSON, W. T. 1955. The seasonal life history of Daphnia in an arctic lake. *Ecology* **36**:439–451.

ERIKSSON, S. 1936. Studien über die Fangapparate der Branchiopoden nebst einigen phylogenetischen Bemerkungen. *Zool. Bid. Upps.* **15**:23–287.

FREY, D. G. 1959. The taxonomic and phylogenetic significance of the head pores of the Chydoridae (Cladocera). *Int. Rev. ges. Hydrobiol.* **44**:27–50.

————. 1961. Differentiation of Alonella acutirostris (Birge, 1879) and Alonella rostrata (Koch, 1841) (Cladocera, Chydoridae). *Trans. Am. Microsc. Soc.* **80:**129–140.

————. 1962. Supplement to: The taxonomic and phylogenetic significance of the head pores of the Chydoridae (Cladocera). *Int. Rev. ges. Hydrobiol.* **47:**603–609.

————. 1965. Differentiation of Alona costata Sars from two related species (Cladocera, Chydoridae). *Crustaceana* **8:**159–173.

————. (organizer). 1971. Symposium on ecology of the Cladocera. (Abstracts only.) *Trans. Am. Microsc. Soc.* **90:**100–121.

————. 1973. Comparative morphology and biology of three species of Eurycercus (Chydoridae, Cladocera) with a description of Eurycercus macrocanthis sp. nov. *Int. Rev. ges. Hydrobiol.* **58:**221–267.

FRYER, G. 1968. Evolution and adaptive radiation in the Chydoridae (Crustacea: Cladocera): a study in comparative functional morphology and ecology. *Philos. Trans. Roy. Soc. Lond., Ser. B, Biol. Sci.* **254:**221–385.

————. 1968a. Tubular and glandular organs in the Cladocera, Chydoridae. *Zool. J. Linn. Soc.* **48:**1–8.

————. 1970. Defaecation in some macrothricid and chydorid cladocerans, and some problems of water intake and digestion in the Anomopoda. *Ibid.* **49:**225–269.

————. 1971. Allocation of Alonella acutirostris (Birge) (Cladocera, Chydoridae) to the genus Disparalona. *Crustaceana* **21:**221–222.

————. 1972. Observations on the ephippia of certain macrothricid cladocerans. *Zool. J. Linn. Soc.* **51:**79–96.

————. 1974. Evolution and adaptive radiation in the Macrothricidae (Crustacea: Cladocera): a study in comparative functional morphology and ecology. *Philos. Trans. Roy. Soc. Lond., Ser. B, Biol. Sci.* **269:**137–274.

GELLIS, S. S., and G. L. CLARKE. 1935. Organic matter in dissolved and in colloidal form as food for Daphnia magna. *Physiol. Zool.* **8:**127–137.

GOULDEN, C. E. 1968. The systematics and evolution of the Moinidae. *Trans. Am. Philos. Soc.* **58:**(6):1–101.

————. 1971. Environmental control of the abundance and distribution of the chydorid Cladocera. *Limnol. Oceanogr.* **16:**320–331.

GOULDEN, C. E., and D. G. FREY. 1963. The occurrence and significance of lateral head pores in the genus Bosmina (Cladocera). *Int. Rev. ges. Hydrobiol.* **48:**513–522.

HARRIS, J. E. 1963. The role of endogenous rhythms in vertical migration. *J. Mar. Biol. Assoc.* **43:**153–166.

HARRIS, J. E., and P. MASON. 1956. Vertical migration in eyeless Daphnia. *Proc. Roy. Soc. Lond.* **145B:**280–290.

HASLER, A. D. 1937. The physiology of digestion in plankton Crustacea. II. Further studies on the digestive enzymes of (A) Daphnia and Polyphemus; (B) Diaptomus and Calanus. *Biol. Bull.* **72:**290–298.

HRBACEK, J. 1959. Circulation of water as a main factor influencing the development of helmets in Daphnia cucullata Sars. *Hydrobiologia* **13:**170–185.

INGLE, L., T. R. WOOD, and A. M. BANTA. 1937. A study of longevity, growth, reproduction, and heart rate in Daphnia longispina as influenced by limitations in quantity of food. *J. Exp. Zool.* **76:**325–352.

JACOBS, J. 1961. Cyclomorphosis in Daphnia galeata mendotae Birge, a case of environmentally controlled allometry. *Arch. Hydrobiol.* **58:**7–71.

————. 1962. Light and turbulence as co-determinants of relative growth rates in cyclomorphic Daphnia. *Int. Rev. ges. Hydrobiol.* **47:**146–156.

JONES, W. H. 1958. Cladocera of Oklahoma. *Trans. Am. Microsc. Soc.* **77:**243–257.

KERFOOT, W. C. 1975. The divergence of adjacent populations. Ecology **56:**1298–1313.

KIANG, H.-M. 1942. Über die Cyclomorphose der Daphnien einiger Voralpenseen. *Int. Rev.* **41:**345–408.

LILLJEBORG, W. 1900. Cladocera sueciae. *Nova Acta Regiae Soc. Sci. Ups., Ser. 3,* **19:**1–701.

MACKIN, J. G. 1930. Studies on the Crustacea of Oklahoma. I. Camptocercus oklahomensis n. sp. *Trans. Am. Microsc. Soc.* **49:**46–53.

McMAHON, J. W., and F. H. RIGLER. 1963. Mechanisms regulating the feeding rate of Daphnia magna Straus. *Can. J. Zool.* **41:**321–332.

McNAUGHT, D. C., and A. D. HASLER. 1963. Rate of movement of populations of Daphnia in relation to changes in light intensity. *J. Fish. Res. Board Can.* **21:**291–318.

MEGARD, R. O. 1965. A chemical technique for disarticulating the exoskeletons of chydorid Cladocera. *Crustaceana* **9:**208–210.

————. 1967. Three new species of Alona (Cladocera, Chydoridae) from the United States. *Int. Rev. ges. Hydrobiol.* **52:**37–50.

MEIJERING, M. P. D. 1975. Notes on the systematics and ecology of Daphnia pulex Leydig in northern Canada. *Ibid.* **60:**691–703.

PACAUD, A. 1939. Contribution à l'écologie des Cladocères. *Bull. biol. Fr. Belg., Suppl.* **25:**1–260.

PEJLER, B. 1973. On the taxonomy of limnoplanktic Daphnia species in northern Sweden. *Zoon* **1:**23–27.

PRATT, D. M. 1943. Analysis of population development in Daphnia at different temperatures. *Biol. Bull.* **85:**116–140.

RINGELBERG, J. 1964. The positively phototactic reaction of Daphnia magna Straus. A contribution to the understanding of diurnal vertical migration. *Neth. J. Sea Res.* **2:**319–406.

SCHINDLER, D. W. 1968. Feeding, assimilation and respiration rates of Daphnia magna under various environmental conditions and their relation to production estimates. *J. Anim. Ecol.* **37:**369–385.

SCOURFIELD, D. J. 1942. The "pulex" forms of Daphnia and their separation into two distinct series represented by D. pulex (De Geer) and D. obtusa Kurz. *Ann. Mag. Nat. Hist.* **9:**202–219.

SCOURFIELD, D. J., and J. P. HARDING. 1966. A key to the British species of freshwater Cladocera. *Sci. Publ. Freshwater Biol. Assoc.* **5:**1–55.

SEBESTYEN, O. 1931. Contribution to the biology

and morphology of Leptodora kindtii (Focke) (Crustacea, Cladocera). *Arb. Ung. Biol. Forsch.-Inst.* **4**:151–170.

SMIRNOV, N. N. 1966. Alonopsis (Chydoridae, Cladocera): morphology and taxonomic position. *Hydrobiologia* **27**:113–136.

————. 1966a. Pleuroxus (Chydoridae): morphology and taxonomy. Ibid. **28**:161–194.

————. 1968. On comparative functional morphology of limbs of Chydoridae (Cladocera). *Crustaceana* **14**:76–96.

————. 1972. Detailed morphology of trunk limbs of some Aloninae. *Hydrobiologia* **40**:393–422.

————. 1974. Chydoridae of the World's fauna. *Fauna of the U.S.S.R. Crustacea* **1**(2):1–644.

STORCH, O. 1924. Morphologie und Physiologie des Fangapparates der Daphniden. *Ergeb. Fortschr. Zool.* **6**:125–234.

————. 1925. Cladocera. *Biol. Tiere Deutsch.* **15**:23–102.

TAPPA, D. W. 1965. The dynamics of the association of six limnetic species of Daphnia in Aziscoos Lake, Maine. *Ecol. Monogr.* **35**:395–423.

THOMAS, I. F. 1961. Review of the genera Pseudosida Herrick, 1884 and Latonopsis Sars, 1888 (Cladocera). *Crustaceana* **3**:1–8.

UÉNO, M. 1927. The freshwater Branchiopoda of Japan. *I. Mem. Coll. Sci. Kyoto Imp. Univ. Ser. B,* **2**:259–311.

VON SAALFELD, E. 1936. Untersuchungen über den Blutkreislauf bei Leptodora hyalina. *Z. vgl. Physiol.* **24**:58–70.

WESENBERG-LUND, C. 1926. Contributions to the biology and morphology of the genus Daphnia with some remarks on heredity. *Mem. Acad. Roy. Sci. Lett. Dan., Sect. Sci., Ser. 8,* **11**:89–251.

WOLTERECK, R. 1913. Über Funktion, Herkunft und Entstehungsursachen der sogen. "Schwebe-Fortsätze" pelagischer Cladoceren. *Zoologica* **26**:474–550.

————. 1932. Races, associations and stratification of pelagic daphnids in some lakes of Wisconsin and other regions of the United States and Canada. *Trans. Wis. Acad. Sci. Arts and Lett.* **27**:487–522.

WOOD, T. R., and A. M. BANTA. 1937. Hatchability of Daphnia and Moina sexual eggs without drying. *Int. Rev. ges. Hydrobiol.* **35**:229–242.

ZARET, T. M., and W. C. KERFOOT. 1975. Fish predation on Bosmina longirostris: body-size selection versus visibility selection. *Ecology* **56**:232–237.

# Chapter 17

# COPEPODA

LIKE THE Cladocera, the Copepoda are almost universally distributed in the plankton, benthic, and littoral regions of fresh waters. They are either absent or present in small numbers in rapid headwater brooks and streams.

**General characteristics.** The body length of the American species ranges from 0.3 to 3.2 mm, but the great majority are less than 2.0 mm long. Most species are drab grayish or brownish, but others, especially littoral species in the spring of the year and at high altitudes, are brilliant orange, purple, or red. Such colorations are usually produced by a wide variety of carotenoids, and are thought to be a means of photoprotection in some species. As a group, the members of the Subclass Copepoda are much more homogeneous in their general structure than the Cladocera, and accurate identification is based largely on anatomical details of the appendages.

The American fresh-water copepods comprise two orders, Eucopepoda and Branchiura, and six suborders: Caligoida, Lernaeopodoida, Arguloida, Calanoida, Cyclopoida, and Harpacticoida. The first three of these suborders are exclusively parasitic, and the morphology is greatly modified and specialized. In the three free-living suborders, however, the body is clearly segmented, more or less elongated, cylindrical, and is divided into a head, thorax, and abdomen. The thoracic region is here considered to be composed of seven segments, but the first one or two are fused with the head to form a cephalothorax, which is covered with a carapace. In addition, the fourth and fifth or fifth and sixth thoracic segments are also occasionally fused. The abdomen consists of three to five segments, typically four. Commonly the last thoracic (genital) segment and the first abdominal segment are fused. Conversely, there is subdivision of some segments in a few species.

Each segment is a rigid, sclerotized cylinder that is attached to adjacent segments by short, flexible, annular portions. One of the articulations is particularly movable, and, for convenience, the copepod body is often divided into metasome and urosome, the former being that part anterior to this articulation and the latter posterior (Fig. 272). The urosome includes all the abdomen, the seventh thoracic (genital) segment, and sometimes the sixth thoracic segment.

**Appendages.** The true head has five pairs of appendages: first antennae, second antennae, mandibles, first maxillae, and second maxillae. The first thoracic segment (fused with the head) bears a pair of maxillipeds, and each of the five subsequent thoracic segments bears one pair of swimming legs. In a few species the seventh thoracic (genital) segment bears a pair of vestigial swimming legs. There are no abdominal appendages.

In Figs. 272A and C the first two thoracic segments are fused with the head; the metasome therefore consists of cephalothorax and free thoracic segments III to V; the urosome consists of thoracic segment VI, thoracic segment VII (fused with abdominal segment I), and free abdominal segments II to IV. In Fig. 272B only the first thoracic segment is fused with the head; the metasome therefore consists of the cephalothorax and free thoracic seg-

FIG. 272.–Typical copepods. A, female *Macrocyclops ater* with egg masses, ×18; B, male *Limnocalanus macrurus*, ×33; C, female *Cyclops*, ×42. *M*, metasome; *U*, urosome. (A modified from Coker, 1938; B modified from Gurney.)

ments II to VI; the urosome consists of thoracic segment VII (genital segment) and abdominal segments I to IV.

Some investigators consider the maxillipeds to be a part of the true head, so that there are only six thoracic segments. Others consider the genital segment to be a part of the abdomen.

In studying species with confusing fusion or subdivision of the thoracic segments, it is easy to orient oneself by locating the first and subsequent swimming legs. They correspond to thoracic segments II to VI. Fundamentally, all head and thoracic appendages are biramous, and a primitive copepod swimming leg consists of a three-segmented basipod having attached at its distal end a median three-segmented endopod and a lateral three-segmented exopod. A typical and relatively unmodified swimming leg of *Cyclops* is shown in Fig. 275.

The appendages of the head are highly modified for various special functions. The first antennae are uniramous and long, consisting of as many as 25 segments; they are sensory appendages but are used also for locomotion. In male cyclopoids and harpacticoids both first antennae are geniculate and modified for copulation (Figs. 274, 276A). In male calanoids only the right is geniculate (Fig. 272).

The second antennae (Fig. 276C) are much shorter, either biramous or uniramous, and are probably most important as sensory structures, although they are prehensile in male harpacticoids. The mandibles, first maxillae, second maxillae, and maxillipeds (occurring in that order) are highly modified for feeding (Figs. 276D–G).

The segmentation of the legs varies considerably from the primitive condition, and the modifications are most pronounced in the last two pairs. In the free-living species the sixth legs are always lacking in the female and are either rudimentary or lacking in the male. The fifth legs are reduced or vestigial in both sexes in the Cyclopoida and Harpacticoida, but in the Calanoida they are well developed and symmetrical in the female and asymmetrical and modified for clasping in the male (Figs. 282–287).

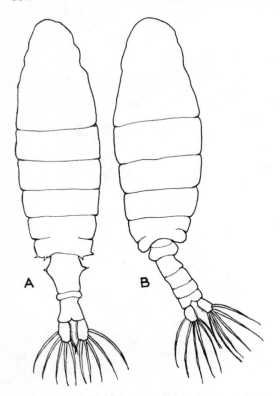

FIG. 273.–Dorsal view of *Diaptomus siciloides* (appendages and most setation omitted). A, female; B, male. (From Comita and Tommerdahl.)

FIG. 274.–Harpacticoid copepods. A, female *Attheyella*; B, male *Attheyella*. (From Coker, 1934.)

The last abdominal (anal) segment bears two posteriorly directed caudal rami. These are simple, more or less cylindrical structures that are neither biramous nor serially homologous with the head and thoracic appendages.

In general, there are five types of slender outgrowths from the exoskeleton. One type, the aesthetasks, presumably function as sensory receptors. They are delicate, elongated, blunt tipped, and occur on the first and second antennae. Aesthetasks are shown in Fig. 276A. The other four types of outgrowths occur on all copepod appendages and less commonly on the body segments; they form a morphological series: spines–spinules–setae–hairs. Spines and spinules are generally short, stout, strong, and inflexible. Setae, on the other hand, are relatively long, flexible, and thin. Hairs are the very finest outgrowths and they us-

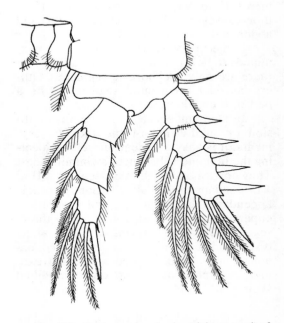

FIG. 275.–Typical swimming leg (right, second) of *Cyclops*, showing two-segmented basipod, three-segmented exopod (right), and three-segmented endopod (left). (Redrawn from Gurney.)

FIG. 276.–Copepod head appendages. A, first antenna of male *Mesocyclops leuckarti*; B, first antenna of female *Macrocyclops fuscus*; C, second antenna of same; D, mandible of same; E, first maxilla of same; F, second maxilla of same; G, maxilliped of same. (Redrawn from Gurney.)

ually occur as fringes or rows on setae and spines. None of the categories spines, spinules, setae, and hairs can be precisely defined to the exclusion of the others, and there are wide variations in size and all possible and imperceptible intergrades. All of them, however, may have one or several functions, depending on their location. Generally they aid in swimming, crawling, and feeding, but some are sensory, and it is possible that the long setae of the caudal rami may act as balancers or stabilizers during locomotion. Sensillae are very short triangular sensory spines found especially on the trunk and legs.

**Feeding.** Harpacticoid mouth parts are adapted from raking, seizing, and scraping food from the bottom. Calanoids feed chiefly by filtration of plankton. The first antennae function as screws and the second antennae beat continuously to produce a current, from which the particles are filtered by the mouth parts, chiefly the maxillae. There is considerable evidence to show that calanoids exhibit some selectivity in the size and kind of algae ingested. There is also some evidence to show that calanoids combine raptorial feeding with filter feeding. Cyclopoids have the mouth parts modified for seizing and biting. The food consists mostly of unicellular plants and animals, small metazoans, and especially other crustaceans, as well as organic debris; and it has now been well established that debris may, under some circumstances, form the majority of material ingested. Cannibalism on immature stages is common. The course of the food through the digestive tract can easily be seen in the living animal under the microscope. The anus is on the last abdominal segment between the bases of the caudal rami. The accumulation of reserve food in the form of oil globules is usually chiefly responsible for the brilliant red coloration of some species of *Diaptomus*.

**Locomotion.** Harpacticoids crawl or run on, and to some extent in, the substrate, and although many cyclopoids and a few calanoids also occur in close association with the substrate, they are chacteristically swimmers. The swimming mechanisms of *Diaptomus* have been carefully analyzed by Storch (1929). A constant, smooth, and relatively slow type of locomotion is produced by the feeding movements of the mouth parts and second antennae. This is punctuated at frequent intervals by a jerky type of locomotion caused by rapid backward movements of the legs. Between beats of the legs the first antennae are kept thrust out stiffly and laterally; they are thus thought to act chiefly as parachutes that greatly retard sinking. A fraction of a second before each beat of the legs, however, the first antennae are bent medially into the general longitudinal plane of the body, the beat of the legs thereby being much more effective. Immediately following each beat of the legs, the antennae are again extended laterally. According to Storch, a single beat of the legs and the accompanying antennal movements are completed in less than one-twelfth of a second. Cyclopoid mouth parts are of little importance, locomotion being brought about by relatively frequent beats of the legs. The accompanying antennal movements are similar to those of *Diaptomus*. In both cyclopoids and calanoids the abdomen is thought to function as a rudder.

**Internal anatomy.** Internal details are generally difficult to study because they are largely obscured by the very complicated system of muscles. A saccular heart occurs only in the Calanoida, and in the other suborders the blood simply circulates about in the hemocoel as the result of the movements of muscles, appendages, and the digestive tract. The oxygen and carbon dioxide exchange occurs through the general body surface and probably to some extent through the posterior part of the digestive tract where water is drawn in and out by extrinsic muscles. Excretion is thought to occur through the maxillary glands near the anterior end, but it is possible that the general body surface and the posterior part of the digestive tract may function in excretion also. The nervous system exhibits considerable fusion and cephalization. Aside from tactile structures, the only recognizable sensory area is the eyespot. In free-living species this is a small, median dorsal, clear or pigmented area at the anterior end of the cephalothorax. With the aid of a scanning electron microscope, however, Strickler (1975) reports an abundance of "sensory pegs" and

"sensory hairs" scattered over the copepod body.

**Reproduction.** Although reproductive habits are generally similar throughout the free-living copepods, the various species differ widely in their detailed behavior and breeding periods. Some species, such as *Cyclops vernalis* and *Eucyclops agilis,* reproduce throughout the year; *E. prasinus* breeds between July and October. Other species are monocyclic and breed for only short periods. *Macrocyclops fuscus* and *M. ater,* for example, reproduce only during the summer months, and some species of *Diaptomus* and *Limnocalanus macrurus* have only one generation per year. Little is known about the breeding habits of harpacticoids. Some have only one generation per year, but others undoubtedly have three or more.

The antennae and, in some genera, the modified fifth legs of the male, are used in clasping the female. The period of clasping may last only a few minutes or it may persist for several days. Sometimes the male clasps the female before she has had her final molt, and such clasping pairs have been observed for as long as 10 days.

Male calanoids have a single pore located asymmetrically on the genital segment, but female calanoids and both sexes in the other free-living suborders have paired genital pores. During clasping, the male transfers the sperm to the female in small, packetlike spermatophores, usually with the aid of the legs. The sperm are stored in a special ventral area of the female genital segment which serves as a seminal receptacle.

Actual fertilization occurs sometime after the two sexes have separated and as the eggs leave the female reproductive tract. This process may be completed within a few minutes or as long as two months after copulation. Fertilized eggs are carried by the female in one or two ovisacs (Fig. 272A). Ovisacs usually contain from 5 to 40 eggs each and are attached to the genital segment ventrally, laterally, or subdorsally. In some species the clutch size varies seasonally, with the largest numbers of eggs being produced in the spring months. Possibly this variation is correlated with temperature or food conditions.

In *Cyclops* the approximate incubation period ranges from 12 hours to 5 days, and when the newly hatched larvae leave the disintegrating ovisacs the female releases another group of eggs from the reproductive tract; these, in turn, are fertilized and retained in a new pair of ovisacs. In this way from 7 to 13 pairs of ovisacs full of eggs may be produced successively at intervals of one to six days, all resulting from the sperm retained from a single copulation. Sometimes unfertilized females release sterile, nonhatching eggs, and a single European species of *Attheyella* is known to reproduce by parthenogenesis.

Although it is believed that ordinary fertilized eggs may occasionally overwinter in an extended incubation period, adverse environmental conditions are usually withstood by special thick-walled "resting" eggs. Such eggs do not occur in the cyclopoids, but they are known to be produced by several species of *Diaptomus* and some harpacticoids, and it is the only type of egg produced by *Limnocalanus macrurus*.

**Metamorphosis.** The copepod egg hatches into a small, compact, active larva called a nauplius, which has three pairs of abbreviated appendages representing the first antennae, second antennae, and mandibles (Fig. 277A). After a period of feeding, it molts and becomes the nauplius II stage, which usually has the first maxillae in addition. In a similar manner there are four additional nauplius stages and five copepodid stages before the last molt, which results in the sexually mature adult. As metamorphosis proceeds, the larvae become progressively larger and more elongated, and acquire additional appendages (Figs. 277B–D). Nauplius VI, for example, usually has all appendages through the second pair of legs, and copepodid I has four distinct thoracic segments and all appendages through the fourth legs. In summary, the typical life cycle consists of the egg, six nauplius stages, five copepodid stages, and the adult. However, in all parasitic species

and some free-living species this series is abbreviated. Thus there are five nauplius stages in some Cyclopoida, and only four or five in certain Harpacticoida.

The time necessary for the complete life cycle from egg to egg is highly variable, depending on the species and environmental conditions. In *Cyclops* it lasts from 7 to about 180 days, whereas some species of *Diaptomus* and *Limnocalanus macrurus* have a one-year cycle.

Some cyclopoids are known to reproduce year round, even in the winter months, although maturation and growth proceed very slowly in cold water. Thus a copepod may have four or more generations during the eight warmest months of the year but only one generation during the four coldest months. Cyclopoid copepods regularly go into diapause on lake and pond bottoms during the cold months. This is simply a nonencysted dormant period found in the copepodid II to the copepodid V stages, especially after the fall overturn. In the spring these stages resume their active existence when the water becomes warmer. Concentrations of more than a million diapausing copepods per square meter of bottom have been reported.

**Parasitic copepods.** Copepod parasites occur on most common species of American fish and they are among the most highly modified and bizarre of all fresh-water animals. They are found on the general body surface, fins, and gills, and obtain nourishment from the tissues of the host.

Only a single genus, *Ergasilus,* of the Suborder Cyclopoida is parasitic and, incidentally, it is the least specialized for its parasitic existence. Only the adult female is parasitic, the immature females and all stages of males being free living. Superficially, the female looks like a *Cyclops* but may be easily distinguished by the greatly enlarged three-segmented clawlike second antennae (Fig. 279) used for clinging to the gills of fish.

The Caligoida is a relatively large suborder composed entirely of parasites. Only one species in one genus and about a dozen species in a second genus occur in

FIG. 277.–Immature copepods. A, nauplius I of *Cyclops*, ×100; B, nauplius IV of *Cyclops*, ×100; C, nauplius VI of *Diaptomus*, ×80; D, diagram of *Cyclops* copepodid, ×90 (only alternate legs shown on each side). (A and B redrawn from Gurney; C modified from Gurney.)

American fresh waters, all others being parasitic on marine fishes. The former, *Lepeophtheirus salmonis* (the sea louse), is scarcely recognizable as a copepod in the adult stage (Fig. 278B); there is a large, broad, flat cephalothorax, and most of the segments are fused, and the legs reduced. This species is only an incidental one in fresh waters; it is found attached to the surface of the body near the anus of salmon which have recently migrated from the sea, and may live only a week or two in fresh water. The males are very rare.

The other genus of the Suborder Caligoida occurring in the United States is *Lernaea*. The nauplii are free-living plankters, but the copepodids seek out a temporary host fish, cling to the gills, and copulate in

this immature stage. Soon thereafter the male copepodid dies, but the female leaves the host and is free living for a short time. She then attaches to the general body surface of any one of a great variety of fresh-water fishes and becomes completely altered morphologically into a long wormlike creature. The anterior half of the body is buried in the superficial host tissues and produces several large anchoring processes (Fig. 278A).

The genus *Argulus* of the parasitic Suborder Arguloida is the only one occurring in the United States. There are about 15 species parasitizing many fresh-water fishes. The adults, familiarly known as fish lice, range from 5 to 25 mm in length and are found attached in the branchial cham-

FIG. 278.–Parasitic copepods. A, ventral view of female *Lernaea cruciata*, ×6.5; B, dorsal view of female *Lepeophtheirus salmonis*, ×6; C, lateral view of female *Salmincola inermis*, ×6; D, dorsal view of female *Achtheres microptera*, ×8; E, dorsal view of female *Argulus flavescens*, ×10. (A and E modified from Wilson, 1914; B modified from Gurney; C and D modified from Wilson, 1915.)

ber or on the general body surface. Fish lice (Figs. 278E; 280) are greatly flattened dorsoventrally, and the head and thorax are covered with an expanded carapace whose lateral areas have a respiratory function. The abdominal segments are fused. The mouth parts are greatly modified or reduced; the second maxillae are completely transformed into curious suction cups; and the region of the mouth has a piercing organ used in obtaining the host blood. The first four pairs of legs are well developed and used for swimming, but the fifth and sixth legs are absent. Dorsally, there are two large movable compound eyes. *Argulus* often leaves its host and swims about freely, especially during the breeding season when the eggs are attached to stones and sticks of the substrate.

Of the parasitic Suborder Lernaeopodoida, only *Achtheres* and *Salmincola* occur in American fresh waters. These two genera are found in the gills and fins of many fishes and are perhaps the ultimate

among Copepoda in modification for the parasitic mode of life. The soft-bodied adult females (Figs. 278C, D) have no legs, little evidence of segmentation, and greatly reduced mouth parts. The second maxillae, however, are large cylindrical structures that have a single saucer- or umbrella-shaped organ at their distal end. The latter is imbedded in the host tissues and functions in absorbing nutriment. Little is known about the males; they are dwarfed, attached to the host fish during the immature stages, but cling to the body of the female before and after copulation. The nauplii stages are passed within the egg, but the first copepodid is a free-swimming planker for a brief period before becoming attached to a fish.

**Economic significance.** Under natural conditions parasitic copepods are rarely present in sufficient numbers to cause serious injury to the host. In hatchery ponds, however, where fish are crowded in a lim-

FIG. 279.–Dorsal view of female *Ergasilus versicolor*, ×70. (Modified from Wilson, 1911.)

Free-living copepods constitute an essential link in the aquatic food chain. They are on an intermediate trophic level between bacteria, algae, and protozoans, on the one hand, and small and large plankton predators (chiefly fish), on the other. In general, however, fresh-water copepods are not as important an element in the fish diet as Cladocera.

Copepods are of further importance as intermediate hosts of parasites of higher animals, particularly some tapeworms of fish, waterfowl, and carnivores; some flukes of fish, amphibians, and birds; and a few nematodes of fish and birds. In Africa, southern Asia, the West Indies, and parts of the Guianas and Brazil, *Cyclops* is of great importance in the transmission of the nematode parasite of man, *Dracunculus medinensis* (the Guinea worm), and some species of both *Cyclops* and *Diaptomus* are intermediate hosts of the broad or fish tapeworm of man and numerous carnivores.

Recently it has been shown that nonparasitic cyclopoid copepods may occasionally be a nuisance in hatcheries. They may merely nibble at the fins of fingerling fish, or they may be so abundant as to feed on and kill the fingerlings.

**Ecology.** Of the free-living copepods, the limnetic cyclopoid and calanoid species are by far the best known and most frequently collected. Sometimes they have been found in almost unbelievable numbers, up to 1000 individuals per liter having been recorded. In most lakes the limnetic copepod plankton is rather monotonous; usually it is composed of only one dominant cyclopoid, such as *Cyclops bicuspidatus*, *C. vernalis*, or *Mesocyclops leuckarti*. Often there is a dominant calanoid present also. In exceptional instances a limnetic population may consist of two or more cyclopoid species and two or more calanoid species all at the same time. Under such circumstances one cyclopoid is the numerical dominant and one calanoid is the numerical dominant. Coexistence of two species in the same genus is usually explained by vertical, seasonal, and food particle size preferences.

ited area, there is much greater opportunity for the free-swimming immature stages to find a host, and, as a result, heavy and serious infections may break out. When firmly established, copepod parasites are difficult to control, chiefly because the sclerotized exoskeleton of the adult is resistant to chemical solutions. Newly attached larval parasites are relatively delicate, however, and sometimes it is feasible to combat infections by giving the fish frequent salt or acid baths. In extreme cases there is no alternative but to get rid of the parasitized fish, clean the hatchery ponds, and start anew.

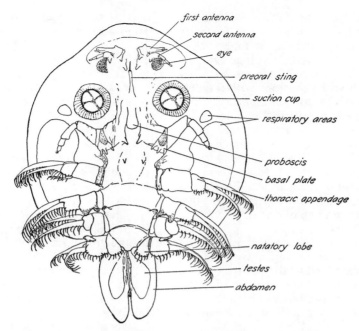

FIG. 280.–Ventral view of *Argulus*, ×23. (Modified from Meehean.)

Perhaps because of the greater variety of ecological niches, the shallow littoral, especially in aquatic vegetation, is much richer in cyclopoid and calanoid species, but the population density is not usually high.

In rivers and lakes the Harpacticoida are restricted to bottom debris of both littoral and benthic regions. In addition, however, there are many Cyclopoida and Calanoida that have become adapted to this habitat. Common bottom forms are *Paracyclops fimbriatus, Eucyclops agilis, Macrocyclops fuscus, M. albidus,* and species of *Canthocamptus, Bryocamptus,* and *Attheyella.* Very few copepods are found in rapid streams.

As ecological groups, the deep-water and limnetic species are somewhat distinct from those occurring in the shallow littoral. The former are generally smaller, slender, and more translucent, whereas the latter are larger, stout, more deeply pigmented, and have more robust appendages.

Harpacticoid copepods have been reported from some unusual habitats. Large numbers (up to 277 per 10 cm³ of sand)

have been found in the interstitial waters of sandy lake beaches, with greatest concentrations at depths of 1 to 6 cm, and at distances of 1.0 to 2.5 m from the water's edge (Pennak, 1940). European workers have described unusual endemic species from springs, underground streams, and cave systems, but little collecting has been done in such habitats in this country. Harpacticoids have also been reported from damp moss in forests far from any body of water.

It is thought that temperature plays an important role in copepod distribution and activity. Some species, such as *Limnocalanus macrurus, Senecella calanoides, Epischura lacustris, Diaptomus minutus, D. sicilis,* and *D. oregonensis,* are definitely cold-water forms occurring only in the northern states and in deep lakes. Others, such as *Diaptomus mississippiensis* and *D. dorsalis,* are restricted to the southern states. The rare species *Cyclops crassicaudis* occurs only in small, temporary, warm pools.

In some interesting experiments, Coker (1933) and Aycock (1942) reared *Cyclops vernalis, C. agilis,* and *C. viridis* under controlled conditions and found that at low temperatures (7.7° to 8.0°) adults were as much as 50 percent longer than adults that had been reared at high temperatures (28.0° to 30.0°). These workers believe that such size variations with temperature are internally controlled and are not dependent on the available food supply.

In general, copepods are much more tolerant of a deficiency of oxygen than are Cladocera. *Cyclops* and *Canthocamptus* have been collected many times from the surface of bottom muds in stratified lakes during summer and winter periods of stagnation and oxygen depletion. Although it is possible for *Cyclops* to swim up into the upper oxygenated layers intermittently, *Canthocamptus,* not being a swimmer, is necessarily restricted to the substrate. The whole problem of the metabolism of copepods and other organisms in anaerobic benthic regions deserves much more attention.

Some adult or advanced copepodids may form cysts or cocoons during unfavorable environmental conditions, and the fact that cysts have been found in abundance on lake bottoms in midsummer is an indication that they may be formed as a response to anaerobic conditions. In *Cyclops* the cysts also constitute an aestivation mechanism and are resistant to drying. The cyst wall is composed of a secreted organic membrane and an enveloping mass of detritus.

Like the Cladocera, some common species of plankton copepods show a daily rhythmic cycle of vertical migrations in lakes, with a greater concentration of individuals in the upper waters during the hours of darkness and correspondingly large numbers in the bottom waters during the hours of daylight. Individuals of some species may move upward at dusk and downward at dawn a vertical distance of as much as 10 or 20 m. It is believed that the primary stimulus for vertical migrations is the daily cycle of subsurface illumination.

**Geographical distribution.** The Copepoda undoubtedly originated in the ocean, and in this environment they have under-

gone much greater evolutionary specialization and speciation than in fresh water. The accompanying physiological divergence has been quite complete, and only a very few American species found in fresh water are known also to inhabit brackish or salt water. Some of these are *Limnocalanus macrurus, Eurytemora affinis, Harpacticus gracilis, Nitocra spinipes,* and *Cletocamptus.*

*Limnocalanus macrurus* is generally considered a relict species, that is, a saltwater form that has gradually become acclimated to fresh water. It is found only in the deep waters of larger lakes such as Green Lake (Wisconsin), the Finger Lakes, and the Great Lakes. It is also widely distributed in similar European lakes and in salt water. *Eurytemora* has close relatives in salt water and is probably a recent migrant. *Senecella* is thought to be of postglacial origin; it has been reported from several localities in Siberia, including some saline lakes. *Epischura* is confined to North America except for two Asiatic species.

*Cyclops* and its relatives have a worldwide distribution in fresh waters, some species, such as *C. bicuspidatus,* being essentially cosmopolitan. The closest marine and brackish relative is probably *Halicyclops.* Europe has about 110 species of cyclopoids, of which about half are known only from subterranean and interstitial waters.

The Diaptomidae are confined to fresh waters, and there are no close marine relatives. Unlike the cyclopoids, they show much evidence of recent speciation, and many of them seem to be confined to small geographic areas; numerous examples are given in the keys. Europe has about 70 species of calanoid copepods. Only 10 of these occur also in the United States.

Most fresh-water harpacticoids belong to the family Canthocamptidae, a group that has a worldwide distribution in salt, brackish, and fresh waters. Many species occur in both North American and European fresh waters, but so little systematic collecting has been done on the other continents that there are insufficient records to warrant the use of the term "cosmopolitan" for them. The great majority of species in the other harpacticoid families covered by this manual are typical of coastal, brackish, and saline waters.

Unquestionably, active migration is responsible for the geographic dispersal of species throughout a single drainage system, but overland transport to adjacent systems presents some difficult questions. Calanoida and Harpacticoida are probably dispersed as resting eggs, and although cysts are produced by some of the latter, they are not resistant to drying. The Cyclopoida, on the other hand, are not known to produce resting eggs, but resistant copepodid cysts are presumably of common occurrence, and it is likely that passive dispersal is brought about in this stage. It is significant that the first cyclopoids to appear in dried mud cultures are in the copepodid stages. Many copepods are found year after year in vernal ponds which are completely dried up during the greater part of the year, and we may safely assume that resting eggs and cysts in the dry mud and debris tide the species over.

Although passive transfer by waterfowl, aquatic insects, and in wind-blown dust explains the extensive distribution of some species, it is difficult to account for the fact that others are restricted to very small geographic areas, sometimes a single pond.

**Collecting.** Littoral and plankton copepods are easily collected with a townet or dipnet. An abundance of species may often be obtained by drawing nets through rooted aquatic vegetation and by lightly skimming the bottom. Collecting harpacticoids is a more tedious procedure. The top centimeter or two of mud and debris should be scooped up, brought into the laboratory, and allowed to settle. If the material is examined by looking toward a light source along the surface of the settled mud, the harpacticoids can be seen moving about at the mud–water interface and can be removed with a long pipette. Sometimes washings of aquatic mosses produce surprising numbers of specimens.

**Preservation.** The best specimens are obtained by killing in 95 percent alcohol.

Seventy percent alcohol is a suitable preservative and much superior to formalin solutions.

**Culturing.** Copepods are much more difficult than Cladocera to maintain as laboratory cultures, and they apparently never do well in dense numbers. Cyclopoids should be fed large protozoans or small metazoans, preferably crustaceans. Calanoids will sometimes thrive if a bit of algal culture suspension is added to the culture twice a week. Most copepods do best in cultures kept below 15°.

**Identification.** It is unfortunate that the identification of species is usually based on minute anatomical details. Some characters, such as the structure of the antennae, first legs, and caudal rami, may be studied from the whole animal, but it is often necessary to dissect the animal in order to study the mouth parts and legs, and it is an imperative procedure in formulating descriptions of new species. Harpacticoids must be dissected more frequently because of their general opacity and smaller appendages. Specimens to be dissected should be placed in a solution of 20 percent glycerin in 70 percent alcohol in a partially covered watch glass. After one to several days, most of the alcohol and water will have evaporated, leaving the undistorted specimens in glycerin. Then they may be easily picked up and transferred with an Irwin loop or on the tip of a fine, flat, toothbrush bristle mounted at the end of a matchstick. The animals should be dissected, one at a time, in a drop of glycerin on a slide on the stage of a high power binocular microscope. The necessary appendages are removed with a pair of sharp, mounted "minuten nadeln." As a fair warning, it should be said that requisite skill and patience in dissection come only with considerable practice! Appendages and whole animals are conveniently and permanently mounted for examination in glycerin jelly under a cover slip ringed with Murrayite. Mounting in fluid glycerin is more of a nuisance and less permanent.

Immature forms of the great majority of species cannot be identified.

If an abundance of specimens is available, the writer has found that all of the necessary anatomical details can usually be seen, even in difficult species, if 5 to 10 whole specimens are mounted, ventral side up, on the same slide. The appendages will become spread out sufficiently in a variety of ways so that all structures can be observed by studying several specimens under the high powers of the compound microscope.

Sometimes it is helpful if the animals are stained before dissection and mounting. From 70 percent alcohol they should be transferred to alum cochineal overnight, washed in 70 percent alcohol for five minutes, and then transferred to the glycerin-alcohol mixture.

Body length extends from the anterior margin of the cephalothorax to the posterior end of the caudal rami. Accurate measurements of body length are of limited use as a taxonomic character because of the fact that the trunk segments may be more or less retracted into each other.

# KEY TO MAJOR GROUPS OF COPEPODA

1. With no constriction, a slight constriction, or a marked constriction between the segments bearing the fourth and fifth legs (Figs. 272A, C; 274; 280); first antennae of female with 5 to 18 segments; depressed or cylindrical; parasitic, commensal, free-swimming, or benthic ...............................6
   With a marked constriction between segments bearing fifth legs and genital segment (Fig. 272B); first antennae of female with 22 to 25 segments; free-living or fixed parasites ..................................... Order **EUCOPEPODA, 2**
2. With a movable articulation between sixth and seventh thoracic segments (Fig. 272B); segmentation well defined; male left antenna geniculate in *Senecella,* male right antenna geniculate in all other genera; free-living. Suborder **CALANOIDA,** p. 406
   Body rigidly fused, without movable articulations, often without segmentation; fixed parasites of fishes ...................................................**3**
3. Adults long and wormlike (Fig. 278A); on gills and general external surface of many common fresh-water fishes; copepodid clings to gills of temporary host fish, then leaves and is free swimming for a short time before becoming attached to final host; adult females 7 to 15 mm long; about a dozen species.
   Suborder **CALIGOIDA,** LERNAEIDAE, **Lernaea**
   Adults not long and wormlike; males rare....................................**4**
4. Cephalothorax forming a broad flat disc (Fig. 278B); first to fourth legs well developed; males not reduced in size, rare; attached to surface of body near anus of salmon that have recently migrated from the sea; may live for a week or more in fresh water; 6 to 16 mm long; sea lice.
   Suborder **CALIGOIDA,** CALIGIDAE, **Lepeophtheirus salmonis** (Kröyer)
   Cephalothorax not forming a broad flat disc; legs absent; males small to minute pygmies clinging to females; early immature stages passed in egg; first copepodid free-living for a brief period before seeking host; attached to gills and fins of host by greatly enlarged second maxillae; adult females 3 to 8 mm long without egg sacs .. Suborder **LERNAEOPODOIDA,** LERNAEOPODIDAE, **5**
5. Posterior end of trunk rounded (Fig. 278C); about eight American species parasitic on Salmonidae and Coregonidae ...................................**Salmincola**
   Posterior end of trunk conical or pointed; segmentation present or absent (Fig. 278D); about 15 American species parasitic on a few species of Coregonidae, Centrarchidae, and Ameiuridae ......................................**Achtheres**

**6.** Body greatly flattened dorsoventrally; abdominal segments fused; no fifth or sixth legs (Fig. 280); fixed parasites in branchial chamber or on general body surface of many species of fish; from 5 to 25 mm long but usually less than 10 mm; fish lice; a single American genus and about 15 species.

     Order **BRANCHIURA**, Suborder **ARGULOIDA**, ARGULIDAE, **Argulus**

  Body not greatly flattened dorsoventrally; abdominal segments not fused; fifth and often sixth legs present; less than 3 mm long; all genera free-living except *Ergasilus* . . . . . . . . . . . . . . . . . . . . . . . . . . . . . . . . . . . . Order **EUCOPEPODA, 7**

**7.** Metasome much wider than urosome; basal segment of fifth legs without inner expansion; first antennae with 6 to 18 segments (Figs. 272A, C).

                  Suborder **CYCLOPOIDA, 8**

  Urosome about as wide as metasome and both more or less cylindrical; basal segment of fifth legs with inner expansion; first antennae with five to nine segments (Fig. 274 ); 0.3 to 1.0 mm long . . . . . . . . .Suborder **HARPACTICOIDA**, p. 414

**8.** Second antennae large, three segmented, and with a large apical claw used for prehension (Fig. 279); adult females parasitic on gills of many common species of fresh-water fishes; 0.6 to 1.0 mm long; males and immature females free-living; about 20 species in the United States. . . . . . . . . . . ERGASILIDAE, **Ergasilus**

  Second antennae small, without a large apical claw; 0.6 to 3.0 mm long.

                  CYCLOPIDAE, p. 401

# KEY TO SPECIES OF CYCLOPOIDA

This key is drawn up specifically for identifying mature females, rather than males, although males can sometimes be successfully run through the couplets because the fifth legs and caudal rami are similar in both sexes. Male cyclopoids often have been misidentified, confused, or not identified at all because the investigator looks at the *sixth* pair of legs and mistakes them for the *fifth* legs. The sixth legs are not present in females. Both of the first antennae are geniculate in the male, neither in the female. Mature females often carry egg sacs.

Immature (copepodid) cyclopoids are difficult to identify, even to the genus level. In plankton populations, however, they may often be identified by association with the adults. In copepodid stages the last body segment is about twice as long as the preceding segment; in adults the last body segment is shorter than the preceding segment.

Our key includes essentially all cyclopoids reported from the 48 contiguous states. According to the number of segments in the first antenna, a copepod will fall under one of the A to K categories. The remainder of the key consists of ordinary numbered alternative couplets.

Some species that "typically" have 17 segments in the first antenna (J in the key) often will appear to have only 14, 15, or 16, owing to partial fusion, complete fusion, or unusual turgidity of adjacent segments. Such variations, however, can be easily checked against the other characteristics given in items G and H in the key. Those species having other variable characters are included in two or more corresponding places in the key. Figure 281 is semidiagrammatic and does not show minute details such as plumose ornamentation on setae and spinules on certain of the spines.

**A.** First antenna six-segmented; last segment of fifth leg with four or five setae and/or spines; several species in brackish coastal waters . . . . . . . . . . . . . . **Halicyclops**

**B.** First antenna eight-segmented; body 0.7 to 0.9 mm long; caudal ramus with a dorsal longitudinal row of spinules; widely distributed in bottom debris of littoral areas . . . . . . . . . . . . . . . . . . . . . . . . . . .**Paracyclops fimbriatus poppei** (Rehberg)

C.  First antenna occasionally 9-segmented (usually 11-segmented, occasionally 10-segmented); fifth leg rudimentary and not distinct from body; in the female in the form of a plate with three stout setae (Fig. 281B); in the male a small plate with two terminal setae plus a stout seta on the body at the base of the plate; 0.7 to 1.3 mm long; a widely distributed but not abundant species of the littoral .................................... **Eucyclops phaleratus** (Koch)

D.  First antenna 10-segmented; littoral species...................................**1**

E.  First antenna 11-segmented ...............................................**2**

F.  First antenna 12-segmented ..............................................**11**

G.  First antenna 14-segmented; inner margin of caudal ramus hairy; length of caudal ramus more than five times the width; 2.5 to 5.0 mm long; rare and poorly known ........................................... **Cyclops insignis** Claus

H.  First antenna 16-segmented; fifth leg composed of three segments (the only U.S. species with this characteristic); 0.7 to 1.3 mm long; common in aquatic vegetation ..............................**Orthocyclops modestus** (Herrick)

J.  First antenna 17-segmented ...............................................**18**

K.  First antenna 18-segmented (rare); 0.8 mm to 1.8 mm long; a variable and common species ........................................ **Cyclops vernalis** Fischer


 1.  Caudal ramus less than twice as long as wide .................................**C**
     Caudal ramus about four times as long as wide; 0.5 to 1.8 mm long; scattered and rare ...........................................**Cyclops bicolor** Sars

 2.  Caudal ramus less than twice as long as wide .................................**C**
     Caudal ramus more than twice as long as wide ..............................**3**

 3.  Exopod and endopod of fourth leg two-segmented ..........................**4**
     Exopod and endopod of fourth leg three-segmented ..........................**8**

 4.  Inner of the two large terminal setae of each caudal ramus at least as long as all abdominal segments and caudal rami combined; 0.5 to 1.0 mm long; widely distributed in weedy ponds ................. **Cyclops varicans rubellus** Lillj.
     Inner of the two large terminal setae of each caudal ramus much shorter than all abdominal segments and caudal rami combined; rare .....................**5**

 5.  Outer apical spine of endopod of fourth leg small and rudimentary (Fig. 281A); 0.5 to 0.8 mm long; a littoral species; second antenna four-segmented.
                                                         **Cyclops bicolor** Sars
     Outer apical spine of endopod of fourth leg more than one-quarter as long as inner apical spine; second antenna three-segmented ..........................**6**

 6.  Body 0.6 to 0.7 mm long; a slender species in coastal brackish waters of the southern tier of states .................................**Cyclops panamensis** Marsh
     Body more than 0.7 mm long.................................................**7**

 7.  Body 0.7 to 0.9 mm long; brackish waters of New Jersey and Delaware.
                                                       **Cyclops spartinus** Ruber
     Body 0.9 to 1.2 mm long; a robust species known only from the Salton Sea, California ............................... **Cyclops dimorphus** Kiefer

 8.  Lateral seta of caudal ramus inserted at about midlength of ramus (Fig. 281C); 0.4 to 0.9 mm long; a rare species of bottom debris ............ **Cyclops nanus** Sars
     Lateral seta of caudal ramus inserted about two-thirds or more from base of ramus. **9**

 9.  Fifth leg consisting of one broad segment armed with an inner spine and two outer setae (Fig. 281F); 0.5 to 0.9 mm long; a rare creeping species of the weedy shallows ...................................... **Paracyclops affinis** (Sars)
     Fifth leg two-segmented; 0.7 to 0.9 mm long .................................**10**

10.  Terminal segment of fifth leg with a seta and a small spur; rare, North Carolina and New York.......................................**Cyclops exilis** Coker
     Terminal segment of fifth leg with a seta and a spine that is longer than the segment; rare, known only from North Carolina well ...**Cyclops jeanneli putei** Yeatman

11.  Caudal ramus with spinules along the outer margin (Fig. 281D); in shallows and littoral ...................................................**12**
     Caudal ramus without such spinules.......................................**14**

12. First antenna not reaching the posterior margin of the cephalothorax; 0.7 to 1.0 mm long; rare, ponds and creeks in a few eastern states.
    **Eucyclops prionophorus** Kiefer
    First antenna reaching beyond the posterior margin of the cephalothorax; 0.7 to 1.6 mm long ........................................................................ 13
13. Length of caudal ramus more than five times the width; widespread but uncommon ...................................... **Eucyclops speratus** (Lillj.)
    Length of caudal ramus less than five times the width (Fig. 281D); common everywhere ...................................... **Eucyclops agilis** (Koch)
14. Fifth leg one-segmented (Figs. 281E, G); 0.5 to 1.0 mm long .................... 15
    Fifth leg two-segmented ...................................................... 16
15. Fifth leg small and cylindrical, with a single apical seta and with or without a tiny spine on the inner margin (Fig. 281E); widely distributed in shore debris and vegetation ................................ **Cyclops varicans rubellus** Lillj.
    Fifth leg broad, with two long setae and one long spine (Fig. 281G); a common and widespread limnetic species ................ **Tropocyclops prasinus** (Fischer)
16. Inner margins of caudal rami with small hairs; 1.5 to 1.9 mm long; rare.
    **Cyclops venustoides** Coker
    Inner margins of caudal rami without hairs .................................... 17
17. Innermost terminal seta of caudal ramus longer than outermost; 0.7 to 0.9 mm long; rare, North Carolina and New York .................... **Cyclops exilis** Coker
    Innermost terminal seta of caudal ramus shorter than outermost; 0.7 to 1.1 mm long; uncommon, in stagnant waters and puddles.
    **Cyclops crassicaudis brachycercus** Kiefer
18. With a hyaline lamella on each of the last two segments of the first antennae (lamellae sometimes difficult to see; use critical lighting and tap the coverslip to turn the antennae if necessary) (Figs. 281M–O) ................................ 19
    Without such lamellae .......................................................... 25
19. Fifth leg composed of one segment bearing one spine and two setae (Fig. 281H); 1.8 to 2.9 mm long; uncommon but widely distributed. **Macrocyclops ater** (Herrick)
    Fifth leg composed of two segments (Figs. 281J, K) .......................... 20
20. Terminal segment of fifth leg with a terminal seta and a long spine (or stout seta) on each side of the seta (Fig. 281K) ...................................... 21
    Terminal segment of fifth leg with one seta and one spine, or two setae ......... 23
21. Inner margin of caudal ramus hairy ........................................ 22
    Inner margin of caudal ramus not hairy; 1.0 to 2.5 mm long; common and widely distributed, especially in vegetation and on bottom. **Macrocyclops albidus** (Jurine)
22. Hyaline lamella on last segment of first antenna toothed (Fig. 281M); 1.2 to 4.0 mm long; common and widely distributed .......... **Macrocyclops fuscus** (Jurine)
23. Hyaline lamella smooth or minutely toothed; 1.2 to 2.2 mm long; widely distributed but not yet reported from North America ... **Macrocyclops distinctus** (Richard)
23. Hyaline lamella of last segment of first antenna distinctly notched (Figs. 281N, O); 0.8 to 1.5 mm long ............................................ 24
    Hyaline lamella of last segment of first antenna not notched; 0.6 to 1.1 mm long; a rare limnetic species ...................... **Mesocyclops dybowskii** (Lande)
24. Inner margins of caudal rami hairy (Fig. 281L); hyaline lamella of antenna with several sharp notches (Fig. 281N); a common limnetic species.
    **Mesocyclops edax** Forbes
    Inner margins of caudal rami not hairy; hyaline lamella of antenna with one deep rounded notch and sometimes several indistinct small notches (Fig. 281O); an uncommon but widely distributed limnetic species. **Mesocyclops leuckarti** (Claus)
25. Terminal segment of fifth leg with both a long seta and a long spine (Fig. 281R); 1.1 mm long; rare, reported only from Arizona ...... **Mesocyclops tenuis** (Marsh)
    Terminal segment of fifth leg with a seta and a short spine or spur, the spine never being greater than one and one-half times the length of the segment (Fig. 281P) ............................................................ 26

FIG. 281.–Structure of cyclopoid copepods (fine setation and ornamentation usually omitted). A, terminal endopod segment of fourth leg of *Cyclops bicolor*; B, fifth leg of female *Ectocyclops phaleratus*; C, caudal ramus of *Cyclops nanus*; D, caudal ramus of *Eucyclops agilis*; E, fifth leg of *Cyclops varicans rubellus*; F, fifth leg of *Paracyclops affinis*; G, fifth leg of *Tropocyclops prasinus*; H, fifth leg of *Macrocyclops ater*; J, fifth leg of *Mesocyclops tenuis*; K, fifth leg of *Macrocyclops albidus*; L, caudal ramus of *Mesocyclops edax*; M, last segment of first antenna of *Macrocyclops fuscus*; N, terminal segment of first antenna of *Mesocyclops edax*; O, terminal segment of first antenna of *Mesocyclops leuckarti*; P, fifth leg of *Cyclops vernalis*; Q, fifth leg of *Cyclops navus*; R, fifth leg of *Mesocyclops tenuis*; S, terminal endopod segment of fourth leg of *Cyclops nearcticus*; T, terminal endopod segment of fourth leg of *Cyclops navus*; U, terminal endopod segment of fourth leg of *Cyclops bicuspidatus*; V, terminal endopod segment of fourth leg of *Cyclops bicuspidatus thomasi*. (R modified from Yeatman, 1964.)

404

26. Three distal segments of first antenna with a dense marginal row of fine hyaline spines; caudal ramus with a longitudinal dorsal ridge and with a hairy inner margin; 1.0 to 1.9 mm long; locally abundant in the hypolimnion of limnetic habitats.

**Cyclops scutifer** Sars

Antenna without such spines; caudal ramus without a longitudinal ridge, inner margin with or without hairs .................................................**27**

27. Inner margins of caudal rami hairy ...........................................**28**
    Inner margins of caudal rami not hairy ......................................**29**

28. Innermost of the four terminal setae of caudal ramus nearly twice the length of the outermost; 1.5 to 2.5 mm long; sporadic and poorly known.

**Cyclops latipes** Lowndes

Innermost of the four terminal setae of caudal ramus about three times the length of the outermost; 1.45 mm long; known only from an Indiana cave.

**Cyclops donnaldsoni** Chappuis

29. Terminal segment of fifth leg with a long seta and a very short spur that is always less than half the length of the segment (Fig. 281P); 0.8 to 1.8 mm long; a highly variable and common species.....................**Cyclops vernalis** Fischer
    Terminal segment of fifth leg with a long seta and a spine that is always half or more than the length of the segment........................................**30**

30. Length of the caudal ramus more than six times the width; 1.1 to 1.4 mm long; a rare species in temporary pools ........................**Cyclops haueri** Kiefer
    Length of caudal ramus less than six times the width ........................**31**

31. Lateral seta of caudal ramus attached at a point three-quarters to four-fifths the distance from base to end of ramus; rare species ......................**32**
    Lateral seta of caudal ramus attached at a point two-thirds or less the distance from the base to the end of ramus .......................................**35**

32. Terminal endopod segment of fourth leg with a short spine on the lateral margin (Fig. 281S); this spine is shorter than the segment bearing it; 0.5 to 0.8 mm long; in small streams and wells........................**Cyclops nearcticus** Kiefer
    Terminal endopod segment of fourth leg with a seta on the lateral margin; this seta is about as long or longer than the segment bearing it .....................**33**

33. Terminal spine of fifth leg only one-half or less as long as the terminal seta ......**34**
    Terminal spine of fifth leg about as long as the terminal seta (Fig. 281Q); 0.8 to 1.2 mm long; in ponds, small lakes, and wells ............**Cyclops navus** Herrick

34. Last endopod segment of fourth leg with a terminal spine and a longer terminal seta; 0.9 mm long; known only from Marengo Cave, Indiana.

**Cyclops jeanneli** Chappuis

Last endopod segment of fourth leg with two terminal spines and one terminal seta; 0.9 to 1.0 mm long; known only from subterranean waters in Tennessee and Illinois .....................................**Cyclops clandestinus** Yeatman

35. Inner terminal spine of endopod of fourth leg about two-thirds the length of the outer terminal spine (Fig. 281U); penultimate thoracic segment with rounded poster-olateral angles; 0.9 to 1.6 mm long; rare in the United States.

**Cyclops bicuspidatus** Claus

Inner terminal spine of endopod of fourth leg about one-half the length of the outer terminal spine (Fig. 281V); penultimate thoracic segment with papillate poster-olateral processes; 0.9 to 1.2 mm long; very common in limnetic habitats.

**Cyclops bicuspidatus thomasi** Forbes

# KEY TO SPECIES OF CALANOID COPEPODA

The critical taxonomic characters of calanoids are usually fine details of the first antennae and the fifth legs of males. Taxonomic characters of the females are less definitive, and in keys they too often amount to unclear judgment decisions. For-tunately, however, when field collections are made there are almost invariably ade-quate numbers of both males and females in the populations, so that the general facies of associated males and females clearly show that they are in the same species

1. Endopod of first leg two-segmented; 0.9 to 4.5 mm long but usually 1.2 to 2.5 mm long .................................... DIAPTOMIDAE, **Diaptomus, 9**
   Endopod of first leg with one or three segments; limnetic ......................2
2. Endopod of first leg one-segmented ..........................................3
   Endopod of first leg three-segmented .....................CENTROPAGIDAE, 5
3. Endopods of second to fourth legs one-segmented; abdomen of male asymmetrical (Figs. 282D, F); 1.1 to 3.6 mm long ............ TEMORIDAE, **Epischura, 6**
   Endopods of second to fourth legs two- or three-segmented; abdomen of male symmetrical ..............................................................4
4. Endopods of second to fourth legs two-segmented; male right antenna geniculate; 1.0 to 1.5 mm long; in salt and brackish waters, as well as fresh-water ponds and lakes along all coasts; also reported from Lake Erie.

   TEMORIDAE, **Eurytemora affinis** (Poppe)
   Endopod of second leg two-segmented, those of third and fourth legs three-segmented; male left antenna not geniculate; 2.4 to 2.9 mm long (Fig. 282A); deep, cold lakes of Great Lakes region and Montana.

   SENECELLIDAE, **Senecella calanoides** Juday
5. Caudal rami short (Fig. 282B); 1.5 to 2.5 mm long; uncommon and erratically distributed over most of the United States ......**Osphranticum labronectum** Forbes
   Caudal rami long (Fig. 282C); 2.0 to 3.2 mm long; occurs in deep, cold lakes in northeast, such as Great Lakes, Finger Lakes, and Green Lake (Wisconsin), but also in Cascade Range lakes in Washington; usually considered a relict marine species ..............................**Limnocalanus macrurus** Sars

FIG. 282.–Structure of calanoid copepods. A, female *Senecella calanoides,* ×26; B, caudal rami of female *Osphranticum labronectum*; C, caudal rami of male *Limnocalanus*; D, abdomen of male *Epischura nordenskioldi*; E, female abdomen of same; F, abdomen of male *Epischura lacustris*; G, female abdomen of same. (A modified from Juday; D to G modified from Marsh.)

FIG. 283.–Structure of male *Diaptomus*. A, fifth legs of *D. oregonensis*; B, fifth legs of *D. reighardi*; C, right fifth leg of *D. mississippiensis*; D, terminal right antennal segments of *D. birgei*; E, right fifth leg of same; F, left fifth exopod of *D. pallidus*; G, fifth legs of *D. tyrelli*; H, fifth legs of *D. coloradensis*; J, terminal right antennal segments of *D. clavipes*; K, terminal right antennal segments of *D. leptopus*; L, right fifth leg of same; M, right fifth leg of *D. virginiensis*; N, antepenultimate and penultimate segments of right first antenna of *D. hesperus*. (A to E, G, and J to L modified from Marsh, 1907; F modified from Light, 1939; H modified from Dodds; M from Wilson and Moore, 1953.)

6. Female abdomen bent to the right (Fig. 282G); deep, cold waters of Great Lakes
     region ...................................... **Epischura lacustris** Forbes
   Female abdomen straight ................................................7
7. Last abdominal segment of male without special processes; terminal segment of female
     fifth leg armed with seven spines; reported only from Massachusetts ponds.
                   **Epischura massachusettsensis** Pearse
   Last abdominal segment of male with special processes ........................8
8. Last abdominal segment of male with two processes, one dorsal and one ventral;
     terminal segment of female fifth leg armed with six spines; Massachusetts and
     western mountainous areas, especially Washington to California.
                     **Epischura nevadensis** Lillj.
   Last abdominal segment of male with one dorsal process (Fig. 282D); terminal segment
     of female fifth leg with five spines; Atlantic coast from Maine to North
     Carolina .................................. **Epischura nordenskioldi** Lillj.
9. Antepenultimate segment of male right first antenna without distinct appendage ..10
   Antepenultimate segment of male right first antenna with lateral or terminal process
     (Figs. 283J, K; 284K) ................................................19

10. Male right and left fifth legs nearly equal in length; terminal hook of right leg symmetrical (Fig. 283A); common and widely distributed, especially in northern states; 1.2 to 1.4 mm long . . . . . . . . . . . . . . . . . . . . .**Diaptomus oregonensis** Lillj.
    Male left fifth leg shorter than right . . . . . . . . . . . . . . . . . . . . . . . . . . . . . . . . . . . . . . . .**11**

11. Male left fifth leg reaching beyond first segment of right exopod (Fig. 283B) . . . . . .**12**
    Male left fifth leg reaching end of first segment of right exopod or only slightly exceeding it (Fig. 283H) . . . . . . . . . . . . . . . . . . . . . . . . . . . . . . . . . . . . . . . . . . . . . . . . . .**14**

12. Endopod of male right fifth leg equal in length to first exopod segment (Fig. 283B); 1 mm long; Great Lakes drainages . . . . . . . . . . . . . . . . **Diaptomus reighardi** Marsh
    Endopod of male right fifth leg longer than first exopod segment (Fig. 283C) . . . . .**13**

13. Terminal claw of right fifth exopod angled (Fig. 283C); 1.2 to 1.3 mm long; Georgia and Florida to Texas . . . . . . . . . . . . . . . . . . . **Diaptomus mississippiensis** Marsh
    Terminal claw of right fifth exopod not angled (Fig. 285A); 1 mm long; lakes and ponds of northeastern states . . . . . . . . . . . . . . . . . . **Diaptomus pygmaeus** Pearse

14. Antepenultimate segment of male right first antenna produced into a blunt point at its distal end (Fig. 283D) . . . . . . . . . . . . . . . . . . . . . . . . . . . . . . . . . . . . . . . . . . . . . . . . . . .**15**
    Antepenultimate segment of male right first antenna not produced into a blunt point at its distal end . . . . . . . . . . . . . . . . . . . . . . . . . . . . . . . . . . . . . . . . . . . . . . . . . . . . . . . . .**16**

15. First segment of right exopod of male fifth leg with marked quadrangular hyaline appendage (Fig. 283E); erratic distribution east of Mississippi River.
                                                                        **Diaptomus birgei** Marsh
    First segment of right exopod of male fifth leg with triangular projection (Fig. 283M); rare; Virginia, Mississippi, and Louisiana . . . . . . **Diaptomus virginiensis** Marsh

16. Inner process of terminal exopod segment of male left fifth leg falciform (Fig. 283F); Mississippi Valley generally; 1 mm long . . . . . . . . . **Diaptomus pallidus** Herrick
    Inner process of terminal exopod segment of male left fifth leg digitiform (Fig. 283H). **17**

17. Lateral spine of second segment of male right fifth exopod strongly curved (Fig. 283H); 1.1 to 1.3 mm long; scattered in high-altitude lakes and ponds of western states . . . . . . . . . . . . . . . . . . . . . . . . . . . . . . . . . . . .**Diaptomus coloradensis** Marsh
    Lateral spine of second segment of male right fifth exopod essentially straight (Fig. 283G) . . . . . . . . . . . . . . . . . . . . . . . . . . . . . . . . . . . . . . . . . . . . . . . . . . . . . . . . . . .**18**

18. Median margin of second basal segment of male left fifth leg with a three-lobed hyaline expansion (Fig. 285B); 1.0 to 1.6 mm long; rare in ponds and lakes of mountains and northern states . . . . . . . . . . . **Diaptomus pribilofensis** Juday and Muttkowski
    Without such an expansion (Fig. 283G); 1.1 to 1.8 mm long; occasional in western mountains . . . . . . . . . . . . . . . . . . . . . . . . . . . . . . . . . . . . **Diaptomus tyrrelli** Poppe

19. Antepenultimate segment of male right antenna with a hyaline lamella (Figs. 283 J, K) . . . . . . . . . . . . . . . . . . . . . . . . . . . . . . . . . . . . . . . . . . . . . . . . . . . . . . . . . . . . . . . .**20**
    Antepenultimate segment of male right antenna with a slender process . . . . . . . . . . .**26**

20. Hyaline lamella broad, extending beyond end of segment (Fig. 283K); 1.2 to 2.4 mm long; widely distributed . . . . . . . . . . . . . . . . . . . . . . . **Diaptomus leptopus** Forbes
    Hyaline lamella narrow, extending beyond end of segment slightly if at all (Fig. 283J). 21

21. Antepenultimate segment of male right first antenna with a short, hook-shaped process (Fig. 283N); 1.1 mm long; Oregon . . . . .**Diaptomus hesperus** Wilson and Light
    Antepenultimate segment of male right first antenna without a hook-shaped process (Figs. 283J, K) . . . . . . . . . . . . . . . . . . . . . . . . . . . . . . . . . . . . . . . . . . . . . . . . . . . . .**22**

22. Basal segment of right fifth leg armed with a sclerotized hook that is as long as the first exopod segment (Fig. 285C) . . . . . . . . . . . . . . . . . . . . . . . . . . . . . . . . . . . . .**23**
    Basal segment of right fifth leg without such a hook . . . . . . . . . . . . . . . . . . . . . . . .**24**

23. Setae on male left antenna segments 17, 19, 20, and 22 hooked; 1.2 to 2.2 mm long; erratically distributed between the Mississippi River and the Continental Divide . . . . . . . . . . . . . . . . . . . . . . . . . . . . . . . . . . . . . **Diaptomus clavipes** Schacht
    Setae on male left antenna segments 17, 19, 20, and 22 not hooked at end; 1.8 to 2.0 mm long; temporary ponds in Oklahoma and Texas.
                                                                        **Diaptomus kingsburyae** Robertson

24. Both terminal processes of left fifth exopod blunt (Fig. 285D); 1.5 mm long; a Eurasian species found in northern Rocky Mountain lakes and ponds.
                                                                        **Acanthodiaptomus denticornis** (Wierzejski)
    Both terminal processes not blunt; 1.3 mm long . . . . . . . . . . . . . . . . . . . . . . . . . . . .**25**

FIG. 284.–Structure of male *Diaptomus*. A, right fifth leg of *D. trybomi*; B, right fifth leg of *D. connexus*; C, fifth legs of *D. judayi*; D, right fifth leg of *D. sicilis*; E, terminal antennal segments of same; F, left fifth leg of same; G, terminal antennal segments of *D. wardi*; H, right fifth leg of *D. caducus*; J, fifth legs of *D. shoshone*; K, terminal antennal segments of same; L, right fifth leg of *D. minutus*; M, right fifth leg of *D. ashlandi*. (A, D to F, K to M modified from Marsh, 1907; B and H modified from Light, 1938; C modified from Ward and Whipple, 1918.)

**25.** One terminal process of left fifth exopod pointed, the other blunt (Fig. 285E); rare in
          ponds of Florida and Louisiana . . . . **Diaptomus lousianensis** Wilson and Moore
    Both terminal processes pointed (Fig. 285E); Louisiana ponds.
                        **Diaptomus bogalusensis** Wilson and Moore
**26.** Slender process generally straight and blunt (Figs. 284E, K) . . . . . . . . . . . . . . . . . .27
    Process curved and usually pointed . . . . . . . . . . . . . . . . . . . . . . . . . . . . . . . . . . . . . . .42
**27.** Process shorter than the penultimate segment . . . . . . . . . . . . . . . . . . . . . . . . . . . . . .28
    Process as long or longer than the penultimate segment . . . . . . . . . . . . . . . . . . . . . .31
**28.** Male right fifth endopod rudimentary (Fig. 284A); Oregon; rare.
                                 **Diaptomus trybomi** Lillj
    Male right fifth endopod not rudimentary . . . . . . . . . . . . . . . . . . . . . . . . . . . . . . . . . . .29
**29.** Posterior face of the terminal right exopod segment of the fifth leg with a large,
          cuticular, spinelike structure (Fig. 285G); 1.3 to 1.7 mm long; Rocky Mountain
          lakes . . . . . . . . . . . . . . . . . . . . . . . . . . . . . . . . . . .**Diaptomus arapahoensis** Dodds
    Posterior face of the terminal right exopod segment of the fifth leg without such a
          structure . . . . . . . . . . . . . . . . . . . . . . . . . . . . . . . . . . . . . . . . . . . . . . . . . . . . . . . . . . . .30
**30.** First segment of male right fifth exopod produced as a rounded lobe on its lateral
          distal margin, its inner margin bearing a rounded hyaline lamella (Fig. 284B);
          0.9 to 1.5 mm long; western states . . . . . . . . . . . . . . **Diaptomus connexus** Light
    First segment of male right fifth exopod not produced on its lateral distal margin, its
          inner margin bearing a triangular hyaline lamella (Fig. 284C); 0.9 mm long;
          Rocky Mountain lakes . . . . . . . . . . . . . . . . . . . . . . . . . . .**Diaptomus judayi** Marsh

FIG. 285.–Structure of male *Diaptomus* (except K is female). A, right fifth leg of *D. pygmaeus*; B, left fifth leg of *D. pribilofensis*; C, right fifth leg of *D. clavipes*; D, left fifth leg of *Acanthodiaptomus denticornis*; E, left fifth leg of *D. louisianensis*; F, fifth legs of *D. bogalusensis*; G, exopod and endopod of right fifth leg of *D. arapahoensis*; H, right fifth leg of *D. schefferi*; J, right fifth leg of *D. kiseri*; K, left caudal ramus of female *D. hirsutus*; L, right fifth leg of *D. kenai*; M, right fifth leg of *D. moorei*; N, tip of right fifth leg of *D. dilobatus*; O, tip of right fifth leg of *D. clavipoides*; P, left fifth leg of *D. marshianus*. (C, D, G, and J modified and redrawn from Edmondson, Ward, and Whipple, 1959; E from Wilson and Moore, 1953; F from Wilson and Moore, 1953a; H, J, K, and P modified from Wilson, 1953; M modified from Wilson, 1954; N modified from Wilson, 1958; O modified from Wilson, 1955.)

31. Process about as long as the penultimate segment (Fig. 284E); 1.1 to 1.5 mm long; common in northern half of the United States, usually in larger lakes.
**Diaptomus sicilis** Forbes
Process longer than the penultimate segment (Figs. 284G, K) ................**32**
32. Antennae at most reaching the proximal end of the caudal rami ................**33**
Antennae reaching beyond the distal end of the caudal rami ..................**40**
33. Process of antepenultimate segment of male right antenna not attaining the distal end of the terminal segment (Fig. 284K) ..................................**36**
Process of antepenultimate segment of male right antenna extending to or beyond the distal end of the terminal segment (Fig. 284G) ..........................**34**
34. Second basal segment of male right fifth leg with one small median lamella (Fig. 285H); 2.5 mm long; rare in northern Rocky Mountain states.
**Diaptomus schefferi** Wilson
Second basal segment of male right fifth leg otherwise ........................**35**
35. Second basal segment of male right fifth leg with two small median lamellae (Fig. 285J); 2.4 mm long; a poorly known species from ponds in eastern Washington ...................................**Diaptomus kiseri** Kincaid
Second basal segment of male right fifth leg with no lamellae at all; 1.2 to 1.6 mm long; ponds in Washington and Montana .............. **Diaptomus wardi** Pearse
36. Dorsal surface of caudal rami of *female* thickly set with hairs (Fig. 285K); 1.8 mm long; California mountain lakes and ponds ....... **Diaptomus hirsutus** Wilson
Dorsal surface of caudal rami of *female* with sparse hairs or no hairs ............**37**
37. Male 1.0 to 1.1 mm long; Nevada, California, and Washington.
**Diaptomus spinicornis** Light
Male 1.5 to 3.3 mm long .................................................**38**
38. Male 1.5 to 2.3 mm long; Louisiana, Georgia, and North Carolina.
**Diaptomus augustaensis** Turner
Male longer than 2.3 mm; western distribution ..............................**39**
39. Terminal hook of right fifth exopod sharply angled (Fig. 284H); 2.4 to 2.6 mm long; Pacific coast ponds ........................... **Diaptomus caducus** Light
Terminal hook of right fifth exopod not sharply angled (Fig. 284J); 2.6 to 3.3 mm long; above 1500 m in western states ................ **Diaptomus shoshone** Forbes
40. Right endopod rudimentary (Fig. 284L); 0.9 to 1.0 mm long; common in cold waters in northeastern states, south to North Carolina and west to Wyoming.
**Diaptomus minutus** Lillj.
Right endopod not rudimentary (Fig. 284M) ..................................**41**
41. Lateral spine of second segment of male right fifth exopod long; lateral claw of terminal right exopod segment near base (Fig. 284M); 0.9 to 1.2 mm long; scattered in northern states .................... **Diaptomus ashlandi** Marsh
Lateral spine of second segment of male right fifth exopod short; lateral claw of terminal right exopod segment subterminal (Fig. 285L); 1.9 to 2.0 mm long; common in western mountain lakes ................ **Diaptomus kenai** Wilson
42. Process equal to or exceeding the length of the penultimate segment .............**43**
Process shorter than the penultimate segment (Fig. 286K) .....................**47**
43. Process about as long as the last two segments ............................**45**
Process not attaining the tip of the last antennal segment ......................**44**
44. Process only slightly longer than the penultimate segment (Fig. 286A); 1.1 to 2.0 mm long; west coast states ....................... **Diaptomus franciscanus** Lillj.
Process reaching to the middle of the apical segment or beyond; 3.2 to 4.0 mm long; a poorly known species reported from the prairies of Nebraska and Saskatchewan .............................. **Diaptomus breweri** Wilson
45. Male left fifth exopod with a long, stiff pinnate terminal seta (Fig. 286B); 1.1 to 1.4 mm long; Pacific coast states .................... **Diaptomus forbesi** Light
Male left fifth exopod without such a seta ...................................**46**
46. Terminal hook of male right fifth leg abruptly angled (Fig. 286C); rare; northern states and west coast; 2.6 to 3.5 mm long .................**Diaptomus eiseni** Lillj.
Terminal hook of male right fifth leg curved, not angled; 3.5 mm long; rare; California, Nevada, North Dakota, Washington; saline lakes. **Diaptomus nevadensis** Light

Fig. 286.–Structure of male *Diaptomus*. A, terminal antennal segments of *D. franciscanus*; B, left fifth leg of *D. forbesi*; C, right fifth leg of *D. eiseni*; D, fifth legs of *D. novamexicanus*; E, fifth legs of *D. bakeri*; F, fifth legs of *D. washingtonensis*; G, right fifth leg of *D. nudus*; H, right fifth leg of *D. albuquerquensis*; J, right fifth leg of *D. signicauda*; K, terminal antennal segments of *D. siciloides*; L, right fifth leg of same. (A modified from De Guerne and Richard, 1889; B modified from Light, 1938; C, E, F, G, H, J, and L modified from Marsh, 1907; D modified from Herrick and Turner; K modified from Dodds.)

47. Both terminal processes of male left fifth exopod digitiform and blunt ...........**48**
    Both terminal processes of male left fifth exopod not digitiform and blunt .......**53**
48. Male right fifth endopod as long as or longer than the first segment of the exopod
    (Fig. 286D) ...................................................**49**
    Male right fifth endopod shorter than the first segment of the exopod (Fig. 286H). **50**
49. Median margin of first exopod segment of right fifth leg with a hyaline lamella (Fig.
    285M); 1.2 mm long; ponds in Florida to Texas ....**Diaptomus moorei** Wilson
    Without such a lamella (Fig. 286D); 1.0 to 1.7 mm long; southwestern Rocky Mountain
    area .................................**Diaptomus novamexicanus** Herrick
50. With hyaline appendages on either the second basal segment of male right fifth leg or
    first segment of male right fifth exopod ...............................**51**
    Without such appendages (Fig. 286G); 1.1 mm long; Rocky Mountain states, rare
    elsewhere ....................................**Diaptomus nudus** Marsh
51. With hyaline appendages on second basal segment of male right fifth leg (Fig. 286H);
    0.9 to 1.5 mm long; Rocky Mountain states but found as far east as
    Oklahoma ..........................**Diaptomus albuquerquensis** Herrick
    With a hyaline appendage on first segment of male right fifth exopod ...........**52**
52. Hyaline lamella on median surface of male right fifth exopod roughly triangular and
    projecting posteriorly (Fig. 286J); 1.0 to 1.3 mm long; occasional in western
    states, rare elsewhere ........................ **Diaptomus signicauda** Lillj.
    Hyaline lamella on median surface of male right fifth exopod not triangular and not
    projecting posteriorly (Fig. 286L); 1.0 to 1.1 mm long; common and widely
    distributed ....................................**Diaptomus siciloides** Lillj.

FIG. 287.–Structure of male *Diaptomus*. A, fifth legs of *D. spatulocrenatus*; B, left fifth leg of *D. conipedatus*; C, terminal antennal segments of *D. lintoni*; D, fifth legs of same; E, left fifth leg of *D. stagnalis*; F, left fifth leg of *D. floridanus*; G, right fifth leg of *D. dorsalis*; H, fifth legs of *D. sanguineus*; J, fifth legs of *D. saltillinus*. (A and E modified from Marsh, 1929; B, G, H, and J modified from Marsh, 1907; C and D modified from Dodds; F modified from Marsh, 1926.)

53. Male left fifth endopod marked with transverse striae (Fig. 287E); 3.0 to 4.0 mm long; eastern states ................................. **Diaptomus stagnalis** Forbes
Male left fifth endopod not marked with transverse striae ......................**54**
54. Male right fifth endopod rudimentary (Fig. 287D) ............................**55**
Male right fifth endopod not rudimentary .....................................**59**
55. Both terminal processes of male left fifth exopod about the same length (Fig. 287B); 1.3 mm long; Louisiana ...................... **Diaptomus conipedatus** Marsh
Terminal processes of male left fifth exopod of unequal length (Figs. 285N, O) ...**56**
56. Male left fifth leg reaching much beyond each of second basal segment of right leg. **57**
Male left fifth leg not reaching much beyond end of second basal segment of right leg (Fig. 287D) ................................................................**58**
57. Terminal spine of right fifth exopod stout (Fig. 285N); 1.6 to 1.7 mm long; rare; Florida.....................................**Diaptomus dilobatus** Wilson
Terminal spine of right fifth exopod slim (Fig. 285O); 2.0 to 2.1 mm long; rare; Louisiana and Florida ...................... **Diaptomus clavipoides** Wilson

**58.** Chiefly in Rocky Mountain lakes; 1.5 to 2.0 mm long ..... **Diaptomus lintoni** Forbes
Reported only from Louisiana and Saskatchewan; 1.2 mm long.

**Diaptomus saskatchewanensis** Wilson

**59.** One of the terminal processes of the male left fifth exopod in the form of a straight or
slightly curved sharp spine (Fig. 287F) ................................**60**
One of the terminal processes of the male left fifth exopod distinctly falciform ....**61**

**60.** Male left fifth endopod not extending beyond end of first exopod segment (Fig. 287F);
0.9 mm long; Florida and Georgia.............. **Diaptomus floridanus** Marsh
Male left fifth endopod longer (Fig. 285P); 1.3 to 1.6 mm long; reported only from
Florida.....................................**Diaptomus marshianus** Wilson

**61.** Male right fifth endopod shorter than first segment of exopod...................**62**
Male right fifth endopod distinctly longer than first segment of exopod (Fig. 287G); 1
mm long; uncommon; southern states .............**Diaptomus dorsalis** Marsh

**62.** Terminal segment of male right fifth exopod slender and elongated (Fig. 287A); 1.1 to
1.3 mm long; Maine to Maryland ........ **Diaptomus spatulocrenatus** Pearse
Terminal segment of male right fifth exopod of the usual proportions ............**63**

**63.** Male left fifth leg not attaining the end of the first exopod segment of the right leg
(Fig. 287H); 1.4 to 2.1 mm long; widely distributed in ponds.

**Diaptomus sanguineus** Forbes

Male left fifth leg extending beyond the end of the first exopod segment of the right
leg (Fig. 287J); Nebraska to Texas ............. **Diaptomus saltillinus** Brewer

## KEY TO GENERA OF HARPACTICOIDA

The following key is to genus only. We now feel that a key to the species of harpacticoids of the United States is a fruitless and misleading effort, chiefly because the group is so poorly known and because there are so many undescribed species in this country. The writer, for example, has seen more than 20 undescribed species during his field work since the publication of the first edition of this book.

Most of the key characters apply to both sexes. When they apply to only one sex, the exception is indicated in the couplet. Body length of harpacticoids ranges from 0.3 to 1.4 mm, but the great majority of species are less than 0.8 mm long. Their small size may be the chief reason they have been neglected. An exceptionally large number of new species are awaiting discovery in the interstitial habitat of sandy beaches and in the phreatic zone of streams.

**1.** Male body composed of 11 segments; female, 10 segments (Fig. 274) .............**2**
Male body composed of 10 segments; female, 9 segments (Fig. 288G).............**3**

**2.** First antenna eight-segmented; a small genus with one widely distributed species
found in many kinds of habitats ......... **Phyllognathopus viguieri** (Maupas)
First antenna seven-segmented; several uncommon and widely distributed species.

**Chappuisius**

**3.** Distal exopod segment of first leg with three to five short clawlike spines; fresh and
brackish water ...............................................**11**
Distal exopod segment of first leg with the usual long spines and setae...........**4**

**4.** Exopod of first leg three-segmented .........................................**5**
Exopod of first leg two-segmented .........................................**12**

**5.** Terminal segment of exopod of first leg with five or six spines and setae (Fig. 289M). **20**
Terminal segment of exopod of first leg with four spines and setae ...............**6**

**6.** Second exopod segment of first leg with an inner seta (Fig. 289C) ..............**10**
Second exopod segment of first leg without an inner seta.......................**7**

**7.** Second exopod segment of first leg with an outer spine .......................**8**
Second exopod segment of first leg without an outer spine; vermiform (Fig. 288A); a
large worldwide genus; usually found in interstitial and subterranean waters.

**Parastenocaris**

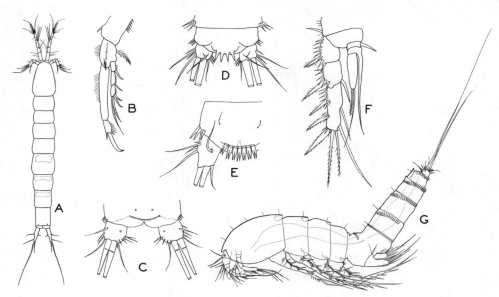

FIG. 288.–Structure of Harpacticoida. A, dorsal view of *Parastenocaris*, ×100; B, female first leg of *Pseudonychocamptus*; C, D, and E, posterior end of *Bryocamptus* spp.; F, male third leg of *Bryocamptus*; G, female *Bryocamptus*, ×85. (B modified from Wilson, 1932; C, D, F, and G modified from Coker, 1934; E redrawn from Gurney.)

8. Endopod of first leg one-segmented .........................................13
   Endopod of first leg with more than one segment ...........................9
9. Endopod of first leg two-segmented ........................................14
   Endopod of first leg three-segmented ......................................24
10. Endopod of first leg two-segmented (Fig. 289C) ...........................25
    Endopod of first leg three-segmented .....................................26
11. Basal expansion of female fifth leg with three or four setae (Fig. 289A); New England
        coast ................................................................ **Harpacticus**
    Basal expansion of female fifth leg with five or six setae; Pacific coast .... **Tigriopus**
12. Endopod of first leg about twice or· more as long as exopod (Fig. 289D); several
        species reported from fresh and inland saline waters .........**Onychocamptus**
    Endopod of first leg no longer than exopod .................................13
13. Endopod of first leg two-segmented (Fig. 289E); in vegetation at margins of lotic and
        lentic waters; uncommon but widely distributed ..............**Maraenobiotus**
    Endopod of first leg one-segmented and small; a marine genus reported from Bear
        Lake, Utah; undoubtedly occurs elsewhere .....................**Huntemannia**
14. Endopod of first leg not extending beyond second exopod segment (Fig. 288B) ...15
    Endopod of first leg longer .................................................18
15. Anterior end of body expanded, tapered posteriorly (Fig. 289G); brackish and fresh
        waters of Atlantic coast............................................**Metis**
    Body slender and vermiform ................................................16
16. First segment of first exopod more than three times as long as wide (Fig. 288B) ..17
    First segment of first exopod no more than twice as long as wide (Fig. 289F); one
        cosmopolitan species in aquatic mosses and other vegetation; 0.3 to 0.5 mm
        long ...................................... **Epactophanes richardi** Mrazek
17. Fifth leg of male unsegmented (Fig. 289H); brackish ponds on northeast coast.
                                                                    **Heterolaophonte**
    Fifth leg of male segmented (Fig. 289J); fresh and brackish ponds on northeast
        coast ......................................... **Pseudonychocamptus**

FIG. 289.–Structure of Harpacticoida (fine hairs and other ornamentation not shown). A, fifth leg of *Harpacticus*; B, terminal segment of exopod of first leg of *Nitocra*; C, first leg of *Mesochra*; D, fifth leg of *Onychocamptus*; E, endopod of first leg of *Maraenobiotus*; F, first leg of *Epactophanes*; G, dorsal view of body of *Metis*; H, fifth leg of *Heterolaophonte*; J, fifth leg of male *Pseudonychocamptus*; K, fifth leg of female *Stenocaris*; L, exopod of second leg of *Moraria*; M, exopod of first leg of *Paradactylopodia*; N, fifth leg of *Tachidius*; O, fifth leg of *Nitocra*. (O redrawn and modified from Edmondson, Ward and Whipple, 1959.)

18. Fifth leg unsegmented (Fig. 289K); vermiform; brackish and fresh waters of northeastern coast . . . . . . . . . . . . . . . . . . . . . . . . . . . . . . . . . . . . . . . . . . . . . . . . . . . .**Stenocaris**
    Fifth leg segmented . . . . . . . . . . . . . . . . . . . . . . . . . . . . . . . . . . . . . . . . . . . . . . . . .**19**
19. Second exopod segment of second to fourth legs without a median seta (Fig. 289L); many species, widely distributed . . . . . . . . . . . . . . . . . . . . . . . . . . . . . . . **Moraria**
    Second exopod segment of second to fourth legs with a median seta (Fig. 288F); many species, widely distributed, very common on all kinds of substrates. **Bryocamptus**
20. Third exopod segment of first leg about one-third as long as the second exopod segment (Fig. 289M); uncommon, euryhaline species of Atlantic coast.
                                                                        **Paradactylopodia**
    Third exopod segment of first leg about as long as the second exopod segment . . .**21**
21. Fifth leg unsegmented (Fig. 290A) . . . . . . . . . . . . . . . . . . . . . . . . . . . . . . . . . . . .**22**
    Fifth leg segmented (Fig. 289O) . . . . . . . . . . . . . . . . . . . . . . . . . . . . . . . . . . . . . . .**23**

FIG. 290.–Structure of Harpacticoida (fine hairs and other ornamentation not shown). A, third exopod segment of first leg of *Tachidius*; B, second leg of *Nitocra*; C, third exopod segment of third leg of *Nitocrella*; D, second leg of *Bryocamptus*; E, fifth leg of *Cletocamptus*; F, first leg of *Bryocamptus*; G, lateral view of *Mesochra* cephalothorax outline; H, lateral view of *Bryocamptus* cephalothorax outline; J, first leg of *Bryocamptus*; K, fifth leg of *Canthocamptus*; L, first leg of *Attheyella*; M, second antenna of *Bryocamptus*; N, second antenna of *Attheyella*; O, second leg of *Bryocamptus*; P, fifth leg of *Attheyella*; Q, fifth leg of *Elaphoidella*. (K, M, N, and P modified from Coker, 1934.)

22. Third exopod segment of first leg with six spines and setae; several euryhaline species of Atlantic coast ..................................... **Microarthridion**
    Third exopod segment of first leg with five spines and setae (Fig. 290A); several fresh-water and brackish coastal species ............................. **Tachidius**
23. Third exopod segment of second and third legs with three lateral marginal spines (Fig. 290B); mostly coastal brackish and fresh-water species ............. **Nitocra**
    Third exopod segment of second and third legs with two lateral marginal spines (Fig. 290C); expect to find this genus in phreatic and subterranean waters. **Nitocrella**
24. Endopod of second leg two-segmented (Fig. 290D); many species, widely distributed, and very common on all kinds of substrates .................. **Bryocamptus**
    Endopod of second leg three-segmented; one species very common in many habitats ............................... **Phyllognathopus viguieri** (Maupas)

25. Exopod of fifth leg separated from base by only a notch or gap (Fig. 290E); several species in brackish and saline lakes and ponds ...............**Cletocamptus**
    Exopod of fifth leg clearly separated from base (Fig. 290K) ....................26
26. Rostrum greatly enlarged (Fig. 290G); endopod of first leg with two or three segments (Fig. 289C); coastal brackish and fresh-water ponds, and inland ponds; several species..................................................... **Mesochra**
    Rostrum small to moderate size (Figs. 288G; 290H) ..........................27
27. Rostrum small (Fig. 288G); exopod of first leg two-segmented (Fig. 290F); many widely distributed species in a variety of fresh-water habitats ... **Bryocamptus**
    Rostrum small to moderate size (Fig. 290H); endopod of first leg three-segmented (Fig. 290J).......................................................28
28. Second seta of basal expansion of female fifth leg greatly reduced (Fig. 290K); several species in a wide variety of fresh-water habitats ............. **Canthocamptus**
    Second seta of basal expansion of female fifth leg not reduced .................29
29. First endopod segment of first leg reaching or exceeding middle of third exopod segment (Fig. 290L); many species in a wide variety of habitats ....**Attheyella**
    First endopod segment of first leg not extending beyond second exopod segment .30
30. Palp of second antenna one-segmented (Fig. 290N) ..........................31
    Palp of second antenna two-segmented (Fig. 290M); endopods of female second and third legs three-segmented (Fig. 290O); many widely distributed species in a variety of fresh-water habitats ............................. **Bryocamptus**
31. Fifth leg of female with rows of fine setae on the ventral surface, and basal expansion with six setae; several species .................................**Attheyella**
    Fifth leg of female without rows of fine setae on the ventral surface, and basal expansion with four setae (Fig. 290Q); several uncommon and widely distributed species ................................................**Elaphoidella**

## COPEPODA REFERENCES

AYCOCK, D. 1942. Influence of temperature on size and form of Cyclops vernalis Fischer. *J. Elisha Mitchell Sci. Soc.* **58**:84–93.

BRANDL, Z. 1973. Laboratory culture of cyclopoid copepods on a definite food. *Vestn. Cesk. Spol. Zool.* **37**:81–88.

BRANDL, Z., and C. H. FERNANDO. 1975. Food consumption and utilization in two freshwater cyclopoid copepods (Mesocyclops edax and Cyclops vicinus). *Int. Rev. ges. Hydrobiol.* **60**:471–494.

CHAPPUIS, P. A. 1927. Freilebende Süsswasser-Copepoden aus Nordamerika. 2. Harpacticiden. *Zool. Anz.* **74**:302–313.

——. 1929. Die Unterfamilie der Canthocamptinae. *Arch. Hydrobiol.* **20**:471–516.

——. 1929a. Copépodes cavernicoles de l'Amérique du Nord. *Bull. Soc. Sci. Cluj* **4**:51–58.

——. 1957. Le genre Parastenocaris Kessler. *Vie et Milieu* **8**:423–432.

COKER, R. E. 1933. Influence of temperature on size of freshwater copepods (Cyclops). *Int. Rev.* **29**:406–436.

——. 1934. Contribution to knowledge of North American freshwater harpacticoid copepod Crustacea. *J. Elisha Mitchell Sci. Soc.* **50**:75–141.

COMITA, G. W., and D. M. TOMMERDAHL. 1960. The postembryonic developmental instars of Diaptomus siciloides Lilljeborg. *J. Morphol.* **107**:297–355.

CRESSEY, R. F. 1927. The genus Argulus (Crustacea: Branchiura) of the United States. *Biota of*

*Freshwater Ecosystems, Identification Manual* **2**:1–14.

DAVIS, C. C. 1959. Osmotic hatching in the eggs of some fresh-water copepods. *Biol. Bull.* **116**:15–29.

DEEVEY, E. S. 1941. Notes on the encystment of the harpacticoid copepod Canthocamptus staphylinoides Pearse. *Ecology* **22**:197–200.

DODDS, G. S. 1915. A key to the Entomostraca of Colorado. *Univ. Colo. Stud.* **11**:265–298.

ELGMORK, K. 1967. Ecological aspects of diapause in copepods. *Proc. Symp. Crustacea* **3**:947–954.

——. 1967a. On the distribution and ecology of Cyclops scutifer Sars in New England (Copepoda, Crustacea). *Ecology* **48**:967–971.

EWERS, L. A. 1930. The larval development of freshwater Copepoda. *Ohio State Univ., Contrib. Franz Theodore Stone Lab.* **3**:1–43.

——. 1936. Propagation and rate of reproduction of some freshwater Copepoda. *Trans. Am. Microsc. Soc.* **55**:230–238.

FORBES, S. A. 1897. A contribution to a knowledge of North American fresh-water Cyclopidae. *Bull. Ill. State Lab.* **5**:27–83.

GURNEY, R. 1931–1933. *British fresh-water Copepoda*. 3 vols. 958 pp. Ray Society, London.

HARDING, J. P., and W. A. SMITH. 1974. A key to the British fresh-water cyclopoid and calanoid copepods. *Sci. Publ. Freshwater Biol. Assoc.* **18**:1–56.

HERRICK, C. L., and C. H. TURNER. 1895. A synopsis of the Entomostraca of Minnesota. *2d Rept. State Zool., Geol. Nat. Hist. Surv. Minn.* 1–337.

HILL, L. I., and R. E. COKER. 1930. Observations on mating habits of Cyclops. *J. Elisha Mitchell Sci. Soc.* **45**:206–220.

HUMES, A. G. 1954. The specific validity of Epischura massachusettsensis Pearse (Copepoda: Calanoida). *Am. Midl. Nat.* **52**:154–158.

JUDAY, C. 1925. Senecella calanoides, a recently described fresh-water copepod. *Proc. U.S. Nat. Mus.* **66**:1–6.

KABATA, Z. 1969. Revision of the genus Salmincola Wilson 1915 (Copepoda: Lernaeopodidae). *J. Fish. Res. Board of Can.* **26**:2987–3041.

KIEFER, F. 1967. Copepoda. *Limnofauna Europaea* 173–185.

LANG, K. 1948. *Monographie der Harpacticiden.* Vols. 1 and 2, 1683 pp. Lund, Sweden.

LIGHT, S. F. 1938. New subgenera and species of diaptomid copepods from the inland waters of California and Nevada. *Univ. Calif. Publ. Zool.* **43**:67–78.

———. 1939. New American subgenera of Diaptomus Westwood (Copepoda, Calanoida). *Trans. Am. Microsc. Soc.* **58**:473–484.

MARSH, C. D. 1907. A revision of the North American species of Diaptomus. *Trans. Wis. Acad. Sci. Arts and Lett.* **15**:381–516.

———. 1926. On a collection of copepods from Florida with a description of Diaptomus floridanus, new species. *Proc. U.S. Nat. Mus.* **70**:1–4.

———. 1929. Distribution and key to the North American copepods of the genus Diaptomus, with the description of a new species. Ibid. **75**:1–27.

———. 1933. Synopsis of the calanoid crustaceans, exclusive of the Diaptomidae, found in fresh and brackish waters, chiefly of North America. Ibid. **82**:1–58.

MEEHEAN, O. L. 1940. A review of the parasitic Crustacea of the genus Argulus in the collections of the United States National Museum. Ibid. **88**:459–522.

PENNAK, R. W. 1940. Ecology of the microscopic metazoa inhabiting the sandy beaches of some Wisconsin lakes. *Ecol. Monogr.* **10**:537–615.

ROBERTS, L. S. 1970. Ergasilis (Copepoda: Cyclopoida): revision and key to species in North America. *Trans. Am. Microsc. Soc.* **89**:134–161.

ROBERTSON, A. 1975. A new species of Diaptomus (Copepoda, Calanoida) from Oklahoma and Texas. *Am. Midl. Nat.* **93**:206–214.

RUBER, E. 1968. Description of a salt marsh copepod Cyclops (Apocyclops) spartinus n. sp. and a comparison with closely related species. *Trans. Am. Microsc. Soc.* **87**:368–375.

RYLOV, V. M. 1948. Freshwater Cyclopoida. *Crustacea. Fauna U.S.S.R.* **3**:(3):1–314.

SANDERCOCK, G. A. 1967. A study of selected mechanisms for the coexistence of Diaptomus spp. in Clarke Lake, Ontario. *Limnol. Oceanogr.* **12**:97–112.

SIEFKEN, M., and K. B. ARMITAGE. 1968. Seasonal variations in metabolism and organic nutrients in three Diaptomus (Crustacea: Copepoda). *Comp. Biochem. Physiol.* **24**:591–609.

SMYLY, W. J. P. 1957. Observations on the life-history of the harpacticoid copepod Canthocamptus staphylinus (Jurine). *Ann. Mag. Nat. Hist.* **10** (115):509–512.

STORCH, O. 1929. Die Schwimmbewegung der Copepoden, auf Grund von Mikro-Zeitlupenaufnahmen analysiert. *Zool. Anz., Suppl. Bd.* **4**:118–129.

STRICKLER, J. R. 1975. Intra- and interspecific information flow among planktonic copepods: receptors. *Proc. Int. Assoc. Theor. Appl. Limnol.* **19**:2951–2958.

WALTER, E. 1922. Über die Lebensdauer der freilebenden Süsswasser-Cyclopiden und andere Fragen ihrer Biologie. *Zool. Jahrb. Abt. Syst.* **44**:375–420.

WILSON, C. B. 1911. North American parasitic copepods.–Part. 9. The Lernaeopodidae. *Proc. U.S. Nat. Mus.* **39**:189–226.

———. 1911a. North American parasitic copepods belonging to the family Ergasilidae. Ibid. 263–400.

———. 1915. North American parasitic copepods belonging to the Lernaeopodidae, with a revision of the entire family. Ibid. **47**:565–729.

———. 1916. Copepod parasites of fresh-water fishes and their economic relations to mussel glochidia. *Bull. U.S. Bur. Fish.* **34**:333–374.

———. 1917. North American parasitic copepods belonging to the Lernaeidae with a revision of the entire family. *Proc. U.S. Nat. Mus.* **53**:1–150.

———. 1918. The economic relations, anatomy, and life history of the genus Lernaea. *Bull. U.S. Bur. Fish.* **35**:163–198.

———. 1932. The copepods of the Woods Hole region, Massachusetts. *Bull. U.S. Nat. Mus.* **158**:1–635.

———. 1944. Parasitic copepods in the United States National Museum. *Proc. U.S. Nat. Mus.* **94**:529–582.

WILSON, M. S. 1941. New species and distribution records of diaptomid copepods from the Marsh collection in the United States National Museum. *J. Wash. Acad. Sci.* **31**:509–515.

———. 1953. New and inadequately known North American species of the copepod genus Diaptomus. *Smithson. Misc. Coll.* **122**:1–30.

———. 1954. A new species of Diaptomus from Louisiana and Texas with notes on the subgenus Leptodiaptomus (Copepoda, Calanoida). *Tulane Stud. Zool.* **2**:51–60.

———. 1955. A new Louisiana copepod related to Diaptomus (Aglaodiaptomus) clavipes Schacht. (Copepoda, Calanoida). Ibid. **3**:37–47.

———. 1956. North American harpacticoid copepods. I. Comments on the known fresh water species of the Canthocamptidae. 2. Canthocamptus oregonensis, n. sp. from Oregon and California. *Trans. Am. Microsc. Soc.* **75**:290–306.

———. 1958. New records and species of calanoid copepods from Saskatchewan and Louisiana. *Can. J. Zool.* **36**:489–497.

———. 1958a. The copepod genus Halicyclops in North America, with description of new species from Lake Pontchartrain, Louisiana, and the Texas coast. *Tulane Stud. Zool.* **6**:176–189.

———. 1958b. North American harpacticoid copepods. 4. Diagnoses of new species of fresh-water Canthocamptidae and Cletodidae (genus Huntemannia). *Proc. Biol. Soc. Wash.* **71**:43–48.

———. 1972. Copepods of marine affinities from mountain lakes of western North America. *Limnol. Oceanogr.* **17**:762–763.

———. 1975. North American harpacticoid copepods II. New records and species of Elaphoidella (Canthocamptidae) from the United States and Canada. *Crustaceana* **28**:125–138.

WILSON, M. S., and S. F. LIGHT. 1951. Description of a new species of diaptomid copepod from Oregon. *Trans. Am. Microsc. Soc.* **70**:25–30.

WILSON, M. S., and W. G. MOORE. 1953. Diagnosis of a new species of diaptomid copepod from Louisiana. *Ibid.* **72**:292–295.

———. 1953a. New records of Diaptomus sanguineus and allied species from Louisiana, with the description of a new species (Crustacea: Copepoda). *J. Wash. Acad. Sci.* **43**:121–127.

YEATMAN, H. C. 1944. American cyclopoid copepods of the viridis-vernalis group (including a description of Cyclops carolinianus n. sp.). *Am. Midl. Nat.* **32**:1–90.

———. 1959. Some effects of temperature and turbulence on the external morphology of Cyclops carolinianus. *J. Elisha Mitchell Sci. Soc.* **75**:154–167.

———. 1964. A new cavernicolous cyclopoid copepod from Tennessee and Illinois. *J. Tenn. Acad. Sci.* **39**:95–98.

# Chapter 18

# OSTRACODA (SEED SHRIMPS)

ALTHOUGH ostracods are abundant and widely distributed, they have received much less attention than the Cladocera and Copepoda. They inhabit all types of substrates in both standing and running waters, including rooted vegetation, algal mats, debris, mud, sand, and rubble. A few species swim about actively above the substrate. Representatives of one family occur only as commensals (or parasites) on the gills of crayfish. Ostracods are comparatively difficult to study, chiefly because of their somewhat opaque bivalve shell (more accurately, a carapace). Identification usually involves dissection.

Superficially, the members of the Subclass Ostracoda resemble miniature mussels, and "mussel shrimps" is an old European vernacular name. However, this name is so easily confused with "clam shrimps," which is used for the Conchostraca, that it does not seem advisable to adopt it. "Seed shrimps" is suggested as an appropriate alternative, for indeed, without a lens ostracods do look much like small seeds.

**General characteristics.** The American fresh-water species are seldom more than 3 mm long and usually less than 1 mm long. A South African fresh-water species reaches a length of nearly 8 mm and the largest marine species is 21 mm long.

Coloration ranges from chalky white through yellow, green, gray, red, brown, and blackish. Light-colored valves are often blotched with darker colors, and species occurring among algae and rooted aquatics are usually gray, green, or brown. Each sclerotized lime-impregnated valve consists of an inner and an outer plate that are fused along the anterior, posterior, and ventral margins. The space between the two plates is occupied by a thin skin fold that secretes the valve material. Dorsally, the skin folds are continuous with the main body of the animal. The valves are connected on the dorsal margin by an elastic band and may be tightly closed by a group of adductor muscle fibers passing transversely through the body of the ostracod and attached to the inner surfaces of the valves (Figs. 299, 301, 302). When the animal is active, however, the valves gape and the locomotor appendages protrude. The outer surface of the valves may be smooth, pitted, papillate, or setose, and the margins are often tuberculate, crenulate, or lipped. There are no concentric growth lines as in some Conchostraca.

All traces of body segmentation are lost (Fig. 292), but the region corresponding to the head bears four paired appendages: first antennae (antennules), second antennae (antennae), mandibles, and maxillae. The five- to seven-segmented first antennae are uniramous, the exopod being lost; they bear short, stiff, clawlike bristles for digging and climbing or long setae for swimming. The four- to six-segmented second antennae are also uniramous, the exopod being reduced to a scale or seta; these appendages are used in locomotion and feeding, and in the male they are modified for clasping the female during copulation. The mouth is surrounded by an upper and a lower lip and two lateral mandibles. Each mandible consists of a strongly toothed and sclerotized base, a branchial plate, and a three-segmented palp. Each maxilla has a

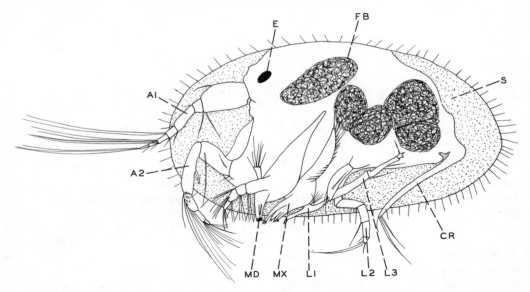

FIG. 291.–Female *Cypricercus reticulatus* (Zadd.), ×80, with left valve removed to show appendages, diagrammatic. *A1*, first antenna; *A2*, second antenna; *CR*, caudal ramus; *E*, eye; *FB*, food ball in digestive tract; *L1*, first leg; *L2*, second leg; *L3*, third leg; *MD*, mandible; *MX*, maxilla; *S*, right valve of shell. (Modified from Hoff, 1942.)

large branchial plate and four basal processes, the outermost of which is largest and palplike.

The thoracic region bears three pairs of legs. In the Limnocytheridae and Entocytheridae all pairs are morphologically similar, in the Darwinulidae the second and third are similar, and in the Cypridae all legs are different. The first legs may be modified for mastication, prehension, copulation, or respiration (respiratory plate). The second legs usually have a long terminal claw. The third legs of the Cypridae are bent dorsally and used in keeping the body and inner surface of the shell free of foreign material.

The abdomen is represented only by two long caudal rami (furcal rami, or furca), which are articulated to the body. Each ramus usually has two terminal claws and two terminal setae. In some species the rami are reduced or lacking.

**Locomotion.** The great majority of individuals are found moving about on the substrate by means of beating movements of the first and second antennae, and to some extent by kicking of the caudal rami.

Such locomotion ranges from creeping and uncertain, weak, tottering movements to rapid bouncing or scurrying. Some of the Candonidae burrow superficially in soft substrates. Those species that leave the bottom and swim about actively are characterized by long, plumose antennules and antennae.

**Food, feeding.** Food consists mostly of bacteria, molds, algae, and fine detritus, but some of the larger Cypridae have been observed feeding on living and dead animals. Ecologically, ostracods are omnivorous scavengers. Beating movements of the setose mandibular palps, maxillary processes, and the branchial plates of the first legs create a current of water between the valves. The current picks up fine particles from the substrate that are strained out by the setae and brought to the mouth. Inedible particles are mostly rejected and removed by the respiratory plates of the maxillae. Large edible bits of food are pulled or pushed toward the mouth by the antennae, mandibles, and first legs. The mandibles are used to rasp and break up the larger pieces. Small balls of finely divided food

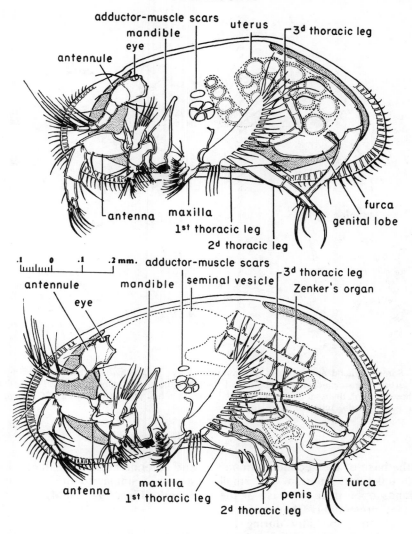

FIG. 292.–General anatomy of *Candona suburbana* Hoff. Upper, female with left valve removed; lower, male with left valve removed. [From Kesling (1956), courtesy Turtox/Cambosco, Macmillan Science Co., Chicago, Ill.]

are swept into the mouth by the mandibular palps.

**Internal anatomy.** The digestive tract consists of a short esophagus, a secretory and absorptive midgut, and a hindgut (Fig. 294). One digestive gland on each side between the lamellae of the valves empties into the midgut. The anus lies at the base of the caudal rami.

Respiration occurs through the general body surface, and a constant supply of oxygenated water is ensured by the movements of the branchial plates.

The hemocoel is filled with a circulating fluid, but no heart has ever been described for fresh-water species.

Three distinct, paired glands are found in ostracods, but for no one of them has a definite function been assigned. The large convoluted shell glands lie between the shell lamellae and in the hemocoel; they

FIG. 293.–Some ostracod appendages. A, mandible of *Cypridopsis vidua,* showing the long, sclerotized, toothed basal portion, the single-segmented branchial plate, and the larger segmented palp; B, maxilla of *Candona acuta* Hoff, showing the four basal processes and the long branchial plate; C, first leg of *C. fluviatilis* Hoff. (A modified from Sars; B and C redrawn from Hoff, 1942.)

open near the base of the second antennae and have an unknown function. The small antennal glands open near the base of the first antennae; presumably they have an excretory function, especially during immature stages. The small maxillary glands are imbedded in the tissues just posterior to the lower lip; some investigators believe that they have an excretory function.

The nervous system consists of a large supraesophageal ganglion (brain), two esophageal connectives, a subesophageal ganglion, and a ventral chain of two paired ganglia.

Two or three prominent eyespots, each with a small lens, and fused in varying degrees, are mounted on a protuberance near the bases of the first antennae. In a few species the eyespots are absent. Many setae of the appendages undoubtedly have a tactile function. In the Cypridae the sec-

ond antenna bears a small clublike sensory structure similar to the aesthetasks of copepods (Figs. 291, 298M).

**Reproduction.** A superficial examination of any field collection of ostracods usually reveals a great majority of females. The various species differ widely in their reproductive habits, depending on the relative occurrence of males, and Hoff (1942) has accordingly recognized four general groups of ostracods. One group, including some species of *Candona* and *Cypricercus,* always reproduces by parthenogenesis, the males being unknown. In some species of *Candona, Cyprinotus, Darwinula,* and *Ilyocypris* males are rare and reproduction is usually parthenogenetic. In some *Cypricercus, Potamocypris, Cypridopsis,* and *Darwinula* males occur in small numbers, and

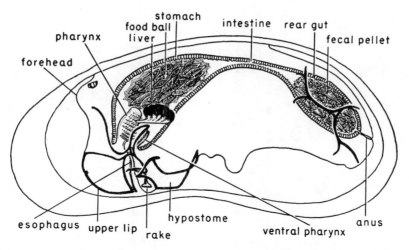

forehead

pharynx
food ball
liver

stomach

intestine   rear gut

fecal pellet

esophagus   upper lip
rake

hypostome

ventral pharynx

anus

FIG. 294.–Digestive system of *Candona suburbana,* left valve removed. Sclerotized body framework of left side is shown in heavy lines. [From Kesling (1956), courtesy Turtox/Cambosco, Macmillan Science Co., Chicago, Ill.]

reproduction is both syngamic and parthenogenetic. A fourth group includes species in which males are always present and reproduction is usually syngamic: *Candona, Cyclocypris, Cypria, Cypricercus, Cyprois, Limnocythere, Notodromas,* and *Physocypria.*

The female reproductive system (Fig. 295A) is simple, consisting of paired tubular ovaries, oviducts, seminal receptacles, and genital openings. In the Cypridae the ovaries lie between the valve lamellae, but in the Cytheridae they are lateral to the midgut. The genital openings are located between the bases of the third legs and the caudal rami.

The paired male reproductive system is more complicated, especially in the Cypridae (Figs. 295B; 296). Each testis consists of four long, tubular branches lying between the valve lamellae. In the body proper these unite to form a vas deferens that enters the dorsal and posterior ejaculatory duct, a spiny, sclerotized cylinder (Zenker's organ) that forces sperm into the penis during copulation. The two penes are large, irregular, lobed, complex, sclerotized structures located near the posterior end of the animal. In the Cytheridae there is no ejaculatory duct, and the testes are lateral to the midgut in the body proper.

The detailed anatomy of the penis is of importance in separating species taxonomically. The sperm are the largest in the animal kingdom.

Reproduction is usually restricted to the summer months, but a few species produce more than one generation per year.

Copulation involves the attachment of the male to the dorsal and posterior margin of the female carapace. The second antennae of the male aid in this attachment, and the penes are inserted between the valves and into the female genital pores. Fertilization occurs in the seminal receptacles.

The careful investigations of Lowndes (1935) have led to some interesting conclusions. He maintains that fertilization of the egg does not actually occur in spite of copulation and highly specialized copulatory apparatus, that all ostracod reproduction is parthenogenetic, and that copulation is merely an instinctive behavior pattern that is a relic of past times when the union of sperm and egg was probably the sole means of reproduction.

*Darwinula stevensoni* retains the fertilized eggs in the dorsal part of the shell cavity until embryonic development is completed, but all other American freshwater species are thought to be oviparous. The spherical eggs have a delicate, double-

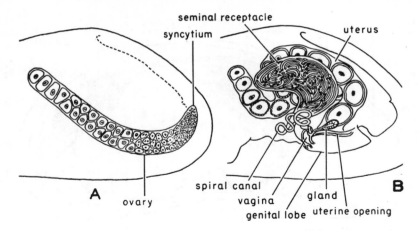

FIG. 295.–Female ostracod reproductive system. A, ovary in position in hypodermis; B, right half of female reproductive system. [From Kesling (1956), courtesy Turtox/Cambosco, Macmillan Science Co., Chicago, Ill.]

walled, limy shell and are usually white, yellow, orange, red, or green. They are deposited singly or in clumps or rows on rocks, twigs, other bits of debris, or aquatic vegetation.

**Development, life history.** Egg development is usually suspended during the

cold months and unfavorable moisture conditions, and there are numerous records of ostracods hatching from eggs kept in dried pond mud in the laboratory for many weeks and months. One report indicates that viable eggs may be kept for more than 20 years in the desiccated condition.

In normal habitats, however, the eggs

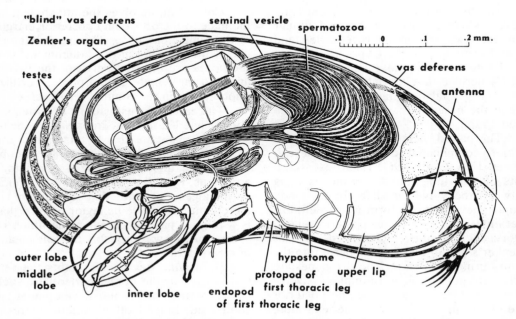

FIG. 296.–Male reproductive system of *Candona suburbana*. Right valve and most appendages removed. Hemipenis slightly lowered from normal noncopulatory position. (From McGregor and Kesling, 1969.)

FIG. 297.–Nauplius larva of *Cyprinotus incongruens* Ramdohr, ×260. (Redrawn from Schreiber.)

usually hatch in a few days to several months. The liberated larva (Fig. 297) is a shelled nauplius with three pairs of appendages, representing the first antennae, second antennae, and mandibles of the adult at intervals of one to three days. Eight molts and eight additional instars occur during the life history, the adult being the ninth instar. Other appendages and increased structural complexity develop with each successive molt. The caudal rami, for example, first appear as two small bristles in the fourth instar. The copulatory organs appear in the eighth instar, but sexual maturity and copulation do not occur until the ninth and last instar.

Many species exhibit a definite seasonal periodicity. Ferguson (1944), working in Missouri, found that *Cypridopsis vidua* was active between February and December, *Potamocypris smaragdina* between March and October, and *Physocypria pustulosa* between March and September. McGregor found that *Darwinula stevensoni* had its reproductive period between May and October. Many species of *Candona* may be collected only in the spring. A few species occur only in the autumn. Aside from eggs and some adults that winter over, the usual life span is completed in several weeks to seven or eight months, depending on the species and environmental conditions. Sometimes the adult instar may last as long as six months. A single generation per year is the common condition in vernal ponds; a few species have two or three generations per year.

**Ecology.** The nature of the substrate and the general type of environment seem to have little influence on the distribution of most seed shrimps. In many cases the same species may be found on algae, decaying vegetation, rooted aquatics, mud, and gravel. *Cyprinotus incongruens* is exceptional, however, and may be found in swift streams, ponds, and puddles. Only a minority of species are restricted to such places as vernal ponds and temporary streams. Out of 31 species collected in Illinois by Hoff (1942), four were restricted to temporary still waters, six were restricted to permanent still waters, two were found only in temporary running waters, and one in permanent running waters. The other 18 species were collected in two or more of these habitats. The largest numbers of species may be collected on mud bottoms where there is little or no current, often in aquatic vegetation; few species occur on bare rocks. Core samples taken in soft substrates show few ostracods deeper than 5 cm. Many forms, especially clamberers and active swimmers, such as *Cyprinotus* and *Cypricercus,* are more active on lighted than on shaded bottoms. Most species occur in water less than 1 m deep, but some are found regularly as deep as 15 m. *Cypridopsis vidua* has been found in depths ranging from 1 cm to 300 m. *Notodromas monacha* is unusual in that it clings to the surface film with the dorsal surface downward.

In general, ostracods tolerate wide ranges of ecological factors usually regarded as limiting for entomostracans. The normal ranges of temperature and water chemistry are of little significance. Though they do not occur in grossly polluted waters, such genera as *Candona* and *Cypris* survive long periods of stagnation and oxygen exhaustion on lake bottoms. It is now known that advanced instars may tide over dry and cold periods by being buried in a torpid state in the mud of dried ponds.

Aquaria and old protozoan cultures sometimes become thick with them. A few hypogean species occur in the waters of underground caves.

The Entocytheridae are common commensals on the gills and articular membranes of crayfishes, sometimes in great densities. They may be removed from their hosts and will live under such artificial conditions for at least several months. However, they will not reproduce unless they are attached to the crayfish gills.

**Geographical distribution.** Active and passive distribution are brought about much as in the Cladocera and Copepoda. Most genera and many species are cosmopolitan or Holarctic, *Chylamydotheca* and the Entocytheridae being the only important North American taxa not found in the Palaearctic region. Even in New Zealand most of the ostracod fauna consists of cosmopolitan species.

In South Africa and New Zealand two species have become specialized for living in the damp humus of forest floors.

Because little intensive collecting has been done in the United States, about half of the reported species are known from only a single state or collecting locality. The known distribution of some species is hopelessly incomplete, for example, "Alaska and Florida"!

**Economic significance.** With occasional exceptions, ostracods are only a minor element in the diet of young and adult fish. A few are the intermediate hosts of Acanthocephala parasitizing fish. Hoff (1942) estimates that 1.0 to 1.5 percent of the ostracods in permanent waters are infected. Ostracods are also the intermediate hosts of some tapeworms of water fowl.

**Collection, preparation.** Perhaps the chief reason for the general neglect of the American Ostracoda lies in the fact that they are nearly always necessarily collected in masses of debris from which they must be laboriously separated. Surface debris of the bottom and its contained ostracods may be scooped up with a dipnet, but

the Birge cone net towed along the bottom, or better, the Birge cone net mounted on a tobogganlike piece of sheet metal is most useful. Ekman dredge samples are equally useful. By washing the debris thoroughly through a fine net or sieve, the smaller particles may be removed, and if the remaining mass is allowed to stand quietly in jars of water, the ostracods soon become active at the debris–water interface, where with a little patience they may be picked up under the dissecting binoculars with a long pipette or Irwin loop. Also, by stirring the contents well, some of the ostracods get a small bubble of air caught between the valves and rise to the surface, where they may be easily removed.

Specimens should be killed in 50 percent alcohol and preserved in 85 percent alcohol. Levinson (1951) gives a good method for anesthetizing and killing with the shell gaping. Formaldehyde makes the animals brittle and may decalcify the valves.

Stained or unstained whole animals may be mounted in balsam or glycerin jelly, but cover-glass supports should be used to avoid crushing. Dissections of adult specimens are usually necessary for accurate identification, and the operation is best carried out in glycerin with fine needles. The valves should be removed first, leaving the body intact, and then the appendages should be carefully dissected off. Valves and appendages are conveniently mounted on separate slides.

**Culturing.** Little is known about culturing ostracods in the laboratory, but some investigators report success by feeding dried yeast and bits of lettuce, celery, or vegetable debris.

**Taxonomy.** The Subclass Ostracoda is divided into four orders: Myodocopa, Cladocopa, Platycopa, and Podocopa. The first three of these are confined to marine waters and are not considered here. The Podocopa are found in both marine and fresh-water environments; the family Bairdiidae is exclusively marine, the Cytheridae contains only a few fresh-water genera. Cypridae are well represented in both environments, and the Darwinulidae are confined to fresh waters.

In the United States, seed shrimps have received more than casual consideration only in Ohio, Massachusetts, Illinois, Florida, and Washington, and each new comprehensive study reveals many undescribed species. Ward and Whipple (1918) listed 54 species from the entire United States, but in 1933 Furtos listed 57 species from Ohio alone. Dobbin (1941) collected 33 species in Washington, of which 14 were new, and Hoff (1942) collected 39 in Illinois, of which 10 were new. The second

edition of Ward and Whipple (1959) includes 157 species from the 48 contiguous states. There are now more than 250 species. Delorme (1967) lists 74 Canadian species. *Candona* is the only large U.S. genus, with about 40 species. Most of the other genera have less than 15 U.S. species. Obviously, it is fruitless to include here a key to the known American species, since such a key would be obsolete in a few years. The key given below therefore goes only as far as genera. It should be borne in mind that it can be used successfully only for specimens in the late instars, preferably the last.

## KEY TO GENERA OF OSTRACODA

1. Exopod of second antenna in the form of a long, hollow seta carrying the secretion from a gland located at the base of the antenna (Fig. 302E); all legs morphologically similar .............................................................29
   Exopod otherwise; all legs not morphologically similar .........................2
2. Second and third legs similar (Figs. 298A,B); caudal rami lacking, body terminating in a single process (Fig. 298C); 0.70 to 0.80 mm long; on mud bottoms of larger bodies of water; widely distributed but rare.
   DARWINULIDAE, **Darwinula stevensoni** (B. and R.)
   Second and third legs not similar (Figs. 298D,E); caudal rami present but sometimes reduced ....................................................................3
3. Terminal segment of third leg short, usually armed with beaklike claw and reflexed seta (Fig. 301H)....................................................................4
   Terminal segment of third leg more or less cylindrical (rarely spherical), armed with three setae and no claw (Fig. 298E) ...................................19
4. Caudal rami well developed, usually with two claws and two setae (Figs. 299C,D)...................................................... CYPRIDAE, **6**
   Caudal rami rudimentary, terminating in a simple flagellum (Fig. 298G); 0.50 to 0.80 mm long ................................................ CYPRIDOPSIDAE, **5**
5. Tumid (Fig. 298H); valves nearly equal in size; widely distributed and very common in many types of habitats ................................... **Cypridopsis**
   Compresed; right valve higher than left (Fig. 298J); common in standing and running waters ..................................................................**Potamocypris**
6. Third leg with a cylindrical terminal segment without a claw and armed with three setae, one of which is reflexed (Fig. 302D) ......... CANDOCYPRINAE, **7**
   Third leg with a short terminal segment, a beaklike claw, and a reflexed seta (Fig. 300D)...................................................... CYPRINAE, **8**
7. Natatory setae of second antenna rudimentary (Fig. 301F); 0.80 to 1.00 mm long; a burrower and creeper; reported from brooks in Ohio. **Candocypria osburni** Furtos
   Natatory setae of second antenna well developed; with two large setae on the penultimate segment of third leg (Fig. 302D); 0.45 mm long; Washington.
   **Cyclocypria kincaidia** Dobbin
8. Shell with reticulate patterns anteriorly and posteriorly; caudal ramus with three claws and one seta (Fig. 299C); 1.10 to 1.20 mm long; rare in ponds and slow streams ..................................... **Ilyodromus pectinatus** Sharpe
   Shell smooth (margins tuberculate in some species) ...........................9
9. Caudal rami slightly different in shape (Fig. 300A); one rare Florida species. **Stenocypris**
   Caudal rami similar ..............................................................10

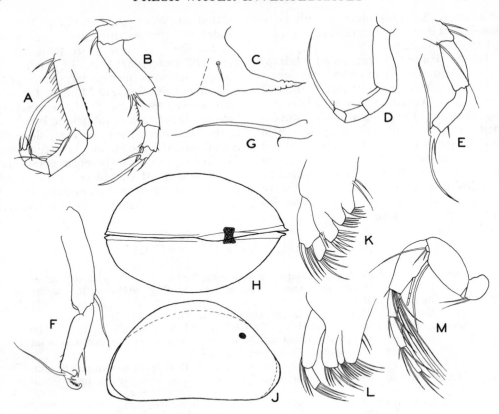

FIG. 298.–Structure of Ostracoda. A, second leg of female *Darwinula stevensoni*; B, third leg of same; C, end of thorax of same; D, second leg of female *Candona punctata* Furtos; E, third leg of same; F, third leg of female *Cypridopsis vidua*; G, caudal ramus of female *Potamocypris smaragdina* Vavra; H, dorsal view of female *Cypridopsis vidua*, ×70; J, lateral view of female *Potamocypris hyboforma* Dobbin, ×40; K, maxilla of *Cyprois marginata* (Straus); L, maxilla of female *Cyprinotus incongruens*; M, second antenna of female *Notodromus monacha*. (A, B, F, and G redrawn from Furtos, 1933; C to E redrawn from Hoff, 1942; H modified from Furtos, 1933; J and L modified from Dobbin.)

10. Natatory setae of second antenna well developed, extending beyond midlength of claws (Fig. 299B) .......................................................11
    Natatory setae of second antenna greatly reduced, not attaining midlength of claws (Fig. 299H,J) .......................................................17
11. Second segment of second leg with two large setae; 2.60 to 3.30 mm long; several uncommon species in southern half of the United States ..... **Chlamydotheca**
    Second segment of second leg with a single large seta (Fig. 299E); 0.50 to 4.20 mm long .......................................................**12**
12. Caudal ramus usually less than one-half as long as valves; males usually absent; common and widely distributed .......................................................**13**
    Caudal ramus usually at least one-half as long as valves; males present; 0.80 to 4.20 mm long .......................................................**16**
13. Subterminal claw of caudal ramus stout, usually nearly as long as terminal claw (Fig. 299D); 1.00 to 2.30 mm long; very common; many species .......................................................**14**
    Subterminal claw of caudal ramus setalike, usually much shorter than terminal claw (Fig. 299F); 0.50 to 0.95 mm long; several uncommon U.S. species .. **Cypretta**
14. Second leg four-segmented, third and fourth segments fused ................**Cypris**
    Second leg five-segmented (Fig. 299E) .......................................................**15**

FIG. 299.–Structure of Ostracoda. A, second antenna of female *Cyprois marginata*; B, second antenna of female *Cyprinotus incongruens*; C, caudal ramus of *Ilyodromus pectinatus*; D, caudal ramus of female *Cyprinotus incongruens*; E, second leg of female *Eucypris virens* (Jurine); F, caudal ramus of *Cypretta turgida* (Sars); G, lateral view of female *Candonocypris pugionis* Furtos, ×15 (anterior and posterior ridges indicated by arrows); H, second antenna of female *Prionocypris longiforma*; J, second antenna of female *Herpetocypris repetans* (Baird); K, spines of third maxillary process of *H. repetans*; L, spines of third maxillary process of *Megalocypris gigantea* (Dobbin); M, end of female second antenna of *Candona caudata* Kaufmann. (B, H, J, and M modified from Dobbin, 1941; C redrawn from Ward and Whipple, 1918; D redrawn from Furtos, 1933; E modified from Sars; F redrawn from Furtos, 1936; G modified from Furtos, 1936; K and L redrawn from Dobbin.)

15. Margins of both valves smooth ......................................**Eucypris**
       At least the anterior edge of one valve tuberculate; about 20 species .....**Cyprinotus**
16. Anterior and posterior extremity of each valve with distinct ridge between inner
       duplicature and submarginal line (Fig. 299G); several scattered and rare
       species .................................................................**Candonocypris**
       Anterior and posterior extremity of each valve without such a ridge; about 15 species;
       widely distributed and common ...............................**Cypricercus**
17. Natatory setae of second antenna very small (Fig. 299H); 1.25 mm long; rare;
       Washington ............................. **Prionocypris longiforma** Dobbin
       Natatory setae of second antenna longer, reaching nearly halfway to tip of terminal
       claws (Fig. 299J); 2.0 to 4.0 mm long; several widely distributed but uncommon
       species.....................................................................**18**
18. Spines of third maxillary process distinctly denticulate (Fig. 299K); less than 2.5 mm
       long .................................................... **Herpetocypris**
       Spines of third maxillary process smooth (Fig. 299L); 2.5 to 5.0 mm long. **Megalocypris**
19. Natatory setae of second antenna lacking (Fig. 299M); shell white when dry; creeping
       and burrowing forms ................................ CANDONIDAE, **20**
       Natatory setae of second antenna present; shell not white when dry .............**22**

Fig. 300.–Structure of Ostracoda. A, caudal rami of *Stenocypris*; B, outline of *Pelocypris* shell; C, third leg of *Candona*; D, tip of third leg of *Herpetocypris*.

**20.** Shell ornamented with polygonal areas and tubercles (Fig. 301D); 0.50 to 0.60 mm long; rare, scattered distribution . . . . . . . . **Paracandona euplectella** (B. and N.)
Shell not ornamented (Fig. 301E) . . . . . . . . . . . . . . . . . . . . . . . . . . . . . . . . . . . . . . .**21**
**21.** Terminal segment of third thoracic leg with three unequal setae (Fig. 300C); 0.60 to 2.00 mm long; unable to swim; widely distributed and very common; about 40 species . . . . . . . . . . . . . . . . . . . . . . . . . . . . . . . . . . . . . . . . . . . . . . . . . .**Candona**
Terminal segment of third thoracic leg with two setae; rare, Florida. **Candocyprinotus**

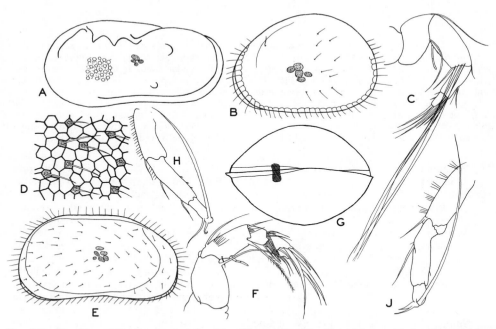

Fig. 301.–Structure of Ostracoda. A, left valve of *Ilyocypris gibba* (Ramdohr), ×47, showing a small portion of sculpturing; B, left valve of *Cyclocypris sharpei* Furtos, ×75; C, second antenna of female *Cypria elegantula* (Lillj.); D, valve sculpturing of *Paracandona euplectella*; E, right valve of female *Candona parallela* Müller, ×55; F, second antenna of male *Candocypria osburni*; G, dorsal view of female *Cyclocypris sharpei*, ×75; H, third leg of female *C. sharpei*; J, third leg of female *Cypria elegantula*. (A, B, D, E, and G modified from Furtos, 1933; F, H, and J redrawn from Furtos, 1933; C modified from Dobbin.)

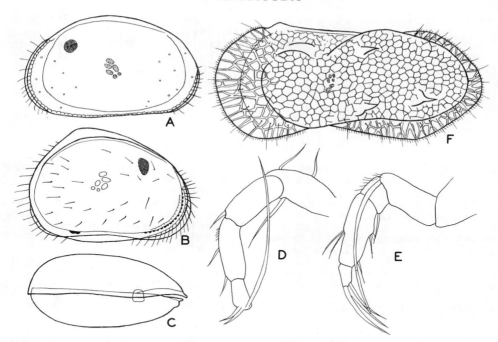

FIG. 302.–Structure of Ostracoda. A, left view of male *Cypria obesa* Sharpe, ×60; B, right view of female *Physocypria pustulosa* Sharpe, ×70; C, dorsal view of same, ×70; D, third leg of female *Cyclocypria kincaidia*; E, second antenna of female *Limnocythere verrucosa* Hoff; F, left valve of male *Limnocythere ornata* Furtos, ×80. (A, C, and F redrawn from Furtos, 1933; B modified from Furtos, 1933; D redrawn from Dobbin; E redrawn from Hoff, 1942.)

**22.** Shell pitted or reticulate . . . . . . . . . . . . . . . . . . . . . . . . . . . . . . . . . . . . . . . . . . . . .**23**
Shell smooth . . . . . . . . . . . . . . . . . . . . . . . . . . . . . . . . . . . . . . . . . . . . . . . . . . . . . . . . . .**25**

**23.** Natatory setae of second antenna used for swimming but extending only slightly
beyond tips of terminal claws . . . . . . . . . . . . . . . . . . . . .**ILYOCYPRIDIDAE, 24**
Antenna stout and used for walking; one species in deep, cold lakes.

CYTHERIDEIDAE, **Cytherissa lacustris** (Sars)

**24.** Margins of shell without mammillary pustules (Fig. 301A); several rare species in
streams . . . . . . . . . . . . . . . . . . . . . . . . . . . . . . . . . . . . . . . . . . . . . . . . .**Ilyocypris**
Margins of shell with numerous mammillary pustules (Fig. 300B); rare . . . .**Pelocypris**

**25.** Third maxillary process with six prominent spines (Fig. 298K).

NOTODROMADIDAE, **26**
Third maxillary process with only two or three prominent spines plus some setae.

CYCLOCYPRIDIDAE, **27**

**26.** Second antenna six-segmented (Fig. 298M); 1.10 to 1.20 mm long; active swimmers;
rare; usually in aquatic vegetation . . . . . . . . . .**Notodromus monacha** (O.F.M.)
Second antenna five-segmented (Fig. 299A); 1.10 to 1.70 mm long; widely distributed
in creeks and vernal ponds . . . . . . . . . . . . . . . . . . . . . . . . . . . . . . . . . . .**Cyprois**

**27.** Shell tumid (Fig. 301B); last segment of third leg at least twice as long as wide (Fig.
301H); 0.80 to 1.40 mm long; widely distributed . . . . . . . . . . . . . . . . **Cyclocypris**
Shell compressed; last segment of third leg less than twice as long as wide (Fig.
301J) . . . . . . . . . . . . . . . . . . . . . . . . . . . . . . . . . . . . . . . . . . . . . . . . . . . . . . . .**28**

**28.** Valves nearly equal in size; margins of both valves smooth (Fig. 302A); 0.40 to 1.00
mm long; many widely distributed species . . . . . . . . . . . . . . . . . . . . . . . . .**Cypria**
Valves unequal in height or length or both; margin of either valve more or less
tuberculate (Figs. 302B,C); 0.40 to 0.70 mm long; widely distributed.

**Physocypria**

**29.** Free margins of valves flattened, with many long pore-canals (Fig. 302F); free-living in a variety of habitats; 0.50 to 0.90 mm long.

LIMNOCYTHERIDAE, **Limnocythere**

Free margins of valves not flattened, with many long pore-canals; commensals on gills and articular membranes of crayfish; 0.30 to 0.70 mm long; about 35 U.S. genera, with the majority of species being restricted to the southern Appalachian area . . . . . . . . . . . . . . . . . . . . . . . . . . . . . . . . . . . . . . ENTOCYTHERIDAE

## OSTRACODA REFERENCES

DELORME, L. D. 1967. Field key and methods of collecting freshwater ostracodes in Canada. *Can. J. Zool.* **45:**1275–1281.

———. 1969. On the identity of the ostracode genera Cypriconcha and Megalocypris. Ibid. **47:**271–281.

———. 1970. Freshwater ostracodes of Canada. Part I. Subfamily Cyprinidae. Ibid. **48:**153–168.

———. 1970a. Freshwater ostracodes of Canada. Part II. Subfamily Cypridopsinae and Herpetocypridinae, and Family Cyclocyprididae. Ibid. 253–266.

———. 1970b. Freshwater ostracodes of Canada. Part III. Family Candonidae. Ibid. 1099–1127.

———. 1970c. Freshwater ostracodes of Canada. Part IV. Families Ilyocyprididae, Notodromadidae, Darwinulidae, Cytherideidae, and Entocytheridae. Ibid. 1251–1259.

———. 1971. Freshwater ostracodes of Canada. Part V. Families Limnocytheridae, Ooxochonchidae. Ibid. **49:**49–64.

DELORME, L. D., and D. DONALD. 1969. Torpidity of freshwater ostracodes. Ibid. **47:**997–999.

DOBBIN, C. N. 1941. Fresh-water Ostracoda from Washington and other western localities. *Univ. Wash. Publ. Biol.* **4:**175–245.

FERGUSON, E. 1944. Studies of the seasonal life history of three species of freshwater Ostracoda. *Am. Midl. Nat.* **32:**713–727.

———. 1957. Ostracoda (Crustacea) from the northern lower Peninsula of Michigan. *Trans. Am. Microsc. Soc.* **76:**212–218.

———. 1958. A supplementary list of species and records of distribution for North American freshwater Ostracoda. *Proc. Biol. Soc. Wash.* **71:**197–202.

———. 1959. A synopsis of the ostracod (Crustacea) genus Cypridopsis with the description of a new species. Ibid. **72:**59–68.

———. 1959a. The ostracod genus Potamocypris with the description of a new species. Ibid. 133–138.

———. 1964. Stenocyprinae, a new subfamily of freshwater cyprid ostracods (Crustacea) with description of a new species from California. Ibid. **77:**17–24.

———. 1964. The ostracod (Crustacea) genus Cypridopsis in North America and a description of Cypridopsis howei, sp. nov. *Trans. Am. Microsc. Soc.* **83:**380–384.

———. 1967. Cyprinotus newmexicoensis, a new cyprid ostracod. *Am. Midl. Nat.* **78:**248–250.

———. 1967a. New ostracods from the playa lakes of eastern New Mexico and western Texas. *Trans. Am. Microsc. Soc.* **86:**244–249.

———. 1968. Recently described species and distributional records for North American freshwater Ostracoda. *Am. Midl. Nat.* **79:**499–506.

FURTOS, N. C. 1933. The Ostracoda of Ohio. *Bull. Ohio Biol. Surv.* **29:**413–524.

———. 1935. Fresh-water Ostracoda from Massachusetts. *J. Wash. Acad. Sci.* **25:**530–544.

———. 1936. Freshwater Ostracoda from Florida and North Carolina. *Am. Midl. Nat.* **17:**491–522.

HART, C. W. 1962. A revision of the ostracods of the Family Entocytheridae. *Proc. Acad. Nat. Sci.* **114:**121–147.

HART, C. W., and D. G. HART. 1969. Evolutionary trends in the ostracod Family Entocytheridae, with notes on the distributional patterns in the southern Appalachians. *Va. Polytech. Inst. Res. Div. Monogr.* **1:**179–190.

HART, D. G., and C. W. HART. 1974. The ostracod family Entocytheridae. *Monogr. Acad. Nat. Sci.* **18:**1–239.

HOFF, C. C. 1942. The ostracods of Illinois. *Univ. Ill. Biol. Monogr.* **19:**1–196.

———. 1942a. The subfamily Entocytherinae, a new subfamily of fresh-water cytherid Ostracoda, with descriptions of two new species of the genus Entocythere. *Am. Midl. Nat.* **27:**63–73.

———. 1943. Seasonal changes in the ostracod fauna of temporary ponds. *Ecology* **24:**116–118.

———. 1944. The origin of Nearctic fresh-water ostracods. Ibid. **25:**369–372.

HOWE, H. V. 1962. *Handbook of ostracod taxonomy.* 386 pp. Louisiana State Univ. Press, Baton Rouge.

KESLING, R. V. 1951. The morphology of ostracod molt stages. *Ill. Biol. Monogr.* **21:**1–324.

——— 1956. The ostracod. A neglected little crustacean. *Turtox News* **34:**82–86, 90–94, 114–115.

———. 1957. Notes on Zenker's organs in the ostracod Candona. *Am. Midl. Nat.* **57:**175–182.

KOSMAL, A. 1968. On the distribution of Ostracoda in the littoral of Lake Kisajno (Masurian Lake District). *Pol. Arch. Hydrobiol.* **15:**87–102.

LEVINSON, S. A. 1951. A technique for anesthetizing fresh water ostracodes. *Am. Midl. Nat.* **46:**254–255.

LOWNDES, A. G. 1935. The sperms of freshwater ostracods. *Proc. Zool. Soc. Lond.* (1935) **1:**35–48.

McGREGOR, D. L. 1969. The reproductive potential, life history and parasitism of the freshwater ostracod Darwinula stevensoni (Brady and Robertson). *In:* Taxonomy, morphology and ecology of recent Ostracoda, ed. J. W. Neale, pp. 194–221, Oliver and Boyd, Edinburgh.

McGREGOR, D. L., and R. V. KESLING. 1969. Copulatory adaptations in ostracods. Part I. Hemipenes of Candona. *Univ. Mich. Contrib. Paleontol.* **22:**169–191.

———. 1969a. Copulatory adaptations in ostracods. Part II. Adaptations in living ostracods. Ibid. 221–239.

SARS, G. O. 1928. Ostracoda. An *Account of the Crustacea of Norway* **9:**1–277. Bergen Museum, Bergen, Norway.

SCHEERER-OSTERMEYER, E. 1940. Beitrag zur Entwicklungsgeschichte der Süsswasserostrakoden. *Zool. Jahrb., Abt. Anat. Ontog. Tiere* **66:**349–370.

SCHREIBER, E. 1922. Beiträge zur Kenntnis der Morphologie, Entwicklung und Lebensweise der Süsswasser-Ostrakoden. Ibid. **43:**485–538.

SOHN, I. G., and L. S. KORNICKER. 1973. Morphology of Cypretta kawarai Sohn and Kirnicker, 1972. (Crustacea, Ostracoda), with a discussion of the genus. *Smithson. Contrib. Zool.* **141:**1–28.

TRESSLER, W. L. 1947. A check list of the known species of North American freshwater Ostracoda. *Am. Midl. Nat.* **38:**698–707.

TURPEN, J. B., and R. W. ANGELL. 1971. Aspects of molting and calcification in the ostracod Heterocypris. *Biol. Bull.* **140:**331–338.

YOUNG, W. 1971. Ecological studies of the Entocytheridae (Ostracoda). *Am. Midl. Nat.* **85:**399–409.

# Chapter 19

# MYSIDACEA (OPOSSUM SHRIMPS)

THE OPOSSUM shrimps form a large order that is almost exclusively marine, only three species having become adapted to fresh waters in the United States. *Mysis oculata relicta* (Loven) (called *M. relicta* by some investigators) is a native plankter in a few deep, cold, oligotrophic lakes of the northern states east of the Great Plains, in the Great Lakes, and in many Canadian lakes. *Neomysis mercedis* Holmes occurs in lakes, rivers, and brackish estuaries of the Washington, Oregon, and California coasts. *Taphromysis louisianae* Banner is known from roadside ditches in Louisiana but may be widely distributed along the Gulf coast.

Superficially, mysids resemble miniature crayfish. A closer examination, however, reveals some striking differences. The carapace for example, is thin and does not completely cover the thorax, the last two segments being exposed dorsally and, to some degree, laterally. In place of the five pairs of walking legs of decapods, mysids have long, thin, setose, biramous, many-segmented appendages. The first thoracic segment bears a pair of maxillipeds, and is fused with the head, but the other seven thoracic segments are distinct. The second thoracic segment bears the second maxillipeds, and each of the remaining six segments has a pair of swimming legs. The stalked compound eyes are extremely large, the scale of the second antenna is large, but the pleopods are proportionately much more reduced than those of decapods. *Mysis oculata relicta* reaches a length of 30 mm, *Neomysis mercedis* reaches 15 mm, and *Taphromysis* only 8 mm.

Mature male mysids may be distinguished from females by their long and specialized fourth pleopods, which may extend as far as the posterior end of the telson, whereas females are characterized by a marsupium consisting of four ventral oostegites originating at the bases of the last two pairs of legs (hence the name "opossum shrimps"). Females are generally larger and more abundant than males.

The exopods of the six pairs of legs project laterally somewhat and their beating produces smooth, rapid swimming. The endopods of these appendages extend more medially, and their movements create a current of water that passes anteriorly over the mouthparts. The two pairs of maxillipeds are particularly efficient in straining zooplankton, phytoplankton, and particulate debris from this current. Such food is then passed on toward the second maxillae, first maxillae, mandibles, and mouth.

Internal anatomy and physiology are generally comparable to conditions found in the crayfish. There are no gills, however, most respiration occurring through the thin lining of the carapace. A current of water is drawn under the carapace by the action of the epipodites of the first maxillipeds. A unique feature is the occurrence of a statocyst in the basal portion of the endopod of each uropod.

Reproduction is restricted to the colder months, and females are gravid between October and May, altough a few gravid specimens may sometimes be found as late as June. A female may produce up to 40 eggs per clutch, depending on her size. Developing eggs and young are carried in the marsupium for one to three months, the young leaving the mother when 3 or 4 mm long. Development is direct and the life cycle is thought to extend through two years in northern latitudes, but only one year farther south. Little is known about

FIG. 303.–Male *Mysis oculata relicta,* ×2.

the number of clutches of eggs that may be produced by a female during her life cycle.

Fresh-water mysids, and especially *Mysis oculata relicta,* are cold-water forms. During the warm months this species is almost restricted to the hypolimnion, where temperatures range as low 4°. It is thought that 14° is the maximum temperature that can be tolerated for any length of time, and certainly *Mysis* has never been reported from lakes where the hypolimnial maximum exceeds this figure.

Of all the fresh-water Crustacea known to exhibit daily vertical migrations, *Mysis* has the most extensive and rapid migrations. Populations are confined to the meter of water just above the bottom during the middle of the day and no amount of sampling above that depth will take specimens. At dusk, however, most of the individuals, expecially the older ones, migrate into the surface waters where temperatures as high as 20° may be tolerated for a few hours. Reverse downward movements begin at dawn.

*M. oculata relicta* has been recorded a few times from water that was only about 20 percent saturated with oxygen, but the great majority of investigations show that 40 or 50 percent saturation is the usual lower limit. In exceptional years the oxygen content of the water just above the bottom of oligotrophic lakes falls below this limit, and populations are then confined to strata above the deepest waters during the daytime.

*M. oculata relicta* has been reported from the Great Lakes (as deep as 270 m in Lake Superior); Geneva, Trout, and Green lakes in Wisconsin; some of the Finger Lakes in New York; a few other lakes in the northern states; and many deep Canadian lakes. It is especially abundant in Waterton Lake on the border between Montana and Canada. Undoubtedly it is much more common and widely distributed in the United States than the published literature indicates. This form is circumpolar and occurs also in the British Isles, the Scandinavian countries, northern Germany, and northern Russia. A few zoogeographers contend that it is a marine relict from glacial times when many northern lake basins were presumably connected with the sea and filled with salt water, but a more acceptable theory, postulating postglacial migration from the sea, is now favored. In addition to being found in fresh waters, *M. oculata relicta* has been reported from northern brackish waters and estuaries.

Variety *relicta* is closely related to *Mysis oculata* (Fabr.), a circumpolar, arctic and subarctic, sublittoral, marine species, from which it is undoubtedly derived. Adults of the two forms differ slightly in the detailed structure of the telson and antennal scale. The immature stages are almost indistinguishable, however.

*Neomysis mercedis* is a species that has apparently evolved from marine ancestry very recently. It occurs in brackish bays and estuaries on the west coast where the salinity is usually less than 20.0 and in strictly fresh waters of rivers and lakes near the coast.

Fresh-water mysids are an extremely important food source for a group of commercially important fishes inhabiting deep, cold waters—namely, lake trout and coregonids. Food studies show that often 80 to 100 percent of the stomach contents of these fishes may be *Mysis*. Because of its value in the trout diet, *Mysis* is a logical artificial transplant, especially because the "*Mysis*-niche" is unoccupied in most lakes. The genus has already been successfully established in several western Canadian lakes and a few Colorado mountain lakes. Experimental plants have also been made in Wisconsin, Minnesota, and New York; in several mountain lakes of California and Nevada; and undoubtedly elsewhere in the western states. Similar transplants have been tried in Sweden and

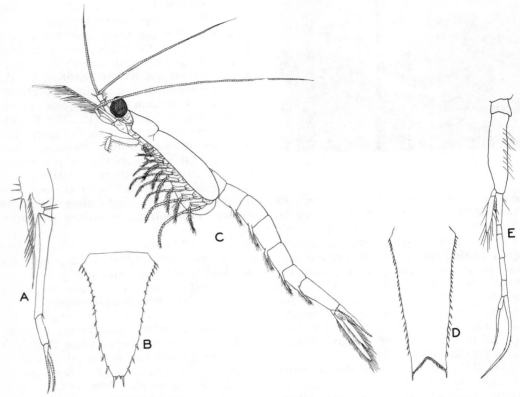

FIG. 304.–Mysidacea. A, male fourth pleopod of *Neomysis mercedis*; B, telson of *N. mercedis*; C, female *Mysis oculata relicta*, ×6; D, telson of same; E, male fourth pleopod of same. (A and B modified from Tattersall; D and E modified from Ekman.)

Russia. Some transplants are known to be successful or provisionally successful; others are still uncertain.

The American species belong to the Subfamily Mysinae in the Family Mysidae. Aside from their distinctive geographic ranges and size differences, they are easily dintinguished morphologically. The telson of *Mysis oculata relicta* and *Taphromysis louisianae* has a wide, bifurcated tip, but that of *Neomysis* has a narrow truncated tip. The exopod of the fourth pleopod of the mature male *Neomysis* is two-segmented; that of *M. o. relicta* is six-segmented; that of *Taphromysis* is indistinctly seven-segmented. Further, in the male *Mysis* the exopod of the third pleopod is well developed and consists of six segments; in *Taphromysis* this ramus is lacking.

## MYSIDACEA REFERENCES

BANNER, A. H. 1953. On a new genus and species of mysid from southern Louisiana. *Tulane Stud. Zool.* **1**:1–8.

JUDAY, C., and E. A. BIRGE. 1927. Pontoporeia and Mysis in Wisconsin lakes. *Ecology* **7**:445–452.

SCHULZE, P. 1926. Schizopoda. *Biol. Tiere Deutschl.* **17**:1–18.

TATTERSALL, W. M. 1932. Contributions to a knowledge of the Mysidacea of California. **II.** The Mysidacea collected during the survey of San Fran-

cisco Bay by the U.S.S. "Albatross" in 1914. *Univ. Calif. Publ. Zool.* **37**:315–347.

——. 1951. A review of the Mysidacea of the United States National Museum. *Bull. U.S. Nat. Mus.* **201**:1–292.

THIENEMANN, A. 1925. Mysis relicta. *Z. Morphol. Okol. Tiere* **3**:389–440.

ZIMMER, C. 1915. Die Systematik der Tribus Mysini H. J. Hansen. *Zool. Anz.* **46**:202–216.

# Chapter 20

## ISOPODA (AQUATIC SOW BUGS)

PILL BUGS and sow bugs are chiefly terrestrial and marine, only about 5 percent of the total known North American species being found in fresh waters. Approximately 80 fresh-water species occur in the United States, and for the most part these are restricted to springs, spring brooks, streams, and subterranean waters. A decided minority are found in ponds and the shallows of lakes. The biology of *Asellus aquaticus* L. and of several other European species has been thoroughly investigated, but relatively little is known about our American species.

**General characteristics.** Unlike amphipods, the members of the Order Isopoda are strongly flattened dorsoventrally. The "head" of an isopod is actually a cephalothorax, since it represents the fusion of the true head and the first thoracic segment. The seven remaining thoracic segments are all similar and are expanded laterally in the form of eavelike lamellae over the basal portions of the thoracic appendages. In all American fresh-water species the last four abdominal segments and true telson are completely fused into a large shieldlike region, often incorrectly referred to as a "telson." The first two abdominal segments are greatly reduced and scarcely visible at the anterior end of the abdomen. In the Sphaeromidae the abdomen consists of two segments, and in *Cirolanides* there are six distinct segments.

Total length, from the anterior margin of the cephalothorax to the posterior margin of the abdomen, usually ranges between 5 and 20 mm.

Coloration may be blackish, brown, dusky, reddish, or yellowish. Some species are variously marked or mottled. Subterranean species are generally whitish or creamy.

The first antennae arise near the median line and anterior margin of the cephalothorax. Each consists of a three-segmented peduncle and a many-segmented flagellum. The second antennae are much longer than the first; they arise ventral and lateral to the first antennae and have five-segmented peduncles.

The eyes are dorsal, unstalked, compound, and usually reduced or absent in subterranean species.

In typical, common species the mouth parts form a compact buccal mass that is covered anteriorly by an upper lip. The sclerotized mandibles are strong, toothed, and may or may not have a palp. Each first maxilla has a basal portion and two elongated, toothed and setose palps. The second maxillae are smaller, weaker, more platelike and have three short, terminal divisions. The maxillipeds, representing the appendages of the fused thoracic segment, are flattened and palped; they fit closely together at the median line, thus effectively forming the lower and posterior surfaces of the buccal mass.

Each of the seven free thoracic segments bears a pair of long walking legs or peraeopods (also spelled pereiopods), all of which are similar except the first pair (gnathopods), which are subchelate and used for grasping. In general, the more posterior legs are the largest. The coxae are completely fused with the body, but the basis, ischium, merus, carpus, propodus, and dactylus are distinct in all the legs. Mature females have large, platelike oostegites attached at the inner bases of several of the anterior pairs of legs. These oos-

FIG. 305.–*Asellus*, ×6.5. (Setation omitted.)

tegites extend inward and collectively form a shallow chamber, or marsupium, on the ventral side of the thorax in which incubating eggs and young are carried. A similar device occurs in the amphipods.

The first five pairs of abdominal appendages (pleopods) are considerably modified and hidden beneath the abdomen. The sixth pair of appendages (uropods), however, are unmodified and project well beyond the posterior end of the body.

In the female the first pleopods are absent, and the second pleopods are reduced and one-segmented. The third, fourth, and fifth pleopods, however, are large, flattened, and biramous. The exopod of the third pleopod forms a sclerotized protective operculum, but the third endopod and both rami of the fourth and fifth pleopods are delicate and respiratory.

The male first pleopods are small, elongated, uniramous, and two-segmented. The second are biramous and greatly specialized for copulation and the transfer of sperm to the female. The third to sixth abdominal appendages are similar to those of the female.

Males may be distinguished from females by their larger body size, larger and more specialized gnathopods, absence of oostegites, and the structure of the first and second pleopods.

Locomotion is restricted to slow crawling. Only the Sphaeromidae are capable of rolling up into a ball as are some of the land isopods.

Species inhabiting subterranean waters are notable for their more elongated body, long weak legs, and long antennae, as well as for their great abundance of tactile hairs.

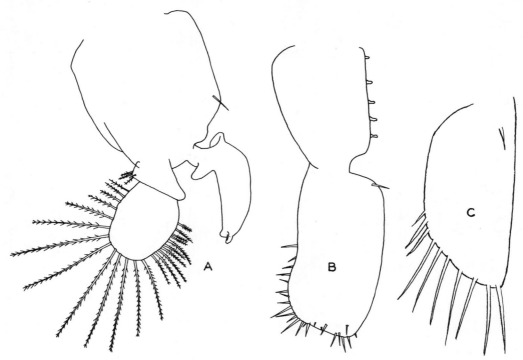

FIG. 306.–*Asellus* appendages. A, second pleopod of male *A. communis*; B, first pleopod of male *A. communis*; C, "first" pleopod of female *Asellus* (actually this is the second pleopod, the true first pleopod being absent in all females.) (A and B from Williams, 1972.)

**Food, feeding.** Isopods are perhaps best characterized as scavengers, since they have been observed eating dead and injured aquatic animals of all kinds and both green and decaying leaves, grass, and aquatic vegetation.

**Internal anatomy, physiology.** The digestive system consists of a short esophagus, a stomach containing a gastric mill, and a long intestine. Four long caeca arise at the junction of the stomach and intestine.

The large heart is located in the posterior part of the thorax. It receives blood from the pericardial chamber via one to three pairs of ostia and sends it out to the hemocoel through a surprisingly large number of arteries (up to 11 in some species). In at least one species, however, the heart has no arteries and no ostia. Most of the carbon dioxide–oxygen exchange occurs through the thin-walled third to fifth pleopods, although it is also possible that the general body surface may be of some respiratory significance.

Two coiled maxillary glands, probably excretory, open at the base of the second maxillae. In addition, other small paired glands in the cephalothorax have sometimes been interpreted as excretory devices.

The nervous system is quite simple in structure; it consists of a brain, circumesophageal connectives, subesophageal ganglia, a double ventral nerve cord with double segmental ganglia in the thorax, and a group of fused ganglia in the anterior portion of the abdomen.

**Reproduction.** Males have three pairs of ovoid testes in the middle of the thorax and dorsal to the intestine. The vasa deferentia open at the tips of two fingerlike projections on the ventral surface of the seventh thoracic segment. (These structures should not be mistaken for the first pleo-

FIG. 307.–Appendages of a male *Asellus*; all in ventral view, from left side, and all to same magnification. A, first leg or pereiopod (gnathopod); B, fourth leg or pereiopod; C, first pleopod; D, second pleopod; E, third pleopod; F, fourth pleopod; G, fifth pleopod; H, uropod.

pods, which immediately follow.) The two ovaries are dorsal, long, and baglike, and the oviducts open through two slitlike genital pores on the ventral surface of the fifth thoracic segment. Just beneath the surface of the body each oviduct is swollen to form a seminal receptacle.

Reproductive habits have been observed for only a few species. In general, breeding may occur throughout the year and does not seem to be governed by temperature, but very few gravid females can be found between October and February. There are one or two broods of young per year.

When ready for copulation, a mature male seizes a female and carries her, ventral side down, beneath his body with his second to fourth legs. Such females either may be in the preadult instar or may already have shed the posterior half of their exoskeleton in the preadult molt. If a male seizes an immature female or one that has

already been impregnated, he releases her almost immediately.

Little is known about the duration of the clasping and copulatory period, but in *Lirceus,* the American genus whose reproductive habits have been most carefully studied, it lasts up to 24 hours.

The female genital pores are not exposed until the preadult exoskeleton has been shed, and if the female has not already lost the posterior half of her exoskeleton, the clasping male usually aids in pulling it off. The male then assumes a copulatory position by sliding sideways so that his ventral surface is pressed against the side of the body of the female. This places the male genital pores and the first and second pleopods in the vicinity of the female genital pore on that side. As sperm are released, the male first and second pleopods undergo rapid vibratory movements that probably aid in transmitting the sperm into the female genital pore and into a seminal receptacle. The process is then repeated on the other side of the female's body, the entire bilateral copulation being completed in less than two hours.

The two individuals then separate, and the female promptly sheds the anterior half of her preadult exoskeleton, the oostegites thereby being transformed from small buds to large functional plates.

After an interval of as long as several days, the mature eggs pass down the oviducts, through the seminal receptacles, where they are fertilized, out the genital pores, and into the marsupium. Depending on the species and size of the female, the number of eggs per brood ranges between 20 and 250. Incubating eggs and newly hatched young are retained in the marsupium for 20 to 30 days. They are aerated by slow up-and-down movements of the oostegites and maxilliped movements that produce an anterior–posterior current of water through the marsupium. The young eventually find their way out of the posterior end of the marsupium by trial and error.

**Development, life cycle.** First instar young have the general characteristics of adults. Little is known about the total number of instars during the isopod life cycle. Presumably there may be at least 15, of which the first five to eight are probably preadult. Casting of the exoskeleton is completed in a few minutes to as much as three days. The process is initiated by a transverse split on the fourth thoracic segment. The posterior half of the exoskeleton is lost first, then, after a variable interval, the anterior half. The life span is thought to be about one year or less. Little specific information is available concerning the number of broods that may be produced during the female life cycle.

**Ecology.** Fresh-water isopods seldom come into open waters but remain secreted under rocks, vegetation, and debris. They are primarily inhabitants of the unpolluted shallows, rarely being found in water more than a meter deep. *Lirceus lineatus* is a notable exception in having been collected at depths up to 55 m, and *A. racov-*

*itzai* has been found in the Great Lakes as deep as 42 m.

Some species are indicators of organic pollution, inasmuch as they may be abundant in the "recovery" zone of streams polluted by domestic sewage.

A single brook or pond almost invariably contains only one species, and it is very unusual to find two species in the same habitat.

A few species, such as *Asellus forbesi*, *A. obtusus,* and *A. scrupulosus,* may occur in temporary ponds, where they burrow into the substrate during periods of drought, but adaptations for withstanding adverse environmental conditions are not generally developed in this order.

Reynoldson (1961), working in Great Britain, has found a positive correlation between the occurrence of *Asellus* and the concentration of calcium and dissolved solids.

Striking masses, or aggregations, of *Asellus,* consisting of scores to thousands of individuals have been observed in small streams. Such aggregations are thought to be formed chiefly as the result of reactions to current velocity. The migration of some individuals upstream as far as possible, or if the current is too swift, being washed downstream until they are able to maintain a footing has the net result of concentrating the isopods in a segment of the stream where the current is neither too fast nor too slow.

Except for *Sphaeroma terebrans,* all of our species of fresh-water isopods are restricted to North America. Furthermore, aside from about 10 species that are widely distributed in this country, they are known mostly from single localities (especially caves and springs) or single states. The common European species *Asellus aquaticus* (L.) does not occur in the United States.

Though the loss of sight is generally characteristic of species confined to subterranean waters, and functional eyes are characteristic of surface water species, there are some interesting exceptions and variations. *Asellus oculata* (Mackin and Hubricht) is found in springs and streams, yet the eyes are reduced. *Lirceus hoppinae,* with functional eyes, occurs in both caves and surface waters. *Asellus hobbsi* (Maloney) is subterranean and has eyes present or absent. *A. spatulata* (Mackin and Hubricht) is a secretive surface form, but the eyes may be present or absent.

**Economic significance.** With few exceptions, isopods are restricted to small lakes and streams, and consequently they are of little importance in the diet of fishes. The writer, however, knows of several small trout lakes where there are large populations of *Asellus communis* and where the rainbow trout populations exhibit extremely rapid growth rates. Economically, *Sphaeroma terebrans* is perhaps the most important species. It is a borer in salt and brackish waters, as well as in fresh-water estuaries of the Gulf coast, and causes extensive damage to wharves and piling. This species has numerous important relatives restricted to salt water. *Lirceus brachyurus* sometimes becomes a pest in commercial beds of water cress. Some isopods serve as intermediate hosts for parasitic nematodes and Acanthocephala of birds and fishes and Acanthocephala of amphibians.

**Collection, prepartion.** Isopods are easily collected by hand-picking, washing out aquatic vegetation, or with a small net. Seventy percent alcohol is a suitable killing agent and preservative. Appendages may be dissected off under the binoculars and permanently mounted in glycerin jelly.

**Taxonomy.** Many of the older descriptions of isopods are useless because they stress highly variable characters such as the number of segments in the antennae and the body length–width ratio. In recent years greater emphasis has been placed on the detailed structure of the mature male second pleopods and gnathopods. These features are constant within each species and there are considerable differences from one genus and species to another.

Most studies in the United States have been scattered and uncorrelated. In 1918 only 21 species were known; now there are about 80, and the several active American investigators in this group have specimens of many more undescribed species in their collections. There are still differences of opinion as to which characters are of generic and specific rank. The status of *Caecidotea* and *Asellus* has been the object of a long controversy; some workers contend that the two should be united under *Asellus,* and this policy has been followed in this manual.

The key to the epigean species of *Asellus* has been modified from Williams (1970). The hypogean species are poorly known and are not included here; most are known only from single localities. It also appears fruitless to attempt a complete key for *Lirceus* until this genus has been more carefully studied; our key includes the six most common species. Unfortunately, identification of most species of *Asellus* is dependent on minute anatomical differences in the sclerotized tip of the endopod of the second pleopod of the male. Furthermore, this structure usually shows morphological variability.

## KEY TO ISOPODA

1. Free-living; morphologically unspecialized ....................................**2**
   Parasitic in branchial chambers of Palaemonidae (*Macrobrachium* and *Palaemonetes*); greatly modified for parasitic existence, appendages reduced, female asymmetrical (Fig. 308); one species.
   Suborder **EPICARIDEA,** BOPYRIDAE, **Probopyrus**
2. Uropods terminal (Fig. 305) ..............Suborder **ASELLOTA,** ASELLIDAE, **6**
   Uropods broad and inserted laterally on abdomen, forming with it a large, horizontally expanded, fanlike structure (Fig. 309B) ........Suborder **FLABELLIFERA, 3**

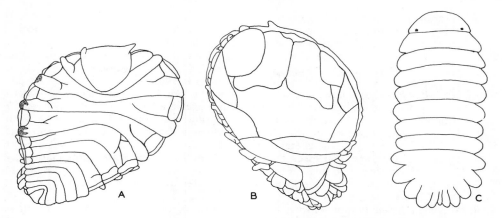

FIG. 308.–*Probopyrus bithynis*, parasitic on *Palaemonetes ohionis*. A, dorsal view of female, ×16; B, ventral view of female, ×16; C, dorsal view of male, ×40. (Modified from Richardson, 1904.)

3. Abdomen with two distinct segments (Fig. 309B); eyes present; up to 10 mm long.

                                                          **SPHAEROMIDAE, 5**

   Abdomen with six distinct segments (Fig. 309A); eyes absent . . . CIROLANIDAE, **4**

4. Exopod of second pleopod and endopods of third to fifth pleopods two-segmented; up to 17 mm long; cave systems of south central Texas. **Cirolanides texensis** Benedict

   Exopod of second pleopod and endopods of third to fifth pleopods one-segmented; up to 12 mm long; found only in Madison Cave, Augusta County, Virginia.

                                                             **Antrolana lira** Bowman

5. Second, third, and fourth segments of palp of maxilliped not produced into lobes (Fig. 309D); a borer in timbers, roots, and mangroves in fresh, brackish, and salt waters; Florida to Texas . . . . . . . . . . . . . . . . . . . . . . . **Sphaeroma terebrans** Bate

   Second, third, and fourth segments of palp of maxilliped not produced into lobes (Fig. 309C); one rare species known from warm springs in New Mexico; a second rare species known from San Nicholas Island, California; a third species, *G. oregonensis* (Dana), is common in fresh-water pools and ponds near the Pacific coast, but it occurs also in the ocean and in brackish waters. **Gnorimosphaeroma**

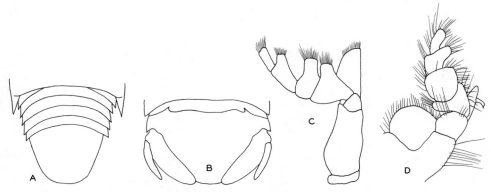

FIG. 309.–Structure of Flabellifera. A, abdomen of *Cirolanides texensis*; B, posterior end of *Gnorimosphaeroma*; C, palp of maxilliped of *Gnorimosphaeroma*; D, palp of maxilliped of *Sphaeroma terebrans*. (A to C modified from Richardson, 1905; D modified from Van Name, 1936.)

6. Anterior margin of cephalothorax with a low but distinct carina (Figs. 310A,B,C.); suture between exopod segments of third pleopod running from the median posterior angle very obliquely toward the lateral margin (Fig. 310H); up to 25 mm long; eyes present; eastern United States as far west as the Great Plains; at least 13 epigean species; usually common in highly restricted ranges; six of these species are known only from single localities in single states; *Lirceus lineatus* (Say), however, is most widespread and has been taken in 10 eastern states; the six most widely distributed species are keyed below ....**Lirceus, 7**

Without a carina on the anterior margin of cephalothorax (Fig. 311F); suture between exopod segments of third pleopod running from the median margin less obliquely toward the lateral margin (Fig. 307E); up to 20 mm long; eyes present or absent; about 60 species are known from the United States; only males may be identified with this key.................................. **Asellus, 14**

7. Mandible with a one- to three-segmented palp, often quite small and stumplike ....**8**

Mandible without a palp .......................................................**9**

8. Abdomen distinctly broader than long (Fig. 310D); reported from streams and springs in Missouri, Arkansas, and Oklahoma ............. **Lirceus hoppinae** (Faxon)

Abdomen only slightly wider than long (Fig. 310F); ponds, springs, and springbrooks in eastern states; common ......................... **Lirceus fontinalis** Raf.

9. Middle and distal propodal processes absent (Fig. 310G); usually in water cress; Pennsylvania and Virginia..................... **Lirceus brachyurus** (Harger)

Middle process and usually also the distal process of the propodus present (Fig. 310J) .........................................................**10**

10. Endopod of each uropod as long or longer than the basal segment (Fig. 310E) ....**11**

Endopod of each uropod shorter than the basal segment (Fig. 310M) ...........**13**

11. Proximal process of propodus as large or larger than the middle process (Fig. 310J); wells and permanent or temporary streams in Missouri, Arkansas, Kansas, and Oklahoma ....................... **Lirceus garmani** Hubricht and Mackin

Proximal process of propodus smaller than middle process (Fig. 310L)...........**12**

12. Uropods flattened (Fig. 310E) ................................................**8**

Uropods cylindrical (Fig. 310M); the most common and widely distributed species in this genus; Great Lakes region and probably in all states east of the Great Plains........................................... **Lirceus lineatus** (Say)

13. Abdomen longer than broad (Fig. 310O); streams, sloughs, ditches, and marshes in Illinois, Missouri, Arkansas, and Louisiana.

**Lirceus louisianae** (Mackin and Hubricht)

Abdomen as broad as long or distinctly broader (Figs. 310D,N) .................**12**

14. Eyes absent; translucent, whitish, or creamy coloration; abdomen longer than broad (Fig. 311A); subterranean springs, wells, and caves; rarely in surface waters; about 46 poorly known species, not included in this key............. **Asellus**

Eyes present; usually gray or brownish coloration; abdomen broader than long (Fig. 305); up to 16 mm long; not subterranean ...................... **Asellus, 15**

15. Palm of propodus of first pereiopod without a triangular process near the midpoint (Fig. 312N); running and standing waters in northwestern states.

**Asellus occidentalis** Williams

Palm of propodus of first pereiopod with a small to large triangular process near the midpoint (Figs. 311C,D) ...............................................**16**

16. First pleopod distinctly longer than second ...............................**17**

First pleopod equal to or shorter than the second pleopod ....................**22**

17. Endopod of second pleopod twisted so that the ventral groove is not visible in ventral aspect (Fig. 312D,L) .......................................................**18**

Endopod of second pleopod not twisted; ventral groove clearly visible in ventral aspect ...........................................................................**19**

18. Endopodial armature of second pleopod forming a terminal spiral structure (Fig. 312L); Arkansas and Oklahoma...... **Asellus montanus** Mackin and Hubricht

Endopodial armature of second pleopod consisting of two large, heavily sclerotized structures showing little torsion (Fig. 312D); known only from Maryland.

**Asellus nodulus** Williams

FIG. 310.–Structure of *Lirceus*. A, cephalothorax of *L. fontinalis*; B, cephalothorax of *L. brachyurus*; C, cephalothorax of *L. lineatus*; D, abdomen of *L. hoppinae*; E, uropod of *L. hoppinae*; F, abdomen of *L. fontinalis*; G, gnathopod of *L. brachyurus*; H, third pleopod of *L. brachyurus*; J, gnathopod of *L. garmani*; K, uropod of *L. garmani*; L, gnathopod of *L. lineatus*; M, uropod of *L. lineatus*; N, abdomen of *L. lineatus*; O, abdomen of *L. louisianae*. (A and C modified from Racovitza, 1920a; D, E, G, and J to O modified from Hubricht and Mackin.)

19. Lateral process at tip of endopod of second pleopod not developed, but medial process large and bifid, and caudal process wide and dentate (Fig. 312B); small creeks in Arkansas and Louisiana ...... **Asellus dentadactylus** Mackin and Hubricht
   Lateral process well developed, and caudal process either absent or broadly rounded. **20**
20. Uropod never more than 0.7 as long as telson; springs and streams in Arkansas, Illinois, Kentucky, and Missouri ............... **Asellus brevicaudus** Forbes
   Uropod about as long as telson ......................................**21**

Fig. 311.–Structure of *Asellus*. A, *A. stygius* (Packard), ×7 (setation omitted), a subterranean species; B, mandible of *Asellus*; C, gnathopod of male *A. communis*; D, gnathopod of female *A. communis*; E, posterior end of *A. brevicaudus*; F, anterior end of *A. intermedius*. (A modified from Hay, 1903; B modified from Huntsman, 1915; C and D modified from Racovitza, 1920.)

21. Medial process at tip of endopod of second pleopod dentate, lateral process sclerotized and pointed, caudal process not developed (Fig. 312C); West Virginia pools .................................... **Asellus scrupulosus** Williams
    Medial process not dentate, lateral process rounded, caudal process developed and broadly rounded with a few irregularities (Fig. 312A); small streams and spring-fed creeks in District of Columbia, Maryland, Pennsylvania, and Virginia.
                                                                 **Asellus kenki** Bowman
22. Medial process absent ................................................... **23**
    Medial process present ................................................... **25**
23. Caudal process absent (Fig. 312J); creeks and ponds in Kentucky and Louisiana.
                                                            **Asellus laticaudatus** Williams
    Caudal process present ................................................. **24**
24. Caudal process usually with acutely pointed apex; cannula (tube) short and wide (Fig. 312H); common in many kinds of waters in the east central states.
                                                              **Asellus intermedius** Forbes
    Caudal process usually broadly rounded; cannula long and narrow (Fig. 312K); very common in northeastern states but known as far west as Colorado.
                                                                 **Asellus communis** Say
25. Cannula long and narrow (Fig. 312G) ....................................... **26**
    Cannula short and wide (Figs. 312E,F) ..................................... **27**

Fig. 312.–Appendage structure of male *Asellus*. A to L, tip of endopod of second pleopod. A, *A. kenki*; B, *A. dentadactylus*; C, *A. scrupulosus*; D, *A. nodulus*; E, *A. obtusus*; F, *A. forbesi*; G, *A. racovitzai*; H, *A. intermedius*; J, *A. laticaudatus*; K, *A. communis*; L, *A. montanus*; M, second pleopod of *A. montanus*; N, gnathopod of *A. occidentalis*. (All redrawn from Williams, 1972.)

26. First and second pleopods about the same length; common in northeastern states but reported also from Washington. ................ **Asellus racovitzai** Williams
First pleopod shorter than second; reported only from Dismal Swamp, Virginia.
**Asellus attenuatus** Richardson
27. Second antennae about as long as body; medial process short and wide, cannula very wide (Fig. 312E); southeastern states ............... **Asellus obtusus** Williams
Second antennae shorter than body; medial process long and narrow (Fig. 312F); common and widely distributed in east central states .**Asellus forbesi** Williams

## ISOPODA REFERENCES

ALLEE, W. C. 1929. Studies in animal aggregations: natural aggregations of the isopod, Asellus communis. *Ecology* **10**:14–36.

BOWMAN, T. E. 1964. Antrolana lira, a new genus and species of troblobitic cirolanid isopod from Madison cave, Virginia. *Int. J. Speleol.* **1**:229–236.

———. 1967. Asellus kenki, a new isopod crustacean from springs in the eastern United States. *Proc. Biol. Soc. Wash.* **80**:131–140.

———. 1974. The California freshwater isopod, Asellus tomalensis, rediscovered and compared with Asellus occidentalis. *Hydrobiologia* **44**:431–441.

CHAPPUIS, P. A. 1957. Un Asellide nouveaux de l'Amerique du Nord. *Notes Biospeolo.* **12**:37–43.

EBERLY, W. R. 1966. A new troglobitic isopod (Asellidae) from southern Indiana. *Proc. Indiana Acad. Sci.* **75**:286–288.

ELLIS, R. J. 1961. A life history study of Asellus intermedius Forbes. *Trans. Am. Microsc. Soc.* **80**:80–102.

———. Notes on the biology of the isopod Asellus

tomalensis Harford in an intermittent pond. Ibid.
90:51–61.

FLEMING, L. E. 1973. The evolution of North
American isopods of the genus Asellus (Crustacea:
Asellidae). Int. J. Speleol. 5:283–310.

HATCHETT, S. P. 1947. Biology of the Isopoda of
Michigan. Ecol. Monogr. 17:47–79.

HENRY, J.-P., and G. MAGNIEZ. 1970. Contribution
a la systématique des asellides (Crustacea Isopoda).
Ann. Speleol. 25:335–367.

HOLSINGER, J. R., and T. E. BOWMAN. 1973. A
new troglobitic isopod of the genus Lirceus (Asellidae) from southwestern Virginia, with notes on its
ecology and additional cave records for the genus
in the Appalachians. Int. J. Speleol. 5:261–271.

HOLSINGER, J. R., and H. R. STEEVES. 1971. A
new species of subterranean isopod crustacean
(Asellidae) from the central Appalachians, with remarks on the distribution of other isopods of the
region. Proc. Biol. Soc. Wash. 84:189–199.

HUBRICHT, L., and J. G. MACKIN. 1949. The fresh-
water isopods of the genus Lirceus (Asellota, Asellidae). Am. Midl. Nat. 42:334–349.

LEVI, H. W. 1949. Two new species of cave isopods from Pennsylvania. Not. Nat. 220:1–6.

MACKIN, J. G., and L. HUBRICHT. 1938. Records
of the distribution of species of isopods in Central
and Southern United States, with descriptions of
four new species of Mancasellus and Asellus (Asellota, Asellidae). Am. Midl. Nat. 19:628–637.

——. 1940. Descriptions of seven new species of
Caecidotea (Isopoda, Asellidae) from central
United States. Trans. Am. Microsc. Soc. 59:383–
397.

MARKUS, H. C. 1930. Studies on the morphology
and life history of the isopod, Mancasellus macrourus. Ibid. 49:220–237.

MENZIES, R. J. 1954. A review of the systematics
and ecology of the genus "Exosphaeroma," with
the description of a new genus, a new species, and
a new subspecies (Crustacea, Isopoda, Sphaeromidae). Am. Mus. Novit. 1683:1–24.

MILLER, M. A. 1933. A new blind isopod, Asellus
californicus, and a revision of the subterranean
asellids. Univ. Calif. Publ. Zool. 39:97–110.

MINCKLEY, W. L. 1961. Occurrence of subterranean isopods in epigean waters. Am. Midl. Nat.
66:452–455.

NEEDHAM, A. E. 1941. Abdominal appendages of
Asellus, II. Q. J. Microsc. Sci. 83:61–89.

RACOVITZA, E. G. 1920. Notes sur les isopodes. 6.
Asellus communis Say. 7. Les pléopodes I and II
dés asellides; morphologie et développement. Arch.
Zool. Exp. Gen. 58:79–115.

——. 1920a. Notes sur les isopodes. 8. Mancasellus tenax (Smith). 9. Mancasellus macrourus
(Garman). Ibid. 59:28–66.

REYNOLDSON, T. B. 1961. Observations on the occurrence of Asellus (Isopoda, Crustacea) in some
lakes of northern Britain. Proc. Int. Assoc. Theor.
Appl. Limn. 14:988–994.

RICHARDSON, H. 1904. Contributions to the natural history of the Isopoda. Proc. U.S. Nat. Mus.
27:1–89.

——. 1905. A monograph of the isopods of North
America. Bull. U.S. Nat. Mus. 54:1–727.

SCHULTZ, T. W. 1973. Digestive anatomy of Lirceus fontinalis (Crustacea: Isopoda). Trans. Am.
Microsc. Soc. 92:13–25.

——. 1973a. Functional morphology of the oral
appendages and foregut of Lirceus garmani (Crustacea: Isopoda). Ibid. 349–364.

STEEVES, H. R., III. 1963. The troglobitic asellids
of the United States: the Stygius group. Am. Midl.
Nat. 69:470–481.

——. 1963a. Two new troglobitic asellids from
West Virginia. Ibid. 70:462–465.

——. 1964. The troglobitic asellids of the United
States; the Hobbsi group. Ibid. 71:445–451.

——. 1965. Two new species of troglobitic asellids from the United States. Ibid. 73:81–84.

——. 1966. Evolutionary aspects of the troglobitic asellids of the United States: the hobbsi, stygius
and cannulus groups. Ibid. 75:392–403.

——. 1968. Three new species of troglobitic asellids from Texas. Ibid. 79:183–188.

——. 1969. The origin and affinities of the troglobitic asellids of the southern Appalachians. Va.
Polytech. Inst. Res. Div. Monogr. 1:51–65.

STEEVES, H. R., III, and J. R. HOLSINGER. 1968.
Biology of three new species of troglobitic asellids
from Tennessee. Ibid. 80:75–83.

STEEVES, H. R., III, and A. J. SEIDENBERG. 1971. A
new species of troglobitic asellid from Illinois. Am.
Midl. Nat. 85:231–234.

STYRON, C. E. 1969. Taxonomy of two populations
of an aquatic isopod, Lirceus fontinalis Raf. Ibid.
82:402–416.

UNWIN, E. E. 1921. Note upon the reproduction
of Asellus aquaticus. J. Linn. Soc. 34:335–343.

VAN NAME, W. G. 1936. The American land and
fresh-water isopod Crustacea. Bull. Am. Mus. Nat.
Hist. 71:1–535.

——. 1940. A supplement to the American land
and fresh-water Isopoda. Ibid. 77:109–142.

——. 1942. A second supplement to the American land and fresh-water isopod Crustacea. Ibid.
80:299–329.

WILLIAMS, W. D. 1970. A revision of North American epigean species of Asellus (Crustacea:Isopoda).
Smithson. Contrib. Zool. 49:1–80.

——. 1972. Freshwater isopods (Asellidae) of
North America. Biota of Freshwater Ecosystems,
Identification Manual 7:1–45.

# Chapter 21

# AMPHIPODA (SCUDS, SIDESWIMMERS)

LIKE THE Decapoda, the Amphipoda are chiefly marine, only about 90 described American species being confined to fresh waters. Worldwide there are about 800 fresh-water species. They occur in a wide variety of unpolluted lakes, ponds, streams, brooks, springs, and subterranean waters. With the exception of one species that may swim about as a plankter in lakes, they are all more or less confined to the substrate.

The layman often calls amphipods "fresh-water shrimp" but, of course, they are only distantly related to (marine) shrimp.

**General characteristics.** The great majority of species are 5 to 20 mm long. The body is laterally compressed and consists of a cephalothorax (first thoracic segment fused with the head), seven free thoracic segments, a six-segmented abdomen, and a small, terminal telson. The pleura of the first four abdominal segments are prolonged ventrally so that these segments are deeper than any of the other body segments. In some species the last three abdominal segments are more or less fused.

Eyes are usually well developed in species living in surface waters, but subterranean species show varying degrees of degeneration or absence of eyes. They are unstalked, compound, and circular, oval, reniform, or elongated.

Both pairs of antennae range from short to long. Each first antenna consists of a three-segmented peduncle and a long flagellum; sometimes there is a very small accessory flagellum (Figs. 314A, B). Each second antenna has a flagellum and a five-segmented peduncle, but the basal segment of the peduncle is fused with the head, and

the second and third segments are very short; only the last two segments are well developed.

The mouth parts are relatively small, compactly arranged, and hidden by the basal segments of the appendages of the first thoracic segment. They include an upper lip; a pair of tearing and cutting mandibles; a pair of laminar and spinous first maxillae; a pair of small, flexible second maxillae; a lower lip; and a pair of maxillipeds. The maxillipeds are homologues of the first maxillipeds of decapods; each consists of a small inner plate, a small outer plate, and a long palp.

The seven pairs of thoracic legs all have seven segments corresponding to the segments of crayfish legs. Beginning proximally, these are as follows: coxa, basis, ischium, merus, carpus, propodus, and dactylus. The coxae are usually called coxal plates; they are greatly enlarged extensions of the coxae, flattened, relatively immovable, and project ventrally at the edges of the body.

The first two pairs of legs, known as gnathopods, are subchelate and adapted for grasping (Fig. 315D), but the third to seventh legs are relatively unspecialized pereiopods (also spelled *peraeopods*). The first two pereiopods are usually flexed forward, the last three backward.

The coxal gills are flattened oval sacs extending downward from the inner surface of the upper posterior corner of the coxal plates. They occur on the second to seventh or second to sixth legs. In addition, there are sometimes very small lateral sternal gills on some of the thoracic segments (Fig. 317B)

The first three abdominal segments

FIG. 313.–*Gammarus lacustris*, ×4.

bear paired pleopods. Each consists of a basal peduncle and two flexible, many-segmented rami. The last three abdominal segments bear paired uropods. These appendages are never very movable, always directed posteriorly, and closely approximated. The peduncles are unsegmented, but the rami are sometimes composed of two segments, the terminal one being small.

Coloration in living amphipods is frequently brilliant, but preserved specimens bleach out so that they are whitish, gray, or cream-colored. Some common species show a wide range in color from one place or time to another. *Hyalella azteca,* for example, is usually light brown or greenish, but bluish, purple, dark brown, or reddish populations are often found. *Synurella dentata* is usually gray-blue but sometimes lavender, brown, or greenish. *Gammarus fasciatus* is whitish, with the body and proximal segments of the appendages banded with green or brown. Very little is known about the causes of color variations within single species, but presumably diet, temperature, and age may be important factors. Subterranean amphipods are almost invariably whitish, cream-colored, gray, or translucent.

The sexes are most readily separated on the basis of large marsupial plates, or oostegites, on the inner surface of the coxal plates of some of the legs (usually second to fifth) of the female. Males often have the larger gnathopods.

**Locomotion.** In general, amphipods are much more active at night than during daylight. The pereiopods are used in crawling and walking but are aided by pushing with the uropods and grasping and pulling with the gnathopods. The last two pereiopods are flexed outward somewhat and are important in a clumsy, skittering sort of locomotion when the animal is on its side. Flexing and extending movements of the entire body aid in crawling and walking. The pleopods are the chief locomotor appendages for rapid undulatory swimming just above the substrate, the body being kept well straightened and the pereiopods directed backward. As an amphipod swims it often rolls over on its side or back (hence the name "sideswimmer").

Especially when disturbed, many amphipods will wriggle into the superficial layers of soft substrates.

**Food, feeding.** Amphipods are voracious feeders, all kinds of animal and plant matter being consumed. Only rarely do they attack and feed on living animals, but freshly killed animals are consumed readily. Species occurring in aquatic vegetation may often be seen browsing on the film of microscopic plants, animals, and organic debris covering leaves, stems, and other substrates (aufwuchs). Like the decapods, then, scuds are omnivorous, general scavengers.

The food mass is held by the gnathopods and anterior pereiopods and chewed directly without being first torn into smaller pieces.

**Internal anatomy, physiology.** Food passes through a short esophagus and into a small stomach containing a gastric mill. The long, undifferentiated intestine opens via the anus just below the telson. Six or seven caeca are usually associated with the digestive tract.

The tubular heart is in the dorsal portion of the thorax. It has three pairs of ostia and anterior and posterior aortas.

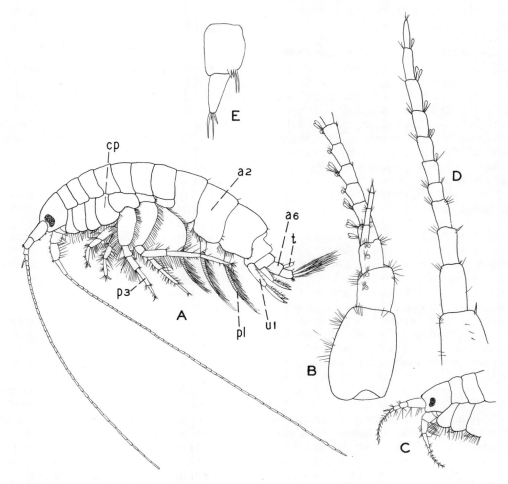

Fig. 314.–Structure of Amphipoda. A, male *Pontoporeia hoyi*, ×9; B, basal portion of first antenna of male *P. hoyi*; C, anterior end of female *P. hoyi*; D, first antenna of female *Hyallela azteca*; E, third uropod of *H. azteca; a2,* second abdominal segment; *a6*, sixth abdominal segment; *cp*, coxal plate; *p3*, third pereiopod; *pl*, third pleopod; *t*, telson; *ul*, first uropod. (A to C modified from Segerstråle; D redrawn from Geisler; E redrawn from Weckel, 1907.)

Although it is possible that some respiration occurs through the general body surface, the thin-walled coxal gills are undoubtedly the chief organs for the oxygen–carbon dioxide exchange. The beating of the pleopods creates a current of water over the gills.

Antennal glands, probably osmoregulatory and excretory, open at the base of the second antennae.

The typical nervous system consists of two ventral nerve cords united at intervals by large segmental ganglia, two circume-sophageal connectives, and a supraesophageal mass, or "brain."

Both pairs of antennae are olfactory and highly sensitive to touch. They sometimes bear minute, stalked, clublike, or wine-glassshaped sensory appendages (Figs. 314B, D), presumably comparable to the aesthetasks of copepods.

**Reproduction.** Testes and ovaries are paired, elongated strands ventral to the heart. The oviducts open at the base of the fifth coxal plates, and the male genital pores open on papillae on the ventral side of the last thoracic segment.

With the exception of *Hyalella azteca* and two or three other species, our knowledge of the details of reproductive behavior is rather sketchy. Syngamic reproduction is the rule, but males are sometimes rare. Most common species breed some time between February and October, depending largely on water temperatures. Mature males pair for the first time when they are in their ninth instar, females in their eighth (nuptial) instar. When two males meet both are active and fail to pair and soon separate, but a female is passive when seized by a male.

In *Gammarus, Hyalella azteca,* and one species of *Synurella,* pairing consists of the males carrying the females on their backs and keeping them in place with their gnathopods. Paired individuals feed and swim about for one to as much as seven days, or until the female is ready to molt to the first adult instar. The two animals then separate for a few minutes to several hours while the female loses her old exoskeleton. A male then returns, the two individuals pair again, and copulation usually occurs within the subsequent 24 hours.

Copulation and transfer of sperm are completed in less than a minute. The male extends the posterior part of his body around and to the ventral side of the female until the tips of his uropods touch the marsupium which is formed by the marsupial plates, or oostegites. Ejected sperm are then swept into the marsupium by movements of the female pleopods. This process of sperm transfer may be repeated several times at intervals of a few minutes, the male holding on to the female all the time.

The animals finally separate, and the female promptly releases her eggs from the oviducts into the marsupium where they are fertilized. The number of eggs released by the female depends on her size and age as well as the particular species. In general, the larger and older females release the larger number of eggs. One species of *Stygobromus* releases only one or two eggs at a time, but the more common species usually average from 15 to 50 eggs per brood. *Hyalella azteca* averages about 18 eggs per brood.

This same species has been shown to have "strains" in different lakes; these do not interbreed.

**Development, life cycle.** The oostegites are bordered with stiff hairs that are hooked distally and entangled somewhat, and the developing eggs are therefore retained securely within the marsupium. In the few species that have been carefully studied, the incubation period ranges from one to three weeks. Newly hatched young are retained in the marsupium an additional one to eight days and are released to the outside when the mother has her first molt following copulation.

Judging from the limited observations that have been made, the females of most species produce only a single brood during the life cycle, but in a few species each female customarily produces a series of broods during the breeding months. *Hyalella azteca,* for example, averages 15 broods in 152 days (Embody, 1911). Copulation is necessary for the production of each brood, so that females pair for the second or subsequent time while they are still carrying their previous brood of eggs or young in the marsupium. These events therefore closely follow each other within a few hours: (1) male leaves female, (2) female molts and releases young, (3) male and female pair again, (4) release of eggs to marsupium, (5) repeated copulation and fertilization, and (6) male leaves female.

*Hyalella azteca* has a minimum of nine instars in its life history (Geisler). As in all other species, development is direct, and the newly hatched young have all the adult appendages. The first five instars form the juvenile period, during which the sexes are indistinguishable. In the sixth and seventh instars, or adolescent period, the sexes can be differentiated; the female has small oostegites and a few small eggs in the ovaries, and the male has slightly enlarged gnathopods. Pairing occurs for the first time in the eighth, or nuptial, instar, and the ninth and subsequent instars form the adult period. The number of molts that may occur during the adult period is variable but may be as high as 15 or 20.

When the old exoskeleton is ready to be cast, a dorsal, transverse split appears halfway around the body between the first and second thoracic segments or occasionally between the cephalothorax and first thoracic segment. Sometimes there are accessory longitudinal splits along the upper margins of the coxal plates. The cephalothorax is withdrawn first and then the rest of the body. Molting is completed in less than an hour.

The interval between molts ranges from a minimum of 3 to a maximum of 40 days, depending on food conditions, temperature, and the species. Immature amphipods molt at much shorter intervals than adults.

Most species complete the life cycle in a year or less. *Pontoporeia hoyi* is unusual in that it is thought to have a life cycle of 30 months or more. This species breeds between December and April, and the young are released from the marsupium in the spring.

**Ecology.** *Hyalella azteca, Gammarus pseudolimnaeus, G. fasciatus,* and *Crangonyx gracilis* constitute the great majority of specimens taken by casual collectors. These species are widely distributed and common in unpolluted clear waters, including springs, spring brooks, streams, pools, ponds, and lakes. Less common species are more restricted to certain types of environments. *Pontoporeia hoyi,* for example, occurs only in deep, cold, oligotrophic, northern lakes. *Gammarus minus* occurs only in caves, springs, and small streams from Pennsylvania, Maryland, Virginia, and West Virginia west-southwest to Illinois, Missouri, and Arkansas. Many species are restricted to seeps, springs, and subterranean waters in one or a few states, or, indeed, to a single cave or cave system.

As a group, amphipods are cold stenotherms, strongly thigmotactic, and react negatively to light. Consequently, during the daytime they are in vegetation or hidden under and between debris and stones. They usually congregate in the corners of culture jars in the laboratory. The true burrowing habit has not evolved in fresh-water species.

Amphipods are sometimes unbelievably abundant. The writer has collected *Gammarus* from spring brooks rich in rooted vegetation where populations have exceeded 10,000 per m². Juday and Birge (1927) reported an average population of 4553 *Pontoporeia hoyi* per square meter at a depth of 50 to 60 m on the bottom of Green Lake, Wisconsin.

Except for *P. hoyi,* which is both a benthic and plankton organism and which has been found as deep as 300 m in Lake Superior, amphipods are restricted to shallow waters. *Hyalella azteca* is about the only other species ever found at depths exceeding 1 m. Large rivers contain few amphipods, except in the shallow backwater and overflow pond areas.

Although it is generally true that the majority of species appear to be restricted to waters of low or medium carbonate content, there are a few notable exceptions. *Gammarus lacustris* is common in hard waters, and *Hyalella azteca* is sometimes found in alkaline and brackish waters.

An abundance of dissolved oxygen appears to be an environmental necessity. The only reported notable exception is *Pontoporeia hoyi,* which has been collected from the bottom waters of lakes where the concentration of dissolved oxygen was less than 7 percent saturation. *Gammarus* might prove to be a useful bioassay organism for studies on pesticides.

The restriction of many species to subterranean waters and springs strongly suggests that they are cold stenotherms.

About 100 species are terrestrial or semiterrestrial on a worldwide basis. Some occur in the debris of the high-tide line on marine shores. Others may be found in commercial greenhouses or in terrestrial habitats in the tropics.

**Geographic distribution, dispersal.** Most of the scuds of the United States are restricted to this continent. In the Gammaridae, all genera except *Crangonyx, Synurella,* and *Gammarus* are restricted to North America. *Hyalella azteca* occurs also in South America. *Gammarus fasciatus* and *Crangonyx gracilis* have recently been reported from England; undoubtedly they have been introduced from the United

States. *Niphargus,* the very large Old World genus, does not occur in the United States.

Very little is known about the passive transport of amphipods from one drainage system to another. Unlike the entomostraca, amphipods are not generally adapted for withstanding drought and other adverse environmental conditions. *Crangonyx gracilis, C. shoemakeri,* and *Synurella bifurca,* however, are inhabitants of temporary as well as permanent ponds and streams, and it has been suggested that these species tide over unfavorable conditions by burrowing into the substrate.

*C. forbesi* undergoes interesting seasonal migrations. In the spring, populations move upstream into spring brooks and springs. There the populations often become so dense that cannibalism results. In the autumn the remnants of the population migrate back downstream. Breeding occurs during the winter months.

*Pontoporeia hoyi* is probably derived from *P. femorata,* an arctic circumpolar and marine species. *P. affinis* is a European and Asiatic fresh-water species also thought to have been derived from *P. femorata.*

**Subterranean amphipods.** The central and south central states, from eastern Kansas and Oklahoma to Indiana, Kentucky, and Tennessee is a region abundant in large caves and cave systems, most of which contain brooks, streams, and pools. It is in such bodies of water that interesting subterranean amphipods are found, but usually as sparse populations. Although the cave habit has evolved in many genera, the species, as a group, are similarly modified. They are generally whitish, creamy, or straw-colored, the antennae and tactile hairs are well developed, the body is often relatively fragile, and the eyes are usually reduced, vestigial, or absent. Their food consists of bits of dead vegetation washed into the caves and the thin bacterial scum covering submerged surfaces. Some subterranean species are generally distributed throughout large areas, but others are rare and have been reported only from single or a few localities.

Subterranean amphipods are often collected just outside of caves and underground streams where the water forms surface seeps, wells, and springs. Some species are represented by two distinct varieties, one subterranean and the other a surface form. The cave variety of *Crangonyx gracilis,* for example, has degenerate eyes and no pigmentation, whereas its pond and stream counterpart has functional eyes and good pigmentation. Comparable differences occur in the varieties of *C. forbesi* and *Gammarus troglophilus* Hubricht and Mackin. *G. minus* is unusual in having three varieties. The one occurring in springs has large eyes, short antennae, and brown coloration. A cave variety has slightly reduced eyes, long antennae, and bluish coloration. Another rare cave variety has a fragile body, greatly reduced eyes, long antennae, and bluish coloration.

**Enemies, commensals, parasites.** Fishes are the chief predators, although only a few species of amphipods occur in streams and ponds large enough to support natural fish populations. The planting of amphipods in small western lakes has, in a few instances, been at least temporarily successful in augmenting the natural food supply of trout. Birds, predaceous aquatic insects, and amphibians probably take an appreciable toll.

Like crayfish, amphipods support an amazing population of algae and sessile Protozoa on the external body surfaces.

Scuds serve as intermediate hosts for a wide variety of parasites, including tapeworms of waterfowl and fishes, and a few nematodes, trematodes, and Acanthocephala of birds, fishes, and amphibians.

**Collection, preparation.** Where specimens are abundant they may be easily taken with a dipnet and by rinsing out masses of aquatic vegetation and bottom debris. Stony bottoms require hand picking with forceps or a small aquarium net. Seventy percent alcohol is a satisfactory killing agent and preservative.

Live specimens may be maintained in aquaria, especially if they are well supplied with aquatic vegetation.

**Taxonomy.** Of the three suborders of the Order Amphipoda, only one, the Gammaroidea, is represented in American fresh waters. The list of species described has grown from 16 in 1907 (Weckel) to about 90 at the present time. Of these, all but two belong in the Gammaridae, *Hyalella azteca* belonging in the Talitridae and *Pontoporeia hoyi* in the Haustoriidae. Our American specialists have representatives of more than 100 undescribed fresh-water species in their possession.

For accurate identification it is important that mature males and females be used, since the keys below are based largely on structures which are best differentiated in the later instars.

*Pontoporeia* has been a particularly puzzling genus, and several species have been described from the United States. The work of Segerstråle, however, has shown that there is only one valid species, *P. hoyi*, which is closely related to *P. affinis* Lindstrom occurring in Europe. The previous confusion resulted from the fact that this species shows marked changes in the later instars, especially with respect to length of the antennae and structure of the uropods.

We use reflected light and watch glasses containing black wax for our dissections under binoculars. Watchmaker's forceps are mandatory. The following key is greatly modified from that of Holsinger (1972).

## KEY TO GENERA AND SPECIES OF AMPHIPODA

1. First antenna with accessory flagellum (Figs. 314A, B) and either longer or shorter than second antenna; third uropod with or without rami; telson cleft or entire. **2**
   First antenna without accessory flagellum (Fig. 314D) and shorter than second antenna; third uropod uniramous (Fig. 314E); telson entire; 4 to 8 mm long; springs, brooks, pools, and lakes; widely distributed and common.
   TALITRIDAE, **Hyalella azteca** (Saussure)
2. First antenna slightly shorter than second antenna, very short in female (Fig. 314C) and very long in mature male (Fig. 314A); accessory flagellum of first antenna consisting of three or four segments (Fig. 314B); fifth pereiopod much shorter than fourth and with second segment greatly expanded; up to 9 mm long; on the bottom and in the plankton of deep, cold lakes, including Great Lakes; Lake Nipigon; Green Lake, Wisconsin, Lake Washington, Seattle; some Finger Lakes, New York; and others. Mature males of variety *typica* have 31 to 57 segments in the flagellum of the first antenna and 42 to 72 segments in the flagellum of the second antenna; mature males of variety *brevicornis* have 14 to 19, and 19 to 24 segments, respectively.
   HAUSTORIIDAE, **Pontoporeia hoyi** Smith
   First antenna either longer or shorter than second, but both antennae long and slender; accessory flagellum very short, consisting of two short segments, or well developed and consisting of from three to seven segments; fifth pereiopod longer or slightly shorter than fourth, and with the second segment only moderately expanded (Fig. 315A) ............................... GAMMARIDAE, **3**
3. Accessory flagellum of first antenna three- to seven-segmented (Fig. 315G); third uropod well developed (Fig. 315E) ....................................**4**
   Accessory flagellum of first antenna small, rudimentary, or consisting of one short and one long segment (Fig. 317D); third uropod usually reduced (Fig. 317G). **8**
4. Coxal gills with cylindrical appendages (Figs. 315B, C); up to 11 mm long; three uncommon species known from brackish waters and coastal streams in Washington, Oregon, and California ...........................**Anisogammarus**
   Coxal gills without cylindrical appendages; up to 25 mm long; common and widely distributed; about six species are rare, are mostly hypogean, and have highly restricted distributions; four species are epigean, widely distributed, and included in this key .......................................**Gammarus, 5**

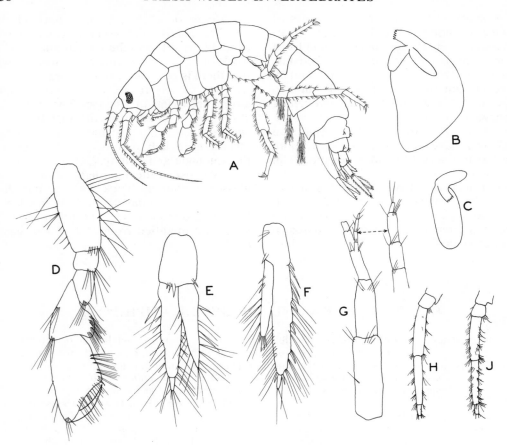

Fig. 315.–Structure of Gammaridae. A, male *Gammarus fasciatus*, ×5; B and C, coxal gills of *Anisogammarus oregonensis* Shoemaker; D, second gnathopod of male *Gammarus lacustris*; E, third uropod of *G. lacustris*; F, third uropod of *G. minus*; G, basal portion of first antenna of *G. lacustris*; H, basal segments of second antenna of *G. minus*; J, basal segments of second antenna of *G. fasciatus*. (A modified from Kunkel; B and C modified from Shoemaker, 1944; D to G modified from Weckel.)

5. Second antenna richly setose (Fig. 315J); up to 14 mm long; common in upper Mississippi drainage, Great Lakes drainage, and the Atlantic coastal plain to North Carolina; lakes and rivers . . . . . . . . . . . . . . . . . . **Gammarus fasciatus** Say
   Second antenna not richly setose (Fig. 315H) . . . . . . . . . . . . . . . . . . . . . . . . . . . . . . .**6**

6. Posterior margin of basal segment of seventh pereiopod with long setae (Fig. 316A); up to 17 mm long; upper Mississippi River and Great Lakes drainages; chiefly in springs and streams . . . . . . . . . . . . . . . **Gammarus pseudolimnaeus** Bousfield
   Posterior margin of basal segment of seventh pereiopod with short setae (Fig. 316B). **7**

7. Posterior angle of second and third abdominal side plates weakly acuminate (Fig. 316C); up to 14 mm long; common in streams and springs from the central Appalachians to the Ozarks . . . . . . . . . . . . . . . . . . . . . . . **Gammarus minus** Say
   Posterior angle of second and third abdominal side plates strongly acuminate (Fig. 316D); up to 22 mm long; a variable species found in a wide variety of habitats over the northern half of the United States . . . . . . . . **Gammarus lacustris** Sars

FIG. 316.–Structure of *Gammarus*. A, base of seventh pereiopod of *G. pseudolimnaeus*; B, base of seventh pereiopod of *G. minus*; C, second and third abdominal side plates of *G. minus*; D, second and third abdominal side plates of *G. lacustris*. (Modified from Holsinger, 1972.)

8. Last segment of sixth and seventh pereiopods with ventral spines (Fig. 317H); two species in hypogean habitats of south central Oklahoma and the Ozark plateau; up to 22 mm long ........................................ **Allocrangonyx**
   Last segment of sixth and seventh pereiopods without ventral spines ............. **9**
9. Second antenna of mature male with paddlelike calceoli (Fig. 318A); chiefly epigean. **10**
   Second antenna of mature male without calceoli; chiefly hypogean ............. **21**
10. Third uropod uniramous, exopod short (Fig. 317J); 5 to 14 mm long; telson cleft (Fig. 317E); epigean ............................................. **Synurella, 11**
   Third uropod biramous, exopod long (Fig. 318G); 4 to 22 mm long; about 20 described U.S. species plus many undescribed species; a difficult taxonomic group; this key includes only the U.S. epigean species that are found in more than one restricted locality ........................................ **Crangonyx, 13**
11. Palmar margin of gnathopod concave (Fig. 318B); ponds, springs, and small streams of southeastern Indiana, southwestern Ohio, and central Kansas.
                                                              **Synurella dentata** Hubricht
   Palmar margin of gnathopod straight (Fig. 318C) .............................. **12**
12. Urosome segments fused; streams, springs, and ponds in Arkansas, Tennessee, south to the Gulf ..................................... **Synurella bifurca** (Hay)
   Urosome segments not fused; small streams and ponds in eastern Virginia, North Carolina, and South Carolina ................. **Synurella chamberlaini** (Ellis)
13. Palmar margin of second gnathopod of female lined with small, weak spines (Fig. 319D) ................................................................ **14**
   Palmar margin of second gnathopod of female lined with strong, notched spines (Fig. 319G) ................................................................ **16**
14. Posterior corner of first abdominal side plate strongly mucronate (Fig. 318E); swamps and pools; Florida to eastern Louisiana ...... **Crangonyx floridanus** Bousfield
   Posterior corner of first abdominal side plate weakly mucronate ................. **15**
15. Mature males without a row of comb spines on outer ramus of second uropod; chiefly in the Great Lakes drainage basin; probably a species complex.
                                                              **Crangonyx gracilis** Smith
   Mature males with a row of comb spines on outer ramus of second uropod (Fig. 318G); uncommon; distribution spotty but probably widely dispersed in the northeastern states; possibly a species complex.
                                                              **Crangonyx pseudogracilis** Bousfield
16. Inner margin of dactyl of female second gnathopod with a row of bladelike spines (Fig. 318H) ....................................................... **17**
   Inner margin of dactyl of female second gnathopod with fine setae only (Fig. 318D). **19**
17. Palmar margin of second gnathopod straight; dactyls of third to seventh pereiopods with two or three short; stiff setae on inner margins (Fig. 318J); cold streams and ponds in lower Michigan, Indiana, Ohio, and Kentucky.
                                                              **Crangonyx setodactylus** Bousfield
   Palmar margin of second gnathopod slightly concave (Fig. 318H); dactyls of third to seventh pereiopods with one stiff seta on inner margin .................. **18**

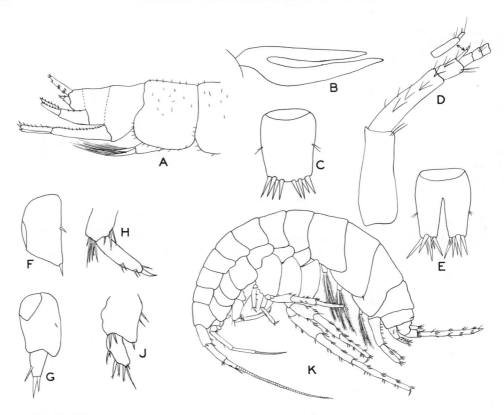

FIG. 317.–Structure of Gammaridae. A, posterior end of *Stygonectes pizzini* (Shoemaker); B, lateral sternal gill of sixth thoracic segment of *S. pizzini*; C, telson of *Stygonectes balconis* Hubricht; D, basal portion of first antenna of *S. flagellatus* (Benedict); E, telson of *Synurella dentata*; F, third uropod of *Apocrangonyx subtilis* Hubricht; G, third uropod of *Stygobromus mackini* Hubricht; H, end of seventh pereiopod of *Allocrangonyx pellucidus* (Mackin); J, third uropod of *Synurella*; K, *Allocrangonyx pellucidus*, a blind species, ×3. (A and B modified from Shoemaker, 1942; C, E, F, and G modified from Hubricht; D redrawn from Weckel; H and J redrawn from Holsinger, 1972.)

18. Mature female with 12 to 15 spines on anterior margin of the basal segment of seventh pereiopod (Fig. 318K); small streams and ponds in Indiana, Illinois, Iowa, and Missouri ................................... **Crangonyx minor** Bousfield
    Mature female with about eight small spines on anterior margin of the basal segment of seventh pereiopod (Fig. 318L); springs, small streams, and bogs in Maryland, District of Columbia, and Virginia.
                                    **Crangonyx shoemakeri** (Hubricht and Mackin)
19. Basal segments of pereiopods five, six, and seven broad and with numerous minute serrations (Fig. 318M); springs and spring-fed streams in adjacent areas of Illinois, Ohio, and Kentucky ................ **Crangonyx anomalus** Hubricht
    Basal segments of pereiopods five, six, and seven not expanded and with few serrations ............................................................**20**
20. Telson short, with shallow cleft and three or four apical spines per lobe (Fig. 318N); a variable species of streams and ponds in Missouri, Illinois, Indiana, Ohio, and Kentucky ................... **Crangonyx forbesi** (Hubricht and Mackin)
    Telson about as long as broad, with two or three apical spines per lobe (Fig. 318O); probably a complex species group; widely distributed in eastern half of the United States in all types of waters ....... **Crangonyx obliquus-richmondensis**

FIG. 318.–Structure of Gammaridae. A, basal segments of male second antenna of *Crangonyx*; B, tip of gnathopod of *Synurella dentata* (all setae and spines omitted); C, tip of gnathopod of *S. bifurca* (all setae and spines omitted); D, tip of second gnathopod of female *Crangonyx*; E, posterior corner of first abdominal side plate of *C. floridanus*; F, posterior corner of first abdominal side plate of *Crangonyx*; G, male uropod of *C. shoemakeri*; H, tip of second gnathopod of female *C. shoemakeri*; J, dactyl of seventh pereiopod of *C. setodactylus*; K, basal segment of seventh pereiopod of *C. minor*; L, basal segment of seventh pereiopod of *C. shoemakeri*; M, basal segment of seventh pereiopod of *C. anomalus*; N, telson of *C. forbesi*; O, telson of *Crangonyx obliquus-richmondensis* group; P, third uropods of *Allocrangonyx*; Q, third uropod of *Stygonectes*. (Mostly modified from Holsinger, 1972.)

**21.** Third uropod biramous, but inner ramus vestigial; outer ramus about as long as peduncle (Fig. 319A); three described hypogean species in Ohio to Kansas and Oklahoma . . . . . . . . . . . . . . . . . . . . . . . . . . . . . . . . . . . . . . . . . . . . . **Bactrurus**

Third uropod uniramous, outer ramus shorter than peduncle and sometimes absent (Figs. 317F, G); three difficult and closely related genera . . . . . . . . . . . . . . . .**22**

**22.** Second gnathopod equal to or larger than first gnathopod; sixth pereiopod usually longer than seventh pereiopod; urosome segments not fused; 10 described species and more than 50 undescribed species; ground waters over much of the Appalachians, eastern interior plateaus, Ozarks, and the far west, but distribution is spotty . . . . . . . . . . . . . . . . . . . . . . . . . . . . . . . . . . . **Stygobromus**

Second gnathopod usually smaller than first gnathopod; sixth pereiopod shorter than seventh pereiopod; urosome segments fused or nearly fused (Fig. 318Q) . . .**23**

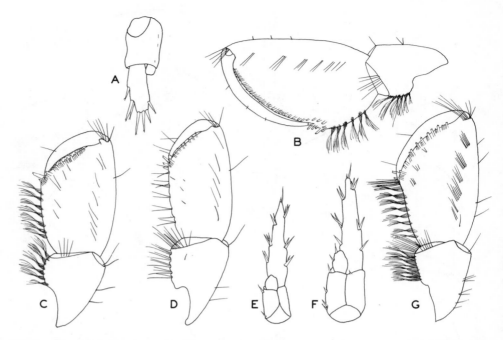

F<small>IG</small>. 319.–Structure of Gammaridae. A, third uropod of *Bactrurus brachycaudus* Hubricht and Mackin; B, second gnathopod of female *Crangonyx obliquus* (Hubricht and Mackin); C, second gnathopod of female *C. shoemakeri*; D, second gnathopod of female *C. gracilis*; E, third uropod of male *C. gracilis*; F, third uropod of female *C. gracilis*; G, second gnathopod of male *C. forbesi* (fine setae of dactyl not visible). (All modified from Hubricht and Mackin.)

23. Second gnathopod equal to or larger than first gnathopod; outer ramus of third uropod vestigial or absent (Fig. 317F); adults 2 to 7 mm long; six described species, but more than six others have been collected but not described; underground waters in Virginia, Illinois, Tennessee, and West Virginia ..... **Apocrangonyx**
Second gnathopod usually smaller than first gnathopod; outer ramus of third uropod small (Fig. 318Q); adults 4.5 to 20 mm long; about 30 described and 10 undescribed hypogean species from Vermont and New York, southwest to Texas and Oklahoma ............................................**Stygonectes**

## AMPHIPODA REFERENCES

A<small>DAMSTONE</small>, F. B. 1928. Relict amphipods of the genus Pontoporeia. *Trans. Am. Microsc. Soc.* **47**:366–371.
B<small>ARNARD</small>, J. L. 1958. Index to the families, genera, and species of the gammaridean Amphipoda (Crustacea). *Occas. Pap. Allan Hancock Found. Publ.* **19**:1–145.
B<small>ARNARD</small>,J.L.,andW.S.G<small>RAY</small>. 1968. Introduction of an amphipod crustacean into the Salton Sea, California. *Bull. S. Calif. Acad. Sci.* **67**:219–232.

B<small>OUSFIELD</small>, E. L. 1958. Fresh-water amphipod crustaceans of glaciated North America. *Can. Field-Nat.* **72**:55–113.
C<small>LAMPITT</small>, P. T. 1965. Dispersal related to density in the amphipods Hyalella azteca and Gammarus pseudolimnaeus. *Proc. Iowa Acad. Sci.* **71**:474–484.
C<small>OLE</small>, G. A. 1970. The epimera of North American fresh-water species of Gammarus (Crustacea: Amphipoda). *Proc. Biol. Soc. Wash.* **83**:333–348.

COOPER, W. E. 1965. Dynamics and production of a natural population of a fresh-water amphipod, Hyalella azteca. *Ecol. Monogr.* **35:**377–394.

CREASER, E. P 1934. A new genus and species of blind amphipod with notes on parallel evolution in certain amphipod genera. *Mus. Zool. Univ. Mich. Occas. Pap.* **282:**1–6.

EMBODY, G. C. 1912. A preliminary study of the distribution, food and reproductive capacity of some fresh-water amphipods. *Int. Rev. (Suppl)* **4:**1–33.

GAYLOR, D. 1922. A study of the life history and productivity of Hyalella knickerbockeri Bate. *Proc. Ind. Acad. Sci.* (1921):239–250.

GEISLER, SISTER F. S. 1944. Studies on the post-embryonic development of Hyallela azteca (Saussure). *Biol. Bull.* **86:**6–22.

HARGRAVE, B. T. 1970. Distribution, growth, and seasonal abundance of Hyalella azteca (Amphipoda) in relation to sediment microflora. *J. Fish. Res. Board of Can.* **27:**685–699.

HOLSINGER, J. R. 1966. Subterranean amphipods of the genus Stygonectes (Gammaridae) from Texas. *Am. Midl. Nat.* **76:**100–124.

———. 1967. Systematics, speciation, and distribution of the subterranean amphipod genus Stygonectes (Gammaridae). *Bull. U.S. Nat. Mus.* **259:**1–176.

———. 1969. The systematics of the North American subterranean amphipod genus Apocrangonyx (Gammaridae), with remarks on ecology and zoogeography. *Am. Midl. Nat.* **81:**1–28.

———. 1969a. Biogeography of the freshwater amphipod crustaceans (Gammaridae) of the Central and Southern Appalachians. *Va. Polytech. Inst. Res. Div. Monogr.* **1:**19–50.

———. 1971. A new species of the subterranean amphipod genus Allocrangonyx (Gammaridae) with a redescription of the genus and remarks on its zoogeography. *Int. J. Speleol.* **3:**317–331.

———. 1972. The freshwater amphipod crustaceans (Gammaridae) of North America. *Biota of Freshwater Ecosystems, Identification Manual* **5:**1–89.

———. 1974. Systematics of the subterranean amphipod genus Stygobromus (Gammaridae), Part I: species of the western United States. *Smithson. Contrib. Zool.* **160:**1–63.

HUBRICHT, L. 1943. Studies in the Nearctic fresh-water Amphipoda, III. Notes on the fresh-water Amphipoda of eastern United States, with descriptions of 10 new species. *Am. Midl. Nat.* **29:**683–712.

HUBRICHT, L., and J. G. MACKIN. 1940. Descriptions of nine new species of fresh-water amphipod Crustaceans with notes and new localities for other species. Ibid. **23:**187–218.

HULTIN, L. 1971. Upstream movements of Gammarus pulex pulex (Amphipoda) in a South Swedish stream. *Oikos* **22:**329–347.

JUDAY, C., and E. A. BIRGE. 1927. Pontoporeia and Mysis in Wisconsin lakes. *Ecology* **7:**445–452.

KARAMAN, G. S. 1974. Contribution to the knowledge of the Amphipoda. Revision of the genus Stygobromus Cope 1872 (Fam. Gammaridae) from North America. *Glas. Repub. Zavoda Zast. Prir.— Prir. Muz. Titograd* **7:**97–125.

MARZOLF, G. R. 1965. Substrate relations of the burrowing amphipod Pontoporeia affinis in Lake Michigan. *Ecology* **46:**579–591.

MATHIAS, J. A. 1971. Energy flow and secondary production of the amphipods Hyalella azteca and Crangonyx richmondensis occidentalis in Marion Lake, British Columbia. *J. Fish. Res. Board of Can.* **28:**711–726.

MINCKLEY, W. L. 1964. Upstream movements of Gammarus (Amphipoda) Doe Run, Meade County, Kentucky. *Ecology* **45:**195–197.

MINCKLEY, W. L., and G. A. COLE. 1963. Ecological and morphological studies on gammarid amphipods (Gammarus spp.) in spring-fed streams of northern Kentucky. *Occ. Pap. C. C. Adams Center Ecol. Stud.* **10:**1–35.

REES, C. P. 1972. The distribution of the amphipod Gammarus pseudolimnaeus Bousfield as influenced by oxygen concentration, substratum, and current velocity. *Trans. Am. Microsc. Soc.* **91:**514–528.

SANDERS, H. O. 1969. Toxicity of pesticides to the crustacean Gammarus lacustris. *Tech. Pap. Bur. Sport Fish. Wildl.* **25:**1–18

SCHMITZ, E. H. 1967. Visceral anatomy of Gammarus lacustris lacustris Sars (Crustacea: Amphipoda). *Am. Midl. Nat.* **78:**1–54.

SEGERSTRÅLE, S. G. 1937. Studien über die Bodentierwelt in südfinnländischen Küstengewässern III. Zur Morphologie und Biologie des Amphipoden Pontoporeia affinis, nebst einer Revision der Pontoporeia-Systematic. *Soc. Sci. Fenn. Comment. Biol.* **7:**1–183.

———. 1954. The freshwater amphipods. Gammarus pulex (L.) and Gammarus lacustris G. O. Sars, in Denmark and Fennoscandia-a contribution to the late- and post-glacial immigration history of the aquatic fauna of northern Europe. Ibid. **15:**1–91.

———. 1971. On summer breeding in populations of Pontoporeia affinis (Crustacea Amphipoda) living in lakes of North America. Ibid. **44:**1–18.

SHOEMAKER, C. R. 1938. A new species of fresh-water amphipod of the genus Synpleonia, with remarks on related genera. *Proc. Biol. Soc. Wash.* **51:**137–142.

———. 1942. Notes on some American fresh-water amphipod crustaceans and descriptions of a new genus and two new species. *Smithson. Misc. Coll.* **101:**1–31.

———. 1944. Description of a new species of Amphipoda of the genus Anisogammarus from Oregon. *J. Wash. Acad. Sci.* **34:**89–93.

SMITH, W. E. 1972. Culture, reproduction, and temperature tolerance of Pontoporeia affinis in the laboratory. *Trans. Am. Fish. Soc.* **101:**253–256.

WECKEL, A. L. 1907. The fresh-water Amphipoda of North America. *Proc. U.S. Nat. Mus.* **32:**25–58.

WILDER, J. 1940. The effects of population density upon growth, reproduction, and survival of Hyallela azteca. *Physiol. Zool.* **13:**439–462.

# Chapter 22

# DECAPODA (CRAYFISHES, SHRIMPS)

OF THE great array of species constituting the Order Decapoda, the vast majority are marine. In the United States only the Astacidae (crayfishes), about 12 species of Palaemonidae (fresh-water prawns and river shrimps), and four species of Atyidae are found in fresh waters. These representatives, totaling about 320 species, are characteristic and common inhabitants of a wide variety of environments, including most types of running waters, shallows of lakes, ponds, sloughs, swamps, underground waters, and even wet meadows where there is no open water. They are absent from the greater portion of the Rocky Mountain region, although one species occurring in Pacific slope drainages has migrated as far eastward as the Great Basin and the headwaters of the Snake, Yellowstone, and Missouri rivers.

To this list should be added at least one grapsoid crab, *Platychirograpsus typicus* Rathbun, which has become well established in the Hillsboro River, Florida. Possibly this river crab occurs also in Gulf coast streams of other states since it is common along the east coast of Mexico.

**General characteristics.** Crayfish, crawfish, crawdads, or crabs, as they are locally and variously known, are all more or less cylindrical, and the body and appendages are strongly sclerotized. The compound eyes are large, stalked, and movable. Total length, not including the antennae, ranges from 10 to 150 mm. The six abdominal segments are all distinct, but the head and thoracic segments are fused to form a large cephalothorax. A carapace covers the cephalothorax, and there is a large gill chamber on each side between the body and the downward extensions of the carapace. The cervical groove of the carapace roughly delimits the head and thoracic regions, and the areola is a narrow more or less hourglass-shaped median area of the carapace just posterior to the cervical groove. The anterior end of the carapace forms an elongated rostrum which bears a short spine (acumen) at its extremity.

The 19 pairs of serially homologous appendages are basically biramous but modified for a wide variety of functions. Detailed accounts of their morphology may be found in most zoology texts and they will be only briefly discussed here. Beginning at the anterior end, each of the first antennae (antennules) has two slender, segmented, sensory flagella. The dorsal surface of the basal segment of the first antenna bears the opening of the statocyst, an organ of balance. The second antenna has a flattened basal scale and a single long flagellum.

The next five pairs of appendages greatly overlap one another and are used chiefly for handling and mincing the food. The heavy, crushing mandibles lie on either side of the mouth. The first maxillae, which follow, are small, flattened, and delicate. Each of the second maxillae has a long, flat extension projecting laterally beyond the point of attachment of this appendage. This is the "bailer"; its rapid beating creates a posterior–anterior current of water through the gill chamber, thereby ensuring a continuous supply of oxygenated water for the gills in the gill chamber. The first, second, and third maxillipeds are progressively more robust and clearly biramous. The third maxillipeds are used for cleaning the antennae.

Fig. 320.–A, dorsal view of *Procambarus*, ×0.7; B, dorsal view of male *Procambarus*, ×0.7.

The last five pairs of appendages of the cephalothorax are large walking legs, or pereiopods (hence the name "Decapoda"). Each consists of seven segments. Beginning at the base, these are as follows: coxa, basis, ischium, merus, carpus, propodus, and dactylus. Sometimes the suffix "podite" is used for each segment; thus: coxopodite, basiopodite, and so on. The coxa and basis are always short and compact. The first three pereiopods are clawed, or chelate, the dactylus being the movable "finger" of the claw, and the propodus constituting the "hand" and immovable finger. The first leg, or chela, is greatly enlarged in the crayfish and is used for crushing the food and as an offensive and defensive weapon. It is of little use in locomotion, walking being chiefly a function of the last four pairs of legs. The second and third legs are also used in handling and mincing the food.

Near the base of the ischium of each walking leg and marked by a double crease is a "breaking joint." When a crayfish leg is seized or irritated, reflex action causes strong contraction of special muscles at the breaking joint, and the whole leg breaks off at this point. Consequently the collector must exercise care if he is to secure suitable specimens. Perfect specimens are uncommon since appendages are often lost as the result of crayfish fighting among themselves. Missing legs are regenerated in miniature at the subsequent molt but later become larger.

The first five abdominal segments bear pleopods, or swimmerets. In the female they are all more or less biramous and are used as places of attachment for the incubating eggs, but in the male the first two pairs are modified and used during copulation. The last abdominal segment bears a flat terminal telson and a pair of flat biramous uropods. The telson and two uropods collectively form the broad tail fan.

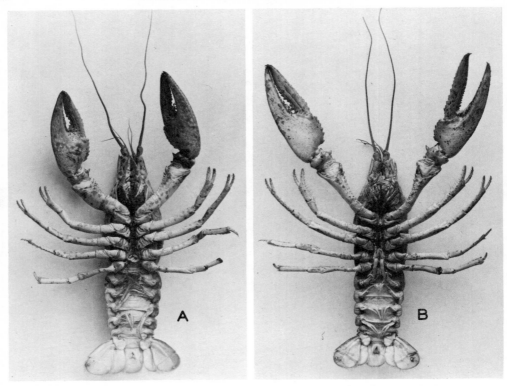

FIG. 321.–A, ventral view of female *Procambarus*, ×0.7; B, ventral view of male *Procambarus*, ×0.7.

Mature crayfish exhibit such sexual dimorphism that there is no difficulty in distinguishing the two sexes. Males usually have the larger chelae and narrower abdomen. In the Cambarine the third segment of some of the male pereiopods bears a small hook used during copulation (Fig. 332E). In the female the genital pores are on the basal segments of the third pereiopods, but in the male they are on the fifth pereiopods. The annulus ventralis, or seminal receptacle, is a grooved, elliptical, calcified area in the midline between the bases of the fourth and fifth pereiopods of the female (Fig. 324). The first pleopods of the female are usually similar to the others, but in the male they have lost their biramous character and are heavily sclerotized, grooved, and specialized at the tip for sperm transfer. The male second pleopods are also somewhat specialized, and both pairs are bent forward so that they lie against the median ventral surface of the body between the bases of the pereiopods.

General body coloration ranges from blackish through brown, red, orange, green, and occasionally blue, with innumerable intermediate shades. Mottling is common, and the pereiopods are often tipped or banded with brighter colors than the rest of the animal. Many species show a wide range of color. *Orconectes immunis*, for example, may be bluish, blackish, brown, greenish, or red. In general, newly molted specimens are more brightly colored than older specimens, especially since the latter usually have an accumulated coat of dirt, debris, and algae.

The coloration of a species often varies in accordance with the coloration of the substrate. In most crayfish such color adaptations are decidedly limited and occur only over a period of weeks or months. In *Palaemonetes paludosus,* however, varia-

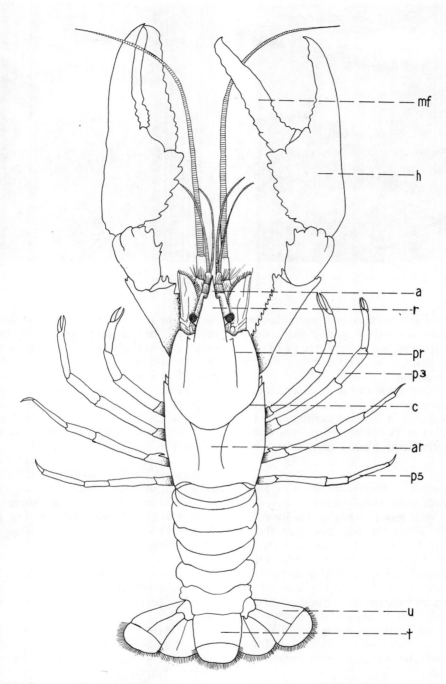

FIG. 322.–Structure of a typical crayfish. *a*, acumen; *ar*, areola; *c*, cervical groove; *h*, hand; *mf*, movable finger of chela; *p3*, third leg (pereiopod); *p5*, fifth leg (pereiopod); *pr*, postorbital ridge; *r*, rostrum; *t*, telson; *u*, uropod. (Modified from Hobbs, 1942a).

Fig. 323.–Fresh-water prawns. Left, *Palaemonetes paludosus,* ×2.5; right, *Syncaris pacifica,* ×1.2.

ble coloration and background resemblance have become developed to a striking degree. This species has four types of chromatophores containing white, red, yellow, and blue pigment granules, respectively, and general body coloration is determined by the relative concentration or dispersion of these granules in various combinations. Color adaptation is completed in less than 24 hours after being placed on a new substrate.

**Locomotion.** Undisturbed crayfish walk or climb about slowly with the pereiopods; they may move forward, backward, or sideways. When alarmed, however, they quickly dart backward by ventrally doubling up the tail fan and the posterior end of the abdomen. They may also leave the substrate and move through the water for short distances by such abdominal contractions. In addition to these two modes of locomotion, the Palaemonidae are distinct swimmers and may move continuously forward through the water by movements of the pleopods.

**Food, feeding.** In general, crayfish are omnivorous but seldom predaceous. They eat all kinds of succulent aquatic vegetation, and animal food is usually a minor part of the diet when there is abundant vegetation. They also prefer fresh to stale meat, and in the laboratory they have been fed raw and cooked meats of all kinds, prepared fish foods, hay, whole seeds, cottonseed meal, and soybean meal. Ecologically, they are usually considered scavengers.

The chelate appendages are used for crushing, picking up the food, and tearing it into pieces. The pieces are then passed forward where they are further cut and masticated by the maxillipeds. The maxillae strain out larger particles and mince the smaller ones further. The mandibles are of limited use in grinding and chewing; mostly they hold food while the maxillipeds tear off fragments.

**Internal anatomy, physiology.** These topics are treated rather completely in most zoology texts and will only be outlined here.

A short esophagus enters a large cardiac chamber of the stomach which, in turn, enters the smaller pyloric chamber. These chambers contain the gastric mill, which is composed of heavy ossicles for grinding the food and rows of stiff setae for straining out larger particles. The long intestine extends to the anus on the ventral side of the telson. Two large glands are associated with the digestive tract in the cephalothorax; they function in digestion, absorption, and food storage.

The pentagonal heart lies in the dorsal portion of the cephalothorax. It receives blood from the surrounding pericardial sinus through three pairs of ostia and sends it out anteriorly, posteriorly, and ventrally through arteries. The blood passes out of the fine terminal endings of the blood vessels and into the various organs and hemocoel. It then circulates back to the sternal sinus, thence to the gills, and back to the pericardial sinus. The blood is almost colorless and contains amoebocytes and a dissolved hemocyanin.

Seventeen or 18 featherlike gills lie within the branchial chamber on each side. They are attached on or near the bases of the maxillipeds and walking legs and extend dorsally. Blood circulates along definite channels through the central stalk and minute lateral processes of each gill.

Excretion and osmotic control are maintained by two complicated, compact green glands which are situated in the anterior end of the cephalothorax and open ventrally at the base of the second antennae. A crayfish does not drink, but quantities of water are continuously diffusing into the blood through the gill surfaces. Blood (minus its proteins) is absorbed by the distal coelomic sac and labyrinth of the green-gland apparatus. As it moves on through the nephridial canal, the useful materials, such as salts, carbohydrates, and some water, are reabsorbed back into the surrounding blood. The material remaining in the canal is a very dilute urine; it passes into the urinary bladder, from which it is periodically voided to the outside through a small pore. There is also some evidence to show that the gills regulate the internal concentration of certain ions, such as sodium.

The nervous system is of the usual crustacean plan, with a ventral nerve cord and chain of ganglia, two circumesophageal connectives, and dorsal brain. The basal segment of each first antenna contains a statocyst, or organ of balance. Taste receptors are especially abundant on the mouth parts and antennae. The antennae are also sensitive tactile organs. The compound eyes are large and consist of hundreds of ommatidia.

In addition to the optic nerve and ganglia, each eyestalk contains a minute sinus gland, an endocrine gland whose secretions influence many important aspects of crayfish behavior and physiology. Among other things, the sinus gland, to a greater or lesser extent, governs: chromatophore contraction, frequency of molting, metabolic rate, growth, viability, and light adaptation of the eyes.

**Reproduction.** With reference to the structure of the first pleopods, there are two distinct types of adult male Cambarinae, first form and second form. The first pleopods of a first form male are corneous, hard, and distinctly sculptured at the tip. In a second form male they are soft and generally lacking in sculpturing. These differences are shown in Figs. 332A, B. Only a first form male is capable of copulating and transferring sperm to the body of a female. Though the instar that precedes the adult first form male is a juvenile instar, the first pleopods are almost indistinguishable from those of a true second form male and for all practical purposes this stage is considered second form. The true second form male, however, is the instar immediately following the first form. Depending on the species and ecological conditions, a true second form male may undergo a further molt to become a first form male again before death. *Orconectes immunis,* for example, is commonly first form during the spring, when copulation occurs, second form during the summer, and first form again beginning in the autumn; copulation may also occur in the autumn. *Pacifastacus* males do not have first and second forms.

Careful work has been done on less than a dozen species in regard to breeding habits, but the available data indicate that time of copulation is variable and occurs between early spring and autumn. In *Orconectes immunis* copulation begins as early as July. *Cambarus diogenes* copulates in the spring. *Palaemonetes paludosus* is thought to copulate in both spring and autumn. *Cambarus bartoni, Orco-*

470    FRESH-WATER INVERTEBRATES

FIG. 324.–Annulus ventralis of female *Procambarus blandingi*. (Redrawn from Hobbs, 1942a).

*nectes propinquus,* and a few other species probably copulate during spring, summer, and autumn, though spring copulation presumably does not occur in the more northern states.

Copulation seems to be more or less a matter of chance, although sex pheromones have been demonstrated in at least one species. The male has no power of sex discrimination, and during the mating season he seizes and turns over every crayfish coming his way. Another male will always resist strongly, but a female will either resist or remain passive and receptive.

The actual process of copulation, sperm transfer, and egg deposition has been described most carefully for *Orconectes limosus* and *Pacifastacus trowbridgi.* The male seizes the female and turns her over on her back. He mounts on her ventral side and holds all her clawed appendages securely with his two chelae. The tips of the first two pleopods are then inserted into the chink of the annulus ventralis, and the tips of the two vasa deferentia are extruded into the bases of the grooves that extend along the first pleopods. Sperm move along these grooves in macaronilike cords and are deposited in the chink. The animals then separate, and either the male or female may copulate later with additional individuals. A single copulation may take from a few minutes to as much as 10 hours. The second pleopods are closely applied to the first during sperm transfer, but their exact function is unknown. After copulation a white waxy plug projects from the chink of the annulus ventralis. In *Pacifastacus* there is no annulus, and the spermatophores are deposited at random on the ventral surface of the female.

The female lays her eggs several weeks to several months after copulation, depending on the season of the year, but before laying them she cleans the ventral side of the abdomen thoroughly with the tips of the pereiopods. Immediately preceding egg extrusion she secretes a sticky, cementlike substance (glair) from ventral glands. The glair covers the ventral surface of the abdomen, tail fan, and pleopods. The sperm plug breaks and sperm are released into the glair. She then lies on her back, curls the abdomen, and releases the eggs from the genital pores. By curious turning movements of the entire body, the eggs become dispersed through the glair, fertilized, and securely attached to the pleopods by a short stalk and surrounding capsule. The female is then said to be "in berry." Most females of nearly all species are seen carrying eggs between March and June. A female may carry as few as 10 eggs and as many as 700. In general, within a species, the larger the female, the greater the number of eggs. Rhythmic movements of the pleopods effectively aerate the developing eggs. Few eggs die.

**Development, life cycle.** The incubation period usually ranges from 2 to 20 weeks, depending largely on temperature, and during this interval the eggs change from dark and opaque to pale and translucent. Hatching involves the rupture and shedding of the embryonic skin and egg membrane, both of which, however, remain attached to the parent pleopod. A newly hatched first instar young clings to the egg stalk with the chelae, and the posterior end remains attached to the cast exoskeleton by a membrane (Fig. 325). Although clearly recognizable as a crayfish, the first instar differs markedly from advanced instars and adults. The cephalothorax is proportionately very large; the rostrum is large, pointed, and bent downward; the eyes are large; the chelae are slender; and there are no first and sixth abdominal appendages. The first instar usually persists for two to seven days, and when it molts the posterior connection with the remains of the egg is lost. The second instar lasts for about 4 to 12 days and remains attached to the pleopods of the mother with its chelae and pereiopods. Third instar crayfish leave the parent pleopods intermittently and then permanently. The young of burrowing species leave the burrow of the mother when they have a body length of 8 to 20 mm. Individuals hatching in the spring usually have a total of 6 to 10 molts by autumn, when growth and molting cease. In the fresh-water Palaemonidae there are five to eight larval molts. During these early instars the body and its appendages gradually assume adult proportions and anatomical details.

Great differences in growth rate may be found within a single pond or stream, the larger specimens being twice or more as long as the smaller ones by autumn. Such differential growth rates are probably due mainly to varying activity and amounts of food consumed.

By autumn many females are sexually mature and many males are first form, so that copulation commonly occurs in the first autumn of life. Some females, however, do not become sexually mature until after a molt early the following spring; similarly, some males do not become first form until after one or two spring molts. Such

individuals copulate in the spring, and the female is in berry after a very short interval. Some females that copulate in the autumn are not in berry until the following spring. Other species, especially burrowers, copulate and are in berry in the autumn. The young leave the burrow some time during the following spring or summer.

Subsequent to the first mating season, most crayfish have only two to four molts before they die. Following copulation, a female does not molt until after her third-instar young have left her. If a male is first form in its first autumn, it usually remains first form during the winter, molts to second form early in the following spring, and after a very short interval molts back again to first form. Such males may therefore copulate again during their second summer or autumn. Among the few species on which life history studies have been made, the normal life span of both male and female crayfish is usually less than 24 months, and a few survive their second winter. Females that pass through a second winter may be in berry for the second time the following spring. Lyle (1938) reports an exceptional longevity for *Procambarus hagenianus* (Faxon) in Mississippi and Alabama, the species attaining an age of six or seven years.

The molting processes are a complex physiological cycle that is modified and controlled chiefly by temperature, light, and hormonal interrelationships.

**Ecology.** Adults remain hidden in their burrows, under stones or debris, or half buried in small depressions in the substrate during the daytime, but between dusk and dawn they feed and move about, even to the extent of coming out on banks of streams and ponds. In shaded streams, however, and especially on cloudy days, adults may venture into open water in daylight. Immature specimens of most species, on the other hand, regularly crawl about actively on the bottom and in vegetation during the daytime.

There is some evidence to show that the 24-hour cycle of activity is governed by an endogenous mechanism. Solar and lunar rhythms have also been suggested.

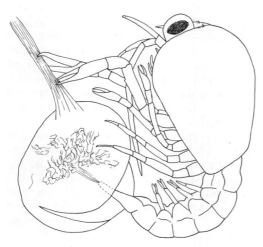

Fig. 325.–Newly hatched first instar of *Orconectes limosus*, ×28. Note claw fastened to stalk of egg shell and abdomen attached to cast skin inside of egg shell. (Modified from Andrews, 1904.)

Fig. 326.–Typical crayfish chimney.

Many crayfish have specific habitat requirements. Some are burrowers in wet meadows and do not enter bodies of water; some occur only in muddy ponds and ditches; some are found only in lakes or slow rivers; others are restricted to swift, stony streams. The preferences of representative species are included in the key that follows.

Closely related species sometimes have similar ranges but are ecologically isolated within these ranges. For example, *Orconectes virilis* and *O. immunis* are often found in the same area but the former is restricted to streams and lake margins, and the latter to ponds and sloughs.

Crayfish are generally inhabitants of shallow waters, seldom being found deeper than a meter. An exceptional record is the occurrence of *Orconectes virilis* at a depth of 30 m in Lake Michigan. Most species tolerate normal but wide ranges in temperature, hydrogen-ion concentration, and free and bound carbon dioxide, though stream species are usually less tolerant than lake and pond species. During winter months crayfish are found in deeper waters of lakes. Similar migrations during the warm months are thought to be associated with gonad maturation. In streams, however, some investigators have found that most individuals have a home range of less than 30 m.

Population densities vary greatly, depending on the species and habitat. Pond populations usually amount to less than 100 lb per acre, but in exceptional cases may attain 500, 1000, or even 1500 lb per acre. In general, stream populations are less dense, although there is one record of 1176 lb of crayfish per acre. Abrahamson and Goldman (1970) calculated an average of 0.9 adult *Pacifastacus leniusculus* per square meter in Lake Tahoe.

Several laboratory studies have shown that in groups of four to eight crayfish, dominance–subdominance relationships soon become established in a linear fashion, and that the dominance order is based on size and learned recognition of individuals. Such work has been done on several species of *Orconectes*, *Procambarus*, and *Cambarellus*.

A few studies have shown that crayfish have a remarkable daily cycle in their oxygen consumption. Fingerman (1955), for example, showed that *Cambarellus shufeldti* had its highest oxygen consumption around 6 A.M., with a secondary maximum at 3 to 6 P.M. Minima occurred from 9 A.M. to noon and from 9 P.M. to midnight.

**Burrows.** Some species, such as *Procambarus gracilis* and *Cambarus carolinus*, habitually burrow in wet pastures and marshy areas where there is no open water.

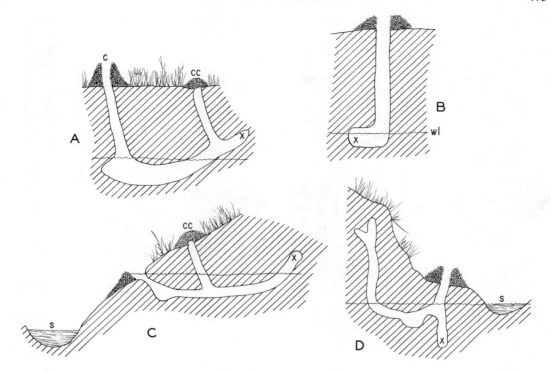

FIG. 327.–Typical crayfish burrows. *c*, chimney and opening of burrow; *cc*, closed chimney; *s*, stream; *wl*, ground water level; *x*, place where crayfish were taken. (A, C, and D modified from Ortmann, 1906.)

Species in a second group live in bodies of water during the greater part of the year, but when streams or ponds dry up in late summer or when the temperature drops in the autumn they construct burrows along the margins and live in them until the water level rises and the weather becomes warmer. *Procambarus simulans, P. blandingi,* and *Orconectes immunis* are included in this group. Species of a third group live continuously in permanent waters and do not make burrows.

Burrows differ widely in construction, depending on the species, the soil, and the depth of the water table (Fig. 327). Usually there is only one entrance, though there may be as many as three. The tunnel leading from the entrance may proceed vertically, at an angle, or almost laterally in a sloping bank. Sometimes the tunnels are branched or irregular, but there is always a chamber at the lower end where the crayfish remains during the hours of daylight. Occasionally a burrow has a lateral chamber. The depth of a burrow ranges from 5 cm to as much as 3 m and is partially determined by the level of the water table, since the chamber must contain water to keep the gills wet. Burrows close to the edge of a pond or stream are shallow, those farther away are deeper.

Except during the breeding season, each burrow houses a single crayfish. Burrows are constructed only at night, and the crayfish brings up pellets of mud and deposits them at the entrance to form a chimney. Such chimneys are usually about 15 cm high, but a few as high as 45 cm have been reported. They do not serve any particular purpose, but are simply the result of the safest and most convenient method of disposing of the mud pellets.

**Geographic distribution, dispersal.** The Cambarinae are restricted to North America, and Ortmann (1905) postulated the origin of this subfamily between Cretaceous and Tertiary times in central Mexico. From

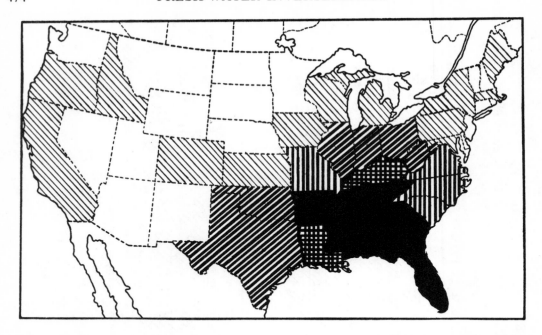

FIG. 328.–Relative distribution of crayfish in the 48 contiguous states. Solid black—more than 40 species and subspecies; cross hatched—31 to 40; vertical lines—21 to 30; coarse diagonal lines—11 to 20; fine diagonal lines—5 to 10; unshaded—less than 5. (Data from Hobbs, 1972.)

this area there was a general spread into the southern United States, where several centers of dispersal arose.

Ancestors of the present species of *Procambarus* are thought to have originated in Mexico and migrated to the general region of Kansas, Oklahoma, Texas, Arkansas, and Louisiana. From there, one group of species migrated northward as far as Wisconsin. A second group migrated eastward to the southern Appalachians where a new large center of dispersal later expanded out extensively up and down the Atlantic coast, as far north as Michigan and Ohio, and eventually as far west as Texas and Oklahoma.

*Orconectes* is thought to have arisen at the junctions of the Ohio, Mississippi, and Missouri rivers and radiated out in all directions as far as Colorado, Wyoming, southern Canada, Lake Superior, the St. Lawrence valley, and the Gulf states. A few species even crossed the divide and reached Atlantic coast drainages.

*Cambarus* is thought to have arisen in Tennessee (Hobbs, 1969). Early migration

occurred mainly in a northeasterly direction at high altitudes, but later some species invaded the lowlands, spread out in all directions, and attained a very wide distribution.

*Cambarellus* originated in Mexico or extreme southern United States and migrated eastward through the Gulf states.

The five American species of *Pacifastacus* are restricted to Pacific slope drainages, although one has migrated over to the Great Basin and headwaters of the Missouri River. The genus probably originated in the Old World, where a total of only about 11 species occur in northern Europe and Asia.

In general, speciation has proceeded most rapidly in the southeastern states, as shown in Fig. 328.

Dry land forms an effective barrier to the migration and geographical spread of lake and stream species, but burrowers such as *Cambarus diogenes* have migrated rapidly and are now found commonly in wet meadows east of the Rocky Mountains.

Male first form *Procambarus clarki* spawn in the autumn and then migrate overland by the thousands. Such exhausted males are weak and soon die; it is doubtful whether they contribute appreciably to the spread of the species.

Restriction to specific aquatic habitats forms a partial barrier for many species. *Procambarus blandingi,* for example, is restricted to sluggish streams and stagnant waters and cannot migrate upstream into rapid water drainage areas.

*Orconectes virilis* and *O. immunis* form an interesting example of ecological isolation. The two species are very closely related and are often in the same general geographic areas. Yet the former occurs only in clear, running waters with stony bottoms, whereas the latter is restricted to stagnant waters and mud bottoms. Very little is known about interspecific competition among crayfishes.

Many species, especially in the southern states, are known only from a single state or single collecting locality.

Several American crayfishes have been intentionally introduced into Europe, dating back to the transportation of *Orconectes limosus* into France as early as 1890; it is now widely distributed in western Europe. *Pacifastacus leniusculus* was brought to Sweden and *Procambarus clarki* into both Hawaii and Japan.

**Cave crayfish.** Perhaps some of the most interesting examples of ecological isolation are to be found among those subterranean crayfish and shrimp that are restricted to the waters of single caves, cave systems, large springs, and sinks.

Cave species are strikingly modified for that environment (Fig. 329). They are mostly small, the body length ranging from 10 to 80 mm. The body is slender, the chelae are not well developed, and the antennae and other appendages are very long and highly specialized as tactile organs. Pigmentation is absent, and the body is translucent or whitish. All are blind, the eyes being atrophied and the eyestalks reduced or rudimentary. About 21 North American crayfish species and subspecies are true troglobites.

In addition to true troglobitic species, there are some which are normally found above ground but have migrated into caves where they have successfully persisted. With the exception of one or two species which have become differentiated into subspecies, these forms are identical with individuals occurring above ground.

**Parasites, commensals, enemies.** The external surfaces of crayfish form a convenient and favorable habitat for microorganisms, and when the exoskeleton has not been shed for a long time it is often covered with debris and a dense growth of algae and sessile Protozoa, especially at winter's end.

The Branchiobdellida (see page 290) are small, leechlike, parasitic or commensal oligochaetes that live on the gills, in the gill chambers, on the general body surface, and at the bases of the legs, antennae, and mouth parts. A genus of ostracods, *Entocythere,* is commensal on the gills (see page 434).

Many species of crayfish east of the Mississippi River may act as the second intermediate host of *Paragonimus westermani,* a lung fluke parasitic in man and many carnivores. The metacercariae of this parasite become imbedded in the muscles and viscera of the crayfish from which they may be transmitted to the definitive host when the raw or poorly cooked crayfish are used as food.

Fish are the most important enemies of crayfish, although wading birds, frogs, turtles, raccoons, otter, and mink consume appreciable numbers.

**Economic importance.** In poorly drained clay agricultural lands of West Virginia, Mississippi, Alabama, and a few other southern states burrowing crayfish become so abundant (as many as 30,000 burrows per acre) that crops cannot be raised because of the fact that the crayfish denude the land of the young grain, sugarcane, and cotton seedlings. Also, their chimneys clog farm machinery. If the land cannot be drained, the best control is the application of some poison to the burrows. Pyrethrum, creosote, cyanide, carbon disulfide, and unslaked lime are some of the more useful poisons. They are most effective when the water table is high. Bait poi-

FIG. 329.–Male *Orconectes pellucidus* (Tellkampf), ×1.7, a cave species. (Modified from Hay, 1893.)

soned with DDT and spread over infested areas is a more recent control measure.

Occasionally crayfish become a nuisance in small reservoirs and irrigation ditches when their lateral burrows through earthen dams and dikes drain the reservoirs.

Europeans use crayfish for the table to a much greater extent than do Americans. Most of the edible crayfish in this country come from the Great Lakes, certain parts of the Mississippi River system, Louisiana, and Oregon. The harvest has greatly declined during the past 30 or 40 years, although in 1960 (Power, 1962) 717,000 lb came from the Gulf coast, 609,000 lb from the Mississippi River drainage, 29,000 lb from Pacific coast drainages, and only 2000 lb from the Great Lakes area. Probably the majority of these animals were dissected in the laboratory in college zoology courses or were used as fish bait.

Small species of crayfish have been raised experimentally at hatcheries for use as fish food, but the practice has not attained any importance.

It has been shown that when it is introduced into weedy trout lakes, at least one species (*Orconectes causeyi*) can keep aquatic vegetation grazed down so that such lakes become much more favorable trout habitats.

**Collection, preparation.** Stream and pond species may be collected with long-handled dipnets, minnow seines, and minnow traps. When crayfish are not abundant, however, it is often necessary to collect by hand and examine overhanging banks, masses of vegetation, and the undersides of submerged logs and stones.

A skillful collector with a headlamp may find it profitable to collect burrowers (as well as open-water species) at night, when they usually leave the burrow and roam about, but often there is no alternative but to dig up the burrow carefully with a spade or trowel until the specimen can be taken in its chamber. Surface traps baited with meat or peanut butter will sometimes take burrowing crayfish.

Crayfish should be killed in 5 percent formalin or 80 percent alcohol and stored in a change to 70 percent alcohol. This preservative keeps the joints pliable. Some workers remove the male first pleopods and the female annulus ventralis, dehydrate in absolute alcohol, clear in xylol, and mount on insect pins.

**Taxonomy.** In 1902 only 66 species of North American Cambarinae were known, but now there are about 300 from the United States alone, most of the additional species having been described from southern states. In addition, some of the common and widely distributed species are represented by several well-defined subspecies.

Characters that are useful for identifying both males and females of certain genera and species include the structure of the rostrum, shape of the areola, structure of the chelae, spines on the cephalothorax, and general body proportions. Unfortunately, however, most species can be identified only from first form males, particularly by the copulatory hooks on some of the legs and the detailed morphology of the first pleopods. In making collections in the field it is therefore essential to get first form males whenever possible.

Beginning with the publication of Hagen's monograph in 1870, various classification schemes for the Cambarinae have been suggested. Most of these publications recognized only a single genus, *Cambarus*, with a series of subgenera or "groups." Beginning in 1942, however, Hobbs proposed a more logical and revised classification in which the Subfamily Cambarinae was subdivided and now contains seven genera. The following key is modified from Hobbs (1972) and includes all genera and the more common species. Total lengths extend from the tip of the acumen to the posterior edge of the telson.

## KEY TO GENERA AND SPECIES OF DECAPODA

**1.** First three pairs of legs chelate; cephalothorax subcylindrical; abdomen more or less flattened dorsoventrally (Figs. 320, 321) .................ASTACIDAE, **2**
First two pairs of legs chelate; cephalothorax and abdomen laterally compressed (Figs. 323, 336) ...............................................................**32**

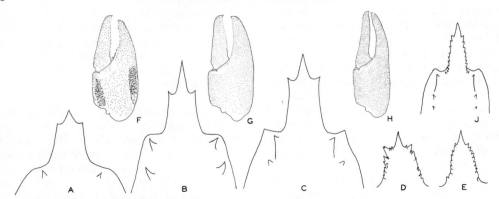

Fig. 330.–Structure of *Pacifastacus*. A to C, anterior end of *P. leniusculus*; D, rostrum of *P. nigrescens*; E, rostrum of *P. gambeli*; F, chela of *P. gambeli*; G, chela of *P. fortis*; H, chela of *P. nigrescens*; J, anterior end of *P. connectens*. (F to H from Hobbs, 1972.)

  2. Ischia of pereiopods of male without hooks; male first pleopods simply rolled at tips; female without first pleopods; up to 110 mm long; except in the upper Missouri River, found only west of the Continental Divide.
      ASTACINAE, **Pacifastacus, 3**
    Ischia of one or more pairs of pereiopods with hooks (Fig. 332E); male first pleopods bifid or toothed at tips (Fig. 331); female with first pleopods; chiefly east of the Continental Divide. (Beyond this point in this key most key characters apply only to first form males; females can be tentatively identified only by "association" with the males) ..............................................7
  3. Rostrum with a single pair of marginal tubercles or spines (Figs. 330A–C); a complex species found in streams and lakes of Washington, Oregon, California, Idaho, and Nevada ...............................**Pacifastacus leniusculus** Dana
    Rostrum with at least three pairs of marginal spines (Figs. 330D, E, J) ............**4**
  4. Palm of chela with two conspicuous dorsal patches of setae (Fig. 330F) ..........**5**
    Palm of chela without patches of setae ......................................**6**
  5. Postorbital ridges with one or two posterior pairs of spines or tubercles (Fig. 330J); Idaho and Oregon streams ................. **Pacifastacus connectens** (Faxon)
    Postorbital ridges without posterior spines or tubercles; streams and lakes of Washington, Oregon, California, Idaho, Nevada, Utah, Montana, and Wyoming.
      **Pacifastacus gambeli** (Girard)
  6. Palm of chela broad (Fig. 330G); streams of Shasta County, California.
      **Pacifastacus fortis** (Faxon)
    Palm of chela slim (Fig. 330H); streams of San Francisco area.
      **Pacifastacus nigrescens** (Stimpson)
  7. Ischia of second pereiopods without hooks .................. CAMBARINAE, **8**
    Ischia of second and third pereiopods with hooks; five small species, usually 15 to 30 mm long; Florida to Texas and north to Illinois, Tennessee, and Arkansas.
      CAMBARELLINAE, **Cambarellus**
  8. Body pigmented; eyes with facets and pigment ...............................**12**
    Albinistic species; eyes rarely faceted and pigment greatly reduced or absent; usually in underground waters .........................................**9**
  9. Ischium of third maxilliped without teeth along inner margin; about 30 mm long; known only from a few subterranean waters in Florida.
      **Troglocambarus maclanei** Hobbs
    Ischium of third maxilliped with teeth along inner margin......................**10**
  10. First pleopod terminating in two large elements that are strongly bent (Fig. 331A); eight species in White River, Missouri, Tennessee, Alabama, Georgia, Oklahoma, and Florida ........................................**Cambarus**
    First pleopod with two or more small terminal elements, bent only slightly (Figs. 331B, C) ....................................................**11**

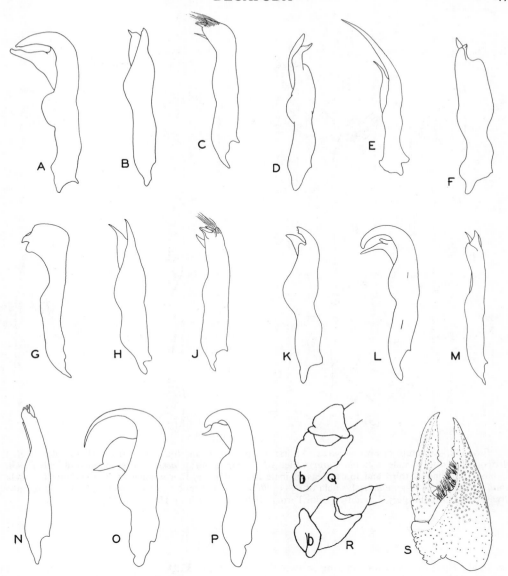

FIG. 331.–Structure of Cambarinae. A to P, first pleopods. A, *Cambarus*; B, *Orconectes*; C, *Procambarus*; D, *Procambarus*; E, *Faxonella*; F and G, *Procambarus*; H, *Hobbseus*; J, *Procambarus*; K, *Cambarus*; L, *Fallicambarus*; M and N, *Procambarus*; O, *Cambarus*; P, *Fallicambarus*; Q and R, base of fourth leg of *Procambarus* showing boss (*b*); S, right chela of *Fallicambarus*. (A to P, S from Hobbs, 1972.)

**11.** First pleopod with two terminal elements (Fig. 331B); four species in Kentucky, Tennessee, Alabama, and Indiana...............................**Orconectes**
First pleopod with two or more elements (Fig. 331C); if only two, then cephalic surface with strong shoulder (Fig. 331D); four species in Alabama and Florida..............................................**Procambarus**
**12.** First pleopod terminating in two elements, of which one is very long and slender and the other is no more than half as long (Fig. 331E); three species in sluggish waters of South Carolina to Florida and west to Oklahoma and Texas. **Faxonella**
First pleopod terminating in two or more elements; if there are two elements, then the shorter element is more than half as long as the other ...................13

FIG. 332.–Structure of *Procambarus*. A, first pleopod of second form male *Procambarus blandingi*; B, first pleopod of first form male of *P. blandingi*; C, left first pleopod of *P. clarki*; D, first pleopod of male *P. simulans*; E, basal portions of third and fourth legs of male *Procambarus*; F, carapace of *P. simulans*; G, chela of *P. simulans*; H, chela of *P. clarki*; J, chela of *P. gracilis*. (A and B modified from Hobbs, 1942a; D redrawn from Creaser and Ortenburger; E modified from Turner, 1926; G and J from Hobbs, 1972.)

13. First pleopod terminating in two elements (Figs. 331A, O. P; 332C, D) . . . . . . . . . . **14**
    First pleopod terminating in more than two elements (Figs. 331C, J, L–N) . . . . . . .**18**
14. First pleopod generally as in Figs. 332C, D; usually with short processes; about 80
    taxa in this genus, mostly with restricted distributions in southeastern states;
    the four most widely distributed and common species are keyed here.
                                                                    **Procambarus, 20**
    First pleopod with two prominent processes, more or less curved (Figs. 331A, O. P). **15**
15. Coxa of fourth pereiopod without a boss . . . . . . . . . . . . . . . . . . . . . . . . . . . . . . . . . . .**16**
    Coxa of fourth pereiopod with a boss (Figs. 331Q, R) . . . . . . . . . . . . . . . . . . . . . . . .**17**
16. In resting position, first pleopods deep along the midline, hidden by a dense mat of
    setae at the base of the pereiopods; five species in Mississippi and
    Alabama . . . . . . . . . . . . . . . . . . . . . . . . . . . . . . . . . . . . . . . . . . . . . . . . . . . . . **Hobbseus**
    In resting position, first pleopods not concealed along the midline; about 60 species,
    mostly with local distributions in southeastern states, but seven widely distrib-
    uted species are keyed here . . . . . . . . . . . . . . . . . . . . . . . . . . . . . . . . . **Orconectes, 23**

Fig. 333.–Structure of *Cambarus* and *Orconectes*. A, first pleopod of male *Cambarus bartoni*; B, first pleopod of male *Orconectes propinquus*; C, carapace of *Cambarus bartoni*; D, chela of *C. bartoni*; E, left first pleopod of *Orconectes virilis*; F, carapace of *Cambarus carolinus*; G, carapace of *C. diogenes*; H, chela of *C. diogenes*; J, chela of *Fallicambarus fodiens*; K, left first pleopod of *Orconectes neglectus*; L, left first pleopod of *O. propinquus*; M, left first pleopod of *O. obscurus*; N, left first pleopod of *O. immunis*. (A to C redrawn from Turner, 1926; D modified from Ortmann, 1906; G redrawn from Hobbs, 1942a; H and J modified from Huntsman, 1915; E, K to N from Hobbs, 1972.)

**17.** Dactyl of chela with a prominent excision on the basal half (Fig. 333J); about 10 species in Louisiana, Arkansas, Tennessee, Mississippi, Florida, Maryland to South Carolina, and one species [*F. fodiens* (Cottle)] more generally distributed east of the Mississippi River .......................... **Fallicambarus**

Dactyl of chela without a prominent excision on the basal half (Fig. 333D); about 55 species, mostly with restricted distributions in southeastern states, but four widely distributed species are keyed here .................... **Cambarus, 29**

**18.** Central projection of first pleopod bladelike, always directed caudally, and bearing a notch (Fig. 331K) (see couplet 17 information) .............. **Cambarus, 29**

Central projection of first pleopod rarely bladelike, but if present then directed laterodistally or lacking a notch (Figs. 331C, F, G, J, L) .....................**19**

**19.** First pleopod with large curved processes (Fig. 331L) (see couplet 17 distribution data)........................................................ **Fallicambarus**

First pleopod with small processes (Figs. 331C, F, G, J) (see couplet 14 information) ...........................................**Procambarus, 20**

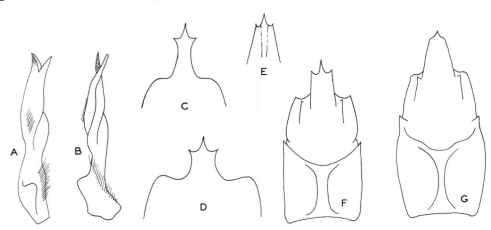

FIG. 334.–Structure of *Orconectes*. A and B, first pleopod of male *O. limosus*; C and D, rostrum of *O. rusticus*; E, rostrum of *O. propinquus*; F, carapace of *O. virilis*; G, carapace of *O. immunis*. (A and B redrawn from Ortmann, 1906; F and G redrawn from Turner, 1926.)

20. Cephalic surface of first pleopod with a prominent shoulder (Fig. 332C); hooks on ischia of both third and fourth pereiopods (Fig. 332E); lentic and lotic habitats from Illinois to Texas and California; introduced in California, Nevada, Virginia, and probably elsewhere; the common "swamp crayfish."
**Procambarus clarki** (Girard)
    Cephalic surface of first pleopod without such a prominent shoulder . . . . . . . . . . . .**21**
21. Hooks on ischia of third periopods only; common burrowers . . . . . . . . . . . . . . . . . .**22**
    Hooks on ischia of third and fourth periopods (Fig. 332E); streams and lentic habitats from Maine to Florida and westward from Minnesota to Texas.
**Procambarus acutus** (Girard)
22. Chela relatively slender (Fig. 332G); lentic and lotic habitats in New Mexico, Colorado, Kansas, Oklahoma, Arkansas, and Louisiana.
**Procambarus simulans** (Faxon)
    Chela relatively stout (Fig. 332J); in muddy streams and ponds; Wisconsin south to Arkansas and Texas . . . . . . . . . . . . . . . . . . . . . . **Procambarus gracilis** (Bundy)
23. Terminal processes of first pleopod less than one-quarter of the total length (Figs. 333B, L, N; 334A, B) . . . . . . . . . . . . . . . . . . . . . . . . . . . . . . . . . . . . . . . . .**24**
    Terminal processes of first pleopod more than one-quarter of the total length (Figs. 333E, K) . . . . . . . . . . . . . . . . . . . . . . . . . . . . . . . . . . . . . . . . . . . . . . . .**27**
24. Terminal processes of first pleopod strongly curved (Fig. 333N); sluggish streams and ponds; New England west to Wyoming and south to Alabama; a burrower; the "mud crayfish" . . . . . . . . . . . . . . . . . . . . . . . . . . . . . **Orconectes immunis** (Hagen)
    Terminal processes of first pleopod not strongly curved . . . . . . . . . . . . . . . . . . . . .**25**
25. Terminal processes of first pleopod divergent (Figs. 334A, B); general color olivegreen to olive-yellow; seldom in burrows; common in larger rivers of Atlantic coastal plain from Maine to Virginia . . . . . . . . . . . . . . **Orconectes limosus** (Raf.)
    Terminal processes of first pleopod not divergent (Figs. 333B, L) . . . . . . . . . . . . . .**26**
26. Rostrum with median keel (Fig. 334E); general color gray to olive-green; streams, rivers, and lakes, especially on stony substrates; Great Lakes crayfish, gray rock crayfish; northeastern quarter of the United States, especially Mississippi, Ohio, and Great Lakes drainages . . . . . . . . . . . .**Orconectes propinquus** (Girard)
    Rostrum without median keel; general color olive-green; Allegheny crayfish; large streams of upper Ohio drainage, New York to Ohio and West Virginia.
**Orconectes obscurus** (Hagen)
27. Sides of rostrum slightly concave (Figs. 334C, D); streams and lakes in New England to Illinois and Kentucky; introduced elsewhere . . .**Orconectes rusticus** (Girard)
    Sides of rostrum not concave (Figs. 334E, F) . . . . . . . . . . . . . . . . . . . . . . . . . . . . .**28**

FIG. 335.–Structure of *Palaemonetes*. A, lateral view of anterior end of carapace of *P. kadiakensis*; B, dorsal view of telson of *P. kadiakensis*; C, lateral view of anterior end of carapace of *P. paludosus*; D, dorsal view of telson of *P. paludosus*; E, basal portion of first antenna of *P. paludosus*; F, basal portion of first antenna of *P. hiltoni*; G, basal portion of first antenna of *P. vulgaris*; H, lateral view of anterior end of *P. vulgaris*; J, lateral view of anterior end of *P. intermedius*; K, lateral view of anterior end of *P. pugio*. (All modified from Holthuis.)

28. Rostrum with median keel (Fig. 334E); coloration yellowish; clear lotic waters in Arkansas, Missouri, Oklahoma, Kansas, Nebraska, and Colorado.
                 **Orconectes neglectus** (Faxon)
  Rostrum without a keel (Fig. 334F); northern crayfish; lakes, streams, and rivers in northeastern states but widely introduced elsewhere. **Orconectes virilis** (Hagen)

29. Areola wide (Fig. 333C); general color green to brownish; burrows only rarely; in springs and small streams, occasional in large streams; common and generally distributed east of Mississippi River except for southern states.
                 **Cambarus bartoni** (Fabr.)
  Areola narrow, linear, or obliterated in middle (Figs. 333F, G) . . . . . . . . . . . . . . . . . .30

30. Areola narrow but not linear (Fig. 333F); the red crayfish; burrows in swampy pastures and fields; Allegheny Mountains and foothills. **Cambarus carolinus** (Erichson)
  Areola linear or obliterated (Fig. 333G) . . . . . . . . . . . . . . . . . . . . . . . . . . . . . . . . . . . .31

31. Areola obliterated at midlength (Fig. 333G); general color greenish to brownish; burrows in wet fields and marshy areas; resorts to ponds and streams only during breeding season; the solitary crayfish; common and generally distributed east of the Continental Divide . . . . . . . . . . . . . . . . . . **Cambarus diogenes** Girard
  Areola linear; lotic waters from New York to Illinois and south to Tennessee, North Carolina, and Virginia . . . . . . . . . . . . . . . . . . . . . . . . **Cambarus robustus** Girard

32. Second chelae larger than first, and without terminal hair tufts (Figs. 336H,J) . . . . . . . . . . . . . . . . . . . . . . . . . . . . . . . . . . . . . . . . . .PALAEMONIDAE, 36
  First and second chelae subequal, with terminal hair tufts (Fig. 336K). ATYIDAE, 33

33. Eyestalks rudimentary, no trace of facets or pigments; translucent; 10 to 23 mm long . . . . . . . . . . . . . . . . . . . . . . . . . . . . . . . . . . . . . . . . . . . **Palaemonias, 34**
  Eyes well developed; usually 20 to 50 mm long . . . . . . . . . . . . . . . . . . . . . .**Syncaris, 35**

34. Rostrum with about 30 dorsal and eight ventral spines; Mammoth Cave, Kentucky . . . . . . . . . . . . . . . . . . . . . . . . . . . . . . . . . . . . .**Palaemonias ganteri** Hay
  Rostrum with 5 to 13 dorsal and zero to two ventral spines; Shelta Cave, Huntsville, Alabama . . . . . . . . . . . . . . . . . . . . . . . . . . . . . . **Palaemonias alabamae** Smalley

35. Upper margin of rostrum with one or two spines, lower margin with five to nine spines; supraorbital spine present (Fig. 336L); small coastal streams north of San Francisco Bay ........................... **Syncaris pacifica** (Holmes)
    Upper margin of rostrum without spines, lower margin with few spines; supraorbital spine present or absent; last recorded from coastal streams near Los Angeles, California, but probably now extinct .......... **Syncaris pasadenae** (Holmes)
36. Second legs only slightly longer than first (Fig. 336A); usually 25 to 45 mm long; fresh-water prawns, glass shrimps ............................ **Palaemonetes, 37**
    Second legs much longer than first (Fig. 336F); river shrimps ... **Macrobrachium, 44**
37. Eyes pigmented, cornea well developed; second legs longer and stouter than first; not subterranean ...................................................... **39**
    Eyes unpigmented, cornea degenerate; first and second legs subequal; up to 18 mm long; subterranean ............................................... **38**
38. Rostrum with teeth on both upper and lower margins; reported only from a small solution sink in Alachua County, Florida ..... **Palaemonetes cummingi** Chace
    Rostrum without teeth on the ventral margin; reported only from subterranean waters near San Marcos, Texas ................. **Palaemonetes antrorum** Benedict
39. Fused portion of the two rami of upper flagellum of first antenna longer than free portion of the shorter ramus (Fig. 335E); carpopodite of second leg longer than claw; fresh waters ................................................ **40**
    Fused portion of the two rami of upper flagellum of first antenna shorter than free portion of the shorter ramus (Figs. 335F, G); carpopodite of second leg shorter than claw; brackish or salt water ..................................... **41**
40. Branchiostegal spine on anterior margin of carapace, just below branchiostegal groove (Fig. 335C); posterior pair of dorsal spines of telson situated midway between anterior pair and posterior margin of telson (Fig. 335D); up to 46 mm long; common in Atlantic coast drainages from New Jersey to Florida; rare in central United States and southern California ...... **Palaemonetes paludosus** (Gibbes)
    Branchiostegal spine removed from anterior margin of carapace, below branchiostegal groove (Fig. 335A); posterior pair of dorsal spines of telson placed close to posterior margin of telson (Fig. 335B); up to 50 mm long; sporadic in central third of the United States, west of Alleghenies, and from Canada to the Gulf ................................. **Palaemonetes kadiakensis** Rathbun
41. Anterior margin of basal segment of first antenna extending farther forward than anterolateral spine of this segment (Fig. 335F); body up to 24 mm long; rare in brackish waters of southern California ......... **Palaemonetes hiltoni** (Schmitt)
    Anterior margin of basal segment of first antenna not extending farther forward than anterolateral spine of this segment (Fig. 335G); Massachusetts to Texas .... **42**
42. Rostrum with first two teeth of dorsal margin posterior to orbit; lower margin of rostrum with three to five teeth (Fig. 335H); body up to 42 mm long; salt and brackish waters ............................. **Palaemonetes vulgaris** (Say)
    Rostrum with only one dorsal tooth behind orbit (Figs. 335J, K) ................ **43**
43. Dorsal teeth of rostrum reaching apex, which is often bifid; lower margin of rostrum with four or five, seldom three teeth (Fig. 335J); up to 37 mm long; brackish waters ............................... **Palaemontes intermedius** Holthuis
    Dorsal teeth of rostrum not reaching apex; lower margin of rostrum with two to four, generally three teeth (Fig. 335K); up to 50 mm long; brackish to nearly fresh waters ................................. **Palaemonetes pugio** Holthuis
44. Carpopodite of second leg shorter than claw; rostrum with about three teeth posterior to margin of orbit and three to five ventral teeth (Figs. 336C–E) ......... **45**
    Carpopodite of second leg about as long as claw (Fig. 336H); rostrum usually with a single tooth posterior to margin of orbit and about six ventral teeth (Fig. 336B); body up to 170 mm long; rivers of Florida to Texas; sometimes in brackish waters ......................... **Macrobrachium acanthurus** (Wiegmann)
45. Claw of second leg without prominent teeth or hairy covering (Fig. 336F); up to 95 mm long; North Carolina to Texas, and Mississippi and Ohio rivers and their main tributaries as far north as Oklahoma, Missouri, Illinois, Indiana, Virginia and Ohio ................................ **Macrobrachium ohione** (Smith)
    Claw of second leg with hair or teeth .......................................... **46**

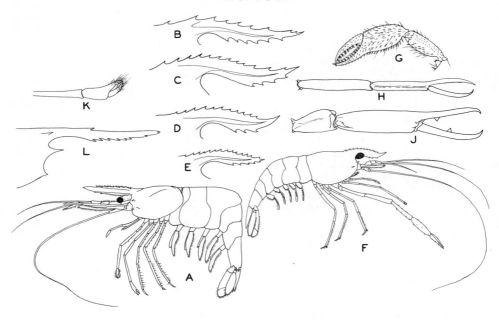

FIG. 336.–Structure of Palaemonidae and Atyidae. A, *Palaemonetes paludosus,* ×1.6; B, rostrum of *Macrobrachium acanthurus*; C, rostrum of *M. carcinus*; D, rostrum of *M. ohione*; E, rostrum of *M. olfersi*; F, *M. ohione,* ×0.6; G, large chela of male *M. olfersi*; H, chela of *M. acanthurus* (spines and setae omitted); J, chela of *M. carcinus* (spines and setae omitted); K, second chela of *Syncaris pacifica*; L, anterior end of carapace of *S. pacifica.* (A modified from Creaser, 1939; B to F redrawn from Hedgpeth, 1947; G to J modified from Hedgpeth, 1949.)

**46.** Claw of second leg similar in both sexes, with a broad triangular tooth on each finger
(Fig. 336J); body up to 240 mm long; rivers, spring brooks, and springs in
Florida and Texas . . . . . . . . . . . . . . . . . . . . . . . . .**Macrobrachium carcinus** (L.)
Claw of second leg on one side in male greatly enlarged, armed with spines and tufts
or bristles (Fig. 336G); body up to 90 mm long; vicinity of St. Augustine,
Florida . . . . . . . . . . . . . . . . . . . . . . . . . . . . . **Macrobrachium olfersi** (Wiegmann)

# DECAPODA REFERENCES

ABRAHAMSON, S. A. A., and C. R. GOLDMAN. 1970. Distribution, density and production of the crayfish Pacifastacus leniusculus Dana in Lake Tahoe, California-Nevada. *Oikos* 21:83–91.

AMEYAW-AKUMFI, C., and B. A. HAZLETT. 1975. Sex recognition in the crayfish Procambarus clarkii. *Science* 190:1225–1226.

ANDREWS, E. A. 1904. Breeding habits of crayfish. *Am. Nat.* 38:165–206.

———. 1910. The young of the crayfishes Astacus and Cambarus. *Smithson. Contrib. Knowl.* 35:5–79.

BLACK, J. B. 1963. Observations on the home range of stream-dwelling crawfishes. *Ecology* 44:592–595.

BOVBJERG, R. V. 1952. Comparative ecology and physiology of the crayfish Orconectes propinquus and Cambarus fodiens. *Physiol. Zool.* 25:34–56.

———. 1953. Dominance order in the crayfish Orconectes virilis (Hagen). *Physiol. Zool.* 26:173–178.

———. 1956. Some factors affecting aggressive behavior in crayfish. Ibid. 29:127–136.

———. 1970. Ecological isolation and competitive exclusion in two crayfish (Orconcectes virilis and Orconectes immunis). *Ecology* 51:225–236.

BROAD, A. C., and J. H. HUBSCHMAN. 1963. The larval development of Palaemonetes kadiakensis M. J. Rathbun in the laboratory. *Trans. Am. Microsc. Soc.* 82:185–197.

CAINE, E. A. 1974. Zoogeography of the Florida troglobitic crayfishes, genus Procambarus. *Am. Midl. Nat.* 92:487–492.

CHACE, F. A. 1954. Two new subterranean shrimps (Decapoda: Caridea) from Florida and the West Indies, with a revised key to the American species. *J. Wash. Acad. Sci.* 44:318–324.

CREASER, E. P.   1931.   The Michigan decapod crustaceans. *Pap. Mich. Acad. Sci. Arts and Lett.* **13**:257–276.

——.   1934.   Age, growth, and sex ratios in the crayfish, Faxonius propinquus. *Pap. Mich. Acad. Sci. Arts and Lett.* **19**:581–585.

CREASER, E. P., and A. I. ORTENBURGER.   1933.   The decapod crustaceans of Oklahoma. *Publ. Univ. Okla. Biol. Surv.* **5**:14–80.

CROCKER, D. W.   1957.   The crayfishes of New York State (Decapoda, Astacidae). *Bull. N.Y. State Mus.* **355**:(1):1–97.

CROCKER, D. W., and D. W. BARR.   1968.   Handbook of the crayfishes of Ontario. *Life. Sci. Misc. Publ. Roy. Ont. Mus.*, pp. 1–158.

DEAN, J. L.   1969.   Biology of the crayfish Orconectes causeyi and its use for control of aquatic weeds in trout lakes. *U.S. Dept. Inter., Bur. Sport Fish. Wildl., Tech. Pap.* **24**:1–15.

ENGLE, E. T.   1926.   Crayfishes of the genus Cambarus in Nebraska and eastern Colorado. *Bull. U.S. Bur. Fish.* **42**:87–104.

FAXON, W.   1885.   Revision of the Astacidae, Part I. The genera Cambarus and Astacus. *Mem. Mus. Comp. Zool.* **10**:1–186.

——.   1914.   Notes on the crayfishes in the United States National Museum and the Museum of Comparative Zoology with descriptions of new species and subspecies to which is appended a catalogue of the known species and subspecies. *Mem. Mus. Comp. Zool. Harvard Coll.* **40**:347–427.

FINGERMAN, M.   1955.   Factors influencing the rate of oxygen consumption of the dwarf crawfish, Cambarellus shufeldtii (Decapoda, Astacidae). *Tulane Stud. Zool.* **3**:103–116.

FINGERMAN, M., and A. D. LAGO.   1957.   Endogenous twenty-four hour rhythms of locomotor activity and oxygen consumption in the crawfish Orconectes clypeatus. *Am. Midl. Nat.* **58**:383–393.

FISHER, A. K.   1912.   Crawfish as crop destroyers. *U.S. Dept. Agric. Yearbook for 1911*, pp. 321–324.

FITZPATRICK, J. F.   1967.   The propinquus group of the crawfish genus Orconectes (Decapoda: Astacidae). *Ohio J. Sci.* **67**:129–177.

FITZPATRICK, J. F., and J. F. PAYNE.   1968.   A new genus and species of crawfish from the southeastern United States (Decapoda, Astacidae). *Proc. Biol. Soc. Wash.* **81**:11–22.

GUNTER, G.   1937.   Observations on the river shrimp, Macrobrachium ohionis (Smith). *Am. Midl. Nat.* **18**:1038–1042.

GUYSELMAN, J. B.   1957.   Solar and lunar rhythms of locomotor activity in the crayfish Cambarus virilis. *Physiol. Zool.* **30**:70–87.

HAGEN, H. A.   1870.   Monograph of the North American Astacidae. *Illus. Cat. Mus. Comp. Zool. Harvard Coll.* **3**:1–109.

HARRIS, J. A.   1903.   An ecological catalogue of the crayfishes belonging to the genus Cambarus. *Kans. Univ. Sci. Bull.* **2**:51–187.

HAY, W. P.   1903.   Observations on the crustacean fauna of the region about the Mammoth Cave, Kentucky, *Proc. U.S. Nat. Mus.* **25**:223–226.

HAZLETT, B., D. RITTSCHOF, and D. RUBENSTEIN.   1974.   Behavioral biology of the crayfish Orconectes virilis I. Home range. *Am. Midl. Nat.* **92**:301–319.

HEDGPETH, J. W.   1947.   River shrimps. *Prog. Fish-Cult.* **9**:181–184.

——.   1949.   The North American species of Macrobrachium (river shrimp). *Tex. J. Sci.* **1**:28–38.

——.   1968.   The atyid shrimp of the genus Syncaris in California. *Int. Rev. ges. Hydrobiol.* **53**:511–524.

HOBBS, H. H., JR.   1942.   A generic revision of the crayfishes of the Subfamily Cambarinae (Decapoda, Astacidae) with the description of a new genus and species. *Am. Midl. Nat.* **28**:334–357.

——.   1942a.   The crayfishes of Florida. *Univ. Fla. Publ. Biol. Sci. Ser.* **3**:1–179.

——.   1945.   Two new species of crayfishes of the genus Cambarellus from the Gulf Coast states, with a key to the species of the genus (Decapoda, Astacidae). *Am. Midl. Nat.* **34**:466–474.

——.   1967.   A new crayfish from Alabama caves with notes on the origin of the genera Orconectes and Cambarus (Decapoda: Astacidae). *Proc. U.S. Nat. Mus.* **123**:1–17.

——.   1969.   On the distribution and phylogeny of the crayfish genus Cambarus. *Va. Polytech. Inst. Res. Div. Monogr.* **1**:93–178.

——.   1972.   Crayfishes (Astacidae) of North and Middle America. *Biota of Freshwater Ecosystems, Identification Manual* **9**:1–173.

——.   1974.   A checklist of the North and Middle American crayfishes (Decapoda: Astacidae and Cambaridae). *Smithson. Contrib. Zool.* **166**:1–161.

HOLMES, S. J.   1900.   Synopsis of California stalk-eyed Crustacea. *Occ. Pap. Calif. Acad. Sci.* **7**:1–255.

HOLTHUIS, L. B.   1949.   Note on the species of Palaemonetes (Crustacea Decapoda) found in the United States of America. *Proc. Konink. Ned. Akad. Wet.* **52**:87–95.

——.   1952.   A general revision of the Palaemonidae (Crustacea Decapoda Natantia) of the Americas. II. The Subfamily Palaemoninae. *Occas. Pap. Allan Hancock Found.* **12**:1–396.

HUXLEY, T. H.   1906.   *The crayfish.* 2d ed. 371 pp. London

LAGLER, K. F., and M. J. LAGLER.   1944.   Natural enemies of crayfishes in Michigan. *Pap. Mich. Acad. Sci. Arts and Lett.* **29**:293–303.

LOWE, M. E.   1956.   Dominance-subordinance relationships in the crawfish Cambarellus shufeldtii. *Tulane Stud. Zool.* **4**:139–170.

LYLE, C.   1938.   The crawfishes of Mississippi, with special reference to the biology and control of destructive species. *Iowa State Coll. J. Sci.* **13**:75–77.

MALUF, N. S. R.   1939.   On the anatomy of the kidney of the crayfish and on the absorption of chlorid from freshwater by this animal. *Zool. Jahrb. Abt. allg. Zool. Physiol. Tiere* **59**:515–534.

MASON, J. C.   1970.   Egg-laying in the western North American crayfish, Pacifastacus trowbridgii

(Stimpson) (Decapoda, Astacidae). *Crustaceana* **19**:37–44.

———. 1970a. Copulatory behavior of the crayfish Pacifastacus trowbridgii (Stimpson). *Can. J. Zool.* **48**:969–976.

———. 1970b. Maternal-offspring behavior of the crayfish, Pacifastacus trowbridgi (Stimpson). *Am. Midl. Nat.* **84**:463–473.

MEEHEAN, O. L. 1936. Notes on the freshwater shrimp Palaemonetes paludosa (Gibbes). *Trans. Am. Microsc. Soc.* **55**:433–441.

MERKEL, E. L. 1969. Home range of crayfish Orconectes juvenalis. *Am. Midl. Nat.* **81**:228–235.

MOBBERLY, W. C. 1963. Hormonal and environmental regulation of the molting cycle in the crayfish Faxonella clypeata. *Tulane Stud. Zool.* **11**:79–96.

MOMOT, W. T. 1966. Upstream movements of crayfish in an intermittent Oklahoma stream. *Am. Midl. Nat.* **75**:150–159.

MOMOT, W. T., and H. GOWING. 1972. Differential seasonal migration of the crayfish, Orconectes virilis (Hagen) in marl lakes. *Ecology* **53**:479–483.

ORTMANN, A. E. 1902. The geographical distribution of the freshwater decapods and its bearing upon ancient geography. *Proc. Am. Philos. Soc.* **41**:267–400.

———. 1905. The mutual affinities of the species of the genus Cambarus, and their dispersal over the United States. Ibid. **44**:91–136.

———. 1906. The crawfishes of the state of Pennsylvania. *Mem. Carnegie Mus.* **2**:343–521.

———. 1931. Crawfishes of the southern Appalachians and the Cumberland Plateau. *Ann. Carnegie Mus.* **20**:61–160.

PEARSE, A. S. 1909. Observations on copulation among crayfishes. *Am. Nat.* **43**:746–753.

PENN, G. H. 1942. Observations on the biology of the dwarf crawfish, Cambarellus shufeldtii (Faxon). *Am. Midl. Nat.* **28**:644–647.

———. 1943. A study of the life history of the Louisiana red-crawfish, Cambarus clarkii Girard. *Ecology* **24**:1–18.

———. 1957. Variation and subspecies of the crawfish Orconectes palmeri (Faxon). *Tulane Stud. Zool.* **5**:229–262.

———. 1959. An illustrated key to the crawfishes of Louisiana with a summary of their distribution within the state (Decapoda, Astacidae). *Tulane Stud. Zool.* **7**:3–20.

PENN, G. H., and J. F. FITZPATRICK. 1963. Inter-specific competition between two sympatric species of dwarf crawfishes. *Ecology* **44**:793–797.

PENN, G. H., and H. H. HOBBS. 1958. A contribution toward a knowledge of the crawfishes of Texas (Decapoda, Astacidae). *Tex. J. Sci.* **10**:452–483.

POWER, E. A. 1962. Fishery statistics of the United States, 1960. *Stat. Dig. U.S. Fish. Wildl. Serv.* **53**:1–529.

RHOADES, R. 1944. The crayfishes of Kentucky, with notes on variation, distribution and descriptions of new species and subspecies. *Am. Midl. Nat.* **31**:111–149.

RIEGEL, J. A. 1959. The systematics and distribution of crayfishes in California. *Calif. Fish and Game* **45**:29–50.

ROBERTS, T. W. 1944. Light, eyestalk chemical, and certain other factors as regulators of community activity for the crayfish, Cambarus virilis Hagen. *Ecol. Monogr.* **14**:359–392.

SCHMITT, W. L. 1933. Notes on shrimps of the genus Macrobrachium found in the United States. *J. Wash. Acad. Sci.* **23**:312–317.

SCUDAMORE, H. H. 1947. The influence of the sinus glands upon molting and associated changes in the crayfish. *Physiol. Zool.* **20**:187–208.

———. 1948. Factors influencing molting and the sexual cycles in the crayfish. *Biol. Bull.* **95**:229–237.

SMALLEY, A. E. 1961. A new cave shrimp from southeastern United States (Decapoda, Atyidae). *Crustaceana* **3**:127–130.

SMITH, E. W. 1953. The life history of the crawfish, Orconectes (Faxonella) clypeatus (Hay). *Tulane Stud. Zool.* **1**:79–96.

STEELE, M. 1902. The crayfish of Missouri. *Univ. Cinci. Bull.* **10**:1–53.

TACK, P. I. 1941. The life history and ecology of the crayfish Cambarus immunis Hagen. *Am. Midl. Nat.* **25**:420–446.

TURNER, C. L. 1926. The crayfish of Ohio. *Bull. Ohio Biol. Surv.* **13**:145–195.

VAN DEVENTER, W. C. 1937. Studies on the biology of the crayfish, Cambarus propinquus Girard. *Ill. Biol. Monogr.* **15**:1–67.

WILLIAMS, A. B. 1954. Speciation and distribution of the crayfishes of the Ozark plateaus and Ouachita provinces. *Univ. Kans. Sci. Bull.* **36**:803–918.

WILLIAMS, A. B., and A. B. LOENARD. 1952. The crayfishes of Kansas, Ibid. **34**:961–1012.

# Chapter 23

# HYDRACARINA (WATER MITES)

THE CLASS Arachnoidea consists chiefly of terrestrial and parasitic members, including such familiar arthropods as spiders, scorpions, ticks, and mites. Only the water mites, forming the Hydracarina (or Hydrachnellae), have become generally adapted to fresh waters. Strictly speaking, "Hydracarina" is a term of convenience, and not a specific taxonomic term. It is an aggregation of families in the Suborder Trombidiformes that are restricted to freshwater habitats and are further characterized by immature forms that differ markedly from adults in form and habits. Furthermore, considering the animal kingdom as a whole, the Hydracarina is one of the few characteristic fresh-water groups, being almost restricted to fresh waters; only a few species are found in brackish and salt waters, and none are terrestrial.

Although Hydracarina are found in almost all types of fresh-water habitats, they are most abundant and characteristic of streams, rivers, ponds, and the littoral region of lakes, especially where there are quantities of rooted aquatic vegetation. Their bright colors, globular to ovoid shape, and clambering and swimming habits identify them unmistakably.

**General characteristics.** Superficially, water mites appear to be minute spiders, but they differ most significantly from the true spiders in having the cephalothorax and abdomen fused into a single mass, all evident segmentation being lost. A decided minority of genera depart from the usual globular or ovoid shape and are dorsoventrally or laterally compressed. Most Hydracarina, and especially the more primitive genera, are soft bodied, but in many forms the cuticle is leathery or thickened to form a series of heavily sclerotized plates. Sometimes the body is almost completely enclosed by two plates, one dorsal and one ventral, whereas in other genera there are numerous smaller plates. The surface of the body is smooth, finely marked, granular, striated, or papillated. A variable number of setae are borne on the body. Total length usually ranges between 0.4 and 3.0 mm.

The six pairs of arachnid appendages are always present, the most conspicuous being the last four pairs, or legs. Each leg is long and consists of six segments that are variously supplied with spines, setae, and long hairs. The last segment usually bears two terminal movable claws. Each of the eight legs originates from a sclerotized ventral plate called a coxal plate, or epimera. At least some of the epimera are adjacent and more or less fused.

The first two pairs of appendages are borne on an anterior and ventral headlike structure called the capitulum, or maxillary organ. The mouth is located at the anterior end of the capitulum, often at the extremity of a straight or curved rostrum of variable length. The ventral surface of the capitulum is termed the maxillary shield. The chelicerae (usually called mandibles in the Hydracarina) are small and, except during feeding, are kept withdrawn into the capitulum. In a few genera they are stilettolike or saberlike (Fig. 341E), but usually there is a separate, terminal, curved, clawlike segment (Fig. 341G). The five-segmented pedipalps (or "palps") are inserted laterally or at the anterolateral angles of the maxillary shield and are customarily curved ventrally.

The only other conspicuous external

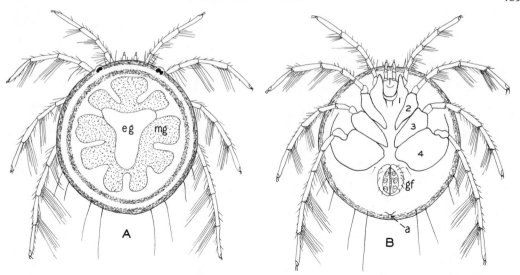

FIG. 337.–*Mideopsis orbicularis* (Müller) female, ×40. A, dorsal; B, ventral. 1, 2, 3, and 4, first, second, third, and fourth epimera; *a*, anus; *eg*, excretory gland; *gf*, genital field; *mg*, midgut. (Modified from Soar and Williamson.)

feature is the genital field, a group of closely associated structures located on the ventral median line between or behind the epimera and sometimes at the extreme posterior end of the body. The genital pore is a small longitudinal slit in the center of the field; it is flanked by two plates that bear few to many curious knoblike or cuplike acetabula of unknown function. Sometimes there is a pair of longitudinal movable or immovable genital flaps that may or may not cover the acetabula (Figs. 337B, 341J).

The two pigmented eyes are near the anterior margin of the body and are usually widely separated, but in a few genera they lie close together along the median line. Each eye is characteristically paired.

The so-called anus is an inconspicuous pore near the posterior end; sometimes it is borne on a special small plate.

The two minute spiracles are located on the dorsal surface of the capitulum near its base and are therefore hidden from view by the body and can be seen only when the capitulum is dissected off.

In contrast to fresh-water invertebrates in general, water mites are particularly striking because of their coloration.

The majority of species are some shade of red or green, but there are many others that are blue, yellow, tan, or brown. The basic body coloration is caused by pigmentation of the body wall, but yellow, brown, or blackish markings and patterns, especially in dorsal view, are produced by the coloration of internal organs, especially the digestive tract and excretory gland (Fig. 337A). *Axonopsis complanata* is one of the most spectacular species; the appendages and general ventral surface are green; the epimera and much of the dorsal surface are blue; the capitulum, genital field, and central part of the dorsal surface are yellowish; and the large excretory gland produces a brown dorsal Y-shaped area. Some species of *Arrenurus* have equally striking combinations of green, blue, and orange. Stream species of water mites are characteristically brownish. Coloration of some species is somewhat variable, especially in *Limnesia,* and different specimens of the same species taken at the same place and time may exhibit different shades of red or green. These variations can be at least partially ascribed to differences in age and varying contents of the digestive tract and excretory gland.

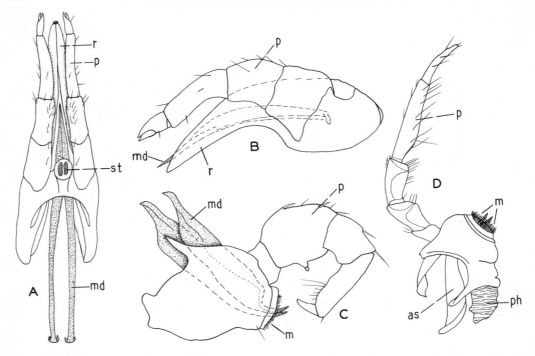

FIG. 338.–Hydracarina capitulum and associated structures. A, dorsal view of capitulum of *Hydrachna*; B, lateral view of capitulum of *Hydrachna* (only left palp shown); C, lateral view of capitulum of *Tyrrellia* (only right palp shown); D, lateral view of capitulum of *Eylais* (only right palp shown). *as*, air sac; *m*, mouth (with projecting mandibles); *md*, mandibles (shaded); *p*, palp; *ph*, pharynx; *r*, rostrum; *st*, stigma (cross hatched). A and D modified from Viets; C modified from Marshall, 1940.)

**Locomotion.** Swimming is effected by relatively uncoordinated flailing movements of the legs, and the ability to swim is variously developed from one genus to another. The best swimmers have rows of long swimming hairs on the legs, especially the more posterior pairs (Fig. 337). At the other extreme are many species that are strictly creepers and crawlers on the bottom or among vegetation; their legs are supplied with only short spines and setae. Swimming ability is lost in many stream forms.

Irrespective of the degree of swimming development, Hydracarina are clearly associated with the substrate and rarely stray far from it. Specific gravity of the body is usually high, and unless they cling to some object, they quickly fall to the bottom when not in motion. *Unionicola crassipes* is probably the only American species that strays far enough from vegetation and a

substrate to be considered an accidental plankton organism.

In addition to locomotion, the legs are used periodically for cleaning debris from the body and from each other.

**Food, feeding.** The great majority of water mites for carnivorous or parasitic, their food consisting chiefly of entomostraca, small insects, various kinds of worms, or host tissues. Sometimes the more active and voracious species are cannibalistic. Sluggish species usually feed on dead animals, and a few investigators have found that they may utilize vegetable material and detritus.

The prey is seized and held with the palps, with or without the aid of the legs, and the body is quickly pierced with the mandibles. Only fluids are ingested, and it is probable that secretions of the several pairs of salivary glands are injected into the prey, where they predigest some of the more solid tissues so that they may be sucked up along with the body fluids. The exoskeleton and indigestible remnants of the prey are then discarded.

**Internal anatomy, physiology.** Ingested fluids pass through the small cavity of the suctorial pharynx and into the midgut, the latter being a capacious, lobed, digestive and absorptive organ filling one-third to one-half of the hemocoel. The midgut usually has about 12 caeca, although there may be as many as 30 in some species. In all the Hydracarina whose anatomy has been carefully studied, it has been found that the midgut and its caeca end blindly, and there is no connection with the "anus."

A heart and blood vessels are lacking, but the blood is circulated about freely in the hemocoel by the movements of the muscles and digestive tract.

Some Hydracarina have a tracheal system. Each of the two minute spiracles opens into an elongated air sac (Fig. 338D). At the posterior end of this sac is a single, short tracheal trunk which branches into many fine, threadlike tracheae ramifying to all parts of the body.

Although the tracheal system is always filled with a gas (air), no adult water mite

FIG. 339.–Modified legs of male Hydracarina. A, middle segments of third leg of *Hydrochoreutes ungulatus*; B, fourth leg of *Forelia*; C, fourth leg of *Acercus*. (A modified from Marshall, 1927; B modified from Marshall, 1935; C modified from Marshall, 1937.)

has ever been observed taking air at the surface film in the manner of many aquatic insects. The spiracles are thought to be covered with gas-permeable but waterproof membranes. When larvae or developing nymphs parasitize insects that leave the water and become aerial, however, it is probable that they take in air through the spiracles. There is also the possibility that air could be taken into the tracheal system when the mandibles and a good portion of the capitulum are thrust into the air-containing tissues of aquatic plants. Nymphs have been observed in this attitude, but it is doubtful whether adults do it, with the possible exception of females of a few species that may assume the attitude as a preliminary to oviposition. Furthermore, mites are found in many habitats where there are no rooted aquatics.

Aside from the question of the physiological significance of the water mite tracheal system and the source of its contained gas, all investigators seem to agree that most of the oxygen utilized in metabolism is absorbed through the general body surface and that carbon dioxide diffuses outward through it. Those species with a thick body wall usually have scattered thin porous areas that presumably facilitate the gaseous exchange.

Although many species survive temporary conditions where the dissolved oxygen concentration may be below 1 ppm, no species are known to remain active under anaerobic conditions.

The excretory gland is a large dorsal T- or Y-shaped organ (Fig. 337A) that connects with the ventral "anus," or "excretory pore," by a duct. Many typical mites have seven pairs of oval or pear-shaped epidermal glands opening over the dorsal and lateral surfaces of the body, and it is possible that these structures have an accessory excretory function.

The nervous system consists of a large central ganglionic mass with little indication of the method of fusion. It is perforated by the pharynx and has radiating nerves. Each of the two lateral eyes consists of two elements that may be clearly separated or more or less fused. An element consists of a pigmented bulb and cuticular lens. Many species have an additional fifth, or median, eye (Fig. 341D). Other senses are poorly developed; the palps are tactile and probably detect substances in solution, and most of the body setae are probably tactile.

In the male there are two testes, two vasa deferentia, and a single penis, which can be extruded through the genital pore. The female has two fused ovaries, two oviducts, and a single vagina, or uterus.

**Reproduction.** Sometimes the two sexes can be distinguished only by slight differences in the anatomy of the genital field, palps, third legs, and fourth legs, but more commonly sexual dimorphism is pronounced. Males frequently have much larger fourth epimera, and genital fields that differ considerably from those of females. The third and fourth legs of males are sometimes specialized for copulation and the transfer of spermatophores; often the fourth legs are elongated, and in a few genera the fourth segment is flattened and platelike (Fig. 339C) or the terminal segment is roughly sickle-shaped (Fig. 339B). The third legs may be modified for clasping the female (Fig. 339A), and sometimes the distal segments form a club for sperm transfer. In *Arrenurus* sexual dimorphism is extreme, the males being characterized by a large posterior prolongation, or cauda (Figs. 343B, C). Unfortunately there is no single general anatomical character or several characters that may be used in distinguishing the sexes throughout the order.

Judging from the few species whose reproductive habits have been carefully described, it appears that Hydracarina exhibit a wide variety of clasping and spermatophore transfer habits. Occasionally the male is carried on the back of the female for a varying time. The males of a few species drag the female about in a haphazard manner. In some genera the genital pores of the two copulating individuals are almost in direct contact during spermatophore transfer, but more commonly the bodies are placed at various angles to each other (often at right angles), while the male securely holds the first two pairs of female legs with his fourth legs. Regardless of the specific copulatory position, the male picks

up the packetlike spermatophores from the tip of his extruded penis with his third legs and transfers them to the region of the female genital pore. Spermatophore transfer takes from less than a minute to as long as an hour.

Statements concerning the breeding season vary widely. Some authorities state that breeding and egg deposition may occur at any time during the year; others maintain that eggs are usually deposited in May, June, and July. It therefore seems logical to assume that the breeding season may vary widely from one species to another and also that it may vary within a single species according to latitude, temperature, and season.

As the female releases the eggs from her genital pore they are fertilized by the sperm contained in the spermatophores previously placed there by the male. Fertilized eggs are rarely deposited singly; usually they are extruded in groups of 20 to 400 onto stones, vegetation, and debris. Each egg may have its own individual gelatinous covering, or the whole group of eggs may be imbedded in a common gelatinous mass. Eggs are usually red. *Hydrachna* oviposits in the tissues of aquatic plants.

**Development, life history.** Depending on temperatures and the particular species, the eggs hatch in one to six weeks. The larvae have functional mouth parts, small epimera, three pairs of legs, and no genital field (Figs. 340A, B). After a short free-swimming period, the larvae become attached to aquatic insects with their capitulum and assume a parasitic existence. Wesenberg-Lund (1919) favors the theory of some broad preference by larvae for certain insect hosts; thus, he states that the Limnocharidae usually parasitize hydrometrids, that Eylaidae mostly parasitize aerial insects, that Hydryphantidae usually occur on culicids, and that several other families appear to be almost restricted to insects that do not leave the water. In view of more recent ecological observations, it is possible that his conclusions may be a reflection of restricted mite and insect faunas in the ponds he studied. It would be highly desir-

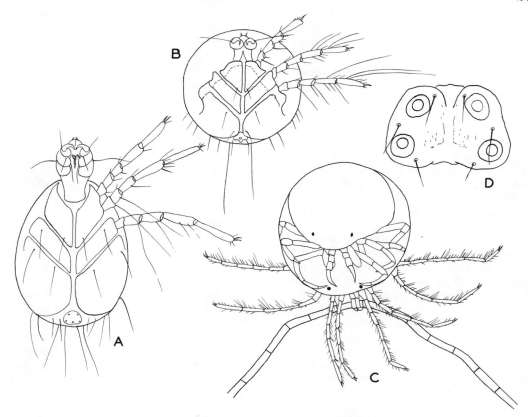

FIG. 340.–Immature Hydracarina. A, larva of *Arrenurus*, ×260; B, larva of *Mideopsis*, ×130; C, adult *Piona* developing within nymphal exoskeleton, attached to filamentous alga, ×40; D, genital field of *Limnesia* nymph. (A and B modified from Soar and Williamson; C modified from Uchida; D redrawn from Viets.)

able to test this question experimentally in order to find out definitely whether or not a particular larval mite has any specific host preference. It is significant that Ephemeroptera and hydrophilid and dytiscid beetles are rarely parasitized, and that Trichoptera are uncommon hosts. The usual hosts are Plecoptera, Odonata, Diptera, and Hemiptera. The larval mite may come in contact with its host on the substrate or at the surface film. Often a single insect may carry 10 or 20 mite parasites.

After a variable feeding period on the host, the larva begins to metamorphose to the nymphal stage. Feeding ceases, and the larva shrinks from its exoskeleton, which then becomes a loose, baglike puparium (still attached to the host). The contained larva loses its definitive features and be-

comes more or less reconstituted to form the nymph stage. Soon the nymph ruptures the puparium and escapes into the water. The period of inactivity between cessation of feeding by the larva and the escape of the nymph is comparable to a pupal stage and is called the nymphophan. The nymphophan stage lasts for periods ranging from five days to six months.

The nymph is considerably larger than the larva and almost as large as the adult. It has the same general structures and proportions as the adult, but there is no genital opening in the genital field. Unlike the larva, the nymph is free-living and has the same carnivorous food habits as the adult.

At the end of a variable period of activity, the nymph attaches itself to an algal filament, rooted aquatic, or bottom debris with its mouth parts and enters a second pupal stage, or teleiophan. Again, the nymphal exoskeleton becomes a baglike puparium with the developing adult within (Fig. 340C). This quiescent period usually lasts only 7 to 10 days, after which the nymphal exoskeleton ruptures and the sexually mature adult emerges.

By way of recapitulation, the stages in the life history of a typical water mite may be outlined as follows: egg, active larva, parasitic larva, quiescent nymphophan, active nymph, quiescent teleiophan, active adult. The active larval and parasitic larval stages are morphologically indistinguishable.

If the larva attaches to an insect that is aquatic until the termination of the nymphophan, the developed nymph simply breaks out of its puparium into the water. If the insect host is an adult beetle or hemipteran, however, it may leave the water intermittently with its attached larval parasite exposed to the air. Furthermore, the host may metamorphose to an adult that leaves the water and is aerial for the rest of its life (Odonata, Diptera, and Plecoptera, for example). In such instances the fully developed nymph breaks out of the puparium and may fall into the water fortuitously, or it may reenter the water when its host oviposits in the water. Nymphs that fall to the ground from an aerial host are presumed to die very shortly.

There are many exceptions to the generalized type of life history outlined in the preceding paragraphs. A few water mites deposit their eggs in the tissues of sponges or the gelatinous matrix of colonial Protozoa. Others are thought to leave the insect host while still in the larval stage and attach to the substrate for the transformation to the nymph. Certain stream species of *Piona* and *Limnesia* do not have a parasitic stage but remain in the gelatinous egg mass until they become nymphs.

The species of *Unionicola* have unusual life histories. The majority pass their entire lives in the tissues or cavities of mussels, but in a few species the adults either are found in mussels or are free-swimming, and one or two are parasitic in sponges. It is thought that eggs are produced the year round; they are inserted into the tissues of the mussel gills by means of a special ovipositor. The larvae are parasitic on the gills, but the nymphs and adults clamber about actively in the gill or mantle cavities. The parasitic adults have short legs and no swimming hairs. Sometimes the great majority of mussels in a bed are infected, and although infestations may be heavy, the mites appear to do little damage to the hosts. It is possible that the nymphs and adults are commensals rather than true parasites. In addition to *Unionicola*, *Najadicola ingens*, an uncommon species, also occurs in mussels.

Complete life histories are known for relatively few water mites, and it is likely that many additional variations, exceptions, and complications will appear as further studies are made.

Almost nothing is known about the duration of the life cycle or number of generations per year, but it is thought that the great majority of species have a life span of less than one year. Overwintering probably occurs most frequently in the adult stage, although parasitic larvae, teleiophans, and nymphs have also been reported.

**Ecology.** Unlike most groups of fresh-water invertebrates, water mites may be collected in all seasons, even under ice, but the greatest numbers of adults are to be found in late spring and early autumn.

They are invariably most abundant in species and individuals among the heaviest growths of rooted aquatics where the water is only a meter or two deep. Populations in excess of 2000 mites per square meter of bottom have been reported from such habitats. For some unknown reason, however, water mites are rare in beds of *Chara* and *Elodea*. Acid lakes, though superficially an ideal collecting ground, contain very few Hydracarina. Wave-beaten sand and gravel shores are also poor places to collect. Many species are capable of clambering and swimming about with surprising agility, whereas others, devoid of swimming hairs, are sluggish bottom creepers. Between these two extremes are all gradations in crawling, swimming, and clambering ability. Mites are active only during the hours of daylight, and sometimes they remain fixed in the same position all night long.

As the water deepens offshore, the fauna becomes progressively depauperate, and even though Hydracarina may be collected from the bottom at depths of 10 to 100 m, such populations are usually scanty and composed of only one to several species. There is some evidence for migration into the weedy shallows in the late spring and back to deeper waters in the autumn, when vegetation disappears, but this problem needs further investigation.

Careful collecting in a favorable lake or weedy pond commonly yeilds as many as 20 to 40 species. Young (1969) collected 99 species in one county in Colorado, of which 72 were new state records and three were new for North America.

Some genera, notably *Thyas, Hydryphantes, Acercus, Piona,* and *Limnesia,* are characteristic of temporary ponds. Perhaps they are capable of withstanding periods of drought by being buried in wet mud and debris of the substrate.

Brook and stream species are often conspicuously modified for withstanding the force of the current. Dorsoventral flattening, small size, strong claws,and the absence of swimming hairs are the usual adaptations. Stream species produce comparatively small numbers of eggs. Few species may be found in both running and standing waters.

Recent studies of the interstitial and phreatic waters of stream gravels have shown a new habitat for Hydracarina. Sometimes these populations are remarkably dense and diverse. Especially in Europe and Japan, new genera and species are being described with great frequency.

Coloration is sometimes correlated with the background, though there is little evidence that the resemblance has any protective value. Elton (1923) found that hungry sticklebacks refused to eat bright scarlet mites, and he postulated possible Müllerian mimicry and warning coloration.

**Geographical distribution, dispersal.** Although the geographical distribution and ecological affinities are well known for many species in Europe, collecting in the United States has been so highly regional and generally neglected that we have little reliable information on the distribution of most species. In view of this fact, it has been largely necessary to omit distributional data for the genera and species included in the key beginning on page 497. The majority of species reported from the United States appear to be restricted to this country, and many are known only from a single locality or two or three widely separated localities. However, only a single rare genus, *Najadicola,* appears to be restricted to North America. On the other hand, a surprising number of American species are cosmopolitan and widely distributed throughout the Northern and even the Southern hemispheres. Furthermore, it is rather striking that in each of about half of the genera occurring in the United States one species (and only one) is widely distributed and common in both North America and Europe. Some of these species are *Piona rotunda* (Koen.), *Unionicola crassipes* (Müller), *Hydryphantes ruber* (De-Geer), *Hydrodroma despiciens, Lebertia porosa* Thor, *Hygrobates longipalpis* (Herm.), *Hydrochoreutes ungulatus* (Koch), and *Mideopsis orbicularis* (Müller).

Dispersal is both active and passive, and those species that are parasitic on insects are undoubtedly easily distributed overland to new drainage systems.

**Enemies.** Hydracarina are preyed on by a wide variety of aquatic invertebrates, especially coelenterates and carnivorous insects. They are not ordinarily an important element in the diet of fishes, but occasionally a fish stomach is found in which mites predominate. Several new species have been described from the stomach contents of trout.

**Collection, preparation.** A successful way to collect quantities of mites is to stir up bottom debris and catch the suspended material with a small dipnet. Hand-picking, dipnetting, and washing out vegetation in an enameled pan are also useful techniques. During July and early August the large majority of specimens collected are immature. Living specimens may be kept in the laboratory and fed entomostraca or nonpredatory aquatic insects, but crowding is disastrous, since they are often cannibalistic.

Because they are so active, it is best to examine living specimens in a compression slide or by anesthetizing and relaxing them with chloretone or in water saturated with chloroform vapor. Binoculars, an opaque white background, and a bright spotlight are essential.

A good killing and preserving agent consists of 5 parts by volume of glycerin, 4 parts water, and 1 part glacial acetic acid. Wolcott recommends the following solution: 2 parts glycerin, 3 parts water, 2 parts glacial acetic acid, and 1 part absolute alcohol.

Suitably translucent whole mounts may sometimes be made by cutting a small incision in the dorsal body wall and pressing out the contents, but it is first necessary to clear dense and hard species with acetic corrosive in order to render them sufficiently translucent for work with the compound microscope. It consists of equal parts (by weight) of glacial acetic acid, chloral hydrate, and water. For critical study and accurate identification, the mouth parts, capitulum, and legs should be dissected off and mounted separately. Some workers prefer permanent euparal or similar mounting media (see Lavers, 1945); others use glycerin or glycerin jelly.

Polyvinyl alcohol and Hoyer's fluid are excellent mounting media that also have clearing properties. See Mitchell and Cook (1952) for a further discussion of making slide mounts.

**Taxonomy.** More than 90 percent of all published information on our American species is based on the work of four careful investigators–Wolcott, whose publications extend from 1899 to 1918; Ruth Marshall, whose numerous papers appeared between 1903 and 1944; Cook, beginning in 1953; and Mitchell, also beginning in 1953. The potential number of species in the United States must be large, Marshall having reported 140 species and varieties from Wisconsin alone. Viets (1936) lists 444 species from Germany, and Soar and Williamson (1925–1929) list 247 for the British Isles.

Mitchell (1954) lists 291 species from North America, and Crowell (1961) lists 457 taxa from North America, but the number of species reported to date for the United States is probably more than 550. Very little is known about the Hydracarina of rapid streams, high altitudes, states west of the Great Plains, and southeastern states.

Identification to genus and species is based primarily on the detailed adult anatomy of the epimera, genital field, capitulum, and palps. The taxonomic status and limits of several families and genera are still controversial, and the following classification of American fresh-water genera used in this manual is modified from the widely accepted one proposed by Viets (1936). It is likely that better limitations of Hydracarina families will be proposed in the future. We have the impression that specialists have been too anxious and zealous to establish new families.

Arrenuridae
  *Arrenurus*
Athienemanniidae
  *Athienemannia, Chappuisides*
Aturidae
  *Aturus, Kongsbergia*
Axonopsidae
  *Albia, Axonopsis, Brachypoda*
Clathrosperchonidae
  *Clathrosperchon*
Eylaidae
  *Eylais*
Feltriidae
  *Feltria*
Hydrachnidae
  *Hydrachna*
Hydrodromidae
  *Hydrodroma*
Hydrovolziidae
  *Hydrovolzia*
Hydryphantidae
  *Hydryphantes*
Hygrobatidae
  *Atractides, Hygrobates*
Krendowskiidae
  *Geayia, Krendowskia*
Lebertiidae
  *Lebertia*

Limnesiidae
  *Kawamuracarus, Limnesia, Neomamersa, Tyrrellia*
Limnocharidae
  *Limnochares*
Mamersopsidae
  *Bandakia*
Mideidae
  *Midea*
Mideopsidae
  *Horreolanus, Mideopsis, Xystonotus, Yachatsia*
Momoniidae
  *Stygomomonia*
Neoacaridae
  *Neoacarus, Volsellacarus*
Omartacaridae
  *Omartacarus*
Oxidae
  *Frontipoda, Gnaphiscus, Oxus*
Piersigiidae
  *Piersigia*
Pionidae
  *Forelia, Hydrochoreutes, Piona, Tiphys, Wettina*
Protziidae
  *Calonyx, Partnuniella, Wandesia*
Sperchonidae
  *Sperchon, Sperchonopsis*

Thermacaridae
  *Thermacarus*
Thyasidae
  *Euthyas, Panisopsis, Panisus, Thyas, Thyasides, Thyopsella, Thyopsis, Trichothyas*
Torrenticolidae
  *Testudacarus, Torrenticola*
Uchidastygacaridae
  *Uchidastygacarus*
Unionicolidae
  *Huitfeldtia, Koenikea, Najadicola, Neumania, Unionicola*

Because of the vagaries of variations within many of the ill-defined families, the following key is highly artificial. Except for a few very rare forms, essentially all the U.S. genera are included, especially where the published literature includes specific collecting records. There are, however, additional potentially new genera in the collections of specialists, and there are also many unpublished U.S. records of species and genera that are well known elsewhere, especially in Europe. Anyone who collects in clean phreatic waters and gravel bars of streams will find many species he cannot easily identify.

## KEY TO GENERA OF HYDRACARINA

1. Lateral eyes of the two sides close together at the median lines and borne on a common plate (Figs. 341B, C); simple, red, soft-bodied species; up to 7 mm long . . . . . . . . . . . . . . . . . . . . . . . . . . . . . . . . . . . . . . . . . . . . . . . . . . . . .**6**
   Lateral eyes widely separated (Figs. 343, 345, 346), or eyes absent . . . . . . . . . . . . . .**2**
2. Body wormlike (Fig. 342A); up to 2 mm long; rare; in hyporheic cold stream gravels; several species. . . . . . . . . . . . . . . . . . . . . . . . . . . . . . . . . . . . . . . . . . . . . **Wandesia**
   Body not wormlike . . . . . . . . . . . . . . . . . . . . . . . . . . . . . . . . . . . . . . . . . . . . . . . . . . . . .**3**
3. Distal extremity of the fourth palp segment produced into a point well beyond the point of insertion of segment five, the two segments together usually resembling a pair of open or closed shears (Figs. 341F, H) . . . . . . . . . . . . . . . . . . . . . . . . . . .**4**
   Distal extremity of fourth palp segment not pointed and produced, or only slightly produced and blunt (Figs. 343A; 344A); segment five, free, tapered, and with the tip pointed, clawed, or toothed . . . . . . . . . . . . . . . . . . . . . . . . . . . . . . . . . . .**19**
4. Mandible one-segmented, the terminal portion straight and stilettolike (Fig. 341E); body globular, soft, and papillated; capitulum produced as a rostrum well beyond anterior end of body (Fig. 341D); with swimming hairs; usually red, orange, or brown; 1 to 8 mm long; common everywhere in standing waters; many species . . . . . . . . . . . . . . . . . . . . . . . . . . . . . . . . . . . . . . . . . . . . . **Hydrachna**
   Mandible one-segmented, the terminal segment curved, clawlike, and often very small (Fig. 341G); capitulum only slightly or not at all produced beyond anterior end of body . . . . . . . . . . . . . . . . . . . . . . . . . . . . . . . . . . . . . . . . . . . . . . . . . . . . . . . . . .**5**

FIG. 341.–Structure of Hydracarina. A, dorsal view of *Limnochares* showing median ocular plate, ×15; B, ocular plate of *Limnochares*; C, ocular plate of *Eylais*; D, dorsal view of *Hydrachna*, ×15; E, mandible of *Hydrachna*; F, palp of *Hydrodroma despiciens*; G, mandible of *H. despiciens*; H, palp of *Hydryphantes*; J, ventral plates of *Hydrodroma despiciens*; K, ventral view of *Protzia*, ×45. (B, C, F, H, J, and K modified from Marshall, 1940.)

**5.** Last two epimera widely separated from first two epimera (Fig. 341K); bottom forms; no swimming hairs; soft-bodied; two species in cold mountain streams (possibly should be called *Calonyx*) . . . . . . . . . . . . . . . . . . . . . . . . . . . . . . . . . . . . . . **Protzia**

 Last two epimera not so widely separated from first two epimera (Figs. 343, 345) . .7

**6.** Eye capsules on either side of an elongated plate in the midline (Fig. 341B); mouth at the tip of a protruding rostrum; usually creepers; several common and widely distributed species in standing and slowly flowing waters . . . . . . **Limnochares**

 Eye capsules connected by a narrow bridge (Fig. 341C); mouth not at tip of a protruding rostrum; swimmers in quiet waters; several species . . . . . . . . . . **Eylais**

7. Distal extremity of fourth segment of palp short (Fig. 341H) ....................8
   Distal extremity of fourth segment of palp long (Figs. 341F; 342B, C) ...........10
8. Median eye present but sometimes unpigmented; 1 to 2.5 mm long; red; not in hot
      springs ........................................................12
   Median eye absent ................................................9
9. Distal portion of fourth palp segment a large rounded cap; rare; known only from
      gravel bars in Wyoming streams ........................... **Chappuisides**
   Distal portion of fourth palp segment otherwise; rare, in western hot springs and their
      effluents ................................................ **Partnuniella**
10. Soft red body; 2 mm long; with long swimming hairs; widely distributed and
      common ............................... **Hydrodroma despiciens** (Müller)
   Body not soft and red; less than 0.8 mm long; several uncommon species in stream
      gravels .......................................................11
11. Fifth segment of palp a long and slender claw (Fig. 342B) ........... **Volsellacarus**
   Fifth segment of palp shorter and more robust (Fig. 342C) .............. **Neoacarus**
12. Swimming hairs present; several widely distributed species in standing waters.
                                                             **Hydryphantes**
   Swimming hairs absent, only short spines on legs ...........................13

FIG. 342.–Structure of Hydracarina. A, ventral view of *Wandesia*; B, palp of *Volsellacarus*; C, palp of
*Neoacarus*; D, dorsal view of male *Thyopsella*; E, dorsal view of male *Euthyas*; F, dorsal view of male *Thyasides*;
G, dorsal view of female *Thyas*; H, median eye region of female *Thyasides*; J, genital field of male *Thyopsis*; K,
genital field of male *Thyopsella*; L, genital field of female *Panisopsis*; M, genital field of female *Thyas*; N, genital
field of female *Panisus*. (A from Lundblad, 1941; B and C modified from Cook, 1963; D to N from Cook, 1959,
*Amer. Midl. Nat.*)

Fig. 343.–Structure of Hydracarina. A, palp of *Arrenurus*; B, lateral view of male *Arrenurus*, ×37; C, ventral view of male *Arrenurus*; D, ventral view of female *Arrenurus*, ×27; E, ventral view of male *Krendowskia similis*, ×33; F, dorsal view of *K. similis*, ×33; G, genital field of female *Geayia ovata*; H, dorsal view of *G. ovata*, ×37. (A to D modified from Lavers; E to H modified from Marshall, 1940.)

13. Dorsal surface covered by a large shield (Fig. 342D) . . . . . . . . . . . . . . . . . . . . . . . . . .**14**
    Dorsal surface not covered by a large shield . . . . . . . . . . . . . . . . . . . . . . . . . . . . . . .**15**
14. Second pair of genital acetabula near posterior end of genital flaps (Fig. 342J); temporary ponds, seepages, and springs; one rare species . . . . . . . . . . . .**Thyopsis**
    Second pair of genital acetabula almost midway between the ends of the genital flaps (Fig. 342K); several uncommon species in springs and seepages . . . **Thyopsella**
15. With a small, spindle-shaped median frontal plate on the dorsal surface (Fig. 342E); one rare species in temporary ponds . . . . . . . . . . . . . . . . . . . . . . . . . . . .**Euthyas**
    Without a small, spindle-shaped median frontal plate . . . . . . . . . . . . . . . . . . . . . . . .**16**
16. Genital flaps extending beyond the first genital acetabula (Figs. 342L, N) . . . . . . .**17**
    Genital flaps not extending beyond the first genital acetabula (Fig. 342M) . . . . . . . .**18**
17. Genital flaps broad at posterior end (Fig. 342N); two species in streams, cold springs, and seepages . . . . . . . . . . . . . . . . . . . . . . . . . . . . . . . . . . . . . . . . . . . . . . . **Panisus**
    Genital flaps narrow at posterior end (Fig. 342L); several species in cold springs, streams, and seepages . . . . . . . . . . . . . . . . . . . . . . . . . . . . . . . . . . . . . . . .**Panisopsis**
18. Median eye surrounded by one large plate (Fig. 342F), or by a very small plate with two adjacent separate plates (Fig. 342H); rare in temporary bog waters. **Thyasides**
    Median eye lying free in integument (Fig. 342G); about eight species in temporary ponds . . . . . . . . . . . . . . . . . . . . . . . . . . . . . . . . . . . . . . . . . . . . . . . . . . . . . . . . **Thyas**
19. Fifth segment of palp pointed, clawlike, and opposable to the projecting margin of segment four (Figs. 343A; 344A) . . . . . . . . . . . . . . . . . . . . . . . . . . . . . . . . . . . .**20**
    Fifth segment of palp not opposable to fourth, and bearing distal claws, setae, or teeth . . . . . . . . . . . . . . . . . . . . . . . . . . . . . . . . . . . . . . . . . . . . . . . . . . . . . . . . .**23**
20. Genital field lying posterior to fourth epimera (Fig. 343C) . . . . . . . . . . . . . . . . . . .**21**
    Genital field lying between fourth epimera (Fig. 343E); running waters . . . . . . . . . .**22**

FIG. 344.–Structure of Hydracarina. A, palp of *Athienemannia*; B, posterior end of *Athienemannia*; C, ventral view of *Omartacarus* (appendages omitted); D, palp of *Uchidastygacarus*; E, terminal segments of first leg of *Stygomomonia*; F, ventral view of male *Thermacarus minuta* Mitchell, ×32; G, ventral view of female *T. minuta*, ×32; H, posterior end of *Aturus* showning distribution of acetabula; J, posterior end of *Feltria* showing distribution of acetabula. (All modified: A, Cook, 1961; B, Cook, 1955; C, Cook, 1963c; D, Cook, 1963d; E, Mitchell, 1959; F and G, Mitchell, 1963; J, Cook, 1963.)

**21.** Males usually with a large posterior prolongation, or cauda (Figs. 343B, C); body wall heavily sclerotized; common everywhere, especially in vegetation; usually red or greenish; the largest American genus; about 120 species ....... **Arrenurus**
Males without a cauda; not red or green; rare in sandy springs ...... **Athienemannia**
**22.** With six genital acetabula (Fig. 343E); dorsal shield large (Fig. 343F); reported from Wisconsin, Illinois, Indiana, and Michigan ........**Krendowskia similis** Viets
With eight genital acetabula (Fig. 343G); dorsal shield smaller (Fig. 343H); uncommon; reported from Wisconsin, Minnesota, and Michigan ... **Geayia ovata** (Wolcott)
**23.** Legs crowded together and inserted at anterior end of body ...................**24**
Legs not crowded together at anterior end of body ..........................**27**
**24.** Body laterally compressed (Figs. 345A, C)..................................**25**
Body not laterally compressed, but elongated (Fig. 344C); rare in gravel bars of clear midwestern streams ...................................... **Omartacarus**
**25.** Without a longitudinal furrow on the dorsal surface; several species in lakes and ponds................................................................ **Oxus**
Dorsal surface of body with a narrow to wide longitudinal furrow (Fig. 345C) ....**26**

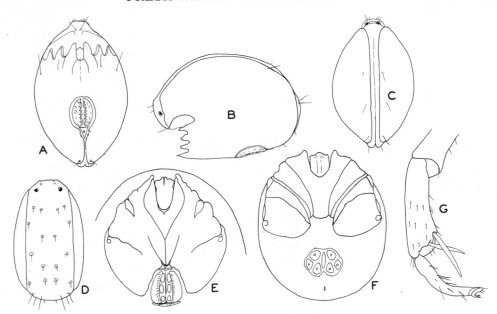

FIG. 345.–Structure of Hydracarina. A, ventral view of *Frontipoda*, ×80; B, lateral view of *Frontipoda*, ×80; C, dorsal view of *Frontipoda*, ×70; D, dorsal view of *Gnaphiscus*, ×47; E, ventral plates of *Libertia*; F, ventral view of *Atractides*, ×45; G, terminal portion of first leg of *Atractides*. (A and C modified from Marshall, 1914; E modified from Marshall, 1932; F and G modified from Marshall, 1943.)

26. Anal plate present (Fig. 345A); sluggish waters . . . . . . **Frontipoda americana** Marshall
    Anal plate absent; rare in lakes and ponds . . . . . . . . **Gnaphiscus occidentalis** Marshall
27. Palp with greatly enlarged second and fourth segments; fifth segment a long claw (Fig. 344D); rare in gravel bars of clear northwestern streams . . . . **Uchidastygacarus**
    Palp otherwise . . . . . . . . . . . . . . . . . . . . . . . . . . . . . . . . . . . . . . . . . . . . . . . . . . . . **28**
28. First epimera completely fused along the median line (Figs. 345E, F) . . . . . . . . . . . .**29**
    First epimera not fused along the median line (Fig. 349) . . . . . . . . . . . . . . . . . . . . . **46**
29. With a large, prominent, sclerotized dorsal plate (Fig. 346B) . . . . . . . . . . . . . . . . . . **34**
    Without a prominent dorsal plate . . . . . . . . . . . . . . . . . . . . . . . . . . . . . . . . . . . . . . . **30**
30. Genital field between fourth epimera (Fig. 345E); widely distributed in many habitats, especially cold waters; about 15 species . . . . . . . . . . . . . . . . . . . . . . . . . **Lebertia**
    Genital field posterior to fourth epimera (Fig. 345F); common and widely distributed . . . . . . . . . . . . . . . . . . . . . . . . . . . . . . . . . . . . . . . . . . . . . . . . . . . . **31**
31. Fifth segment of first leg with two special conspicuous setae (Fig. 345G); several species in mountain streams . . . . . . . . . . . . . . . . . . . . . . . . . . . . . . . . . . . **Atractides**
    Fifth segment of first leg without such setae . . . . . . . . . . . . . . . . . . . . . . . . . . . . **32**
32. Genital field in the posterior half of the ventral surface, sometimes along the posterior margin . . . . . . . . . . . . . . . . . . . . . . . . . . . . . . . . . . . . . . . . . . . . . . . . . . . . . . . . . **33**
    Genital field in the anterior half of the ventral surface; about eight species in running waters . . . . . . . . . . . . . . . . . . . . . . . . . . . . . . . . . . . . . . . . . . . . . . . . . . **Hygrobates**
33. Dorsal surface with many transverse wrinkles; several species in streams. **Kongsbergia**
    Dorsal surface relatively smooth; several species in running waters . . . . . **Brachypoda**
34. Fifth and sixth segments of first leg swollen, with tarsal claw in a large dorsal incision (Fig. 344E); eight rare species in gravels of cold streams . . . . . . **Stygomomonia**
    Fifth and sixth segments of first leg not swollen . . . . . . . . . . . . . . . . . . . . . . . . . . . . **35**
35. Anterior ends of first epimera projecting well beyond the anterior margin of body, leaving a large bay for the capitulum (Fig. 346A) . . . . . . . . . . . . . . . . . . . . . . . **36**
    Anterior ends of first epimera not projecting beyond anterior margin of body (Fig. 346D) . . . . . . . . . . . . . . . . . . . . . . . . . . . . . . . . . . . . . . . . . . . . . . . . . . . . . . . . . **37**

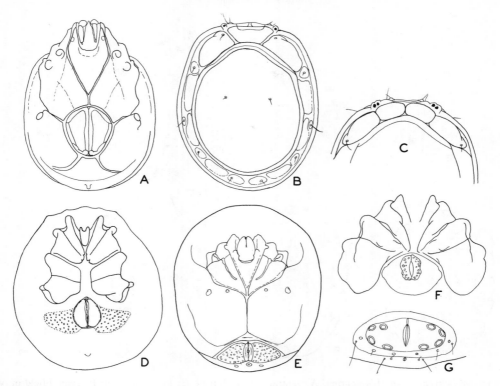

FIG. 346.–Structure of Hydracarina. A, ventral view of *Torrenticola*, ×80; B, dorsal view of *Testudacarus*, ×60; C, dorsal anterior region of *Torrenticola*; D, ventral view of *Koenikea*, ×65; E, ventral view of *Albia*, ×60; F, ventral plates of *Midea*; G, genital field of *Axonopsis complanata*. (A to C modified from Marshall, 1943; D and E modified from Marshall, 1935; G modified from Viets.)

**36.** With four small anterior dorsal plates (Fig. 346C); without swimming hairs; usually in cold streams; widely distributed; about 20 species . . . . . . . . . . . . . .**Torrenticola**

With three small anterior dorsal plates (Fig. 346B); two rare species reported from western streams . . . . . . . . . . . . . . . . . . . . . . . . . . . . . . . . . . . . . **Testudacarus**

**37.** Occurring only in western hot springs; one rare species and one common species (Figs. 344F, G) . . . . . . . . . . . . . . . . . . . . . . . . . . . . . . . . . . . . **Thermacarus**

Not in hot springs . . . . . . . . . . . . . . . . . . . . . . . . . . . . . . . . . . . . . . . . . . . . . . . . . .**38**

**38.** Genital field lying in a bay bounded by all the epimera (Fig. 346F); one rare species reported from Wisconsin . . . . . . . . . . . . . . . . . . . . . . . . . . . . . . . . . . . . . . . **Midea**

Genital field not lying in a bay bounded by all the epimera . . . . . . . . . . . . . . . . . . .**39**

**39.** With numerous acetabula (Figs. 344H, J; 346D, E) . . . . . . . . . . . . . . . . . . . . . . . . . .**40**

With three or four pairs of genital acetabula (Fig. 346G) . . . . . . . . . . . . . . . . . . . . . .**43**

**40.** Genital field near posterior margin of body (Figs. 344H, J) . . . . . . . . . . . . . . . . . . . .**41**

Genital field not near posterior margin of body; fourth epimera not especially large (Fig. 346D); about 10 widely distributed species in rivers and streams. **Koenikea**

**41.** Genital acetabula abundant (Figs. 344H, J) . . . . . . . . . . . . . . . . . . . . . . . . . . . . . . . .**42**

Genital acetabula not abundant (Fig. 346E); several widely distributed species in ponds, lakes, and slow streams . . . . . . . . . . . . . . . . . . . . . . . . . . . . . . . . . **Albia**

**42.** Genital acetabula arranged along the posterior margin (Fig. 344H); less than 5 mm long; several uncommon stream species in eastern states . . . . . . . . . . . . .**Aturus**

Genital acetabula not confined to body margin (Fig. 344J); about 10 species in stream gravels . . . . . . . . . . . . . . . . . . . . . . . . . . . . . . . . . . . . . . . . . . . . . . . . . . . . **Feltria**

FIG. 347.–Structure of Hydracarina. A, ventral view of female *Hydrovolzia*, ×60; B, genital field of *Neomamersa*; C, genital field of *Kawamuracarus*; D, palp of female *Bandakia*; E, dorsal view of *Piersigia crusta* Mitchell; F, ventral view of *P. crusta*; G, anterior ventral surface of *Trichothyas* showing setae of first coxal plate. (A from Mitchell, 1954a; B and C from Cook, 1963; D modified from Cook, 1961; E and F modified from Mitchell, 1955; G modified from Mitchell, 1953.)

**43.** Four pairs of genital acetabula; genital field at extreme posterior end of body (Fig. 346G); 0.45 mm long; brightly colored in green, blue, and yellow; one common species, about 20 rare species; northern lakes and ponds.

**Axonopsis complanata** (Müller)

Three pairs of genital acetabula; genital field not at extreme posterior end of body. **44**

**44.** Swimming hairs present; several rare species in standing waters ........**Xystonotus**

Swimming hairs absent ......................................................**45**

**45.** Third pair of genital acetabula posterior to the edge of the gonopore area; rare; known only from gravel and sand bars of clear streams in Oregon ........ **Yachatsia**

Third pair of genital acetabula in the normal position; about eight species, of which only one is common and widely distributed ......................**Mideopsis**

**46.** Third and fourth legs inserted at periphery of body (Fig. 347A); rare; reported only from Illinois ...............................................**Hydrovolzia**

Third and fourth legs not inserted at periphery of body ........................**47**

**47.** Each genital flap composed of two complete or partial sclerites (Figs. 347B, C) ...**48**

Each genital flap, if present, composed of one sclerite ........................**50**

**48.** Acetabula numerous (Fig. 347B) ............................................**49**

With only six acetabula (Fig. 347C); several hyporheic species in stream gravels.

**Kawamuracarus**

**49.** Ventral surface with six and dorsal surface with 16 large oval latticelike or grid areas; very rare ...........................................**Clathrosperchon**

No such sculpturing; several hyporheic species in stream gravels ......**Neomamersa**

FIG. 348.–Structure of Hydracarina. A, fourth leg of *Tyrrellia*; B, fifth and sixth segments of fourth leg of *Limnesia*; C, ventral plates of *Limnesia*; D, palp of female *Sperchon*; E, palp of male *Sperchon*; F, palp of *Sperchonopsis verrucosa*; G, ventral view of male *S. verrucosa*, ×115. (A modified from Marshall, 1940a; B modified from Viets; C modified from Marshall, 1932; D to G modified from Marshall, 1943.)

**50.** Genital field anterior, at least between fourth epimera; no ancoral process on capitulum (Figs. 347F; 348C) .................................................**51**

Genital field posterior to fourth epimera; ancoral process present on capitulum (Fig. 349) .........................................................................**57**

**51.** With six or seven prominent sclerites (lateroglandularia) along each lateral margin, visible in both dorsal and ventral views (Figs. 347E, F); legs abundantly supplied with pectinate setae; several uncommon species in muddy swamps and marshes ......................................................... **Piersigia**

Without such prominent lateral sclerites, although dorsal and ventral sclerites may be prominent .................................................................**52**

**52.** Mesial margin of first coxa with numerous heavy pinnate setae (Fig. 347G); legs heavy, adapted for crawling; in moss or algal masses on cold, wet rocks; rare, reported only from Illinois .................................... **Trichothyas**

Mesial margin of first coxa not setose .................................................**53**

**53.** Genital acetabula borne on uncovered plates; genital flaps absent (Fig. 348C) .....**54**

Genital acetabula more or less covered by genital flaps (Fig. 348G); swimming hairs absent; sluggish bottom forms .......................................**55**

Fɪɢ. 349.–Structure of Hydracarina. A, ventral view of *Unionicola*, ×36; B, ventral view of *Neumania*, ×35; C, ventral view of male *Hydrochoreutes ungulatus*, ×65; D, ventral plates of *Huitfeldtia rectipes*; E, ventral view of female *Hydrochoreutes ungulatus*, ×40; F, ventral view of female *Tiphys torris* (Müller), ×25; G, ventral view of *Forelia*, ×44; H, ventral plates of *Najadicola ingens* Koen.; J, genital field of *Piona*. (All modified: A and B from Marshall, 1933; C and E from Marshall, 1927; D from Viets; F from Marshall, 1937; G and J from Marshall, 1935; H from Wolcott, 1904.)

**54.** Fourth leg with two terminal claws (Fig. 348A); swimming hairs absent; sluggish; several uncommon species . . . . . . . . . . . . . . . . . . . . . . . . . . . . . . . . . . . . . . **Tyrrellia**

Fourth leg without terminal claws (Fig. 348B); swimming hairs usually present; in a variety of habitats but most common in standing waters; about 20 species.

**Limnesia**

**55.** Fourth segment of palp with two small processes on flexor surface, or processes absent (Figs. 348D); in northern states and mountainous areas; about 15 species in cold streams . . . . . . . . . . . . . . . . . . . . . . . . . . . . . . . . . . . . . . **Sperchon**

Fourth segment of palp with one large process on flexor surface (Figs. 347D; 348F). **56**

**56.** Process on fourth palp segment proximal (Fig. 348F); common and widely distributed in cold lakes . . . . . . . . . . . . . . . . . . . . . . . . . . . . **Sperchonopsis verrucosa** (Protz)

Process distal (Fig. 347D); very rare in cold, sandy creeks . . . . . . . . . . . . . . **Bandakia**

**57.** Genital field usually near posterior margin of body and separated from epimera; posterior margin of fourth epimera transverse (Figs. 349A, B) . . . . . . . . . . . . .**58**

Genital field not near posterior margin of body; posterior median corners or posterior margins of fourth epimera more or less excavated to receive genital field (Figs. 349D–G) . . . . . . . . . . . . . . . . . . . . . . . . . . . . . . . . . . . . . . . . . . . . . . . . . . . . . . . .**59**

**58.** Suture between third and fourth epimera present only laterally (Fig. 349A); most species parasitic or commensal throughout life in gills or mantle cavity of mussels; several species free-living as adults; about 25 widely distributed U.S. species . . . . . . . . . . . . . . . . . . . . . . . . . . . . . . . . . . . . . . . . . . . . . **Unionicola**

Suture between third and fourth epimera complete (Fig. 349B); usually red or bluish with lighter patterns; active swimmers; widely distributed and common; about 20 species in standing or slowly flowing waters . . . . . . . . . . . . . . . . . . **Neumania**

**59.** With eight or nine genital acetabula on each side (Fig. 349D); third leg with a long lateral seta; with swimming hairs; uncommon in northern lakes.

**Huitfeldtia rectipes** Thor

With three or many genital acetabula on each side; third leg without long lateral seta. **60**

**60.** With three or four pairs of genital acetabula (Figs. 349E, F); widely distributed . . .**61**

With many pairs of genital acetabula (Figs. 349G–J) . . . . . . . . . . . . . . . . . . . . . . . . . .**63**

**61.** Palps and legs very long; male with a petiole (Fig. 349C); posterior end of female fourth epimera blunt (Fig. 349E); two species in standing waters. **Hydrochoreutes**

Palps and legs not especially long; male without a petiole . . . . . . . . . . . . . . . . . . . . .**62**

**62.** Posterior end of female fourth epimera pointed (Fig. 349F); about five species in lotic habitats . . . . . . . . . . . . . . . . . . . . . . . . . . . . . . . . . . . . . . . . . . . . . . . . . . . .**Tiphys**

Posterior end of female fourth epimera not pointed; very rare in sandy, cold springs and streams . . . . . . . . . . . . . . . . . . . . . . . . . . . . . . . . . . . . . . . . . . . . . . . . . .**Wettina**

**63.** Fourth epimera pointed medially (Fig. 349G); several widely distributed species in lakes and ponds . . . . . . . . . . . . . . . . . . . . . . . . . . . . . . . . . . . . . . . . . . . . . . **Forelia**

Fourth epimera with longitudinal median margin (Fig. 349H) . . . . . . . . . . . . . . . . . . .**64**

**64.** Posterior margin of fourth epimera convexly rounded (Fig. 349H); parasitic or commensal in gills or mantle cavities of mussels; generally distributed but not common . . . . . . . . . . . . . . . . . . . . . . . . . . . . . . . . . . . . . . . . **Najadicola ingens** Koen.

Posterior margin of fourth epimera not convexly rounded (Fig. 349J); with swimming hairs; brightly colored; common and widely distributed; about 35 species. **Piona**

# HALACARIDAE

The Halacaridae are predominantly a marine family of mites in the Order Acari, and although several of the 30 genera are found in fresh waters, the Halacaridae are not usually considered as belonging in the Hydracarina.

Morphologically, halacarids are distinguished from Hydracarina by the fact that their palps are only three- or four-segmented. In addition, the rostrum and palps project well beyond the anterior end of the body. Body length is less than 0.5 mm. The exoskeleton is leathery and reinforced with four dorsal plates and four ventral plates. There are no separate epimera, and the legs are attached laterally. These mites cannot swim and are usually found creeping about on aquatic plants; on the bottom of ponds, lakes, and streams; in the interstitial waters of sandy and gravel substrates of fresh waters; and in subterranean and hyporheic waters. They are presumed to be predaceous.

In general, halacarids are seldom collected, and their U.S. distribution and ecology are poorly known. The following genera are either known to occur here or are likely to be taken: *Copidognathus, Halacarus, Hamohalacarus, Limnohalacarus, Lobohalacarus, Parasoldanellonyx, Porohalacarus* (Fig. 351), *Porolohmannella,* and *Soldanellonyx* (Fig. 350). *Halacarus* and *Copidognathus* are two genera in transition between fresh and salt waters. They are commonly taken in wells and springs near marine shores.

Until much more information and field collecting records are available for the United States, it seems fruitless to draw up a key based on our fragmentary data.

# ORIBATEI

The oribatids (soil mites) include many terrestrial families, only one very small family, comprising three genera, being restricted to fresh waters. Otherwise, there are a few scattered species throughout eight other families and about 15 genera that

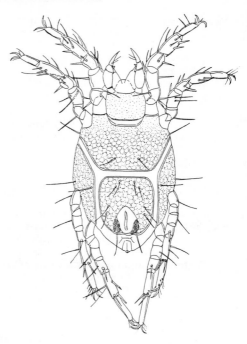

FIG. 351.–Ventral view of *Porohalacarus,* ×275. (From Ramazotti and Nocentini.)

FIG. 350.–*Soldanellonyx chappuisi* Walter. upper, dorsal view, ×85; lower, ventral view (appendages not shown). (From Imamura, 1968.)

either are aquatic or live on moist soil or on *Sphagnum* and other hydrophytes that may be damp or intermittently submerged.

Morphologically, the Division Oribatei is separated most obviously from the Halacaridae and the true water mites by the modified "tear-drop" shape of the body owing to the broad triangular ganthosoma, or capitulum. Oribatids are also more coriaceous and dark-colored.

Undoubtedly, *Hydrozetes* (Fig. 352) (in the Family Eremaeidae) is the most common truly aquatic North American genus. It occurs chiefly in small permanent ponds where the mites are restricted to crevices on submerged logs, twigs, and debris. In the spring it sometimes forms enormous dense aggregations, as large as 2 mm thick, 10 mm wide, and 2 m long! Populations are scattered during the winter months, and individuals appear to exist in a kind of cold narcosis state. Food consists of wood fibers, algae, and detritus. *Hydrozetes* may be easily cultured in the laboratory, where the life cycle usually lasts 30 to 80 days. Instars include larva, protonymph, deutonymph, tritonymph, and adult. Damselfly nymphs (especially *Enallagma* and *Tetragoneuria*) are important predators on *Hydrozetes*.

The American aquatic oribatids are too sketchily known to merit the construction of a key.

## SPIDERS

Among the true spiders, or Araneae, there are no American species that are strictly aquatic, although a European and Asiatic species, *Argyroneta aquatica,* has become curiously adapted to the aquatic environment; it spins a dense, flat, underwater web in vegetation and brings small air bubbles down from the surface film and releases them beneath the web, thus forming a large bell-shaped bubble held in place by the web; the spider spends most of its time within the bubble. Many American species, however, are semiaquatic. They run about along the beach or among shore vegetation and often skitter out over the surface of ponds and marshes, where they may feed on Hemiptera and other insects supported on the surface film. Some even dive beneath the surface when alarmed. Many build their webs on emergent vegetation. Some of the genera having common semiaquatic species are *Dolomedes, Lycosa* (wolf spiders), *Pirata, Pachygnatha,* and *Tetragnatha* (orb weavers). *Dolomedes* is a colorful and spectacular genus, often reaching a diameter of 5 cm. It dives with difficulty and remains submerged by hanging on to objects, but may remain below the surface as long as 45 minutes. Oxygen is probably obtained from air bubbles adhering to the body near the respiratory openings. *Dolomedes* feeds chiefly on aquatic insects, but it has also been reported catching small fish.

FIG. 352.–*Hydrozetes*. upper, ventral view; lower, dorsal view. (All appendages omitted.)

## HYDRACARINA REFERENCES

ARNDT, W., and K. VIETS. 1938. Die biologischen (parasitologischen) Beziehungen zwischen Arachnoideen und Spongien. *Z. Parasitenkd.* **10:**67–93.

BAKER, E. W., and G. W. WHARTON. 1952. *An introduction to acarology.* 465 pp. Macmillan, New York.

BALOGH, J. 1972. *The oribatid genera of the world.* 188 pp. Akadémiai Kiadó, Budapest.

BOETTGER, K. 1970. Die Ernährung der Wassermilben (Hydrachnellae Acari). *Int. Rev. ges. Hydrobiol.* **55:**895–912.

COOK, D. R. 1954. Preliminary list of the Arrenuri of Michigan, Part I. The subgenus Arrenurus. *Trans. Am. Microsc. Soc.* **73:**39–58.

———. 1954a. Preliminary list of the Arrenuri of Michigan, Part II. The Subgenus Megaluracarus. Ibid. 367–380.

———. 1955. A new species of Athienemannia from western North America. *Proc. Entomol. Soc. Wash.* **57:**306–308.

———. 1955a. Two new genera of Hydracarina from a spring in northern Michigan. *Am. Midl. Nat.* **53:**412–418.

———. 1955b. Preliminary list of the Arrenuri of Michigan, Part III. The subgenera Micruracarus and Truncaturus. *Trans. Am. Microsc. Soc.* **74:**60–67.

———. 1955c. Preliminary studies of the Hydracarina of Michigan: The Subfamily Foerliinae (Acarina: Pionidae). *Ann. Entomol. Soc. Am.* **48**:299–307.

———. 1959. Studies on the Thyasinae of North America (Acarina: Hydryphantidae). *Am. Midl. Nat.* **62**:402–428.

———. 1961. New species of Bandakia, Wettina, and Athienemannia from Michigan (Acarina, Hydracarina). *Proc. Entomol. Soc. Wash.* **63**:262–268.

———. 1963. Studies on the phreaticolous water mites of North America: the genera Neomamersa Lundblad and Kawamuracarus Uchida. *Am. Midl. Nat.* **70**:300–308.

———. 1963a. Studies on the phreaticolous water mites of North America: the Family Neoacaridae. *Ann. Entomol. Soc. Am.* **56**:481–487.

———. 1963b. Studies on the phreaticolous water mites of North America: the genus Feltria (Acarina: Feltriidae). Ibid. 488–500.

———. 1963c. Omartacaridae, a new family of water mites from the ground waters of North America. *Entomol. News* **74**:37–43.

———. 1963d. Studies on the phreaticolous water mites of North America: new or unreported genera of Mideopsoidea and Acalyptonotoidea. Ibid. 63–70.

———. 1968. Water mites of the genus Stygomomonia in North America (Acarina: Momoniidae). *Proc. Entomol. Soc. Wash.* **70**:210–224.

———. 1968a. New species of Neoacarus Halbert and Volsellacarus Cook from North America (Acarina: Neoacaridae). Ibid. 67–74.

———. 1969. New studies on the water mite genera Neomamersa Lundblad and Kawamuracarus Uchida (Acarina, Limnesiidae) from North America. *Am. Midl. Nat.* **81**:29–38.

———. 1974. North American species of the genus Axonopsis (Acarina: Aturidae: Axonopsinae). *The Great Lakes Entomol.* **7**:55–79.

CROWELL, R. M. 1960. The taxonomy, distribution and developmental stages of Ohio water mites. *Bull. Ohio Biol. Surv.* **1**:1–77.

———. 1961. Catalogue of the distribution and ecological relationships of North American Hydracarina. *Can. Entomol.* **93**:321–359.

ELTON, C. S. 1923. On the colours of water-mites. *Proc. Zool. Soc. Lond.* (1922):1231–1239.

GREEN, J. 1954. A new species of Lobohalacarus and other porohalacarids (Acari) in Windermere. Ibid. **124**:669–674.

HUSMANN, S., and D. TESCHNER. 1970. Okologie, Morphologie und Verbreitungsgeschichte subterraner Wassermilben (Limnohalacaridae) aus Schweden. *Arch. Hydrobiol.* **67**:242–267.

IMAMURA, T. 1957. Erste Mitteilung über Porohalacaridae aus unterirdischen Gewässern in Japan. *Abh. Naturw. Ver. Bremen* **35**:53–62.

———. 1957a. Subterranean water-mites of the Middle and Southern Japan. *Arch. Hydrobiol.* **53**:350–391.

———. 1959. Check list of the troglobiontic Trombidiidae, Porohalacaridae and Hydrachnellae of Japan. *Bull. Biogeogr. Soc. Jap.* **21**:63–66.

———. 1970. Some psammobiotic water mites of Lake Biwa. *Annot. Zool. Jap.* **43**:200–206.

IMAMURA, T., and K. MITCHELL. 1967. The ecology and life cycle of the water mite, Piersigia limophila Protz. Ibid. **40**:37–44.

LAVERS, C. H., JR. 1945. The species of Arrenurus of the state of Washington. *Trans. Am. Microsc. Soc.* **44**:228–264.

LUNDBLAD, O. 1935. Die nordamerikanischen Arten der Gattung Hydrachna. *Ark. Zool.* **28**:1–44.

———. 1941. Eine Übersicht des Hydrachnellensystems und der bis jetzt bekannten Verbreitung der Gattungen dieser Gruppe. *Zool. Bidr.* **20**:359–379.

———. 1941a. Die Hydracarinenfauna Südbrasiliens und Paraguays. Erster Teil. *K. Sven. Vetenskapsakad. Handl.* **19**:1–183.

MARSHALL, R. 1914. Some new American water mites. *Trans. Wis. Acad. Sci. Arts and Lett.* **17**:1300–1304.

———. 1927. Hydracarina of the Douglas Lake region. *Trans. Am. Microsc. Soc.* **46**:268–285.

———. 1932. Preliminary list of the Hydracarina of Wisconsin. Part II. *Trans. Wis. Acad. Sci. Arts and Lett.* **27**:339–358.

———. 1933. Preliminary list of the Hydracarina of Wisconsin. Part III. Ibid. **28**:37–61.

———. 1935. Preliminary list of the Hydracarina of Wisconsin. IV. Ibid. **29**:273–298.

———. 1937. Preliminary list of the Hydracarina of Wisconsin. V. Ibid. **30**:225–252.

———. 1940. Preliminary list of the Hydracarina of Wisconsin. VI. Ibid. **32**:135–165.

———. 1940a. The water mite genus Tyrellia. Ibid. 383–389.

———. 1943. Hydracarina from California. Part I. *Trans. Am. Microsc. Soc.* **62**:306–324.

———. 1943a. Hydracarina from California. Part II. Ibid. 404–415.

MITCHELL, R. D. 1953. A new species of Lundbladia and remarks on the Family Hydryphantidae (water mites). *Am. Midl. Nat.* **49**:159–170.

———. 1954. Water-mites of the genus Aturus (Family Axonopsidae). *Trans. Am. Microsc. Soc.* **73**:350–367.

———. 1954a. A description of the water-mite, Hydrovolzia gerhardi new species, with observations on the life history and ecology. *Nat. Hist. Misc.* **134**:1–9.

———. 1954b. Check list of North American water-mites. *Fieldiana: Zool.* **35**:27–70.

———. 1955. Two water-mites from Illinois. *Trans. Am. Microsc. Soc.* **74**:333–342.

———. 1955a. Anatomy, life history, and evolution of the mites parasitizing fresh-water mussels. *Misc. Publ. Mus. Zool. Univ. Mich.* **89**:1–28.

———. 1957. Evolutionary lines in water mites. *Syst. Zool.* **6**:137–148.

———. 1957a. The mating behavior of pionid water-mites. *Am. Midl. Nat.* **58**:360–366.

———. 1959. A new water-mite of the genus Stygomomonia (Family Momoniidae). *Trans. Am. Microsc. Soc.* **78**:154–157.

———. 1960. The evolution of thermophilous water mites. *Evolution* **14**:361–377.

———. 1963. A new water mite of the Family

Thermacaridae from hot springs. *Trans. Am. Microsc. Soc.* **82**:230–233.

———. 1964. A study of sympatry in the water mite genus Arrenurus (Family Arrenuridae). *Ecology* **45**:546–558.

———. 1965. Population regulation of a water mite parasitic on unionid mussels. *J. Parasitol.* **51**:990–996.

———. 1967. Host exploitation of two closely related water mites. *Evolution* **21**:59–75.

MITCHELL, R. D., and D. R. COOK. 1952. The preservation and mounting of water-mites. *Turtox News* **30**:169–172.

NEWELL, I. M. 1947. A systematic and ecological study of the Halacaridae of eastern North America. *Bull. Bingham Oceanogr. Coll.* **10**:1–232.

NOCENTINI, A. M. 1961. Primiritrovamenti di Porohalacaridae (Acari) nel Lago Maggiore. *Mem. Ist. Ital. Idrobiol.* **13**:127–138.

PETROVA, A. 1974. Sur la migration des Halacariens dans les eaux douces et la position systematique des Halacariens et Limnohalacariens. *Vie et Milieu* **24**:87–96.

PIECZYNSKI, E. 1960. (Formation of groupings of water mites (Hydracarina) in different environments of Lake Wilkus.) *Ekol. Pol. A,* **8**:169–198.

———. 1961. Numbers, sex ratio, and fecundity of several species of water mites (Hydracarina) of Mikołajskie Lake. *Ibid.* **9**:219–228.

———. 1963. Some regularities in the occurrence of water mites (Hydracarina) in the littoral of 41 lakes in the River Krutynia basin and the Mikolajki District. *Ibid.* **11**:141–157.

RAMAZZOTTI, G., and A. M. NOCENTINI. 1960. Porohalacaridae (Hydracarina) del Lago di Mergozzo. *Mem. Ist. Ital. Idrobiol.* **12**:185–200.

SCHMIDT, U. 1935. Beiträge zur Anatomie und Histologie der Hydracarinen, besonders von Diplodontus despiciens O. F. Müller. *Z. Morphol. Oekol. Tiere* **30**:99–176.

SCHWOERBEL, J. 1955. Über einige Porohalacariden (Acari) aus dem südlichen Schwarzwald. *Zool. Anz.* **155**:146–150.

———. 1959. Ökologische und tiergeographische Untersuchungen über die Milben (Acari, Hydrachnellae) der Quellen und Bäche des südlichen Schwarzwaldes und seiner Randgebiete. *Arch. Hydrobiol. Suppl.* **24**:385–546.

SOAR, C. D., and W. WILLIAMSON. 1925–1929. *British Hydracarina.* 3 vols. 612 pp. Ray Society, London

SOKOLOW, I. 1924. Untersuchungen über die Eiablage und den Laich der Hydracarina. I. *Arch. Hydrobiol.* **15**:383–405.

———. 1925. Untersuchungen über die Eiablage und den Laich der Hydracarina. II. *Zeitschr. Morph. Oekol. Tiere* **4**:301–332.

SZALAY, L. 1949. Ueber die Hydracarinen der unterirdischen Gewässer. *Hydrobiologia* **2**:141–179.

UCHIDA, T. 1932. Some ecological observations on water mites. *J. Fac. Sci. Hokkaido Imp. Univ. Ser. VI. Zool.* **1**:143–165.

VIETS, K. 1936. Wassermilben oder Hydracarina. *Die Tierwelt Deutschl.* **31** and **32**:1–574.

———. 1938. Über die verscheiden Biotope der Wassermilben, besonders über solche mit anormalen Lebensbedingungen und über einige neue Wassermilben aus Thermalgewässern. *Verh. Int. Ver. Limnol.* **8**:209–224.

———. 1950. Porohalacaridae (Acari) aus der Grundwasserfauna des Maingebietes. *Arch. Hydrobiol.* **43**:247–257.

———. 1955. In subterranen Gewässern Deutschlands lebende Wassermilben (Hydrachnellae, Porohalacaridae und Stygothrombiidae). *Ibid.* **50**:33–63.

———. 1955a. Wassermilben aus Nordbayern (Hydrachnellae und Porohalacaridae Acari). *Abh. Bayer. Akad. Wiss. N. S.* **73**:1–106.

———. 1955b. *Die Milben des Süsswassers und des Meeres. Teil I, Bibliographie.* 476 pp. Jena, Germany.

———. 1956. *Die Milben des Süsswassers und des Meeres. Hydrachnellae et Halacaridae (Acari). Teil II und III, Katalog und Nomenklatur.* 870 pp. Jena, Germany.

WESENBERG-LUND, C. 1919. Contributions to the knowledge of the postembryonal development of the Hydracarina. *Vidensk. Medd. Dansk. Naturhist. For.* **70**:5–57.

WOLCOTT, R. H. 1900. New genera and species of North American Hydrachnidae. *Trans. Am. Microsc. Soc.* **21**:177–200.

———. 1905. A review of the genera of water mites. *Ibid.* **26**:161–243.

WOOLEY, T. A. 1969. Two new species of Hydrozetes, extant and fossil (Acari: Cryptostigmata, Hydrozetidae). *J. N.Y. Entomol. Soc.* **77**:250–256.

YOUNG, W. C. 1968. New species of Midea, Piona, and Sperchon (Hydracarina) from Colorado. *Trans. Am. Microsc. Soc.* **87**:165–177.

———. 1969. Ecological distribution of Hydracarina in north central Colorado. *Am. Midl. Nat.* **82**:367–401.

YOUNG, W. C., and A. C. RHODES. 1974. The influence of dissolved oxygen concentrations on three species of water mites (Hydracarina). *Ibid.* **92**:115–129.

# Chapter 24

# GENERAL INTRODUCTION TO THE INSECTA

FROM A BIOLOGICAL standpoint, insects undoubtedly form the most successful group in the animal kingdom. It is estimated that more than 1 million species have been described. Insects vary widely in their habits, they occur in tremendous numbers, and many have become highly specialized and adapted to almost every conceivable habitat. Nevertheless, as a group, insects have not been particularly successful in colonizing aquatic environments. Certainly less than 1 percent of the total number of species occur in or on water at some time during their life histories. Although all the species of Plecoptera, Ephemeroptera, Odonata, and Trichoptera have aquatic stages, these orders are relatively small and are of little numerical significance when compared with the large orders Hemiptera, Lepidoptera, Coleoptera, Hymenoptera, and Diptera, where only a small percentage of the species are aquatic.

Eleven of the 30 to 35 orders of insects contain species that are regularly aquatic or semiaquatic. Among the primitive insects that have no metamorphosis the Order Collembola (springtails) is the only one in which there are aquatic species. A few occur on the surface of ponds and pools.

The Hemiptera (bugs) is the only paurometabolous order containing aquatic forms. In this group the metamorphosis is gradual, and the series of immature forms (nymphs) resemble the adults except in size, body proportions, and wing development. Many species of Hemiptera occur below the surface in both the nymphal and adult stages; others move about on the surface film.

The Ephemeroptera (mayflies), Odonata (dragonflies and damselflies), and Plecoptera (stoneflies) are hemimetabolous insects. The adults are terrestrial, but there is a series of aquatic nymphs (naiads) that usually possess accessory gills.

The other six orders are holometabolous, the stages in development being egg, active larva, quiescent pupa, and adult. A very few Neuroptera (lacewings) and Lepidotera (moths and butterflies), many Coleopotera (beetles) and Diptera (true flies), and all Megaloptera and Trichoptera (caddis flies) have aquatic larvae. All Trichoptera and many Diptera have aquatic pupae.

The major problem in becoming adapted to an aquatic environment seems to be centered around the respiratory mechanisms of insects. The air-filled tracheal system is of course capable of functioning only when the spiracles are in contact with air, and it is significant that in Hemiptera and Coleoptera, the only orders having aquatic adults, the tracheal system is essentially unmodified. Some adult beetles and nymphal and adult bugs come to the surface at intervals where the spiracles are placed in contact with the air, and the supply in the tracheal system is renewed.

The occurrence of bubblelike "air-stores" under the wings or on various parts of the body is common among adult aquatic hemipterans and beetles. Such air stores invariably are in direct contact with certain of the spiracles. The air and water interface of an air store acts as a diffusion membrane or gill, with oxygen entering and carbon dioxide diffusing outward into the water. Carbon dioxide never accumulates in such air stores because of its high solubility in

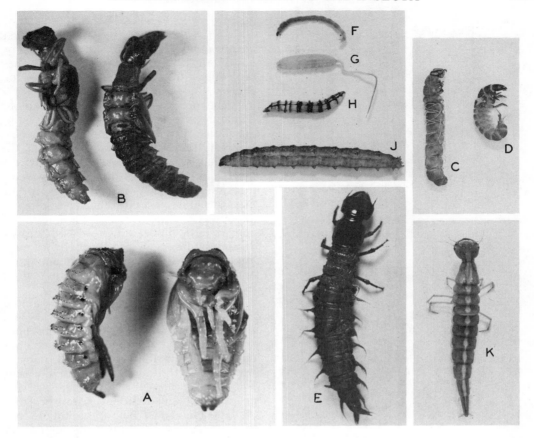

FIG. 353.–Immature aquatic insects. A, dytiscid beetle pupae, ×1.7; B, pupae of the dobson fly, *Corydalus cornutus*, ×1; C, larva of the caddis fly, *Phryganea*, ×1; D, larva of the caddis fly, *Hydropsyche*, ×1; E, larva of the dobson fly, ×1; F, larva of the midge, *Tendipes*, ×1; G, rat-tailed maggot larva, *Eristalis tenax*, ×1; H, larva of the horse fly, *Tabanus*, ×1; J, larva of the crane fly, *Tipula*, ×1; K, predaceous diving beetle larva, *Dytiscus*, ×0.8.

water. However, such air bubbles get smaller the longer the insect remains submerged, chiefly because of the diffusion of nitrogen outward, and it is therefore necessary for the insect to come to the surface periodically to renew the bubble. The renewal interval is highly variable. Sometimes it is only a second or two, sometimes as long as several hours or days, depending on temperature, the amount of oxygen in the water, the particular species involved, and presumably certain physiological variables.

Although similar in function, a plastron differs from an ordinary air store in several ways. The former is a very thin layer of air

in direct contact with large portions of the body surface in certain small aquatic hemipterans and beetles, especially those species that habitually creep about on submerged substrates. The film of air is held in place by "pile," which is an extremely thick growth of fine short hairs. Sometimes there may be more than 2 million such hairs per square millimeter of body surface. Pile hairs are curved at the tip and resist the tendency of water to compress and invade the air space, up to a water pressure of four or five atmospheres. The volume of the air film therefore remains essentially constant, and pile-bearing insects are capable of remaining submerged indefinitely, especially

FIG. 354.–Cases of immature caddis flies, ×1. Top row, cases of *Limnephilus* larvae; second row, cases of larvae: *Pycnopsyche, Pycnopsyche, Phryganea, Phryganea, Glyphopsyche*; bottom row: two larval cases of *Molanna*, three larval cases of *Brachycentrus*, two pupal cases of *Hydropsyche*.

if the water is more than 80 percent saturated with air. In addition to the uptake of oxygen via the spiracles, it has been shown that some oxygen diffuses from the plastron through the cuticle to the internal tissues.

Bubbles of oxygen emitted by aquatic plants and air bubbles in turbulent waters presumably fuse incidentally with air stores and plastrons and thus aid in their maintenance.

In some immature forms, particularly beetle and fly larvae, the aerial mode of respiration has been retained, and functional spiracles persist, usually at the posterior end of the body. From an evolutionary standpoint, however, most larvae have shown more plasticity. They have no spiracles, and most of the oxygen absorption occurs from the water itself through the specialized or unspecialized body surface. Thus they are independent of aerial respiration. Most nymphs of the hemimetabol-

ous orders and larvae of the holometabolous orders have tracheal gills of diverse location and structure. Fundamentally, however, such gills are simply thin-walled projections from the body containing tracheae.

The occurrence of blood gills among immature insects presents some interesting questions. Strictly speaking, a blood gill is a small, thin-walled projection from the body that is devoid of tracheation but contains circulating blood and supposedly functions efficiently in oxygen absorption. Such structures occur in the larvae of some Diptera, Coleoptera, and Lepidoptera. Recent investigations, however, seem to indicate that blood gills are probably of more importance as devices for maintaining the appropriate osmotic relationships within the animal.

There is an increasing tendency among insect physiologists to ascribe considerable respiratory significance to the general body surface in immature aquatic hemimetabolous and holometabolous insects. Compared with adults, the cuticle is relatively thin, and there is often a rich tracheal network just under it. In addition, it seems probable that the blood just below the cuticle may take up appreciable quantities of oxygen directly.

The vast majority of aquatic insects occur in fresh waters, only a very few species having invaded marine and brackish waters. They have become adapted to all types of fresh-water habitats, from the smallest brooks to mountain torrents and sluggish rivers, from puddles to the largest lakes, and from cold to hot springs. With few exceptions, aquatic insects are found near shores, in the shallows, and where there is an adequate supply of oxygen. Only a few Diptera are consistently found in deep lakes and in waters containing a reduced supply of oxygen. The free-swimming plankton habit has been evolved only in a few phantom midge larvae.

The key below is admittedly an artificial one. An effort has been made, however, to utilize the most obvious characteristics for the determination of the various orders. Each order is dealt with individually on subsequent pages.

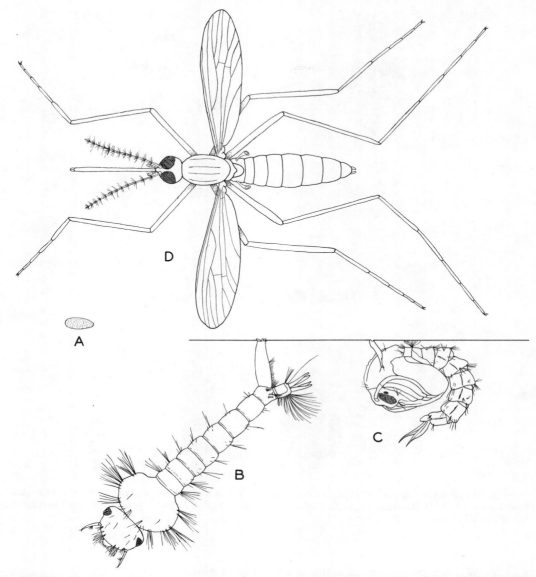

FIG. 355.–Stages in the life history of a typical *Aedes* mosquito, ×10. A, egg; B, mature larva with respiratory opening at surface film; C, pupa with respiratory opening at surface film; D, adult female (setation omitted).


# KEY TO ORDERS OF AQUATIC INSECTS; NYMPHS, LARVAE, PUPAE, AND ADULTS

1. Usually inactive; pupae . . . . . . . . . . . . . . . . . . . . . . . . . . . . . . . . . . . . . . . . . . . . . . . . .2
   Active; nymphs, larvae, and adults . . . . . . . . . . . . . . . . . . . . . . . . . . . . . . . . . . . . .4
2. Maggotlike, but the body shorter, hard, and dark-colored.
                                        Pupae of **DIPTERA** (flies), p. 669
   Mummylike, with the future adult appendages more or less concealed in translucent cases and held close to the body in a fixed position . . . . . . . . . . . . . . . . . . . . . . .3

FIG. 356.–Aquatic nymphs. A, stonefly, *Acroneuria*, ×1.3; B, damselfly, *Enallagma*, ×3.5; C to F, dragon-flies; C, *Anax*, ×1; D, *Boyeria*, ×1; E, *Hagenius brevistylus*, ×1; F, *Libellula*, showing extended labium, ×1.6; G, mayfly, *Hexagenia*, ×1.

 

**3.** Within a case composed of bits of vegetation or mineral matter.

                              Pupae of **TRICHOPTERA** (caddis flies), p. 615

    Without a case, but sometimes in a silken tube or fibrous cocoon.

                                    Pupae of **DIPTERA** (flies), p. 669

**4.** Without jointed thoracic legs; maggotlike . . . . . . . .Larvae of **DIPTERA** (flies), p. 668

    Jointed thoracic legs present . . . . . . . . . . . . . . . . . . . . . . . . . . . . . . . . . . . . . . . . . . . . . .**5**

**5.** With long, segmented, filamentous appendages at the posterior end . . . . . . . . . . . . .**6**

    Posterior filamentous appendages absent, or, if present, then not long and segmented. **7**

 

**6.** With two posterior filamentous appendages; two tarsal claws; usually with fingerlike tracheal gills on ventral side of thorax.

                          Nymphs of **PLECOPTERA** (stoneflies), p. 529

    Usually with three, sometimes two, filamentous posterior appendages; one tarsal claw; with tracheal gills on lateral margins of abdominal segments.

                       Nymphs of **EPHEMEROPTERA** (mayflies), p. 542

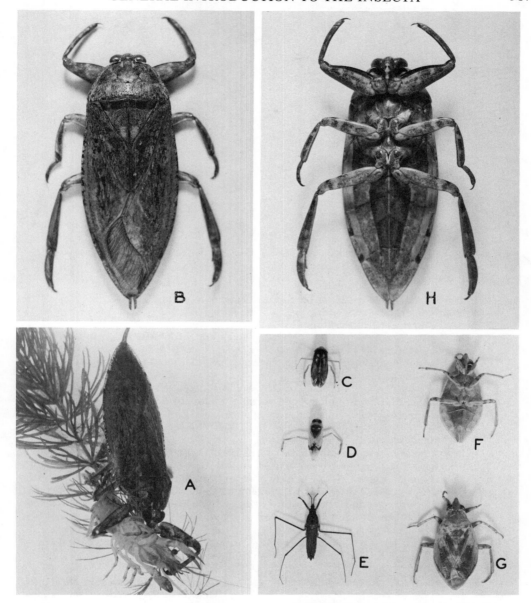

FIG. 357.–Typical aquatic Hemiptera. A, *Lethocerus* feeding on a crayfish, ×1; B, dorsal view of *Lethocerus*, ×1.4; C, *Sigara*, ×1; D, *Notonecta*, ×1; E, *Gerris*, ×1; F, *Belostoma*, ventral, ×1; G, *Belostoma*, dorsal, ×1; H, ventral view of *Lethocerus*, ×1.4.

7. With large hard or leathery forewings covering the abdomen; biting mouth parts.

Adult **COLEOPTERA** (beetles), p. 623

Wings, if present, of another structure . . . . . . . . . . . . . . . . . . . . . . . . . . . . . . . . . . . . . . .8

8. Small insects, usually less than 3 mm long; wingless; with a long forked appendage beneath the abdomen used in springing; on the surface of quiet waters.

Immature and adult **COLLEMBOLA** (springtails), p. 522

Usually more than 3 mm long; wings present or absent; no abdominal appendage for springing; usually submerged . . . . . . . . . . . . . . . . . . . . . . . . . . . . . . . . . . . . . . . . . . . .9

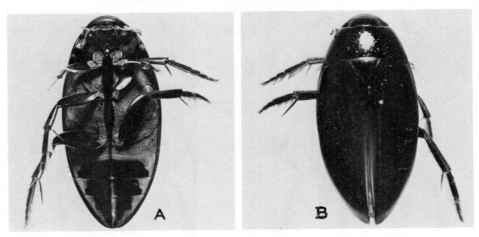

Fig. 358.–Large aquatic beetle, *Hydrophilus,* ×2. A, ventral view; B, dorsal view.

    **9.** With wing rudiments (pads) or functional wings; nymphs and adults . . . . . . . . . . . .**10**
        Without wing rudiments or functional wings; larvae . . . . . . . . . . . . . . . . . . . . . . . . . . .**11**
**10.** Sucking mouth parts in the form of a long jointed beak.
                    Nymphs and adults of **HEMIPTERA** (bugs), p. 568
        Raptorial and chewing mouth parts; labium, when extended, long and scooplike, and
           when folded serving as a mask covering the other mouth parts; with or without
           platelike caudal gills.
             Nymphs of **ODONATA** (dragonflies and damselflies), p. 557
**11.** With slender, decurved, piercing and sucking mouth parts about half as long as the
        body; small larvae living in or on sponges.
                **NEUROPTERA** (spongilla fly larvae), p. 591
        With biting mouth parts . . . . . . . . . . . . . . . . . . . . . . . . . . . . . . . . . . . . . . . . . . . . . . . . . . . . **12**
**12.** With five pairs of abdominal prolegs . . **LEPIDOPTERA** (aquatic caterpillars), p. 619
        Prolegs absent, or confined to the last abdominal segment . . . . . . . . . . . . . . . . . . . . .**13**
**13.** Each abdominal segment with one pair of stout lateral processes.
        **MEGALOPTERA** (hellgrammites, alderfly and fishfly larvae), p. 587
        No stout lateral abdominal processes, but sometimes with long, thin, lateral filamen-
        tous processes; a few beetle larvae with four stout, hornlike processes on each
        body segment . . . . . . . . . . . . . . . . . . . . . . . . . . . . . . . . . . . . . . . . . . . . . . . . . . . . . . . . . . . **14**
**14.** With a pair of terminal abdominal prolegs; usually with small, fingerlike abdominal
        tracheal gills; usually in fixed or portable cases.
                  **TRICHOPTERA** (caddis fly larvae), p. 599
        Without terminal prolegs; rarely with long, thin, filamentous abdominal tracheal gills;
        without cases . . . . . . . . . . . . . . . . . . . . . . . . **COLEOPTERA** (beetle larvae), p. 624

## AQUATIC INSECT ANOMALIES

    In addition to the "usual" fresh-water insect groups treated in this manual, there are isolated examples, on a worldwide basis, of evolutionary curiosities involving highly atypical insects that have success-fully invaded aquatic habitats. Some of these examples are as follows.

    Gravid females of a surprisingly large number of Hymenoptera enter the water only long enough to find and oviposit on the eggs or bodies of other aquatic insects. Some female fairy flies, for example, enter the water, swim with the wings, and seek out and oviposit in the eggs of dragonflies and backswimmers. A European hymenopteran, *Agriotypus,* parasitizes caddis larvae. *Anoplius* is a "diving wasp" that dives below the surface when hunting aquatic and semiaquatic spiders.

In New Zealand there is a trichopteran (*Philaniscus*) which has successfully invaded brackish water having a salinity in excess of 2.5 percent.

In Uruguay there is a semiaquatic grasshopper (*Marellia*) that has oar-shaped hind legs. It lives on the upper surface of floating aquatic vegetation but can swim on or below the water surface.

In Liberia, a species of *Rhabdoblatta,* a genus of cockroaches, lives in water at least part of the time among aquatic vegetation.

Six blind trogloboiontic aquatic beetles have been described from subterranean waters in Japan, central Africa, and France. They belong to the Dytiscidae and Elmidae.

Only one dipteran has become completely specialized for a marine existence. In the shallow coral reef areas of Samoa all the stages in the life history of *Pontomyia natans* are submarine. The adult male uses the first and third legs for swimming; wings are reduced; spiracles and a tracheal system are present. The adult female is vermiform with no appendages except for rudimentary second and third legs. Larvae and pupae are similar to these stages in *Tanytarsus,* a common fresh-water genus.

Otherwise only larval Diptera are generally found below the surface of the sea near the shoreline. It is interesting to note that such marine chironomid larvae have no blood gills.

*Aepophilus,* a marine hemipteran, is found in the intertidal zone along the west coast of Europe. It is in the family Saldidae and is thus closely related to amphibious species.

Sometimes typical fresh-water genera of Hemiptera, Coleoptera, and Diptera may be found on or beneath the surface of the sea. It is thought that these are "accidentals," usually washed in by streams or flown in by themselves. Many beetle larvae and adults inhabit the intertidal zone, however, but little is known of their life histories and habits. Their closest relatives are terrestrial.

Many terrestrial species of insects spend all or part of their life cycles on or in the floating and emergent portions of fresh-water rooted hydrophytes. Such forms are not considered in this manual.

## INSECTA, GENERAL REFERENCES

BERG, C. O. 1949. Limnological relations of insects to plants of the genus Potamogeton. *Trans. Am. Microsc. Soc.* **68:**279–291.

BERTRAND, H. 1954. *Les Insectes Aquatiques d'Europe.* 2 vols. 1103 pp. Lechevalier, Paris.

BORROR, D. J., D. M. DE LONG, and C. A. TRIPLEHORN. 1976. *An introduction to the study of insects.* 4th ed. 852 pp. Holt, Rinehart & Winston, New York.

BRUES, C. T. 1932. Further studies on the fauna of North American hot springs. *Proc. Am. Acad. Arts and Sci.* **67:**185–303.

BRUES, C. T., A. L. MELANDER, and F. M. CARPENTER. 1954. Classification of insects. *Bull. Mus. Comp. Zool.* **108:**1–917.

COLE, A. C. 1942. Collecting and preserving immature insects. *J. Tenn. Acad. Sci.* **17:**166–172.

DODDS, G. S., and F. L. HISAW. 1925. Ecological studies on aquatic insects. IV. Altitudinal range and zonation of mayflies, stoneflies and caddisflies in the Colorado Rockies. *Ecology* **6:**380–390.

FROHNE, W. C. 1939. Semiaquatic Hymenoptera in North Michigan lakes. *Trans. Am. Microsc. Soc.* **58:**228–240.

GAUFIN, A. R., and S. HERN. 1971. Laboratory studies on tolerance of aquatic insects to heated waters. *J. Kans. Entomol. Soc.* **44:**240–245.

KARNY, H. H. 1934. *Biologie der Wasserinsekten.* 311 pp. Fritz Wagner, Vienna.

McGAHA, Y. J. 1952. Limnological relations of insects to certain aquatic flowering plants. *Trans. Am. Microsc. Soc.* **71:**355–381.

MIALL, L. C. 1895. *The natural history of aquatic insects.* 395 pp. Macmillan, New York.

NACHTIGALL, W. 1964. Die Schwimmechanik der Wasserinsekten. *Ergeb. Biol.* **27:**39–78.

NEEDHAM, J. G., and C. BETTEN. 1901. Aquatic insects in the Adirondacks. *Bull. N.Y. State Mus.* **47:**382–612.

NEEDHAM, J. G., A. D. MacGILLIVRAY, A. O. JOHANNSEN, and K. C. DAVIS. 1903. Aquatic insects in New York State. Ibid. **68:**199–517. (Odonata, Diptera, Coleoptera, and Megaloptera only.)

PETERSON, A. 1939. Keys to the orders of immature stages (exclusive of eggs and pronymphs) of North American insects. *Ann. Entomol. Soc. Am.* **32:**267–278.

PORTIER, P. 1911. Recherches physiologiques sur les insects aquatiques. *Arch. Zool. exp. gén., Ser. 5,* **8:**89–379.

ROUSSEAU, E. 1921. *Les larves et nymphes aquatiques des insectes d'Europe (morphologie, biologie, systematique).* Vol. I. 967 pp. J. Lebeque, Brussels. (Hemiptera, Odonata, Ephemeroptera, Plecoptera, Megaloptera, and Neuroptera only.)

SCHWEIBERT, E. 1973. *Nymphs.* 339 pp. Winchester Press, New York.

SNODGRASS, R. E. 1954. Insect Metamorphosis. *Smithson. Misc. Coll.* **122:**1–124.

THORPE, W. H. 1950. Plastron respiration in aquatic insects. *Biol. Rev.* **25:**344–390.

USINGER, R. L., et al. 1956. *Aquatic insects of California with keys to North American genera and California species.* 508 pp. Univ. California Press, Berkeley.

WESENBERG-LUND, C. 1943. *Biologie der Süsswasserinsekten.* 682 pp. Gyldendalske, Copenhagen.

WIGGLESWORTH, V. B. 1974. *The principles of insect physiology.* 7th ed. 827 pp. Dutton, New York.

# Chapter 25

# COLLEMBOLA (SPRINGTAILS)

STRICTLY speaking, none of the Collembola are aquatic since the few species associated with water remain suspended on the surface film and submerge only accidentally. They are small to minute, grotesque insects with primitive metamorphosis. Coloration ranges from whitish and bright metallic hues to drab grayish or blackish. The mouth parts are largely hidden and overgrown by the genae; usually they are adapted for biting, but in some species they are drawn out into stylets enclosed in a cone. The eyes are composed of no more than eight ocelli. There are no wings. The abdomen consists of only six segments and these are sometimes indistinctly separated form each other. The first abdominal segment has a curious ventral tubule for anchorage, water taking, and respiration. The most characteristic abdominal structure is the furcula; it consists of a pair of springlike, partially fused appendages attached to the ventral side of the fourth abdominal segment. On the ventral side of the third segment is a catchlike spring holder. When the furcula is released from the holder and suddenly moved downward and backward, the animal is thrown into the air, sometimes as high as several inches.

All springtails occur in damp surroundings, and the great majority are found in such places as moss, humus, fallen trees, litter of the forest floor, and lake beaches. On the surface of marshes, pools, and the quiet backwaters of lakes and ponds, however, springtails may be found on the surface film in blackish patches composed of thousands of individuals. If disturbed, they leap into the air like flying spray, scattering in all directions and coming down a foot or more away. In many aquatic species the two mucrones at the end of the furcula are broadly spoonshaped and lamellate at the edges and thus exert more force on the water during leaping. The small size and water-repellent body surface prevent collembolans from breaking through the surface film.

Aquatic collembolans are most common in the early spring or late autumn, but some may be found throughout the year and even in the middle of the winter. Reproduction is viviparous in aquatic species. Miall believes that they may hibernate on the bottom, although other investigators doubt this. They feed chiefly on algae, fungi, other plant tissues, and vegetable debris of all kinds, but occasionally they are found feeding on dead worms, mollusks, and crustaceans, as well as microzoans.

Usually where springtails occur on the water they may be found in even greater abundance in the debris and vegetation on the adjacent shore. *Podura aquatica* and *Sminthurides* are the forms most commonly found on the water. The other species indicated in the key below, as well as a few additional rare forms, are encountered on water less frequently by the casual collector.

Although published records indicate a spotty distribution, it is probable that the common species occur all over the United States. About 80 Nearctic genera are known, but few are aquatic or semiaquatic. Collembola may be collected with a glass sucking tube, Berlese funnel, or pipette, and transported alive in small vials containing moist earth or filter paper. Hot 95 percent alcohol is a suitable fixative, and 80 percent alcohol is a satisfactory preservative. Specimens may be mounted in glyc-

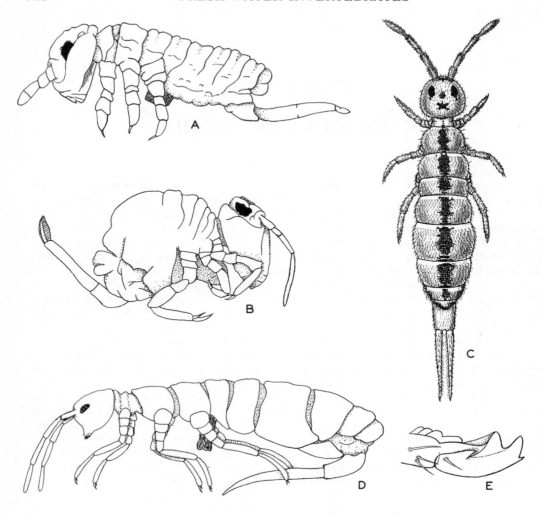

FIG. 359.–Aquatic and semiaquatic Collembola. A, *Podura aquatica*, ×55; B, *Sminthurides aquaticus* (Bour.), ×75; C and D, *Isotomurus palustris*, ×40; E, mucro of furcula of same. (A modified from Willem, 1911; C and E from Folsom, 1937; D modified from Miall.)

erin or glycerin jelly, but clearing in creosote and mounting in euparal is also a good procedure. For distinguishing minute details of light-colored specimens, clear in 20 percent acetic acid and mount in Hoyer's fluid (50 ml water, 30 g gum arabic, 200 g chloral hydrate, and 20 g glycerin). Opaque specimens can be effectively cleared in a cold or warm solution of 50 percent lactic acid.

## KEY TO COMMON AQUATIC AND SEMIAQUATIC COLLEMBOLA

1. Body elongated; thorax and abdomen distinctly segmented.
   Suborder **ARTHROPLEONA, 3**
   Body somewhat globular; thorax and abdomen indistinctly segmented (Fig. 359B) . . . . . . . . . . . . . . . . . . Suborder **SYMPHYPLEONA**, SMINTHURIDAE, **2**

2. Ventral tube without tubercles; 0.5 to 1.0 mm long (Fig. 359B); last segment of antenna long and not subdivided; several aquatic and semiaquatic species. **Sminthurides**
   Ventral tube with tubercles; up to 2.2 mm long; last segment of antenna subdivided into about 12 subsegments; olive, yellow, purple, or brown color.
   **Bourletiella spinata** (MacG.)
3. Pronotum well developed, with bristles (Fig. 359A); cuticle granular. PODURIDAE, **4**
   Pronotum poorly developed, naked (Fig. 359C); cuticle smooth ....ISOTOMIDAE, **5**
4. Furcula long, extending beyond the ventral tube when projecting forward (Fig. 359A); 1.0 to 1.5 mm long; reddish-brown to bluish-black ........ **Podura aquatica** L.
   Furcula shorter, not extending beyond the ventral tube when projecting forward; 1.2 to 1.8 mm long; coloration bluish or greenish gray; several semiaquatic species...............................................**Hypogastrura**
5. Body without sensory hairs; 2 to 7 mm long; coloration variable; several semiaquatic species...............................................................**6**
   Body with fine sensory hairs arising from cuplike pits in the integument; 1.5 to 2.7 mm long (Figs. 359C, D); coloration yellowish or greenish, with blue, purple, or blackish markings ...........................**Isotomurus palustris** (Müller)
6. Anus ventral ......................................**Folsomia fimetaria** (Nicolet)
   Anus terminal ................................................................**Isotoma**

# COLLEMBOLA REFERENCES

BRITT, N. W. 1951. Observations on the life history of the collembolan Achorutes armatus. *Trans. Am. Microsc. Soc.* **70**:119–132.

CHANG, S. L. 1966. Some physiological observations on two aquatic Collembola. *Trans. Am. Microsc. Soc.* **85**:359–371.

FOLSOM, J. W. 1916. North American collembolous insects of the subfamilies Achorutinae, Neanurinae, and Podurinae. *Proc. U.S. Nat. Mus.* **50**:477–525.

———. 1937. Nearctic Collembola or springtails, of the family Isotomidae. *Bull. U.S. Nat. Mus.* **168**:1–144.

FOLSOM, J. W., and H. B. MILLS. 1938. Contribution to the knowledge of the genus Sminthurides Börner. *Bull. Mus. Comp. Zool.* **82**:229–274.

GUTHRIE, J. E. 1903. The Collembola of Minnesota. *Rept. Geol. Nat. Hist. Surv. Minn., Zool. Ser.* **4**:1–110.

JAMES, D. G. 1933. Collembola of the Toronto region with notes on the biology of Isotoma palustris Mueller. *Trans. Roy. Can. Inst.* **19**:77–116.

MAYNARD, E. A. 1951. *A monograph of the Collembola or springtail insects of New York State.* 339 pp. Comtock, Ithaca, N.Y.

MILLS, H. B. 1934. A monograph of the Collembola of Iowa. *Monogr. Iowa State Coll.* **3**:1–143.

MILLS, H. B., and A. R. ROLFS. 1933. Collembola from the state of Washington. *Pan-Pac. Entomol.* **9**:77–83.

SCOTT, H. G. 1961. Collembola: pictorial keys to the Nearctic genera. *Ann. Entomol. Soc. Am.* **54**:104–113.

# Chapter 26

# PLECOPTERA (STONEFLIES)

STONEFLIES are terrestrial insects, but they are seldom found very far from running water, the habitat of the immature stages. The adults are somber-colored, elongated, somewhat flattened, medium to large, and decidedly primitive in structure. At the posterior end there are two cerci; in the North American forms these are usually long and composed of many segments. The legs are well developed. The two pairs of long wings are folded over the back when at rest. In some genera the wings are reduced or rudimentary, especially in the males, and different individuals within the same species may show considerable variation in the degree of wing development. The broad head bears long filiform antennae. Although the mouth parts are of the biting type, they are rather weak, and in some cases the mandibles are reduced, especially in the more northern forms. There are 10 abdominal segments, but the last segment is sometimes reduced or hidden.

Stoneflies have a worldwide distribution, and North America has an especially rich fauna. In mountainous areas of the western states many species are found in rather definite altitudinal zones. They are poor fliers and are usually found resting on objects along the shores of streams or rocky, wave-swept shoals of lakes. Some species are decidedly nocturnal in their activities. In temperate climates the great majority of adults are found between November and August. Some species of Nemouridae are unique in the insect world in that they emerge during the late fall and winter. It is striking to see them moving about on snow or ice in the sunshine of midwinter days. Each species is rather definite in the time of its appearance in the adult stage. As such, they probably do not live more than several weeks.

Oviposition habits vary considerably. Some females drop masses of eggs while flying above the surface of the water; others alight at the surface momentarily and release the eggs; a few have been seen depositing on objects immediately above the surface or actually crawling about beneath the surface.

The nymphs are all strictly aquatic, and, as a group, are remarkably homogeneous in structure. They resemble the adults but may be distinguished from them by the structure of the mouth parts, lack of genitalia, often the presence of filamentous tracheal gills, and wing pads instead of wings. The length of mature nymphs, exclusive of antennae and cerci, ranges from about 6 to 50 mm. Coloration is yellow, tan, brown, or blackish. Some of the nymphs, such as *Isoperla* and *Acroneuria,* are brilliantly decorated with contrasting yellow and black areas on the dorsal surface. Others are quite dull and inconspicuous.

For the most part, stonefly nymphs are sluggish. They occur in debris, in masses of leaves and algae, and under stones in every kind of unpolluted lotic habitat. A few species occur on the wave-swept shoals of lakes. In general, they are found only where there is an abundance of oxygen.

An undescribed species of *Capnia* is unique among stoneflies. It spends its entire life history at depths exceeding 50 m in Lake Tahoe, California. The adult is wingless, and there are no gills on either the nymph or adult.

Many species are quite specific in their

FIG. 360.–Typical adult stonefly, *Isoperla confusa* Frison, ×4.5. (Courtesy Illinois Natural History Survey.)

ecological preferences. Some occur only in small brooks; others, especially the largest forms, occur in the larger rivers. Some are found only where the current is swiftest, others in pools. Most habitats have populations in which four to six species are numerically dominant. But if collections are made frequently and thoroughly from a single stream or stream segment over a full year or two, the populations may be found to be surprisingly complex, with total species lists as high as 20 to 50, most of which are uncommon to rare. In general, stony

rivers have the greatest species diversity. Streams above timber line have few species, often less than 10.

The nymphs may be collected by hand-picking on the undersides of stones or by sorting masses of debris and dead leaves in a shallow pan. If the former method is used, it is wise to place a net or piece of screening downstream in order to catch individuals floating away in the current. Eighty percent alcohol is the best preservative. Pinned specimens are of limited value.

The Perlidae, Perlodidae, and some

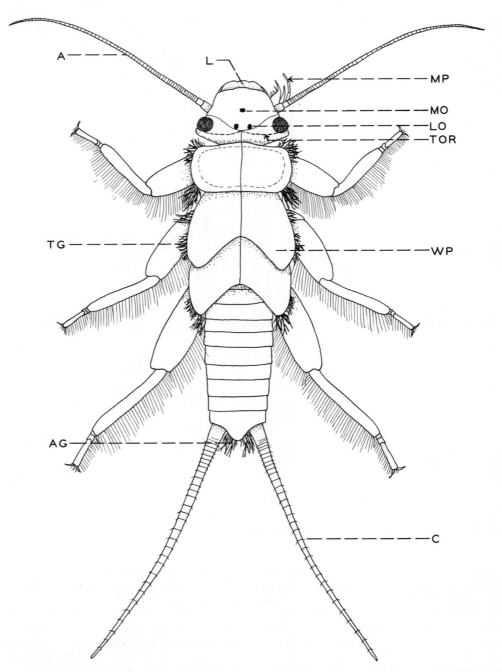

Fig. 361.–Typical stonefly nymph. *A*, antenna; *AG*, anal gills; *C*, cercus; *L*, labrum; *LO*, lateral ocellus; *MO*, median ocellus; *MP*, maxillary palp; *TG*, thoracic gills; *TOR*, transverse occipital ridge; *WP*, wing pad. (Modified from Frison, 1935.)

FIG. 362.–Ventral views of thorax and several abdominal segments of stonefly nymphs showing arrangements and types of gills. Black spots indicate leg attachments. A, *Peltoperla*; B, *Isoperla*; C, *Nemoura*; D, *Perlinella*; E, *Acroneuria*; F, *Pteronarcys*. (Courtesy Ill. Nat. Hist. Surv.)

Chloroperlidae are chiefly carnivorous and feed on other aquatic insects, including mayfly nymphs and Diptera larvae. The other forms feed chiefly on algae, bacteria, and vegetable debris. Strictly speaking, stonefly nymphs are polyphagous, with only the proportions of plant material, animal material, and debris differing from species to species.

The great majority of large nymphs possess filamentous tracheal gills. These customarily occur in tufts and are most abundant on the lateral and ventral surfaces of the thorax, but may also be on the coxae, submentum, and first few abdominal segments. Many species have very delicate, retractile, branched anal "gills." In those without gills the respiratory exchange occurs through the general body surface. It is probable that some cutaneous respiration

occurs in the gilled forms also. Oxygen consumption is influenced by temperature, size, stage in the life history, sex, and genetic makeup.

Some species are known to have special "chloride cells" on the ventral surface of the thorax. Presumably they function in osmoregulation by absorbing salts from water.

Relatively little accurate information is available concerning the number of instars and the duration of nymphal stages. In the few species that have been carefully studied the number of instars ranges from 12 to 36. Under natural conditions the great majority of species are thought to spend from one to three years as nymphs. In some species there is an egg diapause extending from, for example, May to December. Indeed, Harper and Hynes (1970) report that

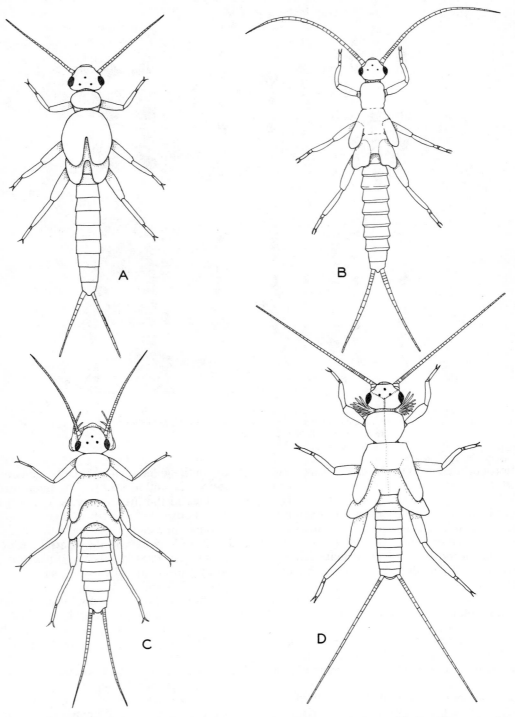

FIG. 363.–Representative stonefly nymphs. A, *Hastaperla brevis* (Banks), ×12; B, *Allocapnia vivipara* (Claassen), ×8.5; C, *Kogotus modesta* (Banks), ×3.3; D, *Nemoura venosa* Banks, ×9. (A, B, and D modified from Frison, 1935; C modified from Frison, 1942.)

early-instar diapausing, especially during the third to seventh instar, may be common during the summer for winter-emerging species. These immatures burrow into porous stream substrates and become inactive for the several warm months. The hemocoel cavity becomes filled with fat globules, the body shape becomes relatively stocky, and the setation pattern becomes greatly altered.

Just before emergence the nymphs crawl out of the water onto stones, brush, or debris. A dorsal split appears in the exoskeleton, and the adult makes its way out. After a short wait while the wings and body structures harden and dry they fly or crawl away. As indicated previously, most species emerge during the fall, winter, and spring. A few species (e.g., *Nemoura*) may emerge year-round from small, cold mountain streams. Sometimes cast skins may be found by the hundreds along the edges of streams.

Nymphs may be artificially reared to the adult stage by keeping them in wire cages in a stream, provided they are supplied with the appropriate debris and food. The cages should project above the surface of the water so that emergence may occur. When kept in ordinary aquaria in the laboratory they die very shortly, presumably because of a lack of oxygen. Under such conditions they exhibit curious rhythmic up-and-down movements of the bodies. If aquaria are supplied with aerators and kept at suitable temperatures, however, many species may be successfully reared indoors. Troughs of running (and recirculating) water are often useful.

Numerous investigations of the food habits of stream fishes, especially trout, have shown that stonefly nymphs form an important portion of the diet.

Authorities are by no means agreed on the taxonomy of this order, even with respect to certain family designations. This situation is undoubtedly largely due to a general neglect of the stoneflies by entomologists. Recently, however, much progress has been made, chiefly through the efforts of Frison, Ricker, Gaufin, and Jewett. There are over 500 species known as adults from North America, and less than half of these are definitely known in the immature stages. Most of the genera found in the United States are quite small, some being monotypic. Relatively few species in each genus are known in the immature stages. Indeed, the nymphs of several genera are rare or unknown.

Several states are known to have 40 to 100 species. About a third of the U.S. genera have a Holarctic distribution. Great Britain has only 34 species.

Several recent investigators, notably Ricker, have distinguished a few to many subgenera within most of the larger genera. Others, (Baumann *et al.*) for example, have raised these subgenera to full generic status. In this manual, we are following the latter alternative.

The key that follows has been greatly modified from several sources. Family designations follow Illies (1962). The approximate size of mature nymphs, exclusive of antennae and cerci, as well as the general geographic distribution in the United States, are included. This key leaves much to be desired, but on the basis of our incomplete knowledge of the nymphs in certain genera, it is the best that can be devised. Whenever possible, advanced nymphal instars should be used for identifications; the early instars often do not demonstrate critical morphological key characters.

## KEY TO FAMILIES AND GENERA OF PLECOPTERA NYMPHS

1. Gills present on the ventral surface of some of the basal abdominal segments (Fig. 362F) . . . . . . . . . . . . . . . . . . . . . . . . . . . . . . . . . . . . . . . . . PTERONARCYIDAE, **16**
   Without abdominal gills . . . . . . . . . . . . . . . . . . . . . . . . . . . . . . . . . . . . . . . . . . . . . . . . . . . .2
2. Ventral surface of thorax covered by large overlapping shieldlike plates (Fig. 362A); flat, broad, and roachlike; less than 10 mm long; several widely distributed species; (sometimes called *Yoraperla*) . . . . . . .PELTOPERLIDAE, **Peltoperla**
   Ventral surface of thorax without overlapping, shieldlike plates . . . . . . . . . . . . . . . .3

FIG. 364.–Structure of stonefly nymphs. A, hind leg of *Taeniopteryx nivalis* (Fitch) showing coxal gill; B, head of *Atoperla ephyre* (Newman); C, wing pads of *Allocapnia*; D, wing pads of *Nemocapnia*; E, ventral view of labium of *Taeniopteryx nivalis* showing similar length of glossae and paraglossae; F, ventral view of labium of *Perlesta placida* (Hagen) showing paraglossae extending farther forward than glossae; G, labium of *Isogenoides* showing gills at base of submentum. (A and F modified from Frison, 1935; E redrawn from Frison, 1935; G redrawn from Frison, 1942; C and D modified from Ricker, 1952.)

3. Labium with paraglossae and glossae extending forward about the same distance (Fig. 364E) ..................................................................4
   Labium with paraglossae extending forward much farther than the glossae (Figs. 364F, G) ................................................................14
4. Second tarsal segment as long as or longer than the first (Fig. 364A); widely distributed ................................. TAENIOPTERYGIDAE, 17
   Second tarsal segment shorter than the first ....................................5
5. Small and robust nymphs; body less than 12 mm long; hairy; hind wing pads extending out from the body at an angle; ventral cervical gills present or absent; detritivores; widely distributed; formerly a single genus (*Nemoura*, now subdivided) ......................................... NEMOURIDAE, 6
   Small and slender nymphs; hairs few, fine, or lacking; hind wing pads approximately longitudinal; no cervical gills ...........................................13
6. Cervical gills present ..........................................................7
   Cervical gills absent ..........................................................9
7. Cervical gills branched; in small permanent brooks ...........................8
   Cervical gills not branched; shredders, usually in vegetable debris; common; about eight Rocky Mountain species ...................................... **Zapada**
8. Gill filaments all originating from one common base; several uncommon species; western .................................................... **Amphinemura**
   Gill filaments originating from two or more separate (but adjacent) bases; several western species .......................................... **Malenka**
9. With gills attached at the lateral margins of the submentum; one rare species in Idaho and Montana brooks ............................................ **Visoka**
   Submental gills absent ........................................................10

10. Pronotum with a fringe of spines on the lateral margins ......................11
    Pronotum without such fringes ............................................12
11. Pronotum rounded at corners; one rare species in northern Rocky
    Mountains................................................**Nemoura**
    Pronotum angular at corners; one rare Rocky Mountain species ..........**Soyedina**
12. First tibiae with fringe of long hairs on outer margin; about three species in lowland
    creeks and rivers.................................................. **Prostoia**
    First tibiae without fringe of long hairs on outer margin; several species in small
    creeks at high altitudes ...................................... **Podmosta**
13. Notch on inner margins of hind wing pads situated on anterior third; lateral margins
    of abdominal segments somewhat rounded; segments widest at posterior mar-
    gin; wing pads present, rudimentary, or absent; all abdominal segments divided
    by a lateral membranous fold........................... CAPNIIDAE, **20**
    Notch on inner margins of hind wing pads situated on posterior third; lateral margins
    of abdominal segments almost straight; abdomen appearing more cylindrical;
    wing pads always present; 10 mm or less long; widely distributed; only the first
    seven or less abdominal segments divided by a lateral membranous
    fold................................................ LEUCTRIDAE, **25**
14. Branched filamentous gills on lateral and ventral surfaces of thorax (Figs. 362D,
    E)...................................................... PERLIDAE, **27**
    Without branched filamentous gills on lateral and ventral surfaces of thorax ......**15**
15. Body with a pigment pattern; cerci at least as long as abdomen. PERLODIDAE, **37**
    Body without a pigment pattern; cerci less than three-quarters as long as
    abdomen ..................................... CHLOROPERLIDAE, **46**
16. With gills on third abdominal segment; less than 25 mm long; several western
    species............................................... **Pteronarcella**
    Without gills on third abdominal segment; 35 to 50 mm long; generally
    distributed ............................................... **Pteronarcys**
17. With a gill on each coxa (Fig. 364A); chiefly eastern ................ **Taeniopteryx**
    Without coxal gills; many species .........................................**18**
18. Cerci densely fringed with long setae; one species in western mountain
    streams .......................................................**Doddsia**
    Cerci without dense fringes of long setae ...................................**19**
19. Basal segments of cerci each with a single long seta; uncommon in large silty
    rivers ............................................... **Oemopteryx**
    Basal segments of cerci without long setae; widely distributed; about eight
    species............................................... **Taenionema**
20. Cerci with prominent fringes of long hairs; about six uncommon species in western
    mountain streams .................................... **Isocapnia**
    Cerci with only one or two bristles per segment ...........................**21**
21. Body and appendages densely covered with bristles; several species east of the
    Continental Divide .......................................**Paracapnia**
    Body with few or no bristles .............................................**22**
22. Each cercus with less than 11 segments; body up to 5 mm long; a rare western
    species............................... **Eucapnopsis brevicauda** (Claassen)
    Each cercus with more than 11 segments ...................................**23**
23. Inner margin of hind wing pad notched close to tip (Fig. 364C) or not at all; common
    east of the Rocky Mountains .............................. **Allocapnia**
    Inner margin of hind wing pad with a notch about halfway from the base to tip (Fig.
    364D)...................................................**24**
24. Cerci with well developed vertical fringes of hairs (Fig. 365A); central and eastern
    states ...................................... **Nemocapnia carolina** (Banks)
    Cerci without well developed vertical fringes of hairs; many species, chiefly in the
    western states; most species small and black.
                  **Capnia** (most common), **Bolshecapnia, Mesocapnia, Utacapnia**
25. Body length much less than eight times the width; springs and seeps; five species in
    northern Rockies, Pacific northwest, and Appalachians ........**Megaleuctra**
    Body long and thin ...................................................**26**

FIG. 365.–Structure of stonefly nymphs. A, lateral view of *Nemocapnia* cercus; B, mesosternal ridge pattern of *Arcynopteryx*; C, mesosternal ridge pattern of certain Perlodidae. (A modified from Harper and Hynes, 1971; B and C modified from Ricker, 1952.)

26. Thorax and abdomen essentially hairless; one rare species in small streams in northern Rocky Mountains .............................**Despaxia augusta** (Banks)
   Thorax and abdomen with moderate to many hairs; usually in springs and spring-fed seeps ........................................ **Paraleuctra, Perlomyia**
27. Compound eyes situated far forward on sides of head (Fig. 364B); widely distributed in the eastern half of U.S. ...........................................**28**
   Compound eyes situated near posterior margin of head........................**29**
28. Anterior ocellus absent (Fig. 364B); less than 12 mm long. **Atoperla ephyre** (Newman)
   Anterior ocellus present; up to 22 mm long ........... **Perlinella drymo** (Newman)
29. Transverse occipital ridge present, with a row of spinules (Fig. 361) .............**30**
   Transverse occipital ridge absent; 20 to 30 mm long; common and widely distributed ...............................................**Acroneuria**
30. Three ocelli ..........................................................**31**
   Two close-set ocelli; up to 13 mm long; several rare species in New Mexico, Arizona, and eastern states .......................................**Neoperla**
31. Abdomen covered with freckle-like spots; up to 10 mm long; several widely distributed species in eastern half of U.S.; rare in Rocky Mountains ............**Perlesta**
   Abdomen without such spots ......................................**32**
32. Abdominal terga with few or no intercalary spinules; widely distributed in western states ................................... **Hesperoperla pacifica** (Banks)
   Abdominal terga with many intercalary spinules ............................**33**
33. Dorsal surface patterned ..........................................**34**
   Dorsal surface uniformly brown; uncommon in eastern states ..........**Acroneuria**
34. Anal gills present (Fig. 361) ......................................**36a**
   Anal gills absent .................................................**35**
35. Common in eastern states ......................................**Paragnetina**
   Found only in the western states ....................................**36**
36. Dorsal surface of thorax and abdomen with a longitudinal row of long setae; two rare Rocky Mountain species .....................................**Doroneuria**
   Without such setae; one rare Rocky Mountain species. **Calineuria californica** (Banks)
36a. Abdomen with conspicuous transverse yellow and black bands; up to 23 mm long; common; eastern................................**Neophasganophora**
   Abdomen without such bands; up to 31 mm long; uncommon; western... **Claassenia**
37. Gills absent; coloration of abdominal terga light or light and dark longitudinal stripes; usually 10 to 14 mm long; widely distributed and common ..........**Isoperla**
   Gills usually present; abdomen without a pattern or with light and dark bands ...**37a**
37a. Maxilla with a single terminal spine and no spines or hairs on the median margin; rare in Rocky Mountain states................................. **Kogotus**
   Maxilla with a large and a small spine, sometimes with additional spinules or hairs on the median margin ............................................**38**
38. Mesosternum with a (faint) median longitudinal ridge which extends anteriorly to the transverse ridge; several western species in rivers and large creeks. **Isogenoides**
   Mesosternum without a median longitudinal ridge ..........................**39**
39. Arms of the Y-ridge of the mososternum meet or nearly meet the anterior corners of the furcal pits (Fig. 365B) ...........................................**40**
   Arms of the Y-ridge meet the posterior corners of the furcal pits (Fig. 365C) .....**42**

**40.** Thoracic gills present; three Rocky Mountain species .................. **Megarcys**
Thoracic gills absent ...............................................**41**
**41.** With numerous denticles on cusps of mandibles; two species in western rivers and
streams ............................................... **Skwala**
Such denticles absent or sparse; one to several common Rocky Mountain
species ...................................................**Arcynopteryx**
**42.** Thoracic gills present ...................................................**43**
Thoracic gills absent ...............................................**44**
**43.** With gills on all thoracic segments; cervical gills present; creeks and small rivers in
Rocky Mountains .............................**Perlinodes aurea** (Smith)
Prothorax without gills; cervical gills absent; rare in creeks and springs of northern
Rocky Mountains .............................**Setvena bradleyi** (Smith)
**44.** Submental gills absent; several Rocky Mountain species ...................**Cultus**
With short submental gills ...............................................**45**
**45.** Pronotum with a longitudinal median row of hairs; tips of cerci dark-colored; uncommon, chiefly Rocky Mountains .............................. **Pictetiella**
Pronotum without such hairs; cerci uniformly light brown; several New Hampshire
and Rocky Mountain species ......................................**Diura**
**46.** Eyes small and set far forward; body slender, about 10 times the abdominal width;
western species .......................................................**47**
Eyes large, not far forward; body not slender ..............................**49**
**47.** Head about as long as wide .............................................**48**
Head longer than wide........................... **Kathroperla perdita** (Banks)
**48.** Ocellar area dark .............................................**Paraperla frontalis** (Banks)
Ocellar area light; one species in northeastern states and one in Rocky Mountain
states ...................................................... **Utaperla**
**49.** Body of mature nymph 5 to 7 mm long; inner margins of hind wing pads almost
straight; one rare and questionable species of **Chloroperla** in the southern
Appalachians; several common and widely distributed species of **Hastaperla** in
eastern half of U.S.
Body of mature nymph 6 to 13 mm long; inner margins of hind wing pads curved or
notched; many species; widely distributed ...........................**50**
**50.** Color usually bright green; widely distributed; many species .............**Alloperla**
Color usually yellowish or yellowish brown; chiefly western; a difficult group of three
genera ................................... **Sweltsa, Triznaka, Naeviperla**

# REFERENCES

BAUMANN, R. W., A. R. GAUFIN, and R. F. SUR-
DICK. 1977. The stoneflies (Plecoptera) of the
Rocky Mountains. *Mem. Am. Ent. Soc.* 31:1–208.
CLAASSEN, P. W. 1928. Additions and corrections
to the monograph on the Plecoptera of North America. *Ann. Entomol. Soc. Am.* 21:667–668.
———. 1931. Plecoptera nymphs of North America (north of Mexico). *Publ. Thomas Say Found.*
3:1–199.
———. 1940. A catalog of the Plecoptera of the
world. *Cornell Univ. Agric. Exp. Sta. Mem.* 232:1–
235.
FRISON, T. H. 1929. Fall and winter stoneflies, or
Plecoptera, of Illinois. *Bull. Ill. Nat. Hist. Surv.*
18:343–409.
———. 1935. The stoneflies, or Plecoptera, of Illinois. Ibid. 20:281–371.

———. 1937. Studies of Nearctic aquatic insects.
II. Descriptions of Plecoptera. Ibid. 21:78–98.
———. 1942. Studies of North American Plecop-
tera, with special reference to the fauna of Illinois.
Ibid. 22:235–356.
GAUFIN, A. R. 1956. An annotated list of the stone-
flies of Ohio (Plecoptera). *Ohio J. Sci.* 56:321–324.
GAUFIN, A. R., A. V. NEBEKER, and J.
SESSIONS. 1966. The stoneflies (Plecoptera) of
Utah. *Univ. Utah Publ. Biol. Ser.* 14:1–93.
GAUFIN, A. R., et al. 1972. The stoneflies (Plecop-
tera) of Montana. *Trans. Am. Entomol. Soc.* 98:1–
161.
HANSON, J. F. 1946. Comparative morphology and
taxonomy of the Capniidae (Plecoptera). *Am. Midl.
Nat.* 35:193–249.
HARDEN, P. H., and C. E. MICKEL. 1952. The

stone flies of Minnesota (Plecoptera). *Univ. Minn. Agric. Exp. Sta. Tech. Bull.* **201**:1–84.

HARPER, P. P., and H. B. N. HYNES. 1970. Diapause in the nymphs of Canadian winter stoneflies. *Ecology* **51**:925–927.

————. 1971. The Capniidae of eastern Canada (Insecta: Plecoptera). *Can. J. Zool.* **49**:921–940.

HEIMAN, D. R., and A. W. KNIGHT. 1975. The influence of temperature on the bioenergetics of the carnivorous stonefly nymph, Acroneuria californica Banks (Plecoptera: Perlidae). *Ecology* **56**:105–116.

HITCHCOCK, S. W. 1969. Plecoptera from high altitudes and a new species of Leuctra (Leuctridae). *Entomol. News* **80**:311–316.

ILLIES, J. 1962. Die Unterordnungen, Familien und Gattungen der Plecoptera. *Verh. XI Int. Kongr. Entomol. Wien* **3**:263–267.

————. 1966. Katalog der rezenten Plecoptera. *Das Tierreich* **82**:1–632.

JEWETT, S. G. 1954. New stoneflies (Plecoptera) from western North America. *J. Fish. Res. Board of Canada* **11**:543–549.

————. 1959. The stoneflies (Plecoptera) of the Pacific Northwest. *Oregon State Monogr. Stud. Entomol.* **3**:1–95.

————. 1960. The stoneflies (Plecoptera) of California. *Bull. Calif. Insect Surv.* **6**:125–177.

————. 1962. New stoneflies and records from the Pacific coast of the United States. *Pan-Pac. Entomol.* **38**:15–20.

————. 1963. A stonefly aquatic in the adult stage. *Science* **139**:484–485.

KAPOOR, N. N. 1972. Rearing and maintenance of plecopteran nymphs. *Hydrobiologia* **40**:51–53.

KERST, C. D., and N. H. ANDERSON. 1974. Emergence patterns of Plecoptera in a stream in Oregon, U.S.A. *Freshwater Biol.* **4**:205–212.

————. 1975. The Plecoptera community of a small stream in Oregon, U.S.A. Ibid. **5**:189–203.

KNIGHT, A. W., and A. R. GAUFIN. 1964. Relative importance of varying oxygen concentration, temperature, and water flow on the mechanical activity and survival of the Plecoptera nymph, Pteronarcys californica Newport. *Proc. Utah Acad. Sci. Arts and Lett.* **41**:14–28.

————. 1966. Oxygen consumption of several species of stoneflies (Plecoptera). *J. Insect Physiol.* **12**:347–355.

————. 1966a. Altitudinal distribution of stoneflies (Plecoptera) in a Rocky Mountain drainage system. *J. Kans. Entomol. Soc.* **39**:668–675.

————. 1966b. Function of stonefly gills under re-

duced dissolved oxygen concentration. *Proc. Utah Acad. Sci. Arts and Lett.* **42**:186–190.

————. 1967. Stream type selection and associations of stoneflies (Plecoptera) in a Colorado river system. *J. Kans. Entomol. Soc.* **40**:347–352.

NEBEKER, A. V., and A. R. GAUFIN. 1967. Geographic and seasonal distribution of the family Capniidae of western North America (Plecoptera). Ibid. 415–421.

NEEDHAM, J. G., and P. W. CLAASSEN. 1925. A monograph of the Plecoptera or stoneflies of America north of Mexico. *Publ. Thomas Say Found.* **2**:1–397.

RICHARDSON, J., and A. R. GAUFIN. 1971. Food habits of some western stonefly nymphs. *Trans. Am. Entomol. Soc.* **97**:91–122.

RICKER, W. E. 1943. Stoneflies of southwestern British Columbia. *Univ. Indiana Publ. Sci. Ser.* **12**:1–145.

————. 1949. The North American species of Paragnetina. *Ann. Entomol. Soc. Am.* **42**:279–288.

————. 1950. Some evolutionary trends in Plecoptera. *Proc. Indiana Acad. Sci.* **59**:197–209.

————. 1952. Systematic studies in Plecoptera. *Univ. Indiana Publ. Sci. Ser.* **18**:1–200.

————. 1959. The species of Isocapnia Banks (Insecta, Plecoptera, Nemouridae). *Can. J. Zool.* **37**:639–653.

————. 1965. New records and descriptions of Plecoptera (Class Insecta). *J. Fish. Res. Board of Can.* **22**:475–501.

RICKER, W. E., and H. H. ROSS. 1968. North American species of Taeniopteryx (Plecoptera, Insecta). Ibid. **25**:1423–1439.

————. 1969. The genus Zealeuctra and its position in the family Leuctridae (Plecoptera, Insecta). *Can. J. Zool.* **47**:1113–1127.

ROSS, H. H., and W. E. RICKER. 1971. The classification, evolution, and dispersal of the winter stonefly, genus Allocapnia. *Ill. Biol. Monogr.* **45**:1–240.

STARK, B. P., et al. 1973. An annotated list of the stoneflies (Plecoptera) of Colorado. Part I. *Entomol. News* **84**:269–277.

————. 1973a. An annotated list of the stoneflies (Plecoptera) of Colorado. Part II. Ibid. 301–305.

SURDICK, R. F., and M. R. CATHER. 1975. The nymph of Utaperla sopladora Ricker (Plecoptera: Chloroperlidae). Ibid. **86**:102–106.

WU, C. F. 1923. Morphology, anatomy and ethology of Nemoura. *Bull. Lloyd Libr.* **23**:1–81.

ZWICK, P. 1973. Insecta Plecoptera. Phylogenetisches System und Katalog. *Das Tierreich* **94**:1–465.

# Chapter 27

# EPHEMEROPTERA (MAYFLIES)

EPHEMEROPTERA are small to medium-sized terrestrial insects with delicate, many-veined, transparent wings that are held together vertically when at rest. Sometimes the hind wings may be greatly reduced or lacking. The head bears inconspicuous antennae, large compound eyes, and vestigial mouth parts. No food is taken during the adult stage. The mesothorax is large, the legs are slender and weak, and at the posterior end of the abdomen there are two or three, long, segmented filaments.

Mayflies have a worldwide distribution but are found only in the vicinity of bodies of fresh water in which the immature stages are passed. Much of the time, and always when a wind is blowing, the adults remain clinging to vegetation, but on calm, sunny spring and summer days or in the evening they take to the air in great hovering swarms. Such swarms are composed almost entirely of males. Each individual flies quickly upward in the swarm and then, spreading out the wings horizontally, it floats downward to the lower part of the swarm "like a bit of thistledown." These movements are repeated over and over. Females enter the swarm singly and emerge almost immediately accompanied by a male. Mating then occurs during flight. Many species are attracted to lights at night, and sometimes mayflies may be present in such numbers as to form dense clouds around lights, and in the morning their bodies may be found piled more than a foot deep on the ground below. Numerous newspaper accounts tell how the millions of dead mayflies make bridges and roads near lakes and streams so slippery as to stop traffic. Such accounts refer particularly to *Ephemera, Hexagenia,* and *Epho-ron*. On the shores of lakes their bodies may be washed up in windrows.

Oviposition habits vary considerably. The eggs may be washed off a few at a time as the female dips her abdomen into the water, or they may be released in large masses. In some species the female actually crawls below the surface and oviposits on submerged objects. The eggs, produced in great numbers, are usually oval, are extremely small, and have a great variety of colors. They are commonly sculptured and viscid, and are sometimes imbedded in a gelatinous material. They often have some additional means of anchorage in the form of knobs or long coiled filaments that become entangled in the debris of the substrate. Depending on the species and water temperature, the eggs hatch in a few days to a few months. Some species of *Callibaetis* are known to be ovoviviparous.

Usually the fully developed aquatic nymph (naiad) merely comes to the surface when it is ready to transform, but in some cases it may crawl out of the water on rocks or emergent vegetation. The nymphal exoskeleton is shed in a few seconds or minutes. The winged insect that appears, however, is not the final adult but a unique "dun," or subimago, which differs slightly from the imago, having a duller appearance and translucent wings. The subimago very soon flies upward and alights on vegetation, where it remains quietly unless disturbed. Some subimagoes are active on warm summer nights. This stage may last only a few minutes, but in the more common species it persists for 24 hours or more. Then a very delicate exocuticle is cast from the whole body, including the wings, and the fully formed imago, or "spinner," is re-

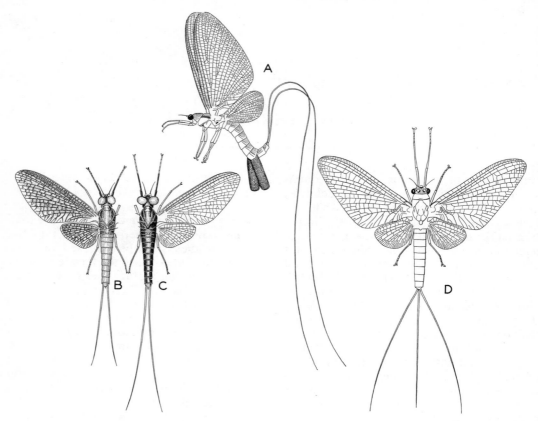

FIG. 366.–Adult mayflies. A, female *Ephoron album* with extruded egg packets, ×2; B, female subimago of *Isonychia sicca,* ×2.5; C, adult female of *I. sicca,* ×2.5; D, *Potamanthus,* ×2.5. (From Needham, 1920.)

vealed. In this condition the wings are usually transparent and the body has a more shiny appearance. In general, the sexually mature adult is notably short-lived. Some species live only a few hours and others a day to a week or more especially if the weather is cool and moist. Seasonal emergence patterns vary widely. Adults of some species may be collected almost daily for two or three months. Others can be taken only during two or three successive days.

In contrast to the uniform structure of the adults, the nymphs show considerable variations and adaptations to their specific habitats. Mature nymphs, however, are all characterized by an elongated body, large head, well-developed mandibulate mouthparts, stout legs, long filiform antennae, large compound eyes, and three rather prominent ocelli. The abdomen consists of 10 segments. Paired tracheal gills on the lateral or dorsal surface of abdominal segments one through seven constitute the most characteristic feature and serve to distinguish mayfly nymphs from all other aquatic insects. Gills may be absent from one or more of these segments. At the tip of the abdomen are usually three, and sometimes two, long, segmented, fringed, caudal filaments. One or two pairs of wing pads are visible in the great majority of species, but in a few nymphs they are hidden by the pronotum. Coloration varies greatly; some forms are dull brown, gray, or blackish; others are pale, greenish, reddish, and variously marked. Many are protectively colored. Schwiebert (1973) contains excellent color plates of many species. Without the caudal filaments, the length range of mature nymphs is about 3

FIG. 367.–Structure of Ephemeroptera nymphs. A, foreleg of *Hexagenia bilineata*; B, *Neoephemera purpurea*, ×3.5; C, *Hexagenia bilineata*, ×2; D, *Ephemera varia*, ×4; E, *Pentagenia vittigera*, ×3; F, head of *P. vittigera*; G, head of *Ephoron*. (A and C to E from Needham, 1920; B modified from Traver, 1931; F modified from Needham, 1920; G modified from Ide, 1935.)

to 28 mm. In general, the burrowers are the largest species.

The tracheal gills show almost endless morphological variations (Fig. 368). Typically, they are leaflike and richly supplied with tracheae connecting with the main tracheal trunks of the abdomen. Most genera have gills on abdominal segments one to seven, but sometimes one or more pairs may be vestigial or absent. Internal muscles vibrate the gills in a rapid, shuttlelike manner, either intermittently or for long periods. Undoubtedly the water currents thus set up ensure an adequate oxygen supply. The relative significance of gills and general body surface in respiration is still a matter

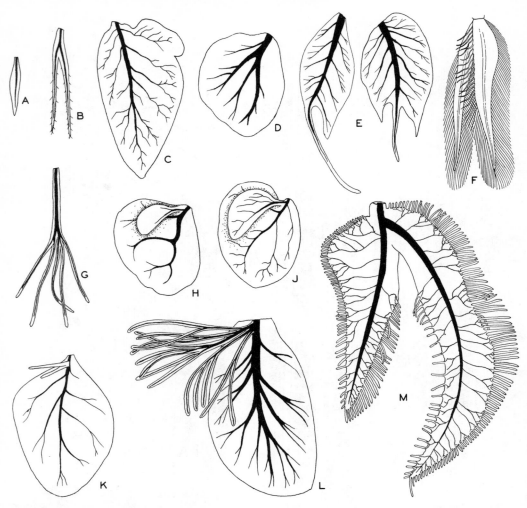

FIG. 368.–Tracheal gills of mayfly nymphs. A, seventh gill of *Stenonema*; B, first gill of *Blasturus*; C, third gill of *Callibaetis*; D, fourth gill of *Neocloeon alamance*; E, third pair of gills of *Blasturus intermedius*; F, second gill of *Hexagenia bilineata*; G, second gill of *Habrophlebia*; H, fourth gill of *Cloeon simplex*; J, fourth gill of *Cloeon*; K, second gill of *Cinygmula*; L, second gill of *Cinygma*; M, fourth gill of *Ephoron*. (C and J redrawn from McDunnough, 1930; G modified from Needham, Traver, and Hsu by permission of the Comstock Publishing Co.; F from Needham, 1920; H modified from Ide, 1937; K and L redrawn from McDunnough, 1933; M modified from Ide, 1935.)

of debate. Recent experimental evidence, however, indicates that a greater percentage of oxygen is absorbed through the general integument in the nonburrowers than in the burrowers. Gills are regenerated after being broken off.

Mayfly nymphs occur in all types of fresh waters, wherever there is an abundance of oxygen. Depending on temperature, 2 to 5 ppm of dissolved oxygen seem

to be the lethal limits. Although they may be found as deep as 15 m, they are most characteristic of the shallows. Those species inhabiting a particular lake, pond, or stream seem to be determined to a large extent by the specific nature of the substrate. Some occur only in vegetation; some only on mud, debris, gravel, or rock bottoms; some are found only between or under rocks; many burrow in mud or debris. Water movements are apparently a further significant ecological factor since many species are confined to quiet ponds and lakes, wave-swept shores, slow streams, rapid streams, or mountain torrents.

In mountainous areas there are nicely defined overlapping limits for many species in accordance with the temperature regime and nature of the substrate.

A few investigators have found a natural, endogenous, rhythmic activity pattern, with greatest activity and mobility at night.

An ecological classification, as suggested by Needham, Traver, and Hsu (1935), follows:

A. Nymphs restricted to the quiet waters of ponds, lakes, and backwaters of streams.
  1. Climbers. These nymphs climb, dart, run, or jump about, usually in submerged vegetation. Their rapid locomotion is due to sudden strong movements of the caudal filaments and gills. Such nymphs are smooth-bodied, are not especially streamlined, and have heavily fringed caudal filaments and platelike gills. Typical genera are *Blasturus, Cloeon, Siphlonurus,* and *Callibaetis* (Fig. 375G).
  2. Bottom sprawlers. These nymphs crawl about slowly on all types of bottoms. They are stiff-legged, hairy, and covered with debris. The legs are spread out laterally, the body is more or less depressed, and the caudal filaments are thinly fringed. The first pair of gills are often differentiated into gill covers that overlap and protect the other gills from silt. Common genera are *Caenis, Ephemerella,* and *Potamanthus* (Figs. 370; 373A; 375H).
  3. Burrowers. These are among the most interesting of all mayfly nymphs. Molelike, they literally plow their way through mud, muddy sand, or debris. The burrow has two openings and is constructed with the flattened front legs and undulations of the long abdomen. In addition, in most species there is a large, tusklike projection from the outer side of each mandible (Fig. 367), and these are probably of some use in digging the burrow. The plumose gills are dorsal in position and their movements maintain a constant current through the burrow that brings in oxygenated water and removes debris. It is also thought that the presence of the current prevents the collapse of the burrow. Usually burrowers are found in the top 5 cm of mud, but they have been observed as deep as 15 cm. Some or all of the species in the following genera are burrowers: *Dolania, Potamanthus, Ephemera, Hexagenia, Litobrancha, Pentagenia, Ephoron, Campsurus,* and *Tortopus.*

B. Nymphs in running waters and on wave-swept shores. Compound eyes dorsal.
  1. Free-ranging species of rapid waters. When at rest, these attractively colored nymphs maintain themselves in the current by clinging to pebbles, but they are able to move about in spite of the current with quick, minnowlike darts. Typical genera are *Isonychia, Ameletus, Paraleptophlebia,* and *Baetis* (Figs. 375E, F).
  2. Clinging species. Unlike the foregoing, these nymphs move about slowly and deliberately. They cling tightly to stones and other objects and may be found in greatest abundance in crevices and on the undersides of stones. The body is very flat and broad anteriorly, and the legs are characteristically flattened. Common genera are *Epeorus, Stenonema, Heptagenia, Rhithrogena,* and *Ephemerella* (Figs. 373A, B; 377F, G). In *Epeorus* and *Rhithrogena* there is, in effect, a ventral suckerlike holdfast. This is composed of the gills that have thick, spiny margins and that are laterally outspread on the substrate, the whole forming a kind of oval ring around the abdomen (Fig. 369). In some species of *Ephemerella* the ventral surface of the abdominal segments is modified to form a sucker. Incidentally, there is some evidence to show that the ven-

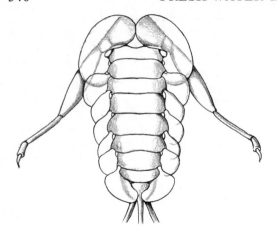

FIG. 369.–*Rhithrogena* abdomen, ventral view. (From Leonard and Leonard, 1962, courtesy Cranbrook Institute of Science.)

tral gill-sucker arrangement is of little or no value in adhering to the substrate, but that the claws are of primary importance.

3. Species inhabiting trash, silt, and moss. These stream-inhabiting nymphs do not occur in swift currents. They are stiff-legged and spiny. Some species of *Ephemerella* and *Neoephemera* are typical representatives.

Mayfly nymphs are chiefly opportunistic feeders. Although they are primarily herbivorous, many species feed on detritus and living animals. In *Isonychia* there are rows of long, stiff bristles set at an angle on the anterior surface of the first legs. These constitute a sieve which strains small particles from the water. Burrowers in hard substrates, as well as *Hexagenia*, are also filter feeders; they frequently leave their burrows to feed on surface debris. Most nymphs feed on fine detritus in surface deposits, including, for example, most Beatidae, some Heptageniidae, most Leptophlebiidae, many *Ephemerella*, the Caenidae, and the Baetiscidae. Periphyton scrapers include such examples as some Baetidae, Heptageniidae, Ephemerellidae, Leptophlebiidae, and Caenidae. Such forms as *Siphlonurus* and *Pseudiron* commonly are carnivorous and feed on chironomid larvae.

The first nymphal stage that hatches

from the egg is a minute creature usually less than a millimeter long, resembling similar stages of the Plecoptera and Zygoptera (Fig. 377A). In some species all the gills appear in the second instar, but usually they appear one pair at a time or irregularly with successive molts. As growth proceeds there is an increase in the number of antennal segments and in the relative size of the compound eyes and wing pads. Just before emergence the body has a silvery appearance owing to gas between the nymphal integument and that of the developing subimago. Very few life histories are completely known. There are numerous nymphal ecdyses, with more than 40 having been recorded for one species. Unlike the adult, then, the nymphal stages constitute a relatively long period in the life history.

FIG. 370.–Dorsal view of *Potamanthus* nymph. (From Burks, 1953.)

Some species have one generation per year, some have two generations per year, and others have a two- or three-year life cycle. During the winter months nymphs may be active or hibernating, and the eggs are usually in diapause. Details of the life cycle for a particular species vary according to latitude and altitude. Many species are active and growing at temperatures as low as 1° to 4°. The serious fisherman often knows precisely when there will be an emergence from his favorite trout stream.

Species occurring in aquatic vegetation may be collected by sweeping with a net or

FIG. 372.–Dorsal view of *Baetis hiemalis* nymph. (From Leonard and Leonard, 1962, courtesy Cranbrook Institute of Science.)

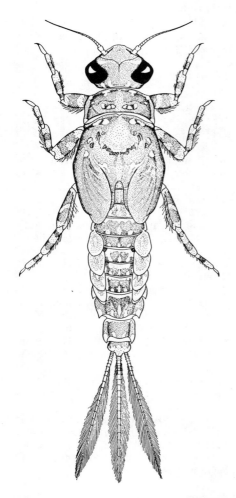

FIG. 371.–Dorsal view of *Ephemerella excrucians* nymph. (From Leonard and Leonard, 1962, courtesy Cranbrook Institute of Science.)

by washing out the vegetation in a suitable container. A sieve net is essential for separating burrowers from the surrounding mud. For stream work a large screen held in the current while rocks and debris upstream are agitated will retain many dislodged specimens. Hand-picking may be used for the species that cling to stones, and in some instances a knife blade is necessary to dislodge the nymphs without injuring them. Ninety-five percent alcohol is a suitable fixative and preservative. Specialists fix nymphs in Kahle's fluid and replace it with 80 percent alcohol in five days. Specimens should be kept in vials completely filled with preservative so that parts will not be broken off because of splashing and movements.

In view of their very slow growth, rearing the immature stages to the imago is a matter of great patience. It is essential, of course, that the nymphs be kept at a suitable temperature in aerated or running water. The burrowing forms may be kept in pans of mud submerged in running water. Some kind of a wire or cloth cage should be arranged to retain the imago at emergence.

As shown by many food studies, mayfly nymphs are often the most abundant and typical trout stream insects. In the riffles especially they form an important item of the trout diet. In many lakes and ponds the nymphs are almost equally important to other types of fishes.

Nearly 600 species of mayflies are known from the United States (in contrast to 44 species in Great Britain). *Ephemerella* is by far the largest genus with about 80 species having been described as adults. *Baetis, Stenonema, Heptagenia, Paraleptophlebia,* and *Isonychia* are also rather large genera. In about half of the American genera, however, less than five species are known. Imagoes are far better known than the nymphs. The key below includes all except a few very rare and poorly known genera. In general, it can be used for any of the late nymphal stages.

The classification system in this key is greatly modified from Edmunds, Allen, and Peters (1963) and from other sources. The serious student will find that the volume by Edmunds, Jensen, and Berner (1976) is indispensable.

## KEY TO GENERA OF EPHEMEROPTERA

1. Gills concealed beneath an enormously enlarged thoracic carapace (Fig. 375A); 4 to 14 mm long; 11 eastern species; rivers and streams. BAETISCIDAE, **Baetisca**
   Gills visible, carapace absent . . . . . . . . . . . . . . . . . . . . . . . . . . . . . . . . . . . . . . . . . .2
2. Mandible with an external projecting tusk visible dorsally (Fig. 367) . . . . . . . . . . . . .3
   Mandible without such a tusk . . . . . . . . . . . . . . . . . . . . . . . . . . . . . . . . . . . . . . . . .**11**
3. Gills lanceolate, not fringed (Fig. 375F); 6 to 10 mm long; about 35 species; generally distributed . . . . . . . . . . . . . . . . . . . . LEPTOPHLEBIIDAE, **Paraleptophlebia**
   Gills lanceolate and fringed (Fig. 368F) . . . . . . . . . . . . . . . . . . . . . . . . . . . . . . . . . . .4
4. Gills dorsal, curving up over abdomen; first tibiae somewhat flattened (Fig. 367); fossorial . . . . . . . . . . . . . . . . . . . . . . . . . . . . . . . . . . . . . . . . . . . . . . . . . . . . . . . . .5
   Gills lateral, heavily fringed; first tibiae slender; mostly sprawlers (Fig. 370); 7 to 13 mm long; eight species. . . . . . . . . . . . . . . . POTAMANTHIDAE, **Potamanthus**
5. Mandibular tusks curved upward . . . . . . . . . . . . . . . . . . . . . . EPHEMERIDAE, **6**
   Mandibular tusks curved downward . . . . . . . . . . . . . . . . . . . . .POLYMITARCIDAE, **9**
6. Mandibular tusks toothed (Fig. 367F); 18 to 24 mm long; central and southern rivers . . . . . . . . . . . . . . . . . . . . . . . . . . . . . . . . . . . . .**Pentagenia vittigera** (Walsh)
   Mandibular tusks not toothed . . . . . . . . . . . . . . . . . . . . . . . . . . . . . . . . . . . . . . . .7
7. Frontal process of head bifid (Fig. 367D); 12 to 20 mm long; generally distributed in lakes and streams; about six species . . . . . . . . . . . . . . . . . . . . . . . . . .**Ephemera**
   Frontal process of head not bifid (Fig. 367C) . . . . . . . . . . . . . . . . . . . . . . . . . . . . . .8
8. Gills of first abdominal segment forked (Fig. 368F); 13 to 32 mm long; burrowers in soft bottom of streams and lakes in eastern half of the United States; about 12 species . . . . . . . . . . . . . . . . . . . . . . . . . . . . . . . . . . . . . . . . . . . . . . . . . . .**Hexagenia**
   Gills of first abdominal segment not forked; 20 to 29 mm long; burrowers in soft bottoms of brooks and small streams; eastern states.
   **Litobrancha recurvata** (Morgan)
9. Mandibular tusks with numerous toothlike tubercles (Fig. 367G); 12 to 17 mm long; often burrow in hard clay substrates of lakes and slow streams; two widely distributed species but not common in west and south. . . . . . . . . . . . . . **Ephoron**
   Mandibular tusks with only one or two toothlike tubercles (Fig. 374B); uncommon. **10**

FIG. 373.–Mayfly nymphs. A, *Ephemerella doris,* ×8; B, *E. allegheniensis,* ×7; C, *Ametropus,* ×4. (Modified from Needham, Traver, and Hsu by permission of the Comstock Publishing Co.)

**10.** Generally distributed east of Rocky Mountains; 20 to 35 mm long; three species.
**Tortopus**
Texas; 10 to 30 mm long . . . . . . . . . . . . . . . . . . . . . . . . . . . . . . . . . . . . . . . . . . . . .**Campsurus**
**11.** Head and thorax with large, dense dorsal pads of spines on each side; 13 mm long; rare in large sandy rivers of southeastern coastal states.
**Dolania americana** Edmunds and Traver
Without such pads . . . . . . . . . . . . . . . . . . . . . . . . . . . . . . . . . . . . . . . . . . . . . . . . . . .**12**
**12.** Forelegs with conspicuous fringes of long hairs (Fig. 375E) . . . . . . . . . . . . . . . . . . . .**13**
Without such hairs . . . . . . . . . . . . . . . . . . . . . . . . . . . . . . . . . . . . . . . . . . . . . . . . . . .**15**
**13.** First abdominal segment with ventral gills; 9 to 12 mm long; sandy rivers.
OLIGONEURIIDAE, **14**
First abdominal segment with dorsal gills; 9 to 16 mm long; active darters and swimmers (Figs. 375D, E); generally distributed in rapid waters; about 25 species. . . . . . . . . . . . . . . . . . . . . . . . . . . . . . . . SIPHLONURIDAE, **Isonychia**
**14.** With two caudal filaments; body depressed; mountain states; two species. **Lachlania**
With three caudal filaments; burrowers; South Carolina to Utah and southward; two species. . . . . . . . . . . . . . . . . . . . . . . . . . . . . . . . . . . . . . . . . . . . . . . . . **Homoeoneuria**
**15.** Gills of second abdominal segment operculate (Fig. 367B) . . . . . . . . . . . . . . . . . . . . .**16**
Gills of second abdominal segment not operculate, or absent . . . . . . . . . . . . . . . . . .**20**
**16.** Gills of second abdominal segment triangular or oval (Fig. 374C).
TRICORYTHIDAE, **17**
Gills of second abdominal segment quadrate (Fig. 367B) . . . . . . . . . . . . . . . . . . . . . . .**18**

FIG. 374.–Structure of Ephemeroptera. A, first gill of *Hexagenia*; B, mandibular tusk of *Tortopus*; C, second gill of *Tricorythodes*; D, femur of *Tricorythodes*; E, femur of *Leptohyphes*; F, head of *Brachycercus* showing tubercles; G, head of *Arthroplea* showing elongated maxillary palps; H, tip of first leg of *Ametropus* showing short claw; J, tip of first leg of *Siphloplecton*; K, second gill of *Siphloplecton*; L, second gill of *Siphloplecton*; M, fourth gill of *Choroterpes*; N, tip of second leg of *Analetris*; O, tip of second leg of *Siphlonurus*. (Redrawn and modified from various sources, and drawn from specimens.)

17. Femora with setae at midlength (Fig. 374D); 3 to 10 mm long; widely distributed.
**Tricorythodes**
    Femora with heavy spines at midlength (Fig. 374E); 3 to 5 mm long; about eight species in large streams. ....................................**Leptohyphes**
18. Operculate gills fused medially (Fig. 367B); 8 to 17 mm long; usually in stream detritus; rare in southeastern states ...........NEOEPHEMERIDAE, **Neoephemera**
    Operculate gills not fused medially ..............................CAENIDAE, **19**
19. Head with three hornlike tubercles (Fig. 374F); 3 to 8 mm long; silty sand substrates; about six species; generally distributed as far west as Idaho and Utah.
**Brachycercus**
    Head without such tubercles; 2 to 7 mm long; widely distributed in ponds and slow streams; about 12 species .......................................**Caenis**
20. With gills on abdominal segments three to seven or four to seven (Figs. 373A, B); paired tubercles usually present on abdominal terga (Fig. 373A); 5 to 15 mm long; a very large (80 species) and complex genus, usually divided into a series of subgenera; found everywhere in a wide variety of habitats ....**Ephemerella**
    With gills on abdominal segments one to five, one to seven, or two to seven; abdominal tubercles rare ....................................................**21**
21. Nymph dorsoventrally flattened, eyes dorsal (Figs. 377G, H) ...................**22**
    Nymph not dorsoventrally flattened, eyes not dorsal ..........................**27**
22. Abdominal gills composed of a large lamella with few to many basal fibrils (Figs. 368K, L) ........................................ HEPTAGENIIDAE, **23**
    Abdominal gills with another structure ................LEPTOPHLEBIIDAE, **60**

23. Maxillary palps enormously elongated and setose (Fig. 374G); 7 to 10 mm long; sluggish waters; northeastern states. .... **Arthroplea bipunctata** McDunnough
     Maxillary palps of normal size .....................................................**24**
24. Claws as long or longer than tarsi; 11 to 15 mm long; sandy bottoms of lotic habitats; rare in eastern states, as far west as Utah ......................**Pseudiron**
     Claws much shorter than tarsi ..............................................**25**
25. All abdominal gills inserted dorsally or laterally, although first and last gills may extend ventrally (Figs. 369, 377E–H); very common ...................**53**
     Abdominal gills on second and third abdominal segments inserted ventrally; rare, in large rivers .....................................................**26**
26. With dorsal tubercles on head, thorax, and abdomen; 9 mm long; Wisconsin, Indiana, and Georgia ...............................................**Spinadis**
     Without such tubercles; 6 to 8 mm long; central states and west to Utah and east to Georgia .................................................**Anepeorus**
27. Claws of forelegs either much shorter than those of second and third legs or bifid (Figs. 374H, J) .....................................................**28**
     All claws similar in structure and size ......................................**30**
28. Claws of forelegs simple; 14 to 18 mm long; rare, one or two species in silty sand of large rivers. ..........................AMETROPODIDAE, **Ametropus**
     Claws of forelegs divided (Fig. 374J); slow streams ...... METRETOPODIDAE, **29**
29. With single and simple gills on abdominal segments one and two; Michigan to Maine; 9 to 10 mm long ............................ **Metretopus borealis** Eaton
     Gills of abdominal segments one and two with one or two recurved flaps (Figs. 374K, L); 8 to 16 mm long; large streams and lakes; about five species. **Siphloplecton**
30. Gills of abdominal segments two to seven: (1) forked, tufted, marginally fringed (Figs. 368B, G, M) or (2) in the form of double lamellae terminating in points (Figs. 374M; 376K) ..................................................**60**
     Gills with a different structure ..............................................**31**
31. Antennae length less than twice the head width............ SIPHLONURIDAE, **32**
     Antennae length more than three times the head width. ........... BAETIDAE, **38**
32. Claws long and thin (Fig. 374N); rare ........................................**33**
     Claws short (Fig. 374O); very common ....................................**34**
33. Each abdominal tergum with a small median tubercle; 20 mm long; rapid streams; reported only from Illinois and South Carolina ............ **Acanthometropus**
     Without such tubercles; 15 mm long; large sandy rivers; Utah and Wyoming. **Analetris**
34. Gills on first and second abdominal segments with double lamellae (Fig. 368J) ....**35**
     Gills on first and second abdominal segments single (Fig. 368D) .................**36**
35. Gills of first and second abdominal segments oval; 15 to 17 mm long; known only from mountain streams in California.......................................**Edmundsius**
     Gills of first and second abdominal segments subtriangular (Figs. 374K, L); 9 to 20 mm long; standing waters and edges of streams; about 15 species; widely distributed..............................................**Siphlonurus**
36. Maxillae with a crown of pectinate spines (Fig. 375J); 6 to 14 mm long; strong swimmers; small streams; widely distributed; about 20 species ......**Ameletus**
     Maxillae without pectinate spines ............................................**37**
37. Mesosternum and metasternum each with a median tubercle; 19 to 20 mm long; very rare in pools in New York ...........................................**Siphlonisca**
     Without such tubercles; 10 to 13 mm long; rare in pools in northwestern states.
                                                                         **Parameletus**
38. Claws spatulate (Fig. 376B); 3 to 10 mm long; rare in silty western streams. **Dactylobaetis**
     Claws pointed .....................................................**39**
39. Without gills on abdominal segments six and seven; 3 to 8 mm long; rare in rapid streams of western states ...........................................**Baetodes**
     Gills present on abdominal segments six and seven .........................**40**
40. Basal two-thirds of caudal filaments with a narrow dark band at every third to fifth segment ...................................................**41**
     Banding absent, or with another arrangement of bands ......................**45**

Fig. 375.–Structure of Ephemeroptera nymphs. A, *Baetisca carolina,* ×7.5; B, protarsal claw of *Ametropus*; C, protarsal claw of *Siphloplecton basale*; D, posterior end of *Isonychia sicca*; E, *I. sicca,* ×2.5; F, *Paraleptophlebia volitans,* ×9; G, *Cloeon mendax,* ×9; H, *Caenis,* ×5.5; J, maxilla of *Ameletus.* (A to C, H, and J modified from Needham, Traver, and Hsu by permission of Comstock Publishing Co.; D and E from Needham, 1920; F and G modified from Ide, 1930.)

**41.** Gills on first and second abdominal segments double (Figs. 368H, J); 4 to 9 mm long; edges of streams; widely distributed; about six species . . . . . . . . . . . . . . .**Cloeon**

Gills on first and second abdominal segments simple or with a small dorsal flap (Fig. 376D) . . . . . . . . . . . . . . . . . . . . . . . . . . . . . . . . . . . . . . . . . . . . . . . . . . . . . . .**42**

**42.** Each gill of first and second abdominal segments with a small dorsal flap (Fig. 376D). **43**

All gills simple . . . . . . . . . . . . . . . . . . . . . . . . . . . . . . . . . . . . . . . . . . . . . . . . . .**44**

**43.** Hind wing pads absent (other data in couplet 41) . . . . . . . . . . . . . . . . . . . . . . .**Cloeon**

Hind wing pads present; 4 to 8 mm long; active species, found in many habitats; about 20 species . . . . . . . . . . . . . . . . . . . . . . . . . . . . . . . . . . . . . . . . . . . . . . . . . .**Centroptilum**

FIG. 376.–Structure of Ephemeroptera. A, gill of first abdominal segment of *Siphlonurus*; B, claw of *Dactylobaetis*; C, gill of first abdominal segment of *Cloeon*; D, gill of first abdominal segment of *Centroptilum*; E, gill of fourth abdominal segment of *Callibaetis*; F, tarsus and claw of *Apobaetis*; G, tarsus and claw of *Paracloeodes*; H, gill of fourth abdominal segment of *Stenacron*; J, dorsal view of head of *Traverella* showing wide labrum; K, gill of fifth abdominal segment of *Leptophlebia*; L, ventral view of abdominal segments of *Habrophlebiodes*. (Redrawn and modified from various sources, and drawn from specimens.)

**44.** Hind wing pads absent (other data in couplet 41) .........................**Cloeon**
Hind wing pads present (other data in couplet 43)....................**Centroptilum**
**45.** Gills folded on one or more abdominal segments (Fig. 368C); 6 to 10 mm long; widely distributed in quiet waters; about 25 species ....................**Callibaetis**
All gills flat.......................................................**46**
**46.** Median caudal filament one-eighth or more as long as lateral filaments (Fig. 372) .**47**
Median caudal filament absent or vestigial ...................................**50**
**47.** Median caudal filament shorter and thinner than lateral filaments (Fig. 372); 3 to 12 mm long; in shallow running waters; very common and widely distributed; about 50 species .........................................**Baetis**
Median caudal filament subequal to lateral filaments ..........................**48**
**48.** Claws half or more as long as tarsi (Figs. 376F, G) ...........................**49**
Claws less than half as long as tarsi (other data in couplet 47)...............**Baetis**
**49.** Each claw almost as long as its respective tarsus (Fig. 376F); 4 mm long; one species known only from the Tuolumne River, California .................**Apobaetis**
Each claw about half as long as its respective tarsus (Fig. 376G); 4 mm long; rare on sandy stream bottoms; widely distributed ....................**Paracloeodes**
**50.** First coxa with a single filamentous gill; 6 to 8 mm long; swift streams in eastern states; three species ...........................................**Heterocloeon**
First coxa without a gill ..............................................**51**
**51.** Nymph greatly depressed; 3 to 6 mm long; widely distributed and common in a variety of habitats; about 12 species..............................**Pseudocloeon**
Nymph not especially depressed ...........................................**52**

Fig. 377.–Structure of Heptageniidae. A, early nymph of *Stenonema*; B, mandible of *Cinygma integrum*; C, mandible of *Heptagenia*; D, maxilla of *Epeorus*; E, ventral view of abdomen of *Epeorus*; F, *Stenonema frontale*, ×4.5; G, *Rhithrogena*, ×4; H, *Epeorus humeralis*, ×4.5. (A and F modified from Needham, Traver, and Hsu; B redrawn from McDunnough, 1933; C redrawn from Needham and Needham, 1938; D modified from Ide, 1930; G modified from Needham, 1940; A, C, F, and G by permission of the Comstock Publishing Co.)

52. Hind wing pads present and small to large (other data in couplet 47) . . . . . . . . **Baetis**
    Hind wing pads absent (other data in couplet 51). . . . . . . . . . . . . . . . . **Pseudocloeon**
53. Median terminal filament rudimentary or absent . . . . . . . . . . . . . . . . . . . . . . . . . . . .54
    Median terminal filament well developed . . . . . . . . . . . . . . . . . . . . . . . . . . . . . . . . .55
54. Paired tubercles on abdominal terga one to nine; 7 to 14 mm long; in swift mountain
    streams; five species; western states . . . . . . . . . . . . . . . . . . . . . . . . . . . . **Ironodes**
    Without such tubercles; 7 to 18 mm long; many species with a ventral suction disc
    formed by the gills (Figs. 377E, H); about 18 species in swift streams; widely
    distributed. . . . . . . . . . . . . . . . . . . . . . . . . . . . . . . . . . . . . . . . . . . . . . . **Epeorus**
55. Enlarged abdominal gills forming a ventral suction disc (Fig. 369); 5 to 12 mm long;
    common everywhere in swift waters; about 20 species . . . . . . . . . .**Rhithrogena**
    Gills smaller, not forming a suction disc . . . . . . . . . . . . . . . . . . . . . . . . . . . . . . . . .56
56. Gills of seventh abdominal segment reduced to thin filaments (Fig. 368A) . . . . . . .57
    Gills of seventh abdominal segment not strongly reduced, similar to preceding pairs. 58
57. Gills of first to sixth abdominal segments pointed (Fig. 376H); 8 to 14 mm long; usually
    in debris of swift streams; central and eastern states; 10 species. . . .**Stenacron**
    Gills of first to sixth abdominal segments not pointed; 6 to 20 mm long; very common
    in many kinds of habitats; about 30 species . . . . . . . . . . . . . . . . . . . .**Stenonema**

58. Fibrillar portion of first few gills reduced to one to four tiny threads (Fig. 368K); 7 to 11 mm long; very common in western mountain streams; rare in eastern states; about 10 species .......................................................... **Cinygmula**
    Fibrillar portion of first few gills well developed (Fig. 368L) ...................59
59. Gill lamella of first abdominal segment less than half as long as lamella of second abdominal segment; 10 to 12 mm long; swift western streams; four species.
    **Cinygma**
    Gill lamella of first abdominal segment more than half as long as lamella of second abdominal segment; 6 to 12 mm long; widely distributed in swift streams.
    **Heptagenia**
60. Labrum very broad (Fig. 376J); 7 to 10 mm long; three species in rapid warm rivers .......................................................**Traverella**
    Labrum narrow .......................................................**61**
61. Gills of second to seventh abdominal segments consisting of clusters of filaments (Fig. 368G); 4 to 5 mm long; in small streams of eastern states.
    **Habrophlebia vibrans** Needham
    Gills of second to seventh abdominal segments with a much different structure ...62
62. Gills of first abdominal segment different from those of succeeding segments .....63
    Gills of first abdominal segment similar to the other gills ......................65
63. Gills of first abdominal segment simple (Fig. 368A); 5 to 8 mm long; in debris of slow streams; 12 species; widely distributed ........................**Choroterpes**
    Gills of first abdominal segment divided (Figs. 374M; 376K) ...................64
64. Gills of second to seventh abdominal segments terminating in a filament and two lobes (Fig. 376K); 7 to 15 mm long; sluggish and standing waters; nine species, chiefly in central and eastern states ................................ **Leptophlebia**
    Gills of second to seventh abdominal segments terminating in three filaments (Fig. 374M) (other data in couplet 63) ............................**Choroterpes**
65. Gills of middle abdominal segments cleft to about midlength ...................66
    Gills of middle abdominal segments cleft more deeply (Fig. 375F) ................67
66. With a row of small spinules on the posterior margins of abdominal terga six to ten, or seven to ten (Fig. 376L); 4 to 6 mm long; usually in debris of swift streams; four eastern species ...................................**Habrophlebiodes**
    With a row of small spinules on the posterior margins of abdominal terga one to ten (other data in couplet 3) ..............................**Paraleptophlebia**
67. Labrum about two-thirds as wide as head; 5 to 12 mm long; five species in streams of New Mexico, Arizona, and Texas ..........................**Thraulodes**
    Labrum less than half as wide as head (other data in couplet 66) ... **Paraleptophlebia**

## EPHEMEROPTERA REFERENCES

ALLEN, R. K., and G. F. EDMUNDS. 1956. A list of the mayflies of Oregon. *Proc. Utah Acad. Sci.* **33**:85–87.

———. 1965. A revision of the genus Ephemerella (Ephemeroptera, Ephemerellidae). VIII. The subgenus Ephemerella in North America.. *Misc. Publ. Entomol. Soc. Am.* **4**:244–282.

BERNER, L. 1941. Ovoviviparous mayflies in Florida. *Fla. Entomol.* **24**:32–34.

———. 1950. The mayflies of Florida. *Univ. Fla. Stud. Biol. Sci. Ser.* **4**:1–267.

———. 1959. A tabular summary of the biology of North American mayfly nymphs (Ephemeroptera). *Bull. Fla. State Mus.* **4**:1–58.

BURKS, B. D. 1953. The mayflies, or Ephemeroptera, of Illinois. *Bull. Ill. Nat. Hist. Surv.* **26**:1–216.

CLIFFORD, H. F. 1970. Analysis of a northern mayfly (Ephemeroptera) population, with special reference to allometry of size. *Can. J. Zool.* **48**:315–316.

CLIFFORD, H. F., M. R. ROBERTSON, and K. A. ZELT. 1973. Life cycle patterns of mayflies (Ephemeroptera) from some streams of Alberta, Canada. *Proc. First Int. Conf. Ephemeroptera*, pp. 122–131.

CRAVEN, R. W., and B. F. BROWN. 1969. Ecology of Hexagenia naiads (Insecta:Ephemerida) in an Oklahoma reservoir. *Am. Midl. Nat.* **82**:346–358.

DODDS, G. S., and F. L. HISAW. 1924. Ecological studies of aquatic insects. I. Adaptations of mayfly nymphs to swift streams. *Ecology* **5**:137–148.

———. 1924. Ecological studies of aquatic insects. II. Size of respiratory organs in relation to environmental conditions. Ibid. 262–271.

———. 1925. Ecological studies on aquatic insects. IV. Altitudinal range and zonation of mayflies, stoneflies, and caddisflies in the Colorado Rockies. Ibid. **6**:380–390.

EDMUNDS, G. F. 1957. The predaceous mayfly nymphs of North America. *Proc. Utah Acad. Sci.* **34**:23–24.

EDMUNDS, G. F., and R. K. ALLEN. 1957. A checklist of the Ephemeroptera of North America north of Mexico. *Ann. Entomol. Soc. Am.* **50**:317–324.

EDMUNDS, G. F., R. K. ALLEN, and W. L. PETERS. 1963. An annotated key to the nymphs of the families and subfamilies of mayflies (Ephemeroptera). *Univ. Utah Biol. Ser.* **13**:1–55.

EDMUNDS, G. F., S. L. JENSEN, and L. BERNER. 1976. *The Mayflies of North and Central America.* 330 pp. Univ. Minnesota Press, Minneapolis.

EDMUNDS, G. F., and J. R. TRAVER. 1954. An outline of a reclassification of the Ephemeroptera. *Proc. Entomol. Soc. Wash.* **56**:236–240.

ELLIOTT, J. M. 1968. The daily activity patterns of mayfly nymphs (Ephemeroptera). *J. Zool.* **155**:201–221.

ERIKSEN, C. H. 1967. Ecological significance of respiration and substrate for burrowing Ephemeroptera. *Can. J. Zool.* **46**:93–103.

FOX, H. M., C. A. WINGFIELD, and B. G. SIMMONDS. 1937. The oxygen consumption of ephemerid nymphs from flowing and from still waters in relation to the concentration of oxygen in the water. *J. Exp. Biol.* **14**:210–218.

FREMLING, C. R. 1960. Biology of a large mayfly, Hexagenia bilineata (Say), of the Upper Mississippi River. *Res. Bull. Agric. Home Econ. Exp. Sta. Iowa State Univ. Sci. Tech.* **482**:841–852.

————. 1968. Documentation of mass emergence of Hexagenia mayflies from the Upper Mississippi River. *Trans. Am. Fish. Soc.* **97**:278–280.

GILPIN, B. R., and M. A. BRUSVEN. 1970. Food habits and ecology of mayflies of the St. Maries River in Idaho. *Melanderia* **4**:19–40.

HALL, C. A. S. 1969. Mortality of the mayfly nymph Ephemerella rotunda (Morgan), at low dissolved-oxygen concentrations. *J. Elisha Mitchell Sci. Soc.* **85**:34–39.

HAYDEN, W., and H. F. CLIFFORD. 1974. Seasonal movements of the mayfly Leptophlebia cupida (Say) in a brown-water stream of Alberta, Canada. *Am. Midl. Nat.* **91**:90–102.

HORST, T. J. 1976. Population dynamics of the burrowing mayfly Hexagenia limbata. *Ecology* **57**:199–200.

HUBBARD, M. D., and W. L. PETERS. 1976. The number of genera and species of mayflies (Ephemeroptera). *Entomol. News* **87**:245.

HUNT, B. P. 1953. The life history and economic importance of a burrowing mayfly, Hexagenia limbata, in southern Michigan lakes. *Bull. Inst. Fish. Res. Mich. Dept. Conserv.* **4**:1–151.

IDE, F. P. 1935. The effect of temperature on the distribution of the mayfly fauna of a stream. *Univ. Toronto Stud. Biol. Ser.* **39**:3–76.

————. 1935a. Post embryological development of Ephemeroptera (Mayflies). External characters only *Can. J. Res.* **12**:433–478.

KOSS, R. W., and G. F. EDMUNDS. 1974. Ephemeroptera eggs and their contribution to phylogenetic studies of the order. *Zool. J. Linn. Soc.* **55**:267–349.

LEONARD, J. W., and F. A. LEONARD. 1962. *Mayflies of Michigan trout streams.* 139 pp. Cranbrook Inst. Sci., Bloomfield Hills, Mich.

LINDUSKA, J. P. 1942. Bottom type as a factor influencing the local distribution of mayfly nymphs. *Can. Entomol.* **74**:26–30.

LYMAN, F. E. 1943. Swimming and burrowing activities of mayfly nymphs of the genus Hexagenia. *Ann. Entomol. Soc. Am.* **36**:250–256.

MACAN, T. T. 1970. A key to the nymphs of British species of Ephemeroptera with notes on their ecology. *Sci. Publ. Freshwater Biol. Assoc.* **20**:1–68.

MAXWELL, G. R., and A. BENSON. 1963. Wing pad and tergite growth of mayfly nymphs in winter. *Am. Midl. Nat.* **69**:224–230.

McCAFFERTY, W. P. 1975. The burrowing mayflies (Ephemeroptera: Ephemeroidea) of the United States. *Trans. Am. Entomol. Soc.* **101**:447–504.

MORGAN, A. H., and M. C. GRIERSON. 1932. The functions of the gills in burrowing may flies (Hexagenia recurvata). *Physiol. Zool.* **5**:230–245.

NEEDHAM, J. G. 1920. Burrowing mayflies of our larger lakes and streams. *Bull. U.S. Bur. Fish.* **36**:265–292.

NEEDHAM, J. G., J. R. TRAVER, and Y. HSU. 1935. *The biology of mayflies.* 759 pp. Comstock, Ithaca, N.Y.

PLESKOT, GERTRUD. 1953. Zur Ökologie der Leptophlebiiden (Ins., Ephemeroptera). *Oesterreich. zool. Z.* **4**:45–107.

RICHARDSON, M. Y., and D. C. TARTER. 1976. Life histories of Stenonema vicarium (Walker) and S. tripunctatum (Banks) in a West Virginia stream (Ephemeroptera: Heptageniidae). *Am. Midl. Nat.* **95**:1–9.

SCHNEIDER, R. F. 1967. Mayfly nymphs from northwestern Florida. *Q. J. Fla. Acad. Sci.* **29**:202–206.

SCHWIEBERT, E. 1973. Nymphs. *A complete guide to naturals and their imitations.* 339 pp. Winchester, New York.

SPIETH, H. T. 1938. A method of rearing Hexagenia nymphs (Ephemerida). *Entomol. News* **49**:29–32.

STUART, A. M. 1958. The efficiency of adaptive structures in the nymph of Rhithrogena semicolorata. *J. Exp. Biol.* **35**:27–38.

SWANSON, G. A. 1967. Factors influencing the distribution and abundance of Hexagenia nymphs (Ephemeroptera) in a Missouri River reservoir. *Ecology* **48**:216–225.

WINGFIELD, C. A. 1939. The functions of the gills of mayfly nymphs from different habitats. *J. Exp. Biol.* **16**:363–373.

# Chapter 28

# ODONATA (DRAGONFLIES, DAMSELFLIES)

WITH THE exception of mosquitoes, the Odonata are perhaps the best-known insects having aquatic stages. The adults are often called darning needles or mosquito hawks because of their size, shape, and habits. They are medium to large insects, often handsomely colored, and have a long, slender abdomen. The two pairs of wings are long, narrow, and net-veined, and the legs are short and used for perching. The head is mobile and bears very large compound eyes. From early morning until late evening dragonflies may be found flying back and forth or darting about erratically, especially along the shores and over the waters of marshes, ponds, rivers, and lakes. The mouth parts are constructed for biting, and the food, consisting of small flying insects, is caught on the wing.

The group is divided into two distinct suborders, the Anisoptera (true dragonflies) and the Zygoptera (damselflies). Dragonflies and damselflies differ in several important ways. The latter are smaller, more slender and delicate, and slower and more uncertain in flight. In the dragonflies the hind wings are broader at the base than the forewings, whereas the two pairs of wings are similar in the damselflies. Also, dragonflies hold the wings horizontally outward when at rest, and damseflies hold them folded parallel with the abdomen or tilted upward.

It is only the series of nymphal stages, or naiads, which are aquatic. These are grotesque creatures, robust or elongated, and gray, greenish, or somber-colored. The body may be smooth or rough and bearing small spines; it is often covered with a growth of filamentous algae and debris. The naiads are commonly found on submerged vegetation and the bottoms of ponds, marshes, streams, and in the shallows of lakes, but are rare in polluted waters and torrential streams. One of their most striking features is the labium, which is greatly modified as a food-getting device (Figs. 379, 380, 387, 391). It is very long, sometimes nearly one-fourth of the body length. Normally it lies folded backward at the base of the submentum and also folded on itself at the base of the mentum; the whole structure lies beneath the head and thorax with the middle hinge resting between the bases of the legs. The distal end of the mentum is more or less enlarged and bears two lateral labial lobes that are usually armed with stout teeth and setae. Damselfly nymphs can always be distinguished from dragonflies by the fact that they have three leaflike tracheal gills at the tip of the abdomen: Also damselflies are much more slender than dragonflies.

Depending on the species, there is a wide range in size. Mature dragonfly nymphs of the more common species usually range between 15 and 45 mm in length; common mature damselfly nymphs range from about 10 to 22 mm in length, exclusive of the gills.

Adult Odonata are often seen mating. This process may occur while at rest or during flight. After fertilization, egg deposition occurs in a variety of ways. In some species the female flies along a short distance above the water and scatters eggs by touching the tip of the abdomen to the surface or by actually dipping much of the abdomen now and then. A few species deposit their eggs in gelatinous masses. Some forms deposit eggs in floating mats of algae, others in sand, mud, or moss near the

551

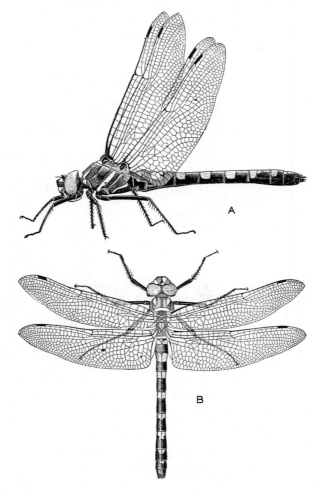

FIG. 378.–Adult dragonfly, *Macromia magnifica*, ×1. A, lateral view; B, dorsal view. (From Kennedy, 1915.)

water's edge (Fig. 383). All female Zygoptera and some Anisoptera have specialized ovipositors with which holes are usually cut in stems of submerged or emergent plants to receive the eggs (Fig. 384). Some damselflies have been seen crawling down along a stem submerged as much as 30 cm, systematically depositing their eggs as they go along.

The newly hatched young is enclosed in a thin, membranous, shroudlike covering, the pronymphal sheath. This is shed within a few seconds or minutes after leaving the egg, and the nymph that emerges is thus in the second instar. At this stage the

nymph is a tiny, long-legged, spidery creature usually less than 1 mm long (Fig. 385). The complete life history has been worked out for only a few species, but it is probable that the great majority of species have from 11 to 14 nymphal instars. The length of each instar varies greatly, depending on the particular species, as well as on the prevailing temperature and food conditions. Sometimes an instar may last only three days; sometimes it may persist for as long as six months. It has been said that a one-year life cycle is the prevailing condition, but there are many exceptions. In some of the Zygoptera, especially *Enallagma* and *Isch-*

FIG. 379.–Nymph of *Macromia magnifica,* ×1.6. A, dorsal view; B, lateral view with labium extended. (From Kennedy, 1915.)

*nura,* there is more than one generation per year. At the other extreme, it has been estimated that some of the large aeschnids may require more than four years for the complete life cycle.

Many important morphological changes occur during the series of nymphal instars. In addition to changes in size and body proportions, there are significant changes in the structure of the labium, a great increase in the relative size of the compound eyes, an increase in the number of antennal segments, and many minor changes in the body setation and spines. Wing covers appear after three to five molts and then grow progressively larger. For a short time after each shedding of the exoskeleton the nymphs are gray or light green and translucent, but thereafter the cuticle becomes more opaque.

FIG. 380.–Lateral view of head and labium of Odonata, semidiagrammatic. A, Aeshnidae; B, Libellulidae. *m*, mentum.

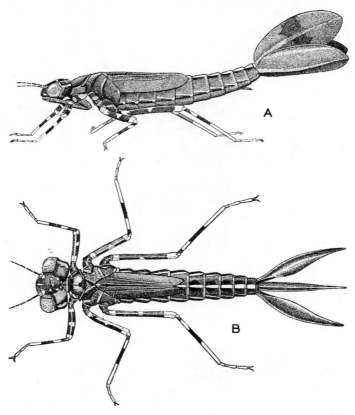

FIG. 381.–Nymph of *Argia emma*, ×3.6. A, lateral view; B, dorsal view. (From Kennedy, 1915.)

Odonata nymphs may be roughly classified into climbers, sprawlers, and burrowers. The climbers move about slowly in dense vegetation or trash in still waters. To this group belong the Coenagriidae and the Aeschnidae. Most of the sprawlers are long-legged, sluggish, dull-covered creatures occurring on many types of bottoms. To this group belong the Agriidae and the Libellulidae. Although not true burrowers, the Cordulegastridae lie almost hidden in sand or silt bottoms. This is accomplished by raking the sand out from beneath the body so that they sink downward. The Petaluridae and the Gomphidae burrow into silt, mud, and sand so that usually only the tip of the abdomen and the eyes are above the surface. The members of the latter family are easily distinguished by their wedgeshaped head and the more or less flattened scraperlike anterior tibiae. Some

FIG. 382.–Gill of typical damselfly nymph.

Fig. 383.–*Cordulegaster dorsalis*. A, female ovipositing in stream bed; B, nymph; C, exuvia. (From Kennedy, 1917.)

of these nymphs are capable of burrowing out of sight in a few seconds.

Although all odonate nymphs are carnivorous, the food-getting habits vary. Some species cautiously stalk their prey; some remain motionless until the food comes within reach. The burrowing forms lie almost completely concealed and may remain immobile for days at a time. In any case, when the prey is within reach it is seized suddenly and effectively by a lightninglike extension and contraction of the labium. Very large nymphs are said to be able to seize prey as much as 25 mm away as the result of the combined action of the labium and a forward lurching movement of the whole body. The labium, with its two lateral lobes, serves as a clamp to hold the food in position at the mouth where it is crushed with the mandibles. The tip of each lateral lobe has a large, movable spine. The real process of mastication occurs in the gizzard, which is supplied with longitudinal, toothed, chitinous ridges. Food consists chiefly of other aquatic insects, annelids, and small Crustacea and mollusks. Very young nymphs consume Protozoa. Although large dragonfly nymphs may be induced to feed on small fish in the laboratory when the normal food is absent, it is

Damselfly nymphs have one median and two lateral flat caudal tracheal gills that are supplied with large tracheal trunks. These gills vary in shape and color. They are easily broken off at their bases but may be regenerated. Unlike the condition in dragonflies, the rectum is unspecialized, and although small quantities of water may be taken into the rectal chamber at frequent intervals in young nymphs, it is thought

FIG. 384.–*Ischnura perparva*. A, in copulation; B, female ovipositing in aquatic plant. (From Kennedy, 1915.)

doubtful whether they attack fish in the normal environment. When crowded under laboratory conditions, cannibalism may result. Very little food of any kind is taken during the winter months in the northern states.

The rectal chamber of dragonfly nymphs is one of the most highly specialized respiratory devices to be found among aquatic insects. This barrel-shaped organ fills much of the abdomen and is set off from the rest of the digestive tract by a constriction. It contains longitudinal rows of minute thin tracheal gills that project into the cavity. Each gill contains an abundance of tracheoles which absorb oxygen from the water in the rectum. The walls of the rectum are provided with muscles that produce regular expansion and contraction movements. In this way water is taken into and expelled from the chamber vigorously by way of the anus. The anus is guarded by three minute valves surrounded by five spinous anal appendages (Figs. 386, 389). One appendage is median and dorsal, two are lateral, and two are ventral. The respiratory pulsations of the abdomen can easily be observed.

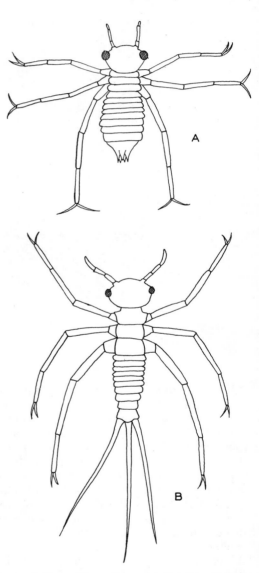

FIG. 385.–Newly hatched Odonata nymphs. A, *Libellula*, ×33; B, *Enallagma*, ×38. (Modified from Wilson.)

that this organ is of negligible respiratory significance, especially in older individuals. In addition to the gills, the general body surface undoubtedly absorbs large quantities of oxygen.

Just before transformation to the imago, the nymph crawls out of the water, usually on emergent aquatic vegetation. The smaller damselflies crawl only a few centimeters above the surface, but other species crawl up higher. Some species, especially sprawlers and burrowers, leave the water on broader objects such as logs, rocks, and trees. Others simply crawl out onto the adjacent shore, and a few individuals have been found wandering more than 10 m from the water. Most Odonata emerge in the early morning or late afternoon; a very few emerge during midday or the hours of darkness.

The actual process of emergence of the imago is heralded by a split in the exoskeleton along the middorsal surface of the thorax. As this rupture becomes longer, the thorax, head, legs, wings, and lastly the abdomen are slowly withdrawn through it. Before flying off, the newly emerged adult clings to the nymph skeleton for an hour or so while the wings become dry and stiff.

Climbing nymphs may be collected by rinsing out masses of vegetation in a suitable container. Sprawling and burrowing forms are found by raking up bottom trash or by pulling a wire sieve net through the surface layers of mud, sand, and debris. When the material is sorted on shore the awkward movements of the nymphs render them easily visible. Seventy or 80 percent alcohol is a satisfactory preservative.

Most of the genera reported in the nymphal stages from the United States are represented by only a few species. The identification of a nymph, even to genus, is often no easy matter because of the fact that morphological differences are so slight. Keys must therefore be used with great care. Furthermore, key characters usually apply only to the more advanced instars. The standard works for American species are the manuals of Needham and Heywood (1929) and Needham and Westfall (1955). Identification is more reliable in the case of questionable species if the nymphs can be reared to the adult stage. Needham recommends simple cylindrical window-screen rearing cages in the laboratory. They should be kept in an upright position about halfway out of the water.

In the following key the general geographic range in the United States is given for each genus. Lengths refer to the last nymphal instars and do not include gills.

## KEY TO GENERA OF ODONATA NYMPHS

1. Gills within the posterior part of the digestive tract; head not wider than thorax and abdomen; dragonfly nymphs .................. Suborder **ANISOPTERA, 2**
Gills consisting of three flat external plates at posterior end; damselfly nymphs.
Suborder **ZYGOPTERA, 67**
2. Labium flat (Fig. 387C); true burrowers and climbers .........................44
Labium is spoon-shaped, covering lower part of face like a mask as far as the base of the antennae (Figs. 380B; 387G) .......................................3
3. Inner edge of lateral lobe of labium coarsely and irregularly toothed (Fig. 387B); hairy species; usually hidden in debris, sand, and silt, but not true burrowers; 31 to 45 mm long; common and widely distributed, especially in eastern states. ......................... CORDULEGASTRIDAE, **Cordulegaster**
Inner edge of lateral lobe of labium evenly and regularly toothed, or without teeth (Fig. 387A); bottom sprawlers, not climbers or burrowers ................4
4. Frontal projection between bases of antennae produced into a prominent median pyramidal horn (Fig. 379); sedentary sprawling species .. MACROMIIDAE, **5**
No such frontal projection ...................................................6
5. Lateral spines of ninth abdominal segment short (Fig. 389A); widely distributed.
**Macromia**
Lateral spines of ninth abdominal segment long, reaching or exceeding tips of abdominal appendages; eastern states..................................**Didymops**

FIG. 386.–Typical dragonfly nymphs. A, *Tachopteryx theoreyi,* ×1.3; B, *Helocordulia uhleri,* ×2.2; C, *Gomphus,* ×1.5; D, *Progomphus obscurus,* ×2; E, *Aeshna,* ×1.3. (A redrawn from Kennedy, 1917; B redrawn from Kennedy, 1924; D redrawn from Kennedy, 1921.)

**6.** Distal margins of palpal lobes with rounded crenations, the highest of which are one-third to more than one-half as high as they are wide (Fig. 389B) ............**7**
Distal margins of palpal lobes straight or with low crenations many times wider than high (Fig. 389C). ..................................LIBELLULIDAE, **17**
**7.** Lateral spines of ninth segment as long as or longer than middorsal ninth segment (Fig. 389N). ..................... LIBELLULIDAE, **Pantala**
Lateral spines of ninth segment shorter than the middorsal ninth segment, or absent (Fig. 386B) ........................................... CORDULIIDAE, **8**
**8.** Well-developed dorsal hooks on some abdominal segments (Figs. 390E,F) .......**12**
Dorsal hooks reduced to knobs, or absent ...................................**9**
**9.** Scallops of distal margin of palpal lobe indistinct or shallow, with each scallop less than one-quarter as long as broad; rare, western states .............. **Belonia**
Each scallop of distal margin of palpal lobe one-third to one-half as deep as broad (Fig. 389F) .........................................................**10**
**10.** Side of thorax with a broad, dark longitudinal stripe ..........................**11**
Side of thorax without a stripe; widely distributed in woodland streams and bogs.
**Somatochlora**
**11.** Dorsal hooks absent or vestigial; 23 mm long; widely distributed.
**Cordulia shurtleffi** Scudder
Dorsal hooks distinct but reduced to stubs; 19 mm long; northeastern states.
**Dorocordulia**

FIG. 387.—Structure of dragonfly nymphs. A, labium of *Plathemis*; B, labium of *Cordulegaster*; C, labium of *Aeshna*; D, lateral labial lobe of *Basiaeschna*; E, lateral labial lobe of *Boyeria*; F, labium of *Perithemis*; G, anterior view of head of *Erythemis* showing masklike labium; H, antenna of *Octogomphus*; J, antenna of *Tachopteryx*; K, antenna of *Ophiogomphus*. 1, lateral lobe of labium; 2, lateral labial setae; 3, mentum; 4, mental setae. (A, B, and F redrawn from Garman, 1927; D and E redrawn from Howe, 1922; G redrawn from Wilson, 1920; H and J redrawn from Kennedy, 1917.)

12. Without lateral spines on eighth segment; rare, northeastern states .... **Williamsonia**
    With lateral spines on eighth segment (Fig. 386B)...............................13
13. Scallops of distal margin of palpal lobe nearly semicircular, or deeper (Fig. 389B). 14
    Scallops of distal margin of palpal lobe more shallow (Fig. 389G)................15
14. Lateral spines of ninth abdominal segment long (Fig. 389E); eastern half of the United
    States........................................................................ **Neurocordulia**
    Lateral spines of ninth abdominal segment short; northeastern states .. **Dorocordulia**
15. Lateral spines of ninth segment more than three times the length of those on eighth
    segment; several widely distributed species ....................... **Epitheca**
    Lateral spines of eighth and ninth segments subequal, or absent.................16
16. With dorsal hooks on segments four and five; widely distributed and common.
                                                                        **Somatochlora**
    Without dorsal hooks on segments four and five (Fig. 386B); eastern .. **Helocordulia**
17. Eyes capping the anterolateral angles of the head, more frontal than lateral (Fig.
    388B) ........................................................................18
    Eyes lateral (Fig. 388E) ....................................................21

Fig. 388.–Dorsal view of head of typical dragonfly nymphs, diagrammatic. A, *Nasiaeschna, Basiaeschna,* and *Boyeria*; B, *Plathemis*; C, *Aeshna* and *Epiaeschna*; D, *Somatochlora*; E, *Leucorrhinia*. (A and C modified from Howe, 1922; B and E modified from Wright and Peterson; D modified from Walker, 1925.)

18. Median lobe of labium evenly contoured (Fig. 389H); hairy species; widely distributed
    and common ............................................................. **Libellula**
    Median lobe of labium crenulated (Fig. 389J) ...............................**19**
19. Without dorsal hooks on middle abdominal segments; southern states.
                                                            **Orthemis ferruginea** (Fabr.)
    With dorsal hooks on middle abdominal segments ..........................**20**
20. With 8 to 15 mental setae (Fig. 389J); widely distributed ............... **Plathemis**
    With none or four mental setae; eastern half of the United States........... **Ladona**
21. Inferior anal appendages strongly decurved (Fig. 390B) ......................**22**
    Inferior anal appendages essentially straight...................................**23**
22. Eleven or 12 lateral labial setae; Florida, Texas, and Oklahoma.
                                                            **Lepthemis vesiculosa** Fabr.
    Seven to nine lateral labial setae; widely distributed.....................**Erythemis**
23. With dorsal hooks on some abdominal segments............................**24**
    Dorsal hooks lacking ....................................................**37**
24. Segment nine with a dorsal hook ......................................**25**
    Segment nine without a hook ...........................................**31**
25. Dorsal hooks curved posteriorly; eastern and southern. ................**Perithemis**
    Dorsal hooks projecting more or less straight upward .........................**26**
26. Dorsal hooks long.........................................................**27**
    Dorsal hooks short and thick ..............................................**29**
27. Abdomen slightly longer than wide; Florida, rare .................... **Tauriphila**
    Abdomen twice as long as wide .........................................**28**
28. Hind wing case reaches midpoint of sixth abdominal segment; southern ...**Cannacria**
    Hind wing case reaches midpoint of seventh abdominal segment; Florida, rare.
                                                                          **Idiataphe**
29. With large teeth on lateral lobe of labium ...................................**30**
    Without teeth on lateral lobe of labium; southern; uncommon ........... **Dythemis**
30. With six lateral setae; Texas, rare ...................................... **Macrothemis**
    With seven to ten lateral setae; rare; Oklahoma, California, Texas.
                                                            **Brechmorhoga mendax** (Hagen)
31. With a dorsal hook on the eighth abdominal segment .......................**32**
    Without such a hook .....................................................**35**

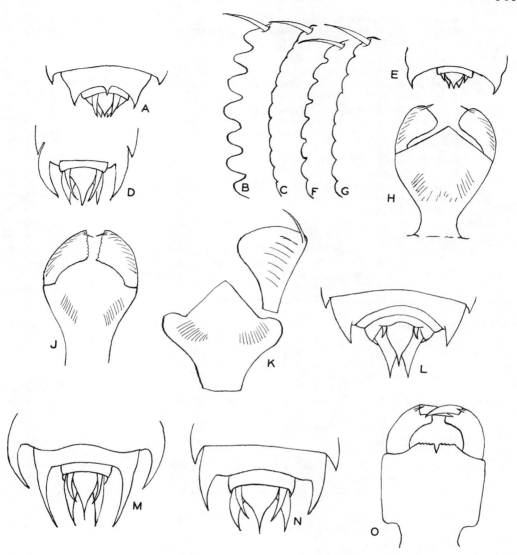

FIG. 389.–Structure of Anisoptera nymphs, semidiagrammatic. A, posterior end of *Macromia*; B, distal margin of palpal lobe of *Neurocordulia*; C, distal margin of palpal lobe of *Libellula*; D, posterior end of *Pantala*; E, posterior end of *Neurocordulia*; F, distal margin of palpal lobe of *Dorocordulia*; G, distal margin of palpal lobe of *Helocordulia*; H, labium of *Libellula*; J, labium of *Plathemis*; K, labium of *Miathyria* showing ten mental setae and seven lateral labial setae; L, posterior end of *Pachydiplax*; M, posterior end of *Tramea*; N, posterior end of *Pantala*; O, labium of *Tachopteryx*. (K modified from Bick, 1953; others semidiagrammatic, all redrawn and greatly modified from various sources.)

32. Labium with 7 lateral and 9 to 11 mental setae (Fig. 389K); Texas, Florida, and Louisiana .................................................**Miathyria**
    Labium with 9 to 12 lateral and 12 to 18 mental setae .........................33
33. Superior abdominal appendage about as long as the inferiors (Figs. 390F,H) .....34
    Superior abdominal appendage much shorter than inferiors (Fig. 390M); common and generally distributed. ........................................ **Sympetrum**

**34.** With 16 or 17 mental setae; rare; Gulf coast states. ... **Macrodiplax balteata** (Hagen)
With 10 to 15 mental setae; common and generally distributed. ....... **Leucorrhinia**
**35.** Lateral spines of ninth abdominal segment longer than the middorsal length of the
segment; eastern half of the United States. .................... **Celithemis**
Lateral spine of ninth abdominal segment shorter ............................**36**
**36.** Teeth of lateral lobe of labium large; southwestern. .... **Paltothemis lineatipes** Karsch
Teeth of lateral lobe of labium inconspicuous; southern and southeastern states; some
species in brackish waters. ............................... **Erythrodiplax**
**37.** Lateral spines of ninth abdominal segment shorter than the middorsal segment length. **38**
Lateral spines of ninth abdominal segment longer than the middorsal segment length
(Figs. 389M,N) ......................................................**42**
**38.** Body 10 mm long; eastern ........................... **Nannothemis bella** (Uhl.)
Body 12 to 20 mm long ....................................................**39**
**39.** Abdomen abruptly rounded, tenth abdominal segment very short; extreme
southwest .................................. **Pseudoleon superbus** Hagen
Abdomen otherwise ......................................................**40**
**40.** Body hairy; eastern half of the United States .................... **Erythrodiplax**
Body not hairy ..........................................................**41**
**41.** Superior abdominal appendage about as long as the inferiors (Fig. 390F); 15 to 21 mm
long; common and generally distributed .................... **Leucorrhinia**
Superior abdominal appendage two-thirds as long as the inferiors; Texas, rare.
**Micrathyria**
**42.** Lateral spines of eighth abdominal segment about half as long as those on segment
nine (Fig. 389L); widely distributed ........ **Pachydiplax longipennis** (Burm.)
Lateral spines of eighth abdominal segment nearly as long as those on segment nine;
widely distributed ....................................................**43**
**43.** Superior abdominal appendage slightly shorter than inferiors (Fig. 389M) ... **Tramea**
Superior abdominal appendage as long as or longer than inferiors (Fig. 389N). **Pantala**
**44.** Antennae four-segmented (Figs. 387H,K); second tarsus two-segmented.
**GOMPHIDAE, 46**
Antennae six- or seven-segmented (Fig. 387J); second tarsus three-segmented ....**45**
**45.** Prementum parallel-sided in distal two-thirds, abruptly narrowed at base (Fig. 389O);
dorsal abdominal appendage not bifid; sluggish species . . **PETALURIDAE, 66**
Prementum widest in distal half but not parallel-sided (Fig. 387C); dorsal abdominal
appendage bifid; climbing species ...................... **AESHNIDAE, 56**
**46.** Tenth abdominal segment greatly elongated (Fig. 390L); Texas, uncommon . **Aphylla**
Tenth abdominal segment normal size .....................................**47**
**47.** Abdomen circular; legs not fossorial; 70 to 90 mm long; eastern and southern.
**Hagenius brevistylus** Selys
Abdomen much longer than wide; legs fossorial (Figs. 386C,D) ................**48**
**48.** Wing cases divergent (Fig. 386D) .'........................................**49**
Wing cases not divergent ................................................**51**
**49.** Fourth antennal segment cylindrical; one species in Florida, one in east and south,
and one in west; burrowers in sand............................**Progomphus**
Fourth antennal segment a spherical rudiment (Fig. 387K) ....................**50**
**50.** Dorsal hooks present on abdominal segments two or three to nine; widely distributed
and common, usually in gravel substrates; 23 to 31 mm long. **Ophiogomphus**
Dorsal hooks present only on abdominal segments two to four; generally distributed
in southern half of the United States; sandy streams. ........ **Erpetogomphus**
**51.** Third antennal segment flat and oval (Fig. 387H) ..........................**52**
Third antennal segment elongated or linear ................................**53**
**52.** Short lateral spines present on abdominal segments eight and nine; burrow in sand;
eastern............................................... **Lanthus**
Short lateral spines present on abdominal segments seven to nine; far western.
**Octogomphus specularis** Hagen
**53.** Ninth abdominal segment with sharp middorsal ridge ending in apical spine ......**54**
Ninth abdominal segment otherwise; widely distributed; burrow in silt .... **Gomphus**
**54.** Without lateral spines on sixth abdominal segment; burrow in silt ........ **Gomphus**
With lateral spines on sixth abdominal segment ............................**55**

FIG. 390.–Abdominal structures of dragonfly nymphs. A to C, lateral view of posterior end; A, *Libellula*; B, *Erythemis*; C, *Nasiaeschna*; D to F, lateral view of abdomen; D, *Neurocordulia*; E, *Sympetrum*; F, *Leucorrhinia*; G to N, dorsal view of posterior end; G, *Neurocordulia*; H, *Macrodiplax balteata*; J, *Pantala*; K, *Coryphaeschna*; L, *Aphylla*; M, *Sympetrum*; N, *Somatochlora*. 1, superior anal appendage; 2, lateral; 3, inferior; 8, eighth abdominal segment; 9, ninth abdominal segment. (B modified from Needham and Needham, 1938, by permission of the Comstock Publishing Co.; C, E, and F modified from Howe, 1922; D and G modified from Byers, 1937; H modified from Needham and Fisher, 1936; J modified from Kennedy, 1923; L modified from Byers, 1930; N modified from Walker, 1925.)

55. Lateral anal appendages as long as the inferiors; southern Texas, rare  .. **Gomphoides**
   Lateral anal appendages shorter than the inferiors; eastern and southern.
                                                            **Dromogomphus**
56. Hind corners of head strongly angular (Fig. 388A) ............................ 57
   Hind corners of head broadly rounded (Fig. 388C) ............................ 61
57. Head elongate-rectangular; southeastern coastal states. ............ **Coryphaeschna**
   Head trapezoidal (Fig. 388A) ................................................ 58
58. Lateral lobe of labium squarely truncate at tip (Fig. 387E); eastern states ... **Boyeria**
   Lateral lobe of labium tapered toward tip (Fig. 387D) ........................ 59
59. Abdomen with a low median dorsal ridge; eastern half of the United States ...... 60
   Abdomen without such a ridge; eastern and central. ....... **Basiaeschna janata** (Say)
60. Low dorsal hooks on segments seven to nine (Fig. 390C).
                                       **Nasiaeschna pentacantha** (Rambur)
   No dorsal hooks on abdomen ......................... **Epiaeschna heros** (Fabr.)
61. With lateral spines on abdominal segments seven to nine ...................... 62
   With lateral spines on abdominal segments five or six to nine .................. 63
62. Antenna longer than distance from its base to posterior margin of head; eastern
       states ...................................................... **Gomphaeschna**
   Antenna much shorter; common and generally distributed .................. **Anax**

FIG. 391.–Structure of damselfly nymphs. A, antenna of Agriidae; B, lateral labial lobe of *Lestes stultus*; C, labium of *Agrion*; D, labium of *Archilestes*; E, labium of *Lestes*; F, tracheal gills, left to right: *Lestes, Ischnura, Chromagrion, Enallagma, Enallagma,* and *Argia*; G, dorsal view of *Coenagrion,* ×4; H, lateral view of *Lestes stultus,* ×3. (B redrawn from Kennedy, 1917; C and E redrawn from Garman, 1927; D and G modified from Kennedy, 1915; H modified from Essig, *College Entomology,* 1942, by permission of the Macmillan Publishing Co.)

63. With raptorial setae on lateral lobes of labium .................................**64**
    Without such raptorial setae ..............................................**65**
64. Lateral setae of labium with uniform length; rare, southeastern states and California ...............................................**Triacanthagyna**
    Lateral setae of labium unequal; Florida and California. **Gynacantha nervosa** Rambur
65. Abdomen with lateral spines on segments five to nine; Arizona and New Mexico.
                                                                    **Oplonaeschna**
    Abdomen with lateral spines on segments six or seven to nine (Fig. 386E); 30 to 48 mm long; generally distributed; very common ..................... **Aeshna**
66. Antennae six-segmented; western states; uncommon ..... **Tanypteryx hageni** (Selys)
    Antennae seven-segmented and thick (Fig. 387J); eastern half of the United States.
                                                            **Tachopteryx thoreyi** (Hagen)

**67.** First segment of antenna longer than the remaining segments combined (Fig. 391A); usually in streams. . . . . . . . . . . . . . . . . . . . . . . . . . . . . . . . . . . . . . . . . . AGRIIDAE, **69**

First segment of antenna much shorter than the remaining segments combined (Fig. 391G) . . . . . . . . . . . . . . . . . . . . . . . . . . . . . . . . . . . . . . . . . . . . . . . . . . . . . . . . . . **68**

**68.** Proximal half, or more, of labial mask very narrow (Figs. 391D,E); usually in ponds, marshes, and bogs . . . . . . . . . . . . . . . . . . . . . . . . . . . . . . . . . . . . LESTIDAE, **70**

Proximal half of labial mask not greatly narrowed (Fig. 391C). COENAGRIIDAE, **71**

**69.** Middle lobe of labium cleft far below base of lateral lobes (Fig. 391C); mostly in eastern half of the United States . . . . . . . . . . . . . . . . . . . . . . . . . . . . . . . . .**Agrion**

Middle lobe of labium cleft only to base of lateral lobes; stream species, eastern states . . . . . . . . . . . . . . . . . . . . . . . . . . . . . . . . . . . . . . . . . . . . . . . . . **Hetaerina**

**70.** With a simple upper notch in the trifid lateral lobe of the labium (Fig. 391D); 20 to 30 mm long; chiefly on the west coast . . . . . . . . . . . . . . . . . . . . . . . . . **Archilestes**

With a serrated upper notch in the trifid lateral lobe of the labium (Fig. 391E); 17 to 25 mm long; generally distributed . . . . . . . . . . . . . . . . . . . . . . . . . . . . . . . **Lestes**

**71.** Gills about half as broad as long (Fig. 381) . . . . . . . . . . . . . . . . . . . . . . . . . . . . . . . . .**72**

Gills not more than one-third as broad as long . . . . . . . . . . . . . . . . . . . . . . . . . . . . .**73**

**72.** With one to four lateral labial setae; standing and slow waters; widely distributed. **Argia**

Lateral labial setae absent (rarely one); far southwestern states.

**Hyponeura lugens** (Hagen)

**73.** Head angular at posterolateral margins . . . . . . . . . . . . . . . . . . . . . . . . . . . . . . . . . . .**74**

Head rounded at posterolateral margins . . . . . . . . . . . . . . . . . . . . . . . . . . . . . . . . . . .**75**

**74.** Gills widest in middle, one-third as broad as long; widely distributed except in far south . . . . . . . . . . . . . . . . . . . . . . . . . . . . . . . . . . . . . . . . . . . . . . . . **Amphiagrion**

Gills widest distally, one-sixth as broad as long (Fig. 391F); usually in springbrooks; northeastern. . . . . . . . . . . . . . . . . . . . . . . . . . . **Chromagrion conditum** (Hagen)

**75.** One or two mental setae . . . . . . . . . . . . . . . . . . . . . . . . . . . . . . . . . . . . . . . . . . . . . . .**76**

Three or more mental setae . . . . . . . . . . . . . . . . . . . . . . . . . . . . . . . . . . . . . . . . . . . . .**77**

**76.** One mental seta; quiet waters; eastern . . . . . . . . . . . . . . . . . . . . . . . . . . . **Nehallenia**

Two mental setae . . . . . . . . . . . . . . . . . . . . . . . . . . . . . . . . . . . . . . . . . . . . . . . . . . . . .**79**

**77.** Six or seven lateral labial setae; total length 14 mm; rare; far southwest but occasional as far east as Florida. . . . . . . . . . . . . . . . . . . . . . . . . . . . . . . . . . . . . . . . . . **Telebasis**

Four to six lateral labial setae; common and widely distributed . . . . . . . . . . . . . . .**78**

**78.** Gills tapering to a fine point (Fig. 391F); length 10 to 15 mm; three to five mental setae; five or six lateral labial setae; still waters . . . . . . . . . . . . . . . . . . **Ischnura**

Gills not tapering to a fine point (Fig. 391F); 16 to 23 mm long; three or four mental setae; four to six lateral labial setae . . . . . . . . . . . . . . . . . . . . . . . . . . . **Enallagma**

**79.** Six or seven lateral labial setae . . . . . . . . . . . . . . . . . . . . . . . . . . . . . . . . . . . . . . . . . .**80**

Four or five lateral labial setae . . . . . . . . . . . . . . . . . . . . . . . . . . . . . . . . . . . . . . . . . . .**82**

**80.** Gills tapering to a slender point; length without gills about 18 mm; east coast states. . . . . . . . . . . . . . . . . . . . . . . . . . . . . . . . . . . . . . . .**Teleallagma daecki** Calvert

Gills bluntly pointed . . . . . . . . . . . . . . . . . . . . . . . . . . . . . . . . . . . . . . . . . . . . . . . . . . .**81**

**81.** Tip of gills obtusely angled; extreme northern states. . . . . . . . . . . . . . . . .**Coenagrion**

Tip of gills rounded; extreme southwest. . . . . . . . . . **Hesperagrion heterodoxum** Selys

**82.** Without lateral spines on terminal abdominal segment; eastern half of the United States . . . . . . . . . . . . . . . . . . . . . . . . . . . . . . . . . . . . . . . . .**Anomalagrion hastatum** Say

With lateral spines on terminal abdominal segment; California.

**Zoniagrion exclamationis** Selys

## ODONATA REFERENCES

BENKE, A. C. 1970. A method for comparing individual growth rates of aquatic insects with special reference to the Odonata. *Ecology* **51**:328–331.

BENKE, A. C., and S. S. BENKE. 1975. Comparative dynamics and life histories of coexisting dragonfly populations. Ibid. **56**:302–317.

BICK, G. H. 1941. Life-history of the dragonfly Erythemis simplicollis. *Ann. Entomol. Soc. Am.* **34**:215–230.

———. 1953. The nymph of Miathyria marcella (Selys). *Proc. Entomol. Soc. Wash.* **55**:30–36.

———. 1957. The Odonata of Louisiana. *Tulane Stud. Zool.* **5**:71–135.

———. 1957a. The Odonata of Oklahoma. *Southwest Nat.* **2**:1–18.

BORROR, D. J. 1945. A key to the New World genera of Libellulidae. *Ann. Entomol. Soc. Am.* **38**:168–194.

BYERS, C. F. 1930. A contribution to the knowledge of Florida Odonata. *Univ. Fla. Publ., Biol. Sci. Ser.* **1**:9–327.

———. 1937. A review of the dragon-flies of the genera Neurocordulia and Platycordulia. *Univ. Mich., Misc. Publ. Mus. Zool.* **36**:1–36.

———. 1939. A study of the dragonflies of the genus Progomphus (Gomphoides), with a description of a new species. *Proc. Fla. Acad. Sci.* **4**:19–85.

CALVERT, P. P. 1934. The rates of growth, larval development and seasonal distribution of dragonflies of the genus Anax (Odonata: Aeshnidae). *Proc. Am. Philos. Soc.* **73**:1–70.

CORBET, P. S., C. LONGFIELD, and N. W. MOORE. 1960. *Dragonflies.* 260 pp. Collins, London.

GARMAN, P. 1917. The Zygoptera, or damselflies, of Illinois. *Bull. Ill. State Lab. Nat. Hist.* **12**:411–587.

———. 1927. The Odonata or dragonflies of Connecticut. *Bull. State Geol. Nat. Hist. Surv. Conn.* **39**:1–331.

GLOYD, L. K. 1959. Elevation of the Macromia group to family status (Odonata). *Entomol. News* **70**:197–205.

HAYES, W. P. 1941. A bibliography of keys for the identification of immature insects. Part II. Odonata. *Entomol. News* **52**:52–55, 66–69, 93–98.

JOHNSON, C., and M. J. WESTFALL. 1970. Diagnostic keys and notes on the damselflies (Zygoptera) of Florida. *Bull. Fla. State Mus. Biol. Sci.* **15**:45–89.

JOHNSON, D. M. 1973. Predation by damselfly naiads on cladoceran populations: fluctuating intensity. *Ecology* **54**:251–268.

KENNEDY, C. H. 1915. Notes on the life history and ecology of the dragonflies (Odonata) of Washington and Oregon. *Proc. U.S. Nat. Mus.* **49**:259–345.

———. 1917. Notes on the life history and ecology of the dragonflies (Odonata) of Central California and Nevada. Ibid. **52**:483–635.

———. 1922. The ecological relationships of the dragonflies of the Bass Islands of Lake Erie. *Ecology* **3**:325–336.

KORMONDY, E. J. 1958. Catalogue of the Odonata of Michigan. *Misc. Publ. Mus. Zool. Univ. Mich.* **104**:1–43.

———. 1959. The systematics of Tetragoneuria, based on ecological, life history, and morphological evidence (Odonata: Corduliidae). Ibid. **107**:1–79.

———. 1961. Territoriality and dispersal in dragonflies (Odonata). *J. N.Y. Entomol. Soc.* **69**:42–52.

LEVINE, H. R. 1957. Anatomy and taxonomy of the mature naiads of the dragonfly genus Plathemis (Family Libellulidae). *Smithson. Misc. Coll.* **134**:1–28.

LUTZ, P. E., and A. R. PITTMAN. 1968. Oviposition and early developmental stages of Lestes eurinus (Odonata: Lestidae). *Am. Midl. Nat.* **80**:43–51.

MARTIN, R. D. C. 1939. Life histories of Agrion aequabile and Agrion maculatum (Agriidae: Odonata). *Ann. Entomol. Soc. Am.* **32**:601–620.

MUTTKOWSKI, R. A. 1910. Catalogue of the Odonata of North America. *Bull. Publ. Mus. Milwaukee* **1**:1–207.

NEEDHAM, J. G. 1941. Life history studies on Progomphus and its nearest allies (Odonata: Aeschnidae). *Trans. Am. Entomol. Soc.* **67**:221–245.

———. 1948. Studies on the North American species of the genus Gomphus (Odonata). Ibid. **73**:307–339.

NEEDHAM, J. G., and E. FISHER. 1936. The nymphs of North American Libelluline dragonflies (Odonata). *Trans. Am. Entomol. Soc.* **67**:107–116.

NEEDHAM, J. G., and C. H. HART. 1901. The dragonflies (Odonata) of Illinois. Part I. Petaluridae, Aeschnidae, and Gomphidae. *Bull. Ill. State Lab. Nat. Hist.* **6**:1–94.

NEEDHAM, J. G., and H. B. HEYWOOD. 1929. *A handbook of the dragonflies of North America.* 378 pp. Thomas, Springfield, Ill.

NEEDHAM, J. G., and M. J. WESTFALL. 1955. *A manual of the dragonflies of North America (Anisoptera).* 615 pp. Univ. California Press, Berkeley.

PAULSON, D. R. 1970. A list of the Odonata of Washington with additions to and deletions from the state list. *Pan-Pac. Entomol.* **46**:194–198.

PENNAK, R. W., and C. M. McCOLL. 1944. An experimental study of oxygen absorption in some damselfly naiads. *J. Cell. Comp. Physiol.* **23**:1–10.

ROBACK, S. S., and M. J. WESTFALL. 1967. New records of Odonata nymphs from the United States and Canada with water quality data. *Trans. Am. Entomol. Soc.* **93**:101–124.

SNODGRASS, R. E. 1954. The dragonfly larva. *Smithson. Misc. Coll.* **123**:1–38.

VASSEROT, J. 1957. Contribution a l'étude du comportement de capture des larves de l'odonate Calopteryx splendens. *Vie et Milieu* **8**:127–152.

WALKER, E. M. 1912. The North American dragonflies of the genus Aeshna. *Univ. Toronto Studies, Biol. Ser.* **11**:1–213.

———. 1925. The North American dragonflies of the genus Somatochlora. Ibid. **26**:1–202.

———. 1953. *The Odonata of Canada and Alaska. Vol. I. Part I: General. Part II: The Zygoptera—Damselflies.* 292 pp. Univ. Toronto Press, Toronto.

———. 1958. *The Odonata of Canada and Alaska. Vol. II. Part III: The Anisoptera—Four Families.* 318 pp. Ibid.

WALKER, E. M., and P. S. CORBET. 1975. *The Odonata of Canada and Alaska. Vol. III. The Anisoptera—Three Families.* 308 pp. Ibid.

WILEY, R. L., and H. O. EILER. 1972. Drought resistance in subalpine nymphs of Somatochlora semicircularis Selys (Odonata: Corduliidae). *Am. Midl. Nat.* **87**:215–221.

WILSON, C. B. 1920. Dragonflies and damselflies in relation to pond-fish culture, with a list of those found near Fairport, Iowa. *Bull. U.S. Bur. Fish.* **36**:182–264.

WRIGHT, M. 1943. A comparison of the dragonfly fauna of the lower delta of the Mississippi River with that of the marshes of the Central Gulf Coast. *Ecol. Monogr.* **13**:481–497.

———. 1943a. The effect of certain ecological factors on dragonfly nymphs. *J. Tenn. Acad. Sci.* **18**:172–196.

WRIGHT, M., and A. PETERSON. 1944. A key to the genera of anisopterous dragonfly nymphs of the United States and Canada (Odonata, suborder Anisoptera). *Ohio J. Sci.* **44**:151–166.

# Chapter 29

# HEMIPTERA (BUGS)

THE TRUE "bugs" may be distinguished from other orders of insects by three outstanding features: (1) the mouth parts are greatly modified to form a segmented piercing and sucking "beak" inserted near the anterior end of the head; (2) the anterior pair of wings are leathery at the base and membranous apically, whereas the second pair are entirely membranous; and (3) metamorphosis is simple and gradual.

In size, they range from minute to very large. Shape varies from oval to very long and cylindrical; many genera are considerably flattened. The prothorax is large and free, and the meso- and metathorax are united. The scutellum is usually prominent. The antennae have only four or five segments. With few exceptions, there are five nymphal instars; these immature forms look and act much like the adults but are smaller and sexually immature. Wing buds usually appear in the second or third nymphal instar. In some species considerable variations occur in the degree of wing development in the adult, and the condition may be macropterous, brachypterous, vestigial, or apterous. Apterous and macropterous individuals may be found in the same aggregation. Thus, the flying ability and geographic migrations are variously developed in aquatic hemipterans.

Although this is a large and important order of insects, relatively few species have become adapted to aquatic habitats. There is, however, a series of semiaquatic and aquatic families that show a gradual transition in their habitats from the damp shores of ponds, swamps, and lakes to the subsurface waters. The Saldidae, Ochteridae, and Gelastocoridae, for example, live on the shore; they run and jump in varying degrees, make short flights, but usually light on the water only by accident. The Hebridae run about at the water's edge on floating vegetation, surface of the water, and the adjacent damp ground. The Hydrometridae, Mesoveliidae, and some Veliidae venture farther out and are almost always found on floating algae and plant rafts. Certain other Veliidae and the Gerridae skate rapidly over the surface of the water. In the Hebridae the body is covered with a velvety pile that effectively sheds water, but in the other surface-living families usually only the legs and especially the tarsi are covered with pile. Six families are truly aquatic and normally found below the surface. Of these, the Nepidae and Belostomatidae usually cling to the substrate but remain more or less in contact with the surface film. The former are modified very little for an aquatic existence, and although the latter have the second and third legs flattened and fringed with hairs, they do not swim a great deal. Both the Pleidae and the Naucoridae clamber about in tangled submerged vegetation, and although they are both swimmers, they are not particularly specialized for such locomotion. The Corixidae and the Notonectidae are swimmers *par excellence*. In both groups the long, flattened, hairy hind legs are used as oars. In the former family the middle legs are long and thin for clinging to the substrate.

Those forms occurring above the surface of the water have the usual unspecialized tracheal respiration characteristic of terrestrial insects. Those that swim below the surface come to the surface at intervals and renew the air in the tracheae. In some Corixidae the pronotum breaks the surface film, but in all other families the tip of the abdomen is brought into contact with the air. In some families, such as the Corixidae, Naucoridae, and Belostomatidae, there is a dorsal reservoir of air between the wings and the body. Also, there may be portions of the general body surface where a film of air is carried by a hydrofuge pubescence; this is especially noticeable in the Corixidae. No tracheal gills are known in the entire order. Many species produce squeaking or stridulatory noises.

Nearly all aquatic Hemiptera are strict predators, the particular prey, depending on the specific habits of the various genera, being chiefly small terrestrial and aquatic insects and entomostraca. The majority have the forelegs more or less specialized for seizing and holding the prey while body fluids are sucked up through the mouth parts with the muscular pharynx.

Although some of the semiaquatic Hemiptera oviposit on sphagnum and shore grasses, the eggs of the aquatic families are customarily laid on the surface or within the tissues of submerged plants. A few Corixidae oviposit on crayfish, snails, and dragonfly nymphs. All ecdyses of the aquatic forms occur under water. The great majority of species winter over as adults hidden in mud, trash, or vegetation at the edges and bottom of their habitat. They may often be seen swimming about under the ice, however.

Aside from the usual nets, no special equipment. is necessary for collecting aquatic Hemiptera. Some species may be reared in aquaria provided they are supplied with suitable food. Either alcoholic or pinned specimens are suitable for identification.

## KEY TO SEMIAQUATIC AND AQUATIC FAMILIES OF ADULT HEMIPTERA

1. Antennae shorter than head . . . . . . . . . . . . . . . . . . . . . . . . . . . . . . . . . . . . . . . . . . . . . . .2
   Antennae as long or longer than head . . . . . . . . . . . . . . . . . . . . . . . . . . . . . . . . . . .9
2. Ocelli present; semiaquatic, shore-living; do not submerge in water . . . . . . . . . . . . . .3
   Ocelli absent; aquatic . . . . . . . . . . . . . . . . . . . . . . . . . . . . . . . . . . . . . . . . . . . . . . . . . .4
3. Antennae concealed, front legs raptorial, eyes protuberant; squat, toad-shaped, mottled bugs found on moist shores of streams, marshes, and ponds; three small but widely distributed genera in the United States; toadbugs.
   GELASTOCORIDAE
   Antennae exposed; front and middle legs similar; resemble Gelastocoridae in appearance and habits; only one small genus in the United States . . OCHTERIDAE
4. Front tarsi consisting of a single spatulate segment . . . . . . . . . . .CORIXIDAE, p. 582
   Front tarsi of the usual form . . . . . . . . . . . . . . . . . . . . . . . . . . . . . . . . . . . . . . . . . . . .5
5. Front coxae inserted at or near the front margin of the prosternum; front legs modified for grasping . . . . . . . . . . . . . . . . . . . . . . . . . . . . . . . . . . . . . . . . . . . . . . . . . . .7
   Front coxae inserted at the hind margin of the short prosternum; legs modified for swimming . . . . . . . . . . . . . . . . . . . . . . . . . . . . . . . . . . . . . . . . . . . . . . . . . . . . . . . .6
6. Hind tibiae and tarsi ciliate; beak four-segmented; eyes very large; body elongated . . . . . . . . . . . . . . . . . . . . . . . . . . . . . . . . NOTONECTIDAE, p. 574
   Hind tibiae and tarsi simple, beak three-segmented; eyes not especially large; body oval . . . . . . . . . . . . . . . . . . . . . . . . . . . . . . . . . . . . . . . . PLEIDAE, p. 575
7. Membrane of upper wings reticulately veined . . . . . . . . . . . . . . . . . . . . . . . . . . . . . .8
   Membrane of upper wings without veins . . . . . . . . . . . . . . . NAUCORIDAE, p. 576
8. Apical appendages of abdomen long and slender; tarsi one-segmented.
   NEPIDAE, p. 577
   Apical appendages of abdomen short, flat, and retractile; tarsi two-segmented.
   BELOSTOMATIDAE, p. 579
9. Head as long as entire thorax; both elongated . . . . . . . . .HYDROMETRIDAE, p. 570
   Head shorter than thorax, including scutellum . . . . . . . . . . . . . . . . . . . . . . . . . . . . .10
10. Tarsal claws preapical . . . . . . . . . . . . . . . . . . . . . . . . . . . . . . . . . . . . . . . . . . . . . . .11
    Tarsal claws apical . . . . . . . . . . . . . . . . . . . . . . . . . . . . . . . . . . . . . . . . . . . . . . . . .12

**11.** Hind femur extending much beyond apex of abdomen; beak four-segmented.
GERRIDAE, p. 572
Hind femur not extending much beyond apex of abdomen; beak three-segmented.
VELIIDAE, p. 572
**12.** Antennae of five prominent segments (except *Merragata* which has four); first and second segments of antennae thicker than the others . . . . HEBRIDAE, p. 569
Antennae four-segmented; two basal segments not swollen . . . . . . . . . . . . . . . . . . . .**13**
**13.** Scutellum distinct behind posterior margin of pronotum; widely distributed . . . . . . .**14**
Pronotum elongated posteriorly; no distinct scutellum; in vegetation and debris close to edges of streams; does not venture out onto water; scattered records in the western states . . . . . . . . . . . . . . . MACROVELIIDAE, **Macrovelia horni** Uhler
**14.** Membrane of upper wings without cells; on floating vegetation.
MESOVELIIDAE, p. 571
Membrane of upper wings with four or five long closed cells; on shore near water's edge; active, erratic bugs somewhat similar to the Ochteridae and Gelastocoridae in their habits; eight small but widely distributed genera in the United States; shore bugs . . . . . . . . . . . . . . . . . . . . . . . . . . . . . . . . . . . . . . . . . . . . . . SALDIDAE

# HEBRIDAE (VELVET WATER BUGS)

Hebridae (velvet water bugs) are minute, the usual length being only 1.5 to 2.5 mm; as a result they are usually overlooked by the casual collector. Aside from the fact that the body is covered with a dense, velvety, water-resistant pile, they are similar in their morphology to terrestrial hemipterans. There are two genera in the United States, including about 12 species of *Hebrus* and two of *Merragata*. The former is common over most of the country, but *Merragata* occurs chiefly east of the Continental Divide. They are found along the margins of bodies of water. *Naeogeus* usually occurs on shore or on plant rafts and is seldom found on the water. *Merragata*, however, is found on the shore less often and runs about on the surface of the water; occasionally it crawls on submerged surfaces at which times it is covered with a film of air. The velvet water bugs feed on small insects.

The two genera may be best distinguished on the basis of the structure of the antennae. The antennae of *Hebrus* are composed of five large segments; those of *Merragata* are composed of four large segments.

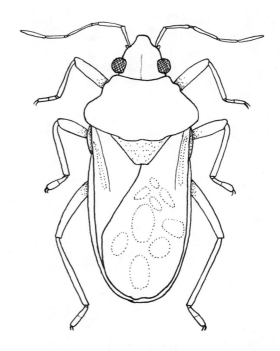

FIG. 392.–Dorsal view of adult female *Hebrus*, ×35. (Redrawn from Hungerford, 1919.)

# HYDROMETRIDAE (MARSH TREADERS, WATER MEASURERS)

The marsh treaders are exceedingly slender brownish or greenish hemipterans with long, thin legs and antennae. The usual length of the body is 8 to 11 mm in adults. They are not rare, but are seldom noticed because of their inconspicuous color and shape and because of their slow, deliberate manner of walking about on shore, on floating vegetation, or on the surface of the water of ponds, and sometimes sluggish stream backwaters. They feed on all kinds of small aquatic metazoans at or near the surface film. The prey is slowly stalked and literally "harpooned" with the tip of the beak and held thus while a pair of thin, flexible stylets are protruded farther into the body, where they are moved about rapidly in the tissues like reamers while the fluids are sucked up. The spindle-shaped eggs are deposited on objects, especially rushes, a little above the surface of the water. Development may occur very rapidly, and under most favorable conditions the entire life cycle may be completed in 15 days, and there may be two to five broods per year. In southern states marsh treaders are active the year round, but in the more northern states the adults and advanced nymphs hibernate during the winter and become active soon after the ice melts in the spring. These hemipterans are easily reared in aquaria if they are supplied with appropriate food organisms. Apterous adults are much more common than the winged forms. *Hydrometra* is the only North American genus, and *H. martini* Kirk. is by far the most common species, being found from coast to coast. Several other species have been reported from scattered localities mostly in the southern states, although one of these forms occurs as far north as Kansas. On a worldwide basis there are about 90 species of *Hydrometra*.

FIG. 393.–*Hydrometra martini*. A, dorsal view of adult, ×12; B, lateral view of head.

## MESOVELIIDAE (WATER TREADERS)

The Mesoveliidae are small hemipterans that occur in bogs, at the edges of ponds, and on floating vegetation and other objects. When disturbed, they run rapidly and often take to the surface of the open water. The adults are usually apterous and a green or yellowish-green, but the silvery winged forms are quite conspicuous. Winged and wingless forms occur together. Food consists of small living and dead insects that fall to the surface and small aquatic organisms that are caught just beneath the surface film. The female oviposits the fertilized eggs in the tissues of emergent or shore plants. It is the adult that hibernates during the winter. *Mesovelia mulsanti* White is common over all the United States; the length of the adult is 4 to 5 mm. Two other species have been described from the eastern states, but they are uncommon and only about half as large as *M. mulsanti*.

FIG. 394.–Dorsal view of adult female *Mesovelia mulsanti*, ×13. (Redrawn from Hungerford, 1919.)

## GERRIDAE (WATER STRIDERS, POND SKATERS, WHERRYMEN)

From early spring until late autumn, the Gerridae, semiaquatic long-legged hemipterans, may be found skating or leaping about on the surface film of ponds and streams everywhere. Many species are gregarious and occur in large blackish masses, especially under overhanging banks or in other shade. When disturbed, they scatter nervously in all directions. The forelegs are relatively short, raptorial, and of little use in locomotion. Water striders feed on a variety of entomostracans and aquatic insects that they catch just below the surface, or on such terrestrial insects as may fall to the water. When food is scarce, however, they are known to be cannibalistic on nymphs and weaker adults of their own species. Wings are polymorphic and often absent. Gerrids are rarely observed in flight. The length range is about 2 to 15 mm.

Of the five genera found in the United States, *Gerris* is everywhere the most common; it is represented by about 20 species,

of which *G. remigis* Say and *G. marginatus* Say are most widely distributed. The usual length is 8 to 15 mm.

Two species of *Limnogonus* are known from the United States; *L. hesione* (Kirk.) seems to be widely distributed east of the Rockies, whereas *L. franciscanus* Stål is a Central American and West Indies form that has been reported from Texas and California. *Limnogonus* is smaller than *Gerris*, being only 4.5 to 8 mm long; it has an abdomen that is proportionately much shorter and a shiny upper surface on the head and thorax; in *Gerris* these areas are dull and pubescent.

Although three species of the genus *Metrobates* have been reported, two of these have been found only rarely in some of the western states. The other species, *Metrobates hesperius* Uhl., however, has been found in scattered localities in most of the states east of the Rockies. The body is black, robust, and 3 to 5 mm long. *Metro-*

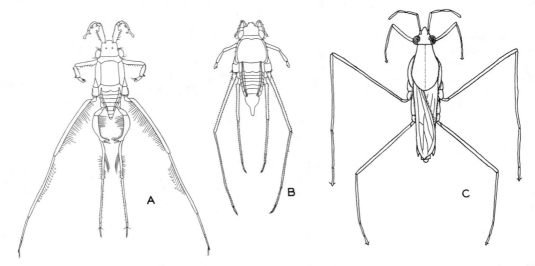

FIG. 395.–Gerridae. A, adult male *Rheumatobates rileyi* Berg, ×7; B, adult female *R. rileyi*, ×7; C, adult *Gerris*, ×3. (A and B from Silvey.)

*bates* can jump several inches into the air and catch mosquitoes in flight.

The members of the genus *Trepobates* are also very small, the body length being only 3 to 4 mm. Coloration is usually yellow and black. Seven species have been reported, and the range seems to be east of the Rocky Mountains. *T. inermis* Esaki and *T. pictus* (H. S.) are the most common and widely distributed.

Since none of the species of *Rheumatobates* are much over 3 mm in length, they are often mistaken for immature stages of larger striders and are usually taken only by the few collectors particularly interested in this group. The males are bizarre creatures; they have curiously curved, spiny antennae, and in many species have curved or deformed hind legs. Judging from the published records, the several American species seem to have a spotty distribution. The most common one, *Rheumatobates rileyi* Berg, occurs east of the Rockies.

This family also includes *Halobates*, which is unique among insects because it is found on the surface of the open ocean.

## KEY TO GENERA OF GERRIDAE

1. Median margin of eye sinuate or concave behind the middle; body long and narrow. 2
   Median margin of eye convexly rounded; body short and broad . . . . . . . . . . . . . . . . . .3
2. Basal tarsal subsegment of forelegs about half as long as second . . . . . . . . **Limnogonus**
   Basal tarsal subsegment of forelegs subequal to second . . . . . . . . . . . . . . . . . . . . . **Gerris**
3. First antennal segment much shorter than the other three taken together . . . . . . . . . . .4
   First antennal segment nearly equal to the remaining three taken together; running
      waters; most common in eastern states . . . . . . . . . . . . . . . . . . . . . . . . . **Metrobates**
4. Abdomen much shorter than remainder of body . . . . . . . . . . . . . . . . . . . . . . **Trepobates**
   Abdomen as long as remainder of body . . . . . . . . . . . . . . . . . . . . . . . . . . . **Rheumatobates**

## VELIIDAE (BROAD-SHOULDERED WATER STRIDERS)

This is a small family of gregarious, plump-bodied surface dwellers. The usual length range is only 1.6 to 5.5 mm, and the color is brown or black, often with silvery markings. The legs are not particularly long and are modified for running and walking

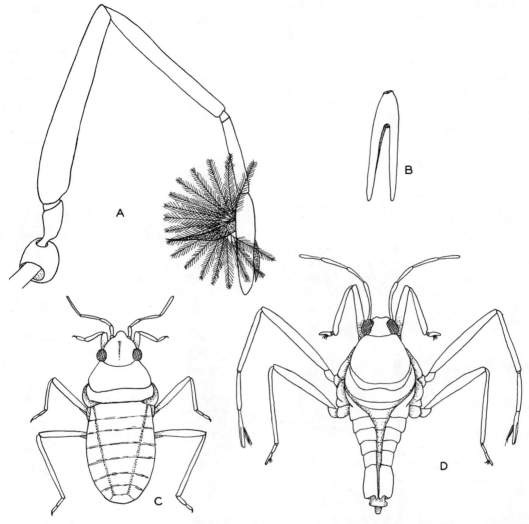

FIG. 396.–Veliidae. A, mesothoracic leg of *Rhagovelia flavicinta* Bueno, showing swimming plume and claws; B, notched second tarsus of *R. flavicinta* from which claws and swimming plume have been removed; C, apterous female *Microvelia borealis* Bueno, ×30; D, apterous female *Rhagovelia obesa* Uhl., ×13. (A and B modified from Coker, Millsaps, and Rice, 1936; C and D redrawn from Hungerford, 1919.)

rather than rowing. These insects are called broad-shouldered water striders because of the fact that the body is broadest in the region of the attachment of the second and third legs. The appropriate names of "ripple bugs" or "riffle bugs" have also been suggested, since the common genus *Rhagovelia* occurs chiefly in or near the ripples and rapids of small streams, where they await food brought by the current. *Microvelia,* on the other hand, is typical of ponds and pools. Food consists of small insects and aquatic Metazoa on or just below the surface. Many species are excellent divers and can swim readily. Overwintering occurs in the adult or egg stage.

*Microvelia* is the most abundant and widely distributed of all American aquatic Hemiptera. At the same time the numerous species in this genus are among the smallest of such forms, the usual length being only 1.6 to 3.7 mm. The hind tarsi have only two segments. *Microvelia* occurs on the rock, sand, and mud borders of streams and ponds as well as on the surface of the water. About 10 species of *Velia* and 10 of *Rhagovelia* have been recorded. Both of these genera have three segments in the hind tarsi. The latter genus is easily identified, however, by a curious tuft of long, featherlike hairs accompanied by long, flat, bladelike, chitinous structures in a deep cleft of the terminal segment of the second tarsus. In locomotion the middle tarsus is thrust through the surface film and the tuft of hairs is spread in a fanlike manner, presumably acting as a paddle. In *Microvelia* the last antennal segment is the longest, but in *Velia* the first antennal segment is the longest. All three genera are widely distributed.

## NOTONECTIDAE (BACK SWIMMERS)

The back swimmers are among the best-known water bugs. Unlike all the preceding families in this chapter, they are aquatic rather than semiaquatic and remain submerged except when in flight. The fact that they swim on their backs readily distinguishes them in their natural habitat. They are more deep-bodied than other Hemiptera and have unusually large eyes. The general dorsal surface of head and thorax is often strikingly colored and patterned with various combinations of white, pearly, yellow, golden, gray, tan, brown, and black. Some of the more common spe-

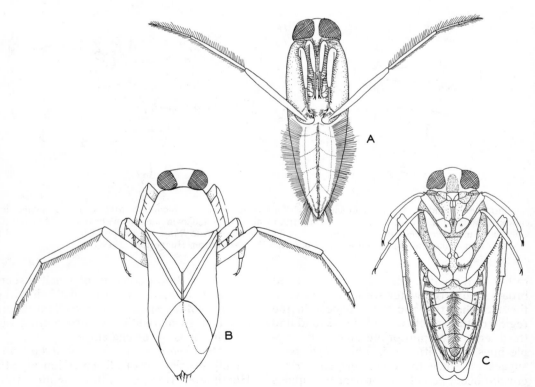

FIG. 397.–Notonectidae. A, ventral view of *Buenoa margaritacea* Bueno showing "crib" formed by first two pairs of legs, ×8; B, dorsal view of *Notonecta*, ×4.5; C, ventral view of *Notonecta*, ×4.5. (A and C modified from Hungerford, 1919; B modified from Britton.)

cies show considerable color variations, especially in the relative amounts of white and black. The antennae are partly concealed in a depression between the head and thorax.

Notonectids are abundant everywhere in ponds, small lakes, and backwaters of streams. They swim powerfully for short distances by means of rapid, oarlike strokes of the densely setose hind legs and often come to rest at the surface, dorsal side downward, with the tip of the abdomen in contact with the air, and the body at an angle. Otherwise they may be found clinging to submerged objects. Air is carried in two troughs on the ventral side of the abdomen. It is held there by three longitudinal fringes of hairs, one median and two lateral. Additional air is carried under the wings and between the head and thorax. During the nymphal stages the food consists mostly of entomostracans, but mature forms may feed on much larger prey such as aquatic insects and even small tadpoles and fishes. If handled carelessly, the notonectids "sting" sharply with the mouth parts and produce a burning sensation.

There are only two North American genera in this widespread family. *Notonecta* is the longer and broader, ranging from 8 to 17 mm in length; the last antennal segment is much shorter than the penultimate. Of the 30 American species, *N. undulata* Say is by far the most common and widely distributed. It is black and white, and the adult ranges from 10 to 13 mm in length.

*Buenoa* is more slender and smaller, the usual length being 5 to 9 mm; the last antennal segment is longer than the penultimate. It differs from *Notonecta* also in that it seldom comes to the surface. The males of this genus can stridulate by rubbing roughened patches on the front legs against the basal segment of the beak, and in both sexes the four anterior legs are margined with long spines that, when folded against the body, form a "crib" to hold the prey. Like the similar Old World genus *Anisops*, *Buenoa* possesses hemoglobin-containing cells in the abdomen. *B. margaritacea* Torre-Bueno and *B. elegans* (Fieb.) are the most common of the 25 American species.

## PLEIDAE (PIGMY BACKSWIMMERS)

The Pleidae are among the smallest aquatic Hemiptera, the adult being only 1.6 to 2.3 mm long. The body is strongly arched, and the color is grayish-yellow. They are found only in dense, tangled vegetation, such as *Chara, Anacharis,* and *Myriophyllum,* where they spend most of their time clinging to the leaves and stems, especially thin-stemmed vegetation in shallow, clear, and permanent waters. By virtue of its physical gill, *Neoplea* can remain submerged for several months when the temperature is below 8°. They swim only for short distances and seem to dodge from stem to stem. Such locomotion is an even, rapid gait, rather than the jerky motion of the notonectids. Food consists mostly of small entomostracans. The eggs are deposited in stems. The single North American

species known in this family, *Neoplea striola* (Fieber), is widely distributed and common. It has several intergrading color variants.

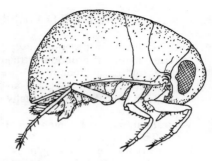

FIG. 398.–*Neoplea striola* (Fieber), ×24. (Modified from Hungerford, 1919.)

## NAUCORIDAE (CREEPING WATER BUGS)

Fig. 399.—Naucoridae. A, dorsal view of *Pelocoris femoratus* P. B., ×6; B, anterior view of head of *P. femoratus*; C, dorsal view of *Ambrysus mormon* Montd., ×5. (A and B modified from Britton; C modified from Usinger, 1946.)

Creeping water bugs are found in a wide variety of habitats. The body is broad, somewhat flattened, and of moderate size (5 to 16 mm long). Coloration is generally dull brown or greenish. The head is exceptionally broad, and the antennae are short and concealed. They feed voraciously on a variety of aquatic Metazoa, and sting viciously when handled carelessly. The anterior legs are modified for grasping the prey, the femora being greatly enlarged. The antennae are shorter than the head and lie concealed. Although these hemipterans are truly aquatic, the legs are but little modified for that habitat. Locomotion consists of a rapid, half-creeping, half-swimming gait in the dense cover of tangled vegetation of ponds, streams, and small lakes. Some species are common on gravel and pebble bottoms of slow streams, and a few occur in warm or cold spring brooks. A supply of air is carried under the wings. Winter is passed in the adult stage. Although naucorids are numerous in the Old World and tropics of the New World, they are not common in the United States.

### KEY TO GENERA OF NAUCORIDAE

1. Anterior margin of pronotum deeply excavated for reception of head (Fig. 399C) . . .2
   Anterior margin of pronotum straight (Fig. 399A) . . . . . . . . . . . . . . . . . . . . . . . . . . . . . .3
2. Ventral surface of abdomen densely pubescent; about 20 species known from the southwestern states, but an additional species occurs as far north as southern Idaho and Montana; usually in clear, flowing waters, some in hot springs.
   **Ambrysus**
   Ventral surface of abdomen naked; two rare species reported from extreme southern Texas . . . . . . . . . . . . . . . . . . . . . . . . . . . . . . . . . . . . . . . . . . . . . . . . . **Cryphocricos**
3. Inner margins of eyes divergent anteriorly; body broadly oval and flattened; one species reported from a stream in Clark County, Nevada . . . . . . . . . . . . . . . . **Usingerina**
   Inner margins of eyes convergent anteriorly (Fig. 399B); body strongly convex; several species common east of the Rockies, rare as far west as Texas and Nevada.
   **Pelocoris**

# NEPIDAE (WATER SCORPIONS)

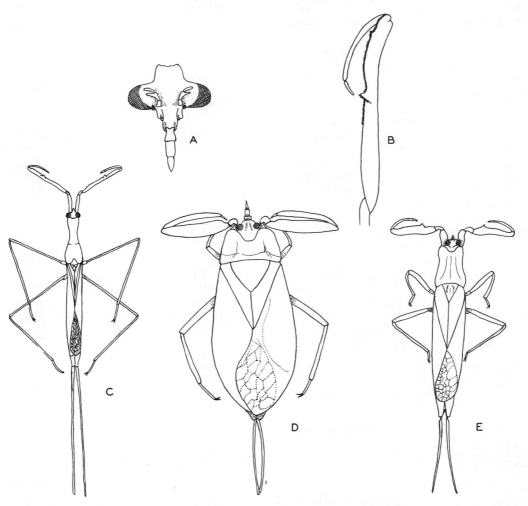

FIG. 400.–Nepidae. A, ventral view of head of *Ranatra*; B, femur, tibia, and tarsus of first leg of *Ranatra fusca* P. B.; C, *Ranatra*, ×1.5; D, *Nepa apiculata* Uhler, ×3; E, *Curicta*, ×2.5. (A, B, and E redrawn from Hungerford, 1922; C modified from Hungerford, 1919; D modified from Britton.)

Although the general body shape varies greatly in this peculiar family, there are certain consistent and striking features. All the species have two long, slender, nonretractile caudal filaments. Each of these has a groove on the median surface, and, when fitted together, the filaments constitute a respiratory tube; at intervals its tip is placed at the surface film so that the oxygen in the tracheal system may be replenished. The Nepidae are called water scorpions because of the fact that the forelegs have a superficial resemblance to the pedipalps of scorpions. The femur of each of these raptorial appendages is long and stout, and the tibia and tarsus may be folded back against the femur, the whole thus acting as a scissors. The eyes are large, the beak is relatively short and three-segmented, and the antennae are small and concealed.

Nepids are inconspicuous, owing to their protective coloration and sluggish movements. They are usually found in trash and mud in the shallows of ponds and slow, grassy streams where they lie in wait for their prey. The forelegs are held out in striking position and are capable of lashing out with great speed. All kinds of aquatic Metazoa, and especially insects, are seized and held in this way while the body fluids are sucked out. Occasional slow swimming movements are effected by alternate motions of the unspecialized second and third legs. Flight occurs at night but has rarely been observed.

On the abdomen are three pairs of peculiar sievelike openings that are in the positions normally occupied by spiracles. Their function is not definitely known, but Hamilton (1931) has shown that they are well supplied with sensory cells and believes that they have a hydrostatic function and aid in keeping the animals oriented in the water. The older theory holds that they are used in obtaining oxygen directly from the water by osmosis.

Of the three American genera, *Ranatra* is the most common and widely distributed. These insects are exceedingly slender and have a striking resemblance to small straws and grasses. The body length, without the respiratory siphon, ranges from 20 to 40 mm. They are usually found clinging to submerged vegetation with the tip of the siphon just above the surface film. *R. fusca* P. B. is the most common of the nine species.

The only representative of the second genus is *Nepa apiculata* Uhl. in eastern states. It is smaller (17 mm), broad, flat, and brown and is found in the trash of the bottom where the water is less than 10 cm deep.

The two species of *Curicta* are confined to several states in the extreme southwest and are seldom encountered by the casual collector. The body shape is intermediate between those of *Nepa* and *Ranatra* and ranges from 16 to 22 mm in length without the respiratory siphon.

The three genera may be separated as follows. In *Nepa apiculata* the body is broadly oval and flat, but in *Curicta* and *Ranatra* the body is elongated. *Curicta* has the prothorax a little broader than the head, and the body is oval-elongate. *Ranatra* has the prothorax narrower than the head, and the body is greatly elongated.

## BELOSTOMATIDAE (GIANT WATER BUGS)

Unlike the preceding family, the giant water bugs are a homogeneous group. They constitute the largest Hemiptera, the usual length of the American species being 20 to 70 mm. The body is flat and oval and a brown or dull greenish color. The four-segmented antennae are hidden beneath the prominent eyes, and there is a pair of short, straplike, retractile appendages at the tip of the abdomen. The forelegs are raptorial, but the other legs are long, flat, and ciliated for swimming. These giant bugs are found on the bottom of shallow ponds and lakes or clinging to some support near the surface with the tip of the abdomen in contact with the air. When submerged, there is a bubble of air between the abdomen and hemelytra. They are fiercely predaceous and feed on all kinds of aquatic organisms, including such relatively large forms as tadpoles, small frogs, and fishes. Occasionally they become nuisances in fish hatcheries. All secrete a toxic salivary substance that kills the prey in a very short time. The layman knows the belostomatids as "electric light bugs" because of their attraction to lights at night.

In two genera, *Abedus* and *Belostoma,* the female cements the eggs to the back of the male, and he carries them about for a week or two during incubation. In some species more than 150 eggs may be carried in this manner.

The majority of species in this family are tropical and subtropical, and, as might be expected, most American forms occur in the southern states. Ten species of *Abedus,* for example, are confined to the southwest; another species, only 12 to 14 mm long, occurs in Florida and Georgia. In the genus *Belostoma* about 10 species are western or southern and three are of more gen-

Fig. 401.–Belostomatidae. A, *Lethocerus americanus*, ×1.5; B, *Belostoma fluminea*, ×3. (A modified from Britton; B from *Insects in Kansas*.)

eral distribution; *B. fluminea* Say is certainly the most common. The large *Benacus griseus* (Say) has a scattered distribution in the southern and southeastern states. In the family as a whole, the most widely distributed and common form is *Lethocerus americanus* (Leidy); there are several other species in this same genus, but they are confined to the south and southwest.

## KEY TO GENERA OF BELOSTOMATIDAE

**1.** Metasternum with a strong midventral keel; membrane of first wing reduced; southwestern states . . . . . . . . . . . . . . . . . . . . . . . . . . . . . . . . . . . . . . . . . . . . . . . . . . . . . . . . **Abedus**
Metasternum without midventral keel; membrane of first wing not reduced; widely distributed . . . . . . . . . . . . . . . . . . . . . . . . . . . . . . . . . . . . . . . . . . . . . . . . . . . . . . . . . . . . .2
**2.** Basal segment of beak longer than the second; less than 30 mm long . . . . . .**Belostoma**
Basal segment of beak shorter than the second; more than 30 mm long . . . . . . . . . . .3
**3.** Anterior femur grooved for the reception of the tibia . . . . . . . . . . . . . . . . . . **Lethocerus**
Anterior femur not grooved for the reception of the tibia . . . . . . **Benacus griseus** (Say)

## CORIXIDAE (WATER BOATMEN)

Water boatmen are the most common of all aquatic Hemiptera, both in species and individuals. They are medium to small insects, usually less than 12 mm long. The body is somewhat flattened above, and the color is dark grayish, customarily mottled or marked with yellow, brown, or black. There is no extended beak, and the mouth parts are fused and built into the head. The stylets are used for piercing and rasp-

Fig. 402.–Structure of Corixidae. A, ventral view of abdomen of a typical female corixid; B, ventral view of abdomen of a typical male corixid; C, dorsal view of abdomen of male corixid showing strigil; D, first tarsus (pala) of a corixid, showing strong setae, scooplike shape, and row of chitinous pegs; E, first tarsus of *Rampho-corixa acuminata*; F, *Sigara,* ×7; G, adult corixid, diagrammatic, ×7; H, first instar nymph of a typical corixid, ×7. (A and B redrawn from Hungerford, 1919; C modified from Hungerford, 1942; D modified from Walley, 1936; F from *Insects in Kansas*.)

ing. What corresponds to the opening at the tip of the beak in other families is a large opening on the anterior surface of the face. The front tarsi are peculiar, being one-segmented, flat, scooplike, and fringed with strong bristles. The middle legs are long, slender, and end in two tarsal claws. The hind legs are also long but are flattened and fringed for swimming.

Corixids occur everywhere in the shallows of ponds, lakes, and streams where they spend most of their time on the bottom; they are even found in muddy stagnant pools. Popham (1943) has found a high correlation between the range of color of any particular species and that of its natural habitat. In their favorite attitude they anchor themselves to some object near the bottom with the tarsal claws of the long second legs. They swim in a quick, darting manner by oarlike movements of the hind legs; at such times the first two pairs of legs lie backward along the sternum.

The body is almost completely enveloped in a film of air, and there is also air beneath the wings. Consequently, when not swimming or clinging to some object, they rise to the surface where the supply of oxygen is renewed. In well-aerated water they may remain submerged indefinitely, obtaining their oxygen by diffusion through the air–water interface of the physical gill.

Most water boatmen are strong fliers and take off easily from the surface of the water. Adults are mainly stimulated to migrate by high temperatures, overcrowding, and an unsuitably colored background. They are sometimes abundant around bright lights at night.

Corixids gather their food from muddy bottoms by sweeping the flocculent material into the mouth with their first tarsi. It consists of debris and a great variety of algae, Protozoa, and microscopic Metazoa characteristic of that habitat. In addition, they feed on algal filaments by piercing each cell with their protrusible stylets and sucking out the contents.

The adult males of some species are able to stridulate, or chirp, by rubbing a patch of pegs on the base of the front femur against a scraper on the side of the head. The males of most species have a curry-comb-like organ, called a strigil, near either the left or right margin on the dorsal side of the sixth abdominal segment; the function of this peculiar structure is unknown, but it may be used during copulation. The males may also be distinguished from the females by the fact that the last few abdominal segments are strongly asymmetrical; with the exception of *Neocorixa snowi* Hungerford, those of the female are perfectly regular.

In most cases the eggs are attached to the stems of aquatic plants. *Ramphocorixa acuminata,* however, habitually affixes its eggs to the body of a crayfish, especially on the first abdominal pleurite. Either the nymphs or adults may winter over. They hibernate in bottom mud and debris, but may sometimes be found actively swimming about, even under ice. Depending on latitude and altitude, corixids may have one, two, or three generations per year. Typically, there are five nymph stages in the life history.

From a taxonomic standpoint, corixids are undoubtedly the most difficult of all the families of aquatic and semiaquatic Hemiptera. There are several reasons for this situation, the chief ones being the great similarity in the various genera and species and the lack of distinctive, easily observed diagnostic features. In addition, many species are quite plastic and show considerable variation in structural details. Identification is based largely on the characters of the males, the females throughout the family being so much alike that it is fruitless to attempt to include them in a key to be used primarily by the nonspecialist. Nevertheless, the females can usually be placed by their resemblance to the males in coloration and structure.

Formerly the generic and subgeneric designations of many American corixids were uncertain and controversial, but the careful monograph of Hungerford (1948) appears to have settled most of these questions in a logical manner. About 120 species are known from the United States. Of these, 50 belong in the genus *Sigara* and 20 in *Hesperocorixa*. The other genera are much smaller, several being monotypic and quite rare.

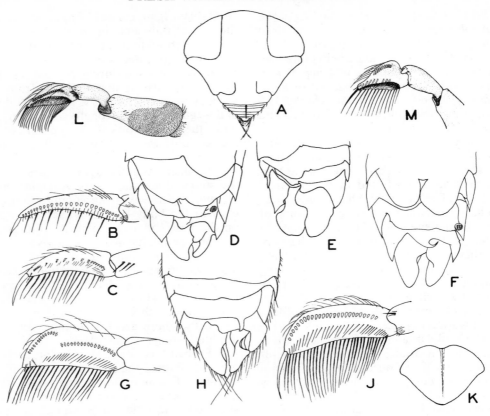

FIG. 403.–Structure of Corixidae. A, frontal view of head of male *Graptocorixa*; B and C, pala of male *Graptocorixa*; D, dorsal view of abdomen of male *Graptocorixa*; E, dorsal view of abdomen of male *Trichocorixa*; F, dorsal view of abdomen of male *Palmacorixa*; G, pala of male *Callicorixa*; H, dorsal view of abdomen of male *Morphocorixa*; J, pala of male *Hesperocorixa*; K, pronotum of *Arctocorisa*; L, first leg of male *Morphocorixa*; M, pala of male *Corisella*. (Modified and redrawn from Hungerford, 1948.)

## KEY TO GENERA OF MALE CORIXIDAE

1. Last three segments asymmetrical ventrally (Fig. 402B) . . . . . . . . . . . . . . . . . males, **2**
   Last three segments symmetrical ventrally (except in *Neocorixa*). . . . . . . . . . .females
2. First tarsus (pala) elongated and subcylindrical (Figs. 403B, C). . . . . . . . . . . . . . . . .**3**
   First tarsus (pala) not subcylindrical (Fig. 403G,L,M) . . . . . . . . . . . . . . . . . . . . . . . .**6**
3. Beak without cross ridges; 6 to 8 mm long; northern . . . . **Cymatia americana** Hussey
   Beak with cross ridges (Fig. 403A) . . . . . . . . . . . . . . . . . . . . . . . . . . . . . . . . . . . . . . . .**4**
4. Palar claw long; not more than 12 to 14 lower palmar hairs; 7.6 to 9.2 mm long; rare;
       known only from northern states . . . . . . . . . . .**Dasycorixa hybrida** Hungerford
   Palar claw short, and pala with 8 to 18 lower palmar hairs (Fig. 403B); or palar claw
       medium to long, and pala with more than 14 lower palmar hairs (Fig. 403C). **5**
5. Strigil absent; abdomen with sinistral asymmetry; female abdomen slightly asym-
       metrical; 6.9 to 8.2 mm long; rare, in Arizona and New Mexico.
                                                        **Neocorixa snowi** Hungerford
   Strigil present; abdomen with dextral asymmetry (Fig. 403D); mostly southwestern;
       about 12 species . . . . . . . . . . . . . . . . . . . . . . . . . . . . . . . . . . . . . . . . . . . **Graptocorixa**
6. Abdomen with sinistral asymmetry (Fig. 403E); pala short and triangular; less than
       5.6 mm long; widely distributed and common, sometimes in saline waters; 12
       species. . . . . . . . . . . . . . . . . . . . . . . . . . . . . . . . . . . . . . . . . . . . . . . . . . **Trichocorixa**
   Abdomen with dextral asymmetry . . . . . . . . . . . . . . . . . . . . . . . . . . . . . . . . . . . . . . . . . .**7**

7. Dorsal lobe of seventh abdominal segment with a projection that is clearly hooked (Fig. 403F); widely distributed from Atlantic coast to Rockies; three species . . . . . . . . . . . . . . . . . . . . . . . . . . . . . . . . . . . . . . . . . . . . . . . . . . . . . . . . **Palmacorixa**
   Dorsal lobe of seventh abdominal segment with or without a projection; if present then never hooklike . . . . . . . . . . . . . . . . . . . . . . . . . . . . . . . . . . . . . . . . . . . . . . . **8**
8. Upper surface of pala deeply incised near middle (Fig. 402E); 5.0 to 5.7 mm long; widely distributed . . . . . . . . . . . . . . . . . . . . . . **Ramphocorixa acuminata** (Uhler)
   Upper surface of pala not deeply incised . . . . . . . . . . . . . . . . . . . . . . . . . . . . . . . . . . . . . **9**
9. Strigil absent . . . . . . . . . . . . . . . . . . . . . . . . . . . . . . . . . . . . . . . . . . . . . . . . . . . . . . . . . **10**
   Strigil present (Fig. 402C) . . . . . . . . . . . . . . . . . . . . . . . . . . . . . . . . . . . . . . . . . . . . . . **12**
10. Body short, broad, and more than one-third as broad as long; one or two rows of palar pegs of which one is never arranged along distal margin of pala (Fig. 403L) . . . . . . . . . . . . . . . . . . . . . . . . . . . . . . . . . . . . . . . . . . . . . . . . . . . . . . . . . . . . . . . . **11**
    Body less than one-third as broad as long; always with two rows of palar pegs of which one is arranged along the distal margin of the pala (Fig. 403G); 6.7 to 8.1 mm long; northern states and at high altitudes; five species . . . . . . . **Callicorixa**
11. Dorsal side of eighth abdominal segment with a slender projection (Fig. 403H); 5.8 to 7.5 mm long; southwestern states; two species . . . . . . . . . . . . . . **Morphocorixa**
    Eight abdominal segment without such a projection; 6.0 to 8.2 mm long; one rare species reported from southwest . . . . . . . . . . . **Centrocorisa nigripennis** (Fabr.)
12. With two distinct rows of pegs on pala (Fig. 403M), or rarely one row of about 12 pegs . . . . . . . . . . . . . . . . . . . . . . . . . . . . . . . . . . . . . . . . . . . . . . . . . . . . . . . . . **13**
    With a single straight to irregular row of 14 or more pegs on pala (Fig. 403J) . . . . .**14**
13. Body width more than one-third of body length; 5.3 to 6.0 mm long; rare; reported only from Arizona . . . . . . . . . . . . . . . . . . . . **Pseudocorixa beameri** (Hungerford)
    Body width less than one-third of body length; 4 to 8 mm long; western states, but one species extending eastward to Pennsylvania; seven species . . . . . **Corisella**
14. First tibia with a group of hairs near the outer margin (Fig. 403J); 6.3 to 11.4 mm long; widely distributed and very common; about 20 species . . . **Hesperocorixa**
    First tibia without such a group of hairs . . . . . . . . . . . . . . . . . . . . . . . . . . . . . . . . . . . .**15**
15. With a well-defined median ridge on pronotum, usually visible for almost the entire length of the pronotum (Fig. 403K); 7.4 to 9.8 mm long; four species in Montana, Wyoming, and Colorado . . . . . . . . . . . . . . . . . . . . . . . . . . . . . . . . . . . . . . . .**Arctocorisa**
    Median ridge absent or visible only on anterior third of pronotum . . . . . . . . . . . . . .**16**
16. Hemelytral pattern not reticulate (Fig. 402F); hemelytra and face not hairy; 2.4 to 9.2 mm long; very common and generally distributed; commonly subdivided into 8 or 10 subgenera . . . . . . . . . . . . . . . . . . . . . . . . . . . . . . . . . . . . . . . . . . . . . . . . **Sigara**
    Hemelytral pattern reticulate; hemelytra and face hairy; 5.2 to 7.8 mm long; widely distributed in northwestern states; 10 species . . . . . . . . . . . . . . . . . . **Cenocorixa**

## HEMIPTERA REFERENCES

Anderson, L. D. 1931. A monograph of the genus Metrobates (Hemiptera, Gerridae). *Univ. Kans. Sci. Bull.* **20**:297–311.

Bacon, J. A. 1956. A taxonomic study of the genus Rhagovelia (Hemiptera, Veliidae) of the Western Hemisphere. *Univ. Kans. Sci. Bull.* **38**:695–913.

Bobb, M. L. 1974. The insects of Virginia: 7. The aquatic and semi-aquatic Hemiptera of Virginia. *Va. Polytech. Inst. State Univ. Res. Div. Bull.* **87**:1–195.

Britton, W. E., et al. 1923. Guide to the insects of Connecticut. Part IV. The Hemiptera or sucking insects of Connecticut. *State of Conn., Bull. Geol. Nat. Hist. Surv.* **34**:1–807.

Caponigro, M. A., and C. H. Eriksen. 1976. Surface film locomotion by the water strider, Gerris remigis Say. *Am. Midl. Nat.* **95**:268–278.

Deay, H. O., and G. E. Gould. 1936. The Hemiptera of Indiana, I. Family Gerridae. *Am. Midl. Nat.* **17**:753–760.

Dodson, V. E. 1975. Life histories of three species of Corixidae (Hemiptera: Heteroptera) from western Colorado. *Am. Midl. Nat.* **94**:257–266.

———. 1975a. The distribution and habitat separation of three corixids (Hemiptera: Heteroptera) in western Colorado. *Freshwater Biol.* **5**:141–150.

Drake, C. J., and H. C. Chapman. 1958. New Neotropical Hebridae, including a catalogue of the

American species (Hemiptera). *J. Wash. Acad. Sci.* **48**:317–326.

DRAKE, C. J., and H. M. HARRIS. 1932. A synopsis of the genus Metrobates Uhler. (Hemiptera: Gerridae). *Ann. Carnegie Mus.* **21**:83–88.

———. 1932a. A survey of the species of Trepobates Uhler (Hemiptera, Gerridae). *Bull. Brooklyn Entomol. Soc.* **27**:113–122.

———. 1934. The Gerrinae of the Western Hemisphere (Hemiptera). *Ann. Carnegie Mus.* **23**:179–240.

DRAKE, C. J., and F. C. HOTTES. 1952. Genus Trepobates Herrich-Schaeffer (Hemiptera; Gerridae). *Great Basin Nat.* **12**:35–38.

DRAKE, C. J., and R. F. HUSSEY. 1955. Concerning the genus Microvelia Westwood, with descriptions of two new species and a check-list of the American forms (Hemiptera: Veliidae). *Fla. Entomol.* **38**:95–115.

FOX, L. R. 1975. Some demographic consequences of food shortage for the predator, Notonecta hoffmanni. *Ecology* **56**:868–880.

GITTELMAN, S. H. 1974. The habitat preference and immature stages of Neoplea striola (Hemiptera: Pleidae). *J. Kans. Entomol. Soc.* **47**:491–503.

———. 1975. Physical gill efficiency and winter dormancy in the pigmy backswimmer, Neoplea striola (Hemiptera: Pleidae). *Ann. Entomol. Soc. Am.* **68**:1011–1017.

GRIFFITH, M. E. 1945. The environment, life history, and structure of the water boatman, Ramphocorixa acuminata (Uhler) (Hemiptera, Corixidae). Ibid. **30**:241–365.

HAMILTON, M. A. 1931. The morphology of the water-scorpion, Nepa cinerea Linn. (Rhynchota, Heteroptera). *Proc. Zool. Soc. Lond.* (1931):1067–1136.

HIDALGO, J. 1935. The genus Abedus (Belostomatidae, Hemiptera). *Univ. Kans. Sci. Bull.* **22**:493–520.

HOFFMAN, C. H. 1924. The life history of three species of gerrids (Heteroptera Gerridae). *Ann. Entomol. Soc. Am.* **17**:419–430.

———. 1932. The biology of three North American species of Mesovelia (Hemiptera, Mesoveliidae). *Can. Entomol.* **64**:88–95, 113–120, 126–134.

HUNGERFORD, H. B. 1919. The biology and ecology of aquatic and semiaquatic Hemiptera. *Univ. Kans. Sci. Bull.* **11**:3–328.

———. 1922. The Nepidae of America north of Mexico (Heteroptera). Ibid. **14**:423–472.

———. 1927. The life history of the creeping water bug, Pelocoris carolinensis Bueno (Naucoridae). Ibid. **22**:77–82.

———. 1933. The genus Notonecta of the world. Ibid. **21**:5–196.

———. 1948. The Corixidae of the Western Hemisphere. Ibid. **32**:1–827.

———. 1954. The genus Rheumatobates Bergroth (Hemiptera: Gerridae). *Univ. Kans. Sci. Bull.* **36**:529–588.

HUNGERFORD, H. B., and N. E. EVANS. 1934. The Hydrometridae of the Hungarian National Museum

and other studies in the family. *Ann. Mus. Nat. Hung.* **28**:31–112.

ISTOCK, C. A. 1973. Population characteristics of a species ensemble of waterboatmen (Corixidae). *Ecology* **54**:535–544.

KUITERT, L. C. 1942. Gerrinae in University of Kansas collections. *Univ. Kans. Sci. Bull.* **28**:113–142.

LARIVERS, I. 1948. A new species of Pelocoris from Nevada, with notes on the genus in the United States (Hemiptera: Naucoridae). *Ann. Entomol. Soc. Am.* **41**:371–376.

———. 1951. A revision of the genus Ambrysus in the United States (Hemiptera: Naucoridae). *Univ. Calif. Publ. Ent.* **8**:277–338.

———. 1971. Studies of Naucoridae (Hemiptera). *Mem. Biol. Soc. Nev.* **2**:1–120.

MACAN, T. T. 1954. A contribution to the study of the ecology of Corixidae (Hemiptera). *J. Anim. Ecol.* **23**:115–141.

———. 1962. Why do some pieces of water have more species of Corixidae than others? *Arch. Hydrobiol.* **58**:224–232.

———. 1965. A revised key to the British water bugs (Hemiptera—Heteroptera). *Sci. Publ. Freshwater Biol. Assoc.* **16**:1–78.

———. 1976. A twenty-one-year study of the water-bugs in a moorland fishpond. *J. Anim. Ecol.* **45**:913–922.

MATSUDA, R. 1960. Morphology, evolution and a classification of the Gerridae (Hemiptera—Heteroptera). *Univ. Kans. Sci. Bull.* **41**:25–632.

MCKINSTRY, A. P. 1942. A new family of Hemiptera-Heteroptera proposed for Macrovelia hornii Uhler. *Pan-Pac. Ent.* **18**:90–96.

MENKE, A. S. 1958. A synopsis of the genus Belostoma Latreille, of American North of Mexico, with the description of a new species (Hemiptera: Belostomatidae). *Bull. S. Calif. Acad. Sci.* **57**:154–174.

———. 1960. A taxonomic study of the genus Abedus Stål (Hemiptera: Belostomatidae). *Univ. Calif. Publ. Entomol.* **16**:393–440.

POPHAM, E. J. 1943. Ecological studies of the common species of British Corixidae. *J. Anim. Ecol.* **12**:124–136.

———. 1960. On the respiration of aquatic Hemiptera Heteroptera with special reference to the Corixidae. *Proc. Zool. Soc. Lond.* **135**:209–242.

RANKIN, K. P. 1935. Life history of Lethocerus americanus Leidy (Belostomatidae, Hemiptera). *Univ. Kans. Sci. Bull.* **22**:479–491.

RICE, L. A. 1954. Observations on the biology of ten notonectid species found in the Douglas Lake, Michigan, region. *Am. Midl. Nat.* **51**:105–132.

SPRAGUE, I. B. 1956. The biology and morphology of Hydrometra martini Kirkaldy. *Univ. Kans. Sci. Bull.* **38**:579–693.

SUTTON, M. F. 1952. On the food, feeding mechanism and alimentary canal of Corixidae (Hemiptera, Heteroptera). *Proc. Zool. Soc. Lond.* **121**:465–499.

TODD, E. L. 1955. A taxonomic revision of the

Family Gelastocoridae (Hemiptera). *Univ. Kans. Sci. Bull.* **37**:277–476.

DE LA TORRE-BUENO, J. R. 1926. The family Hydrometridae in the western hemisphere. *Entomol. Am.* **7**:83–128.

TRUXAL, F. S. 1953. A revision of the genus Buenoa (Hemiptera Notonectidae). *Univ. Kans. Sci. Bull.* **35**:1351–1523.

USINGER, R. L. 1941. Key to the subfamilies of Naucoridae with a generic synopsis of the new subfamily Ambrysinae (Hemiptera). *Ann. Entomol. Soc. Am.* **34**:5–16.

# Chapter 30

# MEGALOPTERA (ALDERFLIES, DOBSONFLIES, FISHFLIES)

MEGALOPTERA were formerly placed in the order Neuroptera, but most authorities now contend that they constitute a small separate order. They are dull colored and medium to large in size, the length ranging from about 10 to 70 mm. The two pairs of wings are similar and are held flat or rooflike over the body when at rest. Flight is weak. The head bears long, slender antennae and biting mouth parts. The order is readily divisible into two families, the Sialidae (alderflies) and Corydalidae (dobsonflies and fishflies). Species belonging in the former family are small, diurnal, and have the fourth tarsal segments dilated and conspicuously bilobed. The Corydalidae, on the other hand, are about 25 to 70 mm long, are nocturnal, and have cylindrical fourth tarsal segments. Although the Megaloptera are widely distributed in the United States, they are rarely found in large numbers. Adults appear mostly in the spring and early summer near streams, ponds, and lakes in which the larval stages are spent. The imagoes live for only a few days and do not feed. Pupation occurs on shore.

The minute elongated eggs are laid in rows forming masses of several thousand on vegetation and other objects overhanging the water, and on hatching, the larvae fall into the water. In most cases the larval stages last for two or three years. Considering this long period of time, there are surprisingly few larval instars, about 10 being the usual number.

Mature Megaloptera larvae are among the most striking of aquatic insects. They can be easily distinguished by the presence of a pair of lateral, cylindrical, simple, or segmented gill filaments on the first seven or eight abdominal segments. These structures are supplied with tracheae and are supposedly of considerable respiratory significance. The body is stout, elongated, from 25 to 90 mm long, dull yellowish, brown, or dusky, and often mottled. The head bears four-segmented antennae, small compound eyes, and strong mouth parts. The legs are well developed. Because they possess functional abdominal spiracles, these larvae may be kept out of water for days at a time, provided the surface of the body is damp. The Corydalidae have a pair of hooked anal prolegs, the Sialidae have a terminal anal filament.

Although larvae have occasionally been collected as deep as 15 m in lakes, they are customarily found along the margins of ponds and lakes and under and between stones in streams, and in stream backwaters. *Sialis* sometimes lies buried in muddy substrates. Although the larvae typically move about by crawling on the substrate, they can swim to some extent by undulations of the body. As indicated by the structure of the mouthparts, they are active predators that feed on all kinds of aquatic organisms, especially insects. In *Sialis* the rectum and gut are osmoregulatory. There are about 10 larval instars.

To the fisherman, hellgrammites are one of the finest of all live baits. They can be kept for days in damp moss and are tough and hardy when placed on a hook.

Just before pupation the larvae crawl out of the water onto the shore, sometimes

FIG. 404.–Larva of female *Neohermes californica* (Walker) exposing spiracles of seventh and eighth abdominal segments above the surface film. *SP*, spiracle. (Modified from Smith.)

as much as 50 m from the water. The pupal chamber may be constructed under stones or debris or up to 5 or 10 cm deep in the earth. Some species pupate in dry stream beds. The pupal stage is short and usually terminates in less than two weeks. The entire life cycle lasts two or three years.

As indicated in the key, the Sialidae and the Corydalidae are easily distinguished. The former family includes only one American genus, *Sialis*. About 23 U.S. species are known. Some are widely distributed over most of the country, whereas others are confined to the far west or Appalachian regions. In the Corydalidae, *Corydalus cornutus* is found throughout eastern North America. The generic affinities of the other species in this family are still unsettled. Some specialists regard them as all belonging to a single widely distributed genus, *Chauliodes*. Others group these species into six different genera, each containing two to six species. Still others consider them subgenera of *Chauliodes*. In this manual we are tentatively adopting the second of these alternatives, while we recognize the strong possibility of a complete revision of the "Chauliodes group" in the future.

## KEY TO GENERA OF MEGALOPTERA LARVAE

1. With seven pairs of lateral segmented abdominal appendages and a long terminal anal filament; anal prolegs absent (Fig. 405B); total length up to 30 mm when mature; alderfly larvae; occasionally burrow in debris.............. SIALIDAE, **Sialis**
    With eight pairs of lateral abdominal appendages, unsegmented or imperfectly segmented; no terminal anal filament; anal prolegs present (Fig. 404); total length up to 90 mm when mature .......................... CORYDALIDAE, **2**
2. With a tuft of hairlike tracheal gills at the base of each lateral abdominal appendage (Fig. 405C); total length up to 90 mm when mature; the true dobson or hellgrammite; under stones in well-aerated streams, but rare in mountainous areas.
                                                                 **Corydalus cornutus** L.
    Without tracheal gills at the base of the abdominal appendages; total length up to 40 mm when mature; fishfly larvae ................... "Chauliodes group," **3**

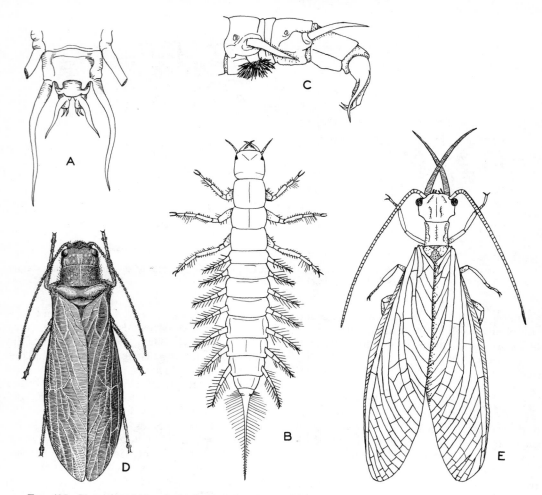

Fig. 405.–Structure of Megaloptera. A, dorsal view of posterior end of *Chauliodes* larva showing prolegs; B, dorsal view of *Sialis* larva, ×3; C, lateral view of posterior end of *Corydalus cornutus* showing prolegs, spiracles, and tracheal gills; D, adult *Sialis*, ×5; E, adult male *Corydalus cornutus* showing enormously developed mandibles, ×1.2. (D from Ross; B modified from Ross; A and C modified from Snodgrass, 1935.)

3. Eighth abdominal segment with two long respiratory tubes extending beyond the posterior end of the living larva; eastern states ..................... **Chauliodes**
    Respiratory tubes of living larva much shorter or absent ........................4
4. Each spiracle of eighth abdominal segment on a low dorsal boss .................5
    Each spiracle of eighth abdominal segment flush with body surface (Fig. 404); lateral abdominal appendages as long or longer than the width of the abdominal segments; **Neohermes** in eastern and western states; **Protochauliodes** in western states (no good separation characters for these two genera).
5. Lateral abdominal appendages about half as long as the width of the abdominal segments; western states ..................................... **Dysmicohermes**
    Lateral abdominal appendages as long or longer than the width of the abdominal segments; sometimes in stagnant waters; east of the Continental Divide. **Nigronia**

## MEGALOPTERA REFERENCES

Azam, K. M., and N. H. Anderson. 1969. Life histories and habits of Sialis rotunda and S. californica in western Oregon. *Ann. Entomol. Soc. Am.* **62**:549–558.

Chandler, H. P. 1954. Four new species of dobsonflies from California. *Pan-Pac. Entomol.* **30**:105–111.

Cuyler, R. D. 1965. The larvae of Nigronia fasciatus Walker (Megaloptera: Corydalidae). *Entomol. News* **76**:192–195.

Maddux, D. E. 1954. A new species of dobsonfly from California. *Pan-Pac. Entomol.* **30**:70–71.

Neunzig, H. H. 1966. Larvae of the genus Nigronia Banks (Neuroptera: Corydalidae). *Proc. Entomol. Soc. Wash.* **68**:11–16.

Parfin, S. I. 1952. The Megaloptera and Neuroptera of Minnesota. *Am. Midl. Nat.* **47**:421–434.

Pritchard, G., and T. G. Leischner. 1973. The life history and feeding habits of Sialis Cornuta Ross in a series of abandoned beaver ponds (Insecta: Megaloptera). *Can. J. Zool.* **51**:121–131.

Ross, H. H. 1937. Studies of Nearctic aquatic insects. I. Nearctic alder flies of the genus Sialis (Megaloptera, Sialidae). *Bull. Ill. Nat. Hist. Surv.* **21**:57–78.

Seitz, W. 1940. Zur Frage des Extremitätencharakters der Tracheenkiemen von Sialis flavilatera L. im Rahmen allgemeiner biologischer Untersuchungen. *Z. Morphol. Oekol. Tiere* **37**:214–275.

Shaw, J. 1955. Ionic regulation and water balance in the aquatic larva of Sialis lutaria. *J. Exp. Biol.* **32**:353–382.

Smith, E. L. 1970. Biology and structure of the dobsonfly, Neohermes californicus (Walker). *Pan-Pac. Entomol.* **46**:142–150.

Tarter, D. C., W. D. Watkins, and M. L. Little. 1975. Life history of the fishfly, Nigronia fasciatus (Megaloptera: Corydalidae). *Psyche* **82**:81–88.

Townsend, L. H. 1935. Key to larvae of certain families and genera of Nearctic Neuroptera. *Proc. Entomol. Soc. Wash.* **37**:25–30.

# Chapter 31

# NEUROPTERA, SISYRIDAE (SPONGILLA FLIES)

ALTHOUGH there are about 40 families of Neuroptera, only one, the Sisyridae, is of interest to the aquatic biologist. In this family, which is very poorly known except to the specialist, the larvae occur in the cavities and on the surface of fresh-water sponges. Hence the name "spongilla flies."

The adults appear during the summer months and probably live for two weeks or more. They are 6 to 8 mm long and brown or yellow and brown. The head bears biting mouth parts and long antennae. The two pairs of wings are somewhat similar.

Eggs are laid in small masses on emergent vegetation and other objects overhanging the water. When the minute larvae hatch they fall into the water where they swim about in an aimless jerking manner. Although it is possible that they are attracted by the currents of water coming out of sponges, it may be that they come in contact with the sponges purely by chance. There are three larval instars.

The mature larva is 4 to 6 mm long. The body is stout and bears long stiff bristles among which bits of sponge become entangled. This condition, in conjunction with their pale green or yellowish coloration, effectively camouflages the larvae. The mouthparts are highly modified, elongated, and grooved to form a needlelike tube that is slightly curved apically. This tube is thrust into the tissues of the sponge and the contents are sucked up into the body. The alimentary canal is closed at the junction of the mid- and hindgut, and any indigestible residue is probably retained in the stomach until the imago stage.

On the ventral side of the first seven abdominal segments in the larger larvae are curious, paired, segmented, tracheal gills. These are moved intermittently in an exceedingly rapid shuttlelike manner.

Two genera and about eight species of spongilla flies are known from the United States. Both *Sisyra* and *Climacia* are widely distributed but seldom collected. The larvae are similar in appearance and hibits and we do not have characters that will separate the two genera. Nevertheless, the following key separates the three most common species.

The larvae are found on most of the common species of sponges, and there is no evidence for host specificity. A few observers have reported them on Bryozoa and algae, but it seems likely that such occurrences are accidental.

Just before pupation the larvae climb out of the water onto the shore, emergent vegetation, or other objects. The silk that is used in constructing the cocoon emerges from the anus. In addition to a close-meshed cocoon that fits tightly around the body, there is an additional loose-fitting outer cocoon, composed of large open hexagons in *Climacia* but close-meshed in *Sisyra*. The pupal stage usually lasts less than 14 days. It is thought that wintering over occurs within the cocoon in the prepupal stage. Two or three broods per year are common.

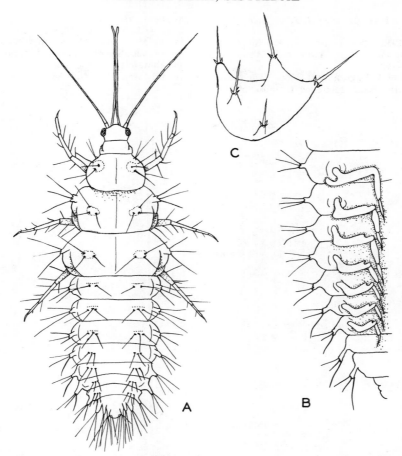

FIG. 406.–Larvae of Sisyridae. A, dorsal view of mature *Sisyra* larva, ×16; B, ventral view of right side of abdomen of same showing tracheal gills, ×30; C, dorsal plate of pronotum of *Climacia areolaris* showing tubercles, spines, and basal teeth. (A modified from Townsend, 1935; B modified from Rousseau, 1921.)

## KEY TO COMMON SISYRIDAE LARVAE

1. Dorsal tubercles long, with the spines of each having small teeth at their bases (Fig. 406C); eastern half of the United States . . . . . . . . . . **Climacia areolaris** (Hagen)
   Dorsal tubercles short, without teeth at bases of their setae . . . . . . . . . . . . . . . . . . . . .2
2. Tenth abdominal segment large, more than half as wide as ninth segment; eastern half of the United States and Oregon and Washington. . . . . . **Sisyra vicaria** (Walker)
   Tenth abdominal segment less than half as wide as ninth segment; Oregon and California . . . . . . . . . . . . . . . . . . . . . . . . . . . . . . . . . . **Climacia californica** Chandler

## SISYRIDAE REFERENCES

ANTHONY, M. H. 1902. The metamorphosis of Sisyra. *Am. Nat.* **36**:615–631.

BROWN, H. P. 1952. The life history of Climacia areolaris (Hagen) a neuropterous "parasite" of fresh water sponges. *Am. Midl. Nat.* **47**:130–160.

FLINT, O. S. 1964. New species and new state records of Sialis (Neuroptera: Sialidae). *Entomol. News* **75**:9–13.

ISOM, B. G. 1968. New distribution records for aquatic neuropterans, Sisyridae (spongilla-flies) in the Tennessee River drainage. *J. Tenn. Acad. Sci.* **43**:109.

OLD, M. C. 1932. Observations on the Sisyridae (Neuroptera). *Pap. Mich. Acad. Sci., Arts and Lett.* **17**:681–684.

PARFIN, S. I., and A. B. GURNEY. 1956. The spongilla-flies, with special reference to those of the Western Hemisphere (Sisyridae, Neuroptera). *Proc. U.S. Nat. Mus.* **105**:421–529.

POIRRIER, M. A., and Y. M. ARCENEAUX. 1972. Studies on southern Sisyridae (spongilla-flies) with a key to the third-instar larvae and additional sponge-host records. *Am. Midl. Nat.* **88**:455–458.

# Chapter 32

# TRICHOPTERA (CADDIS FLIES)

ADULT CADDIS flies are small to medium-sized mothlike insects found near streams, ponds, and lakes, especially between May and September. They are generally an inconspicuous gray, tan, brown, or blackish. The great majority are crepuscular or nocturnal. Flight in most species is rapid, with well-developed dodging movements. The wings are hairy and scaly and are folded rooflike over the body when at rest. The mouthparts are feeble and specialized for liquid foods, the antennae are filiform, and the compound eyes are large. Classification of adults is based chiefly on detailed morphology of the male genitalia.

Metamorphosis is complete, and although the adults are terrestrial insects, the larvae and pupae are aquatic and may be found in most fresh-water habitats. Oviposition habits vary widely. In some species the eggs are dropped into the water during flight; in others they are deposited while at rest. Sometimes the eggs are deposited on objects a short distance above the water, and in such cases the newly hatched larvae are thought to be washed into the water by rain. Usually, however, the females actually go below the surface to oviposit. The eggs may then be enclosed in gelatinous strings or masses in bottom debris or attached to submerged objects. Sometimes the eggs are simply glued to the substrate by a cement substance.

Caddis flies may have one or two generations per year, the former being the rule at high latitudes. The adults are short-lived, and in most species this stage last 30 days or less. The greater portion of the life history is spent as a larva, and it is usually this stage that winters over. The pupal stage lasts only about two weeks.

At least one species of *Philocasca*, reported from Oregon, is an unusual caddis fly because it is terrestrial in all stages of its life history. The European genus *Enoicyla* has similar habits. Several New Zealand species breed in tide pools.

The first encounter with caddis fly larvae in the field is usually a surprise. One detects what appear to be small pieces of debris moving jerkily about on the bottom of a shallow pond or stream. On closer examination these bits of debris are found to be hollow cylindrical cases composed of sand grains, gravel, small pieces of leaves, grass, bark, or twigs. Within, and largely hidden from view, is the elongated caddis worm, or larva.

Although the larval head and thorax may be heavily sclerotized and darkly pigmented, the abdomen is soft and delicately colored, usually green, tan, gray, cream-colored, or whitish. The head bears a pair of very small antennae, chewing mouth parts, and two clumps of black ocelli. In carnivorous species the eyes are set far forward. The three segments of the thorax are distinctly set off from each other, never fused. The prothoracic legs are generally the stoutest and shortest, and are used more for holding the prey and case building than for locomotion.

Each leg consists of the usual five segments, but some of these are subdivided. The trochanters, for example, are composed of two parts, the basal portion sometimes being very short. In some species the middle and hind femora are divided, and in a few cases even the tibiae or tarsi are divided.

In most of the case-building larvae there are three tubercles or "spacing

593

humps" on the first abdominal segment. One is middorsal and the other two are lateral. These prominences maintain a space between the body and the case, so that freshly oxygenated water may come in contact with as much of the body surface as possible. At the posterior end is a pair of small to large prolegs. They bear hooks and function in anchoring the larva to the case or substrate. A lateral line is present in some caddis larvae; it consists of a fringe of hairs on each side of some of the posterior abdominal segments.

Most of the larvae that build portable cases have nonretractile tracheal gills. These occur on most of the abdominal segments, but in a few species they are also present on the thorax. In distribution, number, and morphology they show a wide range of conditions. They are arranged in more or less well-defined rows along the abdomen and may be conical processes or long and filamentous. Usually they are single and simple, but in some genera they are arranged in tufts or are branched. In a few forms the gills are covered with fine hairs. Small, fingerlike blood gills are limited to the anal region and occur much less fre-

FIG. 407.–Adult caddis flies. A, *Hydropsyche*, ×5.5; B, *Rhyacophila*, ×4.5. (From Ross, 1938, courtesy Illinois Natural History Survey.)

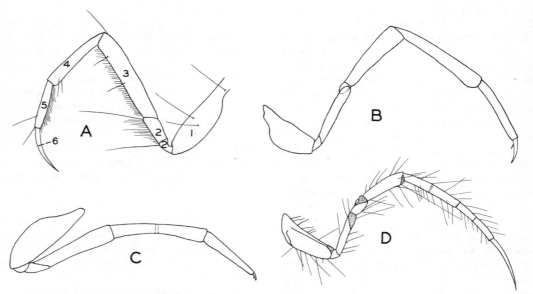

FIG. 408.–Structure of third legs of caddis larvae. A, *Ptilostomis*, showing divided trochanter; B, *Nectopsyche*, showing divided trochanter and femur; C, *Molanna*, showing divided trochanter and tibia; D, *Mystacides*, showing divided trochanter, femur, tibia, and tarsus. 1, coxa; 2, trochanter; 3, femur; 4, tibia; 5, tarsus; 6, tarsal claw. (C modified from Betten; D redrawn from Ross, 1944.)

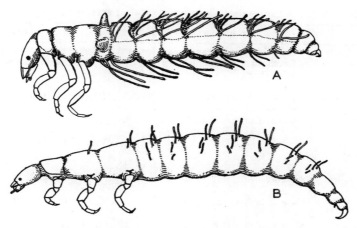

FIG. 409.–Typical caddis larvae, diagrammatic. A, eruciform larva; B, campodeiform larva. (From Dodds and Hisaw, 1925.)

quently; they are of little or no importance in oxygen absorption, but they may be osmoregulatory. In larvae that have no tracheal gills the respiratory exchange occurs through the general body surface. Even in the gilled forms, however, the integument is of much respiratory significance, and experimental work has shown that some larvae are able to obtain sufficient oxygen after all the gills have been removed. In case-building forms undulatory movements of the abdomen and the hairs forming the lateral line create a current of water through the case, and in this way the larvae are assured of an adequate oxygen supply. Actually, it may be said that *all* caddis larvae are surrounded by running water.

With reference to morphology and habits, two general types of larvae have long been recognized: campodeiform and eruciform. As indicated in Table VIII, however, this division is an unnatural one, there being many intermediate types and exceptions, especially in the Phryganeidae.

There are typically five instars between the egg and pupa, although some few species have six or seven. The duration of these instars, and possibly their number, depend on the particular species as well as on such factors as water temperature, amount and type of food, and current velocity. Thus a single particular larval instar may terminate in as little as 15 days, or it

may persist for several months, depending on these conditions.

The great majority of larvae that build portable cases cannot swim but simply crawl about on the substrate when the head and thorax are protruded from the case. Some of the Phryganeidae and Leptoceridae, however, are able to swim well, provided the case is not too heavy. In these larvae the hind legs are modified for swimming. Most of the naked larvae and those that build fixed cases are able to swim, and in such species locomotion is aided considerably by powerful undulations of the body.

On the whole, caddis larvae are omnivorous, but the families may be roughly classified into five groups according to their methods of obtaining food. *Grazers* feed on algae, fungi, detritus, and often very small invertebrates; they pick up material at random that rests on the substrate or is loosely attached to the substrate. This category includes Brachycentridae, Calamoceratidae, Hydroptilidae, Lepidostomatidae, Leptoceridae, Limnephilidae, Molannidae, Odontoceridae, Phryganeidae, Psychomyiidae, and Sericostomatidae. The *scrapers* feed on the same food materials, but their mouthparts are more specialized for actually scraping up attached lithophyton from the substrate; they also undoubtedly ingest much of their food by the grazing process; this group includes Glossosoma-

TABLE VIII.   A COMPARISON OF THE TWO MAIN TYPES OF CADDIS LARVAE

|  | Campodeiform | Eruciform |
|---|---|---|
| Position of head | Head held more or less straight forward, forming a continuation of the long axis of the body. | Head usually bent at a right angle to the long axis of the body. |
| Abdomen | Usually somewhat compressed; middle abdominal segments sometimes wider than the others. | Usually cylindrical; of about equal diameter throughout. |
| Tubercles on first abdominal segment | Absent. | Present in some groups. |
| Lateral line | Absent. | Usually present. |
| Case | Case, if present, not portable. | Case usually portable. |
| Habitat | More common in running water. | More common in standing water. |

tidae, Helicopsychidae, Hydroptilidae, Molannidae, and Odontoceridae. *Suspension feeders* strain all kinds of living and dead particulate materials from the water by means of hairs on the legs, head, and mouth parts; they include Brachycentridae and Psychomyiidae. *Net filter feeders* construct fine nets that strain particulate material from the water; the larvae may eat the whole net and its contents periodically, or they may remove the particles from the meshes. This group includes Hydropsychidae, Philopotamidae, Polycentropodidae, and Psychomyiidae. *Carnivores* feed on small crustaceans, annelids, and insects; they include Phryganeidae and Rhyacophilidae.

Note that some families are included in more than one of the preceding categories because of generic and species feeding behavior differences. Many, perhaps most caddis larvae, feed most actively during midafternoon.

Larvae may be taken in shallow freshwater habitats wherever there is an adequate supply of oxygen, sometimes in very great numbers. They occur on all types of substrates, including rock, gravel, sand, mud, debris, and vegetation. A few genera, such as *Tinodes,* have colonized the thin film of water in hygropetric habitats. With few exceptions, the various taxonomic categories do not seem to be confined to particular types of habitats. Representatives of the same family or genus, for example, may

be found in marshes, ponds, lakes, slow streams, and rapid streams and on a variety of substrates. In general, however, the naked larvae, such as *Rhyacophila,* are restricted to rapid streams and brooks. Also, those larvae that build silken catch nets are confined to running waters. On the other hand, the numerous species that construct rough, clumsy, portable cases are restricted to lentic habitats. It is also usually true that portable cases of larvae inhabiting swift waters are made of heavy materials.

Some species aestivate in debris or the substrate when ponds and streams are temporarily dry during summer or autumn.

Interest in caddis fly larvae has largely been maintained because of their curious habit of net and case construction. From a taxonomic standpoint, it is unfortunate that the identification of most larvae from case characters alone is very difficult and usually impossible. Only a few genera can be positively identified by their unique cases. *Helicopsyche,* for example, builds a case of sand grains in the shape of a snail shell; *Neureclipsis* is found in long, partially coiled, trumpet-shaped silken nets. In most families, and in many genera, the construction of the case is variable, sometimes apparently being largely determined by the specific nature of the materials available to the larva. In the genera of the Limnephilidae the case may be triangular, circular, or flat in cross section; it may be neat and compact or clumsy and loosely con-

TABLE IX. Chief Features of Larval Net and Case Construction in the Families of Trichoptera

| | |
|---|---|
| Beraeidae | Case conical, curved, made of fine sand. |
| Brachycentridae | Conical cases of sand grains, or built of vegetable material and square or circular in cross section (Fig. 418F). |
| Calamoceratidae | Case a bit of hollowed-out twig, or composed of bits of leaves and twigs. |
| Glossosomatidae | Elliptical, portable, gravel case shaped like a turtle shell (Figs. 419D,E). |
| Helicopsychidae | Case composed of sand grains, in the shape of a snail shell (Fig. 414B). |
| Hydropsychidae | No case, or larva lying in a loosely made, immovable case of mineral or vegetable matter, such a case opening into the apical portion of a conical silken net (Fig. 415M). |
| Hydroptilidae | Bean-, purse-, or flask-shaped silken case open at both ends and usually covered with debris, fine sand, or algae (Figs. 416E,F,K,L). No case in early instars of some species. |
| Lepidostomatidae | Smooth conical cases of sand, or built of vegetable material and square or circular in cross section. |
| Leptoceridae | Case conical or cylindrical; made of sand, vegetable matter, or silk (Figs. 417C, F, J). |
| Limnephilidae | Case triangular, circular, or flat in cross section; compact or loosely constructed; composed of bits of a great variety of vegetable or mineral matter (Fig. 422). |
| Molannidae | Straight sand tubes with or without lateral, winglike extensions (Fig. 414C). |
| Odontoceridae | Case cylindrical, tapered, curved, made of sand and fine gravel (Fig. 421B). |
| Philopotamidae | Finger-shaped or saclike silken nets attached to rocks (Figs. 420A, M). |
| Phryganeidae | Case a spirally wound cylinder of bits of vegetation (Fig. 418) or a cylinder composed of rings of bits of vegetation placed end to end (Fig. 418E). |
| Polycentropodidae | Capture nets of several kinds. |
| Psychomyiidae | Silken nets of various shapes; fastened to objects and more or less covered with algae and silt (Fig. 420S). Long debris-covered silken galleries on substrate. Delicate branched tubes of fine sand buried in the substrate except for a small projecting turret. |
| Rhyacophilidae | No case or net. |
| Sericostomatidae | Case conical in early instars, cylindrical later; slightly curved and tapering; made of fine sand. |

structed; it may be built of bits of leaves, twigs, grass, sand, gravel, seeds, mollusk shells, or debris of all kinds. Table IX shows the chief features of larval case and net construction for the various families.

Case construction is usually begun soon after hatching. Materials are selected from the substrate with the legs, and, if it is vegetable material, it may be cut to correct size with the mouthparts. There are large glands in the anterior portion of the body that produce a gluelike substance used for cementing together the particles constituting the case. There is also usually a more or less flimsy silken lining in the case. As the larva grows, additional pieces are added to the case at the anterior end. A few specices tear off the posterior part of the case or leave the old cases and form new ones at intervals. Under normal conditions the same species select the same materials and build cases in the same way, but when the usual materials are not available, substitutes may be utilized (Fig. 410). Experimental work has shown that a vari-

ety of unusual objects, such as paper and egg shells, may be used. Exposed larvae are often able to distinguish their own case from those of others.

There is a large literature covering natural and experimental case and net construction as related to such variables as life history, substrate, and current velocities.

Fig. 410.–Trichopteran case composed almost entirely of bryozoan statoblasts. (Photo courtesy of John Bushnell.)

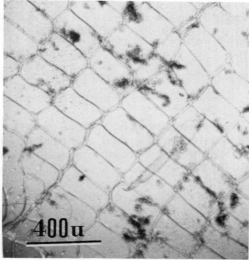

FIG. 411.–Scanning electron micrograph photographs of Hydropsychidae nets. Upper, *Macronemum zebratum*; lower, *Hydropsyche venularis*. (Photos courtesy of J. Bruce Wallace, Univ. of Georgia.)

In the Hydroptilidae the gluelike substance secreted at the mouth is formed into a translucent sheet that forms the bulk of the case. In those larvae that build trapnets, especially Hydropsychidae and Philopotamidae, this material appears as a thin, tough, sticky thread that hardens on exposure to the water. As it leaves the mouth it is woven to form the net.

The meshes are often constructed with astounding accuracy and precision (Fig.

411). Furthermore, each species has a net that will catch food particles of different size ranges (Fig. 412). Wallace and Malas (1976) report that a species of *Dolophilodes* can simultaneously spin 70 fine silken strands. These strands form an exceptionally fine rectangular mesh with openings only 0.5 × 5.5 microns.

In some genera, notably in the family Limnephilidae, cases may differ considerably in shape or construction according to the age of the larvae. An early case, for example, may be built of vegetable material, but a case of the same individual in a later instar may be built of mineral material. Some of the Hydroptilidae and Rhyacophilidae do not begin case construction until they are far along in the larval stage. Sometimes it is built just prior to pupation.

Mecom (1970) has shown that some *Hydropsyche* larvae do not feed or build a net during the winter but remain quiescent in a special winter hibernaculum case (Fig. 413). Some species exhibit a true diapause, either in the larval or adult condition.

Numerous stream and fish food sur-

FIG. 412.–Typical net meshes of mature Hydropsychidae larvae, all drawn to the same scale. a, *Macronema carolina*; b, *Hydropsyche orris*; c, *Diplectrona metaque*; d, *D. modesta*; e, *Parapsyche cardis*. (From Wallace and Malas, 1976.)

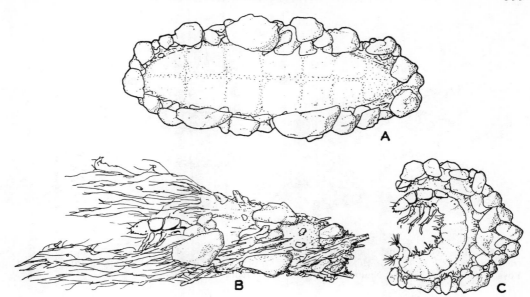

FIG. 413.–Cases of *Hydropsyche occidentalis*. A, loosely woven larval case consisting of gravel and bits of vegetable matter (catch net not present); B, winter hibernaculum with top removed; C, ventral view of pupa and pupal case. (From Mecom, 1970.)

veys establish caddis larvae as an important item in the diet of trout. The fish pick them out of bottom debris or actually scrape them off rocks with the jaws and swallow them, case and all. Occasionally swarms of adults assume pest proportions along shores.

Field collections involve picking the larvae and cases off the substrate with fingers or forceps, or raking or washing them out of drift, debris, or vegetation with a sieve net or large pan. Eighty percent alcohol is a good preservative.

The larvae and pupae are not difficult to rear in the laboratory. They should be kept in running water or in an aquarium supplied with adequate oxygen by photosynthesis or by an aerator. There should also be sufficient food available.

More than 1100 species of adult caddis flies are known from the United States, and the immature stages of less than 20 percent of these have been described. The larvae of

six U.S. genera are still unknown. The great majority of genera are widely distributed over most of the country or over the eastern half. Oregon has 80 genera and 280 species; Kentucky has 175 species; Wisconsin, 208; North Carolina, 164. In contrast, Poland has about 250 species and Great Britain about 200.

This key is modified and rearranged from several sources, and especially from the works of Ross, Anderson, Wiggins, Hickin, and Denning. The serious student cannot do without the superb monograph of Wiggins (1977). Only a few rare and poorly known genera are not included here, especially monotypic genera reported from highly restricted ranges. Because of a renewed interest in caddis flies, we now know the immature stages of a great many genera and species that were undescribed 25 years ago. As a consequence, this key is about twice as long as that which appeared in the first edition of this manual.

## KEY TO GENERA OF TRICHOPTERA LARVAE

1. Case spiral, in the form of a snail shell (Fig. 414B); widely distributed and very common; four species................ HELICOPSYCHIDAE, **Helicopsyche**
Case of another design, or absent ...........................................2

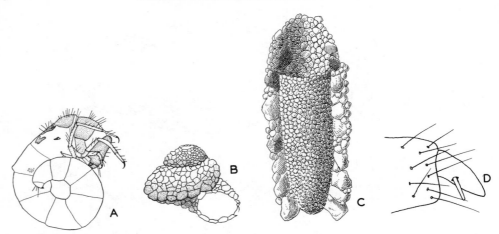

FIG. 414.–Helicopsychidae and Molannidae larvae. A, position of *Helicopsyche* in case, ×8; B, case of *Helicopsyche*, ×7; C, case of *Molanna*, ×2.4; D, tip of third leg of *Molanna*. (A and B from Elkins; C from Ross, 1944, courtesy Illinois Natural History Survey; D redrawn from Betten.)

2. Dorsal surface of each thoracic segment covered by a large sclerotized plate (Fig. 415L) . . . . . . . . . . . . . . . . . . . . . . . . . . . . . . . . . . . . . . . . . . . . . . . . . . . . . .**3**

   Third thoracic segment more or less membranous, often with several pairs of small sclerites (Figs. 421D, 419A) . . . . . . . . . . . . . . . . . . . . . . . . . . . . . . . . . . . . .**4**

3. Abdomen with conspicuous lateroventral gills (Figs. 415L, O); no case, or larva in a loosely made case of mineral or vegetable material, such a case opening into the apical part of a silken net (Fig. 415M); larvae more than 5 mm long; in running waters or in turbulent waters of lake shores. HYDROPSYCHIDAE, **18**

   Abdomen without gills; usually less than 5 mm long; advanced instars in purse-, bean-, or flask-shaped silken cases covered with foreign material; abdomen of advanced instars much wider and (or) deeper than thorax (Fig. 416); lotic and lentic; microcaddis larvae . . . . . . . . . . . . . . . . . . . . . . HYDROPTILIDAE, **28**

4. Antennae at least seven times as long as wide and arising at base of mandibles (Fig. 417K); case portable, conical or cylindrical, curved or straight, made of sand, vegetable matter, or silk; common in standing waters and rivers; omnivorous . . . . . . . . . . . . . . . . . . . . . . . . . . . . . . . . . . . . . .LEPTOCERIDAE, **39**

   Antennae very short, no more than three times as long as wide, often inconspicuous and one-segmented or hidden. . . . . . . . . . . . . . . . . . . . . . . . . . . . . . . . . . . . .**5**

5. Mesonotum without sclerotized plates (Fig. 418A), or with small, scattered sclerites (Fig. 419F) . . . . . . . . . . . . . . . . . . . . . . . . . . . . . . . . . . . . . . . . . . . . . . . . .**6**

   Mesonotum almost completely covered with sclerotized plates; case portable . . . .**11**

6. Last abdominal segment with a dorsal sclerotized plate (Fig. 419C); in swift, cool waters . . . . . . . . . . . . . . . . . . . . . . . . . . . . . . . . . . . . . . . . . . . . . . . . . . . . . .**7**

   Last abdominal segment without a dorsal sclerotized plate . . . . . . . . . . . . . . . . . . . . .**9**

7. With a large ventral prosternal horn (Fig. 418G); case composed of bits of vegetation arranged in a spiral or a series of rings (Figs. 418B–E, H, J); lentic and slow lotic waters. . . . . . . . . . . . . . . . . . . . . . . . . . . . . . . . . . . .PHRYGANEIDAE, **45**

   Prosternal horn absent; tortoise-shell-shaped gravel case (Figs. 419D, E), or case absent; rivers and streams . . . . . . . . . . . . . . . . . . . . . . . . . . . . . . . . . . . . . .**8**

8. Case portable, in the shape of a miniature tortoise shell, composed of gravel and coarse sand (Figs. 419D, E). . . . . . . . . . . . . . . . . .GLOSSOSOMATIDAE, **52**

   Case absent; in cool waters . . . . . . . . . . . . . . . . . . . . . . . . . . .RHYACOPHILIDAE, **57**

9. Labrum soft and expanded laterally (Fig. 420E); in sac- or finger-shaped silken nets on the under sides of rocks in rapid streams . . . . . .PHILOPOTAMIDAE, **59**

   Labrum entirely sclerotized, not expanded laterally . . . . . . . . . . . . . . . . . . . . . . . . .**10**

10. Larvae in flimsy, simple or branched silken nets up to 8 cm long, attached along their entire length; anal prolegs not especially long (Fig. 420L); in running waters and in the littoral of large lakes; small microphagous species. PSYCHOMYIIDAE, 61

Larvae in silken capture nets or in tubes with flared ends (Fig. 420N); anal prolegs very long and diverging (Fig. 420K); predators; running and standing waters. . . . . . . . . . . . . . . . . . . . . . . . . . . . . . . . . POLYCENTROPODIDAE, 63

11. First abdominal segment without dorsal and lateral spacing tubercles; case cylindrical and composed of sand grains or bits of vegetation, or square in section and composed of bits of vegetation (Fig. 418F); very common in running waters . . . . . . . . . . . . . . . . . . . . . . . . . . . . . . . . . BRACHYCENTRIDAE, 68

First abdominal segments with lateral tubercles, and dorsal tubercle usually present; case variable . . . . . . . . . . . . . . . . . . . . . . . . . . . . . . . . . . . . . . . . . . . . . . . .12

12. Claws of hind legs very small (Fig. 414D); those of first and second legs large; case of sand grains, with lateral extensions (Fig. 414C); lentic and lotic. . . . . . . . . . . . . . . . . . . . . . . . . . . . . . . . . . MOLANNIDAE, **Molanna**

Claws of hind legs as long as those of second legs . . . . . . . . . . . . . . . . . . . . . . . . . . .13

13. Labrum with a row of 15 to 20 stout setae across the middle (Fig. 421A); case a bit of hollowed-out twig, or composed of bits of leaves and twigs; uncommon. CALAMOCERATIDAE, 72

Labrum with only about six setae, variously arranged . . . . . . . . . . . . . . . . . . . . . . . .14

14. Anal proleg with a brush of 25 to 30 fine setae (Fig. 421E); hind tarsal claw about twice as long as second tarsal claw; case tapered, curved, made of sand; scattered and rare in eastern states; usually in spring seepages. BERAEIDAE, **Beraea**

Anal proleg without such a prominent brush; hind tarsal claw about the same size as second tarsal claw; case variable; common everywhere . . . . . . . . . . . . . . . . .15

15. Dorsal tubercle of first abdominal segment absent; cases made of sand grains, bark, or leaf bits . . . . . . . . . . . . . . . . . . . . . . . . . . . . . LEPIDOSTOMATIDAE, 74

Dorsal tubercle of first abdominal segment present . . . . . . . . . . . . . . . . . . . . . . . . .16

16. Prosternal horn present (Fig. 422A); case constructed of a wide variety of materials; common everywhere; a large and difficult family . . . .LIMNEPHILIDAE, 75

Prosternal horn absent; case curved, tapered, and made of sand or fine gravel . . .17

17. Stridulator at base of first leg large and slightly hooked (Fig. 421H); not burrowers in substrate; widely distributed in running waters and along lake shores. . . . . . . . . . . . . . . . . . . . . . . . . . . . . . . . . SERICOSTOMATIDAE, 114

Stridulator at base of first leg small and not hooked; usually burrowers in substrate; widely distributed in running waters . . . . . . . . . . . . ODONTOCERIDAE, 116

18. Head with a broad, flat, dorsal area; head dorsoventrally tapered to base of mandibles (Fig. 415J); large rivers, several species, chiefly in eastern half of the United States. . . . . . . . . . . . . . . . . . . . . . . . . . . . . . . . . . . . . . . . . . . . . **Macronema**

Head without such a broad, flat area . . . . . . . . . . . . . . . . . . . . . . . . . . . . . . . . . . . . .19

19. Stridulator at base of front leg forked (Fig. 415B) . . . . . . . . . . . . . . . . . . . . . . . . .20

Stridulator at base of front leg not forked (Fig. 415C) . . . . . . . . . . . . . . . . . . . . . . .22

20. Prosternal plate with a pair of prominent sclerotized plates posterior to it (Fig. 415D); all kinds of permanent streams; about 60 U.S. species . . . . . . . . **Hydropsyche**

Prosternal plate without a prominent pair of sclerotized plates posterior to it; if present, such plates are minute and located at the lateroposterior angles of the prosternal plate. . . . . . . . . . . . . . . . . . . . . . . . . . . . . . . . . . . . . . . . . . . .21

21. Lateral border of mandible with a flange (Fig. 415K); head and thorax light yellowish brown; one species generally distributed in eastern half of the United States . . . . . . . . . . . . . . . . . . . . . . . . . . . . . . . . . . . . . . . . . . . . . **Potamyia**

Lateral border of mandible without a flange; coloration darker; about 35 species; common everywhere; sometimes in warm waters . . . . . . . . . **Cheumatopsyche**

22. Each branched gill with all its branches arising at the distal end of a basal stalk . .23

Each branched gill with its branches arising from sides as well as end of basal stalk (Fig. 415A) . . . . . . . . . . . . . . . . . . . . . . . . . . . . . . . . . . . . . . . . . . . . . . . . .24

Fig. 415.–Structure of Hydropsychidae larvae. A, tracheal gill of *Macronema*; B, stridulator of first leg of *Hydropsyche*; C, stridulator of first leg of *Smicridea*; D, prosternal plates of *Hydropsyche*; E, ventral view of head of *Parapsyche*; F, ventral view of head of *Arctopsyche*; G, dorsal view of head of *Diplectrona*; H, dorsal view of head of *Smicridea*; J, lateral view of head of *Macronema*; K, mandibles of *Potamyia*; L, *Hydropsyche*, ×2.5; M, net and case of *Hydropsyche*; N, treacheal gill of *Diplectrona*; O, tracheal gills of *Hydropsyche*; P, abdominal gills of *Homoplectra*. (A modified from Krafka, 1915; B to F and J to L from Ross, 1944, courtesy of Illinois Natural History Survey; G, H, and N redrawn from Ross, 1944; M modified from Noyes; O redrawn from Thienemann, 1905.)

23. Gula roughly rectangular and of even width (Fig. 415E); cold streams in east and west . . . . . . . . . . . . . . . . . . . . . . . . . . . . . . . . . . . . . . . . . . . . . . . . . . . . . **Parapsyche**
   Gula narrowed posteriorly (Fig. 415F); widely distributed in cold streams. **Arctopsyche**
24. Lateral border of mandible with a flange (Fig. 415K); head and thorax light yellowish brown; one species generally distributed in eastern half of the United States . . . . . . . . . . . . . . . . . . . . . . . . . . . . . . . . . . . . . . . . . . **Potamyia**
   Lateral border of mandible without a flange . . . . . . . . . . . . . . . . . . . . . . . . . . . . . . . .**25**
25. Each abdominal gill with only one to five lateral branches (Fig. 415P); several poorly known species in Oregon and California; cold mountain streams. **Homoplectra**
   Each abdominal gill with more lateral branches . . . . . . . . . . . . . . . . . . . . . . . . . . . . . .**26**

FIG. 416.–Structure of Hydroptilidae larvae. A, tarsal claws of *Stactobiella*; B, tarsal claws of *Ochrotrichia*; D, metanotum of *Hydroptila*; E, case of *Leucotrichia*, ×10; F, case of *Agraylea*, ×7; G, dorsal view of *Hydroptila*, ×17; H, lateral view of same; J, *Leucotrichia*, ×17; K, case of *Oxyethira*, ×13; L, case of *Mayatrichia*, ×20; M, short hind tarsus and long claw of hydroptilid; N, lateral view of two *Ithytrichia* abdominal segments. (A to C and G to L from Ross, 1944, courtesy Illinois Natural History Survey; D redrawn from Ross, 1944.)

26. Frons expanded laterally (Fig. 415G); small, cool streams; several widely scattered species . . . . . . . . . . . . . . . . . . . . . . . . . . . . . . . . . . . . . . . . . . . . . . . . . . . . . . **Diplectrona**
    Frons not expanded laterally (Fig. 415H) . . . . . . . . . . . . . . . . . . . . . . . . . . . . . . . . . . . . . . .27
27. Each abdominal gill of middle segments with more than 15 lateral branches; one species known only from southeastern Texas. . . . . . . . . . . . . . . . . . **Leptonema**
    Each abdominal gill of middle segments with less than 15 lateral branches; several southwestern species . . . . . . . . . . . . . . . . . . . . . . . . . . . . . . . . . . . . . . . . . . . **Smicridea**

**28.** Each abdominal segment with a dark, sclerotized, dorsal area (Fig. 416J); up to 5.5 mm long ........................................................**29**
At least abdominal segments two to seven without dark, sclerotized area; smaller species.....................................................**30**
**29.** Case translucent, ovoid, and flat (Fig. 416E); periphyton feeders; about three widely distributed species ......................................**Leucotrichia**
Case covered with fine sand, purselike, rarely tortoise-shell-like; many species, chiefly in the western half of the United States ............... **Ochrotrichia**
**30.** Hind tarsi about as long as the claws (Fig. 416M)...........................**31**
Hind tarsi about twice as long as claws ....................................**36**
**31.** Body dorsoventrally depressed; abdominal segments with a low tubercle on each side; case of two flat silken valves, or covered with bits of vegetation; several uncommon species in eastern mountains, rare in Rocky Mountains.
**Palaeagapetus**
Body laterally compressed; tubercles absent ...............................**32**
**32.** Tarsal claw stout, with a blunt basal spur (Fig. 416A); case of two symmetrical, purse-shaped valves ....................................................**33**
Tarsal claw slender, with a pointed basal spur (Fig. 416B) ....................**34**
**33.** Valves of case covered with algae; one poorly known local species from North Carolina to Oklahoma .......................................**Dibusa**
Valves of case with few or no algal filaments; several widely distributed species in small streams ...........................................**Stactobiella**
**34.** Second and third legs almost three times as long as first legs; cases flask-shaped, broadest posteriorly (Fig. 416K); many widely distributed species in lakes, ponds, and slow streams......................................**Oxyethira**
Second and third legs not more than one and one-half times as long as first legs; purse-shaped case held vertically ..................................**35**
**35.** Silken case covered with concentric rings of algal filaments (Fig. 416F); several widely distributed species in lakes, ponds, and slow streams .......**Agraylea**
Silken case covered with fine sand grains; many common species; widely distributed ...........................................**Hydroptila**
**36.** Anal prolegs cylindrical, projecting from body ..............................**37**
Anal prolegs short, not projecting from body; silken case; up to 3.5 mm long ....**38**
**37.** Case covered with sand grains; up to 2.5 mm long; about 15 species; widely distributed .................................................**Neotrichia**
Case translucent, dorsal side ridged or fluted (Fig. 416L); rapid waters; several species with local occurrence but widely distributed ........... **Mayatrichia**
**38.** Each abdominal segment with a large dorsal and ventral projection (Fig. 416N); two uncommon species, of which one is widely distributed .......... **Ithytrichia**
Abdominal segments without such projections; about six species, chiefly eastern; among littoral hydrophytes and in slow streams ...............**Orthotrichia**
**39.** Second tarsi slightly bent (Fig. 417N); case a long, tapering, silken cone (Fig. 417C); common in eastern half of the United States. **Leptocerus americanus** (Banks)
Second tarsi straight; case otherwise ....................................**40**
**40.** Case long, tapered, and made of spirally arranged bits of vegetation (Fig. 417J); common and widely distributed.............................. **Triaenodes**
Case not made of spirally arranged bits of vegetation .......................**41**
**41.** Case cylindrical, sometimes slightly curved, formed of small gravel, and with a large posterior opening; often buried in substrates of running waters and along lake shores; several poorly known species in eastern half of the United States. .....................................................**Setodes**
Case without a large posterior opening; widely distributed ....................**42**
**42.** Maxillary palp nearly as long as stipes (Fig. 417L); case cylindrical, composed of bits of gravel and vegetation (Fig. 417A); predators; about 20 species. **Oecetis**
Maxillary palp only about half as long as stipes (Fig. 417M) ....................**43**
**43.** Mesonotum with a pair of sclerotized, narrow, curved, or angled bars (Fig. 417O); case of sand grains, with or without lateral flanges (Figs. 417E, H); many species in lotic and lentic waters.............................. **Ceraclea**
Mesonotum without such bars; common in the littoral of ponds, lakes, and slow streams ........................................................**44**

FIG. 417.—Structure of Leptoceridae larvae. A, case of *Oecetis*, ×6; B, case of *Mystacides*, ×2.5; C, case of *Leptocerus*, ×3.5; D, head of *Ceraclea*; E, case of *Ceraclea*, ×3.5; F, *Nectopsyche*, ×4; G, *Nectopsyche*, ×3; H, case of *Ceraclea*, ×8; J, *Triaenodes*, ×6; K, dorsal view of leptocerid head showing long antennae; L, stipes and maxillary palp of *Oecetis*; M, stipes and maxillary palp of *Ceraclea*; N, second tarsus of *Leptocerus*; O, mesonotum of *Ceraclea*. (A, E, F, and J from Ross, 1944, courtesy Illinois Natural History Survey; C and H from Lloyd, 1921; D redrawn from Ross, 1944; G from Elkins.)

44. Hind tibiae with an indistinct fracture near the middle (Fig. 408D); a few simple abdominal gills present or absent; case cylindrical, made of bits of gravel and vegetation, with twigs or conifer needles extending far beyond the front end (Fig. 417B) .............................................**Mystacides**
    Hind tibiae entire; a few simple abdominal gills present; case long, tapered, made of bits of sand, gravel, and vegetation, and usually built along a long twig or conifer needle ...........................................**Nectopsyche**
45. Case composed of bits of leaves and bark arranged spirally (Figs. 418B–D, H, J). **46**
    Case without spiral construction (Fig. 418E) ..................................**50**
46. With a small, pigmented sternal sclerite between the first coxae (Fig. 418G) .....**47**
    Without such a sclerite; two widely distributed and common species; marshes, ponds, and littoral zone; omnivorous ................................. **Phryganea**

FIG. 418.–Phryganeidae and Brachycentridae. A, anterior end of larva of *Phryganea*; B, case of *Phryganea*, ×1.3; C, case of mature larva of phryganid, ×2; D, case of young larva of *Agrypnia*; E, case *Ptilostomis*, ×2; F, *Brachycentrus*, ×3; G, ventral view of *Agrypnia* prothorax showing sternal sclerite and prosternal horn; H, *Phryganea*, ×3; J, case of *Phryganea*, ×4; K, first coxa of *Agrypnia* showing combs; L, dorsal view of *Brachycentrus*, ×8. (A from Ross, 1944, courtesy Illinois Natural History Survey; B from Wesenberg-Lund, 1911; C to F from Lloyd, 1921; H from Hickin, 1953, by permission; J from Hickin, 1942, by permission; L from Hickin, 1943, by permission.)

47. Frons occasionally with a median black line; about nine species, widely distributed
     in marshes, lakes, and slow rivers; carnivorous .................. **Agrypnia**
     Frons without a median black line .......................................**48**
48. Case with a flaring, bushy appearance; pronotum with only a dark anterior transverse
     line; one or two rare and local species...........................**Fabria**
     Case not bushy, composed of bits of leaves in a spiral arrangement (Fig. 418B);
     pronotum with diagonal lines ..........................................**49**

FIG. 419.–Structure of Rhyacophilidae and Glossosomatidae larvae. A, *Rhyacophila,* ×5; B, prolegs of *Rhyacophila*; C, dorsal view of posterior end of *Glossosoma*; D, dorsal view of case of *Glossosoma,* ×2; E, ventral view of same; F, mesonotum of *Protoptila*; G, dorsal view of *Agapetus,* ×6; H, tarsal claw of *Matriophila*. (A from Ross, 1944, courtesy Illinois Natural History Survey; B modified from Lloyd, 1921; C modified from Krafka, 1924; D and E from Lloyd, 1921; G from Hickin, 1943, by permission.)

49. With well-defined combs on the ventral surface of the first coxa (Fig. 418K); about nine species, widely distributed in marshes, lakes, and slow rivers; carnivorous .............................................. **Agrypnia**
    Coxal combs absent or reduced to irregular rugosities; several common and widely distributed species; marshes, lakes, and sluggish streams ......... **Banksiola**
50. Mesonotum without dorsal sclerotized plates; case composed of rings of leaf bits (Fig. 418E); several widely distributed species ................. **Ptilostomis**
    Mesonotum with dorsal sclerotized plates.................................. **51**
51. Case composed of rings of leaf and bark bits (Fig. 418E); in slow forest streams; two northeastern species ......................................... **Oligostomis**
    Case not composed of rings; constructed of gravel, bark, twigs, and leaves; one uncommon species in mountain streams of California and Oregon ... **Yphria**
52. Mesonotum without sclerotized plates; chiefly western mountains .............. **53**
    Mesonotum with sclerotized plates (Fig. 419G) ............................. **54**
53. Legs attached at anterolateral angles of pronotum; two species east of the Rocky Mountains, but many others are restricted to the west ......... **Glossosoma**
    Legs attached at lateral margins of pronotum; several western species. **Anagapetus**
54. Mesonotum with three sclerites; up to 3.5 mm long .......................... **55**
    Mesonotum with two sclerites (Fig. 419G); larger; common and widely distributed in streams in hilly areas.................................................**Agapetus**
55. Each tarsal claw clearly trifid (Fig. 419H); rare in Tennessee, North Carolina, South Carolina, Georgia, and Kentucky. ......................... **Matriophila**
    Each tarsal claw with two smaller processes or one process and one seta; widely distributed ....................................................**56**

FIG. 420.–Structure of Philopotamidae, Psychomyiidae, and Polycentropodidae larvae. A, catch nets of *Chimarra,* ×1.3; B, head of *Chimarra;* C, head of *Dolophilodes;* D, head of *Wormaldia;* E, labrum of *Chimarra;* F, labrum of *Polycentropus;* G, mandibles of *Phylocentropus;* H, mandibles of *Neureclipsis;* J, case of *Neureclipsis;* K, posterior end of *Neureclipsis;* L, posterior end of *Psychomyia;* M, case of *Polycentropus;* N, net of *Polycentropus;* O, tarsus of *Phylocentropus* (setation omitted); P, anal claw of *Polycentropus;* Q, anal claw of *Polyplectropus;* R, first tibia of *Polycentropus;* S, *Lype* larval retreat. (A modified from Noyes; B to H and K from Ross, 1944, courtesy Illinois Natural History Survey; L modified from Ross, 1944; S from Hickin, 1954, by permission.)

**56.** Larval case with a partial silken collar around each opening, and without a large piece of gravel on each side; several species with sporadic distribution. **Culoptila**
Silken collars absent; large piece of gravel present on each side of case; common and widely distributed . . . . . . . . . . . . . . . . . . . . . . . . . . . . . . . . . . . . . . . . . .**Agapetus**

**57.** With dense tufts of gills on the thoracic and abdominal segments; one species in streams of California, Oregon, and Washington; up to 33 mm long.
**Himalopsyche**
Without such dense tufts of gills; up to 23 mm long . . . . . . . . . . . . . . . . . . . . . . . . .**58**

**58.** First legs chelate; a few rare species in southwestern states. . . . . . . . . . . . .**Atopsyche**
First legs not chelate; many very common and widely distributed species. **Rhyacophila**

**59.** Anterior margin of frons markedly asymmetrical (Fig. 420B); widely distributed . . . . . . . . . . . . . . . . . . . . . . . . . . . . . . . . . . . . . . . . . . . . . . . . . . **Chimarra**
Anterior margin of frons slightly asymmetrical at most; chiefly western but widely distributed . . . . . . . . . . . . . . . . . . . . . . . . . . . . . . . . . . . . . . . . . . . . . . . . . . .**60**

**60.** Frons almost perfectly symmetrical, with posterior portion widened (Fig. 420D) . . . . . . . . . . . . . . . . . . . . . . . . . . . . . . . . . . . . . . . . . . . . . . . . . . **Wormaldia**
Frons slightly asymmetrical, posterior portion not widened (Fig. 420C). **Dolophilodes**

**61.** Anal claw with teeth on ventral margin (Fig. 420L); up to 9 mm long; larvae in long, irregular tubes on rocks; several species, but only one is common and widely distributed . . . . . . . . . . . . . . . . . . . . . . . . . . . . . . . . . . . . . . . **Psychomyia**
Anal claw without teeth . . . . . . . . . . . . . . . . . . . . . . . . . . . . . . . . . . . . . . . . . . .**62**

**62.** One rare species in eastern states; larva in a cylindrical silken chamber covered with bits of debris and up to 10 mm long (Fig. 420S). . . . . . . . . . . . . . . . . . . . **Lype**
Several western species; larva in flattened silken tubes up to several cm long. **Tinodes**

**63.** Tarsi broad and flat (Fig. 420O); larvae in branched silken tubes buried in sandy stream substrates; common east of the Rocky Mountains. . . . **Phylocentropus**
Tarsi not broad and flat; tubes not buried . . . . . . . . . . . . . . . . . . . . . . . . . . . . .**64**

**64.** Anal claw with ventral teeth (Figs. 420P, Q); larva in a cylindrical silken case, open at both ends. . . . . . . . . . . . . . . . . . . . . . . . . . . . . . . . . . . . . . . . . . . . . . . .**65**
Anal claw without ventral teeth . . . . . . . . . . . . . . . . . . . . . . . . . . . . . . . . . . . . . .**66**

**65.** Teeth of anal claw very short (Fig. 420P); several uncommon but widely distributed species; lakes and streams. . . . . . . . . . . . . . . . . . . . . . . . . . . . . **Nyctiophylax**
Teeth of anal claw long (Fig. 420Q); rare, reported from cool streams in Texas.
**Polyplectropus**

**66.** Anal claw with minute spinules on concave margin (Fig. 420K); larva in a trumpet-shaped silken net (Fig. 420J); widely distributed but uncommon. **Neureclipsis**
Anal claw without spinules . . . . . . . . . . . . . . . . . . . . . . . . . . . . . . . . . . . . . . . . . .**67**

**67.** First tibia with one large terminal spine; larva in small depressions on rocks, each depression with a flat silken roof with two holes; one rare species in eastern half of the United States. . . . . . . . . . . . . . . . . . . . . . . . . . . . . **Cyrnellus**
First tibia with three large terminal spines (Fig. 420R); larva in a cylindrical silken tube or bag (Fig. 420M); common and widely distributed in standing and running waters . . . . . . . . . . . . . . . . . . . . . . . . . . . . . . . . . . . . . . **Polycentropus**

**68.** Each tibia produced distally, with stout spurs (Fig. 418L). . . . . . . . . . . . . . . . . . . .**69**
Tibiae not produced . . . . . . . . . . . . . . . . . . . . . . . . . . . . . . . . . . . . . . . . . . . . . . . .**70**

**69.** Case cylindrical, tapered, and composed of fine gravel; rare in running waters of California and Utah. . . . . . . . . . . . . . . . . . . . . . . . . . . . . . . . . . . **Oligoplectrum**
Tapered chimney cases, almost invariably composed of bits of vegetation (Fig. 418F); very common and widely distributed . . . . . . . . . . . . . . . . . . . . **Brachycentrus**

**70.** Tapered chimney cases, composed of ragged bits of plant material; rare in Washington and Oregon. . . . . . . . . . . . . . . . . . . . . . . . . . . . . . . . . . . . . **Eobrachycentrus**
Case cylindrical and tapered, composed of plant material, silk, or sand grains . . .**71**

**71.** With a few scattered abdominal gills; one uncommon species in western states. . . . . . . . . . . . . . . . . . . . . . . . . . . . . . . . . . . . . . . . . . . . . . . .**Amiocentrus**
Without abdominal gills; common and widely distributed . . . . . . . . . . . . . **Micrasema**

**72.** Case a bit of hollowed-out twig; rare in east and in west coast states. **Heteroplectron**
Case with another construction . . . . . . . . . . . . . . . . . . . . . . . . . . . . . . . . . . . . . . .**73**

Fig. 421.–Larvae of Calamoceratidae, Beraeidae, Sericostomatidae, and Limnephilidae. A, labrum of *Heteroplectron*; B, case of *Psilotreta*, ×3; C, case of *Goera*, ×4; D, meso- and metanotum of *Goera*; E, posterior end of *Beraea*; F, tarsal claw of *Neophylax*; G, limnephilid tarsal claw showing short seta; H, lateral view of sericostomatid pronotum showing hooked stridulator. (A redrawn from Ross, 1944; B and C from Lloyd, 1921; D modified from Lloyd, 1921; E from Wiggins, 1954; H modified from Ross and Wallace.)

73. Case composed of a few large bits of leaves or bark; rare in Texas and
    Arizona. . . . . . . . . . . . . . . . . . . . . . . . . . . . . . . . . . . . . . . . . . . . . . . . . . . . .**Phylloicus**
    Case composed of one dorsal and one (smaller) ventral bit of leaf; slow streams; rare
    in eastern states . . . . . . . . . . . . . . . . . . . . . . . . . . . . . . . . . . . . . . **Anisocentropus**
74. Case cylindrical, curved, and composed of fine gravel; a poorly defined genus re-
    ported from a few eastern states. . . . . . . . . . . . . . . . . . . . . . . . . . **Theliopsyche**
    Case variable; usually four-sided and composed of bits of leaf or bark; sometimes
      built of spirally or randomly arranged bits of vegetation, or sand grains;
      springs, streams, and lakes; common and widely distributed . . . **Lepidostoma**
75. Abdominal gills lacking, or with four or eight simple gills. . . . . . . . . . . . . . . . . .76
    With more than 10 abdominal gills . . . . . . . . . . . . . . . . . . . . . . . . . . . . . . . . . . .81
76. Abdominal gills lacking. . . . . . . . . . . . . . . . . . . . . . . . . . . . . . . . . . . . . . . . . . . .77
    With a total of only four or eight simple gills . . . . . . . . . . . . . . . . . . . . . . . . . . .80
77. Head flattened or concave dorsally, bounded by a prominent semicircular carina;
      several species in high western mountain streams. . . . . . . . . . . . . . . . **Imania**
    Head not flattened dorsally . . . . . . . . . . . . . . . . . . . . . . . . . . . . . . . . . . . . . . . . .78
78. Mesonotum with four, five, or six sclerites; case of sand grains, cylindrical, and
      slightly curved; small cold springs in eastern states. . . . . . . . . . . . . . . **Goerita**
    Mesonotum with two sclerites; streams in western states; case composed of sand
      grains, long, tapering, and curved; uncommon . . . . . . . . . . . . . . . . . . . . . . . .79
79. Anterior margin of pronotum weakly dentate. . . . . . . . . . . . . . . . . . . . . **Neothremma**
    Anterior margin of pronotum not dentate . . . . . . . . . . . . . . . . . . . . . . . . . . . . .**Farula**
80. Case composed of gravel with a row of small pebbles along each side; with four gills
      on third abdominal segment, or with four gills on both third and fourth ab-
      dominal segments; cold streams of western mountains. . . . . . . . . . . . **Goeracea**
    Case composed of gravel but without pebbles; third abdominal segment with four
      gills; one species from spring seepages in Oregon and Washington . . .**Lepania**

81. All gills simple. . . . . . . . . . . . . . . . . . . . . . . . . . . . . . . . . . . . . . . . . . . . . . . . . . . . . . . . .82
    At least some gills double, triple, or multiple . . . . . . . . . . . . . . . . . . . . . . . . . . . . .96
82. Mesonotum with four, five, or six sclerites; case curved, cylindrical, composed of
    sand grains. . . . . . . . . . . . . . . . . . . . . . . . . . . . . . . . . . . . . . . . . . . . . . . . . . . . . . . . . . .83
    Mesonotum with two sclerites (Fig. 422F) . . . . . . . . . . . . . . . . . . . . . . . . . . . . . .84
83. Gills present on second abdominal segment; in the substrate of spring seepages; one
    species known from Montana and Idaho. . . . . . . . . . . . . . . . . . . . . . .**Goereilla**
    Gills absent from second abdominal segment; one species from streams in California,
    Oregon, and Washington . . . . . . . . . . . . . . . . . . . . . . . . . . . . . . . . . . **Pedomoecus**
84. More than 80 percent of case consisting of organic material (bits of leaves, bark,
    twigs, needles). . . . . . . . . . . . . . . . . . . . . . . . . . . . . . . . . . . . . . . . . . . . . . . . . . . . .85
    Less than 80 percent of case consisting of organic material . . . . . . . . . . . . . . . . . .89
85. Case constructed of a few bits of leaves with wide lateral flanges on each side of a
    flattened tube; rare in far western states. . . . . . . . . . . . . . . . . . . . . . . **Clostoeca**
    Case without such wide flanges . . . . . . . . . . . . . . . . . . . . . . . . . . . . . . . . . . . . . . . . .86
86. Case a straight tube made of a few pieces of thin bark or leaves with a seam along
    each side; one uncommon species in small streams of western
    mountains. . . . . . . . . . . . . . . . . . . . . . . . . . . . . . . . . . . . . . . . . . . . . . . . . . .**Chyrauda**
    Case with a different construction, consisting of many pieces . . . . . . . . . . . . . . . . .87
87. Case a smooth cylinder; widely distributed in western mountains, but rare.
    **Homophylax**
    Case not smooth; case bulky and irregular, made of wood and leaves (Figs. 422H–
    K, O) . . . . . . . . . . . . . . . . . . . . . . . . . . . . . . . . . . . . . . . . . . . . . . . . . . . . . . . . . . . . . .88
88. With a single small anterior median sclerite on the metanotum; widely distributed in
    small streams. . . . . . . . . . . . . . . . . . . . . . . . . . . . . . . . . . . . . . . . . . . **Heterophylax**
    With two small anterior sclerites on the metanotum, one on each side of the median
    line; widely distributed in streams and small rivers . . . . . . . . . . . .**Pycnopsyche**
89. Anterior opening of case strongly oblique, with the dorsal margin projecting much
    beyond the ventral margin; common in cool mountain streams. . . . .**Apatania**
    Anterior opening of case not strongly oblique . . . . . . . . . . . . . . . . . . . . . . . . . . . . .90
90. Basal seta of tarsal claw about half as long as claw (Fig. 421F). . . . . . . . . . . . . .91
    Basal seta of tarsal claw less than half as long as claw (Fig. 421G) . . . . . . . . . . . .92
91. With lateral gills on some of the basal abdominal segments; case short, heavy,
    composed of sand grains, with larger gravel bits along each side; widely
    distributed and common. . . . . . . . . . . . . . . . . . . . . . . . . . . . . . . . . . . . **Neophylax**
    Without lateral gills on some of the basal abdominal segments; case curved, com-
    posed of sand and gravel particles, without lateral gravel bits; western moun-
    tain streams . . . . . . . . . . . . . . . . . . . . . . . . . . . . . . . . . . . . . . . . . **Oligophlebodes**
92. Case both curved and tapered, built of sand grains. . . . . . . . . . . . . . . . . . . . . . . . . .93
    Case not both strongly curved and tapered . . . . . . . . . . . . . . . . . . . . . . . . . . . . . . . .94
93. Head about as wide as long; rare in western mountain streams. . . .**Ecclisocosmoecus**
    Head clearly longer than wide; widely distributed and common . **Pseudostenophylax**
94. Dorsal surface of head greatly flattened; rare in small western mountain
    streams. . . . . . . . . . . . . . . . . . . . . . . . . . . . . . . . . . . . . . . . . . . . . . . . . . .**Philocasca**
    Dorsal surface of head not flattened; western mountain streams . . . . . . . . . . . . . . .95
95. Ventral surface of first abdominal segment with more than 10 setae; case of small
    gravel particles, occasionally with a few attached evergreen needles; uncom-
    mon in cool western mountain streams. . . . . . . . . . . . . . . . . . . . . . **Ecclisomyia**
    Ventral surface of first abdominal segment with less than 10 setae; case a tube of
    bits of gravel and wood; widely distributed and common in running waters.
    **Psychoglypha**
96. With no lateral gills; case built of gravel with large ballast gravel bits along each side;
    widely distributed. . . . . . . . . . . . . . . . . . . . . . . . . . . . . . . . . . . . . . . . . . . . . . **Goera**
    Some lateral gills present (only one or two on each side in *Psychoronia*) . . . . . . .97
97. Anterior margin of pronotum with a dense, shaggy fringe of hairs; case of bits of
    vegetation arranged transversely; uncommon in western mountain
    streams. . . . . . . . . . . . . . . . . . . . . . . . . . . . . . . . . . . . . . . . . . . . . . . . . . **Cryptochia**
    Pronotum without such hairs . . . . . . . . . . . . . . . . . . . . . . . . . . . . . . . . . . . . . . . . . . .98

Fig. 422.–Structure of Limnephilidae larvae. A, diagrammatic cross section through prothorax of *Limnephilus* showing short prosternal horn; B, *Limnephilus*, ×2.6; C, *Hesperophylax*, ×2.9; D, head of *Limnephilus*; E, head of *Nemotaulius*; F, mesonotum of *Neophylax*; G, case of *Nemotaulius*, ×1; H, J, and K, cases of *Pycnopsyche scabripennis* Rambur, ×1; L, diagrammatic cross section of case of *Pycnopsyche*; M, case of *Hesperophylax*, ×2.6; N, case of *Neophylax*, ×4; O, case of *Hydatophylax*, ×0.6; P–T, cases of *Limnephilus*; U, diagrammatic cross section of *Limnephilus*. (A redrawn from Krafka, 1915; B and C from Elkins; D, E, L, and U modified from Lloyd, 1921; F modified from Ross, 1944; G to J and M to T from Lloyd, 1921.)

98.  At least one-half of the gills with four or more filaments. . . . . . . . . . . . . . . . . . . . . . .99
     Less than one-half of the gills with four or more filaments . . . . . . . . . . . . . .. . . . . . .102
99.  At least some lateral gills of basal abdominal segments with more than four filaments. . . . . . . . . . . . . . . . . . . . . . . . . . . . . . . . . . . . . . . . . . . . . . . . . . . . . . .100
     All lateral gills of basal abdominal segments with one to four filaments . . . . . . .101
100. Pro- and mesonotum with many setae; case of bark, leaves, or sand; temporary pools and streams of eastern states. . . . . . . . . . . . . . . . . . . . . . . . . . . . . . . . **Ironoquia**
     Pro- and mesonotum with few setae; case of bark or leaf fragments; widely distributed but uncommon . . . . . . . . . . . . . . . . . . . . . . . . . . . . . . . . . . . . . . . . . . . . **Lenarchus**

**101.** With only one or two simple lateral gills on each side; case of gravel particles; rare in Colorado and New Mexico. . . . . . . . . . . . . . . . . . . . . . . . . . . . . **Psychoronia**
Lateral gills more abundant, mostly multiple; cylindrical cases of bits of wood or fine gravel; widely distributed in running waters, occasional in mountain lakes . . . . . . . . . . . . . . . . . . . . . . . . . . . . . . . . . . . . . . . . . . . . . . . . .**Hesperophylax**

**102.** Dorsal surface of head uniform in color. . . . . . . . . . . . . . . . . . . . . . . . . . . . . . .**106**
Dorsal surface of head with longitudinal bands of color . . . . . . . . . . . . . . . . . . . .**103**

**103.** Ventral surface of first abdominal segment densely hairy; most gills trifid; cylindrical case built of bits of wood; western mountain streams. . . . . . . . . . . . **Clistoronia**
Ventral surface of first abdominal segment not densely hairy; many gills double; lentic and lotic . . . . . . . . . . . . . . . . . . . . . . . . . . . . . . . . . . . . . . . . . . . . . . .**104**

**104.** Dorsal surface of each abdominal segment with an oval patch of chloride cells; case of gravel or bits of vegetation; northern and Rocky Mountain states. **Asynarchus**
No dorsal patches of chloride cells . . . . . . . . . . . . . . . . . . . . . . . . . . . . . . . . . . . . .**105**

**105.** Dorsal surface of head with a dark-colored median stripe reaching almost to the frontoclypeus (Fig. 422E); pronotum with a dark transverse band just anterior to midlength; case of transverse bits of leaves and twigs (Fig. 422G); one uncommon widely distributed species. . . . . . . . . . . . . . . . . . . . . .**Nemotaulius**
Dorsal surface of head without a stripe, or with diffuse median coloration; pronotum without a distinct dark transverse band; case highly variable, composed of leaves, grass, twigs, sand, gravel, bark, or wood arranged longitudinally or transversely (Figs. 354 top row, 422P–T); a very large and common genus.
**Limnephilus**

**106.** Hind femur with more than two major ventral setae; cylindrical case variously composed of sand, gravel, or vegetable material . . . . . . . . . . . . . . . . . . . . . . .**107**
Hind femur with only two major ventral setae . . . . . . . . . . . . . . . . . . . . . . . . . . . .**109**

**107.** Dorsal surface of head with flattened scale-hairs; rare in small western streams. . . . . . . . . . . . . . . . . . . . . . . . . . . . . . . . . . . . . . . . . . . . . **Allocosmoecus**
Scale-hairs lacking; uncommon . . . . . . . . . . . . . . . . . . . . . . . . . . . . . . . . . . . . . .**108**

**108.** Tibia with only two terminal spurs; streams of western states. . . . . . . . .**Dicosmoecus**
Tibia with several pairs of spurs along ventral margin; northern and Rocky Mountain states; lentic and lotic . . . . . . . . . . . . . . . . . . . . . . . . . . . . . . . . . **Onocosmoecus**

**109.** Prosternal horn projecting well beyond apices of coxae; thick irregular case of fragments of vegetation; streams and ponds of eastern states. **Platycentropus**
Prosternal horn short or absent (Fig. 422A) . . . . . . . . . . . . . . . . . . . . . . . . . . . .**110**

**110.** Lateral abdominal gills all simple; case of gravel and wood fragments; streams in northeastern states; uncommon. . . . . . . . . . . . . . . . . . . . . . . . . . . . . **Frenesia**
At least some lateral abdominal gills branched . . . . . . . . . . . . . . . . . . . . . . . . . .**111**

**111.** Case made of longitudinally arranged pieces of grasses; chiefly in small ponds and sluggish streams of western mountains; uncommon. . . . . . . . . **Grammotaulius**
Case of another form . . . . . . . . . . . . . . . . . . . . . . . . . . . . . . . . . . . . . . . . . . . . .**112**

**112.** Lateral sclerite of proleg with many short, stout setae; case variable, of gravel and bits of vegetation; chiefly in Rocky Mountain waters; rare. . . . **Glyphopsyche**
Lateral sclerite of proleg without such setae . . . . . . . . . . . . . . . . . . . . . . . . . . . .**113**

**113.** Dorsal surface of head with large spots, many partly fused; case of longitudinal bits of vegetation; widely distributed in standing and sluggish waters. . . .**Anabolia**
Dorsal surface of head without such spots . . . . . . . . . . . . . . . . . . . . . . . . . . . . . .**104**

**114.** Rare in southwest and west as far north as Oregon; case long, slender, curved, and tapered, made of sand. . . . . . . . . . . . . . . . . . . . . . . . . . . . . . . . . . . . **Gumaga**
Eastern species; case shorter, made of coarse sand . . . . . . . . . . . . . . . . . . . . . . .**115**

**115.** Dorsal surface of head flat and surrounded by a carina; rare in southeastern states. . . . . . . . . . . . . . . . . . . . . . . . . . . . . . . . . . . . . . . . . . . . . . . . . **Fattiga**
Dorsal surface of head not flat; uncommon, but widely distributed in lotic and lentic habitats of the eastern states . . . . . . . . . . . . . . . . . . . . . . . . . . . . . . . . **Agarodes**

**116.** Ventral surface of first abdominal segment with clusters of gills; tapered case of sand; rare in California and Oregon. . . . . . . . . . . . . . . . . . . . . . . . **Nerophilus**
Ventral surface of first abdominal segment without gills; tapered curved case of sand . . . . . . . . . . . . . . . . . . . . . . . . . . . . . . . . . . . . . . . . . . . . . . . . . . . . . . .**117**

In its general morphology and body proportions, the pupa is somewhat similar to the adult, the antennae, wing cases, and legs being well formed and free from the body (Fig. 423M). The larval tracheal gills are usually persistent, however, especially in the eruciform families. In those pupae without gills the respiratory exchange occurs through the general body surface. Some pupae are quite active in the pupal

FIG. 423.–Structure of Trichoptera pupae. A, left mandible of *Glossosoma*; B, mandible of *Rhyacophila*; C, mandible of *Psilotreta*; D, mandible of *Dolophilodes*; E, apical abdominal processes of *Limnephilus*; F, apical abdominal processes of *Goera*; G, dorsal view of apical processes of *Beraea*; H, lateral view of same; J, lateral view of apical abdominal processes of *Sericostoma*; K, apical abdominal processes of *Banksiola*; L, apical abdominal processes of *Lepidostoma*; M, diagram of typical pupa; N, pupa of *Rhyacophila* in cocoon in case, ×2.5; O, pupal case of *Agrypnia*, ×1.2; P, anterior pupal membrane of *Helicopsyche*; Q, anterior pupal membrane of *Leptocella*; R, anterior pupal membrane of *Limnephilus*. (A to L from Ross, 1944, courtesy Illinois Natural History Survey; N and Q modified from Betten; O from Elkins, 1936; P and R redrawn from Denning; S modified from Ross, 1944.)

chamber, and undoubtedly their rhythmic abdominal undulations aid in obtaining oxygen by the creation of a current through the chamber.

Without exception, the transformation to the pupal stage occurs in some kind of a fixed case, and it is thought that the case-building habit may have arisen at this critical period in the life history. The portable cases of eruciform larvae are fastened to the substrate and modified in a variety of ways to form the pupal case. Frequently it is shortened, but the ends are always closed. This may be effected by loose extensions of the case, by the construction of silken nets (Phyganeidae, Limnephilidae), by silken membranes with holes or slits (Sericostomatidae, Leptoceridae), or by simply plugging the ends with small pebbles or vegetation.

Campodeiform larvae construct a special pupal case at the close of the larval period. This is usually a loosely built mound or corral-like structure of gravel and small pebbles. Within these cases most such larvae form a silken cocoon in which pupation occurs.

Although pupal cases are compact structures, there are always sufficient spaces between the pebbles and in the closing nets and membranes to permit the effective circulation of water over the pupa. Membranes and nets are kept free of debris by means of the sweeping action of long bristles at each end of the body.

Pupation usually occurs in the late spring and early summer. The pupal stage ordinarily lasts only about two weeks. For this reason the average collector encounters relatively few pupae.

Imagoes usually emerge during the late afternoon or night. A mature pupa leaves its case by means of strong undulatory movements of the body that break the closing membranes or the case proper. Some investigators believe that the mandibles aid in this process. In most swift-stream genera the pupae swim rapidly to the surface, where the adult emerges from the pupal integument in a matter of a few seconds. Of those species inhabiting quiet waters, some swim to the surface, where emergence occurs more slowly, and others crawl out of the water and emerge on some exposed object. A very few species have terrestrial pupae.

## KEY TO FAMILIES OF TRICHOPTERA PUPAE*

1. Apex of abdomen membranous, without definite lobes except ventral membranous ones that contain developing genital structures. . . . . . . . . . . . . . . . . . . . . . . . .2
   Apex of abdomen with additional projecting platelike or fingerlike processes (Figs. 423E, L) . . . . . . . . . . . . . . . . . . . . . . . . . . . . . . . . . . . . . . . . . . .5
2. Mandibles without teeth or serrations; pupa less than 5 mm long. HYDROPTILIDAE
   Mandibles with teeth or serrations; pupa more than 5 mm long . . . . . . . . . . . . . . . . . .3
3. Mandibles with teeth grouped near apex (Fig. 423D). . . . . . . . . PHILOPOTAMIDAE
   Mandibles with teeth near middle (Fig. 423A), or mandibles only serrate (Fig. 423B). 4
4. Mandibles minutely serrate and with small teeth (Fig. 423B). .RHYACOPHILIDAE
   Mandibles not serrate and with larger teeth (Fig. 423A) . . . . GLOSSOSOMATIDAE
5. Fifth tergite with only an anterior pair of hook-bearing plates. HYDROPSYCHIDAE
   Fifth tergite with both anterior and posterior hook-bearing plates . . . . . . . . . . . . . . . .6
6. Seventh abdominal tergite without a pair of sclerotized plates. . . . . . . . . . . . . . . .7
   Seventh abdominal tergite with a pair of sclerotized hook-bearing plates . . . . . . . . .10
7. Apical processes of abdomen short, appearing triangular in dorsal view, curved ventrally in lateral view (Figs. 423G, H). . . . . . . . . . . . . . . . . . . . . . . .BERAEIDAE
   Apical processes of abdomen either much longer or not curved . . . . . . . . . . . . . . .8
8. Case shaped like a snail shell. . . . . . . . . . . . . . . . . . . . . . .HELICOPSYCHIDAE
   Case of another design . . . . . . . . . . . . . . . . . . . . . . . . . . . . . . . . . . . . . . . . .9

*Greatly modifed from Ross (1944).

9. Antennae very long, part wound around the abdominal apex. . . . . LEPTOCERIDAE
   Antennae scarcely longer than body . . . . . . . . . . . . . . . . . . . . . . . . . MOLANNIDAE
10. Abdomen without a fringe of hairs. . . . . . . . . . . . . . . . . . . . . . . . . . . . . . . . . . . .**11**
    Abdomen with a lateral fringe of hairs . . . . . . . . . . . . . . . . . . . . . . . . . . . . . . . . .**12**
11. Each mandible with a long terminal "whip" (Fig. 423S). . . . . . . PSYCHOMYIIDAE
    Mandibles without long terminal "whips" . . . . . . . . . . . . POLYCENTROPODIDAE
12. Abdomen with a pair of almost linear transverse lines of hooks between fifth and sixth
    tergites. . . . . . . . . . . . . . . . . . . . . . . . . . . . . . . . . . . . . . . . . . . .BRACHYCENTRIDAE
    Abdomen with these areas of hooks much wider . . . . . . . . . . . . . . . . . . . . . . . . .**13**
13. Apical processes of abdomen platelike (Fig. 423K). . . . . . . . . . . . . PHRYGANEIDAE
    Apical processes fingerlike or styliform . . . . . . . . . . . . . . . . . . . . . . . . . . . . . . . . .**14**
14. Apical processes of abdomen short, widely separated, and bearing long black spines
    (Fig. 423L). . . . . . . . . . . . . . . . . . . . . . . . . . . . . . . . . . . . LEPIDOSTOMATIDAE
    Apical processes either close together or much longer . . . . . . . . . . . . . . . . . . . . . .**15**
15. Mandibles produced at apex into a short, narrow, whiplike process (Fig.
    423C). . . . . . . . . . . . . . . . . . . . . . . . . . . . . . . . . . . . . . . . . . . .ODONTOCERIDAE
    Mandibles pointed but not thus produced . . . . . . . . . . . . . . . . . . . . . . . . . . . . . . .**16**
16. Dorsal surface of abdomen with transverse patches of dense, fine hairs.
    CALAMOCERATIDAE
    Dorsal surface of abdomen with only isolated setae . . . . . . . . . . . . . . . . . . . . . . . .**17**
17. Apical processes with slender terminal appendages (Fig. 423J). SERICOSTOMATIDAE
    Apical processes without terminal appendages . . . . . . . . . . . . . . . . . . . . . . . . . . . .**18**
18. Antennae about twice as long as body; pupal chamber with slits in ends, rather than
    mesh. . . . . . . . . . . . . . . . . . . . . . . . . . . . . . . . . . . . . . . . . . . . . . . .LEPTOCERIDAE
    Antennae much shorter . . . . . . . . . . . . . . . . . . . . . . . . . . . . . . . . . . .LIMNEPHILIDAE

# TRICHOPTERA REFERENCES

ANDERSON, N. H. 1967. Life cycle of a terrestrial caddisfly, Philocasca demita (Trichoptera: Limnephilidae), in North America. *Ann. Entomol. Soc. Am.* **60**:320–323.

———. 1967a. Biology and downstream drift of some Oregon Trichoptera. *Can. Ent.* **99**:507–521.

———. 1976. The distribution and biology of the Oregon Trichoptera. *Tech. Bull. Agric. Exp. Sta. Oreg. State Univ.* **134**:1–152.

ANDERSON, N. Y., and E. GRAFIUS. 1975. Utilization and processing of allochthonous material by stream Trichoptera. *Proc. Int. Assoc. Theor. Appl. Limnol.* **19**:3083–3088.

BETTEN, C. 1934. The caddis flies or Trichoptera of New York State. *Bull. N.Y. State Mus.* **292**:1–576.

CUMMINS, K. W. 1964. Factors limiting the microdistribution of larvae of the caddisflies Pycnopsyche lepida (Hagen) and Pycnopsyche guttifer (Walker) in a Michigan stream. *Ecol. Monogr.* **34**:271–295.

———. 1973. Trophic relations of aquatic insects. *Ann. Rev. Entomol.* **18**:183–206.

DANECKER, E. 1961. Studien zur hygropetrischen Fauna. Biologie und Ökologie von Stactobia und Tinodes (Insecta, Trichoptera.). *Int. Rev. ges. Hydrobiol.* **46**:214–254.

DODDS, G. S. and F. L. HISAW. 1924. Ecological studies of aquatic insects. II. Size of respiratory organs in relation to environmental conditions. *Ecology* **5**:262–271.

———. 1925. Ecological studies on aquatic insects. III. Adaptations of caddisfly larvae to swift streams. Ibid. **6**:123–137.

———. 1925. Ecological studies on aquatic insects. IV. Altitudinal range and zonation of mayflies, stoneflies and caddisflies in the Colorado Rockies. Ibid. 380–390.

ELKINS, W. A. 1936. The immature stages of some Minnesota Trichoptera. *Ann. Entomol. Soc. Am.* **29**:656–689.

FELDMETH, C. R. 1970. The respiratory energetics of two species of stream caddis fly larvae in relation to water flow. *Comp. Biochem. Physiol.* **32**:193–202.

FISCHER, F. C. J. 1960–1973. *Trichopterorum Catalogus.* 15 vols. Ned. Entomol. Ver.

FLINT, O. S. 1958. The larva and terrestrial pupa of Ironoquia parvula (Trichoptera, Limnephilidae). *J. N.Y. Entomol. Soc.* **66**:59–62.

———. 1960. Taxonomy and biology of Nearctic limnephilid larvae (Trichoptera), with special reference to species in eastern United States. *Entomol. Am.* **40**:1–117.

———. 1974. The genus Culoptila Mosely in the United States, with two new combinations (Trichop: Glossosomatidae). *Proc. Entomol. Soc. Wash.* **76**:284.

FREMLING, C. R. 1960. Biology and possible control of nuisance caddisflies of the Upper Mississippi River. *Res. Bull. Agric. Home Econ. Exp. Sta. Iowa State Univ. Sci. Tech.* **483**:853–879.

GALLEPP, G. W. 1974. Behavioral ecology of Brachycentrus occidentalis Banks during the pupation period. *Ecology* **55**:1283–1294.

HICKIN, N. E. 1942–1954. Larvae of the British Trichoptera. 7, 16, 17, 33, 36, 44. *Proc. Roy. Entomol. Soc. Lond., Ser. A.* **17**:134–137, 78–83, 86–88, 39–40, 93–95.

———— 1968. *Caddis larvae.* 480 pp. Fairleigh Dickinson Univ. Press, Rutherford, N.J.

KRAFKA, J. 1924. Morphology of the prolegs of trichopterous larvae. *Ann. Entomol. Soc. Am.* **17**:97–102.

LLOYD, J. T. 1921. The biology of the North American caddis fly larvae. *Bull. Lloyd Libr. Bot. Pharm Mat. Med.* **21**:1–124.

MACKAY, R. J., and J. KALFF. 1973. Ecology of two related species of caddis fly larvae in the organic substrates of a woodland stream. *Ecology* **54**:499–511.

MARSHALL, A. C. 1939. A qualitative and quantitative study of the Trichoptera of western Lake Erie (as indicated by trap material). *Ann. Entomol. Soc. Am.* **32**:665–688.

MECOM. J. O. 1970. Unusual case building behavior of Hydropsyche occidentalis larvae (Trichoptera: Hydropsychidae). *Entomol. News* **81**:33–35.

————. 1970. Evidence of diurnal feeding activity in Trichoptera larvae. *J. Grad. Res. Cent.* **38**:44–57.

————. 1972. Productivity and distribution of Trichoptera larvae in a Colorado mountain stream. *Hydrobiologia* **40**:151–176.

MILNE, M. J. 1938. Case building in Trichoptera as an inherited response to oxygen deficiency. *Can. Entomol.* **70**:177–179.

————. 1939. Immature North American Trichoptera. *Psyche* **46**:9–19.

MILNE, M. J., and L. J. MILNE. 1939. Evolutionary trends in caddis worm case construction. *Ann. Entomol. Soc. Am.* **32**:533–542.

MORGAN, A. H., and H. D. O'NEIL. 1931. The function of the tracheal gills in larvae of the caddis fly Macronema zebratum Hagen. *Physiol. Zool.* **4**:361–379.

NIELSEN, A. 1948. Postembryonic development and biology of the Hydroptilidae. A contribution to the phylogeny of the caddis flies and to the question of the origin of the case-building instinct. *Det. K. Danske Vidensk. Selsk. Biol. Skr.* **5**:1–200.

NOYES, A. A. 1914. The biology of the netspinning Trichoptera of Cascadilla Creek. *Ann. Entomol. Soc. Am.* **7**:251–272.

OTTO, C. 1976. Factors affecting the drift of Potamophylax cingulatus (Trichoptera) larvae. *Oikos* **27**:93–100.

PEARSON, W. D., and R. H. KRAMER. 1972. Drift and production of two aquatic insects in a mountain stream. *Ecol. Monogr.* **42**:365–385.

PHILIPSON, G. N. 1954. The effect of water flow and oxygen concentration on six species of caddis fly (Trichoptera) larvae. *Proc. Zool. Soc. Lond.* **124**:547–564.

RHANE, R. E., and K. W. STEWART. 1976. Life cycles and food habits of three Hydropsychidae (Trichoptera) species in the Brazos River, Texas. *Trans. Am. Entomol. Soc.* **102**:65–99.

ROSS, H. H. 1944. The caddis flies, or Trichoptera, of Illinois. *Bull. Ill. Nat. Hist. Surv.* **23**:1–326.

————. 1956. *Evolution and Classification of the Mountain Caddisflies.* 213 pp. Univ. Illinois Press, Urbana, Ill.

————. 1964. Evolution of caddisworm cases and nets. *Am. Zool.* **4**:209–220.

ROSS, H. H., and J. B. WALLACE. 1974. The North American genera of the family Sericostomatidae (Trichoptera). *J. Ga. Entomol.* **9**:42–48.

SCOTT, D. 1958. Ecological studies on the Trichoptera of the River Dean, Cheshire. *Arch. Hydrobiol.* **54**:340–392.

SIBLEY, C. K. 1926. Studies on Trichoptera. Pp. 185–221 *in:* A preliminary biological survey of the Lloyd-Cornell Reservation. *Bull. Lloyd Libr. Bot., Pharm., Mat. Med.* **27**:1–247.

SLACK, H.D. 1936. The food of caddis fly (Trichoptera) larvae. *J. Anim. Ecol.* **5**:105–116.

SUTCLIFFE, D. W. 1962. Studies on salt and water balance in caddis larvae (Trichoptera). III. Drinking and excretion. *J. Exp. Biol.* **39**:141–160.

THUT, R. N. 1969. Feeding haibts of larvae of seven Rhyacophila (Trichoptera: Rhyacophilidae) species with notes on other life-history features. *Ann. Entomol. Soc. Am.* **62**:894–898.

VORHIES, C. T. 1909. Studies on the Trichoptera of Wisconsin. *Trans. Wis. Acad. Sci., Arts and Lett.* **16**:647–738.

WALLACE, J. B. 1975. Food partitioning in netspinning Trichoptera larvae: Hydropsyche venularis, Cheumatopsyche etrona, and Macronemum zebratum (Hydropsychidae). *Ann. Entomol. Soc. Am.* **68**:463–472.

WALLACE, J. B., and D. MALAS. 1976. The fine structure of capture nets of larval Philopotamidae (Trichoptera), with special emphasis on Dolophilodes distinctus. *Can. J. Zool.* **54**:1788–1802.

————. 1976a. The significance of the elongate, rectangular mesh found in capture nets of fine particle filter feed Trichoptera larvae. *Arch. Hydrobiol.* **77**:205–212.

WALLACE, J. B., and F. F. SHERBERGER. 1975. The larval dwelling and feeding structure of Macronema transversum (Walker) (Trichoptera: Hydropsychidae). *Anim. Behav.* **23**:592–596.

WESENBERG-LUND, C. 1911. Über die Biologie der Phryganea grandis und über die Mechanik ihres Gehäusebaues. *Int. Rev.* **4**:65–90.

————. 1911a. Biologischen Studien über netzspinnende, campodeoide Trichopterenlarven. *Int. Rev.* **4** (Suppl. 3):1–64.

WIGGINS, G. B. 1959. A method of rearing caddisflies (Trichoptera). *Can. Entomol.* **91**:402–405.

————. 1975. Contributions to the systematics of the caddisfly Family Lemniphilidae (Trichoptera) II. *Ibid.* **107**:325–336.

————. 1977. *Larvae of the North American Caddisfly Genera* (Trichoptera). 401 pp. Univ. Toronto Press, Toronto.

WINTERBOURN, M. J. 1971. The life histories and trophic relationships of the Trichoptera of Marion Lake, British Columbia. *Can. J. Zool.* **49**:623–635.

# Chapter 33

# LEPIDOPTERA, PYRALIDAE (AQUATIC CATERPILLARS)

ALTHOUGH there are more than 150 families in this order, in only a few American genera of a single family of moths, the Pyralidae, are the immature stages known to be truly aquatic. The larvae are "aquatic caterpillars," having the characteristic body shape, thoracic legs, and ventral abdominal prolegs of terrestrial species. The adults are small, dull-colored, gray, brown, or blackish moths that may be found flying about on summer evenings near small ponds and streams

There are two general groups of species. In one group the larvae have leaf-cutting mandibles and live in tight cases made of bits of hydrophyte tissue. Cases may be either floating or attached to vegetation. Gills are paired, lateral, and filamentous. In the first larval instar gills are often lacking, but they appear in the second instar and subsequently become more abundant. In the last few instars they are sometimes branched. More than 400 separate filaments have been counted in one species. If the larvae have no gills during any instar, then respiration occurs through functional spiracles; all the body except the anterior end is situated within a large air bubble within the case.

A second group of larvae live under silken nets or in shaggy, feltlike cases on rocks in rapid streams. The mandibles are enlarged and flattened for scraping periphyton. Gills are always present.

Larvae are generally distributed over most of the United States in ponds that are densely overgrown with water lilies, potamogetons, and other vegetation. About 50 species are known, of which *Parapoynx*

*maculalis* (Clemens) is perhaps the most common. The larvae hatch from eggs that have been deposited on the undersides of floating leaves. In most instances they construct flat ovate cases composed of two pieces of leaves fastened together at the edges with silk. With the anterior portion of the body protruding from the case, they crawl about feeding on the undersides of floating vegetation. In some southern localities they are so abundant as to be pests on water lilies. Mature larvae are 20 to 25 mm long, yellow or whitish in color with darker head.

The larvae of *Parargyractis fulicalis* (Clemens) are also especially common. They are found on exposed surfaces of stones in rapid streams. They are protected, however, by a silken canopy that is cemented to the substrate along most of its periphery. The canopy covering the later larval instars may be as much as 25 mm wide and 100 mm long. The larva moves about beneath the canopy feeding on the film of algae covering the rock. Mature larvae are 10 to 12 mm long and straw-brown in color. A total of about 120 filamentous blood gills (apparently devoid of tracheation) are arranged in two lateral rows along the thorax and abdomen. Although the geographic distribution of this common species has not yet been accurately ascertained, it is common in the eastern states.

*Acentropus niveus* (Oliver) is unique among aquatic lepidopterans. Some of the females are brachypterous and are able to swim underwater, especially by means of their hairy second and third legs. The body is covered with a plastron. Such females

618

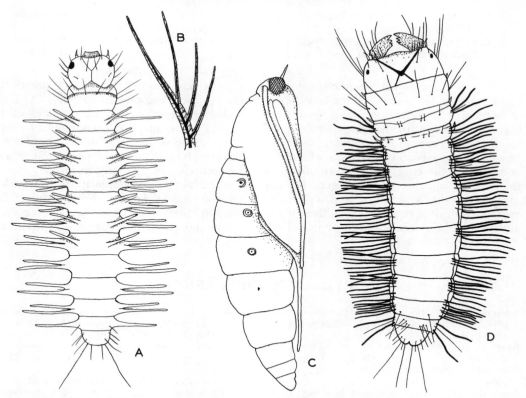

Fig. 424.–Structure of Pyralidae. A, dorsal view of third larval instar of *Parapoynx maculalis* (Clemens), ×20; B, branched tracheal gill of a more advanced larval instar of *Parapoynx*; C, lateral view of pupa of *P. maculalis*, ×6; D, dorsal view of larva of *Parargyractis fulicalis* (Clemens), ×8. (A and C modified from Welch, 1916; B modified from Forbes, 1910; D modified from Lloyd.)

are particularly active at night. Copulation takes place at the surface film. The larva makes a loose case out of bits of vegetation. It is usually attached, especially near the growing tip of a hydrophyte. The case commonly contains an air bubble. Sometimes the larva leaves the case and burrows in the stem of a hydrophyte. *A. niveus* was originally known only from Europe, but is thought to have been imported to the United States. It was first reported in 1938 and has been found many times since.

All species are thought to winter over as immature larvae.

## KEY TO COMMON AQUATIC GENERA OF LEPIDOPTERA LARVAE

1. Mandibles enlarged and flattened, used for scraping periphyton; living under silken or feltlike nets on rocks in clean rapid streams; gills present (Fig. 424D); distribution spotty . . . . . . . . . . . . . . . . . . . . . . . . . . . . . . . . . . . . . . . . . . . . . . . . .**Parargyractis**
   Mandibles small, specialized for leaf cutting; living in cases made from bits of vegetation; gills present or absent . . . . . . . . . . . . . . . . . . . . . . . . . . . . . . . . . . . . . . . . . . .2
2. Tracheal gills present . . . . . . . . . . . . . . . . . . . . . . . . . . . . . . . . . . . . . . . . . **Parapoynx**
   Tracheal gills absent . . . . . . . . . . . . . . . . . . . . . . . . . . . . . . . . . . . . . . . . . . . . . . . . . . .3
3. Larval case roughly spherical, made of 6 to 10 *Lemna* plants held together loosely with silk . . . . . . . . . . . . . . . . . . . . . . . . . . . . . . . . . . . . . . . . . . . . . . . .**Neocataclysta**
   Larval case with another shape; usually not constructed of *Lemna* . . . . . . . . . . . . . . .4

4. Restricted to sphagnum bogs ..................................... **Nymphuliella**
   Not found in sphagnum bogs ............................................... .5
5. Case flat or biconvex, usually made of two bits of leaves. **Nymphula, Synclita, Munroessa**
   Case not flat, made of two or more bits of leaves ..................... **Acentropus**

Pupation habits vary. Some species remain in the water and attach the larval case to submerged vegetation, whereas others leave the water with the case and fasten it to emergent vegetation. In either instance, however, the larva constructs a silken cocoon within the case. Just before pupation the stream species of *Parargyractis* cut away the silken canopy and construct smaller, flat, oval pupal cases in their place and then spin a loose inner cocoon about themselves.

In addition to the genera mentioned above, there are numerous other Pyralidae and a few species in other families of the Lepidoptera that are semiaquatic and are not considered in this manual. These larvae bore and mine in the emergent and submerged tissues of many different kinds of aquatic plants, particularly *Scirpus, Eleocharis,* and *Nelumbo.* For further information concerning these species see especially the papers of Ainslie, Frohne, and Welch.

## PYRALIDAE REFERENCES

AINSLIE, G. G. 1922. Biology of the lotus borer (Pyrausta penitalis Grote). *Bull. U.S. Dept. Agric.* **1076**:1–14.

BERG, C. O. 1950. Biology of certain aquatic caterpillars (Pyralididae: Nymphula spp.) which feed on Potamageton. *Trans. Am. Microsc. Soc.* **69**:254–266.

BERG, K. 1941. Contributions to the biology of the aquatic moth Acentropus niveus (Oliv.). *Vidensk. Medd. Dansk naturh. Foren.* **105**:57–139.

FORBES, W. T. M. 1910. The aquatic caterpillars of Lake Quinsigmond. *Psyche* **17**:219–228.

———. 1911. Another aquatic caterpillar (Elophila). Ibid **18**:120–121.

FROHNE, W. C. 1939. Biology of Chilo forbesellus Fernald, an hygrophilous crambine moth. *Trans. Am. Microsc. Soc.* **58**:304–326.

———. 1939a. Observations on the biology of three semiaquatic lacustrine moths. Ibid. 327–348.

LANGE, W. H. 1956. A generic revision of the aquatic moths of North America: (Lepidoptera: Pyralidae, Nymphulinae). *Wasmann J. Biol.* **14**:59–144.

LAVERY, M. A., and R. R. COSTA. 1972. Reliability of the Surber sampler in estimating Parargyractis fulicalis (Clemens) (Lepidoptera: Pyralidae) populations. *Can. J. Zool.* **50**:1335–1336.

LLOYD, J. T. 1914. Lepidopterous larvae from rapid streams. *J. N.Y. Entomol. Soc.* **22**:145–152.

McGAHA, Y. J. 1954. Contribution to the biology of some Lepidoptera which feed on certain aquatic flowering plants. *Trans. Am. Microsc. Soc.* **73**:167–177.

REICHHOLF, J. 1970. Untersuchungen zur Biologie des Wasserschmetterlings Nymphula nymphaeata L. (Lepidoptera, Pyralidae). *Int. Rev. ges. Hydrobiol.* **55**:687–728.

WELCH, P. S. 1914. Habits of the larva of Bellura melanopyga Grote (Lepidoptera). *Biol. Bull.* **27**:97–114.

———. 1916. Contribution to the biology of certain aquatic Lepidoptera. *Ann. Entomol. Soc. Am.* **9**:159–187.

———. 1919. The aquatic adaptations of Pyrausta penitalis Grt. (Lepidoptera). Ibid. **12**:213–226.

———. 1922. The respiratory mechanism in certain aquatic Lepidoptera. *Trans. Am. Microsc. Soc.* **41**:29–50.

———. 1924. Observations on the early larval activities of Nymphula maculalis Clemens (Lepidoptera). *Ann. Entomol. Soc. Am.* **17**:395–402.

WELCH, P. S., and G. L. SEHON. 1928. The periodic vibratory movements of the larva of Nymphula maculalis Clemens (Lepidoptera) and their respiratory significance. Ibid. **21**:243–258.

# Chapter 34

# COLEOPTERA (BEETLES)

ADULT BEETLES are familiar to everyone. They are minute to large, and the forewings are always modified into horny or leathery elytra that cover the abdomen and meet to form a straight, median, dorsal suture. The hind wings are membranous, folded beneath the elytra, and often reduced or lacking. The mouth parts are adapted for biting and chewing. Metamorphosis is complete; the larvae usually have well-devloped legs and mandibulate mouthparts; the pupae have the wings and legs free from the body.

This is by far the largest order of insects, more than 250,000 species being known, of which about 30,000 occur in the United States. Beetles are chiefly terrestrial insects, and although there are more than 250 familes, only a few are wholly or partly aquatic in the adult or larval stages. Such families occurring in the United States are listed below.

Amphizoidae; very small family; all adults and larvae aquatic.

Haliplidae (crawling water beetles); small family; all adults and larvae aquatic.

Dytiscidae (predaceous diving beetles); largest aquatic family; all adults and larvae aquatic; highly adapted to aquatic habitats.

Noteridae (burrowing water beetles); small family; all adults and larvae aquatic; larvae adapted for burrowing; adults crawl or swim.

Gyrinidae (whirligig beetles); small family; all adults and larvae aquatic; well adapted to aquatic habitats.

Hydrophilidae (water scavenger beetles); large family; majority of species aquatic both as larvae and adults; some terrestrial species.

Hydroscaphidae; very small family; some larvae and adults aquatic.

Limnebiidae; very small family; most larvae and adults aquatic.

Psephenidae; very small family; all larvae and adults aquatic.

Dryopidae; small family; all larvae and adults aquatic.

Elmidae; medium-sized family; except for two genera, all adults are aquatic; all larvae aquatic.

Helodidae; small family; adults terrestrial; larvae aquatic.

Chrysomelidae (leaf beetles); very large family; adults of three common genera found on emergent vegetation; larvae of two of these genera aquatic, the other on emergent vegetation.

Curculionidae (weevils); probably the largest family of insects; adults and immature stages of a few genera feed on emergent aquatic vegetation; adults occasionally found swimming underwater.

Because there is such diversity among the various families of aquatic beetles, the group as a whole will be considered only briefly here, more detailed material being given in the sections dealing with the individual families. In certain families, such as the Elmidae, there are no modifications of the legs for swimming, and the adults simply crawl about on the substrate. Other families, however, such as the Dytiscidae, are good swimmers, and the hind legs may be greatly flattened and hairy. In some families and even genera there is a considerable range of structural modification. Many aquatic Coleoptera are known to fly, and in this way they migrate from one body of

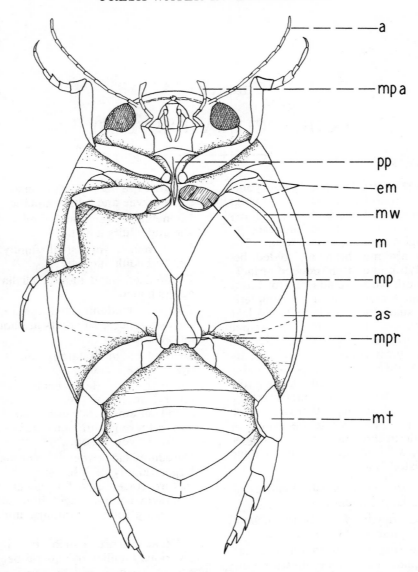

Fig. 425.–Structure of a typical aquatic beetle, *Laccophilus terminalis* Sharp, ×25. *a*, antenna; *as*, first visible abdominal sternite; *em*, episternum of metathorax; *m*, mesocoxa; *mp*, metacoxal plate; *mpa*, maxillary palp; *mpr*, metacoxal process; *mt*, metatibia; *mw*, metasternal wing; *pp*, prosternum and process. (Modified from Leech, 1948.)

water to another. Such flights usually occur at night, and some species are attracted to bright lights where they may be collected in large numbers. Most adult aquatic beetles are fundamentally dependent on atmospheric oxygen. When submerged, some carry a supply of air under the elytra where oxygen diffuses into the spiracles. This supply is renewed at the surface of the water at intervals. Others carry a quantity of air in the form of a thin film (plastron) held to various portions of the body by a hydrofuge pubescence or fine sclerotized granules. Such a film is responsible for the peculiar silvery appearance of these beetles when submerged. Although the air–water interface of a plastron may act as a diffusion membrane through which both carbon dioxide and oxygen may pass to and from the water, respectively, the plastron is usually renewed at intervals at the surface if the water does not contain an abundance of dissolved oxygen. Some species, however, have been kept submerged for several months in aerated water in the laboratory without ill effects.

Adult beetles are found everywhere in streams, rivers, ponds, and protected bays of lakes, even in hot springs. They occur in the shallows near shore, particularly where there are quantities of debris and aquatic vegetation, but are generally absent from wave-swept shores and the deeper waters of lakes and rivers. They may be easily collected with a small dipnet or by washing out vegetation. Many common species are often overlooked by the average collector because of their small size, inconspicuous coloration, and secretive habits. It is usually the adult that winters over by burrowing into debris or mud on the bottom.

Beetles may be kept in satisfactory condition for many years in vials of 80 to 85 percent alcohol containing a few drops of glycerin. Soak and rinse thoroughly in 70 percent alcohol before pinning specimens in an insect box.

Some species, especially members of the Dryopidae and Elmidae, are often covered with tightly attached debris and require cleaning before they can be identified. Nelson (1949) recommends the following procedure. Crimp the metal tip of a small paintbrush to a diameter of about 1.5 mm and cut the bristles down to a length of about 1 mm. Place the beetles in 5 to 10 percent acetic acid for 20 to 30 minutes, and then place them in tap water containing a pinch of trisodium phosphate for 20 or 30 minutes. While carefully holding them in this solution, remove the loosened debris with the brush.

Food habits are quite variable, ranging from a strictly predatory (Dytiscidae) to a vegetarian diet (Haliplidae).

With few exceptions the pupal stage is terrestrial. When the mature larva leaves the water and crawls out upon the adjacent shore, some of the nonfunctional larval spiracles become perforate and begin to function. The pupal chamber is most frequently constructed within 5 m of the water's edge. It may be a hollow chamber at a depth of several inches in the earth, or it may be on the surface constructed of mud pellets or bits of vegetable debris. The pupae are exarate, pale, and covered with a thin, soft cuticle (Figs. 434, 435).

Add adult aquatic beetles have aquatic larvae, the eggs usually being deposited below the surface of the water. These larvae differ from the terrestrial grubs with which everyone is familiar. The former have longer, more efficient thoracic legs, and the body is more elongated and slender, or, in some cases, considerably flattened dorsoventrally. Locomotion includes rapid swimming movements (Dytiscidae), "jumping," walking, active crawling, and sluggish crawling motions (Haliplidae). Most species come to the surface at intervals to obtain a fresh supply of air in the tracheal system via a pair of spiracles at the posterior end, but a few species having prominent lateral gills remain permanently submerged. In addition, some have delicate filamentous anal gills, which may function in respiration. It also seems likely that a portion of the oxygen–carbon dioxide exchange takes place through the general body surface. As in the adults, food habits are variable, ranging from a carnivorous to an herbivorous diet. The mouthparts are well developed for biting and chewing or biting and sucking. In general, the larvae occur in the same habitats as the adults.

Several families have only semiaquatic fresh-water representatives, and these are omitted from this manual, including the Limnichidae, Heteroceridae, Ptilodactylidae, and Chelonariidae. For the most part these species are associated with damp mud and sand along the shores of lakes and streams.

## KEY TO FAMILIES OF ADULT COLEOPTERA

1. Head not prolonged into a beak; common; true beetles . . . . . . . . . . . . . . . . . . . . . . . . . . . . . . . . .2
Head prolonged into a long beak; uncommon in aquatic habitats; weevils.
CURCULIONIDAE, p. 662

2. Eyes completely divided by the lateral margins of the head (Fig. 436D).
GYRINIDAE, p. 637
Eyes not divided . . . . . . . . . . . . . . . . . . . . . . . . . . . . . . . . . . . . . . . . . . .3
3. Hind coxae in the form of large plates (Fig. 427B) . . . . . . . . . HALIPLIDAE, p. 627
Hind coxae normal . . . . . . . . . . . . . . . . . . . . . . . . . . . . . . . . . . . . . . . . .4
4. Tarsi with three segments; 0.5 to 1.5 mm long; southwestern states; uncommon.
HYDROSCAPHIDAE, p. 645
Tarsi with more than three segments . . . . . . . . . . . . . . . . . . . . . . . . . . . .5
5. Hind tarsi apparently four-segmented; third segment broadly bilobed; feeding on
emergent aquatic vegetation . . . . . . . . . . . . . . . . . . CHRYSOMELIDAE, p. 659
Hind tarsi five-segmented; third segment not bilobed . . . . . . . . . . . . . . . . . . . . . .6
6. Antennae clubbed . . . . . . . . . . . . . . . . . . . . . . . . . . . . . . . . . . . . . . . . . . . . .7
Antennae not clubbed . . . . . . . . . . . . . . . . . . . . . . . . . . . . . . . . . . . . . . . .9
7. Prosternum with a process that fits into a groove on the mesosternum (Fig. 445C). 13
Prosternum without such a process . . . . . . . . . . . . . . . . . . . . . . . . . . . . .8
8. Antennal club of five pubescent segments; not more than 2.5 mm long.
LIMNEBIIDAE, p. 645
Antennal club of fewer than five segments; usually more than 2.5 mm long.
HYDROPHILIDAE, p. 641
9. Hind tarsi with two slender, curved claws of equal length . . . . NOTERIDAE, p. 637
Hind tarsi with one straight claw . . . . . . . . . . . . . . . . . . . . . . . . . . . . . . .10
10. Legs much modified for swimming, flattened, with large spurs and small claws (Fig.
428) . . . . . . . . . . . . . . . . . . . . . . . . . . . . . . . . . . . . . . . . . . DYTISCIDAE, p. 629
Legs slightly or not at all modified . . . . . . . . . . . . . . . . . . . . . . . . . . . . . . . .11
11. First sternite completely divided into three parts by the coxae.
AMPHIZOIDAE, p. 625
First sternite not divided . . . . . . . . . . . . . . . . . . . . . . . . . . . . . . . . . . . . .12
12. Prosternum with a process that fits into a groove on the mesosternum (Fig. 445C). 13
Prosternum without such a process; feeding on terrestrial or emergent aquatic
vegetation . . . . . . . . . . . . . . . . . . . . . . . . . . . . . . . . . . . . HELODIDAE, p. 657
13. Entirely aquatic . . . . . . . . . . . . . . . . . . . . . . . . . . . . . . . . . . . . . . . . . . . .14
Not found actually in the water.
ELMIDAE, **Lara** and **Phanocerus clavicornis** Sharp, p. 651
14. With six or seven abdominal sternites . . . . . . . . . . . . . . . . . . . PSEPHENIDAE, p. 648
With five abdominal sternites . . . . . . . . . . . . . . . . . . . . . . . . . . . . . . . . . . . .15
15. Antennae with the apical segments pectinate and forming a close club (Fig.
445A) . . . . . . . . . . . . . . . . . . . . . . . . . . . . . . . . . . . . . . . DRYOPIDAE, p. 650
Antennae usually filiform, but if clubbed, then the segments of the club never pectinate . . . . . . . . . . . . . . . . . . . . . . . . . . . . . . . . . . . . . . . . . . . . . . . . . . . .16
16. Anterior coxae rounded . . . . . . . . . . . . . . . . . . . . . . . . . . . . . . . ELMIDAE, p. 651
Anterior coxae transverse . . . . . . . . . . . . . . . . . . . . . . . . . . . . . DRYOPIDAE, p. 650

## KEY TO FAMILIES OF COLEOPTERA LARVAE

1. Legs six-segmented, with distinct tarsus and one or two claws . . . . . . . . . . . . . . . . . . .2
Legs either five-segmented, with tarsus and claw fused into a single segment, or less
than five-segmented, or vestigial, or absent . . . . . . . . . . . . . . . . . . . . . . . . . .6
2. Tenth abdominal segment armed with four apical hooks . . . . . . . GYRINIDAE, p. 637
No apical hooks . . . . . . . . . . . . . . . . . . . . . . . . . . . . . . . . . . . . . . . . . . .3
3. Ninth abdominal segment present . . . . . . . . . . . . . . . . . . . . . . . . HALIPLIDAE, p. 627
Ninth abdominal segment rudimentary, apparently absent . . . . . . . . . . . . . . . . . . . .4
4. Legs fossorial . . . . . . . . . . . . . . . . . . . . . . . . . . . . . . . . . . . . . . NOTERIDAE, p. 637
Legs specialized for walking or swimming . . . . . . . . . . . . . . . . . . . . . . . . . . . . .5
5. Edges of tergites extended laterally as flattened projections. AMPHIZOIDAE, p. 625
Edges of tergites not extended laterally . . . . . . . . . . . . . . . . . . . . . . DYTISCIDAE, p. 634
6. Body very flat, scalelike, oval, and smooth in outline . . . . . . . PSEPHENIDAE, p. 648
Body shape otherwise . . . . . . . . . . . . . . . . . . . . . . . . . . . . . . . . . . . . . . . . . .7

7. Antennae about as long as or longer than thorax ............HELODIDAE, p. 657
   Antennae clearly shorter than thorax ........................................8
8. Mandibles short, broad, and inconspicuous; feeding on roots and rhizomes of submerged aquatic plants or on upper surface of lily pads.
   CHRYSOMELIDAE, p. 660
   Mandibles prominent; food habits otherwise ...................................9
9. Part or all of ninth sternum forming a movable operculum that usually covers a
   terminal cloacal chamber containing tufts of retractile gills................10
   Movable operculum, cloacal chamber, and retractile gills absent ................11
10. Tracheae never with air sacs; ninth abdominal segment with or without pleural scler-
    ites; with nine pairs of spiracles or with the spiracles only on the eighth
    abdominal segment ................................ DRYOPIDAE, p. 650
    Tracheae with or without air sacs; ninth abdominal segment without distinct pleural
    sclerites; always with nine pairs of spiracles .............ELMIDAE, p. 655
11. With a pair of cercilike filaments on eighth abdominal segement; true cerci absent;
    antennae very short; southwestern ...........HYDROSCAPHIDAE, p. 645
    Filaments absent; cerci two-segmented and well developed; antennae rather long .12
12. With nine complete abdominal segments; the tenth reduced but distinct.
    LIMNEBIIDAE, p. 645
    With eight complete abdominal segments, the ninth and tenth reduced (Fig.
    439) .........................................HYDROPHILIDAE, p. 644

## AMPHIZOIDAE

Only four species of *Amphizoa* are known in this family from the United States. All are rare and seem to be confined to swift, clear streams in the western states. The adults are 11 to 15 mm long, broad, and rough; the antennae are glabrous. Color is reddish-brown to black. These beetles are poorly adapted to an aquatic habitat, the legs being fitted for crawling. They may be found on submerged logs and
The larval stages are somewhat elongated, but the edges of the tergites extend laterally as flattened lamellate projections. The tarsal claws are paired, and there are two short, spinelike cerci. Only the terminal spiracles are functional.

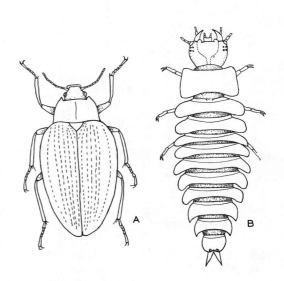

FIG. 426.–Amphizoidae. A, adult *Amphizoa lecontei* Matth., ×4.5; B, larva of same, ×6.5. (B redrawn from Hubbard.)

## HALIPLIDAE (CRAWLING WATER BEETLES)

The crawling water beetles are closely allied to the Dytiscidae. They are all small, the usual length being only 2 to 5 mm, and for this reason are frequently overlooked by collectors. the body is oval, deeply convex, and widest near the anterior edge of the elytra. The color is yellowish or brown, usually marked with black. The antennae are 10-segmented and threadlike, and the elytra have small punctures arranged in longitudinal rows. Of the six ventral segments of the abdomen, the first three to five are covered by the enormously enlarged platelike coxae of the hind legs. The hind femora

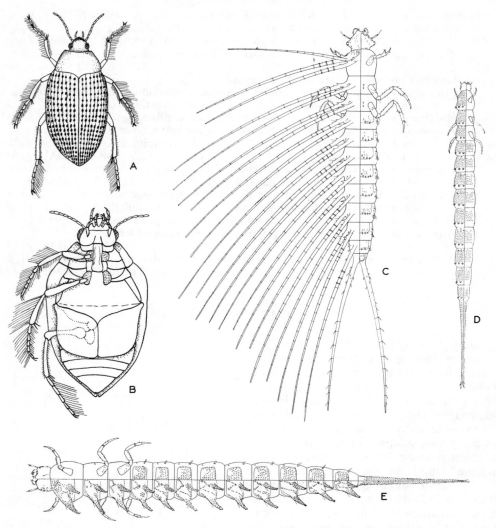

FIG. 427.–Haliplidae. A, dorsal view of *Haliplus*, ×9; B, ventral view of *Haliplus*, ×13; C, mature larva of *Peltodytes*, ×4; D, mature larva of *Haliplus*, ×6; E, mature larva of *Haliplus*, ×10. (C to E show both dorsal and ventral surfaces; from Hickman, 1930.)

are dumbbell-shaped and largely hidden by the coxae; they move between these plates and the abdomen. Except for the long hairs on the tarsi, the legs are unmodified for swimming. Swimming is feeble and consists of alternate movements of the legs. A supply of air is carried under the elytra and coxal plates where it is in direct contact with the thoracic and abdominal spiracles. At intervals these beetles normally take in a fresh supply of air at the surface of the water with the tip of the abdomen. Occa-

sionally they leave the water and fly short distances.

Four genera of this widely distributed family occur in the United States. Several species of *Brychius* are found in the western states. There are about 15 species of *Peltodytes* and 30 species of *Haliplus*, however, and these two genera are common everywhere. *Apteraliplus parvulus* Roberts is the only member of the fourth genus; it appears to be confined to the central California coastal region. Because of their inconspicuous nature, it seems likely that there may be additional, undescribed species in this genus.

Adult haliplids are usually found crawling about on and among masses of filamentous algae and other submerged vegetation in the shallows. *Brychius* is found in running water and occasionally in lakes, but *Haliplus, Apteraliplus,* and *Peltodytes* occur in pools, ponds, sluggish streams, and protected places in lakes. Apparently they feed chiefly on vegetation, although some investigators have observed them eating animal material. Many species are active throughout the winter in situations where the water does not freeze. Mating occurs early in the spring and the fertilized eggs are attached to aquatic vegetation; in some forms the eggs are deposited in the dead cells of algal filaments.

## KEY TO GENERA OF ADULT HALIPLIDAE*

1. Pronotum with sides of basal two-thirds nearly parallel, sometimes slightly sinuate; uncommon; western states ......................................... **Brychius**
   Pronotum with sides widest at base and convergent anteriorly (Fig. 427A) ......... 2
2. Last two segments of palps about the same size; hind coxal plates margined; generally distributed ... ................................................. **Peltodytes**
   Last segment of palps much smaller than second last; hind coxal plates not margined. 3
3. Prosternum evenly rounded from side to side; 1.5 to 2.5 mm long; confined to central California coastal region; rare ................................. **Apteraliplus**
   Median portion of prosternum and prosternal process forming a plateaulike elevation (Fig. 427B); small to large; generally distributed ................... **Haliplus**

The larvae are sticklike, slender, and very sluggish. They are adapted only for crawling and are found in floating masses of algae, as well as in other vegetation or trash in the shallows, where they feed on filamentous algae either by chewing on the cells or by sucking out their contents. Large dorsal spines of *Peltodytes* are well supplied with tracheae and are important respiratory structures. The last segment represents the fused ninth and tenth abdominal segments; it is long and widely bifurcated. *Haliplus* does not have such long spines, but the body has numerous setigerous tubercles. Some species have four dorsal hornlike prominences on each body segment. The abdomen has 10 segments, of which the last is long and attenuated, with a small bifurcation at the tip (Figs. 427D, E). Little is known about the larvae of the American species of *Brychius* and *Apteraliplus.* The three larval instars usually last from three to five weeks, but in cold weather they may persist much longer, even over the winter.

The pupal chamber is constructed in damp earth at edges of bodies of water. The pupal stage lasts two to three weeks.

## KEY TO GENERA OF LARVAL HALIPLIDAE

1. Two, four or six extremely long dorsal and lateral jointed spines on each thoracic and the first eight abdominal segments (Fig. 427C) ..................... **Peltodytes**
   Body without such long spines ............................................... 2
2. Third antennal segment shorter than second .......................... **Brychius**
   Third antennal segment much longer than second .............................. 3
3. Third segment of first leg with two blunt teeth ...................... **Apteraliplus**
   Third segment of first leg without teeth ................................. **Haliplus**

*Modified from Chandler, 1943.

# DYTISCIDAE (PREDACEOUS DIVING BEETLES)

Of the few families of beetles that are exclusively aquatic, the predaceous diving beetles are the most characteristic and best adapted to this environment. Although about 40 genera are known to occur in the United States, most of these are represented by relatively few species. Many species are widely distributed from coast to coast, however.

Adult Dytiscidae range from about 1 to 40 mm in length. They are shiny, usually black or brownish-black, but often marked with dull yellow, green, or bronze. The antennae have 11 segments and are long and threadlike. The second and third legs are widely separated owing to the very large hind coxae. Many species produce sounds by rubbing the abdominal segments and elytra together or by rubbing the legs against the ventral surface of the abdomen. Some genera produce an irritating substance, supposedly defensive, from prothoracic glands.

Dytiscidae may be easily collected by sweeping a net over the bottoms of pools and ponds. They are absent from wave-swept shores and occur in large lakes only where there are shallow, protected bays and small inlets. The presence of a clean substrate and aquatic vegetation seems to be almost indispensable. Few species occur on muddy bottoms, in rapid water, or in springs. One rare blind species, *Haideoporus texas,* has been found in Texas artesian waters.

The first and second legs contribute little to the swimming movements, but the hind legs are more or less flattened, elongated, and hairy; they operate together in an oarlike manner. Throughout the family there is considerable variation in the development and specialization of the hind legs. In *Bidessus* and *Hydroporus,* for example, they are only feebly developed for swimming; in *Agabus* they are more flattened and hairy; and in such genera as *Dytiscus, Acilius,* and *Cybister* they are extemely flattened and densely fringed with swimming hairs. Those genera highly developed for swimming are the most awkward on land.

Many species are known to leave the

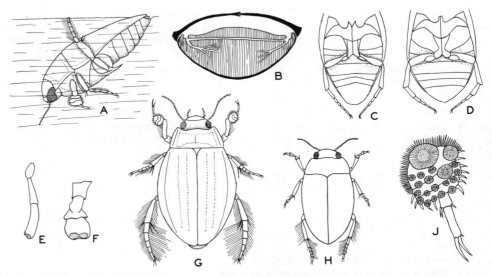

FIG. 428.–Dytiscidae adult structures. A, *Dytiscus* at surface film, ×1; B, diagrammatic cross section through abdomen of same showing elytra, subelytral chamber, and spiracles; C, ventral view of *Agabinus*; D, ventral view of *Agabus*; E, labial palp of *Agabus*; F, same of *Hydrotrupes*; G, *Dytiscus,* male, ×1; H, *Hydroporus,* ×5; J, ventral view of first tarsus of male of *Thermonectus*. (A redrawn from Korshelt; C to F redrawn from Leech, 1942; J redrawn from Wilson, 1923.)

water and fly from pond to pond, some having been found flying more than six miles from any body of water. Sometimes these movements assume the proportions of mass migrations. Dytiscids may often be collected around lights at night.

The group is exclusively carnivorous and voracious. They feed on all kinds of aquatic Metazoa, the larger species commonly attacking dragonfly nymphs, tadpoles, and even small fish. When kept in aquariums, Dytiscidae must be well supplied with food. Such food need not be living organisms; almost any kind of raw or cooked meat will suffice.

There are 10 pairs of spiracles; the first two pairs are on the thorax; the third through ninth pairs are on the dorsolateral portions of the abdominal segments; the last is at the tip of the abdomen. The spiracles open into the subelytral chamber so that when the beetles are submerged they utilize the oxygen of the tracheae and the subelytral chamber (Fig. 428B). It is also thought that some oxygen from the surrounding water diffuses into the subelytral chamber through the air–water interface. At intervals, however, the air supply must be renewed, and dytiscids ordinarily come to the surface every few minutes. The body is maintained head downward at an oblique angle with the tip of the abdomen penetrating the surface film (Fig. 428A). In this way the terminal spiracles are brought into contact with the atmosphere, and the air under the elytra is renewed.

One generation per year is the rule. Copulation occurs during the warm months. In the males of some genera, including *Acilius*, *Hydaticus*, *Thermonectus*, *Cybister*, *Dytiscus*, and others, the first three segments of the anterior tarsi are enormously swollen to form an acetabulum. The ventral surface of this structure is flat, edged with strong bristles, and covered with curious, small, stalked cuplets or sucker discs (Fig. 428J). A few forms have acetabula on the second tarsi also. These structures apparently act as adhesive organs for holding the two individuals together during copulation. Some authorities maintain that a sticky secretion is given off from glands on the acetabulum and that it acts in conjunction with the sucking discs. The female deposits the eggs in trash or under objects along the shore, on floating vegetation, or within the living tissues of aquatic plants by means of a specialized ovipositor. Adults of some species are known to live and reproduce for two or even three summers, and there are a few records of dytiscids that lived for five years. Only one generation is produced each year, and, depending on the species and time of oviposition and hatching, it is usually either the larva or the adult that winters over, the latter condition being more common. They ordinarily hibernate in debris or burrow into the bottom or edges of ponds. It is not uncommon, however, to see the adults swimming about under ice during the winter. Some species aestivate during a portion of the summer.

Adult dytiscids are frequently covered with a tightly adherent layer of grease, dust, and bits of detritus. This can easily be brushed off if the specimens are first soaked in petroleum ether.

## KEY TO GENERA OF ADULT DYTISCIDAE

1. Scutellum fully covered (Fig.428H), or rarely with a small tip visible (in *Celina* entirely visible, but in that case the prosternal process is bent strongly downward) ..2
   Scutellum entirely visible (Fig. 428G) prosternal process not deflected ..........22
2. Prosternal process short, not reaching metasternum; head narrow; rare; one species................................................**Derovatellus**
   Prosternal process long, reaching metasternum ................................3
3. First and second tarsi distinctly five-segmented, the fourth segment approximately as long as the third (Fig. 425) .............................................21
   Fourth segment of first and second tarsi minute and usually hidden between the lobes of the third; usually 2 to 6 mm long ....................................4

FIG. 429.–Dytiscidae adult structures. A, left hind coxal process of *Hydrovatus*; B, metacoxal processes and base of third legs in *Hydroporus*; C, metacoxal processes and base of third legs in *Deronectes*; D, hind femur of *Ilybius* showing group of hairs on inner half of apical angle; E, left metasternum of *Coptotomus*; F, left metasternum of *Rhantus*; G, left metasternum of *Colymbetes*; H, left metasternum of *Acilius*; J, hind coxal processes of *Hydroporus*; K, hind coxal processes of *Hydroporus*; L, hind tarsal claws of *Ilybius*; M, labial palp of *Carrhydrus*.

4. The broad apex of the hind coxal process divided into three parts by two oval emarginations (Fig. 429A); widely distributed ................. **Hydrovatus**
   Hind coxal process otherwise ..............................................5
5. Hind coxal process short, flat, almost in a plane with the ventral segments, and without lateral wings, so that the bases of the trochanters are entirely free ..6
   Hind coxal process not on a level with the first sternite, but somewhat raised, its sides divergent, and more or less produced into lobes that cover the bases of the trochanters ......................................................14
6. Hind claws asymmetrical; hind tibiae straight, of almost uniform width ..........7
   Hind claws symmetrical; base of hind tibiae slightly arched and much more slender than the thickened apical part .......................................8
7. Middle coxae widely separated; rare; Florida ........................ **Pachydrus**
   Middle coxae approximate; about 2 mm long; widely distributed ..... **Desmopachria**
8. Fourth segment of fore and middle tarsi reduced and hidden between lobes of the third segment; 1.5 to 2.5 mm long; widely distributed ....................9
   Fore and middle tarsi distinctly five-segmented, the third segment rounded and not bilobed; eastern; standing waters .......................... **Bidessonotus**
9. Head with a transverse cervical stria or suture behind the eyes ................10
   Head without a cervical stria; eastern states ........................... **Uvarus**
10. Pronotal striae distinct, but elytra without striae; rare; Florida ........ **Brachyvatus**
    Basal pronotal and elytral striae distinct ...............................11

11. Margin of clypeus thickened, upturned, tuberculate, or rimmed ................12
    Margin of clypeus not modified ..............................................13
12. Basal pronotal striae connected by an irregular transverse groove; along sandy stream
        margins; 1.5 to 1.7 mm long; southern states .................. **Anodocheilus**
    Basal pronotal striae distinct, but area between them flat; western mountain
        streams ............................................... **Neoclypeodytes**
13. Anal sternite narrow, impressed on each side; widely distributed in western states.
                                                                    **Liodessus**
    Anal sternite broad, not impressed at sides; southern states ........... **Neobidessus**
14. Elytra acuminate; widely distributed but not common ..................... **Celina**
    Elytra with apex rounded, subtruncate, or acute..............................15
15. The bent-under margin of the elytra with a basal excavation that receives the middle
        knee and is marked off by a diagonal carina; front and middle tarsi four-
        segmented; widely distributed and common ..................... **Hygrotus**
    The bent-under margin of the elytra not excavated; front and middle tarsi five-seg-
        mented, but the fourth segment is very small..........................16
16. Hind femora attaining the metacoxal lobes; eastern states .............. **Laccornis**
    Hind femora not attaining the metacoxal lobes; widely distributed and common...17
17. Median line between lobes of metacoxal processes not abbreviated behind, the apex
        either truncate or more or less angularly prominent at middle (Fig. 429B) ..18
    Median line between lobes of metacoxal processes triangularly excised at middle, the
        lobes more produced posteriorly (Fig. 429C) ..........................20
18. Posterior margins of hind coxal processes angular (Fig. 429J); many common
        species........................................................... **Hydroporus**
    Posterior margins of hind coxal processes not angular (Fig. 429K) ..............19
19. Posterior angles of pronotum rectangular or obtuse; many common species. **Hydroporus**
    Posterior angles of pronotum acute; common ....................... **Deronectes**
20. Pronotum with a line or crease on each side; hind femora with a median row of
        punctures; common and widely distributed...................... **Oreodytes**
    Pronotum without such lines; hind femora punctate over most of surface; about 15
        species; common........................................... **Deronectes**
21. Spines of hind tibiae divided at tip; usually 3 to 6 mm long; widely distributed and
        common ....................................................... **Laccophilus**
    Spines of hind tibiae not divided at tip; rare........................... **Laccodytes**
22. Eyes emarginate (notched) above the bases of the antennae; first three segments of
        male first tarsi widened, but not forming a circular adhesion disc; usually 4 to
        16 mm long.....................................................23
    Eyes not emarginate; first three segments of male first tarsi forming a circular or oval
        adhesion disc (Fig. 428J); usually 9 to 40 mm long ......................35
23. Hind claws of equal length and usually of similar form .......................24
    Hind claws of unequal length, the outer one usually more sharply bent at the tip than
        the inner .....................................................28
24. With a linear group of hairs near the posterior apical angles of the hind femora ...25
    Without such hairs .......................................................27
25. Hind coxal processes in the form of rounded lobes (Fig. 428D)..................26
    Hind coxal processes parallel-sided, lateral margins straight to the apices (Fig. 428C);
        western; rare ................................................. **Agabinus**
26. Labial palps very short, terminal segments subquadrate (Fig. 428F); California moun-
        tain streams; rare .........................................**Hydrotrupes**
    Labial palps approximately as long as maxillary palps, terminal segments linear, not
        subquadrate (Fig. 428E); widely distributed and common ........... **Agabus**
27. Pronotum laterally finely but sharply margined; elytra longitudinally striate in most
        species; widely distributed ................................... **Copelatus**
    Pronotum laterally emarginate; elytral sculpture aciculate; mostly northeastern.
                                                                    **Agabetes**
28. Prosternum flat, with a median longitudinal furrow; eastern and southern .... **Matus**
    Prosternum convex or keeled, without a furrow ..........................29
29. Hind femora with a linear group of small hairs on the inner half of the apical angles
        (Fig. 429D) .....................................................30
    Hind femora without such a group of small hairs ..........................31

30. Penultimate segment of labial palp swollen (Fig. 429L); one rare species. **Carrhydrus**
    Labial palp linear; claws of hind tarsi unequal; mostly east of the Rocky
    Mountains . . . . . . . . . . . . . . . . . . . . . . . . . . . . . . . . . . . . . . . . . . . . . . . . . . . . .**Ilybius**
31. Metasternal wings narrow, linear (Fig. 429E); widely distributed . . . . . . . **Coptotomus**
    Metasternal wings broad, wedge-shaped (Figs. 429F, G) . . . . . . . . . . . . . . . . . . . .**32**
32. Elytra with sharply incised coarse meshwork . . . . . . . . . . . . . . . . . . . . . . . . . . . . .**33**
    Elytra transversely fissured, finely impressed with transverse parallel lines, or finely
    and thickly reticulate; widely distribututed and common . . . . . . . . . . . . . . . . .**34**
33. Depressed; bicolored dorsal surface; woodland ponds; reported from Alabama, Vir-
    ginia, South Carolina, Maryland, and Arkansas; rare . . .**Hoperius planatus** Fall
    Convex; dorsal surface all black; extreme northern states . . . . . . . . . . **Neoscutopterus**
34. Metasternum with a broad and distinct pitlike depression on the anterior border
    between the coxae (Fig. 429F); elytral sculpture various but not of parallel
    transverse grooves; widely distributed, in the vegetation of pools and marshes;
    about 10 species . . . . . . . . . . . . . . . . . . . . . . . . . . . . . . . . . . . . . . . . . . . **Rhantus**
    Metasternum between the coxae flat or with a small, indistinct, longitudinal impression
    (Fig. 429G); elytral sculpture consisting of parallel transverse grooves.
    **Colymbetes**
35. Hind margin of first four segments of the hind tarsi with a coarse fringe of golden,
    yellow, flat hairs along its entire width . . . . . . . . . . . . . . . . . . . . . . . . . . . . . .**36**
    Hind margin of first four segments of hind tarsi without such a fringe, or with hairs
    only on the outer apical angle . . . . . . . . . . . . . . . . . . . . . . . . . . . . . . . . . . . . . .**40**
36. Pronotum margined laterally; Kansas, Colorado, Texas, Arizona, and California;
    rare . . . . . . . . . . . . . . . . . . . . . . . . . . . . . . . . . . . . . . . . . . . . . . . . . . . . . **Eretes**
    Pronotum not margined laterally . . . . . . . . . . . . . . . . . . . . . . . . . . . . . . . . . . . . . .**37**
37. Outer margin of wing of metasternum straight; widely distributed . . . . . . . .**Hydaticus**
    Outer margin of wing of metasternum arcuate (Fig. 429H) . . . . . . . . . . . . . . . . . . .**38**
38. Elytra coarsely punctate, usually fluted in female; widely distributed and common.
    **Acilius**
    Elytra almost smooth . . . . . . . . . . . . . . . . . . . . . . . . . . . . . . . . . . . . . . . . . . . . .**39**
39. Hind margin of middle femora with setae as long as middle tibiae; southwest.
    **Thermonectus**
    Hind margin of middle femora with setae shorter than middle tibiae; widely
    distributed . . . . . . . . . . . . . . . . . . . . . . . . . . . . . . . . . . . . . . . . . . . . **Graphoderus**
40. Hind tibiae distinctly longer than broad; widely distributed and common . . . **Dytiscus**
    Hind tibiae almost as broad as long . . . . . . . . . . . . . . . . . . . . . . . . . . . . . . . . . . .**41**
41. Hind legs of male with two claws, of the female with a long outer and a small
    rudimentary inner claw; Florida; rare . . . . . . . . . . . . . . . . . . . . . . . . **Megadytes**
    Hind legs of male always, of the female usually, with only one claw; widely distributed
    and common . . . . . . . . . . . . . . . . . . . . . . . . . . . . . . . . . . . . . . . . . . . . . **Cybister**

Most dytiscid larvae are elongated and spindle-shaped. The head is large and round, oval, elongated, or with a prominent anterior prolongation. Typically, there is a pair of cerci at the end of the last segment; these may be naked, sparsely setose, or densely setose. Most species are small and inconspicuous, and nearly all our information is based on observations of a few large larvae.

Because of their carnivorous and voracious food habits, they are often called "water tigers," and although a few forms, like *Hydroporus,* will eat pieces of animals that are already dead, this is exceptional.

Food consists of all kinds of aquatic Metazoa, and some of the larger larvae, such as *Dytiscus* and *Cybister,* are of economic importance because they may feed on fish fry in hatchery ponds. They lunge and clutch their prey with their large sickle-shaped mandibles. These mouthparts are peculiarly constructed for piercing and sucking. Each has a groovelike canal that arises near the tip and continues along the inner margin and connects with the mouth cavity at the base of the mandible (Fig. 430H). The canal is effectively, but not entirely, closed off from the outside by close-fitting ridges along the inner surface of the

FIG. 430.–Dytiscidae larval structures. A, head of *Deronectes*; B, outline of head of *Pachydrus*; C, labium of *Thermonectus*; D, labium of *Acilius*; E, labium of *Acilius*; F, larva of *Cybister*, ×6.5; G, cercus of *Deronectes*; H, mandible of *Dytiscus*, showing food channel; J, diagrammatic cross section of same; K, larva of *Acilius*, ×4; L, posterior end of *Dytiscus*, showing anus, spiracles, and cerci. (B modified from Spangler and Folkerts, 1973; C, D, and F redrawn from Wilson, 1923; E modified from Bertrand; L modified from Portier, 1911.)

mandible (Fig. 430J). Food is predigested by a fluid arising in the mouth and given off from the tips of the mandibles. The resulting semifluid material (including the body fluids of the prey) is then drawn into the mouth cavity through the mandibles. The mouth itself apparently remains closed during feeding.

Some dytiscid larvae, such as *Acilius*, are efficient and graceful swimmers; the legs and posterior abdominal segments are heavily fringed with hairs. Also, some are capable of making quick darting movements by throwing the body into sudden curves. A few genera, on the other hand, are sluggish creepers that scarcely swim at all.

Only the two spiracles on the last abdominal segment are functional. Many species swim or crawl to the surface of the water and assume an angle at the surface with these spiracles in contact with the atmosphere. Such larvae as *Dytiscus, Hydaticus,* and *Acilius,* however, are usually lighter than water and float to the surface when they are not clinging to the bottom or to submerged vegetation. Many small and medium-sized larvae probably do not come to the surface at all, but obtain their oxygen by diffusion through the general body surface. *Coptotomus* has six pairs of long, lateral abdominal gills.

## KEY TO COMMON GENERA OF DYTISCIDAE LARVAE*

1. Head with anterior prolongation (Figs. 430A, B) . . . . . . . . . . . . . . . . . . . . . . . . . . . . . . .2
   Head without anterior prolongation (Figs. 430F, K) . . . . . . . . . . . . . . . . . . . . . . . . . .9
2. Anterior prolongation laterally notched (Figs. 430A, B) . . . . . . . . . . . . . . . . . . . . . .3
   Anterior prolongation not notched . . . . . . . . . . . . . . . . . . . . . . . . . . . . . . . . . . . . . . . .7
3. Anterior prolongation with a simple emarginate notch (Fig. 430A) . . . . . . . . . . . . . .4
   Anterior prolongation with spines in a pronounced notch (Fig. 430B) . . . . **Pachydrus**
4. Cerci with six or seven primary hairs (Fig. 431F) . . . . . . . . . . . . . . . . . . . . . . . . . . . .5
   Cerci with a greater abundance of hairs (Fig. 430G) . . . . . . . . . . **Deronectes, Oreodytes**
5. Cerci as long or longer than the eighth abdominal segment (Fig. 432B) . . . . . . . . . . .6
   Cerci very short (Fig. 431F) . . . . . . . . . . . . . . . . . . . . . . . . . . . . . . . . . . . . . . **Laccornis**

FIG. 431.–Structure of Dytiscidae larvae. A, maxilla of *Laccophilus*; B, maxilla of *Cybister*; C, tip of antenna of *Copelatus*; D, ligula of *Acilius*; E, foreleg of *Matus*; F, posterior end of *Laccornis*; G, lateral view of head of *Ilybius*; H, cerci of *Dytiscus*; J, maxilla of *Agabus*. (A and B from Wilson, 1923; D, H, and J from James, 1969; E modified from Spangler and Gordon, 1973; G redrawn from Balfour Browne.)

*Greatly modified from Usinger et al. and other sources.

FIG. 432.–Dytiscidae larvae. A. *Agabus*, ×9; B, *Hydroporus*, ×8; C, *Coptotomus*, ×4; D, *Hydrovatus*, ×11; E, *Laccophilus*, ×8. (A and D modified from Bertrand, 1928; B, C, and E modified from Wilson, 1923.)

6. Eighth abdominal segment one and three-quarters or more times as long as seventh abdominal segment ............................................**Hygrotus**
Eighth abdominal segment proportionately shorter ................... **Hydroporus**
7. Body not especially broad; a group of six genera formerly included in *Bidessus*.
(couplets 9 to 13 in key to adult Dytiscidae).
Body greatly widened at midlength (Fig. 432D) ...............................8
8. Last abdominal segment long; cerci short (Fig. 432D) ................ **Hydrovatus**
Last abdominal segment short; cerci long ............................**Oreodytes**
9. Maxillary stipes stout (Fig. 431J) .........................................10
Maxillary stipes thin (Fig. 431B) .........................................24
10. Seventh and eighth abdominal segments without lateral swimming hairs .........11
Seventh and/or eighth abdominal segments with lateral swimming hairs .........20
11. Last segment of antenna less than two-thirds as long as penultimate segment .....14
Last segment of antenna more than two-thirds as long as penultimate segment ....12
12. Stipes of maxilla with two large setae on internal border (Fig. 431J) ........ **Agabus**
Stipes of maxilla without such setae .......................................13

13. Mature larva less than 25 mm long; claws with spinules .................. **Rhantus**
    Mature larva 27 to 28 mm long; claws sometimes with spinules .........**Colymbetes**
14. Last segment of antenna with a minute accessory basal segment (Fig. 431C). **Copelatus**
    Without such an accessory segment .......................................**15**
15. First and second legs pseudochelate (Fig. 431E) ........................ **Matus**
    All legs normal ..........................................................**16**
16. Cerci densely hairy (Fig. 432E) ..................................... **Laccophilus**
    Cerci not densely hairy .................................................**17**
17. Thorax as wide as long ...........................................**Hydrotrupes**
    Thorax longer than wide .................................................**18**
18. Tibiae and tarsi with apical and subapical spines ..................... **Agabinus**
    Tibiae and tarsi with spines not confined to apical portions (Fig. 432A) .........**19**
19. Head with lateral keels (Fig. 431G) .....................................**Ilybius**
    Head without lateral keels ............................................ **Agabus**
20. Abdomen with slender filaments that serve as tracheal gills (Fig. 432C). **Coptotomus**
    No tracheal gills on abdomen...........................................**21**
21. Ligula short and armed with four spines .............................. **Eretes**
    Ligula long, without spines, or with a few very small spines (Figs. 430D, E)......**22**
22. Ligula bifid, or simple and with a few very short spines (Figs. 430D, E) .....**Acilius**
    Ligula simple, without spines ...........................................**23**
23. Ligula longer than the first segment of the labial palp ................. **Graphoderus**
    Ligula shorter than the first segment of the labial palp, often tipped with two jointed
        spines (Fig. 430C) ...................................... **Thermonectus**
24. Abdominal cerci absent (Fig. 430F) ................................. **Cybister**
    Abdominal cerci present (Fig. 430L) ....................................**25**
25. Cerci fringed (Fig. 430L) ..............................................**26**
    Cerci not fringed ................................................ **Hydaticus**
26. Prothorax longer than wide ...................................... **Dytiscus**
    Prothorax shorter than wide......................................**Hoperius**

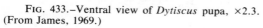

Fig. 433.–Ventral view of *Dytiscus* pupa, ×2.3. (From James, 1969.)

Fig. 434.–Lateral view of pupa of *Cybister,* ×2.3. (Redrawn from Wilson, 1923.)

When the larva leaves the water to pupate, all the spiracles become functional. The pupal cells are formed on shore a short distance from the water, usually under stones, vegetation, or debris. They are constructed of mud pellets on the surface of the ground, or as deep as 10 cm. The pupal stage usually lasts from a few days to two months, although a few species are thought to winter over in this stage.

As in other families of aquatic beetles with terrestrial pupae, this stage in the life history is especially susceptible to drowning. Heavy rains or melting snow may fill the pupal cells with water, resulting in a high mortality rate.

Pupae may be collected around the edges of ponds by turning over logs and masses of debris or by digging in likely areas.

## NOTERIDAE (BURROWING WATER BEETLES)

These beetles are only 1 to 5 mm long and are therefore frequently overlooked. Their affinities are tropical and most species are restricted to the southern states. The predaceous adults swim or creep about on submerged hydrophytes and burrow in bottom debris. Respiratory specializations are similar to those of the Dytiscidae.

The larvae have powerful fossorial legs and dig through mud and debris at a surprising rate. A hollow chitinous spear at the posterior end presumably functions in respiration by piercing intercellular spaces in plants. When kept in shallow water in the laboratory, the tip of the spear is poked through the surface film. The American larvae are poorly known, and no satisfactory key can be devised (see Spangler and Folkerts, 1973).

Mature larvae make pupal cocoons out of bits of vegetation and mud. They are attached to plant roots where a hole has been bitten in the surface tissues.

## KEY TO GENERA OF ADULT NOTERIDAE*

**1.** First tibia with an apical curved spur (Fig. 435); more than 2 mm long . . . . . . . . . . . . .2
Without a spur on the first tibia; 1.25 mm long; rare; Florida and Louisiana. **Notomicrus**
**2.** Spur of first tibia well developed (Fig. 435) . . . . . . . . . . . . . . . . . . . . . . . . . . . . . . . . .3
Spur of first tibia weak; rare, but probably widely distributed . . . . . . . . . . . **Pronoterus**
**3.** Laminate inner plates of the hind coxae subtruncate at apex with an arcuate emargination on each side of the depressed middle; rare; Louisiana and Florida.
                                                        **Suphis inflatus** (LeC.)
Laminate inner plates of the hind coxae with a broad and deep angular excision at apex, leaving a diverging triangular process at each side (Fig. 435); uncommon but widely distributed . . . . . . . . . . . . . . . . . . . . . . . . . . . . . . . . . . . . . . . . . . . . . . . .4
**4.** Apex of prosternal process about twice as broad as it is between the first coxae; less than 3.5 mm long . . . . . . . . . . . . . . . . . . . . . . . . . . . . . . . . . . . . . . . . . . . **Suphisellus**
Apex of prosternal process at least two and one-half or three times as broad as it is between the first coxae (Fig. 435); 4 mm or more long . . . . . . . . **Hydrocanthus**

## GYRINIDAE (WHIRLIGIG BEETLES)

Whirligig beetles occur in colonies of a few to a great many individuals on the surface of lakes, ponds, slow streams, and backwaters of rapid streams. They float quietly or circle and glide about each other in rapid irregular curves near the shore. When alarmed, they scatter in all directions and dive or whirl about so rapidly that they

*Modified from Young, 1954.

FIG. 435.–Ventral view of adult *Hydrocanthus*. First leg shaded, showing spur. (Modified from Young, 1954.)

are exceedingly difficult to catch without a large dipnet. These beetles are black, shiny, oval, and somewhat depressed; the abdomen extends beyond the elytra. They are well adapted for rapid locomotion, the middle and hind legs being greatly flattened, paddlelike, and fringed (Fig. 436F). The compound eyes are divided at the edge of the head by the insertion of the antennae so that in effect there is one pair for aerial vision and another for looking down in the water (Fig. 436D). This is the most distinctive feature of the family. The third segment of the peculiar antennae is much enlarged and earlike, and the following ones form a short, spindle-shaped mass. When handled, many species give off a milky fluid that has a peculiar odor; perhaps this is a protective mechanism. Gyrinids frequently fly, but they are unable to take off from the water and must climb up on some emergent object. Although these beetles are almost always found on the surface, they are good divers. They carry an air supply under the elytra when submerged and are consider-

ably lighter than water, but use their long, hooked forelegs for clinging to the bottom. Although live insects that fall upon the surface of the water probably form the main portion of the diet, there are numerous observations and experiments showing that some species may feed on dead animal matter and vegetation. The conclusion that they are scavengers seems to be a logical one.

Only three genera of Gyrinidae are known from the United States. Both *Dineutus* and *Gyrinus* are widely distributed and common over the entire country, there being about 15 species in the former genus and 40 in the latter. The species of *Gyretes,* however, seem to be confined chiefly to the western states and are especially adapted to swift waters. Small species of *Gyrinus* and *Gyretes* are often found clinging to emergent materials above the water level in swift streams.

Adult Gyrinidae hibernate in mud or trash at the bottom or edges of ponds and streams during the cold months. The eggs are laid on submerged vegetation after activity is resumed in the spring, and these hatch in a few days or weeks. During the middle or late summer the larva builds the pupal case of pellets of earth which are often mixed with sand or debris. Ordinarily it is constructed on vertical plant stems or rocks just above the water or on shore one to several inches above the surface of the ground. In those species that have been studied, the pupal stage lasts about a month. The adults are therefore most abundant in late summer and early autumn. It is thought that there is only one generation per year.

In *Gyretes* the dorsal surface is pubescent, at least at the margins; the last abdominal segment is elongated and conical, with a midventral row of hairs; the body is less than 9 mm long. In *Dineutus* and *Gyrinus,* however, the dorsal surface is glabrous, and the last abdominal segment is rounded and without a midventral row of hairs. *Dineutus* is more than 10 mm long, the metasternal wings are broadly triangular, and the elytra are smooth or with nine striae. *Gyrinus* is less than 9 mm long, the metasternal wings are narrow, and the ely-

FIG. 436.–Gyrinidae. A, ventral view of thorax and abdomen of adult *Gyrinus*; B, ventral view of tip of abdomen of adult *Gyretes*; C, antenna of adult *Gyrinus*; D, lateral view of head of adult *Gyrinus*; E, adult *Dineutus,* ×4; F, mesothoracic leg of adult *Gyrinus*; G, larva of *Dineutus,* ×3.4. 1, metasternal wing; 2, mesocoxa; 3, metacoxa. (A to D modified from Hatch, 1927; E from *Insects in Kansas*; F modified from Bott; G redrawn from Wilson, 1923.)

tra have 11 striae, with the discal striae sometimes obsolete.

The larvae of the Gyrinidae are pale, inconspicuous, elongated, slender, and much flattened. Because of the presence of long, lateral, respiratory filaments on the abdominal segments, they have a superficial similarity to small centipedes (Fig. 436G). There is one pair of these tracheal gills on each of the first eight abdominal segments and two pairs are found on the ninth. The last abdominal segment is small and has two pairs of terminal sickle-shaped

hooks, presumably useful for clinging to the substrate and for holding the larva in place in the pupal case. Unlike the adults, they are independent of the surface for respiration. They are usually found crawling about on submerged vegetation near the shore or swimming in a characteristic sinuous manner. Gyrinid larvae are carnivorous and voracious, feeding on all types of mature and immature aquatic insects. The mandibles are large and sickle-shaped, and have a canal running their length through which the body fluids of the prey are sucked. Mature *Gyrinus* larvae average 10 to 15 mm in length; *Dineutus* average 20 to 30 mm.

*Dineutus* larvae have a subcircular head and a distinct and narrow neck. *Gyretes* and *Gyrinus* larvae have an elongated head, and the neck is about as wide as the head and not distinct. *Gyrinus* has two to four teeth in a transverse row on the anterior median projections of the frons, but there are no such teeth in *Gyretes*.

## HYDROPHILIDAE (WATER SCAVENGER BEETLES)

Although many species in this family are terrestrial and occur in moist earth and dung, the majority are aquatic. As a group, the hydrophilids are characterized by their short, clubbed antennae, which are usually concealed beneath the head; their tactile function is taken over by the long maxillary palps, which are often mistaken for antennae. In addition to this feature, they may be differentiated from the somewhat similar Dytiscidae by their habit of making contact with the surface film with the edge of the body at the anterior end and by the fact that they move their hind legs alternately when swimming. Also, the ventral surface is not strongly convex as it is in the Dytiscidae. The majority of species are blackish, but some are yellow or brown. The length ranges from about 1 to 40 mm. The habits of only the larger species are well known.

Scavenger beetles are common in quiet, shallow pools and ponds, especially where there is considerable vegetation. Only a few, such as *Hydrochara, Hydrophilus, Berosus,* and *Tropisternus* are good swimmers, the others being crawlers. *Laccobius* remains concealed in the mud. A few occur at the edges of streams where the current is not swift. Many leave the water and crawl about on land. Some merely "dabble in the mud at the water's edge." In the spring hydrophilids may be easily collected when they fly to electric lights.

While submerged, oxygen is obtained from air in the tracheal system, and, via the spiracles, from the subelytral chamber and from the silvery film of air (plastron) retained on the ventral side of the body by hydrofuge hairs. The air supply is renewed at intervals in an unusual manner. The beetle comes to the surface with the body slightly inclined to one side so as to bring the cleft between the head and prothorax in contact with the surface film. Then the antenna is introduced into this cleft and raised so that its tip breaks the surface film. The antenna and the cleft in this way form a funnellike tube through which the ventral, subelytral, and tracheal air is renewed.

Formerly it was believed that adult hydrophilids feed exclusively on decaying vegetation (hence the name scavenger beetles), but it is now thought that they eat considerable quantities of living plant material, chiefly algae. Occasionally they eat carrion, and a few species have been known to catch and eat other aquatic insects.

Oviposition occurs in spring and early summer. Although a few species deposit uncovered eggs, the great majority enclose them in cases formed from a hardened, silklike secretion given off from glands that open by a pair of spinnerets at the apex of the abdomen in the female. There may be from 2 to as many as 130 eggs in a single cocoon, depending on the species, but in the case-building species the eggs are enclosed singly. In *Epimetopus, Helochares,* and possibly other genera, the female may carry the cocoon on the hind legs and ventral side of the abdomen. Otherwise the cocoon may be wrapped in a leaf, freefloating, or fastened to submerged aquatic plants or surface debris. The shape of the cocoons varies greatly, but is specific for each species (Fig. 438). The eggs usually hatch in 5 to 10 days, and the young larvae leave the cocoon a few hours after hatching. There are three larval instars. At the termination of the larval period the pupal cell is constructed on shore, either in debris on the surface of the ground or as much as 7 cm below the surface. The pupal stage usually lasts less than three weeks. The adult winters over. In some species there may be two generations per year.

More than 170 species of aquatic Hydrophilidae occur in the United States, and in many areas they are the most abundant beetles. They are grouped in 23 genera, none of which are large. *Helophorus, Hydrochus, Berosus, Tropisternus, Crenitis, Enochrus,* and *Cymbiodyta* all contain between 10 and 25 species each. Because of its large size (35 mm long), abundance, and wide distribution, the best-known American species is probably *Hydrophilus triangularis* Say. Other common genera are *Hydrochara, Tropisternus, Berosus, Helophorus,* and *Hydrochus.*

## KEY TO GENERA OF ADULT HYDROPHILIDAE

1. Pronotum with five longitudinal sulci, or produced anteriorly at middle so as to hide much of the head . . . . . . . . . . . . . . . . . . . . . . . . . . . . . . . . . . . . . . . . . . . . . .2
   Pronotum otherwise . . . . . . . . . . . . . . . . . . . . . . . . . . . . . . . . . . . . . . . . . . . . . . . .3
2. Eyes nearly divided by sides of the head; southwestern; rare . . . . . . . . . **Epimetopus**
   Eyes round, not divided; widely distributed . . . . . . . . . . . . . . . . . . . . . . . . . .**Helophorus**
3. Lateral contours of body uneven; dorsal surface with prominent tuberosities; last segment of hind tarsi as long as the four preceding segments together; (sometimes placed in a separate family, Hydrochidae). . . . . . . . . . . . . . . . **Hydrochus**
   Lateral contours of body even; without prominent dorsal tuberosities; last segment of hind tarsi much shorter than the preceding segments together (except in *Helobata*) . . . . . . . . . . . . . . . . . . . . . . . . . . . . . . . . . . . . . . . . . . . . . . . . . . . . . . . . .4
4. Scutellum usually a long triangle; antennae eight-segmented at most; pronotum narrowed posteriorly . . . . . . . . . . . . . . . . . . . . . . . . . . . . . . . . . . . . . . . . . . . . . . . . .5
   Scutellum not longer, or not much longer than its basal width; antennae nine-segmented at most; pronotum not narrowed posteriorly . . . . . . . . . . . . . . . . . . . . . .6
5. Middle of emargination of fifth sternite toothless; small, narrow, strongly convex, and black species; Louisiana; rare . . . . . . . . . . . . . . . . . . . . . **Derallus altus** (Lec.)
   Middle of emargination of fifth sternite with one or more short horny teeth; yellow or brown species; widely distributed . . . . . . . . . . . . . . . . . . . . . . . . . . . . . . . . . .**Berosus**
6. Mesosternum and metasternum raised in a common median keel, produced behind into a spine (Fig. 437D) . . . . . . . . . . . . . . . . . . . . . . . . . . . . . . . . . . . . . . . . .7
   Mesosternum and metasternum not raised to form a common median keel . . . . . .**11**
7. Prosternum sulcate; metasternal spine long . . . . . . . . . . . . . . . . . . . . . . . . . . . . .8
   Prosternum carinate; metasternal spine short; 13 to 16 mm long . . . . . . . . . . . . . . . .**10**
8. Last segment of maxillary palps shorter than the preceding; at least 25 mm long . . .9
   Last segment of maxillary palps equal to or longer than the preceding; not more than 15 mm long . . . . . . . . . . . . . . . . . . . . . . . . . . . . . . . . . . . . . . . . . . . . . . **Tropisternus**

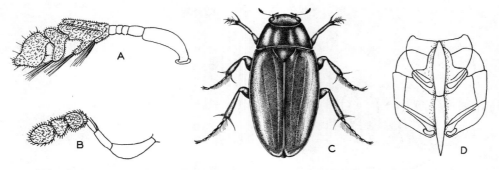

FIG. 437.–Structure of adult Hydrophilidae. A, antenna of adult *Hydrophilus*; B, antenna of *Berosus*; C, *Hydrophilus*, ×1.2; D, ventral view of meso- and metathorax of *Hydrophilus*, showing median keel. (A and B redrawn from Wilson, 1923; C from *Insects in Kansas*; D modified from Trimble.)

9. Prosternal process closed in front, hood-shaped ..................... **Hydrophilus**
   Prosternal process not closed in front, bifurcate ....... **Dibolocelus ovatus** G. and H.
10. Clypeus broadly emarginate along its anterior border, exposing the articulation of the
    labrum, and with its lateral angles protruding in the form of teeth.
    **Neohydrophilus castus** (Say)
    Clypeus more or less truncate .................................... **Hydrochara**
11. The first two sternites on each side with a common excavation and covered by a
    peculiar bilobed hyaline plate; 1 to 2 mm long; widely distributed;
    uncommon ............................................... **Chaetarthria**
    Abdomen of five or six normal segments ...................................12
12. Maxillary palps stout and short, little longer or shorter than antennae ...........13
    Maxillary palps slender, much longer than antennae ........................19
13. Elytra with sutural striae; abdomen with five visible ventral segments ...........14
    Elytra without sutural striae; abdomen with six visible ventral segments; widely
    distributed ..................................................... **Laccobius**
14. More than 4.5 mm long; widely distributed ..............................15
    Not more than 3.5 mm long ...........................................17
15. Second to fifth segments of middle and hind tarsi with a fringe of long, fine hairs;
    widely distributed ......................................... **Hydrobius**
    Without such hairs .................................................16
16. Body strongly convex, almost hemispherical in cross section; rare, eastern states.
    **Sperchopsis**
    Body oval; rare, western states ........................................ **Ametor**
17. Hind femora pubescent basally, at least along the anterior margin ...............18
    Hind femora without pubescence, even along the anterior margin; widely
    distributed ................................................. **Paracymus**
18. Hind femora not pubescent basally except for a short distance along the anterior
    margin; eyes protuberant; eastern; uncommon ..................... **Crenitis**
    Hind femora either with pubescence on their basal two-thirds or only along the
    trochanter and in a narrow band along the anterior border; eyes not protuberant;
    eastern, southern, and California ............................. **Anacaena**
19. All tarsi five-segmented, though basal segment may be very small ..............20
    Middle and hind tarsi four-segmented ...................................22
20. Mesosternum with a longitudinal median lamina; widely distributed ...... **Enochrus**
    Mesosternum at most feebly protuberant .................................21
21. Labrum visible; eastern and southwestern .......................... **Helochares**
    Labrum concealed beneath clypeus; clypeus projecting laterally in front of eyes to a
    great extent; Florida and Louisiana ................. **Helobata striata** Brullé

FIG. 438.–Egg cases of Hydrophilidae. A, *Berosus*; B, longitudinal section through case of *Hydrophilus*; C, *Helophorus*; D, *Helochares*. (A, C, and D from Richmond, 1920; B modified from Wilson, 1923.)

**22.** Mesosternal carina transverse or elevated at middle, forming a pyramidal or dentiform
protuberance; 4 to 5.5 mm long; widely distributed . . . . . . . . . . . . **Cymbiodyta**
Mesosternum with a compressed conical process; 5.5 to 7 mm long; eastern.
**Helocombus bifidus** (LeC.)

In general, the larvae are found in the same specific aquatic habitats as the adults in sand, soil, and debris near the water's edge. They are inconspicuous, elongated, flattened, and have well-developed mouthparts. Color is usually gray, yellowish, brown, or greenish. The great majority are crawlers, and many species are extremely sluggish. A few, such as *Tropisternus lateralis* (Fabr.) and *Hydrophilus triangularis,* swim with undulatory leechlike movements. Sometimes larvae may be found crawling about on the shore just above the water's edge.

The group is predominantly predaceous and carnivorous, even to the point of cannibalism. All types of aquatic Metazoa are eaten. After the food has been seized, the larvae usually crawl up on vegetation

until the head is out of water. The prey is then crushed with the large rapacious mandibles and there may be some preoral digestion. Some species ingest only body fluids; others take in solid tissues as well. It is said that dead vegetation may form a considerable portion of the diet in certain species. Wilson (1923) observed that *Berosus* fed only on living filamentous algae.

With few exceptions, hydrophilid larvae come to the surface at intervals to renew the air in the tracheal system. Since only the posterior pair of spiracles are functional, this renewal occurs with the tip of the abdomen at the surface film. *Berosus,* however, remains submerged since it obtains its oxygen through seven pairs of long, rigid, lateral, abdominal tracheal gills.

FIG. 439.–Larvae of Hydrophilidae. A, *Tropisternus,* ×9; B, *Enochrus,* ×10; C, *Hydrochara,* ×3; D, *Berosus,* ×6. (A, B, and D modified from Wilson, 1923.)

## KEY TO COMMON GENERA OF HYDROPHILIDAE LARVAE

1. Legs vestigial . . . . . . . . . . . . . . . . . . . . . . . . . . . . . . . . . . . . . . . . . . . . . . **Chaetarthria**
    Legs not vestigial . . . . . . . . . . . . . . . . . . . . . . . . . . . . . . . . . . . . . . . . . . . . . . .2
2. Thorax and abdomen with broad lateral prolongations (Fig. 440A) . . . . . . . . .**Crenitis**
    Without such broad prolongations . . . . . . . . . . . . . . . . . . . . . . . . . . . . . . . . . .3
3. With nine complete abdominal segments, the tenth reduced but distinct . .**Helophorus**
    With eight complete abdominal segments, the ninth and tenth reduced (Fig. 439) . . .4
4. Antennae inserted farther from lateral margins of head than mandibles . . . . . . . . . . .5
    Antennae inserted nearer the lateral margins of head than mandibles . . . . **Hydrochus**
5. With seven pairs of prominent tracheal gills on abdomen (Fig. 439D) . . . . . . .**Berosus**
    Tracheal gills reduced or absent . . . . . . . . . . . . . . . . . . . . . . . . . . . . . . . . . . . .6
6. First segment of antennae not markedly longer than the following two taken together;
       femora without fringes of swimming hairs . . . . . . . . . . . . . . . . . . . . . . . . . . .7
    First segment of antennae distinctly longer than the following two taken together (Fig.
       441K); femora with fringes of long swimming hairs (Fig. 441C) . . . . . . . . . . .15
7. Ligula absent; tarsus well developed, about as long as tibia (Fig. 441B) . . .**Laccobius**
    Ligula present (Fig. 441H); tarsus usually much shorter than tibia (Figs. 441A, C). 8
8. Legs reduced . . . . . . . . . . . . . . . . . . . . . . . . . . . . . . . . . . . . . . . . . . . . . . . . .9
    Legs fairly long, not reduced . . . . . . . . . . . . . . . . . . . . . . . . . . . . . . . . . . . . .10
9. Each mandible with two inner teeth; legs not visible from above . . . . . . . . **Paracymus**
    Each mandible with three inner teeth; legs barely visible from above . . . . . **Anacaena**
10. Mandibles symmetrical; abdomen without prolegs . . . . . . . . . . . . . . . . . . . . . . . . .11
    Mandibles asymmetrical (Fig. 441E); abdomen with prolegs on third to seventh
       segments . . . . . . . . . . . . . . . . . . . . . . . . . . . . . . . . . . . . . . . . . . . . . . . . . **Enochrus**
11. Each mandible with three inner teeth, of which one may or may not be small (Fig.
       441F) . . . . . . . . . . . . . . . . . . . . . . . . . . . . . . . . . . . . . . . . . . . . . . . . . . . . . .12
    Each mandible with two inner teeth . . . . . . . . . . . . . . . . . . . . . . . . . . . . . . . . . .14
12. Clypeus with four teeth (Fig. 440B) . . . . . . . . . . . . . . . . . . . . . . . . . . . . . . **Ametor**
    Clypeus with five teeth . . . . . . . . . . . . . . . . . . . . . . . . . . . . . . . . . . . . . . . . . .13
13. Middle tooth of clypeus very small (Fig. 440C) . . . . . . . . . . . . . . . . . . . . . **Sperchopsis**
    Middle tooth of clypeus as large as the others . . . . . . . . . . . . . . . . . . . . . . . **Hydrobius**
14. Anterior sclerites of metathorax with caudal projections . . . . . . . . . . . . . . . **Helochares**
    Anterior sclerites of metathorax without caudal projections . . . . . . . . . . . **Cymbiodyta**

FIG. 440.–Structure of Hydrophilidae larvae. A, middle abdominal segments of *Crenitis*; B, teeth of clypeus of *Ametor*; C, teeth of clypeus of *Sperchopsis*; D, abdominal segment of *Derallus*. (A modified from Van Emden; D redrawn from Bertrand, 1972.)

FIG. 441.–Structure of larval Hydrophilidae. A, mesothoracic leg of *Paracymus*; B, same of *Laccobius*; C, same of *Hydrophilus*; D, mandible of *Tropisternus*; E, mandibles of *Enochrus*; F, mandible of *Hydrobius*; G, labium of *Hydrochara*; H, same of *Paracymus*; J, same of *Tropisternus*; K, head of *Hydrophilus*. 1, mentum; 2, maxilla; 3, labium; 4, antenna; 5, mandible. (A, B, C,F, G, H, and J from Richmond, 1920; D, E, and K modified from Wilson, 1923.)

15. Some thoracic and abdominal segments provided with cylindrical appendages tipped
      with setae (Fig. 440D) ......................................... **Derallus**
    Without such appendages ............................................**16**
16. Each mandible with a single inner tooth (Fig. 441K) .................**Hydrophilus**
    Each mandible with more than one inner tooth, usually two (Fig. 441D) .........**17**
17. Mentum transverse, sides only slightly rounded (Fig. 441J) ......................**18**
    Mentum convex, with its sides strongly rounded (Fig. 441G); poorly developed tra-
      cheal gills present in some species .......................... **Hydrochara**
18. Two thoracic and all abdominal segments each with two lateral setose tubercles on
      each side .............................................. **Tropisternus**
    Without such tubercles ........................................**Neohydrophilus**

# HYDROSCAPHIDAE

Only one aquatic species in this family, *Hydroscapha natans* Lec., is known from the United States. It is uncommon and occurs in the southwest in cold to warm waters. The adult is minute, being only 1 mm or less in length. The hind coxae are widely separated and laminate, and the abdomen is conical and protrudes beyond the tip of the elytra. These beetles crawl about sluggishly on submerged stones in running waters, especially in algal masses.

The larvae are characterized by a pair of cercilike filaments on the eighth abdominal segment and very short, inconspicuous antennae.

# LIMNEBIIDAE

This small family includes a few species of aquatic beetles that are seldom encountered by the general collector. They are distinguished by a five-segmented pu-

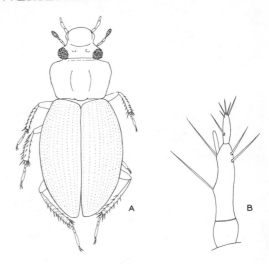

Fig. 443.–Limnebiidae. A, *Ochthebius* adult, ×25; B, larval antenna of *Hydraena*. (B from Richmond, 1920.)

Fig. 442.–Larva of *Hydroscapha natans*, ×50. (From Böving, 1914.)

bescent antennal club and by their small size, the range in total length being only 1 to 2 mm. Adults of the three common genera may be distinguished as follows. In *Limnebius* the second segment of the hind tarsi is longer than the third, the base of the pronotum is as broad as the base of the elytra, total body length is about 1 mm, and the distribution is mostly southern. In *Hydraena* and *Ochthebius* the second segment of the hind tarsi is about as long as the third, the base of the pronotum is slightly or decidedly narrower than the base of the elytra, and the total length is 1 to 2 mm. *Hydraena* is widely distributed and has maxillary palpi that are much longer than the antennae, but *Ochthebius* is southern and has palpi that are shorter than the antennae.

*Hydraena* and *Limnebius* are found along running waters and *Ochthebius* around standing waters. Adults creep and cling to rocks and debris in swift streams as they feed on vegetable material. The ventral surface, except for the head, legs, and tip of the abdomen, is covered with hydrofuge pubescence. Occasionally they replenish this and the subelytral air at the surface film.

The small larvae resemble some of the Hydrophilidae but may be distinguished from the latter by the fact that they have nine complete abdominal segments instead of eight, only the tenth being reduced. In the larvae of *Ochthebius* the cerci are divergent and nearly contiguous proximally. In *Hydraena* and *Limnebius* the cerci are nearly parallel and widely separated proximally. *Hydraena*, however, has the third antennal segment without inner swellings and the second segment with a single antennal appendage. In *Limnebius* the third antennal segment has an inner swelling, and the second segment has two slender antennal appendages.

## PSEPHENIDAE (RIFFLE BEETLES)

The Psephenidae is a very small family of aquatic beetles represented by four genera in the United States. The most common species is *Psephenus herricki* (De Kay), which is widely distributed in the eastern states. The seven additional species in this

FIG. 444.–Psephenidae. A, adult *Psephenus*, ×8; B, dorsal view of larva of *Psephenus*, ×9; C, ventral view of same, ×12; D, dorsal view of larva of *Eubrianax edwardsi*, ×8. (B, C, and D redrawn from Böving and Craighead.)

genus are confined to the western states. *Eubrianax edwardsi* is the only other American representative of the fmaily and it is apparently restricted to the Pacific coast states. *Acneus* is rare in California and Oregon; *Ectopria* is rare in eastern states.

The riffle beetles are appropriately named since they commonly occur on rocky or gravel bottoms along wave-swept shores and in streams where the water is shallow and swift. Incidentally, the swift-water habit is not common among aquatic beetles. The adults are inconspicuous, small, oval, and depressed. Because the body is clothed with fine hairs, these beetles retain a film of air when submerged. Clinging to logs and stones, they creep about in the swift currents, but frequently they emerge from the water to sun themselves on stones.

The adults of the two common genera may be easily distinguished. In *Psephenus* the antennae are distant and inserted at the sides of the frons; the tarsal claws are large and simple; the prosternum is prolonged behind into an acute projection which fits into a narrow groove on the mesosternum; there are six or seven sternites; the color is black; and the length ranges from 3.5 to 6.0 mm. In *Eubrianax edwardsi* the antennae are situated close together on the narrow frons; the tarsal claws have a slender, membranous, basal appendage nearly as long as the claw; the prosternum has no posterior process; there are five sternites; color ranges from orange to black; and the usual length is 3.5 to 5.0 mm.

The eggs, usually deposited on the undersides of stones, hatch into a distinctive type of beetle larva. Because of their curious shape and color, they are often called "water pennies." The body is broadly oval, extremely flattened, limpetlike or scalelike, and a distinct coppery color. The dorsal surface is relatively smooth, but the segments are well defined. The whole body acts in a suckerlike fashion, the larvae adhering very tightly to rocks and pebbles, where they feed on the attached algae. Because of the widely flaring margins, the mouthparts and legs are hidden and may be seen only in ventral view. There are five pairs of ventral, finely branched, white tracheal gills in *Psephenus* and four pairs of tufts in *Eubrianax,* which originate between the abdominal segments. The first thoracic tergite in *Psephenus* is triangular, and the eighth abdominal segment has no lateral expansions; in *Eubrianax* the first thoracic tergite is quadrangular, and the eighth abdominal segment has lateral expansions. *Psephenus* is about 7 mm long.

Pupation occurs beneath the last larval integument. The larvae of *Psephenus herricki* leave the water and pupate under stones and debris in damp places beside streams and lakes. The entire life cycle of this species takes about two years. Only the larvae winter over. *Eubrianax edwardsi* pupates in the water, a rarity among aquatic insects.

## KEY TO GENERA OF ADULT PSEPHENIDAE

1. Posterior margin of prothorax simple ........................................... 2
   Posterior margin of prothorax irregular ....................................... 3
2. Pronotum extending over and concealing the head; 3.5 to 5.0 mm long.
                                                              **Eubrianax edwardsi** (LeC.)
   Pronotum not concealing the head (Fig. 444A); 3.5 to 6.0 mm long ........ **Psephenus**
3. Antennae simple; seldom enters water; usually in streamside vegetation.
                                                              **Ectopria nervosa** (Mels.)
   Antennae of male fanlike ............................................. **Acneus**

## KEY TO GENERA OF PSEPHENIDAE LARVAE

1. With four or five pairs of ventral filamentous gills (Fig. 444C) .................... 2
   Without ventral gills ....................................................... 3
2. First thoracic tergite triangular (Fig. 444B) ............................ **Psephenus**
   First thoracic tergite quadrangular (Fig. 444D) ................. **Eubrianax edwardsi**
3. Posterior end with a small emargination ................................. **Acneus**
   Posterior end without an emargination ................................. **Ectopria**

## DRYOPIDAE

This is a small family of aquatic beetles, there being less than 15 species in the United States. These are grouped into four genera of which *Helichus* is the largest. In their general habits and morphology they are very similar to the Elmidae. They range

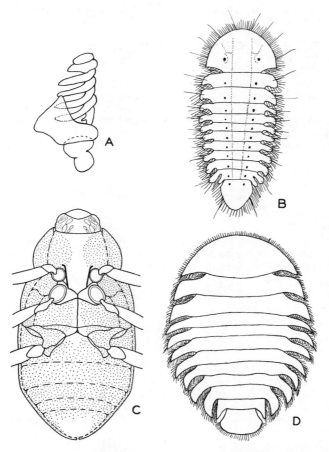

Fig. 445.–Dryopidae. A, antenna of adult *Dryops*; B, larva of *Pelonomus,* ×12; C, ventral view of adult *Helichus,* showing plastron (shaded area), ×5; D, larva of *Helichus,* ×11. (A and D modified from Hinton, 1939; C from Harpster.)

from 2 to 8 mm in length, and the body is covered with a hydrofuge pubescence. In *Dryops, Helichus,* and *Pelonomus* the antennae form a close pectinate club beyond the second or third segment (Fig. 445A), but in *Lutrochus* the antennae are filiform or with the apical segments thickened but never pectinate. *Lutrochus* is sometimes placed in the Family Limnichidae, which also includes several semiaquatic genera. Dryopids cannot swim and the claws are long and adapted for holding on to the substrate. Most species can retract the head into the thorax so that much of the head structure is hidden. A film of air (plastron) covers most of the body; the air–water interface acts as a diffusion membrane. Harpster (1941) has given a complete account of respiration in *Helichus striatus* LeC., including the method of replacement of the ventral plastron at the surface of the stream. Many of the Dryopidae leave the stream and fly about, especially at night. *Helichus* and *Lutrochus* are widely distributed, but the other genera are confined to the south and southwest. Dryopids feed on the algal film of the stream substrate.

## KEY TO GENERA OF ADULT DRYOPIDAE

1. Antennae forming a close pectinate club beyond the second or third segment (Fig. 445A) . . . . . . . . . . . . . . . . . . . . . . . . . . . . . . . . . . . . . . . . . . . . . . . . . . . . . . . . . . .2
   Antennae filiform or with the apical segments thickened but never pectinate. **Lutrochus**
2. Second segment of antennae produced into an earlike process (Fig. 445A) . . . . . . . . .3
   Second segment of antennae not thus produced; seldom enters water.
   **Pelonomus obscurus** LeC.
3. Antennae approximate; thorax with a deeply cut, sharp-edged, longitudinal line on each side; southwestern . . . . . . . . . . . . . . . . . . . . . . . . . . . **Dryops arizonensis** Schaeffer
   Antennae widely separated; thorax otherwise; widely distributed; about 10 species.
   **Helichus**

Unfortunately, little is known about the larval stages, and we are unable to separate certain genera and species on the basis of consistent features. All larvae known from the United States are aquatic, however. Superficially, they are similar to elmid larvae, being cylindrical to onisciform; *Helichus* is so highly modified that it is sometimes mistaken for a psephenid larva (Fig. 445D). It may be distinguished from a water penny by the fact that it has deep lateral notches between the segments. Like the Elmidae, the Dryopidae have a posterior ventral operculum. Anal gills are present in all but *Dryops* and some species of *Helichus*.

## KEY TO GENERA OF MATURE DRYOPIDAE LARVAE

1. Onisciform and flattened (Figs. 445B, D) . . . . . . . . . . . . . . . . . . . . **Pelonomus, Helichus**
   Cylindrical . . . . . . . . . . . . . . . . . . . . . . . . . . . . . . . . . . . . . . . . . . . . . . . . . . . . . . . . . . . . . . .2
2. Stipes and cardo of maxilla completely fused to postmental part of labium; anal gills present . . . . . . . . . . . . . . . . . . . . . . . . . . . . . . . . . . . . . . . . . . . . . . . . . . . . . . . . .**Lutrochus**
   Stipes and cardo of maxilla separate and not fused to postmental part of labium; anal gills absent . . . . . . . . . . . . . . . . . . . . . . . . . . . . . . . . . . . . . . . . . . . . . . . . . . . . . . . **Dryops**

## ELMIDAE (RIFFLE BEETLES)

Of the three closely related families, Elmidae, Psephenidae, and Dryopidae, the Elmidae is by far the largest in number of species. In their general morphology, elmids are rather constant. Few species are more than 3.5 mm long. The color is commonly an inconspicuous blackish; the head is usually partly retractile; and the antennae are filiform except in a few forms where the apical segments form a club. They do not swim but crawl about slowly, clinging to the substrate with their long tarsal claws. Although these beetles are most characteristic of running waters, some species occur in other types of habitats; *Ancyronyx* and *Macronychus,* for example, may be found in ponds or swamps, and a few forms occur in hot springs. Some species may leave the water temporarily at night, but only *Lara* and *Phanocerus* are not true aquatic forms. These two genera occur along the edges of streams; they enter the water only accidentally or when ovipositing. All Elmidae are thought to feed on algae and debris.

During submergence a film of air covers much of the body, and this film is in direct contact with the spiracles. These beetles seldom come to the surface of the water for a renewal of the air supply, but bubbles of air (or oxygen) that are released from submerged aquatic plants may come in contact with the body and fuse with the film of air. There is a strong possibility that bubbles of air being carried along in rapid streams may contribute to the oxygen supply in the same manner. However, some

FIG. 446.–*Limnius*, a typical elmid beetle. (From Holland, 1972.)

species are known to remain permanently submerged in habitats where bubbles of air from any source are negligible, and in such cases some other mechanism must be postulated.

Most Elmidae can be taken near streams at night with light traps. Otherwise the adults and larvae may be picked off rocks and logs, or they may be taken in nets held next to the bottom just below areas where trash or the gravel substrate can be agitated with the hand or foot.

Largely as the result of Hinton's work, it has been found that many species in the United States that had long masqueraded under the genus *Elmis* (=*Helmis*) really belong in other genera. It is now thought that *Elmis* is European and is not represented in America. *Stenelmis* is the only large genus in this country, being represented by about 30 species; a few genera, such as *Phanocerus*, *Ancyronyx*, and *Macronychus*, are monospecific. Most of the 22 genera are confined to the west, southwest, and south. *Stenelmis*, *Macronychus*, *Limnius*, *Promoresia*, *Gonielmis*, and *Ancyronyx*, however, are characteristically eastern and midwestern.

## KEY TO GENERA OF ADULT ELMIDAE*

1. Antennae short, clubbed, and 11-segmented (Fig. 447B); body covered with dense hairs dorsally; found above or just below the water line; 2.5 to 3.5 mm long; Texas . . . . . . . . . . . . . . . . . . . . . . . . . . . . . . . . . . . . . . . . . . . . . . . . . . . . . . . . . . . . . . . **Phanocerus clavicornis** Sharp
   Antennae 7- to 11-segmented, but clubbed only if there are seven or eight segments (Fig. 447A) . . . . . . . . . . . . . . . . . . . . . . . . . . . . . . . . . . . . . . . . . . . . . . . . . . . . . . . . . . . .2
2. Body 5 to 8 mm long; along western streams; three species; usually at water's edge . . . . . . . . . . . . . . . . . . . . . . . . . . . . . . . . . . . . . . . . . . . . . . . . . . . . . . . . . . . . . . . . . **Lara**
   Body less than 4 mm long . . . . . . . . . . . . . . . . . . . . . . . . . . . . . . . . . . . . . . . . . . . . . . . . .3
3. Tarsal claw with a minute basal tooth (Fig. 448A); eastern half of the United States . . . . . . . . . . . . . . . . . . . . . . . . . . . . . . . . . . . . . . . .**Ancyronyx variegata** (Germar)
   Tarsal claw without such a tooth . . . . . . . . . . . . . . . . . . . . . . . . . . . . . . . . . . . . . . . . . . . .4
4. First tibia without tomentum . . . . . . . . . . . . . . . . . . . . . . . . . . . . . . . . . . . . . . . . . . . . . .5
   First tibia with tomentum (Fig. 448B) . . . . . . . . . . . . . . . . . . . . . . . . . . . . . . . . . . . . . . . .6
5. Second elytral stria incomplete (Fig. 448C); antenna 11-segmented; rare; Washington, Oregon, and California. . . . . . . . . . . . . . . . . . . . . . . . **Ordobrevia nubifera** (Fall)
   Second elytral stria complete (Fig. 447G); about 30 species, widely distributed and very common . . . . . . . . . . . . . . . . . . . . . . . . . . . . . . . . . . . . . . . . . . . . . . . . . . . **Stenelmis**
6. With a lobe on the lateral margins of the last abdominal sternite (Fig. 448D) . . . . . . .7
   Without such a lobe . . . . . . . . . . . . . . . . . . . . . . . . . . . . . . . . . . . . . . . . . . . . . . . . . . . .13
7. Second elytral stria very short (Fig. 447F); southwestern states . . . . . . . . . . **Elsianus**
   Second elytral stria reaching posterior end of elytron . . . . . . . . . . . . . . . . . . . . . . . . .8
8. Mandible with a small lateral lobe (Fig. 448E) . . . . . . . . . . . . . . . . . . . . . . . . . . . . . .9
   Mandible without such a lobe . . . . . . . . . . . . . . . . . . . . . . . . . . . . . . . . . . . . . . . . . . . .10

*Modified from Sanderson, 1953, 1954.

FIG. 447.–Structure of adult Elmidae. A, antenna of *Zaitzevia parvula*; B, antenna of *Phanocerus clavicornis*; C, prosternum of *Ancyronyx*; D, anterior end of *Neoelmis*; E, anterior end of *Hexacylloepus*; F, *Elsianus*, ×11; G, *Stenelmis*, ×10; H, *Phanocerus clavicornis*, ×10. (A and C modified from Hinton, 1939; B and F modified from Hinton, 1940; G from Sanderson.)

9. Pronotum transversely depressed at about midlength; southwestern, uncommon.
   **Heterelmis**
   Pronotum transversely depressed before midlength; about 12 species; generally distributed ............................................... **Microcylloepus**
10. Pronotum conspicuously and transversely depressed slightly before midlength (Fig. 447D)....................................................................**11**
   Pronotum not conspicuously and transversely depressed ......................**12**
11. Brown to black; 2.6 to 3.3 mm long; Arizona and Texas; rare.
   **Neocylloepus boeseli** Brown
   Reddish-brown; 1.5 to 1.7 mm long; Texas, Oklahoma, and New Mexico.
   **Neoelmis caesa** (LeC.)
12. With a complete transverse belt of dense pubescence on the turned-under edge of the pronotum; rare, southwestern hard-water streams.
   **Hexacylloepus ferrugineus** (Horn)
   With an incomplete transverse belt of dense pubescence on the turned-under edge of the pronotum; rare, southwestern. ................ **Cylloepus abnormis** Horn
13. Antennae seven- or eight-segmented ........................................**14**
   Antennae 10- or 11-segmented ..............................................**15**
14. Antennae seven-segmented; 2.5 to 3.5 mm long; eastern half of the United States.
   **Macronychus glabratus** Say
   Antennae eight-segmented; 2 mm long; western states. ..... **Zaitzevia parvula** (Horn)
15. Antennae 10-segmented; uncommon; western states ................ **Heterlimnius**
   Antennae 11-segmented (Fig. 446) .........................................**16**
16. Maxillary palp three-segmented ...........................................**17**
   Maxillary palp four-segmented .............................................**22**
17. Total length about 1 mm; rare; Appalachian region ..................... **Limnius**
   Total length 1.5 mm or more ...............................................**18**
18. Pronotum without carinae or swollen areas; western states............... **Narpus**
   Pronotum with carinae or swollen areas (Figs. 448F–J) ......................**19**
19. Prosternum projecting beneath head; 2.5 to 2.6 mm long; California mountain streams; rare ......................................... **Rhizelmis nigra** Chandler
   Prosternum not projecting beneath head; 1.7 to 2.3 mm long ...................**20**

FIG. 448.–Structure of adult Elmidae. A, tarsal claw of *Ancyronyx*; B, first tibia of *Elsianus*; C, elytron of *Ordobrevia*; D, last abdominal sternite of *Elsianus*; E, mandible of *Heterelmis*; F, pronotum of *Ampumixis*; G, pronotum of *Cleptelmis*; H, pronotum of *Cleptelmis*; J, pronotum of *Atractelmis*; K, pronotum of *Ampumixis*; L, prosternum of *Dubiraphia*; M, prosternum of *Gonielmis*; N, prothorax of *Optioservus*. (A–G, L, and M redrawn from Sanderson, 1953.)

20. Pronotal carinae forked at base (Figs. 448G, H); western states; rare .... **Cleptelmis**
    Pronotal carinae not forked ............................................... **21**
21. Sides of pronotum converging slightly from base (Fig. 448J); western states; rare.
                                                          **Atractelmis wawona** Chandler
    Sides of pronotum parallel or slightly divergent from base (Fig. 448K); Washington,
       Oregon, and California .......................... **Ampumixis dispar** Fall
22. Pronotum without basal carinae .......................................... **23**
    Pronotum with two sublateral carinae in basal one-quarter to one-half ........... **25**
23. Prosternum with a faint oblique carina on each side (Fig. 448L); widely distributed
       but rare .............................................. **Dubiraphia**
    Prosternum without such carinae (Fig. 448M) .............................. **24**
24. Pronotum with sublateral carinae extending from anterior to posterior margins; 1.2 to
       1.6 mm long; clear streams in eastern states .... **Oulimnius latiusculus** (LeC.)
    Pronotum with short carinae, or carinae absent; more than 1.6 mm long; eastern and
       southeastern states; rare .................... **Gonielmis dietrichi** (Musgrave)
25. Lateral margins of prothorax finely serrate (Fig. 448N); widely distributed but uncom-
       mon; about 14 species ..................................... **Optioservus**
    Margins of prothorax smooth; eastern and southeastern states; uncommon. **Promoresia**

Relatively little is known about the larval stages of the Elmidae. They are all aquatic, however, and occur in the same specific habitats as the adults. They are correspondingly small, and their shape ranges from parallel-sided and cylindrical to onisciform. Among aquatic beetles as a whole, elmid larvae are especially notable for their complicated setation, sculpturing, and cuticular ornamentation. Some of these finest details are shown in Figure 449. Al-though much of the oxygen–carbon dioxide exchange probably occurs through the general body surface, there are three tufts of retractile anal gills. When withdrawn, these gills lie in a small cavity that is covered by an operculum (Fig. 450A). The larvae are all vegetarians. In the following key there are no comments about geographic distribution and habitat. These may be found in the key to the adults.

FIG. 449.–Structure of mature larva of *Zaitzevia parvula*. Except in K, all surface sculpturing and plates are omitted. Complete setation is shown in B to G and K. A, lateral view showing caudal respiratory filaments completely retracted; B, dorsal view of head; C, ventral view of head; D, ventral view of labium and maxillae; E, mandibles; F, antenna; G, foreleg; H, dorsal view of posterior end showing partially protruded caudal respiratory filaments and opercular claws; J, ventral view of posterior end showing operculum, fully protruded caudal respiratory filaments, and opercular claws; K, detail of a small portion of body surface from anterior to posterior margin of third abdominal segment near middorsal line. (From Pennak, 1953.)

# KEY TO GENERA OF ELMIDAE LARVAE*

1. Abdomen with pleura on first eight segments...............................2
   Abdomen with pleura on first six or seven segments ......................7
2. Body depressed and expanded (Fig. 450C) .............................3
   Body not depressed .......................................................4
3. With abundant large, scalelike spines along lateral margins ................ **Lara**
   Without marginal spines .........................................**Phanocerus**
4. Length of last abdominal segment more than four times the width ......**Dubiraphia**
   Length of last abdominal segment less than four times the width ...............5
5. Anterior margin of head without a prominent tooth on each side ........... **Narpus**
   Anterior margin of head with a prominent tooth on each side (Fig. 450D) ........6
6. Body cylindrical; more than 6.5 mm long ........................... **Cylloepus**
   Body hemicylindrical; less than 6.5 mm long ....................... **Rhizelmis**
7. Sternum of prothorax extending posteriorly (Fig. 450E) ....................8
   Sternum of prothorax not extending posteriorly .........................16
8. Posterior angles of first eight abdominal segments with projecting processes (Fig.
   450F) ............................................................ **Ancyronyx**
   Without such processes....................................................9
9. First eight abdominal segments with dorsal rows of blunt tuberculous spines (Fig.
   450G) .......................................................... **Heterelmis**
   Without such spines ....................................................10

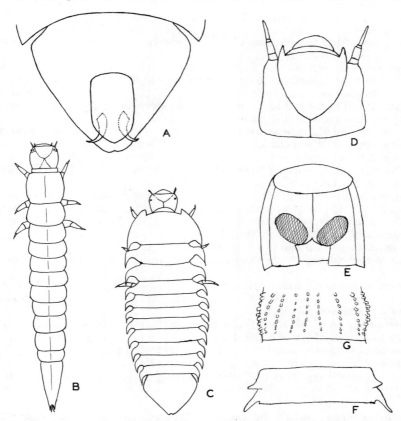

Fig. 450.–Structure of larval Elmidae. A, ventral view of posterior end of *Phanocerus clavicornis,* showing operculum; B, *Stenelmis,* ×18; C, *Phanocerus clavicornis,* ×15; D, anterior end of *Stenelmis;* E, prosternum of *Stenelmis;* F, abdominal segment of *Ancyronyx;* G first abdominal tergite of *Heterelmis.* (D to F modified from Sanderson, 1954.)

*Modified from Brown (1972).

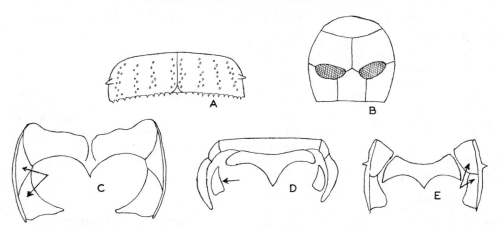

FIG. 451.–Structure of larval Elmidae. A, first abdominal tergite of *Microcylloepus*; B, prosternum of *Elsianus*; C, prosternum and pleurites of *Macronychus*; D, mesosternum of *Optioservus*, showing undivided mesopleuron; E, mesosternum of *Macronychus*, showing divided mesopleuron. (All modified from Sanderson, 1954.)

10. Anterolateral angles of head with triangular processes (Fig. 450D) ...............**13**
    Such processes absent ......................................................**11**
11. With rows of flat tubercles on the dorsal surface of the abdominal segments (Fig. 451A) ...........................................................................**12**
    Tubercles inconspicuous, not arranged in rows ........................**Neoelmis**
12. Last abdominal segment three times longer than wide ..............**Hexacylloepus**
    Last abdominal segment shorter ...............................**Microcylloepus**
13. Tergite of last abdominal segment with three longitudinal ridges ....... **Neocylloepus**
    Tergite of last abdominal segment without ridges. ...........................**14**
14. Second segment of antenna more than twice the length of the first segment. **Ordobrevia**
    Second segment of antenna less than twice the length of the first segment .......**15**
15. Suture from precoxal cavity to lateral margin distinct (Fig. 451B) ......... **Elsianus**
    Suture from precoxal cavity to lateral margin faint or absent (Fig. 450E) .. **Stenelmis**
16. Postpleurite not divided.....................................................**17**
    Postpleurite divided (Fig. 451C) .........................................**18**
17. Body broad, subtriangular in cross section ...........................**Ampumixis**
    Body slender, hemicylindrical ...........................................**Cleptelmis**
18. Mesopleuron small and single (Fig. 451D).................................**19**
    Mesopleuron divided into two (Fig. 451E) .................................**20**
19. Each abdominal segment with one dorsal median boss and two sublateral bosses. **Promoresia**
    Abdominal segments without such bosses...........................**Optioservus**
20. With six abdominal pleura ...................................**Macronychus**
    With seven abdominal pleura .............................................**21**
21. Posterior margin of last abdominal segment emarginate (Fig. 449) ........**Zaitzevia**
    Posterior margin of last abdominal segment without an emargination.............**22**
22. Abdominal segments each with a prominent middorsal hump. ............**Gonielmis**
    Middorsal humps absent .................................................**23**
23. Western distribution; body 4 to 5 mm long.........................**Heterlimnius**
    Eastern distribution; body less than 3.5 mm long .....................**Oulimnius**

Mature larvae crawl out of the water and pupate under loose bark, rocks, and debris near the water's edge. The pupae are small (Fig. 452), are rarely found by the general collector, and are very poorly known. All species appear to have two or more respiratory filaments on the prothorax. Bertrand (1972) has a key to the pupae of some of the common genera. Newly emerged adults fly at night and are often attracted to lights. Indeed, light traps and black light are the most successful collecting techniques for many species. Once the adults enter water, they begin accumulating a surface growth of algae, protozoans, and detritus.

## HELODIDAE

All the adults in this family are terrestrial. They are less than 6 mm long, oval or elongated, and have filiform 11-segmented antennae. The body is covered with a deciduous pubescence and is sometimes spotted. The adults occur on emergent vegetation or on the herbage along shores. There are about 40 species in the United States, including the following genera: *Cyphon, Elodes, Scirtes, Ora, Prionocyphon,* and *Microcara*.

Unfortunately, little is known of the larval stages, all of which are presumed to be aquatic. The following remarks, therefore, are subject to change when more information has been gathered on the American species. There are, however, two features by which these larvae can be distinguished from most other aquatic Coleoptera larvae. First, they have very long filiform antennae; second, they have terminal tufts of "blood gills" that can be withdrawn into a pocket. One investigator has shown that the blood gills are primarily osmoregulatory and have little to do with respiration. The body is broad and somewhat flattened. There are two spiracles at the posterior end above the blood gills and these are brought into contact with the air at intervals. Some species are said to retain an air bubble at the tip of the abdomen when submerged, and, since they are

FIG. 452.–Pupa of *Stenelmis*. (From Holland, 1972.)

lighter than water, they cling to submerged objects. Most species are found on floating or submerged vegetation in ponds, but some move through the water with awkward wriggling movements. *Helodes* may be found on the undersides of stones in swift streams. All helodid larvae are vegetarians. Pupation occurs on shore in damp soil.

## KEY TO COMMON GENERA OF HELODIDAE LARVAE*

1. Head with two anterolateral projections on each side (Fig. 453D) . . . . . . . . . . . . **Helodes**
   Head without two such projections on each side . . . . . . . . . . . . . . . . . . . . . . . . . . . . . . . .2
2. Abdominal segments three to six densely pilose, and with marginal spines . . . . **Scirtes**
   Abdominal segments not especially pilose or spinous . . . . . . . . . . . . . . . . . . . . . . . . . . .3
3. Eighth abdominal segment rounded (Figs. 453C, E) . . . . . . . . . . . . . . . . . . . **Prionocyphon**
   Eighth abdominal segment not so rounded (Fig. 453F) . . . . . . . . . . . . . . . . . . . . . . . . . .4
4. Last segment of maxillary palp short (Fig. 453G) . . . . . . . . . . . . . . . . . . . . . . . . **Cyphon**
   Last segment of maxillary palp longer (Fig. 453H) . . . . . . . . . . . . . . . . . . . . . . .**Microcara**

* Greatly modified from Bertrand, 1972.

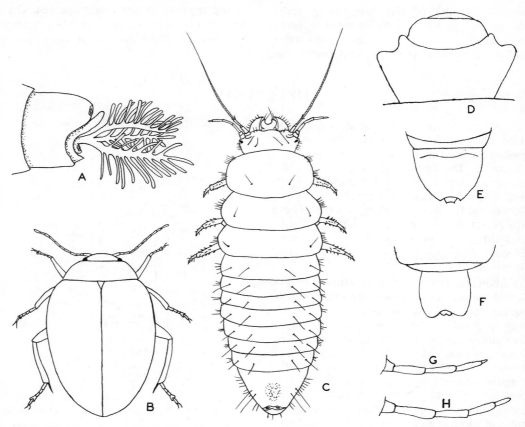

FIG. 453.–Structure of Helodidae. A, posterior end of *Prionocyphon* larva, showing extruded blood gills, anus, and left spiracle; B, *Scirtes* adult, ×15; C, *Prionocyphon* larva, ×16; D, Head of *Helodes* larva; E, last body segment of *Prionocyphon* larva; F, last body segment of *Cyphon*; G, maxillary palp of *Cyphon*; H, maxillary palp of *Microcara*. (A and C redrawn from Böving and Craighead.)

## CHRYSOMELIDAE (LEAF BEETLES)

In this large family of leaf beetles there are no true aquatic adults and only a few semiaquatic species. They occur above the surface of the water, where they walk and fly about among the marginal, floating, and emergent vegetation of ponds and lakes. In this country there are six such genera, all of which are widely distributed. The species of *Donacia* are elongated, have slender antennae, and are of a metallic blue, green, purple, or bronze color; they are about 6 to 13 mm long. *Neohaemonia nigricornis* re-sembles *Donacia* in form; the thorax, elytra, and legs are brownish-yellow, whereas the head and undersurfaces are black; length ranges from 5.5 to 8 mm. *Galerucella,* on the other hand is more oval, brownish or reddish, and only 4 to 6 mm long. The adults feed on a great variety of aquatic plants, but the floating leaves of the yellow pond lily form one of the principal foods. The biology and habits of *Plateumaris, Prasocuris,* and *Hydrothassa* are poorly known.

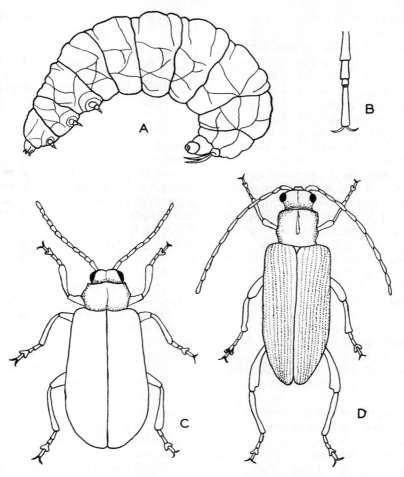

FIG. 454.–Structure of Chrysomelidae. A, larva of *Donacia*, ×6; B, tarsus of *Neohaemonia*; C, *Galerucella* adult, ×10; D, *Donacia* adult, ×6. (A redrawn from Böving and Craighead.)

## KEY TO COMMON GENERA OF ADULT CHRYSOMELIDAE

1. Head not constricted behind the eyes, inserted into the prothorax to the eyes (Fig. 454C) ...................................................................2
   Head necklike, not inserted into the prothorax (Fig. 454D) .....................4
2. Antennae inserted more closely than the length of the first antennal segment.
                                                    **Galerucella nymphaeae** (L.)
   Antennae inserted farther apart than the length of the first antennal segment; poorly known species ..................................................3
3. Basal margin of pronotum with a row of fine beadlike projections; one species in northeastern states ..................................... **Prasocuris**
   Basal margin of pronotum smooth; uncommon ......................**Hydrothassa**
4. Elytra with a stout spine at the outer apical angle; tarsi as in Fig. 454B; common and widely distributed. .........................................**Neohaemonia**
   Without an elytral spine ...........................................................5
5. Sutural margin of elytra sinuate near apex; about 18 species ........... **Plateumaris**
   Sutural margin of elytra straight; about 33 species .......................**Donacia**

The females of *Donacia* and *Haemonia* deposit the eggs in a variety of places. Some species eat holes in the floating leaves of the pond lily and deposit them on the undersurface near the edge of the opening. Others lay their eggs on the submerged surfaces of a great variety of other aquatic plants. A few species deposit the eggs on emergent portions of plants or in the plant tissues below the epidermis. When the eggs hatch the larvae drop to the bottom, where they feed on roots and rhizomes of aquatic plants. The larvae are 8 to 16 mm long, stout, grublike, and white or yellowish in color. The head is minute and almost hidden by the first thoracic segment. The abdomen is 10-segmented with the last three segments usually minute and curved beneath the sixth and seventh. There are nine pairs of spiracles, of which only the last pair are probably functional. These are situated on the base of two stout spines that are located on the dorsal side of the eighth abdominal segment. By pushing these caudal spines into the tissues of the underground portions of plants, the larvae obtain access to the extensive internal air spaces, and by this ingenious method they obtain a continuous supply of oxygen through the posterior spiracles even though they may be in mud under a meter of water. Recently it has been shown that some species that spend a portion of the larval stage surrounded by water rather than mud or sand are capable of obtaining a sufficient quantity of oxygen through the general integument.

The larvae are sluggish and usually while they are feeding the body is bent into a U shape with both the head and posterior end imbedded in the plant tissues (Fig. 454A).

Just before pupation the larva spins a cocoon that is watertight and airtight and is firmly glued to the surface of the plant. Air enters the cocoon from the plant tissues through holes or slits cut through the cocoon and epidermis of the plant where these two are in close contact. The cocoon is completely filled with air, and the adult that breaks out is carried to the surface by the film of air that adheres to the ventral side of the body.

The habits of the immature stages of *Galerucella* differ markedly from those of the two genera described previously. The adult females of *G. nymphaeae,* the only important semiaquatic species, deposit clusters of eggs on the upper surface of yellow pond lily pads. The larvae are about 7 mm long when mature and black with fine whitish lines and spots. They remain on the upper surface of the pads, feeding on the tissues. The pupae are also found on the upper surface of the pads; they are naked, black, and about as long as mature larvae. The pupal stage persists only a few days or weeks.

## KEY TO COMMON GENERA OF CHRYSOMELIDAE LARVAE

1. Dorsal surface of eighth abdominal segment with a pair of prominent pointed spines; abdominal prolegs absent (Fig. 454A); feeding on submerged portions of aquatic plants . . . . . . . . . . . . . . . . . . . . . . . . . . . . . . . . . . . . . . . . . . . . . . . . . . . . . . . . . . . . . . . .2
   No pointed spines on dorsal surface of eighth abdominal segment; abdominal prolegs present; feeding on upper surface of leaves of water lilies and other aquatic plants . . . . . . . . . . . . . . . . . . . . . . . . . . . . . . . . . . . . . . . . . . . . . . . . . . . . .**Galerucella**
2. White or cream-colored; legs small or moderate sized . . . . . . . . . . . . . . . . . . . . .**Donacia**
   Green; legs large; usually on *Potamogeton natans* . . .**Neohaemonia nigricornis** (Kirby)

## CURCULIONIDAE (WEEVILS)

Weevils may be easily identified by the fact that the head is prolonged into a snout with the mouth parts at the tip and the antennae somewhere along its length. This is probably the largest family of insects, but only a relatively few species have developed an incidental semiaquatic habit, and their biology is comparatively unknown.

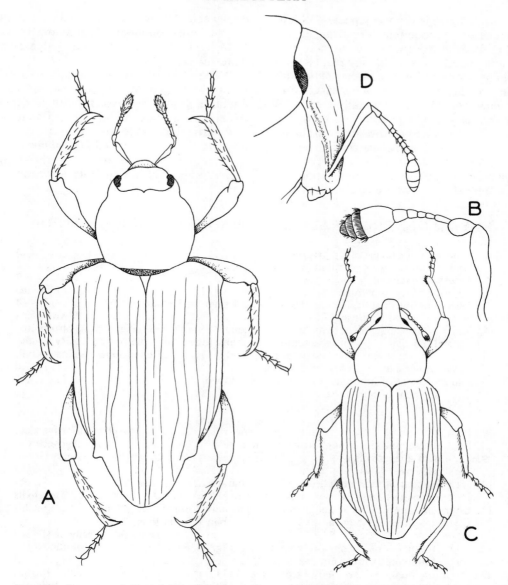

FIG. 455.–Structure of Curculionidae. A, *Bagous,* ×22; B, antenna of *Lissorhoptrus simplex*; C, adult *L. simplex,* ×20; D, anterior end of *Listronotus* showing beak, antenna, and part of compound eye and pronotum. (B and C modified from Tucker.)

About 100 species are associated with a great variety of aquatic plants. The adults may usually be found feeding on the emergent tissues or in low herbage or debris on the nearby shore. Most of these weevils are a dirty brownish color and less than 5 mm long. Aside from a scaly, gummy, waterproof coat in some species, there is little adaptation for an aquatic existence, and although some may dive and swim under water by movements of the hind legs, much the greater portion of the time is spent out of the water. The egg, larval, and pupal stages usually occur on emergent vegetation or on shore.

*Lissorhoptrus simplex,* the rice water

weevil, is the best-known species, chiefly because of its economic importance. The larvae feed on the roots and the adults on the emergent leaves of the rice plant as well as many species of wild aquatics. The adult swims readily on or under the surface. *Phytobius velatus* (Beck), originally a native of Europe, is unusual in that the tarsi bear swimming hairs and all the stages in the life history are found below the surface on *Myriophyllum*, the water milfoil. *Tanysphyrus lemnae*, also a European importation, occurs almost everywhere on *Lemna*, the duckweed. Other plants on which aquatic weevils are commonly found are arrowhead, bulrush, pickerel weed, sedges, and water lilies.

The 100 American aquatic species comprise 14 genera. The largest and most common genus is *Bagous*, with about 30 American species. Other genera that are not particularly rare are *Endalus*, *Lissorhoptrus*, *Listronotus*, and *Phytobius*.

The larval stages are so poorly known that it is useless to construct a meaningful key.

## KEY TO GENERA OF ADULT SEMIAQUATIC CURCULIONIDAE

1. Beak free, not received by prosternum . . . . . . . . . . . . . . . . . . . . . . . . . . . . . . . . . . . . . . . . . . .3
   Beak received by prosternum in repose . . . . . . . . . . . . . . . . . . . . . . . . . . . . . . . . . . . . . .2
2. Anterior coxae contiguous . . . . . . . . . . . . . . . . . . . . . . . . . . . . . . . . . . . . . . . . . . . . . .5
   Anterior coxae separated . . . . . . . . . . . . . . . . . . . . . . . . . . . . . . . . . . . . . . . . . . . . . **Phytobius**
3. Third and fourth sternites together no longer than the second or fifth . . . . . . . . . . . .4
   Sternites not very unequal in size . . . . . . . . . . . . . . . . . . . . . . . . . . . . . . . . **Phytonomus**
4. Second flagellar segment of antenna much longer than the first (Fig. 455D). **Listronotus**
   Second flagellar segment of antenna little if any longer than the first . . . . . **Hyperodes**
5. Beak very short and broad, shorter than head . . . . . . . . . . **Stenopelmus rufinasus** Gyll.
   Beak cylindrical, much longer than head . . . . . . . . . . . . . . . . . . . . . . . . . . . . . . . . .6
6. Third segment of hind tarsi emarginate or bilobed . . . . . . . . . . . . . . . . . . . . . . . .7
   Third segment of hind tarsi simple . . . . . . . . . . . . . . . . . . . . . . . . . . . . . . . . . . . .12
7. Beak curved . . . . . . . . . . . . . . . . . . . . . . . . . . . . . . . . . . . . . . . . . . . . . . . . . . . . . . .9
   Beak straight . . . . . . . . . . . . . . . . . . . . . . . . . . . . . . . . . . . . . . . . . . . . . . . . . . . . . . .8
8. First and second tibiae serrate on inner side . . . . . . . . . . . . . . **Lixellus filiformis** Lec.
   First and second tibiae not serrate on inner side . . . . . . . . . . . . . . . . . . . . **Anchodemus**
9. Tarsi with a single claw . . . . . . . . . . . . . . . . . . . . . . . . . . . . . **Brachybamus electus** Germ.
   Tarsi with two claws . . . . . . . . . . . . . . . . . . . . . . . . . . . . . . . . . . . . . . . . . . . . . . . .10
10. Last segment of tarsi broad, claws well separated . . . . . . . . . . . . . . . . . . . . . . . . .11
    Last segment of tarsi narrow, projecting beyond lobes of the third . . . . . . . **Onychylis**
11. Elytra not appreciably wider than thorax; usually 2 mm or more long . . . . . . **Endalus**
    Elytra much wider than thorax; usually less than 1.5 mm long.
    **Tanysphyrus lemnae** (Fabr.)
12. Club of antenna partly smooth and shining (Fig. 455B). . **Lissorhoptrus simplex** (Say)
    Club of antenna entirely pubescent . . . . . . . . . . . . . . . . . . . . . . . . . . . . . . . . . . . .13
13. Pronotum feebly constricted in front (Fig. 455A) . . . . . . . . . . . . . . . . . . . . . **Bagous**
    Pronotum strongly constricted and tubulate in front . . . . . . . . . . . . . . . . . . . **Pnigodes**

## COLEOPTERA REFERENCES

ARNETT, R. H. 1960. *The beetles of the United States.* 1112 pp. Catholic University Press, Washington, D.C.

BALFOUR-BROWNE, F. 1940. *British Water Beetles. I.* 375 pp. London.

———. 1950. *British water beetles,* Vol. II. 394 pp. London.

BAYER, L. J., and H. J. BROCKMANN. 1975. Curculionidae and Chrysomelidae found in aquatic

habitats in Wisconsin. *The Great Lakes Entomol.* 8:219–226.

BEERBOWER, F. V. 1943. Life history of Scirtes orbiculatus Fabius. *Ann. Entomol. Soc. Am.* 36:672–680.

BERTRAND, H. P. I. 1955. Notes sur les premiers états des Dryopides d'Amérique. *Ann. Soc. Entomol. Fr.* 124:97–139.

———. 1972. *Larves et Nymphes des Coléoptères*

*Aquatiques du Globe.* 799 pp. Henri Bertrand, Paris.

BLACKWELDER, R. E. 1939. *Fourth supplement, 1933 to 1938 (inclusive), to the Leng catalogue of Coleoptera of America, north of Mexico.* 146 pp. Sherman, Mount Vernon, N.Y.

BÖVING, A. G. 1910. Natural history of larvae of the Donaciinae. *Int. Rev. Suppl.* **1**:1–108.

———. 1914. Notes on the larva of Hydroscapha and some other aquatic larvae from Arizona. *Proc. Ent. Soc. Wash.* **16**:169–174.

———. 1929. On the classification of beetles according to larval characters. *Bull. Brooklyn Entomol. Soc.* **24**:55–97.

BÖVING, A. G., and F. C. CRAIGHEAD. 1930–1931. An illustrated synopsis of the principal larval forms of the order Coleoptera. *Entomol. Am.* **11**:1–351.

BROWN, H. P. 1970. A key to the dryopoid genera of the New World (Coleoptera; Dryopoidea). *Entomol. News* **81**:171–175.

———. 1972. Aquatic dryopoid beetles (Coleoptera) of the United States. *Biota of Freshwater Ecosystems, Identification Manual* **6**:1–83.

BROWN, H. P., and R. ARRINGTON. 1967. A new species of Psephenus from Mexico and Texas (Coleoptera, Dryopoidea, Psephenidae). *Coleopt. Bull.* **21**:86–91.

BROWN, H. P., and C. M. MURVOSH. 1974. A revision of the genus Psephenus (water-penny beetles) of the United States and Canada (Coleoptera: Dryopoidea: Psephenidae). *Trans. Am. Entomol. Soc.* **100**:289–340.

CHANDLER, H. P. 1954. New genera and species of Elmidae (Coleoptera) from California. *Pan-Pac. Entomol.* **30**:125–131.

FALL, H. C. 1922. The North American species of Gyrinus. *Trans. Am. Entomol. Soc.* **47**:269–306.

———. 1923. *A revision of the North American species of Hydroporus and Agaporus.* 129 pp. Privately printed.

HARPSTER, H. T. 1941. An investigation of the gaseous plastron as a respiratory mechanism in Helichus striatus Leconte (Dryopidae). *Trans. Am. Entomol. Soc.* **60**:329–358.

HATCH, M. H. 1925. Phylogeny and phylogenetic tendencies of Gyrinidae. *Pap. Mich. Acad. Sci., Arts and Lett.* **5**:429–467.

———. 1927. The morphology of Gyrinidae. Ibid. **7**:311–350.

HICKMAN, J. R. 1930. Life-histories of Michigan Haliplidae (Coleoptera). *Pap. Mich. Acad. Sci., Arts and Lett.* **11**:399–424.

———. 1931. Respiration of the Haliplidae (Coleoptera). Ibid. **13**:277–289.

———. 1931a. Contribution to the biology of the Haliplidae (Coleoptera). *Ann. Entomol. Soc. Am.* **24**:129–142.

HINTON, H. E. 1935. Notes on the Dryopoidea, Col. *Stylops* **4**:169–179.

———. 1939. An inquiry into the natural classification of the Dryopoidea, based partly on a study of their internal anatomy (Col.). *Trans. Roy.Entomol. Soc. Lond.* **89**:133–184.

———. 1940. A synopsis of the genus Macronychus Muller (Coleoptera, Elmidae). *Proc. Roy. Entomol. Soc. Lond. (B)* **9**:113–119.

HOFFMAN, C. E. 1940. Morphology of the immature stages of some northern Michigan Donaciini (Chrysomelidae, Coleoptera). *Pap. Mich. Acad. Sci. Arts and Lett.* **25**:243–290.

———. 1940. The relation of Donacia larvae (Chrysomelidae; Coleoptera) to dissolved oxygen. *Ecology* **21**:176–183.

HOLLAND, D. G. 1972. A key to the larvae, pupae and adults of the British species of Elminthidae. *Sci. Publ. Freshwater Biol. Assoc.* **26**:1–58.

HOSSEINIE, S. O. 1976. Effects of the amount of food on duration of stages, mortality rates, and size of individuals in Tropisternus lateralis numbatus (Say) (Coleoptera: Hydrophilidae). *Int. Rev. ges. Hydrobiol.* **61**:383–388.

———. 1976a. Comparative life histories of three species of Tropisternus in the laboratory (Coleoptera: Hydrophilidae). Ibid. **62**:261–268.

HRBACEK, J. 1950. On the morphology and function of the antennae of the Central European Hydrophilidae (Coleoptera). *Trans. Roy. Entomol. Soc. Lond.* **101**:239–256.

HUBBARD, H. G. 1892. Description of the larva of Amphizoa lecontei. *Proc. Entomol. Soc. Wash.* **2**:341–346.

ISTOCK, C. A. 1966. Distribution, coexistence, and competition of whirligig beetles. *Evolution* **20**:211–234.

———. 1967. Transient competitive displacement in natural populations of whirligig beetles. *Ecology* **48**:929–937.

JACKSON, D. J. 1952. Observations on the capacity for flight of water beetles. *Proc. Roy. Entomol. Soc. Lond. (A)* **27**:57–70.

JAMES, H. G. 1969. Immature stages of five diving beetles (Coleoptera: Dytiscidae), notes on their habits and life history, and a key to aquatic beetles of vernal woodland pools in southern Ontario. *Proc. Entomol. Soc. Ont.* **100**:52–97.

LANDIN, J. 1976. Seasonal patterns in abundance of water-beetles belonging to the Hydrophiloidea (Coleoptera). *Freshwater Biol.* **6**:89–108.

LEECH, H. B. 1940. Description of a new species of Laccornis with a key to the Nearctic species (Coleoptera: Dytiscidae). *Can. Entomol.* **72**:122–128.

———. 1941. The species of Matus, a genus of carnivorous water beetles (Coleoptera: Dytiscidae). Ibid. **73**:76–83.

———. 1942. Key to the Nearctic genera of water beetles of the tribe Agabini, with some generic synonomy (Coleoptera: Dytiscidae). *Ann. Entomol. Soc. Am.* **35**:355–362.

———. 1948. Contributions toward a knowledge of the insect fauna of Lower California. No. 11. Coleoptera: Haliplidae, Dytiscidae, Gyrinidae, Hydrophilidae, Limnebiidae. *Proc. Calif. Acad. Sci.* **24**:375–484.

LENG, C. W. 1920. *Catalogue of the Coleoptera of America north of Mexico.* 470 pp. Sherman, Mount Vernon, N.Y.

LENG, C. W., and A. J. MUTCHLER. 1927. *Supplement 1919 to 1924 (inclusive) to the Catalogue of the Coleoptera of America North of Mexico.* 78 pp. Sherman, Mount Vernon, N.Y.

———. 1933. *Second and third supplements, 1925 to 1932 (inclusive), to Catalogue of Coleoptera of North America, North of Mexico.* 112 pp. Sherman, Mount Vernon, N.Y.

MATHIESON, R. 1912. The Haliplidae of North America, north of Mexico. *J. N.Y. Entomol. Soc.* **20**:156–193.

McGAHA, Y. J. 1954. Contribution to the biology of some curculionids which feed on aquatic flowering plants. *Trans. Am. Microsc. Soc.* **73**:277–282.

MILLER, D. C. 1974. Revision of the new world Chaetarthria (Coleoptera: Hydrophilidae). *Entomol. Am.* **49**:1–123.

MURVOSH, C. M. 1971. Ecology of the water penny beetle Psephenus herricki (DeKay). *Ecol. Monogr.* **41**:79–96.

MURVOSH, C. M., and B. W. MILLER. 1974. Life history of the western water penny beetle, Psephenus falli (Coleoptera: Psephenidae). *Coleopt. Bull.* **28**:85–92.

MUSGRAVE, P. N. 1935. Notes on collecting Dryopidae (Coleoptera). *Can. Ent.* **67**:61–63.

———. 1935. A synopsis of the genus Helichus Erichson in the United States and Canada, with description of a new species (Coleoptera: Dryopidae). *Proc. Entomol. Soc. Wash.* **37**:137–145.

NELSON, H. G. 1949. A method of cleaning insects for study. *Coleopt. Bull.* **6**:89–92.

PENNAK, R. W. 1953. The larva of Zaitzevia parvula (Horn) (Coleoptera: Elmidae). *Trans. Am. Microsc. Soc.* **72**:135–139.

RICHMOND, E. A. 1920. Studies on the biology of the aquatic Hydrophilidae. *Bull. Am. Mus. Nat. Hist.* **42**:1–94.

———. 1931. The external morphology of Hydrophilus obtusatus Say (Coleoptera: Hydrophilidae). *J. N.Y. Entomol. Soc.* **39**:191–250.

ROBERTS, C. H. 1913. Critical notes on the species of Haliplidae of America north of Mexico with descriptions of new species. Ibid. **21**:91–213.

RYKER, L. C. 1975. Observations on the life cycle and flight dispersal of a water beetle, Tropisternus ellipticus LeConte, in western Oregon. *Pan-Pac. Entomol.* **51**:184–194.

SANDERSON, M. W. 1938. A monographic revision of the North American species of Stenelmis. (Dryopidae: Coleoptera). *Kans. Univ. Sci. Bull.* **25**:635–717.

———. 1953, 1954. A revision of the Nearctic genera of Elmidae (Coleoptera). *J. Kans. Entomol. Soc.* **26**:148–163, **27**:1–13.

SCOTT, H. M. 1924. Observations on the habits and life history of Galerucella nymphaea (Coleoptera). *Trans. Am. Microsc. Soc.* **43**:11–16.

SEGAL, B. 1933. The hind wings of some Dryopidae in relation to habitat (Coleoptera). *Entomol. News* **44**:85–88.

SHARP, D. 1882. On aquatic carnivorous Coleoptera or Dytiscidae. *Sci. Trans. Roy. Dublin Soc.* **2**:179–1003.

SINCLAIR, R. M. 1964. *Water Quality Requirements of the Family Elmidae (Coleoptera), with Larval and Adult Keys to the Eastern Genera.* 15 pp. Tenn. Stream Pollution Control Board.

SPANGER, P. J. 1973. The bionomics, immature stages, and distribution of the rare predaceous water beetle, Hoperius planatus (Coleoptera: Dytiscidae). *Proc. Biol. Soc. Wash.* **86**:423–434.

SPANGLER, P. J., and G. W. FOLKERTS. 1973. The larva of Pachydrus princeps (Coleoptera: Dytiscidae). Ibid. 351–356.

———. 1973a. Reassignment of Colpius inflatus and a description of its larva (Coleop: Noteridae). Ibid. 501–510.

SPANGLER, P. J., and R. D. GORDON. 1973. Descriptions of the larvae of some predaceous water beetles (Coleoptera: Dytiscidae). Ibid. 261–278.

SUSSKIND, M. E. C. 1935. A morphological study of the respiratory system in various larval instars of Stenelmis sulcatus Blatchley (Dryopidae; Coleoptera). *Pap. Mich. Acad. Sci. Arts and Lett.* **21**:697–714.

TANNER, V. M. 1943. A study of the subtribe Hydronomi with a description of new species (Curculionidae). *Great Basin Nat.* **4**:1–38.

TREHERNE, J. E. 1954. Osmotic regulation in the larvae of Helodes (Coleoptera: Helodidae). *Trans. Roy. Entomol. Soc. Lond.* **105**:117–130.

TRIMBLE, C. A. 1935. The external morphology of Hydrous triangularis (Hydrophilidae; Coleoptera). *Ohio J. Sci.* **35**:440–450.

TUCKER, E. S. 1912. The rice water-weevil and methods for its control. *U.S. Dept. Agric. Circ. No.* **152**:1–20.

UENO, S. 1957. Blind aquatic beetles of Japan, with some accounts of the fauna of Japanese subterranean waters. *Arch. Hydrobiol.* **53**:250–296.

VAN DYKE, E. C. 1927. The species of Amphizoa (Coleoptera). *Pan-Pac. Entomol.* **3**:197–198.

WALLIS, J. B. 1933. Revision of the North American species (north of Mexico) of the genus Haliplus, Latreille. *Trans. Roy. Can. Inst.* **19**:1–76.

———. 1939. The genus Graphoderus Aubé in North America (north of Mexico) (Coleoptera). *Can. Entomol.* **71**:128–130.

———. 1939a The genus Ilybius Er. in North America (Coleoptera: Dytiscidae). Ibid. **71**:192–199.

WEST, L. S. 1929. Life history notes on Psephenus lecontei Lec. (Coleoptera: Dryopoidea; Psephenidae). *Battle Creek Coll. Bull.* **3**:3–20.

———. 1929a. A preliminary study of larval structure in the Dryopidae. *Ann. Entomol. Soc. Am.* **22**:691–727.

WILSON, C. B. 1923. Life history of the scavenger water-beetle, Hydrous (Hydrophilus) triangularis, and its economic importance to fish breeding. *Bull. U.S. Bur. Fish.* **39**:9–38.

———. 1923a. Water beetles in relation to pond-fish culture, with life histories of those found in fishponds at Fairport, Iowa. Ibid. **39**:231–345.

YOUNG, F. M. 1953. Two new species of Matus, with a key to the known species and subspecies of the genus (Coleoptera: Dytiscidae). *Ann. Entomol. Soc. Am.* **46:**49–55.

———. 1954. The water beetles of Florida. *Univ. Fla. Stud., Biol. Ser.* **5**(1):1–238.

———. 1963. Two new North American species of Hydrovatus, with notes on other species (Coleoptera: Dytiscidae). *Psyche* **70:**184–192.

———. 1967. A key to the genera of American bidessine water beetles, with descriptions of three new genera (Coleoptera: Dytiscidae, Hydroporinae). *Coleopt. Bull.* **21:**75–84.

———. 1969. A checklist of the American Bidessini (Coleop: Dytiscidae—Hydroporinae). *Smithson. Contrib. Zool.* **33:**1–5.

———. 1974. Review of the predaceous water beetles of the genus Anodocheilus (Coleoptera: Dytiscidae: Hydroporinae). *Occas. Pap. Mus. Zool. Univ. Mich.* **670:**1–28.

ZIMMERMAN, J. R. 1960. Seasonal population changes and habitat preferences in the genus Laccophilus (Coleoptera: Dytiscidae). *Ecology* **41:**141–152.

———. 1970. A taxonomic revision of the aquatic beetle genus Laccophilus (Dytiscidae) of North America. *Mem. Am. Entomol. Soc.* **26:**1–275.

ZIMMERMAN, J. R., and R. L. SMITH. 1975. The genus Rhantus (Coleoptera: Dytiscidae) in North America: Part I. General account of the species. *Trans. Am. Entomol. Soc.* **101:**33–123.

———. 1975a. A survey of the Deronectes (Coleoptera: Dytiscidae) of Canada, the United States, and Mexico. Ibid. 651–722.

# Chapter 35

# DIPTERA (FLIES, MOSQUITOES, MIDGES)

THE DIPTERA are highly specialized two-winged flies, including such common insects as the housefly, mosquitoes, crane flies, midges, horseflies, hover flies, and botflies. They all have complete metamorphosis, large compound eyes, and mouth parts that are adapted for lapping or piercing and sucking. The hind pair of wings (halteres) are vestigial, and the thoracic segments are somewhat fused. Many species are of great economic importance.

This is one of the largest orders of insects, there being about 100 families, 2000 genera, and 16,500 species known from North America north of Mexico. Probably less than 2000 species, however, have larval or pupal stages in the life history that are aquatic or subaquatic.

Although the adults are never aquatic, many families have members that have aquatic immature stages. Such larvae and pupae occur in every type of fresh-water habitat, sometimes in enormous numbers. Only a few families, however, such as the Culicidae and Simuliidae, are exclusively aquatic. The egg-laying habits of aquatic Diptera are diverse. The females of some species scatter their eggs just below the surface of the water on vegetation, debris, and rocks. Others oviposit in regular or irregular gelatinous masses or strings below the surface, at the surface, or on objects just above it.

Aquatic Diptera larvae show greater variability in structure and habitat than any other order of aquatic insects. Usually, however, they are distinguished by their elongated, wormlike body, and the absence of eyes and jointed thoracic legs. In the generalized condition there are 12 body segments, that is, three thoracic and nine abdominal, but in many families there is a smaller number owing to fusion or atrophy. The body is usually soft and flexible, and the most common colors are white, gray, yellow, reddish, brown, and black. The surface of the segments may be naked and smooth, or there may be bristles, spines, scales, or tubercles. The antennae are rarely prominent. In some families there are short, stumpy prolegs on some of the segments. In the black-fly larvae, for example, there is a single stout ventral proleg on the prothorax; at the other extreme, some of the shore fly larvae have a pair of prolegs on each of the last eight segments. Many larvae swim by rapid wriggling movements of the body. Creeping on the substrate is facilitated by prolegs, spines, suckers, and sticky secretions of salivary glands. The head and mouth parts may be well developed and complex (Nematocera), but in other larvae (Cyclorrapha) the head is vestigial and the mouthparts peculiarly modified, reduced, and relatively simple. In some families, such as the black flies and mosquitoes, the food consists of minute organisms and particles that are strained from the water by complex fans or mouth brushes composed of setae or bristles. In other families the mouth parts are modified for scraping periphyton from rocks, for feeding on aquatic plants, for predatory food habits, or simply for consuming heterogeneous plant and animal debris.

Because of the great diversity in structure and because many physiological details have not yet been established, it is difficult to characterize briefly the respiratory system of dipterous larvae. Like all other insects, however, they are fundamentally dependent on an internal airfilled tracheal system that branches and ramifies to all the tissues. The spiracles that open into the tracheal system are characteristically reduced in number, modified in their location, and may be absent. Such families as the crane flies and mosquitoes are metapneustic, only the last pair of spiracles being open. Atmospheric air is obtained by contact of these spiracles (usually on a disc or at the end of a special respiratory siphon) with the air at the surface film. The larvae of the moth flies and the flower flies are amphipneustic, and both the prothoracic and last abdominal spiracles are open. In the families where oxygen is derived entirely from the surrounding water, there are usually thin-walled tracheal gills or blood gills that may or may not be situated in areas otherwise occupied by spiracles. Recently, however, several investigators have presented evidence to indicate that blood gills are of little importance in respiration in some dipterous larvae. It is more likely that they are useful in the absorption of dissolved salts; the anal gills of mosquitoes, for example, are believed to be important in the absorption of chloride ions. There is also a growing tendency to attribute greater significance to the general body surface of larvae as a respiratory device. In apneustic forms particularly, such as black-fly and midge larvae, the skin is supplied with a rich network of fine tracheae. A few Diptera have a specialized sharp respiratory siphon for obtaining their oxygen supply from the tissues of submerged aquatic plants.

The larval stage may last for only several weeks or it may persist for at least two years, depending on the species, temperature, and food conditions. Characteristically, the skin is cast three times during growth.

In the Stratiomyidae (soldier flies) the exuviae persist and loosely enclose the pupae. In all other families of the Nematocera and Brachycera the skin is cast at pupation. In the Suborder Cyclorrapha the last larval skin hardens to form an immobile ovoid or barrel-shaped puparium enclosing the pupa.

The pupae of the Nematocera and Brachycera are all somewhat similar in structure. The appendages are free from the body yet more or less fused with each other and in most instances with the body surface.

The important external respiratory organs are found on the thorax and usually project anteriorly. They consist of tufts of fine filaments or a pair of respiratory tubes that range in length from very short tubercles to more than the length of the body. These respiratory structures may be either open or closed at the ends.

Although mosquito and midge pupae are capable of rapid wriggling movements, most other pupae are inactive. Some of the black-fly pupae live in loosely built cocoons. Mountain and net-winged midge pupae remain tightly fastened to the substrate by the flat ventral surface.

The pupal stage usually lasts less than two weeks, although a few types may winter over. The Nematocera and Brachycera imagoes emerge from the pupal case by means of a T-shaped dorsal split; the Cyclorrapha emerge by a caplike annular dehiscence at the anterior end.

Larvae and pupae can usually be killed and fixed in a satisfactory manner by flooding them with boiling water. Seventy-five to 85 percent alcohol or 4 percent formalin are suitable preservatives. Usually the detailed structure of the larval mouth parts and general integument can be more easily studied if the specimens are boiled for a minute or soaked for a day or two in cold 10 percent potassium hydroxide. Such specimens must be passed through dilute acetic acid and several changes of water. Small forms may be permanently mounted on slides in glycerin jelly, balsam, or some substitute. The following families having aquatic immature stages are included in sections of this chapter:

Suborder Nematocera
  Deuterophlebiidae (mountain midges)
  Blephariceridae (net-winged midges)
  Tipulidae (true crane flies)

Ptychopteridae (phantom crane flies)
Psychodidae (moth flies)
Dixidae (dixa midges)
Culicidae
  Culicinae (mosquitoes)
  Chaoborinae (phantom midges)
Simuliidae (blackflies)
Chironomidae (midges)
  Podonominae
  Tanypodinae
  Diamesinae
  Orthocladiinae
  Chironominae
Heleidae (biting midges)
Suborder Brachycera
  Stratiomyidae (soldier flies)
  Tabanidae (horseflies)
  Rhagionidae (snipe flies)

Suborder Cyclorrhapha
  Syrphidae (flower flies)
  Sciomyzidae (marsh flies)
  Ephydridae (shore flies)
  Anthomyiidae

In addition to these families, there are about a dozen other families containing a few rare species, most of which are semiaquatic and found in or on mud and wet moss or on wet stones. In the keys in this chapter all the common genera are included. Also, the great majority of forms are strictly aquatic, very few semiaquatic species being indicated. It should be borne in mind that only the last larval instars are included in the descriptions and keys. In many instances the keys will not apply to immature larvae.

## KEY TO FAMILIES OF DIPTERA LARVAE

1. Head capsule complete, differentiated, sclerotized, and free or retractile into the first thoracic segment ................................................................2
   Head vestigial, not differentiated, membranous, and often apparently lacking ............................... Suborder **CYCLORRHAPHA, 19**
2. Head well developed, with antennae; mandibles opposed to each other horizontally or inclined obliquely downward ............... Suborder **NEMATOCERA, 3**
   Head somewhat incomplete and usually retractile into the first thoracic segment; mandibles or mouth hooks parallel and moving in a vertical plane.
   Suborder **BRACHYCERA, 15**
3. Head, thorax, and first abdominal segment fused; with a row of six ventral suckers for attachment to beds of rapid streams ...... BLEPHARICERIDAE, p. 673
   Head not fused with thorax and first abdominal segment; ventral suckers usually absent (present in *Maruina*) ...............................................4
4. Abdomen with seven pairs of large lateral prolegs supplied with concentric rings of minute claws; antennae branched; on rocks and pebbles in rapid streams ............................. DEUTEROPHLEBIIDAE, p. 670
   With other characters .......................................................5
5. Lobed respiratory disc at the posterior end of body bearing spiracles; head retractile ........................................ TIPULIDAE, p. 676
   No lobed disc at posterior end of body; head not retractile .....................6
6. Body terminating in a very long, conspicuous, respiratory tube.
   PTYCHOPTERIDAE, p. 678
   No long terminal respiratory tube .........................................7
7. Prolegs present ...........................................................10
   Prolegs absent ............................................................8
8. Segments secondarily divided into more or less distinct annuli; amphipneustic .................................. PSYCHODIDAE, p. 678
   Segments not annulated; not amphipneustic ..................................9
9. Thoracic segments fused and distinctly thicker than rest of body.
   CULICIDAE, p. 683
   Thorax and abdomen about equal in diameter .............. HELEIDAE, p. 697

10. Posterior end of body with six long filaments; larvae in wet, sandy soils at streamside; several rare species; not treated in this manual . . . . . . . . . . . TANYDERIDAE
 Posterior end without six long filaments . . . . . . . . . . . . . . . . . . . . . . . . . . . . . . . . . **11**
11. With a single proleg projecting anteriorly from prothorax . . . . . SIMULIIDAE, p. 685
 Prolegs otherwise . . . . . . . . . . . . . . . . . . . . . . . . . . . . . . . . . . . . . . . . . . . . . . . . . . **12**
12. Body flattened, oval in cross section; most segments with long lateral processes; one pair of anterior prolegs . . . . . . HELEIDAE (genus *Atrichopogon* only), p. 697
 Body circular in cross section; no lateral processes . . . . . . . . . . . . . . . . . . . . . . . . . **13**
13. Two prolegs on each of the first one or two abdominal segments; body usually bent into a U shape when at rest . . . . . . . . . . . . . . . . . . . . . . . . . . DIXIDAE, p. 680
 Without such an arrangement of prolegs; body not U-shaped . . . . . . . . . . . . . . . . . **14**
14. One pair of prolegs on prothorax and another pair at the end of the abdomen . . . . . . . . . . . . . . . . . . . . . . . . . . . . . . . . . . . . . . . CHIRONOMIDAE, p. 689
 Prothoracic and posterior prolegs unpaired; larvae in cold streams; four rare species; not treated in this manual . . . . . . . . . . . . . . . . . . . . . . . . . . . . . THAUMALEIDAE
15. Integument with calcium carbonate crystals; prolegs lacking.
 STRATIOMYIDAE, p. 699
 No calcium carbonate deposits in integument; prolegs present . . . . . . . . . . . . . . . . . **16**
16. Last abdominal segment ending in two or four setigerous or fringed appendages . . **17**
 Last abdominal segment otherwise; spiracle at extreme posterior end of body . . . . **18**
17. With one pair of long, fringed terminal appendages, much longer than last prolegs . . . . . . . . . . . . . . . . . . . . . . . . . . . . . . . . . . . . . . . . . RHAGIONIDAE, p. 701
 With one or two pairs of short, setigerous terminal appendages, not longer than last prolegs; a few uncommon species with aquatic larvae; not treated in this manual . . . . . . . . . . . . . . . . . . . . . . . . . . . . . . . . . . . . . . . . . . . . . . . . EMPIDIDAE
18. Posterior spiracle in a vertical slit or a sharply compressed spine; girdle of prolegs on most segments . . . . . . . . . . . . . . . . . . . . . . . . . . . . . . . . . . . . TABANIDAE, p. 701
 Posterior spiracle in a pit surrounded by several unequal pairs of short lobes; a few rare and poorly known species found in aquatic habitats; not treated in this manual . . . . . . . . . . . . . . . . . . . . . . . . . . . . . . . . . . . . . . . . . . . . . . DOLICHOPODIDAE
19. Last segment elongated into a very long telescoping retractile tail.
 SYRPHIDAE, p. 702
 Last segment otherwise . . . . . . . . . . . . . . . . . . . . . . . . . . . . . . . . . . . . . . . . . . . . . . . **20**
20. Larva a miner in petioles of pond lilies . . . . . . . . . . . . . . . ANTHOMYIIDAE, p. 705
 Larva not a miner in petioles of pond lilies . . . . . . . . . . . . . . . . . . . . . . . . . . . . . . . **21**
21. Spiracular disc at posterior end surrounded by several lobes. SCIOMYZIDAE, p. 704
 Without such lobes . . . . . . . . . . . . . . . . . . . . . . . . . . . . . . . . . . . . . . . . . . . . . . . . . . **22**
22. Leaf miners in aquatic plants . . . . . . . . . . . . . . . . . . . . . . . . . . . EPHYDRIDAE, p. 704
 Not leaf miners in aquatic plants . . . . . . . . . . . . . . . . . . . . . . . . . . . . . . . . . . . . . . . **23**
23. Mouth hooks sharp, slender, not dentate below . . . . . . . . ANTHOMYIIDAE, p. 705
 Mouth hooks palmate or digitate . . . . . . . . . . . . . . . . . . . . . . . . . EPHYDRIDAE, p. 704

## KEY TO FAMILIES OF DIPTERA PUPAE

1. Pupa free, not completely covered by last larval skin; cocoon may be present . . . . . **2**
 Pupa remaining wholly within the last larval skin (puparium) . . . . . . . . . . . . . . . . . . **3**
2. Antennal sacs elongated, lying over compound eyes and extending to or beyond the bases of the wing sheaths; prothoracic respiratory organs usually conspicuous. . . . . . . . . . . . . . . . . . . . . . . . . . . . . . . . . . . . . . . . . Suborder **NEMATOCERA, 4**
 Antennal sacs short, not lying over compound eyes; prothoracic respiratory organs lacking or rudimentary . . . . . . . . . . . . . . . . . . . . . . Suborder **BRACHYCERA, 19**
3. Pupa within the last larval skin (puparium), which is unchanged in shape; larval head distinct . . . . . . . . . . . . . . . . . . Suborder **BRACHYCERA**, STRATIOMYIDAE
 Puparium without a distinct head, modified in shape; usually heavily sclerotized, shortened, ellipsoidal, or eggshaped; too poorly known to key to family . . . . . . . . . . . . . . . . . . . . . . . . . . . . . . . . . . . . . . Suborder **CYCLORRHAPHA**

4. Pupa within a fibrous cocoon . . . . . . . . . . . . . . . . . . . . . . . . . . . . . . . . . . . . . . .**5**
   Pupa without a cocoon, though sometimes in a silken tube . . . . . . . . . . . . . . . . . . . . .**6**

5. Cocoon vase-shaped, slipper-shaped, in the form of a wall pocket or simply a structureless mass of matted threads; respiratory organs, consisting of 4 to 60 coarse filaments, projecting from open end; in running water . . . . . . . . SIMULIIDAE
   Cocoon conical or cylindrical; respiratory organ a slender unbranched filament . . . . . . . . . . . . . . . . . . . . . . . . . . . . . . . . . . . . . . . . . . . . . CHIRONOMIDAE

6. Pupa more or less convex and hard-shelled; attached limpetlike to stream bed . . . . .**7**
   Pupa not so attached and not limpetlike . . . . . . . . . . . . . . . . . . . . . . . . . . . . . . . . . .**9**

7. Thoracic respiratory organs leaflike . . . . . . . . . . . . . . . . . . . . . BLEPHARICERIDAE
   Thoracic respiratory organs not leaflike; in western mountain streams . . . . . . . . . . .**8**

8. Thoracic respiratory organs branched and filamentous . . . DEUTEROPHLEBIIDAE
   Thoracic respiratory organs short, simple, and unbranched . . . . . . . PSYCHODIDAE

9. Leg sheaths straight, projecting beyond ends of wing sheaths, in most cases far beyond; caudal end not paddle shaped; usually more than 8 mm long; pupation in sand or mud, rarely in open water . . . . . . . . . . . . . . . . . . . . . . . . . . . . . . . . . . . .**10**
   Leg sheaths often curved or folded, projecting little, if any, beyond ends of wing sheaths, caudal end often ending in a paddle; usually less than 8 mm long; pupation usually in open water . . . . . . . . . . . . . . . . . . . . . . . . . . . . . . . . . . . . . . . . . . .**12**

10. One of breathing horns longer than the body, the other short . . . . . . . . . . . . . . . . .**11**
    Breathing horns less than three-fourths of the body length, subequal in length . . . . . . . . . . . . . . . . . . . . . . . . . . . . . . . . . . . . . . . . . . . . . . . . . . . . . . . TIPULIDAE

11. Head with a high spiny crest . . . . . . . . . . . . . . . . . . . . . . . . . . . . . TANYDERIDAE
    Head without a high spiny crest . . . . . . . . . . . . . . . . . . . . . . . . . . . PTYCHOPTERIDAE

12. Abdominal segments angular . . . . . . . . . . . . . . . . . . . . . . . . . . . . . THAUMELEIDAE
    Abdominal segments not angular . . . . . . . . . . . . . . . . . . . . . . . . . . . . . . . . . . . . . . .**13**

13. Wing sheaths ending about midlength of pupa; leg sheaths short, straight, and superimposed . . . . . . . . . . . . . . . . . . . . . . . . . . . . . . . . . . . . . . . . . . . . PSYCHODIDAE
    Wing sheaths ending distinctly before midlength of pupa when body and leg sheaths are straight, or body arched and leg sheaths undulatory . . . . . . . . . . . . . . . . .**14**

14. Caudal end with two paddles, each with a midrib . . . . . . . . . . . . . . . . . . CULICIDAE
    Paddles, if present, without a distinct midrib . . . . . . . . . . . . . . . . . . . . . . . . . . . . .**15**

15. Paddles narrow, completely fused at base; each with a strong hair on outer margin beyond midlength and several stout spines at tip; minute species. CULICIDAE
    With other characters . . . . . . . . . . . . . . . . . . . . . . . . . . . . . . . . . . . . . . . . . . . . . . . .**16**

16. Caudal paddles long and pointed, fused basally; pupa normally lying on its side in an arched position . . . . . . . . . . . . . . . . . . . . . . . . . . . . . . . . . . . . . . . . . . . . . DIXIDAE
    Caudal paddles absent, or, if present, the pupa differing in other characters . . . . . .**17**

17. Thoracic respiratory organs with open stigmata . . . . . . . . . . . . . . . . . . . . . . . . . . . . .**18**
    Thoracic respiratory organs without open stigmata, or composed of numerous filaments, or lacking . . . . . . . . . . . . . . . . . . . . . . . . . . . . . . . . . . . . . . CHIRONOMIDAE

18. Anal segment ending in a pair of pointed processes . . . . . . . . . . . . . . . . . HELEIDAE
    Anal segment with a two-lobed swimming paddle . . . . . . . . . . . . . . CHIRONOMIDAE

19. Pupa short, stout, and with prothoracic respiratory organs more than one-quarter as long as body . . . . . . . . . . . . . . . . . . . . . . . . . . . . . . . . . . . . . . . . . DOLICHOPODIDAE
    Pupa more elongate; prothoracic respiratory organs shorter . . . . . . . . . . . . . . . . . . .**20**

20. Prothorax with a large aperture connected with the spiracle . . . . . . . . . . . . . . . . . .**21**
    Prothorax without such an aperture . . . . . . . . . . . . . . . . . . . . . . . . . . . . . . EMPIDIDAE

21. Wing sheaths reaching the second abdominal segment . . . . . . . . . . . . . . TABANIDAE
    Wing sheaths not reaching the second abdominal segment . . . . . . . . RHAGIONIDAE

# DEUTEROPHLEBIIDAE (MOUNTAIN MIDGES)

The curious and poorly known Deuterophlebiidae (mountain midges) have been collected in widely separated mountainous areas of Japan, the Asiatic mainland, Canada, and the United States. The adults of only five species are known, but the immature stages of eight species have been adequately described. About eight addi-

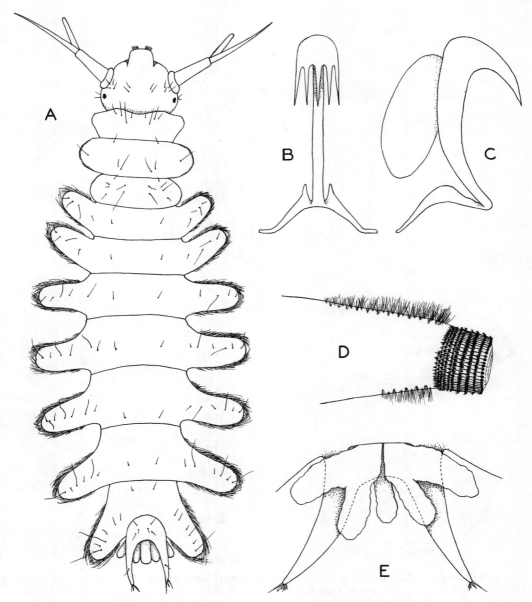

FIG. 456.–Structure of the larva of *Deuterophlebia coloradensis*. A, dorsal view, ×37; B, frontal view of claw of proleg; C, lateral view of claw of proleg; D, ventral view of proleg which has been straightened to show rings of claws; E, ventral view of posterior end, showing the five anal gills. (From Pennak.)

tional species in collections of specialists await description. *Deuterophlebia* is the only genus in the family. The adults are small, the mouthparts are absent, the immense wings have elaborate secondary and concentric transverse folds, and the male has exceptionally long antennae.

The larvae are reminiscent of blepharicerids and creep about sluggishly on the rocky bottoms of clear mountain streams. They are most frequently taken on the upper surface of smooth rocks in small, concave depressions only a millimeter or two deep. The head, thoracic segments,

FIG. 457.–Pupae of *Deuterophlebia coloradensis*. A, ventral view of male; B, dorsal view of female; C, ventral view of female; all ×35. (From Pennak.)

and all eight abdominal segments are distinct and separated from each other. Among the most striking features are the large, blunt, lateral prolegs of the first seven abdominal segments. Each of these has a series of rings of minute sclerotized claws, and the claws, together with the blunt ends of the prolegs, act as imperfect sucking discs for clinging to the substrate.

The head is flat, and the unique branched antennae are long and originate on stout tubercles. The peculiar mouthparts are specialized for scraping diatoms and other algae from rock surfaces. The last abdominal segment is comparatively small and is provided with two long, tapering, sclerotized processes and five delicate blood-gill-like structures originating around the anus.

It is thought that there are four larval instars, the average length of the last being about 4 mm.

The pupae adhere tightly to the substrate. They are broadly oval, only slightly convex dorsally, and flat ventrally. The dorsal surface is strongly sclerotized and dark brown or blackish. On the anterior lateral margins of the thorax are two respiratory processes consisting of several slender filaments. The first, second, and seventh abdominal segments are supplied with stout, thornlike spines along their lateral margins. The eighth and ninth abdominal segments are almost completely enclosed by the projecting seventh segment. On the ventral surface there are three pairs of lateral adhesive pads. The antennae of

the male are enormously elongated, being coiled in large, elliptical rings.

The larval and pupal stages of five American species have been adequately described. *Deuterophlebia coloradensis* Pennak is common in mountain streams in Colorado and also is known from several other western states and Canada. The other species have been reported from Oregon and California. Unfortunately, no larval characters have been found by which species may be identified. The pupae, however, do show distinguishing morphological differences.

Undoubtedly, careful collecting in mountain streams of the west will show that the Deuterophlebiidae are widely distributed and not uncommon.

## BLEPHARICERIDAE (NET-WINGED MIDGES)

The adults are elongated, mosquitolike insects of moderate size, with long legs and broad wings. In addition to veins, the wings have a network of fine lines. These midges are worldwide in distribution, but there are relatively few species. They frequent the borders of rapid mountain streams where they feed on smaller insects. The eggs are deposited on wet rocks at the margins of streams and the larvae move into the water. Both the larvae and pupae are usually found in clusters tightly attached to the rocky bottoms of rushing brooks and streams of ravines and hilly and mountainous areas.

The unique larvae are flattened and usually composed of seven divisions; the first consists of the fused head, thorax, and first abdominal segment; the next five are abdominal segments two to six; the last and smallest division includes three abdominal segments. In a few species the last body division is partially fused with the second last division. Each of the first six divisions has a median ventral sucker by which the larva attaches itself tightly to the substrate. Each division except the last also has a pair of prolegs. There are paired tufts of tracheal gill filaments on abdominal segments two to six. The antennae are slender and

usually short. Total length ranges from 4 to 12 mm, with four instars. Larvae feed on lithophyton.

The pupae are heavily sclerotized, and a shiny brown or black on the dorsal side. The integument of the ventral surface is very delicate and transparent. There are six pads, three of which are on each side near the lower surface of the abdomen. Unlike the larvae, the pupae remain attached in one spot. There are two sets of flat, leaflike, thoracic respiratory organs.

The United States has about 25 described species of blepharicerids, divided into five genera. No satisfactory and reliable key to larval genera can be constructed because of variations in characters ordinarily considered to be taxonomically significant. In mature *Agathon* larvae, for example, some species have no dorsal ornamentation; others have large, flat dorsal plates; and still others have four thornlike structures near the median line of each segment. *Philorus* has four small plates per segment, four tubercles (Fig. 458E), or four fingerlike pseudopods. The number of gill filaments per cluster also varies. *Dioptopsis* has three, four, or five; *Agathon* has five, six, or seven. However, *Dioptopsis, Bibiocephala, Philorus,* and *Agathon* are all

FIG. 458.–Blephariceridae. A, ventral view of *Bibiocephala,* ×11; B, lateral view of pupa of *Bibiocephala,* ×9; C, anterior end of *Blepharicera* pupa showing cephalic sclerite and respiratory lamellae; D, anterior end of *Agathon* pupa showing cephalic sclerite and respiratory lamellae; E, dorsal and ventral composite of *Philorus* larva, ×12; F, dorsal and ventral composite of *Philorus* pupa, ×8. (A redrawn from Johannsen, 1934; B redrawn from Malloch, 1917; C and D from Hogue, copyright © 1973 by The Regents of the University of California; reprinted by permission of the University of California Press; E and F from Hogue, 1966.)

similar in having paired lateral body processes situated immediately and slightly dorsal to the prolegs (Fig. 458E), whereas *Blepharicera* has no such processes. *Blepharicera* is widely distributed over most of the United States in suitable streams, but the other four genera are restricted to the western states.

Unlike larvae, the pupal stages appear to have reliable features at the generic level, and the following key is modified from Hogue (1973).

## KEY TO GENERA OF BLEPHARICERIDAE PUPAE*

1. Respiratory lamellae thin and flexible (Fig. 458F) ......................... **Philorus**
   Respiratory lamellae opaque, rigid, and erect (Fig. 458D) ..........................2
2. Body ellipsoid and strongly convex (Fig. 458B) ..................... **Bibiocephala**
   Body ovate and not strongly convex ......................................3
3. Length of respiratory lamellae never more than one and one-half times the width ...................................................**Dioptopsis**
   Length of respiratory lamellae more than one and one-half times the width ........4
4. Cephalic sclerite triangular (Fig. 458D) ................................. **Agathon**
   Cephalic sclerite broadly rounded (Fig. 458C) ...................... **Blepharicera**

Modified from Hogue; copyright © 1973 by the Regents of the University of California; reprinted by permission of the University of California Press.

# TIPULIDAE (CRANE FLIES)

The crane flies are long-legged, mosquitolike insects commonly found flying singly or in swarms near streams, ponds, or in meadows, especially at twilight. They are attracted to lights and frequently get into houses, where they flutter awkwardly against the windows. They lose their fragile legs easily. In those species with aquatic immature stages, mating occurs during flight, and the females probably deposit the eggs by flying over the water and dipping the tip of the abdomen beneath the surface. The great majority of species have a single generation a year, but a few have two or three generations.

Aquatic crane fly larvae may be easily identified by the spiracular disc at the posterior end. This disc, except in *Antocha*, bears a pair of functional spiracles and may be thrust up to the surface of the water for air, particularly when the supply of dissolved oxygen becomes low. It is customarily lobed, is fringed with hairs, and has a number of delicate anal gills associated with it. Color ranges from brown to whitish, and the integument is often quite transparent. The common species are 10 to 50 mm long.

As shown below, the larvae exhibit a wide range of habitat preferences; many are semiaquatic and occur in damp sand, organic mud, and wet mosses. Some genera, such as *Tipula*, occur in a variety of habitats; others, such as *Antocha* and *Pilaria*, are restricted to a single type of habitat. The family has both carnivorous and herbivorous representatives. Depending on the species and the environment, the larval period may last from about a month to nearly a year. Probably all crane flies in the United States pass the winter as larvae. Most genera have a wide geographic range.

Habitats of aquatic and semiaquatic crane fly larvae of the United States are here summarized; uncommon to very rare genera are indicated by asterisks.

Stream bottoms, but not more or less buried in the substrate: *Antocha*.

Cold springs: *Longurio* and *Pedicia*.

On cliffs or rock faces, in or beneath algal

Fig. 459.–Pupa of *Tipula*, ×5. *BH*, breathing horn.

scum with percolating or flowing water: *Dactylolabis*,* *Elliptera*,* *Limonia*, and *Tipula*.

In sphagnum and other aquatic mosses: *Eriocera*, *Pedicia*, and *Triogma*.*

In sandy, gravelly, or loamy soil—poor in humus, on bottoms of streams and ponds, or along margins: *Erioptera*, *Gonomyia*,* *Helobia*,* *Hexatoma*, *Limnophila*, *Longurio*, *Molophilus*,* *Tipula*, and *Trimicra*.*

In rich mud at edges of bodies of water; swamps and marshes: *Dicranota*,* *Erioptera*, *Elliptera*,* *Gonomyia*,* *Helius*, *Limnophila*, *Limonia*, *Pilaria*, *Phalacrocera*,* *Pseudolimnophila*, and *Tipula*.

On water-logged wood, submerged or in a permanent spray: *Lipsothrix.**

The elongated pupae are formed in the last larval skin, which is usually shed. In some true aquatic species the pupa is enclosed in a silken case, expecially in *Antocha,* but most species pupate in damp earth or sand.

## KEY TO GENERA OF COMMON TIPULIDAE LARVAE

1. Body cylindrical ...................................................2
   Body flattened ............................................**Dactylolabis**
2. Body with very long spines or leaflike projections .........................3
   Body without such structures .......................................4

FIG. 460.–Structure of larvae of Tipulidae. A, spiracular disc of *Limnophila*; B, antenna of *Pseudolimnophila*; C, antenna of *Limnophila*; D, spiracular disc of *Pedicia*; E, spiracular disc of *Helius*; F, spiracular disc of *Pilaria*; G, spiracular disc of *Hexatoma*; H, spiracular disc of *Pilaria*; J, spiracular disc of *Pseudolimnophila*; K, spiracular disc of *Tipula*; L, spiracular disc of *Tipula*; M, lateral view of *Tipula*, ×3; N, dorsal view of *Antocha,* ×7. 1, anal gill; 2, spiracle. (A to C, E to L, and N redrawn from Alexander, 1920.)

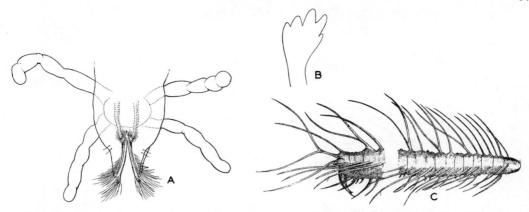

FIG. 461.–Structure of Tipulidae. A, end of abdomen of *Lipsothrix* showing spiracles, four anal gills, and four caudal lobes; B, ventral plate of head capsule of *Erioptera*; C, anterior and posterior ends of larva of *Phalacrocera*. (A from Rogers and Byers; B and C from Johannsen, 1934.)

**3.** Body projections very long (Fig. 461C) ............................ **Phalacrocera**
Body projections in the form of short leaves or tubercles ................ **Triogma**
**4.** Spiracular disc surrounded by six or eight lobes .............................**5**
Spiracular disc surrounded by less than six lobes .............................**7**
**5.** Spiracular disc surrounded by eight lobes (Fig. 460L); very common ........ **Tipula**
Spiracular disc surrounded by six lobes (Fig. 460K).........................**6**
**6.** Anal gills pinnately branched .............................................**Longurio**
Anal gills not pinnately branched ..........................................**Tipula**
**7.** Spiracular disc with two long ventral lobes .................................**8**
Ventral lobes short ........................................................**9**
**8.** Spiracles lacking or vestigial; larva in a silken case in swift waters ........ **Antocha**
Spiracles large; no silken case (Fig. 460D); in cold springs and under moss at edges of streams ................................................. **Pedicia**
**9.** Lobes of spiracular disc indistinct, sometimes apparently lacking.......... **Limonia**
Lobes of spiracular disc distinct .........................................**10**
**10.** Spiracular disc with five lobes (Fig. 460E) ..............................**11**
Spiracular disc with four lobes (Fig. 460G) .............................**13**
**11.** Creeping welts on ventral side of abdominal segments ................... **Helius**
Creeping welts absent .................................................**12**
**12.** Ventral plates of head capsule expanded and with five to eight teeth at anterior end (Fig. 461B) ............................................. **Erioptera**
Ventral plates without such teeth ........**Molophilus, Gonomyia, Helobia, Trimicra**
**13.** Abdominal segments three to seven or nine with dorsal and ventral creeping welts, which are supplied with microscopic hooks ...........................**14**
Creeping welts absent .................................................**15**
**14.** Body depressed...........................................................**Elliptera**
Body cylindrical ......................................................**Lipsothrix**
**15.** Spiracular disc defined by ridge above; hair fringes short (Fig. 460G) .....**Hexatoma**
Spiracular disc not defined by ridge above; hair fringes long ...................**16**
**16.** Disc bare across upper border (Fig. 460G) .............................**Hexatoma**
Disc hairy across upper border ........................................**17**
**17.** Lower border of spiracular disc cross-lined with black (Fig. 460F)...........**Pilaria**
Lower border of spiracular disc little or not at all cross-lined with black .........**18**
**18.** Antennae with two or more elongated apical papillae .......................**19**
Antennae tipped with one or two long setae and a single oval or oval-elongated papilla (Fig. 460C) .............................................**Limnophila**
**19.** Antenna with two elongated apical papillae ..................... **Pseudolimnophila**
Antenna with three or four elongated apical papillae ...................**Hexatoma**

## PTYCHOPTERIDAE (PHANTOM CRANE FLIES)

FIG. 462.–Larva of *Ptychoptera rufocincta,* ×2.5.

FIG. 463.–Anterior end of pupa of *Bittacomorpha clavipes* (Fabr.), ×6.5. (modified from Alexander, 1920.)

Although adult phantom crane flies are somewhat similar to true crane flies, the larval stages are different. They may be easily recognized by the presence of a greatly elongated posterior respiratory tube. There is a similar structure in some of the Syrphidae larvae, but these two larval types may be distinguished by the fact that in the Ptychopteridae there is a well-developed head, whereas the head of a syrphid larva is small, poorly developed, and usually retracted into the thorax.

The immature stages of the Ptychopteridae are typically found in decaying vegetation at the edges of shallow ponds and in marshy areas. Decaying vegetation is the chief food of the larvae. Both the larvae and pupae lie among the debris with the tips of their long breathing tubes thrust up through the surface film. There are about 20 American species, but the two most common aquatic forms are *Ptychoptera rufocincta* O. S. and *Bittacomorpha clavipes* (Fabr.). The larvae of the former are 30 to 35 mm long, whitish or light yellowish in color, and almost smooth; the larvae of the latter are 50 to 60 mm long, brown or reddish brown, and covered with rows of small tubercles. Members of a third genus, *Bit-tacomorphella,* are uncommon but may be identified by their blackish coloration, by the many long horny projections covering the body, and by their small size (less than 20 mm long).

The pupae are similar to those of the Tipulidae, except that one of the pronotal breathing horns is longer than the body and the other is very short (Fig. 463).

## PSYCHODIDAE (MOTH FLIES)

Adult moth flies are very small, usually less than 4 mm long; the body is thickly covered with hairs, and the wings are hairy or scaly. They have a worldwide distribution and occur in shady places near water but are often abundant around lights at night.

Although many species have aquatic stages, those commonly encountered in the United States belong to four genera: *Peri-*

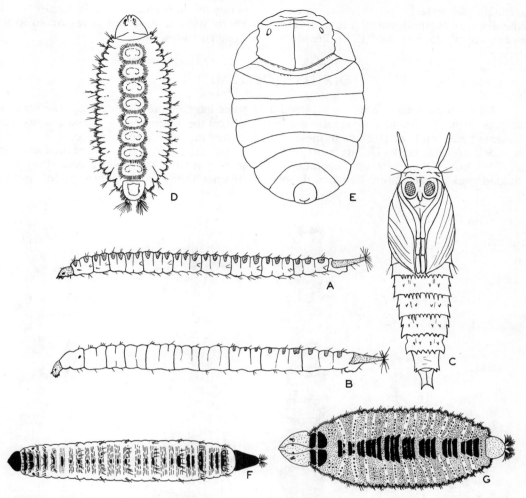

FIG. 464.—Psychodidae. A, larvae of *Pericoma*, ×13; B. larva of *Psychoda*, ×13; C, pupa of *Psychoda*, ×20; D, ventral view of larva of *Maruina*, ×24; E, dorsal view of pupa of *Maruina*, ×24; F, Dorsal view of *Psychoda*; G, dorsal view of *Maruina*. (A and B redrawn from Johannsen, 1934; F and G from Quate, 1955.)

*coma, Psychoda, Telmatoscopus,* and *Maruina.* The elongated amphipneustic larvae are characterized by the lack of prolegs and the subdivision of segments into annuli, some of which bear transverse, hardened, dorsal plates. Food consists of algae and decaying vegetation. Body length is 3 to 10 mm.

The parts of the pupal head, legs, and wings are distinct and closely applied to the body. The prothoracic respiratory organs are slender cylindrical or conical processes into which the tracheae extend.

Larvae and pupae of the more common species usually occur in foul water, sewage, filter beds, and decaying organic matter, but some species of *Pericoma* and all species of *Maruina* inhabit rapid, clear streams. *Psychoda* larvae are cylindrical, grayish-white, and have hardened transverse dorsal plates only on the posterior segments. *Pericoma* and *Telmatoscopus* larvae are also cylindrical, but the coloration is usually brown or blackish and there are dorsal plates on all thoracic and abdominal segments. *Maruina*, however, is strongly depressed, and there are sucker-like discs on the midventral line; coloration is brown or blackish and there are dorsal plates on all segments. Body length is only 1.9 to 3.1 mm. *Maruina* is restricted to the western states.

## DIXIDAE (DIXA MIDGES)

Adult dixa midges are small, slender insects usually found in small mating swarms near ponds or streams in meadows or wood areas at dusk. During most of the daylight hours they rest on vegetation or shaded rocks near water. Females deposit their eggs in the shallows by swishing the tip of the abdomen in the water as they flutter just above the surface.

All the larvae are aquatic, and although they resemble mosquito larvae, they have distinct thoracic segments, paired prolegs

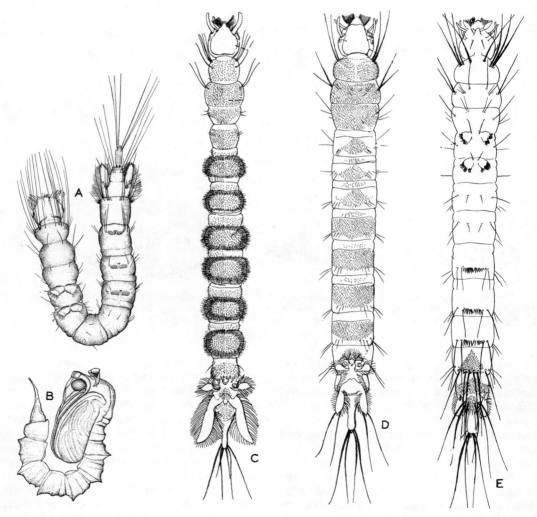

FIG. 465.–Dixidae. A, larva of *Dixa*, ×15; B, pupa of *Dixa*, ×12; C, dorsal view of Dixa; D, dorsal view of *Dixella*; E, ventral view of *Dixella*. (A and B from Johannsen, 1934; C to E from Nowell, 1951.)

on the first and usually also the second abdominal segments. Some species have a definite U shape when at rest. At the caudal end there are two lateral lobes, a long tail process, and two spiracles. Coloration is black or tan. They are found in puddles, ponds, lakes, slow streams, and in the backwaters of rapid streams. Food consists of microorganisms and detritus filtered from the water by means of the mouth brushes. Total length is 4 to 8 mm. Larvae are most abundant on the shaded, downstream, or protected sides of rocks, vegetation, or debris. Because they are always at or near the surface film, the British call them "meniscus midges." Although they may leave the surface when disturbed and swim downward, they return in a few seconds.

Three genera are represented in the United States, each in a different subfamily. The genus *Dixa* contains about 20 species and is generally distributed and very common; the larva has two pairs of abdominal prolegs (Figure 465A). and the dorsal surface of each abdominal segment has a dense corona of setae (Fig. 465C). *Dixella* also has about 20 species; the larva has two pairs of prolegs, but the dorsal surfaces of the abdominal segments are only sparsely setose (Fig. 465D). *Meringodixa chalonensis* Nowell has been collected only in the Pacific coast states; it bears only one pair of prolegs.

In order to pupate, the larvae crawl a few centimeters above the water's edge and affix themselves lightly to the substrate with a gluelike secretion. The pupa is similar to the pupal stage of mosquitoes. It differs from most mosquito pupae, however, in that it is U-shaped, and the posterior end is on a level with the anterior part of the head. Often the pupae are tightly coiled. They are not truly aquatic and are found floating free in the water only fortuitously. Usually, however, they are fastened in a shaded spot where the humidity is high and where they are occasionally splashed with water so that they do not dry out.

## CULICIDAE (MOSQUITOES, PHANTOM MIDGES)

The Culicidae is a large family of worldwide distribution, and because some species are transmitters of malaria and yellow fever, this group has been intensively studied. It is commonly divided into two subfamilies, the Culicinae and the Chaoborinae, the former including the true mosquitoes, the latter the phantom midges. There is much superficial resemblance between these two subfamilies, but the mosquitoes have scaly wings, and the phantom midges have hairy wings, and although many of the female mosquitoes bite, phantom midges do not feed. *Culex* and *Anopheles* are the most common mosquitoes, and *Chaoborus* is the common phantom midge. Aside from the importance of members of this group as disease transmitters and their nuisance as biters, some of the nonbiting Culicidae may occur in such tremendous numbers around lakes as to discourage the use of these bodies of water for summer recreation.

The oviposition habits are diverse but specific for each species. Eggs may be deposited singly, in irregular masses, or in floating rafts, and in such places as tree holes, temporary puddles, rain barrels, marshes, ponds, springs, slow streams and rivers, and lakes.

Culicidae larvae are easily distinguished from other Diptera because of the fact that the fused thoracic segments are thicker than the rest of the body. There are always four instars, the fourth persisting longest. Mature larvae usually range from 3 to 15 mm in length.

Most Culicinae larvae feed on algae, Protozoa, and bits of organic debris by means of the filtering action of the small mouth brushes. A few species have been observed gnawing on submerged surfaces or scraping the periphyton from such objects. Some species of *Psorophora* feed on other mosquito larvae as well as on entomostraca and rotifers.

The larvae usually lie quietly at the surface of the water, but when they are

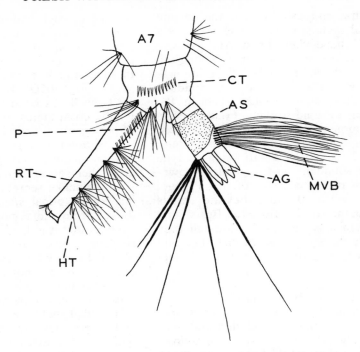

Fig. 466.–Structure of the posterior end of *Culex* larva (somewhat diagrammatic). *A7*, seventh abdominal segment; *AG*, anal gill; *AS*, anal segment; *CT*, comb teeth; *HT*, hair tuft of respiratory tube; *MVB*, median ventral brush of anal segment; *P*, pecten of respiratory tube; *RT*, respiratory tube.

disturbed they swim downward in a characteristic rapid manner that is responsible for their being called "wrigglers." *Anopheles* normally lies horizontally just beneath the surface film, but *Culex* and *Aedes* are inclined at an angle with only the tip of the respiratory tube at the surface. *Mansonia* (both larvae and pupae) is unique in that it breathes by thrusting the specialized tip of its respiratory tube into air-containing tissues of aquatic plants. *Aedes, Psorophora, Orthopodomyia,* and *Toxorhynchites* larvae are usually found in very small temporary ponds, puddles, tree holes, or water held in plants, whereas *Uranotaenia* and *Culiseta* are most common in more permanent ponds and marshes. *Anopheles* is usually found in all types of nonstagnant water, from very small puddles to streams. *Culex* is most frequently encountered in larger, permanent bodies of water. *Wyeomyia* is an inhabitant of small bog pools and the water that accumulates in pitcher plants.

Ecological distribution of the various species shows no correlation with the hydrogen-ion concentration of their habitats. Many forms are able to tolerate a range as great as pH 5.0 to 9.0. The anal gills are osmoregulatory.

Chaoborinae larvae are called phantom larvae because of their transparency. They are capable of moving through the water rapidly by means of jerky, lashing movements of the body. They are all predatory and catch small Crustacea and insect larvae with their prehensile antennae. There are no specialized respiratory organs, the exchange of oxygen and carbon dioxide occurring through the general body surface. *Corethrella* and *Eucorethra* are inhabitants of cold springs and spring pools; *Mochlonyx* occurs most commonly in pools, ponds, and bogs. *Chaoborus* is abundant everywhere in large ponds and lakes; it is easily distinguished from other Chaoborinae by the presence of a pair of particularly

FIG. 467.–Structure of Culicinae. A to G, posterior end of larvae; A, *Psorophora*; B, *Aedes*; C, *Aedes*; D, *Culiseta*; E, *Wyeomyia*; F, *Mansonia*; G, *Anopheles*; H, pupa of *Culex,* ×9; J, larva of *Culex*, ×9; K, rod of larval mouth brush of *Toxorhynchites*. (A to G modified from various sources; H and J from Johannsen, 1934.)

conspicuous pigmented air sacs, or hydrostatic organs, in the thorax and another pair in the posterior end of the abdomen. The air sacs are able to extract oxygen from the water at low concentrations. *Chaoborus* exhibits pronounced daily migratory movements, being confined to the bottom waters and mud during the day and migrating to the surface waters at night.

## KEY TO GENERA OF CULICIDAE LARVAE

1. Antennae prehensile; without mouth brushes ................ CHAOBORINAE, **12**
   Antennae not prehensile; mouth brushes present ................. CULICINAE, **2**

FIG. 468.–Chaoborinae. A, lateral view of larva of *Chaoborus*, ×9; B, lateral view of pupa of *Chaoborus*, ×10; C, dorsal view of larva of *Eucorethra*, ×5.5; D, lateral view of larva of *Mochlonyx*, ×15. (From Johannsen, 1934.)

2. Spiracles sessile on eighth abdominal segment; respiratory tube absent (Fig. 467G); about 12 species; widely distributed and common . . . . . . . . . . . . . . . . **Anopheles**
    Spiracles at tip of a respiratory tube that is at least as long as wide . . . . . . . . . . . . . .3
3. Anal segment with median ventral brush . . . . . . . . . . . . . . . . . . . . . . . . . . . . . . . . . . . . .4
    Anal segment without median ventral brush (Fig. 467E); larva in water of pitcher plants; three rare species in southern Florida and Mississippi, and one common species widely distributed in eastern states . . . . . . . . . . **Wyeomyia smithi** (Coq.)
4. Respiratory tube without pecten . . . . . . . . . . . . . . . . . . . . . . . . . . . . . . . . . . . . . . . . . . . .5
    Respiratory tube with pecten (Fig. 467D) . . . . . . . . . . . . . . . . . . . . . . . . . . . . . . . . . . .7
5. Respiratory tube greatly modified for piercing (Fig. 467F); two rare species confined to Gulf states; a third common and widely distributed.
                                                            **Mansonia perturbans** (Walker)
    Respiratory tube not modified for piercing; in tree holes and water held in plants  . .6
6. Mouth brushes prehensile, each composed of 10 stout rods (Fig. 467K); from New Jersey to Kansas and Texas . . . . . . . . . . . . . . . . . . **Toxorhynchites rutilus** (Coq.)
    Mouth brushes normal; two rare species in southwest, two species common and widely distributed . . . . . . . . . . . . . . . . . . . . . . . . . . . . . . . . . . . . . . . . . . **Orthopodomyia**
7. Respiratory tube with several pairs of ventral tufts of hairs (Fig. 466); widely distributed and common; about 25 species . . . . . . . . . . . . . . . . . . . . . . . . . . . . . . . **Culex**
    Respiratory tube with a single pair of ventral tufts of hairs that are occasionally vestigial or absent . . . . . . . . . . . . . . . . . . . . . . . . . . . . . . . . . . . . . . . . . . . . . . . . . . . . . . .8

8. Head elongated, elliptical; in pools; three species, of which one is common in eastern
   states ..................................................................**Uranotaenia**
   Head nearly circular or transversely oval ......................................**9**
9. Respiratory tube with a ventral tuft of hairs close to the base (Fig. 467D); widely
   distributed; about eight species ...............................................**Culiseta**
   Respiratory tube with a ventral tuft of hairs near the middle or beyond, or the tuft
   may be vestigial or absent ......................................................**10**
10. Head with a prominent triangular pouch on each side; in burrows of marine crabs;
    two rare species in Gulf states .............................................**Deinocerites**
    Head without a prominent triangular pouch on each side; not in burrows of marine
    crabs ...........................................................................**11**
11. Anal segment with a complete sclerotized ring and with the median ventral brush
    piercing the ring (Fig. 467A); widely distributed; about nine
    species.....................................................................**Psorophora**
    Anal segment with a dorsal, saddle-shaped, sclerotized plate; or if completely ringed,
    the median ventral brush is posterior to the ring (Figs. 467B, C); widely dis-
    tributed and common; about 70 species ..........................................**Aedes**
12. Eighth abdominal segment with a single elongated, dorsal respiratory tube (Fig.
    468D) ..........................................................................**13**
    No such tube on eighth abdominal segment .......................................**14**
13. Antennae inserted close together, when at rest folded outward against the head; anal
    brush (fin) not developed; four species; rare, in cold springs; New Jersey to
    California .................................................................**Corethrella**
    Antennae inserted far apart, pendent when at rest; anal brush well developed (Fig.
    468D); widely distributed; three species ......................................**Mochlonyx**
14. Hydrostatic organs (air sacs) present in thorax and in seventh abdominal segment
    (Fig. 468A); widely distributed; six species ....................................**Chaoborus**
    Hydrostatic organs absent (Fig. 468C); widely distributed.
                                              **Eucorethra underwoodi** Underwood

Like the larvae, all culicid pupae are aquatic. The head and thorax are fused into a somewhat rounded triangular mass from which the elongated curved abdomen projects. The pupae breathe atmospheric air by means of a pair of trumpet-shaped structures on the thorax. They are quite active but do not move about much unless they are disturbed. There are two paddlelike devices at the posterior end that are fused basally and are not movable in the Chaoborinae but are free and movable in the Culicinae. Though the larvae are relatively long-lived and may even winter over, the pupae live only a few days. The adult is liberated at the surface of the water by a dorsal splitting of the pupal integument.

## SIMULIIDAE (BLACK FLIES)

The Simulidae, a small family of world-wide distribution, include the black flies, or buffalo gnats, of which about 90 species are known from the United States. They are robust, small insects, seldom being more than 5 mm long. The color is usually gray, brown, or black. Black flies are found near streams and rivers, and in some areas they may be present in such great numbers at certain times of the year as to be almost unbearable. The females are notorious pests and produce irritating bites on warm-blooded animals. Campers, hunters, fishermen, and farmers are particularly well acquainted with them, the last because of the fact that black flies may cause damage to livestock.

Depending on the species and habitat, there may be from one to several generations per year. The eggs are deposited on vegetation, rocks, and logs just under the surface of swift streams, especially where

FIG. 469.–*Simulium venustum* Say. A, dorsal view of larva, ×17; B, lateral view of larva, ×21; C, dorsal view of pupa in cocoon, ×15; D, lateral view of pupa, ×21. (Modified from Jobbins-Pomeroy.)

the current is broken. Overwintering sometimes occurs in the egg stage.

The larvae are unique and easily identified. They are cylindrical, soft-skinned, a dirty yellow, gray, brown, or black, and the caudal third is distinctly swollen. A single stout proleg armed with small hooks projects forward from the prothorax. At the extreme posterior end there is a flat, sessile disc which has 50 to more than 140 radial rows of hooks. Delicate retractile blood gills project from the anus on the dorsal side of the last segment. In addition to the usual mouth parts, there are two prominent fanlike structures located laterally at the extreme anterior end. Each fan consists of

a strong peduncle and 30 to 60 long, thin, curved rays.

Black fly larvae are found in the shallows of streams where the current is especially swift. Sometimes they are so abundant that the substrate is almost obscured. With the head downstream, they are tightly attached by the posterior disc to rocks and vegetation. It has been demonstrated that this adhesion may be attributed to the hooks of the disc and to a sticky salivary secretion deposited on the substrate by the mouth. Apparently the posterior disc exerts little if any suctorial action. By means of both the posterior disc and the proleg, the larvae move about in a series of looping movements, trailing a silken thread as they do so. Sometimes, attached to a strand of silk, they swing free of the substrate and may crawl along the strand with the aid of the mouth parts, proleg, and posterior disc. The anterior fans strain plankton and organic debris from the water for food. The larval stage may last from two to six weeks. Total length ranges from 3 to 15 mm.

Stream predators of black fly larvae include Trichoptera and Coleoptera, as well as fish. Water mites are common parasites.

The generic classification of the Simuliidae is still uncertain, but we recognize five genera in the United States, including 50 species of *Simulium*, about 21 *Prosimulium*, 12 *Cnephia*, 2 *Twinnia*, and a few specimens of one species of *Parasimulium* taken in California and Oregon.

Unfortunately, there are no known larval characters that can be used to differentiate between them. Identification of species is based largely on minute structural characteristics of the mouthparts. Of the numerous species recorded from the United States, *Cnephia pecuarum* (Riley), *Simulium occidentale* Townsend, *S. venustum* Say, and *S. vittatum* Zett. are among the most common.

In at least one species there are seven larval instars. During the last instar the larvae construct silken cocoons in which pupation occurs. The cocoons are firmly cemented to the substrate and may be in the form of a wall pocket, slipper, vase, or simply a matted mass of threads. The pupae are oval, enlarged at the anterior end, and yellowish, reddish, or brown. They have small abdominal hooks by which they remain attached to the cocoon. At the anterior end of the thorax are two groups of long, branched, respiratory filaments. *Cnephia pecuarum* has 40 to 48 filaments in each tuft. *Simulium occidentale* has 22 to 25, *S. vittatum* has 16, and *S. venustum* has six. The pupal stage usually lasts from two to eight days.

Generic determinations can often be made with the pupae. *Prosimulium* pupae have a pair of exceptionally large spines pointing anteriorly on the last abdominal segment. These spines are absent in *Cnephia* and *Simulium*. The cocoons of some species of *Cnephia* are roughly spun and lacking in definite shape, as in *Prosimulium;* in other species of *Cnephia* the cocoons are slipper shaped, loosely woven, and without a definite rim to the aperture. Although the shape of *Simulium* cocoons varies greatly from one species to another, they always have a definite, compact, closely woven shape.

## CHIRONOMIDAE (MIDGES)

The true midges are an exceedingly complex family of about 4000 described species and worldwide distribution. The adults are delicate, nonbiting, and usually less than 10 mm long. They commonly occur in swarms, especially near bodies of water and near lights at night. In some lake localities they swarm in such enormous numbers that they effectively discourage the use of such areas for recreation and summer homes. Some species, however, emerge in the early spring as soon as the ice has melted. The duration of the life cycle is variable; some forms have only one generation in two years, whereas others have several generations in a single year. The majority of species have aquatic larvae. Eggs may be deposited singly, in irregular or regular masses, or in strings on the surface, the bottom, or aquatic vegetation.

A single body of water may support only a few species, but some large lakes and reservoirs may contain as many as 60 species. Some stretches of highly productive stream may harbor more than 30 species.

Chironomids have more marine representatives than any other family of aquatic insects, and the larvae of many species are confined to marine habitats, especially in the intertidal zone and in estuaries where there is an abundance of disintegrating algae.

The larvae are elongated, cylindrical, slender, and range from about 2 to 30 mm in length. They have a pair of prolegs on both the first thoracic and last abdominal segments. Spiracles are absent, but there are sometimes anal gills on the lateroventral surface of the penultimate abdominal segment. Coloration is white, yellowish, greenish, bluish, pinkish, or deep red. This last type of coloration, produced by a series of dissolved hemoglobins in the blood, is characteristic of most of the more abundant species and is responsible for the name "bloodworm."

Chironomid larvae occur everywhere in aquatic vegetation and on the bottoms of all types of bodies of fresh water. Some species are solitary, whereas others occur in great concentrations, over 50,000 per square meter of bottom having been found in certain lakes. Many species construct fragile tubes composed of algae, fine silt, or sand grains cemented together with a salivary secretion. These tubes are open at both ends and a current of water is kept passing through by vigorous undulations of the body. The aestivation habit is rare in this family, but some species overwinter in larval hibernation cocoons. Chironomid larvae are chiefly herbivorous and feed on algae, higher aquatic plants, and organic detritus. Sediment feeding is most common in deep waters. Locomotion consists of a series of creeping or looping movements, although some species are active swimmers.

From an economic standpoint, fish biologists know that chironomid larvae form an important item in the food of young and adult fishes and that without this group, many good fishing lakes might be relatively barren.

Although dipterists are agreed on the higher taxonomic categories, the classification of larvae into genera and species is confused and difficult. This situation is due chiefly to the fact that differences between taxa are sometimes relatively small and that there may be considerable variations within a single species or genus. The situation is further complicated by the fact that in certain groups of adult chironomids there may appear to be close taxonomic affinities, whereas their larval stages may be quite diverse. The opposite situation is equally true. Also, the immature and adult stages of many species have not yet been associated. Among specialists, the "lumpers" use broader anatomical criteria and recognize fewer genera, including such familiar examples as *Tanytarsus* and *Chironomus*. The "splitters," however, break these and other genera into arrays of additional genera. Indeed, the taxa within the Chironomidae, because of their frequent taxonomic manipulations in the "musical chairs" game of systematics, are the most frustrating group to summarize in a reference manual such as this book. In general, we have followed the generic designations of Mason (1973). Unfortunately, new (for North America) genera are being reported frequently.

Frequently it is necessary to make permanent mounts of the head for proper identification. Place the head capsule or entire body in 5 to 10 percent KOH and heat gently until the soft tissues are dissolved and the head capsule is cleared. Rinse in dilute acetic acid, then twice in water. Mount in glycerin jelly or Euparal.

The Family Chironomidae is divided into five subfamilies, of which one, the Podonominae, is rare. The larvae in the Subfamily Tanypodinae are found in ponds, lakes, streams, and rivers. They do not build cases, but are sometimes found in the cases of other chironomids. They are predaceous, and the diet consists of other insect larvae and oligochaetes. *Pentaneura*, *Tanypus*, and *Procladius* are the genera most frequently encountered.

Of the genera in the Subfamily Diamesinae, *Prodiamesa* occurs in quiet, well-aerated water, whereas the others are stream forms. *Potthastia* is the only large genus.

Most Orthocladiinae larvae are found in ponds, lakes, and streams. *Symbiocladius* is a commensal on mayfly and stonefly nymphs, and some species of *Metriocnemus* are found in the water that accumulates in pitcher plants. Some species build cases. *Corynoneura*, *Cricotopus*, and *Orthocladius* are collected most frequently. *Corynoneura* is roughly differentiated from other Orthocladiinae because it is only 2 or 3 mm long.

*Calopsectra* and *Chironomus* are the most abundant of all Chironomidae. These two genera, along with about 20 others, constitute the Subfamily Chironominae. A few species of *Calopsectra* are found in swift water, but the great majority of species in this subfamily are found in sluggish streams, ponds, and lakes, sometimes at great depths. Some species of *Chironomus* that inhabit lake bottoms where there is a deficiency of oxygen have one or two pairs of ventral fingerlike gills on the penultimate abdominal segment, although some investigators have shown that the gills are chiefly osmoregulatory. The hemoglobin dissolved in the blood seems to be most important when the dissolved oxygen of the habitat falls below 3 ppm.

Some of the deep-water species of chironomids are able to live actively for several months under anaerobic conditions. Presumably they have a fermentation type of metabolism under such circumstances. Laboratory work has shown remarkable cryptobiotic features. Some larvae recover after exposure to liquid air, absolute alcohol, and glycerol.

The herbivorous and microphagous habit is characteristic of the Chironominae, as is the building of flimsy tubes of organic detritus, algae, or small sand grains and silt. Such tubes are lined with a silky substance of the salivary secretion. Usually they are attached, but in a very few species they are movable.

Some mud-inhabiting species have a filter feeding mechanism. The larva spins a concave net of salivary secretion across the lumen of the tube, and by anterior–posterior body undulations a current of water passes through the tube, with the result that plankton and detritus are caught by the net. The larva then eats the whole net and its load of food, after which it spins another net. The entire process is completed in several minutes. Other mud-inhabiting species extend their bodies out of the tube and scrape up detritus, either from the surface or from a depth of 5 to 10 mm.

Certain stream species of *Calopsectra* have a case with several radial and upright projections at the upstream end. Salivary sheets strung between these arms catch food particles from the current. Sections of the net and its entrapped material are removed and eaten periodically, and new net material is spun promptly in places from which it is removed.

Chironomid larvae inhabiting the tissues of rooted aquatic plants eat only enough plant material to have sufficient room to build and maintain their silk-lined tubes. Most of their food comes from plankton derived from the outside water and caught on temporary nets extending across the diameter of the tube.

The following key is modified from Mason (1973). A few rare genera are not included.

## KEY TO GENERA OF CHIRONOMIDAE LARVAE

1. Antennae retractile, usually elongated; prolegs long, stiltlike, anterior pair with a common base (Fig. 470A) . . . . . . . . . . . . . . . . . . . . . . . . . . . TANYPODINAE, 8
   Antennae not retractile, usually short . . . . . . . . . . . . . . . . . . . . . . . . . . . . . . . . . .2
2. Premandibles absent; several rare species in cold, swift streams. PODONOMINAE, 3
   Translucent premandibles present, just anterior to the labial plate (Figs. 471A, 473C) . . . . . . . . . . . . . . . . . . . . . . . . . . . . . . . . . . . . . . . . . . . . . . . . . . . . . . . .6
3. Brush pedestals of preanal segment unicolored (these are two long cylindrical processes, one on each side of the anal papillae) . . . . . . . . . . . . . . . . . . **Parochlus**
   Brush pedestals hyaline at base, black distally . . . . . . . . . . . . . . . . . . . . . . . . . .4
4. Middle tooth forming the apex of the triangular labium . . . . . . . . . . . . . . . . . . . . .5
   Middle tooth deeply imbedded in the anterior margin of the labium . . . **Trichotanypus**
5. Labium with seven pairs of lateral teeth . . . . . . . . . . . . . . . . . . . . . . . . **Boreochlus**
   Labium with 12 pairs of lateral teeth . . . . . . . . . . . . . . . . . . . . . . . **Lasiodiamesa**
6. Third antennal segment annulated (Fig. 470G); paralabial plates usually absent, when present they are not striated but are sometimes bearded . . DIAMESINAE, **14**
   Third antennal segment not annulated; paralabial plates, when present, radially striated (Figs. 472E, F) . . . . . . . . . . . . . . . . . . . . . . . . . . . . . . . . . . . . . . . . . . . . . . . . .7

FIG. 470.–Structure of larvae of Tanypodinae, Diamesinae, and Orthocladiinae. A, *Pentaneura*, ×12; B, lingua of *Procladius*; C, lingua of *Anatopynia*; D, mandible of *Coelotanypus*; E, mandible of *Clinotanypus*; F, stellate hair of *Heptagyia*; G, antenna of *Pseudodiamesa*; H, antenna of *Brillia*; J, preanal papilla of *Brillia*; K, antenna of *Corynoneura*; L, *Symbiocladius* under wing covers of mayfly nymph, ×2.5; M, lateral view of *Symbiocladius*, ×7.5; N, labial plate of *Cardiocladius*; O, mandible of *Cricotopus*. (A from Johannsen, 1937; B to G modified from Johannsen, 1937; L and M from Johannsen, 1937a, after Claassen; H to K, N, and O redrawn from Johannsen, 1937a.)

   7. Paralabial plates absent .............................. ORTHOCLADIINAE, 17
      Paralabial plates present (Figs. 472E, F) ................. CHIRONOMINAE, 38
   8. Segments of body with a few scattered bristles; body slender; both pairs of anal gills
         close to anal opening; most species whitish or yellowish and mottled with
         brown ................................................. **Pentaneura**
      Segments of body with a longitudinal hair fringe on each side; head rather broad;
         ventral pair of anal gills attached to base of prolegs, remote from anus ...... **9**
   9. Head never more than one-third longer than broad; antennae one-fourth or one-third
         as long as head ........................................... **10**
      Head about one and one-half times as long as broad; antennae one-half to three-
         fourths as long as head ........................................ **12**
  10. With four anal gills ............................................. **11**
      With six anal gills; bottom dwellers; mud browsers ..................... **Tanypus**
  11. Lingua of hypopharynx with five teeth (Fig. 470B); larva whitish, yellowish, or red-
         dish, and somewhat mottled with brownish spots ............... **Procladius**
      Lingua of hypopharynx with four teeth (Fig. 470C); reddish to greenish, with yellow
         head ................................................. **Anatopynia**
  12. Antennae about three-fourths as long as head; mandibles hooklike (Fig.
         470E) ................................................. **Clinotanypus**
      Antennae about one-half as long as head; mandibles curved (Fig. 470D) ......... **13**

13. Lingua with seven light teeth; several uncommon species ............ **Coelotanypus**
    Lingua with five dark teeth; about 20 species; widely distributed ...... **Ablabesmyia**
14. Labial plate with an odd number of teeth; in quiet waters ............ **Prodiamesa**
    Labial plate with an even number of teeth; some teeth indistinct or lacking; usually
        in swift waters ................................................................**15**
15. Labial plate undulated and smooth, teeth lacking (Figs. 471B, C) ........ **Potthastia**
    Labial plate with some teeth ..............................................**16**
16. Mandible with about three teeth (Fig. 471D) .......................**Monodiamesa**
    Mandible with about five small teeth (Fig. 471E) ................. **Pseudodiamesa**
17. Antennae at least one-half as long as head, second segment usually slightly bent (Fig.
        470K); mature larva less than 5 mm long ..............................**18**
    Antennae shorter, second segment not bent ..................................**20**
18. Labial plate with an odd number of teeth (Fig. 471F); second and/or third antennal
        segments dark colored ..................................................**19**
    Labial plate with an even number of teeth; antennal segments not dark ...... **Brillia**
19. Antennae longer than head capsule (Fig. 470K)..................... **Corynoneura**
    Antennae shorter than head capsule .......................... **Thienemanniella**
20. Living on bodies or under wing covers of mayfly or stonefly nymphs (Figs.
        470L, M)............................................................... **Symbiocladius**
    Not living on aquatic nymphs .............................................**21**
21. Labial plate with an odd number of teeth (Figs. 470N, 471H) .................**22**
    Labial plate with an even number of teeth .................................**30**
22. Eleven teeth of labial plate short and even; middle tooth very wide (Figs. 470N,
        471H); anterior prolegs single, terminating in two crowns of claws; 8 to 10 mm
        long, yellowish or dusky green; running waters ................**Cardiocladius**
    Labial plate with other details .........................................**23**
23. Middle tooth of labial plate very small (Fig. 471G) ........................ **Brillia**
    Middle tooth of labial plate as long as the two adjacent teeth ...................**24**
24. Central tooth or teeth lighter in color than laterals, or middle tooth with a peaked tip
        (Figs. 471J, K, M) ....................................................**25**
    All teeth the same shade; middle tooth without a special tip ...................**27**
25. Labial plate truncate, with an even row of four to seven small teeth projecting above
        the laterals ........................................................ **Smittia**
    Labial plate not truncate ................................................**26**
26. Middle tooth of labial plate dome-shaped, with or without a peaked or emarginate tip
        (Figs. 471J, K)............................. **Eukiefferiella, Psectrocladius**
    Middle tooth of labial plate not dome-shaped........................ **Cricotopus**
27. Outer margin of mandibles finely crenulated (Fig. 470O); larvae in masses of *Nostoc*,
        in silken tubes on stream bottoms, or in mesophyll channels of
        hydrophytes .................................................... **Cricotopus**
    Outer margin of mandibles not crenulated ................................**28**
28. Third antennal segment less than one-quarter as long as second segment .... **Smittia**
    Third antennal segment one-quarter to one-half as long as second segment (Fig.
        471L)..................................................................**29**
29. Labial plate with 7, 11, or 13 teeth (Fig. 471M); base of mandible may have fine
        serrations on inner margin (Fig. 471N) ...................... **Cricotopus**
    Labial plate with 13, 15, 17, or 19 teeth (Fig. 471O); no serrations on mandible
        (includes the genus *Hydrobaenus*)............................ **Orthocladius**
30. Two middle teeth of labial plate fused into a clear wide tooth that often has two
        discrete tips (Figs. 471P, S); lateral teeth dark and partially fused.
                                                    **Nanocladius, Psectrocladius**
    All teeth of labial plate dark-colored ....................................**31**
31. Labial plate with 10 or 12 teeth ........................................**32**
    Labial plate with 14 teeth ..............................................**36**
32. Labial plate with 10 teeth, the middle pair being blunt (Fig. 471Q) ..... **Eukiefferiella**
    Labial plate with 12 teeth (Fig. 471R) ....................................**33**
33. Labial plate with very black teeth, middle pair largest and rarely fused (Fig. 471R);
        oligotrophic, cold water species ...................... **Heterotrissocladius**
    Labial plate with brown middle teeth, partially fused........................**34**

FIG. 471.–Structure of Diamesinae and Orthocladiinae. B, C, F to K, M, O to V are all labial plates. A, labial plate and premandibles of *Diamesa*; B and C, *Potthastia* (toothless); D, mandible of *Monodiamesa*; E, mandible of *Pseudodiamesa*; F, *Thienemanniella*; G, *Brillia*; H, *Cardiocladius*; J, *Eukiefferiella*; K, *Psectrocladius*; L, antenna of *Cricotopus*; M, *Cricotopus*; N, mandible of *Cricotopus*; O, *Orthocladius*; P, *Psectrocladius*; Q, *Eukiefferiella*; R, *Heterotrissocladius*; S, *Psectrocladius*; T, *Trichocladius*; U, *Metriocnemus*; V, *Diplocladius*. (A, B, D to J, M to V simplified from Mason, 1973; C simplified from Saether, 1971; K simplified from Roback, 1957.)

**34.** Middle teeth of labial plate long and almost completely fused (Fig. 471S) . . . . . . . . . . . . . . . . . . . . . . . . . . . . . . . . . . . . . . . . . . . . . . . . . . . . **Psectrocladius**
 Middle teeth not elongated, not fused or fused only basally (Figs. 471T, Q) . . . . . .**35**
**35.** Middle teeth of labial plate spade-shaped (Fig. 471T) . . . . . . . . . . . . . . .**Trichocladius**
 Middle teeth of labial plate rounded (Fig. 471Q) . . . . . . . . . . . . . . . . . . . .**Eukiefferiella**
**36.** Middle four teeth of labial plate light-colored and even in length, much smaller than more lateral teeth (Fig. 471U) . . . . . . . . . . . . . . . . . . . . . . . . . . . **Metriocnemus**
 Middle four teeth of labial plate dark and not much smaller than more lateral teeth (Fig. 471V) . . . . . . . . . . . . . . . . . . . . . . . . . . . . . . . . . . . . . . . . . . . . . . .**37**
**37.** Mandibles dark-colored at least half of length . . . . . . . . . . . . . . . . . . . . . . . **Diplocladius**
 Mandibles dark-colored less than half of length . . . . . . . . . . . . . . . . . . . . . . . .**Zalutschia**
**38.** First antennal segment not long and curved; antennal tubercles much wider than long (Figs. 472B, C) . . . . . . . . . . . . . . . . . . . . . . . . . . . . . . . . . . . . . . . . . . . . . . . . . . .**39**
 First antennal segment long and curved; antennal tubercles longer than wide (Fig. 472A) . . . . . . . . . . . . . . . . . . . . . . . . . . . . . . . . . . . . . . . . . . . . . . . . . . . . . . .**61**

FIG. 472.–Structure of Chironominae. A, antenna of *Calopsectra*; B, antenna of *Cryptochironomus*; C, antenna of *Chironomus*; D, labial plate of *Cryptochironomus*; E, labial and paralabial plates of *Cryptochironomus*; F, labial and paralabial plates of *Pseudochironomus*; G, posterior end of *Pseudochironomus*; H, *Chironomus*, ×10; J, labial plate of *Stenochironomus*; K, labial plate of *Microtendipes*. *1*, antennal blade; *2*, tubercle; *3*, labial plate; *4*, paralabial plate; *5*, preanal papilla; *6*, anal gill; *7*, proleg; *8*, abdominal gill. (A to H modified from Johannsen, 1937a.)

**39.** Antennae five-segmented (Fig. 472C); last segment often vestigial .............. **40**
    Antennae six-segmented ................................ **57**
**40.** Paralabial plates nearly touching in the midline (Fig. 472F) .................... **41**
    Paralabial plates well separated (Fig. 472E) ................................ **42**
**41.** Paralabial plates three times wider than long, and pointed medially. **Xenochironomus**
    Paralabial plates four times wider than long, rounded medially (Fig. 472F) ........................................ **Pseudochironomus**
**42.** Labial plate with 10 low, rounded black teeth (Fig. 472J) .......... **Stenochironomus**
    Labial plate with other characters .................................. **43**
**43.** Labial plate with an odd number of teeth .............................. **44**
    Labial plate with an even number of teeth ................................ **53**
**44.** Middle tooth translucent, flanked by oblique rows of dark teeth (Fig. 473A) (this genus includes *Harnischia*). .................................. **Cryptochironomus**
    Middle tooth dark, if lighter than laterals then laterals are not oblique .......... **45**
**45.** Labial plate with 15 teeth ................................ **46**
    Labial plate with 11 or 13 teeth; middle tooth may be simple or trifid (Fig. 473E) .**47**

FIG. 473.–Structure of Chironominae larvae. A to G, L to W are all labial plates. A, *Cryptochironomus*; B, *Chironomus*; C, *Endochironomus* (showing premandibles); D, *Parachironomus*; E, *Glyptotendipes*; F, *Goeldichironomus*; G, *Kiefferulus*; H, *Einfeldia* mandible; J, *Dicrotendipes* mandible; K, *Glyptotendipes* mandible; L, *Parachironomus*; M, *Polypedilum*; N, *Polypedilum*; O, *Tribelos*; P, *Phaenopsectra*; Q, Endochironomus; R, *Paralauterborniella*; S, *Stictochironomus*; T, *Stictochironomus*; U, *Paratendipes*; V, *Constempellina*; W, *Rheotanytarsus*; X, *Micropsectra* antenna. (Modified from various sources.)

**46.** Middle tooth of labial plate with two small notches, and slightly shorter than first
laterals (Fig. 473C) . . . . . . . . . . . . . . . . . . . . . . . . . . . . . . . . . . . . . . . . . . . . . . . . . **Endochironomus**
Middle tooth of labial plate slightly longer than first laterals (Fig. 473D), sometimes
with a median notch . . . . . . . . . . . . . . . . . . . . . . . . . . . . . . . . . . . . . . . . . . . . . . **Parachironomus**

47. Middle tooth of labial plate low, one-third wider at base than long (Fig. 473E); eleventh body segment without ventral blood gills (lateral blood gills may be present) . . . . . . . . . . . . . . . . . . . . . . . . . . . . . . . . . . . . . . . . . . . . . . .**Glyptotendipes**
 Middle tooth of labial plate longer and simple, notched, or trifid . . . . . . . . . . . . . . .**48**
48. Middle tooth of labial plate trifid or notched at base (Fig. 473B); eleventh body segment with two pairs of ventral blood gills (Fig. 472H) . . . . . . . . **Chironomus**
 Middle tooth simple or with very small lateral notches . . . . . . . . . . . . . . . . . . . . . . .**49**
49. Middle tooth of labial plate with lateral notches (Figs. 473F, G) . . . . . . . . . . . . . . . .**50**
 Middle tooth of labial plate without lateral notches . . . . . . . . . . . . . . . . . . . . . . . . .**51**
50. With two pairs of ventral blood gills . . . . . . . . . . . . . . . . . . . . . . . . . . **Goeldichironomus**
 With one pair of ventral blood gills . . . . . . . . . . . . . . . . . . . . . . . . . . . . . . . . . . . . **Kiefferulus**
51. Third lateral tooth of mandibles unequally divided (Fig. 473H); two pairs of ventral blood gills on eleventh segment; rare . . . . . . . . . . . . . . . . . . . . . . . . . . . . .**Einfeldia**
 Third lateral tooth of mandible equally divided or simple; no ventral blood gills on eleventh segment . . . . . . . . . . . . . . . . . . . . . . . . . . . . . . . . . . . . . . . . . . . . . . . . .**52**
52. Third lateral tooth of mandible equally divided (Fig. 473J) . . . . . . . . . . . . **Dicrotendipes**
 Third lateral tooth of mandible simple (Fig. 473K) . . . . . . . . . . . . . . . . . . **Glyptotendipes**
53. Median labial tooth cleft (Fig. 473L) . . . . . . . . . . . . . . . . . . . . . . . . . . . . **Parachironomus**
 Labial plate otherwise . . . . . . . . . . . . . . . . . . . . . . . . . . . . . . . . . . . . . . . . . . . . . . . . .**54**
54. First lateral teeth of labial plate not longer than second laterals (Figs. 473M, N). **Polypedilum**
 First lateral teeth of labial plate longer than second laterals (Fig. 473O) . . . . . . . . .**55**
55. Four central teeth cleft equally deep (Fig. 473O) . . . . . . . . . . . . . . . . . . . . . . . **Tribelos**
 Two middle teeth cleft not as deeply as first laterals (Figs. 473P, Q) . . . . . . . . . . . .**56**
56. Two middle teeth of labial plate pointed (Fig. 473P) . . . . . . . . . . . . . . . **Phaenopsectra**
 Two middle teeth of labial plate not so distinctly separated (Fig. 473Q). **Endochironomus**
57. Labial plate with 13 teeth; median tooth very wide and translucent (Fig. 473R) . . . . . . . . . . . . . . . . . . . . . . . . . . . . . . . . . . . . . . . . . . . . . . . **Paralauterborniella**
 Labial plate with an even number of teeth . . . . . . . . . . . . . . . . . . . . . . . . . . . . . . . .**58**
58. Labial plate with 12 or 14 teeth (Fig. 472K) . . . . . . . . . . . . . . . . . . . . . . . . . . . . . . .**59**
 Labial plate with 16 teeth . . . . . . . . . . . . . . . . . . . . . . . . . . . . . . . . . . . . . . . . . . . . .**60**
59. Antennae about as long as mandibles . . . . . . . . . . . . . . . . . . . . . . . . . . . . **Microtendipes**
 Antennae about twice as long as mandibles . . . . . . . . . . . . . . . . . . . . . **Lauterborniella**
60. Middle four teeth projecting above second and third laterals (Figs. 473S, T). **Stictochironomus**
 Third lateral teeth longest (Fig. 473U) . . . . . . . . . . . . . . . . . . . . . . . . . . . . **Paratendipes**
61. Paralabial plates pointed and separated medially (Fig. 473V) . . . . . . . . **Constempellina**
 Paralabial plates blunt and meeting at midline (Fig. 473W) . . . . . . . . . . . . . . . . . . .**62**
62. Antennal tubercles with a spur (Fig. 473X) . . . . . . . . . . . . . . . . . . . . . . . . **Micropsectra**
 Antennal tubercle without a spur (Fig. 472A); a complex of genera, sometimes all combined into *Tanytarsus*.
 **Calopsectra, Cladotanytarsus, Paratanytarsus, Rheotanytarsus, Tanytarsus**

Superficially, the pupae resemble those of the Culicidae. The head and thorax form a large mass at the anterior end, and the abdomen is elongated, cylindrical, and strongly curved or straight. Some pupae breathe by means of ovate, trumpet-shaped, or cylindrical thoracic respiratory organs (Fig. 474H); other forms have tufts of fine filaments in a similar location (Fig. 474J). The pupae may remain on the bottom in the old larval tube, where they keep the water in circulation by movements of the abdomen, or they may swim actively near the surface or among aquatic plants. They come to the surface film just before the imago is ready to emerge. Most emergences occur between 6 P.M. and 6 A.M., and especially between 6 P.M. and 8 P.M.

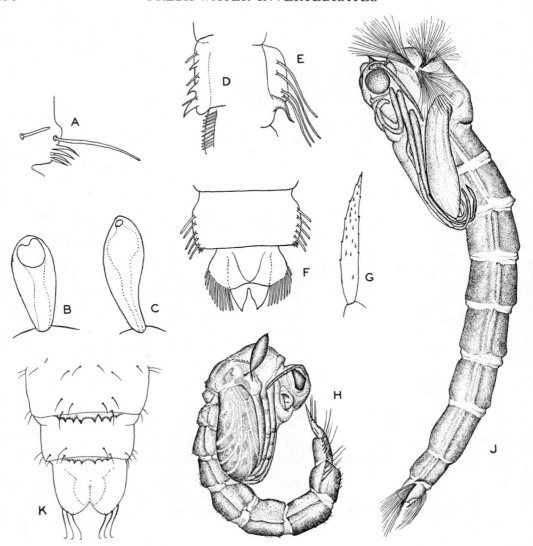

FIG. 474.–Structure of pupae of Chironomidae. A, comb on penultimate abdominal segment of *Cryptochironomus*; B and C, typical abdominal respiratory organs of Tanypodinae; D, comb on penultimate abdominal segment of *Calopsectra*; E, comb and spine on penultimate abdominal segment of *Chironomus*; F, posterior end of *Pseudochironomus*; G, respiratory process of *Brillia*; H, *Pentaneura,* ×12; J, *Chironomus,* ×12; K, dorsal view of posterior end of *Diamesa* pupa. (A, D to F redrawn from Johannsen, 1937a; G redrawn from Johannsen, 1937; H from Johannsen, 1937; J and K from Johannsen, 1937a.)

## KEY TO SUBFAMILIES OF CHIRONOMIDAE PUPAE

**1.** Head and thorax relatively large (Fig. 474H); prothoracic respiratory organs without open stigmata (Figs. 474G, H) ...........................TANYPODINAE
    Head and thorax not especially large (Fig. 474J) ................................**2**
**2.** Thoracic respiratory organs without open stigmata (Figs. 474G, H) ................**3**
    Thoracic respiratory organs with open stigmata .................PODONOMINAE

3. Thoracic respiratory organ a tuft of numerous filaments (Fig. 474J).
   ......................................................CHIRONOMINAE
   Thoracic respiratory organ a slender tubular process, or without thoracic respiratory organ (Fig. 474G) ................................................................4
4. Preanal segment with comb or spines on posterolateral angles (Figs. 474D–F).
   ......................................................CHIRONOMINAE
   Preanal segment without comb or spines on posterolateral angles.................5
5. Posterior margins of abdominal segments with a row of spines (Fig. 474K).
   ......................................................DIAMESINAE
   Posterior margins of abdominal segments without such spines..ORTHOCLADIINAE

## HELEIDAE (BITING MIDGES)

Heleidae (biting midges) are usually less than 4 mm long and are commonly called "sand flies," "no-see-ums," or "punkies." The bite of some species is very irritating, and in certain areas around lakes and along the seashore they are present in such enormous numbers as to be serious pests. The immature stages are chiefly aquatic and semiaquatic in less than half of the species in this family. *Culicoides* and *Leptoconops* are the most common genera, the latter being restricted to the southwest.

Although the elongated larvae may be found in such diverse habitats as springs, mineral waters, psammolittoral, streams, ponds, lakes, and wet mud and debris along shores, they are most abundant in floating masses of algae. Some are herbivorous, others are carnivorous, and a few are even cannibalistic. The last segment has retractile gill filaments. Total length ranges from 3 to 12 mm.

Some American genera are unknown in the larval stages. The key below nevertheless includes those that are most likely to be encountered in aquatic and semiaquatic situations.

The pupae are free except in *Atrichopogon*, where the last larval skin remains attached to the posterior end of the pupa. They are inactive except when disturbed. There are two respiratory trumpets at the anterior end. The pupal stage lasts only three to five days.

Larvae and pupae are most easily collected by washing out masses of algae with a small stream of water, or by examining the filaments in a shallow white pan.

## KEY TO GENERA OF HELEIDAE LARVAE

1. Prolegs present on prothorax .....................................................2
   Prolegs lacking on prothorax .....................................................3
2. Body oval in cross section; lateral processes of body at least as long as segments (Fig. 475J); 12 species ................................................**Atrichopogon**
   Body circular in cross section; lateral processes absent or less than half as long as segments (Fig. 475L); 40 species ...........................................**Forcipomyia**
3. Head well developed; head capsule well sclerotized............................4
   Head not sclerotized but provided with a system of heavily sclerotized rods; mostly western and southwestern states; six species ....................**Leptoconops**
4. Head short and thick, the length not exceeding one and one-half times the width; body segments each slightly longer than head (Figs. 475E, G, H) .................5
   Head long, the length more than twice the width; body segments long and slender (Fig. 475F) .......................................................................8
5. Body curved; larva a climber .....................................................6
   Body straight; larva a swimmer ...................................................7

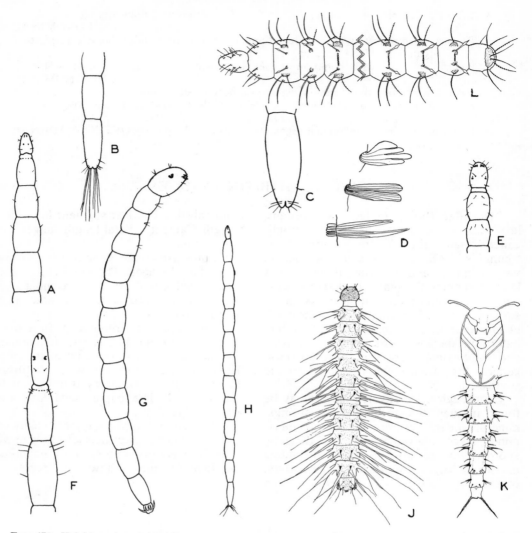

FIG. 475.–Heleidae. A to J larval structures; K, pupa of *Probezzia*, ×13; A, anterior end of *Palpomyia tibialis* (Meigen); B, posterior end of *Alluaudomyia*; C, posterior end of *Stilobezzia*; D, flaplike structures attached on inside of last larval exoskeleton of *Palpomyia*; E, anterior end of *Culicoides*; F, anterior end of *Probezzia*; G, *Dasyhelea*, ×19; H, *Palpomyia*, ×8; J, *Atrichopogon*, ×11; L, dorsal view of *Forcipomyia*. (A to C and E to G modified from Thomsen; D, J, and K from Thomsen: L from Wirth, 1952.)

6. Last segment with hooks; mouth directed ventrally (Fig. 475G); 25 species. **Dasyhelea**
   Last segment without terminal hooks but with short setae (Fig. 475C); mouth parts directed anteriorly; 16 species . . . . . . . . . . . . . . . . . . . . . . . . . . . . . . **Stilobezzia**
7. Head pear shaped; body considerably wider than head (Figs. 475H, L); body 9 to 10 mm long . . . . . . . . . . . . . . . . . . . . . . . . . . . . . . **Palpomyia tibialis** (Meigen)
   Head oval; body about as wide as head (Fig. 475E); 4 to 5 mm long; 100 species . . . . . . . . . . . . . . . . . . . . . . . . . . . . . . . . . . . . . . . . . . . .**Culicoides**
8. Anal hairs as long or longer than last segment (Fig. 475B); body 5 to 6 mm long . . . . . . . . . . . . . . . . . . . . . . . . . . . . . . . . . . . . . . . . . . . **Alluaudomyia**
   Anal hairs shorter than last segment; 7 to 12 mm long . . . . . . . . . . . . . . . . . . . . . . . . . .**9**
9. With flaplike structures inside of cast skin (Fig. 475D); 22 species . . . . . . . . **Palpomyia**
   Without such structures; 30 and 10 species . . . . . . . . . . . . . . . . . . . . **Bezzia, Probezzia**

# STRATIOMYIDAE (SOLDIER FLIES)

Adult soldier flies are small to moderately large insects with bright green or yellow markings. They are chiefly associated with flowers. In those few species having aquatic immature stages, the eggs are deposited most frequently on aquatic plants and debris in shallow ponds, slow brooks, and streams.

The larvae are easily identified: (1) they have a heavy opaque deposit of calcium carbonate in the integument; (2) they are stiff and apparently lifeless, spindle shaped, and somewhat flattened dorsoventrally; and (3) they have a circlet of hairs or bristles around a pair of spiracular openings at the extreme posterior end. These bristles are spread out in a stellate manner on the surface film and act as a float. The larvae may remain submerged for long periods of time, however, utilizing the oxygen contained in the extensive tracheal system. Food includes algae, organic debris, and small Metazoa. Although soldier fly larvae are not common in collections, species of *Stratiomys* and *Odontomyia* are encountered most frequently. Length ranges from 10 to 50 mm.

The pupae remain within the last larval skin, which thus becomes the puparium.

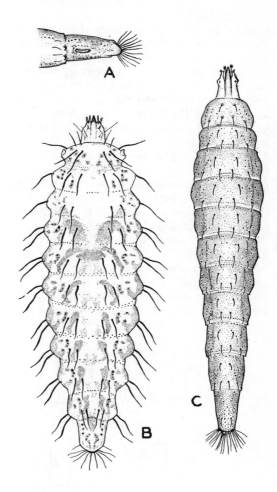

FIG. 476.–Stratiomyidae larvae. A, posterior end of *Odontomyia cincta*; B, *Oxycera*, ×8; C, *Odontomyia cincta*, ×9. (From Johannsen, 1935.)

## KEY TO COMMON GENERA OF STRATIOMYIDAE LARVAE

1. Antennae placed laterally on head (Fig. 476C) ....................................2
   Antennae placed dorsally on head, remote from margin (Fig. 476B) ...............3
2. Caudal margin of penultimate segment with a pair of ventral, stout, curved, hooklike spines (Fig. 476A); antennae more than three times as long as broad; 7 and 30 species ........................................ **Hedriodiscus, Odontomyia**
   Caudal margin of penultimate segment without ventral hooks; antennae less than three times as long as broad; 25 species ............................. **Stratiomys**
3. With a pair of stout, curved, ventral spines on the posterior margin of the penultimate segment; with a transverse ventral row of short, stout spines anterior to the middle of each segment except the last; 12 species .............. **Euparyphus**
   Stout, curved, ventral spines lacking on the posterior margin of the penultimate segment ....................................................................4
4. With four or six long setae on the posterior margin of the last segment; hair fringe of spiracular chamber short; 30 species .........................**Nemotelus**
   No long setae on posterior margin of last segment; fringe of spiracular chamber long (Fig. 476B); six species ......................................... **Oxycera**

## TABANIDAE (HORSEFLIES)

The horseflies are a large family of worldwide distribution, there being more than 400 species in the United States alone. They are large (10 to 25 mm long) and robust. The females of some species bite severely, and many species are serious pests to cattle and other domestic animals as well as to man. Although most species are semiaquatic and pupate in damp earth, the immature stages of some are truly aquatic. The eggs of these are laid in masses on foliage, rocks, or sticks just above the surface of ponds, swamps, pools, and streams.

When the larvae hatch they fall into the water. They are elongated; cylindrical; tapered at both ends; and white, yellowish, greenish, or brownish. The body is divided into a minute head, three thoracic segments, eight abdominal segments, and a short posterior siphon. The first seven abdominal segments bear a pair of dorsal prolegs (often fused and small) as well as a pair of lateral and a pair of ventral prolegs. The eighth abdominal segment has a broad base but tapers distally. At the tip of the siphon the two tracheal trunks either open as a single vertical slit or end in a sharp compressed spine. The usual length is 15 to 40 mm.

Three common genera with aquatic larvae are found in the United States, *Haematopota*, *Chrysops*, and *Tabanus*. The first of these is represented by only five species. *Chrysops* and *Tabanus*, however, are widely distributed and common and are each represented by 75 to 80 species. A few species of *Tabanus* occur in swift water, but most are found in the muddy shallows of ponds and swamps. *Chrysops* feeds on organic debris, whereas *Tabanus* and *Haematopota* are predaceous and devour snails, oligochaetes, and insect larvae.

The duration of the larval stage is variable, but in some instances it is known to

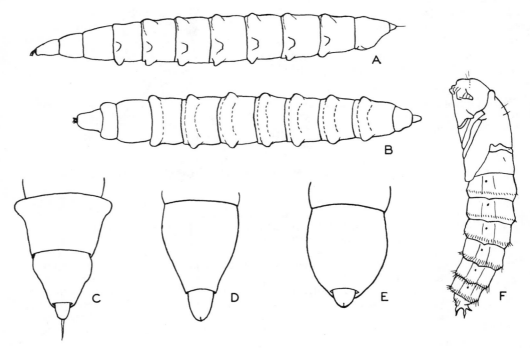

FIG. 477.–Structure of Tabanidae. A to E, larvae; F, pupa of *Chrysops*, ×5; A, *Chrysops*, ×7; B, *Tabanus*, ×3; C, posterior end of *Chrysops*; D, posterior end of *Tabanus*; E, posterior end of *Haematopota*. (B redrawn from Johannsen, 1935.)

last as long as three years. Just before pupation the larvae crawl out of the water to the adjacent soil well above water level, where they burrow into the ground and pupate at a depth of 2 to 8 cm. The entire life cycle lasts one to four years, depending on temperature and other conditions.

## KEY TO GENERA OF TABANIDAE LARVAE

1. Mature larva small, usually less than 20 mm long; tracheal trunks not swollen; body almost entirely striated; terminal (third) segment of antennae as long or longer than second; usually with a protrusile stigmatal spine (Fig. 477A, C). **Chrysops**
   Mature larva usually more than 20 mm long; tracheal trunks usually swollen; ventral and dorsal areas smooth, especially on the thorax; terminal segment of antenna shortest; almost never a protrusile spine at tip of abdomen . . . . . . . . . . . . . . . .2
2. Anal segment rounded; siphon short (Fig. 477E); dark ornamentation only on anal and thoracic segments . . . . . . . . . . . . . . . . . . . . . . . . . . . . . . . . . . . . . . . . . **Haematopota**
   Anal segment tapering; siphon elongated when extended (Figs. 477B, D); dark markings, when present, usually on other abdominal segments also, or confined to prothoracic collar only . . . . . . . . . . . . . . . . . . . . . . . . . . . . . . . . . . . . . . . . . . . . **Tabanus**

## RHAGIONIDAE (SNIPE FLIES)

Snipe flies are Diptera of moderate size that are usually found flying around low bushes, foliage, and tall grasses. Their cone-shaped abdomen is characteristic. A few species are bloodsuckers. Only one American genus, *Atherix,* is known to have aquatic larvae. The female fastens her eggs in masses to twigs and branches which overhang ponds and streams. She dies after oviposition and remains attached to the egg mass. Other females may deposit their eggs on the original mass in the same manner, and in this way eggs and dead females may form a considerable bulk.

On hatching, the larvae fall into the water. They are elongated, cylindrical, slightly flattened, and have the head largely retracted into the thorax. The anterior end is tapered, and there are well developed, paired, spiny prolegs as well as lateral and dorsal pseudopods on the abdominal segments. They may be most easily identified, however, by the presence of two long, fringed, terminal filaments at the end of the abdomen. Respiration is facilitated by two protrusile blood gills situated below the terminal filaments. They are predaceous in their food habits. *Atherix variegata* Walker is the common species. Total length is 10 to 18 mm.

The larva leaves the water and pupates

FIG. 478.–*Atherix variegata.* A, lateral view of larva, ×7.5; B, ventral view of posterior end of larva; C, ventral view of pupa. (A and B redrawn from Greene; C from Neff, 1965.)

in moist soil near the water's edge. The pupa (Fig. 478C) is distinguished by a raised structure bearing the convoluted prothoracic spiracle, by the short wing pads, and by the abundance of setose body projections.

## SYRPHIDAE (FLOWER FLIES)

The members of the Syrphidae are very common brightly colored insects. The majority feed on pollen and nectar, and their habit of remaining poised in the air is responsible for their being called "hover flies." This family is in need of careful taxonomic revision.

The larvae of the majority are found in terrestrial habitats. Others are semiaquatic and are found in such places as water-filled tree holes and wet, decaying logs. Members of a few genera are truly aquatic and occur in sewage, polluted streams, rivulets, and decaying vegetation at the edges of ponds.

Species of the genus *Eristalis* are the only common aquatic larvae in the United States. *E. transversus* Wied., *E. flavipes* Walk., and *E. tenax* (L.) are the species encountered most frequently. The body is covered with fine spinules, and the thoracic and abdominal segments are wrinkled and indistinct. There are seven pairs of ventral prolegs, a pair of short, dorsal, anterior respiratory horns that terminate in a series of minute openings, and an elongated caudal respiratory tube. This tube is three-seg-

mented, telescoping, from two to four times the length of the body proper when extended, and has two spiracular openings at its tip. Respiration is probably further facilitated by a series of delicate retractile anal gills, although some workers believe that these structures are unimportant. The head is small and retracted into the body; it bears reduced mouthparts. *Eristalis* is inactive and feeds on decaying organic material in water that is usually sufficiently shallow to permit the tip of the extended caudal respiratory tube to be projected just above the surface. Because of their peculiar appearance, they have long been called "rat-tailed maggots."

In their habits and general structure, most other aquatic and semiaquatic syrphid larvae resemble *Eristalis*. In some of them, however, the caudal respiratory organ may be strongly sclerotized and relatively short. Sometimes it is less than one-tenth as long as the rest of the body. The total length, exclusive of the respiratory tube, ranges from about 5 to 25 mm.

Fig. 479.–Larva of *Eristalis* with respiratory tube partly contracted, ×2.3.

## KEY TO COMMON GENERA OF SYRPHIDAE LARVAE

1. Extended respiratory tube less than one-fourth as long as body; eight species ........................................................ **Myolepta**
   Respiratory tube longer ................................................. 2
2. Extended respiratory tube shorter than the body; about 12 species ..... **Chrysogaster**
   Extended respiratory tube as long or longer than the body ...................... 3
3. Extended respiratory tube little, if any, longer than the body ............. **Myolepta**
   Extended respiratory tube much longer than body ........................... 4
4. Two longitudinal tracheal trunks undulatory in position; 25 species ....... **Helophilus**
   Two longitudinal tracheal trunks straight ................................. 5
5. Body flattened; 10 species ............................................ **Mallota**
   Body not flattened; 30 species ........................................ **Eristalis**

## SCIOMYZIDAE (MARSH FLIES)

Marsh flies are sluggish yellow or brown flies found at the edges of ponds, streams, and swamps. Although the imagoes of many species are known, the immature stages of relatively few have been studied.

All larvae are aquatic or semiaquatic. They are cylindrical, yellowish to dark brown, and tapered at both ends; each segment has a ring of rounded tubercles. At the caudal end there is a lobed spiracular disc that is somewhat similar to the spiracular disc of crane fly larvae. The head is retracted except for a pair of mouth hooks. The larvae are usually found at the surface of the water among floating vegetation or on the bottom. *Sepedon, Dictya,* and *Pherbellia* are widely distributed American genera. *Tetanocera* is less common, and *Poecilographa* is rare. Total length ranges from 5 to 17 mm.

The puparia are swollen, seedlike, and curved upward at one or both ends, but they still have vestiges of certain larval structures in the integument.

*Pherbellia* and *Sepedon* are unusual because the larvae are carnivorous and feed chiefly on aquatic snails. *Sepedon* kills snails quickly, remains in the snail shell only long enough for a full meal, and then attacks another snail when hungry. *Pherbellia,* however, kills the snail and remains within the shell and feeds on the snail tissues until ready for pupation. In some species the puparia remain within the snail shell.

FIG. 480.–Sciomyzidae. A, puparium of *Dictya pictipes,* ×5; B, larva of *Sepedon fuscipennis,* ×5; C, larva of *Dictya pictipes,* ×6; D, spiracular disc of *Sepedon*; E, spiracular disc of *Dictya*; F, spiracular disc of *Sepedon*; G, spiracular disc of *Pherbellia.* (A to E from Johannsen, 1935; F from Neff and Berg; G from Bratt et al.)

## KEY TO COMMON GENERA OF SCIOMYZIDAE LARVAE

1. Spiracular disc without radiating hairs ............................ **Poecilographa**
   Spiracular disc with radiating hairs ............................................2
2. Spiracular disc with four prominent lateroventral lobes and six small and distinct or
   indistinct dorsolateral lobes (Figs. 480D, F); feeds on snails ......... **Sepedon**
   Spiracular disc otherwise ....................................................3
3. Spiracular disc with eight triangular lobes............................ **Tetanocera**
   Without such triangular lobes ................................................4
4. Spiracular disc with eight broadly rounded lobes extending from dorsal to ventral
   perimeter (Fig. 480E)................................................. **Dictya**
   Spiracular disc with four to eight small lobes restricted to lateral and ventral perimeter
   (Fig. 480G); feeds on snails ...................................... **Pherbellia**

## EPHYDRIDAE (SHORE FLIES)

Shore flies are small, brown, gray, or blackish flies inhabiting moist places on the shores of streams, ponds, lakes, and the ocean. They are especially typical of salt and alkali waters and thermal springs. A few are leaf and stem miners. The immature stages of relatively few species are known.

The cylindrical larvae are characterized by mouth hooks that have a serrate or digitate margin. The caudal respiratory organs are simple paired tubercles or greatly elongated retractile processes. Numerous larval forms have been described in the literature, but the following genera and species are the most common.

*Lemnaphila scotlandae* is a miner in fronds of *Lemna* in the eastern states. The larvae average only 2.25 mm in length and may be identified by the fact that each tracheal trunk ends in a tubercle that terminates in a sharp, hollow spur. The species of *Hydrellia* are somewhat similar to *L. scotlandae* but are larger and mine in the leaves of *Potamogeton, Panicum,* and so on. Both *Lemnaphila* and *Hydrellia* obtain oxygen from intercellular air spaces in their food plants.

*Ephydra* and *Setacera* are similar. They may be recognized by a long, cylindrical postanal process that has two retractile respiratory tubes at its apex. Unlike *Eristalis*, however, they do not obtain their oxygen at the surface film, but swim aimlessly about, sometimes as deep as a meter. There are eight pairs of short, conical, clawed, abdominal prolegs, each pair being fused at the base. The last pair of prolegs are considerably larger than the others. Immature aquatic stages of *Setacera* have been found only a few times in brine and salt pools, but certain species of *Ephydra* are relatively common. *E. gracilis* Packard is extremely abundant in Great Salt Lake and other similar habitats. *E. millbrae* Jones has been found in California salt marshes and the Salton Sea. *E. subopaca* Loew is widely distributed in salt or alkali ponds and lakes. *Hydroporus hians* is common in similar locations in the western half of the United States.

The larva of *Scatella stagnalis* Fall is widely distributed in both cold and hot springs. It may be distinguished from both *Ephydra* and *Setacera* by the fact that prolegs are lacking. The segments are provided with creeping welts, however, the spinules of which are a little longer than those on the adjacent body parts.

*Ephydra, Setacera,* and *Scatella* range from about 8 to 17 mm in length.

The pupae of the shore flies are formed in the last larval integument, which retains many of the larval characteristics but is considerably swollen.

## KEY TO COMMON GENERA OF EPHYDRIDAE LARVAE

1. Leaf miners in aquatic plants; posterior end with two sharp spurs ................2
   Not leaf miners .............................................................3

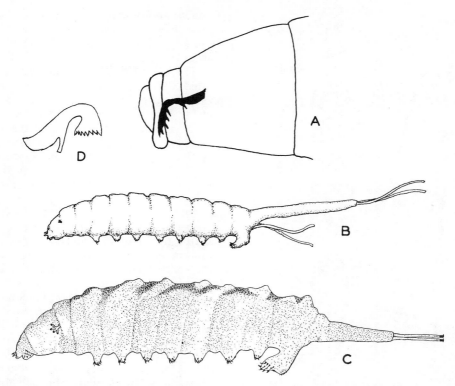

FIG. 481.–Structure of larvae of Ephydridae. A, anterior end of *Ephydra subopaca* showing mouth hooks; B, *E. gracilis,* ×6; C, *E. subopaca,* ×9; D, mouth hook of *Brachydeutera*. (B and C from Johannsen, 1935.)

2. Leaf miner in *Lemna;* body 2.5 mm long; eastern states.
                                        **Lemnaphila scotlandae** Cresson
    Leaf miners in other hydrophytes; many larger species; widely distributed. **Hydrellia**
3. Mud dwellers, usually attached to roots with a posterior respiratory spine; 10 species . . . . . . . . . . . . . . . . . . . . . . . . . . . . . . . . . . . . . . . . . . . . . . . .**Notiphila**
    Not root feeders . . . . . . . . . . . . . . . . . . . . . . . . . . . . . . . . . . . . . . . . . . . . . . . . . . .**4**
4. Mouth hooks palmate, with very short teeth; scavengers (Fig. 481D) . .**Brachydeutera**
    Mouth hooks otherwise (Fig. 481A) . . . . . . . . . . . . . . . . . . . . . . . . . . . . . . . . . . . . .**5**
5. Posterior respiratory tube short, with the basal portion as short as the two distal branches; breeds in pools of crude petroleum and waste oil; two species . . . . . . . . . . . . . . . . . . . . . . . . . . . . . . . . . . . . . . . . . . . . . . **Helaeomyia**
    Posterior respiratory tube long (Figs. 481B, C); not breeding in petroleum areas . . . .**6**
6. With eight pairs of heavily clawed abdominal prolegs (Figs. 481B, C).
        10 species of **Ephydra,** six species of **Setacera,** two species of **Dimecoenia,** and **Hydropyrus hians** (Say) (in highly alkaline lakes)
    Abdominal prolegs absent or poorly developed, without heavy claws . . . . . . . . . . . . .**7**
7. Mouth hooks without teeth; predaceous on small insects; marshy streams; about eight species . . . . . . . . . . . . . . . . . . . . . . . . . . . . . . . . . . . . . . . . . . . . . . . . . **Ochthera**
    Mouth hooks with teeth . . . . . . . . . nine species of **Scatella,** two species of **Neoscatella**

## ANTHOMYIIDAE (ANTHOMYIIDS)

The anthomyiids are closely related to houseflies and are included in that family (Muscidae) by some authorities. There are more than 500 species in the United States. They are usually found on leaves and flowers.

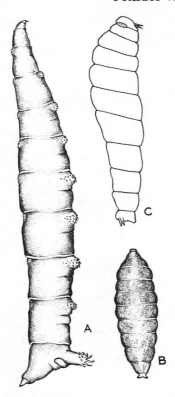

FIG. 482.–Anthomyiidae. A, lateral view of larva of *Limnophora aequifrons,* ×6; B, puparium of *Limnophora torreyae,* ×5; C, larva of *Hydromyza confluens,* ×7. (A and B from Johannsen, 1935; C redrawn from Hickman.)

Of the few genera that have immature aquatic stages *Limnophora* is by far the most common. The whitish or yellowish larvae are cylindrical and tapered anteriorly. The head is wholly retracted except for a pair of black mouth hooks. Ventrally, there are several closely arranged rows of very short setae along the anterior margin of each abdominal segment. Anthomyiid larvae are usually found in shallow brooks, rivulets, or trickles, especially in moss or masses of algae.

There are three common species in the United States. In *L. aequifrons* Stein all the prolegs except the last pair are vestigial, and the last segment ends in a pair of retractile conical projections that have a common base and that bear spiracles at their tips. In *L. discreta* Stein and *L. torreyae* Joh. all the prolegs are vestigial. In the former species the spiracles are borne on two small papillae that are widely separated on the truncate terminal segment. In *L. torreyae,* however, the spiracles are borne at the tips of a pair of tubercles that have a common base at the posterior end of the cone-shaped last segment. Length of the larvae is 7 to 15 mm.

Another group of anthomyiids includes the dung flies, which breed in excrement and decaying vegetation; a few are leaf miners and stem borers. Only one species, *Hydromyza confluens* Loew, is of interest here. The small, dull, whitish larvae are imbedded in the submerged petioles of the yellow water lily, where they feed on the tissues and produce small swellings. The pupae remain within the petiole, and the adults escape from the puparium and leave the petiole through a small trapdoorlike opening in the epidermis and float to the surface and fly off. In the strict sense, the immature stages are not aquatic, since they do not actually come in contact with water.

The puparia are ovoid, reddish-brown, and have 11 visible segments. They have much the same general size and proportions as the larvae, and some larval structures still remain more or less visible.

## DIPTERA REFERENCES

ALEXANDER, C. P. 1920. The crane-flies of New York. Part II. Biology and phylogeny. *Mem. Cornell Univ. Agric. Exp. Sta.* **38**:691–1133.

AUGENFELD, J. M. 1967. Effects of oxygen deprivation on aquatic midge larvae under natural and laboratory conditions. *Physiol. Zool.* **40**:149–158.

BAKER, M. 1961. The altitudinal distribution of mosquito larvae in the Colorado Front Range. *Trans. Am. Entomol. Soc.* **87**:231–246.

BERG, C. O. 1950. Biology of certain Chironomidae reared from Potamogeton. *Ecol. Monogr.* **20**:83–101.

———. 1950a. Hydrellia (Ephydridae) and some other acalyptrate Diptera reared from Potamogeton. *Ann. Entomol. Soc. Am.* **43**:374–398.

BERG, K. 1937. Contributions to the biology of Corethra Meigen (Chaoborus Lichtenstein). *Det Kongelige. Vidensk. Selsk. Biol. Medd.* **13**:1–101.

BOESEL, M. W. 1974. Observations on the Coelotanypodini of the northeastern states, with keys to the known stages (Diptera: Chironomidae: Tanypodinae). *J. Kans. Entomol. Soc.* **47**:417–432.

BRATT, A. D. et al. 1969. Biology of Pherbellia (Diptera: Sciomyzidae). *Mem. Cornell Univ. Agric. Exp. Sta.* **404**:1–247.

BRUNDIN, L. 1949. Chironomiden und andere Bodentiere der südschwedischen Urgebirgsseen. *Rept. Inst. Freshwater Res. Drottningholm* **30**:1–915.

———. 1966. Transantarctic relationships and their significance, as evidenced by chironomid midges with a monograph of the Subfamilies Podonominae and Aphroteniinae and the Austral Heptagyiae. *K. Sven. Vetensk. Handl. Fjärde Ser.* **2**(1):1–472.

CARPENTER, S. J., and W. J. LACASSE. 1974. *Mosquitoes of North America.* 360 pp. Univ. California Press, Berkeley; reprint of 1955 edition.

CARPENTER, S. J., W. W. MIDDLEKAUFF, and R. W. CHAMBERLAIN. 1946. The mosquitoes of the southern United States east of Oklahoma and Texas. *Am. Midl. Nat. Monogr.* **3**:1–292.

COLE, F. R., and E. I. SCHLINGER. 1969. *The Flies of Western North America.* 698 pp. Univ. California Press, Berkeley.

COLLINS, N. C. 1975. Population biology of a brine fly (Diptera: Ephydridae) in the presence of abundant algal food. *Ecology* **56**:1139–1148.

COOK, E. F. 1956. The Nearctic Chaoborinae (Diptera: Culicidae). *Tech. Bull. Univ. Minn. Agric. Exp. Sta.* **218**:1–120.

CRESSON, JR., E. T. 1942. Descriptions of two new Nearctic species of the genus Hydrellia reared from pond-weed (Diptera: Ephydridae). *Entomol. News* **53**:78–79.

CURRAN, C. H. 1965. *The Families and Genera of North American Diptera.* 512 pp. Henry Tripp, Mt. Vernon, N.Y. Reprint of 1934 edition.

CURRY, L. L. 1958. Larvae and pupae of the species of Cryptochironomus (Diptera) in Michigan. *Limnol. Oceanogr.* **3**:427–442.

———. 1961. *A key for the larval forms of aquatic midges (Tendipedidae: Diptera) found in Michigan.* 162 pp. (processed).

DEONIER, D. L. 1971. A systematic and ecological study of Nearctic Hydrellia (Diptera: Ephydridae). *Smithson. Contrib. Zool.* **68**:1–147.

DISNEY, R. H. L. 1975. A key to the British Dixidae. *Sci. Publ. Freshwater Biol. Assoc.* **31**:1–78.

DUNAVAN, D. 1929. A study of the respiration and respiratory organs of the rat-tailed maggot, Eristalis arbustorum L. (Diptera: Syrphidae). *Ann. Entomol. Soc. Am.* **22**:731–753.

DYAR, H. G. 1928. The mosquitoes of the Americas. *Publ. Carnegie Inst.* **387**:1–616.

EWER, R. F. 1942. On the functions of haemoglobin in Chironomus. *J. Exp. Biol.* **18**:197–205.

FEDORENKO, A. Y. 1975. Feeding characteristics and predation impact of Chaoborus (Diptera: Chaoborinae) larvae in a small lake. *Limnol. Oceanogr.* **20**:250–258.

GOUIN, F. J. 1959. Morphology of the larval head of some Chironomidae (Diptera: Nematocera). *Smithson. Misc. Coll.* **137**:175–201.

HALL, H. A., and G. PRITCHARD. 1975. The food of larvae of Tipula sacra (Alexander) in a series of abandoned beaver ponds (Diptera: Tipulidae). *J. Anim. Ecol.* **44**:55–66.

HALL, R. E., and J. J. HARROD. 1963. A method of rearing Simulium ornatum var. nitidifrons (Diptera: Simuliidae) in the laboratory. *Hydrobiologia* **22**:197–201.

HAMILTON, A. L., O. A. SAETHER, and D. R. OLIVER. 1969. A classification of the Nearctic Chironomidae. *Tech. Rep. Fish. Res. Board of Can.* **124**:1–42.

HAYES, W. P. 1938, 1939. A bibliography of keys for the identification of immature insects. Part I. Diptera. *Entomol. News* **49**:246–251; **50**:5–10, 76–82.

HENNIG, W. 1968. *Die Larvenform der Dipteren.* 1271 pp. (three parts). Akademie Verlag, Berlin. (Reprint of 1948–1952 edition).

HICKMAN, C. P. 1935. External features of the larva of Hydromyza confluens. *Proc. Ind. Acad. Sci.* **44**:212–216.

HOGUE, C. L. 1966. The California species of Philorus: taxonomy, early stages and descriptions of two new species (Diptera: Blepharoceridae). *Contrib. Sci. Los. Ang. Cty. Mus.* **99**:1–22.

———. 1966a. A new species of Dioptopsis from California (Diptera: Blepharoceridae). *Contrib. Sci.* **120**:1–5.

———. 1973. The net-winged midges of Blepharoceridae of California. *Bull. Calif. Insect Surv.* **15**:1–83.

———. 1973a. A taxonomic review of the genus Maruina (Diptera: Psychodidae). *Sci. Bull. Nat. Hist. Mus. Los Ang. Cty.* **17**:1–69.

HORSFALL, W. R. 1955. *Mosquitoes. Their Bionomics and Relation to Disease.* 723 pp. Ronald, New York.

JOHANNSEN, O. A. 1934. Aquatic Diptera. Part I. Nemocera, exclusive of Chironomidae and Ceratopogonidae. *Mem. Cornell Univ. Agric. Exp. Sta.* **164**:1–70.

———. 1935. Aquatic Diptera. Part II. Orthorrhapha-Brachycera and Cyclorrhapha. *Ibid.* **177**:1–62.

———. 1937. Aquatic Diptera. Part III. Chironomidae: subfamilies Tanypodinae, Diamesinae, and Orthocladiinae. *Ibid.* **205**:1–84.

———. 1937a. Aquatic Diptera. Part IV. Chironomidae: subfamily Chironominae. *Ibid.* **210**:1–56.

KELLOGG, V. L. 1903. The net-winged midges (Blepharoceridae) of North America. *Proc. Calif. Acad. Sci., Zool., ser. 3,* **3**:187–232.

KENNEDY, H. D. 1958. Biology and life history of a new species of mountain midge, Deuterophlebia nielsoni, from eastern California (Diptera: Deuterophlebiidae). *Trans. Am. Microsc. Soc.* **77**:201–228.

———. 1960. Deuterophlebia inyoensis, a new species of mountain midge from the alpine zone of the Sierra Nevada Range, California (Diptera: Deuterophlebiidae). *Ibid.* **79**:191–218.

KUSTER, K. C. 1934. A study of the general biology, morphology of the respiratory system, and respiration of certain aquatic Stratiomyia and Odontomyia larvae (Diptera). *Pap. Mich. Acad. Sci. Arts and Lett.* **19**:605–657.

LANE, R. S. 1975. Immatures of some Tabanidae (Diptera) from Medocino County, Calif. *Ann. Entomol. Soc. Am.* **68**:803–819.

LEATHERS, A. L. 1922. Ecological study of aquatic midges and some related insects with special reference to feeding habits. *Bull. U.S. Bur. Fish.* **38**:1–61.

MALLOCH, J. R. 1914. American black flies or buffalo gnats. *U.S. Dept. Agric., Bur. Entomol. Tech. Ser.* **26**:1–82.

———. 1915. The Chironomidae, or midges, of Illinois, with particular reference to the species occurring in the Illinois River. *Bull. Ill. State Lab. Nat. Hist.* **10**:275–543.

———. 1915a. Some additional records of Chironomidae for Illinois and notes of other Illinois Diptera. *Ibid.* **11**:301–363.

———. 1917. A preliminary classification of Diptera, exclusive of Pupipara, based upon larval and pupal characters, with keys to imagines in certain families. Part I. *Ibid.* **12**:161–409.

MARCHAND, W. 1920. The early stages of the Tabanidae (horse-flies). *Monogr. Rockefeller Inst. Med. Res.* **13**:1–203.

MASON, W. T. 1973. *An Introduction to the Identification of Chironomid Larvae.* Anal. Qual. Control Lab. Nat. Env. Res. Center, U.S.E.P.A. 90 pp.

MATHESON, R. 1944. *Handbook of the mosquitoes of North America.* 2d ed. 314 pp. Comstock, Ithaca, N.Y.

MILLER, R. B. 1941. A contribution to the ecology of the Chironomidae of Costello Lake, Algonquin Park, Ontario. *Univ. Toronto Stud., Biol. Ser.* **49**:1–63.

MOKRY, J. E. 1975. Studies on the ecology and biology of blackfly larvae utilizing an in situ benthos observatory. *Verh. Int. Ver. Limnol.* **19**:1546–1549.

MUNDIE, J. H. 1957. The ecology of Chironomidae in storage reservoirs. *Trans. Roy. Entomol. Soc. Lond.* **109**:149–232.

NEFF, S. E. 1965. On the pupa of Atherix variegata Walker (Diptera, Rhagionidae). *Entomol. News* **76**:163–167.

NEFF, S. E., and C. O. BERG. 1966. Biology and immature stages of Malacophagous Diptera of the genus Sepedon (Sciomyzidae). *Bull. Agric. Exp. Sta. Va. Poly. Inst.* **566**:1–113.

NICHOLSON, H. P., and C. E. MICKEL. 1950. The black flies of Minnesota (Simuliidae). *Tech. Bull. Univ. Minn. Agric. Exp. Sta.* **192**:1–64.

NIELSEN, A. 1951. Contributions to the metamorphosis and biology of the genus Atrichopogon Kieffer (Diptera, Ceratopogonidae) with remarks on the evolution and taxonomy of the genus. *Det. K. Danske Vidensk. Selsk., Biol. Skr.* **6**:1–95.

NIELSEN, L. T., and D. M. REES. 1961. An identification guide to the mosquitoes of Utah. *Univ. Utah Biol. Ser.* **12**:1–58.

NOWELL, W. R. 1951. The dipterous family Dixidae in western North America (Insecta: Diptera). *Microentomology* **16**:187–270.

PAINE, G. H., JR., and A. R. GAUFIN. 1956. Aquatic Diptera as indicators of pollution in a midwestern stream. *Ohio J. Sci.* **56**:291–304.

PENNAK, R. W. 1945. Notes on mountain midges (Deuterophlebiidae) with a description of the immature stages of a new species from Colorado. *Am. Mus. Novit.* **1276**:1–10.

PETERS, T. M. 1966. The Nearctic Dixidae (Diptera). *Misc. Publ. Entomol. Soc. Am.* **5**:233–278.

QUATE, L. W. 1955. A revision of the Psychodidae (Diptera) in America north of Mexico. *Univ. Calif. Publ. Entomol.* **10**:103–273.

REMPEL, J. G. 1936. The life-history and morphology of Chironomus hyperboreus. *J. Biol. Board of Can.* **2**:209–221.

ROBACK, S. S. 1953. Savannah River tendipedid larvae (Diptera: Tendipedidae (=Chironomidae)). *Proc. Acad. Nat. Sci. Phila.* **105**:91–132.

———. 1957. The immature tendipedids of the Philadelphia area. *Monogr. Acad. Nat. Sci. Phila.* **9**:1–152.

———. 1969. The immature stages of the genus Tanypus Meigen (Diptera: Chironomidae: Tanypodinae). *Trans. Am. Entomol. Soc.* **94**:407–428.

———. 1974. The immature stages of the genus Coelotanypus (Chironomidae: Tanypodinae: Coelotanypodini) in North America. *Proc. Acad. Nat. Sci. Phila.* **126**:9–19.

ROGERS, J. S. 1933. The ecological distribution of the crane-flies of northern Florida. *Ecol. Monogr.* **3**:1–74.

———. 1942. The crane flies (Tipulidae) of the George Reserve, Michigan. *Univ. Mich. Mus. Zool. Misc. Publ.* **53**:1–128.

ROGERS, J. S., and G. W. BYERS. 1956. The ecological distribution, life history, and the immature stages of Lipsothrix sylvia (Diptera: Tipulidae). *Occas. Pap. Mus. Zool. Univ. Mich.* **572**:1–14.

ROSS, H. H. 1947. The mosquitoes of Illinois (Diptera, Culicidae). *Bull. Ill. Nat. Hist. Surv.* **24**:1–96.

ROZEBOOM, L. E. 1942. The mosquitoes of Oklahoma. *Okla. Agric. Exp. Sta. Tech. Bull.* **16**:1–56.

SADLER, W. O. 1934. Biology of the midge Chironomus tentans Fabricius, and methods for its propagation. *Mem. Cornell Univ. Agric. Exp. Sta.* **173**:1–25.

SAETHER, O. A. 1969. Some Nearctic Podonominae, Diamesinae, and Orthocladiinae (Diptera: Chironomidae). *Bull. Fish. Res. Board of Can.* **170**:1–154.

———. 1970. Nearctic and Palaearctic Chaoborus (Diptera: Chaoboridae). *Ibid.* **174**:1–57.

———. 1971. Notes on general morphology and terminology of the Chironomidae (Diptera). *Can. Entomol.* **103**:1237–1360.

———. 1973. Taxonomy and ecology of three new species of Monodiamesa Kieffer, with keys to Nearctic and Palaearctic species of the genus (Diptera: Chironomidae). *J. Fish. Res. Board of Can.* **30**:665–679.

———. 1975. Nearctic and Palaearctic Heterotrissocladius (Diptera: Chironomidae). *Bull. Fish. Res. Board of Can.* **193**:1–67.

WELCH, H. E. 1976. Ecology of Chironomidae (Diptera) in a polar lake. *J. Fish. Res. Board of Can.* **33**:227–247.

———. 1975. Nearctic and Palaearctic Heterotrissocladius (Diptera: Chironomidae). *Bull. Fish. Res. Board Can.* **193**:1–67.

STOCKNER, J. G. 1971. Ecological energetics and natural history of Hedriodiscus truquii (Diptera) in two thermal spring communities. *J. Fish. Res. Board of Can.* **28**:73–94.

STONE, A. 1968. The genus Corethrella in the United States (Diptera: Chaoboridae). *Fla. Entomol.* **51**:183–186.

STONE, A., and H. A. JAMNBACK. 1955. The black flies of New York State (Diptera: Simuliidae). *N.Y. State Mus. Bull.* **349**:1–144.

STONE, A., et al. 1965. A catalog of the Diptera of America north of Mexico. *U.S. Dept. Agric. Handbook* **276**:1–1696.

SUBLETTE, J. E. 1960. Chironomid midges of California. I. Chironominae, exclusive of Tanytarsini (=Calopsectrini). *Proc. U.S. Nat. Mus.* **112**:197–226.

THIENEMANN, A. 1954. Chironomus. Leben, Verbreitung und wirtschaftliche Bedeutung der Chironomiden. *Die Binnengewässer* **20**:1–834.

THOMSEN, L. C. 1937. Aquatic Diptera. Part V. Ceratopogonidae. *Mem. Cornell Univ. Agric. Exp. Sta.* **210**:57–80.

TOWNES, H. K. 1945. The Nearctic species of Tendipedini [Diptera, Tendipedidae (=Chironomidae]. *Am. Midl. Nat.* **34**:1–206.

VAILLANT, F. 1959. The larvae of three Nearctic Diptera of the Family Psychodidae. *J. N.Y. Entomol. Soc.* **67**:39–50.

———. 1963. Les Maruina d'Amérique du Nord (Dipt. Psychodidae). *Bull. Soc. Entomol. Fr.* **68**:71–92.

WALSHE, B. M. 1951. The feeding habits of certain chironomid larvae (subfamily Tendipedinae). *Proc. Zool. Soc. Lond.* **121**:63–79.

WELCH, H. E. 1976. Ecology of Chironomidae (Diptera) in a polar lake. *J. Fish. Res. Board Can.* **33**:227–247.

WIRTH, W. W. 1951. A new mountain midge from California (Diptera: Deuterophlebiidae). *Pan-Pac. Entomol.* **27**:49–57.

———. 1952. The Heleidae of California. *Univ. Calif. Publ. Entomol.* **9**:95–266.

———. 1971. The brine flies of the genus Ephydra in North America (Diptera: Ephydridae). *Ann. Entomol. Soc. Am.* **64**:357–377.

WIRTH, W. W., and J. E. SUBLETTE. 1970. A review of the Podonominae of North America with descriptions of three new species of Trichotanypus. *J. Kans. Entomol. Soc.* **43**:335–354.

WOOD, D. M., et al. 1963. The black flies (Diptera: Simuliidae) of Ontario. Part II. Larval identification, with descriptions and illustrations. *Proc. Entomol. Soc. Ontario* **93**:99–129.

# Chapter 36

# GASTROPODA (SNAILS, LIMPETS)

ON A global basis, only 14 out of a total of 283 families of gastropods are partially or wholly found in fresh waters of the United States. Nevertheless, almost every type of fresh-water habitat, from the smallest ponds and streams to the largest lakes and rivers, has its characteristic population of snails, or univalve mollusks. Only the coldest alpine lakes, grossly polluted waters, and saline inland waters are predictably without snails. Some localities may yield only one or two species, whereas others may contain dozens. Sometimes the collector needs to hunt assiduously in order to find a few specimens; under other circumstances they may be present in enormous numbers. Snails are animals of the substrate and are found creeping about on all types of submerged surfaces, chiefly in water from 10 cm to 2 m deep.

**General characteristics.** The vast majority of fresh-water gastropods have a spiral or discoidal coiled shell. However, in eight American genera (the limpets), the shell is in the form of a very low cone. The range in the maximum dimensions of the shell (length or width) of the mature animal is about 2 to 70 mm.

The muscular portion of the animal which projects from the shell is called the foot. For the most part it is inconspicuously colored, usually being grayish, brownish, or blackish, and often flecked or mottled with yellowish or whitish. The ventral surface of the foot is flat and there is a more or less prominent head at the anterior end. The head bears two tentacles which range in shape from short, blunt, or conical to long and filiform. The eyes are on or near the base of the tentacles. The mouth is on the ventral surface of the head at the extreme anterior end and in contact with the substrate in most species, but in the Viviparidae, Pleuroceridae, Hydrobiidae, and Valvatidae it is at the end of a muscular proboscis, or rostrum. In the Ampullariidae and Neritidae this rostrum is divided into two long, tentaclelike lobes. In the Lymnaeidae the head itself is widened into two flat lateral lobes, constituting the velum, a structure that persists from the larval stage.

The foot consists mainly of muscle tissue, but it contains the anterior portions of the digestive tract and reproductive system, as well as most of the nervous system. The rest of the internal organs form the visceral hump which lies within the shell, where its shape is a counterpart of the coils. Forming a lining for the shell and enclosing the viscera is a thin layer of specialized tissue, the mantle. The shell grows by the addition of the shell material secreted by the edge of the mantle (collar) at the orifice of the shell.

Although a few snails, such as *Valvata,* have a delicate external gill, most fresh-water gastropods have either internal gills that are specialized folds of the mantle for aquatic respiration or an internal air-filled "lung" consisting of a special portion of the mantle cavity surrounded by highly vascularized mantle. The respiratory opening (pneumostome) to either the internal gills or lung is usually situated on the right side at the edge of the shell. In those aquatic snails with a lung the edge of the mantle is often elongated into a respiratory siphon through which air is obtained at the surface film

The exposed portion of the body of a snail is securely fastened to the shell internally by a large columellar muscle, and by the contraction of this muscle the foot may be doubled up and withdrawn from view. Those snails with gills have a discoidal sclerotized (rarely calcareous) operculum attached dorsally on the posterior part of the foot, and when the animal is withdrawn into the shell the operculum fits into the opening and effectively closes it.

In some families external reproductive structures may be seen. In the Hydrobiidae and Valvatidae, for example, more or less laterally in the region of the neck, is the verge, a projecting male copulatory organ of variable structure and size. In the Viviparidae the right tentacle of the male is much larger than the left and serves as a penis sheath.

**Shell.** Compared with marine and tropical land snails, the fresh-water forms are a drab-colored lot. A few species are rich green or yellow with red tinges or bright color bands, but the great majority are nondescript gray, tan, brown, blackish, or "horn-colored," sometimes with indistinct bands or a mottled appearance. The shell proper is covered with a thin organic epidermis in which the pigments are deposited. The epidermis has the important function of protecting the underlying chalky white calcium carbonate from erosion.

In most of the common and widespread species the surface of the shell is superficially smooth, but if it is examined closely, fine longitudinal growth lines and spiral sculpture may be seen. Sometimes these lines can be detected only with the aid of a lens. At the other extreme are a few species whose shells are pronouncedly costate, ridged, carinate, or tuberculate.

When a shell is held with the opening toward the observer and with the tip upward, the shell is said to be dextral if the opening is on the observer's right and sinistral if on the left. The great majority of species are dextral. Some genera contain both dextral and sinistral species, but only in a very few species are both dextral and sinistral specimens known.

The important features of a typical gastropod shell are shown in Fig. 483. The opening of the shell is called the aperture,

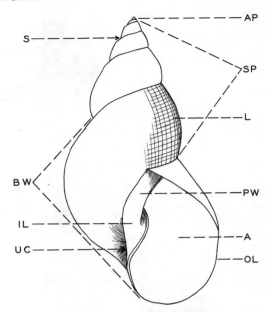

FIG. 483.–Anatomical features of a typical *Lymnaea* shell, ×2. *A*, aperture; *AP*, apex; *BW*, body whorl; *IL*, inner lip reflected over columella; *L*, spiral and growth lines; *OL*, outer lip; *PW*, parietal wall; *S*, suture; *SP*, spire; *UC*, umbilical chink. (Modified from Baker, 1928.)

and the main portion of the shell above the aperture is the spire. The first large coil, or whorl, of the shell is the body whorl, and the nucleus, or protoconch, is the small round knob of from $1^1/_4$ to $1^1/_2$ whorls without distinct sculpturing at the apex of the shell. The whorls are coiled around a central axis, or columella. An inner lip at the columellar margin of the aperture is usually present and reflected over the columellar region. The inner surface of the shell immediately adjacent to the inner lip is termed the parietal wall. The outer lip, or peristome, lies on the opposite side of the aperture; it is often reflected back on itself. The umbilicus may be a small chink or narrow slit between the reflected inner lip and the body whorl; it may be a definite hole one whorl deep; or it may be complete and well developed so that all of the larger whorls revolve around a thin-walled hollow tube occupying the position of the typical solid columella. In many instances the umbilicus is sealed, and the shell is said to be imperforate.

FIG. 484.–Representative American fresh-water gastropod shells. *Top*, *Pomacea* and its operculum, ×1; *second row*, left to right, ×1.5: *Hydrobia*, *Fluminicola*, *Amnicola*, *Pomatiopsis*, *Valvata*, and *Gyraulus* (2); *third row*, left to right, ×1: *Helisoma* (2), *Lymnaea*, *Campeloma*, *Viviparus*, and *Lioplax*; *bottom row*, left to right, ×1; *Lanx* (2), *Carinifex*, *Physa*, *Goniobasis*, *Pleurocera*, and *Neritina*.

Considerable variations in size, shape, shell thickness, and surface markings occur within many genera, and sometimes even within a single species. These variations are particularly striking in the Pleuroceridae. In some cases variations within a species are clearly correlated with certain ecological features of the environment. Thickness of the shell, for example, may be directly related to the amount of calcium in the water. In highly alkaline waters, especially in the western states, many species show increased tendencies toward being ridged,

plicate, or rugose. Specimens in such waters are also generally smaller than those in other habitats. On wave-beaten shores and in rapid streams there is usually an increase in the relative size of the aperture and a decrease in the length of the spire.

**Locomotion.** In spite of many close observations, the detailed mechanism of the usual gliding movements is not well understood. As a snail moves along on the underside of the surface film or on the substrate, it leaves a familiar "slime track," a

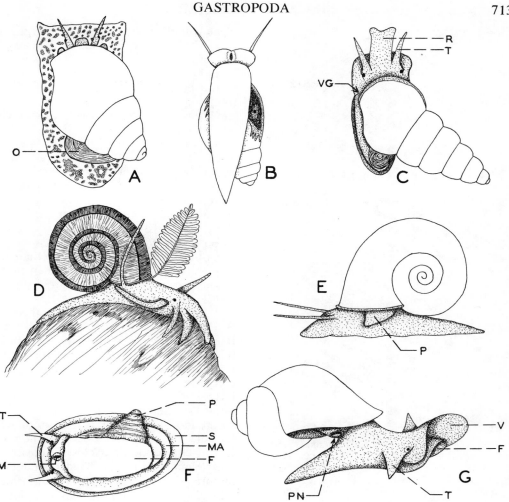

FIG. 485.–External features of typical Gastropoda. A, female *Campeloma*, ×1.2; B, ventral view of *Physa*, ×1.7; C, *Pomatiopsis*, ×.8; D, *Valvata*, ×5, showing plumose left external gill, rudimentary right gill, verge, tentacles, rostrum, and divided foot; E, *Helisoma*, ×1.7; F, ventral view of *Ferrissia*, ×8; G, *Lymnaea*, ×1.5. *F*, foot; *M*, mouth; *MA*, mantle; *O*, operculum; *P*, pseudobranch; *PN*, pneumostome; *R*, rostrum; *S*, shell; *T*, tentacle; *V*, velum; *VG*, vertical groove of foot. (A to F modified from Baker, 1928; G modified from Baker, 1911.)

thin, flat ribbon of mucus secreted by the ventral surface of the foot, especially near the anterior end. The secretion of mucus is apparently necessary for locomotion, perhaps only as a lubricant, but it is not definitely known whether the actual movement of the snail is entirely due to indistinct waves of muscular contraction on the ventral surface of the foot, to ciliary action in the same area, or to both.

Another method of locomotion has been called "hunching." It involves ob-vious muscular contractions of the foot and a jerky pulling forward of the shell. Such movements are not normal, however, and usually occur when the snail is entangled in vegetation or is out of water.

A third method of locomotion, called "spinning," is utilized chiefly by some species of *Physa, Lymnaea,* and *Helisoma;* it occurs when the snail is moving through the water rather than over the substrate. For moving upward in this manner the snail decreases its specific gravity. A thread of

FIG. 486.–Top, diagrammatic longitudinal section through anterior end of a snail; bottom, small central part of the radula ribbon of *Lymnaea*. *BC*, buccal cartilages; *C*, body cavity; *E*, esophagus; *J*, sclerotized jaw; *M*, mouth; *R*, radula; *RS*, radula sac.

mucus is fastened to the substrate at the point of leaving, and the snail moves upward with the lateral margins of the foot brought together and leaving a vertical mucous thread behind. Similarly, a snail at the surface film or on some object above the bottom may fasten a thread and move downward, trailing a mucous track. The same thread may be used a number of times by the same or other individuals, but it soon becomes brittle and breaks. For the most part, those snails that spin have slender, tapered, or pointed feet.

**Feeding, digestive system.** The great majority of fresh-water gastropods are normally vegetarians. The coating of living algae which covers most submerged surfaces forms the chief food, but dead plant material is frequently ingested, and occasionally dead animal material is eaten by some species. *Physa* and *Lymnaea*, for example, are good scavengers and essentially omnivorous. There are even a few records of *Lymnaea* feeding on living animals. When first deposited, mucous trails are sticky and accumulate debris and microscopic organisms, and as snails move about they incidentally utilize it and its contents as food. The entire foot and head areas are chemoreceptive for taste but are decreasingly sensitive laterally and posteriorly. Food in the form of animal tissues elicits responses much more quickly than plant tissues. It has been clearly shown that the higher the temperature, the greater the activity and food intake.

Just inside the dorsal part of the mouth is a set of one, two, or three small sclerotized jaws (Fig. 487), used in cutting off bits of food. One jaw is dorsal and (or) two are lateral. Immediately behind the jaws the digestive tract is swollen to form a large buccal mass. The ventral portion of this organ is greatly thickened and contains stout, movable buccal cartilages to which muscles are attached. Dorsally, the buccal cartilages and their muscles are covered by the radula, one of the most characteristic features of the Gastropoda. It is essentially a longitudinal, toothed, straplike, chitinoid structure which occupies a position analogous with that of the human tongue. The radula is moved back and forth very rapidly by means of the underlying cartilages and muscles, and in this way pieces of food are thoroughly ground between it and the roof of the buccal cavity. The radula wears away as a result, especially at the anterior end, but it is continuously replaced since it is formed in a radular sac at the posterior end of the buccal mass and grows outward much like the human fingernail.

The teeth of the radula are fastened to the flat radular membrane in transverse rows. The number of teeth in a transverse row ranges from 7 to 175 (Fig. 486). The number of transverse rows is usually large, some species having more than 150. Thus the total number of teeth in a radula may

FIG. 487.–Sclerotized jaws of typical Gastropoda. A, *Pleurocera*; B, *Lymnaea*; C, single dorsal jaw of *Aplexa hypnorum*.

range into the thousands. The morphology of the teeth varies greatly from one family and genus to another (Fig. 488), but all teeth are fundamentally similar; each has a base of attachment and a reflected portion bearing the cutting points, or cusps.

In each transverse row three general types of teeth are usually recognized: (1) a single, distinctive, median central tooth, (2) a series of lateral teeth on each side of it, and (3) a series of marginal teeth located outside of the laterals. Thus, in those families having seven teeth in a transverse series, they are named in order: second marginal, first marginal, lateral, central, lateral, first marginal, and second marginal. In the other families there are correspondingly more lateral and marginal teeth, and the morphological gradations between adjacent teeth are very gradual. In the Lymnaeidae it is customary to designate a series of transitional teeth that lie between typical laterals and marginals.

The esophagus, which leaves the buccal mass, is quite long; it passes from the foot into the visceral mass contained within the shell, where it may or may not be dilated to form a crop. A pair of salivary glands may be found along the esophagus or on the crop. Shortly behind the crop is the dilated stomach, which may have a gizzard associated with it. In some genera the gizzard contains sand, presumably to macerate the food further. The stomach is followed by the long intestine, whose posterior end is dilated to form the rectum. The anus opens into the mantle cavity near the edge of the mantle and shell. A very large digestive gland, the so-called liver, empties into the stomach.

**Circulatory system.** The heart is situated in the lower part of the visceral hump,

usually on the left side. In mature individuals with thin shells and in immature individuals the beating may be seen through the shell. The heart consists of one auricle (rarely two) and a ventricle. The ventricle pumps the blood through a short aortic trunk to all parts of the body via a series of arteries and capillaries. From the capillaries the blood passes into spaces, or sinuses, in the tissues collectively called the hemocoel. From the hemocoel it passes into veins and thence back to the auricle.

The blood of gastropods contains a dissolved, complex, copper-containing compound, hemocyanin, which, like hemoglobin, is capable of transporting oxygen. Oxidized hemocyanin imparts a definite bluish color to the blood; in the reduced state it is colorless. In some of the Planorbidae hemoglobin is the respiratory pigment.

**Respiration.** In the Ampulariidae, Bithyniidae, Viviparidae, Valvatidae, Pleuroceridae, Thiaridae, Hydrobiidae, and Neritidae respiration is strictly aquatic and occurs through an internal gill, or ctenidium, to which the surrounding water has easy access. This structure consists of a series of narrow, flat leaflets well supplied with blood and arranged like the teeth of a comb. It is located on the surface of the mantle within the mantle cavity of the body whorl. In some species there are over 100 leaflets in the ctenidium. In *Valvata* the ctenidium is external and plumose (Fig. 485D). The gilled snails may obtain a small amount of oxygen through the general body surface.

Most members of the Physidae, Lymnaeidae, Planorbidae, Ancylidae, Lancidae, and Acroloxidae do not have gills, but obtain oxygen through a "lung," or pul-

FIG. 488.–Radular teeth of typical gastropods. A, *Amnicola* (Bithyniidae); B, *Goniobasis* (Pleuroceridae); C, *Viviparus* (Viviparidae); D, *Valvata* (Valvatidae); E, *Ferrissia* (Ancylidae); F, *Physa* (Physidae); G, *Helisoma* (Planorbidae); H, *Lymnaea* (Lymnaeidae); J, *Neritina* (Neritidae). *C*, central tooth; *L*, lateral tooth; *MI* and *MII*, first and second marginal teeth; teeth designated by number are a few laterals and marginals selected from the complete series. (A modified from Baker, 1928; B to G redrawn from Baker, 1928; H modified from Baker, 1911.)

monary cavity. This is an air-filled, saclike, highly vascularized portion of the mantle cavity that occupies as much as one-half of the body whorl. The pneumostome, a small opening to the pulmonary cavity, is situated where the edge of the mantle and shell meet the foot. In the Lymnaeidae and Physidae the edge of the mantle is frequently drawn out into a long, muscular respiratory siphon around the pneumostome.

At variable intervals most pulmonates come to the surface of the water where the pneumostome is brought into contact with the atmosphere and a fresh supply of air is taken into the pulmonary cavity. In a very quiet laboratory the opening of the pneumostome at the surface may be heard as a faint clicking sound. The migrations to the surface by spinning or on emergent vegetation appear to be largely governed by temperature and the amount of dissolved oxygen in the water, and under average conditions may occur every few minutes to several hours. Under both natural and experimental conditions, however, it has been found that many pulmonates rarely or never come to the surface for air. This is particularly true of certain species of *Lymnaea*, *Physa*, and *Helisoma*, which may pass their entire life cycle without access to the surface. Some pulmonates have been collected in water more than 15 m deep, and Forel collected *Lymnaea* at a depth of 250 m in Lake Geneva, Switzerland. Certainly under such circumstances there are no migrations to the surface for air. Although there seems to be little specific information available (Cheatum, 1934), it appears that pulmonates that occur at great depths and some that remain submerged for protracted periods in the shallows fill the pulmonary cavity with water and use it as a gill. In many species, however, it is well established that all oxygen absorption may occur through the general body surface in both immature and mature individuals. Indeed, in the limpets the respiratory cavity is vestigial. Individuals in this family, as well as in the Planorbidae, have a pseudo-branch. This is a short, blunt to long, conical projection from the dorsal or lateral portion of the foot near the edge of the shell. It is highly vascularized and undoubtedly functions as an accessory gill (Fig. 485F). Under experimental conditions it has been found that few snails can tolerate anaerobic conditions more than 48 hours. Students in the writer's laboratory have found that *Physa gyrina* Say from standing water habitats has a minimum tolerance of 1.8 ppm dissolved oxygen, but specimens from running waters have a minimum tolerance of 1.5 ppm.

**Excretion.** The renal organ is spongy and of varying size and shape. It is situated near the heart and respiratory cavity or gill, and its small duct opens near the anus.

**Muscles.** Aside from the foot, which is composed mostly of muscle tissue, there are several important free muscles. The columellar muscle is attached to the shell

Fig. 489.–Diagrammatic dorsal view of head and visceral mass of *Pleurocera*, showing location of digestive organs. *A*, anus; *BM*, buccal mass; *DG*, digestive gland; *E*, esophagus; *I*, intestine; *M*, edge of mantle; *MO*, mouth; *P*, proboscis; *R*, rectum; *S*, stomach; *SG*, salivary gland; *T*, tentacle. (Modified from Magruder.)

internally and serves to withdraw the animal. Sets of muscles protract, retract, or depress the buccal mass. Those parts of the reproductive system directly concerned with copulation are usually supplied with protractors and retractors.

**Nervous system** The greater portion of the gastropod nervous system (the "brain") usually consists of nine large ganglia, eight of which are paired. They are connected with each other by commissures and are arranged around the esophagus just behind the buccal mass. Large branching nerves originating in these ganglia innervate all parts of the body. Several small accessory ganglia are associated with some of the sense organs.

**Sensory areas and organs.** The eyes, situated at the base of the tentacles, are

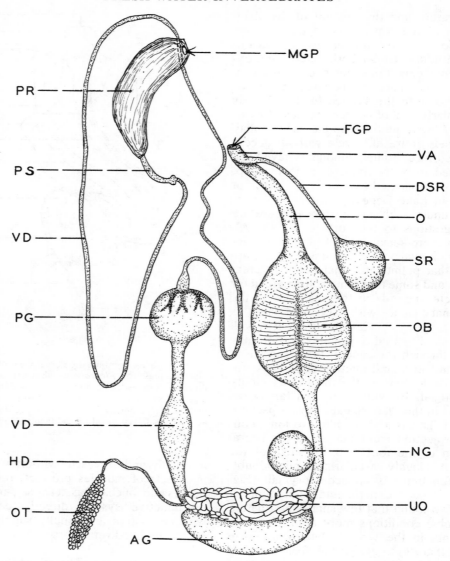

Fɪɢ. 490.–Reproductive system of *Lymnaea stagnalis appressa* Say; protractors and retractors of praeputium and penis sheath not shown. *AG*, albumen gland; *DSR*, duct of seminal receptacle; *FGP*, female genital pore; *HD*, hermaphroditic duct; *MGP*, male genital pore; *NG*, nidamental gland; *O*, oviduct; *OB*, oviducal bulb; *OT*, ovotestis; *PG*, prostate gland; *PR*, praeputium; *PS*, penis sheath; *SR*, seminal receptacle; *UO*, uterine portion of oviduct; *VA*, vagina; *VD*, vas deferens. (Modified from Baker, 1911.)

well developed, although little is known concerning the powers of vision. The ability to detect certain substances in solution is probably centered in the osphradium, a small specialized area of the mantle cavity. The sense of hearing, or perhaps more appropriately the sense of equilibrium and the ability to detect vibrations, is centered in

two statocysts. Each of these is a minute sac closely associated with the central nervous system; it contains a fluid in which are suspended a variable number of calcareous bodies called statoliths. Although the general body surface reacts to touch, the tentacles are especially sensitive. It seems logical to assume that taste is centered in the mouth region where this sense has been attributed to Semper's organ.

**Reproduction.** The anatomy of the reproductive system varies widely in the fresh-water gastropods and is coming to be of increasing taxonomic significance, especially for the separation and identification of difficult species.

The Physidae, Lymnaeidae, Planorbidae, Ancylidae, Valvatidae, Acroloxidae, and Lancidae are hermaphroditic, both the male and female reproductive organs being in the same individual, but in all other fresh-water families the sexes are separate. Figures 490–493 illustrate the reproductive systems of some typical species. The basal portions of the ducts lie in the foot and body whorl; the distal organs, however, occur in the smaller whorls, with the ovotestis, ovary, or testis being more or less imbedded in the digestive gland at the tip of the spire.

The male genital pore is usually located near the base of the right tentacle. It is commonly situated at the end of a muscular, protrusible, intromittent copulatory organ, or penis, which is withdrawn into the body except during copulation. In the Viviparidae the right tentacle is modified as a penis sheath. In the Hydrobiidae and Valvatidae the copulatory organ, usually called a verge, remains protruded and cannot be retracted. Sometimes the verge is long and thin; in other genera it is blunt, lobed, or divided. There is no male copulatory organ in the Pleuroceridae and the male genital pore lies at the edge of the mantle cavity.

The female genital pore is unspecialized and usually lies at the base of the neck near the pulmonary aperture or at the edge of the mantle cavity.

Although surprisingly little accurate work has been done, the available information seems to indicate that a variety of conditions exist regarding fertilization in the hermaphroditic fresh-water Gastropoda. In some species isolated individuals have been observed to produce young; under such circumstances both mature sperm and mature eggs are produced simultaneously, and self-fertilization, rather than self-copulation, occurs in the reproductive tract. In other cases two such individuals may copulate and exchange sperm, each animal acting as male and female during the process; this is thought to be the common condition. In still other instances the ovotestis may produce eggs at one time and sperm at another, and therefore an individual may act as either male or female during copulation, but not both.

Parthenogenesis is uncommon, but it is known to occur in *Hydrobia* and in *Campeloma,* especially in the northern states.

Oviposition usually occurs in the spring, although it may continue into the summer and early fall. Some species produce few eggs; others hundreds at a time. They are almost invariably deposited in a gelatinous mass on some substrate.

The early developmental stages occur within the egg mass, and by the time the young snail leaves, it has taken on the basic morphological features of the adult, and the shell has one to two whorls. The Viviparidae are ovoviviparous, the individuals being well developed at birth.

It is thought that in the great majority of species the usual length of life is 9 to 15

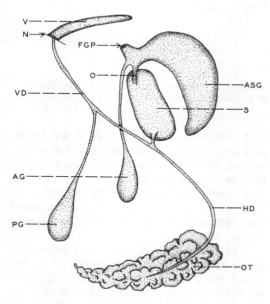

FIG. 491.–Reproductive system of *Valvata tricarinata. ASG,* accessory shell gland; *N,* wall of neck; *S,* spermatheca; *V,* verge; see legend of foregoing figure for other structures. (Modifed from Bernard.)

FIG. 492.–Reproductive systems of male and female individuals of *Bithynia tentaculata* L. *F*, flagellum; *OV*, ovary; *T*, testis; *U*, uterus; see legends of foregoing figures for other structures. (Modified from Baker, 1928.)

months. Some species, however, have two or three generations per year, especially in southern states, and notably among limpets. Length of life is often determined by period(s) of enforced aestivation. Some of the Lymnaeidae, Planorbidae, and *Goniobasis* are known to live as long as two to four years.

**Predators.** Perhaps the greatest natural enemies of snails are the fishes. It has been estimated that about 20 percent of our fresh-water species feed to a greater or lesser extent on mollusks. For only a few forms, however, do snails form a significant portion of the diet; some of these are the suckers, perch, sheepshead, pumpkinseed,

and whitefish. Some ducks, shore birds, and occasional amphibians may eat snails. Among the invertebrates their most important predators are leeches, beetle larvae, and Hemiptera and Odonata nymphs. At least in the laboratory, it has been found that ostracods will attack small snails and destroy their eggs.

Many species of snails are known to serve as the intermediate hosts of trematodes, but it is thought that such infections are seldom fatal, although the reproductive capacity may be greatly decreased and the digestive gland severely damaged.

**Ecology.** In the words of Boycott (1936), it is difficult to "disentangle the im-

portance of quality of water from geographical distribution, the physical character of
the habitat, and available food materials.''
Nevertheless, it is possible to point out certain ecological factors of the environment
that have a pronounced influence in the
determination of the habitat and activities.

One of the most important of these factors is the amount of dissolved salts in the
water, especially calcium carbonate, which
is the essential material for shell construction. It is generally true that soft waters
contain few species and individuals,
whereas hard waters contain many species
and individuals. The majority of Lymnaeidae, for example, occur in water high in
carbonates (more than 15 ppm of bound carbon dioxide). A few species, however, are
striking in their ability to thrive in soft
waters that are low in carbonates. The Valvatidae are most common in waters containing less than 8 ppm. *Campeloma* has
been found in abundance in water containing only 1 ppm. It is difficult to understand
how calcium carbonate can be utilized at
such low concentrations. Many species are
of course adapted to a wide range of carbonate content; *Amnicola limosa porata*

FIG. 494.–Verges of typical gastropods. A, *Somatogyrus*; B, *Amnicola*; C, *Hydrobia*; D, *Amnicola*;
E, *Amnicola*; F, *Amnicola*; G, *Pomatiopsis*. (A and C
to G modified from Berry, 1943; B modified from
Baker, 1928.)

FIG. 493.–Reproductive system of male *Campeloma integrum*. *R*, rostrum; *RT*, right tentacle; see
legends of foregoing figures for other structures.
(Modified from Baker, 1928.)

has been collected from lakes having a
bound carbon dioxide content ranging from
1 to 30 ppm; and other species undoubtedly
have still wider limits. Some investigators
have shown that on substrates composed
of mixed high- and low-carbonate rubble
that the majority of individuals will select
the high-carbonate pieces.

Hydrogen-ion concentration is closely
associated with, and partly determined by,
the carbon dioxide content, and lakes low
in carbonates are usually toward the acid
side of the scale (below pH 7.0), whereas
those high in carbonates are almost always
alkaline. It follows, then, that the great

majority of species and the largest numbers of individuals occur under alkaline conditions. All the Valvatidae and nearly all the Lymnaeidae, for example, are confined to waters having pH readings of 7.0 or above. Nevertheless, there are some striking exceptions in other families. *Ferrissia parallela* has been found in waters ranging from pH 6.0 to 8.4, and *Amnicola limosa porata* from pH 5.7 to 8.3. In general, however, snails are uncommon in lakes and streams whose surface waters are more acid than pH 6.2. They are never found in true acid sphagnum bogs.

Dissolved oxygen is another important limiting factor, most pulmonate and gilled species requiring rather high concentrations. For this reason severely polluted rivers and the deeper parts of lakes that become oxygen deficient during the summer and winter are usually devoid of gastropods. Limpets seem to be found only where the water remains almost saturated.

The great majority of species and individuals occur in the shallows, especially in water less than 3 m deep. At greater depths river and lake faunas tend to become more and more depauperate. The fact that the shallows are a favorite habitat is probably correlated with the abundance of food in this zone. Although a few genera, such as *Lymnaea,* occur in a wide variety of habitats, many forms are restricted to particular types of substrates. *Pleurocera* is usually found on rocky or sandy shoals, the Viviparidae are most common on sandy bottoms, and the Ampullariidae are mud lovers. *Physa* occurs in greatest abundance where there is a moderate amount of aquatic vegetation and organic debris, and it is rare among dense mats of vegetation. The Hydrobiidae are usually found among aquatic plants, sometimes in enormous numbers. *Hydrobia nickliniana,* the "water cress snail," is restricted to the dense mats of water cress and other vegetation of cool springs. Swift streams with sand or gravel bottoms and wave-swept beaches are generally poor places for collecting.

Large bodies of water usually have many species and small bodies have few, the reason presumably being the fact that the former have a greater variety of specific subhabitats suitable for the individual species. A few snails have become isolated in caves and underground streams, especially *Physa* and some Hydrobiidae. Such species are blind.

Although some gastropods may be active down to the freezing point of water, such conditions are not favorable, and perennially cold lakes and streams and bodies of water in high, mountainous areas contain few species and individuals. At the other extreme, only a few U.S. species can tolerate a continuous temperature of 30°. Some lake pulmonates exhibit seasonal migrations correlated with temperature; in the fall they move into deeper waters and in spring into the shallows.

**Hibernation, aestivation.** Populations in ponds that freeze solid are able to overwinter by burrowing into the mud and debris on the bottom and hibernating. In intermittent streams and ponds that are dry for a short period in the summer many pulmonates burrow into the mud up to a depth of several inches and aestivate during the unfavorable period. The most effective seal and protection is afforded by a mud bottom that has a high percentage of clay. In *Lymnaea* the formation of an epiphragm has been studied closely. This structure is usually produced when the snail is imbedded in the mud. It is a thin sheet of mucus which is formed just within the aperture by the foot. On drying, it hardens and forms an effective seal that aids in protecting the an- imal during the drought period. This device may account for the presence of *Lymnaea* in some waters to the exclusion of other genera. Viable aestivating *Planorbis* and *Lymnaea* have been kept in the laboratory for more than three years.

**Geographic distribution, dispersal.** The fresh-water gastropod fauna of the United States is rich in species, rich in individuals, and rich in diversity. Not counting additional varieties, Baker (1928) lists 95 species from Wisconsin; Goodrich and van der Schalie (1944) list 99 from Indiana; Harman and Berg (1970) report 38 species from the Finger Lakes region of New York; and Winslow (1926) lists 142 from Michigan.

Even Texas, which is by no means a favorable area for the development of an extensive fauna, has 96 species (Murray and Roy, 1968). It is estimated that more than 90 percent of the species and half of the genera found in North American waters are endemic.

Some genera, such as *Lymnaea, Helisoma, Gyraulus,* and *Ferrissia,* occur almost everywhere from coast to coast. The Pleuroceridae are confined largely to the states east of the Mississippi except for a few species in the Pacific coast states. Native species of Viviparidae are not found west of the Mississippi drainage, but two imported species are found in California. The Neritidae occur only in Alabama, Florida, and along the Gulf coast, and the fresh-water species of the Ampullariidae are found only in Florida and Georgia. Some genera are similarly restricted. *Lanx* occurs only in the west coast states, *Aplexa* in the northern states, *Lyogyrus* in the Atlantic coast states, and *Tulotoma* only in the Alabama River and its tributaries. Perhaps the most interesting case of all, *Gyrotoma, Amphigyra,* and *Neoplanorbis* are (were) confined to the Coosa River, Alabama.

*Bithynia tentaculata,* a small introduced euryokous European species, is spreading very rapidly over the United States. It is now the dominant species in Oneida Lake, New York, where the snail fauna dropped from 36 species in 1918 to 31 species in 1970.

Many species in the Mississippi drainage and in other eastern drainages undoubtedly would find suitable ecological conditions in many areas west of the Continental Divide, but their rate of geographic spread across the central plains and over the Divide since the last glaciation has been much too slow, except where man has made intentional transplants.

Because of increasing levels of pollution during the past 50 years, populations of many of our American stenokous and unusual species have been slowly disappearing, so that many forms that were formerly abundant in restricted geographical ranges are now uncommon or rare and difficult to find. Many species now have ranges that are more and more restricted to

headwater streams. Clark (1970) reports that out of 103 species in the Ohio River drainage, 41 are rare and endangered, and probably eight of these are extinct. This problem is especially acute in some of the Texas and southeastern drainages, such as the Coosa River, Alabama, where *Amphigyra, Neoplanorbis,* and other exotic forms have undoubtedly become extinct. The information on geographic ranges in this chapter should not therefore be accepted at face value.

The general problem of an explanation of the present geographic distribution of American fresh-water snails is extremely complicated, poorly understood, and beyond the scope of this volume. It involves, among other things, a careful consideration of past geological, geographic, and climatic changes.

Presumably it is relatively easy for a species to migrate slowly and extensively throughout an entire, connected drainage system provided that unfavorable environmental conditions are not encountered during such migrations. Movements between normally isolated bodies of water, or between inaccessible parts of the same drainage system, however, are necessarily passive and dependent on outside agencies. Occasional flood waters may leave their normal channels and carry eggs or adults to distant places. There are numerous instances recorded in the literature where small snails have been found on the feathers or in mud on the feet and legs of ducks and shore birds, and most authorities are agreed that this is a most important means of increasing the geographical range. Goodrich and van der Schalie (1944) have aptly summarized the essentials of distribution: "Whatever the mode of distribution, it has to be remembered that continued existence of a mollusk in any spot to which it may penetrate depends upon whether that spot is environmentally favorable, particularly for reproduction. It is to be suspected that in times without number migration has proved a failure."

Several species native to Europe, Japan, and the general Pacific area have been introduced into the United States by aquarium fanciers and have "escaped" to natural habitats. *Bithynia tentaculata,* the "faucet snail, " was imported to the Great Lakes region from northern Europe in the late 1870s. *Tarebia* is native to the Far East and western Pacific islands, but was introduced into Florida, where it is now locally abundant. *Viviparus stelmaphorus* is a Japanese species in springs, lakes, and streams near San Francisco, Boston, Philadelphia, Niagara Falls, St. Petersburg, Fla., and other areas. Several other introduced freshwater species have been collected in various parts of the country, and the list will undoubtedly grow with time. Many unreported tropical species have "escaped" into the wild but are not yet common or abundant.

**Collection, preparation.** The nature of collecting apparatus depends on the type of environment being visited. In the shallows of lakes and streams simple hand-picking may be used. In deeper waters a long-handled net or tin strainer is effective. In water more than a meter or two deep it is usually necessary to work from a boat with a dredge. Bottom debris and vegetation should be sifted and examined on shore. Limpets should be carefully removed from the substrate with a small knife blade. Wide-mouth bottles may be used to transport specimens to the laboratory.

For anatomical work the animal should preferably be killed and fixed in boiling water, although 75 to 95 percent alcohol is also useful. In the Hydrobiidae and Valvatidae, where species identification may be based on the morphology of the undistorted verge, it is best first to narcotize the animal by sprinkling menthol or magnesium sulfate crystals on the surface of the water and wait until it becomes very sluggish (which may be a whole day later), then kill and fix in Bouin's solution. Sixty to 75 percent alcohol is a suitable perservative. Formaldehyde should not be used, as it makes the specimens brittle and damages the shell.

Either freshly killed or alcoholic specimens may be used for dissection. The foot and the attached visceral hump should be kept intact by carefully pulling the latter from the shell with a pin or hairpin. If the specimen is small, the shell may be broken away from the underlying parts bit by bit, or the shell may be dissolved in dilute hydrochloric or sulfuric acid. The only instruments necessary for the dissection itself are a fine scalpel, forceps, scissors, and needles. First, the foot should be pinned down in a small dish containing a thick layer of paraffin on the bottom. Beginning at the head, a median, dorsal, longitudinal cut should be made through the body wall; it should be carried well into the mantle area, using great care not to injure the underlying parts. The dorsal flaps of the body wall and mantle may then be pinned back, thus exposing most of the viscera.

The radula may be isolated and cleaned by simply placing the whole buccal mass in cold 10 percent potassium hydroxide for several hours to a day or by heating the solution for a few minutes. A quicker method of preparing the radula for mounting involves dropping a few drops of household Clorox on the isolated buccal mass. Within a few minutes the radula will be free of tissues and is ready for further processing. After a thorough rinsing in dilute acetic acid and twice in distilled water, the radula should be placed between two slides with a strip of paper on each side of the radula to prevent crushing. The two slides should be bound together with string. While in this flattened position, the radula should be dehydrated in alcohol and cleared. One slide is then removed and the radula is covered with mounting fluid and a cover slip. It is sometimes advantageous to stain it in strong chromic acid or carmine. It is wise to mount the radula with the teeth up and to make several transverse cuts so the surface of the teeth can be more closely examined at the ends of the cuts. The teeth at the anterior end of the radula are too worn to be diagnostic.

If the dry shell is to be preserved, the animal should first be pulled out and then the shell cleaned. It should be rubbed internally with a bit of sponge on a wire and then rinsed with a syringe. The external surface is often encrusted with algae, debris, and calcium carbonate or iron oxide deposits, and the appearance may be much improved by scrubbing with a stiff toothbrush and water, or by placing the shell in a weak solution of oxalic acid for a half hour or longer. Finally the shell should be well rinsed and dried before storage. It is not necessary to remove the animal from the shell in the minute species, but the whole specimen should be kept in 70 percent alcohol for a day or two and then simply allowed to dry without any resulting offensive odor. Some workers place the live snail in a stoppered shell vial in the freezing compartment of the refrigerator. After it is frozen solid, thaw it; the whole visceral mass then can be easily pulled out of the shell.

Opercula can be cleaned in oxalic acid, dried, and then placed in the shell whose aperture is plugged with cotton.

Suggestions for storing, arranging, and cataloging a shell collection are given in *How to Collect Shells* (1955).

**Taxonomy.** Three orders of Gastropoda are represented in American fresh waters. The Mesogastropoda includes the families Ampullariidae, Thiaridae, Bithyniidae, Hydrobiidae, Viviparidae, Valvatidae, and Pleuroceridae. All these gastropods except the Valvatidae are dioecious and have an internal gill; all have an operculum, a heart with a single auricle, and a radula with few teeth in a transverse series; the two visceral nerves are crossed, forming an 8-shaped loop. The Order Archaeogastropoda, including the single Family Neritidae, is similar to the preceding except that the heart has two auricles and the radula has many teeth in a transverse series. The Basommatophora, on the other hand, consisting of the Physidae, Lymnaeidae, Planorbidae, Acroloxidae, Lancidae, and Ancylidae, are hermaphroditic and have an internal pulmonary cavity, a heart with a single auricle, and a radula consisting of many teeth in a transverse row. The operculum is absent, and the visceral nerves do not cross, but form a simple loop.

Much of the generic and specific nomenclature of the past is confused because

of descriptions based on one or a few shells taken from one or a few localities, but even with our present knowledge there are many species that are still troublesome to the specialists. This situation is due mainly to individual variations, age differences, and ecological variations within single species. The shells of some species of Pleuroceridae, for example, are said to be "infinitely variable." Basch (1963) has shown a wide range of shell distortions in *Ferrissia* kept in aquariums for long periods.

It has become increasingly apparent that more accurate, critical identifications can be made by using the anatomical details of the radula and the internal and external reproductive organs as criteria. Since none of these structures show any considerable variations within a species, they are proving to be particularly valuable in such families as the Hydrobiidae, where the shells are minute and not particularly distinctive.

Some investigators divide the Lymnaeidae of the United States into eight genera, including *Lymnaea, Stagnicola, Fossaria, Radix, Pseudosuccinea, Bulimnaea, Polyrhytis* and *Acella,* but this division has not been generally accepted, and most workers consider them subgenera of the single genus *Lymnaea.* This practice has been followed in the present manual.

Most of the species in the genus *Amnicola* are known only by their shell characteristics. In a few forms, however, the radula and reproductive organs have been studied, and they indicate a wide range of conditions. On the basis of these morphological differences some investigators have placed a few of the species of *Amnicola* in new genera. Nevertheless, pending a careful investigation of many species of *Amnicola* in order to establish relationships more completely, it seems judicious to retain the original broad limits of the genus. These same general remarks also apply to the genus *Somatogyrus.*

The key that follows includes essentially all the known genera occurring in the United States; only a few very rare and poorly known forms are omitted. Only fresh-water forms are indicated, those restricted to brackish waters being omitted.

## KEY TO FAMILIES AND GENERA OF GASTROPODA

1. Without an operculum; mantle cavity a lung .....................................3
   Operculum present; with gills ...............................................2
2. Radula small, with few teeth (usually seven) in a transverse series (Fig. 488A–D);
       widely distributed ....................................................6
   Radula large, with many teeth in a transverse series (Fig. 488J); Alabama, Florida,
       and Gulf coast ...................................... NERITIDAE, 13
3. Shell spiral and sinistral (Figs. 496D–H) ........... PHYSIDAE (pouch snails), 14
   Shell not both spiral and sinistral ..........................................4
4. Shell spiral, elongated, and dextral; spire more or less elongated (Figs. 484, 485B);
       about 12 species; usually in quiet waters; common and widely distributed; often
       split into eight subgenera .......... LYMNAEIDAE (pond snails), **Lymnaea**
   Shell discoidal, patelliform, or rarely with a low spiral (Figs. 498, 499) ...........5
5. Shell discoidal and orblike, or with a low spiral ...PLANORBIDAE (orb snails), 15
   Shell patelliform; not found in torrential streams; limpets.......................24
6. Operculum concentric (Fig. 500A) .........................................7
   Operculum spiral (Fig. 497C) ............................................10
7. Shell medium and discoidal, yellowish-brown to greenish-brown, and with a flaring
       aperture; an introduced common tropical aquarium species in
       Florida.................................................AMPULLARIIDAE, **Marisa**
   Shell spiral .............................................................8
8. Shell very large, the largest American fresh-water snails (Fig. 484); both gill and lung
       present; proboscis divided into two tentaclelike structures; usually on muddy
       substrates; several species in Florida and Georgia.
                              AMPULLARIIDAE (apple snails), **Pomacea**
   Shell smaller; animal with gill only ..........................................9

FIG. 495.–Typical Lymnaeidae. A, *Lymnaea* (= *Pseudosuccinea*) *columella* Say, ×3; B, *L.* (= *Acella*) *haldemani* ("Desh." Binn.), ×1.3; C, *L.* (= *Radix*) *auricularia* (L.), ×2; D, *L. stagnalis*, ×1.5; E, *L.* (= *Bulimnaea) megasoma* Say, ×1.5.

9. Shell less than 13 mm long (Fig. 502C); introduced from Europe; in rivers and lakes of the Great Lakes region; usually in vegetation.

BITHYNIIDAE, **Bithynia tentaculata** (L.)

Shell more than 15 mm long; usually on sandy bottoms of lakes and rivers .......................................... VIVIPARIDAE, **31**

10. Operculum circular and multispiral (Fig. 497C); gill external (Fig. 485D); shell generally less than 7 mm in diameter; several species; generally distributed in a variety of habitats, but especially in large lakes.

VALVATIDAE (round-mouthed snails), **Valvata**

Operculum not circular; paucispiral (Fig. 502F) or multispiral; gill internal .......**11**

11. Shell more than 15 mm long, thick, and heavy; male without external verge ......**12**

Shell less than 10 mm long; male with external verge.......... HYDROBIIDAE, **40**

12. Shell elongate, with many transverse ridges basally and rows of small bosses or spinules distally; occurs locally in Florida; introduced from western Pacific islands. ...................................... THIARIDAE, **Tarebia**

Shell with other characters; in clean running waters.

PLEUROCERIDAE (river snails), **34**

13. Shell globose, thick, and solid; columellar region expanded and flattened (Fig. 496A); operculum calcareous; few species in fresh and brackish waters of Florida and Gulf coast. ............................................... **Neritina**

Shell small and thin; columellar region concavely flattened (Figs. 496B, C); operculum corneous; one rare species in the Coosa and Cahaba rivers of Alabama. .................................... **Lepyrium showalteri** (Lea)

FIG. 496.–Typical Neritidae (A to C) and Physidae (D to H). A, *Neritina*, ×1.5; B and C, *Lepyrium showalteri*, ×6.5; D, *Physa gyrina*, ×1.7; E, *P. parkeri*, ×2; F, *P. sayi*, ×2; G, *P. integra*, ×2.5; H, *Aplexa hypnorum*, ×2.5.

FIG. 497.–Valvatidae. A, *Valvata sincera*, ×8; B, *V. tricarinata*, ×11; C, operculum of *V. tricarinata*. (C modified from Baker, 1928.)

14. Shell with body whorl somewhat inflated; inner edge of mantle digitate or lobed and extending over shell (Figs. 496D–G); many variable species inhabiting all types of waters, especially in northern states; often the only mollusk to be found in polluted waters . . . . . . . . . . . . . . . . . . . . . . . . . . . . . . . . . . . . . . . . . . . . **Physa**
   Shell more elongated (Fig. 496H); inner edge of mantle simple, not extending over the thin shell; in swales, intermittent streams, and stagnant pools; generally distributed in northern states . . . . . . . . . . . . . . . . . . . . . . . **Aplexa hypnorum** (L.)
15. Shell discoidal . . . . . . . . . . . . . . . . . . . . . . . . . . . . . . . . . . . . . . . . . . . . . . . . . . . .**16**
   Shell with a low spiral; western . . . . . . . . . . . . . . . . . . . . . . . . . . . . . . . . . . . . . . .**23**
16. Interior of aperture armed with several lamellae or teeth (Fig. 498J) . . . . . . . . . . . . .**17**
   Interior of aperture without lamellae or teeth . . . . . . . . . . . . . . . . . . . . . . . . . . . . . .**18**
17. In eastern half of the United States; several species (Fig. 498J) . . . . . . . . . **Planorbula**
   Several uncommon species in southern Texas and Louisiana. . . . . . . . . . . **Tropicorbis**
18. Shell large, greatest diameter more than 12 mm; lip usually thickened (Figs. 498F, G); shell ultradextral or ultrasinistral; many species in all types of habitats, but most common in quiet waters; widely distributed. . . . . . . . . . . . . . . . . .**Helisoma**
   Shell small, greatest diameter less than 9 mm; lip sharp; dextral . . . . . . . . . . . . . . . . .**19**
19. Base of body whorl somewhat flattened; one rare species in southern Texas . . . . . . . . . . . . . . . . . . . . . . . . . . . . . . . . . . . . . .**Drepanotrema cultratum** (Orb.)
   Base of body whorl convex (Figs. 498B–D); common and widely distributed . . . . .**20**
20. Shell costate, less than 3 mm in diameter (Fig. 498E); one or two species in northern states . . . . . . . . . . . . . . . . . . . . . . . . . . . . . . . . . . . . . . . . . . . . . . . . . . . . . . . **Armiger**
   Shell not costate . . . . . . . . . . . . . . . . . . . . . . . . . . . . . . . . . . . . . . . . . . . . . . . . . . . . .**21**
21. Shell rounded, or with carinate or subcarinate periphery (Figs. 498A–D); many species in a great variety of habitats . . . . . . . . . . . . . . . . . . . . . . . . . . . . . . . . . . . .**Gyraulus**
   Shell with acutely carinate periphery (Fig. 498H); usually in quiet waters; widely distributed but common only east of the Rockies . . . . . . . . . . . . . . . . . . . . . . .**22**
22. Penial gland sausage-shaped; northern California . . . . . . . . . . . . . . . . . . . . . . . **Menetus**
   Penial gland flattened; several species more widely distributed . . . . . . . . . **Promenetus**
23. Shell imperforate (Fig. 498L); several western species. . . . . . . . . . . . . . . . .**Parapholyx**
   Shell deeply umbilicate (Fig. 498K); several western species . . . . . . . . . . . . . **Carinifex**
24. Apex of shell sharply acute and directed posteriorly (Figs. 499N, O); a rare species known from Lake Eldora, Colorado, and other isolated mountain lakes in the United States and Canada.
            ACROLOXIDAE, **Acroloxus coloradensis** (Henderson)
   Apex otherwise . . . . . . . . . . . . . . . . . . . . . . . . . . . . . . . . . . . . . . . . . . . . . . . . . . . . . . .**25**
25. Apex of shell in front of center (Figs. 499E, F); gills absent; mature shell up to 18 mm long; Pacific coast states . . . . . . . . . . . . . . . . . . . . . . . . . . . . . . . LANCIDAE, **26**
   Apex of shell behind center (Figs. 499J, K); shell usually less than 10 mm long . . . . . . . . . . . . . . . . . . . . . . . . . . . . . . . . . . . . . . . . . . . . . . . ANCYLIDAE, **27**

FIG. 498.–Typical Planorbidae. A and B, *Gyraulus circumstriatus*, ×6; C, *G. deflectus*, ×6; D, *G. altissimus*, ×5; E, *Armiger crista*, ×6; F, *Helisoma antrosa*, ×1.7; G, *H. trivolvis*, ×1.2; H, *Promenetus exacuous*, ×4; J, *Planorbula*, ×4; K, *Carinifex*, ×.9; L, *Parapholyx*, ×4. (A and B redrawn from Baker, 1928.)

26. Muscle scar incomplete (Fig. 499G); shell apex forward of middle; anterior slope concave; several species in the Columbia River drainage ..........**Fisherola**
    Muscle scar complete (Fig. 499H); shell apex subcentral; anterior slope not concave; several species in coastal streams south of the Columbia River........ **Lanx**
27. Shell with a horizontal septum (Fig. 499Q); a rare and problematical genus; several species, widely distributed ...................................**Gundlachia**
    Shell without a horizontal septum ............................................**28**
28. Shell elevated; apex in midline, with faint pink or red coloration (Figs. 499J, K); southeastern states; three species, of which two are probably extinct ................................................... **Rhodacmea**
    Shell elevated or depressed; apex in midline or to the right, not pinkish or red....**29**
29. Shell elevated (Fig. 499B); apex with fine radial striations (Fig. 499A); about six species; widely distributed in standing and running waters .......... **Ferrissia**
    Shell depressed (Figs. 499D, M); apex smooth; chiefly in standing waters; eastern and southern states .........................................................**30**
30. Apex obtuse (Fig. 499D); east of the Mississippi River; two species ...... **Laevapex**
    Apex subacute, to the right of the midline (Fig. 499L); Florida to Texas.
    .................................................**Hebetancylus excentricus** (Morelet)
31. Operculum wholly concentric (Figs. 500A, C) ...............................**32**
    Center of operculum subspiral (Fig. 500B); several species east of Mississippi River ...............................................................**Lioplax**
32. Whorls of shell somewhat flattened and nodulous; inner margin of operculum reflected, forming an elevated marginal fold (Fig. 500G); several species; restricted to the Alabama River and its tributaries ............................... **Tulotoma**
    Whorls of shell not flattened, smooth; inner margin of operculum simple ........**33**
33. Shell subconic, thin (Fig. 500D); several species, chiefly eastern; most common in lakes and streams of the Mississippi Valley ..................... **Viviparus**
    Shell turreted (Fig. 500F); numerous species; generally distributed from the Mississippi Valley to the Atlantic coast ................................. **Campeloma**
34. Aperture canaliculate below (Figs. 501D, E) ...............................**35**
    Aperture not canaliculate below ...........................................**38**
35. Shell fusiform, large; canal long (Fig. 501D); in rapid streams of eastern Tennessee and western Virginia .......................................................**Io**
    Shell conical; canal short ...................................................**36**
36. Spire elongated (Figs. 501F, G); numerous and extremely variable species; from Great Lakes and Mississippi Valley south to Kentucky, Tennessee, and Alabama, in which states it is most common.............................. **Pleurocera**
    Spire short ...................................................................**37**

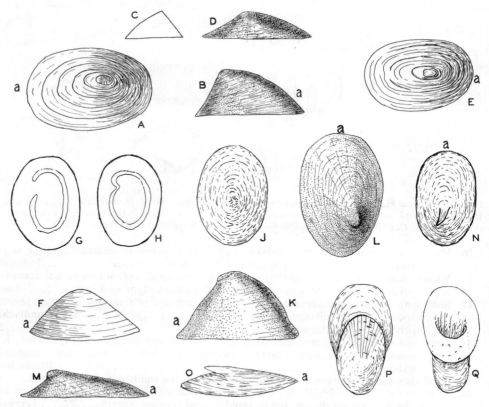

FIG. 499.–Typical Ancylidae, Acroloxidae, and Lancidae. A, dorsal view of *Ferrissia*, ×9; B, lateral view of *F. rivularis*, ×6; C, cross section of *F. rivularis*; D, lateral view of *Laevapex*; E, dorsal view of *Lanx newberryi*, ×3; F, lateral view of *L. newberryi*; G, ventral surface of shell of *Fisherola* showing muscle scar; H, same for *Lanx*; J, dorsal view of *Rhodacmea*; K, lateral view of *Rhodacmea*; L, dorsal view of *Hebetancylus*; M, lateral view of *Hebetancylus*; N, dorsal view of *Acroloxus coloradensis*; O, lateral view of *A. coloradensis*; P, dorsal view of *Gundlachia*; Q, ventral view of *Gundlachia. a*, anterior. (B, D, K, L, and M from Basch, 1963.)

37.  Parietal wall callously thickened above and below (Fig. 501E); several species; Ohio River system and Arkansas . . . . . . . . . . . . . . . . . . . . . . . . . . . . . . . . . .**Lithasia**
     Parietal wall callously thickened above (Fig. 501B); several species in Tennessee River drainage . . . . . . . . . . . . . . . . . . . . . . . . . . . . . . . . . . . . . . . . . . . . . . . . .**Eurycaelon**
38.  Shell ovate-conic to elongated (Fig. 501H); numerous species; most common in rivers of Tennesse and Alabama, but extending north to Great Lakes, St. Lawrence River basin, and western tributaries of the Mississippi River; a few species in the Pacific coast states, and two species reported from northwestern Nevada; absent in the Rocky Mountain region . . . . . . . . . . . . . . . . . . . . . . . . . **Goniobasis**
     Shell more globose . . . . . . . . . . . . . . . . . . . . . . . . . . . . . . . . . . . . . . . . . . . . . . . . . .**39**
39.  Aperture entire; shell heavy, ridged or smooth, and with a low to high spire (Fig. 501C); numerous highly variable species; from New York west to Kansas and south to Alabama and Arkansas; especially abundant in the Coosa River, Alabama; a difficult genus, here interpreted to include *Spirodon, Mudalia, Leptoxis,* and *Nitocris* . . . . . . . . . . . . . . . . . . . . . . . . . . . . . . . . . . . . . . .**Anculosa**
     Aperture with a sutural fissure above (Fig. 501A); about a dozen highly variable species in the Coosa River, Alabama. . . . . . . . . . . . . . . . . . . . . . . . . . .**Gyrotoma**

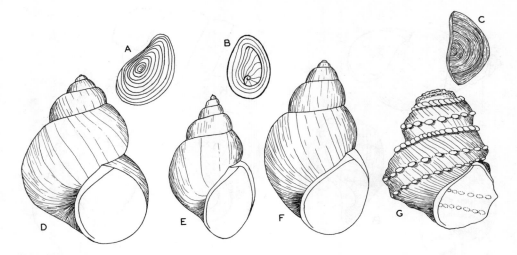

FIG. 500.–Typical Viviparidae. A, operculum of *Viviparus*; B, operculum of *Lioplax subcarinata*; C, operculum of *Tulotoma*; D, *Viviparus subpurpureus*, ×1.5; E, *Lioplax subcarinata*; F, *Campeloma decisum*, ×1.7; G, *Tulotoma magnifica*, ×1.

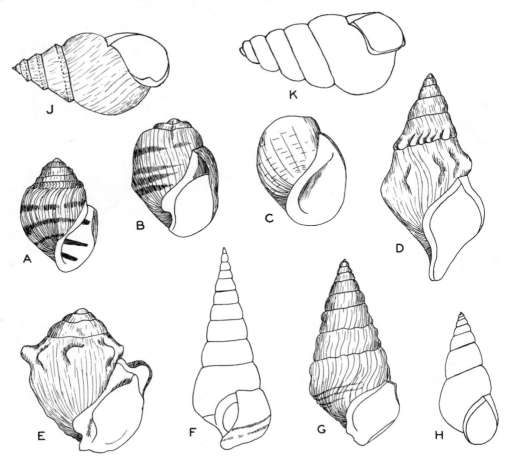

F<small>IG</small>. 501.–Typical Pleuroceridae. A, *Gyrotoma amplum,* ×2; B, *Eurycaelon anthonyi,* ×1.5; C, *Anculosa picta,* ×2; D, *Io spinosa,* ×1.2; E, *Lithasia,* ×2.2; F, *Pleurocera acuta,* ×2; G, *Pleurocera,* ×1.5; H, *Goniobasis livescens,* ×2; J and K, *Anculosa,* ×2. (A redrawn from Goodrich, 1924; C modified from Goodrich, 1922; F modified from Goodrich and van der Schalie.)

52. Edge of aperture sinuous, not in the same plane (Fig. 502J); in rapid streams; several
       species west of Continental Divide . . . . . . . . . . . . . . . . . . . . . . . . . . **Fluminicola**
     Edge of aperture not sinuous . . . . . . . . . . . . . . . . . . . . . . . . . . . . . . . . . . . . . . . . . .**53**
53. Edge of aperture in a horizontal plane . . . . . . . . . . . . . . . . . . . . . . . . . . . . . . . . . . .**54**
     Edge of aperture oblique . . . . . . . . . . . . . . . . . . . . . . . . . . . . . . . . . . . . . . . . . . . . . .**55**
54. New Jersey to South Carolina . . . . . . . . . . . . . . . . . . . . . . . . . . . . . . **Gillia altilis** Lea
     Rivers of northern Florida and Georgia; up to 9 mm long. . . . . . . . . . . . . . . **Notogillia**
55. Each lateral tooth of radula with a prominent cusp flanked by an equal number of
       smaller cusps on each side (Fig. 502R); one rare species in Wisconsin and
       another in the Potomac drainage . . . . . . . . . . . . . . . . . . . . . . . . . . . . . . . . . . .**Clappia**
     With an unequal number of cusps on each side of the prominent central cusp of the
       lateral tooth of radula; about 20 species east of the Mississippi River and mostly
       south of the Ohio River; up to 8 mm long; a difficult genus; some investigators
       divide it into several genera such as *Marstonia, Rhapinema,* and *Spilochlamys*
       (Fig. 502D) . . . . . . . . . . . . . . . . . . . . . . . . . . . . . . . . . . . . . . . . . . . **Somatogyrus**

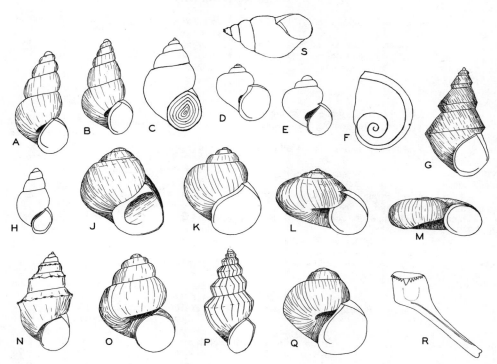

FIG. 502.–Typical Hydrobiidae and Bithyniidae. A, *Hydrobia nickliniana*, ×7; B, *Pomatiopsis lapidaria*, ×4; C, *Bithynia tentaculata* with operculum, ×2.5; D, *Somatogyrus subglobosus*, ×2; E, *Amnicola limosa*, ×4; F, operculum of *A. limosa* with fine striations and growth lines omitted; G, *Pyrgulopsis nevadensis*, ×5; H, *P. letsoni*, ×5; J, *Fluminicola columbiana*, ×2.5; K, *Gillia altilis*, ×2.5; L, *Cochliopa riograndensis*, ×3; M, *Horatia micra*, ×8; N, *Lyrodes*, ×10; O, *Lyogyrus browni*, ×10; P, *Tryonia clathrata*, ×5; Q, *Clappia*, ×8; R, lateral tooth of *Clappia*; S, *Littoridina*, ×10. (R redrawn from Baker, 1928.)

# GASTROPODA REFERENCES

ABBOTT, R. T. (ed.). 1955. *How to Collect Shells. A Symposium.* 75 pp. American Malacological Union, Buffalo, N.Y.

ADAMSTONE, F. B. 1923. The distribution and economic importance of Mollusca in Lake Nipigon. *Univ. Toronto Stud. Biol. Ser.* 22:67–119.

AHO, J. 1966. Ecological basis of the distribution of the littoral freshwater molluscs in the vicinity of Tampere, South Finland. *Ann. Zool. Fenn.* 3:287–322.

BAKER, F. C. 1911. The Lymnaeidae of North and Middle America. *Spec. Publ. Chic. Acad. Sci.* 3:1–539.

———. 1916. The relation of mollusks to fish in Oneida Lake. *N.Y. State Coll. For. Tech. Publ.* 4:1–366.

———. 1918. The productivity of invertebrate fish food on the bottom of Oneida Lake, with special reference to mollusks. Ibid. 9:1–233.

———. 1918a. The relation of shellfish to fish in Oneida Lake, New York. *N.Y. State Coll. For. Circ.* 21:1–34.

———. 1928. *The fresh water Mollusca of Wisconsin. Part I. Gastropoda.* 507 pp. Wis. Acad. Sci., Arts and Lett. Madison, Wis.

———. 1945. *The molluscan family Planorbidae.* 530 pp. Urbana, Ill.

BASCH, P. F. 1959. The anatomy of Laevapex fuscus, a freshwater limpet (Gastropoda: Pulmonata). *Misc. Publ. Mus. Zool. Univ. Mich.* 108:1–56.

———. 1959a. Status of the genus Gundlachia (Pulmonata: Ancylidae). *Occas. Pap. Mus. Zool. Univ. Mich.* 602:1–9.

———. 1963. Environmentally influenced shell

distortion in a fresh-water limpet. *Ecology* **44**:193–194.

———. 1963a. A review of the recent freshwater limpet snails of North America (Mollusca: Pulmonata). *Bull. Mus. Comp. Zool.* **129**:401–461.

BERG, K., and K. W. OCKELMANN. 1959. The respiration of freshwater snails. *J. Exp. Biol.* **36**:690–708.

BERRY, E. G. 1943. The Amnicolidae of Michigan: distribution, ecology, and taxonomy. *Mus. Zool. Univ. Mich. Misc. Publ.* **57**:1–68.

BOSS, K. J. 1974. Oblomovism in the Mollusca. *Trans. Am. Microsc. Soc.* **93**:460–481.

BOVBJERG, R. V. 1968. Responses to food in lymnaeid snails. *Physiol. Zool.* **41**:412–423.

———. 1975. Dispersal and dispersion of pond snails in an experimental environment varying to three factors, singly and in combination. Ibid. **48**:203–215.

BOYCOTT, A. E. 1936. The habitats of freshwater Mollusca in Britain. *J. Anim. Ecol.* **5**:116–186.

BRANSON, B. A. 1970. Checklist and distribution of Kentucky aquatic gastropods. *Ken. Fish. Bull.* **54**:1–20 (processed).

BRYCE, G. W. 1970. Rediscovery of the limpet, Acroloxus coloradensis (Basommatophora: Acroloxidae), in Colorado. *Nautilus* **83**:105–108.

BURKY, A. J. 1971. Biomass turnover, respiration, and interpopulation variation in the stream limpet Ferrissia rivularis (Say). *Ecol. Monogr.* **41**:235–251.

CARRIKER, M. R. 1946. Morphology of the alimentary system of the snail Lymnaea stagnalis appressa Say. *Trans. Wis. Acad. Sci. Arts and Lett.* **38**:1–88.

CHAMBERLIN, R. V., and D. T. JONES. 1929. A descriptive catalog of the Mollusca of Utah. *Bull. Univ. Utah* **19**:1–203.

CHEATUM, E. P. 1934. Limnological investigations on respiration, annual migratory cycle, and other related phenomena in fresh-water pulmonate snails. *Trans. Am. Microsc. Soc.* **53**:348–407.

CLAMPITT, P. T. 1970. Comparative ecology of the snails Physa gyrina and Physa integra (Basommatophora: Physidae). *Malacologia* **10**:113–151.

CLARKE, A. H. (ed.). 1970. Papers on the rare and endangered mollusks of North America. Ibid. 1–56.

———. 1973. The freshwater mollusks of the Canadian interior basin. Ibid. **13**:1–509.

CLENCH, W. J., and R. D. TURNER. 1956. Freshwater mollusks of Alabama, Georgia, and Florida from the Escambia to the Suwanee River. *Bull. Fla. State Mus. Biol. Sci.* **1**:97–239.

DANIELS, J. M., and K. B. ARMITAGE. 1969. Temperature acclimation and oxygen consumption in Physa hawnii Lea (Gastropoda: Pulmonata). *Hydrobiologia* **33**:1–13.

DAWSON, J. 1911. The biology of Physa. *Behavior Monogr.* **1**:1–120.

DAZO, B. C. 1965. The morphology and natural history of Pleurocera acuta and Goniobasis livescens (Gastropoda: Ceritheacea: Pleuroceridae). *Malacologia* **3**:1–80.

DeWITT, R. M. 1954. Reproduction, embryonic

development, and growth in the pond snail, Physa gyrina Say. *Trans. Am. Microsc. Soc.* **73**:124–137.

GILLESPIE, D. M. 1968. Population studies of four species of Molluscs in the Madison River, Yellowstone National Park. *Limnol. Oceanogr.* **14**:101–114.

GOODRICH, C. 1922. The Anculosae of the Alabama River drainage. *Mus. Zool. Univ. Mich. Misc. Publ.* **7**:1–57.

———. 1924. The genus Gyrotoma. Ibid. **12**:1–32.

———. 1936. Goniobasis of the Coosa River, Alabama. Ibid. **31**:1–60.

———. 1941. Distribution of the gastropods of the Cahaba River, Alabama. *Mus. Zool. Univ. Mich. Occas. Pap.* **428**:1–30.

GUNTER, G. 1936. Radular movements in gastropods. *J. Wash. Acad. Sci.* **26**:361–365.

HANNA, G. D. 1966. Introduced mollusks of western North America. *Occas. Pap. Calif. Acad. Sci.* **48**:1–108.

HARMAN, W. N. 1972. Benthic substrates: their effect on fresh-water Mollusca. *Ecology* **53**:271–277.

HARMAN, W. N., and C. O. BERG. 1970. Freshwater Mollusca of the Finger Lakes region of New York. *Ohio J. Sci.* **70**:146–170.

———. 1971. The freshwater snails of central New York with illustrated keys to the genera and species. *Search, Agriculture* **1**:1–68.

HARMAN, W. N., and J. L. FORNEY. 1970. Fifty years of change in the molluscan fauna of Oneida Lake, New York. *Limnol. Oceanogr.* **15**:454–460.

HENDERSON, J. 1924. Mollusca of Colorado, Utah, Montana, Idaho, and Wyoming. *Univ. Colo. Studies* **13**:65–223.

———. 1929. Non-marine Mollusca of Oregon and Washington. Ibid. **17**:47–190.

———. 1936. Mollusca of Colorado, Utah, Montana, Idaho, and Wyoming—supplement. Ibid. **23**:81–145.

———. 1936a. The non-marine Mollusca of Oregon and Washington. Supplement. Ibid. 251–280.

HOFF, C. C. 1940. Anatomy of the ancylid snail, Ferrissia tarda (Say). *Trans. Am. Microsc. Soc.* **59**:224–242.

HUBENDICK, B. 1951. Recent Lymnaeidae. Their variation, morphology, taxonomy, nomenclature, and distribution. *K. Svenska Vetenska. Handl.* **3**:1–225.

JONES, W. C., and B. A. BRANSON. 1964. The radula, genital system, and external morphology in Mudalia potosiensis (Lea) 1841 (Gastropoda: Prosobranchiata: Pleuroceridae) with life history notes. *Trans. Am. Microsc. Soc.* **83**:41–62.

MACAN, T. T. 1950. Ecology of fresh-water Mollusca in the English Lake District. *J. Anim. Ecol.* **19**:124–146.

MAGRUDER, S. R. 1935. The anatomy of the freshwater prosobranchiate gastropod, Pleurocera canaliculatum undulatum (Say). *Am. Midl. Nat.* **16**:883–912.

MALONE, C. R. 1965. Dispersal of aquatic gastropods via the intestinal tract of water birds. *Nautilus* **78**:135–139.

McNEIL, C. W. 1963. Winter survival of Stagnicola palustris nuttalliana and Physa propinqua. *Ecology* **44**:187–191.

MORRISON, J. P. E.   1932.   A report on the Mollusca of the northeastern Wisconsin lake district. *Trans. Wis. Acad. Sci. Arts and Lett.* **27**:359–396.

———.   1955.   Notes on the genera Lanx and Fisherola. *Nautilus* **68**:79–83.

MURRAY, H. D., and E. C. ROY.   1968.   Checklist of freshwater and land mollusks of Texas. *Sterkiana* **30**:25–42.

NEKRASSOW, A. D.   1928.   Vergleichende Morphologie der Laiche von Süsswasser-Gastropoden. *Z. Morphol. Oekol. Tiere* **13**:1–35.

NOLAND, L. E., and E. REICHEL.   1943.   Life cycle of Lymnaea stagnalis completed at room temperature without access to air. *Nautilus* **57**:8–13.

PILSBRY, H. E.   1934.   Review of the Planorbidae of Florida, with notes on other members of the family. *Proc. Acad. Nat. Sci.* **86**:29–66.

SHOUP, C. S.   1943.   Distribution of fresh-water gastropods in relation to total alkalinity of streams. *Nautilus* **56**:130–134.

TAYLOR, D. W., and N. F. SOHL.   1962.   An outline of gastropod classification. *Malacologia* **1**:7–32.

THOMPSON, F. G.   1970.   Some hydrobiid snails from Georgia and Florida. *Q. J. Fla. Acad. Sci.* **32**:241–256.

WALKER, B.   1918.   A synoposis of the classification of the freshwater Mollusca of North America, north of Mexico, and a catalogue of the more recently described species, with notes. *Mus. Zool. Univ. Mich. Misc. Publ.* **6**:1–213.

WENZ, W.   1938–1944.   *Gastropoda. Band 1: Prosobranchia und Allgemeiner Teil.* 1639 pp. Koeltz, Koenigstein-Taunus, Germany.

———.   1960.   *Gastropoda. Band 2: Euthyneura.* 834 pp. Ibid.

WINSLOW, M. L.   1926.   A revised check list of Michigan Mollusca. *Mus. Zool. Univ. Mich. Occas. Pap.* **181**:1–28.

WURTZ, C. B.   1956.   Fresh-water mollusks and stream pollution. *Nautilus* **69**:96–100.

# Chapter 37

# PELECYPODA (CLAMS, MUSSELS)

UNLIKE THE Gastropoda, the bivalve mollusks are all aquatic, and although they occur in nearly all types of fresh-water environments, they are most abundant and varied in our larger rivers.

**General characteristics.** The mussels, or clams, of our inland waters range from about 2 to 250 mm in length. The two valves of the shell are securely attached to each other dorsally by an elastic hinge ligament, and under natural conditions the valves gape slightly to permit the protrusion of the muscular hatchet- or axe-shaped foot at the anteroventral margin and the inhalent and exhalent siphons at the posterior margin. There are no tentacles, head, or eyes. The animal lies obliquely with the ventral half (or more) hidden in the substrate; in some species the shell may be entirely hidden from view with only the siphons appearing at the surface.

**Locomotion.** Mussels move over and through the substrate by means of a series of contractions of the intrinsic muscle fibers of the foot. The foot is first elongated and thrust forward in the substrate; then the distal portion of the foot becomes more or less swollen transversely so that it obtains a purchase, and at the same time the entire foot is shortened; as a result the main portion of the body and its enclosing shell are pulled forward slightly. These repeated muscular contractions therefore result in locomotion that is essentially a series of short "hunching" movements. Some species are known to move several feet per hour and the resulting long, troughlike tracks of larger mussels may often be seen on sandy lake bottoms where there is little wave action. The stimuli responsible for extensive movements of clams are not generally known, but it is thought that stagnation and fall in water level are of primary importance. Thin-shelled species are generally more active than heavy-shelled species.

**Shell, muscles.** Mussel shells exhibit a variety of shapes. Some are decidedly elongated or oval; others are subcircular, rhomboidal, quadrate, trapezoidal, or subtriangular. At the dorsal margin of each valve, just anterior to the hinge ligament, is a raised area, the umbo or beak, which denotes the point at which growth began in the juvenile mussel. Surrounding each umbo and extending out to the edges of the valves is a series of concentric lines which are formed at the edge of the shell as the animal grows. At intervals these rings are more closely grouped, forming a more or less distinct ridge. In many species it can be shown that these markings clearly denote limits of annual growth and winter rest periods, especially if an adequate sample from a particular locality is studied. The annual growth-ring picture is often confused, however, by the presence of accessory rings formed in response to a variety of temporary unfavorable environmental conditions, such as lack of food, low oxygen supply, and fall in water level. In addition to these concentric markings, many genera bear pustules, rays, knobs, or wrinkles.

External coloration is whitish to brown in the Sphaeriidae, and light yellow, light green, dark green, brown, or blackish in other families. In older shells, especially near the umbones, the outer protective col-

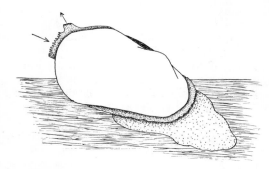

FIG. 503.–Female *Lampsilis siliquoidea* (Barnes) in natural position in river bottom, ×3. Arrows indicate currents of water. (Modified from Baker, 1928.)

teeth which aid in keeping the two valves in juxtaposition. In the Unionidae the pseudocardinal teeth are in the anterior part of the shell below the umbones, and the long, narrow, ridgelike lateral teeth are more posterior and below the region of the ligament. In the Sphaeriidae there are lateral teeth both anterior and posterior to the true cardinals.

The hinge teeth serve as a fulcrum, and the springlike hinge ligament normally keeps the shell slightly open. When the foot and siphons are withdrawn, however, the shell may be tightly closed by the contraction of the two large but short transverse muscles fastened to the inner surface of the valves, the anterior and posterior adductors.

In addition to the scars produced by the attachment of the adductor muscles, each valve typically contains the scars of three other muscles. Above, and more or less closely associated with the posterior adductor scar, is a small scar produced by the attachment of the posterior retractor of the foot. The anterior adductor has a comparable associated scar for the anterior retractor of the foot, as well as an additional scar for the protractor muscle of the foot. There are also some small and indistinct scars in the cavity of the umbo from muscles that aid in holding the visceral mass in place.

ored layer (periostracum) is often eroded away, exposing the chalky white calcium carbonate layer underneath. The internal surface of the shell is thickly coated with nacre, or mother-of-pearl, which ranges in color from silvery white through pink to dark purple; it is composed of extremely thin alternating laminae of calcium carbonate and an organic substance. Between the nacre and the periostracum is the prismatic layer; it consists of minute, closely packed, prismlike blocks of calcium carbonate (Fig. 505).

The important features of the inner surface of a typical shell are shown in Fig. 506. Near the dorsal margin there is usually a series of projecting and interlocking hinge

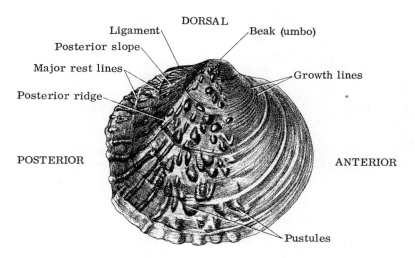

FIG. 504.–Shell structure of *Cyclonais*. (From Burch, 1973.)

FIG. 505.–Small section of mussel shell. *PER*, periostracum; *PL*, prismatic layer; *N*, nacre.

Except where muscles are attached, the inner surface of the shell is completely lined with a sheet of glandular tissue, the mantle. This structure is securely fastened near the edges of the valves along the muscular pallial line. Such an attachment prevents foreign particles from getting between mantle and shell. An indentation in the pallial line may be present near the posterior end of the shell; it is called the pallial sinus and is produced by intrinsic muscles that retract the siphons. The entire lateral surface of the mantle secretes the nacre, but the periostracum and prismatic layer are formed only by the border of the mantle at the periphery of the shell.

**Gross visceral anatomy.** When one valve of a mussel is removed, the underlying mantle can be seen covering the viscera. At the posterior end of a typical animal the edges of the two lobes of the mantle are modified to form three slitlike openings. Uppermost is the smooth supra-anal opening; below this is the anal (exhalent) opening, which may be smooth or crenulated; lowermost is the distinctly papillose branchial (inhalent) opening. In the Unionidae and Margaritiferidae the edges of the mantle around the branchial opening project to form a more or less distinct siphon. Some Sphaeriidae have long, cylindrical, protrusible anal and branchial siphons (Fig. 508); in other species only the anal siphon is prominent. Neither the Margaritiferidae

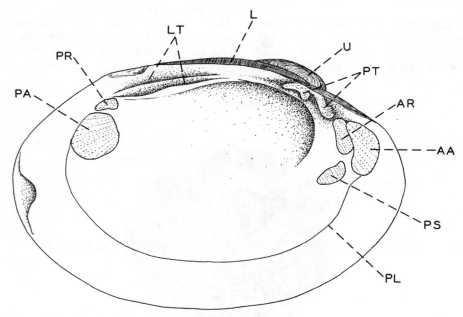

FIG. 506.–Diagrammatic view of inner surface of left valve of *Elliptio*, ×1. *AA*, anterior adductor muscle scar; *AR*, anterior retractor muscle scar; *L*, ligament; *LT*, lateral teeth; *PA*, posterior adductor muscle scar; *PL*, pallial line; *PR*, posterior retractor muscle scar; *PS*, scar of protractor muscle of foot; *PT*, pseudocardinal teeth; *U*, umbo.

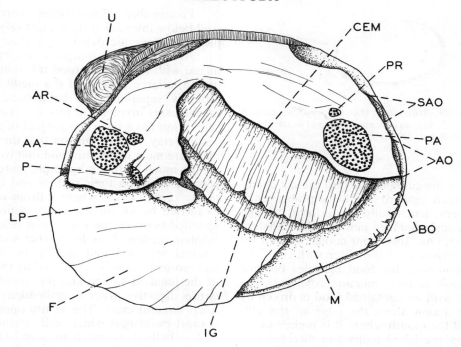

FIG. 507.–Diagrammatic partial dissection of *Fusconaia,* ×1.4. *AA*, anterior adductor muscle; *AO*, anal opening; *AR*, anterior retractor muscle; *BO*, branchial opening; *CEM*, cut edge of mantle; *F*, foot; *IG*, inner gill; *LP*, labial palps; *M*, mantle; *P*, protractor muscle of foot; *PA*, posterior adductor muscle; *PR*, posterior retractor muscle; *SAO*, supra-anal opening; *U*, umbo. (Modified from Lefevre and Curtis, 1910.)

nor the Sphaeriidae have a supra-anal opening.

When the mantle is removed from one side, the two long flat gills of that side are exposed to view. Each gill is composed of two lamellae that are united at the lower but not the upper margin, the two gills together being roughly W-shaped in cross section. The outer gill is connected at the outside and top to the mantle, and the inner gill is attached at the inside to the outer surface of the main median visceral mass; the base of the inner lamella of the outer gill and the base of the outer lamella of the inner gill are attached to each other. The cavity between the two lamellae of each gill is subdivided by vertical partitions into many narrow chambers or water tubes, closed below but opening above into a longitudinal space along the dorsal portion of the gill called the suprabranchial chamber. At the posterior end of the animal the suprabranchial chambers are fused to form a single cavity, the cloacal chamber. Near the anterior end of the gills and surrounding

the small slitlike mouth are two flat labial palps on each side. The upper lip is continuous with the left and right outer palps, and the lower lip is continuous with the left and right inner palps. The greater portion of the foot lies between the gills in the anterior part of the mantle cavity. It tapers posteriorly, and the median visceral mass of the posterior part of the animal is confined to the dorsal part of the mantle cavity.

**Feeding, digestive system** The food of a mussel consists of zooplankton, phytoplankton, and organic detritus, the feeding processes being specialized for the removal of these suspended microscopic particles from the water. It has been found that some Sphaeriidae can remove particles as small as 1 micron from the water. The inner surface of the mantle, the gills, and the visceral mass are covered with cilia that beat in such a coordinated way as to draw a stream of water in through the branchial siphon. This water passes into the mantle cavity and enters the many minute openings, or

FIG. 508.–*Musculium,* showing branchial and anal siphons, ×2. Arrows indicate currents of water. (Modified from Baker, 1928.)

ostia, of the gill lamellae into the gill chambers, then upward to the suprabranchial chambers, and finally posteriorly through the cloacal chamber and out the exhalent opening. As this continuous stream of water passes over the outer surface of the gills, however, the food particles become entangled in their mucous covering. The mucus with its contained food is driven by ciliary action along the edge of the gills toward the mouth where it is picked up by cilia on the labial palps and directed into the mouth in a constant ribbonlike stream

Presumably Sphaeriidae burrowing well below the mud surface must rely completely on organic detritus for their food.

Although some inorganic silt may be mixed with the organic food taken into the mouth, a large portion of the inedible material is separated out beforehand. The mechanisms involved in this selection and separation have been the subject of a long controversy, and it appears that the labial palps are most important, and that by some means much of the indigestible material is separated out on their surface and carried to the ventral edges where it drops off and is carried backward by ciliary action and expelled between the valves just below the inhalent siphon. It is likely that some additional selection and separation of food and inorganic debris is effected by the edge of the inhalent siphon and the mouth. The entire digestive tract is imbedded in the main visceral mass. The mouth opens into a short esophagus which leads to the more or less bulbous stomach situated in the anterior dorsal portion of the foot. The stom-

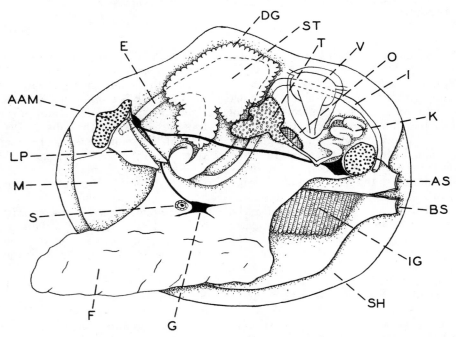

FIG. 509.–Diagrammatic longitudinal section of *Musculium,* ×12. *AAM,* anterior adductor muscle; *AS,* anal siphon; *BS,* branchial siphon; *DG,* digestive gland; *E,* esophagus; *F,* foot; *G,* pedal ganglion; *I,* intestine; *IG,* inner gill; *K* kidney; *LP,* labial palp; *M,* mantle; *O,* ovary; *S,* statocyst; *SH,* shell; *ST,* stomach; *T,* testis; *V,* ventricle of heart.

ach is surrounded by a large green gland, or "liver." The long narrow intestine has several coils behind and below the stomach before it proceeds to the dorsal region and runs posteriorly above the posterior adductor muscle and opens into the mantle cavity through the anus just above the exhalent opening of the mantle cavity.

The anterior part of the intestine of the Unionidae has a lateral diverticulum, or groove, containing the curious crystalline style. This is a cylindrical structure of a hyaline, milky, or brownish color and of a dense gelatinous consistency. During normal feeding activities it is revolved on its long axis by the ciliary epithelium of the style sac. The anterior end of the style usually projects into the stomach, where it rubs against a cartilagelike shield and is constantly being eroded away. This erosion liberates a polysaccharide-digesting enzyme and is thought to function also in separating food from foreign particles. The style disappears during periods of starvation but is regenerated as a response to ingestion. It is formed only slowly at low temperatures.

**Circulation.** The circulatory system consists of a single ventricle, two auricles, blood vessels, and spaces or sinuses in the tissues. Dorsally and posterior to the stomach is the thin-walled pericardial cavity, containing the heart and through which the posterior part of the intestine passes longitudinally. The ventricle is an oval organ surrounding the intestine, and the two flat auricles lie at the sides of the ventricle and open into it just below the middle of each side.

Arising from the ventricle are an anterior and a posterior artery whose branches supply all of the soft parts of the animal, the mantle and gills being supplied with a particularly large quantity of blood. From the smaller arteries the blood passes into numerous sinuses in the tissues, and thence into veins and back to the auricles.

The blood is colorless or slightly bluish owing to dissolved hemocyanin, a respiratory pigment. The heart rate is usually less than 20 beats per minute, but a rate as high as 100 beats has been recorded.

**Respiration.** Although the entire body surface is in contact with water and probably functions in respiration, the greater portion of the oxygen–carbon dioxide exchange undoubtedly occurs in the mantle and gills.

**Excretion.** The two kidneys, or organs of Bojanus, lie in the visceral mass immediately below or behind the pericardial cavity. Each kidney is a dark-colored more or less convoluted tubule with the opening at one end in the pericardial cavity and the opening at the other (external) in a suprabranchial chamber.

**Nervous system.** Unlike snails, mussels have a simple nervous system, with only three pairs of ganglia. The cerebropleural ganglia lie immediately posterior to the anterior adductor muscle, one on each side of the esophagus, and are connected by a short commissure passing over the esophagus; the pedal ganglia are deeply imbedded in the foot and are more or less fused; the visceral ganglia lie just anterior to the posterior adductor and are also partially fused. Connecting the cerebropleural ganglia with the pedal and visceral ganglia are two pairs of long commissures. Each ganglion is the source of nerve fibers to the adjacent organs.

**Sense organs.** Maintenance of equilibrium is effected by a pair of minute statocysts situated near the pedal ganglia. Each statocyst is an ovoid or spherical fluid-filled cavity lined with sensory cells and containing a spherical concretion, the statolith.

The osphradia are two small areas of specialized epithelium on the roof of the cloacal chamber. Their function has never been successfully established, but most writers assume that they are useful in detecting dissolved foreign materials in the water.

In addition to being sensitive to touch, the projecting edges of the mantle are capable of detecting pronounced changes in light intensity, and the valves can be caused to shut by casting a shadow or bright light on the mantle.

Fig. 510.–Outer gill of female *Lampsilis ventricosa* (Barnes), showing posterior marsupium.

**Reproduction.** The Sphaeriidae are uniformly hermaphroditic, but in the Unionidae the sexes are separate except for a few species that are sporadically or consistently hermaphroditic. The ovaries and testes are imbedded in the upper part of the foot and are connected with the suprabranchial chambers by short ducts.

The details of reproduction differ markedly in these two families. In the Sphaeriidae it is thought that self-fertilization occurs in the reproductive ducts. The zygotes pass into the suprabranchial chambers and then downward into the water tubes of the inner pair of gills. Here they develop and grow, and the gills, becoming greatly distended, are then called marsupia. An adult may contain from one to an astounding 60 young in various stages of development. When released from the marsupia, the immature individuals are fully formed, having the shell and all morphological features of adults; sometimes they are surprisingly large, often one-quarter to one-third as long as the parent. Reproduction is thought to continue throughout the year, although very few young are released during the winter months.

In the Unionidae the unfertilized eggs pass into the suprabranchial chambers and then downward into the water tubes of the gills. Depending on the species, all four gills, the two outer gills, or only special parts of the outer gills (Fig. 510) are utilized. Sperm of the male are swept out of the animal through the exhalent opening into the surrounding water. Some of the sperm are then drawn fortuitously into the incurrent siphon of a mature female in the vicinity; they pass through the ostia of the gill lamellae and fertilize the eggs in the water tubes. The embryos are retained only for the early stages of development, but growth is pronounced, and the gills (marsupia) soon become distended. The number of embryos present at one time ranges from several thousand in the smaller species to more than 3 million in some of the largest mussels.

Depending on the species, breeding may begin in the first to eighth year of life. The Ambleminae are short-term breeders and are gravid between April and August; the Unioninae are long-term breeders, the eggs being fertilized in midsummer and carried until the following spring or summer.

Marine bivalves and *Corbicula* have characteristic ciliated free-swimming larvae, but all other American fresh-water mussels have an entirely different type of larva, the glochidium, which becomes a temporary and obligatory parasite on a fish. The mature glochidium which is released from the marsupium of the female mussel ranges from 0.05 to 0.50 mm in diameter. Superficially, it appears to be a small edition of an adult in its general morphology. There are two chitinoid valves joined at their bases along a hinge, lined by a layer of cells comprising the larval mantle, and held together by a single adductor muscle. The mantle bears several tufts of sensory hairs. In species of *Unio, Anodonta,* and *Quadrula* the glochidium has a peculiar long thread that is thought to be useful in becoming attached to the host fish (Fig. 511A). The general shape of the valves may be simple and oval or rounded, roughly triangular, or ax-head shaped (in *Proptera* only). Sometimes the periphery of the shell opposite the hinge bears teeth.

In the Ambleminae and some Unioninae the glochidia leave the female via the suprabranchial chambers and exhalent siphon; they may be free or more or less imbedded in mucus. In other Unioninae irregular masses break through temporary openings in the water tubes. In either case the glochidia become scattered and sink to the bottom where they remain with the valves gaping upward. If they do not come in contact with the body of a fish they us-

FIG. 511.–Immature Pelecypoda. A, end view of glochidium of *Anodonta,* ×130. B, lateral view of juvenile stage of *Actinonaias,* ×150. *AM,* adductor muscle; *HI,* hinge; *LM,* larval mantle; *LT,* larval thread; *SH,* tuft of sensory hairs; *VA,* valve. (A modified from Tucker; B modified from Lefevre and Curtis, 1912.)

ually die within several days. Fish become infected by brushing against the bottom, by stirring up the bottom with fin movements, and by taking in water that contains the glochidia in temporary suspension. The larvae are exceedingly sensitive and clamp tightly to the superficial tissues immediately on contacting the fish. The hookless species usually become attached to the gills, hooked species to the fins or general body surface. Some forms are host-specific and infect only one species of fish; others are capable of infecting several to many species of fish. Sometimes the glochidia become attached to an unsuitable host but soon leave voluntarily.

Within a short time the tissues of the fish begin to grow over the glochidium, and in a day or two the latter is completely encased and forms a small projecting nodule. This parasitic stage usually lasts from 10 to 30 days, although some records indicate as long as 190 days; undoubtedly water temperatures influence the duration of the parasitic period.

During encystment the glochidial structures change markedly, and most of the adult organ systems become more or less definitely formed. The single adductor muscle is replaced by two; the mouth and intestine are present; the gills, kidneys, heart, and foot are represented by functional rudiments; and the mantle has taken on a more definitive structure. Usually, however, there is little increase in size.

At the close of the parasitic period the young mussel breaks out of its cyst, falls to the bottom, and enters a period appropriately called the juvenile stage (Fig. 511B). The organ systems begin to develop rapidly, and the beginning of the adult shell appears beneath the glochidial shell. The foot is long and ciliated and provides a means of locomotion. A long, sticky, hyaline thread, or byssus, is secreted by the posterior part of the foot in many species; it apparently facilitates attachment to the substrate and is usually shed in a few weeks. The smaller juvenile mussels burrow into the bottom and for this reason are seldom collected. As growth proceeds, however, the adult habits are assumed, and the organs take on their adult characteristics. Strictly speaking, the juvenile stage lasts from one to as much as eight years, that is, until the animal is sexually mature.

Several species are known to be able either to complete development to the juvenile stage in the brood chamber or to leave the parent as a glochidium and parasitize a fish in the usual manner. One species, *Simpsoniconcha ambigua,* parasitizes *Necturus,* the mud puppy.

Even though more than 3000 glochidia have been found parasitizing a single adult fish, there is little evidence that they do any direct harm in natural habitats. Nevertheless, heavy infections (100 or more) have been shown to kill 30-mm fingerling trout by causing secondary bacterial infections.

**Growth, longevity.** The period of growth extends from about April to September, and the actual rate of growth is dependent on numerous factors, including temperature, food supply, current, and the specific chemical nature of the water. Mussels usually grow to a length of 30 to 80 mm in two growing seasons. Some of the Anodontidae live for 10 to 15 years, but the Sphaeriidae are thought to live no longer than 12 to 18 months.

**Enemies.** The Sphaeriidae are eaten regularly by numerous fishes, including the gizzard shad, whitefish, buffalo, sucker, redhorse, and perch, and soft-shelled species of the Anodontidae are eaten to a limited extent by catfish and sheepshead. Muskrats are undoubtedly the most important mammalian enemy of mussels. They usually select thin-shelled forms and either let them die on shore when the shell gapes, or force the shell open with their teeth. Piles of discarded shells near muskrat colonies are said to be an excellent source for some of the uncommon species. Mussels are also occasionally eaten by mink, otter, raccoon, turtles, and hell benders (*Cryptobranchus*).

The branchial and mantle cavities are often infested with parasitic or commensal Hydracarina. Larval flukes are sometimes found in the branchial and pericardial cavities. Both of these groups may be responsible for the production of small irregular pearls and blisters on the inner surface of the host shell, and sometimes the nacre may be discolored.

**Economic importance.** As a result of the utilization of marine shells, satisfactory synthetic substitutes, and the gradual depletion of mussel beds, the fresh-water pearl button industry has been declining in importance for many years, although the value of the products has held up well. The industry was founded in 1891, and by 1912 there were 196 factories in 20 states along the larger rivers of the Mississippi system and a few rivers entering the Gulf east of the Mississippi. In that year these plants produced $6,173,486 worth of merchandise. In 1941, with far fewer factories, the corresponding figure was about $2,500,000, but in 1944 it was $4,306,353, and in 1949 it was $3,696,452. About 20,300 tons of shell were harvested in 1944 with a value, before processing, of $892,915; Tennessee, Kentucky, and Arkansas rivers yielded 78 percent of the total.

There are about 40 useful species and 17 species of first importance in the manufacture of buttons; these are included in the following genera: *Fusconaia, Megalonaias, Amblema, Quadrula, Actinonaias, Plagiola, Legumia,* and *Lampsilis.* The mussels are collected in several ways. One widely used device is the crowfoot dredge. It consists of a long iron bar to which are attached 100 to 200 four-pronged hooks on short lengths of cord. When the dredge is lowered from a flat-bottomed boat and dragged along the bottom, the hooks become lodged between the open valves of mussels, and the animals clamp tightly on them. At intervals the dredge is raised and the mussels are removed. Other devices include rakelike tongs, stout rakes with large attached bags or nets, and forks for shallow water collecting. Some states outlaw forking in the interests of conservation.

The mussels are killed by steaming in a cooker, and the meat is removed. The shells are then sold by the ton to the buyers. In the factories or along the river's edge they are sorted and soaked in water before the blanks are cut with a tubular saw. The blanks are ground to uniform thickness, drilled, finished, sorted, and carded or packed for sale.

The beginning of World War II marked the demise of the pearl button industry, and subsequently plastics began to be used almost exclusively for buttons. In the early 1950s, however, the cultured pearl industry of Japan found that small pellets from American thick-shelled mussels formed excellent nuclei for cultured pearls, and the U.S. mussel industry had a revival, especially in the Ohio, Tennessee, and Green rivers. In the 1950s Tennessee, Alabama, Arkansas, Kentucky, and Indiana were the chief shell-producing states. During the 1950s and 1960s musselmen overharvested the natural production, so that by the 1970s the industry again had a demise. In the 1960s mussel shells sold for as much as $100 to $240 per ton. In 1966 the commercial mussel shell harvest in Illinois rivers amounted to more than 3500 tons.

Mussels are seldom collected primarily for their pearls, the fresh-water pearl industry being carried on in conjunction with, and in addition to, the preparation of shells for the button factories. The pearls are more or less imbedded in the soft tissues, and after removal from the shell these parts are examined visually and slipped between the fingers to detect hidden pearls. Small pearls are sometimes recovered by allowing the meats to rot. When reduced to a pulp, the mass is rubbed through a fine sieve that retains the pearls.

Pearls are formed by the secretion of nacre around a foreign body that becomes lodged against the mantle or other tissues. This secretion takes place in a sac lined with epithelium physiologically and histologically similar to the shell-secreting epidermis of the mantle. The foreign body may be a bit of debris, sand grains, or even some kind of a parasite. Though the layman usually thinks of pearls as being "balls," "pears," or "buttons," there are many other irregular shapes habitually produced by certain species. Some of these are called "petal," "lily," "leaf," and "arrowhead," according to their shape. Such curious but natural shapes are determined by pressures and movements of surrounding organs during their formation. Spherical pearls, on the other hand, occur only in a part of the body that is free from unequal pressures and extensive movements; button pearls are formed near the outer surface of the mantle, where they are pressed against the shell while nacre deposition is occurring.

The formation of real freak pearls, or "baroques," is usually instigated by the presence of a parasite or by a button or ball pearl becoming lodged in a new location. Baroques may be either attached to the shell or free. They are of irregular shape, but rare specimens may simulate a bird, insect, other object, or even a face. Single unusual and large baroques and perfectly formed regular pearls command high prices, hundreds and even thousands of dollars having been paid for many specimens. One Arkansas pearl, weighing 3.4 grams, is reputed to have been sold for $6750. Unfortunately, the finding of really fine pearls is an event of increasing rarity because of the great depletion of our mussel resources.

The reported total value of mussel pearls collected in the entire Mississippi River drainage system in 1931 was only $11,436.

In view of our rapidly declining mussel populations, United States government research workers have intermittently been trying to develop effective and economical methods of artificially propagating mussels ever since 1894.

*Corbicula manilensis,* introduced from Asia, sometimes is so abundant as to be a nuisance by plugging waterways in pumping plants, irrigation systems, and the production of sand and gravel. There has been some success in eradicating this species by the addition of 1 ppm of chlorine to the water. In some areas the juveniles are consumed by crayfish.

**Ecology.** Fresh-water bivalves occur in all types of unpolluted habitats but they are most abundant and varied in the larger rivers. Small creeks and spring brooks are devoid of mussels, although they contain Sphaeriidae. Similarly, small lakes, especially seepage lakes, contain few species, and large drainage lakes contain many. Lake Pepin, for example, which is really a wide place on the Mississippi, contains 32 species of mussels.

Like snails, bivalves are most abundant in the shallows, especially in water less than 2 m deep. In the largest rivers and some lakes, however, mussels occur as deep as 7 m. The record depth collection is

*Anodonta,* which was taken at 30 m in Lake Michigan. The specimens were 7 to 14 years old but less than 53 mm long. Sphaeriidae are regularly found in great abundance on some lake bottoms more than 30 m below the surface. These small bivalves are often active burrowers and have been taken up to 25 cm deep in soft substrates.

The occurrence of the largest species and largest numbers of mussels in rivers where there is a good current has not yet been satisfactorily explained from an ecological standpoint. It is possible that abundant food supply, the specific type of substrate, an abundance of oxygen, water chemistry, or a combination of factors may be significant. River genera have thicker shells than lake genera, and individuals of a single species inhabiting both types of environments usually have heavier shells in running waters. Also, in a single species, flatter and less inflated varieties may occur in upper tributaries, more swollen varieties in the lower parts of a river system. Mussels inhabiting exposed lake shoals may be somewhat stunted and more heavy-shelled than specimens from protected waters.

Bare rock bottoms and shifting sands and muds, with their accompanying high turbidities, are unsuitable for bivalves, whereas stable gravel, sand, and substrates composed of sand or gravel mixed with other materials support the largest populations, some such beds having more than 50 mussels per square meter. Though soft mud bottoms are generally uninhabited, there are some common "mud-loving" species of *Anodonta.* Customarily, mussels inhabit substrates free of rooted vegetation, but there are numerous exceptions. The Sphaeriidae are less specific in their occurrence and are found on all types of bottoms except clay and rock; in favorable situations populations of more than 5000 individuals per square meter may be counted.

To a large extent the geographical distribution of the fresh-water bivalves appears to be determined by the chemical features of waters. The Anodontidae are rarely found in acid waters (pH below 7.0) or in waters having a bound carbon dioxide content of less than 15.0 mg per liter. Decidedly alkaline waters and an abundance of

calcium carbonate for shell construction favor large numbers of individuals and species. The Sphaeriidae, on the other hand, have become adapted to a wider range of conditions, and some species are common in lakes having a pH as low as 6.0 and a bound carbon dioxide content of only 2.0 mg per liter. It is difficult to understand how a calcium carbonate shell can be secreted and maintained under such unfavorable conditions. Salts appear to be actively absorbed directly from the water. Potassium seems to be relatively toxic, and waters having more than 7 mg per liter of potassium are generally devoid of mussels.

Because of the apparent disappearance of mussels from the shallows during the winter months, it was formerly inferred that they migrated to deeper waters in the fall. It is now believed, however, that migrations are unimportant and that most individuals simply burrow more deeply into the bottom of their summer habitat so that only the inconspicuous edges of the siphons project. The siphons are opened infrequently, and the animals remain in a dormant state throughout the winter. Ten degrees is thought to be an average critical hibernation temperature.

Many Sphaeriidae are known to burrow into the drying substrate in times of drought, and among the Unionidae, species of *Uniomerus, Carunculina, Ligumia,* and *Amblema* have all been found buried in substrates which were moist or dry for several months.

Fresh-water mussels are thought to have first developed in the New World, and, more specifically, in the general area of the Mississippi drainage basin, for it is here that the greatest diversity of species occurs. *Anodonta* is found also in Europe and Asia, but all other U.S. genera of Anodontidae are endemic. The Margaritanidae are widely distributed throughout the Northern Hemisphere, and the Sphaeriidae are worldwide. The other families mentioned in this chapter are predominantly marine, only a few species having invaded brackish waters and the coastal areas of rivers.

The Mississippi drainage includes more than half of the area of the United

States, from the Continental Divide on the west to the Atlantic region on the east, and from Canada to the Gulf. It has an extremely rich naiad fauna. The Pacific region includes those drainages entering the Pacific Ocean and is characterized mainly by the presence of *Anodonta, Gonidea,* and *Margaritifera.*

Not counting many additional varieties, there are about 220 species of Unionidae and perhaps 40 species of Sphaeriidae known from the 48 contiguous states. The Cumberland River has (had) more than 80 species of Unionidae; Michigan has 66 Unionidae; Dane County, Wisconsin, has 34; Ohio has 70; Texas has 78. The known naiad fauna of the Great Lakes comprises six species from Lake Superior, ten from Michigan, 17 from Huron, 40 from Erie, and six from Ontario. The Atlantic coast states, Great Plains, Rocky Mountain states, and the Pacific coast area have few species of Anodontidae.

By migrating naturally and extensively into suitable habitats, a species may, over a long period of time, come to occupy much of a large drainage area. More rapid migration is undoubtedly effected by fishes carrying the glochidial stage of mussels, and possibly by birds transporting Sphaeriidae and immature Unionidae overland in mud or debris on their legs and feet. There is, however, little actual evidence for the latter mode of transport.

Greater numbers of species are usually found in the lower waters of river systems rather than in the small tributaries. The greater abundance of species in large, shallow lakes is probably due to the fact that such environments have a greater variety of subhabitats or niches than small lakes.

Although sphaeriids are common, there are no mussels in high Rocky Mountain lakes, probably chiefly because these lakes do not contain the proper host fishes for the glochidia. Fundamentally, however, such lakes are usually poor in calcium and could not support mussels anyway.

Pollution, silting of rivers, shell harvesting, and the construction of dams are decidedly inimical to our American mussel fauna. Many of the less common species are fast disappearing, and reduced populations appear to be unsuccessful in increasing their present restricted geographical distribution.

Recent surveys, compared with early surveys, give some idea of the rate at which our fauna is become depauperate. Isom (1969), for example, found that annual harvests in the Tennessee River decreased from 10,000 tons of shells in the 1940s and 1950s to 2000 tons from 1964 through 1967. The present mussel fauna in this river now consists of only 44 species, as contrasted with 100 species before the 1936 Tennessee Valley Authority impoundment. Matteson and Dexter (1966) report a "drastic decline" in the mussel fauna of the Big Vermilion River between 1918 and 1962. Isom and Yokley (1968) report only 48 species in the Duck River, Tennessee, as contrasted with 63 reported originally by Ortmann. In the Illinois River, Starrett (1971) found only 24 species in 1966–1969 (five species represented by single specimens) as contrasted with 45 in 1906–1912. Only three mussel beds in the Kentucky River are now said to be commercially valuable. Since it usually takes a long time for field data to make their way into the literature, it is probable that the mussel situation in the United States is much more serious than we realize.

**Collection, preparation.** Little special apparatus is necessary for field collecting. The larger species may easily be hand-picked in the shallows; small forms may be washed from vegetation or sifted from bottom debris. A long-handled rake may be used for collecting mussels in water of moderate depths, and dredges are necessary for sampling in deep lakes.

If mussels are placed in warm water and heated to boiling, the valves will separate, the viscera can be easily removed, and the epidermis will not crack so easily. The judicious use of dilute oxalic or hydrochloric acid and a toothbrush are valuable for removing surface incrustations and restoring the natural brilliance of the nacre. After treatment with acid, shells should be rinsed thoroughly in clear water. The epidermis of study specimens should be varnished or greased lightly with petroleum jelly before the two valves are tied together. The Sphaeriidae should be placed in 40 percent alcohol for a day or two, the viscera should then be removed, and the shell wrapped in tissue paper to prevent gaping while they are allowed to dry thoroughly.

Preservation for the study of soft parts should be in 70 or 80 percent alcohol, not formaldehyde.

**Taxonomy.** Except for *Margaritifera* and a few representatives of marine families that have invaded brackish waters and coastal regions of rivers, the fresh-water bivalves of the United States are all included in the Unionidae and Sphaeriidae. In the former family, the subfamilies and the great majority of genera and species are well established, although some forms have a lengthy synonymy dating back a century. Many species have several subspecific designations, some of which are useful ecol-

ogically. According to Baker (1928), for example, *Strophitus rugosus* (Swainson) occurs in large and medium rivers, *S. rugosus pavonius* (Lea) is a creek form, *S. rugosus pepinensis* Baker a river-lake form, *S. rugosus winnebagoenis* Baker a small river-lake form, and *S. rugosus lacustris* Baker a small lake form. *Quadrula quadrula* (Raf.) is even more variable.

To the pearl fisherman and button industry, mussels are known by highly descriptive vernacular names. Some of these are niggerhead, pimple back, pig toe, washboard, pocketbook, elephant's ear, slop bucket, spectacle case, paper shells, three-ridge, maple-leaf, warty-back, monkey face, lady finger, floater, and snuff box.

During the past 25 years many of the long-standing taxonomic and nomenclatural problems of our fresh-water bivalves appear to have been resolved. In general, this key follows the suggestions of Burch and other workers, but is highly modified and simplified from these sources.

## KEY TO GENERA OF PELECYPODA

1. Ligament external . . . . . . . . . . . . . . . . . . . . . . . . . . . . . . . . . . . . . . . . . . . . . . . . . . . . . . . . . . . .2
   Ligament internal; in mild to strongly brackish waters  . . . . . . . . . . . . . . . . . . . . . . .8
2. Shell with true cardinal teeth (Figs. 512B, 534) . . . . . . . . . . . . . . . . . . . . . . . . . . . . . .5
   Shell with well-developed pseudocardinal teeth, occasionally vestigial or absent (Figs. 512A, 517A, 518A) . . . . . . . . . . . . . . . . . . . . . . . . . . . . . . . . . . . . . . . . . . . . . . . . .3
3. Shell elongated, laterally compressed (Fig. 512A); dorsoposterior mantle margins not united to form a separate anal opening; epidermis blackish; 80 to 175 mm long; lotic. . . . . . . . . . . . . . . . . . . . . . . . . . . . . . . . . . . . MARGARITIFERIDAE, 4
   Shell subcircular, oval, subtriangular, or elongated; dorsoposterior mantle margins forming one or more separate openings; edge of mantle thickened between incurrent and excurrent openings; lotic and lentic; pearly mussels or naiads.
   UNIONIDAE, 9
4. Shell thin and elongated (Fig. 514B); Cumberland and Tennessee river systems, and Ohio, Illinois, Iowa, Wisconsin, and Nebraska. **Cumberlandia monodonta** (Say)
   Shell thicker, not elongated (Fig. 512A); *M. margaritifera* (L.) in northern third of states from Pennsylvania to upper Missouri River system; *M. falcata* (Gould) in Pacific drainages; *M. hembeli* (Conrad) in Alabama and Louisiana.
   **Margaritifera**
5. Hinge with anterior and posterior lateral teeth (Figs. 534F,G; 512B) . . . . . . . . . . . . . .6
   Hinge without lateral teeth; shell circular and thin; 10 to 15 mm long; a single species in brackish waters of Florida . . . . CYRENELLIDAE, **Cyrenella floridana** Dall
6. Shell thin and fragile, length ranging from 2 to 20 mm but rarely more than 10 mm; concentric growth rings not prominent; pallial line simple; widely distributed and common; seed shells, pea, pill, and fingernail clams. SPHAERIIDAE, 66
   Shell heavy, more than 10 mm long, with prominent concentric growth rings (Figs. 512B, 514A); pallial line sinuate . . . . . . . . . . . . . . . . . . . . . . . . . . . . . . . . . . . . . . . .7

FIG. 512.–Representative Pelecypoda. A, *Margaritifera margaritifera*, ×0.7; B, *Polymesoda caroliniana*, × 0.8; C, *Rangia cuneata*, ×0.8; D, *Mytilopsis leucophaeta*, ×1.4.

7. More than 25 mm long (Fig. 512B); a single species in streams and brackish waters near the coast from South Carolina to Texas.
   CYRENIDAE, **Polymesoda caroliniana** (Bosc)
   Ten to 50 mm long; periostracum blackish (Fig. 514A); introduced from Asia and spreading in a phenomenal fashion; sloughs and streams; from California north to Washington and east to Florida, and also in the greater Mississippi River drainage; sometimes called *C. fluminea* or *C. laena*.
   CORBICULIDAE, **Corbicula manilensis** (Philippi)
8. Hinge with cardinal and lateral teeth; 25 to 70 mm long (Fig. 512C); shell thick; Maryland to Florida to Texas .........MACTRIDAE, **Rangia cuneata** Gray
   Hinge without distinct teeth; shell mytiliform; with a byssus; 10 to 15 mm long (Fig. 512D); Maryland to Florida. DREISSENIIDAE, **Mytilopsis leucopheata** Conrad
9. Marsupium formed of all four gills, swollen in gravid females .. AMBLEMINAE, **10**
   Marsupium formed of only the outer gill on each side, swollen in gravid females.
   UNIONINAE, **22**
10. Hinge teeth well developed ................................................**11**
    Hinge teeth rudimentary or lacking; shell smooth, elongated, and usually with a high, sharp, posterior ridge (Fig. 517A); Pacific coast drainages.
    **Gonidea angulata** (Lea)

FIG. 513.–Representative Unionidae. A, *Anodonta*, ×0.7; B, *Arcidens confragosus*, ×0.7.

11. Shell corrugated posteriorly (Fig. 514C) ......................................**12**
    Shell not corrugated posteriorly (Figs. 514D, 517B) ...........................**20**
12. Posterior edge steep and short (Fig. 514C); Alabama .......... **Quadrula stapes** Lea
    Posterior edge not especially steep and short (Fig. 515) ......................**13**
13. Shell pustulated (Figs. 514E, 516A) .........................................**14**
    Shell not pustulated (Fig. 514D) but may be ridged ...........................**16**
14. Shell essentially circular (Fig. 516A); Tennessee River. **Quadrula intermedia** (Conrad)
    Shell elongated ..............................................................**15**
15. Shell with a well-developed posterior ridge; pustules small (Fig. 515); Mississippi and
    Gulf drainages. .................................**Tritogonia verrucosa** (Raf.)
    Posterior ridge low; with a row of large pustules (Fig. 514E); Ohio, Cumberland, and
    Tennessee river systems, but west to Nebraska and Oklahoma.
                                                        **Quadrula cylindrica** (Say)

FIG. 514.–Representative Pelecypoda. A, *Corbicula manilensis*, ×1.3; B, *Cumberlandia monodonta*, ×0.5; C, *Quadrula stapes*; D, *Plectomerus dombeyanus*, ×0.5; E, *Quadrula cylindrica*, ×0.5. (C from Burch, 1975, by permission; A, B, D, and E from Burch, 1973.)

FIG. 515.–*Tritogonia verrucosa*. A, female, ×0.6; B, male, ×0.6.

FIG. 516.–Representative Unionidae. A, *Quadrula*, ×0.9; B, *Megalonaias gigantea*, ×0.9.

**16.** Shell elongated, rhomboidal (Fig. 514D); nacre violet to bronze ................**17**
Shell elongated, oval to circular (Figs. 516B, 518A); nacre white ...............**18**
**17.** Anterior adductor muscle scar smooth; Georgia and Florida.
                                    **Elliptoideus sloatianus** (Lea)
Anterior adductor muscle scar rough; Alabama to Tennessee and Texas.
                                    **Plectomerus dombeyanus** (Val.)
**18.** Shell less than 7 cm long, smooth; Florida to Texas; three species .....**Quincuncina**
Shell large and corrugated (Fig. 516B) .......................................**19**
**19.** Beak sculptured with strong zigzag lines; shell elongate-quadrate, very heavy; 80 to
        250 mm long (Fig. 516B); in large, deep rivers; Mississippi system generally
        and from Alabama to Texas ..................**Megalonais gigantea** (Barnes)
Beak not sculptured (Fig. 518A); eastern half of the United States; small to large
        rivers; two species ......................................... **Amblema**
**20.** Shell rhomboidal, with or without a posterior ridge (Fig. 514D) ................**17**
Shell circular, triangular, or oval (Figs. 514E, 517B) .........................**21**
**21.** Shell pustulose (Fig. 514E); Mississippi drainage as far west as Minnesota and Texas;
        about eight species .......................................... **Quadrula**
Shell smooth (Fig. 517B); common and generally distributed in eastern half of the
        United States; about 12 species ................................**Fusconaia**

FIG. 517.–Representative Unionidae. A, *Gonidea angulata*, ×0.9; B, *Fusconaia*, ×0.8.

Fig. 518.–Representative Unionidae. A, *Ambelema*, ×0.8; B, *Cyclonaias tuberculata*, ×1.

26. Shell circular (Fig. 518B); nacre purple; Mississippi and St. Lawrence drainages.
**Cyclonais tuberculata** Raf.
Shell more or less oval (Fig. 519A); nacre white or pinkish; Ohio, Cumberland, Tennessee, and Mississippi river systems north to Minnesota; two species.
**Plethobasus**
27. Pseudocardinal teeth poorly developed to vestigial (Figs. 520B,C) ...............**28**
Pseudocardinal teeth well developed ......................................**29**
28. Pseudocardinal teeth poorly developed (Fig. 520B); Mississippi drainage north to the Ohio River, west to Colorado and in Florida to Texas (Fig. 524A).
**Uniomerus tetralasmus** (Say)
Pseudocardinal teeth vestigial (Fig. 520C); Ohio, Cumberland, and Tennessee river systems ........................................ **Hemistema lata** (Raf.)

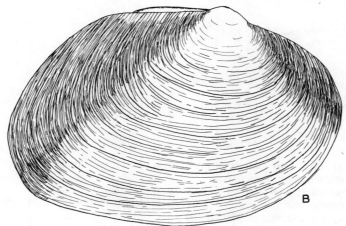

FIG. 519.–Representative Unionidae. A, *Plethobasus*, ×1; B, *Lexingtonia*, ×1.8.

29. Shell elongate, rhomboidal; beak low, not arched forward (Figs. 526B, C); many species in a wide variety of lotic and lentic habitats throughout the eastern half of the United States; about 20 species ............................. **Elliptio**
Shell another shape; beak high, arched forward (Figs. 519B, 520D) .............**30**
30. Outer gills (marsupia) swollen, orange or red; Tennessee River drainage and North River, Virginia; two species ................................. **Lexingtonia**
Outer gills not swollen; white, gray, yellow, or pale orange; about 30 species, mostly in the southeastern states, but a few in drainages in the northeastern quarter of the United States .......................................... **Pleurobema**
31. Hinge without teeth, or only with pseudocardinals present (Figs. 513A, 520E, F); shell thin, fragile .......................................................**32**
Hinge teeth present, occasionally poorly developed (Fig. 521B); shell not fragile ..**41**
32. Pseudocardinal teeth absent (Figs. 513A, 520E) .............................**33**
Pseudocardinal teeth rudimentary (Fig. 520F) ...............................**37**
33. Restricted to drainages east of the Continental Divide ........................**34**
Restricted to Pacific drainages ........................................ **Anodonta**

FIG. 520.–Structure of Unionidae. A, horizontal section of a bit of marsupium of *Lasmigona* showing each main water tube divided into three chambers; B, teeth of *Uniomerus tetralasmus*; C, teeth of *Hemistema lata*; D, *Pleurobema,* ×0.6; E, teeth of *Anodonta*; F, teeth of *Alasmidonta*; G and H, teeth of *Lasmigona*; J, *Anodonta,* ×0.5. (A modified from Burch, 1973; B–E, G–J from Burch, 1973; F redrawn from Burch, 1975.)

**34.** Umbos extending only slightly or not at all above the dorsal margin (Fig. 520J); widely distributed and common . . . . . . . . . . . . . . . . . . . . . . . . . . . . . . . . . . . . . . . **Anodonta**
Umbos extending well above the dorsal margin (Fig. 513A) . . . . . . . . . . . . . . . . . . . . **35**
**35.** Beak sculpture double-looped (Fig. 522A); widely distributed and common. **Anodonta**
Beak sculpture concentric (Fig. 522B) . . . . . . . . . . . . . . . . . . . . . . . . . . . . . . . . . . . . . . **36**
**36.** Beak sculpture coarse (Fig. 522C); widely distributed. . . . **Strophitus undulatus** (Say)
Beak sculpture fine (Fig. 522D); widely distributed. **Anodontoides ferussacianus** (Lea)
**37.** Pseudocardinal teeth thin, bladelike (Fig. 520F) . . . . . . . . . . . . . . . . . . . . . . . . . . . . **38**
Pseudocardinal teeth tubercular (Fig. 521D) . . . . . . . . . . . . . . . . . . . . . . . . . . . . . . . . **39**
**38.** Shell rhomboidal, with a posterior ridge (Fig. 522F); St. Lawrence River to South Carolina . . . . . . . . . . . . . . . . . . . . . . . . . . . . . . **Alasmidonta varicosa** (Lamarck)
Shell elongated (Fig. 521A); Alabama, Georgia, and Florida.
**Anodontoides radiatus** (Conrad)
**39.** Posterior slope slightly corrugated (Fig. 522F); eastern states; common. **Alasmidonta**
Posterior slope not corrugated . . . . . . . . . . . . . . . . . . . . . . . . . . . . . . . . . . . . . . . . . . . . . **40**
**40.** Shell about twice as long as high (Fig. 523B); Ohio River system, extending to Arkansas, Iowa, Michigan, and Tennessee . . . . **Simpsoniconcha ambigua** (Say)
Shell length/height ratio 1.8 or less (Fig. 521D); Florida to Mississippi.
**Strophitus subvexus** (Conrad)
**41.** Shell with large corrugations on either or both the central disc or posterior slope (Figs. 513B, 522H) . . . . . . . . . . . . . . . . . . . . . . . . . . . . . . . . . . . . . . . . . . . . . . . . . . . **42**
Shell without large corrugations in these areas (Figs. 521B, C) . . . . . . . . . . . . . . . . **43**
**42.** Central disc not sculptured (Fig. 522H); Arkansas and Oklahoma.
**Arkansia wheeleri** (Ortmann and Walker)
Central disc sculptured (Fig. 513B); states adjoining Mississippi River, Texas, and Alabama . . . . . . . . . . . . . . . . . . . . . . . . . . . . . . . . . . . . . . . **Arcidens confragosus** (Say)

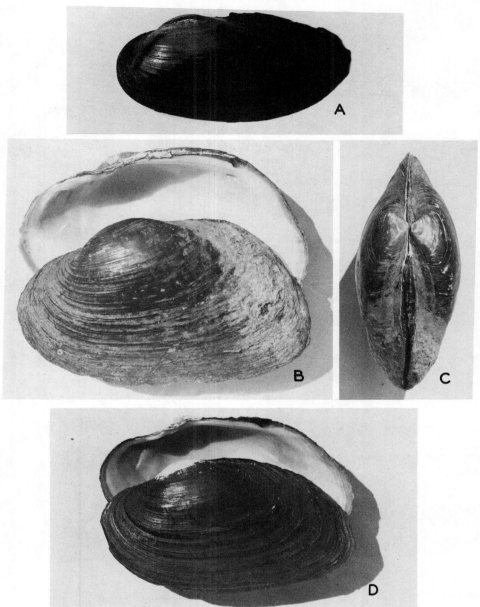

FIG. 521.–Representative Unionidae. A, *Anodontoides,* ×0.9; B, *Alasmidonta,* ×0.9; C, *Alasmidonta,* dorsal, ×0.7; D, *Strophitus,* ×0.9.

**43.** Beak sculpture concentric (Fig. 522B); widely distributed east of the Continental Divide, but especially abundant in southeastern states; about 12 species (Figs. 521B, C) ...............................................**Alasmidonta**
Beak sculpture double-looped (Fig. 522A); six widely distributed species in eastern half of the United States (Fig. 523A) ...........................**Lasmigona**

FIG. 522.–Structure of Unionidae. A, double-looped beak sculpture of *Anodonta*; B, concentric beak sculpture; C, coarse beak sculpture of *Strophitus*; D, fine beak sculpture of *Anodontoides ferrusacianus*; E, pseudo-cardinal teeth of *Alasmidonta*; F, *Alasmidonta varicosa*, ×0.8; G, *Alasmidonta*, ×0.5; H, *Arkansia wheeleri*, ×0.3. (From Burch, 1973.)

FIG. 523.–Representative Unionidae. A, *Lasmigona*, ×0.7; B, *Simpsoniconcha ambigua*, ×1.7.

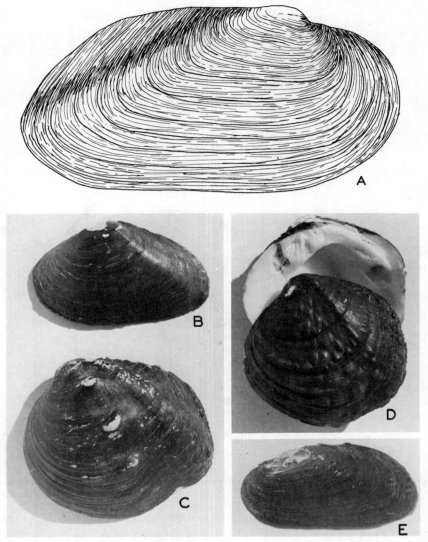

FIG. 524.–Representative Unionidae. A, *Uniomerus*, ×1.7; B, *Ptychobranchus*, ×0.8; C, *Oliquaria reflexa*, ×0.8; D, *Cyprogenia*, ×1; E, female *Medionidus*, ×1.3.

**44.** Entire outer gill serving as a marsupium . . . . . . . . . . . . . . . . . . . . . . . . . . . . . . . . . . . . . **45**
    Marsupium confined to the central or posterior part of the outer gill, as shown by
        swollen portion . . . . . . . . . . . . . . . . . . . . . . . . . . . . . . . . . . . . . . . . . . . . . . . . . . . **46**
**45.** Ventral edge of marsupium not folded; southeastern Texas.
                                                **Cyrtonaias tampicoenis** (Lea)
    Ventral edge of marsupium folded; five species; Ohio River system and south to
        Florida and west to Oklahoma (Fig. 524B) . . . . . . . . . . . . . . . . . . **Ptychobranchus**
**46.** Marsupium confined to middle part of outer gill . . . . . . . . . . . . . . . . . . . . . . . . . . . . **47**
    Marsupium confined to posterior part of outer gill (Fig. 510) . . . . . . . . . . . . . . . . . . . **48**
**47.** Shell with several large lateral tubercles (Fig. 524C); Mississippi River system.
                                                **Obliquaria reflexa** Raf.
    Shell without such large tubercles (Fig. 524D); two species; Ohio, Cumberland, and
        Tennessee river systems, and west to Oklahoma and Kansas . . . . . **Cyprogenia**

FIG. 525.–*Lampsilis*. A, male, ×1; B, female, ×1.2.

**48.** Marsupium confined to lower part of posterior part of outer gill; Tennessee and
　　　Cumberland river systems ......................... **Dromus dromas** Lea
　　Marsupium in both upper and lower halves of posterior part of outer gill ........**49**
**49.** Posterior slope corrugated or radially grooved (Fig. 527A) .....................**50**
　　Posterior slope smooth (Figs. 528A, D) .......................................**51**
**50.** Shell with radiating grooves attaining the posteroventral margin; Tennessee River
　　　drainage ......................................... **Lemiox rimosus** Raf.
　　Shell with another kind of sculpturing (Figs. 524E, 527A); Alabama, Florida, and
　　　Mississippi; five species ................................... **Medionidus**
**51.** Posterior half of pseudocardinal teeth forming a series of deep, parallel, rough lamellae
　　　(Fig. 527C); slow streams; Florida to Texas .....**Glebula rotundata** (Lamarck)
　　Without such deep lamellae ...............................................**52**
**52.** Shell high, compressed, and with a smooth arc (Fig. 528A); hinge teeth very large and
　　　heavy; Pennsylvania to Minnesota and south to Alabama and Oklahoma.
　　　　　　　　　　　　　　　　　　　　　　　　　　　**Ellipsaria lineolata** Raf.
　　With another combination of characters ...................................**53**
**53.** Females with a wartlike caruncle on the inner edge of each side of the mantle in front
　　　of the branchial opening; total length of adults less than 45 mm (Fig. 528D);
　　　probably two species; New York to Minnesota and south to Florida and
　　　Arkansas ................................................. **Carunculina**
　　Females without such a caruncle; total length of adults less than 45 mm ........**54**

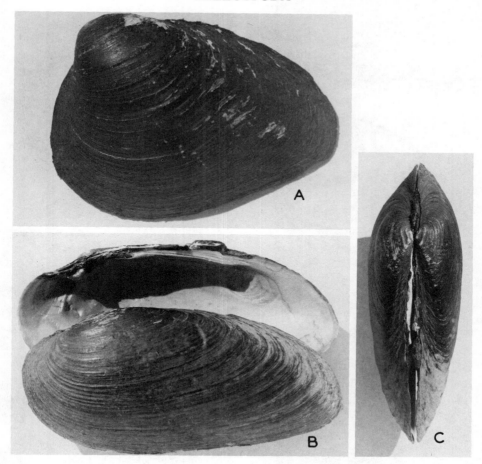

Fig. 526.–Representative Unionidae. A, *Pleurobema*, ×0.7; B, *Elliptio*, ×0.9; C, dorsal view of *Elliptio*, ×0.8.

54. Shell twice or more as long as high ......................................... 55
    Shell less than twice as long as high ........................................ 56
55. Inner edge of mantle with a ribbonlike flap (Fig. 532A); Mississippi drainage system
    and Florida to Texas; two species (Fig. 532F) ................... **Lampsilis**
    Inner edge of mantle papillate (Fig. 532C); generally distributed in eastern half of the
    United States; probably two species (Fig. 531B) ................. **Ligumia**
56. Shell circular or high-oval (Fig. 531C); teeth heavy; generally distributed in eastern
    half of the United States; six species .......................... **Obovaria**
    Shell with another shape; teeth heavy or not ................................. 57
57. Shell of mature mussel less than 6 cm long; sexually dimorphic (Figs. 527D, E);
    posterior end of some species with raised radiating ridges; about 18 species;
    generally distributed in eastern half of the United States but most species
    restricted to the Tennessee and Cumberland river drainages........ **Dysnomia**
    Shell with another combination of characters................................ 58
58. Posterior ridge angular (Figs. 528B, 525) ..................................... 59
    Posterior ridge rounded or absent (Fig. 529B) ................................ 60

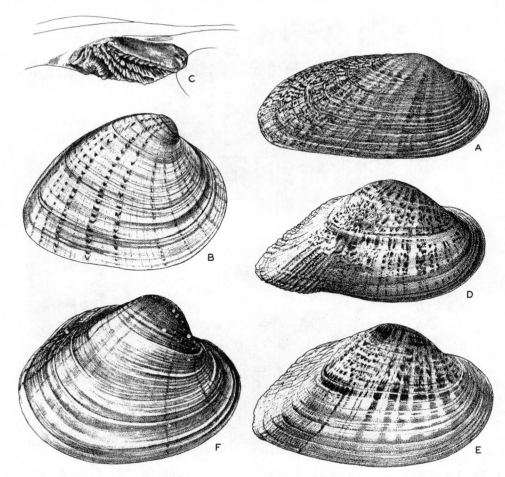

FIG. 527.–Representative Unionidae. A, *Medionidus*, ×1.2; B, *Ellipsaria*, ×0.6; C, left pseudocardinal teeth of *Glebula rotundata*; D, female *Dysnomia*, ×1; E, male *Dysnomia*, ×1; F, *Lampsilis*, ×0.7. (From Burch, 1973.)

**59.** Shell compressed; beak cavities shallow; color rays with or without V-shaped markings (Fig. 528B); 5 cm long; three species; Mississippi and St. Lawrence river
drainages, and Texas and Oklahoma ..............................**Truncilla**
Shell inflated; beak cavities deep; color rays present or absent (Figs. 525, 532F); about
seven species; Mississippi and St. Lawrence drainages, and southeastern
states. ........................................................ **Lampsilis**
**60.** Pseudocardinal teeth poorly developed (Fig. 529B); four species in eastern half of the
United States ................................................**Leptodea**
Pseudocardinal teeth well developed (Fig. 529A) ...........................**61**
**61.** Shell with a well-developed wing (Fig. 529A); three species in a genus distributed
widely in eastern half of the United States..............**Proptera alata** (Say)
Wing lacking or poorly developed.........................................**62**
**62.** Shell extremely inflated ..................................................**Proptera**
Shell not extremely inflated ..............................................**63**
**63.** Shell up to 115 mm long; purple nacre...................................**Proptera**
Nacre white; if nacre is pinkish-purple, then shell is less than 60 mm long.......**64**

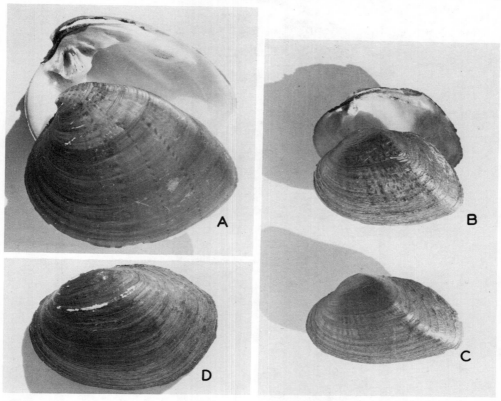

FIG. 528.–Representative Unionidae. A, *Ellipsaria lineolata*, ×0.9; B, *Truncilla*, ×1; C, *Dysnomia*, ×1; D, *Carunculina*, ×1.2.

**64.** Posterior inner mantle margin smooth or crenulated, not papillate or ribbonlike; three
species in eastern half of the United States (Fig. 530) ........... **Actinonaias**
Posterior inner mantle margin papillate or ribbonlike (Figs. 532A–C) ............. **65**

**65.** Posterior inner mantle margin papillate (Figs. 532B, C); a poorly defined genus consisting of about 15 species; mostly southeastern, but at least one species extending as far north as Virginia and Michigan (Fig. 532E) ............. **Villosa**
Posterior inner mantle margin ribbonlike (Fig. 532A); about 20 species in the eastern
half of the United States (Figs. 527F, 532F) ..................... **Lampsilis**

**66.** Shell with two cardinal teeth in one valve, and one cardinal tooth in the other valve
(Figs. 534F, G); generally distributed ................................... **67**
Shell with only one feeble cardinal tooth in each valve, shell subrhomboidal and
mottled (Fig. 533D); 7 mm long; North Carolina to Texas.
                                                                     **Eupera cubensis** (Prime)

**67.** Shell sculptured with coarse striae or widely spaced striae (Fig. 534A); nepionic valves
not inflated and separated from subsequent portion of shell; three species.
                                                                     **Sphaerium**
Shell sculptured with fine striae; nepionic valves usually inflated and separated from
subsequent portion of shell by a sulcus (Figs. 534B, E) ................... **68**

**68.** Mature shell more than 8 mm long ........................................... **69**
Mature shell less than 8 mm long ........................................... **70**

**69.** Beaks prominent (Fig. 533C); three species .......................... **Musculium**
Beaks not prominent (Fig. 534D); three species ...................... **Sphaerium**

FIG. 529.–Representative Unionidae. A, *Proptera,* ×0.9; B, *Leptodea,* ×0.7.

FIG. 530.–*Actinonaias,* ×0.8.

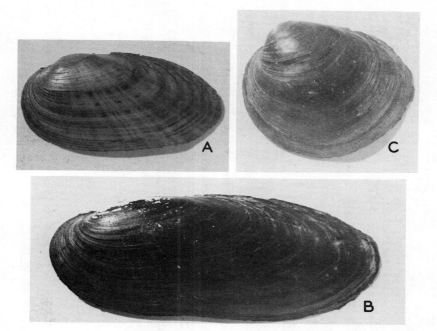

FIG. 531.–Representative Unionidae. A, *Villosa*, ×0.9; B, *Ligumia*, ×0.8; C, *Obovaria*, ×0.9.

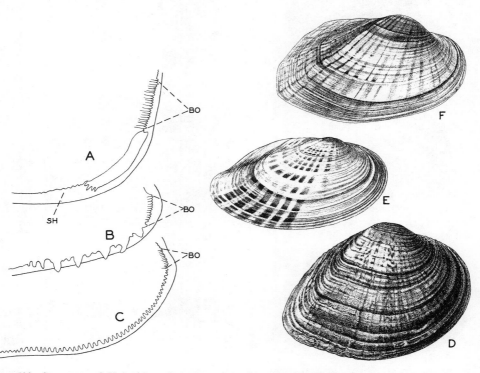

FIG. 532.–Structure of Unionidae. A, ventro-posterior edge of mantle and shell in a female *Lampsilis ventricosa*; B, same for *Micromya iris*; C, same for *Ligumia recta*; D, *Truncilla*, ×1; E, *Villosa*, ×0.6; F, *Lampsilis*, ×0.6. (D–F from Burch, 1973.)

FIG. 533.–Representative Sphaeriidae. A, *Pisidium*, ×1.5; B, *Musculium*, ×1.5; C, *Musculium*, dorsal, ×1.5; D, *Eupera*, ×1.7.

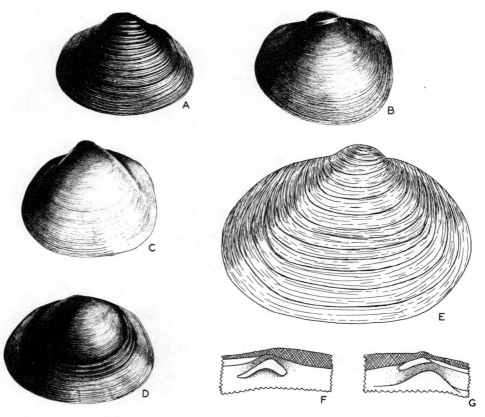

FIG. 534.–Structure of Sphaeriidae. A, left valve of *Sphaerium*, ×4; B, left valve of *Sphaerium*, ×4; C, left valve of *Musculium*, ×3; D, left valve of *Sphaerium*, ×3; E, right valve of *Sphaerium simile*, ×5; F, cardinal tooth of right valve of *S. simile*; G, cardinal teeth of left valve of *S. simile*. (A–D from Burch, 1973; F and G modified from Baker, 1928.)

766

**70.** Posterior end nearly at right angles to the dorsal margin; two species .... **Musculium**
Posterior end and dorsal margin rounded or forming an obtuse angle ............ **71**
**71.** Beaks swollen; one species ........................................ **Musculium**
Beaks not swollen; three species.................................. **Sphaerium**

# PELECYPODA REFERENCES

ALLEN, W. R. 1921. Studies of the biology of freshwater mussels. Experimental studies of the food relations of certain Unionidae. *Biol. Bull.* **40**:210–242.

AREY, L. B. 1932. The formation and structure of the glochidial cyst. Ibid. **62**:212–221.

BAKER, F. C. 1898. The Mollusca of the Chicago area. The Pelecypoda. *Bull. Nat. Hist. Surv. Chica. Acad. Sci.* **3**:1–130.

———. 1916. The relation of mollusks to fish in Oneida Lake. *N.Y. State Coll. For., Tech. Publ.* **4**:1–366.

———. 1918. The productivity of invertebrate fish food on the bottom of Oneida Lake, with special reference to mollusks. Ibid. **9**:1–233.

———. 1918a. The relation of shellfish to fish in Oneida Lake, New York. *N.Y. State Coll. For., Circ.* **21**:1–34.

———. 1928. *The fresh water Mollusca of Wisconsin. Part II. Pelecypoda.* 495 pp. Wis. Acad. Sci, Arts and Lett. Madison, Wis.

BEDFORD, J. W., et al. 1968. The freshwater mussel as a biological monitor of pesticide concentrations in a lotic environment. *Limnol. Oceanogr.* **13**:118–126.

BOYCOTT, A. E. 1936. The habitats of fresh-water Mollusca in Britain. *J. Animal Ecol.* **5**:116–186.

BROOKS. S. T., and H. B. HERRINGTON. 1944. The Sphaeriidae, a preliminary survey. *Nautilus* **57**:93–97.

BROWN, C. J. D., C. CLARK, and B. GLEISSNER. 1938. The size of certain naiades from western Lake Erie in relation to shoal exposure. *Am. Midl. Nat.* **19**:682–701.

BURCH, J. B. 1972. Freshwater sphaeriacean clams (Mollusca: Pelecypoda) of North America. *Biota of Freshwater Ecosystems, Identification Manual* **3**:1–31.

———. 1973. Freshwater Unionacean clams (Mollusca: Pelecypoda) of North America. Ibid. **11**:1–176.

———. 1975. *Freshwater sphaeriacean clams (Mollusca: Pelecypoda) of North America.* 99 pp. Malacological Publications, Hamburg, Mich.

———. 1975a. *Freshwater unionacean clams (Mollusca: Pelecypoda) of North America.* 204 pp. Malacological Publications, Hamburg, Mich.

CHAMBERLIN, R. V., and D. T. JONES. 1929. A descriptive catalog of the Mollusca of Utah. *Bull. Univ. Utah* **19**:1–203.

CHURCHILL, E. P., JR., and S. I. LEWIS. 1924. Food and feeding in fresh-water mussels. *Bull. U.S. Bur. Fish.* **39**:437–471.

CLARKE, A. H. (ed.). 1970. Papers on the rare and endangered mollusks of North America. *Malacologia* **10**:1–56.

CLARKE, A. H., and C. O. BERG. 1959. The freshwater mussels of central New York. *Mem. Cornell Univ. Agr. Exp. Sta.* **367**:1–79.

COKER, R. E. 1919. Freshwater mussels and mussel industries of the United States. *Bull. U.S Bur. Fish.* **36**:13–89.

COKER, R. E., A. F. SHIRA, H. W. CLARK, and A. D. HOWARD. 1921. Natural history and propagation of fresh-water mussels. Ibid. **37**:76–181.

DUNDEE, D. S. Catalog of introduced molluscs of eastern North America (north of Mexico). *Sterkiana* **55**:1–37.

FOSTER, T. D. 1932. Observations on the life history of a fingernail shell of the genus Sphaerium. *J. Morphol.* **53**:473–497.

FRIERSON, L. S. 1927. *A classified and annotated check list of the North American Naiades.* 111 pp. Baylor Univ. Press. Waco, Texas.

GALE, W. F., and R. L. LOWE. 1971. Phytoplankton ingestion by the fingernail clam, Sphaerium transversum (Say) in Pool 19, Mississippi River. *Ecology* **52**:507–513.

GILMORE, R. J. 1917. Notes on reproduction and growth in certain viviparous mussels of the family Sphaeriidae. *Nautilus* **31**:16–30.

GOODRICH, C., and H. VAN DER SCHALIE. 1939. Aquatic mollusks of the Upper Peninsula of Michigan. *Mus. Zool. Univ. Mich. Misc. Publ.* **43**:1–45.

———. 1944. A revision of the Mollusca of Indiana. *Am. Midl. Nat.* **32**:257–326.

HANNA, G. D. 1966. Introduced mollusks of western North America. *Occas. Pap. Calif. Acad. Sci.* **48**:1–108.

HEARD, W. H. 1962. Distribution of Sphaeriidae (Pelecypoda) in Michigan, U.S.A. *Malacologia* **1**:139–160.

———. 1965. Comparative life histories of North American pill claims (Sphaeriidae: Pisidium). Ibid. **2**:381–411.

———. 1975. Sexuality and other aspects of reproduction in Anodonta (Pelecypoda: Unionidae). Ibid. **15**:81–103.

HENDERSON, J. 1924. Mollusca of Colorado, Utah, Montana, Idaho, and Wyoming. *Univ. Colo. Studies* **13**:65–223.

———. 1929. Non-marine Mollusca of Oregon and Washington. Ibid. **17**:47–190.

———. 1936. Mollusca of Colorado, Utah, Montana, Idaho, and Wyoming–supplement. Ibid. **23**:81–145.

IMLAY, M. J. 1973. Effects of potassium on survival and distribution of freshwater mussels. *Malacologia* **12**:97–113.

ISOM, B. G. 1969. The mussel resources of the Tennessee River. Ibid. **7**:397–425.

ISOM, B. G., and P. YOKLEY. 1968. The mussel

fauna of Duck River in Tennessee, 1965. *Am. Midl. Nat.* **80**:34–42.

JONES, R. O. 1949. Propagation of fresh-water mussels. *Prog. Fish-Cult.* **12**:13–25.

KUNZ, G. F. 1898. The freshwater pearls and pearl fisheries of the United States. *Bull. U.S. Fish Comm.* **17**:373–426.

LEFEVRE, G., and W. C. CURTIS. 1912. Studies of the reproduction and artifical propagation of fresh-water mussels. *Bull. U.S. Bur. Fish.* **30**:105–201.

MATTESON, M. R. 1955. Studies on the natural history of the Unionidae. *Am. Midl. Nat.* **53**:126–145.

MATTESON, M. R., and R. W. DEXTER. 1966. Changes in pelecypod populations in Salt Fork of Big Vermilion River, Illinois, 1918-1962. *Nautilus* **79**:96–101.

MEIER-BROOK, C. 1969. Substrate relations in some Pisidium species (Eulamellibranchiata: Sphaeriidae). *Malacologia* **9**:121–125.

MONK, C. R. 1925. The anatomy and life-history of a fresh-water mollusk of the genus Sphaerium. *J. Morphol. Physiol.* **45**:473–501.

MORRISON, J. P. E. 1932. A report on the Mollusca of the northeastern Wisconsin lake district. *Trans. Wis. Acad. Sci. Arts and Lett.* **27**:359–396.

MURPHY, G. 1942. Relationship of the fresh-water mussel to trout in the Truckee River. *Calif. Fish and Game* **28**:89–102.

MURRAY, H. D., and E. C. ROY. 1968. Checklist of freshwater and land mollusks of Texas. *Sterkiana:* **30**:25–42.

NELSON, T. C. 1918. On the origin, nature, and function of the crystalline style of lamellibranchs. *J. Morphol.* **31**:53–111.

ORTMANN, A. E. 1912. Notes upon the families and genera of the Najades. *Ann. Carnegie Mus.* **8**:222–365.

———. 1919. A monograph of the Naiades of Pennsylvania. Part III. Systematic account of the genera and species. *Mem. Carnegie Mus.* **8**:1–384.

REIGLE, N. J. 1967. An occurrence of Anodonta (Mollusca, Pelecypoda) in deep water. *Am. Midl. Nat.* **78**:530–531.

ROSCOE, E. J., and S. REDELINGS. 1964. The ecology of the fresh-water pearl mussel Margaritifera margaritifera (L.). *Sterkiana* **16**:19–32.

SEPKOSKI, J. J., and M. A. REX. 1974. Distribution of fresh-water mussels: coastal rivers as biogeographic islands. *Syst. Zool.* **23**:165–188.

SIMPSON, C. T. 1914. *A descriptive catalogue of the naiades, or pearly freshwater mussels.* 1540 pp. Bryant Walker. Detroit, Mich.

SINCLAIR, R. M., and B. G. ISOM. 1963. *Further studies on the introduced Asiatic clam (Corbicula) in Tennessee.* Tenn. Dept. Public Health, Tenn.

Stream Pollution Control Board, 76 pp. (processed).

STARRETT, W. C. 1971. A survey of the mussels (Unionacea) of the Illinois River, a polluted stream. *Bull. Ill. Nat. Hist. Surv.* **30**:266–403.

STERKI, V. 1916. A preliminary catalog of the North American Sphaeriidae. *Ann. Carnegie Mus.* **10**:429–474.

———. 1916a. Some directions and suggestions for collecting the Sphaeriidae and aquatic gastropods. Ibid. 478–486.

STRECKER, J. K. 1931. The distribution of the naiades or pearly fresh-water mussels of Texas. *Baylor Univ. Spec. Bull.* **2**:3–71.

SURBER, T. 1912. Identification of the glochidia of freshwater mussels. *U.S. Bur. Fish. Doc.* **771**:1–10.

THIELE, J. 1935. *Handbuch der systematischen Weichtierkunde.* Zweiter Band, pp. 779–1154. Gustav Fischer, Jena.

UTTERBACK, W. I. 1915–1916. The naiades of Missouri. *Am. Midl. Nat.* **4**:41–53, 97–152, 181–204, 244–273, 311–327, 339–354, 387–400, 432–464.

VAN CLEAVE, H. J. 1940. Ten years of observation on a fresh-water mussel population. *Ecology* **21**:363–370.

VAN DER SCHALIE, H. 1938. The naiad fauna of the Huron River, in southeastern Michigan. *Mus. Zool. Univ. Mich. Misc. Publ.* **40**:1–83.

———. 1940. Aestivation of fresh-water mussels. *Nautilus* **53**:137–138.

———. 1945. The value of mussel distribution in tracing stream confluence. *Pap. Mich. Acad. Sci. Arts and Lett.* **30**:355–373.

———. 1970. Hermaphroditism among North American freshwater mussels. *Malacologia* **10**:93–112.

VAN DER SCHALIE, H., and A. VAN DER SCHALIE. 1950. The mussels of the Mississippi River. *Am. Midl. Nat.* **44**:448–466.

WALKER, B. 1918. A synopsis of the classification of the freshwater Mollusca of North America, north of Mexico, and a catalogue of the more recently described species, with notes. *Mus. Zool. Univ. Mich. Misc. Publ.* **6**:1–213.

WILLIAMS, J. C. 1969. *Mussel fishery investigation. Tennessee, Ohio, and Green rivers.* Final Report. Ken. Dept. Fish and Wildl. Res. 107 pp. (processed).

WILSON, C. B., and H. W. CLARK. 1914. The mussels of the Cumberland River and its tributaries. *Bur. Fish. Doc.* **781**:1–63.

WOOD, E. M. 1974. Development and morphology of the glochidium larva of Anodonta cygnea (Mollusca: Bivalvia). *J. Zool. Lond.* **173**:1–13.

# Appendix A

# FIELD AND LABORATORY APPARATUS

CERTAIN pieces of efficient and time-saving field and laboratory apparatus are frequently unfamiliar to the beginning investigator who is interested in collecting and working with fresh-water invertebrates. In addition, the advanced researcher is sometimes unaware of the advantages inherent in some kinds of equipment that could easily be adapted to his special needs. For these reasons it seems appropriate to include this brief pictorial and explanatory appendix. The following photographs are by no means a catalogue of field and laboratory apparatus used in working with fresh-water invertebrates. They represent merely a selection of a few items that the writer and his students have found especially useful. Most of them are mentioned in one or more places in the appropriate chapters of this volume. Some items are standard in many laboratories; others are seldom seen. Some are expensive; others are trivial in cost.

The size and design of containers used for bringing specimens back to the laboratory are of infinite variety and depend to a large extent on the size, nature, and numbers of organisms collected and transported. Regardless of the size of the container, however, it is best to fill it almost to the top with water or preserving fluid. If the container is only one-half or two-thirds full, the fluid and specimens will be sloshed about as they are carried by hand or on the floor of an automobile, and the softer and larger organisms are thereby often damaged or ruined.

If live specimens are being transported over long distances, the lid of the container should be removed at intervals or a portion of the water should be changed in order to renew the supply of oxygen.

Field collecting is often a long, hard, and tedious task. Especially for taxonomic work, the beginner should bear in mind that he must collect large, representative samples consisting of an abundance of individuals. *Specimens without complete accompanying data are worthless.* They should have attached notations of the precise location and habitats (understandable to any colleague), date, name of collector, and any special notes on associated organisms, weather, and water conditions.

With few exceptions, specimens once collected should be attended to promptly in the laboratory. Fluids should be changed, and specimens should be properly killed and fixed where necessary. Much hard-earned material is worthless if the tired collector postpones caring for it until the following day.

FIG. 535.–Field collecting apparatus. An ordinary long-handled dipnet is shown at the bottom of the photograph. A scraper net is shown in the upper left. It is used for scraping along the bottom of ponds and streams for aquatic insects and other macroscopic forms. The four sides are made of galvanized sheet metal, and the bottom is fine-meshed brass screening. The apron net (right) is perhaps the best single tool for collecting larger aquatic invertebrates. It is pointed at the front so that it may be pushed through vegetation and bottom debris. The wide-meshed cover allows animals to enter while keeping out coarser materials. The curved bottom is made out of heavy brass screening that permits fine debris to pass through. A final vigorous push of the apron net lands the catch toward the rear of the net where it may be removed through a hinged door. Materials should be sorted in a white enameled pan.

FIG. 536.–Various types of collecting nets. Two "pond-life dipnets" with 3-foot handles are shown at the bottom of the photograph. One has a very fine weave suitable for Protozoa (173 meshes to the inch) and a detachable glass vial at its tip; the other has a coarse weave (38 meshes to the inch). A standard plankton townet is shown at the top. The mouth has a diameter of 10 in. and the bag is made of fine (number 20) bolting silk (173 meshes to the inch). In the left center are two small aquarium nets. These are useful for collecting in the shallows and in puddles; they are also handy for sorting and washing specimens. A Birge cone net is shown at right center. The conical front end is made from coarse brass screening, and the rear end consists of a shallow cup with a screw cap at the bottom. The two are connected with a tapered bolting silk net. If properly weighted, the cone net may be towed behind a boat. It may also be thrown from shore at the end of a long line. The coarse screen keeps out vegetation and debris but allows small organisms to enter. When the net is retrieved it should be held upright so that the organisms are concentrated in the cup. The screw cap is then carefully removed and the contents emptied into a collecting vial or jar.

FIG. 537.–Dredge net. This is a strong, lightweight net for bottom collecting from a boat. It consists of a D-shaped frame mounted on runners about 20 in. long. The net has a relatively coarse mesh. Appropriate weights attached to the line several feet in front of the net permit effective use as it is towed along in deep water. When properly used, the dredge net will take organisms living on the surface of the substrate and just above the surface.

FIG. 538.–Zooplankton collecting tube. This simple device consists of a rubberized fabric tube with a continuous imbedded spiral wire to maintain constant diameter (about 8 cm). Such tubing can be obtained commercially and is priced reasonably. It is absolutely unexcelled for taking top-to-bottom quantitative zooplankton samples in water from 1 to 10 m or more deep, depending on the length of the tube used. The tube is fitted with a recovery line and a piece of fine bolting silk tied with cord over the opposite end. A sample can be taken in less than a minute, as follows: (A) Lower the tube *quickly* into the water, open end down. (B) Hold the upper end in place and pull the open end of the tube above the water by means of the recovery line. (C) Let go of the end that is covered with bolting silk and let it dangle in the water. (D) Pull the tube up vertically, slosh the last 50 cm up and down to settle the sample on the bolting silk, and pull the bolting silk end out of the water. Carefully untie the piece of cord to release the bolting silk and rinse off the retained organisms into the sample vial. In this figure the water is 2.3 m deep. The sampler has the great advantage of being usable in weed beds.

FIG. 539.–Mud-sucker. A semiquantitative instrument used for taking a surface sample of mud and its contained microorganisms in deep water. The photograph on the left shows the mud-sucker as it is lowered to take a sample. When it touches the bottom a brass weight is allowed to slide down the line and trip the catch. The photograph on the right shows the sampler after being tripped. Mud is sucked up into the rubber bulb. (Photo courtesy of George M. Moore.)

FIG. 540.–Bottom sampling materials. The Peterson dredge is a heavy instrument that is especially useful for taking quantitative bottom samples from sand and gravel substrates. Accessory cast iron weights can be attached to make the dredge as heavy as 60 lb. The dredge covers about one-thirteenth of a square meter of bottom. Samples should be mixed and rinsed several times with portions of water in a large metal pan, the supernatant being quickly poured through a sieve to catch the organisms. The piece of brass screening with two wooden handles shown on the left is useful for collecting stream bottom organisms. It should be held obliquely and just downstream from the point where silt, debris, pebbles, and rubble are dislodged and worked over with the fingers or a short stick.

FIG. 541.–Ekman dredge and sieve. This dredge is used for taking quantitative samples from soft, muddy bottoms; it is useless for sand, gravel, rock, and debris substrates. The photograph shows the jaws set for release; they are closed by sending a brass messenger down the taut line to trip the spring catch. This model takes a sample 9 in. square, but a smaller model takes a sample 6 in. square. The depth to which the sampler sinks into the substrate depends partially on the speed with which it is allowed to strike bottom. The brass screen across the top prevents bottom animals from being lost when the sampler sinks into the substrate. If the mud sample is diluted with quantities of water as it is washed through the sieve, the organisms can be separated out relatively quickly.

FIG. 542.–Water "telescope," or viewing box. This device is made of galvanized sheet metal and has the shape of a truncated pyramid. The upper end is open, but the lower end is covered with a piece of heavy glass which is carefully cemented in place so that the box is watertight. The underwater view through this box is surprisingly clear and revealing. It is useful for observing the activities of clams, snails, and crayfish, as well as for locating lost instruments. In the photograph it is being used at the edge of a dam, but it is equally advantageous in deeper water from the side or stern of a boat.

FIG. 543.–Stream bottom sampler. This device is essentially a modification of the well-known square-foot sampler, and the area within the brass or stainless steel frame covers 25 by 40 cm (one-tenth of a square meter). The mouth of this quantitative sampler is faced upstream so that the conical net bellies downstream. In swift currents the sampler must be held down firmly to prevent shifting. When the gravel, debris, rubble, sand, or silt within the frame are worked over thoroughly with the fingers, the organisms are dislodged and float back with the current into the net. They may then be emptied into a collecting jar or enameled pan for sorting. The model shown in the photograph is fastened together with six wingnuts so that it may be easily disassembled and carried in a more compact manner. The net has a light canvas collar and is made from number OOOXX bolting silk.

FIG. 544.–Plankton counting materials. An ordinary pipette or Hensen-Stempel pipette (left) is used for placing exactly 1 ml of a plankton sample in the shallow Sedgwick-Rafter counting cell (center), and the cell is then carefully covered with a large cover slip. The cell consists simply of a thin brass or plastic frame cemented to an extra large glass slide. Since the depth of the chamber plus the cover slip thickness is only about 1.5 mm, an 8 mm microscope objective can be used for identifying and counting the organisms in the cell.

FIG. 545.–Irwin loops. Upper photo, ×2.6; lower photo, ×0.6. The Irwin loop is a highly successful but simple device for picking up and transferring micrometazoans from one fluid to another while working with dissecting binoculars. It consists of a loop at the end of a double strand of fine, twisted, stainless steel wire, the whole being mounted in a slender wooden handle. The loop owes its special usefulness to the fact that it is small, flattened, and bent at an angle of 30 degrees. By sliding the loop under a specimen, the latter may be easily lifted up and through the surface film, usually on the first trial. It is much more efficient than a bristle or fine pipette. Several sizes are available in which the transverse inside diameter of the loop ranges from about 0.3 to 0.8 mm. Irwin loops may be obtained from Sargent-Welch Co., Catalog number S-44362.

FIG. 546.–Materials used in making glycerin jelly mounts of small invertebrates. Included are electric hot plate, small jar of glycerin jelly, slide labels, cover slips, mounted bristles and "minuten nadeln" (upper right), slides, Syracuse watch glass containing specimens, Irwin loop, needles, forceps, and pipette. (See p. 183 for method of making mounts.)

FIG. 547.–Materials for sealing slide mounts. Shown are turntable, Murrayite cement, and camel's hair brush. In general, only round cover slips should be used with glycerin, glycerin jelly, CMC, and similar mounting media. The slide should first be centered on the turntable so that the center of the cover slip is over the center of the turntable. Then the wheel is given a moderate spin, and while it is in motion a partial brushful of Murrayite should be held at the edge of the cover slip. In this way the edge of the cover slip is neatly and effectively sealed to the slide with an airtight seal. If too much Murrayite is applied or if the wheel is turned too rapidly, centrifugal force will cause the cement to flow out over the edge of the slide. A needle thrust through the handle of the camel's hair brush will fit across the top of the Murrayite jar so that the brush will not be immersed too deeply.

FIG. 548.–Microscope lamp. Most commercial high intensity lamps for compound and dissecting microscopes are out of the student's price range. This one can be made easily and reasonably, and it serves the purpose admirably. A 75 watt reflector spot bulb will fit an ordinary gooseneck lamp if the front part of the shade is taken off with a hacksaw. The bulb has a life of about 2000 hours. We suggest that a piece of heat filter glass be used between the lamp and the microscope.

# Appendix B

# REAGENTS, SOLUTIONS, AND LABORATORY ITEMS

FOR THE most part, this brief appendix lists only those reagents and solutions that are mentoned more than once in the text portion of this volume. Information concerning additional reagents and procedures, including fixation, imbedding, sectioning, staining, and so on, can be obtained by consulting any of the standard microtechnique handbooks.

In the writer's laboratory all transfers of small specimens from one solution to another are performed in the same vial. When solutions are added they are squirted into the vial with a pipette so that there is thorough mixing; when solutions are removed they are sucked up with a pipette after the specimens have all settled to the bottom of the vial. Although two or three such portions are usually necessary to effect a complete change of solutions in a vial, the small additional time is well compensated for by the convenience and compactness of the method. Furthermore, there is little danger of drying, spilling, or loss of specimens.

The following list includes a variety of anesthetics. In general, such solutions should be slowly and gradually added to the water containing the specimens. Experience will determine proper amounts.

**Acetic acid.** Usually supplied as glacial acetic acid which is 99.5 percent $CH_3COOH$. Two to 10 parts of glacial acetic acid are often added to 100 parts saturated mercuric chloride as a fixative.

**Alcohol.** Wherever "alcohol" is indicated in this manual, ethyl alcohol, or $C_2H_5OH$, is meant. It is used in varying concentrations as a fixative and preserva-tive. Alcohol is usually supplied commercially in about 95 percent concentration (190 proof). All alcohol dilutions are made by measuring out the number of milliliters of 95 percent alcohol equivalent to the percentage of alcohol desired and diluting to 95 ml with water. For example, to make a 60 percent solution add 35 ml water to 60 ml of 95 percent alcohol. Absolute (essentially 100 percent) alcohol is expensive to buy but may be easily made in the laboratory by dehydrating 95 percent alcohol with anhydrous copper sulfate. Crystals of copper (cupric) sulfate should first be heated in an evaporating dish until the water of crystallization is driven off and a white powder remains. Place some of this powder in a bottle and add 95 percent alcohol. The water in the alcohol immediately unites with the copper sulfate, turning it blue. Add more anhydrous copper sulfate until it no longer turns blue. Then quickly filter the alcohol into a dry bottle and stopper with a tight cork or ground glass stopper.

**Alum cochineal.** An excellent whole-mount stain for many small invertebrates. Add 6 g potassium alum and 6 g powdered cochineal to 90 ml distilled water and boil for 30 minutes. Allow the fluid to settle, decant the supernatant, add a little water, and boil until about 90 ml of solution remains. Filter when cool and add 0.5 g thymol to inhibit molds. Depending on size and density of specimens, stain for 4 to 30 hours. After staining, wash specimens in several changes of water for 15 to 30 minutes to extract the alum. The material is then dehydrated and mounted in balsam, permount, or some similar nonaqueous material.

777

**Balsam** (Canada balsam). A general permanent mounting medium for dehydrated whole specimens or microtome sections. It is easiest to buy a thick solution and dilute with xylol (xylene) to the proper consistency. Add a marble chip to keep the solution neutral.

**Benzamine hydrochloride, benzamine lactate.** Anesthetics for certain small metazoans; usually used in 2 percent solutions.

**Bismarck brown.** An intravitam stain useful for protozoans. Boil 1 g of the stain in 100 ml water and filter.

**Borax carmine.** This is a most useful stain for whole mounts of small metazoans. Boil 2 g carmine in 100 ml of 4 percent borax until dissolved. Then add 100 ml of 70 percent alcohol; filter after 24 hours. Stain objects for 10 hours to several days, depending on size and density. Transfer to 70 percent acid alcohol and keep there until the stain no longer forms clouds. Wash the specimens in neutral alcohol.

**Bouin's fluid.** A general fixative consisting of 75 ml saturated aqueous picric acid, 25 ml formalin, and 5 ml glacial acetic acid. The normal fixing time is 2 to 16 hours, but tissues are not harmed if left in the fluid up to several weeks.

**Butyn, butyn sulfate.** Anesthetics for certain small metazoans; usually used in a 0.1 to 2 percent solution.

**Carmine.** (See Gower's carmine.)

**Carnoy's fluid.** Especially useful for killing and fixing fragile immature insects. Consists of 10 percent acetic acid, 60 percent alcohol, and 30 percent chloroform. Fix for 12 to 24 hours; wash in 70 percent alcohol; store in 70 percent alcohol.

**Chloral Hydrate.** A general anesthetic for small metazoans. Make up as a 10 percent solution.

**Chloretone.** A common anesthetic (chlorbutanol) usually used in 0.1 to 0.6 percent solution.

**Chloroform.** Occasionally used as a saturated aqueous solution (1.0 percent) for anesthetizing small metazoans. Chloroform vapors are sometimes useful if the organisms are concentrated in a small amount of water under a bell jar beside a small beaker of chloroform.

**Chloroplatinic acid.** This compound, $H_2PtCl_6 \cdot 6H_2O$, is especially valuable to preserve and keep osmic acid solutions stable. A gram should be added to every 100 ml of osmic acid solution.

**Clorox.** A commercial caustic useful for isolating small sclerotized structures from musculature and connective tissues, and especially for isolating trophi of rotifers. Usually diluted 1 to 10 with water.

**CMCP (nonresinous mounting medium).** This is a series of permanent mounting material useful for whole mounts of aquatic insects, crustaceans, and possibly certain other small metazoans. It is available in a thick, syrupy solution in which specimens may be mounted directly and satisfactorily from water, formalin preservative solutions, alcohols, and glycerin. It dries hard (but slowly) and has the additional advantage of being a clearing agent. For real permanency, however, cover slips should be ringed with Murrayite or some similar cement after the mounts have dried for several days. CMCP may be thinned with water. It is just as permanent as balsam, and is indeed an important contribution to biological technique and slide making. The product is marketed by the Macmillan Science Co., Chicago, Ill.

**Cocaine, Novocain.** Excellent anesthetics for small metazoans but extremely difficult to obtain because of narcotics regulations. Best used as a 1 percent solution in 95 percent alcohol or water.

**Eosin.** General purpose cytoplasmic stain for small metazoans. Usually used as a 0.5 percent solution in 95 percent alcohol or water.

**Euparal.** A permanent slide mounting medium. Specimens may be transferred directly from 95 percent alcohol into euparal.

**FAA (formalin-aceto-alcohol).** A general-purpose fixative in which material may be kept for several days without harm. Numerous modifications of this fixative are used; a typical one consists of 40 ml distilled water, 2 ml glacial acetic acid, 50 ml of 95 percent alcohol, and 10 ml formalin.

**Formalin.** A common and cheap preservative consisting of a 37 to 40 percent aqueous solution of formaldehyde, $H_2CO$. Depending on the nature of the preserved material, 2 to 6 percent solutions of formalin (*not* 2 to 6 percent formaldehyde) are usually used. Commercial formalin is slightly acid and may be neutralized by maintaining a slight deposit of magnesium carbonate or household borax in the bottom of the reagent bottle. When formalin dries it forms a whitish irreversible polymer.

**Fuchsin (basic).** A nuclear stain sometimes useful in temporary whole mounts of micrometazoans. Make up a 0.5 percent aqueous solution.

**Gilson's fluid.** (See p. 128.)

**Glycerin.** An excellent medium for dissecting and for temporary and permanent mounts for many kinds of micrometazoans. Directions for making the latter are given on pages 183-184. Glycerin is miscible with water and alcohol at all concentrations and has the advantage of being a slight clearing agent. Because glycerin is nondrying, the writer regularly adds about 5 percent of it to stored vials of alcoholic and formalin specimens. If such vials should break, or the water and alcohol should dry, the specimens are still available in good condition. Specimens to be used in concentrated glycerin should first be placed in a 5 to 20 percent solution of glycerin in 50 to 95 percent alcohol. If the container is uncovered (but protected from dust), the alcohol and water evaporate in a few days, leaving the specimens in pure glycerin.

**Glycerin jelly, glycerin jelly slide mounts.** A valuable permanent mounting medium that is solid at ordinary temperatures. It is sold by most biological supply firms, but may be easily made in the laboratory. Soak 1.5 g clean gelatin overnight in 100 ml water, then dissolve with gentle heat. Add half its volume of clean glycerin and 0.5 g carbolic acid. Warm *gently* and stir for 10 minutes until homogeneous. Store in a small wide-mouth bottle with a screw cap. Specimens to be mounted in glycerin jelly should first be in at least 50 percent glycerin. Melt the glycerin jelly gently in warm water or on a hot plate. (If it is heated too much it polymerizes and is useless.) Place the specimen on a slide in a droplet of glycerin, drop on one to several drops of liquid glycerin jelly with a thin glass rod, and quickly orient the specimen with a warm needle. Then pick up a clean circular cover slip with a forceps, breathe on the undersurface, and gently put it in place on top of the fluid. Set the mount aside to congeal for at least 30 minutes. Later the excess glycerin jelly may be removed from the edge of the cover slip with a razor blade and clean cloth. For real permanence the cover slip should be ringed on a turntable with several coats of Murrayite.

**Gower's carmine stain.** This stain is especially useful for staining small freshwater invertebrates to be mounted in glycerin or glycerin jelly. It will not "bleed" into the mounting medium. Add 10 g of carmine to 100 ml of 45 percent acetic acid. Heat to a boil, cool, filter, dry, and save the residue. Then to 1 g of dry residue add 10 g of alum and 200 ml distilled water. Heat to dissolve, cool, filter, and add one crystal of thymol. (See staining with Gower's carmine.)

**Helly's fluid.** (See p. 129)

**Hematoxylin.** Delafield's hematoxylin is a general purpose nuclear stain. Dissolve

1 g of hematoxylin crystals in 10 ml absolute alcohol and add it drop by drop to 100 ml of a saturated aqueous solution of aluminum ammonium sulfate. Expose this mixture to air and light for several weeks to "ripen." Then filter, add 25 ml glycerin, and 25 ml methyl alcohol.

**Hertwig-Schneider's fluid.** (See p. 109)

**Hydroxylamine hydrochloride.** Anesthetic for certain small metazoans; usually used in a 2 percent aqueous solution.

**Isopropyl alcohol.** Occasionally useful as an anesthetic, especially for certain protozoans. Sometimes used in histological work as a substitute for ethyl alcohol.

**Jeweler's forceps.** These are extremely fine and well-made forceps that are indispensable for dissections. Obtainable from your local jeweler or jewelers supply house.

**Kahle's fluid.** Useful for killing and fixing fragile immature insects. Consists of 11 percent formalin, 28 percent alcohol, 2 percent glacial acetic acid, and 59 percent water. Drain off after a week, rinse in 70 percent alcohol, and store the specimens in 70 percent alcohol.

**Lactophenol.** A special mounting medium with index of refraction especially favorable for cuticular details. Made up of 20 g phenol crystals, 40 g glycerin, 20 g lactic acid, and 20 ml distilled water.

**Lugol's solution.** An excellent fixative and preservative for microzoans, especially for cellular details. Consists of 5 g iodine, 10 g potassium iodide, 10 g glacial acetic acid, and 100 ml water. Add 1 ml of this solution to each 100 ml of water containing the specimens.

**Magnesium sulfate.** Occasionally used as an anesthetic for fresh-water invertebrates but more useful for marine forms.

**Menthol.** An anesthetic occasionally used for fresh-water invertebrates. Sprinkle fine crystals on the surface of the water containing the specimens.

**Menthol–chloral hydrate narcotic.** General-purpose narcotic for small invertebrates. Grind 48 g menthol and 52 g chloral hydrate with a mortar and pestle until an oily fluid results. Place a few drops of this liquid on the surface of the water containing the animals.

**Methyl cellulose.** A fluffy white substance, easily soluble in water, and especially useful for slowing the movements of protozoans. Usually sold as 1 or 10 percent syrupy water solutions. Add a drop or two to water containing protozoans on a slide, mix with a needle, and add a cover slip. Keep it away from the end of the microscope objective!

**Methylene blue.** An excellent intravitam stain for translucent forms. Make up a stock of 0.01 g of methylene blue in 100 ml absolute alcohol. Add enough of this solution to the water containing the organisms to tinge it a light blue.

**Monk's fluid.** This is an aqueous mounting medium that is useful for making permanent slides of copepods and other small arthropods. It consists of 5 ml white corn syrup, 5 ml Certo (fruit pectin), and 3 ml water. Add a crystal of thymol as a preservative. The mixture sets in a few minutes. Dry to hardness over gentle heat, preferably a hot plate.

**Murrayite.** A synthetic cement that is dissolved in benzol to a thin, syrupy consistency. Since it is permanently waterproof, alcohol proof, and glycerin proof, it is an excellent sealing cement for museum jars and cover slips. If circular cover slips are ringed on a turntable, several coats should be applied with a camel's hair brush, allowing at least 10 hours between coats. It is sold by G.B.I. Industries, Ltd., Heaton Mills, Heaton St., Denton, Manchester, England.

**Neosynephrin hydrochloride.** Anesthetic for small metazoans; usually used in a 1 percent water solution.

**Neutral red.** An intravitam stain useful for protozoans. Dissolve 1 g of the powder in 100 ml water.

**Newcomer's fixative.** A good general fixative for small invertebrates. Six parts isopropyl alcohol, 3 parts propionic acid, 1 part petroleum ether, 1 part acetone, and 1 part dioxane. Specimens may be stored in this fixative.

**Nicotine sulfate.** This salt is occasionally used as an anesthetic for small freshwater invertebrates in about 2 percent solution.

**Nitric acid.** Concentrated nitric acid is used in cleaning and isolating sponge spicules and gemmules. Two percent nitric acid is useful for fixing turbellarians, and a 1 percent solution is used for dissociating tissues of hydras.

**Osmic acid.** Really osmium tetroxide, $OsO_4$, this compound is poisonous and extremely volatile. Used in a 1 percent solution in distilled water, it is an excellent and rapid fixative for a variety of small metazoans. Prepare the solution by crushing the cleaned hermetically sealed glass container in an appropriate amount of water and allowing the released osmic acid crystals to dissolve. This compound is easily oxidized by light and dust and should therefore be kept in a blackened dropping bottle. Solutions have much greater permanence if they contain 1 percent chloroplatinic acid. If specimens are in a drop of water on a slide, fixation is accomplished in a few seconds if the slide is inverted over the mouth of the osmic acid bottle. A few drops of osmic acid are sufficient for fixing specimens in 5 ml to 10 ml of water. All fixed material should be washed in several changes of water. If the material is colored dark brown or black by the action of the osmic acid, place in commercial hydrogen peroxide until sufficiently bleached. Osmic acid is unfortunately very expensive.

**Potassium hydroxide.** A 2 to 10 percent solution of potassium hydroxide is often used for clearing opaque chitinous insects and other arthropods. Specimens may be heated gently in the solution for a few minutes or left in it cold for 8 to 48 hours. Specimens should then be neutralized with 10 percent acetic acid and washed with several changes of water.

**Schaudinn's fixative.** A general fixative consisting of 2 parts saturated mercuric chloride and 1 part 95 percent alcohol. Fix for 5 minutes to 3 hours, depending on size and density of the objects. Remove all the salt by washing in several changes of 70 percent alcohol for a total of three to eight days. Salt removal may be greatly speeded by adding a small amount of tincture of iodine to the alcohol. The action of this fixative is enhanced by the addition of sufficient glacial acetic acid to make a 1 percent solution immediately before using.

**Staining with Gower's Carmine.** Transfer specimens to water. Add Gower's carmine solution to make 20 to 90 percent of the total volume. Let stand a half hour to 24 hours. Wash twice in water. If necessary, destain in 70 percent alcohol. Transfer to dilute glycerin in readiness for further processing.

**Terpineol (synthetic oil of lilac).** A good clearing agent, readily miscible with 90 percent alcohol. Does not make specimens brittle.

**Watchmaker's forceps.** (See jeweler's forceps.)

**Zut.** Trade name of a cement that is especially useful for tacking or ringing temporary or permanent slides, especially glycerin jelly mounts. Thin with butyl acetate. Apply with a turntable and a small camel's hair brush. Obtainable from Bennett Paint Products, Salt Lake City, Utah.

# REFERENCES

HULINGS, N. C., and J. S. GRAY. 1971. A manual for the study of meiofauna. *Smithson. Contrib. Zool.* **78:**1–83.

LIND, O. T. 1974. *Handbook of common methods in limnology.* 154 pp. Mosby, St. Louis.

NEEDHAM, J. G., et al. 1937. *Culture methods for invertebrate animals.* 590 pp. Dover, New York.

SAUR, J. F. T., et al. 1964. Sources of limnological and oceanographic apparatus and supplies. (3rd rev.) *Limnol. Oceanogr. Spec. Publ.* **1:**i–xxxi.

SCHWOERBEL, J. 1966. *Methoden der Hydrobiologie.* 207 pp. Franckh'sche Verlagshandlung, Keller, Stuttgart.

TURTOX/CAMBOSCO, MACMILLAN SCIENCE CO., 8200 South Hoyne Ave., Chicago, Ill. 60620.

WARD'S NATURAL SCIENCE ESTABLISHMENT, INC. P.O. Box 1712, Rochester, N.Y. 14603.

WELCH, P. S. 1948 *Limnological methods.* 381 pp. Blakiston, Philadelphia.

# INDEX

The main entries of this index include all names of genera and higher taxonomic categories used in this volume, as well as important anatomical and ecological terms. Where two or more species names in a genus are used in this book, then such species are sublisted alphabetically under the appropriate genera.

Entries are based chiefly on the earliest and/or most significant page references. There is no attempt to list *all* pages on which a particular item is mentioned.

Roman type page numbers indicate key or text locations. **Boldface** page numbers indicate the location of pertinent figures. An *italicized* page number means that both a figure and a text and/or key reference appear on that page.